FIRST PRINCIPLES
OF ECONOMICS

FIRST PRINCIPLES OF ECONOMICS

Second Edition

Richard G. Lipsey

Professor of Economics, Simon Fraser University
Vancouver, Canada

Colin Harbury

Emeritus Professor of Economics,
City University, London

OXFORD UNIVERSITY PRESS

Oxford University Press, Great Clarendon Street, Oxford OX2 6DP

Oxford New York

Athens Auckland Bangkok Bogota Bombay
Buenos Aires Calcutta Cape Town Dar es Salaam
Delhi Florence Hong Kong Istanbul Karachi
Kuala Lumpur Madras Madrid Melbourne
Mexico City Nairobi Paris Singapore
Taipei Tokyo Toronto
and associated companies in
Berlin Ibadan

First published 1988
Reprinted 1989
Reprinted 1990
Second edition 1992
Reprinted 1994
Reprinted 1997

ISBN 0 297 82120 2 paperback

Filmset in Sabon by
Selwood Systems, Midsomer Norton

Printed and bound in Great Britain by
Butler & Tanner Ltd, Frome and London

Contents

Preface to the Second Edition

PART 1   INTRODUCTION

Preface to Part 1

1 The Nature of Economics   3
The Boundaries of Economics – Economic Issues – Factors of Production – Resource Allocation – Opportunity Cost – Production Possibility Curves – Three Basic Economic Questions

2 Basic Questions and Answers   14
The Three Questions in Everyday Life – Economic Systems – Command Economies – The Failures of Central Planning – Market Economies – *Laissez-Faire* – How Markets Work – The Functions of Prices – Market Failure – Inefficiency – Inequity – Mixed Systems

3 How Economists Work   26
Positive and Normative Statements in Economics – Scientific Method – A Science of Human Behaviour – The Nature of Economic Theory – Economic Models – Testing Economic Models – Economic Statistics – Why Economists Disagree

PART 2   ELEMENTARY MICROECONOMICS

Preface to Part 2

4 Demand and Price   37
Consumer Demand – What Determines Quantity Demanded? – Demand by a Single Consumer – A Demand Curve – Diminishing Marginal Utility – The Rule for Maximizing Utility – Market Demand – Consumer Surplus – The Paradox of Value

5 Demand, Income and Other Determinants   46
Income – Normal Goods – Inferior Goods – Substitutes – Complements – Income Distribution – Demographic Changes – Shifts in Demand Curves and Movements Along Them – Time and Demand – The Law of Demand and Exceptional Demand Curves – Giffen Goods

6 Supply   53
The Nature of Supply – What Determines Quantity Supplied? – Supply and the Own Price of the Commodity – What Lies Behind the Supply Curve? – Marginal Cost – The Rule for Profit Maximization – Market Supply – Shifts in Supply Curves and Movements Along Curves – Time and Supply – Three Conventional Time-Periods

7 Elasticity of Demand and Supply   62
Price Elasticity of Demand – Ranges of Elasticity – Elasticity of Demand and Consumers' Total Outlay – Arc Elasticity of Demand – Simplifying the Formula for Elasticity – Determinants of Elasticity of Demand – Time and Elasticity – Income Elasticity of Demand – Cross Elasticity of Demand – Supply Elasticity – Determinants of Elasticity of Supply

8 Market Price Determination   72
Equilibrium Price – Disequilibrium Prices – The Working of Market Forces – What Equilibrium is *Not* – Desirability of Equilibrium – Achievement of Equilibrium – Stability of Equilibrium – Changes in Equilibrium – The Laws of Supply and Demand – Shifts *versus* Movements Along Curves Again – The Nature of Economic Laws

9 Market Efficiency and Market Failure **81**

General and Partial Equilibrium – The Nature of Economic Efficiency – The Case for *Laissez-Faire* – Market *versus* Non-Market Allocations – Market Failure – Public Goods – Merit and Demerit Goods – Externalities – Information Deficiencies – Dynamic Considerations – The Cobweb Theorem – Equity or Fairness

10 How to Use Supply and Demand Analysis **94**

The A–F Framework: A 5-Step Procedure – Step AB (Appropriate Because) – Step C (Causes) – Step D (Direction) – Step E (Effects) – Step F (Finale) – Applying the A–F Procedure – Application 1: the Imposition of a Tax on Sales of a Commodity – Application 2: A Maximum Price for Bread – Using the A–F Procedure – Agriculture

PART 3 INTERMEDIATE MICROECONOMICS

Preface to Part 3

11 Indifference Curves **111**

The Budget Line – Consumers' Tastes – An Indifference Curve – Diminishing Marginal Rate of Substitution – The Indifference Map – Indifference Curves with Special Shapes – Consumer Equilibrium – Utility Maximization – Shifts in the Budget Line – Indifference Curve Analysis and the Conventional Demand Curve – Income and Substitution Effects of a Price Change

12 Business Decisions **125**

Output Decisions – Input Decisions – The Determinants of Business Decisions – Market Considerations – The Number of Sellers – The Size of Sellers – Type of Product – Entry Conditions – Factor Markets – Internal Organization of the Business – Types of Business Organization – Mergers – Owners *versus* Controllers – Goals of Owners – Government and Business Decisions

13 The Productivity of Factors of Production **134**

The Short Run and Long Run – Short-Run Returns to a Variable Factor – Total, Average and Marginal Products of a Variable Factor – The 'Law' of Diminishing Returns – The Long Run: Returns to Scale – The Compatibility of Diminishing Returns to a Variable Factor and Increasing Returns to Scale – The Determinants of Returns to Scale – Indivisibilities – The Very Long Run: Changes in Techniques – Inventions and Innovations

14 Costs of Production **142**

The Nature of Costs – Imputed Costs – Depreciation – Accounting *versus* Opportunity Costs – Costs and Output in the Short Run – Cost Curves in the Short Run – Size of Plant and Capacity – Costs and Output in the Long Run – Cost Minimization and Factor Prices – Cost Curves in the Long Run – Learning-by-Doing – Internal and External Economics of Scale – The Continued Existence of Small Firms – Product Cycles – Non-Profit-Maximization

15 The Profit-Maximizing Firm and Perfect Competition **152**

The Firm in Any Market – Normal Profit – Two Rules for the Profit-Maximizing Firm – Rule 1: The Shut-Down Rule – Rule 2: The Rule for Maximum Profit Output – Equilibrium of the Firm Under Perfect Competition – Long-Run Equilibrium of the Firm – Equilibrium of the Industry Under Perfect Competition – Entry and Exit of Firms – An Alternative Analysis Using Total Revenue and Cost Curves

16 Monopoly **161**

Profit-Maximizing Output of a Monopolist – Monopoly Equilibrium in the Short Run and the Long Run – Barriers to Entry – Monopoly Power – Optimum Output of a Discriminating Monopolist – Monopoly and Economic Efficiency – Output and Price Under Monopoly and Perfect Competition Compared – Monopoly and the Price Mechanism – Market Failure and Monopoly – Marginal Cost Pricing – Natural Monopoly

17 Imperfect Competition **172**

Concentration of Industry – Types of Imperfect Market – Monopolistic Competition: Short-Run Equilibrium – Long-Run Equilibrium – Excess Capacity under Monopolistic Competition – The Relevance of Monopolistic Competition – Oligopoly: The Nature of Cost Curves under Oligopoly – The Basic Dilemma of Oligopoly – Price Stickiness – Kinked Demand Curve – Oligopoly and Efficiency – Contestable Markets – Government and Industry – Competition Policy

18 Competitive Factors Markets 185
Who Gets It? – The Size Distribution of Income – The Functional (or Factor) Distribution of Income – Market Explanations of Income Differences – The Marginal Product of a Factor – Elasticity of Demand for a Factor – Supply of a Factor – Factor Mobility – Backward-Sloping Supply Curve – Equilibrium in Perfect Factor Markets – Economic Rent and Transfer Earnings – Land and Economic Rent – Quasi-Rent

19 Labour and Capital 196
Labour – The Population Base – The Labour Force – Imperfect Labour Markets – Monopsony Employers – Monopoly Trade Unions – Bargaining Power of Trade Unions – Capital – The Two Prices of Capital – Compound Interest – Demand for Capital by a Firm – The Supply of Capital – Human Capital – Risk, Profit and Interest on Capital – Income Differences

20 International Trade 208
Interpersonal and Interregional Trade – The Special Features of International Trade – The Gains from Trade – A Special Case: Absolute Advantage – The General Case: Comparative Advantage – Limits to the Gain from Trade – The Gains from Economies of Scale – Learning-by-Doing – The Terms of Trade – International Trading Equilibrium – The Case for Free Trade – Protectionism – Tariffs – Quotas – Non-Tariff Barriers – Arguments for Protection – International Co-operation – A Free Trade Area – A Customs Union – A Common Market – Trade Creation and Trade Diversion

21 Government and Microeconomic Policy 223
The Goals of Economic Policy – Economic Efficiency and Market Forces – Optimal Allocation of Resources and the Second Best – The Goal of Equity – Market Failure – The Methods of State Intervention – Government Income – The Role of Taxes – Government Expenditure – Non-Budgetary Policies – Rules and Regulations – Cost-Benefit Analysis – State Ownership – The Case for Nationalization – The Case for Privatization – The Costs of Intervention: Government Failure – The Proper Balance

PART 4   ELEMENTARY MACROECONOMICS

Preface to Part 4

22 An Introduction to Macroeconomics 241
What is Macroeconomics? – Key Macro Variables – Employment and Unemployment – Total National Product – The General Price Level – The Interest Rate – The Balance of Payments and Exchange Rates – The Goals of Macroeconomic Policy – Early Goals – Modern Goals – Policy Instruments – Macroeconomic Theories and Economic Policies

23 The Circular Flow and National Income Accounting 254
The Circular Flow of Income – Major Types of Production – Consumption Commodities – Investment Goods – Government Production – Output, Expenditure and Income in the Circular Flow – The Output or Product Method – The Expenditure Method – The Income Method – The Identity of Output, Income and Expenditure – National Income Statistics – Various Measures of Total Expenditure – Interpreting National Income Measures – Money Values and Real Values – Total Output and Per Capita Output – Measurement Problems – Omissions from Measured National Income – Does the GDP Measure Living Standards? – Which Measure is Best?

24 Consumption and Investment 269
The Keynesian Model – A Two-Sector Model – Categories of Expenditure in the Two-Sector Model – Characteristics of Expenditure Flows – The Determinants of Investment Expenditure – Fixed Investment – Investment in Stocks – Residential Housing – Consumption Expenditure – The Aggregate Expenditure Function

25 Equilibrium National Income 283
The Income-Expenditure Method – The Leakages-Injections Method – The Equivalence of the Two Methods – How General are the Results? – A Link Between Saving and Investment?

26 Changes in National Income 291
Movements Along Curves and Shifts of Curves – Why National Income Changes – A Change in Desired Investment – A Change in Desired Consumption and Saving – The Paradox of Thrift – The Multiplier, or How Much Does National Income Change? – The Definition of the Multiplier – The Determination of the Multiplier

27 Government and the Circular Flow   **300**

The Income-Expenditure Method – The Behaviour of Desired Expenditure – Equilibrium National Income – The Effects of Changes in Government Taxes and Expenditures – The Leakages-Injections Method – The Multiplier with a Government Sector – The Size of the Multiplier – The Balanced Budget Multiplier – An Application

28 Income Fluctuations and Fiscal Policy   **310**

Types of Fluctuation – The Trade Cycle – The Terminology of the Trade Cycle – Explanations of the Trade Cycle – Fiscal Policy – Three Gaps – The Government's Budget – The Goals of Fiscal Policy – A Policy-Induced Cycle – Discretionary and Automatic Policies

29 The Balance of Payments and National Income   **322**

International Payments and Exchange Rates – The International Payments Accounts – The Balance of International Payments – The Exchange Rate – Foreign Trade in the Theory of Income Determination – The Theory of Income Determination – The Size of the Multiplier – The International Transmission of Income Changes – Imports and Exports: Good or Bad?

30 Money and the Price Level   **334**

Money – The Functions and Characteristics of Money – The History of Money – Modern Money – Money Values and Relative Values – The Relation Between Money and Prices: the Classical Quantity Theory of Money – The 'Equation' of Exchange – From the Equation of Exchange to the Quantity Theory

31 Banks and the Supply of Money   **346**

Types of Financial Assets – The UK Banking System – The Retail Banks – The Bankers' Clearing House – Other Institutions in the UK Financial System – The Creation of Money by the Retail Banks

PART 5 INTERMEDIATE ECONOMICS

Preface to Part 5

32 The Demand for Money   **355**

Bonds, Bills and the Rate of Interest – What is a Bond? – The Market Value of a Bond – The Market Rate of Interest – Present Value – Bills – The Concept of Liquidity – Money and Wealth – Kinds of Assets – Money and Bonds – The Demand to Hold Money and Bonds – The Transactions Motive – The Precautionary Motive – The Speculative Motive

33 Money, Interest and National Income   **364**

The Liquidity Preference Theory of Interest – The Monetary Transmission Mechanism – An Increase in the Supply of Money – Other Monetary Changes – Monetary Shocks at Various Income Levels – Unemployed Resources – Full Employment – The Automatic Elimination of an Inflationary Gap – Conclusion

34 The Bank of England and Monetary Policy   **372**

The Bank of England – The Issue and Banking Departments – Functions of the Bank of England – Monetary Policy in a Closed Economy – Instruments, Targets and Goals – The Instruments of Monetary Policy – The Intermediate Targets of Monetary Policy – Policy Variables

35 Aggregate Demand and Aggregate Supply   **388**

Limitations of the Basic Keynesian Model – The Demand Side of the Economy – Equilibrium National Income when the Price Level Changes – Derivation of the Aggregate Demand Curve – Movements Along and Shifts of the *AD* Curve – The Supply Side of the Economy in the Short Run – Equilibrium of Aggregate Demand and Aggregate Supply in the Short Run – Shifts in the *AD* and *SRAS* Curves – The Slope of the *SRAS* Curve Further Considered – Two Asymmetries in Aggregate Supply – The Supply Side of the Economy in the Long Run – Effects of an *Increase* in Aggregate Demand on the *SRAS* Curve – Effects of a *Decrease* in Aggregate Demand on the *SRAS* Curve – The Long-Run Aggregate Supply Curve

36 Economic Growth and Development   399

The Timescales for Assessing Growth – Kinds of 'Growth' – The Short- and Long-Run Effects of Investment on National Income – The Short- and Long-Run Effects of Saving on National Income – Theories of Growth – Growth Without Learning – Growth With Learning – Additional Factors Affecting Growth Rates – Benefits and Costs of Growth – Growth as a Goal of Policy – Growth and the Environment – Growth in Less Developed Countries – The Uneven Pattern of Development – Barriers to Economic Development – Some Basic Choices – Some Controversial Unresolved Issues

37 Employment and Unemployment   420

Kinds of Unemployment – Demand-Deficient Unemployment – Frictional Unemployment – Structural Unemployment – Real-Wage Unemployment – Is the NAIRU All Voluntary Unemployment? – The Measurement of Unemployment – Cures for Unemployment – Conclusion

38 Inflation   430

Causes of Inflation – Supply-Shock Inflation – Demand-Shock Inflation – Issues Concerning Inflation – Is Inflation a Monetary Phenomenon? – Does Inflation Reduce Excess Demand? – Are Rising Interest Rates Anti-Inflationary? – What is the Relation Between Desired Saving and Inflation? – What is the Relation Between Investment and Inflation? – The Phillips Curve, or How Fast Does the *SRAS* Curve Shift?

39 Macroeconomic Policy in a Closed Economy   441

Demand Management Policies – Fiscal Policy – Monetary Policy – Fiscal *versus* Monetary Policy – Goals of Demand Management: Full Employment and Stable Prices – Limitations of Demand Management Policies – Supply-Side Policies – Prices and Incomes Policies – Market-Oriented, Supply-Side Policies – Policy Trade-Offs: a Concluding Word

40 Exchange Rates   460

Two Important Distinctions – The Mechanism of International Transactions – The Determination of the Exchange Rate – The Exchange Rate Determined Graphically – Structural Changes – Capital Movements – The Relation Between the Exchange Rate and the Balance of Payments – The Value of the Exchange Rate in the Long Run – Different Exchange-Rate Concepts

41 Exchange-Rate Regimes   471

Two Main Types of Regime – Twentieth-Century Regimes – Fixed Exchange Rate Regimes – Advantages of Fixed Exchange Rates – Problems with Fixed Exchange Rates – Flexible Exchange Rate Regimes – A Regime of Managed Floats

42 Macroeconomic Policy in an Open Economy   480

Goals and Instruments – Policy Goals: Internal and External Balance – Policy Instruments: Expenditure-Changing and Expenditure-Switching – Internal and External Balance with a Fixed Exchange Rate – Policy Combinations – Lags in the Adjustment Process – Expenditure-Switching Under Fixed Exchange Rates – Macroeconomic Policy and the Capital Account – Fiscal and Monetary Policy Compared

43 Macroeconomic Controversies   496

Alternative Views – Different Diagnoses – The Trade Cycle – The Price Level – Growth – The Different Prescriptions – Market-Oriented Prescriptions – Interventionist Prescriptions – The Long-Run Prospects for Growth – A Tentative Verdict

Appendix 1: Graphs in Economics   504

Appendix 2: The Derivation of Elasticity of Demand at a Point on a Demand Curve   511

Appendix 3: Derivation of Equilibrium Values for Simple Micro and Macro Models   512

Appendix 4: Choice of Techniques: An Alternative Analysis Using Isoquants   514

Appendix 5: The Basic Dilemma of Oligopoly Using Game Theory   516

Answers to End-of-Chapter Questions   517

Index   521

Preface to the Second Edition

This is a new edition of an introduction to economic principles for complete beginners. The main users of the first edition have been students preparing for examinations in A-level economics, and first-year undergraduates – especially those without A-level economics and those taking non-specialist degrees. The book is suitable also for students taking the economics examinations of the major professional bodies, such as the Institutes of Chartered Accountants, of Bankers, of Actuaries, of Chartered Surveyors, etc.

There is no shortage of introductory economics texts. The distinctive features of ours are not to be found in colour, pictorial illustrations or similar novelties, but in relevance and clarity of content. Our aim is to provide an authoritative, up-to-date treatment of elementary, mainstream economics. We do not try to pass on complex wisdoms in simplified forms; nor to be comprehensive. We give top priority to writing understandable explanations of basic economic principles. Doing this thoroughly, sometimes means writing at length. We take as much space as we need to expound each topic properly, rather than make a ritualistic bow to it.

The coverage of economic theory in the book is full, as may be seen from the summaries which end every chapter, and from the table of contents.[1] Moreover, while the main text calls for only minimal mathematical background, we have written an ultra-elementary guide to the use of graphs and mathematics in economics, which appears in an appendix. A few other optional extras, e.g. technical material included in the syllabuses of only one or two examining bodies, appear in other appendexes.

There are plentiful illustrations of the economist's approach to economic problems (including a unique chapter on 'How to Use Supply and Demand Analysis'). A major feature of the new edition is the introduction of a large number of 'Boxes' where economic theory can be applied to current problems. However, we do not pretend to provide a full or complete coverage of material on the UK economy. To do so would take excessive space; such material also tends to date rapidly, and there are other books which concentrate on applied economics. The reader will not be surprised to hear that we recommend our own

Introduction to the UK Economy (3rd edition, Pitman, 1989; 4th edition, Blackwell, forthcoming 1993).[2]

We are fortunate in that a substantial number of users of the first edition have made comments, some spontaneous, others responses to a survey carried out by our publishers, and these have significantly affected the preparation of the new edition. One major addition is the inclusion of typical A-level examination questions at the end of every chapter (with the answers at the back of the book). These provide practice for the short-answer, multiple-choice and other 'objective test' papers. The applied Boxes also contain questions designed to provide practice for essay papers and 'Data Response'.[3]

Bold type is used to highlight key passages throughout the book, and the first appearance of each technical term is denoted by capital letters and a definition.

Every page of every chapter has been reconsidered; many have been rewritten, some drastically. The changes are too extensive to itemize. Material has been added on many topics. Some of it to cover developments in economic theory – for example in oligopoly and stabilization policy. Other additions reflect changed relevance of topics – for example privatization, taxation, international economic unions, human capital, location of industry, monetary integration, unemployment policies and fixed versus flexible exchange rates. Some material has been quite heavily rewritten to improve clarity, for example the chapters on elasticity of demand and macroeconomic policy in an open economy.

While rewriting occasionally adds length, we have been at pains to ensure that the book has not been lengthened, by abbreviating in appropriate places. The two chapters on indifference curves, for example, have been telescoped into a single chapter by eliminating some frills in the previous treatment. Some re-ordering has taken place, mainly to highlight important principles, sometimes involving deferment of more difficult material to later pages. (For example, the analysis of income and substitution effects of price changes using indifference curves now comes after the derivation of the conventional demand curve.) One place where re-ordering has brought a rich reward is in the treatment of microeconomic policy. Prin-

---

1 The book stops well short of the coverage and depth of Richard Lipsey's *Introduction to Positive Economics* (Weidenfeld and Nicolson, 7th edn 1989, 8th edn 1993).

2 Other suitable books include P. Curwen (ed.), *Understanding the UK Economy* (Macmillan) and M. J. Artis (ed.), *Prest and Coppock's The UK Economy* (Weidenfeld and Nicolson, 13th edn, 1992). Current periodicals, bank reviews, etc. are also often useful.

3 We recommend you to supplement the questions in the text with one or other of the many Workbooks on the market – such as Colin Harbury, *Workbook in Introductory Economics* (Pergamon, 4th edn, 1987). *Workbook for the seventh edition of An Introduction to Positive Economics* by Richard Lipsey, David Forrest and Wendy Olsen, contains some questions and problems which are equally within the scope of a reader of this book.

ciples and Problems are no longer treated in separate chapters, but are now integrated.

The structure of the book is designed to allow flexibility in the order of reading. There are five parts:

Part 1 Introduction
Part 2 Elementary Microeconomics
Part 3 Intermediate Microeconomics
Part 4 Elementary Macroeconomics
Part 5 Intermediate Macroeconomics

All routes through the book begin with Part 1, and continue with either Part 2 or Part 4. Thus, micro- or macro-economics can come first. There are several possible routes – Parts 1, 2, 3, 4, 5; Parts 1, 2, 4, 3, 5; Parts 1, 4, 2, 3, 5; Parts 1, 4, 2, 5, 3. We would, however, advise against Parts 1, 4, 5, 2, 3, because Part 5 uses, as does all of modern macroeconomics, many microeconomic concepts. Without a good mastery of elementary price theory, a student would find much of Part 5 a complete mystery.

We are grateful to all readers who have written to us with many useful comments and suggestions (mainly teachers, but some students), including the 35 who responded to a questionnaire sent out by our publishers, and especially to C. G. Bamford (Chief Examiner for the Cambridge A-level, U.C.L.E.S.), D. H. Cutting (of Derby College of F.E.), M. J. Farrer (of Sir John Leman High School, Beccles), Shaun Lang (of Lancashire Polytechnic), and Richard Lown (of Colchester High School for Girls) who completed extended reports on the first edition of this book. We hope readers – students as well as teachers – will continue to write in with comments and suggestions. We should also like to thank Diana Lipsey for reading the text, and Robyn Willis for coping with masses of typing, cutting and pasting.

As we wrote in the preface to the first edition, we hope that the reader who masters the principles of economics presented here will do more than pass his or her examinations successfully. Even at this elementary level, economic principles are extraordinarily powerful tools. They allow the significance of many current events to be appreciated in a new light. They aid, too, in reasoning sensibly and arguing persuasively about the pros and cons of policies proposed to deal with the economic problems of the day.

Richard Lipsey
Colin Harbury
January 1992

PART

1

Introduction

Preface to Part 1

The main Preface, on page xii, explains how this book is divided into five Parts. This, the first Part, is designed to give you a quick 'feel' for the subject by setting out in three chapters (i) the nature of economics, (ii) the main questions that economics seeks to answer, and (iii) how economists study their subject. This Introduction takes you quite deeply into some areas of economics. Do not worry if you do not fully understand all at a first reading. You will meet virtually everything in this Part again somewhere in the rest of the book – often many times. When you have finished the last chapter you will find these early ones seem quite easy, and it will even be helpful to reread them. But make a start – now!

1 The Nature of Economics

Capitalism versus Communism, *alias* free markets *versus* state control, the battle of the centuries appears to be over. Capitalism has won the most resounding victory. Western economies have swept more and more public sectors into the market net since privatization and deregulation became the flavours of the month in Britain and other European countries. Even in the Soviet Union and other nations in the old communist bloc, a swing away from planning to free markets has been heralded as the way out of economic backwardness and low living standards.

How well do markets work? Are they all they have been cracked up to be? Are there worries on the debit side, that the world and the UK might in some ways be worse places if the power of the state continues to decline? Can governments improve market performance?

Will living standards rise faster? Will inflation be more easily controlled? Will unemployment fall? Will pollution and global warming disappear? Will standards of housing, health-care and education rise? Will poverty decline in Britain and in the developing Third World? What will happen to wage differentials? Will sterling appreciate or depreciate against the currencies of the rest of the world? Will the European Community flourish or languish? Will the growing strength of market forces see improvements on these fronts? Or will the pendulum swing back, perhaps, with the state regaining some powers it has currently given up?

These questions carry important implications for all of us. So do others; for instance, what policy instruments are there which can help the government lead a market economy towards wealth and prosperity? They can be sensibly answered only if one first understands *how* markets work. That is partly what this book is about. Of course, you must not expect to find all the answers in one introductory textbook. To be honest, many of the questions are still unsettled, despite long, intensive and careful study by many of the world's greatest thinkers. But even a single introductory book, like this one, should give you real insight, both into the issues involved and into tentative answers to many leading questions of economic policy.

THE BOUNDARIES OF ECONOMICS

Economics is one of a group of subjects known as the social sciences. (Other social sciences include anthropology, social psychology, sociology and political science.) These subjects all deal with how people behave in society. As with any closely related group of subjects, the topics covered by each often overlap. Let us consider a simple example.

Most people know that economics deals with supply and demand. An example is the demand for ice-cream. What determines the number of ice-creams that the public will buy in one particular week in July? Although a complete answer could fill several pages, here are four important determinants.

First, the number of ice-creams people will buy depends on the price of ice-creams; for example, at 30p each the quantity bought will be more than at a price of £1. Second, the number depends on people's incomes; for example, if many people are unemployed and feeling pinched for funds, the number of ice-creams will be less than if they are not. Third, the weather will have a major influence; cold and rainy days will see fewer ice-creams sold than hot and sunny days. Finally, people's tastes will matter; if ice-creams are popular, sales will be larger than if apples are thought to be tastier, and/or better for the health.

The first two determinants listed above, price and income, are explained within the subject of economics. The last two, weather and tastes, are not. Weather is understood – if at all – by meteorologists, and tastes – if at all – by psychologists.

So we now have something that we wish to explain – ice-cream sales – and four possible determinants of those sales – price, income, weather and tastes. How do economists proceed when some of the influences in which they are interested are explained within economics while others lie outside it? Simply, economists seek to explain the factors that lie within their expertise, such as price and income, and they take as given those that do not, such as weather and tastes.

When we say that we take things such as weather and tastes as *given* we mean that, although we are interested in the *effects* of these things on what we are trying to explain, we do not, as economists, try to explain what *causes* them to change. So when we say, for example, that the state of the weather is given, we mean it has a particular state – say, a very warm summer – which we accept without trying to explain why it occurred. We are, however, interested in the question 'what will happen to the demand for ice-cream if the weather changes?', but we do not try to explain *why* such changes in the 'givens' occur.

Some terms to learn

A variable: A VARIABLE is a magnitude that can vary in quantity. It may relate to some aspect of economic behaviour that economists wish to explain, or to one which helps to determine behaviour.

Price is an important economic variable, people's incomes are another. The price of ice-cream, in the example considered earlier, might fall into a range varying between say, 10p and £2.50, while people might have incomes varying between say, £50 and £5000 per week.

Endogenous and exogenous variables: Variables that are explained within the theory we are studying are called ENDOGENOUS VARIABLES, while variables that are taken as given, because they are explained outside the theory (possibly even outside economics), are called EXOGENOUS VARIABLES. To illustrate, recall our example of the price of ice-creams, which is an endogenous variable because it is determined within our economic theory. In contrast, the weather is an exogenous variable. It is not affected, as far as we can tell, by economic conditions. Exogenous variables are important. At times the weather can significantly affect the demand for ice-creams. But the weather is not itself influenced by the price of ice-creams or by any other economic variable.

Economic Issues

One main lesson to be learned from the above discussion of boundaries is that there are few problems whose complete solution lies within economics – or for that matter, within any one social science. For complete explanations of social phenomena, social scientists need to help each other. For example, to explain such 'economic' behaviour as sales of ice-creams more fully, economists need help from specialists in other subjects. Psychologists study how tastes are formed and changed. Sociologists study the influence of such institutions as the family. Social and economic historians help to put contemporary matters and tastes into a longer-term perspective. Many specialists in subjects outside the social sciences may also contribute to the understanding of so-called economic issues – for example, accountants, philosophers, meteorologists, and engineers.

The above discussion helps with the question: what is economics? A useful definition that will serve us well enough for the moment is that 'economics is what economists do'. This will be sufficient, provided we understand that what economists do is to study questions that can be handled with their own expertise.

When all of the jargon and technical apparatus has been stripped away, what economists are really interested in is people's living standards – i.e. in their material well-being. Economists assume that people have certain wants, and they then study how particular societies are organized so as to satisfy people's wants. In doing so they ask such questions as: Is one way of organizing the economy more efficient for satisfying wants than another? Can government intervention improve the society's ability to satisfy wants?

One key aspect of wants is that, for all practical purposes, they are unlimited. Most of us want rising living standards, and most of us would like some goods that we do not now have and more of those that we do have – better living accommodation, more holidays, faster and more comfortable cars, more rock concerts or visits to the theatre, possibly just more or better food; indeed the list is endless. The country's ability to satisfy wants depends on:

- how much is produced
- how many people there are to consume what is produced, and
- how the production is divided up among those who wish to consume it.

The nation's total output measures how much is produced. That output is divided into two broad categories – physical GOODS, such as television sets, handbags and cars, and SERVICES, such as permanent waves, pop festivals and theatrical performances. The word 'goods' is sometimes used loosely to mean both goods and services, which are also termed COMMODITIES.

Total output divided by the number of people available to consume it determines average output per person, which is usually called output per head (or sometimes *per capita output*). It determines the country's *average* standard of living.

How evenly output is divided up determines whether there are great or small divergencies between the amounts going to the 'better-off' and the amounts going to the 'less well-off' members of the population. This concerns the distribution of living standards among the people in society.

FACTORS OF PRODUCTION

The first question in the above list is 'how much is produced?' The answer depends on the quantity of resources available to produce commodities which satisfy wants and on how efficiently the resources are used.

Economists find it useful to divide resources into four categories which they call LAND, LABOUR, CAPITAL, and ENTREPRENEURSHIP. Collectively these are referred to as FACTORS OF PRODUCTION.

Land: Land includes everything commonly called natural resources. It includes the surface of the earth itself, in the condition that nature provided it, and all the other resources provided by nature such as minerals, waterfalls and trees.

The nation's total endowment of land, as we have broadly defined it, is inherited from the past. This inheritance can be used now and/or passed on to the future. Some resources are *non-renewable*. If they are used now, they will not be available in the future. Examples are oil and coal deposits. Other resources are *renewable*. They can be used today and, under appropriate circumstances, can also be used in the future. Examples are forests and fish. The current interest in such issues as conservation and pollution is centred on the *use* of non-renewable resources and the *destruction*, by over-exploitation, of resources that would otherwise be renewable.

Modern production techniques often involve recycling waste products, which can reduce the depletion of natural resources. For example, paper is manufactured from pulp derived from softwood, so that salvaging wastepaper conserves conifer forests; while recycling glass in the bottle banks which we see around us, preserves sand, limestone and salt, as well as energy. (A tonne of glass requires half a tonne of coal or 1000kw of electricity.)

Notice that renewable resources are living things that will reproduce themselves naturally, while non-renewable resources are inanimate things that, once removed, will not reproduce themselves.

Labour: The term 'labour' refers to all human resources that could be used in the production of goods and services. The basic determinant of the amount of the nation's labour is its population. The size of the population is itself determined by three factors: (i) birth rates, (ii) death rates, and (iii) the balance of migration movements into and out of the country.

Of course, the whole population is not available for use in production. First, only people of working age – roughly identified as being between 16 and 65 years old – are currently available as a productive resource. Second, many of those who are of working age choose not to work. This latter group includes, for example, those who stay on at school beyond 16, those who choose to retire early, and those who stay at home to look after their families.

The total number of persons available for work is referred to collectively as the LABOUR FORCE, or the WORKING POPULATION, and the fraction of the total population who are in the labour force defines what is called the ACTIVITY RATE or the PARTICIPATION RATE. For example, about one half of the women between 16 and 25 are in the UK labour force, so the participation rate of that group is about 0.5.

Capital: Capital refers to man-made aids to further production. Factories and equipment are capital. So also are the tools that workers use, as well as equipment such as word-processors and computers used by office staff. Capital is a produced factor of production. Its production requires effort: the pay-off to such effort comes because much more can be produced with capital than without it.

Capital can take either of two forms, fixed or circulating. FIXED CAPITAL provides a stream of services during its lifetime, and comprises mainly plant and equipment. All of a country's stock of factories, warehouses, machine tools and equipment are a part of its fixed capital. CIRCULATING, or WORKING, CAPITAL circulates through the production process. Stocks of raw materials that a firm is waiting to use, all goods in the process of being produced and all stocks of finished goods waiting to be sold are part of a country's circulating capital. For example, a dress manufacturing firm would regard its dress-making machines as fixed capital, while its circulating capital would consist of stocks of partly finished dresses awaiting processing, and of stocks of completed dresses waiting to be sold.

Notice, therefore, that 'fixed' does not necessarily mean capital that is 'bolted to the floor'. It means that equipment can be used over and over again in the production of many units of output. Considering our dress manufacturing firm

again, needles are part of its fixed capital even though they can be moved around in an everyday sense.

The basic meaning of capital is clear enough, but the concept can be a tricky one, as is shown by the following two examples.

First, when resources are used to preserve, or improve, the productivity of land, this is correctly regarded as increasing the quantity of capital rather than that of land. When resources are used in education to improve the productivity of labour, this is also correctly regarded as increasing the amount of the nation's capital. Such capital is so important that a special term, HUMAN CAPITAL, is used to describe it. This refers to the skills that labour acquires through education and training (both on and off the job) as opposed to abilities that are inherited.

Second, in ordinary speech, people refer to money as capital. A widow with £1 million in the bank might refer to that sum as her 'capital'. In economics, however, capital refers to the *real* assets (factories etc.) and the skills that exist to aid further production. It does not refer to sums of money, although it is often convenient to value capital assets in money terms.

Entrepreneurship: There is one special kind of human activity that is close to, but different from, management. Managers are employees, though usually well-paid ones. Therefore, management is a part of labour as defined above. In a well-established firm where years of experience in producing and selling some standard product, such as saucepans, have been acquired, managers may have little more to do than supervise routine tasks. When a new venture is being contemplated, however, risks arise. They involve the unknown future. Will a new product appeal to consumers? Can it be effectively marketed? Will its costs of production turn out to be as predicted? And so on.

Someone must assess these risks and make judgements about whether or not to undertake them. The people who do so are called ENTREPRENEURS, and the factor of production is known as ENTREPRENEURSHIP (or, sometimes, as ENTERPRISE).

Often in the past, and sometimes today, colourful individuals, as Henry Ford and Richard Branson, initiate new products or new ways of producing old ones. Today, much effort goes into the research and development (R&D) that lies behind new products and new processes, much of which is called 'knowledge-intensive'. Many of these increasingly important entrepreneurial functions are carried out by the staff of large corporations such as IBM, Sony, and General Electric. Indeed, most firms selling consumers' goods are in constant competition to make new and better products, called *product innovation*. Most large manufacturing businesses compete to find better and lower-cost methods, called *process innovation*.

Factor services

So far we have talked about the factors of production themselves – land, labour, capital and entrepreneurship. Each of these factors is owned by someone, though workers are, of course, owned by themselves (unless slavery exists).

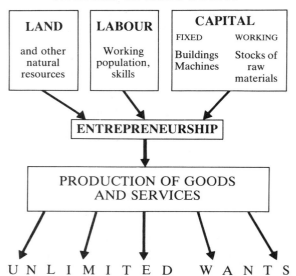

FIGURE 1.1 **Factors of Production.** Land, labour and capital are combined by entrepreneurs to produce goods and services that satisfy some of our unlimited wants.

The owners of factors provide the services of factors to businesses. Workers, for example, provide work effort to the firm that hires them; they do not sell themselves. Landowners provide the services of their land to tenant farmers (or to themselves if they farm their own land). For this reason we speak of *factor services* being sold on markets. These services are sold *by* those who own the factors *to* those that wish to use them in production.

Figure 1.1 summarizes our discussion of the four factors of production and shows how they may be used to produce goods and services that go to satisfy some of the unlimited wants of consumers.

RESOURCE ALLOCATION

What is often called 'the central economic problem' is the allocation of resources to satisfy human wants. The problem exists because of three characteristics of our society:

- Wants are, for all practical purposes, unlimited.
- The resources (land, labour and capital) that are available to produce goods and services to satisfy those wants are limited.
- Most resources have alternative uses: for example, land can be used to grow wheat, rye or barley, or as a site for a factory, or for a block of flats; labour can be employed on a farm, or in a factory, or in a pop band, and so on.

The first two of the above characteristics give rise to the basic economic problem of SCARCITY: there are not enough resources to satisfy all of the people's wants for consuming all goods and services. Scarcity, in conjunction

with the third characteristic noted above, gives rise to the basic need for CHOICE: how are resources to be allocated among their competing uses? How much labour, for example, should go into producing wheat, how much to eggs, how much to assembly-line work, and how much to recording pop music on compact discs?

The central 'economic problem' is often defined as the allocation of scarce resources among competing uses for the satisfaction of consumers' wants.

Opportunity Cost

A sacrifice is involved in choosing to use scarce resources to produce one commodity *rather than another* – for example, certain amounts of land, labour and capital that could have made 20 pocket calculators might be used to make one word-processor. The sacrifice in making the word-processor would then be 20 pocket calculators. Consider a second example. We might plant more tomatoes in our kitchen garden, cutting back on runner beans to create the needed space. The sacrifice is then of runner beans. Or, to put it another way, we *trade off* runner beans for, say, tomatoes. Note, that we cannot avoid this choice by deciding to have more tomatoes *and* more runner beans. Our kitchen garden has limited space that is already fully used. So the decision to grow more tomatoes implies a decision to grow less of something else, and that reduction in the output of the 'something else' can be regarded as the cost of the extra tomatoes.

To capture this basic idea of choice, economists use the concept of OPPORTUNITY COST (sometimes called economic cost or real cost), which measures the cost of something that one attains measured in terms of the sacrifice of the next best alternative.

Thus, in our kitchen garden, the opportunity cost of tomatoes is measured in terms of the runner beans that we could have grown instead. In precise terms, the opportunity cost of a pound of tomatoes might be $\frac{3}{4}$ of a pound of runner beans. In our other example, the opportunity cost of a word-processor was 20 pocket calculators.

Measuring opportunity cost

Notice two important things about opportunity cost.

First, opportunity cost is measured in physical, not monetary, units. Indeed, it is sometimes called *real* opportunity cost to distinguish it from money cost. For example, you might ask what is the cost of one more personal computer. To be told that it is £500 is not revealing unless you know what else £500 would purchase. Of course, we state costs in money terms constantly, but this is meaningful only because we know other prices and hence can make real, opportunity cost comparisons implicitly, as soon as we hear a money price. Thus, if you feel £25,000 is a high cost for a particular car, it is because you know other prices and realise that to spend £25,000 on the car would imply the sacrifice of what you might otherwise have bought with the £25,000.

BOX 1.1 Closure of Rail Crossings Expected after Three Die

'British Rail is likely to increase its attempts to close many of the 2000 unmanned railway footpath crossings after a woman and two children were killed by a high speed train ... Attempts by BR to close footpath crossings, often a public right of way protected by law, have met with determined resistance from ramblers' groups and local authorities ... but the accident on Tuesday night seems certain to lead to a renewed campaign to phase out many of the crossings ... Providing footbridges instead would be highly expensive; in the case of Potteric Carr, near Doncaster, where the accident happened, it would cost between £250,000 and £500,000.

'The deaths occurred on Tuesday as Janet S ... was returning with her children, Daniel, 4, and David, 6, and a friend Emma, 7, from Potteric Carr nature reserve near their homes.'

(*The Times*, 21 June 1990)

This news item provides a dramatic illustration of the fundamental scarcity of resources and the nature of opportunity cost. The alternatives which are sacrificed when resources are used in any particular way always deserve consideration. Here, replacing unmanned rail crossings with footbridges would involve sacrificing other goods and services which could have been produced instead.

Questions

1 What relevance, if any, has the cost of construction of the footbridge to the question of whether or not it should be built?
2 What limit is there, if any, to the amount of resources that are justified to save a human life?

Second, notice that opportunity cost normally involves giving up some positive amount of one commodity in order to get more of another. We therefore describe this cost as being *positive*.

Can opportunity cost ever be zero?

Opportunity cost is, as we have said, positive with economic goods. Normally, the production of one commodity necessitates giving up some positive amount of some other commodity. There are, however, three important exceptions:

- Free goods
- Single-use factors
- General unemployment

Free goods: There are a very few things that nature provides in such abundance that no opportunity cost is involved in their use. In many rural areas, wild fruit grows on moors and in hedgerows. The fruit is there for the picking. Since it does not grow on cultivated land that could be used for other purposes, its 'production' by nature implies no sacrifice of alternative crops (though the actual picking does involve opportunity cost: if I spend time picking fruit, I give up watching television, for example). Oxygen is another example. There is no real cost in breathing it, for (at least at present) there is more than enough for everyone to breathe with plenty left over for the filling of oxygen cylinders.

Note, however, that a good may be free at one time, but not free at another. For example, fresh drinking water was once a free good but is now costly to produce in most areas; oxygen, now a free good, may cease to be one if depletion of the world's forests reduces the natural production of oxygen so much that we have to use scarce resources to produce it artificially.

Single-use factors: Positive opportunity costs occur when resources have alternative uses. Where such alternatives do not exist, there is no opportunity cost. For example, a scenic site in the Scottish highlands may have only one use. It is either used for the enjoyment of sightseers, or it is not used at all.

Such examples are most often encountered with capital equipment, which does often have only one use. For example, a hydroelectric plant can produce electricity and nothing else; a coalmine produces coal or is left idle; a road tunnel through the Alps is used to allow cars and lorries to get from one side of the mountain to the other, or it is not used at all. Resources that have only a single use are said to be *product specific*; they are specific to the production of the product in question and not useful for anything else. Thus a dam is specific to the production of electricity, a coalmine to the production of coal, and a road tunnel to the production of transportation services. The resources that were used to build the specific capital had alternative uses *in the past* but, once the capital has been constructed, it has none.

General unemployment: Opportunity cost exists because factors of production have alternative uses. If a factor is used to produce one good, it cannot be used to produce another. Thus, if factors which were used to build schools are now used to build hospitals, the opportunity cost can be measured as so many schools forgone per hospital built. For much of the last 50 years, something close to full employment has existed. In these circumstances, opportunity cost certainly was positive: producing more of one thing required taking resources away from producing something else. At times, however, there are unemployed supplies of all resources and, at such times, opportunity cost may, strictly, be zero. If, for example, there are unemployed building labourers, cranes, bricks and mortar, and everything needed in the building trade, it may be possible to build more hospitals without having to build fewer schools – or fewer of *anything* else.

Such situations of zero opportunity cost occur only during periods of *general* unemployment of *all* resources. Note the condition that there be unemployment of *all* relevant factors. If there is unemployed labour, but no unemployed equipment, then the decision to produce more hospitals would not require that labour be taken from any other job (since the unemployed could be put to work), but it would require that the equipment be moved from some other use. Production would, then, have to fall in the use from which the equipment was withdrawn. Thus, positive opportunity cost requires that there be full employment of at least one, but not necessarily all, of the factors of production needed to make the commodity whose output is to rise.

In the first half of this book we shall assume that the unemployment situation is such that opportunity cost is positive. There are two reasons why we do so. First, full employment of at least some resources may exist, as it often has in the past. Even when the general level of unemployment in the labour force has been high, there have been shortages of labour with special skills or in some parts of the country. Second, the government may decide, as a matter of policy, to maintain a certain level of unemployment of resources. (This could be part of its macroeconomic policy, to be discussed in Parts 4 and 5 of this book.) If so, the resources needed to produce more of something will have to be drawn from other lines of employment. Opportunity cost will then, in effect, be positive in spite of the existence of unemployed resources.

Production Possibility Curves

We are now going to illustrate our discussion using a graph. Graphs are used extensively in elementary economics, both to display information and, more importantly, as a reasoning device. A facility with graphs is, thus, a necessity for any student of economics. Since we know that some of you will have had trouble with geometry, and possibly not learned as much of it as you were supposed to, we have prepared an Appendix telling you what you need to know about the use of graphs in order to read this book. This Appendix starts on page 504. Everyone should look at it by way of revision, but those who find they do not already know some of the material in the Appendix must study it with care.

Several aspects of the important concept of opportunity cost can be illustrated with the aid of a graph. In Figure 1.2 we show the way in which resources can be deployed in an ultra-simple economy, one in which the nation is capable of producing only two goods, jeans and kebabs, abbreviated to *j* and *k*.

On the vertical axis we measure the number of kebabs produced. On the horizontal axis we measure the number of jeans. We shall soon portray on the graph all the combinations of jeans and kebabs that the economy is capable of producing when all of its resources are fully employed in the most efficient manner.

Suppose that the possible combinations of output are those listed in Table 1.1. This Table tells us that, when all of the nation's resources are devoted to kebab production,

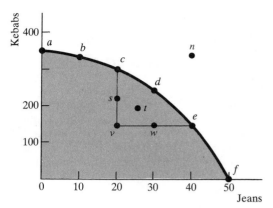

FIGURE 1.2 A Production Possibility Curve (ppc). This curve shows all combinations of commodities that are just attainable when all resources are fully and efficiently employed, e.g. those at points *a*, *b*, *c*, *d*, *e* and *f*. All combinations within the shaded area, such as *t* and *v*, are also attainable but inefficient; those to the right and above the curve, e.g. at *n*, are unattainable. All combinations within the area *vce* are greater than at *v*.

the maximum total output is 350*k*. It also tells us that, when all resources go to jean production, output is 50*j*. These two points appear on the graph and are labelled *a* and *f*. They lie on the two axes.

TABLE 1.1 Alternative Production Combinations

Kebabs	Jeans	Reference letter
350	0	a
330	10	b
300	20	c
250	30	d
150	40	e
0	50	f

Next we plot the intermediate points corresponding to the other four combinations of outputs shown in the Table. In these cases, factors of production are used to produce some of both goods. These points are the *combinations* (*b*) 330*k* and 10*j*, (*c*) 300*k* and 20*j*, (*d*) 250*k* and 30*j*, and (*e*) 150*k* and 40*j*.

We then join the points we have just plotted with a line called a PRODUCTION POSSIBILITY CURVE. It describes all the possible combinations of jeans and kebabs that the economy is capable of producing, using all resources with maximum efficiency. Note the use of the word 'efficiency'. To be on the curve it is not enough that all resources be used, they must be used as efficiently as possible. Note also that the curve slopes downwards because of the underlying scarcity of resources – having more of one good *necessitates* having less of another.[1]

1 The slope of a curve is usually described as *positive* when the variables on the two axes move in the same direction, or *negative* when they move in opposite directions. Economists often read graphs from left to right and hence describe positive, and negative, curves as upward, and downward, sloping, respectively.

Some terms to note

In the above section, we introduced some important terms. We pause now to say a little more about each of these.

Combinations: First, note the use of the word 'combinations'. Whenever economists refer to quantities of two or more commodities, such as 30 pairs of jeans *and* 250 kebabs, they speak of COMBINATIONS, or BUNDLES, or BASKETS of commodities. Thus one bundle of commodities might be 20 units of food and 40 units of clothing, while another combination might be 30 units of food and 10 units of clothing.

The production possibility curve: Second, note the various terms used to describe the line drawn in Figure 1.2. We have called it a 'production possibility curve'. In practice, a bewildering number of terms is used to describe this simple construction. Look first at the last word that we use. We use the term 'curve'. We might also have said 'boundary'. Both of these words can be used to indicate the line or curve shown on the diagram.

The term 'boundary' emphasizes that the points on the curve are maximum points. It is always possible to produce at points *within* the curve by not employing some factors of production, or by using them inefficiently. (We shall investigate this possibility in more detail below.)

Now look at the first part of the term. We have used the words 'production possibility', but the term 'transformation' is also used. The idea behind the term transformation is that you can, in effect, 'transform' one commodity into another by moving resources from the production of one commodity into the production of the other. The idea of transforming one commodity into another stresses the idea of opportunity cost.

You can make up six terms by combining the words listed below. All six terms mean the same thing:

	Curve
Production Possibility	
	Boundary
Transformation	
	Frontier

We shall also use the abbreviation ppc.

Aspects of production possibilities

Figure 1.2 can be used to illustrate some important features of the economy's production possibilities. We shall look at four of these: inefficient output combinations, unattainable combinations, the representation of opportunity cost, and the representation of changes in the country's production possibilities.

Inefficient output combinations: While it is possible to produce combinations shown by points *on* the curve, it is also possible to produce combinations shown by points *inside* the curve (i.e. in the shaded part of Figure 1.2). Such points would indicate less of both goods than can be produced at some points on the curve. Production inside

the curve occurs if one or more factors of production are either being used inefficiently or are not being used at all (i.e. unemployed labour, idle machines, or half-used factories).

Consider, for example, point *v* in Figure 1.2, representing the output combination 150*k* and 20*j*. It is clearly possible to produce more jeans or kebabs without having less of the other good. To see this on the diagram, draw lines from point *v* horizontally and vertically to meet the production possibility curve at *c* and *e*. This defines the area *vce* enclosing all combinations which are greater than that at *v*, either in jean production (e.g. points *w* and *e*), in kebab production (e.g. points *s* and *c*), or in both jean and kebab production (e.g. points *t* and *d*).

Unattainable output combinations: All output combinations represented by points lying outside the shaded portion of Figure 1.2 are unattainable. Society's resources are insufficient to allow, for example, the production of 350*k* and 40*j*, indicated by point *n* in Figure 1.2. If 350 kebabs are produced, there are no resources free to make jeans; while if 40 jeans are produced, there are only enough resources to make 150 kebabs.

The graphical representation of opportunity cost

The opportunity cost of changing output can be represented on the production possibility boundary. To see what is involved, we reproduce the curve of Figure 1.2 in Figure 1.3. Suppose the economy is producing only kebabs, i.e. is at point *a* on its production possibility curve. Output is 350*k*. We then decide to produce 10 jeans. What is the opportunity cost, in terms of kebabs given up, of making this change? From the Table we know that kebab output

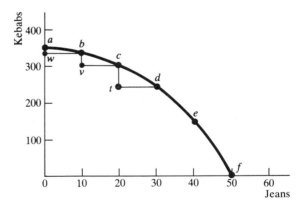

FIGURE 1.3 The Representation of Opportunity Cost. Moving along the production possibility curve (ppc) indicates how much of one good must be given up to obtain quantities of the other, e.g. moving from *b* to *c* involves sacrificing *bv* kebabs in order to produce *vc* extra jeans.

When the ppc is, as here, bowed out from the origin, marginal opportunity cost rises as output increases (e.g. as jeans output rises by equal amounts, from *a* to *b* to *c* to *d* on the ppc, quantities of kebabs sacrificed increase: *aw* < *bv* < *ct*).[1]

---

1 The mathematical symbols > and < stand for 'greater than' and 'less than', respectively.

must fall from 350k to 330k. So the opportunity cost of the extra 10 jeans is 20 kebabs: 10 more jeans *cost* – i.e. require the sacrifice of – 20 kebabs. If we want to find the opportunity cost *per pair of jeans*, we need to divide the 20 'lost' kebabs by 10 – the number of jeans 'gained'. This gives us the opportunity cost of each additional pair of jeans, i.e. 2 kebabs.

The graphical expression of the opportunity cost of the first 10 jeans produced is simply the vertical drop in kebab production of 20k. As we move from a to b on the production possibility curve in Figure 1.3, this drop is the distance aw, which we can read off the vertical axis as equal to 20k. If we increase jean production further and so move downwards further along the curve to point c, we produce another 10 jeans. The opportunity cost of these extra jeans is the reduction in output of kebabs from 330k to 300k. This is again given by the vertical distance, which is bv or 30 kebabs.

There are two important points to be noted about the conclusions we have reached on the measurement of opportunity cost.

- The first is to learn a new term which economists use to describe the change in cost that occurs when output changes by a single unit. It is MARGINAL COST. We shall use this term extensively later (see page 144 for a fuller explanation). But we can begin to use the new term, marginal cost, immediately to describe changes in opportunity costs. For example, as jeans output rises from 0 to 10 (as explained above), the opportunity cost of 10 jeans is 20 kebabs. The cost of each of the 10 units of jeans is one tenth of the 20 kebabs given up. Hence, we may describe the marginal cost of a unit of jeans as 20/10 kebabs, ie 1j=2k.
- The second observation relates to the relationship between the *shape* of the production possibility curve and the behaviour of marginal opportunity cost. The curve in Figures 1.2 and 1.3 are 'bowed out' from the origin of the graph. Such curves depict marginal opportunity cost rising with increasing output. For example, as jeans output grows from 0 to 10, to 20, to 30 and to 40, the quantity of kebabs that must be sacrificed grows progressively from aw to bv, to ct, and so on.

Rising costs are quite a normal phenomenon, though we shall have to wait until Chapter 14 before we offer a satisfactory explanation for it. We can, however, provide a contrasting case, that of constant marginal opportunity costs, which occurs whenever the production possibility curve is a straight line (*linear*, to use mathematical jargon).

Straight-line production possibility curves: Consider Table 1.2 and Figure 1.4, which depicts the corresponding production possibility curve as a graph. If we repeat the exercise of describing marginal opportunity cost by increasing the output of jeans from 0 to 10, to 20, to 30 and to 40, we find that the quantity of kebabs that must be given up does not rise, but is constant, at 10. In the Figure, $ah = bk = cm = dn$. This constancy arises from the fact that the production frontier is linear. *Marginal*

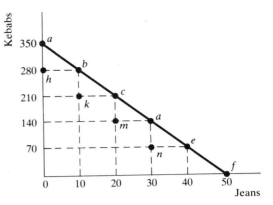

FIGURE 1.4 A Production Possibility Curve where Opportunity Costs are Constant. When the ppc is a straight line, marginal opportunity cost is constant. As jeans output rises by equal amounts, from a to b to c to d on the ppc, quantities of kebabs sacrificed do not alter: $ah = bk = cm$.

opportunity costs do not vary as output changes on a straight-line production possibility curve.[1]

TABLE 1.2 Alternative Production Combinations when Marginal Cost is Constant

Kebabs	Jeans	Reference letter
350	0	a
280	10	b
210	20	c
140	30	d
70	40	e
0	50	f

Shifts in the production possibility curve: Changes in the efficient allocation of resources are represented by *movements along* the production possibility boundary; e.g. from point b to point c in Figures 1.2 or 1.3.

A production possibility curve is drawn to represent the situation that exists at a particular point in time. If anything happens to alter production possibilities, this will cause the whole ppc to *shift*. Changes in the productive capacity of the economy may be caused by rises (or falls) in the supplies of factors of production, or by changes in their productivity. An increase in productive capacity, which allows more of both commodities to be produced, pushes the ppc outwards (i.e. upwards and to the right). An example is shown by the shift from af to $a'f'$ in Figure 1.5. Some things that could cause such a shift are a rise in the size of the working population, in the amount of capital, in labour productivity, or technological advance.

1 There is a third case which, for the time being, must stay as a footnote – the case of decreasing costs (see pages 147–8), where the production possibility curve is bowed inwards, as in the accompanying diagram.

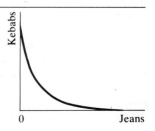

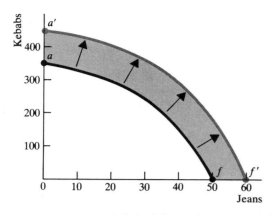

FIGURE 1.5 An Outward Shift of the Production Possibility Curve. An increase in productive capacity makes it possible to produce more of both goods. It is represented by a shift in the ppc from *af* to *a'f'*. All the output combinations inside the area *Oaf*, which were previously unattainable, are now attainable.

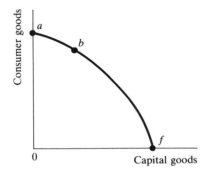

FIGURE 1.6 A Production Possibility Curve Showing a Choice between Consumer Goods and Capital Goods. The point chosen *now* on this ppc will affect the position of the ppc *in the future*. If the economy chooses combination *b* rather than *a*, this will tend to shift the ppc outwards, as in Figure 1.5.

As we have seen, increases in the total resources available to an economy are often associated with investment in capital goods which aid future production. A choice has, therefore, to be made between the production of capital goods and that of consumer goods. The choice is similar, in principle, to that between different consumer goods, such as jeans and kebabs. Figure 1.6, for example, depicts the choice facing an economy between devoting resources to capital goods or to consumer goods for immediate use.

Note, however, the important implications of this decision for the position of the production possibility curve, later. If the economy chooses, say, position *a*, where all resources are used for current consumption, the ppc will not move. If, in contrast, resource allocation is at *b*, output potential will rise and, when the new capital is ready for use, the production boundary will shift outwards, as in Figure 1.5. Indeed, so long as the extra capital lasts, the further to the right along this ppc the economy settles, the larger the outward shift is likely to be.

Rising productivity is the most common experience in modern economic systems. However, declining pro-

ductivity is also sometimes met. If it is, then the production possibility curve would shift inwards (i.e. downwards and to the left) – in Figure 1.5 *from a'f'* (if that were its starting position) *to af*. Some things that could cause such a shift are a fall in the size of the population, a drop in worker efficiency or the depletion of a non-renewable resource, such as oil.

The new curve *a'f'* in Figure 1.5 was drawn in a particular way. It showed a change in productive capacity of the economy that is proportionately the same for the outputs of both jeans and kebabs; i.e. if *j* output rises by 10 per cent, *k* output rises by 10 per cent as well. This is not, however, always the case. Changes often affect productivity relatively more in the production of one commodity than another.

Suppose, for example, a new machine were introduced which raised productivity in the jean industry. There is no reason to suppose that it would also affect productivity in the kebab industry. In such a case the new production possibility curve would not be parallel to the old curve. Both would start from exactly the same point, *a*, on the kebab axis. But the new curve would be to the right of the old one at every other point, as is shown by the curve *af''* in Figure 1.7. Notice that it is now possible to have more

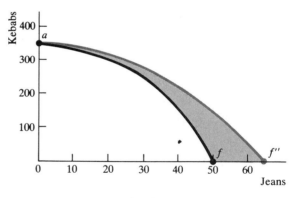

FIGURE 1.7 A Shift in the Production Possibility Curve when Productivity Change is Limited to One Industry. Productivity rises only in jean production, thereby shifting the ppc from *af* to *af''*. If all resources are devoted to kebabs, no more kebabs can be produced. But if *some* jeans are produced, more of both goods becomes possible – all output combinations inside the area *Oaf*, previously unattainable, are now attainable.

kebabs, as well as more jeans, even though productivity has not increased in the kebab industry. The reason is that the increase in productivity in jeans production, means that any given quantity of jeans can be produced with fewer resources. If some of the resources that are no longer required to make the original output of jeans are devoted to making more jeans and some to making more kebabs, output of both commodities can be increased. Only in the case of zero jeans output is there no benefit from the rise in productivity in jeans production.

THREE BASIC ECONOMIC QUESTIONS

Earlier in this chapter we said that economics was about what determines people's living standards. We can now take our study of the determinants of living standards a step further by asking three key questions that relate to how the economy does determine these living standards.

Question 1: Will the economy use its resources so that production is, in a sense, at a maximum in that it takes place somewhere on, rather than inside, the production possibility curve? This question entails two separate considerations – (1) will all resources be fully employed? and (2) will factors of production be used efficiently?

The issue of full employment will be dealt with in the second half of this book. Here, we concentrate on the second question. It involves efficiency in choice of techniques. As a rule there are several alternative ways of producing a certain output – for example, using different, relative amounts of land, labour and capital in agriculture. Choosing any technique other than the best will result in production inside the production possibility curve rather than on the frontier.

Question 2: Which of the combinations of outputs represented by all the points on the production possibility curve is to be selected? Choosing one particular point means producing one particular bundle and this, in turn, implies one particular allocation of resources among their competing uses. Choosing another point means producing another bundle of goods which, in turn, implies another allocation of resources.

Question 3: How are the chosen outputs to be divided among all the members of society? This question involves consideration of the distribution of income among the nation's inhabitants.

Our discussion of the concept of opportunity cost and the production possibility curve makes it natural to ask these questions in the order listed above. An alternative order allows us to restate the three basic questions of economics as follows:

What to produce? (question 2)
How to produce it? (question 1)
For whom is output produced? (question 3)

We shall use this order in the next chapter.

Summary

1 Economics is one of a group of subjects known as the social sciences which study the behaviour of human beings in society.

2 Economists seek to explain the behaviour of variables such as prices and incomes which lie within their expertise, and which are called endogenous variables. They take as 'given', variables such as the weather and tastes, whose explanation is outside their field of study, and which are called exogenous variables.

3 A nation's resources, its factors of production, fall into three main groups: land, labour and capital. Land includes everything commonly called natural resources; labour refers to human resources; and capital refers to man-made aids to production. A fourth factor, entrepreneurship, referring to the undertaking of business risks, is also sometimes distinguished.

4 What is often called the central economic problem is the allocation of resources to satisfy human wants. It arises from the scarcity of factors of production, which have alternative uses. Since resources are limited and wants are infinite, choices have to be made on how to allocate the scarce resources.

5 The opportunity cost of producing a commodity is the sacrifice involved in NOT using the required resources in the next best alternative line of production.

6 Opportunity cost is normally positive. It may, however, be zero in three special cases: (i) where there is abundant supply in nature, (ii) where a factor of production has only a single use, and (iii) where there is general unemployment.

7 The production possibility curve is a graphical expression of all combinations of goods and services that can be produced when all resources are fully and efficiently employed.

8 The slope of a production possibility curve reflects the opportunity costs which are incurred when output changes.

9 The production possibility curve is a straight line when marginal costs are constant. It is bowed out from the origin (as in Figure 1.3) when marginal costs rise as output increases.

10 Three basic economic problems are:
- What assortment of goods and services should be produced?
- How should the economy ensure that the techniques it uses in production are efficient in the sense that it operates on, rather than inside, the production posssibility curve?
- For whom should output be produced?

Questions

(For answers see page 517.)

1 All except one of the following would be classed as capital. Which is the exception?
  (a) factories producing nuclear missiles
  (b) stocks of shirts and skirts at Marks & Spencers
  (c) risk-taking entrepreneurs
  (d) secretarial skills acquired by a course in typing

2 Is the following statement True or False?
  'Should a time arrive when there are enough resources to produce all the food and housing, and as many cars, items of clothing and durable household goods as people would like to have, there will be no more economic problems.'

3 Which One or More of the following statements are correct?
  (a) An exogenous variable is one which is not explained within an economic theory.
  (b) Variables whose effects are studied in economics are endogenous variables.
  (c) Resources of an economy are known as factors of production.
  (d) If the activity rate in a country is 0·25, then every fourth adult of working age is unemployed.

4 Refer to Figure 1.2. Which One or More of the following combinations is the economy *in*capable of producing?
  (a) $25j + 300k$, (b) $100k + 50j$, (c) $200k + 30j$.

5 If the economy is at point t in Figure 1.3, which One or More of the following statements is/are correct?
  (a) At least one factor of production must be unemployed.
  (b) More j *or* more k could be produced, but not more of *both* j and k.
  (c) Factors of production must be inefficiently used.
  (d) More of j is possible at zero opportunity cost.
  (e) All of the above are correct.

6 Refer to Figures 1.3 and 1.4 (and Tables 1.1 and 1.2). In which of the two is the opportunity cost of increasing jeans production from 10 to 20 greater, and by how much?

2 Basic Questions and Answers

In the previous chapter we listed three of the basic questions of economics – what?, how?, and for whom?. Just by looking around we can see examples of these questions every day.

THE THREE QUESTIONS IN EVERYDAY LIFE

What to produce?

Travel to your nearest shopping area and you will see an enormous variety of goods and services available for purchase. Breakfast cereals are sold (and hence must be produced) in a wide variety of types and in very large quantities, while herrings are sold (and hence must be produced) in fewer varieties and in smaller quantities. Many shops offer to style your hair, while only a few offer to repair your shoes.

Now ask your grandparents what they would have noticed if they had also been making similar observations? First, they would tell you that, when they were young there were no supermarkets and, in the grocery stores of their day, they would not have found the current vast array of prepared breakfast foods – but they would have found herrings. Also there were, they would tell you, far fewer hairdressing establishments and far more shoe repair shops then than now.

These observations, and a myriad others like them, illustrate the WHAT question: What goods and services are to be produced and in what quantities?

How to produce it?

Read any newspaper or visit any factory town and you will hear of factories closing and, in some towns at least, of new factories being built. The new ones will almost always use production techniques that differ from those in factories about to close.

Talk to the careers officer at any school. You will quickly learn that the skills required of school leavers change dramatically from decade to decade. Before the invention of the computer and the desk calculator, the ability to add long columns of figures rapidly and accurately, and to write clearly, was essential for an office worker (who in the words of W.S.Gilbert could 'rise to the top of the tree' merely by 'copying all the letters in a hand so free'). With the invention of the typewriter and the desk calculator came a need for different skills. No one then gained rapid promotion for penmanship or for prodigious feats of dreary calculations which the new machines could do faster and more accurately than people. Today, with the advent of the word processor and the computer, an ability to communicate with the computer in its own language is becoming more important for office staff than are the more conventional office skills.

These observations illustrate our economy giving changing answers to the HOW question: By what method is the nation's output of goods and services to be produced?

For whom is output produced? (Who gets it?)

Now walk around your home town and see some people living in large houses and others in small ones; some people driving large new cars, others small old ones and yet others walking; some people buying the expensive luxuries on supermarket shelves, others confining their purchases to bread-and-butter items; some people taking skiing holidays in Switzerland as well as Mediterranean cruises in the summer, while others make do with a whizz down the hill of the local heath, if snow comes in winter, and with staying at home to tend to the garden during the summer.

If you had made the same observations at the beginning of the century, you would still have seen different expenditure patterns for different income groups. You would have observed, however, much larger differences between the amounts of money spent by skilled and unskilled workers and between factory managers and foremen than you would today.

In all of these observations we see the economy dealing with the WHO question: Who receives larger and who receives smaller proportions of the economy's total production (i.e. how is that production distributed among the population)?

Notice that the set of observations just given, highlights people's tastes as well as their incomes. On the one hand, while a rich person can take many expensive holidays abroad, which many do, some others choose not to because they do not like foreign travel. On the other hand, while poorer persons find foreign holidays stretching their meagre means, some like foreign travel so much that they stint on other lines of expenditure in order to be able to afford an occasional trip abroad. Thus, while the market economy determines people's purchasing power – by determining their incomes – it leaves everyone free to spend the income that they do receive according to their own tastes and, hence, to decide on the 'bundle' of goods that will best satisfy their own wants.

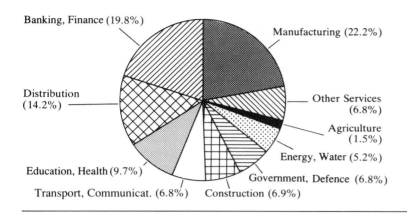

FIGURE 2.1 What is Produced? Many commodities may be produced with the resources available. The allocation of resources among alternative uses in the UK, 1989. (*Source*: *UK National Accounts*, 1990, HMSO)

Aggregate observations

When we look around us, as we have just imagined doing, we see illustrative details of how our economy provides answers to the three basic questions. We can also see how these questions are answered by examining economic data. Figure 2.1 relates to question 1, what is produced? It shows the current allocation of resources in the UK, i.e. about 22 per cent of total output consists of manufactured goods, 20 per cent is of financial services, 10 per cent is of education and health, and so on, as shown in the Figure. Finer breakdowns are available so that we could show, for example, how resources were allocated to produce outputs of many dozens of different groups within the manufacturing sector.

Part of the answer to question 2 'How is it produced?' is illustrated in Figure 2.2. It shows for some major British industries the proportions of total expenditure accounted for by capital and by labour. We can see from the diagram

that the relative amounts of capital and labour used vary greatly from one industry to another. Among the industries included in the Figure, energy and chemicals use relatively large amounts of capital and are said to be highly *capital-intensive*, whereas construction and textiles, at the opposite end of the scale, are more *labour-intensive*.

Figure 2.3 helps to answer question 3: 'For whom is output produced?' This diagram shows the percentage shares of total household income received by each of the five 'quintile' groups (a quintile means a fifth). Thus, we see that the richest 20 per cent of households received about half of total income, while the poorest 20 per cent of households received only just over 2 per cent. Note, these are *gross*, pre-tax, incomes, which also exclude sums provided by the state, such as retirement pensions, unemployment benefit and social security payments to the poor. We consider the distribution of *net* incomes after these matters are taken into account in Chapter 21.

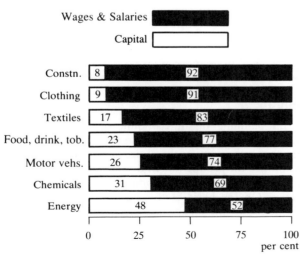

FIGURE 2.2 How to Produce? Factors of production can be combined in many ways to produce different commodities. The relative importance of capital and labour in certain industries in the UK, 1988. (*Source*: Census of Production, 1988 (*Business Monitor*, PA 1002, 1990, HMSO))

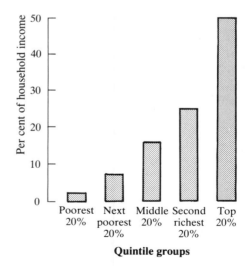

FIGURE 2.3 For Whom is Output Produced? The nation's output can be distributed among the population in many ways. The distribution of income among households in the UK, 1987: percentage shares of total income received by quintile groups (a quintile is a fifth). (*Source*: *Economic Trends*, 1990, HMSO)

Coverage of the three questions

Virtually all of the basic issues that concern economists are covered by the three questions we have just illustrated. This may not, however, always be obvious. 'Where', for example, you might ask, 'does unemployment fit in?'

It comes under question 1. Other things being equal, the higher unemployment is, the lower will be the nation's total output of goods and services.

'Well, then, what about economic growth – isn't it ignored?' Growth raises aspects of all three questions! Economic growth usually involves an increased total output of goods and services, changes in the methods of production, and changes in the distribution of income (since there are almost always winners and losers from the process of growth).

ECONOMIC SYSTEMS

An economic system is a distinctive method of providing answers to the three basic economic questions.

In its entirety, each country's economic system is a very complex engine. It includes laws – such as those relating to the ownership of property – rules, regulations, taxes and subsidies, and everything that governments use to influence what is produced, how it is produced, and who gets it. It includes firms, both large and small, both publicly and privately owned, those that are owned or controlled by residents of a country and by foreigners. It includes consumers of every sort, both young and old, both rich and poor, and both working and non-working. It also includes customs of every conceivable kind, and the entire range of contemporary mores and values.

Social organization is a particularly important part of any economic system because it can influence the use of resources. Three aspects need to be distinguished. One relates to *ownership*, the second to *control*, and the third to the *objectives* of those who do exercise control.

Consider, for example, the factor of production, land. Its *ownership* may be in the hands of the state or of private individuals. In the latter case, there may be a few large landowners, numerous small peasant farmers, or anything in between. *Control* of the current uses of land may lie with the owners or be devolved onto tenant farmers. *Objectives* (often called *goals*) of those who have control over the land may vary enormously. Some people may be very money-conscious and cultivate crops that yield the largest return. Others may grow mainly for their own consumption. Some may go for immediate return at the expense of the long-term fertility of the land, while others may be concerned to preserve its productivity.

So, the idea of an economic system encompasses many different institutional arrangements and behaviour patterns. It is helpful, however, to suppress many of the details of particular systems in order to distinguish three major types, called *traditional*, *command*, and *market*.

Traditional Economic Systems

A *traditional economic system* is one in which behaviour is based on tradition, custom and habit. The characteristics of traditional systems are fairly obvious. Young men follow their fathers in choice of occupation: hunting, fishing, fighting, etc. There is little change in the pattern of goods produced from year to year, other than those imposed by the vagaries of nature. The techniques of production also follow traditional patterns, except when the effects of an occasional new invention are felt. Finally, production is distributed according to long-established traditions of hierarchy, or communality. The answers to the economic questions of what to produce? how to produce it? and how to distribute it? are based on tradition.

Such a system works best in an unchanging environment. Prehistoric studies show that the systems did change, but only occasionally, and usually only when large external shocks made some form of adaptation unavoidable. A climatic change, the introduction of a new crop, or the invention of a new tool, are obvious examples. But where conditions are static, a system that does not continually raise problems of choice may be efficient on economic as well as on social grounds.

Economic systems which were predominantly organized on a traditional basis were common in earlier times. Today, only a few small, isolated, self-sufficient communities still retain wholly traditional features. In many countries, however, some aspects of behaviour are still governed by traditional patterns.

Command Economies

In command economies, questions about resource allocation are decided by some *central* authority, which makes all the necessary decisions on what to produce, how to produce it, and who gets it.

Such economies are characterized by the *centralization* of decision-taking. However, since centralized decision-taking requires plans for the desired outcomes, the terms *command economies* and *centrally planned economies* are used to refer to the same type of economic system.

Planning

Central planning of all economic decisions in a large modern industrial nation is an extremely complex business. Planners need to know the entire range of technological possibilities for production, and to have full details of the supplies of all factors of production with their characteristics. On the basis of this information, the planners must settle on their choice of goods and services to be produced and how to produce them. Planning the allocation of commodities may be done by decree: e.g. by rationing. However, planners often use prices for distribution. In this case they set the prices of consumers' goods and leave individuals to buy what they wish at the state-controlled prices. Even then, however, the planners must predict the pattern of consumers' demand in order to issue the correct production orders. Whenever they get the quantities wrong, there are queues for some scarce goods and unsold surpluses of others.

The countries of the USSR, Eastern Europe and China were command economies for much of the present century and called themselves socialist or communist. Centralization of decision-taking appeared to make sense politically in the context of socialist principles. But it was also maintained that a command economy was an efficient system for the allocation of resources. The apparent successes of the Soviet Union and China in the early stages of industrialization seemed to support this conclusion, though a great debate continued for many years on this matter.

The debate took a dramatic course, however, as the decade of the 1980s drew to a close. Indeed it appears to be, to all intents and purposes, ended as, starting in 1989, an amazed world watched as Poland, East Germany, Czechoslovakia, Hungary, Bulgaria, Romania and even the USSR itself, rejected their centrally planned economies. Those countries of Africa that experimented with central planning have not been far behind in abandoning their system.

The failures of central planning

To a considerable extent the changes reflected political as much as economic matters – the wholesale dissatisfaction with systems based on single-party government, and the popular clamour for multiparty democracies. However, there can be no doubt that the command-style system of economic organization had also failed in many ways.

Four failures were particularly significant:

- **Failure of organization**
- **Failure of quality control**
- **Lack of incentives**
- **Environmental degradation**

Failure of organization: The sheer quantity of data required for the central planning of an entire economy is enormous, and the task of analysing it to produce a fully integrated plan can hardly be exaggerated. Moreover, the plan is not once-and-for-all. It must be a rolling process, continually changing to take account, not only of current data, but also of future trends in labour supplies, in technological developments, and in tastes of the population for different goods and services.

Long experience in Eastern Europe confirms that co-ordination with any reasonable degree of efficiency has not been possible. Bottlenecks in production, shortages of some goods and gluts of others plagued the Soviet economy for decades. For example, in 1989 much of a bumper harvest rotted on the farms because of shortages of storage and transportation facilities; and for years there was an ample supply of black and white television sets, and severe shortages of toilet paper and soap.

Failure of quality control: Central planners can monitor *quantities* produced, rewarding those who over-fulfil their targets and punishing those who fall short. But monitoring *quality* of output is much harder, especially since factory managers can easily let quality slip in order to meet quantity quotas. A constant Soviet problem, therefore, has been the production of low quality goods, as the crop of jokes about Lada cars, made in the USSR, confirms. (How to double the value of your Lada? Fill it with petrol. Etc, etc.)

Lack of incentives: In command economies, the planners have limited power to use wage incentives to encourage labour to move from job to job and to work hard. Workers usually have complete job security. Industrial unemployment is rare. Even when it does occur, new jobs are usually found for those thrown out of work. Although the high level of security has attractions, it proved impossible to provide sufficient incentives for reasonably hard and efficient work under such conditions. In the words of the historian Timothy Ash, who wrote eye-witness chronicles of the events in Eastern Europe in the 1980s, the prevailing relationship between workers and government may be summed up as 'we pretend to work and you pretend to pay us'.

The most important incentive failure related to innovation. In market economies, private entrepreneurs accept the risks of introducing new products and new production processes. If they succeed, they hope to earn large profits; if they fail, they expect to make losses. Thus, innovation is the engine of long-term growth that has raised living standards over the centuries since the first industrial revolution.

In planned economies there are no profits and losses to reward successful innovators and penalize unsuccessful ones. The result has been a lack of the long-term technological dynamism that characterizes many advanced market economies. The long-term failure of planned economies was, substantially, a failure to produce satisfactory economic growth.

Environmental degradation: Fulfilling production plans became the all-embracing incentive in planned economies, to the exclusion of most other considerations, including the environment. As a result, environmental degradation occurred in all the countries of Eastern Europe on a monumental scale. A particularly disturbing example took place in central Asia where high quotas for cotton output led to indiscriminate use of pesticides and irrigation. Birth defects involving almost one child in three ensued, and the vast Aral Sea was nearly drained, causing incalculable environmental effects.

Market Economies

In the third type of economic system, decisions about resource allocation are made without any central direction but, instead, as a result of innumerable independent decisions taken by individual producers and consumers. Such a system is known as a MARKET ECONOMY.

Decentralized decision-taking

In a market economy, decisions relating to the basic economic issues are decentralized. They are nonetheless co-ordinated. The main co-ordinating device is the set of market-determined prices – which is why the free-market system is often also called a PRICE SYSTEM. Much of our study in this book will be of how prices are determined and of how they act to co-ordinate decentralized decisions.

A MARKET is an institution defined as any convenient arrangements whereby persons can communicate with each other in order to buy and sell goods, services or factors of production. Markets are sometimes located physically in particular buildings or streets. The Stock Exchange and the London Metal Exchange in the City of London are specialized markets where buyers and sellers of shares in companies and of non-ferrous metals, respectively, meet to deal with each other. Petticoat Lane in the East End of London and the Bull Ring in Birmingham are popular street markets where many stallholders offer a range of goods from antiques to fruit and vegetables.

The term 'market' must not, however, be thought as necessarily pertaining to particular sites. We speak of the 'foreign exchange market', which has no more specific location than the international telephone network and computer hook-ups, by which dealers buy and sell pounds, dollars, francs, yen and other currencies. Markets may indeed use all conceivable means of communication, including the press, as in the case of many second-hand goods such as motorcars. If you have a car to sell, or want to buy one, you will find that 'the market' comprises the local press, specialized magazines such as *The Motor* and *Exchange and Mart*, as well as car dealers' showrooms.

Market economies are characterized by two key features:
(i) specialization in production, accompanied by freedom to exchange what is produced among individuals, and
(ii) market-determined prices.

Specialization and exchange

Small, isolated, traditional societies in the pre-agricultural stage of history were (and where they now occur, are) self-sufficient. Such societies are characterized by a

'relative simplicity of material culture (only 94 items exist among Kung bushmen); the lack of accumulation of material wealth (and mobility) ... Subsistence requirements are satisfied by only a modest effort – perhaps two or three days a week by each adult; they do not have to struggle over food resources; the attitudes towards ownership are flexible and their living groups open.' [1]

Only a few nomadic societies, of the type referred to in the above quotation, survive today. They were, however, typical societies about 10,000 years ago, before the first agricultural revolution which put an end to wandering self-sufficiency. This revolution, which came when man learned how to plant and cultivate crops, brought with it surplus production; the new farming methods meant that farmers

could produce substantially more than they needed in order to survive. As a result, some of the population was freed from the need to work on the land. New occupations then appeared: artisans, soldiers, barbers, entertainers, priests and government officials. The age of specialization had begun.

Specialization must be accompanied by trade. People who produce only one thing must trade most of it in order to obtain all the other things that they require. Early free-market economies used BARTER, the trading of goods directly for other goods. But barter is costly in terms of time spent searching out satisfactory exchanges. To avoid its cumbersome nature, another institution, known as money, evolved. Money eliminates barter by separating transactions. If a farmer has wheat and wants a hammer, he or she does not have to find someone who has a hammer and who wants wheat. They merely have to find someone who wants wheat. The farmer takes money in exchange, then finds another person who wishes to sell a hammer, and then gives up money for the hammer. Money becomes the 'medium of exchange.'

By eliminating the cumbrousness of barter, money greatly facilitates trade and specialization.

Specialization by individuals in the production of only one commodity was accompanied by a tremendous increase in productivity. Rising output was aided by another aspect of specialization generally known as the *division of labour*: the specialization on a single task within the process of making one commodity. The most efficient way of building a house is not to employ a dozen workers who share all the necessary tasks, *each* doing some brick-laying, some plastering, some painting and decorating, some electrical wiring, some plumbing, and so on. It is, instead, to employ specialist bricklayers, plasterers, painters and decorators, electricians, plumbers, etc. Skilled craftspeople are more effective if each chooses the occupation in which he or she has some natural, or acquired, advantage and then concentrates on the skill in which continual practice and experience raises efficiency.

The combination of specialization and division of labour proved to be the most powerful instrument of economic progress that the world had ever seen. Its power reached unprecedented heights during the first industrial revolution which began in the early eighteenth century.

Market-determined prices

We have seen that an economic system in which people specialize in the production of goods and services necessitates the exchange of commodities. Perhaps the most remarkable feature of the market system is that it requires no planning authority, no bureaucracy, to allocate resources. The price mechanism works as a result of millions of decisions made by individual producers and consumers acting in their own self-interest.

The key to the whole process is to be found in the role of prices, which perform the crucial function of providing signals that help to determine the allocation of resources.

1 *The Times Atlas of World History*, ed. G.Barraclough (London: Times Books, 1978), p. 35.

That they do it remarkably well (though not without some deficiencies, to which we return later) is clear because what some groups want to sell usually matches what other groups want to buy.

A co-ordinator of decisions: Every day millions of people make millions of decisions concerning production and consumption. Most of these decisions are not motivated by a desire to contribute to the social good, or to make the whole economy work well, but by considerations of self-interest. The price system co-ordinates these decisions, so that the economic system as a whole is sensitive to the wishes of the individuals who compose it.

The basic insight into how this system works is that decentralized private decision-takers, acting in their own personal self-interests, respond to *signals*, which are the prices of what they buy and sell. Economists have long emphasized price as a signalling agent. When a commodity, such as oil, becomes scarce, its price tends to rise. Firms and households that use oil are led to economize on it and to look for alternatives. Firms that produce oil are led to discover more of it and bring higher-cost sources, such as tar sands, into production. This system works best, as we shall see, where prices are flexible and determined in markets where there are many buyers and sellers. The prices that give signals about scarcities and surpluses are then set by the impersonal forces of demand and supply and are acted upon by individuals.

Lack of conscious overall direction: The market economy fulfils its function of co-ordinating decisions without anyone having to understand how it works. For example, the dairy farmer does not need to know how many people eat butter (let alone who they are), how many people drink milk, how many other dairy farmers there are, or whether more money is spent on beer than on milk. What he needs to know are the prices of different kinds of fodder, the characteristics of different cows, the price of milk, the cost of hired labour relative to that of farm machinery, and what his net earnings might be if he sold his cows and raised sheep instead.

By responding to such public signals as the costs and prices of what he buys and sells, the dairy farmer helps to make the whole economy fit together, to produce what people want and to provide it where and when they want it.

Laissez-faire: The ability of impersonal market forces to co-ordinate economic decisions led early economists to speak of a policy of *laissez-faire*. This French expression indicates a belief that the nation's commerce functions best when it is free from government intervention and left to be governed by what the great eighteenth-century Scottish economist, Adam Smith, called the 'invisible' hand of market forces.

In later times, the term *laissez-faire* came to be used to describe a callous policy of ignoring all concerns about social welfare. Originally, however, it merely described the belief that the market economy would perform most efficiently if left free from government intervention.

HOW MARKETS WORK

The great bulk of this book is about how markets work. But it is useful to begin with a brief synoptic overview of the basic market mechanism. We limit ourselves to two illustrations. These are a change in tastes, and a change in costs.

A change in tastes: First, consider how markets react to a change in consumers' tastes. Assume, at the outset, that producers find it equally profitable to produce Wensleydale or Cheddar cheese, and that consumers are prepared to buy the quantities of each that are being supplied at prevailing market prices.

Now, suppose that consumers experience a greatly increased desire for Wensleydale and a diminished desire for Cheddar cheese. The precise reason is not important. It could be anything from the discovery of the delicious flavour of Wensleydale following holidays in Yorkshire, to the establishment by the medical profession of the fact that eating Wensleydale while watching television reduces the risk of contracting dandruff.

What will be the effects of this change? First, consumers will buy more Wensleydale and less Cheddar. With production unchanged, a shortage of Wensleydale and a glut of Cheddar will develop. In order to unload their surplus cheddar, merchants will reduce its price, on the principle that it is better to sell it for less than not to sell it at all. In contrast, merchants will find that they cannot keep Wensleydale on their shelves. It has become scarce. People will be prepared to pay more for it and its price will rise. As the price rises, people will buy less expensive Cheddar instead. Thus, the quantity demanded will adjust itself to the available supply.

The price changes brought about in the shops will filter through to the cheese factories. They will reallocate their resources from Cheddar to Wensleydale production since, provided costs of production have not altered, it will be profitable to do so. Thus, the change in consumer tastes, working through the price mechanism, causes resources to be reallocated to meet the change.

A change in costs: For our second example, consider a change originating not with consumers, but with producers. Begin, as before, with a situation in which producers find it equally profitable to produce Wensleydale and Cheddar, and that consumers are prepared to buy, at prevailing market prices, the quantities of these two cheeses that are supplied. Now imagine that a technological change occurs; an improved Wensleydale-making process is developed and this lowers the cost of Wensleydale production. Since costs fall, Wensleydale production becomes more profitable. Everything else is unchanged, including consumers' tastes and the costs of making Cheddar cheese.

What will happen now that Wensleydale production is more profitable than it used to be? Clearly, if they are at all interested in increasing their profits, producers will begin to switch resources from Cheddar to Wensleydale. Soon the quantities of the two cheeses coming on to the market will change. A shortage of Cheddar and a glut of Wensleydale will result. The price of Cheddar will start to rise and that of Wensleydale to fall. As the former becomes more expensive, less of it will be bought by consumers. The opposite will happen with Wensleydale. The lower price will encourage consumers to buy and eat more of it. At the same time, there will be an incentive for producers to move some resources back into Cheddar production as its price rises relative to that of Wensleydale.

The functions of prices

The price mechanism operates to allocate resources in such a way as to answer the three basic questions of what is to be produced, how it will be produced, and how it will be distributed among the population. Prices do so by acting as signals to consumers and producers in two sets of markets:

(i) markets for commodities, i.e. for goods and services (often called goods markets for short)

(ii) markets for factors of production (often called factor markets for short)

Markets for goods and services

Goods markets help to determine the answer to our first question: 'What is to be produced?' We described the functioning of the price mechanism in the market for Wensleydale and Cheddar cheeses. These two goods, chosen for illustrative purposes, may be regarded as typical of the markets for *all* goods and services. The signalling function of prices in the goods market was implicit in our explanation of the ways in which changes in production and consumption of Cheddar and Wensleydale cheese responded to movements in their prices.

Prices signal to producers which goods are most profitable to produce. Prices signal to consumers which goods give most value for the money they must pay to purchase them.

Resources are rechannelled in new directions following price changes brought about by changes in tastes, or in costs of production.

Markets for factors of production

We now need to look at the part played by factor markets in answering the three basic questions: What is produced? How is it produced? and Who gets it?

The operation of the price mechanism in factor markets closely parallels that in goods markets already described. The services of each factor – land, labour, and capital – are bought and sold, just as are goods and services for consumption. The price of labour is the wage that is paid for employing it. The price of land is its rent, and so on. The price of any factor of production is influenced by two forces: the amount offered for sale on the market and the amount firms wish to purchase.

What is produced?   This question, as we have seen, concerns the allocation of resources among the production of Cheddar or Wensleydale cheese and all other products? We have seen that part of the answer to this question comes from goods markets, where signals go to consumers and firms. However, if firms are to respond to a signal to produce more of one product and less of another, resources must be released from firms which are contracting production and persuaded to move to firms which are expanding production. A signal for such reallocation of resources comes from changes in factor prices. These prices are set in factor markets.

A rise in the demand for factors in some productive use, or geographical area, will tend to raise the prices of factors in that use or area. A fall in the demand for factors in other productive uses, or geographical areas, will tend to lower the prices of factors in those uses or areas. The owners of factors – workers, capitalists and landowners – respond to these signals by moving their factors out of uses where prices are falling and into uses where prices are rising.

When a factor responds to changing price signals by moving from one use to another, that factor is said to be MOBILE. Factor mobility relates to movements between occupations, industries, or regions. A rise in wage rates, for instance, acts as an incentive for labour to move. The relative strength of the demand for accountants in recent years led to high earnings for accountants, which, in turn, encouraged increasing numbers of school leavers to train for the accountancy profession. The fact that wage rates are, on average, higher in London than in Sheffield or Glasgow helps to cause a southward migration of labour. These movements are responses to the signals provided by prices. Factors move as long as it pays them to do so. The movement of factors, however, tends to reduce the disparities between factor prices in different regions, in different occupations and in different industries.

How is it produced?   Consider next how factor markets help to answer the second basic economic question, How?, i.e. 'What methods of production are to be used?' Because factors of production are to some extent interchangeable, there is usually more than one way in which a given output can be produced. Labour, capital and other factors can be combined in different proportions. As we saw in Figure 2.2, some industries, such as energy and chemicals, are relatively capital-intensive, others, such as construction and clothing, are relatively labour-intensive, with yet others in between. Why should these differences in factor proportions exist among industries?

The answer has two strands, one technical and one economic. A simple example will illustrate. How does a farmer consider the best method of producing a given quantity of, say, cauliflowers? We assume he uses only three inputs – land, labour and fertilizers.

Consider, first, the technical side of the matter as seen by a single producer, whom we call farmer Brown. The farmer knows from experience how the productivity of land changes as the amount of labour and fertilizer employed is varied. If all these factors of production were free, farmer Brown would clearly use all the labour and fertilizer needed to secure the maximum possible yield from the land. He would be looking only for technical efficiency – maximizing the yield from every square metre of land. He would do this without regard for how much labour and capital he used, because all he wanted was freely available.

Labour and fertilizers are not, however, freely available. They are scarce, and they have alternative uses. Each commands a price which is influenced by market forces. The most *economically* efficient combination of factors produces a given quantity of output at minimum cost. To achieve it, regard must be given to the prices of inputs. Farmers who are trying to run their businesses as profitably as possible will consider the prices of the factors that they use.

To see how changing factor prices affect farmer Brown's choice of techniques, imagine that, after he has selected his minimum-cost method, the price of one of the factors alters. Suppose, for instance, that fertilizers fall in price because of technical progress in the chemical industry, while the price of labour remains the same. Brown will rethink his situation, recalculate his costs of different production methods and will substitute fertilizers for labour. He will do this by using less labour, but more fertilizer, to produce cauliflowers. If, in contrast, the price of labour falls because of an influx of farm workers from overseas, he will substitute labour for fertilizers. In all this, he is reacting to the signals he receives of relative prices, and he is adjusting his input combinations to minimize his production costs. Because he is trying to make as much profit as possible, he reacts in a predictable way to price changes.

The significance of cost minimization: We have seen that factor prices influence producers in their decisions of what methods of production to adopt. What is the significance of this for the whole economy? The answer is that cost minimization when factor prices are set by demand and supply, tends to lead to *efficient production*. Let us see how this comes about.

The prices of factors of production reflect, by and large, their relative scarcities. In a country with a great deal of land and a small population, for example, the price of land will be low while, because labour is in short supply, the wage rate will be high. In such circumstances, firms producing agricultural goods will tend to make lavish use of (cheap) land and to economize on (expensive) labour: a production process will be adopted that is land-intensive. On the other hand, in a small country with a large population, the demand for land will be high relative to its supply. Thus land will be relatively expensive and firms producing agricultural goods will tend to economize on it by using a great deal of labour per unit of land. In this case, producers will prefer labour-intensive methods of cultivation.

In general, the prices of abundant factors will be lower than those of factors that are scarce. Profit-seeking firms will then be led to use much of the factors with which the whole country is plentifully endowed, and to economize on factors that are in scarce supply.

This example illustrates how the price system co-ordinates decentralized decision-taking. No single firm need be aware of national factor surpluses and scarcities, because they will be reflected in prices determined on the competitive market. Individual firms that never look beyond their own private profit are, nonetheless, led to economize on factors that are scarce in the nation as a whole.

We should not be surprised, therefore, to discover that methods of producing the same commodity differ in different countries. In the United States, where labour is highly skilled and very expensive, a steel company may use elaborate machinery and economize on labour. In China, where labour is abundant and capital scarce, a less mechanized method of production may be more appropriate. The Western engineer, who feels that the Chinese are backward because they are using methods long abandoned in the West as inefficient, may be missing the point about economic efficiency in the use of resources.

The price system tends to produce an efficient use of resources. The common sense of this is that *any* society interested in getting the most out of resources should take account of relative scarcities in deciding what production processes to adopt, which is what the price system leads individual producers to do.

For whom is output produced?   The final basic question of resource allocation – how the output of goods and services is divided up among the population – is also answered by a market system. This is the question of the distribution of income, and we must now see how factor markets answer it.

The prices of factors provide a twofold signalling function, one on the demand and another on the supply side. On the demand side, users of factors are induced by considerations of profit maximization to economize on expensive factors and, wherever possible, to make more use of cheap factors. On the supply side, a high price for a factor encourages the supply of that factor, while a low price discourages it. For example, high prices for computer programmers and low wages for filing clerks will encourage people to stay on in school to train as computer programmers, rather than to leave school early to become filing clerks.

As a result of the interaction of demand and supply, all factors of production get priced. The income earned by any factor depends on the price paid for it: wages for labour, rent for land, etc. Those factors which command high prices for their services will also be able to earn high incomes. For instance, workers with scarce skills that are in strong demand will tend to be paid more than other less skilled workers for whose services demand is weak and the market price is low. Owners of land in cities receive higher rents than owners of marginal hill farms.

Prices play their part in the determination of individual incomes. Thus, the market system helps to determine the distribution of income going to the owners of each and every factor of production.

The Eighth Wonder of the World?

The allocation of resources through a market system has

many attractive features which were extensively praised by early economists. As we remarked earlier, the great Scottish economist Adam Smith wrote in his classic *The Wealth of Nations*, published in 1776, of 'the invisible hand' guiding resources into their most profitable, and at the same time socially effective, uses. He called the hand invisible because it was, and still is, precisely that. Decisions taken by millions of individual producers and consumers match each other as a result of the working of the price mechanism.

Without any centralized planning, the efforts of private individuals to maximize their own satisfaction as buyers, and their profits as sellers, causes the quantity of each good and service to match the quantity that people want to buy. All this is brought about by price movements responding to any changes that occur in conditions prevailing in the market, such as changes in consumer tastes or in costs of production. The price system is, moreover, an automatic, flexible and self-regulating device which provides, with no conscious overall direction, answers to the basic question of how to allocate resources among competing uses. It appealed to Adam Smith and many of his contemporaries because of the prevailing philosophy of the time and, in particular, because it relegated the role of government to a relatively small number of matters such as defence of the realm and the administration of justice. Perhaps, then, the market economy should be regarded as the eighth wonder of the world? In this book we will look at that question in some detail.

Capitalism and the market system

It is not a matter of chance that the market system reached its heights under the organization known as capitalism. The main feature of a capitalist system lies in the institutions of private property and, in particular, the private ownership of capital by persons, or organizations, called capitalists.

Early economists saw that capitalists' pursuit of profits might be beneficial, not only to the capitalists themselves but also to the rest of the community. The motivation of profit was seen as the necessary incentive for producers to concentrate on the provision of those commodities most valued by consumers. In our own day, the advantage of the profit motive has again been seen by those living in the command economies of the Soviet Union and eastern Europe, which suffered from bureaucratic inefficiencies and the lack of effective incentives.

At the same time, however, ownership is in some respects a side issue. The price mechanism can operate in principle, and does operate in practice, where ownership is collective rather than private – i.e. where firms belong to the state but the managers respond to the price signals provided in markets. The nationalized industries in the UK provide examples. Many of these were transferred from public to private ownership after 1980, as the renewed belief in market forces was reflected in the programme of privatization. However, even before privatization, industries such as gas, electricity and the telephone service were much influenced both by the prices of their products as well as by the prices of the factors of production that they used.

The remaining nationalized industries, such as the railways, still take account of market prices when making decisions on what to produce and how to produce it.

Market Failure

Despite the unquestioned merits of the price mechanism, the system is not entirely without blemish. As we recognized failures of the command economy, so we must also recognize certain causes of MARKET FAILURE – circumstances which lead to the questioning of the allocation of resources that a pure market system brings about.

Criticisms of a laissez-faire market system fall into two main categories, related to

- **Efficiency, i.e. resource allocation may be inefficient.**
- **Equity (fairness), i.e. resource allocation may be unfair.**

Inefficiency

The first set of causes of market failure relates to the fact that the price mechanism may fail to allocate resources efficiently. There are certain goods and services that a pure *laissez-faire* system would not produce at all, or not in the most appropriate quantities, and others that it would produce, but which might be better not produced at all or in smaller quantities.

We cannot provide a comprehensive list of the causes of market failure at this early stage in the book. Suffice, for the moment, to mention the following:

Collectively consumed commodities: There are certain goods and services that collectively benefit the community as a whole. Remember that producers only supply goods that *individuals* want to buy, and that can be sold to the users. So it is not surprising that private businesses will not supply a county police force, which benefits everyone (except criminals) by its very existence. No one can be excluded from enjoying the benefit provided by the police force once it exists, despite the fact that he or she might not be prepared to pay for it. Neither would private suppliers produce the lighting in the streets of Glasgow which, again by its very existence, benefits all Glaswegians and cannot be denied to those who will not pay for it.

The earliest supporters of the market system recognized that there were goods with this collective characteristic, which economists call PUBLIC GOODS. They saw, at the same time, the need for some intervention in markets to remedy this kind of market failure.

Merit (and demerit) goods: A rather different cause of market failure concerns goods which the market would supply in inappropriate quantities because individuals might not always act in their own best interests. Some people might like to buy goods which would harm them, or they may fail to purchase other goods which would turn out to have greater benefits than had been realized. Intervention to remedy market failure arising in these ways is often described as 'paternalistic', though 'parentalistic' might be a less sexist term. Examples of its use to justify interfering with the decisions of individuals in the amounts of goods they wish to purchase are seatbelts and glue (for sniffing). The former is an example of what is called a MERIT GOOD. The latter falls into the class of so-called DEMERIT GOODS.

Commodities with 'spillover' effects: Similar in some ways to our first category of public goods are commodities whose benefit (or detriment) spills over to consumers and/or producers who are not *directly* involved in market transactions. Consider two examples – vaccinations against disease, and pollution. When individuals are vaccinated they benefit, but so do persons who are *not* vaccinated and who enjoy diminished risk of disease because of *other people's* consumption. Spillover effects (known as EXTERNALITIES) can be negative as well as positive. For example, some people suffer indirectly from the adverse consequences of production, or consumption, by others – from the spreading smoke, for example, that spills over from a factory chimney to affect neighbouring houses. There is no reason to expect that profit-motivated private businesses should take account of *externalities* unless some action is taken, e.g. by the state, to ensure they are included in their own private costs and revenues.

Concentrations of economic power: A final cause of market failure arises because of the existence of organizations which possess the power to influence markets. The relevance of this point to the UK is without doubt, since nearly half of total output in the manufacturing sector of industry lies in the hands of a mere 100 giant producers.

The consequences of the concentration of economic power in relatively few hands are important both politically and economically. The economic implications are related, in particular, to the extent to which producers compete with each other. We shall return to this matter later in the book. We shall also deal with other criticisms of the market system, such as the existence, at times, of mass unemployment, in the second half of the book.

Additional market shortcomings: The major categories listed above are formally known as causes of market failure. There are also other reasons for thinking that markets are not working well. Two are worth mentioning now: inadequacies due to poor information about the products available on the market, and deficiencies arising from the behaviour of markets over time. The latter are noticeable when markets are especially sluggish or volatile – taking a long time to induce changes in supply or demand, or overreacting and causing large movements in prices and/or quantities. For example, markets for some agricultural products are rather sluggish, and the market for houses is at times rather volatile.

Inequity, or unfairness

The causes of market failure discussed above all relate to inefficiency that can occur under certain conditions. A second reason why a completely free market economy may lead to an allocation of resources which is regarded as less than satisfactory relates not to questions of efficiency but to those of equity, that is of fairness.

The price mechanism ensures the production of commodities that consumers want to buy. But people's ability to buy goods and services depends on their incomes. A market system may be likened to an election in which votes are cast, not for political candidates, but for goods and services. The 'votes' are not ballot papers but money, the notes and coins we have to spend. Consumers 'vote' for a good by spending money on it. Producers pocket the money consumers spend when they provide the commodities people wish to buy. However, unlike parliamentary elections, where votes are distributed equally and everyone has a single vote, in market elections votes are distributed unequally. Those with high incomes have more votes than those with low incomes.

Thus, in a *laissez-faire* market system, the distribution of income affects the allocation of resources. If the distribution changes, the allocation of resources changes. For example, if the distribution becomes more unequal, say with relatively more rich people and fewer poorer ones – one would expect there to be more luxury goods produced, and vice versa.

Be careful here not to identify equity with equality. The fairness of the distribution of income is an ethical question on which we all (economists as well as others) are entitled to our opinions. However, as economists, we have no special rights to pronounce on such an issue as fairness. All we can do (apart from studying the *effects* of changes in income distribution) is to conclude that *if* the distribution is generally regarded as being equitable, or fair, then the resulting allocation of resources may be regarded as satisfactory.

Mixed Systems

Our discussions of market and command economic systems lead to the clear conclusion that neither is perfect. Each suffers from different deficiencies. At the time of writing, the evidence suggests, pretty emphatically, that command economies perform less satisfactorily, as nations all over the world have moved increasingly towards greater freedom for market forces. However, it would be rash to rely totally on either.

As it happens, no pure command nor pure market economies exist in the real world. Even in the Soviet Union at the height of its reliance on central planning, prices were allowed to play some part in resource allocation. Information about rising and falling prices was allowed to help planners decide what commodities to produce. Even decisions on how to produce can be left to be influenced to an extent by market forces. For example, state factories may be set profit targets and left to make their own decisions rather than being given directives on what to produce and how to organize production.

If a complete command economy does not exist, neither does a pure *laissez-faire* market system. Governments intervene with a host of policies, from laws and directives to taxes and subsidies. (They are the subject matter of Chapter 21.) In the UK, such interventionist activities are

BOX 2.1 Gorbachev's Perestroika and Adam Smith

'The purpose of the current economic reforms which are a most important part of *perestroika* is to make socialism work by introducing into the present system considerable elements of market competition and disciplines. Since the restoration of the market, competition and profit motivation have been proclaimed as the basic principles of the reforms, some Smithian concepts are entering, if only implicitly, high level statements on economic policy. One can find examples in speeches by both Chairman of the Supreme Soviet (President) Mikhail Gorbachev and Prime Minister Nikolai Ryzhkov at the session of the Congress of People's Deputies in May and June 1989. Gorbachev said in fact that humanity has not invented a more efficient and more democratic instrument of economic management than the market. Ryzhkov echoed him by saying that a most important condition for the efficient development of the market is 'overcoming monopolism'. Adam Smith would have readily underwritten both these statements. Both Gorbachev and Ryzhkov stressed, however, that the state should defend the population from the vicissitudes of the market by means of social policy.'

(Professor Andrei Anikin (Institute of World Economy and International Relations, Moscow), 'Adam Smith, Russia and Soviet Economics', *Royal Bank of Scotland Review*, No. 166, June 1990)

In 1989 Gorbachev unveiled *perestroika* (restructuring), to try to shift the Soviet economy from a command to a market-oriented basis of the kind associated with Adam Smith. Until then an article by a Soviet economist like Professor Anikin, would have been unthinkable in the journal of a British bank.

The failure of central planning in the USSR is seen in low living standards – low outputs of poor-quality goods delivered sporadically to shops. The causes of failure are of organization, of quality control and of incentives.

Note, however, that unfettered market economies also fail on some counts. The case for mixed economic systems rests partly on the failures of central planning, but also on the conclusion that competition is a necessary ingredient for efficiency in market economies.

Questions

1 List some of the difficulties in turning a command into a market economy.
2 Professor Anikin believes that Adam Smith would have agreed with the statements by Gorbachev and Ryzhkov. Does that mean that market and command economies have any similar deficiencies?

---

often associated more with Labour than with Conservative administrations. Nevertheless, even the strongly pro-market Conservative governments under Prime Minister Margaret Thatcher in the 1980s, continued with many policies which involve interference with private-sector decision-taking. In every country some production activities are run by the state. Outstandingly, during major wars, central planning is widely adopted even in essentially free-market economies. In such times, the overriding national aim is to bring hostilities to a successful conclusion. Priority to military needs is generally accepted and consumer interests take second place. Even rationing of such essentials as food and clothing may be introduced without popular complaint. In mixed economies, such as that of the UK, there are also intermediate sectors, where economic decisions are taken neither by maximizing sellers and buyers, nor by the state, but, for example, by charities.

It is common to distinguish two different types of sectors in mixed economies: (i) a *market sector*, where commodities are bought by consumers and sold by producers, who must cover their costs from the revenues from sales, and (ii) a *non-market sector*, where the costs of production are met by the government or, in the case of charities, from voluntary subscriptions.

Some people argue that central planning can be useful in achieving major structural changes more rapidly than a market system might achieve. It has been claimed that

planning has been used to bring about speedy industrialization of poor agricultural countries in the Third World. At the same time, there are cases of failure, e.g. in Africa, which have been attributed to the difficulties of central planning – especially hard for countries which have few reliable sources of the essential statistical data required. Partial planning, comprising centralized decision-taking for a limited number of sectors of the economy which are regarded as of key importance, is also practised sometimes. Governments sometimes take on the role of central planners, in a few key industries, organizing production in areas such as postal services and rail transport.

Thus, although it is helpful to study pure types to gain insight into various issues, it is important to remember that *all real economies are mixed economies*. Each country differs only in the proportion of the mix between reliance on markets to co-ordinate decentralized decisions, and reliance on centralized decision-taking using the command principle. What distinguished the economies of such countries as the USSR and the USA was never the complete absence of markets in the former and the complete absence of government intervention in the latter. It was that there was much more central planning and less use of markets in the USSR than in the USA. Today the differences between them are diminishing.

What is the proper mix? We should not mislead you into thinking that we, or anyone else, knows the answer, or

Summary

1 The three basic questions of economics are: What to produce? How to produce it? and For whom is output produced? The term 'economic system' describes a distinctive set of social and institutional arrangements that provides answers to the three basic questions.

2 There are three major types of economic system: (i) traditional economies, where resources are allocated by custom; (ii) command economies, where resources are allocated by central planners; and (iii) market economies, where resource allocation is determined through the price mechanism.

3 A market is any institution which allows buyers and sellers to communicate with each other about the exchange of commodities (or factors). Market economies are characterized by decentralised decision-taking, exchange, specialization and the division of labour.

4 What is produced is determined by prices in markets for goods and services. How output is divided up amongst the population is determined by markets for factors of production.

5 In market economies the self-interest of individual producers and consumers is mobilized in an automatic, flexible and self-regulating system for the allocation of resources. A market economy which operates with minimum government intervention is called *laissez-faire*.

6 Market failure refers to situations where resource allocation through the price mechanism is inefficient. Market allocations may also be regarded as inequitable (unfair).

7 The main causes of market failure due to inefficiency are associated with (1) commodities that are consumed collectively (public goods); (2) commodities with spillover effects (externalities); (3) merit and demerit goods; (4) markets which under- or over-react; and (5) concentrations of economic power.

8 The failures of central planning include failure of organization and of quality control; lack of incentives; and environmental degradation.

9 All real economies are mixed economies, relying to a greater or lesser extent on market forces and on central planning.

that one answer is correct for all times and all places. It is, of course, as much a political issue as an economic one, and personal opinions are unavoidable. We hope that our explanation in this book of how markets work will help you form your own judgement.

Questions

1 For each of the following, can you identify which relates primarily to the basic economic questions What? (W), How? (H) and For whom? (F)?
  (a) Male–female wage differentials.
  (b) The size of the NHS.
  (c) Traditional *versus* command economic systems.
  (d) Private *versus* public ownership of resources.

2 What is generally thought to have been one of the most important causes of economic progress?

3 Which of the following is essential for the existence of a market for a commodity?
  (a) A distinct physical area.
  (b) All producers and consumers buy and sell in the market.
  (c) Buyers and sellers communicate with each other.
  (d) All of the above.
  (e) None of the above.

4 If the distribution of income changed so that the share of young persons rose and that of the old fell, what would be the implications for resource allocation in a market economy?

5 How can it be said that prices act as signals guiding producers to offer commodities wanted by consumers for sale? Would it not be better to say profits were the signals?

6 'A command economy may not be as efficient as a market economy but it guarantees that proper attention is paid to the environment.' Is this statement True or False?

3 How Economists Work[1]

Economists often give advice on a variety of problems. If you read a newspaper, watch television or listen to the radio you will often notice some economist's opinions being reported. Perhaps it is on the prospects for unemployment, inflation or interest rates, on some new tax, on the case for privatization or regulation of an industry, on the efficiency of the National Health Service, or some other topic.

POSITIVE AND NORMATIVE STATEMENTS IN ECONOMICS

Economists do not always agree on the advice that they give, and we shall shortly discuss the reasons for this. First, we must appreciate a vital distinction between two kinds of statement that economists make, called *positive* and *normative* statements. The distinction between them is fundamental to all scientific enquiry, not only that of economics. Indeed, the success of modern science rests partly on the ability of scientists to separate their views on *what does, or might, happen* in the world, from their views on *what they would like to happen*. For example, until the nineteenth century almost everyone believed that the earth was only a few thousand years old. Evidence then began to accumulate that the earth was thousands of millions of years old. This evidence was hard for some people to accept since it ran counter to a literal reading of many religious texts. Those people did not want to believe the evidence. Nevertheless, scientists, many of whom were religious, continued their research because they refused to allow their feelings about what they wanted to believe to affect their search, as scientists, for the truth.

Distinguishing what is true from what we would like to be, or what we feel ought to be, depends partly on being able to distinguish between positive and normative statements.

NORMATIVE STATEMENTS depend on value judgements. They involve issues of personal opinion, which cannot be settled by recourse to facts. POSITIVE STATEMENTS, in contrast, do not involve value judgements. They are statements about what is, was or will be, i.e. statements that are about matters of fact.

Many, but not all, positive statements are testable. A testable statement is one that is, in principle, refutable. Let us consider some examples.

- The statement that unemployment is such a bad thing that governments should try to reduce it at all costs, is a normative statement depending on our value judgements.
- The statement that there is an association between the rate of inflation and the rate of unemployment, such that increasing inflation will reduce unemployment, is a positive, testable, statement.
- The statement that at some time in human history there will exist a society with zero unemployment is a positive statement, since it does not depend on value judgements. It is irrefutable. No matter how much time passes without the advent of the zero-unemployment society, true believers can say 'just wait, it is around the corner'. Not until the last second of human history could we say the statement had been refuted – and then it would be too late, since there would be no one around to know about it.

It is important to appreciate that testability refers to testability *in principle*. All we mean by this statement is that it is possible to *design* a test which, if it could be perfectly carried out, could disprove it.

To make sure you fully understand the distinction between positive and normative, consider the ten statements set out at the top of the next page.

All five statements listed as positive, assert things about the nature of the world in which we live. In contrast, the five statements listed as normative cannot be answered without making value judgements.

Notice, too, that statements A to E are not only positive, they are testable. Given enough evidence, the probability of their being false could be established. In other words we could design tests, collect evidence and decide if the statements were wrong.

Statement A, for example, could be tested by collecting data to see whether, in the past, high rates of interest were associated with high saving and vice versa. (In fact existing evidence tends to support the statement.) In contrast, statement F can in no way be tested by recourse to facts. It is 'correct' if saving is 'a good thing' and if good things ought to be encouraged; otherwise not. But whether or not saving is good in itself is a question which depends on a value judgement about the desirability of saving. It is clearly a matter on which opinions can differ from one person to another. Therefore the statement is normative.

We leave the reader to analyse the remaining eight statements to decide precisely why each is either positive or normative. Remember to apply the two tests: (1) Is the statement about actual or alleged facts? If so, it is a positive one. (2) Are value judgements necessary to assess the truth

---

1 Students may omit this chapter without immediate loss of understanding, but should return to it at a later stage when they can relate it to the economics they will have learned by then.

Positive	Normative
A Raising interest rates encourages people to save.	F People should be encouraged to save.
B High rates of income tax encourage people to evade paying taxes.	G Governments should arrange taxes so that people cannot avoid paying them.
C Rising wage rates cause people to work harder.	H Firms should raise wage rates to encourage people to work harder.
D Lowering the price of coffee causes people to buy less of it.	I The government should put a tax on coffee so that people will consume less coffee.
E The majority of the population would prefer a policy that lowered the level of unemployment to one that brought inflation down.	J The government ought to be more concerned with reducing unemployment than inflation.

of the statement? If so, it is normative.

Several points need to be noted about the positive/normative distinction. First, positive statements need not be true. Statement D is almost certainly false. Yet it is positive, not normative.

Second, the inclusion of a value judgement in a statement does not necessarily make the statement normative. Statement I is about the value judgements that people hold. It is possible to try to find out whether people really do prefer inflation to unemployment. One can ask them and one can observe how they vote. There is no need to introduce a value judgement in order to establish the validity of the statement itself.

Third, not all statements are necessarily classifiable into positive or normative. There is a class of statements, called 'analytic', which involve conditional theorizing and are neither factual nor involve value judgements. For example, the statement 'if all men are immortal and if you are a man you are immortal' is true by the rules of logic. It involves no value judgement to assess its truth. Nor is it a statement about the real world. It is a conditional statement which is logically unfalsifiable. Such statements often occur in economic reasoning.

The Nature of Positive Economics

It should now be understood that positive economics is concerned with the development of understanding about how economies work. The way that economists develop this understanding involves the testing of theories against evidence of factual behaviour in the real world.

The theories may be based on assumptions about human motivation, or on observations, called *empirical evidence*.

For example, it is known that consumers tend to buy smaller quantities of goods and services when their prices rise, or when the incomes of consumers fall. These observations led economists to propose theories about the nature of the relationship between quantity demanded and prices and income. Insofar as they turn out to fit the facts that we already know, and allow us to predict things we do not yet know, they are useful theories.

Scientific Method

Economics shares some things in common with the natural sciences. Both try to develop theories that explain behaviour. In the case of physics, the behaviour is that of inanimate matter. In the case of economics, the behaviour is social, or human. Both seek to identify consistent behaviour patterns of the kind we have mentioned. Both employ what is known as *scientific method*.

A great deal has been written on the question of whether or not economics is a fully-fledged science. We shall not enter into the controversy because it would not be profitable at this stage of your studies. However, economics does share at least one important characteristic with natural science: they both attempt to relate theory to evidence in a *systematic way*. In economics the evidence in which we are interested is that of human behaviour – how men and women react to changing circumstances.

Experimental and non-experimental sciences

Much work in economics consists of the collection of empirical evidence about human behaviour, the propounding of theories based on that evidence, and the testing of theories against new evidence. The two main purposes of economic theories are: (1) explaining observed behaviour, and (2) predicting as yet unobserved behaviour.

To understand how economists go about their jobs, we must first deal with a distinction between *experimental* and *non-experimental* sciences. In such fields as physics and chemistry, laboratory experiments are used to generate observations against which to test a theory. Such sciences employ what is known as the EXPERIMENTAL METHOD.

Economists, in common with most other social scientists (other than some psychologists) and astronomers, are denied the luxury of experimentation in much of their work. This is a notable disadvantage. (Indeed, this is one reason why some people have contended that economics is not even a science.) The ability to conduct experiments carries two outstanding advantages, replication and control.

The advantage of laboratory experiments

Experiments can be repeated: A physical scientist may continue to repeat his experiments over and over again – no first result is convincing until he has repeated it enough times to be satisfied with it. Furthermore, other scientists who are sceptical can, and will, replicate the experiment. Generally, no new result gains wide acceptance until many independent scientists have verified it.

Experimental conditions can be controlled: The behaviour of many substances is liable to be affected by a number of influences. Laboratory conditions can often be used to create conditions which isolate a single determinant of behaviour. Consider, for instance, an example from the field of biology. The rate at which a plant grows may be affected by several factors, including the amount of sunlight received, the moisture and the nitrogen content of the soil. Suppose we desire to ascertain the importance of nitrogen content. We can create conditions in a greenhouse (laboratory) in which the amount of sunlight and moisture in the soil is held constant. We then use two sets of plants. Both sets are given the same amount of sunlight and water. However, one set has more nitrogen than the other set, which is used as a 'control'. We may then attribute any observed differences in plant growth to the only difference between them – the nitrogen content. We have ourselves created the difference in our laboratory.

One of the reasons why scientists want to duplicate experiments before accepting a result is the worry that, no matter how hard they tried, the original experimenters may have failed to hold constant all of the factors other than the one they were consciously varying.

The inapplicability of laboratory experiments in economics

The reasons why economists usually cannot make controlled experiments, fall into two categories, non-controllability and the purposeful nature of human behaviour.

Non-controllability: The determinants of human behaviour are complex. Consider how to design an experiment to isolate the determinants of investment decisions made by businesspersons. Suppose that we suspect (rightly, as it happens) that the amount of investment that businesses undertake depends, among other things, on their expectations of the profitability of their investment and on the rate of interest that they have to pay on money they borrow to finance the investment. How can we possibly generate conditions in a laboratory wherein we incarcerate a number of business executives and hold constant everything else, while we vary the rate of interest and observe how much they spend on investment?

The answer is that we cannot. We might try to get them to play a game like Monopoly with 'pretend' money. But we would be rash to imagine that, in the complex real world, they would behave as they do when playing games. In a word, we cannot usually generate laboratory conditions that simulate the real world sufficiently well to derive useful results from our experiment.[1]

Human behaviour is consciously determined: Human beings differ from inanimate objects and plants in that their reactions to stimuli are *consciously* thought out. We are not lumps of matter who will always react identically to identical circumstances. You can bombard a set of atoms using a linear accelerator, and the atoms will just 'sit there' while their neighbours are smashed one by one. But try doing the same using a weapon from a concealed position on a group of humans. The first person 'smashed' might seem a mystery to the others and cause little movement from the rest. But smash a few, and very soon the rest will *deduce* the presence of a malevolent force – even though they cannot see it – and they will take evasive action.

Moreover, individuals may react differently to the same stimulus. For example, if you put a match to any dry piece of paper the paper will burn. If you try to extract vital information from human beings by torture, some will yield it while others will not. More confusingly still, the same individual may react differently at different times. While the response of inanimate objects to stimuli is consistent, that by human beings may be less so.

A Science of Human Behaviour

Economists can apply the scientific method, even though they are usually unable to make controlled, and repeatable, laboratory experiments. Other methods of confronting theories with evidence must be used.

Economists cannot often generate data in controlled experiments. But of course they do have data. A mass of data about human behaviour is generated naturally in the real world. Every day, for example, consumers are comparing prices and deciding what to buy. Firms are comparing prices and costs of production and deciding what to offer for sale. All these acts can be observed and recorded. They then provide the observations against which to test theories about the effects of different prices on the amount bought by consumers and on the amount offered for sale by producers.

Peculiarities of economic behaviour

The difficulty of conducting laboratory experiments is one characteristic that makes life difficult for economists. There are two others: the variability of human behaviour, and the complexity of the determinants of social behaviour.

The variability of human behaviour: It is often argued that social science is impossible because it attempts to deal with people who have free will and cannot be made subject to inexorable laws. Such a view implies that it is impossible to develop laws which will determine *precisely* how an individual will *always* react to any situation. There is a strong element of truth in this view. This does not mean, however, that human beings behave in a totally capricious and unpredictable way. It may be hard to say when, or

---

1   There are a few areas in economics, such as the attitudes of individuals to risk and uncertainty, that have been investigated by laboratory experimentation. Opinion in the profession is divided on the usefulness of such experiments in understanding the behaviour of people to risk in the real world.

why, any particular person will buy an ice-cream, but we can observe a stable response pattern from a large group of individuals: the higher the number of people visiting the beaches, the greater the sales of ice-cream.

Many other examples come to mind, where we cannot predict the behaviour of any one individual with certainty, but can do so with remarkable accuracy for a *group* of individuals. No one can predict with certainty when Betty Smith will die, or whether James Jones will have a motoring accident. But for large groups of men and women, we can know with a remarkable degree of certainty how many will die in any particular year and how many will have car accidents. Moreover, the larger the number of people in our group and the more information we have about them, the greater the accuracy with which we can make predictions.[1]

The complexity of the determinants of social behaviour: The second problem arises from the large number of determinants of human behaviour and from the ways in which they can interact with each other. Consider, for example, the hypothesis that one's health as an adult depends upon one's diet as a child. Clearly, all sorts of other factors affect the health of adults – heredity, conditions of childhood other than nutrition, age, sex, exposure to infections, and other environmental factors. The complexity of the determinants of social behaviour means that we should not be too ambitious about developing 'laws' about all types of behaviour. We must also be prepared to accept partial explanations of behaviour which may work better at some times than at others. They will usually be better than nothing, but they will always be subject to some degree of error.

THE NATURE OF ECONOMIC THEORY

Economists develop theories in an effort to understand and predict the behaviour we see around us. Because of the complexity of the determinants of economic behaviour, it is impossible to work with all possibly relevant considerations.

The method used by economists is to construct what is described as a 'model' of the economy, or of that part of it which they wish to study. The model is no more than a simplified representation of what are believed to be the major factors influencing the behaviour in question. Economists are basically no different from workers in other disciplines in their use of models. For instance, civil engineers use models of bridges to study such factors as metal fatigue and the effects of wind on structural stability; car manufacturers work with models of new designs, to study various performance characteristics. The word model as used here has the same meaning as theory, or hypothesis.[2]

Models deliberately ignore some factors in order to concentrate on others. Thus, an economic model of the determinants of the savings made by the population of the UK might concentrate on things such as the level of income, the rate of interest that may be earned on savings, and the total amount of savings accumulated in the past. The model might exclude other potential determinants of savings, such as the age distribution of the population, the expectation of life, the rate of inflation, and people's existing wealth.

When economists exclude some matters that might affect the subject they are studying from their model, we say that they are abstracting from reality. Abstraction is acceptable because a model is not intended to be a duplication of the real world but a useful simplification of it.

The variables listed in the theory are assumed to be the important ones, while the omitted variables are assumed to be unimportant. Since any theory must abstract from the potentially infinite number of influences, the inclusion of a small number of variables and the exclusion of many is necessary. The test of whether or not all the important variables are included and only unimportant ones are excluded, is whether the theory correctly predicts events that are yet to be observed. Consider, for example, the demand for carrots. If the important determining variables have been included in the behavioural relation, then virtually all observed variations in demand for carrots will be associated with these variables. If important influencing factors have been omitted, then variations in demand for carrots will occur that cannot be associated with the variables included in the model.

Economic Models

Economic models contain two types of variables, dependent variables whose behaviour is to be explained, and independent, or explanatory, variables that provide the explanation.

They also contain *behavioural assumptions* that explain how the dependent and independent variables are related to each other.

The meaning of each of these components of an economic model can best be explained with an example. Consider an extremely simple model which explains the savings behaviour in an economy as being determined by a single variable, the level of income. Here, the dependent variable is savings, the independent, or explanatory, variable is income; while the behavioural assumption is that a change in the level of income *causes* a change in the level of savings.

Properties of a good economic model

Two desirable features of an economic model are that the variables in it should be clearly defined, and that the

---

1 This is because of the properties of what is known as the 'law' of large numbers. See R.G. Lipsey, *An Introduction to Positive Economics*, Chapter 2 (Weidenfeld & Nicolson, 8th edn 1993). All subsequent references to this book are made to 'IPE'.

2 Note that some economists reserve the word model to describe certain more complicated kinds of relationships that interact with each other in a complete system. Our use of 'model' includes these interactive models, but also includes simpler theories and individual behavioural relations.

relationships in the model are quantifiable.

The first point is simple, but not perhaps too obvious. In our example, it is important that the variables, income and savings, should be unambiguously defined; for instance, there should be a clearly stated period of time to which they relate (e.g. a week, a month or a year), and it should be clear that we are talking about the income and savings of, say, persons, rather than total national savings and income, which would include also business and government.

The second point is that a model is usually more useful if it can be quantified. Some models may simply state that one variable depends positively or negatively on another. But quantification of an economic model tells us the extent of the influence. Let us return yet again to our savings model. The form in which it has been expressed so far is not quantified. It becomes quantified when we state by *how much* savings change when income changes. For example, if we state that savings are always 20 per cent of income, we quantify the income-savings relationship. Such a model yields more information than one which is not quantified.

Alternative expressions

There are four ways in which an economic model or behavioural relation may be expressed: (i) verbal statement; (ii) illustration by schedule (i.e. table); (iii) mathematical statement (i.e. using algebra); and (iv) geometrical statement (i.e. using graphs).

Verbal statement: With a verbal statement, the dependence of one variable on another is expressed in words. This is the only form that we have used so far.

Consider the savings model that we are using for purposes of illustration. In a quantified form, the verbal statement of the theory might be: 'Savings depend on income in such a way that 20 per cent of income is always saved'. This statement gives us enough information to enable us to calculate the level of savings *given* the level of income. For example, if income is £100, savings are 20 per cent of £100, i.e. £20. If income is £200, savings are 20 per cent of £200, i.e. £40, and so on.

Schedules: Economists sometimes present the information relating to theories in the form of tables or schedules. For example, our savings model can be illustrated in tabular form as in Table 3.1.

Such tabulations, or *schedules*, are less complete than other ways of expressing a model because they present only a select number of observations of the variables.

TABLE 3.1 The Relation Between Income and Savings

Income (Y)	Savings (S)	Reference letter
100	20	a
200	40	b
300	60	c
400	80	d

Mathematical statement: Students are sometimes frightened by mathematical expressions. Mathematics, however, is only a language. It uses symbols to make statements much as written languages use words to make sentences, and it does so very economically.

Using the symbols S for saving and Y for income, our model of savings behaviour can be expressed concisely as:

$$S = 0.2Y$$

This statement is in the form of an algebraic equation. It gives us exactly the same information as the verbal statement of the theory. We can calculate S for every level of Y. For example, if $Y = 100$, $S = 20$; if $Y = 200$, $S = 40$, and so on.

Geometrical statement: The fourth method of expressing an economic model is by the use of graphs, which are commonly used in this book. You must fully understand graphical methods if you are to read, and appreciate, major parts of later chapters. We assume here that you are able to use and interpret graphs. (If you are not, you should carefully study Appendix 1, which begins on page 504.)

Figure 3.1 is the graphical representation of our savings model, which we expressed verbally as savings are 20 per cent of income, and algebraically as $S = 0.2Y$. The vertical axis in the graph measures savings, and the horizontal axis measures income. Any *point* on the graph represents the value of savings that is associated with a particular value of income. For instance, point a represents savings of 20, associated with income of 100 as shown in the first row of Table 3.1. The other points marked with reference letters b, c and d are shown on the graph, and the line marked $S = 0.2Y$ on the graph joins all points where savings are 20 per cent of income. It is thus the graphical expression of our model.

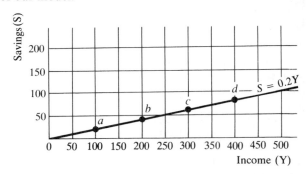

FIGURE 3.1 **A Graphical Expression of a Relationship Between Income and Savings.** The line marked $S = 0.2Y$ joins all points on the graph where savings are 20 per cent of income. This is the same model as that given by the above equation. The 4 points listed in Table 3.1 can also be identified in the diagram.

Complex economic models

Our description of economic models has been illustrated by one which has only two variables, the relationship between which can be expressed verbally, geometrically or mathematically. The real world, however, is more complex and economists often need to consider numerous variables. This is why professional work uses mathematical models, which cannot be expressed in the graphical terms on which we rely heavily on in this book.

One technique, commonly employed by economists in their analysis of complex models, is that of considering the influence of individual variables one (or a few) at a time. In order to do this the other variables in the theory are assumed not to change while the influence of a particular variable is analysed. Such a procedure involves what is known as a CETERIS PARIBUS assumption, the Latin expression meaning 'other things being equal'. You will meet this term frequently in this book – the next time on the second page of the very next chapter, where we assume all determinants of the demand for a commodity other than its price are held constant, *ceteris paribus*, while we examine, in some detail, the effect of price on quantity demanded.

TESTING ECONOMIC MODELS

We have seen that economists construct theories and then seek to test them against facts. We have already discussed the construction of theories and we turn now to their application to empirical evidence.

Economic Statistics

Modern statistical analysis has been developed to test economic theories when evidence is generated in an uncontrollable fashion. To some extent, statistical techniques used by economists are common to those used in other scientific subjects. However, there are also problems peculiar to economics, for which a special branch of statistics has grown up. It is called ECONOMETRICS.

Testing theories by confronting them with evidence is a procedure with the following steps:

1 State the theory in a testable form.
2 Collect data to test the theory.
3 Compare the predictions from the theory with the evidence.
4 Ask if any associations discovered are causal.

These steps may be illustrated by applying them to our model of savings behaviour.

Step 1. State the theory in a testable form

One can test a theory which states that one (or more) specified variables depends on another (or others). Our example of the theory of savings is in such a form, i.e. that savings is a constant 20 per cent of income. Given any level of income, the theory predicts the level of savings.

Step 2. Collect data to test the theory

For our test we need observations of past savings behaviour at different income levels. It is obvious that we cannot obtain data about all past income-savings relationships for all people for all time. Hence we select some data which we believe to be representative of the total. Such partial data is known as a sample (of the total population). To test our savings theory we could, for example, obtain records of the savings of persons of different income levels. If those we selected were representative of people in general, we would be satisfied that we could draw general conclusions about the population as a whole. Standard statistical theory deals with the question of how to choose a representative sample.

Step 3. Compare the predictions of the theory with the evidence

Statistical theory has well-developed procedures for deciding whether the evidence is consistent with the theory. Since nothing can ever be certain in our world of experience, these statistical tests give *probabilities* that the theory is correct, *given* the observations that have been made.

Statisticians use the term STATISTICAL ASSOCIATION (or CORRELATION) to describe the extent to which a theory they are testing is consistent with the facts. Consider a theory that says two variables are positively associated. If the observed facts show no statistical association between the variables, the theory is said to be not supported by the test. If a positive correlation is shown, the theory is said to be consistent with the facts. In the latter case, there are statistical methods of ascertaining the strength of the association.

These matters can best be made clear by an example. Imagine that we have drawn a sample of people in different income groups whose savings behaviour we then study. We are faced with the task of judging whether there is some correlation or association between their savings and their income levels. One of the most useful starting points is to plot the observations on a graph to give a visual representation of the relationship between the two variables. Such a graph is called a *scatter diagram*.

In Figure 3.2 we show three scatter diagrams based on hypothetical data on the savings and income of three different groups of people. Let us ask whether we can detect any statistical association in the three cases and how much confidence we would have in them.

To see whether there is an association we inspect the graphs for any clear pattern. In Figure 3.1(i) there is no obvious pattern in the scatter of points. At any level of income, savings vary over a wide range. In Figure 3.1(ii), in contrast, a very clear pattern is observable. The points on the graph all lie close to a line which we have drawn showing the average relationship between income and savings of all the people in the sample.[1]

The confidence we can have in a statistical correlation, such as that of Figure 3.2(ii), depends on two considerations, the variability of the observations around the line showing the average relationship, and the actual

---

1 The line representing the average relation between any two variables can be found precisely by using well-known statistical procedures – the simplest of which is known as 'least-squares regression analysis'.

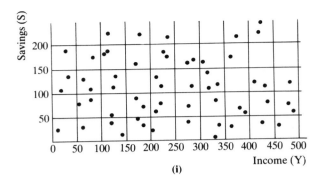

(i)

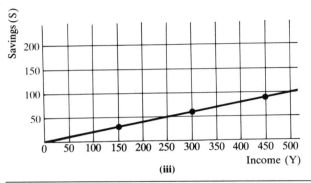

(iii)

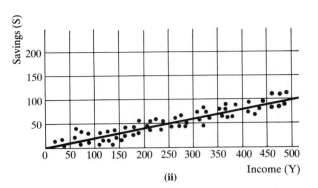

(ii)

FIGURE 3.2 Three Scatter Diagrams Showing the Relationship Between Income and Savings for 3 Groups of People. In part (i) of the diagram there is no obvious correlation between the two variables, while in parts (ii) and (iii) there are clear positive associations between income and savings.

In (ii) there are enough observations to suggest that the correlation is positive, but the variability exhibited makes it difficult to quantify precisely by visual inspection alone.

In (iii) there is no variability around the linear relation, but with only 3 observations the correlation might rather easily be due to chance.

number of observations. In Figure 3.2(iii), for example, there are only three observations. Therefore, despite the fact that savings are exactly 20 per cent of income for the three people in the sample, one would hesitate to draw a general conclusion that income and savings were positively correlated. With so small a sample, the results could all too easily be a matter of pure chance.

Chance and confidence: Statistical techniques have been developed to estimate the probability that any observed correlations are the result of chance. They are based on the two characteristics of sample data already mentioned – variability, and sample size.

Data reliability: In addition to being cautious about assessing statistically observed associations, one must take care over the data themselves, which are not always as reliable as they sometimes seem to be. Many statistics, official and other, have the appearance of reliability, sometimes because they are given to one or more places of decimals. The data on personal savings, discussed earlier in the chapter, for example, happen to be amongst the least reliable of all official statistics. The figures for particular years are usually heavily revised later, and should thus be regarded as subject to large errors of measurement.[1]

Working economists must assemble the best data available, and apply the most efficient techniques for assessing whether an economic model is, or is not, supported by the evidence. At several stages in the testing process, judgement will be called for before conclusions are reached.

1 For a discussion of data reliability, see C. Harbury and R.G. Lipsey, *An Introduction to the U.K. Economy* (see page xi above for details).

Step 4. Ask if any associations discovered are causal

Let us say we have a theory that X is the cause of Y, and our tests show that variations in X are accompanied by variations in Y. The data is consistent with our theory of causation, but it does not prove it. Consider what else might be the explanation of the observed relation between X and Y.

- Y might be the cause of X.
- The observed relation between X and Y might have arisen by chance.
- X and Y might be unrelated to each other but both might be affected by some common, third, variable.

Let us consider these in turn.

In the first case there is a causal relation but it is the reverse of the theory – Y causes X, rather than X causes Y. Identifying the correct causal direction may be difficult, especially if the events which are correlated are close to each other in time, even chasing each other in chicken-and-egg fashion. For example, business confidence appears to increase as businesses increase their spending on capital investment. Which comes first?

In the second case there is no causal relation. The statistical relation occurred by pure chance. One may never be certain that this is not the case, but statistical tests are designed to assess the probability of chance happenings.

The third case is a very common cause of incorrectly inferring a causal correlation. To illustrate, consider a simple case. If you look at statistics of the annual numbers of deaths by suicide and of marriages in England and Wales since the turn of the century, you will observe a strong

BOX 3.1 Treasury Blocks Reform on Statistics

'A Royal Statistical Society working party, which included Sir Claus Moser, former head of the Government Statistical Service, has suggested changes in the system for collecting figures.

'Its nine-month investigation found "a serious erosion of public confidence in UK official statistics". It said the organisation of the statistical service allowed a "potential for political influence"; the quality and accuracy of some publications had created "unease"; some figures, notably on the balance of payments, were seriously deficient; and ministers manipulated the release of statistics so that bad news received minimum exposure. The working party was set up after repeated criticisms of government statistics by academic as well as opposition politicians. Since 1979, there have been 30 changes in the way unemployment figures are calculated, of which 29 have reduced the total ... Members of the working party say that, even if the Government is satisfied with its statistics, users in industry and the City are not.'

(*The Independent on Sunday*, 10 September 1990)

Economists work by constructing models of the economy which they test by confronting those models with data from the real world. The reliability of the tests depends, among other things, on the reliability of the statistical data themselves. Doubts about the quality of official statistics have long been expressed by economists, such as the American Professor Oskar Morgenstern, whose classic book *On the Accuracy of Economic Observations* was published as long ago as 1950.

Questions

1 Statistics of the distribution of personal income can be obtained in several ways, e.g. by studying the income-tax returns of individuals or by conducting surveys, asking people how much they earn. What biases would you expect to find in these methods?
2 Identify two kinds of economic data which you would want to manipulate in one direction if you were a supporter of the present government, and in another direction if you were a supporter of the opposition?
3 Economic data based on official statistics forms the basis of a number of tables in this book. Have a look at those on pages 15, 172, 228, 243 and 247. Which would strike you as being the more reliable and the less reliable?

statistical association. Both suicides and marriages were about 35 per cent higher in 1988 than in 1900.

Is the statistical association causal, in the sense that marriages *cause* suicide? Surely not. The circumstances that drive people to take their own lives are more complex than the simple correlation would suggest. The basic cause of this statistical association is to be found in the rise in the total population (from 33 to 50 million), which pushed up the numbers of both marriages and suicides.

Causation is difficult to prove. In the real world, events follow each other in sequence. We try to explain the sequences with theories. The more events a theory appears to explain satisfactorily, the more naturally one would expect it to explain another.

WHY ECONOMISTS DISAGREE

Economics uses scientific method, confronting theories with evidence about the real world, in a manner comparable with other sciences. This does not, however, prevent economists from disagreeing, as the media sometimes take delight in pointing out.

Basically, there are two reasons why economists may disagree. To understand them we must go back to the distinction between positive and normative economics discussed at the beginning of this chapter.

First, there are all the positive issues which involve interpreting historical events and predicting the effects of adopting different policies. If you follow the debate about some proposed change in policy, such as the effect on savings of lowering the rate of personal income tax, you will find some disagreement among economists. Even more disagreement surrounds the forecasts of the economic models made by economists in government, in universities, in research institutes and elsewhere. Their forecasts, e.g. for inflation, economic growth, or UK exports, not infrequently differ, sometimes by rather wide margins. Such differences stem from varying theories that economists hold about *how the economy works*. They follow simply from the problems involved in drawing conclusions from statistical testing of economic hypotheses, the more important of which were mentioned earlier.

The second cause of differences among economists relates not to positive, but to normative economics – affecting questions of economic *policy*. We may, for example, find some economists who favour one policy rather than another because of its effects on the distribution of income, because it involves less (or more) government intervention in the activities of private business, or because it is likely to reduce unemployment faster than it brings inflation down. Such differences may reflect the value judgements held by individuals, i.e. a preference for more or less inequality in income distribution, a repugnance for things which give more power to governments, etc., etc.

Economists should do their utmost to make clear when

they are engaging in positive economics, and when letting their personal value judgements affect their writings and sayings. When they do this, the task of choosing between alternative policy proposals is eased. Of course, it does not help resolve differences in positive economics – e.g. which economic forecast to believe on where the economy is going to be next week, next month or next year. The extent of disagreements among economists is, however, often exaggerated in the media, which search for conflicting views. There are many areas of consensus, for example on the general effects of taxes, price controls, international trade and the creation of monopoly powers, and you will learn about them in the course of your study of this book.

Summary

1 Economists distinguish between positive and normative statements. Positive statements are about matters of fact; many are testable, in principle, against empirical evidence. Normative statements involve opinions (or value judgements) and cannot be settled, even in principle, by appeal to facts.

2 Scientific method relates theories to evidence in a systematic way. Economics is, in this sense, a science – one which studies human behaviour.

3 Most natural sciences, e.g. physics, can test theories in laboratory experiments, holding constant one or more variables in order to study the influence of others. Non-experimental sciences, such as economics, mainly relate theories to evidence gathered in everyday life, when many variables are changing at the same time.

4 Economic theories (also called models or hypotheses) contain two types of variables – *independent*, or *explanatory*, variables which explain the behaviour of *dependent* variables. They also contain behavioural assumptions, which link the two types of variables causally. Many economic theories may be expressed verbally, geometrically or mathematically.

5 Testing an economic theory involves (i) stating it in a testable form, (ii) collecting relevant data, and (iii) confronting the theory's predictions with the evidence.

6 Testing economic theories involves the use of statistical techniques (econometrics). If a test implies that variables are correlated (associated statistically), a separate question of whether they are also *causally* linked requires careful consideration.

7 Disagreements among economists may be attributed to either positive considerations (e.g. different views as to how the economy functions), or to normative considerations (e.g. personal preferences for different policies).

Questions

1 Which of the following statements are Positive (P), Normative (N), and neither positive nor normative (A)? (i) People save more when their income rises. (ii) If people save more as their income rises, a statistical association between income and savings will be observed. (iii) People should behave rationally and save less as their incomes fall.

2 Reword the following statement so as to make it testable. 'The government should lower the rate of income tax because it encourages people to work harder.'

3 Is the following statement True or False? 'Economics is regarded as a (social) science because theories about economic behaviour can be confronted with evidence from the real world.'

4 Given the following simple economic model, identify the dependent variable (DV), the independent variable (IV) and the behavioural assumption (BA). 'When confidence is low, businesses will choose to build few new factories.'

5 You are told that consumers spend a constant proportion of their income (Y) on consumption (C), and that two points on a graph are $Y = 100$, $C = 80$, and $Y = 200$, $C = 160$. Draw the relationship on Figure 3.1 and express it in the form of an equation.

6 Which One or More of the following conclusions can be drawn from the data given below?

Year	Income (Y)	Expenditure (E)
1	1000	500
2	1300	600
3	1500	750

(a) Y and E are statistically correlated.
(b) E is a constant proportion of Y.
(c) A rise in Y causes a rise in E.
(d) A rise in E causes a rise in Y.
(e) All of the above.

PART

2

Elementary
Microeconomics

Preface to Part 2

In this second Part, you will learn how to use some elementary tools of economic analysis. These concern the well-known forces of supply and demand. You should not find them too difficult to master. They will enable you to see many real-world problems in a new light and with greater understanding.

The content of this Part 2 and the next Part 3 of this book constitute what is known as *microeconomics,* in contrast to the *macroeconomics* of Parts 4 and 5 which looks at the broad features of the economy as a whole. MICROECONOMICS is the name given to the part of our subject which studies economic behaviour 'in the small'. It looks at the details of the economy and at the relationships among its constituent parts, dealing with such matters as prices, costs and quantities in thousands of individual markets for goods, services and factors of production. It is, in a way, as if we are looking at parts of the economy through a microscope.

In Chapter 2, we described how a market system allocates resources among alternative uses. Buyers and sellers interact in markets where goods and services are bought and sold. The prices at which these transactions take place help to determine the allocation of resources, and movements in these prices help to motivate the reallocation of the resources.

Part 2 of this book is about the determinants of quantities of commodities bought and sold and the prices at which these sales take place. We start with two chapters devoted to a study of demand – the behaviour of buyers. They are followed by a chapter on supply – the behaviour of sellers. Finally we look at how supply and demand come together in markets to determine actual quantities and prices.

4 Demand and Price

Consider those who buy goods and services for their own consumption – in economics they are called consumers. (They are sometimes also called buyers, purchasers or households.) The quantity of a good that consumers want to buy per period of time is referred to as their *demand* for that commodity. What are the main determinants of demand?

Before outlining the theory of demand, we must carefully define our terms and lay out our assumptions.

CONSUMER DEMAND

Consumers: These are the people who make decisions about buying goods and services. Some consumers are individuals acting for themselves alone; others are members of households buying on behalf of their group.[1]

Consumer motivations: We assume that consumers seek to allocate their expenditures among all the goods and services that they might buy so as to gain the greatest possible satisfaction.

We say that consumers try to maximize their satisfaction, or their utility. When they succeed we say that they have achieved an OPTIMUM position (using the Latin word meaning the best possible result).

Durables and non-durables: We have earlier drawn a distinction between goods and services. Another distinction is also important. Some goods are only used once. They are consumed and are of no further use – a lamb chop or a baby's disposable nappy for example. Many other goods are durable and are useful over an extended period of time. This book, a television set and a ballpoint pen are examples of such durable-use goods. The former type of goods are called NON-DURABLES while the latter are called CONSUMER DURABLES or sometimes just DURABLES.

Time: To describe consumers' behaviour we need to know how much they wish to purchase – how many bottles of wine, concert tickets, etc. – *per period of time.*

This means that demand is a flow, it takes place over time measured as so much per period of time.

The unit of time chosen is merely a matter of convenience. After all, it means exactly the same thing to say that a consumer buys oranges at a rate of *one per day*, or *seven per week*, or *365 per year*.

Effective demand: Demand theory is about the quantities of a good that consumers *desire to buy* over a period of time. The phrase 'desire to buy' is critical. It is not just 'desire' in the sense of 'would like to have', it is 'desire *to buy*' in the sense of 'prepared to spend the necessary money to make the purchase'.

Thus, demand means EFFECTIVE DEMAND, in the sense of being able and willing to buy.

Price-taking behaviour: At the outset we consider markets that contain a large number of buyers. There are so many of them that no one of them can have an appreciable effect on the market by altering his or her own behaviour. Each consumer buys so small a fraction of the total being sold, that an increase, or a reduction, in the quantity each purchases, would go unnoticed. Clearly, many real world markets are like this. Even complete withdrawal by any one buyer from the market has no noticeable effect on the price.

We shall consider markets in which buyers have significant price influence later in this book. For now, we confine ourselves to situations in which buyers are so numerous that they must take the market price as they find it, being unable to influence it. We say such buyers are *price-takers*.

WHAT DETERMINES QUANTITY DEMANDED?

How much of some commodity will consumers be willing to buy, say, per month? The amount will be influenced by many variables including: the commodity's own price, the prices of related commodities, average income and its distribution among consumers, tastes, expectations, the size of the population, and social and psychological factors.

We can neither develop a simple theory, nor understand the separate influence of each variable, if we start by trying to consider what happens when everything changes at once. Fortunately, there is an easier way. We can consider the influence of the variables one at a time. To do this, we hold all but one of them constant, i.e. we make the assumption that they do not change.

For example, when examining the relationship between quantity demanded and *price*, we assume that consumers' incomes, tastes, and *all the other determinants* of quantity demanded are unchanged. We then let price vary, and study how it affects quantity demanded. We then do the

---

1 Because we are not yet considering businesses' demand for factors of production, we neglect purchases by firms of commodities to use in their production processes.

same for each of the other variables in turn. In this way we are able to understand their importance by studying their influences one at a time. Once this is done, we can aggregate the separate influences of two or more variables to discover what would happen if several things changed at the same time – as they often do in practice.

As we said in Chapter 3, holding all other influencing variables constant is often described by the words 'other things being equal' or by the equivalent Latin phrase, CETERIS PARIBUS. When economists speak, for example, of the influence of the price of wheat on the quantity of wheat demanded, *ceteris paribus*, they refer to what a change in the price of wheat would do to the quantity demanded, if all other factors that influence the demand for wheat do not change.

In this chapter, we discuss exclusively the relationship between the quantity demanded of a good and one of these variables – the price of the good itself, known as its OWN PRICE. We return, in the next chapter, to consider other variables.

DEMAND BY A SINGLE CONSUMER

Holding all other influences constant, how do we expect the quantity of a particular commodity demanded to vary as its own price varies? *In the case of almost all commodities, this quantity increases as the price of the commodity falls* – all other influences being held constant, by our *ceteris paribus* assumption.

To illustrate the relation between price and quantity demanded, we consider a particular good, lamb chops. Table 4.1 presents data showing the quantities in column (i) that one consumer, whom we call Alan, would be prepared to buy per month at 6 selected prices. The Table is called a demand schedule. It shows, for example, at a price of £2.00 per lb. his quantity demanded is 2 lbs. per month; at a price of £1.00 his quantity demanded is 6 lbs. per month and so forth. Each of the price-quantity combinations in the table is given a letter for easy reference.

TABLE 4.1 Alan's Demand for Lamb Chops

Reference letter	Price (£s per lb.) (i)	Quantity demanded (lbs. per month) (ii)
a	2.50	0
b	2.00	2
c	1.50	4
d	1.00	6
e	0.50	8
f	0.00	10

The data in Table 4.1 can also be presented in the form of a graph. In Figure 4.1, we measure price on the vertical axis and quantity on the horizontal axis. We choose our scales in order to accommodate the numbers in the table and then plot each point, one at a time.

The first point, labelled *a*, represents 0lbs. of lamb chops demanded at a price of £2.50 per lb. It conveys identical information to that of the top line in the Table. Point *b* represents 2 lbs. of lamb chops demanded per month at a

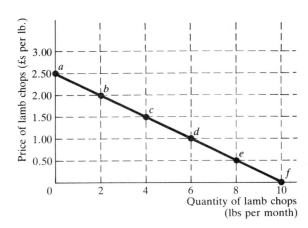

FIGURE 4.1 A Demand Curve for an Individual Consumer. Each point on the curve shows the quantity of lamb chops that Alan would buy at each particular price.

price of £2.00 per lb. Points labelled *c*, *d*, *e* and *f* on the graph correspond to the price-quantity combinations shown in the corresponding rows in the Table. Point *f* tells us how many lamb chops Alan would consume per month if they were free.

A Demand Curve

We now draw a continuous line through all these points. This is called a *demand curve* for lamb chops. It is more general than the schedule in the table, which shows only six price-quantity combinations. The demand curve shows the quantities demanded not only at all the prices in the table, but also at *all* intermediate prices. For example, to find quantity demanded at a price of £1.75 per lb., we locate the price £1.75 on the price axis and follow that price over to the demand curve. We then run down to the quantity axis to find that the associated quantity is 3 lbs. per month. We can do this for any price. For example at a price of £0.75, quantity demanded is 7 lbs. per month.

The DEMAND CURVE describes the complete relationship between price and quantities demanded.[1]

The slope of the demand curve

The demand curve in Figure 4.1 is consistent with the statement made earlier that the quantity of any commodity that is demanded increases as its own price falls. To put it the other way, quantity decreases when its own price rises. This type of relationship, when one variable moves in the opposite direction to another, is known in mathematics as a negative relationship.

It means simply that the two variables, here price and quantity, move in opposite directions to each other. So, the demand curve is said to have a negative slope. Econ-

---

1 Geometrically, a demand curve may take the shape of either a curved or a straight line. By convention, the demand relation is referred to as a demand *curve* in either case.

omists often read graphs from left to right and thus often refer to the demand curve as 'being downward-sloping', rather than as 'having a negative slope'.

Why should the slope be negative? One reason is that, when a good's own price falls, the good becomes cheaper *relative to* other goods. It is, therefore, easier for the good to compete against other substitute commodities. At £0.50 a lb., lamb chops are cheap relative not only to steak but relative to minced beef and other low-priced meats. At prices higher than £2.50 a lb., lamb chops look expensive, relative to these other kinds of meat, and Alan will tend to buy these other kinds instead of lamb chops. Do not forget that our *ceteris paribus* assumption means that all other influences, including the prices of other kinds of meat, do not change.

Utility

A deeper explanation of the negative slope of demand curves is given by what is called utility theory. The satisfaction that consumers derive from the goods they buy is called their UTILITY. We use this concept, although consumers may never have heard of it, because it enables us to construct a theory of consumer behaviour.

Consider the utility that one consumer, call her Kate, derives from purchases of a good such as ice-cream. If only one ice-cream is consumed each week, it will be enjoyed greatly, the second perhaps a little less, the third, fourth, fifth and subsequent ice-creams will each give less pleasure still. Indeed, once a dozen or two are consumed each week, Kate may have had her fill and want no more, even if the ice-creams are free.

Diminishing marginal utility

Let us examine the relationship between utility and the quantity consumed for an individual. First, we must make an important distinction between the total utility derived from the consumption of all of the goods consumed over some period of time and the change in utility derived from a change in consumption of one unit over that period of time, often called its marginal utility. MARGINAL UTILITY is defined as the difference in utility arising from a change in the rate of consumption per period of time. If TU_n stands for the total utility from consuming n units of a good, and TU_{n-1} stands for the total utility from consuming one less of the good over the period of time in question, then marginal utility is the difference, TU_n minus TU_{n-1}.

The more of a good that any individual consumes, per time-period, the greater the TOTAL UTILITY that he or she enjoys. But consider what happens to marginal utility, i.e. the *increases* in total utility that occur as consumption increases. Suppose Kate's consumption rises from one ice-cream per week to two. Total utility from two ice-creams will be greater than from one. Suppose a third ice-cream is bought each week. Total utility rises again, but the *extra* or *marginal utility* from the third ice-cream is less than that from the second, which is less again than that from the first.

Diminishing marginal utility (from consumption of ice-creams in this case) means that, while total utility rises with consumption, marginal utility, in contrast, falls. In other words, the extra satisfaction obtained from eating more and more ice-creams leads to smaller and smaller rises in satisfaction. To put this point yet another way, the rate at which total utility rises, diminishes as consumption of any one commodity increases.

If all this sounds forbidding, read on and soon you will find the idea becoming quite clear.

Utility schedules and graphs

Table 4.2 sets out hypothetical data illustrating the assumptions that have been made about utility. Column (ii) of the table shows Kate's total utility rising as the number of ice-creams she eats each week rises. *Ceteris*

TABLE 4.2 Kate's Total and Marginal Utility Schedules. Total utility rises but marginal utility declines as Kate's consumption increases.

Number of ice-creams eaten per week (i)	Total utility (ii)	Marginal utility (iii)
0	0	
1	60	60
2	100	40
3	130	30
4	150	20
5	166	16
6	178	12
7	186	8
8	192	6
9	196	4
10	198	2

paribus the more ice-creams she eats each month the more satisfaction she gets – at least over the range shown in the table.

Now consider the marginal utility, shown in column (iii) of the table – for example, the marginal utility of 40, shown against an increase in consumption from 1 to 2 ice-creams per week. This arises because total utility increases from 60 to 100 – a difference of 40 – with the second ice-cream. The marginal utility of 2, shown in the last row of the table, arises because total utility rises only from 196 to 198, when consumption rises from 9 to 10 ice-creams per month. Marginal utility is associated with the *change* from one unit of the good to another. To indicate this, the figures for marginal utility are recorded half-way between the other rows.

Now, notice that although total utility is rising as the number of ice-creams Kate consumes each week rises, her marginal utility associated with each extra ice-cream consumed per month is falling.

The same data can also be shown graphically, as in Figure 4.2, parts (i) and (ii) of which depict total and marginal utility, respectively. Note that the curve showing total utility rises continuously. But the amount of the rise is less and less as more and more ice-creams are consumed.

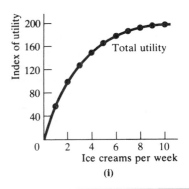 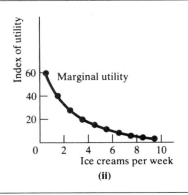

FIGURE 4.2 Curves of Total and Marginal Utility.
The total utility that Kate derives from ice-creams rises as the quantity consumed increases, but it rises at a diminishing rate. Thus the marginal utility falls as consumption increases.

Thus the marginal utility curve is declining: *each successive ice-cream adds to total utility, but each adds less than its predecessor*. Note, too, that the figures for marginal utility are plotted at the midpoints of the intervals over which they are calculated. This is because marginal utility is associated with changes in utility – exactly the same reason as for utility schedules (see above).

How universal is diminishing marginal utility?

This is a question of fact (often called an EMPIRICAL question). Experiments have been designed to test it in various situations and, although such tests are difficult to design, the evidence suggests marginal utility does indeed tend to decline, and is likely at some point to reach zero.

Take apples as an example. Even for the most ardent apple lover, at some point eating additional apples ceases to add to utility. Beyond that point where marginal utility is zero, apples could be said to have a negative marginal utility (or, as it is sometimes called, a marginal disutility), though an individual would not voluntarily consume apples or any other commodity when marginal utility became negative. The same is true of most other goods and services, though we cannot be sure that marginal utility diminishes for every single commodity for everybody in the world.

There are bound to be exceptions. Alcoholic drink and cigarettes, which have addictive properties, may be examples for some people. The second, or third drink, for instance, may give more satisfaction than the first, though marginal utility will eventually fall off as further amounts give less and less satisfaction, quite apart from the fact that you may become ill.

Marginal utility and the demand curve

We have explained the downward slope of demand curves with the idea of diminishing marginal utility – that as an individual consumes additional quantities of a good, the *extra* satisfaction derived from them gradually falls. There is, however, another way of looking at the reason for the downward slope, which arises from the fact that many commodities can be used for several purposes.[1] Each use

is itself subject to diminishing marginal utility. When price is relatively high, the good is bought mainly for the uses ranked high by the consumer; when the price falls, the good will then be bought for less important uses, and for which marginal utility is lower.

Consider, for example, champagne. Its most obvious use is for drinking on special occasions, such as weddings, or for smashing at the launch of ocean liners! Champagne can also be drunk as an aperitif; it can be served as a table wine with a meal; it can even be used for cooking. The fact that marginal utility from some uses is lower than from others helps explain the downward slope of the demand curve for champagne. When the price of champagne is £20 or more a bottle, it will be bought principally for celebrating special occasions. At £10 or £12 a bottle

---

BOX 4.1 Art in the Market-Place

'Van Gogh's portrait of his doctor fetches almost £50m at an auction in New York. Renoir's *Au Moulin de la Gallete* is likely to go for nearly as much tonight. Monstrous! cry the killjoys. How can one painting be worth so much? Shame! cry the publicly-funded museums. How shall we ever be able to afford a masterpiece?'

(*The Times*, 17 May 1990)

The idea that demand is essentially willingness to pay regardless of the reasons for someone wanting to do so is illustrated by this news item. (Incidentally, the forecast for the Renoir was not far out. It fetched £46.5 million.)

Questions

1 If the purchaser was a collector who owned 99 other works of art, what if anything can be inferred about (i) the total utility, (ii) the marginal utility, of his collection?
2 What would the marginal utility have been of the highest unsuccessful bidder when he dropped out of the auction?

---

1 The demand for commodities which can be used for several purposes is known as COMPOSITE DEMAND, but the term is rarely used nowadays.

some may be bought for somewhat more humble parties. If the price were to fall well below £10 it might be bought to serve as a table wine, or even for cooking. All of this suggests why the demand curve for champagne has a negative slope.

Marginal utility and the quantity demanded

The argument so far has been largely intuitive. Now we consider more formally the relationship between marginal utility and the quantity demanded.

Consider Table 4.2, which shows Kate's total and marginal utility schedules for ice-creams. Given some price of ice-creams, say 40p each, how many would she buy?

To answer this question, we recall our assumption that Kate, and all other consumers, seek to maximize their total utilities from consumption.

The principle for doing so is that they should distribute their expenditures among all available commodities until the last penny spent on each commodity yields the same marginal utility.

This has an immediate appeal to common sense. If the last penny spent on ice-creams yielded more utility than the last penny spent on apples, then total utility could be increased by transferring a penny of expenditure from apples to ice-creams. Say, for example, the last penny spent on ice-creams yielded 100 units of utility, while the last spent on apples yielded only 70. By spending a penny less on apples, 70 units of utility are lost; by spending that penny on ice-creams, 100 units are gained. The net gain from the transfer is thus 30 units of utility.

Let us suppose that Kate is in this situation, and that she starts reallocating her spending as suggested. As she buys less apples, their marginal utility will rise; as she buys more ice-creams, their marginal utility will fall. She goes on, gaining the difference between the two marginal utilities each time she transfers a penny, until the marginal utility of a penny spent on apples is the same as the marginal utility spent on ice-creams. Say the marginal utility of ice-creams has fallen to 90, while that for apples has risen to 90. There is now nothing to be gained from further reallocations of expenditures between the two products.

The Rule For Maximizing Utility

The condition for dividing expenditures between apples and ice-creams can now be stated in an equation. We do this by letting MU stand for marginal utility, calling apples 'good A' and ice-creams 'good B'. Now we can write:

$$MU \text{ of 1p spent on } A = MU \text{ of 1p spent on } B \quad (1)$$

Next we ask: 'how do we know the marginal utility of a penny spent on any commodity, say ice-creams, when all we are given is the marginal utility of a unit of the commodity?' Table 4.2, for example, tells us that the marginal utility of the third ice-cream is 30. What, however, is the marginal utility of a penny spent on ice-creams when consumption goes from two or three? The answer depends

on how much ice-creams cost. If the third ice-cream costs 30p and yields 30 units of utility, then the utility per penny is 30/30p = 1 unit of utility per penny spent. If ice-creams cost only 15p, then the marginal utility per penny spent is 30/15p = 2; if the price is 60p, then the marginal utility per penny spent is 30/60p = 0.5.

In general, then, the marginal utility of a penny spent on some commodity is the marginal utility of a unit of that commodity divided by its price per unit. Now we can rewrite equation (1), the condition of maximizing utility, into a new form:

$$\frac{MU \text{ of } A}{\text{price of } A} = \frac{MU \text{ of } B}{\text{price of } B} \quad (2)$$

Now let us consider the demand for one of these products, commodity A. Rearrangement of (2) produces the following result:

$$\frac{MU \text{ of } A}{MU \text{ of } B} = \frac{\text{price of } A}{\text{price of } B} \quad (3)$$

Equation (3) tells us that in equilibrium the consumer will adjust purchases of any two goods until their marginal utilities are proportional to their prices. This is not a new condition, it is just another way of putting the point made in (2). The consumer wants the same marginal utility per penny spent on A and on B. This means that, if a unit of A costs twice as much as a unit of B, the marginal utility from the last unit of A must provide double that from the last unit of B.

Changes in equilibrium

Consider, now how a consumer reacts to changing prices. *Ceteris paribus*, which in this case means holding the price and consumption of commodity B constant, let the price of A fall. The consumer restores equilibrium by consuming more A until its marginal utility falls in the same proportion as its price has fallen. For example, if the price of A falls by 10 per cent, the consumer increases her purchases of A until the marginal utility of A falls by 10 per cent. Then the ratio given in (3) will be re-established.

This demonstrates why the demand curve for A has a negative slope and by a similar argument why so has every other commodity. Notice that the consumer adjusts purchases of A until its marginal utility changes in proportion to the change in its price. This does not mean changing the quantity of A in that proportion. If the marginal utility of A falls quickly, only a little more A will be bought; if the marginal utility of A falls slowly, then a lot more A will be bought.

MARKET DEMAND

So far we have looked at a single consumer's demand for a good. To explain market behaviour we need to know the *total demand* for a good from all consumers.

To obtain the market demand, we add together the

demands of all individuals. To illustrate, we take a simple case where there are only two consumers, Alan and Jill. Alan's demand schedule and demand curve we have already encountered. We repeat it in column (ii) in Table 4.3 and in Figure 4.3(i) below, adding Jill's demand schedule in column (iii) of the table, and putting her demand curve alongside Alan's in Figure 4.3(ii).

Market Demand Schedule

Let us deal, first, with the market demand *schedule*. This is obtained by adding the quantities demanded by Alan and Jill at each price to give a total quantity demanded in column (iv). Since Jill likes lamb chops more than Alan, we see that when price is between £2.50 and £3.50 per lb., only Jill buys them. Since Jill is then the only consumer in the market, the market demand schedule corresponds exactly to Jill's schedule at these high prices. As soon as price falls below £2.50 per lb., however, Alan wants to buy lamb chops too. The market demand at these prices is, therefore, the sum of both persons' positive demands. For example at a price of £2.00 per lb. the demand is 2 lbs. from Alan plus 3 lbs. from Jill, which equals 5 lbs. for the two of them. When price is £1.00 a lb. the market demand is 6 plus $4\frac{1}{2} = 10\frac{1}{2}$ lbs., and so on.

Market Demand Curve

Now consider the derivation of the market demand *curve*. This can, of course, be constructed by plotting the market demand schedule in column (iv) of Table 4.3, which we derived in the previous paragraph. The geometrical equivalent of this is to add horizontally the demand curves of the two individuals. This process is illustrated in Figure 4.3. By taking a common price on each curve, and adding the corresponding quantities, we discover the total quantity demanded at each price. For example at a price of £1.50 a

TABLE 4.3 Individual and Market Demand Schedules for Lamb Chops

PRICE	QUANTITIES DEMANDED		
(£s per lb.)	Alan (lbs. per month)	Jill (lbs. per month)	Market demand (lbs. per month) (Alan *plus* Jill) (ii)+(iii)
(i)	(ii)	(iii)	(iv)
4.00	0	0	0
3.50	0	$\frac{3}{4}$	$\frac{3}{4}$
3.00	0	$1\frac{1}{2}$	$1\frac{1}{2}$
2.50	0	$2\frac{1}{4}$	$2\frac{1}{4}$
2.00	2	3	5
1.50	4	$3\frac{3}{4}$	$7\frac{3}{4}$
1.00	6	$4\frac{1}{2}$	$10\frac{1}{2}$
0.50	8	$5\frac{1}{4}$	$13\frac{3}{4}$
0.00	10	6	16

lb. the two curves tell us that Alan will demand 4lbs. while Jill will demand $3\frac{3}{4}$ lbs. This makes a total of $7\frac{3}{4}$ lbs. which is plotted as the total market demand associated with a price of £1.50 per lb.

In practice, we seldom obtain market demand curves by summing the demand curves of individual consumers. Our knowledge of market demand is usually derived by observing total quantities directly. We have shown the way to do it here, because we wish to understand the relationship between curves for individual persons and the market curve. Of course, market demand curves express the demands for many more than two people – in some cases it is millions of people. We have used two persons merely to illustrate the procedure.

Distinctive features of market demand

Predictability: Individuals are not perfectly predictable machines. They sometimes do erratic things that we are

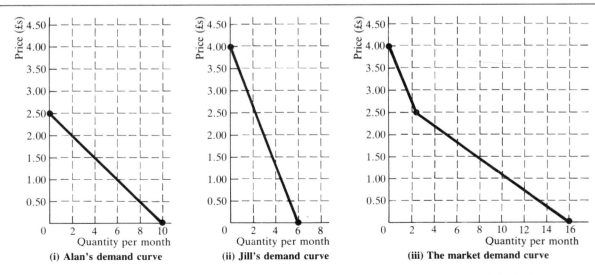

FIGURE 4.3 Individual and Market Demand Curves. The market demand curve is derived by the horizontal summation of the individual demand curves.

unable to explain in rational terms. As long, however, as this behaviour is random, it will tend to cancel out when each individual's behaviour is aggregated to obtain the market demand curve. If, for example, some individual for no apparent reason decides to increase his purchases of lamb chops this week, a second individual may, equally inexplicably, decide to reduce her purchases. Thus, occasional erratic behaviour on the part of any one person will not upset the normal systematic relations between market demands and the factors that influence them. As long as erratic behaviour is unrelated across consumers (i.e., everyone does not do the same erratic thing at the same time), the market as a whole will behave normally.

Price and quantity demanded: Because the extra satisfaction consumers derive from consuming additional units of a commodity tends to fall as more of it is consumed, people will only buy more of a commodity (*ceteris paribus*), when its price falls. Thus, a fall in price stimulates individuals already buying a good to buy more of it. This is the explanation of the downward-sloping demand curve for individual consumers. But individuals have different tastes and, therefore, enjoy different levels of utility from consumption of a good. When we consider the whole market, we should expect a fall in price to encourage *new* consumers to enter the market – i.e. those whose marginal utility was previously too low to consider purchases. Thus, normally market demand curves show larger changes in quantity when price rises, or falls, than the demand curves of individual consumers.

We can observe this in Figure 4.3 (or Table 4.3). When price falls from £3 to £2, Jill increases her consumption from $1\frac{1}{2}$ to 3 lbs. Alan, however, who bought no chops when price was £3, enters the market and buys 2 lbs. when price falls to £2. Market demand (Jill *plus* Alan) rises by $1\frac{1}{2} + 2 = 3\frac{1}{2}$ lbs.

Consumer Surplus

Consider an individual buying strawberries. Call him Harold. Table 4.4 shows part of his demand schedule. Suppose that market price is 60 pence per pound and that Harold maximizes his satisfaction when he buys 5 lbs., costing him £3.00.

Now let us ask what is the money value of the total satisfaction that Harold enjoys when he consumes 5 lbs. of strawberries? Harold's demand schedule can provide us with the answer, because we can deduce from it the marginal utility of each additional pound of strawberries. If we add together the marginal utilities of all 5 lbs., we end up with their total utility.

TABLE 4.4 Harold's Demand for Strawberries

Price (pence per lb.)	Quantity demanded (lbs. per month)
80	1
75	2
70	3
65	4
60	5

The marginal utility of the first pound must be worth 80p to Harold, because he would be prepared to pay that amount for it. The marginal utility of the second pound, by similar reasoning, is worth 75p, that of the third is worth 70p, and so forth. The total utility derived by Harold from 5 lbs. is made up of the sum of the marginal utilities of the 1st, 2nd, 3rd, 4th and 5th lbs. – i.e. 80p + 75p + 70p + 65p + 60p = 350p.

As we observed, however, 5 lbs. of strawberries do not cost Harold 350p. but only 300p. The difference between Harold's total outlay of 300p and his total satisfaction of 350p is 50p. This difference is known as CONSUMER SURPLUS. It is made up in this example of a surplus of 20p on the first pound (80p – 60p) plus surpluses on the second, third and fourth pounds of 15p, 10p, and 5p. Of course there is no consumer surplus on the fifth pound, which Harold values at 60p which is also the market price paid.

The concept of consumer surplus defined as the difference between total utility and total outlay can be applied to a whole market as well as to a single individual; and it may be depicted graphically.

In Figure 4.4 we show a market demand curve for strawberries. Suppose that market price is p_0 and the quantity bought is q_0. Total consumer outlay is given by the area Op_0eq_0, representing price times quantity. Total utility is represented by the area under the demand curve, $Oaeq_0$, showing the sum of the marginal utilities[1] derived from q_0 strawberries. The difference between these two areas, which is the shaded area aep_0, is the consumer surplus which accrues to all consumers, variously as individuals depending on how much each values intra-marginal units of strawberries.

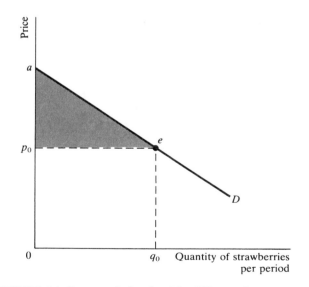

FIGURE 4.4 Consumer's Surplus. The difference between total utility ($Oaeq_0$) and total outlay (Op_0eq_0) is the shaded area (aep_0), which is the consumer's surplus.

1 See Appendix 1, p.508.

A helpful way of thinking about consumer surplus is to describe it as the difference between the amount that a consumer *actually pays* when he buys a number of units of a good, and the *maximum amount he would be prepared to pay* if he were charged a different price for each unit. In Harold's case in Figure 4.4, one might imagine charging him 80p for one pound of strawberries. This is the value he places on one pound, you then offer him a second. How much would he pay for that? The answer is 75p when 2 lbs. are bought. So one could go on, charging Harold a price equal to the value that he places on each unit. The total you extracted from him would be the full value that he places on his total consumption. He would not be left with any consumer surplus. You would have drained it all away, by charging him differential prices per unit. But the difference between the amount you extracted and the amount he would have had to pay if he had bought all 5 lbs. at the market price of 60p, would add up to the same figure of 50p as we obtained by our first method, comparing total utility and total outlay.

Another way to think of consumer surplus is to ask how much you would have to pay Harold to compensate him for not allowing him to buy *any* strawberries at the market price. He would be no worse, nor better off, than before he started buying strawberries, if you gave him 50p to compensate for complete strawberry deprivation. He would still have the 300 pence, which he would have spent on them. Add this to the 50p compensation, and Harold has 350 pence altogether, which is equal to the total utility he would have gained from consuming 5 lbs. of strawberries.

The Paradox of Value

Commodities which confer utility on a consumer are not necessarily 'useful' in the conventional sense of being practically helpful for specific purposes. A carpenter buys tools because the utility he derives from them happens to be useful, but an art lover buys a painting for the utility derived from aesthetic enjoyment, regardless of its lack of conventional usefulness.

There is, however, a special aspect of the difference between utility and usefulness that deserves attention. It concerns what is known as the 'paradox of value'. It was noticed by Adam Smith, over 200 years ago, that some

'useful' commodities, such as water, had very low values in exchange, while other, less useful ones, such as diamonds, had much higher exchange values. (By exchange values Smith meant market prices.)

Most people's emotional reactions to many goods reflects a certain unease which is related to the paradox that Smith pointed out. Yet there is really nothing paradoxical about his observation. The paradox may be resolved using the distinction between total and marginal utility, which we emphasized when explaining the concept of consumer surplus. The high value that people put on water refers to the total utility that is derived from it, not to its marginal utility.

A good such as water has a high total utility; hence, consumers gain a large consumer surplus from it. A good such as diamonds has a lower total utility; hence, consumers gain a lower consumer surplus from it. If you doubt this, compare the amounts of money consumers would accept to persuade them to give up their total consumption of water and of diamonds. Since water is a necessity of life itself, a vast – even infinite – sum would not be enough to compensate most people for giving up all water.

But water is plentiful and cheap, so it is consumed to the point where its marginal utility is low. Diamonds are scarce and expensive, so consumers stop buying them when their marginal utility is still high. Thus there is no paradox in a good with a high total utility having a low price and low marginal utility, as long as it is plentiful.

A note on the use of the concept of the margin in economics

The reader may have noticed that this is the second chapter in which we used the adjective 'marginal' in this book. Here we have talked about marginal utility; earlier we wrote about marginal cost (see above, p.10).

Economic theory makes much use of these 'marginal' concepts. Marginal means on the margin, or on the border. The concept refers to what would happen if there were a small change from the present position. We shall find that many important results of economic theory about consumer and producer behaviour, and about the conditions for the attainment of economic efficiency, run in marginal terms.[1]

---

1 Marginal and incremental values are further discussed in Appendix 1 (see pp.508–10).

Summary

1 Demand in economics is effective demand – i.e. it refers to quantities of a good, or service, that consumers wish to buy per period of time.

2 Quantity demanded has several determinants, which are helpfully considered one at a time, holding others constant by *ceteris paribus* assumption. A major determinant is the (own) price of the good itself. The relationship between (own) price and quantity demanded is represented graphically by a demand curve.

3 As consumption of a good increases total utility, or satisfaction, usually increases and marginal utility (defined as the change in utility derived from a unit change in consumption) also increases, but at a diminishing rate. Demand curves for individual consumers slope downwards (i.e. have negative slopes) reflecting diminishing marginal utility.

4 A market demand curve is constructed by (horizontal) summation of the demand curves of all consumers. Market demand is more predictable than individual demand. An additional reason why market demand curves slope downwards is that new consumers enter the market when price falls.

5 Consumer surplus is the excess of total utility derived from consumption of a good over total outlay by consumers on it (or, the difference between the amount consumers pay for the quantity purchased and the maximum they would be prepared to pay to obtain that quantity).

6 Goods which provide utility to consumers are not necessarily 'useful'. The 'paradox of value' is resolved by recognition that the total utility from water exceeds that from diamonds, while the marginal utility from diamonds exceeds that from water.

Questions

1 Which One or More of the following helps to explain why market demand curves slope downwards?
  (a) Total utility from a good rises at a diminishing rate as consumption increases.
  (b) The principle of diminishing marginal utility is not universal.
  (c) Most goods have multiple uses.
  (d) Some consumers quit the market when price rises.

2 What is the total utility enjoyed by Alan in Figure 4.1 if lamb chops are free?

3 Is the following statement True or False? 'If one consumer's ratio of marginal utility/price for peaches is greater than that for pears, she is buying too many pears relative to peaches to maximize her satisfaction.'

4 Refer to Figure 4.3 or Table 4.3. Market price is £3.50. (i) How many lamb chops are bought by (a) Alan and (b) Jill? (ii) Jill buys 3 chops. What is total market demand?

5 A consumer is buying 2 goods, X and Y. Which of the following describes consumer equilibrium? (Abbreviations: mu = marginal utility, tu = total utility, p = price.)
  (a) $mu_a = mu_b$
  (b) $mu_b/mu_a = mu_a/mu_b$
  (c) $tu_a = tu_b$
  (d) $mu_b/mu_a = p_b/p_a$
  (e) none of the above.

6 A consumer maximizing her satisfaction buys 4 rabbits at the price ruling in the market. The marginal utility derived from the 1st, 2nd and 3rd rabbits are £8, £6, and £5 respectively. She also enjoys a consumer surplus of £10. How much does she pay for each rabbit?

5 Demand, Income and Other Determinants

This chapter continues our discussion of the determinants of the quantity of a good that consumers wish to buy. In the previous chapter, we concentrated on the influence of the price of the commodity itself (called its *own price*.) In this chapter, we consider other determinants of demand, first from the viewpoint of the individual consumer, and afterwards for the market as a whole.

OTHER DETERMINANTS OF DEMAND

To consider other determinants of quantity demanded, the *ceteris paribus* clause must now include the good's own price. In what follows, therefore, we assume a certain fixed price for the good in question. The influences we shall then discuss are: (1) income, (2) prices of other goods, (3) expectations, and (4) other factors.

Remember that quantities demanded are still to be regarded as so much *per period of time*. We shall continue to label diagrams 'per period' on the quantity axis in this and the next chapter until it becomes second nature for you to think of demand in this way. Later we shall take this as understood.

Income

Consider, first, the effect of changes in income on quantity demanded.

Normal goods

Usually, we would expect an individual to buy more of a good when his or her income rises, and to buy less of it when his or her income falls. This positive association between price and income is common, and the goods which obey this rule are called NORMAL GOODS. Two exceptions need to be noted.

Goods subject to satiation

The first is where the quantity demanded remains unchanged once the consumer's income reaches some critical level. This is the case for commodities for which the desire is completely satisfied after a certain level of income has been reached. For example, the demand for salt is not much affected by an increase in a consumer's income from £25,000 to £26,000 per annum or by a decrease within the same range (though the demand for salt might conceivably fall if a consumer's income sank to £500 per annum).

Inferior goods

The second exception relates to goods where the association is *negative*, i.e. a rise in income is associated with a fall in quantity demanded, and vice versa. Goods in this category are known as INFERIOR GOODS. They are often those which are regarded as cheap, inferior, substitutes for other commodities. In many countries, potatoes and bread provide examples. As incomes rise above some critical level, consumers switch to more expensive foodstuffs. A black and white television set is also an inferior good for those persons who replace it with a colour set when their incomes rise. Notice that *inferiority is relative to income*. Goods cannot be inferior at *all* income levels, or they would never be bought at all. They must be normal over some income range, and only then become inferior.

In Figure 5.1 we show the relationship between one consumer's income and her demand for a good under the assumption that all factors other than income remain constant. Note that the vertical axis is different from that in diagrams used for conventional demand curves, such as in Figure 4.1. We still measure quantity demanded along the horizontal axis, but we now measure income on the vertical axis.

Quantity demanded and income are positively related with normal goods and negatively related with inferior goods. Curve 1 illustrates the case in which an increase in income brings about an increase in purchases at all levels of income. Such a commodity is normal at all income levels.

Curve 2 illustrates the case in which the commodity is a normal good up to some level of income, here y_1, while, for higher levels of income, demand does not respond at all as income varies. The same quantity, q_1, is demanded at income levels y_1 and y_3, for example.[1]

Curve 3 illustrates the case in which a commodity is an inferior good after a certain income level is reached, here y_2. Until that income is attained, the good is a normal one. However, increases in income beyond y_2 are associated with decreases in quantity demanded. For instance q_3 is demanded at income y_2, but only q_2 at income y_3. You can now see why a good cannot be inferior at *all* levels of income. If you try to draw the curve for such a good it will

---

1 There are two ways of describing graphical values such as the quantity represented by the point q_1 or the income represented by the point y_1 in Figure 5.1. The other way would be to call them Oq_1 and Oy_1. We use the 'point' style (common to some other books, such as IPE, but not to others). Thus, when we refer to changes, such as when income goes from y_2 to y_1 in Figure 5.1, we describe it as y_1-y_2, i.e. the difference between y_1 and y_2. To make sure you understand this, refer to Appendix 1, pp.505–6.

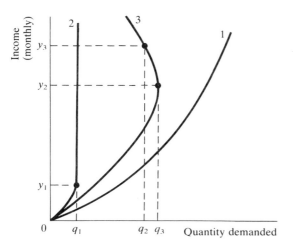

FIGURE 5.1 Income and Demand. Curve 1 shows a normal good (income and quantity demanded are positively associated). Curve 2 shows a normal good for income levels below y_1. Curve 3 shows a good which is normal and inferior for income levels below and above y_2 respectively (income and quantity demanded are negatively associated above y_2).

lie below the quantity axis. This would mean a negative quantity consumed, which makes no sense.

Note that very poor people do not buy many of the goods commonly purchased by middle- and higher-income persons. Although not shown in the Figure, the curve relating a consumer's income to quantity demanded for such commodities would cut the vertical (income) axis in Figure 5.1, showing that there is a range of incomes between zero and some positive amount over which the good is not purchased at all, then a further range over which increases in income lead to increases in purchases of the commodity.

The Prices of Other Goods

When the price of one good changes, this may affect the demand for other goods, because of a change in their *relative* prices. The demand for different commodities may be related, or unrelated. If unrelated, then a change in the price of one will leave the demand for the other unaffected. With related goods, there are two types of relationship to be distinguished, referred to as:

• Substitutes
• Complements

Substitutes

If a fall in the price of one good causes a fall in the quantity demanded of another good, the two goods are said to be SUBSTITUTES. The relationship is the one shown by the curve Subs in Figure 5.2, where goods X and Y are substitutes. A rise in the price of good X leads to an increase in the purchases of good Y as people switch purchases from the increasingly expensive good X to its substitute that has not risen in price.

BOX 5.1 Video Records Huge Rises in Income

'Video as a medium is beginning to rival cinema ... In the early '80s the major Hollywood studios were slow to appreciate the potential of video ... They derived only 0.6% of their income from it, and regarded it as a threat. By 1988 that figure stood at 43% ...

'In 1985 7.7 million homes had video recorders; by the end of this year [1990] it will be 14 million ... The acceleration in machine purchase is partly because of improved availability of films. Blockbuster movies are no longer milked at the box office for as long as possible. Instead they are moved smartly on to the small screen, freeing the UK's limited big screen space for the ever increasing number of films being released. Popular TV series are now being sold on video, while record shops have had to find yet more shelf space for the growing business in musical video tapes.'

(*The Independent on Sunday*, 22 April 1990)

The extract tells of recent developments in a dynamic market, where the level of demand was under the influence of changes in consumer income, in relative prices, and also probably in tastes.

Questions

1 Can you identify substitutes and complements mentioned in the article?
2 Which of the changes in demand referred to (if any) would be represented by shifts of a demand curve, and which (if any) by movements along a demand curve?

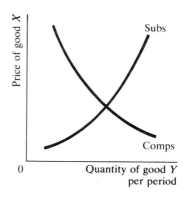

FIGURE 5.2 Substitutes and Complements. When X and Y are substitutes, a rise in the price of either good leads to an increase in the quantity demanded of the other, as with the curve Subs. When X and Y are complements, a rise in the price of either good leads to a fall in the quantity demanded of the other, as with the curve Comps.

Examples of substitutes are butter and margarine, carrots and cabbage, cinema tickets and theatre tickets, bus rides and taxi rides. However, substitutability need not be as close or as obvious as with these examples. Whenever a consumer weighs up the relative merits of buying two goods, they are potential substitutes for that consumer. If a rise in the price of food leads a poor family to spend less on entertainment, because it must spend more on food, then, for that family, food and entertainment are substitutes. Do not be confused by the fact that sausages and visits to the cinema are not substitutes in the everyday sense of the word.

Complements

If a fall in the price of one commodity raises the demand for another, the two are said to be COMPLEMENTS. When the price of one such commodity falls, more of it is consumed and more of other commodities that are complementary to it are also consumed, as illustrated by the curve Comps in Figure 5.2.

Goods that are complements are those which tend to be consumed together. Examples are skis and ski boots, strawberries and cream, needles and sewing thread, and cameras and film. These goods are sometimes said to be in JOINT DEMAND, or to be jointly demanded. All this means is that if you decide you want more of one, this usually implies wanting more of the other.

Expectations

We have seen that changes in prices and changes in incomes cause consumers to change the quantities that they demand of various goods. If these changes happen unexpectedly, people cannot react until the change has occurred. But sometimes the changes are foreseen. Then people can, and often do, react to the expectation that changes in prices or incomes will occur in the future. If people expect some price to rise, they may rush to buy now while the commodity is still cheap, relative to what they expect it to cost in the future. If people expect their incomes to rise in the future they may borrow and spend now, intending to repay the loan out of the increase of income that they expect in the future.

Other Factors

Many other factors affect the demand for a good. We have grouped them into four subgroups.

Sociological and demographic factors: Here we include age, sex, marital status, health, education, social class, place of residence (particularly whether urban or rural) and moral and religious values whether induced by family, peer group or political allegiance.

Psychological factors: This head covers all the influences, inherited and acquired, that affect personality and therefore *tastes*. We here include fads and fashions and the effects of new knowledge and rumours, whether or not well-founded, such as the effects of smoking on health or the risk of eating beef after an outbreak of 'mad cow' disease.

'Acts of God':   This term describes such factors as the weather, earthquakes, the incidence of disease of man, beasts or crops. It also covers strikes, war, riots, etc which insurance companies call acts of God, but which are, generally acts of man.

Acts of the state: Government legislation can affect the demand for a commodity in a great variety of ways, such as when it makes rules and regulations requiring the wearing of car seatbelts and regulating advertising standards. The state can also influence the price received by sellers, by imposing taxes or subsidizing a commodity.

MARKET DEMAND

As in the previous chapter, we must point out certain distinctive features which apply to market demand rather than to the demand of any one individual.

In the first place, our earlier remarks about predictability are equally applicable to the determinants of quantity demanded other than the own price of a good. Erratic behaviour from some individuals tends to cancel out in aggregate market demand. For example, a large number of people may find their incomes rising and decide to buy a few more lamb chops. Some may, however, decide to reduce their purchases for all sorts of individually peculiar reasons. Others might even decide to buy no meat except lamb chops for reasons that seem good to themselves. But the erratic behaviour of these few consumers will tend to cancel out, and the market as a whole will show a stable relation, with the demand for lamb chops increasing moderately as incomes rise.

In the second place, when considering market as opposed to individual demand we need to take certain distributional factors into account. Two are of particular importance – the distribution of income, and the distribution of the population.

Income Distribution

Income, which influences individual demand, gets an extra dimension when we are considering market demand. The new dimension is distributional. Even if total income is constant, a change in the distribution of that income can shift the demand curves for many products.

Consider, for example, two societies with the same total income. In one society, there is a fair number of very rich households, many very poor ones, but hardly any in the middle income range. In the second society, most households have incomes that do not differ much from the average income for all households. Income is distributed more unequally in the first society than in the second.

Even if the influence of all other factors affecting demand is exactly the same in the two societies, they will have different patterns of demand for goods and services. In the first, there will be relatively large demands for goods bought by the rich, such as solid silver cutlery, and also for goods bought by the poor, such as plastic knives and forks. In the second society, demand for both these types of good will be relatively small, but there will be larger demands for goods bought by middle-income households, e.g. stainless steel cutlery. Thus, the pattern of demand for particular goods will change if the distribution of income changes.

Demographic Changes

Any shift in the populations between groups that have different tastes and needs will tend to alter the pattern of demand for different goods and services. One example is a change in the age distribution of the population, such as might be brought about by a decline in the birth rate, accompanied by fall in the death rate of people over 60. Two other examples are a rise in the proportion of the population living in the towns rather than in the country, and a fall in the proportion of married couples in the population, such as may occur with a rise in the divorce rate.

In so far as people of different ages buy different goods, townsfolk buy different goods from country dwellers, and single and divorced persons buy different goods from married couples, so the pattern of market demand will change with these distribution shifts in the population.

SHIFTS IN DEMAND CURVES AND MOVEMENTS ALONG THEM

It is important to distinguish between two types of change affecting demand curves. One causes a movement along a demand curve, while the other induces a shift of the whole curve. The distinction is, in principle, straightforward, but be warned that even quite experienced students sometimes have difficulty in putting it into practice.

Remember that the demand curve shows the relationship between own price and quantity demanded on the assumption of *ceteris paribus* – that is to say that all influencing factors other than own price do not change. These other factors cannot cause quantities demanded to alter unless they themselves change. It follows, therefore, that

the effect of a change in price on quantity demanded is to be read along a demand curve.

Discovering the effects of movements in price involves moving along the demand curve to ascertain the effect on quantity demanded. Such movements are also sometimes described as EXTENSIONS or CONTRACTIONS of demand. An extension is a downward movement to the right along a demand curve in response to a fall in price; a contraction is an upward movement to the left along the demand curve in response to a rise in price. It follows that:

the effect of a change in any factors other than price on quantity demanded, involves a shift in the demand curve itself.

In other words, at any given price the quantity demanded changes; a different quantity is bought because something else has changed. The 'something else' will be any of the determinants of demand other than price. A change in income, or in its distribution, in the prices of other goods, in expectations or in sociological factors cause the whole demand curve to shift. Such changes are often referred to as changes in the CONDITIONS OF DEMAND. For example, consider the demand for lamb chops discussed in Chapter 4. If Alan's income rises he may buy more lamb chops even though their price is unchanged.

Changes in the conditions of demand shift the demand curve – to the right if demand increases and to the left if demand falls – showing different quantities demanded at every price.

This is illustrated in Figure 5.3, which shows two demand curves, D and D'. An increase in demand causes a shift to the right of the demand curve, from D to D', a larger quantity being demanded at each and every price. For example, at price p_0, quantity demanded rises from q_0 to q_1. In contrast, a fall in price causes a movement downward along a single demand curve. For example, when the demand curve is D', a fall in price from p_1 to p_0 increases the quantity demanded from q_0 to q_1.

Now let the original demand curve be D'. A shift in the demand curve to D indicates a decrease in demand; less is demanded at each price. For example, at price p_0 quantity demanded falls from q_1 to q_0. In contrast, a rise in price causes a movement upwards along a single demand curve, i.e. a decrease in the quantity demanded. For example, when the demand curve is D', a rise in price from p_0 to p_1 reduces the quantity demanded from q_1 to q_0.

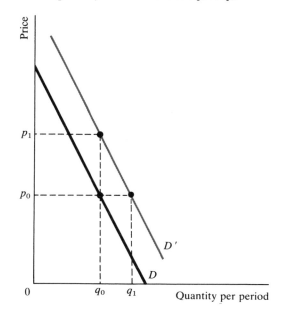

FIGURE 5.3 Shifts of a Demand Curve. When any determinant of demand, other than the own price of the good, changes, the demand curve shifts. A different quantity is demanded at every price. See Table 5.1 for examples of when the demand curve shifts to the right or left.

Some terminology to learn

Economists have no universally accepted terminology to distinguish between the two types of change we have described. In particular the phrases 'increase in demand' and 'decrease in demand' are sometimes used to refer to a movement along a curve and sometimes to refer to a shift of a curve. This is unfortunate. Moreover, there are several terms that are used to describe shifts in the demand curve. These include (1) shifts to the right or left, (2) upward or downward shifts, (3) shifts to the North East or to the South West.

The first refers to the fact that a different quantity is bought at each price; the second refers to the fact that each quantity is associated with a different price; the third draws an analogy with a map where a journey upwards and to the right on the map is a journey towards the N.E. while a journey downwards and to the left is a journey to the S.W., and vice versa. Sometimes one term is more descriptive than another. In this book we shall avoid the use of the compass directions of NE and SW, and stick mainly to leftward and rightward shifts.

All of the terminological distinctions are summarized in Table 5.1, which covers most of the important factors affecting demand.

Time and Demand

Note that the response of demand to a change in price can vary as the time period over which the response can take place is lengthened.

One reason is that most of us are to an extent creatures of habit. Hence, the fall in price of a good that we are unaccustomed to buying may not have any immediate impact on our spending behaviour. However, if the price fall persists, we may in time reconsider the relative merits of the good compared to others. Take, for example, the case of trout. Some years ago a pound of trout cost at least double that of a pound of cod. Today the two fish cost about the same. When the price of trout first fell, relative to that of cod, many people did not consider it as an alternative fish. The lower price has, however, persisted. In consequence, the demand for trout has grown, though it has taken time to do so.

A second reason why demand may respond slowly to price changes is that we are not always as price-conscious as we might be. We do not immediately realize that changes in relative price have occurred, but only after they have lasted for some time. This is particularly likely to be the case in the kind of inflationary world that we have lived in for many years. When all prices are tending upwards, changes in relative prices may be difficult to discern. When they are discerned, quantities demanded will increase when relative prices have fallen, and decrease when relative prices have risen.

A third reason for the slow initial response of demand to price changes – by far the most important in fact for many commodities – is that they are consumed together with other *durable* goods. It is only after the stock of durables is fully adjusted that the price change becomes fully effective. For example, when the action of the OPEC group of nations raised the price of petrol dramatically in 1973 and 1979, the quantity of petrol demanded fell substantially only when time had elapsed sufficiently for replacement of cars with large engine sizes by those with smaller engines.

The greater response of quantity demanded to a price change the longer the period under consideration, is illustrated in Figure 5.4, which shows two demand curves for a product, Z. D_S is a short-run demand curve, while D_L is the demand curve for the same product when time is sufficient for people to make a full adjustment to a price change. If price falls from p_0 to p_1, the quantity demanded increases only to q_S in the short term, but to q_L in the longer term.

TABLE 5.1   The Terminology of Demand Curves

Change	Terms Used to Describe the Change
(A) A change in the own price of the good causes a MOVEMENT ALONG a demand curve	
1 Price of the good rises.	1 A decrease, fall or reduction in the quantity demanded. A contraction in demand.
2 Price of the good falls.	2 An increase, or rise, in the quantity demanded. An extention of demand.
(B) A change in any influence other than own price causes a SHIFT OF a demand curve	
1 A rise in income, if the good is normal. A fall in income, if the good is inferior. A rise in the price of a substitute good. A fall in the price of a complementary good. A change in tastes in favour of the good.	1 A rightward, upward or northeasterly shift of the demand curve. An increase in demand. An improvement in the conditions of demand.
2 A fall in income if the good is normal. A rise in income if the good is inferior. A fall in the price of a substitute good. A rise in the price of a complementary good. A change in tastes against the good.	2 A leftward, downward or southwesterly shift of the demand curve. A decrease in demand. A deterioration in the conditions of demand.

Note: The terms we employ most commonly in this book are given first.

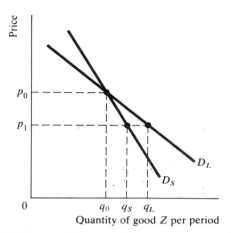

FIGURE 5.4 Time and Demand. The longer the time allowed the greater the probable effect of a change in price on quantity demanded. D_S is a short-run demand curve; D_L is a long-run demand curve. A price fall, from p_0 to p_1, causes a bigger increase in quantity with D_L than with D_S.

The Law of Demand and Exceptional Demand Curves

The tendency for the quantity demanded of any good to vary in the opposite direction to that good's own price, and its graphical expression in the negatively sloped demand curve, is sometimes called the LAW OF DEMAND.

There are cases where the law of demand does not hold, in the sense that more is demanded at high prices than at low. We deal with four of the most common types, though we shall show that the first is not so much an exception to the law as a confusion of movements along a demand curve with shifts of the entire curve. They are: speculative demand, snob demand, judging quality by price, and Giffen goods.

Speculative demand: The first, alleged, exception to the law of demand occurs when the price of a good rises, but that rise is expected to be followed by a further rise. We may *observe* an association of rising price with rising quantities bought in such cases. However, the real reason for the rise in demand is not the rise in price, but the new expectation that a further rise will follow. In other words our standard *ceteris paribus* assumption does not hold. One 'other thing' has changed. Expectations are different; now price is expected to rise in the future.

These circumstances mean that the *demand curve shifts* to the right, reflecting the extra demand at the existing (and every other) price because people expect that, whatever today's price, tomorrow's price will be higher. What we observe is not a movement along a perverse, upward-sloping demand curve, but a rightward shift of a normal downward-sloping curve. For an example of this case see Box 9.2 on page 91.

Snob demand: The second exception to the law is of a good which is wanted, not for the satisfaction it intrinsically gives, but *because* it is expensive. Goods in this category are sometimes said to have snob appeal.

Assume, for example, that a consumer's satisfaction depends not only on how much is consumed of some commodity, but also on the price he or she is known to have paid for it. Some consumers may, for example, buy diamonds not because they really like diamonds, but because they wish to display their wealth in an ostentatious, but socially acceptable, way. These consumers value diamonds precisely because they are expensive; thus, a fall in price might lead them to stop buying diamonds and switch to a different object for ostentatious display.

No doubt there are some consumers of this type. They have positively sloped individual demand curves for this particular good: the lower the price, the fewer they will buy. This is a genuine exception to the law of demand for particular groups of consumers. It occurs because the utility from the good rises when the price rises, and vice versa.

But what of the demand curve for the market as a whole? If enough consumers act similarly, the market demand curve for diamonds would slope upwards as well. But an upward-sloping market demand curve for diamonds, and other similar products, has never been observed. Why?

The most obvious explanation is that most existing and potential purchasers do not buy diamonds just for their snob value but because they like them. The behaviour of the masses of lower-income consumers who would buy diamonds if they were cheap enough would swamp that of the minority of consumers who buy for ostentatious display. Hence, the demand curve for the market as a whole slopes downwards, and the exceptional snob-based demand is a rarity, if it exists at all.

Judging quality by price: Another reason why demand curves may slope upwards for some individuals is that they may mistakenly judge quality by price. When the price of a certain good falls, consumers may, incorrectly, assume that its quality has fallen as well, and switch to other, more expensive, close substitutes. This behaviour will show up as an upward-sloping demand curve – when the price falls less, rather than more, is bought.

The same comment applies here as to snob demand. It is easy to imagine some consumers behaving in this way but, for the market to do so, these consumers must be in the majority. It is more likely that the normal behaviour of the majority will swamp the behaviour of the smaller group, who judge quality solely by price.

Note that the above argument applies only to consumers who incorrectly assume that quality has changed because price has changed. There is, however, evidence – for example from *Which?* magazine, published by the Consumers' Association – that at least some cheaper goods *tend* to be of lower quality than more expensive goods of the same type. If the quality of a good does change then it is not quite the same good and its demand curve will shift. Thus the observation that a fall in price is accompanied by a fall in quantity demanded of a good whose quality has changed is not an observation of two points on one positively sloped demand curve. Instead it represents two points on two different demand curves.

Giffen goods: Another genuine exception to the downward-sloping demand curve for a commodity is called a 'Giffen good', after the Scottish economist, Sir Robert Giffen, who is alleged to have observed such a case in the nineteenth century.

Two conditions must be fulfilled for a Giffen good to exist. First, it must be an inferior good, the demand for which rises when income falls. Second, it must be a staple commodity on which the poor spend a high proportion of their incomes – so high in fact that when impoverished by the rise in the price of the good, they must severely cut down on their consumption of their few luxuries and buy more of the staple for their very subsistence. This rare exception to the law of demand is further discussed later in the book, after we have developed the theory needed to understand it more deeply (see Chapter 11, pp.123).

Summary

1 Determinants of demand other than the own price of a good are assumed constant by *ceteris paribus* assumption. They include income, prices of substitutes and of complements, tastes and expectations.

2 Normal goods are those where quantity demanded is positively associated with income. Inferior goods are those where the association is negative.

3 Goods are substitutes if a change in the price of one leads the quantity demanded of the other to change in the same direction. Goods are complements if a change in the price of one leads the quantity demanded of the other to change in the opposite direction.

4 Quantity demanded at a given price by individual consumers may be affected by changes in consumer income, by expectations of future prices, or by other variables.

5 Quantity demanded by the market may be affected by changes in the distribution of income among consumers and by demographic changes.

6 Changes in any of the *ceteris paribus* assumptions (i.e. other than the own price of a good) cause the demand curve to SHIFT. Changes in the own price of the good cause MOVEMENTS ALONG the demand curve.

7 Demand tends to respond more to price changes the longer the time allowed.

8 The Law of Demand is the tendency for quantity demanded to vary in the opposite direction to its price. Exceptions to the Law of Demand may arise from speculation about future price, snob value attached to a good, incorrect association of price and quality, and the rare case of a Giffen good.

9 A Giffen good exists only if the good is both inferior and takes up a high proportion of consumer expenditure.

Questions

1 List THREE *ceteris paribus* assumptions made when drawing a conventional own price demand curve.

2 Select from the following alternatives to describe what happens to the demand curve for plastic cups under the circumstances listed below: (L) demand curve shifts to left, (R) demand curve shifts to right, (N) no shift in the demand curve.
  (i) The price of china cups rises.
  (ii) The price of plastic cups falls.
  (iii) The price of plastic saucers rises.
  (iv) The price of plastic cups is expected to fall.
  (v) Picnics become less popular.

3 What change in the axes of the graph would turn the Subs curve in Figure 5.2 into a demand curve for a normal good?

4 What names are given to the following?
  (i) A good the demand for which is negatively related to consumer income.
  (ii) Two goods such that when the price of one rises the quantity demanded of the other falls.

5 Is the following True or False? 'When the price of a good rises, demand will usually fall off more in the short run than in the long run, because consumers will economize on it to start with, but later discover that they needed it more than they realized.'

6 What would characterize a consumer's demand curve for a good which she buys only for its snob value?

6 Supply

In the two previous chapters, we outlined the elementary theory of the demand for a good. We now turn to the supply side of the market to present a parallel elementary theory of supply. Our treatment of supply is shorter than that of demand because much of the discussion concerning supply is broadly similar to what we have already said about demand, and does not need to be repeated in full.

THE NATURE OF SUPPLY

This chapter is about business behaviour – in particular about the quantities of a good that suppliers wish to produce and offer for sale. We describe the elementary theory of supply in a manner similar to that of the previous chapter on demand. We explain first who the suppliers are, the kind of goods they are supplying and the forces determining their behaviour.

Suppliers: The organizations which make decisions about how many goods to supply are variously known as suppliers, sellers, producers, businesses, firms and enterprises. These terms are often used interchangeably, although it is not always correct to do so. The word 'producer', for example, usually describes someone who makes a product such as a motorcar. It is not strictly applicable to second-hand car dealers – although both are suppliers. Some of the terms, such as enterprises, have technical meanings which will be explained in a later chapter (see p 130). For present purposes we employ the words seller, supplier, or producer when we wish to refer to the organizations responsible for supply.

Who within the organization actually makes decisions to produce? This is an important question which we shall address in Part 3. For now, we ignore it, and assume that each supplier makes decisions as if these decisions were made by a single individual. This allows us to take the supplier as the basic unit of behaviour on the supply side of markets, just as the consumer is treated as the basic unit of behaviour on the demand side.

Sellers' motivation: We assume, to start with, that suppliers make their decisions with respect to a single goal or objective – to make as much profits as possible.

When a supplier reaches a situation where profits are maximized, that position is said to be optimal from the supplier's point of view. This goal of PROFIT MAXIMIZATION is analogous to the consumer's goal of utility maximization.

There is a difference, however: although consumer satisfaction cannot be directly observed and measured, a seller's profits can be.

Goods and services: Parallel to the decision taken with demand, we deal mainly in this chapter with supplies of goods. We thereby exclude other areas of supply, such as that of factors of production (for which see Chapters 18 and 19).

Time: As with demand, the theory of supply is concerned with the quantities offered for sale *per period of time*. Thus quantity supplied is always to be taken as a *flow*, so many lamb chops *per month* or ice-creams *per week*, etc. In all the diagrams in this chapter, we shall continue to label the quantity axes 'per period'. For the rest of the book, to avoid cluttering diagrams, we shall assume that this is understood and that we do not need to write it every time.

Price-takers: We deal at this stage with markets that contain many sellers. We assume that they are so many that no one of them can have any appreciable effect on the market price. No alteration in one producer's own behaviour, even by withdrawing from the market completely, will affect the market price of what the producer sells.

Many real-world markets are of this type. For example, one supplier more or less would scarcely be noticed in most retail shopping areas and in most agricultural markets. Within manufacturing, however, this is not often the case. There are only a few car manufacturers and makers of household detergents. Each is quite large. One supplier more or less in either industry would cause a noticeable change that would appreciably affect the car and detergent markets, as would a significant change in the output of any one or more manufacturer. For the moment, however, we shall confine ourselves to situations where the sellers are so numerous that they must take the market, including the price, as they find it, and cannot influence it. We say such sellers are *price-takers*. In Part 3, we shall extend our study to producers who *can* influence the price of the products.

WHAT DETERMINES QUANTITY SUPPLIED?

How much of some commodity will each producer be willing to make and offer for sale per period, say per month? The amount will be influenced by the following variables: (1) the own price of the commodity; (2) the prices of related goods; (3) the costs of production, which depend on (a) the prices of factors of production, and (b) the state of technology; (4) the goals of producers; (5) producers' income; (6) expectations of the future; (7) other relevant factors.

Supply and the Own Price of the Commodity

To keep our study simple to begin with, we concentrate on a single major influence determining supply: the price of the good itself, its own price. We therefore adopt the assumption to which you should by now have become accustomed, of *ceteris paribus*, i.e. we assume that all other possible influences on the producer's output decision do not enter the picture. They are assumed unchanged in order that we may concentrate on the first influence from the above list.

Our basic hypothesis on the supply side is that the quantity that a producer will supply is positively associated with the commodity's own price: quantity rises when price rises and falls when price falls. This hypothesis is derived formally later. For now, we can note its commonsense appeal: the higher the price of a good, the greater are the prospects for making profits and, thus, the greater the incentive to produce more. In sharp contrast to the theory of demand, exceptions are very important; they will be considered at length in Part 3.

We illustrate the relationship between price and quantity supplied with hypothetical data for a producer of lamb chops. The data can, as we know from our earlier consideration of the demand side of this market, be presented either in the form of a schedule or graphically. Table 6.1 is a supply schedule. It shows in column (ii) the quantities supplied at each price shown in column (i). For example, the producer will offer 300 lbs. for sale each month when the price is £1.00 a lb. If the price rises to £1.50 a lb., 600 lbs. will be supplied, and so forth. Each of the price-quantity combinations in the schedule is given a letter for easy reference.

TABLE 6.1 A Producer's Supply Schedule for Lamb Chops

Reference letter	Price (£s per lb.) (i)	Quantity supplied (lbs. per month) (ii)
t	0.50	0
u	1.00	300
v	1.50	600
w	2.00	900
x	2.50	1200
y	3.00	1500
z	3.50	1800

The data in Table 6.1 can be presented in the form of a graph, exactly as the demand schedule was so presented (see pp.38).

The graphical presentation is given in Figure 6.1. In similar fashion to Figure 4.1 where we drew a demand curve, price is plotted on the vertical axis and quantity on the horizontal axis, and the scales are chosen to accommodate the numbers in the table. For example, point *v* on

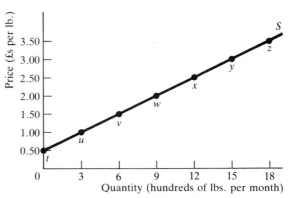

FIGURE 6.1 A Producer's Supply Curve for Lamb Chops. Each lettered point refers to a price-quantity combination in Table 6.1.

the graph corresponds to the third line of the table. Both indicate that 600 lbs. will be supplied each month when the price is £1.50 a lb. Similarly, we plot points *t, u, w, x, y* and *z* on the graph corresponding to the combinations with the same reference letters in the table.

Note that the supply curve cuts (or INTERCEPTS) the vertical price axis at a positive price (i.e. a price above zero). This positive intercept is the geometrical expression of a basic property of the production of most goods. Some minimum price is needed to call forth any supply at all; below that minimum price, quantity supplied is zero. In the present case, nothing at all is supplied at a price of £0.50 or less. A price in excess of 50p is needed to bring forth any output. The supplier could not even cover its costs if it had to sell for £0.50 (or less), so it would rather produce nothing.

We now draw a smooth line through the points *t* to *z*.

This line is the producer's supply curve. It shows the quantity offered for sale at every price in the table and at all other prices covered by the graph.

For example, to find the quantity supplied at a price of £2.75 per lb., we locate £2.75 on the vertical axis, run over to the curve at that price, then drop vertically down to the quantity axis and discover that the quantity associated with a price of £2.75 is 1350 lbs.

What Lies Behind the Supply Curve?

The justification for drawing an upward-sloping supply curve, such as the one shown in Figure 6.1, is that sellers are likely to feel they can profitably offer more of a good for sale the higher is its price. This parallels the justification that we initially offered for the downward-sloping demand curve: that people are inclined to buy more of a good the lower is its price. Both arguments are plausible, but they are not theoretically tight explanations.

In the case of the demand curve, we were able to derive its downward slope from the theory of diminishing marginal utility, combined with the hypothesis of utility maximization. The utility-maximizing consumer, faced with the market price of a commodity, buys that quantity at which the marginal utility of the last unit purchased is equal to its price. A parallel theory explains the upward-sloping supply curve. Whereas the consumer is assumed to seek to maximize utility, the producer is assumed to seek to maximize profits. Because, in the elementary theory in this part of the book, we are assuming that producers and consumers are all price-takers, both face a market price that they are unable to influence. To complete the story, all we need is the producer's counterpart of diminishing marginal utility. This is the concept of *increasing marginal cost*, which we must now explain.

Each level of output that could be produced implies some level of total cost. No one will be surprised to hear that, the greater the producer's output, the greater will be its total costs of production. To produce more requires more labour and more of all other factors of production, all of which must be paid for. Thus total costs rise as output rises (just as the consumer's total utility rises as total consumption of a commodity rises). But how fast do costs rise as output is increased? To answer this question we need the concept of *marginal cost*, which is analogous to the concept of the consumer's marginal utility.

Marginal cost

The MARGINAL COST (MC) of producing an extra unit of output is defined as the increase in total costs incurred by the producer as a result of producing an extra unit of output.

Say, for example, that to produce 10 units of output costs £200, and to produce 11 units costs £225. Then, the marginal cost of producing the 11th unit of output is the difference between the total cost of 11 units and the total cost of 10 units, i.e. £225 minus £200 = £25.[1]

So, now we know what marginal cost is, the next thing to ask is, how does marginal cost behave as output varies? The answer is given in much more detail in a later chapter, where it is shown to depend on a famous law called the Law of Diminishing Returns. At this stage we can only assert the result and offer an intuitive explanation for it. The basic result is that, as output is increased, marginal cost must sooner or later start to rise. The reason for rising MC lies in the fact that, in the short run, the producer has to operate with a given, fixed, size of plant (factory and equipment) which cannot, for the time being, be altered. In such circumstances, the *marginal cost of producing extra output rises*. In other words, each unit produced adds more to total costs than did each preceding unit produced. To illustrate using our previous example, the producer might decide to produce a 12th unit and find that costs rose to £255. Since 11 units cost £225, the marginal cost of the 12th unit is £30 (£255 − £225). Thus marginal costs are rising since the marginal cost of the 11th unit was only £25. The intuitive reason for rising marginal cost is that

production becomes less and less efficient the more output is squeezed from its existing plant and equipment.

The rule for profit maximization

So now we have a producer trying to maximize profits, faced with a given market price and a marginal cost curve which rises as output increases. How much should be produced? The answer can be presented in the form of a Rule which must be followed if profits are to be maximized.

The Rule for all price-taking producers is that production should be at that level of output for which marginal cost (MC) is equal to price (p):

$$MC = p$$

Let us see how the $MC = p$ Rule works for a producer. First, say that, at the present level of output, marginal cost is *less than* price. This means that an extra unit can be produced at a cost less than it can be sold for. Its production will thus add to profits so that the unit should be produced.

Whenever, at the present level of output, marginal cost is less than price, output should be increased.

Now assume that, at the present level of output, marginal cost *exceeds* price. This means that the last unit produced adds more to costs (marginal cost) than it adds to the producer's revenue (the price at which the unit is sold). Thus, there is a loss on producing the last unit of output, and it should not be produced.

Whenever, at the present level of output, marginal cost exceeds price, output should be reduced.

Since output should be increased when MC is less than price, and reduced when MC is greater than price,

it follows that only when marginal cost equals price is there no profit incentive to alter output.

The argument may be clarified with the use of a diagram. In Figure 6.2, the curve labelled MC shows marginal costs

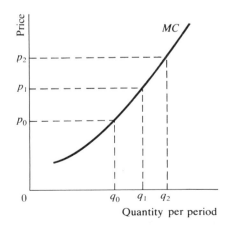

FIGURE 6.2 A Producer's Rising Marginal Cost Curve. A price-taking producer maximizes profits by producing output up to the level at which marginal cost equals price – e.g. if price is p_1, output should be expanded up to q_1.

---

1 Marginal values can be written mathematically. Let us use subscripts to denote values of total cost of producing units, e.g. TC_1, TC_2, and TC_n, for the total cost of 1, 2 and n units respectively. Then TC_n minus TC_{n-1} generally stands for the marginal cost of producing n units, i.e. one more unit than $n-1$ units.

rising with output. If market price is p_0, additions to output up to q_0 are worth producing, because the extra (marginal) cost of producing them is covered by the price of the product. If market price rises to p_1, outputs between q_0 and q_1, which were not previously profitable, are now worth producing. If price rises still higher to p_2, output can profitably be expanded up to q_2, at which point marginal cost is equal to price.

We have now discovered how to derive the producer's supply curve. Since the profit-maximizing level of output is where marginal cost equals price, the producer's marginal cost curve *is* his supply curve.

Going back to our previous example, the marginal cost of the 11th unit of output was £25 and the marginal cost of the 12th unit was £30. If the price of the product is £30, the producer should produce 12 units of output. Thus, as soon as we know the producer's marginal costs, we know what will be produced at each market price. It follows that *the supply schedule* shown in Table 6.1 *is also the producer's marginal cost schedule*. For example, the marginal cost of producing the 1,200th unit must have been £2.50. Otherwise the producer would not have produced 1,200 units when the price was £2.50.

We shall return to this discussion in Chapter 15, when our Rule will come in for modification to deal with other situations. In the meantime, all that you need to remember is that any producer who is a price-taker facing a market price he cannot change and who is seeking to maximize profits will produce that level of output where marginal cost equals price. *And since we are assuming that marginal cost increases as output increases, this explains why supply curves are upward-sloping.*

Other Determinants of Supply

We studied the relationship between the quantity of a good supplied and its own price using the assumption that all other influencing forces were held constant. We now examine the influence of each of the factors listed on pages 53–4 by letting them change one at a time on the assumption that all other influencing forces, including the product's own price, are held constant.

Prices of other goods

Prices must be viewed *relative* to one another. When the price of x falls, while the price of y remains the same, x has become *relatively* cheaper while y has become *relatively* more expensive. As relative prices change, what matters on the supply side is *substitutability in production*.

When considering the effect of a change in the price of other goods on the supply of a product, therefore, we consider price changes of those other goods which can most easily be produced with the resources at the firm's disposal. For example, a manufacturer of steel roof-racks for cars could probably switch production to steel frames for chairs without too much difficulty. If the price of such chairs were to rise, while the price of roof-racks was unchanged, there might well be a reduction in the output of racks, accompanied by a rise in the output of chairs.

If factors of production are used in the output of a given commodity, it is normally the case that less of other commodities are produced. However, this is not always the case. For technical reasons, output of one good happens, sometimes, to be a by-product of another good. In such cases, the commodities are said to be in JOINT SUPPLY, to distinguish them from the normal case of COMPETITIVE SUPPLY. Examples are beef and leather, or fish fingers and cod liver oil. Thus, a rise in the price of beef will increase the quantity of leather supplied because the quantity of skins available for tanning into leather increases automatically as the output of meat increases. They are *jointly supplied*.

Costs of production

We have seen that producers will offer goods for sale so long as the extra revenue received is greater than the marginal cost of production. Thus any change in production costs will, *ceteris paribus*, affect quantity supplied.

To illustrate, return to Table 6.1 on p.54 where the supply schedule may now be understood as a marginal cost schedule. Suppose marginal cost rises by 50p at all the output levels shown in the Table – possibly because some input has become more expensive. The quantities offered for sale now fall. For example, 300 units would now be supplied only if the price were £1.50 instead of at £1.00, 600 would be supplied at a price of £2.00 instead of at £1.50, and so forth.

We now study two important reasons why production costs may change: changes in the prices of factors of production and changes in technology.

Factor prices:　If the price of a factor of production rises, costs of production must rise. If the market price of the good produced by the factor of production is unchanged (as it is under our *ceteris paribus* assumption), its output becomes less profitable, and less will be produced. A fall in the price of a factor of production has the opposite effect.

The state of technology:　Costs of production depend not only on the prices of the factors of production, but also on their productivity. At any given moment of time, productivity may be taken as given – determined by the state of technology (or 'the state of the art', as it is sometimes called).

Over time, however, technology advances. Indeed, the enormous increase in production per worker in industrial societies over the last 200 years is largely due to improved methods of production. Discoveries in chemistry have led to lower costs of production of well-established products such as paints, and to a large variety of new products such as plastics and synthetic fibres. The modern electronics industry based on the microchip has revolutionized production in television, hi-fi equipment and computers. Nuclear energy may be used to produce fresh water from saltwater. At any time, what is produced, and how it is produced, depends on what is known. Over time, knowledge changes and so therefore do the costs of producing, and hence the supplies of, commodities.

Sellers' goals

We noticed earlier, that individual suppliers may strive after various goals. We start by assuming that the prime objective is to maximize profits, and we postpone alternative hypotheses until a later chapter. For the present it is sufficient to indicate the nature of some of them.

A supplier may aim, for example, at a high growth rate for sales as well as at profitability. A business may be run by an individual who enjoys taking big risks for big returns, or by someone who is cautious. A small supplier, moreover, may be controlled by a man or woman whose personal lifestyle exerts an influence over its activities – e.g., the local record shop may be closed every Wednesday so that the owner can play squash. Some businesses may be run on Scrooge-like principles, others with worker satisfaction playing a dominant role. All these are examples of different goals at which a producer may aim. We must note that *quantity supplied is affected by the producer's goal*.

Producers' income

Producers' net income are their profits. Thus, income enters as a determinant of supply through the assumption of profit maximization.

It may be worth noting, however, that the owners of some small businesses may have target incomes. If the prices of the goods they sell rise, *ceteris paribus*, the producers' incomes also rise. They may elect, instead of producing more, to produce and sell less. By doing so they maintain their target income, and reduce the amount that they have to work.

Expectations of the future

Supply can be affected by changes in expectations. If there is an unexpected change in any of the determinants of supply, producers will react after the change has occurred. If, however, the change is foreseen, producers may react to the expectations of the change. Many changes in supply can only be understood as responses to an expected change in one of the variables that influence supply.

'Acts of God'

Such forces as disease and weather, which are largely outside the control of man, can sometimes be of immense importance to supply. For example, *ceteris paribus*, a drought will reduce the supply of corn while excellent growing weather will increase it.

Acts of the state

Government regulation can affect supply conditions in a variety of ways. Rules relating to smoke pollution, for instance, control the types of boilers that may be used; while laws prescribing working conditions affect the productivity of labour. Many government taxes (and subsidies) also affect sellers' marginal costs, and therefore influence supply decisions.

Social and psychological determinants

Under this heading we include all influences on producer behaviour not elsewhere mentioned, e.g. the state of business confidence, political considerations, etc.

MARKET SUPPLY

To obtain market supply, we need to sum the supplies of all producers in an industry. Let us take a simple case where there are only two producers. We shall call them producer A and producer B. Both producers supply lamb chops.

Figure 6.3(i) and (ii), using data in Table 6.2 columns (ii) and (iii), show the supply curves for each producer. Note that the minimum price required before producer B will provide anything to the market is higher than that for A.

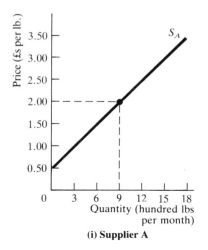
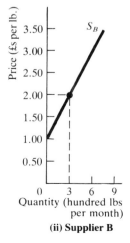
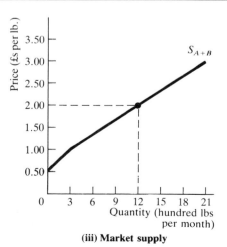

FIGURE 6.3 Individual Producer and Market Supply Curves. The market supply curve is derived by the horizontal summation of the supply curves of individual producers.

TABLE 6.2 Individual and Market Supply Schedules

PRICE	QUANTITIES SUPPLIED		
(£s per lb.)	Producer A (lbs. per month)	Producer B (lbs. per month)	Market supply (lbs. per month) (ii)+(iii)
(i)	(ii)	(iii)	(iv)
0.50	0	0	0
1.00	300	0	300
1.50	600	150	750
2.00	900	300	1200
2.50	1200	450	1650
3.00	1500	600	2100
3.50	1800	750	2550

The derivation of the market supply schedule is by simple addition of quantities supplied at each price by the two producers.

We see, therefore, that market supply when price is £1.00 per lb. is identical with supply by producer A. At this low price, producer B (which presumably has higher production costs than producer A) does not offer any lamb chops for sale at all. However, at the price of £1.50 a lb., producer A supplies 600 lbs. and producer B supplies 150 lbs. Market supply is therefore 600 + 150 = 750 lbs. The market supply at each of the prices in the table is the sum of columns (ii) and (iii).

Consider next the MARKET SUPPLY CURVE. This can be plotted directly from the combined supply schedule in column (iv) of Table 6.2. But we can also use the geometric method explained in connection with the construction of the market demand curve (see Chapter 4, pp.42). Just as we added, horizontally, the demand curves of two consumers to get the market demand curve, so we can add, horizontally, the supply curves of two producers to get the market supply curve. As the two methods are identical, we shall not repeat the explanation in full. Consider, however, market supply at the price of £2.00 per lb. This is the sum of the 900 and 300 for producers A and B respectively. To find the appropriate point on the market supply curve, we mark off a distance equal to the sum of these two quantities, i.e. 1200, and plot it against £2.00 in the Figure. Repeating the exercise for other prices and joining up the points yields the market supply curve, S_{A+B}.

Shifts in Supply Curves and Movements Along Curves

The supply curves with which economists mainly work are those relating quantity supplied to price. As with demand curves, it is important to make the same distinction between a movement along a curve and a shift of the entire curve.

A change in quantity supplied resulting from a change in price is read as a movement along a supply curve. A change in supply resulting from a change in anything other than a change in price involves shifting the whole curve.

The shift means that a new and different quantity is sup-

plied at each market price. Such shifts, arising from changes in one or more of the *ceteris paribus* assumptions, are often referred to as changes in the CONDITIONS OF SUPPLY.

Little further needs to be said in explanation of movements along a supply curve. They are simply readings of quantities supplied at different prices *ceteris paribus*. But it may be helpful to provide a few illustrations of causes of shifts in supply curves, and to explain also the *direction* of the shifts.

Figure 6.4 shows the original supply curve S and a new curve, S', which shows that larger quantities are supplied at each and every price. For example, at price p_0, the quantity goes from q_0 to q_1.

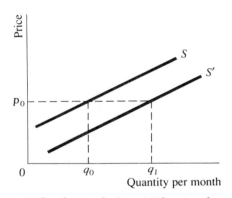

FIGURE 6.4 Shifts of a Supply Curve. When any determinant of supply other than the own price of the good changes, the supply curve shifts. A different quantity is supplied at every price. See Table 6.3 for examples of when the supply curve shifts to the right or left.

Any of the following changes could explain the shift to S': a fall in the price of any input, e.g. a fall in the wage rate of workers in sheep farming; a change in technology, e.g. a cheaper method of slaughtering lambs is introduced; a fall in the price of an alternative product, e.g. if pork chops lose popularity and fall in price, producers may increase their output of lamb because pork is less in demand; or a government subsidy on lamb chop production.

Any of the following changes could cause a shift in the opposite direction, from S' to S, implying fewer lamb chops supplied at each and every price: a rise in the wages of shepherds; a decline in productivity of workers in abattoirs; a rise in the price of pork chops; spreading of sheep tick disease; or a government tax on the output of lamb chops.

The terminology used to describe shifts of supply curves and movements along them by economists is no more standard than in the case of demand. Table 6.3 summarizes the main terms used, and covers the most important factors affecting supply.

Time and Supply

The length of time under consideration can have important

TABLE 6.3 The Terminology of Supply Curves

Change	Terms Used to Describe the Change
(A) A change in the (own) price of the good causes a MOVEMENT ALONG a supply curve	
1 Price of the good rises.	1 An increase or rise in the quantity supplied. An extension of supply.
2 Price of the good falls.	2 A decrease, fall or reduction in the quantity supplied. A contraction of supply.
(B) A change in any influence other than (own) price causes a SHIFT OF a supply curve	
1 A fall in the price of a substitute product. A fall in the price of a factor of production. An improvement in the state of technology (a rise in productivity).	1 A rightward, downward or southeasterly shift of the supply curve. An increase in supply. An improvement in the conditions of supply.
2 A rise in the price of a substitute product. A rise in the price of a factor of production. A deterioration in the state of technology (a fall in productivity).	2 A leftward, upward or northwesterly shift of the supply curve. A decrease in supply. A deterioration in the conditions of supply.

Note: The terms we use most commonly in this book are given first.

implications for the response of suppliers to changes in the price of a good. In general, the longer the time that passes, and the longer a change is expected to last, the greater the likely response.

BOX 6.1 Mad Cow Disease Hits Sales of Cattle

'Cattle sales have dropped by 38 per cent in Britain as farmers withhold their animals from market in anticipation of a fall in demand and prices because of fears that "mad cow" disease, bovine spongiform encephalopathy, could pass to humans through infected meat. "Farmers are making commercial judgement as to what they think the market will bear and keeping their animals at home until they see how things are going," Mr Vic Robertson, spokesman for the Meat and Livestock Commission, said.'

(*The Times*, 23 May 1990)

The news that some British cattle were suffering from 'mad cow' disease affected both the supply and demand sides of the market. It frightened many regular beef-eaters, even causing several European countries to ban imports of beef from this country. It also led some farmers to think again about the quantity of beef cattle they would take to market.

Questions

1 Does the information given in the news item suggest shifts or movements along (i) the supply curve, (ii) the demand curve?
2 Would you judge the effects to be different in the three different time-periods mentioned in the text?
3 Fortunately for farmers, the scare subsided. But had it continued, what do you think beef farmers would have done?

Note, too, that the time pattern of response may vary from one good to another. In cases where factors of production can be easily switched to alternative outputs, less time is needed for a substantial change than where it is difficult to do so. An example of easy switching is a producer of carrots, who can use his land to grow other crops (though the time between sowing and harvesting provides a lower limit to the time needed for output to change). An example of difficult switching is an aircraft manufacturer with a great deal of specialist equipment. Many years would be needed to switch into the easiest alternative type of production.

Three conventional time-periods

The responsiveness of quantity supplied to a change in price usually increases as time passes. To capture this in a useful but simplified way, economists use three conventional time-periods. They are called momentary (or instantaneous),[1] short run and long run.

The first of these, the MOMENTARY period, does not imply the passage of a particular time-span. It refers to situations when there is insufficient time to alter quantities offered for sale. The term is appropriate in a street market, for example, when all available goods are on display. The momentary period can, however, be much longer in agriculture; once planted, crop size cannot as a rule be changed until the following season.

The second, the SHORT RUN, refers to a period over which production can be varied within the confines of the producer's existing productive facilities. A farmer will have a fixed size of farm and a manufacturer fixed plant and equipment. It is possible for producers to take on or lay off labour, and to buy more or fewer materials. But production is constrained by the given productive facilities.

The third, the LONG RUN, refers to a period long enough to alter everything that producers wish to alter in response to a change in price. New factories can be built, land can be brought in from other uses, and more or less labour and other factors of production may be employed.

---

1 Also sometimes called the 'market period'.

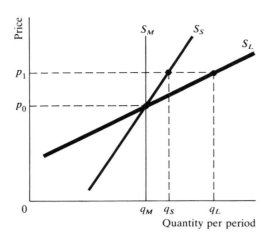

FIGURE 6.5 Time and Supply. The longer the time allowed the greater the probable effect on quantity supplied. S_M is a momentary supply curve, S_S is a short-run and S_L is a long-run supply curve. When price rises from p_0 to p_1, quantity supplied rises most with S_L and least with S_M.

Figure 6.5 illustrates the different shapes of the supply curve over these three periods. The curves S_M, S_S and S_L are the momentary, the short-run and the long-run supply curves. Assume that we start with a market price of p_0. The quantity supplied is q_M in all three cases. All three curves go through the same price-quantity combination because they are meant to describe reactions over various periods of time starting from one situation.

Consider, now, how quantity supplied varies over time in response to a change in price, resulting perhaps from a switch in consumers' tastes in favour of the commodity. Suppose the new price is p_1. In the momentary period, supply cannot be changed. The quantity offered for sale remains at q_M, so that the supply curve is the vertical line S_M. In the short run, the quantity can be changed somewhat. S_S is the appropriate supply curve and the quantity offered for sale rises from q_M to q_S. In the long run, S_L is the relevant supply curve. Sufficient time is available for the producers to make a full response to the price change. A further increase in supply takes the quantity supplied from q_S to q_L.

Supply Curves which are Not Upward-Sloping

We concluded our discussion of the elementary theory of demand with a section on exceptional demand curves that did not slope downwards as do most demand curves. We conclude this chapter on the same note, with a mention of supply curves which do not have the usual slope. Note, however, we do not use a heading 'Exceptional Supply Curves' as we did with demand. The reason is that, while upward-sloping supply curves are common in the short run, other slopes are by no means exceptional. In the long run, when producers have time to adjust fully to changes such as rising demand, costs need not rise. They may be constant, or even fall, when supply curves need not slope upwards. We deal with these cases at length in Chapter 14.

Summary

1 Supply in economics refers to the quantities of a commodity that sellers wish to offer for sale per period of time. In the elementary theory of supply, sellers are assumed to seek to maximize their profits and to be price-takers.

2 The determinants of quantity supplied include the own price of the good, the prices of other goods, costs of production, producers' goals, income and expectations. Costs depend on the prices of factors of production and the state of technology.

3 The relationship between own price and quantity supplied, *ceteris paribus*, is represented graphically by a supply curve. If the marginal cost of production rises as output increases, the supply curve will be upward-sloping. A profit-maximizing seller will offer more for sale as price rises.

4 The rule for a profit-maximizing seller is that output should be where *marginal cost is equal to price*.

5 Goods are substitutes in production if a change in the price of one good leads to a change in the opposite direction in the supply of another (competitive supply). Goods are in joint supply if a change in the price of one leads to a change in the same direction in the supply of another.

6 A market supply curve is constructed by the horizontal summation of the supply curves of individual producers.

7 Changes in any *ceteris paribus* assumptions (i.e. other than changes in the own price of the good) cause the supply curve to *shift*. Changes in the own price of the good cause *movements along* the supply curve.

8 Three time-periods are conventionally recognized for supply: momentary, short run and long run – reflecting the greater ease of altering quantity supplied as time passes.

Questions

1 Refer to Figure 6.3, or Table 6.2, and estimate the quantities that would be supplied by (i) the market, and by (ii) A and (iii) B at the following prices: (a) 50 pence per lb., (b) £1.75 per lb.

2 Which of the following would, *ceteris paribus,* cause the supply curve for bread to shift to the right (R), to shift to the left (L), not to shift at all (N)?

(i) A rise in the productivity of labour in baking.
(ii) A rise in the price of bread-making machinery.
(iii) A rise in the price of bread.
(iv) A rise in consumers' income.
(v) A rise in the price of cakes (due to increased demand).

3 What relationship identifies profit-maximizing output for a price-taking producer?

4 You are given the following information about total costs of production: at output 50 they are £1000; at output 60 they are £1200. Calculate marginal costs.

5 What would be the shape of a market supply curve if marginal costs did not vary with output?

6 Extend the straight-line supply curves S_S and S_L in Figure 6.5 so that they cut the axes. Why does the latter seem more plausible than the former?

7 Elasticity of Demand and Supply

Smoking damages your health. The government has tried to discourage cigarette smoking by banning television advertising and requiring warnings on cigarette packets. What about trying to use the price mechanism? What about a swingeing increase in the tax on cigarettes? How effective would it be? What would happen to consumption, market price and government revenue?

The government could easily raise tobacco tax to any level it desired. However, the effectiveness of such a measure would depend on the responsiveness of demand to price rises. If smokers continued to smoke nearly as much as before, the main impact would be a large rise in government tax revenue. In contrast, if the price rise led smokers to cut cigarette consumption drastically, the government would achieve its purpose. Between the two rather extreme cases just described, there might be *some* fall in consumption and *some* rise, or fall, in government revenue. Obviously, the government would like to estimate the likely outcome before introducing such a measure. What the government needs to know in order to predict the outcome of its tax is the *elasticity of demand* for cigarettes. Let us see what is involved.

Economists have a special measure for the response of one variable, such as quantity demanded, to changes in another variable, such as price. It is called ELASTICITY and it has many uses, as we shall find out in this chapter and beyond. In the present chapter we deal with the responses of two main variables, quantity demanded and quantity supplied, and we refer to these as demand elasticity and supply elasticity.

We have seen that many variables influence quantity demanded. The response to change in each influencing variable is measured by a separate elasticity. We start with the most common elasticity, price elasticity of demand.

PRICE ELASTICITY OF DEMAND

The measure of the responsiveness of the quantity demanded of a good to changes in its own price is known as PRICE ELASTICITY OF DEMAND, though we shall follow normal practice and drop the word 'price' when no ambiguity is involved.

A Formal Definition

Price elasticity of demand, sometimes symbolized by the Greek letter η (pronounced eeta), is defined by the following formula:

$$\text{Demand elasticity } (\eta_d) = \frac{\% \text{ change in quantity demanded}}{\% \text{ change in price}}$$

This formula tells us that the elasticity of demand is calculated by dividing the percentage change in quantity demanded by the percentage change in price which brought it about.

The result of the division process is a number, which is larger the greater is the percentage change in quantity demanded compared to the percentage change in price.[1] If the value of elasticity calculated from the formula is high, then demand is relatively responsive to price change. If the value of elasticity is low, then demand is relatively unresponsive to price changes.

We can see what is involved by applying the formula to a commodity, X, the price of which falls by 2 per cent and the quantity demanded rises by 4 per cent. Our measure of the elasticity of demand for good X is:

$$\eta_{dX} = \frac{4\% \text{ change in quantity}}{2\% \text{ change in price}} = 2$$

Ranges of Elasticity

The meaning and significance of the concept of elasticity of demand may be appreciated by showing that the value of elasticity for any good must lie in one of three ranges according to whether (i) the percentage change in quantity is greater than the percentage change in price, (ii) the percentage change in quantity is less than the percentage change in price, or (iii) the percentage change in quantity is equal to the percentage change in price.

Range I. Demand is elastic: Percentage changes in quantity demanded are larger than percentage changes in price. Demand in this range is relatively responsive to price changes. The numerical value of elasticity in the formula is greater than 1 but less than infinity. For illustration we need look no further than two paragraphs back, where we described a commodity, X, where a 2 per cent fall in price led to a 4 per cent increase in quantity demanded, and where elasticity of demand was therefore 4/2 = 2.

Range II. Demand is inelastic: Percentage changes in quantity demanded are smaller than percentage changes in price. Demand in this range is relatively unresponsive to price changes. The numerical value of elasticity in the formula lies between 0 and 1. To illustrate, consider a commodity, Y, the price of which falls by 2 per cent

---

1 The careful reader will have noticed that we have avoided the problem that the *sign* of the number is negative when quantity and price are negatively associated. We deal with this shortly.

while the quantity demanded rises by only 1 per cent. Our measure of the elasticity of demand for good Y is:

$$\eta_{dY} = \frac{1\% \text{ change in quantity}}{2\% \text{ change in price}} = 0.5$$

The demand for good Y is inelastic.

Range III. Demand is unit elastic: Percentage changes in quantity demanded are equal to percentage changes in price. Demand is neither elastic nor inelastic. The numerical value of elasticity of demand is exactly unity. To illustrate, consider a commodity, Z, the price of which falls by 2 per cent while the quantity demanded also rises by 2 per cent. Our measure of the elasticity of demand for Z is:

$$\eta_{dZ} = \frac{2\% \text{ change in quantity}}{2\% \text{ change in price}} = 1$$

Elasticity of demand and consumers' total outlay

How does consumers' total outlay react when the price of a product changes? Total outlay is price times quantity. When price changes, quantity changes in the opposite direction to price.

Thus, what happens to total outlay depends on the relative strengths of these opposing forces – a price fall and quantity increase (or a price increase and quantity fall).

The simplest example will show that total outlay may either rise, fall or stay the same in response to a price change. Suppose 100 units sell at a price of £1. If price is cut to £0.90 and quantity *rises* to 120, total outlay rises to £108. If, however, the same price change increases quantity only to 105, then total outlay *falls* to £94.50.

What happens to total outlay is related to the elasticity of demand, which is the percentage change in quantity divided by the percentage change in price. If the percentage change in quantity is precisely the same as the percentage change in price (i.e. elasticity equals 1), the two influences will exactly balance out, and total outlay will not change

when price changes. If the percentage change in quantity exceeds the percentage change in price (i.e. elasticity is greater than 1), total outlay will rise if price falls. If the percentage change in quantity is less than the percentage change in price (i.e. elasticity is less than 1), total revenue will fall if price falls.

The three cases described in the previous paragraph are illustrated diagrammatically in Figure 7.1. Each section of the diagram corresponds to one of the three ranges of elasticity, greater than unity (written in symbols as $\eta > 1$), less than unity (in symbols, $\eta < 1$) and equal to unity, which were described in the previous section.

Total revenue is measured on a graph as an area – that described by multiplying price by quantity. Thus, in all sections of the diagram, total outlay at the higher price is given by the rectangle Op_0aq_0, while total outlay at the lower price is given by the rectangle Op_1bq_1. If we imagine price falling from p_0 to p_1, consumer outlay is *reduced* by the amount indicated by the size of the rectangle labelled A. At the same time, the lower price results in consumer outlay being *increased* by the darker rectangle labelled B. If B is greater than A, total outlay is greater at the lower price. If area A exceeds area B, total outlay is greater at the higher price. If areas A and B are equal, total outlay is equal at higher and lower prices.

Part (i) of the diagram shows relatively elastic demand. Elasticity is greater than unity – in symbols $\eta > 1$. Area B is greater than area A; total outlay is larger at the lower price; demand elasticity is greater than unity. Part (ii) of the diagram shows relatively inelastic demand. Elasticity is less than unity – in symbols $\eta < 1$. Area A is larger than area B; total outlay is larger at the higher price; demand elasticity is less than unity.

In part (iii) of the diagram, areas A and B are equal; total outlay is the same at the higher and lower prices; demand elasticity is equal to unity.[1]

---

1 Demand curves of constant elasticity equal to unity are known mathematically as rectangular hyperbolas, because the rectangles formed by dropping perpendiculars to the two axes (representing total consumer outlays) from any points on the curve, are equal in area.

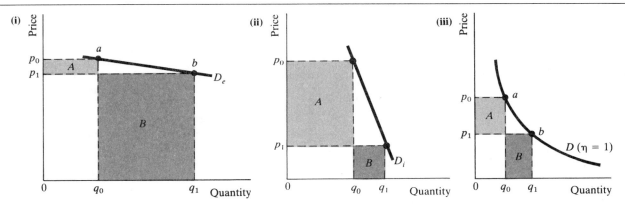

FIGURE 7.1 Demand Curves with Elasticities Greater Than, Less Than and Equal to Unity. (i) When elasticity is greater than 1, total outlay is greater at the lower of two prices ($Op_1bq_1 > Op_0aq_0$); (ii) when elasticity is less than 1, total outlay is greater at the higher of two prices ($Op_0aq_0 > Op_1bq_1$); (iii) when elasticity is equal to 1, total outlay is the same at different prices ($Op_0aq_0 = Op_1bq_1$).

Two extreme cases

We have seen that the elasticity of demand can vary from inelastic to elastic. At the extreme ends of these ranges lie two limiting cases of zero and infinite elasticity.

Zero elasticity: Zero elasticity arises when a change in price has no effect on quantity demanded. The same amount is demanded at all prices, so the change in quantity brought about by a change in price is zero. In this case, demand is said to be PERFECTLY or COMPLETELY INELASTIC.

A demand curve of zero elasticity is a straight vertical line,

such as that in Figure 7.2, which shows that q_0 is demanded whatever the price.

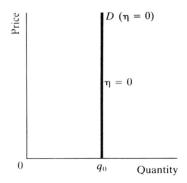

FIGURE 7.2 Perfectly Inelastic Demand. When elasticity of demand is zero, the quantity demanded is the same (q_0) at all prices.

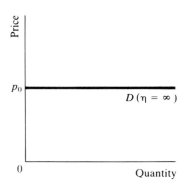

FIGURE 7.3 Perfectly Elastic Demand. When elasticity of demand is infinite, nothing is bought at a price above p_0, but at that price consumers will buy any amount that is offered for sale.

Infinite elasticity: Infinite elasticity arises when a small decrease in price raises quantity demanded from zero to an infinitely large amount. Put another way, nothing at all is bought if price is above a certain amount, say p_0, while consumers will buy any amount that is available as soon as price falls to p_0. In this case, demand is said to be PERFECTLY, COMPLETELY or INFINITELY ELASTIC.

A demand curve of infinite elasticity is a straight horizontal line

such as that in Figure 7.3, which shows that consumers are prepared to buy all they can obtain at a price p_0, but zero at any higher price.

The relationship between elasticity and total revenue is summarized in Table 7.1.

TABLE 7.1 The Terminology of Elasticity

Description	Numerical value	Total outlay
INFINITELY ELASTIC	equal to infinity ($\eta = \infty$)	Zero for a price rise Infinity for a price fall
ELASTIC	greater than 1 ($\eta > 1$)	Decreases for a price rise Increases for a price fall
UNIT ELASTIC	equal to 1 ($\eta = 1$)	Remains the same whether price rises or falls
INELASTIC	less than 1 ($\eta < 1$)	Increases for a price rise Decreases for a price fall
ZERO ELASTIC	equal to 0 ($\eta = 0$)	Increases for a price rise Decreases for a price fall

Note: ∞ is the mathematical symbol for infinity.

Two technical problems

In our discussion of elasticity so far, we have avoided two small technical issues that we must now deal with. These concern the sign of our measure of elasticity, and the method of calculating percentages on which it depends.

Demand elasticity is negative (i.e. less than 0): This arises from the fact that price and quantity demanded normally vary in opposite directions, i.e. demand curves have negative slopes – they slope downwards.

Consider the two parts of the fraction in the formula for elasticity. They must, for all normal demand curves, have the opposite signs. The denominator is the percentage change in price. If price rises, then the percentage change in price is positive. However, in that case, quantity falls, so the percentage change in quantity must be negative. Hence the whole expression for elasticity has a negative sign. The same result occurs if price falls and quantity rises. This time, the numerator is negative and the denominator is positive, so the whole expression is negative. For convenience, we ignore the negative sign for elasticity most of the time and treat it as a positive number.[1]

Percentages: It is possible to calculate percentages in more than one way. We have to decide on the base to use in the calculation.

---

1 Note that in practice real estimates of price elasticities are often reported with their correct, negative, signs. One reason is that price elasticities are often given alongside other elasticities (such as income elasticities, see below p.68), which can be either positive or negative.

TABLE 7.2 Two Price-Quantity Points on a Demand Curve for Apples

Price (pence per lb.)	Quantity (lbs.)	Total outlay (£s) (i)×(ii)
(i)	(ii)	(iii)
100	10,000	10,000
50	10,100	5,050

Consider the data in Table 7.2 which gives two price–quantity points on a demand curve for apples. Let the price of apples fall from £1 to 50p. We could show this as a change of 50 per cent by calculating the change as a percentage of the original price of £1: (0.5/1.0)100 = 50 per cent.

However, we could just as well have been considering the effects of a rise in price from 50p to £1. The original price would then have been 50p. In this case the 50p change in price would be 100 per cent: (0.5/0.5)100 = 100 per cent of the price of 50p.

The problem arises with percentage changes in quantity as well as in price. We see from the Table that the quantity demanded rises by 100lbs. when price falls from £1 to 50p per lb. This change in quantity may be taken as a percentage of quantity demanded at the higher price (10,000) or of the amount demanded at the lower price (10,100). The former would give a percentage rise of 1 per cent: (100/10,000)100 = 1 per cent. The latter would give a percentage change of 0.99 per cent: (100/10,100) 100 = 0.99 per cent.

Arc elasticity of demand

None of this is very satisfactory, since it makes the elasticity between any two points on the demand curve depend on the direction of movement. To avoid this problem, we can take the price changes as percentages of the *average* of the higher and the lower price; and we can take the quantity changes as percentages of the *average* of the higher and the lower quantities. This gives us a single value of elasticity of demand between any two points on a demand curve. It is known as the ARC, or average, ELASTICITY.

We are now able to calculate the elasticity of demand for apples, between the price of £1.00 and £0.50 from the data given in Table 7.2. Note first that the *average* price is 75p while the price change is 50p. This makes the percentage change in price: (50/75)100 = 66.7 per cent. Similarly, the change in quantity is 100 units and the *average* quantity is 10,050, making the percentage change in quantity: (100/10,050)100 = 0.995 per cent. Thus the arc elasticity is

$$\text{Arc } \eta = \frac{0.995\%}{66.7\%} = 0.015$$

This shows that the demand for apples is inelastic over the price range 50 to 100 pence. It has a value well below unity. Notice, too, that since demand is inelastic, we expect a fall in price to reduce total expenditure on the product. The calculations in the last column of the table confirms this. Total outlay at the lower price is barely more than half of total outlay at the higher price.

Simplifying the formula for elasticity

The formula for elasticity (on page 36) can be rewritten

$$\text{Arc } \eta = \frac{\left(\dfrac{\Delta q}{q}\right)100}{\left(\dfrac{\Delta p}{p}\right)100}$$

where p and q stand now for average price and average quantity, and the Greek letter Δ is used to mean 'change in'.

We shall find it useful to simplify this formula, by cancelling out the 100s from the numerator and the denominator to give

$$\eta = \left(\frac{\Delta q}{q}\right)\bigg/\left(\frac{\Delta q}{p}\right)$$

The only difference between this and the original formula is that elasticity is now expressed as the *proportionate* change in quantity divided by the *proportionate* change in price, instead of the ratio of the two *percentage* changes. A further simplification is to invert the denominator so as to be able to multiply by it, to give

$$\eta = \left(\frac{\Delta q}{q}\right)\left(\frac{p}{\Delta p}\right)$$

Since the order in which we write the terms is of no consequence, we can write the formula finally as

$$\eta = \left(\frac{\Delta q}{\Delta p}\right)\left(\frac{p}{q}\right)$$

which will be a useful form for considering the elasticity of graphs of demand curves, and particularly convenient for the calculation of elasticity.[1] This way of writing the formula is so widely used in economic analysis that we shall give you another example. Suppose two points on a demand curve are (i) price £10, quantity sold 550, and (ii) price £9, quantity sold 590. The arc elasticity is then

$$\text{Arc } \eta = \left(\frac{\text{change in quantity}}{\text{change in price}}\right)\left(\frac{\text{average price}}{\text{average quantity}}\right)$$

$$= \left(\frac{590-550}{10-9}\right)\left(\frac{(10+9)/2}{(590+550)/2}\right)$$

$$= \left(\frac{40}{1}\right)\left(\frac{9.5}{570}\right) = \frac{2}{3}$$

---

1 Note that the formula can be used to calculate not only the elasticity of demand, but also the effects of a change in price for a given elasticity, if sufficient other information is also provided. Thus, suppose you are told that a certain good has a demand elasticity of 2 and that price is lowered by 1 per cent. You can use the formula to find the new quantity demanded, provided you are given the old quantity. If elasticity of demand is 2, the percentage change in quantity is double the percentage change in price, i.e. two times 1 per cent equals 2 per cent. So quantity demanded increases by 2 per cent when price falls by 1 per cent. If you are given the old quantity demanded, you can calculate the new quantity demanded. Say the old quantity is 50; the new quantity at the lower price will be 50 plus 2 per cent of 50, which is 54.

Demand is therefore inelastic in the price range £9–£10, with a numerical value of 2/3.

Measuring the elasticity of a demand curve

The careful reader will have noticed that in the previous two sections we did not refer to demand *curves* as being elastic and inelastic but to *portions* of demand curves *between the two prices* we were considering. This is because the elasticity of demand normally varies among different points on one demand curve.

Linear demand curves: This may be illustrated by showing that the elasticity of a straight-line (called a LINEAR) demand curve is different at all points along it.

Consider the elasticity formula $\eta = (\Delta q/\Delta p)\,(p/q)$. The first term, $\Delta q/\Delta p$, is in fact the reciprocal of the slope $\Delta p/\Delta q$ of the demand curve. Since the demand curve is a straight line, the *slope* of the curve, and hence its reciprocal, must be the same all along it. Thus the slope $\Delta p/\Delta q$ in Figure 7.4 is the same when price goes from p_0 to p_1 (and quantity from q_0 to q_1) as when price goes from p_2 to p_3 (and quantity from q_2 to q_3).

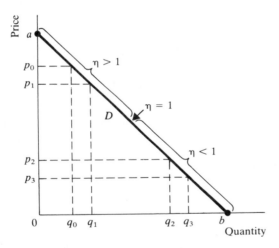

FIGURE 7.4 Elasticity Varies Along a Linear Demand Curve.
Elasticity is infinite at the point of intersection of the demand curve with the price axis (at *a*); it is zero at the point of intersection with the quantity axis (at *b*); it is unity at the mid-point of the demand curve.

The elasticity of demand is *not*, however, the same everywhere on the curve. Recall that the formula is $(\Delta q/\Delta p)\,(p/q)$. It is true that the *first term* in the formula is constant along the demand curve, but there is a second term, p/q, price divided by quantity. This term varies along the demand curve. Near its upper end, p is high and q is low so the ratio p/q is large. Near the lower end p is low and q is high, so the ratio p/q is small. It follows that *elasticity falls as we move downwards to the right along a linear demand curve*.

Finally, consider the two end-points of the curve. Where it cuts the quantity axis p is zero, so p/q is zero, so elasticity is zero. Where it cuts the price axis q is zero, so p/q

is infinite, so elasticity is infinite.[1] We conclude that the elasticity of a straight-line demand curve varies from infinity, where the curve cuts the price axis, to zero where it cuts the quantity axis.

Figure 7.4 shows the sections of the demand curve labelled with their corresponding elasticities. Notice that at the mid-point along the curve, demand elasticity is exactly unity. Below that point, demand elasticity varies between 0 and 1; it is inelastic – marked as $\eta < 1$. Above that point, demand elasticity varies between 1 and ∞; it is elastic, marked in Figure 7.4 as $\eta > 1$.

The intuition of the variable elasticity is that while the constant slope of a straight line indicates a constant absolute reaction of quantity (Δq) to a constant absolute change in price (Δp), elasticity refers to percentage changes. If we move down the demand curve making equal absolute changes in price and quantity, these represent small percentage changes in p and large percentage changes in q near the top of the curve (elasticity high) and large percentage changes in p and small percentage changes in q near the bottom of the curve (elasticity low).

Curvilinear demand curves: If you draw a non-linear demand curve at random, it will very probably also have an elasticity that varies over its length. There are, however, non-linear curves with constant elasticities. We already know one. The demand curve when elasticity is equal to unity is a rectangular hyperbola because pq is constant.

Determinants of Elasticity of Demand

The actual values of elasticity of demand differ from commodity to commodity. Some generalizations about the determinants of elasticity may however be made, under two heads – the nature of the good, and the length of time under consideration.

The nature of the good

Two aspects must be dealt with: first, the availablity of substitutes, and second, the definition of the good.

Substitutes: By far the most important generalization to make about the determinants of demand elasticity is that the more and the better substitutes there are for a commodity, the higher the elasticity of demand will be.

Some commodities, such as margarine, cabbage, pork and Ford cars have quite close substitutes – butter, cauliflower, beef and Toyota cars, for example. A change in the price of such commodities, *the prices of substitutes remaining constant*, will cause quite substantial substitutions. A fall in the commodity's price will lead consumers to buy much more of the commodity in question, and much less of the substitute; a rise in the commodity's price will lead consumers to buy much less of the commodity, and much more of its substitute. Demand is

---

1 Division by zero is an inadmissible operation. But as q gets smaller and smaller, the ratio p/q increases without limit – which is what we mean when we say loosely that its value is infinite when q is zero.

responsive to price changes, and elasticity is, therefore, high. Other commodities, such as salt, housing, and all vegetables taken as a group, have few, if any, satisfactory substitutes. A rise in their prices will cause a smaller fall in quantities demanded than if close substitutes had been available. In these cases, demand is relatively unresponsive to price changes and elasticity of demand is, therefore, low.

Note that the argument has *not* been couched in terms of a division of commodities into two sets called 'luxuries' and 'necessities'. Demand studies do not show commodities falling clearly into these two categories. Instead, there is a continuous spread of values of measured elasticities, running from high to low. Moreover the definition of 'necessity' and 'luxury' varies from one individual to another, and can be closely associated with income. Thus, there are goods which could be thought of as luxuries but which may have low demand elasticities. Rolls-Royce cars, for example, are certainly 'luxury' items for most of us, but for the relevant (high) income groups who buy them, a rise in price may not discourage purchases by a large amount.

Definition of the good: The elasticity of demand depends on how closely a good is defined. The reason for this is related to the question of the availability of substitutes, just discussed. Consider, for instance, the examples we used to illustrate goods with elastic demands – cabbages and cauliflowers. Compare them with all vegetables taken as a group, which we cited as illustrative of inelastic demand. What this comparison illustrates is the narrower the definition, the more likely it is that a good will have close substitutes and, therefore, will have an elastic demand. For example, elasticity of demand is very high for $1\frac{1}{2}$ litre black Ford Escorts. Substitutes include all other-colour Escorts, other-engine-size Fords, and all other makes of car. The elasticity of demand for $1\frac{1}{2}$ litre Ford Escorts, of all colours, taken as a group, must be less than that for $1\frac{1}{2}$ litre black Escorts because the closeness of substitutes is less – red Escorts are no longer possible substitutes. The elasticity of demand for a Ford Escort of any engine size or colour must be less still, because other-engine-size Escorts are also excluded from the possible substitutes.

You can continue the chain at your will, defining the commodity more and more widely, with the effect that you reduce the number of substitutes and also, therefore, the elasticity of demand. You may end up considering the elasticity of demand for all cars, which will be lower than the average elasticity for all sub-groups of cars. Why? Because there are fewer close substitutes for cars in general than for any single model.

We are not just inventing distinctions for their own sake. How widely or narrowly a good is defined depends on the problem at hand. For example, a general blight that destroys all vegetable crops will make its effects felt against a relatively inelastic demand for vegetables. But a cauliflower worm that attacks only that vegetable, will make its effects felt against a relatively elastic demand for that one vegetable.

The irrelevance of the proportion of consumers' expenditure on the good: It is sometimes argued that the smaller the percentage of consumers' expenditure on a good, the lower the elasticity of demand for it. Examples selected are goods such as matches and salt. The impression is given that demand is unresponsive because no one notices price changes with goods that take up little of one's expenditure.

Both matches and salt happen to have low elasticities. The reason, however, is the one already given: they have few, if any, satisfactory substitutes. It does not follow that such goods have low elasticities *merely because* they take little of consumers' income. In the case of matches, there are some substitutes (e.g. gas lighters), but they are few and not very satisfactory for all purposes. That is why the elasticity of demand for matches taken as a whole is relatively low. However, the elasticity of demand for any one brand of matches, expenditure on which is an even lower proportion of consumers' total expenditure, is likely to be high because consumers can switch to other brands of matches.

Consider another example. Polo mints unquestionably take up a very small proportion of consumer expenditure. But does anyone doubt that a significant rise in their price would lead to a large fall in purchases as mint suckers switched to other cheaper sweets? Evidently, the producers of Polo mints do not think they face a low demand elasticity! (If they did, they would raise their price and enlarge their profits, since their revenues would increase if the elasticity of demand was really less than unity.)[1]

Time and elasticity

In Chapter 3, we pointed out that the longer the period of time under consideration, the greater we would expect the effect of a change in the price of a good to be on the quantity demanded. All we need to do now is to couch this same discussion in terms of elasticity. We suggested several reasons why demand responds more in the long term than in the short term.

First, news of price changes takes time to percolate through the whole community. Second, habits take time to be broken. Third, the commodity itself may be durable, so that the full reaction does not occur until all of the existing stock has been replaced. Fourth, full adjustments require a lot of time whenever the commodity in question is used along with a durable complement (as, for example, petrol is with cars). *For these reasons, elasticities of demand for many goods tend to be greater the longer the time-period considered.*

For example, a large fall in the price of imported cars will not make everyone discard their domestic-made cars immediately, but as these cars are replaced, more buyers may switch to imported cars. The result may be a small response to the price reduction over a month, quite a large response over a year and a massive response over five years.

---

1 For a full discussion see Colin Harbury, 'Price Elasticity of Demand and Consumers' Income: A Conventional Folly', *Economics*, 1986.

OTHER DEMAND ELASTICITIES

The concept of elasticity of demand can be broadened to measure the response of quantity demanded to *any* of the factors that influence demand. Besides the price of the good itself, we often need to know how changes both in income and in the prices of other commodities affect quantities demanded.

Income Elasticity of Demand

As incomes rise, consumers increase their demands for many commodities. In richer countries, the demand for food and basic clothing does not increase with income nearly as much as does the demand for many durable goods and many kinds of service.

The responsiveness of demand to changes in income is measured with a concept called the income elasticity of demand, denoted by η_y and defined as

$$\eta_y = \frac{\% \text{ change in quantity demanded}}{\% \text{ change in income}}$$

The sign of income elasticity is usually positive. This is the case with normal goods, defined as those the demand for which is positively associated with income (see above, p.46). It is only with inferior goods, where the association is negative, that income elasticity is negative.

We explained earlier that a good cannot be inferior at all levels of income. (Refer back to p.46 if you need to.) The same argument holds for income elasticity, which has to be positive at some low incomes. It may also be helpful to refer back to Figure 5.1 on p.47 to confirm the signs of the income elasticities of the income demand curves in that diagram. They are as follows: Curve 1, positive; Curve 2, positive up to income y_1 (zero at higher incomes as quantity demanded remains unchanged with rising income); Curve 3, positive up to income y_2, and negative at higher incomes.

It is necessary to add only that the relationship between income elasticity and consumers' total outlay does not parallel that between price elasticity of demand and total outlay. It is as follows: when income elasticity is positive, total outlay rises with income, regardless of the numerical value of elasticity; when income elasticity is negative, total outlay falls as income rises, and vice versa.

Cross Elasticity of Demand

We have already seen that the quantity demanded of a good can be affected by changes in the price of other goods. The responsiveness of demand to changes in the price of *another* good is known as

the cross elasticity of demand. It is denoted by η_{xy} and defined as

$$\eta_{xy} = \frac{\% \text{ change in the quantity of good X}}{\% \text{ change in the price of good Y}}$$

The value of cross elasticity of demand can vary between minus infinity and plus infinity. Goods which are sub-stitutes for each other have positive cross elasticities. Goods which are complements to each other have negative cross elasticities. One would, therefore, expect butter to have a positive cross elasticity of demand with respect to changes in the price of margarine, because a fall in the price of margarine would lead consumers to substitute it for butter. In contrast, the cross elasticity of demand for ski boots with respect to the price of skis is likely to be negative. A fall in the price of skis would lead to an increase in demand for ski boots.

BOX 7.1

Estimates of Elasticities of Demand for Selected Household Foods, UK, 1988

	Price elasticity	Income elasticity
Beef and veal	−1.23	0.03
Bread	−0.16	−0.28
Meat	−1.17	0.03
Cheese	−1.19	0.25
Fresh fruit	−0.77	0.53
Mutton and lamb	−1.75	0.22
Oranges	−1.44	0.28
Potatoes	−0.16	−0.53
Pork	−1.57	−0.10

Source: Annual Report to the National Food Survey Committee, Ministry of Agriculture, Fisheries and Food, *Household Food Consumption and Expenditure* (1989).

The relative values of these official estimates of demand elasticities for selected foods are probably more reliable than their absolute values.

Questions

1 Re-order the commodities according to their price elasticities of demand. Does the order make any kind of sense? Why is the price elasticity of demand for beef greater than for meat?
2 Can you find two other commodities where a similar relationship holds to that between beef and meat?
3 Additional information on cross elasticities of demand (for 1981–88) are:

	with respect to the price of:		
	Beef (and veal)	Mutton (and lamb)	Pork
Beef (and veal)	−1.23	0.04	0.02
Mutton (and lamb)		−1.75	−0.11
Pork			−1.57

Questions: Which pairs of goods are the closest sub-stitutes for each other? Are any pairs complements?

SUPPLY ELASTICITY

Just as elasticity of demand measures the response of quantity demanded to changes in any of the factors that influence it, so *elasticity of supply* measures the response of quantity supplied to changes in any of the factors that influence supply. Because we are focusing mainly on the commodity's own price as the factor influencing supply, we shall be concerned mainly with *price elasticity of supply*. We follow the usual practice of dropping the adjective 'price' and referring simply to 'elasticity of supply' wherever there is no ambiguity in this usage.

Supply elasticities are very important in economics. We shall devote less space to the elasticity of supply than we have to elasticity of demand, however, because the two elasticities have much in common.

A Formal Definition

ELASTICITY OF SUPPLY is defined as the percentage change in quantity supplied divided by the percentage change in price which brought it about.

Letting the Greek letter epsilon, ε, stand for elasticity of supply, its formula is:

Elasticity of supply (ε) = $\dfrac{\text{\% change in quantity supplied}}{\text{\% change in price}}$

With the upward-sloping supply curves that we have used so far, the numerator and denominator of the fraction both have the same sign – a rise in price is associated with an increase in quantity supplied, and vice versa. The value of elasticity of supply in such cases is therefore positive. As with demand, it is best to calculate percentages on the average of higher and lower prices and quantities, and to use the concept of arc elasticity (see above, p.65).

Note that the relationship between elasticity and total outlay which we observed in the case of price elasticity of demand does *not* apply to supply curves which are positively sloped. Such supply curves show that price and quantity are positively associated, i.e. when price rises quantity also rises; when price falls quantity also falls. It follows that sellers' total receipts (i.e. prices times quantity) must always rise when price rises, and vice versa, whatever the value of the elasticity of supply. However, total receipts rise more, for a given change in price, the greater is the elasticity of supply.

Graphical Interpretation of Elasticity of Supply

Figure 7.5 illustrates the two limiting cases of supply elasticity. The vertical supply curve (labelled $\varepsilon = 0$) is perfectly inelastic, i.e. has zero supply elasticity. The same quantity q_0 is offered for sale regardless of price. The horizontal supply curve (labelled $\varepsilon = \infty$) has infinite elasticity. Suppliers would be prepared to offer an unlimited amount at the price p_0, but even the smallest fall in price would reduce the quantity supplied to zero. Such a curve is often described as being perfectly (or completely) elastic.

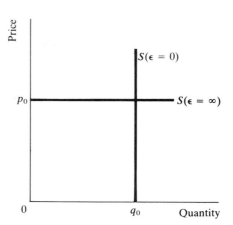

FIGURE 7.5 Perfectly Elastic and Perfectly Inelastic Supply Curves. When elasticity is infinite, the supply curve is horizontal. When elasticity is zero, the supply curve is vertical.

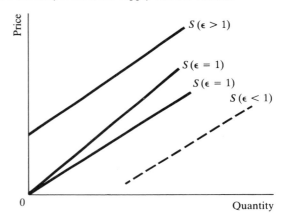

FIGURE 7.6 Supply Curves with Varying Elasticities. A linear supply curve has an elasticity > 1 if (projected) it would cut the price axis, an elasticity < 1 if (projected) it would cut the quantity axis, and equal to 1 if (projected) it would pass through the origin of the graph.

Figure 7.6 shows four supply curves. The two labelled $\varepsilon = 1$ have unit elasticity, as do *all* straight-line supply curves passing through the origin. This is because the proportionate changes in price and quantity are the same at all points on such curves. The curve labelled $\varepsilon > 1$ is relatively elastic, as is any straight-line supply curve intersecting the price axis. The curve labelled $\varepsilon < 1$ is relatively inelastic, as is any straight-line supply curve which would, if projected, intersect the quantity axis.[1]

Determinants of Elasticity of Supply

What determines the response of producers to a change in the price of the commodity that they supply? The size of the response depends, in part, on the same two factors that determine demand elasticity – the nature of the good and

1 In Figure 7.6, if the supply curve $\varepsilon < 1$ were extended to intersect the quantity axis at a positive quantity, this would carry the implication that such an amount is supplied, as it were, 'free', but that a positive price must be paid to call forth supplies greater than this.

the time-period under consideration. However, they require slightly different interpretation.

The nature of the good

The major consideration here is the availability of substitutes, though the word 'substitutes' does not have quite the same meaning as it did in the case of elasticity of demand. In the case of supply, substitute goods are those to which factors of production can most easily be transferred, not those goods which are substitutes in the minds of consumers. For example, a producer may easily move from producing spanners to producing screwdrivers, even though consumers will not regard these products as close substitutes. The more easily factors can be transferred from the production of one good to that of another, the greater the elasticity of supply.

Exactly the same point may be made about supply elasticity and the definition of a good, as was made about demand elasticity. The more narrowly the commodity is defined, the greater the elasticity. For example, it is easier to transfer resources from producing red skirts to green skirts than from skirts in general to trousers.

Time and elasticity

It is as true of supply as it was of demand that elasticity tends to be greater the longer the time-period over which it is measured. The longer the period, the easier it is to shift factors of production among products, following a change in their relative prices. This argument has particular force for many agricultural products, because of the natural time-lag between planting and harvesting of crops. The argument is also strong when long-lasting and costly capital equipment may continue to be used after a fall in demand, but will not be replaced when it wears out.

We end by adding that elasticity of supply is strongly influenced by the way costs change with output – a subject we shall cover in Chapter 15.

Summary

1 Elasticity is the economist's measure of the response of one variable to changes in another. Price elasticity of demand is percentage change in quantity demanded divided by percentage change in price. It varies between zero (perfectly inelastic) and infinity (perfectly elastic).

2 When demand elasticity equals 1, consumers' total outlay is the same at all prices. When demand elasticity is less than 1, total outlay and price change in the same direction. When elasticity is greater than 1, total outlay and price change in opposite directions.

3 Perfectly inelastic demand is where quantity does not respond to price changes; the demand curve is a vertical line. Perfectly elastic demand is where the quantity demanded is indefinitely large at the going price and zero at any lower price; the demand curve is a horizontal line.

4 Arc elasticity relates price and quantity changes to the average prices and quantities. Elasticity varies at every point on straight-line demand curves, other than when the line is vertical or horizontal.

5 Elasticity of demand tends to be greater the more substitutes there are for a commodity, the more narrowly a commodity is defined, and the longer the time-period.

6 Income elasticity of demand is the percentage change in quantity demanded divided by percentage change in income. It is positive for normal goods and negative for inferior goods.

7 Cross elasticity of demand is the percentage change in quantity of one good divided by the percentage change in price of another. It is positive for substitutes, and negative for complements.

8 Elasticity of supply is percentage change in quantity supplied divided by percentage change in price.

9 Perfectly elastic supply is where quantity supplied is indefinitely large at the given price and zero at any lower price; the supply curve is a horizontal line. Perfectly inelastic supply is where quantity supplied does not respond to price changes; the supply curve is a vertical line.

10 Linear supply curves have elasticity greater than 1 if they intersect the price axis, less than 1 if they intersect the quantity axis, and equal to 1 if they pass through the origin of the graph.

11 Elasticity of supply for a commodity tends to be greater the more good substitutes there are among which factors of production can be transferred, the more narrowly the commodity is defined, and the longer the time-period.

Questions

1 Estimates of the elasticity of demand for good X are greater than that for good Y. Why could this be?

2 Refer to the statistics on elasticities in the Box on p.68. Which, if any, commodities listed are inferior goods?

3 Good W has an income elasticity of demand equal to unity. Which, if any, of the following statements is necessarily correct?
    (a) If price falls by 10 per cent, quantity will rise by 10 per cent.
    (b) If income rises by 100 units, quantity demanded will fall by 100 units.
    (c) W is neither a normal nor an inferior good.
    (d) Total consumer outlay is the same at all prices.
    (e) Consumer expenditure on W is the same at all incomes.

4 Refer to Figure 4.1 on page 38. Estimate the values of elasticity of demand at points a, b, c, d and e.

5 (i) What is the value of the cross elasticity of demand between perfect substitutes? (ii) What is the minimum value that the cross elasticity of demand between two commodities can take?

6 Which of the supply curves in Figures 6.1, 6.4 and 6.5 (on pages 54, 58 and 60) have elasticities (a) $\varepsilon > 1$, (b) $\varepsilon = 1$, (c) $\varepsilon < 1$, (d) $\varepsilon = 0$, (e) $\varepsilon = \infty$.

8 Market Price Determination

In Part 1 of this book we gave an intuitive description of how a market system allocates resources through the price mechanism. So far in Part 2 we have built up separate theories of demand and of supply. Now, in this and the next two chapters, we put supply and demand together to analyse how they interact in market situations. We remind you of two concepts which you have already encountered, that of a market and *ceteris paribus*.

The market: The key concept in this chapter is the market.

A market is any kind of institutional arrangement whereby buyers and sellers communicate with each other to buy and sell a commodity.

The market is our stage. The players on the demand side are consumers who wish to buy goods, and on the supply side are producers who offer goods for sale. We have already made the key assumptions about the behaviour of these two groups. Consumers aim to maximize the satisfactions that are derived from their purchases, while producers attempt to maximize their profits. We have also assumed that both groups are price-takers, being unable, individually, to affect market prices by changing the quantities they supply or demand.

Ceteris paribus: The analysis uses the *ceteris paribus* assumption, that everything that affects the quantity of a good demanded and supplied is held constant except the price of the good itself. We have called this the 'own price' of the commodity. Later we shall drop the assumption, so that we can study the effect of other influences.

PRICE DETERMINATION

Table 8.1 sets out hypothetical data for market demand and market supply for bottles of cider. This is a market that contains thousands of buyers and scores of sellers, no one of whom is important enough to influence the market price by altering his or her own behaviour.

Notice that if cider costs only 40p per bottle, consumers in this market would drink 19 thousand bottles each month. As the price of cider rises over the range shown, the quantity that people buy falls continuously.

On the supply side, no one will offer any cider for sale until the price is at least £1 per bottle. As the price rises above that amount, over the range shown, more and more bottles of cider are offered for sale.

TABLE 8.1 Demand and Supply Schedules for Bottles of Cider

PRICE (£s per bottle)	QUANTITIES (Thousand bottles per month) Demanded	Supplied	
(i)	(ii)	(iii)	
0.40	19	0	Excess demand
0.60	18	0	
1.00	16	4	
1.40	14	8	
1.80	12	12	Demand equals supply
2.00	11	14	Excess supply
2.50	8.5	19	
3.00	6	24	
3.50	3.5	34	

Equilibrium Price

First consider the price £1.80 in the table. At that price the quantity demanded is 12 thousand bottles per month; the quantity supplied is also 12 thousand bottles per month. At this price the quantity that consumers wish to buy is exactly the same as the quantity that producers wish to sell. Notice, also, that there is no other price shown in the table at which this is the case.

This price is known as the *equilibrium price,* and the quantity bought and sold at that price, 12,000 bottles per month in this example, is known as the *equilibrium quantity.*

EQUILIBRIUM occurs when supply and demand are balanced, when the quantity suppliers want to offer for sale balances the quantity consumers want to purchase. At this price there are no unsatisfied buyers or sellers. The market is exactly cleared.

Now look at Figure 8.1, which plots both the demand and the supply data from Table 8.1. The demand curve is plotted from columns (i) and (ii), which together show how much is demanded at each of the prices covered in the table. The supply curve is plotted from columns (i) and (iii), which together show how much is supplied at each of the prices. (If you are in any doubt about how to plot these curves from the data in the table, refer back to Chapter 4, page 38, which explains how to do it in detail.)

The equilibrium price and the equilibrium quantity occur at the *intersection* of the demand and supply curves. At the intersection point, the quantity demanded, which is read off the demand curve, is the same as the quantity supplied, which is read off the supply curve.

Thus, graphically, the equilibrium price is the price at which the demand and the supply curves intersect. When

the market price is equal to the equilibrium price, there will be neither unsatisfied demanders nor unsatisfied suppliers in the market. The market is said to be exactly cleared.

Disequilibrium Prices

The *equilibrium price* is the price at which demand equals supply. It is the price at which there are neither unsatisfied buyers nor unsatisfied sellers. The MARKET PRICE (which is sometimes called the 'actual price') is the price that actually rules at any point in time. The equilibrium price does not change unless the demand or supply schedules shown in Table 8.1 change. But the actual market price can change continually. Thus, for example, given the schedules in Table 8.1, the equilibrium price remains at £1.80. The actual market price may, however, be above the equilibrium price or below it.

Let us consider what happens when the market price does *not* equal the equilibrium price. Looking at the data in Table 8.1 or the curves in Figure 8.1, it is clear that, when the market price is above the equilibrium price, the amount demanded is less than the amount supplied. For example, at a price of £3.00, both the table and the diagram indicate a quantity of 6 thousand bottles demanded, and a quantity of 24 thousand bottles supplied. In such circumstances, the quantity sellers offer for sale exceeds the quantity consumers wish to demand.

Graphically, the supply curve lies to the right of the demand curve at that price. Notice, also, that at market prices below the equilibrium price, both the table and the diagram indicate that the quantity demanded exceeds the quantity supplied. Graphically, the demand curve lies to the right of the supply curve at those prices.

When the quantity demanded is greater than the quantity supplied, there is said to be EXCESS DEMAND.

This is the case for all prices below £1.80 in both Table 8.1 and Figure 8.1.

When the quantity supplied is greater than the quantity demanded, there is said to be EXCESS SUPPLY.

This is the case at all prices above £1.80 in both the figure and the table.

The Working of Market Forces

We now consider the forces that act on the market price when it is not the equilibrium price. On the one hand, when there is excess demand, consumers will not be able to buy all they wish to buy. There simply is not enough supplied for them to be able to do so. On the other hand, when there is excess supply, suppliers will not be able to sell all they wish to sell. Demand is insufficient for them to be able to do so.

In the cases of excess demand and excess supply, therefore, some people are not able to do what they would like to do. We would expect some action to be taken as a result. That action is described as the working of market forces.

Excess demand: Suppose, first, that market price is *below* the equilibrium price of £1.80. Say market price is £1.00 in Figure 8.2. The quantity demanded is 16 thousand bottles per month, while the quantity supplied is 4 thousand. Thus, there is *excess demand* of 12 thousand bottles. What will then happen?

Market price will begin to rise. On the one hand, some consumers, finding themselves unable to buy as much as they wish to buy, offer higher prices in an attempt to get more of what is available for themselves. On the other hand, suppliers, finding themselves easily able to sell all of their total production, begin to ask for higher prices for the quantities that they have produced. Thus market forces – the response by producers to the competition among consumers for goods – tend to push the price up. These

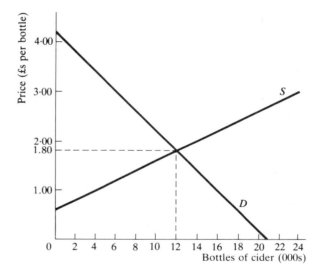

FIGURE 8.1 Market Equilibrium. The point of intersection of the supply and demand curves identifies the equilibrium price, at which the quantities demanded and supplied are equal.

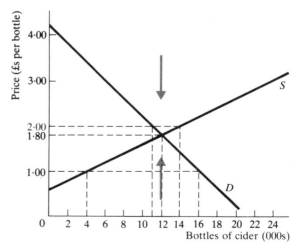

FIGURE 8.2 Excess Demand and Supply. When market price is above equilibrium, competition among sellers drives price downwards. When market price is below equilibrium, competition among buyers drives price upwards.

market forces are illustrated by the upward-pointing arrow in Figure 8.2, indicating an upward pressure on the market price whenever it is below the equilibrium price of £1.80.

Excess supply: Suppose now that market price is *above* equilibrium. Say it is at £2.00 in Figure 8.2. Quantity supplied is now 14 thousand bottles, while quantity demanded is only 11 thousand. Thus, *excess supply* of 3 thousand bottles develops. Market price will now fall. Suppliers will find themselves unable to sell all of their output. As a result they will begin to ask lower prices for what they sell. Buyers will observe the glut of unsold output and will begin to offer lower prices in response. Both of these pressures, coming from sellers and from buyers, will push the market price down. This market pressure is illustrated by the downward-pointing arrow in Figure 8.2, indicating a downward pressure on the market price whenever that price is above the equilibrium price of £1.80.

Summary of market-price determination

The theory just outlined explains why price in the market for bottles of cider tends towards equilibrium at the point of intersection of the supply and demand curves. At prices above equilibrium, market forces tend to push price down, with the consequence that excess supply is eliminated. At prices below equilibrium, market forces tend to push price up, with the consequence that excess demand is eliminated. Only when market price is at its equilibrium value is the market exactly cleared in the sense that consumers *want* to buy exactly the same amount that producers *want* to sell. The equilibrium price is, therefore, sometimes called the MARKET-CLEARING PRICE, leaving no unsatisfied buyers or sellers.

This equilibrium price is also the price at which there are no market forces – brought into play either by excess demand or by excess supply – to cause the price to change. At any other than the market-clearing price, DISEQUILIBRIUM is said to exist.

What Equilibrium is *Not*

We have said something about the nature of equilibrium. It is equally important to be clear that equilibrium does *not* imply certain things. Equilibrium is (1) *not* defined as the situation where the quantity bought is equal to the quantity sold; (2) *not* necessarily desirable; (3) *not* necessarily achieved; and (4) *not* necessarily stable.

Equilibrium and the quantity bought and sold

Our first point about equilibrium is that it is not the only position where the quantity bought is equal to the quantity sold. Indeed, these two quantities are equal *at every price*. You cannot buy from me more (or less) than I sell to you. By the same token, all that is bought by purchasers must have been sold by sellers.

To drive the point home, consider again Figure 8.2 (and Table 8.1), where we know the equilibrium price and quantity are £1.80 and 12,000 bottles. Suppose, that the

market is in disequilibrium, because actual price is £2.00. At this price, sellers would like to sell 14,000 bottles, but buyers are only willing to buy 11,000. How many will be bought and sold?

What no one will buy cannot be sold. So actual sales will be the same as actual purchases, 11,000. True, there will be excess supply, of 3,000 bottles, which will remain unsold. Thus the actual quantities bought and sold are equal, even though in this case the market price exceeds the equilibrium price. Desired sales, however, exceed desired purchases.

What distinguishes the equilibrium price from any other price is not any difference between the actual quantity bought and the actual quantity sold. The points are distinguished by whether the quantity consumers want to buy is equal to the quantity that suppliers want to sell.

It is only in equilibrium that the wants of suppliers and consumers are simultaneously, and fully, met, so that there are neither unsatisfied buyers nor unsatisfied sellers.

What is actually bought and sold is also referred to as the realized (or the *ex post*) quantity. Realized purchases and sales are necessarily always equal to each other by virtue of the two-sided nature of transactions. What buyers want to buy and what sellers want to sell are referred to as desired, planned, or *ex ante* quantities. These are equal only in equilibrium and are unequal at all other prices.

Desirability of equilibrium

Market equilibrium has a purely technical meaning – that price is such that quantities supplied and demanded are equal. It must not be taken to imply any judgement that the equilibrium situation is either desirable or undesirable. In other words, whether or not a market is in equilibrium is a question of positive economics (in the sense that we explained the term 'positive' in Chapter 3, p.26). Whether a particular market equilibrium is, or is not, desirable is a normative question. To answer it we need to make value judgements.

Later, we shall see that the market system results in an allocation of resources that is, in certain circumstances, likely to be judged efficient. We consider this matter further in the next chapter, as well as that of market failure – the circumstances which imply less than satisfactory market allocations. For the present, we emphasize only that

there is nothing necessarily good or bad about equilibrium.

Achievement of equilibrium

Our explanation of the means by which equilibrium was reached, in the market for bottles of cider, was based on a simple model of a market where price was determined by supply and demand. We should not jump to the conclusion that all markets in the real world behave like that one. Although some markets work in a similar fashion, others do not. There are many reasons for this, which we shall consider later. Two may be mentioned now.

First, market forces do not work instantaneously. It

takes time for excess supplies and/or excess demands to stimulate quantity adjustments to price movements. In some cases, the time-lags are considerable.

Second, the world is a place where many things are continually changing. Market forces may tend towards equilibrium but, as conditions change, the equilibrium itself may change before it is reached. Thus equilibrium may never be reached. Instead, market behaviour may be a perpetual chase towards an ever-moving target.

Stability of equilibrium

A market equilibrium is said to be STABLE if any movement of the market price away from the equilibrium price is self-restoring, i.e. market forces are set up which return market price to its equilibrium level.

An analogy may help to clarify the distinction between a stable and unstable equilibrium. Imagine two bowls, one the right way up, and the other upside down. Now place a marble in the bottom of the first bowl, and balance another on the top of the second bowl. Both are in equilibrium. However only the first is in *stable* equilibrium. If you push it away from the bottom of the bowl with your finger, it will roll back. But if you push the marble balanced on top of the upside-down bowl in any direction, it will not return to the top. It is (or rather it was) in an *unstable* equilibrium, before you disturbed it.

For an equilibrium to be stable, two conditions are necessary.

(1) When the market price is not equal to the equilibrium price, forces should be set up to push it back in the direction of the equilibrium price.

(2) These forces should not be so strong as to continually push the market price past the equilibrium, thus setting up a series of gyrations in which, although the price is pushed towards the equilibrium, it overshoots and never gets to its equilibrium value.

If both these conditions are fulfilled, the market may be stable in much the same way as was one of those old-fashioned toy clowns with a weighted bottom (known to connoisseurs as Kelly toys). You cannot knock the clown over: however hard you push it, it always comes back upright – its behaviour is stable.

If either of these conditions is not fulfilled, the market is said to be UNSTABLE because if an equilibrium is disturbed, market forces will not restore that equilibrium. There are two types of unstable equilibrium, depending on which of the above necessary conditions for stability are not fulfilled. We leave the discussion of the case where the second condition is not fulfilled until the next chapter. Here, we discuss the case where the first condition is not fulfilled.

The first condition for equilibrium was fulfilled in the cider market. To illustrate, look again at Figure 8.1. Assume the price in equilibrium is at £1.80. *Any* fall in price would create excess demand and set up market forces pushing price back up again towards the equilibrium price. Conversely, any rise in price above the equilibrium value would cause quantity supplied to exceed quantity

demanded. The excess supply would then set up market forces pushing price down towards equilibrium.

The market shown in Figure 8.3, however, does not meet this necessary condition for stability. The intersection of the supply and demand curves produces an equilibrium price, p_0, and an equilibrium quantity, q_0. At this price, desired purchases and desired sales are equal.

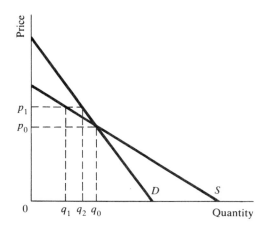

FIGURE 8.3 An Unstable Equilibrium. Any departure from equilibrium sets up market forces leading further away from equilibrium. For example, at prices above (or below) p_0 there is excess demand (or excess supply).

So far this is all very familiar. Now consider, however, what would happen if price rose above p_0, say to p_1. The rise in price reduces the quantity demanded to q_2, but it reduces the quantity supplied, by even more, to q_1. Thus, *excess demand* of $q_2 - q_1$ develops. Excess demand pushes the market price upwards. But that leads price *away* from its equilibrium value, so that market forces here do not restore equilibrium, as they did in Figure 8.2.

It is beyond the scope of this book to probe far into the conditions that are sufficient for market equilibrium to be stable. But we wonder if you can spot a crucial difference between Figures 8.3 and 8.2. One difference is that in Figure 8.2 the supply and demand curves have their normal slopes, while in Figure 8.3 The demand curve has the same (negative) slope as Figure 8.2 but the supply curve also slopes downward.[1]

Changes in Equilibrium

So far in this chapter we have focused attention on the meaning of equilibrium in a market when supply and demand are given. We now need to study how equilibrium changes when supply and/or demand changes.

We know that demand (and/or supply) curves shift whenever there is any change in any determinant of the quantity demanded (and/or supplied), other than the own

---

1 We should, however, tell you that a negative supply curve is not sufficient, by itself, for instability. It may also be flatter (i.e. less steep) than the demand curve. Equilibrium will also be unstable if the demand curve is upward-sloping. Try drawing these curves and prove for yourself what happens to market price out of equilibrium.

price of the good, held constant by *ceteris paribus* assumption. Both curves can shift in either of two directions. Shifts to the *right* mean that more is demanded (or supplied) at every price; shifts to the *left* mean that less is demanded (or supplied) at every price.

THE LAWS OF SUPPLY AND DEMAND

The effects of shifts in the supply and demand curves are so important that they are sometimes referred to as 'laws' of supply and demand. There are four primary 'laws' relating to rises and falls in demand and supply, and two supplementary 'laws' which involve the concept of elasticities.

A rise in demand

We start by considering a rise in demand. In Figure 8.4 the original demand curve is D and the original supply curve is S. The original equilibrium price is p_0. The original quantity supplied and demanded is q_0.

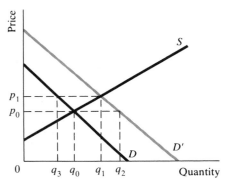

FIGURE 8.4　A Shift of the Demand Curve. A rightward shift, from D to D', raises equilibrium price and quantity. A leftward shift, from D' to D, lowers equilibrium price and quantity.

Assume now a change in the conditions of demand, say a rise in consumers' income. This increases the quantity that consumers wish to buy at every price. The demand curve shifts to D'. As a result, excess demand develops, because at the original price of p_0 the quantity demanded is now q_2. There is excess demand of $q_2 - q_0$,[1] which sets up market forces which raise the equilibrium price. The process continues until price rises from p_0 to reach a new equilibrium p_1. Quantity sold rises from q_0 to reach the new equilibrium level of q_1.

This analysis establishes our first 'law':

(1) A rise in the demand for a commodity (a rightward shift of the demand curve) causes an increase in the equilibrium price and quantity.

---

1 This is the way in which we describe *differences* between two values in this book. Refer to Appendix 1, pp. 505–6, for a full explanation.

A fall in demand

Next consider the effects of a fall in demand. Assume a change in the conditions of demand which leads consumers to want to buy smaller quantities at every price. For example, there might be a fall in the price of a substitute for the good in question.

The fall in demand shifts the demand curve leftward. To study the effects, let D' in Figure 8.4 be the original demand curve and D the new lower demand. The original equilibrium price and quantity are now p_1 and q_1. When the demand curve shifts to D, however, *excess supply* of q_1–q_3 develops. Market forces push price downwards towards the new equilibrium price of p_0. The new equilibrium quantity bought and sold is q_0. This gives our second 'law':

(2) A fall in the demand for a commodity (a leftward shift of the demand curve) causes a decrease in the equilibrium price and quantity.

A rise in supply

Let the original demand and supply curves be D and S in Figure 8.5. This yields an equilibrium price and quantity of p_0 and q_0. Now consider a change in the conditions of supply which increases the quantities that producers are prepared to offer for sale at every price. Say, for example, that there is an increase in the productivity of factors of production following from a technological advance, which lowers costs of production. The supply curve in Figure 8.5 shifts rightward from S to S'.

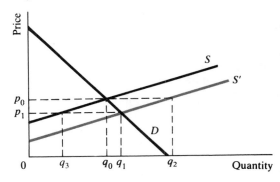

FIGURE 8.5　A Shift of the Supply Curve. A rightward shift, from S to S', lowers equilibrium price and raises equilibrium quantity. A leftward shift, from S' to S, raises equilibrium price and lowers equilibrium quantity.

On this occasion, the increase in supply causes excess supply to develop at the old equilibrium price. At that price the quantity demanded is still q_0, but suppliers now offer q_2 for sale. The excess supply of $q_2 - q_0$ sets up market forces which depress price. Price continues to fall until the new equilibrium price of p_1 is reached. At that new price the quantity supplied and demanded are equal, at q_1. This gives our third 'law':

(3) A rise in the supply of a commodity (a rightward shift of the supply curve) causes a decrease in

the equilibrium price and an increase in equilibrium quantity.

A fall in supply

Reasoning parallel to that of the previous paragraph can be applied to the effects of a fall in the supply, such as might result from a rise in the price of a factor of production, or any other appropriate change in the conditions of supply. This would lead producers to offer smaller quantities for sale at every price. It is illustrated in Figure 8.5 by letting S' be the original supply curve, yielding an equilibrium price and quantity of p_1 and q_1. Now let the supply curve shift leftward to S. At the old equilibrium price of p_1 there is now excess demand, of $q_1 - q_3$, because consumers still wish to buy q_1, but sellers are only willing to offer q_3 for sale. Market forces now push price upwards until the new equilibrium price p_0 is reached, at which price the quantity supplied and demanded are equal at q_0. This leads to our fourth and final 'law':

(4) A fall in the supply of a commodity (a leftward shift in the supply curve) causes an increase in the equilibrium price and decrease in equilibrium quantity.

Shifts versus Movements along Curves Again

In previous chapters we stressed the difference between shifts of curves and movements along curves. We warned that it is easy to confuse the two. The mistake is serious and common. So before dealing with the two supplementary laws of supply and demand, we devote a little space here to illustrate the trap. Someone who fell into it wrote in answer to an examination question:

'*An increase in income causes demand to rise. The rise in demand causes an increase in price. The increase in price causes an increase in supply, which pushes price back towards its original level.*'

There is a serious mistake in this quotation. Can you spot it?

   Consider the quotation step by step. It begins well enough. The increase in income certainly shifts the demand curve to the right. It is also true that the rise in demand puts upward pressure on price. Even the start of the next step in the argument is correct. The rise in price does tend to increase the quantity supplied. Then, however, comes the error. Supply only increases *along the supply curve*. What would really happen with a simple rise in demand is what was described on page 76 and illustrated in Figure 8.4. *There is no shift in the supply curve.*

   The mistake lies in confusing a movement along the supply curve, as a result of a change in price, which does happen, with a shift in the supply curve, which does not happen. The confusion led the student to argue as if the increase in price shifts the supply curve to the right. Compare the student's incorrect statement with the following *correct* version of the effects of a change that occurs

BOX 8.1 Surfeit of Shops has put Retail Sector in Trouble

'Britain has too many shops, according to Mr Richard Eassie, chairman of Verdict, the market research organization which specializes in retailing. ... Over-confidence in the boom years lay at the root of many of the trade's current problems. ... The explosion of retail space had led to a decline in the productivity of some retailers in terms of sales per square foot. ... jewellers, chemists and toy and sports retailers had increased their productivity in terms of sales per square foot since 1988, while DIY, electrical, furniture and menswear retailers had seen it drop dramatically.'

(*The Times*, 11 May 1990)

Market equilibrium is liable to change in different ways for different markets as time passes. The above extract identifies different sectors of the retail trade where supply and demand conditions have been altering.

Questions

1 In which direction, and why, have any demand and supply curves been shifting for each of the retail sectors mentioned in the article?
2 What implications do you find for the volume of sales and for profit margins from your analysis? Remember to make some judgements about variables that can, in principle, influence demand and supply, but which you choose to hold constant (*ceteris paribus*).

only in the conditions of demand, the conditions of supply being unchanged.

'*An increase in income causes demand to rise. The rise in demand induces an increase in price. The increase in price induces an increase in the quantity supplied. Price settles at a new equilibrium level above the old price, where the quantity consumers want to buy equals that which producers want to sell, which is higher than the old equilibrium quantity.*'

Shifts in supply and demand curves and elasticity

We are now ready to consider our two 'supplementary laws of supply and demand'. These in no way alter the primary laws just outlined, but show the *extent* to which price and quantity are affected when there are changes in supply and/or demand. This turns out to depend on the elasticities of demand and supply which, as we warned you, have important implications for economic theory.

   All we shall now do is to reconsider the effects of shifts in demand and supply curves of different elasticities. We shall show that the greater the value of the elasticity, the greater will be quantity changes and the smaller will be price changes, following a shift in the supply and/or demand curves.

A shift in demand: Consider, first, the effects of a shift in demand with supply curves of different elasticity. Figure 8.6 shows two supply curves, S_e which has elasticity greater than unity, and S_i, which has elasticity less than unity. There are also two demand curves: D, the original curve, and D', which is a new demand curve – shifted to the right, due to any change in the *ceteris paribus* assumptions on which demand curves are drawn, such as a rise in income for a normal good, a greater preference for the commodity by consumers, etc.

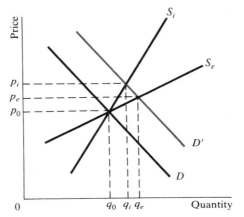

FIGURE 8.6 **Demand Shifts and Elasticity of Supply.** Demand shifts from D to D'. Supply curve S_e is more elastic than S_i. Market price rises less and quantity supplied rises more with the more elastic supply curve.

The effects of the shift in demand are seen in the diagram. Starting from the equilibrium price of p_0 and quantity of q_0, we observe the two new equilibria at the intersections of D with each of the supply curves. Quantity demanded increases and price rises in both cases, but the rise in quantity, to q_e, is the greater with the more elastic demand curve, S_e; while the rise in price, to p_i, is the greater with the less elastic supply curve, S_i.

The argument of the previous paragraph can, of course, be reversed to deal with a leftward shift of the demand curve, simply by calling D' the original and D the shifted demand curves. This allows us to reach the general conclusion:

A shift in demand will cause a larger change in equilibrium quantity and a smaller change in equilibrium price, the greater is the elasticity of supply.

The conclusions in the previous paragraph are general. But it is worth extending them to the two limiting cases of supply curves with extreme values, zero and infinity. In Figure 8.7, we draw these two supply curves, S_0 and S_∞, together with the two demand curves D and D' as in Figure 8.6. When the demand curve shifts, the rise in quantity

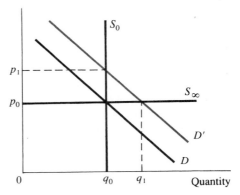

FIGURE 8.7 **Demand Shifts when Supply is Completely Elastic and Inelastic.** Demand shifts from D to D'. Market price is not affected when supply is perfectly elastic, S_∞; quantity supplied is not affected when supply is perfectly inelastic, S_0.

remains the greater with the perfectly elastic supply curve, but there is an important difference. It is that there is *no rise at all in quantity with the perfectly inelastic supply curve* (quantity supplied remains at q_0). Likewise, the rise in price remains the greater with the perfectly inelastic supply curve, but the difference here is that *price does not rise at all with the perfectly elastic supply curve* (price remains at p_0). This result has many applications, so we state it again in a general form:

A shift in demand will have no effect on equilibrium market price if supply is perfectly elastic, and will have no effect on equilibrium quantity sold if supply is perfectly inelastic.

A shift in supply: Finally, we go through precisely the same analysis for a shift in the supply curve as we did in the previous section for a shift in demand. The relevant diagram, Figure 8.8, shows the effects of the supply curve

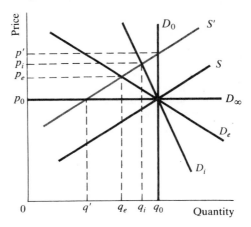

FIGURE 8.8 **Supply Shifts and Elasticity of Demand.** Supply shifts from S to S'. When demand is perfectly elastic, D_∞, market price is unaffected. When demand is perfectly inelastic, D_0, quantity is unaffected. In the intermediate cases, quantity is affected more, and price less, the greater is the elasticity of demand. Compare the effects of the shift of the relatively elastic D_e with the relatively inelastic D_i.

shifting to the left, from S to S', due to any change in the *ceteris paribus* assumptions on which supply curves are drawn, such as a fall in labour productivity, a rise in the cost of capital, etc.

Figure 8.8 includes four demand curves of different elasticity: D_e and D_i, where demand is relatively elastic and relatively inelastic, respectively, as well as the two limiting cases of perfectly elastic demand D_∞, and perfectly inelastic demand D_0.

The effects on price and on quantity in the four cases can be seen from the diagram. Since the reasoning exactly parallels that in the previous section on demand shifts, we shall merely state the conclusions, leaving it to you, the reader, to supply the verbal explanations:

A shift in supply will cause a larger change in equilibrium quantity and a smaller change in equilibrium price, the greater the elasticity of demand.

A shift in supply will have no effect on equilibrium market price if demand is perfectly elastic, and will have no effect on equilibrium quantity sold if demand is perfectly inelastic.

You will certainly need to use these results on numerous occasions when you apply the principles of supply–demand analysis to various situations. It is worth reminding you that elasticity of both supply and demand, tends to increase the longer the time-period under consideration. Hence, the above results could be stated in terms of time lapsed. The supply and demand curves in Figures 8.6, 8.7 and 8.8 of zero elasticity could be called 'very short run' (or 'momentary'); those which are relatively inelastic could be called 'short run'; those which are relatively elastic could be called 'long run', etc.

THE NATURE OF ECONOMIC LAWS

We have now completed a comparatively extensive survey of 'laws of supply and demand', because it is essential to understand them in order to put these elementary, but powerful, economic tools to work. Two points should be made before concluding.

First, the analysis has, almost without exception,[1] been based on the assumptions about consumer and producer behaviour that we outlined at the very start of Chapters 4 and 6 (see pp.37 and 53). These included maximizing behaviour (of satisfaction and of profits) by large numbers of price-taking consumers and producers. More complex, and more realistic, analysis is just round the corner in Part 3 of this book.

Second, it is right and proper to emphasize that our economic laws are similar neither to moral laws which relate to 'right' and 'wrong' ethical values, nor to legal rules which tell us about what may lawfully be done according to the criminal code or the laws of cricket.

In so far as they exist at all, economic laws are *scientific* laws. They are no more and no less than observations about the behaviour of people and institutions in the

(continued on next page)

---

1 'almost' because of the need to introduce a downward-sloping supply curve in Figure 8.3 in order to explain why equilibrium is not necessarily stable.

Summary

1 A market is in equilibrium when price is such as to clear the market, so that the quantity offered for sale equals the quantity consumers wish to buy. Graphically, this is at the intersection of the supply and demand curves.

2 When market price is above equilibrium, excess supply exists and competition among sellers leads to downward pressure on price. When market price is below equilibrium, excess demand exists and competition among buyers leads to upward pressure on price.

3 Equilibrium price is not defined as the price at which the quantities actually bought are equal to the quantities actually sold. Market equilibrium is not, in itself, necessarily desirable or undesirable. Market equilibrium is not necessarily stable in the sense that movements away from equilibrium are self-restoring.

4 A rise in demand causes an increase in the equilibrium price and an increase in the equilibrium quantity. A fall in demand causes a decrease in the equilibrium price and quantity. A rise in supply causes a decrease in the equilibrium price, and an increase in the equilibrium quantity. A fall in supply causes an increase in the equilibrium price and a decrease in the equilibrium quantity.

5 A shift in either the supply or demand curve will have a greater effect on quantity and a smaller effect on price, the greater the value of the elasticities of demand and supply.

6 Neither a rise nor a fall in demand will affect equilibrium market price if supply is perfectly elastic. Neither a rise nor a fall in supply will affect equilibrium market price if demand is perfectly elastic.

7 Neither a rise nor a fall in demand will affect the equilibrium quantity if supply is perfectly inelastic. Neither a rise nor a fall in supply will affect the equilibrium quantity if demand is perfectly inelastic.

economy. They reflect conclusions from the testing of hypotheses about economic behaviour that have, so far, stood up successfully when set against the facts of the real world (along the lines of the scientific method described in Chapter 3).

Looked at in this way, these so-called laws will often prove helpful in understanding and predicting the effects of changing situations, arising from economic policies, etc. But we stress that the laws are in no sense immutable. Those that fail to help predict correctly will need to be amended or even discarded, as economic science continues to accumulate new evidence on which better theories may be based.

Questions

1 Refer to Figure 8.1 or Table 8.1 and answer the following:
(i) At what price is excess demand equal to excess supply?
(ii) What are sellers' total receipts in equilibrium?
(iii) What price would clear the market if only 6000 bottles were offered for sale?
(iv) What difference is there in the price needed by sellers to offer 18,000 bottles for sale and the price that would clear the market of that quantity?

2 What errors, if any, occur in the following statement? 'In a market where supply curves are upward-sloping and demand curves are downward-sloping, if price is below equilibrium, excess demand will be present, the quantity bought will be equal to the quantity sold, and competition among consumers will drive price upwards towards equilibrium.'

3 Which curve or curves shift in which direction in the cases listed below: Demand curve to right (DR), to left (DL), Supply curve to right (SR), to left (SL)?
(i) Labour productivity falls.
(ii) Consumer income rises.
(iii) Price of a complementary good falls.
(iv) The own price of the good rises.

4 Which of the following continuations most correctly finishes the sentence?
'The laws of supply and demand tell us . . .
(a) what rules may legitimately be used in economic analysis.'
(b) the likely effects of changes in demand on market price.'
(c) how people always behave in market situations.'
(d) how to choose between different market allocations.'

5 Refer to Figure 8.7. Assume one of the curves is long run and the other is short run, and answer the following:
(i) Given a rise in demand how much more, or less, does price rise in the long run than in the short run?
(ii) What is the change in equilibrium quantity in momentary market situations, following a fall in demand?
(iii) What change takes place in equilibrium price when supply elasticity equals infinity, following a rise in demand?

6 If there is an increase in the supply of a commodity the demand for which is perfectly elastic, what happens to (i) market price, (ii) total receipts by sellers?

9 Market Efficiency and Market Failure

In the previous chapter we considered the way in which the forces of supply and demand operate in a market system and the nature of the equilibrium price which exactly clears the market. We now complete our analysis of the workings of the price mechanism in simple market situations with a consideration of the interrelationships between different markets and the efficiency of the system as a whole in the allocation of resources.

GENERAL AND PARTIAL EQUILIBRIUM

The major purpose of supply and demand analysis is to understand the way in which a market system allocates resources. Yet most of the analysis so far in this book has been concerned with behaviour in a single market.

The study of behaviour in markets taken one at a time is known as PARTIAL EQUILIBRIUM ANALYSIS, because it deals with only a part of the economic system. It is based on *ceteris paribus* assumptions. One of these is that prices in markets other than the one under consideration are unchanged (i.e. the prices of other goods are held constant). In order to see the full working of a market system, however, we must look at interactions among markets and follow the ways in which the forces of supply and demand push prices towards equilibrium in all markets. The study of such reactions is known as GENERAL EQUILIBRIUM ANALYSIS.

The theory of general equilibrium is an advanced subject. It employs complex mathematical techniques and cannot be fully explained by the use of two-dimensional diagrams showing supply and demand in individual markets. We can, however, take you a little way along the road to understanding it.

Interactions in markets for two goods

Consider, for purposes of illustration, two goods: boots and shoes. The goods are, incidentally, carefully chosen. They are *related* to each other on both supply and demand sides, i.e. they are substitutes in both production and consumption. Changes in relative prices can lead both consumers to switch purchases, and producers to switch production, between boots and shoes. Let us now consider the effect of a single disturbance on the equilibrium of both markets.

These effects cannot be *fully* explained with supply-demand diagrams. We can, however, observe something of what is involved with the aid of a diagram. In Figure 9.1 we show the original supply and demand curves in the market for shoes and in the market for boots. Both are in initial equilibrium with prices p_0 and quantities bought and sold q_0.

Next, imagine that some change takes place to disturb the equilibria. It could be a change in any one of several supply or demand influences that are held constant by the *ceteris paribus* assumption. Suppose it is a change in the state of technology, lowering the production costs of boots.

We can show the immediate impact of the change in Figure 9.1(i) by a rightward shift in the supply curve for boots from S to S'. The result is a downward movement in the price of boots towards a new equilibrium of p_1 and an increase in the quantity bought and sold, tending towards q_1.

However, boots and shoes are substitutes for consumers, and the demand curve for shoes is drawn on the assumption that the prices of other goods are constant. Since the price of boots has fallen, the conditions under which the demand curve for shoes was drawn are no longer applicable. Shoes are now relatively more expensive compared to boots, so consumers demand fewer at every price of shoes. In other words, the demand curve for shoes shifts from D to D', as shown in Figure 9.1(ii). This change will have the effect of depressing the price of shoes, which moves towards the new equilibrium price of p_1.

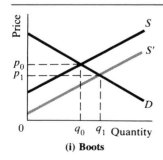

(i) Boots

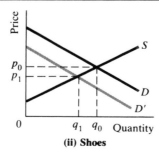

(ii) Shoes

FIGURE 9.1 Market Interactions. Price changes in the market for boots will generate a shift in the demand curves for shoes if boots and shoes are substitutes.

Chain reactions

This is not the end of the story. The fall in the price of shoes just referred to, means a change in the conditions under which the demand curve for boots was constructed. We should therefore draw a new demand curve for boots, lower than the old one. We refrain from doing so because the process we have started to describe is a chain. Every time there is a change in the price of boots, the demand curve for shoes shifts; every time there is a change in the price of shoes, the demand curve for boots shifts.

Moreover, we have not yet mentioned the possibility of shifts on the supply side. They are likely to happen as well. Supply curves are also drawn on the *ceteris paribus* assumption that the prices of other goods to and from which resources might shift are constant. Factors of production making shoes could, without much difficulty, be transferred to boot production, and vice versa. When the price of boots changes relatively to the price of shoes, therefore, resources are attracted from the production of one good to that of the other. When the price of boots falls relative to the price of shoes, therefore, resources are attracted from the production of one good to that of the other. When the price of boots falls relative to the price of shoes, suppliers produce more shoes. The supply curve for shoes shifts rightwards.

You may now appreciate why we said that supply and demand curve analysis cannot fully track the process by which equilibrium is reached even in two markets. Our diagrams would become immensely complicated as we drew shifting supply and demand curves every time there was a change in the price of a related good. As the number of markets we consider rises, such a procedure is out of the question. That is why mathematical techniques are essential for the general equilibrium analysis of all the markets in the economy.

We shall not try to take you along any further steps in the analysis. We have shown that any change which affects a single market in the first place, spills over and generates effects in other markets, on both the supply and demand sides. General equilibrium occurs when the relative prices of all goods are such that there are no excess demands or excess supplies in any markets and, hence, no economic forces encouraging changes in quantities supplied or demanded.

THE NATURE OF ECONOMIC EFFICIENCY

Very early in this book we offered an intuitive explanation of how a *laissez-faire* market system may produce an efficient allocation of resources. We also referred to reasons why markets may not always work well, described as market failures.

Now that we have some tools of economic analysis at our disposal we may review the arguments more rigorously, though we still do so within the framework of our elementary analysis, wherein buyers and sellers are assumed to be price-takers. Moreover, we shall not yet

concern ourselves with issues of economic policy – on how one might try to improve the behaviour of markets, or even to replace them. These matters will be discussed later, when we can drop the restrictive, price-taking assumption.

We must, first, be more explicit about what we mean by an EFFICIENT ALLOCATION OF RESOURCES. A definition will be helpful:

Resources are said to be allocated efficiently if it is not possible to produce more of any one good without producing less of another or, by any reallocation, to make any one person better off without making at least one other person worse off.

We should note, incidentally, that an efficient resource allocation is often referred to as an OPTIMAL ALLOCATION, and sometimes as a Pareto-optimal allocation, after the great Italian economist, Vilfredo Pareto, who first worked out the conditions necessary for economic efficiency about a hundred years ago.[1]

Note, too, that there are two distinct components of economic efficiency, implicit in the above definition:

- Productive efficiency
- Allocative efficiency

PRODUCTIVE EFFICIENCY obtains when it is not possible to produce more of any one good without producing less of any one other good.

ALLOCATIVE EFFICIENCY involves choosing between productively efficient bundles. Resources are said to be allocatively efficient when it is not possible to produce a combination of goods, different from that currently being produced, which will allow any one person to be made better off without making at least one other person worse off.

We defer full consideration of productive efficiency until Part 3 of this book, after we have studied the ways in which producers employ factors of production in order to minimize costs. It may, however, be helpful to think of productive efficiency obtaining whenever production takes place somewhere *on*, rather than *inside*, the production frontier (see above pp. 8–9). We now focus on the way in which a *laissez-faire* market system may cause output of goods and services to be allocatively efficient, i.e. so that production is at the 'right' point on the production possibility curve and thus the combination of goods and services produced is optimal in the sense which we have explained.

The Case for *Laissez-Faire*

One aspect of the case for leaving market forces to settle resource allocation is that they will do so efficiently, provided certain important conditions are fulfilled. The argument, which we outlined only intuitively earlier, is as follows.

Buyers are assumed to maximize their satisfactions and

---

1 Although the word 'optimal' comes from the Latin meaning 'best', as used in economics it has the more limited meaning of 'most efficient', i.e. not necessarily best from all conceivable viewpoints.

sellers to maximize their profits. In doing so, they adjust their demands and supplies of goods and services in response to signals produced by changing market conditions. The signals that they react to are the market prices of the goods they buy or sell.

Recall that buyers maximize their satisfactions when the last unit of each good that they buy yields as much satisfaction as it costs. In other words, the marginal utility (*MU*) of each commodity purchased is equal to its price. Recall also that suppliers maximize their profits when the last unit of any good produced yields as much revenue as it costs to produce the good. Since the revenue that price-taking suppliers receive from the sale of each unit of a good is the price for which that unit sells, profit maximization requires that price is equal to marginal cost (*MC*).

We have also seen that market forces produce equilibrium situations where price is equal to marginal utility for each consumer and to marginal cost for each producer.

It is but a small step, therefore, to conclude that, if all markets are in equilibrium as a result of the working of the price mechanism, marginal utility for each and every consumer must be equal to marginal cost for each and every producer in each and every market – since both *MC* and *MU* are equal to price.

Thus, when equilibrium is reached in all markets, the marginal utility of bread, for example, is equal to the marginal cost of bread, the marginal utility of lamb chops is equal to the marginal cost of lamb chops, and so on for every good and service.

Next, consider the meaning of the term 'cost' in the sense used by economists. This we have understood as real, opportunity, cost. The opportunity cost of producing a good is the sacrifice of another good that could have been produced with the same resources. If all resources used to produce a good are valued by producers so as to reflect their true opportunity costs, we can measure marginal opportunity cost in money terms. This means that in equilibrium – when marginal costs are equal to prices – an extra pound spent by a producer of one good correctly measures the market value of the other goods that this pound's worth of resources could have produced instead. Since marginal utilities are equal to prices, it follows that these market values also measure the marginal utilities that consumers attach to the goods.

All of this tells us that the equality of marginal utility and marginal cost, brought about by the price system, has a special significance. It means that the extra utility that consumers derive from an additional unit of a good is equal to its opportunity cost, measured by the sacrifice of not having extra quantities of other goods in its place. If this condition holds in the markets for all commodities, the allocation of resources is efficient in the sense defined above.

An illustration: So far the discussion has been rather abstract. We can give it more appeal by considering an example using only two goods. We shall call them food and clothing. The markets for these goods are shown in the two parts of Figure 9.2. When the two markets are in equilibrium, the price and quantity of food are p_0 and q_0, while the price and quantity of clothing are P_0 and Q_0. (To distinguish the prices and quantities in the two markets, we use lower-case letters for the food market, and capital letters for the clothing market.)

We now consider the efficiency of equilibrium, bearing in mind that the supply and demand curves are also the curves of marginal cost and marginal utility, respectively. The best way to show the efficiency of an equilibrium situation is to show the *inefficiency* of any alternative allocation of resources.

To do this, let us assume that *more* than the equilibrium quantity of resources is allocated to *food*, and *less* than the equilibrium quantity is allocated to *clothing*. Say, for example, that the output of food is q_1 while that of clothing is Q_1. If people are consuming q_1 of food, the marginal utility of food must be p_1 (since the demand curve tells us that p_1 is all that people would be prepared to pay to purchase q_1 units of the commodity). However, if producers are producing q_1 units of food, the marginal cost of producing the last unit is p'_1. Thus, *in the food market, marginal cost exceeds marginal utility*; it costs more to produce the last unit of food than the value consumers put on it (as shown by the amount they would be prepared to pay for it).

Now consider the clothing market. Here the reverse situation holds. Output is only Q_1, which is less than the equilibrium output of Q_0. Since consumers are consuming

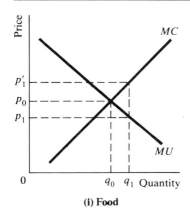

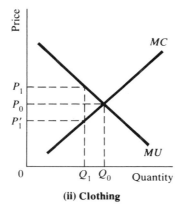

(i) Food   **(ii) Clothing**

FIGURE 9.2 Economic Efficiency. Since marginal utility lies behind the demand curve and marginal cost lies behind the supply curve, a market is efficient in equilibrium where the two curves intersect, so that marginal cost equals marginal utility.

only Q_1 of clothing, its marginal utility must be P_1 (since the demand curve tells us that P_1 is what they would be prepared to pay for it). Producers, however, have a marginal cost of only P'_1 (which is read off the marginal cost, or supply, curve at the quantity Q_1). Thus, *in the clothing market, marginal utility exceeds marginal cost*; it would cost less to produce another unit of clothing than the value that consumers would put on that unit.

Next, consider transferring £1's worth of resources from food to clothing production. On the one hand, the extra utility of the additional clothing output is worth more to consumers than the extra cost of producing it. On the other hand, in the food industry, the lost utility from reduced food output is worth less than the marginal cost of producing the food – whose reduction in production released the resources for the additional clothing production. So there is a gain in transferring these resources: all consumers can be made better off by this transfer, because *every* consumer values the lost food at *less* than its marginal cost, and *every* consumer values the additional clothing at *more* than its marginal cost. Indeed, efficiency can be continually improved if resources are transferred from food to clothing, as long as the marginal cost of food exceeds its marginal utility, while the marginal cost of clothing is less than its marginal utility.

Thus, when free-market equilibrium is not achieved, it is always possible to transfer resources from industries where marginal cost exceeds marginal utility into industries where marginal cost is less than marginal utility, and make all consumers better off. The source of this gain is the extra value that can be created by moving resources from uses where marginal utility is less than marginal cost and into uses where marginal utility is greater than marginal cost.

When these two markets (and all others) are in equilibrium, there is no further gain in transferring resources. Consumers now value the forgone production in the market that loses the resources the same as they value the additional production in the market that receives the resources. There is no way that resources can be transferred among markets to make everyone better off. Since there is no reallocation that will create extra value, it is not possible to make a reallocation that has the potential of making everyone better off. (Since additional value cannot be created for everyone by reallocating resources, the only way to make some people better off is by taking income from others who are, therefore, made worse off.)

The argument in previous paragraphs is a restatement, using the technical tools now at our disposal, of the intuitive reasoning in the section called 'Eighth Wonder of the World' on page 21 above. We explained there why the 'invisible hand', as Adam Smith described the price mechanism, had its great appeal. He saw it as an automatic, flexible and self-regulating device which answers the basic question of how to allocate resources among competing uses. Further, it does this without any conscious direction by any person or persons. The market system works without anyone even having to understand how it works! Producers need only to know relative prices of goods and services to decide on their most profitable outputs, and

consumers, likewise, need only to know relative prices to decide what goods and services to buy in order to maximize their satisfaction. Moreover, we have now seen that the allocation of resources brought about through the operation of the price mechanism can be considered optimal, in the strict sense of efficient, as we defined that term at the beginning of this section.[1]

Market *versus* Non-Market Allocations

In order to evaluate market allocations of resources, it may be helpful to compare them with allocations made in ways which do not use the market system.

Suppose that the government decides to impose a maximum price on a particular commodity, interfering with economic forces. If the price ceiling is set below equilibrium, there will be excess demand (so long as demand curves slope downwards and supply curves slope upwards). Consider Figure 9.3, which shows hypothetical supply and demand curves for umbrellas. Equilibrium price is p_0, and quantity q_0.

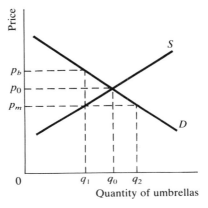

FIGURE 9.3 **Maximum-Price Control.** If a price ceiling of p_m is imposed, excess demand $q_2 - q_1$ will be present. Only q_1 will be supplied, but consumers would be prepared to pay p_b, the black market price for q_1.

If a maximum price of p_m (below equilibrium) is imposed by the government, suppliers will supply only q_1, while consumers will want to buy q_2. There will be excess demand equal to $q_2 - q_1$. The question arises who, among the persons who would like to buy, will be included in the 'lucky ones' who do buy? The answer is, 'it all depends'. It depends on what system is used to allocate the limited supply.

There are many possibilities, among which we suggest five are common.

Queues: Queues may form, with those consumers in the front of the queues getting the umbrellas. Note that

---

1 Market allocations are sometimes said to demonstrate 'consumer sovereignty', i.e. to imply that the consumer is king and decides what shall be produced. We think the analogy is a misleading half-truth, since both supply and demand sides of the market are equally important.

queuing does not have to consist of getting physically in line. Queuing can be by putting one's name on a waiting list for a commodity where there is excess demand.

Rationing: The government, realizing that its action in imposing a price ceiling will leave some consumers unsatisfied, may introduce some form of rationing. Rations do not have to be egalitarian, as was food rationing in wartime. Rationing can favour selected (targeted) groups; subsidized housing, for example, tends to be allocated to people thought most deserving according to such criteria as family size, income, length of time in the area, etc.

Sellers' preferences: A third, alternative, allocative system involves a kind of unofficial rationing by sellers. Owners, or managers, of shops selling umbrellas may choose to allow preferred customers to have them at the low price. Who such preferred persons may be is a matter for speculation – friends, customers of long standing, or perhaps those who buy some other goods which are proving difficult to sell.

Black markets: It is to be expected that some umbrellas will reach the black market, i.e. the maximum price limit is illegally broken. The incentive to break the law is present. In Figure 9.3 we see that consumers would be prepared to pay as much as p_b for q_1 umbrellas (more than the free-market equilibrium). If the price ceiling is weakly enforced, one would also expect the quantity supplied to increase.

Chance allocations: In the absence of any of the above methods, resource allocation might be, in a sense, haphazard. For example, in Eastern European planned economies, supplies of highly valued 'luxury foods' such as bananas used to suddenly and unexpectedly appear in some shop or other. Those persons who happened to be present at the moment of arrival would then be likely to benefit. We describe such haphazard results as chance allocations.

The discussion in this section has been illustrative rather than comprehensive, because this book is basically about markets, and because the number of alternative methods that might occur is, in principle, enormous. We should, however, point out one particular restriction of our analysis. It has been limited to the demand side.

Were we to have written about alternatives to market allocations in the case of a *minimum* price, rather than a maximum, the emphasis would have been on the supply side. Where there is excess *supply*, the question arises of which *sellers*, among the many who would like to sell at a *price above equilibrium*, are the lucky ones. We shall not go into this matter further now, though we shall meet some examples later.

There is, however, one other point to make. The title of this section, market *versus* non-market allocations, might suggest to you that we are about to make a general judgement favouring one or the other. Sorry to disappoint you. For the moment, we wish only to emphasize that market allocations cannot be seen in isolation. They have to be compared with other, non-market, allocations. The general

case for the market allocation has been made already. In the case of umbrellas a major advantage of leaving the price mechanism to work is that it ensures that those people who put a high enough value on umbrellas, and are prepared to pay for them, will be the ones who are satisfied. You will probably find the argument pretty strong, for umbrellas. There are, however, other circumstances, and commodities, which may not appear to favour market allocations so strongly, if at all. It is time to take a more critical look at the market system.

MARKET FAILURE

When we looked first at the advantages of the market system (in Chapter 2) we followed with an intuitive outline of its disadvantages. Certain of these are formally known as market failures, in addition to which there are other reasons for thinking that markets are not working well. We now return to the subject, making use again of the same tools of economic analysis that we employed in expanding the case for *laissez-faire*.

Criticisms of market systems, you may recall, fall into two categories, efficiency and equity. We deal with efficiency first.

Let us start by reminding ourselves of the four sources of market failure mentioned in Chapter 2 (see pp.22–3):

(1) collectively consumed commodities (public goods)
(2) merit (and demerit) goods
(3) externalities
(4) concentrations of economic power.

Discussion of the last of these is, however, deferred until Part 3, where we analyse the behaviour of the price-makers, as distinct from the price-takers that we have considered so far.

Public Goods

We remind you that public goods are those which are consumed collectively – which, if produced at all, are available to the community as a whole.

Pure public goods have two distinctive characteristics – they are non-rival and non-excludable.

A public good is said to be NON-RIVAL in consumption, in the sense that there is no less available for any one person because another person is enjoying it. It is also NON-EXCLUDABLE in that, if provided for one person, it is automatically available for everybody.

Street lighting is an example. You either light a street, which automatically benefits all who pass along it, or you don't light it at all. The lamp shines no less brightly for me because you walk down the street too. It is non-rival. Further it is non-excludable. There is no way to stop me from benefiting from the street lighting even if I am unwilling to pay for it. Compare an 'ordinary' private (i.e. non-public) good, such as an ice-cream. If you eat it, I cannot. The private good is rival. Furthermore the ice-cream seller can deny me the ice-cream if I am unwilling to pay for it. The private good is excludable.

The market system is inefficient in supplying public goods, such as street lighting, because producers cannot sell quantities of light to individual passers-by, who wish to buy it. The decision on whether to allocate resources to the provision of such collective consumption goods is usually taken outside the market system. (The actual provision of the public goods, however, may still be left to private enterprise – under contract from the government which pays the bill.)

Merit and Demerit Goods

MERIT GOODS are those the government compels or encourages people to consume, mainly because individuals are said to be unaware of the true benefit from consuming them. DEMERIT GOODS are those which the state forbids people to consume, mainly because individuals are said to be unaware of the true harm they would suffer by consuming them. Examples are car seatbelts as merit goods, and addictive drugs as demerit goods. By analogy with collective consumption commodities, the market system does not efficiently provide appropriate quantities of merit and demerit goods.

The market works by producers responding to the demands of individual consumers. But if we believe that individuals do not appreciate the true benefits to be derived from consumption, we cannot expect the market system to provide the quantities of merit goods that individuals would really benefit from, as distinct from the lesser quantities they thought they would. Furthermore, the market, responding to individual demands, would supply demerit goods which ought not to be offered for sale.

Whether or not such paternalistic attitudes are proper is, of course, a value judgement, about which economists, in their professional capacity, can make no special claims for their opinions.[1] But, presumably, as long as there are thought to be merit and demerit goods, there will be a need for decisions to be taken outside the market system on whether or not they should be produced, and in what quantities. (Though, as with public goods, if merit goods are to be provided, it is another matter whether their actual provision should be by private enterprise.)

Externalities

There are certain goods which are said to have what we earlier called spillover effects, in that their production, or consumption, *indirectly* affects persons other than those who do the actual producing or consuming.

Inoculations, for example, benefit *directly* individuals

---

[1] To those who believe that individual adults are the best judges of their own self-interests, there are no merit goods, only autocratic attempts to ram the tastes of some down the throats of others, or to justify the elitist tastes of the minority who control public spending. For others, merit goods represent genuine cases where people do not appreciate the true value of certain goods and services and the state is justified in having more of them produced and consumed than individual choice would dictate.

BOX 9.1 Lords Debate: Drink Driving 'Costs' £365m

'The cost to Britain of drink-driving accidents was incalculable in terms of human suffering, Lord Clinton-Davis said in the Lords yesterday . . .

'In financial terms, the cost had been estimated at £365 million a year, he said, during the committee stage of the Road Traffic Bill . . . the latest available figures showed that in 1989 1 in 6 road deaths were in accidents which were drink-related. Such accidents had killed 840 people and injured 22,000.'

(*Daily Telegraph*, 3 May 1991)

This is a report of a speech made in the House of Lords in support of a motion calling for the introduction of random roadside breath-tests (which was, incidentally, defeated by 87 votes to 41). It illustrates a clear divergence between private and social values, since motorists who drink and drive may assess the cost only to themselves if they are involved in accidents.

Questions

1 List as many as you can of the social costs that are involved in drink-related driving accidents. Do not forget to include private as well as external costs.
2 What do you think of the proposal for random breath-testing? Why do you think it was rejected by the House of Lords?
3 Can you think of any other ways of narrowing the gap between private and social costs?

---

who have them. But they may also *indirectly* benefit others who do not have them. The reduced risk of contracting infectious disease may spill over from persons who have been inoculated to the rest of the community. The benefits accruing to society *as a whole* are then greater than the benefits accruing to the individuals who obtain them directly. Economists say that the value of social benefits exceeds the value of private benefits – the difference between them being known as external values. In such cases markets, which supply services for the people who want to buy them, do not supply as much as is needed for an efficient allocation of resources from *society's* point of view. This is because purchasers take no account of the external benefits conferred on other non-consumers.

In the above example, social benefits exceeded private benefits. There are, however, other cases where private benefits exceed social benefits. These cases occur when *negative* externalities are present and external costs are imposed on other individuals. An example is pollution of rivers and waterways by the discharge of sewage or factory

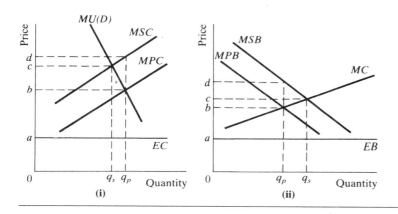

FIGURE 9.4 **A Market with Externalities.** In (i), output causes external costs (*EC*) which added to private costs (*MPC*) give total social costs *MSC*. Private optimum output exceeds social optimum output ($q_p > q_s$). In (ii), output creates external benefits (*EB*) which added to private benefits (*MPB*) give total social benefits. Social optimum output exceeds private optimum output ($q_s > q_p$).

waste. This may impose costs on water users, but will not feature in the private costs of the polluters. Free markets supply goods with such excess of public over private costs in overlarge quantities, compared with socially efficient output.

The argument may be clarified with the aid of Figure 9.4, which is in two parts. Part (i) shows a case where, as output rises, costs to the producer rise along the upward-sloping curve labelled *MPC*, standing for marginal private costs. However, increasing output creates indirect costs which spillover to other producers (or consumers). They are shown by the curve *EC* (standing for EXTERNAL COSTS), which assumes a constant unit cost equal to *a*. Total costs, known as SOCIAL COSTS (private costs + external costs), are shown along the *MSC* curve (standing for marginal social costs) which is derived by adding the external cost (per unit), equal to *a*, to the marginal private cost curve.

A free-market system would result in an output of q_p, where private producers just cover the cost of production, *b*, of the last unit produced. The benefit to the community of the last unit is the marginal utility (read off the demand curve). But the social marginal cost to all and sundry, including direct and indirect costs, is not *b* but *d*. Resource allocation is not efficient because the social cost of producing the good, at the margin, *d*, is greater than the benefit, at the margin, to consumers which is *b*. The market fails to achieve the socially optimum output of q_s, where marginal social cost is equal to marginal utility. The reason is that social costs are greater than private costs.

Part (ii) of Figure 9.4 shows a case where the externalities are on the benefits side. As output increases, consumers of the product benefit (as shown by the marginal private benefit curve *MPB*), but so also do non-consumers. The external benefit is *a* per unit of output. Social benefit, direct plus indirect, is the sum of private and external benefit (*MPB* + *a*), shown by the *MSB* curve. Socially optimum output is therefore q_s, which is identified by the intersection of the *MSB* curve with the *MC* curve. It is greater than the output that a free-market system would supply, q_p. The reason is that social benefit is greater than private benefit.

Thus, there is force to the criticism of a free-market system based on the existence of externalities. The market may underprovide or overprovide, compared to the outputs that would be socially optimal.

Underprovision occurs where social benefits exceed private benefits – health, education and the arts, for example. Overprovision occurs where social costs exceed private costs – pollution and traffic congestion are examples.

Other Market Shortcomings

The three types of market deficiencies discussed above are well-defined and relatively easy to classify, if not always to remedy. They are known formally as market failures. There are, however, other circumstances where it may appear that a market is not working well, though none of our standard causes of failure seem to be operating. Two such circumstances are especially worthy of mention, (1) those relating to deficiencies in the quality or quantity of *information* on which consumers base their decisions, and (2) those relating to dynamic considerations – i.e. how markets work *over time*.

Information deficiencies

We shall discuss the second kind of inadequacy about markets at some length, but a few words need to be said about the first. Information deficiencies are sometimes blamed for the fact that certain goods and services are not available on the market, even though consumers would be prepared to buy them if they fully appreciated all the relevant facts. Merit goods, discussed earlier, fall into this category, but there are others which do not have 'paternalistic' associations but where criticisms are sometimes levelled at the way in which markets work.

A common example concerns insurance, where individuals, unaware of the true risks involved, fail to buy fire or accident insurance. Moreover, in a world of rapidly changing technology, and persuasive advertising, there are many situations where consumers feel they have insufficient relevant information for making the choice of product to best satisfy their needs. For example, do you feel you know enough about the advantages and disadvantages of the range of fabrics and fabric mixtures for clothing and furnishing, or the merits of all the CD players on the market? Market forces do, of course, supply information, but it is not always complete, reliable or accessible.

Dynamic considerations

What we choose to call by the somewhat fancy name 'dynamic considerations' concerns the ways in which markets behave over time. There is evidence that markets sometimes take longer to operate, i.e. to reach equilibrium, than might be regarded as satisfactory. The evidence relates, on the one hand, to sluggish markets, where the forces of supply and demand are not very sensitive to price changes and, on the other hand, to volatile markets, where economic forces are highly sensitive to price changes, so that the market witnesses excessive fluctuations in price and sometimes in quantity.

Probably the most serious worry under this head relates to the behaviour of the economic system as a whole and, in particular, to the labour market. The distinguished English economist John Maynard (later Lord) Keynes is credited with early recognition of the excessive time that the labour market can take to reach equilibrium. Keynes was concerned at the persistence of heavy general unemployment throughout the UK economy for almost two decades – the 1920s and 1930s – and he was critical of the time the 'economic juggernaut', as he called it, took to work. One of his most famous remarks was that 'in the long run we are all dead'. Criticisms of the working of the economic system as a whole are, however, part of the subject matter of macroeconomics, which we leave to Parts 4 and 5 of this book.

Within microeconomics, there are plenty of examples of markets where undershooting or overshooting occurs. We distinguish them by the terms 'sluggish' and 'volatile' markets.

Sluggish markets: These are markets which, by definition, take a long time to react to changes, because prices are 'sticky' or because buyers and/or sellers adjust slowly to price changes. Such markets clear slowly, or even not at all. Some of the prime reasons for the presence of sluggish markets are 'institutional', in that they derive from forms of business organization which operate in manufacturing and other industries. We consider this subject in Part 3 of this book.

All we say now is that, where price does not act swiftly to clear the market, the price mechanism may seem not to be working efficiently. If price is held down in the face of an increase in demand, for example, the limited quantity supplied will, somehow or other, be allocated. Queues or waiting lists may build up for underpriced scarce new sportscars, for example, thereby defeating the objectives of a market system – allocation to those prepared to pay the highest prices.

Volatile markets: These are markets which overreact to changes. We may observe large fluctuations in market prices, taking a long time reaching, and even temporarily moving away from, equilibrium.

There are many reasons why price fluctuations may

appear excessive, not all of which can be thought of as indicating markets failing to work properly. As we showed in Chapter 8, for example, shifts in either supply or demand cause larger price movements the smaller are the values of elasticities of demand and or supply (see p.78). Wherever demand or supply elasticities are, therefore, low, we may observe large price movements as the conditions of demand or supply change. For example, a raspberry crop failure can cause price in a particular year to be well above the 'norm'. However, the high price shows the price mechanism *working* to allocate a given supply.

There are two circumstances in which volatility in market prices might, nonetheless, mean that the market is not working efficiently. The first case is associated with what is known as the 'cobweb theorem'; the second is related to the role of expectations in market price determination.

The cobweb theorem

The reason for this curious name to the second explanation of price volatility will become clear as we examine the diagrams which will be used to explain it. The distinguishing feature of this case is not in its name, but in the nature of the supply curve.

Turn to Figure 9.5, which portrays the supply and demand curve for potatoes. The demand curve is the one we are used to. It shows how the quantity of potatoes demanded varies with current market price. It is downward-sloping, indicating that the lower the price of potatoes, the greater will be the quantity currently demanded. The supply curve, S, is the short-run supply curve for potatoes. It also has the familiar shape, indicating that more potatoes will be offered for sale the higher is their price. However, the curve differs in one important way from those we have considered so far. It explicitly takes account of a *time-lag* in adjusting supply to the

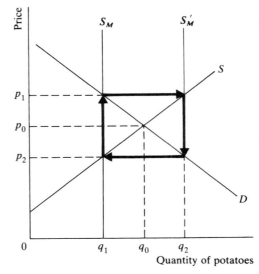

FIGURE 9.5 A Volatile Market with a Stable Cobweb. Quantity supplied depends on price in the previous period. Price and quantity fluctuate repeatedly around the equilibrium.

current market price. We assume that, if farmers wish to vary the quantity of potatoes that they produce and offer for sale, it takes a year for the new crop to be planted, harvested and brought to market.

Thus, the supply curve relates the quantity produced in any one year to the price ruling *in the previous year*. This year's output of potatoes was planted last year and thus depends on last year's price.[1] Putting the same point in another way, next year's quantity of potatoes depends on *this year's price*.

The equilibrium price and quantity are determined in the usual way at p_0 and q_0. If the price p_0 has ruled for several years, farmers will plant q_0 potatoes each year and, when the crop comes onto the market the following year, it will be sold at a price of p_0. This price will clear the market and will lead farmers to plant the same quantity for the following year. Unless something happens to disturb it, equilibrium will continue unchanged from year to year.

Now, suppose that something new does happen. Assume, for example, that, as a result of a temporary epidemic of potato blight, this year's output falls to q_1, which is below the equilibrium quantity. What will happen?

As a result of the blight, this year's crop is fixed at q_1. The momentary supply curve (which in this case persists for a year until a new crop comes onto the market) is S_M, which is perfectly inelastic at quantity q_1. To find the price at which the quantity q_1 will be bought, we go to the temporary equilibrium at the intersection of S_M with the demand curve. This tells us that the price that clears the market, i.e. the price at which the output q_1 will be sold, is now p_1. As a result of the shortage of potatoes, the market price rises.

How might the market return from its temporary equilibrium at p_1 to its equilibrium of demand and supply at p_0? If the quantity produced were to expand slowly and continuously from q_1 to q_0, as it would in many markets, the price would fall slowly and continuously from p_1 to p_0. However, this is not the case in our potato market.

The momentary equilibrium price persists for a year, i.e. until next year's crop is planted, raised and harvested. While it does persist, farmers know only the current market price at which the present crop is being sold, but they must now make their plans for how many potatoes to plant for sale next year. The signal they see is a rise in the market price from p_0 to p_1. Their supply curve tells us that at p_1, the amount they would like to supply is not q_1, but q_2. If they behave as we described earlier, relating their current plantings, and hence next year's output, to the current price, they will plan to produce q_2 the following year.

What happens the following year when q_2 potatoes come on the market? There is then another momentary supply curve, S_M', which is vertical at the new output of q_2. At the old price of p_1 there is, now, an excess supply of potatoes $q_2 - q_1$. This will bring potato prices plummeting down.

Price falls below the old equilibrium value of p_0. There is a new momentary equilibrium price which clears the market, p_2 (which is the intersection of the demand curve and the new momentary supply curve, S_M').

This, then, becomes the temporary equilibrium that persists until another new crop comes onto the market. But, at the new price p_2, farmers will only want to produce q_1. Say they plant that amount. When q_1 comes onto the market in the following year, excess demand recurs at the price of p_2 and the market is cleared at a momentary equilibrium of p_1 and q_1. Farmers respond now again to the price p_1, by producing q_2 next year; but when this comes onto the market, price falls to p_2 and so on ...

Thus, a series of temporary equilibria recur with price oscillating around its equilibrium value. This is because the quantity coming onto the market in any year is the response to the price ruling in the previous year. The case shown in Figure 9.5 is called a *stable* cobweb because the fluctuations repeat themselves without increasing or decreasing in magnitude.

What we have just described is a model, or theory, of the behaviour of a market where supply adjusts to price with a specific time-lag. This model is usually referred to as the COBWEB THEOREM.

Two observations may be made about the cobweb theorem. First, the reason for the 'cobweb' part of its name may now be understood. Figure 9.5 looks a little like a cobweb, and Figures 9.6 and 9.7 look much more so. Second, and more importantly, we conclude that with some time-lags on the supply side, market forces may not tend towards equilibrium, even in theory. In the language which we used on p.75 of the previous chapter, equilibrium may be unstable, in that a departure from equilibrium is not self-restoring, i.e. changes in quantities supplied and/or demanded do not lead us back to equilibrium.

Convergent and divergent cobwebs: In Figures 9.6 and

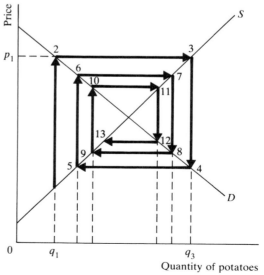

FIGURE 9.6 A Less Volatile Market with a Convergent Cobweb. Quantity supplied depends on price in the previous period. Price and quantity converge on the equilibrium.

---

1 To be more precise, this year's supply depends on what farmers expected this year's price to be when they planted their crop last year. In this simple treatment we are assuming that farmers expect next year's price to be the same as this year's price.

9.7 we show two more versions of the cobweb theorem. Each shows behaviour which differs from the repeated, steady, oscillations of the stable cobweb in Figure 9.5.

Convergent cobwebs: Consider the case of Figure 9.6, which is described as a *convergent cobweb*. We shall not retrace each step of the argument. The process is similar to that described in the previous section. If you are not clear about it, we suggest you read the earlier description again before proceeding.

We start as before, with a crop failure which takes the momentary supply to q_1 in the diagram and the momentary equilibrium to point 2, where the price p_1 clears the market. Price and quantity movements follow the pattern shown in the diagram, going in the direction of the arrows from points 2 to 3, to 4, etc. Just to remind you, position 3 occurs when farmers supply q_3 in response to price p_1; but this forces price down until position 4 is reached; but then when output contracts, position 5 is reached, and so on.

The distinguishing feature of Figure 9.6 is that the oscillations become smaller and smaller every period. Price and quantity do not cycle repeatedly and steadily around equilibrium as they did in Figure 9.5. In Figure 9.6 the oscillations get smaller each year and gradually approach the equilibrium. This version of the cobweb theorem is described as convergent, which means that the oscillations converge on the equilibrium price and quantity.

Divergent cobwebs: Consider finally Figure 9.7. Starting once more with a crop failure that reduces output temporarily to q_1 and produces a momentary equilibrium at point 2, we follow the price and quantity movements represented by points 2, 3, 4, 5 and so on, in the direction of the arrows. Note that on this occasion the oscillations become greater and greater every period. This is the divergent case. The process is explosive.

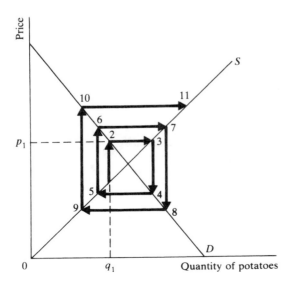

FIGURE 9.7 A Very Volatile Market with a Divergent Cobweb. Quantity supplied depends on price in the previous period. Price and quantity progressively diverge from equilibrium.

Evidence on cobwebs: We need not bother you with the precise nature of conditions which lead to the different cobweb cases. You may wonder, though, whether there is any basis in fact for this cobweb-type behaviour or is it just a piece of abstract economic theory without supporting empirical evidence?

The cobweb theory was first propounded in the 1930s by an American economist called Mordecai Ezekial. He noticed price oscillations in the hog (pig) market in Chicago and developed the theory to explain it. Today, cobweb tendencies are still sometimes observed. They are, however, rather less pronounced than might be suggested by the crude theory given here.

The main reason is that producers learn, by experience, not to link supplies *mechanically to past prices*. Such intelligent learning from experience is no more than we would expect. Such learning explains, for instance, why explosive cobwebs do not persist indefinitely. Producers do not ignore historical patterns in the price of the good they produce. Nonetheless, to look ahead and anticipate cobweb-type fluctuations is much more sophisticated behaviour than merely reacting to current prices. Furthermore, whenever the conditions of demand or supply change, the nature of the potential cobweb fluctuations will change, thus rendering past experience, to an extent, obsolete. But because producers cannot perfectly anticipate market forces, many agricultural products do exhibit cycles, with periods of low output and high prices alternating with periods of high output and low prices. Because producers can partially anticipate market forces, explosive or even stable cobwebs do not persist for ever.

Expectations

Our final explanation for some markets being volatile turns around the part that can be played by expectations. For example, a price rise (or fall) can, of itself, generate the expectation of a further price change in the future. A good example can be found in the way in which the housing market in the UK has sometimes behaved (see Box 9.2).

We met this case early in our discussion of the theory of demand, when we suggested that the observation of closely associated movements in price and quantity may not be evidence of upward-sloping demand curves, but of shifting demand engineered by price changes. Consider, for example, the experience of the housing market. An initial increase in demand pushed prices up, and as this led people to expect a further price rise, it shifted demand upwards again. The rate of increase in house prices accelerated towards the end of the 1980s, and then fell off. Demand stopped rising because the very reason for it increasing earlier had vanished. In fact, expectations became those of stable, and eventually of falling, prices with demand falling in consequence.

In the context of market failure, with which we are currently concerned, all that needs to be said is that price ceased to function as a housing market-clearing mechanism in the mid-to-late 1980s. Even very volatile price movements were unable to achieve market-clearing because, in the booming conditions, rises did not lead to falls in quan-

BOX 9.2 House Price Booms and Slumps –
The Record Over Two Decades

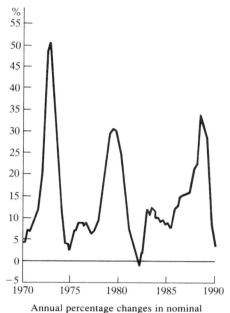

Annual percentage changes in nominal
house prices 1969–1990, UK

(*Source*: M.C. Fleming and J.G. Nellis, 'The Rise and Fall of House Prices: Causes, Consequences and Prospects', *National Westminster Bank Quarterly Review*, November 1990.)

Market forces act more speedily and efficiently to adapt to shifts in supply or demand in some cases than in others. Price can then appear to be volatile. One market where price fluctuations have, at times, been especially large is that for houses. The graph shows three periods of volatility between 1970 and 1990.

The house price boom of the mid-1980s resulted from an upward shift in demand for houses and was itself due, in turn, to a combination of circumstances including low mortgage interest rates, income-tax cuts and institutional changes increasing the supply of credit for house purchase. Rising house prices generated expectations of further price rises and an upward price spiral developed. The bubble burst with the realization that the accelerating process could not continue indefinitely.

Questions

1 Draw supply and demand curves to illustrate the behaviour of the market for houses in the last years of the decade of the 1980s.
2 Can you explain why there were several years of relative price stability in both the 1970s and 1980s?
3 Would you expect the analyses of *downward* price movements to be symmetrical to those explaining upward movements in the text above?

---

tity demanded but to expectations of further price rises. In such times, houses were so 'scarce' that buyers had to act quickly to snap up the few that came on to the market. When the boom was over, the opposite situation occurred. Sellers had exceptional difficulty in disposing of houses while prices were falling and buyers held back in the hope of further price falls. The case of the housing market is not, of course, unique. Another example of a market which has been at times volatile is oil.

Equity or Fairness

The price system allocates resources efficiently (given the assumptions we have made so far). But *efficiency* is not the same thing as *equity* (and equity, you will recall, is not the same thing as equality – equity means fair while equality means equal). It is possible to have an efficient allocation of resources in a society in which there are a few very rich citizens and the rest are very poor.

It is also possible to have an efficient allocation in a society in which most people have incomes close to the average. All that efficiency guarantees is that it is not possible to make some people better off without making some others worse off. *Given the distribution of income*, there is an advantage in avoiding an inefficient allocation – because

when allocation is inefficient *everyone* can be made better off by an appropriate reallocation of resources. But what can we say about two societies, both of which have efficient allocations, but very different distributions of income? To judge between the two, we need to bring in value judgements about these different distributions.

When we first discussed this issue in Chapter 2, we likened the market-place to an 'election' for goods and services, with notes and coins representing 'votes'. Because those with high incomes have more 'votes' than those with low incomes, the results of 'elections' are bound to be influenced by the distribution of income. If people regard the distribution as inequitable (meaning unfair, not, we would remind you, unequal), the allocation of resources may not be regarded as *satisfactory*, even if it is *efficient*.

We are now ready to take the argument a little further. Recall what we said in Chapter 2 under the heading 'Who Gets It?' (see pp. 14, 23): the working of the *laissez-faire* market system *determines* the distribution of income. People earn their incomes by selling on the market either the services of the factors of production that they own or the goods that they produce.

When the market determines the prices and quantities of goods and factor services, it also determines the incomes of those who sell them. People who sell goods and factor services that the market values highly will tend to earn large incomes, and people who sell those that have low market values are likely to earn low incomes. We shall have a lot more to say about this aspect of the working of the market in Chapters 18 and 19. In the meantime, we merely note that allowing the *laissez-faire* market mechanism to determine the allocation of resources, also means allowing it to determine the distribution of income.

The second point to consider is that the collection of goods produced will differ between societies with different distributions of income. Consider a society that produces only two goods, caviar and hamburgers, and assume that the workings of the free market produces a very unequal distribution of income. Most of the income is concentrated in the hands of the few rich, and much less finds its way into the hands of the many very poor citizens.

As a result there will be a large demand for the caviar that the rich can afford to consume and a smaller demand for the hamburgers that are the fare of the poor. In response to this pattern of demand, caviar production will be high and hamburger production low. As long as the market works efficiently, so that marginal cost is equated to marginal utility in both the hamburger and the caviar industries, the allocation of resources will be efficient: it will be impossible to make any citizen better off without making at least one other citizen worse off.

Most citizens are unlikely, however, to judge such a distribution of income as equitable. Let us suppose that in response to such judgements, a government is elected on a platform of egalitarianism. It uses the tax and expenditure system to reduce income inequalities; the rich are made less rich and the poor less poor. Now the demand for caviar falls and the demand for hamburgers rises. Production will respond so that more hamburgers and less caviar will be produced than in the pre-election situation. Once again, however, as long as the market works efficiently so that marginal cost is equated to marginal utility in both industries, the allocation of resources will be efficient: it will be impossible to make any one citizen better off without making at least one other citizen worse off.

Since resources are efficiently allocated in both the pre- and the post-election situations, there is no way of choosing between the two output combinations on efficiency grounds alone. We can only make such a choice on the basis of our value judgements about which distribution of income is preferable.

This example illustrates the important proposition that efficiency in resource allocation and equity in income distribution are distinct concepts. The desire for efficiency is a desire to avoid waste, to avoid situations where everyone could be made better off. The desire for equity is a desire for fairness. We might have a fair distribution of income with resources allocated inefficiently, and we might have an unfair distribution of income with resources allocated efficiently. Of course, the ideal situation is one in which the distribution of income is judged equitable and resources are allocated efficiently.

It is important to note that the argument has assumed that income can be redistributed without affecting efficiency. Usually this is not the case. The very taxes and expenditures that are used to redistribute income may make it impossible to achieve an efficient allocation of resources. Thus, by redistributing the economic pie (i.e. total output) we may make the pie smaller. If this is the case it is necessary to trade off efficiency against equity considerations.

Even if we thought a completely equal distribution of income was the most equitable distribution, however, we might hesitate to go that far with government redistribution policies because the effects of such policies in reducing efficiency might shrink the available economic pie too drastically. The important, but very complex, issue of the interrelation between redistributive policies and efficiency is taken up briefly later in Chapter 21.

Concluding Remarks

At the time of our first comparison of resource allocations under *laissez-faire* and central planning, we emphasized that the choice is not a black and white one. There are shades of grey — mixed economies of many kinds.

Views of the overall merits of more or less government intervention are, inevitably, taken at particular historical moments. There seems to be a popularity pendulum that swings between more or less state intervention, reflecting, one suspects, not so much fashion as unsatisfactory experiences with one or the other. The grass always seems greener on the other side of the fence.

Currently, popular opinion the world over is strongly anti-interventionist pro-market, not least because of disillusion with 'socialist planning' as in Eastern Europe, and disappointment with governments' apparant inability to improve resource allocations by interventionist activities in countries such as the UK. Just after the end of the Second World War, popular opinion was quite the opposite, following the failures of market systems in the Great Depression of the 1930s. The nationalization era of the late 1940s contrasts with the privatization era of the 1980s.

Finally, we would remind you that we have deliberately avoided discussion of what to do about market failure. It is easier to point out a market inefficiency than it is to design an effective way of removing it. However, there are alternative economic policies available. For example, externalities may be treated by the taxation system, or by rules and regulations, while retaining the basic free-market system, or even by 'clubs' where groups of people join together and 'internalize' them. These matters are discussed in Chapter 21 when we shall have added new theoretical instruments to our toolbag.

Summary

1 General equilibrium occurs when prices are such that there are no excess demands or supplies in any markets.

2 Economic efficiency obtains when resources are optimally allocated, i.e. in such a way that it is not possible to make any one person better off without making at least one other person worse off.

3 Economic efficiency comprises two components: (i) productive efficiency, which obtains when it is not possible to produce more of any one good without producing less of another good; (ii) allocative efficiency, which obtains when the combination of goods available is optimal.

4 Under certain conditions a free-market system achieves an efficient allocation of resources. This happens when the activities of profit-maximizing sellers and satisfaction-maximizing buyers bring about the equality of marginal utility and marginal cost in every market.

5 Non-market allocations include the following: allocation by queues, by rationing, by the exercise of 'buyers' or 'sellers' preferences', through black markets, or by chance.

6 Market failure arises in the case of (1) public goods, (2) merit and demerit goods, (3) externalities, (4) concentrations of economic power.

7 Public goods are consumed collectively, are non-rival and non-excludable. Merit (and demerit) goods are where consumers are said to be unaware of their true benefit (or harm). Externalities exist when the direct private costs (or benefits) of production or consumption indirectly spill over to others. Private costs (or benefits) plus external costs (or benefits) equal social costs (or benefits).

8 Markets may suffer from lack of availability of complete, reliable and relevant information.

9 The way in which markets operate over time may not be satisfactory. Some markets may be sluggish, taking a long time to clear. Others may be volatile, causing large oscillations in price.

10 The cobweb theorem shows that price and quantity may oscillate around, progressively diverge from, or gradually converge on, equilibrium.

11 When price changes lead to expectations of further price changes, price movements may be large and volatile.

12 Different income distributions may lead to different efficient allocations. Resources may be allocated efficiently without the distribution being fair and equitable.

Questions

1 There are two goods A and B. When the demand for A falls, there is a rightward shift in the supply curve for B. What can be said about the relationship between the two goods?

2 Is the following statement True or False? 'An economy can be enjoying resource allocation which is productively efficient but is not allocatively efficient.'

3 A certain good is consumed in smaller quantities than consumers would choose to buy if they were aware of the true satisfaction it would bring. Is it (a) a merit good, (b) a public good, (c) a demerit good, (d) any of the above?

4 Which One or More of the options correctly completes the sentence beginning: 'If it is known that marginal social cost is greater than marginal private cost for good X, and marginal private benefit is greater than marginal social benefit for good Y, then a free market will result in the production of . . .

   (a) the optimum amount of X and Y.'
   (b) too much X and too little Y.'
   (c) too little X and too little Y.'
   (d) too little X and too much Y.'
   (e) None of the above.

5 The following questions relate to Figure 9.5. (i) If market supply became an amount indicated on the quantity axis by a point half way between q_0 and q_1, how much would be supplied next year? (ii) What could you do to turn Figure 9.5 into a convergent cobweb?

6 Why does economic theory not teach that if income distribution becomes more equal, the allocation of resources will become more equitable?

10 How to Use Supply and Demand Analysis

The tools of supply and demand described so far in this book are simple but powerful. If you have understood them, you can apply them to novel situations; they will help you to understand many things you see around you and to answer examination questions such as

Are the people who sell 'black market' tickets outside Wembley Stadium parasites or benefactors?

What merit is there in the idea of a bread subsidy to help the poor?

One problem is that you may feel that you have almost too many analytical tools. In this chapter we show you how to select from them, to deal effectively with the relevant aspects of situations that you are confronted with. We suggest a 5-step procedural framework to help you organize your analysis.

THE A–F FRAMEWORK: A 5-STEP PROCEDURE

Our procedural framework starts with an equilibrium situation which is disturbed by some change or other. The five steps are labelled: AB, C, D, E and F.

- AB stands for APPROPRIATE BECAUSE. It asks if the procedure is appropriate to use (i.e. whether the elementary tools we already know are good enough).
- C stands for CAUSES. It asks about the cause of the change in the situation.
- D stands for DIRECTION. It asks about the direction of the change, i.e. whether it is positive or negative.
- E stands for EFFECTS. It traces the effects of the change, looking for example at their size and nature.
- F stands for FINALE. It comments finally on the efficiency of resource allocations, etc.

The procedure is best understood by using it and we shall shortly try out some illustrative cases. However, first, let us go through each step in turn (though not every single step, or sub-step, is always needed in every problem).

Step AB (Appropriate Because)

The first step is to check that the procedure is appropriate for the problem. The procedure uses only the elementary supply-demand analysis covered in previous chapters. It is appropriate for all cases where the assumptions of the elementary theory hold. These are that buyers and sellers are price-takers, trying to maximize satisfaction and profits respectively, demand curves slope downwards and supply

curves slope upwards. In such conditions, a free-market equilibrium exists, and you have the green light to proceed to the next step, C.

The procedure cannot normally be used if the assumptions mentioned above do not hold, for instance if buyers or sellers are price-makers, not price-takers. There is, however, one major exception to note. The A–F procedure *is* applicable if sellers set an *arbitrary* price, which prevents the attainment of a free-market equilibrium, even though this means that one of the assumptions of the elementary theory does not hold.

An example would be where the price of tickets for the Cup Final at Wembley are set (as they are) at an arbitrary level below free-market equilibrium. Sellers possess a degree of monopoly power and are not price-takers. If they set price to maximize their profits, for example, we would need monopoly theory. But since they do not set a profit-maximising, but an arbitrary, price, the elementary tools of supply and demand are adequate. The A–F framework is appropriate.

The problems we have chosen to illustrate the A–F procedure are all assumed to pass the first step, AB, so you can concentrate on learning how to use the other steps.

Step C (Causes)

This step in the procedure is a critical one. It asks you to distinguish between two types of causes of change. You should not have any difficulty with it because the distinction is a familiar one. It rests on the difference between changes arising from shifts in supply or demand curves, and those where there are no such movements. To illustrate, suppose a market is in equilibrium and you want to analyse the effects of something happening that affects the equilibrium. We call the two types of change C1 and C2.

Change type C1 is where equilibrium changes. Something happens which shifts one of the curves, thereby creating a new market equilibrium.

Examples would be where a rise in productivity shifts the supply curve to the right, or a fall in consumer income shifts the demand curve, for a normal good, to the left. Both will influence market price and quantities bought and sold.

Change type C2 is where equilibrium is prevented. Something happens which interferes with the market mechanism so that price is held above, or below, equilibrium.

Neither supply nor demand curve shifts, but the equilibrium is prevented. For example, the government may impose a maximum, or minimum, price different from that which would equate supply and demand.

We make this distinction in the procedure because the entire focus of attention in the two cases is different.[1]

With C1, where equilibrium changes because of a shift in demand or supply, the focus of attention is straightforward comparisons of two equilibrium situations, the old and the new. For example, following a rise in demand, the comparison is likely to cover such matters as whether price is higher or lower in the new equilibrium, whether quantities bought and sold are greater or less than in the old equilibrium, etc.

With C2, where equilibrium is prevented, the focus of attention is different. We cannot compare new and old equilibria, because equilibrium is prevented. The focus of attention is, therefore, on the difference between the market allocation, in the equilibrium, and the alternative non-market allocations that take over when equilibrium is prevented.

If you refer back to the section 'Market Versus Non-market Allocations' in the previous chapter (see p.84), you will find a discussion of non-market alternatives. We considered the case of the imposition by the government of a maximum price below equilibrium. We mentioned a number of ways in which scarce resources might be allocated in the case of excess demand which accompanied a price ceiling, e.g. by queues or rationing. One of the comparisons we made was between the persons who buy when free-market equilibrium obtains and those who are lucky enough to be satisfied (e.g. those at the front of the queue) when others who would like to buy are prevented from doing so by the price control. Remember, if resources are not allocated through the price mechanism they *must* be allocated in some other way.

When we deal with a type C2 change we will need to make comparisons between market allocations, and allocations brought about by other means. In the illustrative case we dealt with earlier of a maximum-price control, the alternatives were:

1 Queues, when those at the head are the lucky ones;
2 Rationing, if the government introduces it;
3 Sellers' preferences, if a sort of unofficial 'rationing' by sellers is possible;
4 Black markets, when those prepared to ignore the legal price limit are successful;
5 Chance, if the allocation turns out to be haphazard.

These are the alternatives we shall need to analyse when we deal with type C2 changes.

Step D (Direction)

Step D requires you to determine the direction of change. This is a straightforward application of the principles outlined in Chapters 4 to 9. The precise procedure needs, however, to be varied slightly for the two types of change, C1 and C2, described in Step C.

Type C1 changes: For changes involving shifts in either the supply or the demand curve, you must decide not only which curve shifts, but also in which direction it moves. Thus, for example, a fall in the price of a good which is a substitute for the good under consideration will shift the demand curve to the left; a rise in factor productivity will shift the supply curve to the right, and so on.

Type C2 changes: For changes which make equilibrium unattainable, you must first note whether the change is in price or quantity. (The examples we consider here are of the imposition of disequilibrium prices.) But quantities may also be controlled arbitrarily, as for example when output is restricted by the imposition of quotas while price is left to be determined on a free market.

In the case where a disequilibrium price is imposed, you must then decide whether price is above equilibrium, in which case there will be excess supply, or below equilibrium, in which case there will be excess demand. Thus, for example, state legislation setting a commodity's maximum permitted price below its equilibrium price will cause excess demand; a minimum price set above the equilibrium price will cause excess supply.

In taking Step D, two pairs of concepts which you have learned will be particularly useful: substitutes and complements, and normal goods and inferior goods. For example, to determine the effect of a change in the price of one good on the price of another good, you must decide whether the goods are substitutes or complements. To determine the effect of a change in consumer income on market price, you must decide whether the good is normal or inferior.

Step E (Effects)

This step is normally the longest in the procedure. In it, you should attempt an assessment of the effects of changes, the directions of which you identified in Step D. Usually, such assessment will include the magnitude of the effects, whether due to shifts in supply or demand, or to the presence of excess demand or excess supply.

We suggest three substeps as guides to the kind of analysis required when considering effects are discussed below:
   (i) Effects on prices and quantities.
   (ii) Effects over time.
   (iii) Primary and secondary market effects.

(i) Effects on prices and quantities: An attempt should be made to examine the likely effects on the following variables:
   (a) the own price of the good (p)
   (b) the quantity of the good bought and sold (q)
   (c) total revenue (or outlay) on the good (pq)
A major determinant of these effects are the relevant elasticities – price and income elasticities of demand, and elasticities of supply. You might wish to refer back to Chapter 7 to refresh your memory on the determinants of these elasticities when you come to a particular problem.

In the case of type C2 changes, you should try to quantify the amount of excess demand or supply. (Here again elas-

---

1 Some complex situations can involve both C1 and C2 causes; see below, p.104.

ticities are relevant.) Since excess demand or excess supply mean that some people cannot succeed in buying or selling all that they wish to at the prevailing price, you may have to consider which consumers actually succeed in buying, and which sellers actually succeed in selling. This is the point at which comparison of market and non-market allocations probably needs to be made. The list of alternatives mentioned earlier, including queues, rationing, black markets and sellers' preferences, will prove helpful.

(ii) Effects over time: It will often be relevant to consider whether effects of the kind described above differ as time passes. The distinction between short-run and long-run time-periods will be helpful; sometimes also the very-short-run (momentary) equilibrium.

(iii) Primary and secondary market effects: With some changes, it will be necessary to examine not only *direct* effects on the primary market, but also *indirect* effects on related, or secondary, markets. For example, suppose you are faced with the problem of examining the effects of the introduction of a tax on sales of good *x*. Our procedure suggests that you should examine, first, the effects of the tax on the price, quantity and total outlay on good *x*. You should then consider the effects on *related* markets. For example, if *x* is ballpoint pens, you should consider what will happen in the market for *pencils* when ballpoints are taxed, as well as what will happen in the market for ballpoints. Exactly the same considerations will arise in secondary markets – i.e. elasticities and time-periods – and you would be well advised to think about cross elasticities (see p.68) when discussing secondary markets.

Step F (Finale)

As a final step, you may be asked to comment on the results of applying economic analysis, particularly if a question of policy is involved – for example, maximum-price control.

Your comments should relate to resource allocations, and particularly to the extent to which they may be assessed according to the criteria of (1) efficiency and (2) equity. The content of Chapter 9 is relevant here, and you should refresh your understanding of the implications of economic efficiency, defined as the situation when no one can be made better off without anyone else being made worse off. Also frequently invaluable will be the principal causes of market failure. Those which come within our present scope are public goods, merit and demerit goods, externalities and dynamic, sluggish or volatile markets. Finally, questions of equity and income distribution often need to be faced, when you should try to keep separate positive statements about effects on the distribution of income, and normative statements about which distributions are preferable.

When you are asked to comment on a particular policy measure, you should do so in the light of the expressed object of the measure, i.e. how well does it achieve its target? That should not preclude you from commenting on any side-effects. For example, if asked to consider the desirability of rent controls to protect tenants, you should consider both whether tenants are protected and also relevant side-effects, e.g. the effects of rent control on the supply of houses and flats for rent. You might also ask, on grounds of equity, why tenants should be singled out for special treatment.

Finally, whenever you are faced with a particular policy proposal, you should consider, in principle, whether there are alternative policy measures which might be more efficient in achieving a stated objective. There may not be time to make a complete analysis of all possible policy alternatives in every case you come across, but one should never make a final judgement on any one proposal without considering alternative policy measures.

APPLYING THE A–F PROCEDURE

We shall now illustrate the procedure by taking you through two problems in some detail. Those we have chosen require the application of most of the steps in the procedure in full. That is why we chose them. But when you come to tackling problems of your own, it is important to appreciate that all steps may not be necessary. It depends on the nature of the problem.

For example, you might be asked to analyse the effects of a government subsidy on potatoes *on the price of potatoes*, or of the effects of a tax on sugar *on government tax revenue*. These are *limited* questions, and you would only be expected to use the appropriate parts of the A–F framework to do your analysis. It would be wrong to use the parts of the framework which deal, for example, with redistributive effects. They would be irrelevant. The framework is not intended to be applied, indiscriminately, for all purposes. Think of it as your servant, not your master.

Our first application of the A–F framework relates to the imposition of a tax on the sales of a commodity, and it involves a C1 type change. The second application is the imposition of a maximum price for a commodity, and it involves a C2 change.

Application No. 1: The Imposition of a Tax on Sales of a Commodity

Governments impose taxes on goods and services for many reasons – e.g. to raise revenue, to redistribute income, or to reduce consumption of a good. Suppose we are invited to analyse and comment on a proposal to place a tax of 10p a tube on glue. Let us apply our A–F procedural steps.

Step AB (Appropriate Because)

We assume the procedure is appropriate because the AB conditions discussed earlier in this chapter apply in this case.

Step C (Causes)

This step calls on us to decide whether the imposition of the tax will lead the market towards a new equilibrium or merely prevent the attainment of equilibrium. This test, you will recall, is whether or not the initial disturbance, here the tax, causes the supply or demand curve to shift. If so, equilibrium changes, and we are dealing with a C1 type problem. If not, equilibrium is prevented, and the problem is type C2.

A little reflection will suggest that if the government requires glue sellers to charge their customers 10p tax on every unit sold, this will affect the quantity that sellers want to offer for sale at every market price. Therefore, it will shift the supply curve and there is nothing in the question to prevent market price from reaching equilibrium.[1] Thus we have a C1 type change to analyse.

Step D (Direction)

On this step, we must determine the direction of the shift of the supply curve. To find this, note that the 10p tax must be paid to the government on every tube of glue sold. It may be regarded as an increase in the marginal costs of production. As well as paying all their factor costs that went to determine the supply curve, S, producers must pay an additional 10 pence per unit to the government.

Hence, the tax shifts the supply curve upwards and to the left. This is illustrated in Figure 10.1. The original supply and demand curves are labelled S and D. The effect of the tax is to shift the supply curve upwards, and hence to the left, to $S + T$. The vertical distance between the two curves (T) is equal to the tax that has to be paid.

To understand this, consider, for example, point c on the supply curve S. This point tells us that q_1 will be offered for sale if suppliers receive a price of p_2. If the tax, $b - c$ (equals T equals $p_1 - p_2$), is added to the price that sellers receive, they will, in fact, supply q_1. This is because consumers will pay p_1 for q_1 units. Sellers, of course, must pass $b - c$ per unit to the government, leaving them with p_2. Hence, a *market* price of p_1 induces sellers to supply q_1 and, thus, point b must be on the new supply curve $S + T$.

Note that b lies above c by an amount exactly equal to the tax per unit. All other points on the new supply curve also lie vertically above the old supply curve by an amount equal to the tax. Hence $S + T$ is parallel to S. (Had the tax been a percentage tax, the new supply curve would lie to the left of the old supply curve, but the vertical difference between them would have been a constant percentage of the price received by sellers. It would lie a constant percentage above the original supply curve and, therefore, by an increasing absolute amount.)

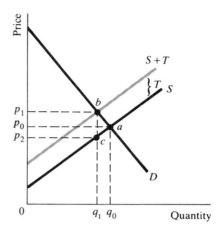

FIGURE 10.1 The Effects of a Tax on the Sales of a Commodity. In the general case, price rises by less than the full amount of the tax. A tax of bc ($p_1 - p_2$) per unit shifts the supply curve from S to $S + T$. Post-tax price p_1 is higher, by $p_1 - p_0$, than pre-tax price. Government revenue is p_1bcp_2; sellers' receipts, net of tax, are $0p_2cq_1$.

Step E (Effects)

Now we come to the meat of the analysis, and ask the question what happens to market price, quantity bought and sold, and total outlay. Remember, relevant considerations include the elasticities of demand and supply and the time-period.

It is sometimes helpful to consider the effects in four limiting cases of elasticities of both demand and supply, where each is equal to zero and to infinity. This allows you to draw conclusions about intermediate cases: the higher the actual elasticity, the closer will the result be to the infinite-elasticity case, and the lower the actual elasticity, the closer the result will be to the zero-elasticity case. First, however, let us analyse a general case where the elasticity of both supply and demand are greater than zero and less than infinity, as in Figure 10.1.

The general case: The original equilibrium is at the intersection of the supply curve S and the demand curve D; market price is p_0, the quantity bought and sold is q_0 and total consumer outlay (which when there are no taxes is also the sellers' revenue) is $0p_0aq_0$. The government now imposes a tax of T per unit sold, which shifts the supply curve upwards and to the left, to $S + T$. The new equilibrium price is p_1, the new equilibrium quantity is q_1 and the total outlay at the new equilibrium is $0p_1bq_1$. Let us compare the new situation with the old.

First, consider price. This has risen as a result of the tax. Note, however, that *the price rise is less than the tax*. The price rise is $p_1 - p_0$, which you can see from the diagram is less than $b - c$, which is the amount of the tax. This is an important conclusion. We shall shortly examine special circumstances when the price change is equal to the tax, but in the case where *neither* demand *nor* supply has an elasticity of zero or infinity, sellers do not pass the full

---

1 Note, it would be satisfactory to analyse this problem by shifting the demand curve rather than the supply curve. If we deduct the tax from the demand curve then both the D and S curves indicate the after-tax price received by sellers. If we add the tax to the supply curve, then both the D and the S curve indicate the pre-tax market price paid by buyers. Deducting the tax from the demand curve would indeed be the more obvious way of approach if the state were to collect the 10p tax directly from consumers instead of from sellers. Some textbooks analyse tax incidence in this fashion (drawing a new demand curve net of tax). The results are the same regardless of approach. You can test this for yourself by trying the alternative method *after* you have read to the end of the section.

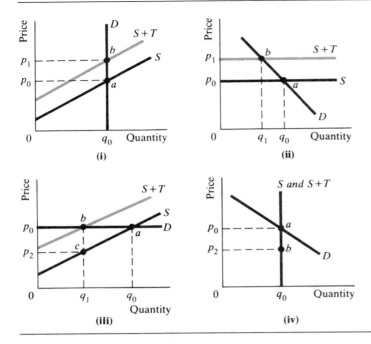

FIGURE 10.2 Two Limiting Cases. The effects of a tax on sales of a commodity can leave market price unchanged, or it may rise to the full extent of the tax. Market price rises by the full extent of the tax if (i) demand is perfectly inelastic or (ii) supply is perfectly elastic. Market price is unaffected by the tax if (iii) demand is perfectly elastic or (iv) supply is perfectly inelastic.

amount of a tax on to consumers. They cannot do so if market forces are allowed to work.

Consider, next, the change in quantity. This falls as a result of the tax from q_0 to q_1. This is a second general conclusion (though, again, we examine exceptions below in the next diagram). The imposition of a tax on a commodity lowers the quantity bought and sold. Finally, consider the change in total consumer outlay and sellers' revenue. Whether consumer outlay rises or falls depends, of course, on the value of the elasticity of demand. If the elasticity is greater than unity, the rise in price reduces consumers' total outlay; if it is less than unity, total outlay rises.

Total outlay by consumers is not, however, in this case, the same as total receipts by sellers, because part of sellers' revenue must be passed to the government. Sellers' total receipts, net of tax, are shown by the area Op_2cq_1 in Figure 10.1. Government tax revenue is the new equilibrium quantity, q_1, multiplied by the tax, $b-c$, which is the area, p_1bcp_2.

Extreme cases: The conclusion that the imposition of a tax on a commodity causes market price to rise, but by less than the full amount of the tax, does not hold in four extreme cases, which are illustrated in Figure 10.2. That diagram is in four sections, two of which show price rising by the full tax and two which show price unchanged despite the tax. *Price rises exactly as much as the tax if either demand elasticity is zero or supply elasticity is infinite.* These cases are illustrated in Figure 10.2(i) and (ii), and are self-explanatory.

The remaining sections of Figure 10.2 (iii) and (iv) show the cases where the tax does *not* affect market price. This occurs when *either demand is perfectly elastic or supply is perfectly inelastic.* Section (iii) of the diagram is again self-explanatory, but it is worth pointing out the reason why there is only one supply curve in the case of section (iv) because it may not be immediately obvious.

The reason is that, when supply elasticity is zero, sellers offer the same quantity for sale regardless of the price they receive. Hence, there is only one supply curve, which is labelled both S and $S + T$. The quantity q_0 is offered for sale before and after the tax, though sellers' total receipts are, of course, different in the two cases. Without any tax, total receipts are Op_0aq_0 (which is equal to total outlay by consumers). With the tax, however, sellers only retain Op_2bq_0. The remainder, p_0abp_2, is handed over to the government as tax revenue.[1]

There is one more question to ask about these exceptional cases. How does quantity bought and sold after the tax compare with quantities in the original equilibrium? In the typical case (i.e. when the elasticities of supply and demand are greater than 0 and less than infinity), quantity falls after the tax is introduced. This conclusion holds also in two of the exceptional cases – when either the demand or the supply curve is perfectly elastic, as in sections (ii) and (iii) of Figure 10.2.

In the two other exceptional cases, the conclusion does not hold. If either the demand or the supply curve is perfectly inelastic, the quantity bought and sold does not change after the tax is introduced (see Figure 10.2 (i) and (iv)). It is not difficult to understand why this is so. If changes in price leave either quantity supplied or demanded unaffected, it is not surprising that market equilibrium pre- and post-tax shows the intersection of the supply and demand curves at the same quantity.

Effects in different time-periods: Recall that our Step E requires consideration of what happens when we vary the

---

1 You may like to notice that this case is not an exception to our rule that the tax shifts the supply curve vertically upwards by the amount of the tax. If you take any point on a vertical supply curve and shift it upwards by any amount, you will still get the same vertical curve.

time-period under consideration. We can make certain generalizations about such differences on the basis of the diagrams in Figures 10.1 and 10.2. These show demand and supply curves with elasticities varying between zero and infinity. As we know that elasticities tend to be greater the longer the time-period, we can also make use of the diagrams to indicate the probable differences in effects in the short and long run. Thus, we can take the demand and supply curves with low elasticities as representing shorter-run curves than those with high elasticities. Let us apply the three-fold classification of time-periods – momentary, short run and long run – in this analysis.

(i) *Momentary period.* The instantaneous markets situation is that of Figure 10.2(iv) – supply is perfectly inelastic.

(ii) *Short run.* Compared to the momentary period, in the short run both demand and supply tend to be more elastic; hence Figure 10.1 may better represent the situation than Figure 10.2(iv).

(iii) *Long run.* In the long run, both demand and supply tend to be even more elastic than in the short run. The limiting cases are where supply is perfectly elastic, as in Figure 10.2(ii), and where demand is perfectly elastic, as in Figure 10.2(iii). As we shall see when we come to study costs of production (Chapter 14), the former case is quite common in the long run, when constant costs of production imply that the supply curve is perfectly elastic. The latter case, in contrast, is exceptional, even in the long run. Elasticity of demand equal to infinity is rarely found. Figure 10.2(iii) might, however, come close to representing the effects of a tax on a commodity such as red bicycles, for which almost perfect substitutes – black, green and purple bicycles – exist. Consumers would switch their purchases to bicycles of other colours, leaving market price of red bicycles almost unchanged. (Even in this case, however, we would not expect demand to be perfectly elastic. If people have colour preferences we would expect them to be willing to pay some amount to exercise those preferences.)

The four limiting cases illustrated in Figure 10.2, and the general case shown in Figure 10.1, show the different effects a tax can have on market price, sellers' receipts and tax revenue as demand and supply elasticities differ. In a real problem, it would be useful to obtain some empirical evidence on the values of supply and demand elasticities over various time-periods.

Secondary market effects: So far in Step E, we have concentrated on effects in the primary market – i.e. the market for glue – on which the tax was levied. In principle, one should next look to see whether there are any secondary markets closely related on the demand and/or the supply side. This is the point at which cross elasticities are relevant.

Sometimes the effects on secondary markets are small enough to be safely ignored. At other times the effects are large and it would be dangerous to ignore them.

For an extreme example of the latter case, assume that initially the government is levying a tax on all new cars, and that it then elects to double the tax on red cars only. The main primary result will be a large drop in sales of cars of that colour with a large drop in government revenue

from the initial proceeds of the tax on all cars. If you looked only at the primary market, that would be the end of your story. But those who would have bought red cars will now buy cars of other colours. So there will be an increase in the demand for all other cars approximately equal to the fall in sales of red cars. Tax revenues will rise on the resulting extra sales to more or less balance the loss of tax revenue on red cars. In this case an analysis of the effect on the government's revenue from the increased tax on red cars based solely on the demand and supply curves for red cars would have been hopelessly in error.

Step F (Finale)

In the final step of our procedure, we need to evaluate the potential success of the government's policy. We can, of course, comment generally on the efficiency and equity aspects of the resource allocation. It will be more helpful to apply these criteria in the light of any known specific objective the government had for imposing the tax. As we have not been told what it is, we must now consider a number of alternative objectives, such as raising revenue, discouraging consumption and redistributing income.

If the main purpose of the tax is to raise revenue for the state, the conclusion is clear. A given unit tax will produce more income for the government the less elastic is demand or supply (e.g. Figure 10.2(i) or (iv)). If, in contrast, the prime purpose is to discourage consumption (perhaps because, for example, of health hazards from sniffing glue), the answer is equally clear, though different. The fall in the quantity bought and sold is greater the greater is the elasticity of demand or supply (see Figure 10.2(ii) and (iii)). If the government's aim is redistributive, the analysis is much more complex, and we cannot consider it in detail here.

Suffice to say that we should need to know whether the objective is to give most help to the buyers or the sellers of glue. If we are told this, we can attempt an assessment of the redistributive effects of the tax by reference to whether the facts of the situation were such as to cause the tax to fall more heavily on the one or the other group (though it is pretty obvious that a tax on glue is a very poor instrument for redistribution).

Provided there are no reasons to suspect the existence of externalities or of volatile or sluggish markets, and that glue is a neither a public good nor a merit good, there remains a single final observation on the efficiency of resource allocation. If resources were believed to have been efficiently allocated in the pre-tax situation, then we should be more content with the tax, the closer market conditions resembled those of Figure 10.2(i) or (iv). These are the cases where either supply or demand is perfectly inelastic, because in neither of them is there any change in the quantity bought and sold. Hence, if resource allocation was efficient before the tax, it will remain efficient after the tax. Having said that, one should be warned that it does not follow that taxes on goods in highly inelastic demand or supply are always to be preferred to taxes on other goods. There are other considerations to be taken into account. We discuss some of these in Chapter 21.

Application No. 2:
A Maximum Price for Bread

Many goals of economic policy have been pursued through the use of controls, of which one type is the setting of legal maximum and minimum prices. For our second illustration of the application of the A–F procedure, we shall analyse and comment on a hypothetical government proposal to introduce a price ceiling for bread. In this case we are given a reason for the measure – to help the poor. Let us apply our procedure, beginning at Step C, because, as previously stated, we assume that the problem has passed through Step AB, and that our framework is appropriate to use.

Step C (Causes)

In this step, we ask whether the introduction of a price ceiling is a type C1 or a type C2 problem. Type C1 changes involve the market moving towards a new equilibrium because of a shift in either the demand or supply curve. Type C2 changes prevent equilibrium being attained. Price controls do nothing to shift demand or supply curves. They affect price, but not quantities demanded or offered for sale at every possible price. Therefore, a type C2 analysis is called for – equilibrium prevented.

Step D (Direction)

The third step in the procedure calls for an indication of the direction of change to be expected. For changes which do not involve any shifts in supply or demand curves but prevent equilibrium being attained, you must decide whether excess supply or excess demand develops. In order to answer the question, a diagram may be helpful.

The analysis from here on follows the discussion of price controls in Chapter 9 (see pp.84–5). Fig 10.3, in fact, is basically a reproduction of Figure 9.3. The diagram depicts the market for bread, with equilibrium price p_0 and equilibrium quantity bought and sold q_0. Notice that the imposition of a price control does not necessarily interfere with the operation of market forces. If the maximum price is

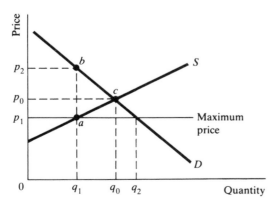

FIGURE 10.3 A Price Ceiling. The imposition of a maximum price (p_m) below equilibrium creates excess demand ($q_2 - q_1$). The black market price would be p_b.

set *at or above* the equilibrium price, there would be no reason why that price should not continue to prevail. There would, then, be no effect to be analysed, and we need not proceed any further. Equilibrium is attainable.

It would, of course, be rather pointless for the state to set a price ceiling at a level which had no current effect (though such a policy might be introduced to prevent price rising above existing levels in the future). More commonly, price ceilings are set below equilibrium market prices. In this case, we assume the legal maximum price for bread to be p_1 in Figure 10.3.

We can see from the diagram that at price p_1 consumers wish to buy q_2 bread, while sellers are only prepared to offer q_1 for sale. In the absence of the control, market forces would tend to push price upwards. However, this is illegal and, provided the maximum price can be enforced (see below), there will be an excess of quantity demanded over quantity supplied. That is the direction of change, and we move to Step E to consider the effects that might follow the appearance of excess demand.

Step E (Effects)

We are now ready to take the biggest step in our procedure and examine the effects of the excess demand for bread that follows the imposition of a price ceiling.

We ask, first, what happens to price, quantity and total outlay, according to the proposed framework for analysis. These questions cause little problem if we assume that 'policing' arrangements are completely effective, so that no bread is sold at prices above the legal limit. Price falls from p_0 to p_1, quantity bought and sold falls from q_0 to q_1, and consumers' outlay, and sellers' revenue, falls from Op_0cq_0 to Op_1aq_1.

When equilibrium is prevented and excess demand created, in this case by a price ceiling, we know that some alternative way of allocating resources other than through the price mechanism will, inevitably, occur. We have suggested five alternatives: queues, rationing, sellers' preferences, black markets and chance allocation.

Queues: The first possibility is that queues will develop for the product in relatively short supply. The length of the queue will be directly related to the amount of excess demand, $q_2 - q_1$. In the case of a product such as bread, the probability is that the queues will take the form of physical lines of people outside bakers' shops and at bread counters in supermarkets.

Rationing: The second possible way of allocating a short supply is by rationing. The government can issue ration books containing coupons which must be surrendered, as well as cash, to obtain bread. The state can control the supply of coupons to equal the available supply.

Sellers' preferences: The third possible means whereby limited supplies may be allocated is where the sellers decide whom to sell to. There are many ways in which they might do this. For example, shopkeepers might choose to sell on a first-come, first-served basis. Under such circumstances since sellers are not effectively exercising any preferences, the allocation is that of the first alternative described on the previous page, namely by queues. Alternatively, sellers might store bread 'under the counter' and give preference to regular customers, for example, or to those who also buy their cakes and pastries. In the case of some commodities subject to price ceilings, sellers may opt to give preference to whomsoever they choose.

Black markets: The fourth possibility is that the law will be broken and some bread sold on the black market at prices in excess of p_1. It is bound to be profitable for sellers to do this because, as we can see from Figure 10.3, consumers would be prepared to pay p_2 per unit for the amount q_1.

Whether or not black markets develop, and what proportion of total supply finds its way to them, are questions beyond the realm of economics. The answers depend on such matters as the strength of the incentive to break the law described in the previous paragraph, the efficiency of compliance measures taken by the government, including the severity of penalties imposed on offenders, and the willingness of consumers to pay black-market prices. It is unlikely that all available output is ever put on the black market, but human nature appears to be such that some black-market activity is usual.

Chance allocation: For completeness, we should mention a fifth way in which supplies may be allocated, which is simply haphazard. This is most likely to occur if supplies appear on the market irregularly and the product is very perishable. Bread is a fair example of such a commodity, though it would be a better one if we were considering bread in France, where quality deteriorates so rapidly that many French people buy their bread twice daily. Chance allocations could then work to the advantage of any person who happened to pass a baker's shop at the moment that loaves were just being taken out of the oven.

Effects in different time-periods: In the present case, we cannot take the economic analysis much further on the question of different expected effects as the time-period under consideration lengthens. Any of the five allocative mechanisms described above may persist in the long term as well as in the short. However, the short-run demand and supply curves may shift as a result of the enforced disequilibrium price, making the analysis more complex. We could then be faced with a C1 type problem as well as that of the C2 type we have been following. Equilibrium is prevented alright, but equilibrium also changes.

We shall not follow the analysis far along this road, but can give some idea of how it runs. Some consumers, deprived of the opportunity of buying as much bread as they would like, may decide to bake their own, or turn to substitutes for which they may acquire a taste. This means a leftward shift in the demand curve for bread. Sellers, faced with the low controlled price of bread, begin by cutting back on production to equate marginal cost with the new lower price. But a lower level of production means that there will be excess capacity in terms of too many

bakers, too many ovens and too many shops in the bread industry.

As time passes, thought will be given to alternative ways of utilizing underused resources. Some bakers will switch to other occupations and some equipment will not be replaced when it wears out. Thus, the supply curve of bread will shift to the left as the size of the bread industry shrinks. Supply-side forces work to moderate the shortage as consumers switch their purchases to substitutes for bread. The net effect on excess demand cannot therefore be predicted in the absence of further quantitative knowledge.[1]

Secondary-market effects: As suggested in the previous sections, the imposition of a price ceiling for bread might well have significant impacts on related markets. The legal maximum price for bread disturbs the previous equilibrium between that price and the price of bread substitutes. Sellers will be encouraged by the relative price differential to turn to the production of goods such as cakes and other flour confections. Buyers, too, will turn to substitute products because of the shortfall in supplies of bread caused by the price ceiling.

We cannot tell whether the end result will be that of a rise in the price of cakes, etc. That will depend on whether there is a larger switch on the demand or on the supply side. If the former exceeds the latter, the price of cakes will rise, and vice versa. But whatever happens, the allocation of resources will be different from what would occur under a freely working price mechanism.

If people spend less money on bakery products in general, then they will have more to spend on all other goods. Presumably much of this will go to buy other food products. The effect, however, is likely to be spread over the markets for so many products that the effect in any one will be negligible. If so, effects in secondary markets can be ignored.

Step F (Finale)

In this final step in our procedure, we comment on the efficiency and equity aspects of the resource allocation. We have been told that the object of the price ceiling was to benefit the poor, so we must consider if it does so, and how effectively.

Consider, first, efficiency. Let us compare the new allocation of resources with that brought about by free-market forces. The equilibrium price, before the price control was introduced, cleared the market at an output which ensured the equality of marginal cost and marginal utility. The

---

1 It may be worth noting a difference between supply and demand in this case. On the supply side, bakers can sell all they want so their responses are the ones we analysed in general terms in earlier chapters – more elastic the longer the time-span under consideration. Demanders cannot buy all they wish so their response is something we have not analysed previously. Their demand curves are shifting in response to a new variable, the probability of being able to buy the good when they want it. When dealing with unhindered markets we did not need this variable because in equilibrium there were no unsatisfied demanders (or suppliers).

legislation removed that equality and led to an output at which marginal utility was greater than marginal cost (the difference between them being *ab* in Figure 10.3). We know, however, that market allocations are preferable only under certain conditions, one of which is that no redistribution is considered to be worth the cost.[1] So although there may be efficiency losses, these may be judged acceptable if they are small and the measure helps the poor enough.

Let us proceed by asking two questions: (1) whether the price ceiling fulfils its purpose of helping the poor, and (2) whether there might be better ways of doing this.

Consider the first question which asks, in effect, whether redistribution of income in favour of those at the bottom of the scale results from the price ceiling. The answer depends on which of the five methods of allocation discussed in Step E are actually adopted. Let us consider them one by one.

Queues:　Suppose, first, queues form outside bakers' shops. Will this achieve the objective of helping the poor? The answer can only be yes if the poor are in the front of the queues. If they have less time to spare for queuing, the answer will be no. Allocation by queuing gives preference to people with most time available for standing in queues; for example, households with retired and unemployed members.

So, for example, wealthy families with retired parents living in or nearby will gain at the expense of single-parent families with children in school. Some rich people have even been known to pay others to stand in queues for them. In other words, redistribution may be haphazard by income or even perverse, in the sense that most of the cheap bread goes to the rich while the poor account for most of the unsatisfied demanders.

Rationing:　Second, suppose the government supports its price control with a coupon rationing scheme. What then? If rations are set to be equal per head of the population, the poor will certainly benefit in being able to buy cheaper bread, though probably less of it than they would wish to buy. Note, too, that the favourable income distributive effect (in terms of the stated objective of greater equality) is not frustrated by allowing coupons to be freely transferable. Indeed, the poor may be even better off if they can sell their ration coupons for cash, and use the money to buy things they value even more highly than bread.

Sellers' preferences:　Third, allocation might be according to sellers' preferences. We cannot deal with all the possible outcomes here. They are as many as the different preferences that might motivate sellers. However, let us consider two examples, both possible. In the first case, assume

bakers decide to ration supplies unofficially, and equally, to each of their regular customers. The effects would be rather similar to official rationing by the government, except in so far as the customers of bakers with relatively few regular customers do better than others. In contrast, if there are customers who are not regulars at any shop, they will get no bread at all.

In the second case, assume that bakers favour customers who buy other goods from them – cakes, pastries, etc. In so far as other goods are more expensive commodities, less affordable by the poor, the stated objective of helping lower income groups may be frustrated. Indeed bakers could raise the price of the cakes sold along with the bread, so that the total price of cakes plus bread was what it would have been in the absence of the price cutting.

Black markets:　The fourth alternative we considered was allocation through black markets. If this were to happen, the objective of helping the poor would certainly be hindered. Insofar as the black-market price exceeds the free-market equilibrium price without a price ceiling, the poor are *less* able to afford bread than before, and there is less bread to go around as well.

Chance allocation:　Lastly, allocation may be what we have called chance or haphazard. However, since some rich and some poor will be lucky, and other rich and other poor unlucky, the most likely outcome will be no redistribution, on average, among income groups – although there will be redistribution between the lucky and unlucky groups.

Secondary effects:　The analysis has concentrated on effects in the market for bread. In so far as there is any general conclusion, it must be that whether or not the objective of helping the poor is served, depends on how the shortfall in supply is allocated. There will certainly be redistribution, but without rationing it is unlikely to be from rich to poor. Note also that all purchasers of bread gain from the low price. The poor may be helped, but so are others including the rich who also get bread at the controlled price.

Secondary market implications may work in many ways. For purposes of illustration consider just one. Suppose there is a bigger transfer of demand than of supply to one close substitute for bread – namely cakes – which causes the price of cakes to rise. Indeed, it is commonly found that price ceilings have the effect of pushing up the prices of substitute goods. This may frustrate, at least partially, the stated objective of the government, however effective are the measures used to enforce a fair allocation of the limited supplies of the price-controlled commodities.

For example, during the Second World War, 'meat' was rationed, as well as being price-controlled. One consequence was that those who could afford it bought unrationed poultry and game at high free-market prices. This is not to say that the system was completely ineffective, simply that it was not 100 per cent egalitarian in impact. Nor could it be. It is almost impossible (and very costly) to control all prices and ration all goods and services.

---

1 Market allocations can only be regarded, strictly speaking, as ideal if the distribution of income is fair and equitable. Since we are never likely to encounter such a situation in real life, the condition is stated as in the text. We do not inhabit an ideal world and the only useful consideration is this operational one. Market allocations may not be distributively fair, but if the cost of deviating from them is greater than the gain in equity, then they are preferable; otherwise, not.

BOX 10.1 Not Quite Tennis

'More people want to watch the tennis at Wimbledon than there are seats to accommodate them. Rationing used to work through privilege, luck, patience – and price. Now the Wimbledon authorities have announced that those rationing by price are to be threatened with prosecution and jail.

'The most privileged winners of Wimbledon tickets each year are the club's 2100 debenture holders. They automatically receive a centre court ticket for every day of the two-week tournament. Debentures, for 1991–95, which officially cost £19,250, are already fully sub-scribed. Debentures covering the last two years of the current period can be bought on the Stock Exchange for around £35,000.

'Cheaper . . . is to become a member of the All England Club which runs Wimbledon. Only top tennis players need apply. Membership is fixed at 375 people and another 800 are on the waiting list . . . . Most others have to win tickets in ballots . . . turn up at dawn on the day . . . or buy from any of the above groups or via ticket "touts".

'Wimbledon tickets, like those for the cup final, Covent Garden opera and certain big West End shows are in short supply. Tickets therefore fetch high prices. The only question is who is to benefit from this price, those supplying the service or the middle men?'

(Leader in *The Times*, 28 September 1990)

Any commodity can be allocated through the market or by other means. When the Wimbledon authorities decide to bypass the market they lay themselves open to a variety of charges. For example, they do not raise as much as they could to support the game of tennis in the UK; they discriminate among tennis lovers by allocating tickets through local tennis clubs; and they encourage black market activity by persons described as 'touts'.

Questions

1 Five methods of allocating supply other than through the market are mentioned in the chapter. Which do you think applies to the allocation described above?
2 Which of the following allocation methods would raise most money for supporting tennis: (i) selling all tickets at the market-clearing price? (ii) offering all tickets for sale by auction? (iii) limiting ticket sales to persons with incomes above a lower limit?
3 Might there be anything to be said in favour of allo-cating tickets by national lottery, with resale per-mitted?

So far, we have considered only the effects on consumers. Bakers will be affected as well as their customers. If the demand switches to substitutes made by bakers, they may not be seriously affected. But if the demand switches to other products, e.g. imported Norwegian biscuits, bakers lose sales and some may be driven out of business. Thus, bakers as a whole suffer, and it is important to include them in the redistributive effects.

The final assessment, which includes the benefit to bread consumers and other redistributive effects discussed above, should include the effects on producers' incomes as well. If some bakers are poorer than their customers, the redis-tribution, on this account, could be from poor to rich.

Alternative policies: When we outlined our A–F pro-cedure for the application of supply and demand analysis, we stressed the importance of considering alternative policy measures for achieving a stated objective. Such a step is essential before forming a final judgement on a particular policy proposal, such as the imposition of a price ceiling for bread, which we have analysed.

Since the maximum-price control was designed to help the poor, we ought to compare our results with analyses of alternative policies having the same aim. To do so in full would be an enormous task simply because of the multitude of redistributive policies that can be adopted.

We may, however, mention here two alternatives to a price ceiling on bread, for purposes of illustration.

One method would be to allow a free market to operate for bread but to subsidize bread purchases by the poor. Coupons, valued at so much money when spent on bread, could be given to those below a certain income. (Bakers who accepted these could redeem them for cash from the government.) Such a measure would have two main advantages over the price ceiling. In the first place, the benefits would be restricted to the poor; and in the second place, there would be no decline in bread production.

Another policy alternative would be to forgo all direct intervention in the bread market and give all poor people a straightforward income supplement, thereby increasing their purchasing power. There is a lot to be said in favour of this alternative, which benefits all poor people, regard-less of how much they happen to like bread.

USING THE A–F PROCEDURE

We believe you should find the A–F procedure useful for applying supply and demand analysis to a wide range of problems, similar to those illustrated. To remind you of the major steps and sub-steps we have provided a Checklist (see Table 10.1 on page 105).

Although we illustrated the procedure with only two problems, they were carefully chosen to cover the two different types of situation that crop up – described in Step C (Causes) as type C1 (Equilibrium Changes) when a supply or demand curve shifts, and type C2 (Equilibrium Prevented). It may be helpful to give you some general ideas on applying the A–F procedure in slightly different situations without going into the full details as in the two problems covered in the main body of the chapter.[1]

One area which crops up concerns the allocation of a commodity the supply of which is fixed and cannot be increased, certainly in the short run and often in the longer run, too. Examples are the supply of tickets for the Cup Final at Wembley stadium or the Centre Court at Wimbledon (see Box 10.1). Another area is agriculture.

Agriculture

Supply-demand analysis is frequently applied to agriculture, for which it is well suited. We shall look briefly at some of the policy issues that arise here. To make sense they need to be seen, however, in context. Hence a short diversion to provide some background is necessary.

The agricultural sector looms larger in importance in the Western world than is, perhaps, justified by its relative size. In the UK, as you may confirm by referring back to Figure 2.1, agriculture accounts for approximately 1.5 per cent of total output of the whole economy. Although the agricultural sector is particularly small in the UK, it is also one of the smallest sectors in most Western countries. Its importance in economic policy is partly political, related to the voting power of farm lobbies, and partly social, because of countryside-preservation lobbies, which depend, to an extent, on the farming industry.

There is, however, a clear economic basis to the interventionist activities of governments in agricultural markets. This is to be found in the historical pressures leading to a decline in the size of the farm sector.

These pressures stem from both demand and supply sides. On the demand side, one notable feature is that the proportion of income spent on food has tended to fall as income has risen. Some foodstuffs are inferior goods with negative income elasticities of demand, while income elasticities are low, if positive, for many others. Further, the price elasticity of demand for foodstuffs as a whole is low. There is an obvious limit to the amount we can eat, however low prices may fall. On the supply side, farm problems have been aggravated by the very rises in productivity from technological advance that have helped to

keep in check the numbers of the starving among the world's population.

The problems faced by farmers can be viewed as stemming from the shifts in supply and demand curves implied in the previous paragraph, all of which are type C1 causes in the terminology of our A–F procedure. Consider first the rightward shift in the supply curve. Ask what effect this has on (1) the price of the product, (2) quantities sold and (3) producers' total incomes?

The answers to these questions will surely vary between the short and the long run, as your A–F procedure will expect you to consider. The effect on price will be unambiguously downwards and on quantity unambiguously upwards, but the magnitude of the effects will depend on the value of the price elasticity of demand. If, as we expect, demand elasticity is low, quantity will not increase very much and price will fall considerably. Indeed if the price elasticity of demand is less than unity, quantity increases less than proportionately when price falls.

The answer to the third question, what happens to producers' total income, is that, given the inelastic demand, it falls. One of the two major problems that government agricultural policies seek to alleviate is, therefore, the secular decline in farm incomes that has accompanied productivity advance in an industry with demand conditions as they have been described.

The second major farm problem, which has not yet been mentioned, concerns not so much the trend towards declining incomes as the fact that incomes tend to fluctuate more than they do in other sectors. We need not look far for explanations of such fluctuations. In the first place, low price elasticities of demand with shifts of the supply curve (such as occur when output varies with weather conditions or the incidence of crop disease) bring lower farm incomes at times of bountiful harvests and low prices, and bring higher incomes when crops are poor and prices are high. The second explanation of price instability is the existence of conditions described in the cobweb theorem, where quantity supplied is related to past rather than current market price (see above, pp.88–90).

Supply-demand analysis may be especially helpful in the evaluation of policies towards agriculture. There is no shortage of alternatives available. How do you deal with them using the A–F procedure? Without going into detail, we may make a few comments to help you organize your thoughts on the matter.

Price controls

There are two types of policy that a government may adopt aimed at directly influencing prices. One involves supporting farm prices by means of an output-related subsidy. The second consists of a minimum price floor.

If you think of applying the A–F procedure to these policies, you should recognize the first as a C1-type policy. A subsidy shifts the supply curve to the right, as sellers receive a sum from the state for each unit sold. Your analysis can parallel that of the first example, of the tax on glue, in the chapter (see pp.96–9). The main difference lies in Step D, direction of change. But the diagrams could

---

1 The distinction between type C1 and type C2 causes will be appropriate for many of the problems you will encounter in introductory economics. You should, however, be alert in case you encounter a complex problem where the event requiring analysis contains elements of both C1 and C2 type causes. We met such a case earlier (see p.101). Here is another example: 'In the face of a failure of the wheat crop, the government decides to freeze the price of bread.' Here the crop failure is a C1 type cause, because the supply curve shifts. The price freeze is a C2 type cause, because equilibrium is prevented. In this case, you would be advised to address yourself first to the effects of the crop failure, and later take in the effects of the price freeze.

TABLE 10.1

STEP AB (APPROPRIATE BECAUSE)   *Tick boxes*
1. Demand curves slope downwards   ☐
2. Supply curves slope upwards   ☐
3. Buyers and sellers are maximizers   ☐
4. Buyers and sellers are price-takers (*or* price is arbitrary) ☐

STEP C (CAUSES)

    CHANGE TYPE **C1** (equilibrium changes)   ☐
        Demand/supply curve shifts

    CHANGE TYPE **C2** (equilibrium prevented)   ☐

STEP D (DIRECTION)

		to right	to left
CHANGE TYPE **C1**	Demand curve shifts:	☐	☐
		above equilibrium	below equilibrium
CHANGE TYPE **C2**	Market price held:	☐	☐

STEP E (EFFECTS)

Primary effects

Indicate size in boxes: (L) Large, (S) Small

		Short-run	Long-run
CHANGE	**PRICE** (*p*)	☐	☐
TYPE **C1**	**QUANTITY** (*q*)	☐	☐
	PRICE times QUANTITY (*pq*)	☐	☐

CHANGE TYPE **C2**	Non-market allocation method:	queues	☐
		rationing	☐
		sellers'/buyers' prefs.	☐
		black market	☐
		other	☐

Secondary effects   (related goods)

Demand side   ☐
Supply side   ☐

STEP F (FINALE)

EFFICIENCY	Pro-market considerations	☐
	Market failure:	
	public goods	☐
	externalities	☐
	merit/demerit goods	☐
	sluggish/volatile markets	☐
	other	☐
EQUITY	Distributive effects	☐
POLICY	Targets	☐
	Alternatives	☐

probably serve well enough if you interchanged the original and the shifted curves. In Figures 10.1 and 10.2 the (shifted) *S* + *T* curves would be the original ones, and the (original) *S* curves would represent the shifted supply curves resulting from the state subsidy.

The second policy, of a price floor, would not involve any shifts in supply or demand curves. We recognise it as a C2-type change, preventing equilibrium. Figure 10.4 would help discussion of the issue. This diagram is similar to Figure 10.3, which depicted a price ceiling below equilibrium. Figure 10.4, in contrast, deals with a price floor, p_f, above equilibrium. In this case there is excess supply in place of excess demand. The quantity that sellers cannot find purchasers for at the high price is represented by $q_2 - q_1$. Analysis similar to that of the effects of the maximum price for bread can follow (see pp.100–3.)

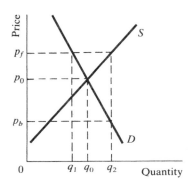

FIGURE 10.4 A Price Floor. The imposition of a minimum price (p_f) above equilibrium for the whole supply of q_1 creates excess supply $(q_2 - q_1)$. The black market price for the whole supply of q_2 would be p_b.

It remains true that, if resources are not allocated by the price mechanism, then some other way of allocating them must obtain. Instead of asking who are the actual consumers who are lucky enough to be able to buy bread at its high price, we ask who are the lucky *sellers* who can get the insufficient customers? The alternative categories you will need to consider will not be very different from those for allocating excess demand. When we have excess supply, the queues will be of frustrated *sellers* wishing to dispose of surplus stocks; black markets will be where sellers *undercut* the price floor (p_b in Figure 10.4 is the market price at which they could sell their output of q_2); rationing will be some system whereby sellers are allocated *output quotas*; buyers' preferences will refer to a situation where *consumers* choose which sellers they wish to buy from.

One can go a last step further to throw light on how the accumulations of so-called mountains and lakes of food and drink associated with the Common Agricultural Policy of the European Community occurred. They resulted from the intervention of governments buying up output which the private sector did not buy at the controlled prices.

Other controls

Price controls, as discussed above, relate mainly to the goal of preventing farm incomes from falling below certain levels. There are other policies which may be likewise targetted, for example quantity controls, reducing output by quota (also included in the EC Common Agricultural Policy as 'Set Aside' acreage reductions).

Straightforward price and quantity controls are generally less effective in trying to achieve the goal of reducing fluctuations in farm incomes. Indeed, minimum price floors may cause farm incomes to vary more than they would in a free market, in so far as incomes then rise and fall

Summary

This chapter sets out a 5-step A–F procedure for the application of elementary supply and demand analysis to solve problems you might face.

AB (Appropriate Because): The first step is to check that the procedure can be applied to the particular problem – i.e. that free-market equilibrium exists or is possible. This will be the case if the following assumptions hold: (1) demand curves slope downwards, (2) supply curves slope upwards, (3) buyers and sellers are maximizers, and (4) buyers and sellers are price-takers. The A–F procedure is also appropriate even if an arbitrary price is imposed preventing the attainment of free-market equilibrium, as long as all the listed assumptions hold.

C (Causes): The second step is to identify the cause of change. Two types are distinguished – type C1 where equilibrium changes (because of a shift in a supply and/or demand curve), and type C2 where equilibrium is prevented (e.g. because of the imposition of a price control). The focus of attention in type C1 changes is on comparisons between equilibrium before and after a change. In type C2 changes, the focus is on comparisons between equilibrium market allocations and non-market allocations.

D (Direction): The third step is to decide on the direction of the change that will take place. For type C1 changes, this means deciding on whether supply and/or demand curves shift, and whether to the right or the left. For type C2 this means deciding on whether excess demand or excess supply will develop. Relevant concepts are substitutes/complements, and normal/inferior goods.

E (Effects): The fourth step calls for analysis of the size of the effects of the change on such matters as price, quantity, and total outlay. Relevant concepts are elasticities of demand and supply, and the time-period. For type C2 causes, the question of how excess supply or demand is allocated should be considered (e.g., whether by queues, black markets, rationing, sellers' or buyers' preferences, or by other means). Secondary effects on related markets may sometimes be important.

F (Finale): The final step is for comments on the efficiency and equity aspects of resource allocations. Arguments in favour of the price mechanism and causes of market failure are likely to be relevant. Economic policies should be judged against their objectives, and alternative policies considered. Positive and normative aspects should, as far as possible, be separated.

in direct proportion to changes in output. Buffer stock schemes – whereby the state sells to offset price rises, and buys to offset price falls – can be analysed using simple supply and demand analysis. We cannot spare the space for it here.[1]

Questions

1 Which of the following problems would be classed as C1 or C2 problems?
  (i) Introducing a price floor above free-market equilibrium.
  (ii) Fixing a legal maximum price above free-market equilibrium.
  (iii) Paying 50 per cent of all charges for tooth extractions in the NHS.

2 Under what circumstances would a unit tax on a good leave both market price and quantity bought unaltered?

3 Is the following statement True or False? 'If the state imposes a maximum price below free-market equilibrium, the excess demand will have to be allocated by queues, rationing, sellers' preferences, or haphazardly.'

4 A local government authority sends officials to a vegetable market with instructions to collect an immediate and once-for-all £25 poll tax on every trader for that day only. Which of the seven diagrams in the chapter would be most useful for analysing its effects?

5 Under what circumstances would a unit subsidy on a good lead to a fall in market price exactly equal to the subsidy?

6 Which of the following policies is most appropriate for dealing with problems affecting farmers which arise out of the cobweb theorem?
  (i) price floors, (ii) buffer stocks, (iii) production quotas, (iv) price ceilings, (v) production-related subsidies.

---

1 See 1PE8.

PART

3

Intermediate Microeconomics

Preface to Part 3

Part 3 of this book takes the subject-matter of micro-economics further in several ways. We delve deeper into what is called the theory of the firm. We look more closely at the costs and revenues of businesses and consider how they affect their behaviour. We drop some of the simplifying assumptions of Part 2, in particular that buyers and sellers are price-takers, and look at behaviour under monopoly (single seller), and other business forms, such as oligopoly (few sellers). We also analyse markets for factors of production.

The first two chapters in Part 3 extend the analysis of the demand side of the market, introducing a new analytical technique which provides a better understanding of individual consumer behaviour, and which does not depend on the assumption that marginal utility can be measured.

11 Indifference Curves[1]

In this chapter we look at the theory of consumer behaviour in greater depth than we did in Chapters 4 and 5. We avoid the assumption that marginal utility can be measured or compared, though the final conclusions we reach are similar to those based on that assumption.

We begin by studying the behaviour of a single consumer, whom we call Chris, who has a given money income and wants to allocate that income between two goods, which we call eggs and bacon. Before we can proceed, we need to know (i) what Chris *can* buy, and (ii) what she *would like* to buy. What Chris can buy depends on her income and the prices of eggs and bacon. What she would like to buy depends on her tastes.

THE BUDGET LINE

First, we show how to represent graphically the choices open to the consumer by constructing what is called a budget line. This shows all the combinations of the two goods that Chris can purchase, given her income and given the prices of the goods that she buys. To illustrate, we assume that Chris's money income is £10 per day, that eggs cost 50p per dozen while bacon is £1 per lb.

Table 11.1 shows some of the alternative combinations of eggs and bacon that can be bought with Chris's £10 income. If all of it is spent on bacon, 10lbs. can be bought. If all of it is spent on eggs, 20 dozen can be bought. Alternatively, any of the combinations listed in the table can be purchased, e.g. 9 lbs. of bacon and 2 dozen eggs, 1 lb. of bacon and 18 dozen eggs, and so forth.

TABLE 11.1 Maximum Available Quantities of Goods for a Consumer with a Given Income

Reference point	Eggs (dozen) (i)	Bacon (lbs.) (ii)
a	20	0
b	18	1
c	16	2
d	14	3
e	12	4
f	10	5
g	8	6
h	6	7
i	4	8
j	2	9
k	0	10

The data in Table 11.1 are plotted in Figure 11.1. We measure quantities of eggs and bacon on the two axes.

1 This chapter may be omitted by students following a syllabus that excludes indifference curve analysis.

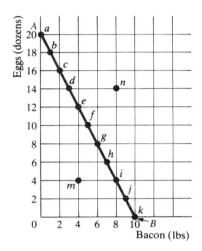

FIGURE 11.1 The Consumer's Budget Line, *AB*, shows all combinations of two goods that can be purchased with given prices and income. Given a price of eggs of 50p per dozen, and a price of bacon of £1 per lb., the consumer with an income of £10 can buy all combinations of eggs and bacon along *AB*.

Each point in the diagram, labelled *a* to *k*, corresponds to a row in the table. If the consumer is at point *a*, all income is spent on eggs; at point *k*, all income is spent on bacon; at point *b*, 18 dozen eggs are bought *and* 1 lb. of bacon, and so forth.

Next we join all the points in the figure with a straight line. The resulting line is called the consumer's BUDGET LINE (or CONSUMPTION POSSIBILITY LINE). It shows all of the combinations of the two commodities – those shown in the table and intermediate ones as well – that the consumer can buy by spending all of her income.

Attainable and unattainable combinations: But what about other points on the graph? Point *m*, inside the budget line, for example, shows an *attainable* purchase of 4 dozen eggs and 4 lbs. of bacon. However, at point *m*, Chris would not be using all her income. At the stated prices and assumed income, it would be possible to buy more of one or both goods.

Point *n*, beyond the budget line, on the other hand, shows an *unattainable* combination, 14 dozen eggs and 8 lbs. of bacon which Chris simply cannot purchase with an income of £10 a day when faced with the stated prices.

Changes in Income

What happens to Chris's budget line when her income changes, *while prices remain constant*? We consider this question with the aid of Figure 11.2, where the line *AB* repeats the budget line in Figure 11.1. Suppose, for example, Chris's income falls from £10 to £5, while the prices of eggs and bacon are unchanged. The quantities of the two goods that she can buy are cut in half. If she buys no bacon, only 10 dozen eggs can be bought. Alternatively, if she buys no eggs then she can purchase only 5 lbs. of bacon. All the new combinations of eggs and bacon now available to our impoverished consumer are given on the new budget line *CD* in Figure 11.2. Note that this line is *parallel* to the old budget line *AB*, but closer to the origin, O, of the diagram.

Now, consider what happens to the budget line if Chris's income doubles to £20. Twice as much bacon and eggs become attainable. If only eggs are bought, at the unchanged price of 50p per dozen, 40 dozen are now in range. If only bacon is bought, 20 lbs. can be purchased. Indeed, any combination of the two goods shown by points on the new budget line *EF* are now available. Note again that *EF* is *parallel* to both *AB* and *CD*, but is further from the origin, O, of the diagram.

We conclude that variations in a consumer's income shift the budget line in a parallel fashion, inwards towards the origin when income falls, outwards away from the origin when income rises.

Changes in Relative Prices

Consider, next, what happens to the budget line when relative prices change while the consumer's money income remains constant. We show this with the aid of Figure 11.3, which reproduces the original budget line *AB*.

Suppose we change the price of eggs while holding the price of bacon and consumer income constant. Let us say that the price of bacon is halved, to 50p per lb. Chris's £10 income will now buy twice as much bacon – 20 lbs. instead of 10 lbs., provided she buys no eggs. So point B_1 is a point on her new budget line, replacing point B. Since Chris's income and the price of eggs are unchanged, however, she can still buy only 20 dozen eggs, the same number of eggs as before, provided she buys no bacon at all. So point A is on both the old and the new budget lines. To complete Chris's budget line after the fall in the price of bacon, we simply join points A and B_1. She can buy any of the combinations of eggs and bacon represented by points on the line B_1.

Suppose now that instead of the price of bacon falling, it rises – say it doubles, to £2 per lb. (money income and the price of eggs remaining unchanged as before). If she spends all her income on bacon, Chris can now only buy 5 lbs. Hence point B_2 is on her second new budget line. Point A is, of course, still on the new budget line. So to complete this budget line we need only to join points A and B_2.

We now have three budget lines, each representing a different relative price of bacon to eggs, *AB*, AB_1, and AB_2. Note that the three lines have different slopes; the 'steepest' line, AB_2, shows the highest relative price of bacon, where 1 dozen eggs 'buys' $\frac{1}{2}$ lb. of bacon; while the 'least steep' line, AB_1, shows the lowest price of bacon, where 1 dozen eggs 'buys' 20 lbs. of bacon.

The slope of the budget line measures the quantity of eggs you must sacrifice to get a unit of bacon. Thus, if bacon costs twice as much per unit as eggs, you have to sacrifice two units of eggs to get one unit of bacon. This is the price of bacon in terms of eggs.[1]

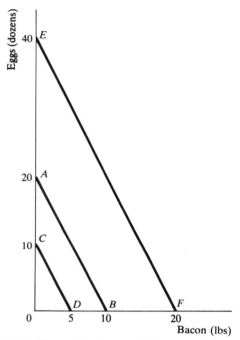

FIGURE 11.2 **Changes in Consumer's Income,** with constant *relative* prices, *shift* the budget line in a *parallel* fashion. Consumer income along *EF* is double that along *AB*, which is double that along *CD*.

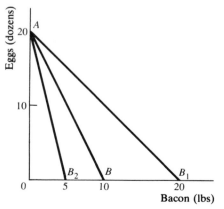

FIGURE 11.3 **Changes in Relative Prices,** with constant money income, alter the *slope* of the budget line. With an income of £10 and an egg price of 50p per dozen, the budget lines for bacon prices of 50p, £1 and £2 per lb. are AB_1, *AB*, and AB_2, respectively.

---

1 The slope of the budget line is given by the price of bacon/the price of eggs. Thus, if bacon costs £1.00 per lb. while eggs cost 50 pence per dozen, the slope is £1/50p = 2. The slope of the budget line is the same, 2, if the price of bacon is £2 per lb. and the price of eggs is £1 per dozen.

Each line in Figure 11.3 shows the quantity of bacon that can be bought instead of 20 dozen (*A*) eggs, i.e. the quantity of one good that has to be given up to be able to buy units of the other good. Thus, when the money price of bacon equals the money price of eggs – i.e. the price of 1lb. of bacon is 1 dozen eggs – the budget line has the slope of AB_1. When the price of bacon halves, so that only half the quantity of bacon has to be given up in order to buy a given quantity of eggs, the budget line, AB_1, is less steep than that of *AB*. Finally, when the price of eggs in terms of bacon doubles, so that twice as much bacon has to be given up in order to buy a given quantity of eggs, the budget line, AB_2, is steeper than that of *AB*. (It may help you to know that the argument is exactly the same as that used to explain why the slope of the production possibility curve showed the opportunity cost of one good in terms of the other. See Chapter 1, pp.9–10.)[1]

Note that the slope of the budget line depends only on the relative prices of eggs and bacon. Changes in consumer income (or equal proportionate changes in the prices of both goods) leave the slope of the budget line unchanged – they merely shift it, in parallel fashion, as we showed in the previous section.

CONSUMERS' TASTES

In order to analyse consumer behaviour we said that we needed two pieces of information: (i) what the consumer can buy, and (ii) what the consumer would like to buy. We already know how to deal with the first of these, by means of a budget line. We now turn to the second. What the consumer would like to buy depends on his or her tastes.

In this treatment, we use the concept of indifference curves to display the consumer's tastes. This treatment has two advantages over the familiar demand curves.

(1) Indifference curves do not need to rely on all the *ceteris paribus* assumptions of demand curves. Indifference curves allow us to consider the behaviour of consumers when they are faced with combinations, or 'bundles', of more than one commodity. For example, one bundle might be 3 oranges and 5 apples, while another bundle might be 6 oranges and 2 apples.

(2) Indifference curve analysis avoids the need to measure utility in *absolute* terms (called a CARDINAL measure) and requires only that the consumer be able to state his rank order of preference for goods (called an ORDINAL measure). This means that our analysis will be based on a consumer preferring one bundle of goods to another. It will not require the rather unrealistic assumption that a consumer can tell us *how much better off* he or she feels from consuming one bundle of goods rather than another.

An Indifference Curve

Now let our consumer, Chris, have some quantity of each of the two goods, say 18 units of eggs and 10 units of bacon. Now offer Chris an alternative bundle of goods, say 13 units of eggs and 15 units of bacon. This alternative has 5 fewer units of eggs and 5 more units of bacon than the first one. Which bundle Chris prefers depends on the relative valuation that she places on 5 more units of bacon and 5 fewer units of eggs. If she values the extra bacon more than the forgone eggs, she will prefer the new bundle to the original one. If she values the additional bacon less than the reduced eggs, she will prefer the original bundle.

There is a third alternative. If Chris values the extra bacon the same as she values the forgone eggs, she would gain equal satisfaction from the two alternative bundles of bacon and eggs. In this case, Chris is said to be *indifferent* between the two bundles.

Assume that, after much trial and error, a number of bundles have been identified, each of which gives equal satisfaction. These are shown in Table 11.2. The table shows that Chris gets equal satisfaction, and is thus indifferent, among bundle *a* (30 eggs and 5 bacon), bundle *b* (18 eggs and 10 bacon) and so on down to bundle *f*.

TABLE 11.2 Alternative Bundles Giving a Consumer Equal Satisfaction. These bundles all lie on a single indifference curve

Reference point	Eggs (dozens)	Bacon (lbs.)
a	30	5
b	18	10
c	13	15
d	10	20
e	8	25
f	7	30

Now consider Figure 11.4. This shows points *a* to *f* plotted from Table 11.2. There will, of course, be combinations of the two commodities, other than those set out in the table, that will give the same level of satisfaction to

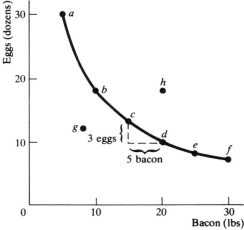

FIGURE 11.4 An Indifference Curve. Points on the curve, e.g. *a* to *f*, show combinations of eggs and bacon which yield the same level of satisfaction. Combinations such as *g* yield less, and as *h* yield more, satisfaction. The slope of the curve indicates the marginal rate of substitution between the two goods.

---

1 If we vary the price of eggs and hold constant money income and the price of bacon, all budget lines will start from the same point on the horizontal (bacon) axis – the steeper the line, the lower the price of eggs (the higher the price of bacon, as before).

the consumers. All of these combinations are shown in Figure 11.4 by the smooth curve that passes through the points plotted from the table.

This curve is an INDIFFERENCE CURVE and it shows all combinations of goods that yield the same satisfaction to the consumer.

In other words, a consumer is *indifferent* between the combinations indicated by all the points on one indifference curve.

Any points above and to the right of the curve show combinations of bacon and eggs that the consumer would prefer to combinations indicated by points on the curve. Consider, for example, the combination of 18 eggs and 20 bacon, which is represented by point *h* in the figure. Although it may not be obvious that this bundle must be preferred to bundle *f* (which has more bacon but less eggs), it is obvious that it will be preferred to bundle *c* because there is both less eggs and less bacon at *c* than at *h*.

Inspection of the graph shows that *any* point above the curve will be superior to *some* points on the curve in the sense that it will contain both more bacon and more eggs than those points on the curve. But since all points on the curve are equal in the consumer's eyes, the point above the curve must be superior to *all* points on the curve. By a similar argument, points below and to the left of the curve represent bundles of goods that are inferior to bundles represented by points on the curve.

Slope of an indifference curve

The indifference curve that we have drawn in Figure 11.4 has two basic characteristics. First, it slopes downward to the right – i.e. it has a negative slope. Second, its slope gets flatter and flatter as we move downwards along it to the right.

The slope was no accident. It reflects the basic assumptions of indifference theory. To see these assumptions we must first define a new term.

Marginal rate of substitution: We have seen that all the points on one indifference curve indicate combinations of the two commodities that give the consumer equal satisfaction. If we now compare two nearby points on an indifference curve, we can answer another question: how much of one commodity could the consumer give up in return for an additional unit of the other commodity, while her level of satisfaction stays the same?

The answer to this question measures what is called the marginal rate of substitution of eggs for bacon. The MARGINAL RATE OF SUBSTITUTION (MRS) is the amount of one commodity a consumer could give up to get one more unit of another commodity while leaving the level of satisfaction unchanged.

We are now ready for the first of the three basic assumptions of indifference theory.

(1) The first basic assumption of indifference theory is that the marginal rate of substitution is negative.

This means that to gain an *increase* in consumption of one commodity, the consumer is prepared to *reduce* her consumption of a second. Graphically, the negative marginal rate of substitution is shown by the downward slope of indifference curves.

Diminishing marginal rate of substitution: A basic idea of indifference theory is that the marginal rate of substitution between any two commodities depends on the amounts of the commodities currently being consumed by the consumer. Consider a case where the consumer has a lot of eggs and only a small amount of bacon. Common sense suggests that the consumer might be willing to give up quite a few of her plentiful eggs to get one unit more of very scarce bacon. Now consider a case where the consumer has only a few eggs and quite a lot of bacon. Common sense suggests that the consumer would be willing to give up only a few of her scarce eggs to get one more unit of already plentiful bacon.

(2) This example illustrates the second main assumption of indifference theory, the assumption of the DIMINISHING MARGINAL RATE OF SUBSTITUTION. In terms of our bacon-and-egg example, the assumption states that the fewer eggs (and the more bacon) the consumer has already, the smaller will be the number of eggs she will be willing to give up to get one further unit of bacon.[1]

TABLE 11.3 The Marginal Rate of Substitution Between Eggs and Bacon. The marginal rate of substitution of eggs for bacon declines as the quantity of bacon increases

Movement	Change in eggs (dozens)	Change in bacon (lbs.)	Marginal rate of substitution (i) ÷ (ii)
	(i)	(ii)	(iii)
a to *b*	− 12	+ 5	− 2.4
b to *c*	− 5	+ 5	− 1.0
c to *d*	− 3	+ 5	− 0.6
d to *e*	− 2	+ 5	− 0.4
e to *f*	− 1	+ 5	− 0.2

The assumption says that the marginal rate of substitution changes systematically as the amounts of two commodities consumed vary. Take any two commodities, A and B. The more A and the less B the consumer currently has, the less B that consumer will be willing to give up to get a further unit of A.

The assumption is illustrated in Table 11.3, which is based on the example of bacon and eggs in Table 11.2. When the consumer moves from *a* to *b*, she gives up 12 units of eggs and gains 5 units of bacon: she remains at the same level of overall satisfaction. The consumer at point

---

1 The student may wonder what relationship, if any, there is between the 'law' of diminishing MRS and that of diminishing marginal utility (MU) which we met in Chapter 4. The answer is that both are based on the idea that the value of units of a commodity to an individual tends to decline with increasing quantities of them. However, the two laws are in another way different, because diminishing MU is based on a cardinal measure of utility, while diminishing MRS is based only on an ordinal measure (see p.113, above).

a was prepared to sacrifice 12 eggs for 5 bacon, which is 2.4 units of eggs *per unit of bacon* obtained ($-12/5 = -2.4$). (Notice that the ratio is negative because the change in eggs is negative while the change in bacon is positive.) When she moves from *b* to *c*, she sacrifices 5 units of eggs for 5 units of bacon (a rate of substitution of 1 unit of eggs per unit of bacon). Column (iii) of the table shows the rate at which the consumer is prepared to sacrifice units of eggs per unit of bacon obtained. At first she will sacrifice 2.4 units of eggs to get 1 unit more of bacon, but as consumption of eggs diminishes and that of bacon increases, the consumer becomes less and less willing to sacrifice further eggs for more bacon.

Graphical representation of the MRS: The graphical representation of the marginal rate of substitution is also shown in Figure 11.4. The figure plots points *c* and *d* from Table 11.2. It shows that, in moving from *c* to *d*, the consumer needs 5 bacon to compensate for the loss of 3 eggs. Over this range, the rate at which the consumer will substitute eggs for bacon is 3/5 which, as Table 11.3 shows, is 0.6. In other words, she is prepared to give up 0.6 units of eggs for every additional unit of bacon that she gets over this range. Thus, the *MRS* is the slope of the line joining the two points in question.[1]

Now that you know that the marginal rate of substitution is given by the slope of the indifference curve, you may see that the graphical representation of the assumption of the diminishing marginal rate of substitution is that an indifference curve becomes flatter as the consumer moves downward to the right along the curve. In terms of the indifference curve in Figure 11.4, the *MRS* diminishes as the consumer moves down the curve because she is prepared to sacrifice fewer and fewer eggs to get one more unit of bacon. The gradually diminishing absolute value of the slope of the indifference curve reflects just this.

The Indifference Map

So far we have constructed a single indifference curve, a curve that relates to a particular level of satisfaction. To represent consumer tastes at higher and lower levels of satisfaction, we need other indifference curves. The whole range of tastes is expressed by a set ('family') of indifference curves known as an INDIFFERENCE MAP. On each curve, the level of satisfaction remains constant, but at a different level from every other curve. To relate one curve to the other, we introduce:

(3) the third basic assumption of indifference curve theory that more of any good is usually preferred to less of that good.

Now let us see how indifference curves order the level of satisfaction associated with various consumption bundles. Consider, for example, point *h* in Figure 11.5, which represents a combination of e_0 eggs and b_0 bacon. Compare it

1   This *MRS* is the average slope of the indifference curve, over this range of consumption. For a very small movement along the curve, the MRS becomes very close to being the slope of the curve. At any *point* on the curve, the *MRS* is the slope at that point.

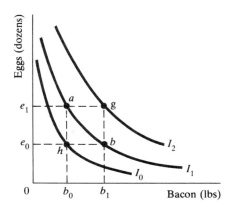

FIGURE 11.5 An Indifference Map. The further from the origin of the graph, the higher the level of satisfaction represented by an indifference curve.

with combination *a* on indifference curve I_1, which represents e_1 eggs and b_0 bacon. Combination *a* has more eggs and the same amount of bacon as combination *h* and, given our assumption that more of any good is preferred to less, *a* must be preferred to *h*. Point *h* cannot be on the same indifference curve as *a*, and the indifference curve I_0 that does pass through *h* must represent a lower level of satisfaction than the curve I_1, that passes through *a*. Any points on I_0 represent combinations of eggs and bacon which yield the same satisfaction as any other points. They all yield less satisfaction than any points on I_1.

Consider, in similar fashion, point *g* in Figure 11.5, which represents e_1 eggs and b_1 bacon. Compare it with a point such as *b* on I_1. Clearly *g* is preferable to *b*, because it represents more eggs and the same amount of bacon as *b*. Therefore *g* must lie on a different, higher, indifference curve than I_1. We have drawn this preferred curve through *g* on the graph, and labelled it I_2. Each point on I_2 yields equal satisfaction to any other point on it. They all yield higher satisfaction than any points on I_1.

Inspection of the graph shows that any point above and to the right of any indifference curve will be superior to some points on that curve, in that it contains more eggs and more bacon than those points on the curve. But, since the bundles represented by all points on a curve are equal to each other in the eyes of the consumer, the point above the curve must be superior to all points on the curve.

Hence, we may conclude that indifference curves represent higher levels of satisfaction the further they are from the origin of the graph. All points on I_2 are superior to all points on I_1, which are in turn superior to all points on I_0. Conversely, of course, indifference curves represent lower levels of satisfaction the closer they lie to the origin of the graph.

Indifference curves cannot intersect each other: A final point which needs stating about the indifference map is that no two indifference curves can intersect (or touch) each other. In Figure 11.6, we draw two intersecting indifference curves. We have written WRONG over it, because it is an impossible situation.

The argument is brief. Point *g* on I_B is preferred to *h* on

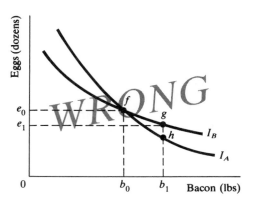

FIGURE 11.6 Indifference Curves Cannot Intersect Each Other. The combination at f cannot yield the same satisfaction both at g and at h.

must be superior to h. So we have a contradiction: g cannot be both equal to, and superior to, h.

Therefore, indifference curves cannot intersect. If they did it would mean that some combinations of goods were simultaneously superior to, as well as equal to, other combinations.

Indifference curves with special shapes

It may help you to become familiar with indifference curves to think about the meaning of some which have special shapes, though this should not be taken to mean that all are necessarily rare. Figure 11.7 shows six of them.

(i) Perfect substitutes: Goods which are identical to each other in the mind of the consumer are perfect substitutes – e.g. pins that come in green packs and pins that come in red packs for a colour-blind consumer. *Indifference curves for perfect substitutes are straight lines.* The slopes of the lines indicate the rate at which a consumer can substitute units of one good for units of another, while holding total utility constant. Consider our example of pins in coloured packs: 500-pin red packs would be substituted by the consumer at different rates for 500-pin green packs and for 1000-pin green packs, because the larger packs give greater total satisfaction. Thus, in Figure 11.7(i), I^β shows an

I_A by the assumption that more is preferred to less (g has more eggs and the same bacon as h). But h must give the same satisfaction as f (representing e_0 eggs plus b_0 bacon), since they are both on indifference curve I_A. However, g must also give the same satisfaction as f, since they are both on indifference curve I_B. It follows, therefore, that g and h should give the same satisfaction, since both give the same satisfaction as f. But we started by showing that g

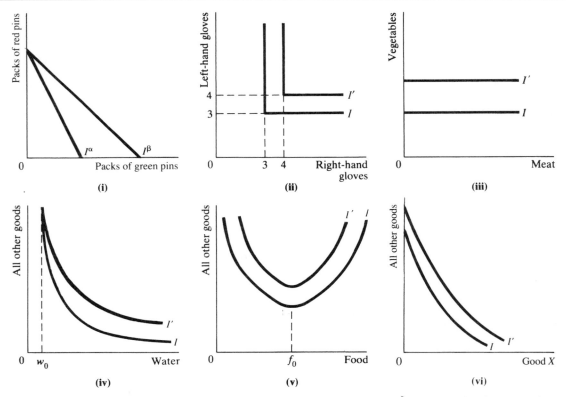

FIGURE 11.7 Indifference Curves with Special Shapes. (i) Perfect substitutes: I^β is where red and green packs contain the same number of pins; I^α is where green packs contain twice as many pins as red packs. (ii) Perfect complements: goods needed in fixed proportions. (iii) One good (meat) gives zero utility. (iv) An absolute necessity: a minimum of w_0 of one good (water) is needed to sustain life. (v) Forced consumption of one good (food) gives negative utility beyond quantity f_0. (vi) One good (X) is not consumed at all.

indifference curve for packs of equal size, while I^a shows an indifference curve when green packs contain twice as many pins as red packs. (Note, in this diagram only, all points on both indifference curves yield the same satisfaction. That is why we have labelled them I^a and I^β, in contrast to all other diagrams where, e.g., one curve I gives less satisfaction than a higher curve, I'.)

(ii) Perfect complements: Goods which are needed in fixed proportions are perfect complements, e.g. left-hand and right-hand gloves. No additional unit of one of them raises the level of consumer satisfaction, without an additional unit of the other. *Indifference curves for perfect complements are 'L-shaped'*, as in Figure 11.7(ii).

(iii) A good which gives zero utility: When a good gives no satisfaction at all, the consumer will not give up any quantity of another good for it, e.g. meat for a vegetarian. *Indifference curves in such cases are straight lines parallel to the axis measuring quantities of the unwanted good.* In Figure 11.7(iii), consumer satisfaction is entirely dependent on vegetable consumption.

(iv) An absolute necessity: When a minimum amount of a good, such as water, is regarded as an absolute necessity, the quantity of other goods a consumer would accept in return for cutting down on the necessity would become increasingly vast – approaching infinity at the minimum level necessary, for instance, to sustain life itself. *Indifference curves in such cases become vertical (as in Figure 11.7(iv)) at the minimum level (w_0)*, at which point also the marginal rate of substitution reaches infinity.

(v) A good that confers negative utility after some level of consumption: Some goods may give positive satisfaction up to a point, after which they are so disliked that utility would be negative if a consumer were *forced* to consume them. *Indifference curves in such cases would slope upwards from the point at which disutility sets in*, as in Figure 11.7(v) beyond f_0 food consumption. The positive slope indicates that more of both goods gives the same satisfaction as less of both of them, the extra utility from one cancelling out the extra disutility from the other. Many goods would fall into this category if consumption was compulsory, e.g. all foods if forced feeding were practised, but such cases are usually ignored as it is rare to find a commodity that consumers cannot reject if they want to.

(vi) A good that may not be consumed at all: If a consumer consumes a zero amount of a commodity, one or more *indifference curves must cut the axis measuring quantities of other goods*, as in Figure 11.7(vi).[1] Many commodities are of this kind. Think of all the thousands of goods your family does not buy – hundreds of different kinds of foodstuffs, brands of toothpaste, etc., etc.

There is one other special feature about Figure 11.7(vi). It is not restricted to showing only two commodities. The vertical axis measures quantities of 'all other goods' (sometimes called the COMPOSITE COMMODITY). This is a convenient way of overcoming the fact that indifference curves have to be drawn on two-dimensional paper, and it will prove very useful at times.

CONSUMER EQUILIBRIUM

We are now ready to bring together the budget line and the indifference map, to show how a consumer trying to maximize satisfaction will allocate income between two commodities.

In Figure 11.8 we portray four of Chris's indifference curves superimposed on the diagram from Figure 11.1, which shows her budget line on the original assumption that she has an income of £10 and is faced with prices of eggs and bacon of 50p and £1 respectively. Chris can attain any point in the area bounded by her budget line and the two axes. However, we already know that points *inside* the area mean that she is not spending all her income.

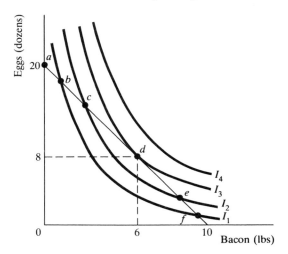

FIGURE 11.8 Consumer Equilibrium. With given income and prices, represented by the budget line, the consumer maximizes satisfaction by moving to the highest indifference curve, I_3, where it is tangent to the budget line, at point d.

Suppose Chris starts at point a in Figure 11.8, spending all of her income on eggs. Remember, all the points on her budget line are available to her. Imagine that she considers buying some bacon and reducing her purchases of eggs. In the graph, this means she moves downward to the right along her budget line. Let us compare her levels of satisfaction at points a, b, c, d, e and f.

As Chris moves down her budget line she reaches higher and higher indifference curves which represent higher and higher levels of satisfaction – until she reaches point d. If she moves beyond that point, to e for example, she arrives at lower indifference curves and hence achieves lower levels of satisfaction.

---

1 For this result to hold, strictly, the budget line must be steeper than the indifference curve at the point of intersection of the axis.

Utility Maximization

The customer's highest level of satisfaction is at point *d*.

Graphically, consumer equilibrium is identified at the point where the budget line just touches but does not cut, i.e. is tangent to, an indifference curve.

To understand this, consider a situation where Chris is *not* maximizing her satisfaction. For instance suppose that she is at *h* in Figure 11.9. The slope of her indifference curve, I_1, at point *h* is different from the slope of the budget line. We know from Chris's indifference curve that she would be as well off if she gave up $h-k$ eggs and received $m-k$ bacon in return. But we know from the budget line that she could obtain more than $m-k$ bacon by reducing her consumption of eggs by $h-k$. In effect, she is *exchanging*[1] $h-k$ eggs for $y-k$ bacon, landing up at point *y* on the budget line. Because *y* is on a higher indifference curve than *h*, Chris has raised her level of satisfaction by buying more bacon and less eggs than at point *h*.[1]

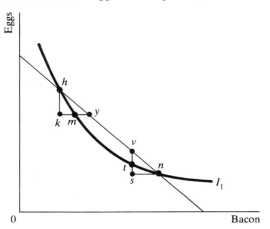

FIGURE 11.9 Consumer Disequilibrium. The consumer cannot be maximizing satisfaction at any point where the budget line cuts an indifference curve; for example she would be better off at *y* than at *h*.

Alternatively, consider why Chris would not choose to remain at another point, *n*, on the budget line. The slope of her indifference curve through *n* tells us that she would be as well off if she gave up $n-s$ bacon in return for $t-s$ eggs. But the slope of the budget line shows that she could exchange $n-s$ bacon for $v-s$ eggs, which is greater than $t-s$. Therefore, when Chris is at *n*, she would prefer to exchange bacon for eggs at the price available in the market.

It is only when the budget line is tangent to the highest attainable indifference curve that the consumer is in equilibrium, maximizing her satisfaction.

The argument as expressed in terms of Figure 11.9 is perfectly satisfactory, but it may be helpful also to explain consumer maximizing behaviour without the use of a graph. The explanation runs in terms of the relationship between the marginal rate of substitution between commodities and the ratio of their prices.

Let us return to our example of eggs and bacon, and start again with a disequilibrium situation. So long as the price of bacon in terms of eggs differs from Chris's valuation of extra bacon in terms of eggs sacrificed (given by her marginal rate of substitution between eggs and bacon), Chris would find her satisfaction increases if she exchanges one commodity for the other.

Consider the simplest case, where Chris's marginal rate of substitution of eggs for bacon is equal to unity (MRS = 1), i.e. she is indifferent between her present bundle and another bundle containing one more bacon and one less egg. Now suppose that the price of eggs is 50p and the price of bacon is £1. Chris can increase her satisfaction by exchanging bacon for eggs. She can get 2 eggs for 1 bacon, which must make her better off, given that she would be exactly as well off with only 1 extra egg instead of the unit of bacon.

Now, suppose that Chris's MRS stays the same, but the price of eggs is £1 and the price of bacon is 50p. In these circumstances, Chris can raise her level of satisfaction by giving up 1 egg in exchange for 2 bacon.

Only when the marginal rate of substitution of eggs for bacon is equal to the price of bacon in terms of eggs, is the consumer in equilibrium, maximizing her satisfaction.[1]

Shifts in the Budget Line

We deal now with two changes which can affect the consumer's equilibrium position: a change in income and a change in relative prices. We assume that the consumer's tastes, i.e. the indifference map, is unchanged.

A change in income

As we saw in the previous chapter, variations in income lead to *parallel* shifts of the budget line. For each level of income there will, of course, be an equilibrium position at which an indifference curve is tangent to the relevant budget line. Each such equilibrium position means that the consumer is doing as well as she possibly can for that level of income.

An example is shown in Figure 11.10. As Chris's income increases, the budget line moves outwards from *AB* through *CD* to *EF*. The combinations of eggs and bacon that she selects can be found by reading off the quantities of the two goods corresponding to the points of tangency of each budget line with an indifference curve. If we move the budget line through all possible income levels and join

---

1 When we talk of Chris 'in effect exchanging quantities of one good' for another, we do not mean that she literally takes some of one good to the market and barters them for quantities of another good. We mean that she reduces consumption of one good and uses the income saved to buy another.

1 As stated earlier, the slope of the budget line measures the price of bacon in terms of eggs (i.e. the quantity of eggs you must sacrifice for a unit of bacon), and is given by the price of bacon/the price of eggs. Thus, if bacon costs £1.00 per lb. while eggs cost 50 pence per dozen, the slope of the budget line is £1/50p = 2. The consumer will be in equilibrium if the marginal rate of substitution of eggs for bacon is also 2.

up all the points of equilibrium, such as x, y and z, we trace out what is known as an INCOME-CONSUMPTION LINE. This line shows how consumption changes as income changes, with relative prices held constant.

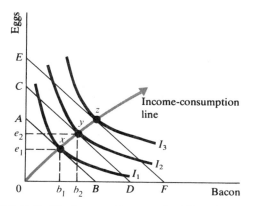

FIGURE 11.10 **The Income-Consumption Line.** As income changes, prices remaining constant, the consumer finds equilibrium where parallel budget lines are tangent to indifference curves, e.g. at points x, y and z. Bacon and eggs are normal goods, since consumption of both is greater on higher than on lower indifference curves (i.e. at higher real incomes).

The shape of the income-consumption line depends on the nature of the goods. In particular, it depends on whether a good is normal or inferior. In Figure 11.10, bacon and eggs were assumed to be normal goods, so the consumption of both rises as the consumer moves to higher indifference curves, i.e. real income increases. For example, with an outward shift of the budget line from AB to CD, consumption of bacon increases from b_1 to b_2 and consumption of eggs increases from e_1 to e_2. In Figure 11.11, we show the case of an inferior good, sausages, and a normal good, steak. The outward shift of the budget line from AB to CD in this case leads to a *fall* in the quantity of sausages purchased from q_1 to q_2.[1]

A change in relative prices

We saw earlier in this chapter that a change in the relative prices of two commodities causes the slope of the budget line to change. We illustrate a change in the price of bacon in the upper section (i) of Figure 11.12.

Assume the consumer has an income which allows the purchase of either A eggs and no bacon, or B bacon and no eggs. Given the budget line AB, the consumer chooses point 1 on the graph, buying q_0 bacon. The money price of bacon now falls, while income and the price of eggs remain unchanged. The budget line pivots, to AC. A further fall in the price of bacon pivots the line to AD. Two more points of equilibrium, labelled 2 and 3 in the Figure, can be identified as tangents of AC and AD with indifference curves I_1 and I_2. The quantity of bacon con-

1 In order to avoid cluttering the diagram with too many lines, we have not shown that steak is a normal good in Figure 11.11. You should be able to do so by dropping perpendiculars from the equilibrium positions to the vertical axes.

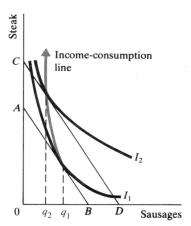

FIGURE 11.11 **The Income-Consumption Line for an Inferior Good.** Sausages are an inferior good, since the quantity consumed, q_4, is less on indifference curve I_2, which represents higher real income, than on I_1 (q_3).

sumed rises to q_1 and then to q_2 at these lower prices of bacon.

If we move the budget line through all possible prices of bacon and join up all the points of equilibrium, we trace out what is known as a PRICE-CONSUMPTION LINE. This line shows how consumption of bacon changes as the price of bacon changes, with income and the price of eggs held constant.

Indifference Curve Analysis and the Conventional Demand Curve

The price-consumption line provides information which can be used to construct a conventional demand curve, such as we encountered in Part 2 of this book. We can do this with Figure 11.12, exactly as it stands, if we assume that there are only two goods, eggs and bacon, or if we let eggs stand for 'all other goods' (the composite commodity, see above, p.117).

The lower part of the diagram, Figure 11.12(ii), derives the demand curve for bacon which, you will remember, shows the quantities of bacon demanded at different bacon prices, with money income and the prices of other goods being held constant. If we assume the consumer has a money income which allows the purchase of A eggs, while we vary only the price of bacon, we get, as you know, the price-consumption line, which contains exactly the information which we need to plot the demand curve. Each point on the price-consumption line corresponds to one price of bacon and one quantity demanded. The price of bacon is given by the slope of the budget line, while the quantity demanded is found by simply dropping a perpendicular to the bacon axis.

Note that the *horizontal* axis of Figure 11.12(i) is exactly the same as Figure 11.12(ii) – both measure the quantity of bacon. The *vertical* axis is, however, different. In the upper part (i), we show the price of bacon, indirectly, by

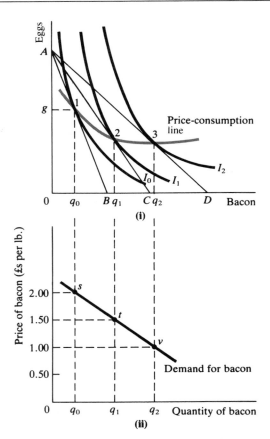

(i)

(ii)

FIGURE 11.12 A Price-Consumption Line and the Conventional Demand Curve. In part (i), as the price of eggs and money income remain constant, a falling price of bacon pivots the budget line around A in an anti-clockwise direction. The resulting points (1, 2, 3) of tangency of budget lines with indifference curves, trace out the price-consumption curve.

In part (ii) the conventional demand curve is derived from information in part (i). The quantity axes of the two parts of the diagram are the same. The vertical axis in (ii) measures the price of bacon which is only indirectly determined from the slope of the budget line in (i).

the slope of the budget line. In the lower part (ii), we measure the price of bacon directly on the axis.

Given the budget line AB, Chris finds her equilibrium at position 1 in Figure 11.12(i) where indifference curve I_0 is tangent to the budget line. At the given price, she uses $A - g$ of her income to buy q_0 bacon (spending g, therefore, on all other goods). To derive a point on Chris's demand curve, all we need to do is to plot point s in the lower part of the diagram, showing that q_0 bacon is demanded at a price of £2.00. To find other points on the demand curve, we pivot the budget line around A and read off the quantity of bacon demanded at different prices. For example, when the price of bacon is £1.50 per lb., the budget line is AC. At this lower price, q_1 bacon is demanded. We can then plot a second point, t, on the demand curve in the lower part of the diagram showing the price of £1.50 directly and the same quantity, q_1, on the horizontal axis. If we perform this exercise for all possible points on the price-consumption curve, we trace out the conventional demand

curve, showing directly the relationship between prices and quantities demanded for bacon.

We showed the effect of a change in relative prices in Figure 11.12(i), when we derived the price-consumption curve. However, we can now take the analysis further. Indifference curves can be used to divide the effects of a price change into what are called the 'income' and 'substitution' effects. First, we shall explain the nature of these two effects.

Income and Substitution Effects of a Price Change

Reconsider what happened in Figure 11.12(i). Figure 11.13 reproduces a part of that diagram without the indifference curves. As before, we assume an initial money income and the relative prices of eggs and bacon as given by the budget line AB. Now, the price of bacon falls, *ceteris paribus*, so that the budget line becomes AC.

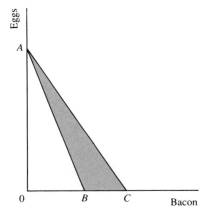

FIGURE 11.13 A Change in Relative Prices. A fall in the price of bacon shifting the budget line from AB to AC brings all combinations of eggs and bacon in the shaded area within the range of the consumer.

The effect is to increase the quantities of both eggs *and* bacon within Chris's reach. All combinations represented by points within the shaded area between the two budget lines, become available for her to buy. All points in that area, except for those along the horizontal axis, give the consumer more of either good with no less of the other good than before. Yet only the price of bacon has fallen. How can we explain the other points as being now available? The answer is that when the price of bacon falls, although *money* income remains constant, *real* income rises – more goods can be bought with the unchanged money income. Consequently, the consumer can buy more of both goods. The effect on the demand for bacon of the rise in real income induced by the fall in the price of bacon is known as the INCOME EFFECT of the price change.

The substitution effect of the price change is easier to explain. It refers to the effect on demand of the change in relative prices, pure and simple – in our example, of the fact that bacon is cheaper *relative* to eggs.

To summarize: the income effect of a price change results from the change in real income that automatically occurs when the price of a good changes, while money income is held constant. The substitution effect of a price change results from the change in relative prices.

In order to identify the income effect, we need to hold relative prices constant. To identify the substitution effect, we need to hold real income constant. Indifference curve analysis allows us to separate out these two effects. Let us see how it works.

In Figure 11.14, we show our consumer, Chris, faced with a budget line AB. Her equilibrium is at point 1, where q_1 bacon is consumed. Now let the price of bacon fall, while money income and the price of eggs remain the same. Her new budget line is AC and her new equilibrium is at point 3 on indifference curve I_2, where q_3 bacon is purchased.

The substitution effect

We can isolate the substitution effect of the price change in the following manner. We hold Chris's real income constant, and see what she would do if just relative prices changed.

Chris would remain on indifference curve I_1, but she will not maximize satisfaction at point 1, because relative prices have changed. They are no longer given by the slope AB, but by the slope AC. So, to find her best combination of eggs and bacon, we ask where on her indifference curve,

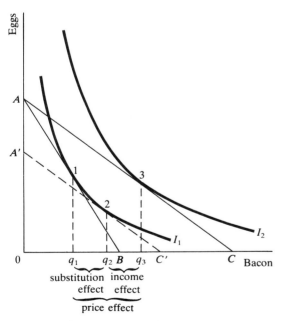

FIGURE 11.14 The Income and Substitution Effects of a Price Change. The consumer, faced with the budget line AB, starts in equilibrium at point 1. The price of bacon falls, shifting the budget line to AC. The substitution effect consists of the move from 1 to 2, where relative prices change while real income is held constant. The income effect consists of the move from 2 to 3, where real income changes while relative prices are held constant.

BOX 11.1 UK Household Expenditure

selected items (percentage of total expenditure)

	1981	1985	1989
Food	16.3	14.4	12.4
Alcohol & tobacco	10.9	10.7	8.9
Clothing	6.7	7.0	6.2
Fuel	5.1	4.9	3.6
Household goods & services	6.9	6.7	6.8
Transport & communication	17.2	17.4	18.1
Recreation & education	9.4	9.4	9.4

Source: Social Trends, 1991 (HMSO, 1991).

Over a hundred years ago, the German statistician Ernest Engel (contemporary with, but not the same person as Friedrich Engels, famous for his association with Karl Marx) studied the relationship between income and expenditure on certain classes of commodities. Engel's Law, named after him, states that the proportion of income spent on food tends to fall as income rises.

The table above reports details collected annually in the government's Family Expenditure Survey. Additional information about the level of real income over the years 1981–89 is as follows: 1981 = 100, 1985 = 111, 1989 = 127.

Questions

1 Does the data in the table support Engel's Law? Are there other commodities that might be subject to the 'law'?

2 Do the reported facts suggest that any commodity groups are more likely to be normal rather than inferior goods? What extra data would help you answer this question with more confidence?

3 Between 1981 and 1989, prices rose by the following: food +33 per cent, alcohol and tobacco +60 per cent, clothing +16 per cent, fuel +36 per cent, the general price level +43 per cent. Does this information give you any idea of the likely income and substitution effects of price changes for food, and other commodities?

I_1, she will settle. The answer is that she will choose the point on that curve where the new relative price of bacon in terms of eggs is equal to her marginal rate of substitution of eggs for bacon. As we know, this is where the indifference curve is tangent to the line representing the ratio: price of bacon/price of eggs.

To find this point, we construct the line $A'C'$, parallel to AC, and tangent also to I_1. Since $A'C'$ and AC are parallel, they have the same slope; and, since the point of tangency of $A'C'$ with I_1 is Chris's equilibrium position, we can say that she will maximize her satisfaction at point 2, buying q_2 bacon, if the price of bacon falls and her real income is held constant. The difference between her consumption of bacon before the price fall, q_1, and her consumption after the price fall, q_2, is $q_2 - q_1$, which is the substitution effect of the price change.

The income effect

We have divided the full price effect into two parts – the income and substitution effects. We could, therefore, deduce the size of the income effect immediately as $q_3 - q_2$ bacon, being the difference between the total increase in quantity $q_3 - q_1$ minus the substitution effect, of $q_2 - q_1$ bacon. However, it is important to understand how the income effect is derived. Conceptually, the pure income effect of a price change is the extent to which a change in real income affects quantity purchased, while relative prices are held constant.

When we isolated the substitution effect we held real income constant by confining Chris to her original indifference curve, I_1. Now, to identify the income effect, we release her from this restriction and allow her to attain I_2. We want to observe her behaviour when we allow her income to rise but no change occurs in relative prices, because we are now interested only in the income effect of the price change.

All we need to do to isolate the income effect is to observe the difference in Chris's consumption of bacon

when the relative price of bacon is held constant, but her real income is allowed to rise as much as it would from the fall in price. This is done by holding the money prices of the two goods constant and raising her real income. In other words, we must compare her bacon consumption at point 3 with that at point 2, because the relative price of bacon is the same at both points, and only her real income has gone up from I_1 to I_2.

We can see from Figure 11.14 that Chris increases her consumption of bacon from q_2 to q_3, when the price of bacon is held constant but her real income rises. So the income effect of the price change is $q_3 - q_2$.

The last few paragraphs have been rather technical. It may be useful to summarize them. The effect of a change in the own price of a good on the consumer's purchases may be *conceptually* divided into two parts.

One part is due to a change in the purchasing power of the consumer's income caused by the price change with constant money income. The other part is due to the effect of the change in relative prices.

The former effect is the income effect. It shows the effect on quantity demanded of a move from one indifference curve to another (representing the change in real income). The latter effect is the substitution effect. It shows the change in quantity demanded as a result of moving along an indifference curve as relative prices change, while real income is held constant. The sum of the income and substitution effects may be described as the *net*, total, or price effect.[1]

Price effects with inferior goods

The example we have used to illustrate the breakdown of a price change into an income and a substitution effect concerned a normal good, i.e. one where quantity demanded is positively associated with income. With such goods, both the income and the substitution effect move *in the same direction*. The fall in the price of bacon led to a rise in quantity demanded, both because Chris substituted bacon for eggs and because her higher real income led her to buy more bacon.

When we are dealing with an inferior good, we must allow for an income effect which operates *in the opposite direction to the substitution effect*. If such a good falls in price, the substitution effect will still cause an increase in quantity purchased. But the income effect will cause a decrease in quantity. This is because the fall in price raises a consumer's real income which, for an inferior good, means that less will be demanded.

Economic theory alone cannot predict definitely whether

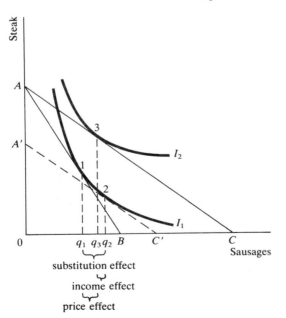

FIGURE 11.15 **The Income and Substitution Effect of a Change in Price for an Inferior Good.** This diagram is similar to Figure 11.14 except that the latter depicted a normal good and this Figure shows an inferior good. In this case the income effect (from 2 to 3) of a fall in the price of sausages (from the slope of AB to that of AC) works in the opposite direction to the substitution effect (from 1 to 2). The substitution effect is greater than the income effect, so that the demand curve is negatively sloped.

1 Income and substitution effects occur in practice simultaneously. It is only possible to isolate them conceptually. We have chosen to identify the substitution effect before the income effect, as do many textbooks. It is equally valid to reverse the process and show the substitution effect by comparing points of tangency at the new and the old relative prices on the indifference curve reached after the price change rather than on the initial indifference curve. Such a procedure would be likely to show some (small) difference in the relative sizes of the income and substitution effects, but not of the overall price effect. Neither approach is more correct than the other.

the income or substitution effect will predominate. Their relative strength is a question of fact, not of theory. But we can analyse the two cases.

In Figures 11.15 and 11.16 we distinguish two cases to show income, substitution and full price effects of the fall in the price of the (inferior) good, quantities of which are measured along the horizontal axis.

Case 1. The substitution effect exceeds the income effect: In Figure 11.15 the substitution effect is the stronger of the two. The goods we choose for illustrative purposes are the same as those for Figure 11.11 – steak, as the normal good, and sausages, as the inferior good.

The original equilibrium is at point 1. The consumer buys q_1 sausages. The price of sausages now falls, as indicated by the shift of the budget line from AB to AC. The substitution effect then shifts the consumer from point 1 to 2. It results in an increase in the quantity bought of $q_2 - q_1$. When the income effect is brought in, however, equilibrium moves from point 2 to point 3. Because sausages are assumed to be inferior goods, there is a decrease in quantity of $q_2 - q_3$, as a result of the income effect alone. The full price effect is for an increase in quantity of sausages bought of $q_3 - q_1$. This is made up of an *increase* of $q_2 - q_1$ and a *decrease* of $q_3 - q_2$. The substitution effect more than offsets the income effect.

Case 2. The income effect exceeds the substitution effect (Giffen goods): Figure 11.16 illustrates the extreme case of an inferior good where the income effect is greater than the substitution effect. As forewarned in Chapter 5, there is a special name for goods in this category. They are called

GIFFEN GOODS. The diagram is, as it happens, a little tricky to draw, but no more difficult to explain than Figure 11.15.

The original equilibrium is at point 1 with quantity q_1 consumed. The fall in price of the Giffen good shifts the budget line from AB to AC as before. The substitution effect of the price fall, as it must, leads the consumer to buy more of it, $q_2 - q_1$ in this case. However, the income effect with this inferior good, $q_2 - q_3$, is so large that it more than offsets the substitution effect.

The full effect of the fall in the price of a Giffen good is, therefore, a fall in the quantity demanded. This was one of our examples of exceptions to the 'law' that demand curves slope downwards, that we discussed in Chapter 5. However, we should remind you that there is no evidence that Giffen goods are any more than extremely rare phenomena, if they exist at all. We include them here for theoretical completeness.

Questions

1 Which One or More of the following are identified as being points on a consumer's budget line?
   (a) Combinations of goods which yield the same satisfaction to the consumer.
   (b) Combinations of goods which the consumer can purchase using all his income.
   (c) Prices of one of the goods in terms of the other.
   (d) The price of one of the goods in money terms.

2 What would happen to the consumer's budget line AB in Figure 11.2 in the following circumstances (assume *ceteris paribus*)?
   (i) Consumer's income changes to £15.
   (ii) The price of eggs changes to £1 per dozen.

3 Is the following statement True or False? 'An indifference curve has a negative slope which gets steeper and steeper as we move upwards to the left because of "diminishing marginal rate of substitution".'

4 In Figure 11.5, what represents the quantity of eggs that the consumer would sacrifice to have a level of satisfaction indicated by indifference curve I_1 while losing $b - h$ bacon?

5 A consumer whose indifference curves are those of Figure 11.8, has a money income which will allow the purchase of 10 lbs. of bacon or 7 dozen eggs. What (approximate) quantities of bacon and eggs will maximize satisfaction? What indifference curve will the consumer attain?

6 Consider the effect of the change in the price of bacon when the budget line shifts from AC to AD in Figure 11.12.
   (i) What is the sum of the income and substitution effects?
   (ii) Can you say from the information in the diagram whether bacon is a normal, inferior, or Giffen good? How can you tell, or why can you not?

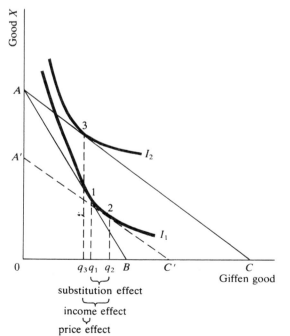

FIGURE 11.16 The Income and Substitution Effects of a Change in Price for a Giffen Good. This diagram is similar to Figure 11.15 except that the income effect is greater than the substitution effect, so that the demand curve has a positive slope.

Summary

1 Indifference curve analysis avoids the need for cardinal (absolute) measures of utility and rests on ordinal (preference ranking) measures only.

2 A budget line shows combinations available to a consumer with a given money income and given prices of two goods. The slope of the budget line measures the price of one good in terms of the other. A change in income causes a parallel shift of the budget line.

3 Consumer tastes are represented by indifference curves, each of which shows combinations of goods that yield the same satisfaction. The further from the origin of the graph, the greater the level of satisfaction represented by an indifference curve. Indifference curves cannot intersect.

4 The slope of an indifference curve measures the marginal rate of substitution between two goods – the amount of one good that a consumer would give up in return for a unit of another good, while retaining the same level of satisfaction. The marginal rate of substitution diminishes as consumption of a good increases.

5 A consumer maximizes satisfaction by buying that combination of goods for which the budget line is tangent to an indifference curve – i.e. where the marginal rate of substitution between, e.g., eggs and bacon equals the price of bacon in terms of eggs.

6 An income-consumption line, derived from the points of tangency of indifference curves with parallel budget lines, shows how consumption changes when income changes, while relative prices are held constant.

7 A price-consumption line, derived from points of tangency of indifference curves with budget lines of varying slope, shows how consumption changes when the price of one good changes, while money income and the prices of other goods are held constant.

8 The effects of a change in the (money) price of a good may be broken down into an income effect and a substitution effect. The income effect isolates what happens to quantity demanded when real income changes while relative prices are held constant. The substitution effect isolates what happens to quantity demanded when relative prices change, while real income is held constant.

9 The substitution effect of a price change always causes quantity bought to move in the opposite direction to the price change. The income effect can work in either direction. With a normal good, the income effect works in the same direction as the substitution effect; with an inferior good, in the opposite direction.

10 The income effect is found by holding relative prices constant, and varying the position of parallel budget lines. The substitution effect is found by holding real income constant, along a single indifference curve, and varying the slope of the budget line.

11 The net effect of income and substitution effects is always to cause quantity bought to move in the opposite direction to the price change (other than in the exceptional case of a Giffen good, where the 'perverse' income effect is greater than the substitution effect).

12 Business Decisions

The previous chapter took demand theory to the intermediate level. We now turn to supply, where the simplifying assumptions of our elementary theory in Part 2 of
this book severely restricted the analysis. In this Part, we
shall deal with business behaviour in circumstances where
these simplifying assumptions do not hold. In particular
we shall consider: (1) markets where sellers are price-
makers rather than price-takers, in that they are large
enough not to have to take market price as given; (2) supply
curves which do not slope upwards, because marginal costs
do not increase as output increases; and (3) sellers who are
not necessarily profit-maximizers.

In this chapter we begin our study of these matters by
examining the background to business decisions. Consider
Figure 12.1. It portrays the types of decision that must be
made by those who run businesses, and the main considerations that determine those decisions. The upper
portion of the Figure shows the types of decision. They are
divided into two groups: (1) those relating to outputs and
(2) those relating to inputs.

OUTPUT DECISIONS

There are four interrelated matters to consider: (1) what
to produce, (2) how much to produce, (3) what price to
charge for the products, and (4) how to market them.

For a business engaged in producing more than one
product, the first two of these questions concern the *mix*
of various kinds of product of different qualities that
should be produced. Most businesses sell a range of products, and some of the most interesting questions in this
area of economics relate to product mixes. Their analysis
is, however, complicated and difficult to handle in non-
mathematical terms. Hence, most of our discussion will
deal with single-product businesses that make a product
of given quality.

The third question, what price to charge, is one that we
now meet for the first time, because we have so far assumed
sellers to be price-takers. We shall consider price setting at
length in later chapters, but it may be stated now that the
power of sellers to determine the selling price of their
product is never unlimited. Even the strongest monopolist
(as a single seller is called) is constrained by the demand
for its product. Other large firms which possess sufficient
market power to influence the selling prices of their products, are constrained additionally by the behaviour of rival
competing businesses. What each can charge depends,
among other things, on what its competitors charge.

INPUT DECISIONS

A separate set of decisions must be taken by a business
about its inputs. Two types of decision are distinguished
in Figure 12.1 – (1) relating to the use of factors of production, and (2) relating to location.

The decision about the best combination of factors of
production to employ – the *factor mix* – is of fundamental
importance to the minimization of costs. A business must
choose from among several different techniques of production that are usually available. Some are likely to be
relatively *labour-intensive*, for example, others relatively
capital-intensive, i.e. some techniques use relatively more
labour than capital, others more capital than labour. This
question of *how* to produce a given output is one of the
basic questions of economics to which we referred as
far back as Chapter 2. It has two aspects, technical and
economic.

**TECHNICAL EFFICIENCY means avoiding production
methods that use more of all factors of production than
others.**

For instance, technological advances created by the microchip mean that it is not today efficient to construct radios
and other electronic equipment with valves. To take
another example, computer-controlled robotics have
opened up major new production possibilities in a wide
range of industries. A profit-maximizing firm necessarily
minimizes costs by being technically efficient. But it must
also choose among alternative methods of production on
economic grounds.

**Different techniques usually employ different factor pro-
portions. The most efficient will be that which, again,
minimizes costs, and it will depend on factor prices.**

Labour-intensive techniques may, for example, be better
than capital-intensive techniques in an economy where the
price of labour is low relative to that of capital. That is
why it may be sensible for some industries in developing
countries in the Third World to use methods of production
that seem 'backward'. If labour is plentiful and cheap,
while capital is scarce and dear, costs are kept down by
adopting labour-intensive rather than capital-intensive
techniques.

To illustrate this important point from another industry,
farmers have to decide the best combinations of land,
labour and capital to employ in agriculture. It is no accident
that one finds highly land-intensive methods in land-rich
countries, such as Australia, Canada and the USA; while
in land-scarce countries, such as the UK and the Netherlands, the available land is farmed more intensively, using

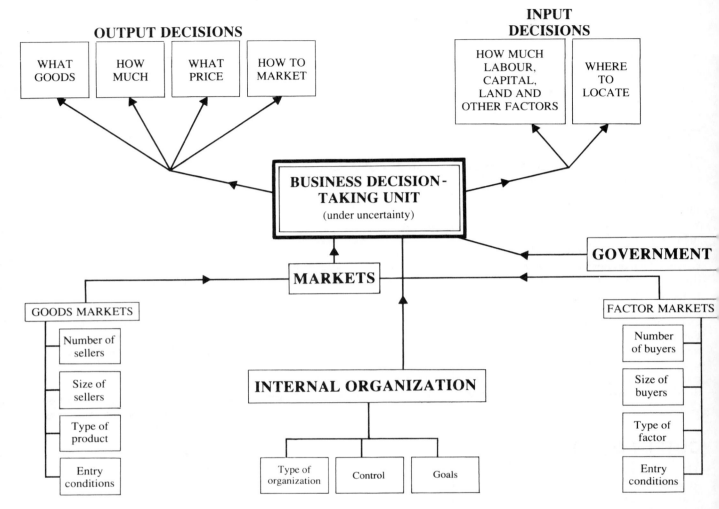

FIGURE 12.1 Business Decisions. The upper portion of the diagram indicates two types of decisions that businesses need to make about their outputs and inputs. The lower portion shows the prime determinants of those decisions.

relatively more labour and capital which are comparatively cheap. Such responses to factor prices are encouraged by the market mechanism. It is no accident that crop yields *per acre* in the UK are among the highest in the world.

Scale of output: Factor use is not solely a matter of the proportions of factors of production to adopt. It is also a matter of the *scale* of output. Should output capacity be large or small? The answer to this question is likely to depend, in part, on the planned time horizon for production – on whether the business is looking to take quick advantage of a new opportunity, for example, or planning for the long-term future. Capital investment in plant and equipment should be undertaken only if the period over which it can be used is expected to be long enough. Similar considerations apply to research and development (R & D), which is a form of investment. R & D is undertaken in order to develop new products and/or more efficient methods of production. Both may be important to attain, or retain, competitive advantage over other businesses.

There are many subsidiary decisions to be made by a business on the input side, such as what stocks of raw materials to hold, and how to raise the finance to develop the business. One area of particular importance for a new business about to start production, or one about to expand, is where to locate.

Location: Consider, for example, a new business on the point of starting up production of electric guitars. Economic considerations are not the only ones determining choice of location – many a factory has been located because of its 'amenity value' to the owner, in pleasant surroundings, for example, or close to home to cut time spent commuting. However, for most large business organizations, the prime considerations are economic. The best location is the one that minimizes costs of production.

Economic theory of location focuses on the 'pulls' of the various elements in cost minimization. Some of these locational pulls often tug against each other. Thus, there are pulls to be close to a market, to labour supplies, to supplies of raw materials, to other similar businesses in order to draw on certain services that the business may be too small to provide for itself. In all these considerations transport costs inevitably feature. Calculations are required on whether it is cheaper to locate near to main markets, to raw materials, to sources of cheap labour, to supplies of expertise, and so on.

The most efficient site is that which minimizes total production costs, including transport costs, having regard to any special considerations. For instance, climate dominates the location of some agricultural production. Sources of power can also affect choice of location. In the nineteenth century, the need for proximity to coalfields virtually dictated the siting of most heavy industries, such as iron and steel, in the UK. The advent of electricity drastically diminished the pull of the coalfields. However, the massive hydroelectric power needs of the aluminium industry still dominate its location – concentrated in Canada, the USA and similar areas which are able to provide for such requirements.

Returning to our illustration, our guitar producer may do well to spend time researching the cost advantages and disadvantages of different locations. Since transport costs of guitars are not likely to be great, the choice of site may, perhaps, be dominated by labour supply. Or, if production methods involve sophisticated electronic equipment, the proximity of a skilled service network to deal with technical problems may assume importance. It is all a question of weighing the pros and cons of all cost components in calculating what looks like the best site.

Business Decisions under Uncertainty

Business decision-taking can be an exciting, even a nerve-racking affair. Virtually all the issues on which decisions must be taken involve the uncertain future. Decisions about what to produce and how to produce it, even whether to produce at all, inevitably require that the producer take some view about the future course of events. For example, what will the demand for electric guitars be in a year or two's time, when a new factory gets rolling, what will competitors be doing, both at home and overseas, how much will it cost to employ labour in Telford, Tonypandy or wherever?

Running a profitable business is the result of efficient management and reasonably accurate forecasting of demand and costs of production, as changes occur in tastes and advances in technology. The ability to move speedily into expanding areas and out of declining ones, depends on being able to recognize them early. For example, in the UK in recent years, growing markets have included personal computers, low-fat food products, double-glazing, and video recorders; while declining markets have included typewriters, clockwork watches, high-cholesterol foods, and film projectors. Businesses which profit from developments are those which enter expanding sectors in advance of their competitors, and others which switch production to take advantage of correctly predicted changes.

All business decisions are taken in an atmosphere of some uncertainty. There exist modern techniques which can reduce the risks in certain kinds of venture, but they can never be eliminated entirely. The reward for successful business operation in conditions of uncertainty is profits, which accrue to the factor of production we have earlier described as entrepreneurship. The reward for failure is losses.

THE DETERMINANTS OF BUSINESS DECISIONS

The lower portion of Figure 12.1 illustrates schematically the major determinants of business decisions. We concentrate here on two – markets and internal organization – touching finally and briefly on one other, the influence of government.

Market Considerations

A business's ability to make decisions that we have discussed depends on conditions prevailing in two kinds of markets – those in which it sells its product, and those in which it buys the services of factors of production, known as GOODS MARKETS and FACTOR MARKETS, respectively.

It would be, perhaps, too strong a word to describe the competition between businesses as battles for markets. But competitive forces can be cut-throat in that losers may be forced out of business. Freedom for individual producers to manoeuvre depends, to a substantial extent, on the degree of competition that they face in the markets in which they operate. The strength of competition in turn depends on four characteristics depicted in the lower portion of Figure 12.1, which are (1) the number of sellers in the industry, (2) the size of sellers, (3) the type of product, and (4) entry (and exit) conditions. These market characteristics influence the firm's ability to make independent decisions on such matters as what price to charge for its product.

Goods markets

Consider, first, the importance of these four characteristics in the markets for the products of a business.

The number of sellers: This is a prime determinant of the freedom of individual businesses to make decisions. The smaller the number of sellers, the greater the chance that any one of them can choose what it wants to do. In the extreme case, there may be industries where only a single monopolist seller operates. Pure monopolies are rare. More common are markets, known as 'oligopolies', where there are a *few* sellers. If the number of producers is very large, the industry is likely to be very competitive and the freedom of manoeuvre for any one producer, in consequence, to be small.

The size of sellers: A very large number of sellers in an industry is not sufficient to ensure that none of them can influence market prices by its actions. If all sellers are to be price-takers, it is also necessary that no single seller should be large. Obviously, one giant business surrounded by a large number of small ones is constrained more than if it were the sole supplier, since it may well have to consider what the other firms may do, before taking some actions itself.

Type of product: The power of a seller to make decisions on the price it charges for its product depends not only on the number and size of all the producers in the industry, but also on the nature of its product. It is usual to distinguish between two groups of products, called homogeneous and heterogeneous.

In an industry where all firms are producing identical products, these are described as HOMOGENEOUS (meaning of the same sort). Where products are differentiated, the term is HETEROGENEOUS (meaning of different sorts).

For example, English-grown Granny Smiths apples are virtually homogeneous. One trader's stock does not differ significantly from that of another. On the other hand, the car industry produces heterogeneous products since each model of car is different from every other model – although they all share a set of basic common characteristics that make them cars.

If a producer sells a good which is (or is thought by consumers to be) identical to that of every other producer, its freedom to set price will be more limited than that of a producer whose product is differentiated from those of its competitors.

A greengrocer is constrained in the price he can charge for King Edward potatoes by prices charged by other greengrocers, whose King Edwards are regarded as identical to his own. On the other hand, restaurateurs are less constrained in the prices they can charge, because of differences in menus offered, quality of food, imagination of the chef, 'ambiance', location or other distinctive features. They cannot, however, get their prices too far out of line from those of other similar restaurants.

Entry conditions: The final market consideration affecting the ability of a business to make independent decisions is entry conditions into the market. These determine the length of time that power over the market lasts. A business may possess a degree of monopoly power in the short run, but as new producers (or new products) enter the industry, that power weakens and may disappear altogether. There are, however, BARRIERS TO ENTRY of new producers.

Barriers can be of many types – artificial or natural, legal, locational or related to cost conditions. They are of immense importance in deciding the long-run competitiveness of different industries. In some cases barriers restricting the *exit* of producers from an industry can also affect business behaviour too.

Factor markets

We have described the determinants of the degree of competition in the markets in which a business sells its product. A similar set of considerations determine the competitiveness of the markets in which businesses buy their inputs. We deal with them briefly (they are discussed at length in Chapters 18 and 19) under the same headings as those used for the markets for products (see Figure 12.1).

The number of buyers: This consideration parallels that of the number of sellers in goods markets. Businesses are buyers of the services of factors of production. The smaller the number of buyers, the greater the freedom for a single one of them to do what it wants to do. In the extreme case of a market where there is a single buyer, it is a MONOPSONIST; where there are only a few buyers, they are 'oligopsonists'.

The size of buyers: Just as we specified the need for all sellers to be small in the goods market for all to be price-takers, for the same reason so also should no single buyer be large in the factor market. One powerful purchaser may not be constrained, even by a large number of other buyers, if all are small.

Type of factor: In goods markets, we noted that the freedom of sellers depends on whether or not their products are homogeneous, or differentiated from each other. In factor markets, a similar consideration arises.

Some inputs are, of course, homogeneous – one steel ingot, for example, is the same as another; but markets for the factor of production 'labour' are liable to be highly differentiated, e.g. by skill, or geographically. Labour available in South Wales is not easily available in London, for example.

Entry conditions: The final consideration affecting factor markets concerns entry conditions. Just as barriers to entry (and exit) in goods markets affect business decisions, so barriers in factor markets have similar effects. Factor mobility is impeded by such barriers, which will be described later.

Internal Organization of the Business

Market considerations apart, the decisions taken by a business depend on its internal structure and objectives. Decisions are made by people (whether individuals or committees) whose identity and goals may affect the way they act. The extent to which decision-takers have freedom of manoeuvre depends, among other things, on: (1) the type of business organization, (2) the identity of those who own and control the business, and (3) the business's goals.

Types of business organization

There are four principal forms of private business organization in the UK: (1) single proprietorships, (2) partnerships, (3) co-operatives, and (4) joint-stock companies.

State-owned industries in the public sector are discussed in Chapter 21.

Single proprietorships: As its name implies, this category covers businesses which are owned and controlled by a single person, whether run by that person or by a hired manager. The owner being solely responsible for everything done by the business, and accountable only to himself, can make all the decisions, subject only to what is technically feasible and to market forces, as discussed in the previous section. Single proprietorships are common in most sectors of the UK economy, especially in retailing.

With a few notable exceptions, virtually all businesses in this category are small – a feature which may give flexibility. Growth is, however, hampered by limited availability of capital, and single proprietorships have been declining in relative importance for a very long time.

Partnerships: In a partnership, as its name implies, there are two or more joint owners of the business. Each of the partners is jointly, and personally, responsible for what is done by the firm. Capital availability is usually a little greater in partnerships than in sole proprietorships, though most partnerships are small, and often consist of members of the same family. Exceptions are in certain professions, such as accountancy and the law where the ruling associations prohibit the company form of organization (see below).

Co-operatives: Some business activity, especially in the retail trade but also in farming, is organized on co-operative lines. There are two types of co-operative – those where production is organized by *workers* and those run by, or on behalf of, *consumers*. The distinctive feature of co-operatives is that any profits of the business are shared among workers, or consumers.

The first consumer co-operative, in Rochdale in 1844, began a movement which flourished in the nineteenth century, but which has been declining in the twentieth. Today co-operative societies account for little more than 5 per cent of total retail trade, though they are still important in milk distribution. Worker co-operatives are less common, appearing from time to time when employees band together to rescue a business threatened with closure.

Joint-stock companies: Joint-stock companies – also called corporations – are owned by individuals who buy shares in them. The corporation, however, is regarded in law as having an identity of its own, separate from owners who are not personally liable for anything done in the name of their company.

This form of business organization has grown to dominate most sectors of the UK economy, especially manufacturing industry, since the principle of limited liability was introduced in a series of Company Acts going back to the 1860s. LIMITED LIABILITY refers to the release from responsibility for the debts of the firm for owners, known as SHAREHOLDERS, whose liability is limited to the amount they have invested in the business. This confers an immense advantage for companies wishing to

raise large sums of capital, and explains the dominance of the corporate form of organization in the UK today.

Companies wishing to acquire finance offer shares in the business for sale to individuals (and institutions), who are able to sell them for cash in a specialized market – the Stock Exchange. There are several types of shares. Prime importance attaches to ORDINARY SHARES (or EQUITIES), which give the owners shares in profits and, as a rule, voting rights at company meetings.

Capital can also be raised by the sale of securities called debentures (or 'loan stock'). A DEBENTURE is a financial asset which promises a *fixed* rate of interest annually. Debenture holders are not owners of the business and have no say in how it is run. The higher the proportion of capital raised by fixed interest securities, the greater is said to be its GEARING. A highly geared company is more vulnerable than a low geared one during unprofitable periods. When a firm is making losses, it can cut distributions to shareholders but, if it is to stay in business, it cannot default on fixed interest payments to debenture holders or other creditors of the business.

There are hundreds of thousands of companies organized on a joint-stock basis in modern Britain. The vast majority are small private companies, similar in many ways to partnerships or to single proprietorships. They are organized as joint-stock companies for tax and other advantages, accruing from the fact that the company is a separate entity from its owners. *Private* companies are barred from offering shares on sale to the general public – a privilege reserved to public companies, which must display the letters p.l.c. after their name.

Almost all large-scale businesses are organized as public companies. Some own other companies, known as 'subsidiaries', which may, in turn, own subsidiaries of their own. The main parent organization may be called a 'holding company', owning a pyramid of other companies which can number many hundreds. The Sears group, for example, operates in many different markets from shoes and jewellery to second-hand cars and betting shops through its ownership of Dolcis, Mappin & Webb, Selfridges and William Hill (Racing) Ltd. It is one of the 50 largest company groups in the UK, controlling more than 400 companies through five pyramidal tiers.

Special terms are used to denote the role of individual parts of such giant businesses. The whole entity of companies under a single ownership (including ownership of a controlling interest in other companies) is called an ENTERPRISE. Subordinate companies within the empire are subsidiaries, which may operate one or more ESTABLISHMENTS or 'plants', comprising individual factories on specific sites. Some of the very largest enterprises have interests in many countries in the world. They are termed TRANSNATIONALS (formerly MULTINATIONALS).

Very large businesses do not necessarily rely on highly centralized decision-taking at head offices. Decentralization of the managerial structure can allow autonomy to divisions, and to even smaller segments of a business, especially where companies operate over a widely diversified product range. However, financial constraints are usually placed by Head Office of the principal, parent, company on the use of capital by subsidiary companies.

It is among the giant corporations that we find oligopolists (and monopolists), for which the assumption that sellers are price-takers is inappropriate. Giant enterprises are not, of course, necessarily free from competition from other giants, but their freedom of manoeuvre is usually different from that of small businesses in industries consisting of large numbers of small companies. Moreover, decision-takers in large enterprises may pursue somewhat different goals from those of small companies.

Mergers

Businesses grow in size in two distinct ways – by internal growth, and by MERGER (or 'amalgamation'), when two or more separate businesses join up to become a single enterprise. Three types of merger are commonly distinguished: (1) horizontal, (2) vertical, and (3) conglomerate mergers.

When mergers are among companies producing the same product they are termed HORIZONTAL MERGERS; when they are among businesses at different stages of the production process they are called VERTICAL MERGERS; and when they are among firms without any common interest they are termed CONGLOMERATE MERGERS.

An example of a horizontal merger is that between Dolcis and Saxone shoe retailers. Examples of vertical mergers are the acquisition of public houses by breweries (called *forward integration*), or the purchase of a printing works by a publishing company (called *backward integration*). Conglomerate mergers, between unrelated businesses, are common. They are often made in order to spread risks by diversification, though there may sometimes be certain hidden advantages.

Mergers between companies can be amalgamations by mutual agreement, or the subject of 'hostile' takeovers of one company by another. Since World War II, there have been several periods of merger booms, though recently a certain amount of 'demerger' activity has also occurred, when some large diversified corporations decided to divest themselves of less attractive subsidiaries. Such events can involve the sale of a subsidiary to its managers who, usually with outside financial help, make a Management Buy Out (MBO) which, incidentally, may or may not prove a good idea. For instance, the MBO of the Lewis's group of department stores from the Sears group in 1987 was followed by the bankruptcy of the Lewis's group in 1991.

The concept of a firm

Economists use the term FIRM to cover all types of business organization discussed above. It refers to *any* organization that makes decisions on how to organize inputs to produce commodities. In other words, the firm makes all of the decisions listed in the top half of Figure 12.1 and is influenced by all of the forces shown in the bottom half of the figure.

Owners versus controllers

In order to explain the behaviour of businesses, economists construct theories of the firm. To understand the ways in which firms behave, and to be successful in predicting how they react to changing circumstances, we need to know who controls the firm, as well as who formally owns it.

There is, usually, no difficulty on this matter in the case of single proprietorships, partnerships and small private companies, especially when the owners take an active role in running the business. Even when owners are inactive, differences between the decisions they would have made and those made by employed managers are unlikely to persist, since a manager can be replaced.

In giant corporations, in contrast, the situation may be quite different. The owners of joint-stock companies are the shareholders. They elect the Boards of Directors, who are answerable, in principle, to the shareholders at company meetings, especially at the annual general meeting (a.g.m.) when accounts for the past year, and forecasts for the future, are presented for approval. The directors, in turn, appoint salaried managers to run the business. The chief executive is usually the managing director, or the chairman of the company.

The power that the owners of a business have over directors may, however, be quite limited in practice. Many investigators of corporate behaviour hold the view that, often, a minority of shareholders exercises effective control over the decisions of the company.

Dispersion of share ownership: The power of small groups of shareholders depends, among other things, on the distribution of share ownership. It may be slight if ownership is widely dispersed. To understand why this is so, it is necessary to appreciate that each ordinary share normally carries one vote. Any individual, or group, owning 51 per cent of the voting shares clearly controls a majority of votes. But, suppose one group owns 30 per cent, with the remaining 70 per cent distributed so widely that few of the dispersed group bother to vote. In this event, 30 per cent may be the overwhelming majority of shares *actually voted*. Often a small fraction of the shares actually voted may be the dominant influence at shareholders' meetings.

Dispersed ownership and minority control are common in giant companies. The separation of ownership and control was first pointed out in the United States more than 50 years ago by Berle and Means. They concluded that nearly half of the largest 200 US corporations were effectively under the control of managers because no individual or group owned as much as 25 per cent of voting shares.

The power of directors is reinforced by their peculiarly favourable position for acquiring proxy voting rights. It is the directors who call the annual general meetings, and they usually include, in the mailing forms, offers to exercise proxy rights on behalf of shareholders who are unable or unwilling to attend company meetings. Hence, the divorce of ownership from control in many corporations leaves the Board of Directors in a strong position.

BOX 12.1 A Part Exchange at Burton Group

'Two million pounds to pay off Sir Ralph Halpern may not sound like value for money to the 50,000 owners of the company; the army of small shareholders who backed the very man being paid off, and the institutions who wanted him out, but not necessarily at any price.

'Halpern has increasingly turned the Burton Group's most valuable asset into something of a liability ... Burton, which owns Debenhams, Dorothy Perkins, Principles, and Top Shop, yesterday announced £133 million pre-tax profits for the year to end September, down 39 per cent ... Faltering performance is only one of the reasons advanced for the dumping of Halpern. More important is that he tried to run Burton as if it were a proprietorial, or at best family, business.'

(*The Times*, 16 November 1990)

If economic theory is to help understand how firms behave, it must be based on proper assumptions on what motivates business decisions. The traditional assumption of profit maximization is a useful first approximation. But the modern giant corporation with thousands of owners (shareholders) may depart from this model. The separation of ownership from control can cushion directors who control the firm, and who may strive less for the largest profits, because of their interest in other goals.

Shareholders' interests can rarely be neglected indefinitely. In particular, financial institutions who own large numbers of shares in major companies can wield plenty of clout if they choose to. The news item provides an illustration of a spectacular move to unseat a director who was felt to have underperformed.

Questions

1 There is an implication in the quotation that institutional shareholders have more influence than small shareholders, even if there are large numbers of the latter. Why do you think this is likely to be true? When might it be, perhaps, false?
2 Can you think what the implications for the goals of the Burton Group might have been if there was any truth in the allegation that Sir Ralph Halpern had been trying to run it as a family firm?

The power of directors, even in companies where share ownership is widely dispersed, is not, however, unlimited, especially in the long run. In the first place, over half of ordinary shares in the UK today are owned by financial institutions (especially insurance companies and pension funds) who comprise most of the large shareholders. Although these 'institutional' shareholders are reluctant to involve themselves in the day-to-day running of the business, they can exert considerable influence, especially if they decide to act together.

The most common constraint on company directors, however, is probably the threat of takeover by other powerful companies. Mismanagement and poor performance by directors rarely goes unnoticed for long. It is a spur to outside interests, which may seek to take over the firm by making offers to existing shareholders to buy their shares on favourable terms. If successful, the new owners can replace the directors and attempt to run the company more efficiently.

Takeover bids are usually made on attractive terms, relative to the current market price of the shares. If the firm is not currently well managed, such prices can be offered in the expectation of being able to increase the firm's profits after the takeover. Sometimes directors engage in a battle with the predators, as they see them, for control of the company. Shareholders receive letters from would-be takers-over, and from defending management, urging them to sell, or not to sell, their shares. The outcome can go either way. The important point, however, is that the threat of takeover action is a constraint on manager-controllers, even when share ownership is widely dispersed.

Goals of the firm

The third set of factors which ranks high in importance in understanding the decisions made by a firm is the goals or objectives of those who control it.

In the elementary theory of supply in Part 2 of this book, we assumed that firms try to *maximize their profits*. The assumption has much to commend it. There are many competitive markets where it motivates firms' behaviour. It is, however, not universally applicable. The extent to which firms can and do try to maximize profits depends on three circumstances: (1) the goals of owners, (2) the power of owners *vis-à-vis* controllers, and (3) market conditions.

The goals of the business: There is no reason for believing that all businessmen are interested in profitability as the sole aim. Some decisions in single proprietorships confirm this, e.g. the location of a factory close to agreeable surroundings despite high production costs, or the decision to close down on Wednesdays to allow for a regular game of tennis. Co-operatives also have objectives other than profit maximization. Worker co-operatives generally seek maximum opportunities for employment, especially where the establishment of worker control has followed the threat of the closure of an unprofitable business. Consumer co-operatives claim to operate in the interests of customers, but retail co-operative societies in the UK happen also to be politically motivated and associated with the Labour Party, and this can affect some of their business decisions.

Large joint-stock companies may well be, as we have seen, characterized by the divorce of ownership of the company from control by directors and managers. Nonetheless, whenever the latter seek to make the company as profitable as possible they are serving the interests of shareholders.

Directors and managers, however, may have other objectives. The chief of these are probably job security and remuneration (i.e. salary and other 'perks'), which are often more important than any share of profits. The salaries of directors are usually related to the size of a business, whether measured in terms of output, sales, employment or other variables. Hence, maximizing the growth of sales may loom large in the goals that boards of directors strive after. That is not to say that directors are likely to ignore profitability entirely. A sufficient level of profits to keep shareholders quiet, and/or keep takeover bidders at bay, must be a consideration. However, the goal of profit *maximization* may not be an appropriate assumption.

The power of owners vis-à-vis controllers: There are several theories of the firm based on different assumptions of motivation. One set which cover situations where directors are the dominant force are described as MANAGERIAL THEORIES of the firm. Another set, called BEHAVIOURAL THEORIES of the firm, stresses that a firm is not always run entirely in the interests of its owners or managers, but represents a diversity of interests, all of which may play a part in decision-taking. These interests include, of course, owners and managers, but also workers, customers and inhabitants of the area where the firm is located. Behavioural theories consider the bargaining process within the firm among all relevant interests on such matters as production, profits, growth, location, and so on. The objectives need not conflict with profit maximization – for example good catering and sports facilities can aid productivity. The voluntary inclusion of national economic targets may also pre-empt governments from forcing them on a firm.

In conclusion, it must be admitted that individual firms may have objectives which are complex and which vary from time to time. Appreciation of this led the American economist and Nobel Prizewinner Professor Herbert Simon to invent the term SATISFICING, to describe the totality of goals pursued by a firm.

Market conditions: Our discussion of business goals has emphasized what decision-takers would like to do. The extent to which they are able to do what they would like depends substantially on market conditions and, in particular, on the degree of competition facing an individual firm.

All the four determinants of competitiveness discussed earlier in this chapter – number and size of firms, type of product and entry conditions – are relevant. There is no need to go over them again. It is enough to appreciate that a firm possessing a high degree of market power is freer to depart from the aim of profit maximization than a small firm in a fiercely competitive industry, where profits are kept low by competitive forces, and where the pursuit of other objectives may mean extinction. We should, however, be careful not to jump to the conclusion that large firms always have great market power. Strength depends on more than mere size. We shall discuss this subject further in Chapter 17.

Government and Business Decisions

If you return for a final look at Figure 12.1, you will see that we included government as a separate force which can affect business decisions.

The state intervenes at various levels and in many ways to influence the behaviour of firms. Its goals are often different from those of private businesses. We discussed economic policy earlier and we shall take the subject further in later chapters. The instruments of government policy are many and varied. They include a wide range of taxes and subsidies, price controls, quality regulations, etc. Most of them affect business decisions, sometimes in complex ways. There is nothing very useful of a general nature to be said now about the influence of government on business decisions. There will be plenty to say about individual policy instruments when we come to study them in Chapter 21.

Summary

1 Businesses make decisions about their outputs and inputs. The prime output decisions are what and how much to produce, what price to charge, and how to market the products. The prime input decisions are related to the quantities of each factor of production to employ.

2 Locating production so as to minimize costs involves calculating the advantages of proximity to markets and to input sources, as well as the costs of transport required by being distant from them.

3 Business decisions are made in conditions of uncertainty and are influenced by the type of market in which the business operates and by its internal organization.

4 The influence of market type is felt on competitiveness, and depends on the numbers and size of buyers and sellers, on whether outputs and inputs are homogeneous or heterogeneous, and on entry conditions.

5 The principal forms of private business organizations are single proprietorships, partnerships, co-operatives and joint-stock companies.

6 The main advantage of the company form of organization is that limited liability for shareholders enables capital to be raised relatively easily. Companies can grow by borrowing through the sale of debentures, by raising more ownership capital through the sale of equities, by internal growth or by merger with other firms.

7 Most large businesses are organized as public companies owned by shareholders, and run by a Board of Directors.

8 The goals of owners and controllers are not necessarily identical. Where share ownership is dispersed among a large number of shareholders, directors may pay less attention to profit maximization than to other goals.

9 Directors and other managers may be inefficient or may not try to maximize profits. They may be constrained by threats of takeover by other powerful firms, and by the large institutional shareholders.

10 The goals of a business may include profit maximization, growth, sales maximization, and 'satisficing'. They are affected, in turn, by the goals of the owners, the powers of owners *vis-à-vis* controllers, market conditions, and the activities of government.

Questions

1 What is the name given in economics to a market characterized by (i) a small number of sellers, (ii) a single buyer?

2 Which of the following most affects a firm's decision on whether to employ labour-intensive rather than capital-intensive production methods?
   (a) The price of the product.
   (b) The prices of factors of production.
   (c) The power of shareholders *vis-à-vis* controllers.
   (d) The number and size of sellers in goods markets.
   (e) The number and size of buyers in factor markets.

3 What is the significance of the distinction between homogeneous and heterogeneous products for decision-taking in a firm?

4 What is the principal reason why it is easier for a p.l.c. to raise large sums of capital than a partnership?

5 Which One or More of the following (i) give company directors and managers some freedom to ignore the interests of shareholders, (ii) act as constraints on the freedom of directors to ignore shareholders' interests?
   (a) Large number of personal shareholders.
   (b) Wide dispersion of ordinary share ownership.
   (c) Increasing size of institutional shareholders.
   (d) Linking directors' pay to profits.
   (e) The threat of takeover bids.
   (f) Highly competitive product markets.

13 The Productivity of Factors of Production

We continue the intermediate theory of supply by examining the firm's decision about what level of output it is most profitable to produce. The answer depends partly on demand and partly on costs. In this and the next chapter we start by considering costs, which depend on two influences. The first is the technical relation of how outputs vary as inputs vary, i.e. factor productivity. The second is what it costs the firm to obtain its factor inputs, i.e. factor prices.

This chapter is devoted to a consideration of how output varies as inputs vary. The next chapter uses the conclusions from this one and deals with costs of production.

Factor Productivity

The ability of a factor of production to produce output is known as the factor's PRODUCTIVITY. It is a technological relationship, between what is fed into the productive apparatus by way of inputs of factor services, and what is turned out by way of product. In stating this relationship, it must be remembered that production is a flow: it is not just so many units: it is so many units *per period of time*. If we speak of raising the level of monthly production from 100 to 101 units, we do not mean producing 100 units this month and 1 unit next month, but going from a *rate* of production of 100 units per month to a rate of 101 units per month.

In this chapter we shall consider the relationship between factor inputs and output in a simple example. We shall assume that there are only two factors of production, labour and capital. Output of the firm's product, per period, depends on the quantities of these factors that are used by the firm. This simplification will not materially affect the conclusions we shall reach, but it will enable us to get quickly to the essential aspects of the problem.

Suppose that the firm wishes to increase its rate of output. To do so it must increase the inputs of one or more factors of production. However, the firm cannot usually vary both of its factors with equal ease. Labour, for example, can be taken on, or laid off, at fairly short notice (a week or a month). But a longer time is needed to vary the quantity of some other factors, for example to install more capital.

To allow for different speeds with which different inputs can be varied, we think of the firm as making decisions within two time-periods, the short run and the long run.

Any factor of production that cannot be varied over the time-period under consideration is called a FIXED factor. Any factor that can be varied over the time-period under consideration is called a VARIABLE factor.

THE SHORT AND LONG RUNS

The SHORT RUN is defined as the period of time when at least one factor of production is fixed.

In practice, the factor that is fixed in the short run is usually an element of capital (such as plant and equipment) or land, but it might be the services of management or even the supply of skilled labour. As we are dealing with a simplified case with only two factors, we let capital be the fixed factor and labour the variable factor. If the firm wishes to vary its production in the short run, it can do so only by changing its labour input. Since capital is fixed, this necessitates changing the *proportions* in which labour and capital are combined.

The LONG RUN is defined as that period long enough for all factors of production to be varied, within the confines of given technology.

The long run is the period that is relevant when a firm is either planning to go into business or to expand, or contract, its entire *scale* of operations. The firm can then choose those quantities of all factors of production that seem most suitable. It can opt for a new factory of any feasible size. However, once the planning decision has been carried out – the plant built, machines purchased and installed, and so on – the firm acquires fixed factors: it is operating in the short run.

The boundary between the short and the long runs is not defined by reference to calendar time. It varies from industry to industry, and from one time to another, defined only in terms of the fixity of at least one factor of production. In the electric power industry, for example, it takes three or more years to acquire and install a steam-turbine generator. Thus, an increase in the demand for electricity cannot immediately be met by increasing capital equipment. Existing machines must supply as much of the extra demand as they can. In contrast, a courier service can meet an increase in demand by acquiring an extra one or more motorcycles and riders in a matter of days or even hours.

The length of the short run is influenced by technological considerations, such as how quickly equipment can be manufactured or installed, and by economic matters, such as the price the firm is willing to pay for equipment.

We turn now to consider how the productivities of factors of production vary with output in the short and in the long run.

The Short Run: Returns to a Variable Factor

In the short run we are concerned with the behaviour of output as more units of a variable factor are applied in conjunction with a given quantity of a fixed factor. We continue to assume that our firm employs two factors of production – capital which is fixed, and labour which is variable.

TABLE 13.1 Total, Average and Marginal Products of a Variable Factor (Labour) used with a Fixed Factor (Capital) in the Short Run

INPUTS		OUTPUT		
Labour	Capital	Total product (TP)	Average product (AP) (iii) ÷ (i)	Marginal product (MP)
(i)	(ii)	(iii)	(iv)	(v)
1	10	4	4	4
2	10	10	5	6
3	10	21	7	11
4	10	40	10	**19**
5	10	55	**11**	15
6	10	60	10	5
7	10	63	9	3
8	10	**64**	8	1
9	10	63	7	−1

Table 13.1 presents hypothetical figures for the behaviour of outputs and inputs. The same data are shown graphically in Figure 13.1. We can look at the effect of changing the quantity of inputs on total product, average product and marginal product. These three are described in the output columns (iii), (iv) and (v) in Table 13.1 and in Figure 13.1.

Total, average and marginal products of a variable factor

Total product (TP): Total product is given in column (iii). It means just what it says: the total volume of output resulting from the employment of all factors of production.

Average product (AP): Average product is given in column (iv). It shows the *output per unit of the variable factor*. It is calculated by dividing *TP* in column (iii) by the quantity of labour employed in column (i). For example, output with 9 units of labour is 63, so *AP* of 63/9 = 7.

Marginal product (MP): Marginal product is given in the final column (v). It is defined as the *change* in total output resulting from a *unit change* in the input of the variable factor. For example, when the first unit of labour is employed, total product rises from zero to 4; hence *MP* is 4 (because 4 divided by 1 is 4). When a second unit of labour is added, *TP* rises from 4 to 10; hence *MP* = 6 (10 minus 4 divided by 1 = 6). Note that the marginal products in column (v) do not refer to particular input levels but to

changes in input levels. They are shown, therefore, in between the rows. (For the same reason, in Figure 13.1, *MP*s are plotted between the inputs of labour.)

The 'law' of diminishing returns

Although the data used for Table 13.1 and Figure 13.1 are hypothetical, the relationship shown between total, average and marginal products is widely applicable. We use the word 'law' to describe the relationship, in the same way as we used that term in connection with the 'laws of supply and demand' earlier. The relationship would be more accurately described as a hypothesis, which is valid if consistent with the facts. However, it is sufficiently well tested for us to refer to the 'law of diminishing returns'.

The LAW OF DIMINISHING RETURNS states that when increasing quantities of a variable factor are used, in combination with a fixed factor, both the marginal product and the average product of the variable factor will eventually decrease.

The operation of the law is illustrated in Table 13.1. Total product increases as the number of men working with the fixed amount of capital rises from 1 to 8. Average product increases until 5 men are employed. Thereafter, average product declines. Marginal product rises until 4 men are employed. Then it diminishes.

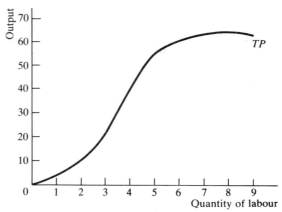

(i) Total product

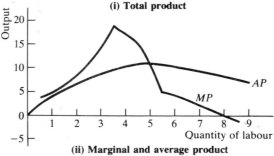

(ii) Marginal and average product

FIGURE 13.1 The Productivity of a Variable Factor Used in Combination with a Fixed Factor in the Short Run. The variable factor is here, by assumption, labour. Part (i) shows *TP* rising at an increasing, then at a diminishing rate until 8 men are employed. Part (ii) shows *AP* rising to a peak until 5 men are employed and then diminishing; and *MP* peaking before *AP*, but equalling *AP* when *AP* is at its maximum.

The same data are plotted graphically in Figure 13.1, which is in two parts. The upper part (i) shows *TP* rising, at a varying rate, first increasing then diminishing, until the 9th man is employed, when total output declines. The lower part (ii) of the diagram shows *MP* rising to a peak until the input of the 4th unit of labour, after which it declines. *AP* rises until a 5th man is employed, after which it, too, declines. *MP* becomes *negative* as a 9th unit of labour is taken on – because *TP falls*, i.e the *change* in total product is negative.

Note that the *MP* curve cuts the *AP* curve at the maximum *AP*. This is a straightforward mathematical property of the curves which is important to appreciate. It may help you to understand the reasoning by considering what the addition of an amount to the total product does to the average. That depends on whether the amount added (marginal product) is greater or less than the existing average product. If the *MP* is the same as the existing average, *AP* stays the same. If the *MP* is greater than the existing *AP* then the *AP* rises as a direct result of the additional *MP*. If the *MP* is less than the existing average, then this must bring the average down. As can be seen in Figure 13.1, when *AP* is rising, *MP* is greater than *AP*; when *AP* is falling, *MP* is less than *AP*; when *AP* is neither rising nor falling, but is at a maximum, *MP* equals *AP*.[1]

The basis of the 'law':

In order to understand why the 'law' of diminishing returns operates, it is essential to remember that the application of varying quantities of one factor to a fixed quantity of another, *changes the proportions* in which the two factors are combined.

This key consideration lies behind the alternative name sometimes used for the law – THE LAW OF VARIABLE PROPORTIONS. Some factor combinations are more efficient than others. As we increase the inputs of the variable factor towards the best combinations, productivity rises. As we move beyond it, diminishing returns set in.

The common sense of diminishing marginal productivity is that the presence of a fixed factor limits the amount of

additional output that can be realized by adding more of the variable factor. Were it not for the law of diminishing returns, there would be no need to fear that the world's population explosion will cause a food crisis. If the marginal product of additional workers applied to the fixed amount of land in the world were constant, then world food production could be expanded in proportion to the increase in population, merely by keeping the same proportion of the population on the farms.

The working of the 'law':　We can illustrate the working of the law within the context of agriculture, by looking at the situation of a single farmer. Assume he uses only two factors, a fixed amount of land – say 10 acres – and a variable amount of labour. If he has only a single worker, the labourer will have to do all the tasks required. At harvest time he must cut the corn, gather it into piles, load them on to a cart, thrash the corn, fill sacks with the grain, dispose of the chaff, etc., etc. There is no opportunity for specialization. One worker must do everything.

Suppose the farmer now takes on a second worker. He can divide the different duties between the two men, increasing their skills, and reducing the time they must spend moving from job to job. Each man can, to an extent, perform specialist functions. When three men are employed, the possibilities for specialization increase. Average product will again tend to rise, as a result of such specialization.

Why then, you may wonder, do diminishing returns ever set in? The answer is because the men are, by definition, being employed *in conjunction with a fixed amount of land*. With only 10 acres to farm, the opportunities for specialization gradually diminish as more men are employed.

Division of labour is likely to be extremely effective when a second man is taken on – one drives the cart around while the other loads the corn. But as more and more men are working, the opportunities for efficient division of functions fall. Indeed by the time, say, 20 men have been taken on, each is already doing a single specialist task. The only work the farmer can think of for a 21st man might be to carry beer round to the others when they are thirsty. Hence, the scope for raising productivity by increasing specialization will be great when only a few are employed, but eventually a level of employment will be reached where 'diminishing returns' set in.

Indeed, if the farmer were silly enough to continue to add more and more workers to his 10 acres of land, the point would finally be reached when additional workers had a *negative* marginal product: they would cause total product to fall, because, for example, there were so many of them that they got into each other's way – as happens after 8 men are employed in Figure 13.1 (or Table 13.1). Such a situation is not of any economic significance. No profit-maximizing producer would consider employing so many men.

The reason for diminishing returns is the presence of a fixed factor of production, with which the variable factors have to work.

If the farmer bought more acres of land whenever he

---

1 An illustration from cricket may help in seeing this relationship working. Consider a cricketer, Ian Botham perhaps. He goes in to bat every week, scoring a certain number of runs. His latest score is his marginal score. His average score is the total number of runs he has made to date, divided by the number of innings when he was batting (we ignore the possibility that he was 'not out', even though he probably would not like that!).

Suppose, then, that Botham has played in three matches so far this year and scored 25, 50 and 75 runs. His average is 50. In this fourth match he scores 62, i.e. his marginal score fell (from 75 to 62). However his average score is now 53. It is still rising, because his marginal score of 62 is above his previous average score of 50. Suppose, however, he goes on to score 53 in his fifth match. This is exactly equal to his average score, which does not change. But if in his sixth match Botham gets only 47 runs, his average starts to fall (it is now 52), because his marginal score is less than his previous average score.

This example illustrates the general proposition that when marginal values exceed the average value, then the average value must be rising, but when the marginal value falls below the average value that must drag the average value down.

hired more labour, the law would not be applicable because we would not be considering the application of varying quantities of one factor with a fixed factor. We would be varying both of them. The law does not apply.

The law of diminishing returns refers only to the effect of varying factor proportions, in the short run.

THE LONG RUN: RETURNS TO SCALE

In the short run, the only way to change output is to alter the inputs of the variable factor, changing thereby factor proportions. The long run is defined as a period long enough for *all* factors of production to be varied. When this is done, holding factor proportions constant, we talk about RETURNS TO SCALE. A firm might for example double, or triple, the amount of labour used in production and double, or triple, the amount of capital at the same time.

When the scale of operations is increased, or decreased, the law of diminishing returns does not apply. No factor of production needs to be fixed. Capital, land and all other factors may be varied in quantity.

We use the term 'returns to scale' to describe the relationship between output and inputs when the scale changes, but factor proportions are held constant. Returns to scale can be increasing, constant or decreasing.

To illustrate, consider a firm employing two factors of production, capital and labour. If the firm doubles its use of *both* labour and capital, and output more than doubles, there are *increasing* returns to scale. If the same doubling of inputs causes a doubling of output, returns to scale are *constant*. If, finally, doubling inputs causes a rise in output that is less than double, then *decreasing* returns to scale are operating.

The three cases are illustrated in Figure 13.2. All three sections of the diagram show the short-run average and marginal product curves as variable amounts of labour are employed *in two plants of different sizes*. In the short run, the firm is restricted to one or other plant so that output changes can come only from changing the input of the variable factor, shown by moving along either set of short-run curves. In the long run, the firm can elect to operate either plant. Long-run changes, therefore, consist of *moving from one set of short-run curves to another*. This must mean altering the amount of capital. The short-run curves are labelled SAP_1 and SMP_1 for the smaller plant; and SAP_2 and SMP_2 for the larger plant, which is assumed to employ exactly twice the number of units of capital as the smaller plant.

Constant returns to scale: Let us begin with the topmost part (i) of Figure 13.2, which deals with constant returns to scale. Suppose the firm is operating on its short-run average product curve SAP_1 at point c, where AP is at a maximum, i.e. labour input is l_1 and average output per worker is c. It then builds a new plant of double the size of the original plant, and double the amount of labour is

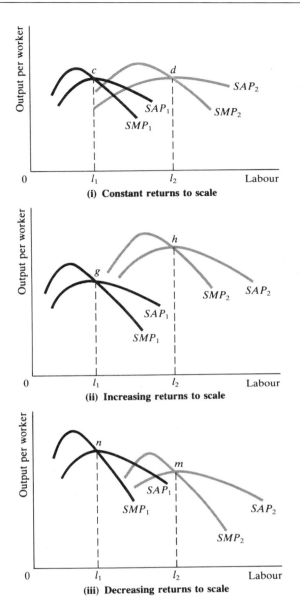

FIGURE 13.2 Returns to Scale in the Long Run, under conditions of (i) constant, (ii) increasing and (iii) decreasing returns. SAP_1 and SMP_1 are the short-run AP and MP curves for one size plant, SAP_2 and SMP_2 for another plant of double the capital. When labour input is also doubled (from l_1 to l_2), AP is measured by the vertical distance from the labour axis to the AP curve (e.g. $c = d$ when returns to scale are constant in (i); $h > g$ with increasing returns in (ii); $m < n$ with decreasing returns in (iii)).

also employed (i.e. l_2 is double l_1).

What happens to output? It doubles also. We can deduce from this that output per unit of input stays the same. Thus, in Figure 13.2(i) $c = d$ and output changes in direct proportion to inputs: returns to scale are said to be constant.

Increasing returns to scale: Figure 13.2 (ii) shows *increasing* returns to scale. The argument is unchanged. We suppose the firm moves from the smaller plant to the larger plant, thereby doubling its amount of capital. It also doubles its input of labour from l_1 to l_2. This time, average product rises: h is greater than g. If average product per unit of labour rises when labour and capital inputs double, then total product must more than double. Returns to scale are increasing.

Decreasing returns to scale: Figure 13.2(iii) shows *decreasing* returns to scale. The argument is again the same. But in this case a doubling of the size of the plant and of labour input, lowers average product from n to m and hence less than doubles output.

The Compatibility of Diminishing Returns to a Variable Factor and Increasing Returns to Scale

There is no reason why a firm cannot experience diminishing returns to one of its variable factors alongside increasing returns to scale. Diminishing returns relate to the short run, when there is at least one fixed factor; returns to scale relate to the long run, when all factors are variable. The mutual compatibility of diminishing returns with constant, increasing, or decreasing returns to scale is shown in Figure 13.2. However, students sometimes have difficulty in grasping this important point. To help, we offer a numerical example to supplement the diagram.

Table 13.2 shows total output that results from the use of different inputs of labour and capital. The table can be used to derive the marginal product of capital, the marginal product of labour and returns to scale.

Consider first the marginal product of labour. To derive this, we examine the behaviour of total output going down any of the *columns* in the table, which means increasing labour inputs with capital held constant. The first column, (i), can be used to calculate the marginal product of labour when 1 unit of capital is employed, column (ii) the marginal product of labour when 2 units of capital are used, and so forth.

To illustrate, let us find the marginal product of labour working with a fixed single unit of capital. To do so we read the figures of total output down column (i), which show it to be 100 and 130 for 1 and 2 units of labour respectively. The marginal product of labour is therefore 30 (130 minus 100). Now increase labour input by another unit, still holding capital constant at one unit. Output becomes 150. The marginal product of labour is therefore 20 (150 minus 130). Thus the *marginal product of labour is diminishing* (from 30 to 20).

The marginal product of capital is derived in a similar way. We now need to hold constant the quantity of labour and vary capital inputs. Hence we inspect the figures of output going across the *rows* of the table. The first row provides the basis for calculating the marginal product of capital working with 1 unit of labour; the second row for calculating the marginal product of capital working with 2 units of labour, etc.

Now consider returns to scale, holding factor proportions constant. For these we need to look at the figures in the diagonal cells. From them we see that output is 100 when 1 unit of capital and 1 of labour are employed. It is 220 when 2 units of capital and 2 units of labour are employed. In other words, inputs double and output more than doubles, from 100 to 220. *Returns to scale are increasing.* Now increase labour and capital again. This time raise *both* of them by 50 per cent, i.e. from 2 to 3. The table tells us that output goes from 220 to 335. In this case we have increased inputs by 50 per cent, while output rises by just over 52 per cent. *Returns to scale are still increasing.*

Although the arithmetic of this section may be tedious, the lesson to be learned is important. Exactly the same output figures can yield diminishing returns to each factor in the short run, and increasing returns to scale in the long run. Whether you understand this as a result of verbal argument, arithmetic or graphs is of secondary importance.

The Determinants of Returns to Scale

Increasing, constant and decreasing returns to scale are all found in many industries. We need to explain why this is so. It is simplest to ask, first, why returns to scale should be increasing.

The bases of increasing returns to scale

The major source of increasing returns lies in the existence of INDIVISIBILITIES. Many other determinants will be seen as being related in some way to indivisibilities, or pertaining to a period we have not yet mentioned – the very long run. There are also certain advantages that accrue to large-scale organization. They relate to marketing, financial and other considerations, and we discuss them in the next chapter.

Indivisibilities: The idea of 'indivisibility' is a simple one. It is that certain productive techniques can only be used if output is large enough. To illustrate, consider a step in the production process of a soft-drink manufacturer – that of putting caps on bottles once they have been filled. Capping may be done by hand or with an automatic bottle-capping machine. The smallest such machine will have a certain capacity of caps that it can put on each day, and it is not possible to have one with a smaller daily capacity. If you want an automatic bottle-capper, you must buy a machine with the minimum capacity that technology will allow. If you want to cap fewer bottles per day, either you buy the machine and leave it idle for part of the time, or you resort to labour-intensive capping by hand. Thus, it is only worthwhile to apply certain production techniques if output

TABLE 13.2 Outputs from Various Inputs of Labour and Capital

		UNITS OF CAPITAL		
		1	2	3
		(i)	(ii)	(iii)
UNITS	1	100	120	135
OF	2	130	220	290
LABOUR	3	150	300	335

exceeds a minimum level dictated by the capacity of a particular technique.

It is not difficult to find examples of capital equipment which are indivisible, in the sense in which we are using the term. Computer-controlled cylinder boring machines in engine manufacture are one example. Electricity generation is another. Inputs other than capital may also be indivisible. A small firm may have a single *general* manager in charge of production, sales, purchases of raw materials, and personnel. A large firm may be able to appoint several *specialized* managers in each of these departments. The existence of indivisible equipment means that the average (and marginal) product curves for higher outputs lie above and to the right of those for lower outputs – as do SAP_2 (and MAP_2) lie above and to the right of SAP_1 (and MAP_1) in Figure 13.2(ii).

Increased dimensions: One special kind of indivisibility worthy of mention is known as the principle of INCREASED DIMENSIONS. It is best illustrated by containers; for it is a fact that the capacity of a container increases more than proportionately to the quantity of material used in its construction.

To illustrate, compare two oil storage tanks, one of which has sides (in metres) 2×2, and the other 4×4. Each tank has six sides, so the *surface area* of the larger tank

$(4 \times 4 \times 6 = 96$ sq. metres) is *four* times the surface area of the smaller tank, which is $(2 \times 2 \times 6 = 24$ sq. metres). However the *capacity* of the larger tank $(4 \times 4 \times 4 = 64$ cubic metres) is *eight* times larger than that of the smaller tank $(2 \times 2 \times 2 = 8$ cubic metres).[1] A fourfold increase in material content raises capacity eightfold. Output volume must, of course, be sufficient to warrant use of the larger container, but the principle is of widespread application, as witness the long-term growth in the sizes of container lorries, oil tankers, and many factory buildings and supermarkets, to mention but a few.

The bases of constant and decreasing returns: In the previous sections, we described some reasons for the existence of increasing returns to scale. We look now at why constant and even decreasing returns to scale are sometimes present.

Our discussion can be brief, since the explanation of the appearance of constant returns to scale lies simply in the exhaustion of the bases for increasing returns. Sometimes the cause may be purely technological – larger machines may be more efficient up to a certain point, but there is no reason why larger and larger machines will always be so.

---

1 The surface area of the sides of a cube is related to the *square* of one of its sides; its capacity is related to the *cube* of a side.

BOX 13.1 The Lean Production Revolution

Production techniques are currently being revolutionized by the most fundamental change to occur since the introduction of mass production … a technique based on specialization and division of labour, identified by Adam Smith in the 18th century, and brought to full development by Henry Ford in the early 20th century.

Lean production methods combine the flexibility and high quality standards of craft production with the low cost of mass production techniques. They are 'lean' because they use less of all inputs, and the cost of switching is relatively low. Workers are organized as teams, using less specialized equipment than in mass production. Each team member can stop the assembly line when a fault is discovered. This leads to high worker morale and job satisfaction. Although stoppages are frequent when lean production methods are first introduced, they diminish markedly after some time, becoming fewer than the typical mass production line.

Japanese automobile firms using lean production methods have been able to achieve lower unit costs than those of mass-production-based North American car factories operating at double their volume levels. The major Japanese cars have also acquired the highest reputation for quality of the finished product.

(Adapted from R.G. Lipsey *et al.*, *Economics*, 9th edn, Harper & Row, New York, 1990)

To understand the 'lean production revolution', pioneered by the Japanese, one must contrast it with the two other production methods used today – craft methods and mass production techniques. Craft methods employ skilled workers to make non-standard products, which are of high quality but expensive, though providing considerable job-satisfaction for craftsmen. Mass production techniques employ relatively unskilled labour to produce standardized parts, and assemble them using highly specialized machines. The cost of switching equipment to vary the product is high. The result is long runs of standardized products of moderate quality but low cost. Job satisfaction is generally low.

Lean production methods are expensive in product design, but combine the flexibility and high quality standards of craft production with the low cost of mass production techniques.

Questions

1 Are the input-output relationships with lean production methods compatible with the law of diminishing returns, and returns to scale?

2 What, if anything, is the relevance of the very long run period to the lean revolution?

3 Can Figure 13.2 be used to illustrate the introduction of lean production methods?

A common explanation for eventually decreasing returns to scale relates to management. Experience suggests that increasing the entire scale of operations creates problems of management co-ordination, so that efficiency declines as top management loses touch with some sections of a business.

THE VERY LONG RUN: CHANGES IN TECHNIQUES

In the long run, factor inputs are varied within the confines of given techniques. Over time, however, knowledge changes, so that capital (and labour) may become more productive. This means that the long-run product curves such as those in Figure 13.2 shift upwards, indicating that given amounts of labour and capital become more productive, as a result of the invention of new and superior techniques of production.

The period of time over which these changes occur, sometimes called the VERY LONG RUN, is important when the rate of economic growth is being studied. Although economic growth is related to economic efficiency and is increasingly understood to be a microeconomic issue, it is traditionally considered part of macro rather than microeconomics, and is dealt with in Chapter 37 of this book.

In the meantime, we note that changes in the techniques of production are a potent source of long-term increases in living standards. Indeed, in the last few decades the material standard of living of the typical family has risen substantially in all the world's industrialized countries. Much of this increase has been due to the invention of improved ways of making products.

It is, for example, rare for a firm to replace an existing piece of capital equipment with another which is exactly the same. The new equipment usually incorporates some technical advance, which may be of outstanding significance, as with developments triggered by silicon microchips in computers and other electronic equipment. Or, it may be relatively modest as with cameras, or petrol-driven engines.

Inventions and Innovations

Productivity increases can follow the discovery of new ideas and their application in productive processes.

An INVENTION is defined as the discovery of something new, such as a production technique or a new product. An INNOVATION is defined as the introduction of an invention into use.

There is little of general relevance to be said about the process of innovation. It may result from the activities of the firm itself, through its own research and development, or from those of other firms or institutions, such as universities. The legal and institutional framework may play a part, for example, through the operation of patent laws and the tax structure.

It may, however, be a matter of importance whether an invention happens to be spontaneous, or occurs as a response to economic signals – i.e. movements in relative prices of inputs or outputs. For example, in many high-technology firms, research is continuous and no one knows exactly what it may lead to. It may result in inventions which need to be used in conjunction with other scarce, skilled and costly labour. Other inventions may be *induced* by factor prices, and the availability of relatively abundant factors, such as labour with existing skills. We should, therefore, be more likely to expect to find shocks to the economic system when inventions are spontaneously determined, than when they are as a result of responses to market forces.

Summary

1 The productivity of a factor of production is the relationship between inputs of the factor and outputs resulting from its use.

2 The average product of a factor is total output divided by all the units of the factor employed. The marginal product is the change in total product divided by the change in the quantity of the inputs of the factor employed.

3 In the short run, the quantity of at least one factor of production is, by definition, fixed, while inputs of other factor(s) are variable. In the long run, all factors can, by definition, be varied.

4 The Law of Diminishing Returns states that when increasing quantities of a variable factor are used together with a fixed factor in the short run, the marginal and average products of the variable factor will eventually decrease. The law follows from the fact that the proportions in which the factors are employed change in the short run.

5 When the marginal product of a factor is (i) equal to, (ii) greater than, or (iii) less than the average product, then average product is (i) constant, (ii) rising, or (iii) falling.

6 The relationship between inputs and outputs in the long run when factors proportions are constant is called returns to scale. Returns to scale are said to be (i) constant, (ii) increasing, or (iii) decreasing when total output increases (i) proportionately, (ii) more than proportionately, or (iii) less than proportionately to total inputs.

7 Diminishing returns to a variable factor in the short run are compatible with constant, increasing, or decreasing returns to scale in the long run.

8 The major source of increasing returns to scale is the existence of productive techniques which employ factors of production that are *indivisible*, and cannot be used unless output is greater than a certain minimum.

9 The very long run is the period when technical changes are possible as a result of the introduction into the production process (innovation) of new discoveries (inventions).

Questions

1 What distinguishes the short run, the long run and the very long run in the theory of production?

2 A business increases its inputs, one at a time, of a variable factor (working with a fixed factor) and finds the marginal products to be: 15, 25, 35, and 25. (i) What are the corresponding average products? (ii) What level of output for a 5th unit of the variable factor would cause the average product to be 22?

3 Given that 3 units of a variable factor give total output of 180, while 5 units give total output of 200. What are (i) average product when 3 units are used, (ii) marginal product when the variable factor increases from 3 to 5? (iii) What would be the total product from using 6 units of the variable factor if average product of 6 units was 35?

4 Refer to Figure 13.2(i). If a new firm is building a plant, what minimum level of output makes it sensible to install the larger size plant?

5 Which One or More of the following is a correct statement of the law of diminishing returns?
  (a) As more of a variable factor is added to a fixed factor, total product rises at a diminishing rate.

  (b) As more of all factors are used in constant proportions, average and marginal product eventually decline.
  (c) As an individual consumes more of a product, the marginal utility derived from it diminishes.
  (d) When average product of a variable factor is rising, marginal product is rising faster.
  (e) As more of a variable factor is added to a fixed factor, total product eventually falls.

6 Given the following relationship between inputs of capital and labour:

		Units of Capital		
		1	2	3
Units	1	100	150	170
of	2	140	180	210
Labour	3	x	200	230

  (i) Are returns to scale constant, increasing or decreasing?
  (ii) What is the marginal product of labour working with 2 units of capital?
  (iii) What is x if the marginal product of the 2nd unit of capital is 30?

14 Costs of Production

In the previous chapter we looked at the productivity of factors of production and at the relationship between physical inputs and outputs. The next step, in this chapter, is to translate productivity into costs by bringing in the prices that have to be paid for the use of factors of production.

THE NATURE OF COSTS

The cost to the firm of employing a factor is normally expressed in money terms. However, if a firm is to make profit-maximizing production decisions, those money values should reflect real opportunity costs. We met the concept of opportunity cost in the first chapter of this book, where we saw it as the sacrifice of the next best alternative when one chooses to use resources in a particular way.

Opportunity cost is always positive when resources have alternative uses.

You should remember that opportunity cost can be zero (see p.7). This would arise with any factor that has only a single use. For example there might be some highly specialized machine tool used in the construction of a particular body panel in a particular model of a particular motorcar. It is true that the cost of purchasing the tool was a genuine real cost, *when the initial decision to buy it was made*. At that time, its money cost represented what the firm could have bought instead of the machine tool. But once the tool was purchased and in situ, its opportunity cost falls to zero. Since it has, by assumption, a single use, there is nothing else it can do. As the well-known expression has it, 'bygones are bygones'. Such instances of zero opportunity costs are sometimes called *sunk costs*.

For correct decision-taking, the money values of costs should reflect real current sacrifices, regardless of the amounts actually paid out by the firm in the past.

Opportunity cost is a simple enough concept, but applying it is sometimes less simple. Consider the following applications.

Imputed Costs

No payments are made for the use of resources that are already owned by a firm. Yet a cost must be assigned to their use if they could have been productively employed in other ways. Such costs are known as IMPUTED COSTS. They should be reckoned at values reflecting what the firm could earn by shifting them to their next best alternative use. Take three examples.

The cost of money

Consider a firm that uses £100,000 of its own money that could have been loaned to someone else at 15 per cent interest per year. £15,000 should, therefore, be accounted for by the firm as the cost of funds used in production. If, for example, the revenue after paying for all other costs was £14,000, it should show a loss of £1,000. This is because the firm could have closed down, and loaned its money to someone else, yielding £15,000.

Special advantages

Suppose a firm owns a patent giving the sole right to use a new industrial process, or a highly desirable location, or that it makes a product with a popular brand-name, such as Coca-Cola, Nescafé, or Hoover. Each of these involves an opportunity cost to the firm. Whether or not the patent or trademark was acquired free, the firm could always sell, or lease, it to others. Hence a real sacrifice is involved, if the firm decides to use it itself. Typically, the value of assets such as these, differs from the cost at which the firm originally acquired them, which is called HISTORICAL COST, and which must be clearly distinguished from current opportunity cost.

Depreciation

The employment of capital equipment, such as building and machinery, usually involves a cost, which is called DEPRECIATION. It may arise simply because the asset wears out with use or because it becomes obsolete. To illustrate, successive generations of more powerful computers are replacing older ones, which lose their value even though working perfectly. The depreciation that should be allowed for is the reduction in the value of the assets, whatever the cause.

Depreciation should be calculated using the principle of opportunity cost. This principle requires careful consideration of the appropriate alternatives open to a firm. The precise nature of the asset, and the firm's intentions, are relevant to the calculation. However, as the following example will show, the historical cost of the asset is rarely an appropriate starting point.

Consider the case of Claire Vue, a window cleaner. Her only capital equipment is a ladder, which cost £150 when she bought it last year. Claire is a bit heavy on ladders and only keeps them for two years, when they are replaced.

How much depreciation should Claire allow at the end of the first year?

The answer is that the depreciation should be the *replacement cost of the ladder minus its second-hand price*. Say, for example, that new-ladder prices have held constant at £150 but that the market price of a one-year-old ladder is only £30. She should then charge herself £150 minus £30 = £120 depreciation for using the new ladder over its first year. Why charge £120? Why not just charge £75, on the grounds that she only half-used up the £150 ladder, which she intends to use for two years? The reason is that, instead of buying a new ladder for £150 at the beginning of the year, she could have bought a one-year-old ladder on the second-hand market for £30 and used the remaining £120 for other purposes. Her use of a new ladder for a year did indeed cost her £120, i.e. it entailed the sacrifice of £120 worth of other things.

Accounting versus Opportunity Costs

Accounting practices that are used to provide for depreciation vary. Some are conventionally based on historical costs. When this happens, two unfortunate consequences may ensue. In the first place, as we have shown, profits may be misstated. In the second place, errors may be made in the decisions a firm makes about its best course of action.

To understand why this is so, you must appreciate that a business's decision whether or not to produce a commodity for sale should have regard to the real costs incurred in production. Depreciation is such a real cost, so long as a sacrifice is involved in using an asset – i.e. there is a positive opportunity cost. However, historical costs do not necessarily reflect real costs.

Consider, for instance, a slight variation of the case we already met on the previous page where opportunity costs are zero. Suppose a firm has just spent £250,000 on machines for making fishing rods. Suppose, too, that the machines cannot be used to make anything else, that their expected life is 5 years, and that they have negligible scrap value. *Once the firm has bought the machines*, there is no cost at all in using them. Remember, bygones are bygones!

What is the most profitable (or least unprofitable) policy for our fishing-rod manufacturer should there be a decline in the demand for fishing rods such that sales revenues just cover labour and all other costs, but will not cover the depreciation of the machines, based on what the firm paid for them? Should they be used, or should the business be shut down?

The answer is that the machines should indeed be used, so long as their use is profitable, in that they yield *any* net revenue over all variable costs. The machines exist and have no other use. The decision to install them may have been wrong – with hindsight – but historical costs are irrelevant to current decisions.[1]

The principle brought out by this example may be stated in general terms:

---

[1] That is not to say that positive depreciation should not be deducted from revenue to assess the profitability of past decisions.

current decisions should be based on current costs; past costs should have no influence on what is currently the most profitable course of action.

The principle has widespread applications, within economics and outside. The notion that bygones are bygones simply means that, at any moment of time, the best thing to do depends only on current alternatives. Past mistakes are irrelevant. The principle is simple and very important, but is not intuitively obvious to everyone. So, we shall give you one final example.

We have an old friend who inherited some money and decided to buy a small flat in London. It cost him £100,000. Unfortunately, he bought at the top of the property boom and could not let the flat at a rent which covered his out-of-pocket expenses. We suggested that he should consider selling the property if he could earn more on his capital by lending it elsewhere, for example to a building society. This he refused because, he told us, the resale value of the flat was only £80,000 and he had paid £100,000 for it. He acknowledged that the purchase had been a mistake, but could not see the *irrelevance* of that *past* mistake for his current position – that bygones are bygones. So he held onto the property and made less money than if he had sold it and put £80,000 into a building society account. Our friend's behaviour shows his failure to appreciate the significance of the way in which economists calculate costs – that the best course of action always depends only on *current* alternatives. Bygones are bygones.

COSTS AND OUTPUT IN THE SHORT RUN

We have argued that the cost for any given output must be based upon real opportunity costs, including imputed costs, where a firm uses resources that it owns, and allowing for depreciation with proper regard to the alternatives to which resources may be put. To discover which of its possible levels of output is the most profitable, a firm needs to know how costs vary with output.

From Productivity to Costs

We know from the previous chapter how the returns to a variable factor working with a fixed factor behave in the short run, and how returns to scale operate in the long run. We now wish to derive short- and long-run cost curves for the firm. To do this, we merely value all factors at their opportunity costs, according to the principles outlined in the previous sections.

To illustrate, let us reconsider the output data in Table 13.1 (on page 135) which showed the variations in output from using increasing units of labour with a fixed quantity (10 units) of capital. Assume that the price of a unit of labour is £20, and the price of a unit of capital is £5. We can now derive 2 sets of figures of costs of production. See Table 14.1.

Columns (i), (ii) and (iii) in Table 14.1 reproduce from Table 13.1 details about inputs of capital and labour, and total output respectively. The remainder of the Table shows the costs of producing the different levels of output. Three measurements are shown: (i) total cost, (2) average cost, and (3) marginal cost.

Total cost (TC): This is the total cost of producing any given rate of output. Total cost is divided into two parts: TOTAL FIXED COST (TFC) and TOTAL VARIABLE COST (TVC). *TFC* does *not* vary with output. 10 units of capital are employed at a price of £5 per unit. Therefore total fixed cost, which is the opportunity cost of using the 10 units of capital, is £50 at all outputs (see column (iv)). Fixed costs are often referred to as OVERHEAD COSTS, and sometimes as INDIRECT COSTS or UNAVOIDABLE COSTS. (They are unavoidable because they are incurred whether or not the plant is operating.)

All costs that vary directly with output are called VARIABLE COSTS, often known as DIRECT COSTS, as PRIME COSTS, and occasionally as AVOIDABLE COSTS. (They are *avoidable* because they do not have to be paid if the plant is not operating.)

In Table 14.1, the only variable cost is that of using the variable factor, labour. Column (v) in the Table is calculated by multiplying the inputs of labour (column (i)) by the price of labour (£20 per unit). So, in the top row of the Table, 1 unit of labour is used, giving a figure of £20 for total variable costs. In the second row, 2 units of labour give total variable costs of £40, and so on.

Column (vi) in the Table is the sum of total fixed and total variable costs. It is calculated by adding the figures in columns (iv) and (v).

Average cost: The average cost of producing any given output is the cost of producing it divided by the number of units produced. AVERAGE TOTAL COST (ATC), sometimes known as UNIT COST, may be divided into AVERAGE FIXED COST (AFC), and AVERAGE VARIABLE COST (AVC).

Average fixed cost must decline as output increases, since the fixed total is divided by larger and larger outputs. This is a process popularly known as 'spreading one's overheads'. In column (vii) of Table 14.1, *AFC* is calculated by dividing *TFC* (column (iv) by total output (column (iii)). In the top line of the Table, the *AFC* of producing 4 units of output is £50 divided by 4 = £12.50. In the second row, *AFC* is £50 divided by 10 = £5, and so on.

Average *variable* cost may rise, fall or remain unchanged as output varies. As production grows, *AVC* will rise if *TVC* rises more rapidly than output, and vice versa. *AVC* will be constant if *TVC* rises at the same rate as output rises.

AVC, shown in column (viii) of Table 14.1, is calculated by dividing *TVC* (column (v)) by total output (column (iii)). So, the top row in the Table shows *AVC* as being £5. This figure is the result of dividing £20 by the output of 4. In the second row, *AVC* is £40 divided by 10 = £4, and so on.

ATC, column (ix) in the Table, is the sum of *AVC* and *AFC*, obtained by adding the figures in columns (vii) and (viii) or by dividing the figures in column (vi) by those in column (iii).

Marginal cost (MC): This is shown in column (x) in the Table and is defined as the difference in total cost resulting from a unit change in output. The MARGINAL COST is, therefore, calculated by dividing the increase in total

TABLE 14.1 Short-run Cost Schedules. (The figures are based on output data in Table 13.1 valued at a price of labour of £20 per unit and a price of capital of £5 per unit)

INPUTS (units)		OUTPUT (total)	TOTAL COST			AVERAGE COST			MARGINAL COST (MC)
Labour (i)	Capital (ii)	(iii)	Fixed (TFC) (iv)	Variable (TVC) (v)	Total (TC) (vi)	Fixed (AFC) (vii)	Variable (AVC) (viii)	Total (ATC) (ix)	(x)
1	10	4	£50	£20	£70	£12.50	£5.00	£17.50	£5.00
2	10	10	50	40	90	5.00	4.00	9.00	3.33
3	10	21	50	60	110	2.38	2.86	4.94	1.82
4	10	40	50	80	130	1.25	2.00	3.25	1.05
5	10	55	50	100	150	0.91	1.82	2.73	1.33
6	10	60	50	120	170	0.84	2.00	2.84	4.00
7	10	63	50	140	190	0.80	2.22	3.02	6.67
8	10	64	50	160	210	0.78	2.50	3.28	20.00

Col. (vi) = col. (iv) + col. (v).
Col. (vii) = col. (iv) ÷ col. (iii).
Col. (viii) = col. (v) ÷ col. (iii).

Col. (ix) = col. (vi) ÷ col. (iii) = col. (vii) + col. (viii).
Col. (x) = change in output from col. (iii) divided by change in variable cost from col. (v).

cost by the change in output. Looking at the Table, we see that an increase in output from 4 to 10 units results in an increase in total costs from £70 to £90. The difference in total cost is therefore £20. The change in output is 10 − 4 = 6 units. Marginal cost is, therefore, £20 divided by 6, or £3.33, which is the figure in the last column of the Table. When output rises from 10 to 21 units, total cost rises from £90 to £110. Marginal cost is then £20 divided by 11 = £1.82.

We have calculated marginal cost from the figures of total (fixed *and* variable) cost in column (vi). We could equally have used the figures in column (v) of total variable cost alone. If you perform the calculations in the previous paragraph substituting column (v) for column (vi), you will find that they give exactly the same results. This is because

'fixed' costs do not enter into marginal costs. They are fixed and do not change when output changes. In other words, marginal fixed costs are bound to be zero, so that marginal costs are marginal variable costs.

Marginal costs may rise, fall or remain constant as output varies. They are determined by the rate of change of total cost, as output increases, or decreases, one unit at a time.

The three measures of cost are merely different ways of looking at the same data. They are interrelated, as we have seen. Sometimes it is convenient to use one, and sometimes another.

(Note that in Table 14.1 marginal costs are recorded in the intervals between rows, because they relate to changes in costs, which are given by differences between adjacent rows. The reason is the same as that for showing marginal product in the intervals between rows in Table 13.1.)

Cost Curves in the Short Run

The cost schedules in Table 14.1 are represented graphically in Figure 14.1. Part (i) of the figure displays the total costs of producing different outputs. Part (ii) shows the unit average and marginal cost of producing the same outputs. The scales of the two sections are, therefore, identical on the output (horizontal) axis, but differ on the vertical axis, which measures costs.

Figure 14.1(i) shows total fixed costs as a horizontal straight line at a figure of £50, because that cost is incurred at all outputs. The curves TVC and TC are parallel to each other. The vertical distance between them is £50, which is TFC.

In Figure 14.1(ii) AFC is a downward-sloping curve because total fixed costs are spread over larger and larger outputs. TFC for any output is average fixed cost times the quantity of input, which is the area enclosed by dropping perpendiculars from a point on the AFC curve to the two axes. For example, when output is 20, AFC is £2.50 and TFC is 20 × £2.50 = £50; when output is 25, AFC is £2 and TFC is 25 × £2 = £50. These areas are equal because TFC is always £50. (AFC is, therefore, a rectangular hyperbola for the same reason as is a demand curve of unit elasticity – see Chapter 7, p.63)

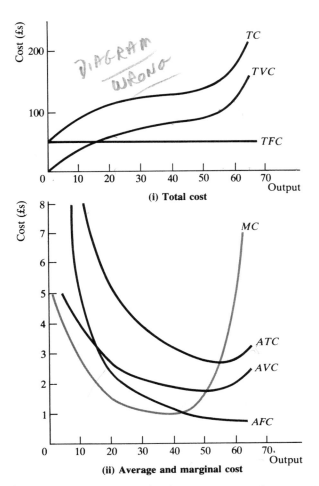

FIGURE 14.1 Cost Curves in the Short Run. Part (i) shows Total Variable Costs (*TVC*), Total Fixed Costs (*TFC*) and Total Costs (*TC*); *TVC* + *TFC* = *TC*. Part (ii) shows unit costs: Average Variable costs (*AVC*), Average Fixed Costs (*AFC*), Average Total Costs (*ATC*) and Marginal Costs (*MC*).
AVC + *AFC* = *ATC*. *AVC* and *ATC* are U-shaped; each is cut at its minimum point by *MC*.

There is an alternative way of showing AFC in the diagram. Since TC is made up of fixed and variable cost, AFC is the (vertical) *difference* between AVC and ATC. Since average cost is measured for any output as the height of the cost curve at that output, the vertical distance between AVC and ATC must measure AFC. Moreover, as AFC falls continuously as output increases, AVC and ATC must become vertically closer to each other as output rises. AVC, ATC and MC curves fall at first as output increases, reach minima, and then start to rise. They are sometimes described as ∪-shaped. This shape is due to the 'law' of diminishing returns, which applies because these are short-run cost curves.

If you turn back and compare Figure 14.1 with Figure 13.1 on page 135, you will notice a striking similarity between them. The one is an inverted image of the other. The cost curve is ∪-shaped, the product curve is ∩-shaped. Average product rises at first, reaches a maximum and starts to fall. Average cost falls at first, reaches a minimum and starts to rise.

The common sense of this cost-product relationship is that each new worker adds the same amount to cost, but a different amount to output. When output per unit of labour is rising, the cost per unit of output is falling, and vice versa. The same argument applies to the relationship between average total product and average total cost, and also to that between marginal product and marginal cost.

Notice that MC cuts ATC and AVC at their lowest points. This is another example of the relationship between average and marginal curves. The reason was explained fully with regard to average and marginal product curves. (Refer back to page 136, if you are unsure about this.) Note, too, that the ATC curve slopes downward as long as the MC curve is below it. It makes no difference whether the MC curve itself is sloping upward or downward. The reason is that if marginal cost is less than the average cost, then the average must be falling.

Size of plant and capacity

The short-run cost curves in Figure 14.1 are drawn for a given quantity of the fixed factor – say a plant of given size. There will be a different, ∪-shaped, set of short-run cost curves for each plant.

The output that corresponds to the minimum of the average total cost curve is called FULL CAPACITY, or sometimes just CAPACITY.

Note that capacity output is not an upper limit to output, merely minimum average cost output. Nor is it necessarily maximum profit output. To determine its best output, a firm has to consider demand as well as costs. In this chapter we discuss costs; demand considerations are added in the next chapter.

COSTS AND OUTPUT IN THE LONG RUN

In the short run, at least one factor of production is fixed. Output can be changed only by adjusting the input of the variable factor. Thus, in the short run, once the firm has decided on its output, there is only one technically possible way of achieving it.

In the long run, all factors are variable. A firm, then, has an additional decision to make: by which of the various methods should any given output be produced? Usually, there are many ways of producing a given output. Some are relatively more labour-intensive than others, some more capital-intensive, some more land-intensive, and so on. How should the firm decide which is best?

Assuming that the firm's prime objective is to maximize profits, the answer must be to choose the technique that incurs the lowest possible cost. This is called cost minimization.

Long-run planning decisions affect future profits. Today's variable factors are tomorrow's fixed factors.

Once a new factory is built or new equipment installed, it is fixed – perhaps for a long time to come. If the firm makes a mistake now, it must live with the consequences.

Long-run decisions are difficult, because the firm must anticipate what methods of production will be the most efficient in the years ahead. This depends on the future prices of labour, capital and raw materials and on the demand for its product. New products may emerge, and new production techniques may be developed. A firm that is shrewder in estimating future trends in costs and demand than others will reap the rewards of larger profits. Other firms, through bad judgement, bad luck, or a combination of both, will earn smaller profits. They may even make losses and close down.

Cost Minimization and Factor Prices

The alternative methods of production open to the firm in the long run, involve different amounts of the inputs of labour, capital and other factors of production. The cost of each method will differ according to the quantities of the different inputs and of the prices of these inputs. Hence, the least-cost method must include consideration of *factor prices*.

There is a general principle to guide the firm in its search for the minimum-cost method. It is that the last pound spent on each and every factor of production should yield the same extra output.

To illustrate, assume, as we did previously, that a firm has two factors, capital costing £5 per unit and labour costing £20 per unit. Suppose, now, that the marginal product of capital is 50 units of output and that the marginal product of labour is 200 units of output. Since the last unit of capital yields 50 units and costs £5, its output *per pound* spent on it is $50/5 = 10$ units. Since the last unit of labour yields 200 units and costs £20, its output *per pound* spent on it is $200/20 = 10$ units. They are equal. The condition is satisfied and costs minimized.

The principle of substitution

To demonstrate why the principle illustrated in the previous paragraph is necessary for cost minimization, let us consider the implications of a choice of techniques where the condition does *not* hold.

Assume, as before, that the prices of labour and of capital are £20 and £5 per unit respectively. However, assume now that the marginal products of capital and labour are both 200. The last unit of capital employed costs £5 but yields 200 units of output. Therefore, the yield of the last pound spent on capital is $200/5 = 40$ units per £1 spent. The last pound spent on labour however is still, as before, $200/20 = 10$ units per £1 spent. Thus, each pound spent on labour yields only a quarter of the output of each pound spent on capital. In this case, the firm could lower the cost of producing the *same output*, by substituting capital for labour. It would pay the firm to switch to a more capital-intensive technique of production, so long as the productivity of capital *relative to the price of capital* was greater than the productivity of labour *relative to the price of labour*.

We can now state the principle of equality of marginal products per pound spent on each factor generally. All we did in the above example was to divide the marginal product of each factor by its price, and ensure that the results were equal:

$$\frac{\text{marginal product of capital}}{\text{price of capital}} = \frac{\text{marginal product of labour}}{\text{price of labour}}$$

or,
$$\frac{MP_K}{P_K} = \frac{MP_L}{P_L}$$

(using symbols K for capital, L for labour and P for price.)

Expressing the condition for cost minimization this way emphasizes that the condition for cost minimization relates to the *ratios* of each factor's marginal product divided by its price.

Be careful not to make the common error of stating the principle for cost minimization as the equality of marginal products. Marginal products are defined in terms of physical inputs of factors of production. The condition for cost minimization runs in terms of marginal products *per unit of money* spent on them.

Changes in techniques of production

The rule for cost minimization can be used to show how a profit-maximizing firm responds to changes in cost conditions. Such changes can arise in two ways – from changes in factor prices, or from changes in marginal products of factors. Either can affect the choice of technique. Thus, it pays a firm to substitute labour for capital if the marginal product of labour rises, or the price of labour falls, relative to that of capital.

This proposition is central to the theory of the allocation of resources. It lies behind all the arguments about the way in which a market economy reallocates resources in response both to changes in the supplies of factors – which are reflected in factor prices – and to changes in productivity – which reflect developments in technology. Firms tend to use less of factors that become relatively expensive in terms of their productivity, and more of those which become relatively cheap.

Cost Curves in the Long Run

There is a best, least-cost, method of producing each rate of output when all factors are free to vary. If factor prices and productivities are given, a minimum cost can be found for each possible level of output. If this minimum achievable cost is expressed as an amount per unit of output, we obtain the long-run average cost of producing each level of output. When this information is plotted on a graph, the result is the LONG-RUN AVERAGE TOTAL COST (LATC) CURVE. An example is shown in Figure 14.2.

$LATC$ is determined from the technology of the industry

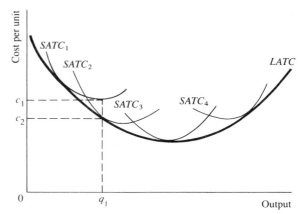

FIGURE 14.2 The Long-Run Average Total Cost Curve (LATC). *LATC* shows the average costs of different outputs when all factors are variable. The cost of producing q_1 is c_1 with plant $SATC_1$, but only c_2 in the long run with plant $SATC_2$.

and the prices of factors of production. It is drawn on the assumption that the firm has a choice among all possible plant sizes. In Figure 14.2, we show four short-run average cost curves (each labelled $SATC$). Thus, in the short run a firm might be operating with a small plant, $SATC_1$, and producing q_1 at an average cost of c_1. In the long run, however, the larger plant, $SATC_2$, could be installed, which would lower average costs to c_2.

If we let the firm choose between plants of many sizes, we can derive the long-run average cost curve shown in Figure 14.2. The $LATC$ curve is sometimes described as the ENVELOPE curve that encloses the family of $SATC$ curves which just touch (are tangent to) it. Each $SATC$ curve shows how costs vary if output changes in the short run. For each such curve the amount of the fixed factor is that which is needed, when the plant being used is optimal. The $LATC$ curve shows how costs vary if output changes when all factors can be varied.

The shape of the long-run average cost curve

The long-run average cost curve that we drew in Figure 14.2 shows long-run average cost falling at first as output increases, reaching a minimum, and then rising. It is ∪-shaped, as are the short-run cost curves. It is important to appreciate, however, that the 'law' of diminishing returns to a variable factor used with a fixed factor, cannot explain the shape of the long-run average cost curve because, in the long run, all factors may be varied.

The ∪-shape of the $LATC$ curve consists of three regions, with average costs first decreasing, then increasing, with an intermediate stage when they bottom out (i.e. are constant). We shall explain the reasons for each region in turn.

Decreasing long-run costs

Since we have ruled out changes in factor proportions to account for changes in costs, we must associate decreasing long-run costs with increasing returns to scale. As long as factor prices are not affected by the amount that the firm buys, increasing returns to scale imply decreasing long-run costs. Several sources of falling costs can be noted, though the borderlines between them are not always clear-cut.

Technical economies of scale: These refer to the techniques of production itself. Included among them are the matters we described under the heading of 'increasing returns to scale' (see pp.138–9). The chief source of such economies are the indivisibilities that accounted for increasing returns – for example, for the fact that it is only worthwhile installing expensive, highly specialized and efficient machinery if the scale of production warrants it.

Firms in many industries produce a range of different products. For example, a modern paper manufacturer may produce over 400 different types and grades of paper. Each product may have development costs and require some specialized machinery. These are fixed costs. The longer the production run of each product, the lower the average total costs, because these fixed costs are spread over more and more units. Modern research has shown that in many industries, production-run economies are a more important source of falling costs than the traditional scale economies referred to in the previous paragraph.

Managerial economies of scale: These are those economies which arise from the opportunities for division of labour and specialization among management. A large firm, for example, can provide full-time activity for those with specialist managerial skills such as accountants, lawyers, buyers, personnel, marketing, production and other managers.

Marketing economies of scale: These arise because the principle of the employment of specialists can be extended to marketing arrangements on both the buying and selling sides. A large enough firm can use the services of specialized buyers of its raw materials – perhaps even a specialist for each raw material. It can also employ personnel trained in the peculiarities of the market, or markets, in which it sells its product. There are technical economies to be reaped in marketing, too (which could as well be included under our first heading). Bulk purchases or sales may be made at lower unit costs, as for example is the case with much packaging, invoicing, delivery and so on.

Financial economies of scale: These arise when a firm needs to borrow to expand its scale of operations. The cost of borrowing is normally lower, the larger the sums involved. This is because there are certain minimum charges made by financial institutions, and thus average costs will fall if they are spread over larger amounts than over small ones.

Risk-bearing economies of scale: This is the final category. These arise because larger firms can *diversify*, and doing so reduces risks. To an extent, risk reduction is a cause of the lower cost of borrowing money, which we have already dealt with. There are, however, other cost

advantages of diversification. A firm which is operating in many markets is less vulnerable to a slump in any one market than is another firm selling only in a single market. The argument applies to firms selling the same goods in different markets, say at home and overseas. It applies, too, to diversification in the types of goods that the firm sells – i.e. not keeping all one's eggs in one basket.

Learning-by-doing

The discussion of economies of scale, so far, has concerned the relationship between two variables – costs and output. But there is a variable other than the level of output that may cause costs to change. It is experience.

Early economists placed great importance on what we now call *learning-by-doing*. They felt that as businesses specialize in particular tasks, workers, and managers, gradually become more efficient in performing them. As people acquire expertise, or know-how, costs tend to fall *as experience accumulates, rather than because the rate of output grows*. Research, moreover, suggests that this really does happen.

It is important to distinguish carefully the implications of learning-by-doing and of economies of scale for the cost curves of a firm. Changes in costs traceable to changes in the level of output, due, e.g., to technical, managerial and other economies of scale, involve *moving along a downward-sloping long-run cost curve*. Changes in costs that happen over time, as a result of learning by doing, cause the *long-run cost curve to shift downwards*.

Internal and external economies of scale

There are two kinds of economies of scale, those internal and those external to the firm. Economies mentioned so far have been

INTERNAL ECONOMIES (of scale), so-called because they are within the firm's own control. EXTERNAL ECONOMIES are sources of falling costs, outside the firm's control, and related to events in an industry – often that in which the firm operates but also in related industries.

As an industry expands, the costs of each firm may fall. For example, the supply of skilled labour may increase, relieving the individual firm of some part of training costs, which are shared with other firms (and with the government which may subsidize vocational courses in the area).

As an industry expands, its firms may find their costs fall because firms *in related industries* are subject to increasing *internal* economies of scale. For example, aluminium production is subject to increasing returns to scale. An expansion of the aircraft industry, which is a consumer of aluminium, reduces the cost of producing aluminium, thereby lowering costs in the aircraft industry.

The two sources of external economies of scale described above – increased factor efficiency and lower costs of inputs supplied by other industries – are likely to have particular strength when an industry is concentrated geographically. Information spreads quickly locally, which is conducive to efficiency and helps explain why geographical concentration of industry is common – for example, motor-vehicle assembly and manufacture of vehicle parts in the West Midlands.

Constant long-run costs

The opportunities for specialization, division of labour, and the resulting falling production costs are not unlimited. When a firm reaches the size at which opportunities for economies of scale are exhausted, costs per unit cease to fall. The *LATC* curve becomes horizontal, as illustrated in Figure 14.3. The level of output at which production costs cease to fall is called the *MES* (MINIMUM EFFICIENT SCALE); it is shown by output q_0 in this figure.

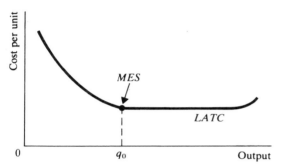

FIGURE 14.3 **Minimum Efficient Scale (MES).** MES is the level of output, q_0 here, beyond which costs cease to fall in the long run.

It is useful to relate *MES* to the size of the industry as a whole, in order to know how many firms of minimum efficient size an industry can accommodate. Evidence for the UK shows that there are many sectors where the *MES* is high as a proportion of total sales, especially in manufacturing.

For example, the ratio of *MES* to total industry sales is over 30 per cent for aluminium semi-manufactures, over 50 per cent for diesel engines and refrigerators, and 100 per cent or over for TV tubes and electronic calculators. In this last case, production at the lowest possible cost would require that the industry contain only one firm. Such a firm would be called a 'natural monopoly'. We shall consider the implications of the existence of natural monopolies in Chapter 16.

Increasing long-run costs

The long-run average total cost curves shown in both Figures 14.2 and 14.3, eventually turn up. The upward-sloping portions of the curves mean that as output increases unit costs rise, even in the long run. They correspond to the range of decreasing returns to scale.

The sources of rising long-run costs may be internal or external. Significant internal diseconomies of scale tend to be associated with management or with geography.

It is hard to find firm evidence on the subject, but firms can get so large that managerial problems become excessive. Rising costs associated with management problems may more than offset other economies of large-scale production, so that overall costs rise as output increases. However efficient a management may be, it may eventually lose touch when a business grows beyond a certain size.

Delegation to subordinates and decentralization may give rise to problems of co-ordination and control. Transport costs per unit of output may increase as businesses spread further from head office. Moreover, industrial relations may deteriorate as firms reach giant size. Low morale and a feeling of alienation, not to mention more industrial disputes, may lower productivity on the shop floor, thereby raising costs of production.

External diseconomies shift the entire set of cost curves upwards for all firms in an industry. For example congestion pushes up transport costs for all firms in areas of

---

BOX 14.1 Arms Firm Turns to Cricket Bats

'South Africa's giant arms manufacturer Armscor has developed a peaceful sideline on the swords-for-ploughshares theme by adapting machinery used for shaping wooden rifle stocks to make cricket bats.

'The Armscor subsidiary Musgrave Manufacturers is importing from England the special willow used to make top-quality cricket bats. It hopes to seize a share of the 50,000 bats which are imported by South Africa each year.'

(*Daily Telegraph*, 31 August 1990)

Costs of production depend on factor prices and technology. The proper basis for calculating costs must always be that of opportunity cost, reflecting the next

best use to which factors of production may be put. If a factor has only a single use then its opportunity cost must be counted as zero, even in the face of a drastic decline in demand for the product. However, as the news item shows, a little ingenuity can sometimes lead to revision of previous thought about alternative uses of factors.

Questions

1 Do you think the above quotation relates to one time-period rather than another? If so, which?
2 Can you think of another product that Armscor might turn to if South Africans stopped playing cricket?
3 What implications, if any, do you think the above might have for the persistence of small firms in South Africa?

heavy industrial concentration. There are also pressures which lead to increasing prices of factors of production as industries grow.

The Continued Existence of Small Firms

We are used to living in an economy where economies of scale favour large firms. However, although small-scale production sometimes occurs in plants which are owned by large multi-plant businesses, small independent firms persist in some sectors, for a variety of reasons.

Cost conditions: Costs rise sharply as output increases in some industries, giving advantage to small size.

Market limits: A much-quoted saying of Adam Smith's is that the division of labour is limited by the extent of the market. This can explain the persistence of small firms in markets with very limited demand. The total number of tuning forks demanded, for example, is hardly likely to be great enough for even a single manufacturer to become very big.

A more general point is that, while costs may fall for standardized products, there is often a demand for variety, which can involve large firms in exceptionally high costs. This sometimes allows small, flexible, firms producing a few differentiated products to survive.

Product cycles: New products appear continually, while others disappear. At the early stage of a new product, total demand is typically low, costs of production are high and many small firms try to get ahead of their competitors by finding the twist that appeals to consumers, or the technique that slashes their costs. Some new products never get past that stage. In other cases, the successful firms grow to dominate the industry, often eliminating their rivals by merging with them or by forcing them out of business. Eventually, at the mature stage of the industry, a few giant firms may become dominant.

Sooner or later, however, new products appear that erode the position of the established large firms, which run into financial difficulties and/or switch to other industries, including those where small firms are already present. The cycle starts again. At any moment of time, industries can be found in all phases, helping to explain the persistence of small firms.

Non-profit maximization: As stated earlier, not every business tries to maximize profits. In some cases, firms do not grow because their owners prefer to keep them small for reasons unrelated to profit maximization. We should note incidentally that non-profit maximization may also work to *increase* the size of firms if they strive to grow beyond the most efficient size in pursuit of other objectives.

The discussions in this chapter and the previous one have been concerned with the cost conditions facing firms, and with reasons why both small and large firms persist in a market economy. In the next three chapters we shall put cost and demand conditions together to construct theories of the firm which can help explain their behaviour, especially with regard to the choice of output and price.

Summary

1 The costs that are relevant to business decisions are opportunity costs. They should include imputed costs for the use of resources owned by a firm, for example money, special advantages and depreciation.

2 Historical costs may not be the same as opportunity costs. Bygones are bygones; past costs are irrelevant to current decisions.

3 Short-run average total cost is the sum of average fixed cost and average variable cost. Marginal cost is the difference in total cost resulting from a unit change in output.

4 In the short run, average variable and average total cost curves may be drawn for a given size plant. They are ∪-shaped reflecting the law of diminishing returns. Each is cut at its minimum point by the marginal cost curve. Output where average total cost is minimal is called (full) capacity output.

5 In the long run, the firm has a choice of plant size. The long-run average cost curve is derived from the set of short-run cost curves for different size plants. It is an envelope curve.

6 The condition for long-run cost minimization is that a firm should employ factors of production up to the points at which the marginal products of every factor *per unit of money spent on them* are equal; in other words the marginal product of each factor is proportional to its price.

7 In the long run, costs may decrease, remain constant or increase. Decreasing costs may be attributed to technical, managerial, marketing, financial, or risk-bearing economies of scale.

8 Economies of scale may be internal, i.e. within the firm's control, or external, i.e. outside its control and arising from conditions in the industry, or in other industries.

9 The Minimum Efficient Scale (MES) of plant is that beyond which long-run costs stop falling, i.e. stay constant, or start to rise.

10 The persistence of small firms in the economy is explained by rising costs (especially managerial and geographically related costs), market limits, product cycles and non-profit-maximizing behaviour.

Questions

1 Which One or More of the following considerations (which could affect business decisions) would you include as examples of the principle that 'bygones are bygones'?
  (a) The need to count the use of a firm's own money as a cost.
  (b) The fact that past, historical costs must be recovered if the firm is to continue in business.
  (c) Disregarding the cost of building a factory when deciding whether to use it.
  (d) The fact that sunk costs should be disregarded, even if they are positive.
  (e) Taking account of the fact that a factory built last year was unprofitable when deciding whether to build another one this year.

2 Refer to Figure 14.1(i). (i) What is the meaning of the difference between the slopes of TC and TVC? (ii) Refer to Figure 14.1(ii). Call the point of intersection of MC and ATC 'a'. Drop a perpendicular from a to the output axis and call the point at which your line cuts AVC 'b'. What is the meaning, if any, of the distance $a - b$?

3 Distinguish between 'capacity' and 'MES' (minimum efficient scale).

4 Are the following statements True or False? (i) average variable cost may be constant, rise or fall as output is varied, but average fixed costs must fall in direct proportion to output increases; (ii) a firm minimizes costs when the marginal products of all factors are equal.

5 A firm is operating under the following conditions: the price of a unit of labour is £25 and a unit of land is £50. Employing an extra unit of labour would produce £1000's worth of commodities, and an extra unit of land would produce £2000's worth. Which of the following would be the most profitable acts?
  (a) employ more labour
  (b) employ more land
  (c) employ more labour and less land
  (d) employ less labour and more land
  (e) employ no more nor less labour or land.

The Profit-Maximizing Firm and Perfect Competition

This chapter is the first of three in which we examine the behaviour of profit-maximizing firms in different market situations. Our analysis will take up the next three chapters. First, however, we must develop some general rules that apply to all maximizing firms, regardless of the kind of market in which they operate.

THE FIRM IN ANY MARKET

In anybody's language, profits are the difference between revenues and costs. However, as we saw in the previous chapter, costs can be thought of, and measured, as either historical accounting costs or opportunity costs.

The opportunity cost of capital

We shall, of course, use the definition that is based on opportunity costs. We include in costs everything which involves a real sacrifice, whether or not it involves the actual payment of monies by the firm. Moreover, we include among costs a new category called the OPPORTUNITY COST OF CAPITAL. This represents the return that the capital of a business would earn if it were lent out at the market rate of interest, or were used in another industry – that which earned it the 'next best' rate of return.

Normal profit

The economic profits of a firm are the result of deducting from total revenues all real opportunity costs, including the opportunity cost of capital, as defined in the previous paragraph. We shall say that a firm is earning NORMAL PROFIT if its economic profits are zero. In such a case the firm earns no more and no less than it could by using all of its resources not in their present, but in their next best, use.[1]

The cost curves of the firm are drawn to include normal profits. We shall use the terms SUPERNORMAL, and SUBNORMAL, profits when firms are earning more, and less, than the opportunity cost of employing all their resources elsewhere.

Various revenue concepts

Profits are maximized when the difference between total costs and total revenues is at its greatest. In the previous chapter, we armed ourselves with a set of clearly defined cost concepts. We must now do likewise with revenues.

We can look at revenues in three ways, as we did with costs in the previous chapter.

TOTAL REVENUE (TR) means just what it says, the total receipts of money that the firm obtains from all sales. Total revenue is equal to the quantity of goods sold multiplied by their selling price.

AVERAGE REVENUE (AR) is total revenue divided by the number of units sold. *Average revenue is the same as the price of the product.*

MARGINAL REVENUE (MR) is the *change* in total revenue resulting from a *change of one unit* in the rate of sales (per period of time). If the total revenue from the sale of 9 units is £15, and the total revenue from the sale of 10 units is £17, marginal revenue is equal to £17 − £15 = £2.

Two points to note: Note, first, that marginal revenue is defined as the change in revenue resulting from the production and sale of *one more* (or *one less*) unit. Sometimes, however, we only have data for changes covering more than one unit. In such cases, we have to strike an average over the range of output for which information is available. For example, if TR from 9 units is £15, and from 11 units is £23, then MR is £$(23 − 15)/(11 − 9) = 8/2 = £4$. To accommodate such possibilities, we define MR as $\Delta TR / \Delta Q$, where Δ stands as usual for 'change in'.

The second point to note is that marginal revenue refers to different values of output *at the same period of time*. Do not think that 9 units are sold at one time, and 11 units at some later time. Marginal revenue refers to what would happen during any one period if different amounts were sold.

TWO RULES FOR THE PROFIT-MAXIMIZING FIRM

We now give two rules that any firm should follow if it is to produce the output which maximizes profits. The rules answer two questions. First, should the firm produce at all? Second, if it is profitable for the firm to produce, what is its best, or optimum, output?

Rule 1. The Shut-Down Rule

The first Rule states that output should be positive only if total revenue is equal to, or greater than, total variable cost.

---

1 The concept of normal profit is widely used in economics at an introductory level. Note, however, that in a good deal of more advanced work (including IPE), the concept of normal profit is not employed.

This is often called the shut-down rule, because it shows that a firm which is currently producing, should shut up shop if there is no output for which total variable cost is less than total revenue. The name is, perhaps, a little misleading, for it might just as well be called the 'start-up' rule, because it also tells when a firm, currently shut-down, should commence production.

The reason for the rule is that the firm's variable costs can be avoided by ceasing production. Hence, it only pays to produce if revenues from sales at least cover these avoidable (i.e. variable) costs. We can state this condition in either of two ways. First, we can say that total revenue should be equal to, or greater than, total variable cost.

A second way of stating exactly the same condition is to put it in terms, not of total, but of average variable cost and average revenue. Average revenue is total revenue divided by output, and average variable cost is total variable cost divided by output. Therefore, the condition for producing a positive output may also be stated as that average revenue should be equal to, or greater than, average variable cost.

Different costs are avoidable in the short and the long runs. Rule 1 has, therefore, two applications. It is important to distinguish between them.

Shut-down conditions in the short run: When a firm is considering whether or not to close down in the short run, its decision depends only on short-run variable costs and is unrelated to fixed costs, which are unavoidable since they have to be met even if the firm produces no output at all.

An example may clarify this important principle of the irrelevance of fixed costs. Consider a hotel business at a seaside resort. During the winter, demand is slack so that only a few rooms may be occupied daily. Should the hotel close down for the winter, or rub along trying to cover some of its costs?

The hotel has both fixed and variable costs. The unavoidable fixed costs may, for example, include business rates payable to the local authority, interest on capital used to buy the hotel (or perhaps the annual rent on a lease that cannot be cancelled at short notice). The variable costs include all avoidable expenses of running the hotel, such as wages, heating and lighting, laundering, etc. If the hotel cannot earn enough revenue to cover the variable costs of keeping open for the few guests who will come during the winter, the most profitable course is the one that minimizes winter losses – shut down for that period.

Indeed, many hotels do just this. However, some hotels may find that, by staying open, they can earn enough revenue to cover all variable costs and make some contribution to fixed costs. It then clearly pays to keep going in the winter, in spite of the fact that they do not cover total costs. They would be worse off if they closed down, *because they still have to meet fixed costs.* That is why you will see some hotels in holiday resorts open in the winter. Many offer special low rates out of season, usually just enough to cover variable costs, and make some contribution, however small, towards fixed costs.

Shut-down conditions in the long run: Because in the long run all costs are variable, a profit-maximizing firm will stay in business in the long run, *only* if it can cover its total costs. Covering short-run variable costs is not sufficient. To return to our seaside hotel, it is only sensible to remain open in winter, covering the variable costs of doing so, if the revenue in summer and winter together is sufficient to cover total costs *of the year as a whole.* If this is not possible, the firm should close down in the long run.

To illustrate these conditions, consider as an example, the Esplanade Hotel at Brightpool. Its revenues and costs of operating during the in-season and off-season periods are shown in Table 15.1 on page 154. When charging the profit-maximizing price for its rooms, the hotel earns a return over its total variable costs of £24,000 during the in-season, as shown in the final column of the table. This surplus goes towards meeting the hotel's fixed costs, which are assumed to be £26,000.

The hotel discovers that, by charging lower prices during the off-season, it can let some rooms for a total revenue of £20,000 at a cost of staying open of £18,000, as shown in the second row of the table. This surplus, though small, can help to cover part of the fixed costs. Therefore the hotel should stay open the whole year round. Indeed, if it were to close in the winter, it would have to close in the summer too, since it could not then cover its total fixed and variable costs.

Now assume that the off-season total revenue falls to £19,000 (everything else the same). The short-run condition for staying open, $TR > TVC$, is met in the in- and the off-seasons. But the long-run condition is not, since the excess of TR over TVC over the whole year of £25,000 is less than the fixed costs of £26,000. The hotel will remain open as long as it can do so with its present capital. But it will not pay the owners to replace the capital as it wears out.

The hotel will get run down, and guests will ask 'why don't they do something about this place?' But the owners' behaviour is sensible. They are operating the hotel as long as it covers its variable costs but they are not putting new investment into it since it cannot cover its fixed costs. Sooner or later the fixed capital will become too old to attract customers, and the hotel will close.

Rule 2. The Rule for Optimum Output

The second Rule states that if a firm is to produce at all, then the output that maximizes profits is that where marginal cost is equal to marginal revenue.[1]

The logic behind this rule can best be appreciated by considering what happens to the profits of a firm which does *not* follow the rule. Consider two cases.

First, suppose a firm finds that, at its present level of output, the cost of making another unit per month (marginal cost) is less than the revenue that would be gained by selling that unit (marginal revenue). In this case, total profit could be increased by producing another unit.

---

1 In more advanced economics we should recognize that, strictly speaking, there is a third rule, which states that the marginal cost curve must cut the marginal revenue curve from below. (See IPE7, p.205.)

Second, suppose the firm finds that, at its present level of output, the cost of making the last unit exceeded the revenue that was gained from selling it. Total profit could be increased by not producing the last unit each month. Thus, whenever a firm whose objective is maximizing profits, finds that, at the current level of output, marginal revenue exceeds marginal cost, output should be expanded; whenever marginal cost exceeds marginal revenue, output should be contracted. Its profit-maximizing output is, therefore, where *marginal cost* is neither greater nor less than *marginal revenue* but equal to it, or in symbols, where

$$MC = MR$$

The output that maximizes a firm's profits is called its OPTIMUM OUTPUT. The two rules tell us how to find it. If the condition set out in Rule 1 is not fulfilled, the optimum output is zero; if that condition is fulfilled, then Rule 2 tells us that the optimum output is where marginal cost equals marginal revenue.

TABLE 15.1 The Esplanade Hotel, Brightpool. Total costs and revenues (£s)

Season	Total revenue (TR)	Total variable costs (TVC)	Net revenue ($TR - TVC$)
In	60,000	36,000	24,000
Off	20,000	18,000	2,000

Note: Total fixed costs per annum are £26,000.

Profit Maximization in Different Markets

The application of the rules for a profit-maximizing firm varies slightly according to the market in which the firm operates. We shall distinguish four market structures in this and the next two chapters: (1) perfect competition, (2) pure monopoly, (3) monopolistic competition, and (4) oligopoly. We deal with the first of these in this chapter; the others later.

PERFECT COMPETITION

Perfect competition provides the theory that lies behind the supply curves we used in Part 2. We shall now do the first thing that we promised for an intermediate theory of supply: go behind the supply curve of Part 2 and explain the behaviour that gives rise to it. Note, first, that the word 'perfect' in the term 'perfect competition' does not carry a connotation of desirability. When used together with the word 'competition', perfect means the most *complete*, or *highest*, degree of competition conceivable.

The Assumptions of Perfect Competition

A market is said to be **PERFECTLY COMPETITIVE** when all firms regard themselves as price-takers – i.e., they can sell all they wish at the going market price, and nothing at any higher price. A set of conditions that is sufficient to guarantee this result (sometimes known as the assumptions of perfect competition) are: (1) a homogeneous product, (2) many sellers, (3) perfect information, and (4) freedom of entry and exit.

(1) **A homogeneous product:** A product which is the same for every firm in the industry is called a homogeneous product. One farmer's brussels sprouts are indistinguishable from those of any other farmer. They are homogeneous. By contrast, the Ford 'Escort' differs from all other manufacturers' cars, and from Ford's other models. It is a differentiated product.

(2) **Many sellers:** For firms to be price-takers, the number of sellers must be large enough that no single firm acting alone can exert any perceptible influence on the market price of its product by altering the quantity that it offers for sale. This is another key distinction between, for example, the car industry and the brussels sprout industry. Any one farmer's contribution to the total production of sprouts is a tiny portion of the total. He could double his production, or switch completely to some other crop, with no perceptible effect on the total market supply, and therefore on the price of sprouts. In contrast, Ford's car output is a significant part of total car production. Ford does have the power to influence price by varying the number of cars it produces. The power is not unlimited, but it exists.

(3) **Perfect information:** When buyers of the product are fully informed about the prices and qualities of goods offered for sale, we say that there is perfect information. An important consequence is that, if any firm raises the price of its (homogeneous) product above the prices charged by other producers, it will lose *all* its customers. This is because people will not buy a commodity from a firm at one price if they know that the identical commodity can be purchased at a lower price from another firm. Hence only one price can prevail.

(4) **Freedom of entry and exit:** Assumptions 1, 2 and 3 relate to individual *firms*. The fourth assumption relates to the *industry*. Freedom of entry means that a new firm is free to start up production if it so wishes. There are no barriers to entry. There are no legal or other restrictions on entry. Freedom of exit means that any existing firm is free to cease production and leave the industry if it so wishes. There are no legal, or other, restrictions on exit.

The Equilibrium of the Firm under Perfect Competition

To develop a theory of the behaviour of a firm under perfect competition, our first step is to derive the demand curve facing the firm.

The firm's demand curve

In perfect competition a firm is a *price-taker*. This follows from the fact that the product is homogeneous and the firm is too small to affect market price.

The graphical expression of the demand curve for a firm which is a price-taker, is a horizontal straight line drawn at the going market price.

In Figure 15.1 we show the perfectly competitive firm's demand curve. We assume for the moment that price has been determined at p_0 by the market forces of supply and demand. The firm can sell any quantity it wishes at price p_0. If it tries to raise its price above p_0, its sales will fall to zero, since all its customers realize that they can buy the identical product elsewhere at price p_0. In other words the demand curve is *perfectly elastic* at price p_0.

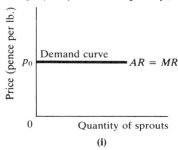

FIGURE 15.1 The Demand Curve for a Firm under Perfect Competition. The firm is a price-taker and faces a perfectly elastic demand curve. $MR = AR =$ Price.

A perfectly elastic demand curve has an important characteristic: the average revenue from the sale of every unit will be equal to the marginal revenue from the sale of an extra unit. Average revenue (AR), you will remember, is another term for the price at which the firm sells its product. Marginal revenue (MR) is the change in total revenue resulting from the sale of an additional unit of the product. Since the firm can sell as much or as little as it wants at the going price, MR must be equal to AR.

Consider for example, a producer who faces a market price of 25 pence per pound for brussels sprouts. Since every pound of sprouts he sells brings in 25p, $AR = 25$p. Also, since price is *given* at 25p, each *additional* pound sold will bring in 25p, i.e. $MR = 25$p. This is the key point: $MR = AR$ *for the firm under perfect competition*. The demand curve facing the firm is, thus, identical to both the average and the marginal revenue curves. All three coincide in the same straight line, showing that price $= AR = MR$. As far as the producer is concerned, all are constant regardless of the quantity offered for sale.

Optimum output for the firm

Earlier, we derived the shape of the cost curves that apply to any firm. Now we know the revenue curves facing any firm in perfect competition. If we put these cost and revenue curves together we can use the two rules developed earlier to derive a firm's profit-maximizing, or optimum, output.

Consider, first, Rule 2: if the firm is to produce at all, it should produce the output for which $MC = MR$. In the case of perfect competition, $MR = AR =$ price. So, in this *special case*, the rule becomes *equate marginal cost to price*. (Note, this special form of the $MC = MR$ rule applies *only* in perfect competition. We shall not be able to use it in other markets situation in the following chapters.)

Now look at Figure 15.2, which shows the cost curves of a firm in perfect competition. The diagram shows four demand curves which the firm might face. All are perfectly elastic, i.e. horizontal straight lines. If the firm faces demand curve D_1, it can sell as much as it wants at price p_1; if the demand curve is D_2, it can sell as much as it wants at the price p_2, and so forth.

Rule 2 tells us that, if the firm is to produce at all, its optimum output is found from the intersection of the marginal cost curve with the demand curve, which shows the price at which output can be sold. Hence, if the demand curve is D_1, the optimum output is q_1; if the demand curve is D_2, the optimum output is q_2, and so forth.

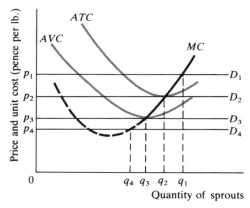

FIGURE 15.2 Optimum Output for a Firm under Perfect Competition is where $MR = MC$ and AR is equal to or greater than AC. If price is p_1, the firm sells q_1 and makes supernormal profits. If price is p_2 the firm sells q_2 and just makes normal profits. If price is p_3 the firm stays in business in the short run, covering its variable costs. If price is p_4 the firm shuts down.

Now apply Rule 1 to determine whether the firm should produce at all or shut down. Remember the rule is based on whether total revenue is sufficient to cover total variable costs.

Consider, first, the demand curve D_1. When the firm sells q_1, at the price p_1, AR exceeds AVC, and the firm is not just earning normal profits, since AR exceeds ATC. It is earning supernormal profits, and should certainly not shut down. Next, assume that the demand curve is D_2. Now the firm equates MC to price, and is just earning normal profits. Hence, the firm should stay in business in this case too. Now, consider the situation of the firm when faced with the demand curve D_3. Optimum output for the firm, q_3, where $MC = MR$, puts the firm on the margin of indifference as to whether or not to remain in production. AVC are just covered by AR, but the firm is earning nothing towards the fixed costs.

Finally, let the demand curve be D_4. The best that the

firm can do if faced with a price of p_4 is to produce q_4, *if it is to stay in production*. But at q_4 output, AR is less than AVC. The firm is not even covering its avoidable costs, so it would be better off shut-down. Optimum output is zero.

The firm's supply curve

We now wish to derive the firm's short-run supply curve, which shows the relation between market price and desired output. We saw in the previous section that a profit-max-imizing firm under conditions of perfect competition produces the output which equates marginal cost to price. For example, in Figure 15.2 the firm produces output q_1 when price is p_1, output q_2 when the price is p_2, and output q_3 when price is p_3. It follows that the marginal cost curve of a perfectly competitive firm is that firm's supply curve.

Recall that at any price below p_3, such as p_4, the firm produces nothing, since if it did produce where $MC = p$, it could not even cover its variable cost.

Thus, the *MC* curve is the supply curve only for prices at or above the minimum point on the firm's *AVC* curve.

The firm's short-run supply curve in Figure 15.2 comprises that part of the MC curve drawn with a solid line – i.e. to the right of, and above its intersection with, AVC. It slopes upwards because the law of diminishing returns causes marginal cost to rise as output increases.

Note that we have derived only the short-run supply curve of the firm. The long-run supply curve is derived on the same principle of identifying the marginal cost of production – but in the long run. As we know, a firm is able to vary its techniques of production in the long run, when all factors are variable. It can choose among plants of different sizes. The long-run marginal cost is the cost of changing output by one unit using the most efficient plants all the time.

The Equilibrium of the Industry under Perfect Competition: The Long Run

So far, we have examined the equilibrium of an individual firm. Next we look at the industry as a whole.

In order to see what is happening in the market as a whole, we need market demand and supply curves. The market demand curve is the ordinary demand curve for a product, such as we used all through Part 2 of this book.

The market supply curve is scarcely more of a problem. We showed, in Chapter 6, how to derive the market supply curve by the horizontal summation of the supply curves of individual firms. We now know that each firm's short-run supply curve is the portion of that firm's marginal cost curve that lies above its AVC curve. *Hence if we sum these marginal cost curves horizontally, we get the industry supply curve.*

In Figure 15.3 we set the market supply and demand curves shown in part (ii), beside the cost curves for a typical firm shown in part (i), which is one of the many firms in this perfectly competitive industry. The vertical scales of the two parts of the diagram are identical – price per lb. of sprouts. The horizontal axes both measure quantities of sprouts. However, the horizontal *scales* are different. We have chosen to calibrate the quantity axis in the diagram for the individual firm in lbs.; while that for the industry has been calibrated in tonnes. The difference reflects the fact that each individual firm supplies only an insignificant part of the whole market. The firm in the diagram is taken as the typical firm in the industry. In particular it is typical in the sense that potential new entrants may expect to do about as well, or as poorly, as this firm does.

Long-run equilibrium

Figure 15.3 shows the firm's position when the industry is in long-run equilibrium. Equilibrium market price (p_0) is determined at the intersection of the *market* supply and demand curves, in part (ii) of the diagram. *At this price the demand curve facing the price-taking firm is perfectly elastic*; it is the horizontal line labelled $AR = MR$ in part (i). The firm's maximum-profit output is where $MR = MC$, namely output q_0. At price p_0 and output q_0, the total revenue of the firm covers, and only just covers, its total costs, including 'normal profits'. This is shown in the diagram by the fact that $AR = ATC$. You will recall that normal profits are included in the cost curve, and must be earned if the firm is to remain in the industry.

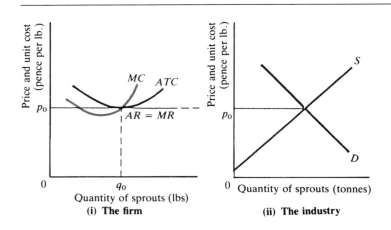

FIGURE 15.3 Firm and Industry in Long-Run Equilibrium. The typical firm in the industry is just covering its total costs (including normal profits).

0   q_0
Quantity of sprouts (lbs)
(i) The firm

0   Quantity of sprouts (tonnes)
(ii) The industry

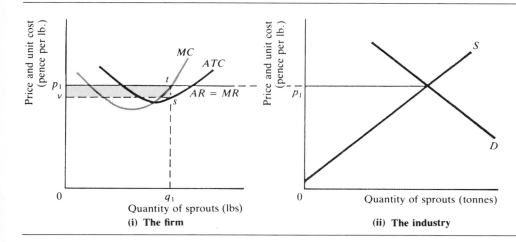

FIGURE 15.4 **Industry in Long-Run Disequilibrium.** Supernormal profits attract the entry of new firms.

Entry and exit of firms: The key to long-run equilibrium for a perfectly competitive *industry* is entry and exit. So long as firms are just breaking even, they are doing as well as they could if they employed their capital elsewhere. They have no incentive to leave the industry. Nor will there be any incentive for new firms to enter the industry. Long-run equilibrium has been achieved. If, however, existing firms are earning supernormal profits after meeting all costs, including the opportunity costs of capital, new firms will enter the industry to share in these profits. If existing firms are making subnormal profits, firms will leave the industry, because a better return can be obtained elsewhere in the economy.

Long-run disequilibrium

Figures 15.4 and 15.5 show industry in long-run disequilibrium. Both diagrams show the same typical firm as was shown in Figure 15.3. The difference between the three figures is that the industry demand curves are different; hence so are market prices. Let us consider them in turn.

In Figure 15.4 the intersection of the market supply and demand curves determines a market price of p_1. The perfectly elastic demand curve for the individual firm is at market price p_1. Profit-maximizing output for the firm is at q_1, where marginal cost is equal to marginal revenue. The firm's total revenue now exceeds its total cost – average

revenue (AR) exceeds average total cost (ATC). The firm is, therefore, making supernormal profits of $p_1 - v(= t - s)$ per unit. Over its whole output, supernormal profit is $p_1 - v$ multiplied by output, which is shown by the shaded area p_1vst in the diagram.

This industry is not in long-run equilibrium; the presence of supernormal profits will attract new firms into the industry to share in these profits.

Before considering the way in which equilibrium is reached, consider Figure 15.5. This is similar to Figure 15.4 in every respect, except that market price of p_2 is such that the firm is not able to cover all its costs at its profit-maximizing output. It makes subnormal profits, equal to the deficiency of average revenue from average cost, i.e. $w - p_2(= t - s)$ per unit, or a total deficiency of the shaded area p_2wts.

Long-run shifts in the supply curve

The entry and exit of firms provides the mechanism by which an industry moves into equilibrium when super- or subnormal profits are present. Changes in output by any *one* individual firm cannot affect market price, but the entry or exit of *many* firms will do so.

The short-run supply curve is the summation of the cost curves of those firms that are currently in the industry. If new firms enter the industry because of the presence of

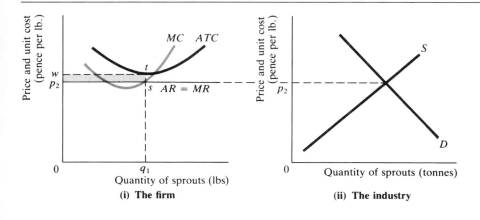

FIGURE 15.5 **Industry in Long-Run Disequilibrium.** Subnormal profits lead to exit of firms.

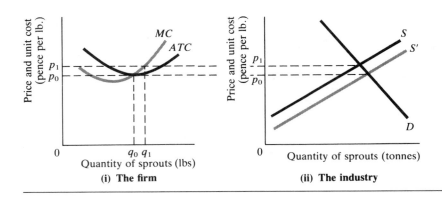

FIGURE 15.6 The Effect of New Entrants on the Industry Supply Curve. New entrants shift the industry supply curve to the right, which causes the market price to fall.

supernormal profits (such as are shown in Figure 15.4), the *industry* supply surve will shift to the right. Market price will fall, which in turn causes a downward shift in the horizontal demand curve *facing each firm*. (Do not forget that the individual firm's demand curve is horizontal at the prevailing market price.) Both old and new firms will adjust their outputs to this new price.

Figure 15.6 shows this process in operation. The original disequilibrium situation is that of Figure 15.4.

Market price p_1, determined in the right-hand portion of the diagram, provides firms with supernormal profits. New firms enter the industry, and this shifts the supply curve, S, to the right, to S' in Figure 15.6(ii). Market price falls, lowering thereby the horizontal demand curve facing each existing firm, as well as each new entrant. Each firm adjusts output to new profit-maximizing positions, where marginal cost equals marginal revenue. Firms will continue to enter the industry so long as supernormal profits can be earned. Each new entrant increases market supply and lowers market price. Eventually, there are enough entrants to push the supply curve to S'. Price has now fallen back to its initial level of p_0, where only normal profits are made. The industry is in long-run equilibrium, similar to that in Figure 15.3.

The use of space in a textbook for one purpose has a real opportunity cost in that it cannot be used for another. We shall, therefore, leave you to fill in for yourself the parallel argument to show how, when market price leads to subnormal profits, as in Figure 15.5, the *exit* of firms continues until a new long-run equilibrium is reached.

The equilibrating process summarized

The process by which long-run equilibrium is reached has been outlined in the previous section. It may be summarized as follows. Supernormal or subnormal profits in a competitive industry lead to the entry or exit of firms. On the one hand, an increase in demand, following a change in tastes for example, raises market price, lifts the demand curve facing individual firms, increases optimum outputs and the level of profits. New firms enter the industry to restore equilibrium (as in Figure 15.6). On the other hand, a reduction in demand lowers market price, shifts the demand curve facing individual firms downwards, reduces optimum outputs, and produces subnormal profits. Given

free entry and exit, long-run equilibrium will occur where firms are just covering total costs, including normal profits, and there is no incentive for the size of the industry to change.

An Alternative Analysis using Total Revenue and Total Cost Curves

Our analysis of the firm under perfect competition has been expressed mainly in terms of *unit* cost and revenue curves – i.e. based on average and marginal cost and

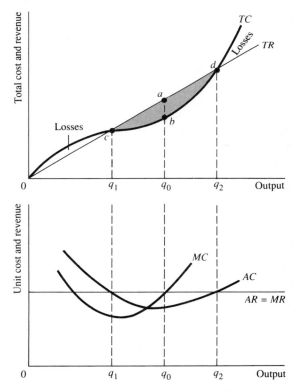

FIGURE 15.7 Total Revenue and Cost Curves for a Firm under Perfect Competition. Optimum output is where the vertical difference between *TR* and *TC* is greatest, at output q_0, where the firm makes supernormal profits $(a - b)$. This corresponds to output where $MC = MR$. Losses occur at outputs below q_1 and above q_2.

revenue. This is the most common approach, but the same results can be obtained using total cost curves, dealt with in Chapter 14 (see page 145), and total revenue curves. To keep the analysis simple we restrict ourselves here to the long run, when all costs are variable.[1]

Figure 15.7 shows the long-run total cost curve (TC) for the firm. The curve goes through the origin of the graph, because all costs are variable in the long run. The TR curve in the diagram shows total revenue at different outputs. It is new to us, but it is not a difficult curve to understand. A firm in perfect competition is a price-taker. Therefore, total revenue changes in direct proportion to quantity sold and, thus, TR curves must be straight lines going through the origin of the graph – the steeper the line, the higher the price. We draw one such TR curve in Figure 15.7. Price is constant throughout (given by any of the ratios c/q_1, a/q_0, or d/q_2).

Consider now the optimum output for the firm. This will be where the difference between total cost and total revenue is greatest. Both TR and TC are measured by the vertical distances between each curve and the quantity axis. Thus, at output q_1, TR and TC are both equal to c. They are equal also at output q_2 (to d). At outputs below q_1 and

greater than q_2, TC exceeds TR and the firm is making losses. Between outputs q_1 and q_2, the firm makes profits, indicated by the shaded area. The greatest (vertical) difference between TR and TC is $a - b$, which occurs at output q_0, which is maximum profit output. Note that it corresponds exactly to the output derived in our more familiar way in the lower portion of the diagram.[1]

q_0 is the equilibrium output for the firm. Is the industry also in equilibrium? The answer is no, because the firm is covering more than normal profits, included in the TC

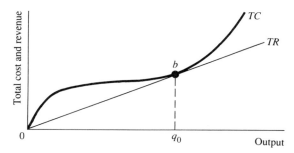

FIGURE 15.8 Industry Equilibrium Using Total Cost and Revenue Curves. Optimum output for the firm is q_0, where total cost (including normal profit) and total revenue are equal to b.

---

1 To analyse the short-run equilibrium of the firm, you would need to relabel the TC curve in Figure 15.8 as TVC, and to draw a new TC curve, to include fixed costs (see Figure 14.1). Short-run equilibrium output would be where TR exceeded TVC by the greatest amount. Long-run equilibrium would still be determined by the relationship between TR and long-run TC.

---

1 An alternative way of looking at the TR and TC diagram is to compare the *slopes* of these curves, which measure marginal revenue and marginal cost, respectively. At optimum output, where $MR = MC$, the TR and TC curves have the same slope.

BOX 15.1 Tory Landladies Force Rethink over Guest-House Rates

'Hoteliers and guest-house keepers have forced the Government to rethink its unified business rate because it was creating an incentive for them to close down for most of the year.

'The rules give exemption to premises open for less than 100 days a year, regardless of their size. The idea was to make things easier for the seaside landlady who offers a few bedrooms for holidaymakers in her home during the summer. . . . Established guest-house keepers argued that the rule allowed "amateurs" to open for a few weeks in the summer, to charge lower prices and thus take the cream of the holiday trade ... Stanley Andrews, who runs the Scotsgrove Guest House in Shanklin with his wife Dorothy, said: "I make all my money between the last week in June and the first week in September. Staying open the extra few weeks is costing me £1,400 and it's just not worth it. I only get a few people in but I'd have to cover my costs and there's no way I'm going to do that." '

(*The Independent on Sunday,* 29 July 1990)

Rates are a tax on businesses levied by local government. They are, therefore, costs to a business. If there

were no exemption rules, such as that described in the news item, they should be regarded by hoteliers as *fixed* rather than variable costs, since they would have to be paid so long as the guest-house was open whether for 1 or 365 days per year.

However, the exemption rule means that the tax needs to be paid only after 'output' occurs for more than 100 days a year. Guest-house owners consider the tax to be a variable cost, and take it into consideration when deciding whether or not to open for more or less than 100 days.

Questions

1 Are guest-house owners right to include their rates as a variable cost, under the circumstances?
2 Does the exemption rule relating to the business rate affect Rule 1 or Rule 2 in the text, or both?
3 What difference would it make to the Andrews if the exemption rule was changed so that rates were paid only after rental income exceeded a stated minimum, instead of coming into force only when income was received for more than a minimum period? What effects would it have on resource allocation?

curve. It is making supernormal profits, equal to $a - b$ in Figure 15.7. For industry equilibrium, we must allow for the entry of firms, which pushes price down, and causes the TR curve to move down and to the right. When the TR curve is tangent to the TC curve, the firm will be making only normal (though maximum) profits, as at output % in Figure 15.8. For completeness, we suggest you draw another diagram to show when firms would leave the industry. (See question 6 at the end of the chapter.)

Summary

1 Profit is the difference between costs and revenues. Costs should be calculated on opportunity cost principles. Revenues may be expressed as totals, or in average or marginal terms. Average revenue (AR) = Total revenue (TR) divided by output. Marginal revenue (MR) is the change in TR resulting from a unit change in sales.

2 The treatment in this book uses the concept of normal profit, which is what the firm could earn in the next most profitable industry after all costs are included.

3 The Shut-down Rule for profit maximization states that output should be greater than zero only if total revenue is equal to, or greater than, total variable costs. In the long run, this means that total revenue should be equal to or greater than total costs.

4 The Optimum Output Rule for profit maximization states that output should be where marginal cost is equal to marginal revenue ($MC = MR$). It applies only where total revenues are equal to, or greater than, total variable costs ($TR \geq TVC$).

5 Perfect competition is a market form which exists where there is a homogeneous product, many sellers, perfect information, and freedom of entry into, and exit from, the industry. The firm is a price-taker and faces a perfectly elastic demand curve, in which average revenue equals marginal revenue equals price.

6 Optimum output for a firm under perfect competition is where marginal cost equals marginal revenue which is also equal to average revenue or price (and where AR at least equals AVC).

7 Long-run equilibrium of the industry under perfect competition occurs when average revenue of existing firms just covers average total cost, including normal profits. The presence of supernormal and subnormal profits result in firms entering into, and exiting from, the industry, causing shifts in the industry supply curve and changes in market price, towards equilibrium.

8 Equilibrium conditions under perfect competition can alternatively be expressed in terms of total cost and total revenue curves.

Questions

1 What is the difference between the shut-down conditions for a firm in the short and the long run?

2 Are the following statements True or False? (i) Normal profits include the opportunity cost of capital. (ii) The short-run supply curve of a firm in perfect competition is its marginal cost curve for outputs greater than where $MC = AVC$. (iii) A profit-maximizing firm must make at least normal profits if it is to stay in business in the long run.

3 Which One or More of the following would indicate that a firm was operating under conditions of perfect competition?
  (a) The firm's demand curve is perfectly elastic.
  (b) Marginal cost equals marginal revenue.
  (c) Average revenue equals average variable cost.
  (d) Average total cost equals average revenue.
  (e) Average revenue equals price.

4 Refer to Figure 15.2. Which One or More of the following statements is correct?
  (a) Optimum output if price is p_4 is q_4.
  (b) In the long run, price must be greater than p_2 for the firm to stay in business.
  (c) If price is p_3 the firm will be making supernormal profits.
  (d) Unless cost or demand conditions change, the firm will never find it profitable to produce output q_4.

5 What is indicated by the fact that firms are seen leaving a perfectly competitive industry?

6 Refer to Figure 15.8. Assuming the TC curve is unchanged, (i) what would need to happen to the TR curve to cause firms to leave the industry? (ii) what are average costs at output q_0? (iii) what is average revenue at output q_0?

16 Monopoly

In the previous chapter, we described two rules for a profit-maximizing firm in any market. We applied the rules to a firm operating in a market structure where all sellers are price-takers, called perfect competition. Now for the first time in this book we drop the price-taking assumption and study the market structure at the opposite extreme from perfect competition – pure monopoly.

A MONOPOLY is defined as an industry where there is only a single seller. (Where there is only a single *buyer*, it is a 'monopsony', which we discuss in Chapter 19, see p.199.) The firm and the industry are one and the same. Whether a complete monopoly can exist is a question that has worried some people. In one sense, the answer is no – because all products compete for consumers' limited income. In another sense, the answer is yes – a single seller of one particular product is perfectly conceivable, although the *market power* of such a monopolist is never absolute. We shall look at market structures between perfect competition and pure monopoly in the next chapter. Meanwhile it is convenient to contrast the theory of the firm in the two extreme market forms.

PROFIT-MAXIMIZING OUTPUT OF A MONOPOLIST

Any profit-maximizing firm must follow the two rules set out in the previous chapter – the shut-down rule, and the optimum output rule. For a monopolist, the former rule applies in a straightforward manner, but the optimum output rule requires a different interpretation.

Under perfect competition, we saw that the latter rule, $MC = MR$, could also be expressed as MC = price because for any price-taking firm, average and marginal revenues are equal. This form of the rule does *not* apply to monopoly because, as we shall shortly see, a monopolist's price does not equal its marginal revenue. The profit-maximizing rule, $MC = MR$, is unchanged but its application differs.

Marginal revenue under monopoly

We know that, in perfect competition, marginal revenue is equal to price. This is because an individual firm can sell as much or as little as it wishes at the going price. A monopolist is unable to do the same.

Because it is the sole supplier of the industry's product, the demand curve facing the monopoly firm is the market demand curve of the industry. Since market demand curves are downward-sloping, a monopolist that wishes to sell an extra unit of output must lower its price. The reduction in price applies to all units of output. Therefore, the marginal revenue from the sale of an extra unit is less than the price at which all units are sold.

An example will help to clarify this point. Suppose a monopolist is selling 3 units of output per week at a price of £6 each for a TR of £18. Suppose, too, that in order to sell 4 units per week, price must be lowered to £5 yielding a TR of £20. The difference in TR from selling 4 rather than 3 units is thus only £2. This is less than the new price of £5 at which the increased sales of 4 units take place.

Another way of looking at the reason for MR being less than price, is to consider the change in TR when sales rise from 3 to 4 units as being the result of two components. In the first place, there is an *increase* in TR of £5, resulting from the sale of one extra unit at the price of £5. In the second place, there is a *decrease* in TR, resulting from the lower price now charged on the 3 units that formerly sold for £6 each and now sell for only £5. The decrease in TR is therefore £3. We can now calculate MR as:

Change in units sold	Change in TR
plus 1 @ £5	+ £5
minus 3 @ £1	− £3
Net change	+ £2

Table 16.1 sets out the average and marginal revenues for a monopolist at five prices at which various quantities can be sold. Note that MR is less than AR throughout the table (except for the first output where $TR = MR$). Note too that MR is negative after 4 units are sold. This arises from the relationship between elasticity and total revenue, that we explained earlier, and that you may find easier to recall with a diagram.

TABLE 16.1 Average and Marginal Revenue under Monopoly

Output (units)	Average revenue (price) (£s)	Total revenue (£s)	Marginal revenue (£s)
1	8	8	+ 8
2	7	14	+ 6
3	6	18	+ 4
4	5	20	+ 2
5	3	15	− 5

Marginal revenue and elasticity of demand

The relationship between the AR and MR curves is portrayed graphically in Figure 16.1, which makes it clear that MR lies below AR for every output.

Figure 16.1 shows also the varying values of the elasticity

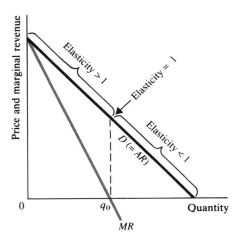

FIGURE 16.1 The Relation between Elasticity of Demand and Average and Marginal Revenue. MR is positive for outputs less than q_0, when elasticity >1; MR is negative for outputs greater than q_0, when elasticity <1; $MR = 0$ when elasticity = 1, at output q_0.

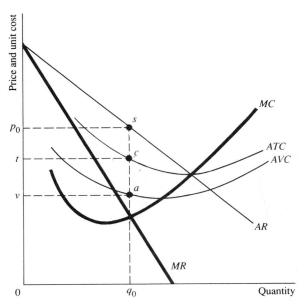

FIGURE 16.2 Monopoly Equilibrium occurs where $MC = MR$ at output q_0. Market price is p_0. Supernormal profits are tp_0sc in the short run and tp_0sc in the long run.

of demand for the portions of the straight-line demand curve which we explained in Chapter 7 (see Figure 7.4 and text on page 66). It is important to understand the relationship between marginal revenue and demand elasticity because it affects the sign of marginal revenue. This is shown in the diagram.

Note, that MR is positive only when demand elasticity is greater than unity, in which case a fall in price causes a proportionately larger rise in quantity demanded. This means that TR rises when price falls – i.e. MR (which is defined as the change in TR) must be positive. The MR curve lies above the horizontal axis.

The corollary is, of course, that MR is negative whenever elasticity of demand is less than unity, when a price fall causes a proportionately smaller rise in quantity demanded. This means that TR falls when price falls – i.e. MR is negative. The MR curve lies below the horizontal axis.[1]

Monopoly Equilibrium in the Short Run

Now that we have derived the marginal revenue curve for a monopolist, we can apply the two rules for profit-maximizing behaviour from Chapter 15.

Consider Figure 16.2 which shows a firm's AR and MR curves (as in Figure 16.1), together with its average and marginal cost curves.

The optimum output rule identifies the profit-maximizing (or loss-minimizing) output as that where $MC = MR$.

This is q_0, the level of output at the intersection of the MC and MR curves. q_0 can be sold at price p_0, because the demand curve indicates that consumers are prepared to pay p_0 for q_0.

The shut-down rule can be stated in either of two ways – that total revenue is at least sufficient to cover total variable costs, or that average revenue is equal to, or greater than, average variable costs.

Consider, first, the latter formulation, AR is equal to or greater than AVC. Is it satisfied in the diagram? The answer is yes. At output q_0, AVC is v (the vertical distance above 0) while AR is p_0. The excess of AR over AVC is $p_0 - v$, and is available to cover fixed costs and profits.

The formulation of the optimum output rule in terms of total revenues and total variable costs can be checked in the diagram by a comparison of areas. TR is AR multiplied by output q_0, or the area Op_0sq_0. TVC is AVC multiplied by output, or $Ovaq_0$. Clearly Op_0sq_0 is greater than $Ovaq_0$, so $TR > TVC$. The difference is the area vp_0sa, which is available to cover fixed costs and profits.

Monopoly Equilibrium in the Long Run

We may now apply the same two rules for a profit-maximizing firm to find monopoly equilibrium in the long run. Rule 2 states that as long as output is positive, the profit-maximizing output occurs where $MC = MR$, i.e. output is q_0 and price is p_0.

The application of Rule 1, however, leads to results that may differ in the two time-periods. In the long run, all costs are variable. The application of the shut-down rule in the long run differs from the short run only in that we must have regard to the total costs rather than to short-run variable costs. If total costs are at least equal to total revenue the firm should not shut down in the long run. On inspection of Figure 16.2, we find that at optimum output, q_0, AR is greater than ATC, by $s - c$ per unit. In total

---

1 When elasticity of demand is equal to unity, TR is by definition constant. MR, which is the change in TR, is therefore zero. The MR curve cuts the quantity axis at the output where elasticity equals unity.

cost and revenue terms, $Op_0sq_0 > Otcq_0$. The firm should certainly not shut down. It is making supernormal (monopoly) profits, equal to tp_0sc.

Analysis using total cost and revenue curves: In the previous chapter, we showed two ways of analysing the long-run behaviour of a profit-maximizing firm under perfect competition. The main technique involves *unit* cost and revenue curves, such as we used in the previous section. The alternative method uses *total* revenue and cost curves. We can apply this, second, technique to a monopolist.[1] Figure 16.3(i) is drawn on similar lines to Figure 15.8. The total cost curves (TCs) in the two diagrams are identical. Both curves pass through the origins of their respective graphs, because they refer to the long run, when all costs are variable.

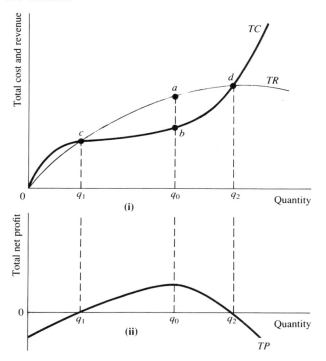

FIGURE 16.3 Monopoly Equilibrium using Total Cost and Total Revenue Curves. Optimum output is at q_0, where the vertical distance between TR and TC is greatest, i.e. $a - b$ in part (i). Part (ii) shows net profits (TP) as TR minus TC, which are negative at outputs less than q_1 and greater than q_2.

The total revenue curves, however, are different. TR in Figure 15.8 was a straight line because, under perfect competition, firms are price-takers and TR must, therefore, be proportional to quantity sold. The TR curve in Figure 16.3, in contrast, is a curve the slope of which declines as output increases because, under monopoly, price must be lowered to sell larger quantities.

The rest of the analysis is unchanged. Profits are maximized when the difference between TR and TVC is greatest. In Figure 16.3(i) this is at output q_0, where the

1 To adapt the analysis to the short run, see the footnote on page 159 in the previous chapter.

vertical distance between the two curves is seen to be at a maximum. Part (ii) of the diagram shows the curve of (net) total profits, TP. Net profits are negative at outputs less than q_1, and greater than q_2. They are at their maximum at output q_0.

Barriers to entry

Under perfect competition the presence of supernormal profits, such as tp_0sc in Figure 16.2, would lead to entry of firms until long-run equilibrium of the industry was reached, where only normal profits were earned by the typical firm.

Under monopoly, in contrast, there is only a single producer. If the monopolist is to retain its position as the only seller, there must be BARRIERS TO ENTRY, which protect the monopolist's position by preventing other firms from entering the industry. Barriers may be natural or man-made.

Natural barriers

Three important natural barriers are based on (1) cost advantages, (2) uniqueness, and (3) location.

Cost advantages: In an industry subject to increasing returns to scale and falling long-run costs, the larger the firm the lower are its costs. Any industry where there is room for only one firm producing at minimum efficient scale (*MES*) (see p.149) is a NATURAL MONOPOLY. In such an industry, a single firm serving the whole market tends to emerge, because the largest firm always has lower costs, and hence can undersell any smaller competitors. We return to consider the special case of natural monopoly later in the chapter.

Uniqueness: A second natural barrier (which may be a prime cause of cost advantages described in the previous paragraph) is uniqueness. A firm may possess sole access to the supply of a major input, such as a raw material; or it may have an exceptionally talented employee on its staff. For example, Alcoa Corporation of Canada owns the major areas of land beneath which aluminium is found; the Beatles were a unique group with exceptional talents; the Louvre museum in Paris owns the only painting of the *Mona Lisa* by Leonardo da Vinci, etc.

Locational advantages: Particular locations often give firms special advantages which make it difficult for less privileged potential entrants to compete. For example, corner sites offer twice the window space of other sites; newsagents' shops adjacent to bus stops can expect larger sales than those more remote; and so forth. Note, however, that some locational advantages could be classified under cost advantages. For example, proximity to a river lowers costs of waste disposal for firms located there, compared to other firms. We treat locational advantages as a special case because they are common.

Man-made barriers

In contrast to natural barriers, are those created by people. Three types may be distinguished – barriers created (1) by businesses, (2) by law and (3) by the government.

Barriers created by businesses: Firms may build barriers to restrict the entry of other firms. Many are related to marketing. Some arise from product differentiation – the creation of a product which is distinctive from others on the market – for example, a new car model or almost any brand of domestic electric appliance. To be effective as an entry barrier conferring a degree of monopoly power, product differentiation does not have to consist of real distinctive characteristics, as long as consumers regard the product as if it does.

Legal barriers: The chief legal restrictions on the entry of new firms are patents on processes and copyrights on publications. For example, photocopying was the monopoly of Rank-Xerox in the UK and lawnmowers based on the 'hover' principle were the monopoly of Flymo, until the patents ran out. The D'Oyly Carte Opera Company enjoyed a monopoly of commercial performances of Gilbert and Sullivan operas until 1950, though Sir Arthur Sullivan died in 1900.

Barriers created by government: Akin to patent monopolies, governments can create monopoly situations by granting legal rights to single firms. For example, the Acts of Parliament setting up the nationalized industries after World War II included provisions protecting them from some competition. More recently, transfers of the same industries to the private sector as part of the privatisation programme, have transferred monopoly powers to the newly formed private companies, e.g. British Gas.

The persistence of entry barriers

Barriers to entry are essential to the persistence of monopoly power.

Some, such as cost advantages arising from economies of scale, can endure for long periods of time. Others, such as patents, run out, and differentiated products tend to last for shorter periods.

The evidence, however, strongly supports the view that barriers to entry can last for long enough for monopolists to enjoy supernormal profits. This creates an incentive for other firms to challenge the existing monopoly in order to share in any supernormal profits. The greater the monopoly profits, the more powerful the incentive for new firms to enter an industry.

The distinguished economist, the late Joseph Schumpeter, viewed the drive by some firms to create monopoly profits, and by other firms to share them, as vital elements in the generation of economic progress. Firms outside a monopolistic industry strive to enter, and existing monopolists strive continually to create *new* monopoly situations as challenges from other firms gather strength.

Schumpeter called this process 'creative destruction'. He saw the attempt of firms to seize the monopoly profits of existing firms, and to acquire their own monopolies by inventing new products and new, cheaper, ways of producing old products, as *the* great engine of growth in market societies.

Barriers to exit

For completeness, we should mention the existence of barriers preventing firms from leaving an industry, when profits fall below the opportunity cost of capital. Many such exit barriers can be traced to government regulation, on behalf of consumers (e.g., postal services in remote country areas), or of workers in regions of heavy unemployment (such as N. Ireland).

MONOPOLY POWER

The analysis of monopoly so far, has focused on the equilibrium of a monopolistic firm and the sources of monopoly power. Certain conclusions arising from the analysis need to be emphasized.

A monopolist can control price or output

A monopolist has the power to set *either* price *or* output. If it chooses to set price, the quantity it will be able to sell is fixed by the demand curve. If it chooses to set output, the price at which that output can be disposed of is also fixed by the demand curve. The monopolist cannot set *both* price *and* output.

A monopolist will not operate in the range where the elasticity of demand is less than unity

The reason is clear from Figure 16.1. When demand elasticity is less than unity, marginal revenue is negative. Since costs are always positive, the intersection of MR and MC could not occur under such conditions.

A monopolist need not earn supernormal profits

The analysis of monopoly equilibrium allows for the possibility of supernormal profits; it does not guarantee them. Figure 16.4 shows the optimum position of a monopolist who is earning only normal profits, because $ATC = AR$, at profit-maximizing output q_0. Whereas long-run equilibrium under perfect competition is *always* that equilibrium where only normal profits are earned, such an equilibrium would be a coincidence for a monopoly. The ATC and AR curves just happen to touch but not to intersect. A monopolist may also earn subnormal profits in the short run. This occurs if the ATC curve is everywhere above the AR curve. As long as variable costs are covered, the monopolist will remain in the industry for the short run. In the long run, however, it will exit and the product will no longer be produced.

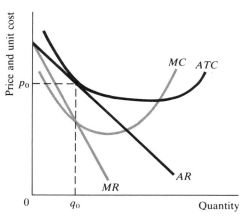

FIGURE 16.4 A Monopolist Earning only Normal Profits. At optimum output q_0, AR only just covers ATC.

A monopolist need not maximize profits

Monopoly firms can often earn supernormal profits. However, they are under no obligation to *maximize* profits. There is even a common misconception that if such firms are not maximizing their profits, they must be making subnormal profits. This certainly does not follow. In Figure 16.2, for example, tp_0sc supernormal profits are earned by a profit-maximizing monopolist. But a monopoly might choose to produce output other than q_0 and would still remain in business over the long run so long as total revenue was equal to, or greater than, total cost.

A monopolist may be able to charge different prices for a single product

The final point to make about monopoly is that, under certain circumstances, the firm's power over its market is greater than so far suggested.

If a monopolist charges different prices for the same product, it is engaging in PRICE DISCRIMINATION, an activity that can improve its profitability.

Types of price discrimination: There are two types of price discrimination. One type involves the sale of different quantities of a good at different prices *to the same consumer*. Car-parking spaces, for example, are often charged at different rates for long and for short stays. Another example is where consumers pay different prices for individual units of electricity according to whether consumption is during the day or night. This type of price discrimination often requires keeping track of sales of each unit to individual consumers.

The second type of price discrimination involves the sale at different prices of identical products to *different* consumers. This may happen within one market, as when a trader charges rich clients more than poor ones for the same service. It may also happen between markets, as when EC goods are sold at one price within the EC and at another to countries outside.

Conditions for price discrimination:

There are two conditions which must hold before price discrimination takes place among markets. One is to do with the possibility of discrimination, the other with its profitability.

BOX 16.1 What Price a Golf?

Prices quoted by main dealers for a 5-door VW Golf 1.8 litre*

Country	Price (£s)	Tax rate (%)
Britain	10,100	26
Belgium	7,855	25
France	9,700	25
Ireland**	12,000	23
Italy**	8,415	19
West Germany	8,000	14

*On-the-road prices, including taxes; exact specifications vary from country to country. **1.6 litre model.

(*The Independent on Sunday*, 13 May 1990)

'There is some concern that car buyers are being denied the advantages of the Common Market, because of the way in which the manufacturers are alleged to dictate resale conditions to their dealers and divide up the Community into discreet markets, according to the price which each national market will bear.' (Sir Leon Brittan, a vice-president of the European Commission.)

(*The Times*, 2 June 1990)

Economic theory identifies the conditions which make price discrimination possible and profitable. One should not jump to the conclusion that the differences referred to in the extract are necessarily due entirely to price discrimination. However, the evidence from the news items is suggestive, at the very least.

Questions

1 What are the 'conditions' referred to in our comment?
2 If the reported price differences are due to price discrimination by the manufacturer, are there forces which might work to reduce, or even eliminate them?
3 What other explanations for the reported differences can you suggest?

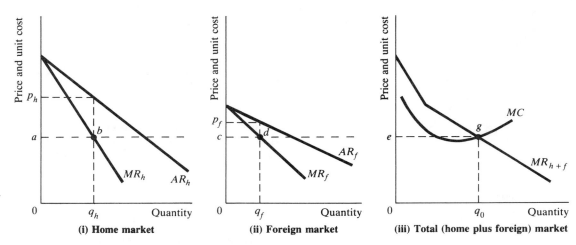

FIGURE 16.5 Price Discrimination under Monopoly. Optimum total output q_0 is where MC = the combined MR_{h+f}. Sales are q_h in the home market at price p_h; and q_f in the foreign market at price p_f.

First, the markets must be separate. Consumers in the market where price is relatively low must be *unable* to resell to consumers in other markets. Unless this condition holds, flows of goods between markets will erode any attempt to maintain different prices. Discrimination will not be possible.

Second, the demand curve in each market must be different. To show that price discrimination is profitable as well as possible when this condition holds, consider the following illustration.

Suppose that a firm sells a single product in two markets, home and foreign. We show the average and marginal revenue curves in each market in Figure 16.5(i) and (ii). How should the profit-maximizing firm decide how much to sell, and what price to charge in each market?

Optimum output for a discriminating monopolist: Any profit-maximizing monopolist equates MC with MR. MC poses no new problem here. The firm merely needs to know what each extra unit of product adds to costs. MR, however, is more complicated to calculate for a discriminating monopolist. The firm may, for example, sell in two markets – home and foreign. What is its overall MR? The answer lies in realizing that

the profit-maximizing firm will allocate any given output between the two markets so as to maximize total revenue.

Were this not done, MR would be greater in one market than the other. It would be possible to switch sales of a given output between home and overseas and increase total revenue.

To discover the firm's overall marginal revenue we need to construct a marginal revenue curve for the two markets combined, MR_{h+f}. This curve is drawn to show total overall MR from the sale of all possible outputs, allocated in such a way that TR is maximized by equating MR in the two markets. To find the overall marginal revenue that

applies to each output, therefore, we sum the separate quantities in each market that correspond to each particular MR. If, for example, the 10th unit sold in the home market and the 15th unit sold in the foreign market both have MRs of £1 then the MR of £1 corresponds to overall sales of 25 units. The overall MR curve, MR_{h+f} is therefore derived by horizontal summation of MR_h and MR_f. At prices p_h and above, MR_{h+f} is identical to MR_h; at lower prices, MR_f has to be added to it.

Point g on the combined marginal revenue curve, for example, is constructed by measuring eg equal to $ab + cd$. (The procedure is similar to that used to construct the market demand curve from the demand curves of two individuals.)

Having derived the overall marginal revenue curve MR_{h+f} in Figure 16.5(iii), we find its point of intersection with the MC curve. This gives optimum output for the firm.

The second step in the process of determining the equilibrium of the price-discriminating monopolist is to divide total output between home and foreign markets. To find the best allocation we apply the principle that *marginal revenues must be equal in the two markets*. Finding the split between markets involves, as it were, retracing the steps we took to construct MR_{h+f}. So, we move leftwards along the horizontal grid line drawn from g to a, selling q_h in the home market and q_f in the foreign market. This must ensure equality of MR_h and MR_f, and of MC and MRs.

To determine the price to be charged in each market, we move up from the points b and d to the demand curves. The quantity q_h will sell at price p_h in the home market; the quantity q_f will sell in the foreign market at the price p_f. The prices are different, because the demand curves are different in the two markets.[1]

---

1 The difference relates to demand elasticity. Profit-maximizing price is higher in the less elastic market (see IPE8).

MONOPOLY AND ECONOMIC EFFICIENCY

To complete this chapter we look at the implications of monopoly behaviour for economic efficiency. To provide a benchmark for comparisons, we contrast the behaviour of a profit-maximizing monopoly firm with that of a firm in perfect competition. Two substantial differences are explained in Figure 16.6. This is virtually identical to Figure 16.2, which we used to demonstrate monopoly equilibrium, with certain additions which we shall use later. We do, however, now give the product a name, balium, which will make it easy to refer to.

Output and Price under Monopoly and Perfect Competition Compared

(1) Output:

Monopoly output is less than perfectly competitive output for any given set of cost and demand conditions.

In both markets, of course, profit-maximizing output is found from the intersection of the MC and MR curves. In Figure 16.6, we know monopoly output to be q_m. Now consider what output would be if the industry were perfectly competitive. Under those conditions, the demand curve AR in Figure 16.6 would be the demand curve of the

industry. The *firm's* demand curve would be perfectly elastic at every market price. For each firm, $MR = AR$ (or price). The optimum output for the firm, where $MC = MR$ is, therefore, where $MR = AR = MC$. In Figure 16.6 perfectly competitive output is q_c, which is greater than q_m, monopoly output. This difference arises from the monopolist's power to restrict output to raise price.

(2) Price:

Monopoly price is higher than perfectly competitive price for any given set of demand and cost conditions.

This follows from the fact that MR is less than AR under monopoly, while $MR = AR$ under perfect competition. In Figure 16.6 monopoly price is p_m, which is higher than perfectly competitive price, p_c.

Bearing in mind the differences in output and price under monopoly and perfect competition, we may now address the question of the relative efficiency of the two market structures. We shall be concerned with both allocative and productive efficiency, starting with the former.

Allocative Efficiency under Perfect Competition

You should remember that allocative efficiency exists when it is not possible to reallocate resources so as to make any one person better off without making at least one other person worse off. When we first met this concept we associated it with the market mechanism and the equality of marginal cost and marginal utility ($MU = MC$). When this equality obtains in every market, 'it means that the extra utility that consumers derive from an additional unit of a good is equal to its opportunity cost, measured by the sacrifice of not having extra quantities of other goods in its place'. (We quote verbatim from page 83, to encourage you to refresh your memory on the argument that led to this conclusion if you are in any doubt about it.)

We have emphasized that the price mechanism might produce such an efficient allocation of resources if certain conditions were present. We have reached the point in this book where these conditions can be described more fully – because it so happens that they occur automatically in perfectly competitive markets but not under monopoly. The key feature of perfect competition in this connection is that all sellers are price-takers. We showed in the elementary theory of demand that consumer equilibrium occurs when the marginal utilities of all goods are equal, per unit of money spent on them, i.e where the ratio MU/price is the same in all markets in the economy. We know, however, that:

under perfect competition firms maximize profits equating MC to MR, which is the same as AR or price. Since consumers and producers face the same prices, this means that we can substitute MC for price in the ratio MU/price, giving MU/MC. The equality of the ratio MU/MC in all markets is, moreover, the condition for allocative efficiency, as described in the previous paragraph.

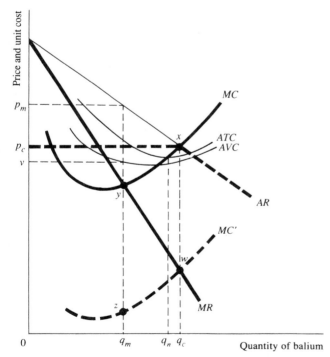

FIGURE 16.6 Devices to Persuade a Profit-maximizing Monopolist to Produce Optimum Output (q_c, where $MC = AR$). Any of the following: (1) A price ceiling of p_c makes demand perfectly elastic (when $MR = AR$) for outputs up to q_c. (2) A requirement to charge a price $= MC$, makes q_c the most profitable output. (3) An output-related subsidy could shift the MC curve to MC'.

We can observe the condition for allocative efficiency in Figure 16.6. Perfectly competitive output q_c sells at a price p_c, which is equal both to MC and to MU (determined by the demand curve).

Allocative Inefficiency under Monopoly

A profit-maximizing monopolist produces that output which equates MC and MR. The demonstration of allocative *inefficiency* under monopoly, merely requires recognition that MR is not equal to, but is less than, AR – i.e. less than price and marginal utility. Thus, under monopoly, the equality of MC and MR does *not* mean the equality of MC and MU. Hence, the condition for allocative efficiency is not satisfied.

In Figure 16.6, our monopolist is in equilibrium producing q_m, at which output $MC = MR$. The market-clearing price, at which the firm sells q_m, is read off the demand curve as p_m, which also indicates marginal utility. This means that the valuation put by consumers on the last unit of balium is worth p_m in money terms. Notice, however, that the MC of q_m balium is less than p_m and, therefore, less than MU.

We thus derive the important result that marginal utility exceeds marginal cost under monopoly.

This suggests that resource allocation could be improved if more balium were produced. Consumers value it, at the margin, as worth more than it costs to produce. Since marginal cost in real terms measures the value of the other goods sacrificed for the sake of balium, consumers would be better off with fewer of them and more balium.

We conclude that perfect competition leads to an allocation of resources which is efficient, while monopoly leads to one which is inefficient.

We stress that this result follows from the assumption of profit-maximizing behaviour by the monopolist, in the face of a downward-sloping demand curve for the product.

Productive Efficiency under Perfect Competition

Productive efficiency exists when it is not possible to produce more of any one good without producing less of any other. We have thought of it as obtaining when production takes place on, rather than inside, the production frontier (see Chapter 1, p.8).

In the context of an industry, the interpretation of productive efficiency is that firms are operating so that costs are minimized.

Under conditions of perfect competition, market forces bring about productive efficiency in long-run equilibrium. There is no change in the size of the industry when, at the margin, neither subnormal nor supernormal profits are being earned. When this occurs, average revenue is equal to average total costs, which are at their minimum level. To put the above statement in terms of a diagram, refer

back to Figure 15.3 on page 156. When market price is p_0, the industry is in long-run equilibrium. The firm equates MC and MR at output q_0, which is the minimum level of average cost. (This situation is sometimes described as where 'the AC curve is sitting on top of the AR curve'.)

Productive Efficiency under Monopoly

A profit-maximizing monopolist minimizes the costs of producing a given output. However, restriction by a monopolist may result in a level which is less than that where AC are at a minimum as they are under perfect competition, because of output restriction. Figure 16.2, for example, shows monopolist equilibrium output q_0, below the point of minimum average cost. There are, however, two aspects of costs that call for attention. They have conflicting implications for the productive efficiency of monopoly relative to perfect competition.

Managerial efficiency

In the first place, there is the question of how likely a monopolistic firm is to pursue cost minimization. While in the long run under perfect competition firms make only normal profits, under monopoly many make supernormal profits. The *scope* for managerial slack is, therefore, greater for a monopoly. Moreover, while firms in perfect competition are small, some monopolies may be organized in large joint-stock companies, where we know that the separation of management from ownership may lower the priority of the goal of profit maximization, especially in the short run.

Managerial inefficiency (which is sometimes called X-INEFFICIENCY) shows up in the position of the firm's cost curves. If a firm is minimizing the costs of producing given outputs, it is operating on the lowest set of cost curves attainable. The real cost of not doing so is wasted resources, in that more of all goods could be produced if costs were lower.

Economies of scale

The conclusion so far must be that monopoly may suffer from managerial inefficiency as well as allocative inefficiency. However, there is one special case which suggests higher productive efficiency under monopoly. The countervailing argument is based on the presence of economies of large-scale production, and it applies with special force to the case of so-called 'natural monopolies' – i.e. those whose very existence is derived from their falling cost curves.

Consider the firm in Figure 16.7. Its average total costs fall over the range of output for which demand is positive, so that the total cost of producing any output in this range is minimized if there is only a single firm in the industry.

To show this, imagine that output is to be q_1. Compare cost if there is one firm with that of two firms, say, of equal size. Total costs for the single firm are c_1 times output q_1. Total costs for each of the two firms are c_2 times output

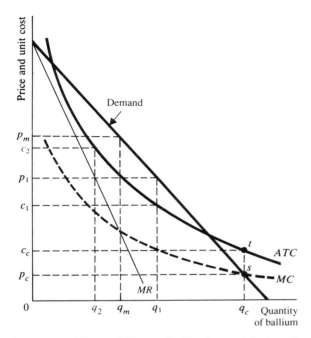

FIGURE 16.7 A Natural Monopoly. Total costs (of q_c) are less for one firm ($c_1 \times q_1$) than two firms (twice $c_2 \times q_2$). If price is set $= MC$ at optimum output, q_c, the firm makes a loss of $p_c c_c ts$.

q_2. Since output q_1 is equal to two outputs of q_2, and since average costs c_2 are clearly greater than c_1, total costs are lower for the single firm than for two firms of equal size (or of any number of firms producing the same total output). The existence of extensive large-scale economies, therefore, opens up the possibility that productive efficiency is potentially greater under monopoly than under competition.

MONOPOLY AND THE PRICE MECHANISM

Attempts to defend monopoly against a charge of economic inefficiency might succeed on some counts and fail on others. The best defence probably lies in the argument of the previous section – that monopoly power allows the enjoyment of economies of large-scale production, though there may also be some stimulus to cost reduction from Schumpeter's argument about the drive to invent and inno-vate to continue to enjoy monopoly profits (see p.164 above). The best of the anti-monopoly arguments lie differ-ently, in the allocative inefficiency of profit-maximizing behaviour, and the scope for productive inefficiency that can accompany easy enjoyment of supernormal profits.

Market Failure and Monopoly

Whatever the verdict in individual cases, there is clearly a case to be made against monopoly on grounds of market failure, in the sense in which we have used that term.

Indeed, if you turn back to page 85, you will see that we

forewarned you that we would later introduce a category of market failure associated with the concentration of economic power. That later moment has now arrived.

While the price mechanism under perfect competition leads to allocative and productive efficiency, under profit-maximizing monopoly it does not necessarily do so. The reason for failure on grounds of allocative efficiency, stems from output restriction by a monopolist in order to raise price. To this one might add a scope for productive inef-ficiency when competition is weak.

The potential danger from monopoly is, therefore, a subject that has long interested government. Official policy towards monopoly has varied over the years and from country to country. At present in the UK, there are a number of strands to what is, these days, called 'competition policy'.

In the first place, there are certain special institutions which were established for the control of monopolistic firms and practices: the Monopolies and Mergers Com-mission, the Restrictive Practices Court, and the Office of Fair Trading. In the second place, there are policies designed to strengthen the competitive nature of business environment, through the reduction of entry barriers, e.g. so-called 'de-regulation' measures, such as the opening up of the right to do conveyancing (legally transferring the ownership of dwellings), previously restricted to solicitors. Thirdly, there are a number of sectors with special prob-lems, where close supervision of a monopoly (and/or trans-fer to public ownership) is thought helpful for the promotion of economic efficiency, both allocative and pro-ductive. The 'public utilities' of electricity, gas and tele-phones are prime examples.

When we reach the final chapter in this book on micro-economic policy, we shall discuss the measures mentioned in the previous paragraph further. There are, however, additional ways of approaching some of the problems associated with monopoly which involve merely using the price mechanism to persuade a profit-maximizing mon-opolist to produce optimum output. Although the admin-istrative feasibility of some of these measures may be doubtful, it is an instructive exercise to show how the price mechanism might be set to work in this way. We end this chapter by looking at four cases. All rely on the assumption that the monopoly seeks to maximize profits, by equating MR and MC. We shall examine ways in which the price system can be used to produce the level of output that would obtain under perfect competition.

Price controls

One way of inducing a monopolist to produce optimum output would be to impose a maximum price at which the product could be sold. In Figure 16.6 we assume that the government rules that the maximum price that may be charged for balium is p_c. The effect would be to change the demand curve facing the firm, for all outputs below q_c. If the firm cannot charge more than p_c for any quantity that it puts on the market, its demand curve becomes perfectly elastic at that price, and for all quantities at which the firm would otherwise have charged higher prices. For quantities of balium for which the firm would charge prices below the legal maximum, demand is unchanged.

The new demand curve facing the monopolist, therefore, is shown by the heavy dashed line in Figure 16.6 running from p_c to x and then following the original demand curve below and to the right of x. Note that, since the demand or average revenue curve is horizontal up to output q_c, the marginal revenue curve is now the same as the demand curve up to that point.

Recall that, on a perfectly elastic demand curve, $MR = AR$. It follows that the profit-maximizing output of the monopolist shifts to q_c, because this is now the output that equates cost with the new MR. The common sense of this result is that the monopolist restricts output below q_c only in order to raise the price of his product. If market price cannot be raised, there is no sense in restricting output.

This policy requires the government to know enough about cost and demand curves to set the price at the proper level, and to keep it there as conditions change. (Some price controls would even worsen resource allocation. See question 5 at the end of the chapter.) The political and administrative problems can be enormous.

Marginal cost pricing

An alternative to price control to induce a monopolist to produce the perfectly competitive output is to require that the firm charges a price equal to its marginal cost.

Look again at Figure 16.6. How much balium would a profit-maximizing monopolist produce under that rule? The answer is the output corresponding to where the MC curve cuts the demand curve AR, i.e. q_c, which is optimum output.

The marginal-cost-pricing rule has been used for determining output policy of publicly owned (i.e. nationalized) industries, where it has proved useful but not always easy to implement.

An output-related subsidy

A third method of persuading a monopolist to produce the perfectly competitive output is to offer a subsidy related to output, thereby shifting the marginal cost curve downwards.

In Figure 16.6, we show this by shifting the MC curve to MC', representing a subsidy equal to the vertical distance between z and y at monopoly output, which is the same as the distance between w and x at perfectly competitive output. (The procedure is comparable to the shifting of an output-related *tax* except that a tax raises, while a subsidy lowers, the MC curve. See above, p.97.)

The new MC' curve has been drawn to intersect the (unchanged) MR curve at q_c, thereby making optimum output also that of maximum profit for the monopolist.

This device suffers from the same problems as the price control mentioned earlier. The government may not know MR and/or MC, either or both of which may be changing. There is, moreover, an additional problem here that does not occur with a price control. The subsidy has the effect of increasing the monopolist's profits – a result which may be politically unacceptable if not positively noxious.

The total cost of the subsidy to the government is the subsidy per unit multiplied by the output produced. In Figure 16.6 this is xw times q_c. If the state introduced legislation allowing balium to be produced only under licence,[1] it could set a price on the licence at a figure exactly equal to the cost paid out in subsidy.

Natural monopoly

Our final example of using the price mechanism to persuade monopolistic firms to produce perfectly competitive output concerns natural monopoly. The difficulties in this case are severe. Indeed we mention it partly because of the nature of the difficulties.

Let us return to examine Figure 16.7, which reminds us, in the first place, that a natural monopoly is characterized by falling costs of production such that unit costs are minimized if there is only a single firm. Profit-maximizing monopoly output, at which $MR = MC$, is q_m, which would sell at the price p_m, leaving an excess of AR over ATC. Optimum output is q_c, where $MC = MU$.

So far, the situation resembles that of Figure 16.6, where a price control, or a requirement to charge a price equal to marginal cost, might persuade the monopolist to produce optimum output. However, the important difference here is that when the firm is a natural monopoly, producing the optimum output would involve it in a loss, whereas a monopoly with *increasing* costs would earn at least normal profits, as in Figure 16.6.

The explanation of the difference is clear from the diagram. At optimum output, q_c, ATC is greater than AR. Hence, the firm would make a loss (of $t-s$ per unit).[2] This follows from the relationship between average and marginal curves that we discussed earlier. When average value is falling, marginal value must be less than average.

This characteristic of natural monopolies makes the problem of finding a policy for them very difficult. They are commonly treated differently from other firms, and have often been prime candidates for public ownership and/or regulation. We reconsider them in Chapter 21.

---

1 An alternative to selling licences is to tax *profits*. So long as firms do not regard a profits tax as affecting their variable costs, output is not affected by the tax.

2 One way of avoiding the problem is for the firm to levy two charges – a fixed sum unrelated to output, and a price related to cost. An example is the quarterly fixed rental for a telephone installation, combined with a unit charge for each call.

Summary

1 A monopoly is an industry where there is a single seller; the industry and the firm's demand curve are the same.

2 Marginal revenue under monopoly is less than average revenue; it is positive, zero, and negative for outputs where demand elasticity is greater than, equal to, or less than unity.

3 Monopoly equilibrium is found where marginal cost equals marginal revenue, and average revenue is at least equal to average variable costs. Any excess of total revenue over total costs is supernormal, or monopoly, profits.

4 Barriers to entry under monopoly eliminate the distinction between short and long-run equilibrium that obtains under perfect competition.

5 Entry barriers may be natural, i.e based on uniqueness, cost or locational advantages; or man-made, i.e. created by business, government or legal restrictions.

6 A monopoly (i) cannot control both price and output; (ii) will not operate where demand elasticity is less than unity; (iii) may earn no more than normal profits; (iv) need not maximize profits.

7 A monopoly may be able to charge different prices for a single product; price discrimination is possible when markets are separate; it is profitable when demands are different in each market. Optimum output is where marginal revenues are equal in all markets, and equal to marginal costs.

8 Profit-maximizing monopolists produce less and sell at a higher price than perfectly competitive firms.

9 Resources are inefficiently allocated under profit-maximizing monopoly because marginal utility is greater than marginal cost. In contrast under perfect competition, marginal revenue equals marginal cost equals marginal utility, and resource allocation is efficient.

10 Productive efficiency under monopoly may be affected by managerial slack (X-inefficiency), but also by economies of scale.

11 Market failure under monopoly is associated with allocative inefficiency.

12 A profit-maximizing monopolist might be persuaded to produce the same output as a firm in perfect competition by (1) price control, (2) an output-related subsidy, or (3) marginal cost pricing. Such measures are less suitable for a natural monopoly which would make losses at optimum output.

Questions

1 Which One or More of the following indicates that a profit-maximizing firm is operating in (i) a perfectly competitive market, (ii) a monopolistic market?
 (a) In equilibrium, average revenue is greater than price.
 (b) The marginal cost curve cuts the average cost curve at its lowest point.
 (c) In equilibrium, marginal cost is less than average revenue.
 (d) Marginal revenue is less than average revenue.
 (e) The demand curve of the firm is perfectly elastic.

2 What are the maximum outputs that a firm can produce while making no more than normal profits (i) in Figure 16.2, (ii) in Figure 16.3?

3 Does a monopolist choose to operate on the part of his demand curve that has an elasticity greater or less than unity? Why?

4 Which kind of barrier to entry results in a monopoly which would not be able to cover normal profits if it produced optimum output and charged a price equal to marginal cost?

5 Refer to Figure 16.6. Suppose the government wished to set a price ceiling to try to induce optimum output from a monopolist in this market. Market price and monopoly output are known but not the cost nor demand curves. What maximum prices would lead to (i) more, and (ii) less, efficient output than monopoly equilibrium?

6 A monopolist serving two separate markets, called N and S, maximizes profits. Which One or More of the following is correct?
 (a) Combined MR in N + S = MC.
 (b) MR in N = MR in S.
 (c) $MC = MR$ in N.
 (d) Combined MC in N + S = MR.
 (e) AR in N = AR in S.

17 Imperfect Competition

This is the final chapter in the group of three outlining theories of the firm in different market situations. We have dealt with the limiting cases of perfect competition and pure monopoly which approximate some real-world markets. Basic raw materials and foodstuffs, for example, are sold on highly competitive world markets. There are also a few commodities produced by a single firm, for example insulin; and certain sectors, such as the supply of gas and electricity, where monopoly power is regionally strong.

The two extreme market forms do not, however, cover important segments of the economic activity that we see today. Many firms involved in the production of both consumer goods and capital goods operate between the two extremes. These intermediate market forms fall into the category known as IMPERFECT COMPETITION. Firms there do not operate under perfect competition because they are not price-takers. Nor are they monopolies because there is more than one firm in the industry. However, they are monopolistic, in that they have power to set their own prices; they are competitive, in that they actively compete with each other.

CONCENTRATION OF INDUSTRY

There are two ways of looking at business concentration. The first examines *overall concentration* – the share of output controlled by large companies; the second focuses on individual industries in what is termed *market* (also known as industry, seller or sectoral) *concentration*.

Overall concentration

The modern large corporation typically produces a variety of goods and services spread over different industries. The share of total output[1] in all industries which is in the hands of large businesses is a measure of OVERALL CONCENTRATION.

The dominant position of large firms is very much a twentieth-century phenomenon, though their increasing importance was greatly helped by the legislation granting limited liability to joint-stock companies that we mentioned earlier.

The one hundred largest corporations, commonly referred to as *giants*, now control a substantial proportion of total output. Restricting ourselves to the manufacturing sector, where most applied research has been done, we can

obtain a good idea of the level of overall concentration and of past trends from the share of the 'top 100' in total output. The number of companies of all sizes in manufacturing is well over 100,000, so the top 100 represent less than one-tenth of one per cent of the total. They include companies such as ICI, Unilever, Sainsburys, Ford, General Electric, British Steel, IBM, Guinness and Rolls-Royce, as well as less familiar names like Rio Tinto Zinc, Thorn EMI, Hanson, and Trafalgar House. Even the smallest of the top 100 could boast of a turnover, in 1989–90, of £1.5 billion.

Figure 17.1 shows the share in total manufacturing output of the largest 100 enterprises since the first decade of the century. Their share rose from less than 20 per cent at that time, to over 40 per cent by 1970, falling off slightly towards the late 1980s.

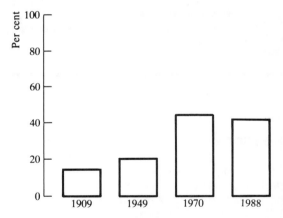

FIGURE 17.1 **Overall Concentration in the UK: Share of the 100 Largest Enterprises in Manufacturing Industry** (*Sources*: S. J. Prais, *The Evolution of Giant Firms in Britain* (Cambridge University Press, 1981), and Census of Production 1988 (see Table 17.1 for details).

Growth by merger became a matter of public concern in the 1960s, with the first of a series of merger waves. Activity expanded greatly, peaking at a figure of over 1,500 in 1987, when almost 10 per cent of the total capital value of UK companies was involved. All three types of merger mentioned earlier – horizontal, vertical and conglomerate (see above, p.30) – took place. Horizontal and vertical mergers have been the most and least common. The most rapidly increasing type of merger, accounting for over a third since 1980, has been the conglomerate, where diversification of interests is the prime motive.

---

1 Other indices of concentration measuring shares of total employment, sales, and capital values, are also used.

Market concentration

One characteristic of giant companies in the UK is their diversified interests. The typical giant operates in several distinct markets. For example, the Sears group, mentioned earlier, has interests in shoe shops, betting shops, department stores, and engineering; while the Pearson group controls Penguin Books, Royal Doulton China, *The Financial Times*, and Madame Tussauds, among many others.

To see the extent of concentration in particular markets in the hands of large company organizations, we have to look, therefore, at market shares. This is usually done with the help of statistics known as market CONCENTRATION RATIOS (CRs). These are the shares that the largest companies have in either output or employment. Often the shares of the 5 largest enterprises are used. This measure, called CR5, shows the proportion of total output, or employment, in the hands of the largest 5 enterprises.

In Table 17.1, we show statistics of CR5 for a selection of industries, chosen to illustrate the wide range of concentration in the UK. Thus, there are sectors, such as asbestos, man-made fibres and tobacco, where the largest 5 enterprises produce over 90 per cent of total output, and others, such as toys, clothing and tools, where the percentage is low. Note, that the table shows the total number of firms in each industry as well as the concentration ratio.

TABLE 17.1 Concentration Ratios, UK Manufacturing Industry 1988. Percentage shares in total (net) output by the 5 largest enterprises (CR5), and total number of enterprises in selected industries.

INDUSTRY	CR5 (per cent)	ALL ENTERPRISES (number)
Machine tools	9	3854
Hand tools	11	8549
Clothing	15	8851
Toys, sports	19	978
Motor vehicle parts	24	1289
Paints	39	369
Brewing	38	138
Footwear	40	788
Glassware	54	747
Elec. appliances, domestic	58	531
Spirit distilling	68	47
Steel tubes	72	112
Motor vehicles	83	159
Cement	88	131
Asbestos	93	28
Man-made fibres	95	21
Tobacco	99	21

Source: Census of Production, Summary Tables, 1988 (Business Monitor, PA 1002, HMSO 1990).

Market power does not depend only on concentration, as simply measured by CR5. It is affected also by matters such as the number and size of the firms below the Top 5, and how intensely they all compete with each other. Look, for example, at two sectors, brewing and glassware. The latter is more heavily concentrated, with a CR5 of 54 per cent compared to 38 per cent for brewing. However, in brewing the Top 5 enterprises operate in a sector with only 138 firms, while in glassware there are over five times that number. Note, we do not want you to draw a conclusion that either glassware or brewing is the more competitive industry, only that concentration ratios, alone, do not tell the whole story about industrial structure. We shall have more to say on the determinants of competitive behaviour later in the chapter.

TYPES OF IMPERFECT MARKET

Market structures between perfect competition and pure monopoly are classed as imperfect competition, the term used to describe non-monopoly markets where at least one of the assumptions of perfect competition is not present. These concern the number of firms, the type of product, and entry conditions.

Under *im*perfect competition, there must be one or more of the following conditions – a relatively small number of firms, a differentiated product, and restricted entry into the industry. Two types of imperfect market are commonly distinguished – monopolistic competition and oligopoly.

MONOPOLISTIC COMPETITION refers to situations where an industry contains many firms, and there are no barriers to entry. Monopolistic competition is distinguished from perfect competition because the product of each firm is differentiated from those of other firms. The concept was developed in the 1930s by the American economist Edward Chamberlin, reacting to the inapplicability of the theories of perfect competition and monopoly to large sectors of the economy.[1]

OLIGOPOLY refers to a market where there are *few* sellers (the word oligopoly means precisely that in Greek).

MONOPOLISTIC COMPETITION

The major characteristics of monopolistic competition are: (i) a large number of firms, (ii) each firm has a distinctive, or differentiated, product, and (iii) there is freedom of entry into, and exit from, the industry.

The first characteristic, a large number of firms, is the same as under perfect competition. It means that each firm in a monopolistically competitive industry makes its decisions with no thought to reactions from other competing firms. Any one firm is too small for its actions to have a significant effect on the others.

The second characteristic is that the products of firms are differentiated from each other. This means that, although the products have enough in common to be grouped together as one commodity (e.g. ready-to-eat breakfast foods), they are sufficiently different from one another to be regarded by consumers as not perfect substitutes for each other.

Note that it does not matter if the products are physically

---

1 The British economist Joan Robinson was also involved in developing the theory of imperfect competition. Although her work greatly advanced the theory of monopoly, it did not prove useful in explaining behaviour in intermediate markets.

identical so long as they are perceived as differentiated in the minds of consumers. Because the products of the firms in an industry are imperfect substitutes for each other, the typical monopolistically competitive firm is not a price-taker. It can raise price without losing all of its sales to competitors; and it can lower price in order to sell more. The demand curve facing the firm slopes downwards; it is not perfectly elastic, as in perfect competition.

The final characteristic of monopolistic competition, freedom of entry and exit, likens the industry to perfect competition rather than to monopoly. If supernormal profits are being earned by existing firms, newcomers will enter the industry. If subnormal profits are being made, firms will leave.

Equilibrium Conditions

Consider now the conditions for equilibrium under monopolistic competition in the short and long runs.

Short-run equilibrium

Assuming that firms are profit-maximizers, the short-run equilibrium of the firm in monopolistic competition is exactly the same as under monopoly. Maximum-profit output is found where $MC = MR$ (provided TVC are not greater than TR) at all levels of output. Figure 17.2 shows equilibrium output q_0 with market price p_0. Supernormal profits are given by the shaded rectangle ap_0st – price *minus* ATC *times* output. Notice, incidentally, that the diagram is similar to Figure 16.4 in the previous chapter, except that the demand curve is here drawn flatter, to allow for the large number of substitutes under monopolistic competition.

Long-run equilibrium

So far, we have seen that the short-run equilibrium of the firm under monopolistic competition is the same as under monopoly. Because of barriers to entry, monopoly equilibrium is the same in the long and short runs. This is not so under monopolistic competition because there is freedom of entry into the industry.

If existing firms are making supernormal profits, as in Figure 17.2, new firms are attracted into the industry, adding to total industry supply, and depressing the demand for the product of every existing firm. This is because the existing market demand must be shared out among more and more firms. The effect is to shift the demand curve of each existing firm to the left, as its market share is reduced. The process continues until the typical firm in the industry is making only normal profits, i.e. when the demand curve is tangent to the average cost curve at the most profitable output.

The long-run equilibrium of each firm under monopolistic competition is the same as was shown in Figure 16.4 on page 165 for a monopolist who was just covering its total costs. The only difference is that for a monopolist, this result would be a coincidence, while for a monopolistic competitor this result necessarily follows from the entry of

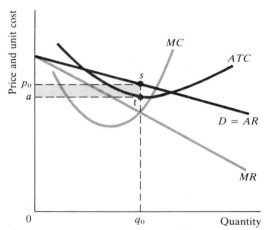

FIGURE 17.2 A Firm in Monopolistic Competition. The firm will be in short-run equilibrium, selling q_0 at price p_0, and earning ap_0st supernormal profits. Firms enter the industry, shifting the demand curve down until only normal profits are earned (as in Figure 16.4 on page 165).

new firms to enjoy supernormal profits (or exit of firms where profits are subnormal) at optimum output. Market price is p_0. At output q_0 and price p_0, average revenue exactly equals average cost. The only profits are normal profits, which are included in the cost curve.

Excess capacity under monopolistic competition

Note, in Figure 16.4, that the equilibrium output of the firm is at output q_0 where the ATC curve is falling.[1] Average cost is minimized at the output where the MC curve cuts the ATC curve. This is a larger output than q_0. In other words, firms under monopolistic competition do not achieve full productive efficiency. They do not produce at minimum average costs, as occurs under perfect competition.

The difference between equilibrium output and minimum-cost output is called EXCESS CAPACITY. Such excess capacity is associated with long-run equilibrium under monopolistic competition.

It was regarded for many years as a sign of the relative inefficiency of this market form. (Under perfect competition, in contrast, excess capacity can only occur in the short run.)

The modern view of the excess-capacity argument is less critical of monopolistic competition. While unit costs are higher than under perfect competition, consumers have the benefit of a wider range of products to choose from. In judging the efficiency of resource allocation under monopolistic competition, the costs have to be weighed against the benefits.

---

1 The AC curve is tangent to the downward-sloping demand curve at output q_0. Therefore, as the two curves must have the same slope at that point, the AC curve must also be downward-sloping.

The relevance of monopolistic competition

The theory of monopolistic competition, described in the previous paragraphs and developed in the 1930s, began later to fall out of favour as it was perceived that there were few sectors in the economy where large numbers of firms compete in the sale of differentiated products.

At first sight, this may sound surprising. A visit to any department store or supermarket will reveal that there are many industries where a large number of slightly differentiated products compete for the buyer's attention. In most such cases, however, the industries contain only a few firms, each of which usually sells a large number of products. For example, you may find a dozen different brands of instant coffee on the supermarket shelves. But the number of different blends of coffee bean, of roasting processes and of packagings greatly exceeds the number of different companies producing instant coffee.

Retail shopkeeping is another sector where monopolistic competition might seem applicable. In every city you will find a large number of shops selling a particular range of products. But any one individual store is not in *effective* competition with *all* of them, only with those in reasonable geographical proximity. The boutiques in London's Kings Road compete with each other far more than they do with dress shops in Hampstead, Watford, or Nottingham. Moreover, several of the shops selling one line of goods may belong to a single business enterprise, e.g. Saxone, Dolcis and Manfield shoe shops, mentioned earlier.

The current view of applied economists, therefore, is that the theory of monopolistic competition among *large numbers* of small firms producing differentiated products does not apply to major sectors of the economy. Attention has shifted to competition among *small numbers* of firms which are in close competition with each other. They are the subject of the theory of oligopoly.

OLIGOPOLY

Oligopoly is the market form where few sellers compete with each other. It is the most common type of market structure outside agriculture. In a typical oligopolistic industry, there are anything from two to a dozen dominant firms,[1] at least one of which produces a significant fraction of total industry output.

Characteristics of Oligopoly

The prime distinguishing feature of markets with few sellers is that the behaviour of any individual firm is affected by the actions, both actual and anticipated, of other firms. This characteristic, described in the word RIVALROUS, distinguishes oligopoly from other market forms – from perfect and monopolistic competition where all firms are individually too small to have a significant effect on the market; and from monopoly, where a single seller is protected from potential rivals by barriers to entry.

A major consequence of the rivalrous behaviour mentioned in the previous paragraph is that firms under oligoply are not price-takers. Each faces a downward-sloping demand curve for its product.

Like a monopolist, the oligopolist can determine *either* the price of its product *or* the quantity it sells. When the oligopoly firm chooses to set its prices, these are said to be 'administered'.

The firms which dominate an industry classed as an oligopoly, mostly produce a range of differented products, though this is not an essential feature. The UK steel industry is considered oligopolistic because it comprises a number of firms each of which is large enough to influence market price, although some products, such as steel sheet, are virtually homogeneous and do not differ in quality from one producer to another.

Oligopoly has been the subject of much theoretical and applied work in economics, and the results are complex, because rivalrous behaviour can take many forms. A firm finding its market share falling after a price cut by its rivals can react, for example, by cutting its own price, by differentiating its product in countless ways, or by spending more on advertising, packaging, etc. Moreover, the intensity and nature of rivalrous activity varies greatly from industry to industry and from one period of time to another.

The Basic Dilemma of Oligopoly

Oligopolists face a basic dilemma, whether to compete or to co-operate with their rivals. There should be no difficulty about appreciating the advantage of co-operation. If all the firms in the industry get together and agree to behave exactly as if they were a monopoly, they will be able to restrict their joint output and enjoy monopoly profits. They will have set up what is known as a CARTEL. It is in their joint interests to do this, though the way in which the members of the cartel divide the monopoly profits among themselves creates plenty of scope for disagreement.

The room for dispute over the division of the 'spoils' is one reason for the oligopolist's dilemma. Those cartel members who feel they have too small a share in group profits are liable to think they might do better by competing, expanding output by selling at a price below that agreed by the 'loyal' firms. However, the dilemma is much more firmly based than that.

It is always in the interest of any one firm to break away from the agreement with others provided they do not retaliate. However, retaliation may soon follow one firm's breaking out of the cartel, because the profits of the rest are reduced. Thus, any other one of the remaining firms will also find it worthwhile dropping out – again provided others do not retaliate.[1]

The result may be that one by one firms quit, the cartel

---

1 The conclusion is known as the 'Prisoners' dilemma' because it was first set in the context of two prisoners bargaining with their captor over sentences.

falls apart, with all firms worse off than before. This conclusion can be reached using the techniques of a branch of mathematics called game theory which analyses the optimum strategies for games in which players compete, while knowing that they need to take account of each other's reactions to anything they do. Advances in understanding oligopoly have been made in recent years with the use of game theory. It is beyond the scope of this book to describe it in the text, but see Appendix 5 for an illustration.

Cartels which agree to restrict joint output to enforce the monopoly price are in many cases illegal in the UK and other advanced countries, though laws require policing and are not always observed. Moreover, tacit agreement by the firms in an industry can have the same effect as explicit cartelization, without any illegal agreement necessarily taking place. If all the firms in the industry appreciate the advantages of co-operation, they may behave as if they were a monopoly. The oligopolist's dilemma is, however, unaffected. It remains in the interest of each firm to co-operate, provided other firms do so, but any one firm gains by 'cheating,' provided other firms do not cheat too.

Oligopolistic industries may, therefore, pass through alternative periods of stability and instability as cartels (which may be explicit or tacit) form, break up and reform – not unlike the history of the international oil producers' cartel, OPEC. In 1973–4, OPEC, whose members together accounted for nearly three-quarters of the world's oil supply, first managed, by means of jointly agreed output quotas, to quadruple the price of oil. After years of enjoying exceptionally high incomes, and in the face of a decline in the world demand for oil, some members of OPEC were tempted to cheat and exceed their quotas. Matters came to a head in 1984 when, despite attempts by the dominant producer, Saudi Arabia, to re-establish output quotas, the cartel more or less collapsed.

To collaborate or to compete? That is the question

What makes firms in an oligopolistic industry decide to collaborate or to compete? This is a question to which there is no single answer, because there are too many complex factors at work. However, the results of applied economic research suggest that whether firms see their best policy as competition or co-operation is likely to depend on the following:

The number of sellers in the industry: The fewer they are, the greater the probability of collaboration. Tacit co-ordination is easier and the chance of cheating without incurring retaliation is lower.

The nature of the product: In some cases certain products lend themselves to differentiation and firms may choose to compete in this way, suppressing competition on price. Moreover, the more homogeneous the product, the less scope there is for any one firm to steal a march on others by price-cutting without provoking retaliation.

The number of dominant firms: When an industry contains a single dominant firm, often also a price leader, co-operation is more likely than when there is a group of more or less equal competitors.

Trends over time in the size of the industry: When an industry is growing, firms can produce at full capacity without any need to steal from rivals. When the market is dwindling the temptation to compete and undercut rivals' price increases.

Barriers to entry: The higher the barriers to entry, the longer the profits of co-operative action can persist without encouraging the entry of new firms. Hence, also, the less temptation to cheat and compete.

Later in the chapter we return to consider the implications of the analysis of the oligopolist's dilemma of whether to collaborate or compete. Meanwhile, we must note another characteristic of oligopoly – that prices tend to be fairly stable, or 'sticky'. They fluctuate less with changes in the conditions of demand and supply than they are observed to do under perfect competition. We shall suggest a number of reasons for this price stickiness. In order to do so fully we have, first, to appreciate the nature of cost curves under oligopoly.

The Nature of Cost Curves under Oligopoly

Ever since economists began estimating firms' costs, they reported that average variable cost curves were flat, rather than U-shaped. The evidence is overwhelming that in manufacturing, and some other industries, cost curves have the shape shown in Figure 17.3, with a long flat middle portion and sharply rising sections at either end. Over the flat range, from q_0 to q_1, average variable and marginal costs are constant. At outputs below q_0, AVC is declining, so MC is below it. At outputs above q_1, AVC is rising, so MC is above it. Such cost curves are sometimes described as *saucer-shaped*.

Minimum average cost occurs over a *range* of outputs, rather than at a single point, as with U-shaped curves. The firm, normally, hopes to operate at some output below output q_1 where unit costs start to rise. This might be output q_2 in Figure 17.3. Output q_1 is called FULL CAPACITY OUTPUT, while output q_2 is called NORMAL CAPACITY OUTPUT. The gap between q_2 and q_1 allows a margin of spare capacity on which the firm may draw in periods of peak demand, but does not use in periods of average or slack demand.

At first sight, the saucer-shaped short-run average variable cost curve might appear to violate the 'law' of diminishing returns. This 'law' formed the basis for the U-shape that we previously encountered. There is, however, no contradiction. The explanation for the falling and rising portions of the AVC curve is the presence of a fixed factor of production. The falling portion of the curve occurs because the fixed factor is less than optimally employed;

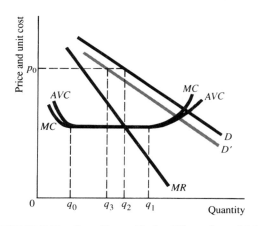

FIGURE 17.3 Flat Cost Curves Under Oligopoly and Sticky Prices. $AVC = MC$ and is constant over the range q_0 to q_1. Optimum long-run output is q_2 with price p_0. Short-run demand shift to D' causes output to fall, to q_3, with price remaining at p_0.

the rising portion occurs because there is not enough of the fixed factor to provide the optimal combination with the variable factor. We earlier attributed the falling short-run average costs to the fact that the fixed factor is *indivisible*. However, it can happen that the fixed factor is *divisible, in the sense that all of it need not be used all of the time.*

Consider, as a simple example, a 'factory' that contains 10 sewing machines, each of which requires only one operator. Whatever output is required, the best way of producing it is by using a combination of operators to machines of one-to-one. This implies that not all the machines will be employed if demand is below the full capacity of the plant, i.e. demand can be met by less than 10 sewing machines. Thus, at a time of low demand, only 6 machines may be used, and only 6 operators hired (rather than having, say, 6 operators dashing around trying to keep 10 machines working). Idle machines will be brought into use only if demand warrants it. When that happens, extra staff will be engaged, one for each extra machine used.

Clearly, in such cases, the marginal cost of altering output will be *constant*. It is constant because the 'fixed' factor, capital (sewing machines in this case), is divisible. Thus, the ratio of *employed* capital to *employed* labour does not vary as output varies (at least over the range from zero to the normal output possible from 10 machines). Hence, there is no conflict between the law of diminishing returns, *which applies when factor proportions are varied*, and the saucer-shaped constant short-run average and marginal cost curves, commonly found in manufacturing industries, *which apply when factor proportions are constant.*

Price Stickiness

We have already said that prices tend to be sticky under oligopoly. What we mean by this is that firms do not alter the price of their product every time cost or demand

conditions change. They are price-makers, because they face downward-sloping demand curves. However, they prefer to follow a policy of ADMINISTERED PRICES, i.e. holding price relatively steady, and adjusting the quantity they offer for sale if there are short-term shifts in demand. Why should they do so? Four possible explanations will be considered. The first suggests that firms are not short-run profit maximizers. The other three are consistent with short-run profit maximization and explain price stickiness by forces that are omitted from the simplest theories of the firm. We consider the explanations in turn.

Full cost pricing

According to the ideas of Hall and Hitch, two pioneering Oxford economists writing in the 1930s, businessmen calculate the average total cost of operating at full capacity – which they call their 'full costs' – and then add a conventional 'mark-up' to determine price. They then sell whatever they can at that price, so that fluctuations in demand cause quantity, rather than price, to fluctuate.

Hall and Hitch explained full cost pricing as showing businessmen to be uninterested in profit maximization. Instead they were seen as creatures of habit, who added conventional mark-ups to costs calculated at their typical output, and were then reluctant to change the prices that resulted from such calculations.

The cost of changing prices

What seems like full cost pricing behaviour may, however, be consistent with profit maximization. For example, the 'conventional' mark-up may correspond to the one that maximizes profits at normal output, and it may be costly to alter prices frequently. The first point is illustrated in Figure 17.3. Having built a plant, whose normal capacity is consistent with profit-maximizing output, say at q_2 in the diagram, the mark-up can be set to achieve maximum profits in normal times – i.e. p_0. Fluctuations in demand, e.g. to D', cause fluctuations in quantity sold, to q_3, at the fixed market price of p_0.

The second point is that there is a significant cost involved when any modern industrial firm changes its selling prices. Such a firm often sells thousands of different products, and changing prices across the whole range is a costly affair. New price lists must be printed; price tags must be changed; salesmen must be informed; and the firm's customers must make adjustments. The changes also require extra book-keeping and there is the worry of losing consumer goodwill if prices are liable to change all the time. If there were no cost of changing prices, profits would be maximized by altering prices every time demand shifted, no matter how short-lived the change was expected to be. If the cost of changing prices is great enough, the most profitable policy will be to set the profit-maximizing price for the average level of sales expected, and then hold price constant as demand varies in the short term.

Non-price competition

The next explanation of price stickiness under oligopoly has something in common with that of full cost pricing. Both rest, to an extent, on the real cost to a firm of continuously changing selling prices.

Given that a business finds it profitable not to change price, there are, in imperfect markets, a number of alternative policies that it can engage in, following a change in demand. These are embraced under the general term NON-PRICE COMPETITION. For example, a fall in demand can be met by increased advertising, by 'free gifts' of goods (e.g. glass storage jars, free bingo entry forms, etc.) or by differentiating the product. The choice of policies facing a multi-product oligopolist, with respect to price- and non-price-competitive methods, is usually great.

Kinked demand curve

An alternative explanation of price stickiness under oligopoly, also developed in the 1930s, predicts price stability in the case of changing *costs* as well as changing demand.

The theory is known as that of the 'kinked demand curve' because it assumes that the demand curve facing the firm is 'kinked' at the current price-output combination, such as at point *a* in Figure 17.4. The kink arises because of two key assumptions. First, the firm is assumed to believe that, if it *cuts* its price, rival firms *will follow suit*. The firm's own sales will expand, but only slowly along the relatively steep portion of the demand curve below and to the right of *a*. Second, the firm is assumed to believe that, if it *raises* its price, its rivals *will not follow suit*. Its own demand will, therefore, fall off rapidly along the relatively flat part of the demand curve above and to the left of *a*.

The flat demand curve above the current price and the steep curve below it, mean that the curve facing the firm is kinked at the going price. As a result, a major change in either cost or demand conditions may be necessary before the firm will consider changing its price.

The stickiness of price following cost changes may be demonstrated by inspecting the MR curve in the diagram. Because of the kink in the demand curve, the curve marginal to it is discontinuous. (This should be clear to those readers who also study mathematics.)

The discontinuity may be explained by considering that the demand curve, Baf, consists of portions of two distinct demand curves. One is the portion Ba of the demand curve Bac, which describes the firm's demand on the assumption that rival firms match any price change. The other is the portion af of the demand curve Eaf, which describes the firm's demand on the assumption that rivals do not follow any price change. The two MR curves, Bgk and Emh, correspond to these two demand curves. The portions of those MR curves appropriate to the demand curve Baf make up the MR curve $Bgmh$, which is discontinuous between g and m.

The effect of the discontinuity in the MR curve at the current price-output combination is that a change in MC, within the range m to g, has no effect on market price for a profit-maximizing firm. If the MC curve varies between MC and MC' in the diagram, for example, marginal cost stays equal to marginal revenue *without any change in price or output*.

Although the kinked-demand-curve explanation of price stickiness under oligopoly is intuitively plausible, it suffers from two major disadvantages. First, it denies not only price but also output fluctuations in response to cost changes, a stability unsupported by evidence. Second, the theory offers no explanation for how the current price (at which the demand curve is kinked) is arrived at.

Prices in practice

Most modern industrial economists believe the short-run stickiness of industrial prices is consistent with profit-maximizing behaviour. The reasons are: price changes are costly, and non-price methods of competition may be superior to price-cutting when conditions change temporarily.

Under these circumstances, profit maximization requires only that price (which is another way of saying the mark-up over full costs) should be set so as to maximize profits at the firm's average levels of output and sales. Of course, when changes in demand or costs are permanent, oligopolists do change their prices; their prices are just sticky, not stuck.

Oligopoly and Efficiency

In the previous chapter we compared monopoly and perfect competition from the standpoint of economic efficiency, and earlier in this chapter we made some observations about resource allocation under monopolistic competition. It remains to consider oligopoly and efficiency.

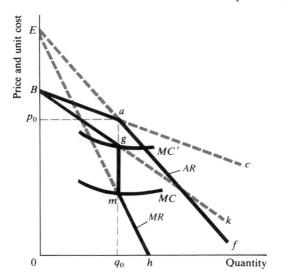

FIGURE 17.4 The Kinked Demand Curve under Oligopoly. At optimum output q_0 and price p_0, demand is much more elastic for a price rise than for a price fall. Shifts in the point of intersection of MR and MC curves between m and g do not alter optimum output nor market price.

This is a far from simple task, not least because of the complex nature of oligopolistic behaviour that we referred to previously. Moreover, rather like our conclusions on efficiency under monopoly, there is something to be said on both credit and debit sides. In so far as oligopolists collaborate in order to act as if they were a monopolist, resource allocation is liable to be less satisfactory than if they compete, when allocation should be closer to what would happen under perfect competition.

Although prices tend to be sticky under oligopoly, that does not mean that firms do not respond to market forces. It is just that the market-signalling system works in a slightly different way. Under perfect competition, changes in market conditions (i.e. in demand or costs) are signalled by changes in market prices. Under oligopoly, the same changes are signalled by changes in the quantities firms can sell. Moreover, the more intensely firms in oligopolistic markets compete, the closer they are likely to come to perfectly competitive output.

BOX 17.1 British Airways Warns New Deal Will Hit Profits

'British Airways has given warning that the agreement to open up transatlantic air routes to and from Heathrow will lower profits. ... Industry analysts agree. ... The company will be very sorry to have lost the battle over transatlantic flights in and out of Heathrow. The agreement reached with the American authorities allows Pan Am and TWA to sell their routes to United Airlines and American Airlines ... and means that a second British airline would be allowed to fly from Heathrow to America in addition to British carriers being granted the right to fly to America via continental Europe.

'A jubilant Richard Branson celebrated by cutting all Virgin fares by 15 per cent.'

(*The Times*, 12 March 1991)

Monopoly and oligopoly power rests on barriers to entry, some of which result from acts of governments. Deregulation is the term applied to lowering entry barriers, such as that following the opening up of the transatlantic air travel market described in the news item.

Questions

1 In which of the standard categories of market structure would you class the airline industry? To what extent do they sell a homogeneous or differentiated product? How do they compete?

2 The deregulation measure referred to above is only a partial one. Have you any idea what further could, and perhaps should, be done?

Barriers to entry

Earlier in the chapter we suggested some considerations which would influence firms in oligopolistic markets to compete or to collaborate. One of the prime considerations we mentioned is the strength of barriers to entry. The stronger are entry barriers, the longer any profits from co-operative action can persist without new firms entering the industry.

We have discussed barriers to entry several times. One barrier is of particular relevance in oligopoly. It is product differentiation, especially when it consists of the proliferation of new products whose introduction is accompanied by heavy advertising expenditure. Such activity creates high entry, or set-up, costs for new firms merely to establish themselves in the industry. Anything which places newcomers at a disadvantage compared to established firms probably means that resource allocation will be closer to that under monopoly, and further from that under perfect competition.

We should, therefore, not be surprised to learn that economists view the raising of barriers to entry into an industry as weakening market forces, which work most powerfully under competitive conditions.

Advertising and the consumer

Advertising serves purposes other than acting as a barrier to entry. Its valuable function most often mentioned is that of spreading information on the availability and quality of products, especially new ones. Moreover, advertising plays an important role in the competitive process as an alternative to price competition.

However, advertising has been the focus of attack by some people, outstanding among whom is Professor John K. Galbraith of Harvard University. Galbraith's thesis is that modern firms actively manipulate market demand by spending vast sums on advertising – persuading consumers to buy what they want to sell, rather than producing what consumers want to buy.

Whether or not Galbraith is right in presenting consumers as victims of the giant corporations is a controversial matter. There is no dispute on the enormous volume of advertising expenditure, especially on certain products, such as motorcars. Nor is it contested that advertising is successful in shaping demand. Firms would hardly spend money on advertising if they thought it did not pay. The force of the Galbraithian view is probably greatest when restricted to the success of competing brands of *similar* products. If Ford stopped advertising, for example, it would surely lose sales to Vauxhall.

On the other hand, it can be forcibly argued that the strength of demand for *different* products is the result of many basic needs, fads and fashions as well as advertising. Moreover, it is hard to believe that advertising could succeed in selling products that consumers really disliked. How much advertising would persuade you to buy a slide-rule instead of a pocket calculator, or an album from the eighties instead of a current one. There is no reason to think the arguments are all on one side or the other. You must make up your own mind on how strong you think they both are.

Contestable markets

The more responsive established firms are to economic forces and the easier it is for new firms to enter an industry, the more efficiently resources are likely to be allocated. As we have stressed, this is very much a matter of the strength of barriers to entry. It is also, to some extent, a matter of barriers to *exit*. Firms are more likely to move into an industry if they can leave easily, i.e. without losing much money in the process.

The question of ease of exit lies behind a recent idea of so-called CONTESTABLE MARKETS, defined as those where sunk costs are low. SUNK COSTS are historical costs which cannot be recovered when a firm leaves an industry. In a contestable market, a firm contemplating entering an industry where supernormal profits are being earned, incurs few or no expenditures which are not recoverable on exit.

Note, a contestable market is not one where entry costs are small. They can be quite high; the point is that they can be recovered on exit. Contestable markets include those where capital needed to get established, can easily be switched to other markets. An example might be transatlantic air travel. One needs aircraft to enter the market for flights between Europe and America. An existing airline may decide to move aeroplanes into the transatlantic market in the knowledge that it can transfer them to, say, Far Eastern routes without too great expense.

Some markets are, of course, more contestable than others. In many manufacturing industries, there are substantial set-up costs, involving the installation of highly specific plant equipment, and even factories. In such cases, freedom of exit is absent. However, where markets are contestable, new entrants may be easily tempted by supernormal profits. Moreover, established firms may even react to the threat of entry, as if it had actually taken place.

An Assessment

No clear-cut or simple assessment of the efficiency of oligopoly is possible, but oligopoly is so important a market structure in the economy that some general concluding comment is called for.

The most that can really be said is that there are both efficient and inefficient oligopolistic industries, and that one of the prime determinants of efficiency is the degree of competitiveness in the industry.

It must not be overlooked that competition can be national and international. The strength of international competition has been increasing substantially in recent years, partly as a result of the process of globalization of production that is described in Box 17.2. Competitiveness at the national level depends to a considerable extent on

---

BOX 17.2 Globalization of Production and Competition

'A mere 100 years ago people and news travelled by sailing ship, so that it took months to communicate across various parts of the world. Advances in the first 60 years of this century sped up communications and travel, and in the past two decades the pace of change has accelerated, due to such technological developments as direct telephone dialling, faxes, satellite links, fast jet travel and computer networks. The world has witnessed a communications revolution that has drastically changed the way business decisions are made and implemented.

'The communications revolution has caused an internationalization of competition in the majority of industries. National markets are no longer protected for local producers by high costs of transport and communication or by the ignorance of foreign firms. Walk into a local supermarket or department store today and you will have no trouble finding products representing most of the United Nations.

'Consumers gain by being able to choose from an enormous range of well-made, low-priced goods and services. Firms that are successful gain world-wide sales. Firms that fall behind even momentarily may, however, be wiped out by competition coming from many quarters. Global competition is fierce competition, and firms need to be fast on the uptake – either of other people's new ideas or of their own – if they are to survive.'

(R.G. Lipsey *et al.*, *Economics*, 9th edn, Harper & Row, New York, 1990)

Economic theory has always recognized that the degree of competition in a market depends on the number and size of firms and the ease of entry into and exit from an industry. The nature of competition has been transformed in the present century by the revolution that has taken place in communications referred to in the quotation.

Questions

1 Has the communications revolution affected some market forms more than others?
2 How has the growth in importance of TNCs (transnational corporations) been affected by the developments described above?
3 What implications does the communications revolution have for the location of production?

government policy, which we now examine in the final section of this chapter.

GOVERNMENT AND INDUSTRY

There are many ways in which the state can intervene in industry and many reasons for doing so. In the previous chapter, we showed how economic theory could be used in an attempt to induce a monopolist to produce the perfectly competitive output. We now look at a wider range of policies designed to improve the performance of privately owned firms operating under imperfect competition, i.e. under oligopoly and monopolistic competition, and under monopoly. We shall, however, leave until the final micro-economic policy chapter (Chapter 21), the special case of natural monopoly, where a single firm emerges as the lowest cost producer. The special problems in this case call for special remedies, and we shall look at the alternatives of nationalization and regulated privatization.

The conclusions suggested by our analysis are that there is no simple policy rule to raise the levels of productive and allocative efficiency in imperfect markets. A flexible approach has much to commend it. If each case of market imperfection is treated on its merits, one can take all relevant considerations into account. These include:

- whether productive and/or allocative inefficiency is present;
- why the market is imperfect – what entry barriers exist, and whether they are natural or man-made;
- the strength of monopoly power;
- whether there are substantial Schumpeterian-style, dynamic (i.e. innovating, growth-promoting) advantages to be gained from allowing firms to enjoy some monopoly power;
- what policy instruments are available, and how effective they might be;
- what the costs of alternative courses of action are, and whether they are politically feasible.

Competition Policy

The set of policies we shall now consider are referred to as COMPETITION POLICY. (It used to be called monopoly policy.) We have not the space to describe it in detail in this book, but shall refer briefly to its main strands.

Three government-created agencies operate UK competition policy. They are the MONOPOLIES AND MERGERS COMMISSION (MMC), the RESTRICTIVE PRACTICES COURT, and the OFFICE OF FAIR TRADING (OFT). The MMC is charged with making recommendations on monopolies and mergers, the Court rules on cases of collusion among firms, while the OFT, under its Director-General of Fair Trading (DGFT), operates in all three areas. The DGFT plays a key role, under the Secretary of State for Trade and Industry, in selecting industries and practices to be given priority for investigation. The annual report of the Director-General of Fair Trading is an excellent source of details on the current state of competition policy (see the extract we give in Box 17.3).

Monopolies: The Monopolies and Mergers Commission is told to regard a firm as a 'monopoly', and hence within its terms of reference, if it has a minimum share of 25 per cent of industry output. In other words, it is concerned with oligopolies as well as what we have called monopolies. This apparently simple guideline is not a simple test for the strength of monopoly power. A lot may depend on how narrowly a product is defined. For example, is mail-order trade a distinct industry, or part of the whole retail trade? Depending on the answer, the largest mail-order firm will, or will not, be a monopoly under the 25 per cent rule.

Provided it finds that the market share exceeds 25 per cent, the MMC is then required to decide whether or not the firm has been operating against the public interest. This can involve profound difficulties. The Commission is given some guidance on the meaning of the public interest, and told of the desirability of maintaining and promoting competition. This, nevertheless, allows the MMC considerable flexibility in making recommendations, which are usually, though not always, adopted.

Mergers: The procedure on mergers is similar to that on monopolies. Merger proposals may be referred to the MMC for report, the criteria for investigation being either a 25 per cent market share, or that gross assets after the merger would exceed £30 million.

As with monopolies, so with mergers, the MMC is asked to make recommendations on whether any proposed merger is likely to affect the public interest adversely, and it is, again, instructed to have regard to the potential implications for competition in the UK if the merger is allowed to proceed. In so far as this means predicting the future, it is inherently an even more difficult task than that of forming a view about past behaviour, as the Commission has to do with monopolies.

The official view is that the vast majority of mergers raise no competition or other objections, and the number of merger proposals referred to the MMC for report has remained small (between 1 and 5 per cent of all qualifying mergers in the 1980s). Nevertheless, a few important amalgamations have been stopped (see Box 17.3).

Restrictive practices: The third strand of competition policy concerns what are termed *restrictive practices*. The principal target has been collusive agreements among firms acting as a cartel, to operate practices such as joint price-fixing (including resale price maintenance, RPM) and measures to support it, e.g. collective boycott of businesses who do not adhere to fixed prices, and market-sharing arrangements by cartel members. However, the DGFT may also take action against anti-competitive practices by individual firms.

Most collective agreements involving restrictive practices must be registered with the OFT, and are deemed to be contrary to the public interest and therefore unlawful. The Restrictive Practices Court was established in

BOX 17.3 How Does Competition Policy Protect Consumers?

'Let us look at the various ways in which the operation of competition policy promotes consumers' interests. Cartels are the most obvious way in which the frustration of the process of competition denies choice to consumers. In this country cartels are unlawful if not notified to me as required by the Restrictive Trade Practices Act. Secret cartels continue to be discovered and brought before the Court. Some of these agreements have been directly harmful to consumers, for example agreements on ferry fares across the Irish Sea, or on estate agents' commission in Southend. Others affect consumers less directly, examples being agreements on glass and ready-mixed concrete. When such agreements come to light it is my role to bring them before the Restrictive Practices Court to be struck down. Some of these have been price-fixing cartels; others sought to share out markets (with the effect of allowing their members to charge whatever prices they liked). All aimed to deprive consumers of the benefits brought by freedom of choice. They also affected consumers in a more insidious way: when competition is restricted the spur to improve efficiency is blunted; and when that spur is blunted the cost mounts cumulatively.

'The Resale Practices Act prohibits imposing minimum resale prices on dealers. ... I took action against suppliers of a wide range of consumer goods, including suppliers of perfume, alcoholic drinks, vacuum cleaners, home computers and domestic power tools. In all these cases, consumers were wrongly being deprived of the benefit of price competition between retailers ... Other restrictions concerned not so much with price but with other conditions of supply, have been at the centre of recent monopoly investigations by the Monopolies and Mergers Commission, notably of beer and of petrol, both products of keen interest to consumers. Here, there was

no lack of brewers or refiners capable of providing competition. It was disquiet about their involvement in the *retailing* of their products, both through their ownership of outlets and through exclusive supply agreements, that led me to make the references to the Commission.

'Finally mergers ... in 1989, my Office scrutinised more than 300 mergers to see whether they risked impairing competition ... If I see any risk that competition will be reduced by a merger I am likely to advise the Secretary of State to refer the merger to the Commission. In 1989 they found the proposed merger between Elders and Scottish & Newcastle Breweries against the public interest, and it was not allowed to proceed. Later in the year they investigated a major merger in textiles, between Coats Viyella and Tootal: they found that it would lead to a serious reduction in competition in the market for domestic sewing thread; they recommended that it should be allowed to proceed only if Coats would divest itself of its domestic thread business.'

(Extracts from *The Annual Report of the Director-General of Fair Trading, 1989* (HMSO, 1990))

The Director-General's annual report provides a very useful summary of the government's competition policy.

Questions

1 Which of the three areas of policy seem to have (i) occupied most time, (ii) produced the most effective results?
2 How far do the items mentioned in the box correspond with the ideas in the body of the chapter?

1956 to consider exemptions for individual cases. To obtain exemption, an agreement must pass through at least one of eight so-called 'gateways', e.g. that it protects the public against injury, and on balance operates in the public interest.

On one count, the restrictive practices legislation might be judged effective – of over 8500 agreements registered, the vast majority have been abandoned, undefended; only 12 had survived the Restrictive Practices Court by the end of the 1980s. However, at that time the government viewed the legislation as too weak, partly because of lack of observance (see Box 17.3) and partly because of the costs of administration.

Other policies

So far we have not considered the implications of the

European Community's competition policy, where articles 85 and 86 of the Treaty of Rome deal with restrictive practices and dominant firms, and restrict the freedom of member nations to operate policies to deal with imperfect markets.

There is, too, a wide variety of government policies which impinge on economic efficiency and the competitive process. There are also many of them, including for example measures directed at consumer protection from misleading, not to mention fraudulent, advertising, and other sales practices. These are the responsibility of the Director-General of Fair Trading, but operated also by the locally organized inspectorate of weights and measures. A final area of government activity of importance concerns the law regarding patents, which encourage innovation at the same time as discouraging competition. Decisions have to be made on such questions as – How long should a patent provide protection? Should patent-holders be obliged to allow competitors to produce their patented product under licence? If so, what price should they be permitted to charge licensees in order to provide a reasonable balance between encouraging innovation and stimulating competition?

Summary

1 Markets between the extremes of perfect competition and monopoly are classed as imperfect competition.

2 The degree of concentration varies from industry to industry. Its growth since the beginning of the century is due to both amalgamations among firms and internal growth.

3 In monopolistic competition, a large number of firms compete in the sale of differentiated products in markets where there is freedom of entry and exit.

4 The equilibrium of the firm under monopolistic competition is the same as under monopoly in the short run, but different in the long run when the entry of firms competes away supernormal profits.

5 Monopolistic competition is characterized by excess capacity (in that equilibrium output is less than cost-minimizing output), which may or may not be outweighed by the variety of differentiated products for consumers to choose from.

6 Oligopoly exists in markets which have only a few sellers, whose behaviour is rivalrous. Each firm is affected by the actions of others. Oligopolists are price-makers, but may produce homogeneous or differentiated products.

7 The basic dilemma for an oligopolist is whether to co-operate with other firms or compete with them. Co-operation implies behaving as a monopoly, and is preferable for all firms, provided all 'play the game'; but it pays any one firm to 'cheat' provided the others do not cheat too. The probability that firms will co-operate rather than compete depends on the number of sellers, the nature of the product, the number of dominant firms, barriers to entry, and whether or not the industry is growing.

8 Cost curves under monopoly typically have a long flat middle section, where average and marginal costs are constant, described as 'saucer shaped'.

9 Prices under oligopoly are usually administered, and tend to be 'sticky'. This may be due to (i) full cost pricing, i.e. charging a price which includes a standard percentage mark-up over costs; (ii) the fact that the very act of changing price is itself costly; (iii) a preference for non-price competition, e.g. product differentiation, advertising, etc; (iv) the nature of the demand curve, which may be 'kinked', resulting in a discontinuous marginal revenue curve.

10 Resources under oligopoly are likely to approach the efficient allocation under perfect competition if firms compete, but to approach that under monopoly if firms co-operate.

11 Advertising creates barriers to the entry of new firms; it has a persuasive function but provides information about product availability for consumers.

12 Contestable markets are those where there is freedom of exit from an industry because 'sunk costs' are low, so that firms can recover most of the costs of entry if they decide to leave.

13 Competition policy seeks to improve economic efficiency where privately owned firms operate in imperfect markets. The advantages and disadvantages of existing market arrangements are often best weighed against each other in individual cases, though some universal guidelines can be recognized.

Questions

1 Which One or More of the following are found in markets described as (i) oligopoly, (ii) monopolistic competition, (iii) perfect competition, (iv) imperfect competition?
    (a) Many sellers and a differentiated product.
    (b) Few sellers and a differentiated product.
    (c) Few sellers and a homogeneous product.
    (d) Many sellers and a homogeneous product.
    (e) Freedom of entry into the industry.

2 Which type, or types, of merger would you be most likely to associate with raising (i) the concentration ratio in an industry, (ii) the level of overall concentration in the economy without changing the concentration ratios of any industries?

3 Referring to Figure 17.2, would you conclude that a firm in monopolistic competition which wished to earn only normal profits would produce more or less than q_0?

4 Given the assumptions about rivals' price behaviour in Figure 17.3, under what circumstances would the firm charge a price (i) higher than, (ii) lower than p_0?

5 Place each of the following into one of three categories according to their most likely effect on competition: (i) strengthening it, (ii) weakening it:
    (a) Requiring the Restrictive Practices Court to show that registered practices are against the public interest.
    (b) Changing the rule defining monopoly to 25 per cent of total sales.
    (c) Putting a heavy tax on advertising.
    (d) Lowering exit barriers from industries.

6 What kind of behaviour in what kind of market results from the existence of a discontinuous marginal revenue curve?

18 Competitive Factor Markets

So far in this book, we have been studying how the price mechanism operates in markets for goods and services – to answer two of the three basic questions of economics posed in Part 1 – *What to produce*? and *How to produce it*? Now, we turn to the third question – *Who gets it*? This takes us to the study of markets for factors of production, the branch of economics called the THEORY OF DISTRIBUTION. In this chapter, we study competitive factor markets. In the next chapter, we see how factor markets work under imperfect competition.

WHO GETS IT?

People's incomes, together with their wealth, are key determinants of what they are able to consume. Incomes, therefore, determine who gets it. Two interrelated ways of looking at the way income is divided up are the distribution of income (1) according to size, and (2) according to source. The former is called the size distribution of income, and the second is called the functional (or factor) distribution of income.

The Size Distribution of Income

The distribution which is most talked about is that related to size, i.e. how much the rich receive compared to middle income groups and the poor. We took a preliminary look at the size distribution of income in Chapter 2 (see Figure 2.3 on page 15). Now, however, we employ a different kind of diagram, which provides a neater way of representing the extent of equality and inequality. This makes use of what is called a LORENZ CURVE, and it shows the percentages of total income accounted for by different percentages of the population.

Figure 18.1 contains a Lorenz curve for the UK for 1988. The vertical axis measures (cumulative) percentages of total income and the horizontal axis (cumulative) percentages of the total population. We read directly from the graph to find the income shares of any percentage of the poorest members of the population.

Thus, we see, for example, that the poorest 20 per cent of the population received about 4 per cent of total income, the poorest 50 per cent received about 20 per cent of total income, and so on. (Note, the shares of the richest income groups are not *directly* readable from the Figure. They are residuals – what is left by subtracting the shares of the poorest from 100 per cent. Thus, the share in total income of the richest 80 per cent of income recipients is 96 per cent – 100 per cent minus the 4 per cent received by the bottom 80 per cent of the population.)

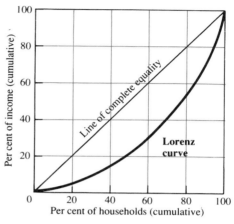

FIGURE 18.1 The Size Distribution of Income, UK, 1988. The Lorenz curve shows the percentages of total income received by different percentages of the population of households. (*Source*: S. P. Jenkins, 'Income Inequality and Living Standards', *Fiscal Studies*, Vol. 12, No. 1, 1991.)

In Figure 18.1 note the diagonal in the diagram, labelled the 'line of complete equality'. This line, which makes an angle of 45° with the axes, shows how a completely equal distribution would appear on the Figure. Every point on this line represents complete equality, because it shows that any given percentage of the population would receive exactly the same percentage of total income. The line of complete equality serves as a useful benchmark against which any distribution can be compared – the further from the diagonal is the Lorenz curve, the greater the degree of inequality. Thus, we can see that income is indeed unequally distributed in the UK, as it is in all countries.

People receive incomes from two sources: (1) as rewards for the services of factors of production, and (2) as transfers, especially from the state in the form of retirement pensions, unemployment benefit, etc. We shall discuss government transfer payments and how they affect income distribution in Chapter 21. In this chapter and the next, we concentrate on factor incomes.

The Functional (or Factor) Distribution of Income

Market-determined factor prices can explain some of the inequality we have seen. This is for two reasons:

In the first place, some people have more sources of factor incomes than others.

In the second place, all factors do not earn the same amount.

The second explanation is concerned with the questions why some members of the labour force earn higher wages than others, why some owners of capital earn more than others, why some entrepreneurial profits are higher than others, and so on. We shall return to this question shortly as it forms the bulk of the subject-matter of this and the next chapter.

The first explanation of inequality of income among persons – that some individuals have more *sources* of factor incomes than others – is another way of saying that some people own more factors of production than others. Someone may own some land let out to tenants, some shares in a business, have some money in a building society account, and work for a wage or salary. Each of the above components comprises a return from the ownership of a factor of production – rent, profits, interest, and labour income.

By far the largest component of income accrues to labour. But something like a quarter of the total of all factor incomes consists of rent, interest and profit, and most individuals derive income from more than one source. However, the bulk of investment income is received by the top income groups. Interest on capital provides a much higher proportion of their incomes than it does of those with average incomes, let alone of those near the bottom of the income scale.

The basic reason for inequality in the distribution of income from investment is, of course, that personal wealth, from which this income is derived, is itself unequally distributed. The richest 10 per cent of the population own about 40 per cent of all personal wealth, compared with well under 20 per cent owned by the poorest half of the population.

There are many reasons why the distribution of wealth is unequal. These include the institution of inheritance, and differences in saving habits among individuals. Although *wealth* distribution explains some of the inequality of *income* in Britain, it is not the only cause. Within each functional share of the total income, there are also substantial variations. Paul Gascoigne, George Michael, Nick Faldo and the chairmen of the major industrial and financial companies, receive incomes from their labour services greatly in excess of those of unskilled workers, especially if they are black, female and live in Northern Ireland, for example.

Sometimes it is said that people earn according to their ability. But note that labour incomes are distributed more unequally than any measured index of ability, such as IQ or physical strength. Is George Michael 5, 10, 20 or more times more able than a promising new pop singer? In what sense is a lorry driver more able than a school teacher, or a football player than a boxer? If answers couched in terms of ability seem superficial, so are answers such as 'It's all luck,' or 'It's just the system.' Can economic theory explain income differences better than glib 'explanations'?

MARKET EXPLANATIONS OF INCOME DIFFERENCES

The services of factors of production are bought and sold in the market-place. Wages, salaries, rent, interest and profit are no more than the prices of factors of production. Hence, we would expect the forces of supply and demand for the various factors of production to play at least some part in determining their prices.

To explain the market determination of incomes, we apply to the case of factor services the principles we learned about the operation of market forces. There are some key distinctive features of factor markets that we shall encounter later, but we can go quite a long way just using our existing demand and supply techniques.

Note that we should always talk of the prices of *services* of factors of production, not the prices of the factors of production themselves. This is because it is the services that are supplied and demanded. Firms, which own factors of production, buy them only for the services that they provide. Incidentally, the buying of a labourer, as opposed to just the buying of his or her services, implies the existence of a slave market! However, for convenience, we shall talk of the price of labour and the prices of other factors, when we really mean the prices of their *services*.

Factor Prices in Competitive Markets

The reader should be familiar enough, by now, with the practice of economists of starting to analyse problems with simple models. We make no excuse for doing so again. We start with a theory, based on unrealistic assumptions, which would explain a world in which all incomes were equal. We shall then be able to see why the inapplicability of some of the assumptions helps to explain why incomes differ.

You may recognize this theory as resembling perfect competition. Suppose there is a factor of production, whose price is determined by market forces. The factor could be land, labour, or capital, but we shall call it labour, and its price wages. We now make the following six assumptions:

- Buyers and sellers are price-takers.
- Labour is a homogeneous factor of production, i.e. there is no difference in ability, or in any other characteristic, between one worker and another.
- Every buyer and seller is fully informed about the price of labour, and knows that it is homogeneous.
- Wages fluctuate so as to equate the demand for labour with its supply.
- There is complete mobility of labour. This assumption parallels that of freedom of entry and exit of firms under perfect competition. It means that there are no barriers to movement of labour between regions of the country, occupations or industries.
- Finally we have our maximizing assumptions. Employers seek to use labour in pursuit of profit-maximization. Workers seek to work in industries where wages are highest.

Given these assumptions, market forces ensure that workers earn the same wages, regardless of the industries in which they work. To illustrate, suppose there are two industries, employing homogeneous and mobile labour. Let us call them clothing and textiles. Assume that markets for both clothing and textiles are in equilibrium, and that the wage rate is the same in both industries. Assume, now, that the demand for clothing rises while that for textiles falls. The demand for labour will rise in the clothing industry, and fall in the textile industry. The new demand conditions will have an immediate effect of raising wages of clothing workers, and of lowering wages of textile workers.

This wage difference cannot, however, persist. Textile workers, aware of the higher earning opportunities in the clothing industry, will pack up and move. This migration from one industry to the other will cause a shortage of textile workers, which will raise wage rates in textiles. It will also increase the supply of clothing workers, causing their wage rates to fall. Labour will continue to flow between the two industries until there is no incentive for workers to move from one to the other. This will be when wage rates are again the same in clothing and textiles, but now there will be more workers in clothing and fewer in textiles than in the original equilibrium. The transitory difference in wages served the purpose of reallocating workers between the industries but, in the final equilibrium, wage rates returned to equality.

The simple model outlined above is not, of course, a mirror of the world in which we live. But market forces exercise a powerful influence on the distribution of incomes. In this chapter we investigate more closely the working of market forces under perfect competition. We examine, first, the demand for and, second, the supply of, some factor of production, in order to understand more about the way in which the market price of a factor is determined.

The Demand for a Factor

Firms require land, labour, raw materials, machines and other inputs to produce the goods and services that they sell. The demand for any input depends on there being a demand for the goods that it helps to make. We say that the demand is a DERIVED DEMAND. In other words, factors are demanded, not for themselves, but for the goods they can produce.

Obvious examples of derived demand abound. The demand for computer programmers is growing as firms turn increasingly to the use of computers in production and offices; demand for shipyard workers declines as the ship-building industry declines, and so forth. Moreover, a factor is typically used for making several goods rather than just one. Agricultural land is used to grow many crops; the services of carpenters are used to make many products. Total demand for a factor will be the sum of its derived demands in all uses.

The marginal product of a factor

In Chapter 14 we showed how a profit-maximizing firm

decides how much to employ of the various factors of production available to it. The rule for cost-minimization was expressed as that the last pound spent on each and every factor should yield the same extra output. Another way of putting this rule is to say that a profit-maximizing firm will employ units of each variable factor up to the point where the marginal cost of employing it is equal to the addition to the firm's *total revenue from selling the factor's marginal product*. This last concept is called the MARGINAL REVENUE PRODUCT, defined as the marginal product (in physical terms) multiplied by the marginal revenue derived from it.

The general rule for deciding how much of a factor to employ, known as MARGINAL PRODUCTIVITY THEORY, can then be expressed as:

$$MC \text{ of factor} = MRP \text{ of factor}$$

If there were any factor for which this did not hold, the firm could increase its profits by varying the employment of that factor. If *MC* were greater than *MRP*, the firm should decrease its use of that factor, and vice versa.

Having explained the above rule, which holds in equilibrium for every factor employed by every profit-maximizing firm, our next step is to apply it to firms operating under different market conditions for their product.

Different market structures

In this chapter we are confining our attention to perfectly competitive *factor markets*. We need, however, to consider various types of *goods markets*. This is because the firm's demand for factors will be influenced by the type of market in which it sells its output. To demonstrate this, we show the derivation of the demand for a factor, first by a firm which sells its output in a perfectly competitive market, second by a firm which sells its output in a monopolistic market. Let us start with the perfectly competitive case.

Perfect competition in the goods market: You will recall that firms selling their output in perfectly competitive markets are price-takers facing perfectly elastic demand curves for their product. Under such circumstances, the demand curve for a factor can be directly derived from the curve of the factor's marginal product. Figure 18.2 shows *both* the marginal product of a variable factor and the firm's demand curve for labour! We put an exclamation mark after the previous sentence to emphasize that we have not, by mistake, forgotten to draw one of the curves.

There are, however, two scale markings on the vertical scale axis. The one on the left is marked in units of physical output. This is the one that applies to the curve of marginal product, which is given the full name of MARGINAL PHYSICAL PRODUCT (MPP). This curve is drawn in exactly the same way as was the curve of the marginal product of a variable factor, in Figure 13.1 on page 135. You should refer to the text there if you are in any doubt about it. The scale on the right is MPP multiplied by the price of the product (£2 per tonne in this case). It is, thus, a constant multiple of the scale on the left.

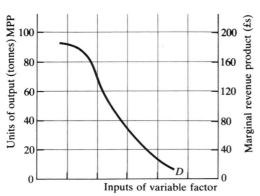

FIGURE 18.2 A Firm's Demand Curve for a Variable Factor of Production. This curve is the same as that in Figure 13.1, which shows the marginal product of a variable factor using the left-hand vertical scale. Additionally, using the right-hand scale *MP*s are here multiplied by the price of the product to give this marginal revenue product, or demand, curve.

Imperfect competition in the goods market: If a firm is not operating in a perfectly competitive market for its product, it is a price-maker, not a price-taker. It faces a downward-sloping demand curve, so that, in order to sell additional units, it has to lower the price of its product. We explained earlier that, under these conditions, the marginal revenue from additional sales is less than the price of the product.

This divergence of price from *MR* for firms which are price-makers has important implications for the demand curve for a variable factor.

Suppose, for example, a firm is producing 100 units of output which are sold at a price of £50 each. Total revenue of the firm is £5000. Now assume that an extra unit of a factor of production is employed, and output increases by 4 to 104. Since the firm is not a price-taker, it must lower the price of its product in order to sell more. Say, the price at which 104 can be sold is £49 per unit.

First, consider what the sale of the extra production of 4 units brings in to the firm. This is called the VALUE OF THE MARGINAL PRODUCT (VMP), defined as the marginal physical product multiplied by price (*MPP* × price). In the example, the 4 units of *MPP* sell at £49 each, making *VMP* = £196.

Next consider the marginal revenue product (*MRP*), defined on page 187. Total revenue from the sale of the original 100 units at £50 per unit was £5000. The total revenue from the sale of the 104, at a price of £49, is £5096. The *change* in total revenue from the employment of an extra factor of production is therefore £96. This is the *marginal revenue product* of the extra unit of the factor. It is less than the value of the marginal product of that unit of the factor (*MRP* < *VMP*).

There is no mystery about this. The value of the marginal product is the extra output multiplied by the price at which it is sold. This calculation takes no account of the cut in price that is needed to sell the extra output, and which reduces the revenue gained from all the units that were already being sold.

Thus, the contribution of an extra unit of a factor of production to increased revenue is equal to the extra revenue resulting from the sale of the additional amount it adds to output *minus* the loss in revenue resulting from the cut in price on units already being sold. This is the change in total revenue resulting from the employment of another unit of the factor of production. This result holds whenever the firm faces a downward-sloping demand curve, so that more sales mean a lower price on all units sold.

However, this result does not hold when the firm is in perfect competition in the market for its product. In this case the firm is a price-taker, and can sell all that it wishes at the going market price. There is no loss of revenue on units already being sold. It follows, therefore, that the value of the marginal product is equal to the net addition to the firm's revenue, i.e. the marginal revenue product (*VMP* = *MRP*), under perfect competition.

There are three summary points to this discussion:

All profit-maximizing firms will hire each factor up to the point at which the marginal revenue product is equal to the cost of the factor.

Under perfect competition, the marginal revenue product is equal to the value of the marginal product, so the price of the factor will in equilibrium be equal to the value of the factor's marginal product.

Whenever the firm faces a downward-sloping demand curve for its product, the factor's marginal revenue product will be less than the value of its marginal product.

Industry demand for a factor

When we derived the market demand curve for a commodity in Chapter 4, we merely added horizontally the demand curves of all the individuals in the market. We cannot adopt such a simple procedure in the case of the demand for a factor of production. The reason is as follows.

When the price of a factor of production falls, a firm will use more of it. *But so will other firms.* The result will be that output sold by all firms in the industry will rise, leading to a fall in the price of a product. This price fall will be reflected in a decline in the marginal revenue product for all firms in the industry. Hence, the industry demand curve cannot be derived by straightforward addition of the demand curves of each of the firms in the industry. It is a more complicated procedure, which we do not include in this book.[1]

Elasticity of demand for a factor

We conclude our general discussion of the demand for a factor with four propositions concerning the determinants of the elasticity of demand for a factor of production, i.e. the determinants of the responsiveness of the demand for a factor to changes in that factor's price.

1 For details see IPE8.

(1) The elasticity of demand for a factor will be greater the more elastic is the demand for the industry's output.

This follows from the fact that the demand for a factor is derived. So if the price of a factor falls, costs of production fall. The supply curve *of the product* shifts to the right. More of the product will be offered for sale at a lower price than before. If the demand for the product is relatively elastic there will be relatively large increases in sales and also, therefore, a relatively large increase in the demand for the factor of production.

(2) The elasticity of demand for a factor will be greater the easier it is to substitute other factors for the one in question.

This depends on the technological conditions of production. In agriculture, for example, wheat and other crops may be produced by varying combinations of land, labour, machines and fertilizers. A substantial change in the price of one of these factors, relative to another, may result in a considerable shift in the use of resources. Production may become more land-intensive, more labour-intensive or more capital-intensive, depending on relative factor price changes.

(3) The elasticity of demand for a factor will be greater the longer the time-period allowed.

This is merely an extension of the general conclusions we drew in Chapter 7 about elasticity of both supply and demand in the goods market. All we add here is that, the elasticity of demand for a factor will be greater the longer the time-period allowed for demand to respond to a given change in the factor's price. The longer the time allowed, the easier substitution becomes among factors.

(4) The elasticity of demand for a factor will be smaller the less the proportion of total cost accounted for by that factor.

The reason for this is not difficult to appreciate. A fall in the price of a factor, for example, lowers the marginal costs of production and shifts the supply curve to the right. With any given demand curve, the rise in output that follows depends on how large or small is the shift of the supply curve.

Consider, for example, the use of two factors of production, A and B, where expenditure on A accounts for 2 per cent, and on B for 50 per cent of total costs. Suppose there is a 1 per cent fall in the price of each factor. The fall in the price of A will shift the supply curve much less than the fall in the price of B. Therefore output, and hence the derived demand for the factor, will increase less when factor A's price falls, than when factor B's does. We may conclude that the elasticity of demand for a factor is smaller the less the proportion of total costs accounted for by that factor.

The Supply of a Factor

Note, first, that there are sometimes different determinants of supply of a factor at the local and at the national levels.

Just as in the case of demand, where we distinguished between the firm and industry demand, so we should differentiate supply according to the level at which we wish to study it. In particular we distinguish: (i) *total* supply of a factor, (ii) supply of a factor *for a particular use*, and (iii) supply of an *individual unit of a factor*.

Total supply of a factor

When we talk of the total supply of a factor, such as land or labour, we mean the total quantity that is offered for sale at different prices, throughout the entire economy. At first glance, it may seem that the total supply of most factors is fixed. After all, there is only so much land in the country and in the world as a whole. There is an upper limit to the number of workers. There is only so much coal, oil, copper and iron ore in the earth. These considerations certainly put maxima upon the supplies of each factor. But, in virtually every case, current use is far from the upper limits, and the determinants of the *effective* supply of land, labour, natural resources or capital need to be considered.

Take land, for example. If by 'land' we mean the total area of dry land, then its supply is pretty well fixed. However high the price may rise, no more than a marginal increase can be obtained by reclamation of land from swamp or sea. The traditional assumption in economics has, therefore, been that the total supply of land is perfectly inelastic. However, if by 'land' we understand all the *fertile* land available for cultivation, then the supply of land is subject to large fluctuations. There is no doubt that a high return to land provides incentives for irrigation, drainage and fertilization that can greatly increase the total supply offered on the market. When, in contrast, the return to land is low, such incentives are weak and the supply is also low.

Labour supply offers a different illustration of the same point. In so far as the size of the workforce depends on the numbers of adults in the population, this, too, is fixed for longish periods. However, the total number of persons offering to work, the *effective* supply, or the labour force, is also variable with respect to the price of labour. ACTIVITY RATES (or PARTICIPATION RATES) are defined as the proportions of the total number of persons, in various groups, seeking employment. These proportions certainly vary with the level of wages and other factors, as witness the substantial rise in activity rates for married women during the second half of this century.

Supply of a factor for a particular use

Most factors have alternative uses. It would, therefore, still be necessary to allocate them among competing uses, even if the total supply were fixed. A given amount of land, for example, can be used to grow a variety of crops; it can be subdivided for a housing development, given over to parkland, factory or airport construction, etc. A mechanic from Coventry can work in a garage in almost any part of the country, and in many different industries which run their own transport.

It follows that the supply of factors of production to any particular use is likely to be more elastic than the total supply of that factor. Moreover, when we use the term 'particular use', we should think of it in a broad sense to refer to the supply to a particular firm, to a particular occupation, to a particular industry, or to a particular region in the country.

Factor mobility

A key role in the determination of factor prices is played by factor MOBILITY. A factor is said to be mobile if it responds to movements in the prices paid for its services in various uses. If a factor is highly mobile, in that owners will quickly shift from use A to use B in response to a small change in relative factor prices, then the supply will be relatively elastic. If, in contrast, factor owners are 'locked in' to some use or other, and so do not respond quickly, the supply of the factor to a particular use will be relatively inelastic.

Mobility among factors of production is very much a question of the circumstances of time and place, and the specific factor under consideration. One of the few generalizations that can be made about factor mobility is that it is normally greater the longer the time allowed for movement to take place.

Factor prices are liable to be materially affected by factor mobility. The greater the mobility, the faster any divergencies in the rewards paid by different firms for a given factor will be competed away, as factors move from the low-payers to the high-payers. This is generally true, and in the next chapter we shall see that it has important implications for the labour market, where questions of geographical mobility among regions of a country, and occupational mobility among jobs, will be considered.

The factor land, although the least mobile factor of production in a *physical* sense, is highly mobile in an *economic* sense. For example, a farmer can switch his crops from one harvest time to another, agricultural land can be turned into a golf course, and urban land can be switched from residential to commercial use. The time-scale needed for transfer is variable.

Individual supply of a factor

Finally, we consider the response of the individual owner of a productive factor to the price offered for its services. This analysis is in terms of labour, but could equally apply to other factors.

The response that individual workers make to a change in the wage rate depends on the alternative uses of time that are available. This idea is, of course, none other than our old friend, opportunity cost. The opportunity cost of an hour's work is the leisure that is given up by working. Hence the supply of work, sometimes called the SUPPLY OF EFFORT, is dependent on the desire for leisure.

We can even put a price on leisure time. It is the cost to the individual of not working. The higher the wage rate, the higher the cost of leisure, because more potential income has to be given up for idling away an hour. Conse-

quently, a change in the wage rate implies a change in the price of leisure in terms of earnings sacrificed.

Consider Figure 18.3, which depicts the options open to an individual worker, whom we call Mary. Mary has a choice of how to spend the 24 hours in the day. The axes on the diagram represent the two things she can do with her time – earn income by working (as measured on the vertical axis), or take time off enjoying hours of leisure (as measured on the horizontal axis).

Suppose Mary can earn £10 an hour. Then her options are represented by the line AB, which is one form of the budget line we first met in Chapter 11. AB is the line which shows the ways in which Mary can allocate the 24 hours in the day between work and leisure. We can think of it as a kind of 'choice line'. The *slope* of the line AB indicates the *rate* at which she can earn income by giving up hours of work.

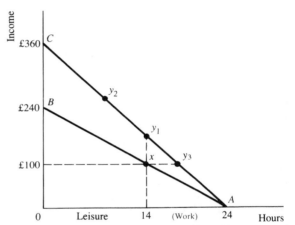

FIGURE 18.3 **Individual Factor Supply.** The choices available are given by the line AB, the slope of which is the rate of pay (£10 an hour). The factor chooses 14 hours leisure and 10 hours work, earning £100. A rise in the rate of pay to £15 an hour shifts the choice line to AC, when the supply of effort may rise to any point to the left of y_1, fall to any point to the right of y_3, or remain the same, at exactly y_1.

To see this, suppose Mary decided not to work at all. She would have chosen to be at point A in the diagram, taking 24 hours of leisure and not earning anything. The opposite extreme for Mary would be to work for 24 hours. Though unrealistic, this option helps understand the meaning of the choice line, AB, that Mary faces. If Mary took no leisure, but worked 24 hours, she could earn £240, and would be at point B in Figure 18.3. The intermediate points between A and B represent other choices for Mary of dividing her time between work and leisure. Suppose she chooses point x. She would have chosen to take 14 hours' leisure, working the other 10 hours, earning £100.

A change in the wage rate: Consider, now, the effects of a change in the wage rate. Suppose this rises from £10 to £15 an hour. Mary's new options are now represented in Figure 18.3 by the line AC. The extremes available are (1) to work 24 hours and earn £360, point C, and (2) to take

24 hours leisure and no income, point A. Intermediate options are the points along AC, such as y_1, y_2, and y_3.

Mary's choice is a matter of considerable importance to her. If she decides on point y_1, it means she takes exactly the same number of hours leisure and, therefore, also works the same number of hours, despite the fact that the wage rate has gone up by 50 per cent! However, she might choose not y_1, but a point such as y_2 or y_3. In the former case, y_2, Mary would be working longer hours; in the latter case, y_3, she would be working shorter hours. Are all these options reasonable possibilities?

The answer is that they are. To understand why, we have to remember that a price change has both a substitution effect and an income effect (see above, pp.120–22). Here, they pull in opposite directions.

Consider first the substitution effect of the rise in the wage rate. It encourages Mary to work longer hours – to give up some leisure time in order to work and earn more income. The opportunity cost of leisure time for Mary has risen, in the sense that she has to sacrifice £15 rather than £10 for every hour of leisure (i.e. of not working). She would be tempted to move to points such as y_2, to the left of y_1, substituting income from work for time taken as leisure, as a result of the rise in her wage rate.

However, we have still to take account of the income effect of the price change. The income effect of the rise in Mary's wage rate occurs because she is *better off*. Any given number of hours worked bring her a higher income than before. If, for example, she worked the same number of hours, she could earn a larger total income, choosing point y_1. Alternatively, Mary could work fewer hours than previously while still earning the same income, choosing the point y_3. Finally, Mary could work even more hours, because the wage rate is better for her, choosing a point such as y_2.

We cannot take this analysis much further here.[1] However, there are some important conclusions from this analysis.

First, we cannot assume that raising people's wage rates will make them work longer hours. If they are earning what they consider is more or less enough before their wage rate rises, they may work no more, even perhaps fewer, hours.

Backward-sloping supply curve: Second, the supply curve of the factor, labour, may appear 'backward-sloping', as in Figure 18.4. The meaning of this somewhat unusual-looking curve is that, as the wage rate increases up to w_1, the worker works more hours, giving up more leisure – e.g. at w_0 she works h_0 hours, at w_1 she works h_1 hours. However, at wage rates higher than w_1, hours worked decrease; e.g. at wage rate w_2, hours worked fall to h_2.

There is plenty of evidence that some labour supply curves are backward-sloping over at least part of the range. At low wage rates, the supply of labour tends to behave 'normally', responding to a wage rate rise by working longer hours. When rates become higher, however, a 'perverse' backward-sloping portion of the curve may become

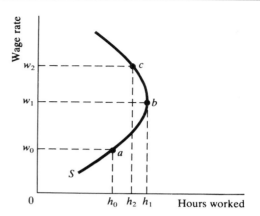

FIGURE 18.4 A Backward-Sloping Supply Curve. Hours worked increase as the wage rate rises to w_1, but at higher wage rates they decrease.

relevant, showing that an increase in the wage rate causes the supply of effort to decrease as the income effect outweighs the substitution effect.

Equilibrium in Perfect Factor Markets

It is useful at this point to consider what has been said about equilibrium in perfectly competitive factor markets, in the light of what was said about perfectly competitive goods markets earlier in the book.

Consider Figure 18.5, which shows the supply and demand curves for a variable factor of production. (Only the upward-sloping part of the supply curve is included here.) The operation of market forces is broadly similar, in this case, to that in the market for goods. But recall that the demand curve for a factor is *derived* and should be interpreted as the curve of the MRP of the factor (whether or not there is perfect competition in the *goods* market).

The supply curve must be interpreted as the units of factor services offered for sale at different prices. Equilibrium market price is p_0 and equilibrium quantity is q_0.

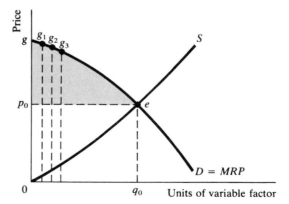

FIGURE 18.5 Factor Market Equilibrium under Perfect Competition. The market is cleared at price p_0, with q_0 units of the variable factor supplied and demanded. Area Oq_0ep_0 is total factor earnings. Area p_0eg is remaining revenue available for all other factors.

---

1 See, however, IPE8.

Total factor earnings are equal to the area Op_0eq_0 (quantity of factor used times its price). The shaded area, p_0ge_0, represents the revenue remaining to the firm to pay for all other inputs, including profit. This, perhaps, needs a word of explanation.

The total revenue of a firm can be viewed as the sum of revenues it receives from selling each unit of output – i.e. the sum of its marginal revenues. Equally, the total revenue from employing additional units of variable factor can be viewed as the revenue it receives from the employment of each unit of factor employed – i.e. the sum of its marginal revenue products.

The diagram shows the value of the total revenue from employing a given amount of the variable factor. To see this, let us mark out units of that variable factor on the horizontal axis of the graph. If we do, we can describe the total revenue from, say, 3 units of the factor as $g_1 + g_2 + g_3$ in Figure 18.5.

Extending this approximation to the general case, we can find the total revenue from employing any number of units of a variable factor, as the *area under the demand curve for the factor*. Thus, in the present case, when q_0 units are employed, total revenue is given by the area $Ogeq_0$. However, as we have already explained, Op_0eq_0 is the total paid to the variable factor. Therefore, the remainder, p_0ge, is the amount available for all other factor payments.

All the conclusions we reached in Part 2 of this book, on price determination in the market for goods, can be applied to this factor market. The same principle for distinguishing shifts and movements along curves is as valid as before. If, for example, any change occurs other than in the price of a factor, then either the demand curve or the supply curve shifts. If the price of the factor itself changes, this represents a movement along the relevant supply or demand curve.

Thus, an increase in labour productivity following training would shift the MRP, i.e. the demand curve for labour, to the right; immigration of workers from overseas would shift the supply curve of labour to the right. Similar generalizations may also be made about the responsiveness of demand and supply to price changes, in the short- and long-run factor markets.

ECONOMIC RENT AND TRANSFER EARNINGS

Because of its importance in explaining income differentials, we make a distinction between two components that together comprise the total earnings of a factor of production. A part, called TRANSFER EARNINGS, represents the amount that a unit of a factor must earn in order to prevent it from transferring to another use.

Thus, transfer earnings are essentially the opportunity cost of employing a factor in its present use. They are the minimum necessary to retain it. The second part of factor earnings is called ECONOMIC RENT. This is the excess over transfer earnings that a factor receives.

An example will help to illustrate this important point. Assume a machinist is earning £10 an hour in his present occupation, and could earn £8 in his next best occupation. His total earnings are £10 per hour, his transfer earnings are £8, and the £2 remainder is economic rent.

Let us return to re-examine Figure 18.5, which is reproduced as Figure 18.6 except that a different area is shaded. We know that the total income of all the units of the variable factor in Figure 18.6 is the price per unit, of p_4, multiplied by the quantity of q_4, which is the area Op_4eq_4. How much of that total is transfer earnings and how much is economic rent? The key to the answer is contained in the supply curve.

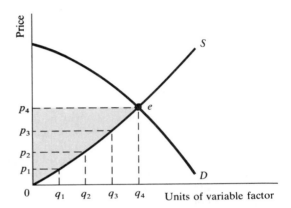

FIGURE 18.6 Economic Rent and Transfer Earnings. In equilibrium with a market price of p_4, factor earnings consist of economic rent of Oep_4, and transfer earnings of Oeq_4.

As we know, 4 units of the factor are employed in equilibrium. We can see from the supply curve how much each unit *needs to be paid* to attract it into the industry. The first unit requires a price of p_1. Only the fourth and final unit needs to be paid the market price of p_4.

Hence, the total earnings of the fourth factor unit are wholly transfer earnings, but there is an element of economic rent in the incomes of all other units. That element, in the case of the first unit, is the price of p_4 that it received, less its transfer earnings p_1. Thus its economic rent is $p_4 - p_1$. By similar reasoning the economic rents of the second and third units of the factor are $p_4 - p_2$, and $p_4 - p_3$, respectively. If we assume that there is a smooth supply curve, we can partition the total factor income, of Op_4eq_4, into transfer earnings of Oeq_4 (the area under the supply curve) and economic rent of Op_4e (the area above the supply curve and below the equilibrium price of the factor).

Land and Economic Rent

The concept of economic rent was first developed by the great British economist of the early nineteenth century, David Ricardo. During the Napoleonic Wars both the rent that tenants had to pay landlords for agricultural land and the price of corn (the term used to describe all cereal grains) rose greatly. Were the high rents being paid for land, driving up the price of corn, or was the high price of corn driving up the price of the land?

BOX 18.1 Top Dough for Janet's Big Entrance

'It began in Richard Branson's hot air balloon, and ended in hot air. No one at Virgin Records will confirm exactly how much they agreed to pay Janet Jackson to join the company this week – the estimates range from £17m to a world record £27m – but they will outdo each other's superlatives in claiming that she is a bargain: "The most talented ... the biggest potential ... the finest cheekbones."

'At 24, the singer has even been compared to a Rembrandt by a beaming Mr Branson, the company's chairman.... When the Beatles signed for EMI in 1962 they received a royalty of just one penny per record sold.... Bruce Springsteen received a royalty of 37 per cent in the mid-eighties, and the Rolling Stones, an advance of £28m when they signed for the same company in 1983.'

(*The Independent on Sunday*, 17 March 1991)

Economic rent is the name given to the excess of income received over and above earnings that could be obtained in the next most lucrative occupation, or as the extra paid to a factor of production over and above the sum that he or she would be prepared to offer their services for. One imagines that there are some elements of rent in at least some of the payments mentioned in the news item.

Questions

1 If Janet Jackson might have been offered a virtually identical contract by EMI, would there be any element of economic rent accruing to her?
2 Could any rents referred to above be likened at all to quasi-rents?
3 The average gross weekly pay in April 1990 of shop assistants was £177 and that of crane drivers was £296. Why cannot you deduce the sizes of rents and transfer earnings from this information? What assumptions about the nature of the supply of labour to these occupations would enable you to do so?

Ricardo argued for the latter alternative – because corn was expensive, there was keen competition among farmers for land, which in turn bid up the level of farm rents. Rents were high because the price of corn was high. Ricardo thus rebutted the popular view that the high price of corn was the consequence of rapacious landlords profiteering from the war. The high rents followed the shortage of land, not vice versa.

Ricardo's argument assumed that land had only one use, growing corn, and that the amount of land available was perfectly inelastic. This is illustrated in Figure 18.7 where q_0 amount of land is assumed to be available, regardless

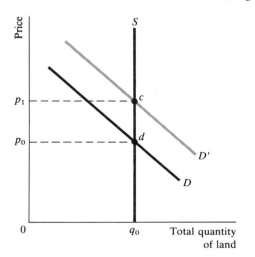

FIGURE 18.7 A Factor Earning Only Economic Rent. All the income of a factor in perfectly inelastic supply consists of economic rent.

of the price of land. Even if the price were zero, q_0 would be supplied. When D is the demand curve for land, the price is p_0. Total earnings of landlords, Op_0dq_0, would consist of economic rent, because nothing was needed to be paid in order to attract the land into use. If the price of corn rises, and the derived demand for land rises, say to D', the new price of land, p_1, merely increases economic rent (by p_0p_1cd).

Note that the argument of the previous paragraph applies only where the supply of land is very inelastic. But as we have emphasized, the amount of land available *for any particular use* is, normally, highly elastic to relative price changes. In so far as a farmer can switch easily among different crops, the supply for any one use approaches the perfectly elastic, as in Figure 18.8. A price of p_0 in Figure 18.8 will call forth any required quantity, because land can easily be switched from one crop to another. The entire amount paid for the land consists of transfer earnings. An increase in the demand for land, shown by the rightward shift in the demand curve from D to D', raises transfer earnings from Op_0dq_0 to Op_0sq_1, and does not cause any economic rents.

The Modern View of Economic Rent

The modern view of economic rent is that it is a form of surplus paid to *any* factor over and above the minimum necessary to keep it in its current use. Economic rent forms a part of the income of every factor which is *not in perfectly elastic supply*. The intermediate case is common and was illustrated in Figure 18.6.

Most factors earn some economic rent, at least in the short run. To illustrate, consider labour in an industry which is experiencing an increase in the demand for its product. More workers are needed and, in so far as it is necessary to pay a higher rate of wages to attract extra workers, *existing* employees will also be paid more. To these existing workers, the rise in wages is an economic rent. They were already in the industry; hence they did not need further inducement to work there. Of course, the new workers do not receive an economic-rent component in their income. The higher wages represent their transfer earnings, needed to attract them into the industry.

Quasi-rent

The concept of economic rent can be applied to capital. The price paid to keep a piece of capital equipment in one use rather than another is its transfer earnings. However, some equipment has only a single use. In this case, any income that is received from its operation is economic rent. Assume, for example, that when a machine was installed it was expected to earn £5000 per annum in excess of operating costs. If the demand for the product falls, so that the machine can earn only £2000, it will still pay to keep it in operation rather than scrap it. Indeed, it will pay to do so as long as it yields any return above its operating costs. It has no alternative use to which it can be put. Hence all the return earned by the machine, *once it has been installed*, is economic rent.

Machines, however, wear out eventually. When they do, they will not be replaced, unless they are expected to earn a return, over their lifetime, sufficient to make them worthwhile investments.

Thus, in the long run (defined as the expected life of a machine) some part of the earnings of a machine are transfer earnings. If they are not covered, a machine will not be replaced when it wears out.

Whether a payment made to a depreciating factor of production, such as a machine, consists of economic rent or of transfer earnings, depends on the time-span under consideration. In the short run, once a machine which has a single use has been installed, all its earnings are economic rent because no payment is needed to stop the machine from transferring to another use. It has none. In the long

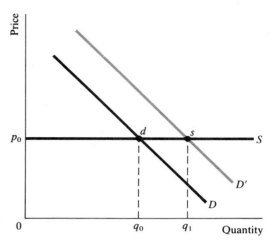

FIGURE 18.8 A Factor Earning Zero Economic Rent. All the income of a factor in perfectly elastic supply consists of transfer earnings.

run, some of its earnings (possibly all) are transfer earnings because this amount must be earned or the machine will never be replaced. Factor payments which are economic rent in the short run and transfer earnings in the long run are called QUASI-RENTS.

Implications of the existence of economic rents

Transfer earnings serve a function in allocating resources to uses where they are most productive. Economic rent serves no allocative purpose. It is a surplus. The idea of taxing the owners of factors of production which receive *only* economic rent once had great appeal. Such factors would be supplied at any price. Why not tax them? Supply will not fall. No one has, however, yet devised a scheme that can tax the economic rents, but not the transfer earnings, of such divergent factors as land, top football players, High Court judges, or the owners of patent rights. Until this can be done, it will be impossible to tax rents without also taxing transfer earnings, which would affect the allocation of resources among alternative uses.

Summary

1 The size distribution of income, which can be portrayed using a Lorenz curve, is related to the functional (or factor) distribution of income. Personal incomes depend on factor prices, factor ownership and transfers.

2 Market forces set factor prices. In perfectly competitive markets, factor prices tend to equality. Factor price differences are due to the absence of one or more assumptions necessary for perfect competition.

3 The demand for a factor is derived from its marginal revenue product (MRP), which is marginal physical product (MPP) times marginal revenue. Under perfect competition in the goods market for the firm's product, MRP equals the value of the marginal product (VMP), which is MPP times the price of the product. Under imperfect competition in the goods market, MRP is less than VMP.

4 A profit-maximizing firm equates the MRP of each factor with the MC of employing it.

5 Elasticity of demand for a factor is greater (i) the more elastic the demand for the firm's product, (ii) the easier it is to substitute the factor for other factors, (iii) the longer the time-period, (iv) the greater the proportion of total cost accounted for by the factor.

6 The total supply of a factor, the amount offered for sale for all uses, tends to vary with the factor's price.

7 The supply of a factor for a particular use tends to be more elastic than its total supply, and depends on factor mobility among uses.

8 The individual supply of labour involves a choice between work and leisure. Hours worked depend on the wage rate. A change in the wage rate will have a substitution and an income effect, which normally pull in opposite directions. If the former predominates, the supply curve slopes upwards (i.e. positively). If the latter predominates, the supply curve becomes backward-sloping.

9 A factor's earnings comprise (i) transfer earnings, needed to secure its employment, and (ii) economic rent – the surplus over transfer earnings.

10 The earnings of a factor in perfectly inelastic and perfectly elastic supply are all economic rent and all transfer earnings, respectively. In intermediate cases, earnings are part rent and part transfer earnings.

11 Factor earnings for single-use capital equipment may be quasi-rent – which is economic rent in the short run only.

Questions

1 What is the difference between the marginal physical product of a variable factor and the demand curve for the factor, under (i) perfect, (ii) imperfect competition in the market for the firm's product?

2 In Figure 18.1, (i) what percentage of total income goes to (a) the bottom 30 per cent, (b) the top 10 per cent of the population? (ii) How would you interpret a Lorenz curve which starts at the origin of the graph, runs full length along the horizontal axis and then up the vertical axis?

3 What is the significance of factor mobility in explaining income differences?

4 Which One or More of the following would tend to make the elasticity of demand for factor X greater than for factor Y?
  (a) Y accounts for a larger percentage of total costs than X.
  (b) Substitutability between Y and factor Z is greater than between X and Z.

  (c) Less Y is offered on the market when its price rises than of X when its price rises.
  (d) Y has more uses than X.
  (e) Y is mainly used to produce good A; X is used mainly to produce good B; demand elasticity for B is greater than for A.

5 Which One or More of the following characteristics would apply to a factor of production whose income consisted partly of economic rent?
  (a) It is in perfectly elastic supply.
  (b) It is in perfectly inelastic supply.
  (c) Its elasticity of supply is less than infinity but greater than zero.
  (d) It would offer its services on the market for a price between zero and the market price.
  (e) Its transfer earnings are negative.

6 Refer to Figures 18.7 and 18.8. Assume the factor price is p_0. Use letters in the diagrams to describe (i) economic rent, and (ii) transfer earnings, in each case.

19 Labour and Capital

In the previous chapter, we concentrated on factor markets under competitive conditions. In this chapter, we take account of some important imperfections in the markets for labour and capital.

LABOUR

All markets have a common characteristic: demand and supply interact to determine equilibrium price and quantity. The labour market is, however, distinct from the markets for other factors of production, and for commodities. Other factors are owned by people, but the labour force is, itself, human. This has an important consequence for our standard maximizing assumptions. Although workers can be thought of as maximizing the satisfaction they get from earning by working, they do not always seek employment in industries, or occupations, which pay the highest wages. However, this can still be maximizing behaviour. Workers care about other things too, such as working conditions, and choose the job which gives the highest net satisfaction.

The Population Base

The size of the labour force, sometimes known as the active or occupied population (or even by the sexist term manpower), depends on the size of the population itself. Nearly two hundred years ago, the Reverend Thomas Malthus, an economist, discussed the determinants of the size of the population in his *Essay on the Principle of Population* (1798). Malthus was living at a time when population growth was accelerating at an unprecedented rate. He took a pessimistic view and forecast that the rate of population growth would slow down as a result of disease, famine, war and other pestilence, unless steps were taken to keep it in check. The reasons for Malthus's gloom were his belief in an ever-widening disparity between the natural rates of growth of population and of the means of subsistence.

Malthus held that the supply of land in the world was limited, and that the 'law' of diminishing returns operated. As a result, he saw no way in which supplies of foodstuffs could keep pace with the accelerating population growth of the late seventeenth and early eighteenth centuries, which had had its roots in the control of disease and rising birth rates. He therefore advocated 'preventative checks', especially the postponement of marriage, and the use of birth-control techniques (then in their infancy), to avoid impending disaster.

Malthus's pessimism has not been confirmed for countries in Western Europe, North America and other 'advanced' countries, largely because of massive improvements in the application of technology to agriculture, and of a fall in fertility rates (due at least partly to the spread of Malthus's own proposal for voluntary family limitation). His message retains applicability today to some less-developed countries, many of which actively seek to discourage large families. (There is a related, broader notion of an 'optimum population' – that which maximizes income per head of the population – which we discuss in Chapter 36, pages 403–4.)

Forecasting future population trends is a subject for demographers rather than for economists. We may note, however, that whoever does the job needs to predict birth rates, death rates and the balance of migratory movements. Birth rates depend on such factors as the age of marriage, and the typical number of children per family. Over long periods, these social forces are notoriously changeable. Over short periods, the number of births is relatively easy to predict, since it is heavily dependent on the numbers of women of child-bearing age, which – immigration and emigration aside – is known for twenty or more years in advance, because all such women are alive now.

Death rates depend chiefly on the success of medical science. Over the past half century, the expectation of life at birth in Britain has risen from 59 to 72 years for men and from 63 to 78 for women. Future improvements in mortality rates will have to come from extending the lives of older people. Migration movements, which were high before the war, fell drastically as a result of worldwide governmental restrictions on immigration, from the 1950s. More recently, population movements began to grow again, for example as a result of mass migration from Eastern Europe, and from Latin America into the USA. However, in the decade of the 1980s the numbers migrating into and out of the UK were roughly equal.

The labour force

The UK population at the beginning of the 1990s was about $57\frac{1}{2}$ million, and the best estimates are for a small increase by the end of the century. Of this total, we need to ask how many should be included in the factor of production called labour?

The size of the labour force expressed as a proportion of the total population, the activity rate, depends on a variety of economic, social and demographic factors. They may be grouped into two categories: (i) the age distribution of the population, and (ii) the numbers of persons seeking employment.

Age distribution of the population: This is the prime

demographic determinant. At present about two-thirds of the population are in the age bracket from which the labour force comes. However, not all in that bracket choose to work, so that the UK labour force is under 30 million.

Numbers seeking employment: Several million people of working age do not enter the labour force for various reasons. The principal one is that many are married women, staying at home to raise families. A second important category comprises young persons continuing full-time education, and there is a small number of others who choose not to seek employment.

The overall activity rate reflects social attitudes, legal requirements and economic incentives, which are liable to change, so that the activity rate changes in consequence. For example, there has been a substantial increase since World War II in the numbers of married women choosing to work. The numbers in full-time education are directly affected by such matters as the minimum school-leaving age, and the size of funds allocated for tertiary education.

The social factors mentioned in the previous paragraph must be seen within an economic context. Many individuals in the DEPENDENT POPULATION (those *not* in the labour force) choose not to seek employment because they find alternatives more attractive. The incentive to work must be strong enough to encourage participation. Incentives fall into two classes – the rate of pay and job opportunities. Both tend to move together. In prosperous times, wage rates are relatively high and there are ample job opportunities. The reverse is true in times of depression. Economic incentives also affect those outside what is

regarded as the 'normal' working age group, as people take early retirement when the economy is in recession, or may be induced to work above the age of 60 or 65 in periods when there are shortages in certain occupations.

Characteristics of the labour force

The labour force, or the working population, consists of individuals who differ from each other in ways which can affect earnings and unemployment. The chief differences relate to (i) age, (ii) sex and race, (iii) ability and skill, (iv) attitude to work and risk, (v) location.

Age: A distinct pattern is to be found in the age-earnings profile for most workers. Earnings rise with age, reach a peak, and then decline. The peak varies for different categories of workers. In the manual category, highest weekly earnings appear around the mid-thirties, when physical productivity is greatest. In contrast, top non-manual earnings continue to rise until the age of about 60. This can reflect productivity rising with experience in managerial occupations.

Sex and race: Women and non-whites have always earned less, on average, than white males in the UK and in many other countries. No one is entirely certain why.

One explanation of earnings differentials is differences in productivity. Women tend to leave the labour force while raising families, and both women and non-whites are often less well-trained, all of which can lower their marginal products relative to male white workers.

BOX 19.1 Gap Between High and Low Pay Greatest Since 1886

'The gap between the pay of high and low-paid employees is now wider than at any time since records began in 1886, the Government's *New Earnings Survey* shows. Over the last decade the best paid group has enjoyed a real pay rise 16 times as large as the worst paid group.... The divergence is remarkable because pay differentials were so stable before Margaret Thatcher came to power in 1979.

'The breakdown of traditional values is most apparent among high earners, said Professor A.B. Atkinson of the London School of Economics. Between 1968 and 1979, the highest paid 10 per cent of all men earned between 157 per cent and 161 per cent of the average. They now earn 181 per cent.... "We have had a shift in values whereby pay is much more market-oriented and less constrained by accepted customs, values and differentials," Professor Atkinson said. "There has also been a large structural change. Manufacturing has been in decline, and services have grown rapidly."'

(*The Independent on Sunday*, 30 September 1990)

Wage rates are determined in the market for labour, and differentials arise from the strength of demand and supply for labour of different skills. The quotation shows that substantial changes have occurred in these differentials both over the very long and short term, though the causes are not fully understood.

Questions

1 Does the suggested explanation of the trends in the extract imply changes on the supply side, the demand side, or both supply and demand sides of the labour market?
2 What can you say about the nature of differentials in the manufacturing sector of the economy in the light of the comments above?
3 If market forces continue to play a large part in the determination of wages, what would you expect to happen to earnings over the next decade?
4 What conclusions, if any, can be drawn from the evidence in the extract about trends in (i) the distribution of income, (ii) wage-rate differentials (as distinct from the distribution of earnings)?

A further explanation of differences is that women, and non-whites, are discriminated against in the labour market. DISCRIMINATION is said to exist when factors with equal productivity receive different rewards for their work. It requires the SEGMENTATION of the market with largely NON-COMPETING GROUPS of workers, e.g. men and women, blacks and whites, who are unable to compete away wage differences.

Ability and skill: A third characteristic of the labour force which affects earning power, is ability and skill. There is no doubt that both genetically inherited ability, and skill acquired by training, are important determinants of work performance and pay. Assessing the relative importance of each of these is difficult.

Economists have spent much time researching the influence on earnings of extended education and on-the-job training. This aspect lies within the scope of economic analysis, because people have some choice in the amount of education and training they will undergo. Every individual is faced, in principle, with a decision to seek employment immediately after reaching the minimum school-leaving age, or to acquire additional qualifications through further education. A similar decision continues after starting paid employment – whether to forgo current earnings in the hope of raising future earning power by further training. The process involves the acquisition of what may be called 'human capital'. We shall find it easier to discuss this after we have dealt with the factor, capital, later in the chapter.

Attitude to work and risk: As we explained in the previous chapter, an individual faces a choice between earning by working and taking leisure. Differences in attitudes towards work can explain a significant part of earnings differentials. Although the opportunity for varying hours worked is not available to all individuals, there remains plenty of choice. Some people 'moonlight' (take a second job in their spare time). Others choose to work part-time, or even to live on social security.

Attitudes to risk are a second source of income differences, arising from distinctive personal attitudes. We are not referring here so much to the higher earnings of people such as steeplejacks and stunt men, as to the expected *variability* of earnings in different occupations. Some careers are relatively 'safe', carrying limited but secure lifetime income prospects, including pension rights after retirement. Others offer much higher rewards for the really successful, matched by much lower prospects for others. Individuals differ in their preferences for undertaking risks of this kind. They may be said to have different degrees of *risk aversion*, or *risk preference*, and this may affect their earnings.

Risk averters tend to seek employment in occupations which offer a high degree of job security, which is often accompanied by relatively low pay. Risk preferrers, who value the chance of well-above-average incomes more than they fear the chance of well-below-average earnings, tend to go into careers that yield a few high incomes despite the risk of earning low ones – e.g. in self-employment.

A third source of income differences, traceable to distinctive personal attitudes, is to be found in what are termed the NON-MONETARY or NON-PECUNIARY ADVANTAGES of different occupations. These, as their name implies, are advantages of a non-monetary kind, which attach to particular jobs and which make them more or less attractive than other jobs. Such advantages often appeal because they overlap with leisure interests, e.g. for dancing instructors or sales assistants in hi-fi music shops, or because they involve work in congenial surroundings, e.g. in the open air. There are also jobs earning high monetary rewards to compensate for NON-PECUNIARY DISADVANTAGES, where a job is boring or dirty – for example, in refuse collection.

Individuals differ in the extent to which they value the non-monetary advantages of different occupations. Those who place high values on such advantages often earn *monetary* incomes which are lower than those attached to jobs without such non-pecuniary advantages. Market forces tend to equate the *net* advantages, monetary and non-monetary, of different occupations – *ceteris paribus*, of course.

Location: A final characteristic of the labour force which affects earnings is its geographical location. Wage rates and earnings vary regionally for workers with similar degrees of skill, and in similar occupations. Average earnings of adult males in Greater London, for example, are near to 50 per cent above those in Northern Ireland, to take the highest and lowest regional groups.

Were the geographical mobility of labour high, one might expect market forces to reduce, if not eliminate, regional earnings differences. Workers would move from areas where wages were low to those where they were high. However, geographical labour mobility is limited, especially in the short run, by social and psychological barriers, and by housing availability. This is particularly so in the UK compared, say, with the USA, where large-scale geographical shifts of the population occur quite speedily, as job opportunities and earnings vary among regions.

The social and psychological barriers call for little comment. Most people are not like nomads of the past, who moved around with their tribes. Many, especially settled older and married workers, are naturally reluctant to pack up and leave family and friends for work reasons, unless forced by very adverse circumstances.

The geographical distribution of the existing housing stock is a second major barrier to mobility. There are some 22 million dwellings in the UK, to which net annual additions have rarely added more than 1 per cent in recent years. The time taken to build new houses severely limits the prospects of any speedy matching of housing supplies to regional changes in the supply and demand for labour.

Moreover, the nature of the UK market in second-hand houses is far from conducive to labour mobility. There are long-winded rigmaroles of legal and institutional barriers in the buying and selling of houses, not found in many other countries. The alternative of renting accommodation was severely restricted for many years by legal rent controls, though this market has much eased recently.

Labour mobility is substantially greater in the long run than in the short. During the present century there has been plenty of movement, mainly from Scotland, Wales and the north of England towards the south. It has, however, been very much a long-term response to earnings differentials and job opportunities, and much of it has taken the form of new generations of young people moving away from home at the start of their adult lives, before settling down with their own families. Notice, however, that regional differences in earnings may fall without labour mobility, but as a result of firms choosing to locate in low-cost areas of the country. Neither the mobility of labour nor of firms has been sufficient to prevent regional inequalities from developing.

Nor are earnings the only regional labour market differential attributable to immobilities. Unemployment rates also vary greatly among regions. For many years, Northern Ireland has suffered from an unemployment rate double, and more, the rates in southern England and East Anglia. Moreover, the regions with relatively high unemployment rates (including also Scotland, Wales and northern England) happen also to be those with relatively low average earnings.

In consequence, the government has, since before the Second World War, adopted a variety of measures to try to lessen these inequalities. They have come to be called 'regional policy', and we shall discuss them later, in Chapter 21.

Imperfect Labour Markets

Our discussion of factor price determination in the previous chapter was based on the assumption that buyers and sellers were price-takers. We now drop this assumption and study labour markets where either employers, employees, or both, can exert some degree of monopoly power. First, we look at the demand side.

Monopsony employers

A single firm which is the only buyer of labour in a particular market is known as a MONOPSONIST (from the Greek *mono*, one, and *opsonia*, purchase). In the same way as a monopolist can affect the price of the product that it *sells* by restricting the quantity offered on the market, a monopsonist can affect the price of the labour that it *buys* by restricting the amount that it purchases.

As we analyse the behaviour of a profit-maximizing monopsonist in the labour market, you will see how closely it parallels the behaviour of a profit-maximizing monopolist. Consider Figure 19.1, which shows the marginal revenue product curve (MRP) of a monopsonist buyer of labour services and the labour supply curve, S. We know that firms in a perfectly competitive industry would go on hiring labour until the wage rate was equal to the MRP, i.e. they would employ q_c labour. The equilibrium wage rate would be w_c. At that wage rate the MRP of the factor is equal to the wage rate.

Competitive firms, however, are price-takers. A mon-

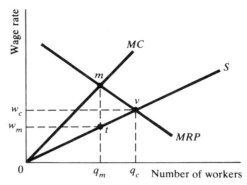

FIGURE 19.1 A Monopsony Employer. Marginal cost of an extra worker is greater than average cost (the wage rate). Monopsonist employs q_m workers at wage rate w_m (compared to q_c at w_c under perfect competition).

opsonist is a price-maker. When it employs more workers, it must pay them all a higher wage rate. When it employs fewer workers, the wage rate is driven down. It follows that *the marginal cost to a monopsonist employer is greater than the wage rate paid.*

For example, if 10 workers are employed at a wage of £20 per day, the total cost is £200. If 11 workers are employed and the wage rate is driven up to £21 per day, the total cost becomes £231. The average cost *per worker* is £21, the wage rate; but the marginal cost to the firm of hiring one more worker is £31 (£231–£200). (The argument is similar to that which explains why marginal revenue is less than average revenue, or price, for a monopolist.)

All this is shown in Figure 19.1. The MC curve lies above the supply curve of the factor. The profit-maximizing monopsonist will equate the MC of labour with its MRP. In other words, it will go on buying the factor until the last unit purchased increases total cost by as much as it increases total revenue. This is at point *m* in the Figure, which gives an equilibrium quantity q_m. The price paid for q_m units is read off the supply curve. It is w_m. To achieve this equilibrium, the monopsonist offers a wage of w_m which produces a supply of q_m workers, who have an MRP of *m*.

The equilibrium price and quantity under monopsony can be compared with that under competition, which would be w_c and q_c.

Therefore, monopsony results in a lower level of factor employment, and a lower wage rate, than under competition.

Monopoly trade unions

The counterpart to the monopsony power of employers is the monopoly selling power of trade unions. Early in the history of unions, their organizers perceived that ten or a hundred men acting together had more influence than one acting alone. The union was the organization that would provide a basis for confronting the monopsony power of employers with collective monopoly power of the workers. But employers did not accept unions passively. Union organizers were sometimes sacked, physically assaulted and even murdered. The 'right' to organize was won as a result of a number of Acts of Parliament, beginning in the 1820s; after that the trade union movement grew from strength to strength. Over half the labour force were members of a union by the end of the 1970s, though a decade later membership had fallen to about 40 per cent.

In the early years the successful unions were of highly skilled specialist workers, but nowadays there are several very large general unions, such as the Transport and General Workers' Union, as well as others organized on an industry basis, such as the National Union of Railwaymen. Unions negotiate with employers, especially on wages and employment. Their strength derives, basically, from solidarity and the right to strike – concerted refusal to work, backed at times by picketing. It depends also on the general economic climate, and on the prevailing legal framework, which became markedly less favourable to unions in the 1980s.

Economic analysis can be applied to union actions directed at wages and employment levels – objectives which may be conflicting, as we shall see. We look at labour markets where employers are (i) competitive, (ii) monopsonistic.

Trade unions versus competitive employers: A union enters the competitive labour market as shown in Figure 19.2, where the wage rate, w_c, is determined by the forces of supply and demand, with q_c workers employed. We assume that the union has the power to set the wage rate. This it does, at a rate of w_u, above the market rate of w_c.

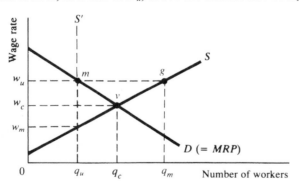

FIGURE 19.2 Trade Union Bargaining with competitive employers, shifts the supply curve to $w_u mgS$, raising the wage rate from w_c to w_u and reducing employment from q_c to q_m.

The effect of setting this wage rate is to change the supply curve of labour. No worker is allowed to offer his or her services for less than w_u. Firms can hire up to q_m workers at this rate (i.e. the amount that will be voluntarily supplied), but to employ more than q_m workers they would have to pay higher rates. The new industry supply curve of labour is $w_u mgs$. It is horizontal, or perfectly elastic, up to point g.

The profit-maximizing firm equates the MC of employing labour to its MRP at m where q_u workers are taken on.

The trade union succeeds in raising the wage rate, but at the cost of reducing the level of employment, from q_c to q_u.

Notice that the number of workers who would offer their services at the union-fixed wage rate of w_u is q_m. Hence, there is an excess supply of $q_m - q_u$ workers over the quantity demanded. Some of these workers would be prepared to work for a wage even below w_c, the old pre-union rate.

It is clearly to the employers' advantage to hire some of these workers at less than the going rate and, given the chance, they will do so. This implies that the union can succeed in effectively raising the wage rate only if it can strictly enforce the set wage. If not all employees are parties to the collective agreement (i.e. if there are people who would work for less than the union rate), this will be difficult. If the union and employers agree to a rule that only members of the union may be taken on, it is easier to enforce the agreed wage rate. Hence, the importance attached to CLOSED SHOP agreements which limit employment to union members. They cause problems, however, even from the union side, because some workers are bound to want employment at less than the union wage rate. Over 5 million workers were in closed shops at their peak, at the end of the 1970s. A decade later, the number had halved, with legal changes and a political climate which had moved against the closed shop.

Another point to notice is that the union could, in principle, achieve the same result if, instead of fixing the wage rate, it decided to restrict the supply of labour. Suppose in Figure 19.2 the union reaches agreement that only union members will be taken on by employers (i.e. a closed shop agreement), and the union also restricts membership of the union to q_m workers. The effect will be that only q_u workers can offer themselves for employment. The supply curve to the firm now follows the original supply curve up to the wage w_m at which q_u workers would want employment. At that point the supply becomes perfectly inelastic, $q_u S'$, intersecting the demand curve at m to determine an equilibrium wage of w_u.

The method of restricting the supply of labour by the trade union secures an increase in the wage rate at the cost of a lower level of employment, exactly as does a directly negotiated rise in the wage itself. The only difference is that, when the wage is negotiated, there is excess supply of labour ($g - m$ in the Figure) while, when supply is restricted, no excess need occur.

We have not yet discussed how the union decides on its optimum policy for the wage rate or employment. To maximize the total wage bill would require the union to behave as any monopolist seller, equating marginal cost and marginal revenue. There are, however, two problems to be faced. One is how (and if) the total 'monopoly profit' should be divided among all union members, including any who lose their jobs. The other problem is that aggressive union bargaining can cause employers to collude and act as a monopsony.

Trade unions versus a monopsonistic employer: In Figure 19.1 we showed that a monopsonistic employer facing a competitive (i.e. non-unionized) labour supply will pay a lower wage rate and employ fewer workers than do perfectly competitive employers.

We now show that a trade union negotiating with a monopsonist employer may be able to increase the wage rate *and* achieve a rise in the level of employment. We can follow this by looking at Figure 19.1.

We saw that before the union was formed, the monopsonist faced a supply curve of labour, S, and a marginal cost curve of labour, MC, which lies above it. Optimum employment for the firm is found where MC equals MRP, q_m workers being employed at a wage rate of w_m. Suppose now that the trade union sets a wage rate of w_c. The supply curve facing the firm now becomes perfectly elastic at the set wage rate, i.e. it is given by $w_c vs$ in Figure 19.1. Moreover, since the supply curve is horizontal until q_c workers are employed, the marginal cost of employing additional workers becomes the same as the average cost (the wage rate). Hence, the monopsonist maximizes profits by employing q_c workers at the wage rate w_c, just as in the competitive case.

Monopoly versus monopsony in the labour market: We have seen what a monopolist trade union seller might like, if faced with competitive employers; and what a monopsonist employer might like if faced with an unorganized competitive labour supply. What if the two meet head on?

Economic theory has no single answer. The situation is one called BILATERAL MONOPOLY, and there is a range of possible outcomes. They may be illustrated in Figure 19.2. Let us assume that the union wants a wage rate of w_u, while the employer wants a wage rate of w_m. Who will win? We cannot say anything more than that the wage rate will settle in the range between w_u and w_m, being closer to the limit desired by the group with the stronger bargaining power.

Bargaining power of trade unions

So many factors come into the picture that generalization about the outcome of union-employer wage bargaining is difficult. All we can suggest are the kinds of circumstance which might favour one side or the other. We put our suggestions in the form of circumstances favouring unions, and leave you, if you wish, to reverse the arguments to present them from the employers' point of view.

Trade-union bargaining strength will tend to be high under the following circumstances.

- *When there is little scope for substituting other factors of production for labour.* This gives doctors, for example, strong bargaining power, and unskilled labourers little clout.
- *When the demand for the product is relatively inelastic.* If this is the case, a rise in wages, and therefore in costs of production, depresses the quantity demanded relatively little. For example, this gives electric power workers strength, but shopworkers in a single department store weakness.

- *When labour costs are a small proportion of costs.* If this is the case, a given rise in wages shifts the firm's marginal cost curve by only a small extent. Equilibrium output of the firm is, therefore, reduced by only a small amount, and there is little reduction in the demand for labour.
- *When the union itself is strong.* A union will tend to be stronger, the higher the proportion of workers in the industry that are union members; the greater the support of the membership; the higher the financial resources to withstand prolonged strike action; and the more a union can count on the support of other unions in a struggle with employers.
- *When the employer earns substantial profits.* There is obviously little scope for unions to raise wages in industries which are on the margin of profitability. Where employers enjoy high profits, however, a union's prospects for raising wages are better. This means that both employers and employees may gain if a firm can monopolize the market for its products.
- *When the union offers productivity 'deals'.* Many wage settlements have been reached by unions accepting productivity changes which they had previously opposed. In this age of rapidly advancing technology, such productivity changes frequently involve mechanisation and reduction in the industry's workforce. While unions are, understandably, reluctant to agree to the sudden unemployment of their members, they are often realistic enough to accept that they cannot stand for ever opposed to the introduction of new production techniques. Hence, we see agreements for *gradual* phasing-in of new processes.

CAPITAL

To many Marxists, capitalists are villains. To many Conservatives, they are heroes, who steer the economy to higher living standards. To an economist, capitalists are simply those who own capital, which we defined earlier as man-made aids to further production. If there are capital goods, someone must own them, though that 'someone' may be private individuals or it may be the state.

Our interest in this chapter is not with the ownership of capital, but with its price as a factor of production. A key characteristic of capital is that it is durable and yields a return over its useful life. This means that it has not one, but two, *prices*, although, as we shall see, they are closely related to each other.

The Two Prices of Capital

The two prices of capital are its YIELD (or rental value) and its *purchase price*. The yield is the price paid for the use of the factor's services for a period of time, say one year. The price at which a capital good is bought and sold, reflects the present value of the future flow of services that can be obtained from the good over its whole lifetime. The distinction is the same as between renting a flat (paying, say, monthly, for the flow of services it gives) and buying the flat, thereby acquiring the right to all its future services.

For this reason the income derived from the ownership of capital is sometimes called its 'rental value' as well as its yield, the term we shall use, while what the capital good could be bought or sold for is called its 'purchase price'.

The relationship between the yield and purchase price

Consider a machine that costs £100, if bought today. Suppose, if put to use to produce plastic dolls, it yields a net revenue in a year's time of £110, at which time it reaches the end of its life and is scrapped. The yield of the asset may be expressed as a percentage, known also as the RATE OF RETURN ON CAPITAL:

$$\text{yield} = \frac{110}{100} = 10 \text{ per cent}$$

Now look at the capital asset from a different viewpoint. Let us assume that we know only that it will yield a return of £110, one year from now. That yield must be worth something, even today, because the asset could be sold for cash to someone who wanted £110 next year. Whatever that person was prepared to pay for the asset gives us the PRESENT VALUE of the capital – its purchase price.

The present value of a capital asset, therefore, represents the (purchase) price that an individual will be prepared to pay at present to enjoy its yield in the future.

Note, too, that this yield is something to be obtained, not now, but in the future. The benefits are postponed. Not unnaturally, therefore, future yields are worth less today than when they accrue. The *present value* of a future yield (even if quite certain) is less than the yield itself.

There is a standard method of finding the present value of a future yield. It involves DISCOUNTING, by which is meant scaling down, by a factor which quantifies the sacrifice involved in postponement. For any individual the value he or she places on such a sacrifice depends on his or her preference for the present over the future, a subject we shall shortly discuss. It will suffice, for the present, to use the market rate of interest, which measures the market valuation of such sacrifices. For example, if the market rate of interest is 10 per cent, I can enjoy £110 next year by lending out £100 today. I sacrifice £100 today, but get £110 in a year.

Returning to our example of finding the present value of £110 in a year's time, when the rate of interest is 10 per cent, we discount using the formula:

$$\text{present value (PV)} = \frac{\text{yield}}{1 + r}$$

where r is the rate of interest expressed as a decimal fraction, rather than a percentage.

As the yield is £110 and r is 10 per cent (0.1), this gives

$$PV = \frac{110}{1.1} = £100$$

Compound interest[1]

Students of mathematics will recognize the formula at the end of the previous paragraph as that for simple interest. For assets that continue to yield returns over several years, we need the formula for compound interest. For a stream of yields over t years, this is

$$P = \frac{A}{(1 + r)^t}$$

where P stands for Principal, A for Amount, r for the Rate of interest expressed as a ratio, and t for the Time, in periods, over which compounding takes place. In economic usage, the term P stands for Present Value and A for the Yield, while r and t have the same meanings as in the compound interest formula. Note, too, that the present value P is sometimes called the Discounted Cash Flow (DCF). This term is particularly descriptive, since it conveys the idea that converting future yields to a present value involves discounting, by means of the rate of interest.

The reason why the rate of interest is used to convert future sums into values in the present is that present amounts of money become greater if invested at the ruling market rate of interest. If, at a rate of interest of 10 per cent, £100 becomes £110 in a year's time, then the present value of £110 a year from now is £100. Or, using the formula to make this calculation:

$$PV = \frac{100}{(1 + 0.1)^1}$$

The example just given is of the present value of an asset which produces a yield for only a single year. The formula can be used to calculate the present value of an asset lasting any number of years. Suppose, for example, the asset lasts two years and yields £220 next year and £242 the year after. Assuming, still, that the rate of interest is 10 per cent, the yields must be discounted over the different periods, as follows:

$$PV = \frac{220}{(1 + 0.1)^1} + \frac{242}{(1 + 0.1)^2}$$

$$PV = \frac{220}{1.1} + \frac{242}{1.21} = 400$$

In other words the present value of £220 next year plus £242 the following year is £400 when the rate of interest is 10 per cent.

Notice that the formula can be used to calculate any one of the four variables, P, A, r or t, given the other three – i.e. the present value of £x in t years' time if it earns at the rate of r per cent; the rate of interest earned if a sum £x yields £y over t years; and how many years a sum £x will take to yield £y at r rate of interest.

---

1 This section on compound interest may be omitted without loss of the main argument of the chapter. For a fuller treatment, see 1PE8.

Demand for Capital by a Firm

In what sense is capital productive? Rarely, if ever, do we make consumer goods directly with the aid of such simple tools as nature provides. Productive effort goes, first, into the manufacture of capital – tools, machines and other goods that are desired not in themselves, but as aids to making other commodities. The capital goods are then used to make consumer goods. Capital renders the production process ROUNDABOUT. The roundaboutness is, moreover, efficient, because more consumer goods can be produced in future years by making capital goods in the current year.

When capital is productive, it eventually yields a return over all other costs of production, though it is necessary to wait for this return to accrue.

It is convenient to think of a firm as having a stock of capital, which may be measured in physical units – so many machines, factories, etc. As with any other factor of production, there is an average and a marginal product of capital. The marginal product of capital is the contribution made to total output when the quantity of capital is increased by a single unit, the quantities of all other factors of production being held constant.

Marginal product is a physical measure. We need, however, to obtain a measure of the value of the marginal product in money terms. To do so we value the output at its market price. The MARGINAL EFFICIENCY OF CAPITAL (*MEC*) gives the monetary return on each extra pound's worth of capital added. In the short run the amounts of other factors are held constant, so that the *MEC* tends to fall, reflecting the law of diminishing returns.

A firm's *MEC* curve is shown in Figure 19.3. The horizontal axis measures the value of the firm's capital stock, while the vertical axis measures the yield expressed as a percentage of the capital. The *MEC* curve slopes downwards, because of the law of diminishing returns. Thus, we can read from the diagram that, when the firm adds a unit of capital to a £30,000 stock of capital, the *MEC* is 12 per cent; when the stock is £50,000, the *MEC* is 8 per cent, and so on.

We now explain why we have focused attention on the *MEC* curve.

It is because the demand for capital by a firm is the marginal efficiency of capital of the firm. In other words, its *MEC* curve is its demand curve for capital, and shows the amount of capital that a firm would choose to employ at different costs.

To understand this, recall that the cost of capital is the rate of interest that has to be paid by a firm to borrow funds to acquire capital (or, for a firm that has funds of its own, the rate of interest that could be earned by lending them elsewhere).

Consider again Figure 19.3 and suppose the rate of interest (the cost of capital to the firm) is 12 per cent. How much capital will the firm employ? It will certainly employ all capital up to £30,000 because the *MEC* is greater than the cost of capital to the firm. At the same time, it will not pay the firm to employ, say, £50,000 capital, because the *MEC* is less than the rate of interest.

It will not be profitable for the firm to employ *any more* than £30,000 capital. This is the optimum amount of capital for the firm when the rate of interest is 12 per cent.

The equilibrium amount of capital is that where the marginal efficiency of capital is equal to the rate of interest.

The important principle established above may be illustrated in another way. Consider the arithmetic example used above of a machine making plastic dolls which produced a yield of 10 per cent (see p.202) If the firm faces a rate of interest of 10 per cent or less, it will be profitable to install the machine. If the rate of interest is more than 10 per cent, it will not.

The Supply of Capital

We looked at the demand for capital as demand by firms to borrow money for the expansion of their capital stock. So, we can view one of the determinants on the supply side of the capital market, as the quantities of funds that are available for borrowing. This enables us to draw a supply curve in Figure 19.4.

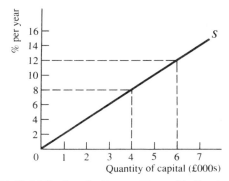

FIGURE 19.4 The Supply Curve of Loanable Funds. Loanable funds supplied on the market rise as the rate of interest rises.

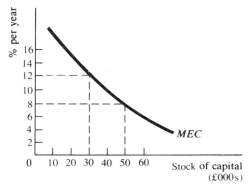

FIGURE 19.3 A Firm's Demand for Capital. Desired capital investment rises as the rate of interest falls. It is the curve of the marginal efficiency of capital (*MEC*).

In order to understand why anybody should offer funds for lending, let us recall the discussion of discounting. The reason we gave for scaling down benefits to be received in the future in order to put a value on them in the present,

BOX 19.2 Non-Renewable Resources: How Much Should We Conserve?

'In practice few, if any, resources are completely non-renewable. Although there is only a fixed stock of oil, coal, or iron ore that is known to exist at any moment in time, new discoveries add to the known stock, while extraction subtracts from it.... The answer to the question, 'How much of a non-renewable resource should be consumed now?' was provided many years ago by the American economist, Harold Hotelling. His answer is very simple, yet it specifically determines the optimum profile of prices over the years. The answer applies to all non-renewable resources. It does not matter whether there is a large or small demand, or whether demand is elastic or inelastic. In all cases the answer is the same:

'The rate of extraction of any non-renewable resource should be such that its rate of price increase is equal to the interest rate, and this is the rate of extraction that will be produced by a competitive industry.'

(R.G. Lipsey, et al., *Economics*, 9th edn, Harper & Row, New York, 1990)

The conclusion in the extract is perhaps surprising. It suggests that, if markets are competitive, government intervention to conserve any non-renewable resource is unnecessary. The rate of interest measures the value to society of any investment. As stocks of a resource are used up, its price is pushed up. The price rise over a year is the return that accrues if the resource is not used up. If its price is expected to rise by more than the rate of interest, it will pay a firm to hang on to the resource, and vice versa.

Of course, markets may fail to achieve the socially optimal conservation for any of the standard reasons discussed elsewhere in the book (see especially Chapters 9 and 21), perhaps because of ignorance about future scarcities and because of divergencies between private and social values.

Note, however, the desirability of allowing the price of a scarce non-renewable resource to rise. It encourages conservation and stimulates innovation and the development of substitutes.

Questions

1 Make two lists, one of 6 renewable and the other of 6 non-renewable natural resources.
2 How is the rate of exploitation of a non-renewable resource affected by the demand for the product?

was that people prefer a given sum of money to enjoy now, to the *same sum* tomorrow, or later. By lending, people sacrifice today's enjoyment for enjoyment in the future, when they are repaid.

It follows that people can be expected to lend a given amount now if they are repaid more than the sum lent later. The extra amount that is needed to induce people to lend depends on what is known as their marginal rate of TIME PREFERENCE, defined as the rate at which future goods are valued in terms of present goods.

An example will help to make this clear. If someone values, say, £100 given up today as being worth £110 at the end of the year, that person's marginal rate of time preference is 10 per cent. If the rate of interest that can be earned in the market is over 10 per cent, that person will be prepared to lend.

Thus, the supply of funds for lending will depend on the rate of interest (though it will depend also on other important variables). What is more, the amount of funds offered for lending will, *ceteris paribus*, be greater the higher the rate of interest. The supply curve in Figure 19.4 is for this reason upward-sloping. At a rate of interest of 8 per cent, £4000 of funds are offered for lending. If the rate of interest is higher at 12 per cent, the supply of funds is £6000.

Our discussion in this section has been about the supply and demand for capital, and we have seen that both depend on the rate of interest. We cannot proceed further at this point to discuss the determinants of the rate of interest itself, because there are important monetary forces to be studied in macroeconomics first. So we must leave the question of interest-rate determination until then (see Chapter 33). Meanwhile, there is a distinctive type of capital to be dealt with.

Human capital

Capital goods are usually discussed in terms of tangible assets, such as machines and buildings, but the idea of capital can also be applied to the factor labour. You may remember that earlier in the chapter we raised this possibility when we were discussing characteristics of the labour force which might affect earnings. The acquisition of skills as a result of education and training can be regarded as creating what we may call human capital. Current expenditure which increases the quality and productivity of the labour force and yields a future return may be regarded as capital investment.

Acquiring human skills is costly – the real cost is measurable in terms of the sacrifice of current income. The higher the skill the more its acquisition is likely to cost. At the same time, higher skills must yield higher rewards if the investment in training is to be worthwhile.

How should anyone decide whether or not to invest in

human capital? The technique we outlined in the previous section is as applicable to human as to any other form of capital. Compare the present value of the enhanced future earnings with the costs, which must be measured in opportunity cost terms – i.e. including any lost earnings during the time spent training. If the former exceed the latter, the expenditure pays off. We may look separately at human capital investment decisions by individuals and by firms.

Investment by individuals: At each stage in one's educational career, a choice must be made between stopping and continuing. For example, a 16-year-old school leaver faces the choice of staying on at school to take A-levels; an 18-year-old, the choice of going on to higher education; a 21-year-old who has just completed a BSc, the choice of going further to acquire a specialist professional qualification, by taking the examinations necessary to practise as an accountant or a solicitor, and so on.

Both costs and benefits must be assessed. The costs are the easier of the two, partly because most benefits are further away in time as well as, hopefully, lasting longer. The benefits lie not only in prospective higher earnings, but also in lower risks of unemployment, and wider job choice. Some monetary value has to be put on these – a difficult task, given the weakness of some of the evidence, which suggests also that a wide range of returns is possible.

Investment by firms: Many firms engage in substantial expenditure on the acquisition of human capital for their employees – both on-the-job training and more general education. However, a firm paying for its employees to acquire skills must realize that it risks losing them to other firms. In so far as firms are, therefore, inhibited from spending on education and training it may fall to the government to subsidize education in the public interest.

Risk, Profit and Interest on Capital

The uncertainty surrounding the returns to investment in human capital mentioned in the previous section, applies to other capital investments too, though to varying extents. Future yields are not certain, they must be estimated. For example, a machine is ordered today, or contracts signed for the construction of a new factory. But there is a waiting time, not only before the machine arrives or the factory is built, but also for the duration of its life, before one can know whether the extra capital yields as much as was hoped for. The same can be said about the uncertainty of the reward from investment in education and training.

The fact that there is an element of uncertainty about the future yield of capital investment means that such investment performs more than one economic function. The rate of return on capital provides the incentive for forgoing present consumption, but it also provides a reward for undertaking the risk that investment may prove less profitable than hoped for. Part of the earnings of capital, therefore, is a reward for risk-taking.

No one knows precisely what the future will bring. Even if the physical productivity of a machine is thought to be fairly certain at the time the decision is made to install it, events may reveal that one has been unduly optimistic or pessimistic.

Still greater uncertainty attaches to the profitability of investment *in money terms*. Not only must physical productivity be estimated but one needs also to forecast the prices at which the output of a machine can be sold.

We opened the section on capital in this chapter by referring to a view that capitalists might, perhaps, be regarded as heroes, because of the role they play in leading the economy towards higher living standards. In so far as the prospect of profits and losses from investment induces owners of capital to make risky investments which promote economic growth, there may be force in that contention. In so far as the prime stimulus for economic progress comes from increases in the amount of capital investment of a relatively riskless nature, the heroic image weakens. There is plenty of evidence on this subject, but it is controversial and beyond the scope of this book.

INCOME DIFFERENCES – A SUMMARY

This chapter and the previous one have enquired into the reasons why incomes differ. We end now with a summary statement. Personal incomes depend on factor ownership, factor prices and transfers.

Factor ownership is relevant because, although most people receive the bulk of their income as a wage or salary, a few receive substantial income in the form of rent, interest and profits.

Factor prices differ because of imperfect competition in factor markets and in goods markets, and because factors of production are not homogeneous.

Perfect mobility of factors would diminish, if not eliminate, differential factor earnings. However, the mobility of labour among geographical locations, among occupations and among economic sectors is naturally limited by physical, psychological and sociological barriers. Immobility of other factors also aids in the preservation of factor price differentials – e.g. higher rates of return on capital in some sectors than in others. The longer the time allowed, the greater factor mobility tends to be.

How much inequality is desirable or undesirable is partly a normative question, calling for value judgements. However, the evidence is also strong that substantial inequalities are needed for the efficient working of an economic system. An important question follows, therefore, on how much an increase in equality would lead to a reduction in efficiency. We shall consider the question of *re*distribution of income in Chapter 21 on microeconomic policy.

Summary

1 The total supply of labour depends on population size, itself dependent on birth rates, death rates and net migration. The activity rate depends on the age distribution of the population and on the numbers seeking employment.

2 Individual characteristics affecting earnings and unemployment rates include age, sex and race, ability and skill, attitude to work and risk, and location.

3 There is an age-earnings profile which varies among occupations; women and non-whites earn less than men and whites. Differences may be due to productivities and/or discrimination. Average earnings are higher among skilled than unskilled workers – differences are partly due to innate abilities and partly to education and training; earnings are affected by how long people work and their attitude to risk; geographical differences in average earnings are also great. Restricted labour mobility maintains wage differences.

4 The degree of competition in the labour market affects the level of wage rates. A monopsony employer will employ fewer workers and pay a lower wage than under perfect competition.

5 A monopoly trade union facing competitive employers may succeed in raising wages only at the cost of a lower level of employment. Facing a monopsonist, a union may succeed in raising both wage rates and the level of employment.

6 The bargaining power of a trade union will be greater the less scope there is for substituting other factors of production for labour; the less elastic the demand for the product; the lower the proportion of total costs accounted for by labour; the stronger the union; the more profitable the employer; the better the productivity deals the union can make.

7 The factor of production, capital, has two prices: (i) a yield, and (ii) a purchase price, which is the value placed on the enjoyment of a stream of future yields.

8 The relationship between the present value and future yield of a capital asset is calculated by discounting, using the standard formulae for (compound) interest.

9 Capitalistic production methods raise output in the future. The marginal efficiency of capital is the monetary yield of an addition to the capital stock. Expressed as a percentage, the *MEC* is the demand curve for capital; it slopes downwards, showing that the lower the rate of interest the more a firm would wish to invest in capital.

10 The supply of capital depends, among other things, on the rate of interest earned by lenders. People have a time preference for present over future consumption; the higher the rate of interest, the more funds may be offered to borrowers.

11 The productivity of the workforce may be raised by education and training, which are described as investment in human capital. Such investment may be made by firms for their employees, by individuals for themselves, or by the government. The assessment of costs and benefits of such investment is, in principle, similar to that in the case of any other capital expenditure.

12 Market-determined income differences among individuals stem from factor ownership and factor prices, which differ because factors are not homogeneous, some markets are more competitive than others, and factor mobility is incomplete.

Questions

1 Distinguish between the working population, the dependent population and the labour force.

2 What difference would you expect between income distribution of two groups of persons who are (A) risk-averters, and (P) risk-preferrers?

3 Refer to Figure 19.2. If the union secures a wage rate of w_u, will the total earnings of all employees be greater or less than the competitive level before the union deal?

4 Which One or More of the following is likely to (i) increase, (ii) decrease the power of a trade union to raise wages in an industry?
  (a) The firm switches production to a product with a higher demand elasticity.
  (b) There is a fall in the degree of substitutability between labour and capital.
  (c) The employers form a buyer's monopsony for labour.
  (d) Production methods change so that relatively more capital and less labour are used.

5 Using the formula for simple interest, calculate (i) the value in 12 months' time of a capital asset with a present value of £1000 and a yield of $12\frac{1}{2}$ per cent, (ii) the present value of £210 twelve months from now, when the market rate of interest is 5 per cent, (iii) the market rate of interest which gives the present value of £360 in twelve months' time as £300.

6 Which One or More of the following are of direct relevance to maximizing individuals who are considering whether to undertake additional education?
  (a) Their stock of human capital.
  (b) The value of the time spent in studying.
  (c) The money cost of courses to be taken.
  (d) The relative satisfaction derived from purchases in the future compared to the present.
  (e) The value derived by time spent in past education.

20 International Trade

The British buy Volkswagens, Germans take holidays in Italy, Italians buy spices from Tanzania, Arabs buy Japanese cameras, and the Japanese depend heavily on American soy-beans as a source of food. International trade refers to exchanges of goods and services that take place across international boundaries. We have ignored it so far, in order to simplify our study of production and distribution in a national context. However, international trade is of major importance in the modern world; it has been expanding very much faster than has world production.

For the UK, trade now accounts for over a quarter of national output, and we must ask why countries engage in trade with each other, what they gain by so doing, and why obstacles are sometimes placed on international trade. Later, in Parts 4 and 5 of the book, we shall deal with macroeconomic aspects of trade, including the balance of payments, exchange rates and capital transactions.

Interpersonal and Interregional Trade

Economists have long recognized that the *principles* governing the gains from international trade are the same as those governing trade within a single country.

In Chapter 2, we explained that a major source of economic growth and rising living standards throughout the world derives from specialization and division of labour. Reaping the gains from specialization requires trade – trade among individuals, and trade among regions. Let us remind you of the argument.

First, consider trade among individuals. If there were none, each person would have to be self-sufficient, producing all the food, clothing, medical services, entertainment and other things that he or she required. It does not take much imagination to realize that living standards would be very low in such a self-sufficient world. Trade among individuals allows people to specialize in those activities they can do well, and to exchange their surpluses with other people, who specialize in different activities. Poor carpenters but good doctors can specialize in medicine, providing physicians' services not only for themselves but also for good carpenters who have neither the training nor the talent for medicine. Thus, trade and specialization are inter-connected. With trade, everyone can specialize in what they do relatively well, and all can gain.

Exactly the same principle applies to regional specialization. Without interregional trade, each region would have to be self-sufficient, producing all the agricultural products, manufactured goods and services that the people in the region require. With trade among regions, however, specialization is possible. Plains regions with suitable cli-

mates can specialize in growing grain crops; mountainous regions can specialize in timber and mining; cool regions can produce crops that thrive in temperate climates; hot regions can grow tropical crops such as coffee and bananas; regions with abundant power sources can specialize in manufacturing; and so on. With trade, each region can concentrate its efforts on what it does relatively well. And with exchange among specializing regions, all regions can gain. The same arguments apply to nations. International trade leads to specialization, and thus gain.

The Special Features of International Trade

Although identical principles apply to international, interregional and interpersonal trade, there are two characteristics that distinguish the first from the other two. They relate to factor immobility and to the existence of national currencies.

Factor immobility: Land is, of course, totally immobile, while labour is a great deal more mobile among regions than among countries, because of the existence of national frontiers. Not only do many nations have their own languages, they have different traditions and lifestyles, which impede factor mobility. For example, workers in Scotland face much more severe adjustment problems if, in search of higher wages, they migrate to Switzerland than if they move to England. They not only need to understand one of the Swiss languages, they have to be prepared to change their diet rather drastically, not to mention missing *Eastenders*.

Even if the Scottish worker is willing to make the adjustments involved in going to Switzerland, he may find legal restrictions on his mobility. Outside economic unions, such as the EC (see below), many nations restrict the rights of foreign nationals to work in their countries.

Capital is highly mobile, and has become particularly so in recent years, as knowledge of world markets and the ability to communicate quickly and cheaply among them has risen. In the 1980s, for example, foreign direct investment grew at a much faster rate than did trade in goods and services.

National currencies: Trading nations mostly have their own currencies – francs, dollars, pounds, yen, etc. As a result, an extra element of uncertainty is involved for a firm exporting to another country, compared to exporting to another part of its own country. For example, a Welsh firm selling in England is paid in pounds sterling which are the currency unit in both Wales and England. But if it exports to the USA it will be paid in dollars, and there is an element of uncertainty about the rate at which dollars will exchange for pounds, when payment is received.

National sovereignty: The freedom for a nation to pursue independent economic policies is affected by its international economic relations. Two powers which protect its sovereignty are (1) that of determining the exchange rate between its own and other currencies and (2) that of imposing restrictions on import and export trade. Many feel that these powers give a national government a degree of freedom to pursue independent economic policies – a freedom it is often reluctant to lose, as witness the UK government's attitude (especially under Prime Minister Margaret Thatcher in 1990) to joining the European Community's Exchange Rate Mechanism (ERM) with the prospect of the (eventual) replacement of pounds sterling, German marks, French francs and all the other national currencies by a single European currency unit. We shall, however, have to wait until Chapter 41 before we can appreciate the full significance of the argument about loss of sovereignty.

THE GAINS FROM TRADE

We now look more closely at the three sources of the gains from trade: (i) specialization, (ii) economies of scale, and (iii) learning-by-doing.

The Gain from Specialization

To isolate the gains from specialization, we assume that costs of production are independent of the level of output – i.e. they are constant. To keep the analysis simple, we assume also that the world consists of only two countries, that only two commodities are produced, and that transport costs are negligible. The conclusions that can be reached using this simple model have general applicability. Later, we shall refer briefly to some necessary modifications, when the theory is applied to real-world situations.

A special case: absolute advantage

Our first approach to demonstrating the gains that can result from specialization compares the amounts of two commodities that can be produced in each of two countries when both use the same quantity of inputs. One country is said to have an ABSOLUTE ADVANTAGE over the second country in the production of a commodity, say wheat, if the first country can produce more wheat using a given quantity of inputs than can the other.

Table 20.1 provides a simple example, on the assumption that, with a given unit of resources, America (A) can produce *either* 10 bushels of wheat (w) *or* 6 yards of cloth (c); while the same quantity of resources in Britain (B) can produce *either* 5w *or* 10c. In this case America has an absolute advantage in wheat and Britain in cloth.

TABLE 20.1 Gain from Specialization with Absolute Advantage. A and B each have 10 units of resources. In A, each unit can produce 10w *or* 6c. In B, each unit can produce 5w *or* 10c.

| (i) | PRODUCTION | | |
	America (ii)	Britain (iii)	World (ii) + (iii) (iv)
Self-sufficiency (half resources used for w and half for c)	50w + 30c	25w + 50c	75w + 80c
Specialization A produces only w B produces only c	100w + 0c	0w + 100c	100w + 100c
Gain from specialization			25w + 20c

Suppose that each country has 10 units of resources, and that, under self-sufficiency, A and B each devote half their resources to producing w and half to producing c. (The assumption of a fifty-fifty allocation is arbitrary, and does not affect the argument.) Row 1 of the Table shows self-sufficient output, in A of 50w + 30c (col. ii), in B of 25w + 50c (col. iii). World output is the sum of the outputs of A + B and is shown in col. (iv), namely 75w + 80c.

Row 2 of the Table shows what happens if both countries specialize in the production of the good in which they have an absolute advantage. A produces 100w (and no c), while B produces 100c (and no w). World output becomes 100w + 100c, as shown in col. (iv).

Row 3 of the Table shows the gain from specialization, as the difference in total world output under specialization from that under self-sufficiency, i.e. the difference between rows 1 and 2 of col. (iv). This is (100w + 100c) minus (75w + 80c).

The gain from specialization is therefore 25w + 20c. There is both *more wheat and more cloth available* for world consumption when A and B specialize, and a potential gain from trade for both countries. This is hardly surprising. If one country can make more of one good than another, while the second country can make more of the other good, their joint production will increase if they specialize.

These gains result from specialization in the two countries. Note now that America is producing all wheat and Britain all cloth. If the inhabitants of each country are to consume a balanced bundle including both commodities, as they did when each country was self-sufficient, trade must take place. Britain must export cloth and import wheat while America does the opposite.

Trade allows countries to specialize and the world to reap the gains from specialization. Thus, economists use the terms 'gains from trade' and 'gains from specialization' synonymously.

The general case: comparative advantage

What if one country has an absolute advantage in the production of *both* goods? Suppose, for example, that America is more efficient in both wheat and cloth production than Britain. This was the question that the English economist, David Ricardo, posed and answered more than 150 years ago. Ricardo showed that a gain from specialization was possible, even if one country had an absolute advantage over another country in the production of all commodities, *provided that its margin of advantage was not the same in all lines of output.*

This condition amounts to saying that a gain can result when one country has a relatively greater, or *comparative*, advantage in the production of some goods than of others. Ricardo's proposition is, therefore, known as the principle of comparative advantage (also, sometimes, as the principle of comparative costs).

We can demonstrate Ricardo's Principle of Comparative Advantage with the aid of another simple arithmetical example. In Table 20.2 we assume that American efficiency is greater than British in *both* wheat and cloth production – that a unit of resources in A produces 20w *or* 10c, while in B the same unit produces only 10w *or* 8c. Britain no longer has an absolute advantage in the production of either commodity. You might imagine that efficient America has nothing to gain from trading with such an inefficient partner as Britain. You would, however, be wrong. *Both* countries can gain from trade.

In the top row of Table 20.2 we can see, as in Table 20.1, the production that takes place if A and B are self-sufficient, and each devotes half its resources to cloth and half to wheat. This assumption is again, of course, arbitrary. There must be *some* allocation of resources when each country is self-sufficient, and this one is as good as any other for purposes of illustration. Total production in A and B is shown in columns (ii) and (iii) respectively. A produces 100w + 50c, while B produces 50w + 40c.

TABLE 20.2 Gain from Specialization with Comparative Advantage. A and B each have 10 units of resources. In A, each unit can produce 20w *or* 10c. In B, each unit can produce 10w *or* 8c.

| (i) | PRODUCTION | | |
	America (ii)	Britain (iii)	World (ii) + (iii) (iv)
Self-sufficiency (half resources used for w and half for c)	100w + 50c	50w + 40c	150w + 90c
Specialization A uses 80% of its resources for w and 20% for c. B produces only c.	160w + 20c	0w + 80c	160w + 100c
Gain from specialization			10w + 10c

Now, let us see what happens to total production if each country specializes, to some extent, in the production of the commodity in which it has *comparative advantage*. The data in the Table show that, although America has an absolute advantage over Britain in both wheat and cloth, her *margin* of advantage is not the same in the two goods. America can produce twice as much wheat as can Britain, using the same quantity of resources, but only twenty-five per cent more cloth.

Therefore, we can say that America has a *comparative advantage* in the production of wheat (and a *comparative disadvantage* in the production of cloth), because Britain is *relatively less inefficient* than America in cloth than in wheat production.

If we now allow America to devote more resources to wheat, and Britain to specialize in cloth production, we can show the gain in total world output. Suppose Britain produces only cloth, while America increases its resources devoted to wheat – allocating 8 out of its total 10 units of resources to wheat, and only 2 units to cloth production. A's output is then 160w + 20c. B's output is 80c. Total world output is, therefore, 160w + 100c.

Row 3 in Table 20.2 shows, in precisely the same way as in the case of absolute advantage, the gain from specialization, i.e. the difference between world output in rows 1 and 2 of column (iv). The gain in this case is 10w and 10c. There is still *more wheat and more cloth* available for consumption with specialization, and a potential gain therefore, for both countries.

Comparative advantage summarized: Two important conclusions can be drawn from the example we have been studying:

- **The gains from specialization depend on comparative advantage. World production can always be increased if trade takes place between countries which have different relative efficiencies in the production of any goods or services. If each concentrates on those commodities in which it is relatively more efficient, or relatively less inefficient, a gain is there for the taking.**
- **Without comparative advantage, there is no reallocation of resources within countries that will increase total world production.**

The second proposition follows directly from the first. There are no gains from specialization without comparative advantage, and no reallocation of resources within countries will increase total production of both commodities. For example, if one country is exactly twice or three times as efficient as another in every line of output, there will be no gain if they do specialize. To show this for yourself, construct a third table, similar to Tables 20.1 and 20.2, for the case where one unit of resources can produce 20w *or* 14c in A, or the same unit can produce 10w *or* 7c in B. You will find that world output of both commodities cannot be increased by specialization. In other words, comparative advantage is necessary, as well as sufficient, for gains from specialization.

Limits to the gain from trade

The gains from trade may be more limited than might be concluded from the previous section. There are two reasons for this. One relates to transport costs, and the other to increasing costs of production.

Transport costs: Our demonstration of the principle of comparative advantage made no reference to transport costs. They were assumed to be zero. If, more realistically, we assume that there are positive costs of transporting commodities among countries, this will clearly limit the gain from trade. The higher the transport costs, the less the scope for gain. In the limit, if transport costs are equal to or greater than the cost difference among countries, trade will not be profitable, so there will be no gain.

One reason why trade has risen so fast in recent years is rapidly falling transport costs. Together with improved methods of preserving perishables, the impact has been to make virtually all goods 'tradeable'.

Increasing costs of production: The second limit to the scope for gain from trade occurs if costs of production increase with output. In our example of trade between Britain and America, we explicitly assumed constant costs. In consequence, trade continued until Britain was completely specializing in the production of cloth. However, if the British cloth industry was working under conditions of increasing costs, the cost differences between the two countries, which are the source of the gain from trade, would gradually diminish. Moreover, it is likely that trade would come to an end at a lower level.[1]

Comparative advantage and opportunity cost

The principle of comparative advantage, as we have set it out, is expressed in terms similar to those used by David Ricardo in 1817. We made use of the concept of a unit of resources, which could be equated across different countries in the world. However, techniques and factors of production differ so much among countries that the concept of a common measure of resource inputs is suspect.

The principle of comparative advantage can be stated without reference to the real, or absolute, cost of resources, using the idea of opportunity cost. To do this, return to the example of Table 20.2 and calculate the opportunity cost of wheat and cloth in the two countries. These are shown in Table 20.3. The calculations in the table are based on the original assumption that one unit of resources can produce *either* 20w *or* 10c in A, and *either* 10w *or* 8c in B.

TABLE 20.3 The Opportunity Cost of 1 Unit of Wheat and 1 Unit of Cloth in Countries A and B In A, 1 unit of resources can produce 20w *or* 10c. In B, each unit can produce 10w or 8c.

	Country A	Country B
Opportunity cost of 1w	$\frac{10}{20} = 0.5c$	$\frac{8}{10} = 0.8c$
Opportunity cost of 1c	$\frac{20}{10} = 2w$	$\frac{10}{8} = 1.25w$

Consider, first, the opportunity cost of a unit of wheat in the two countries. In A, the opportunity cost of 20w is 10c. So the opportunity cost of a single unit of w must be one-twentieth of 10c. In other words, the opportunity cost of 1w is 10c/20c = 0.5c. In B, the opportunity cost of 10w is 8c. So the opportunity cost of 1w in B is 8c/10c = 0.8c. The opportunity costs of 1w differ in the two countries. In A, one unit of w involves the sacrifice of 0.5c, while in

B the sacrifice is 0.8c. The sacrifice is greater in B. Hence, A enjoys a comparative advantage in the production of wheat, while B has a comparative *dis*advantage in the production of that commodity.

Consider, next, the opportunity cost of a unit of cloth in each country. In A, the opportunity cost of 10c is the sacrifice of 20w given up. So, the opportunity cost of a single unit of c must be one-tenth of that of producing 10c. In other words the opportunity cost of 1c is 20w/10w = 2w. In B, the opportunity cost of 8c is 10w. So, the opportunity cost of a single unit of c must be one-eighth of 10w. Therefore the opportunity cost of 1c is 10w/8w = 1.25w.

The opportunity costs are different in the two cases. In A, one unit of cloth involves the sacrifice of 2w, while in B the sacrifice is only 1.25w. This gives us the definition of comparative advantage:

one country has a comparative advantage over another in the production of one commodity if its opportunity cost of producing that commodity is less than another's.

In the above example, country B has a comparative advantage in the production of cloth, while country A has a comparative *dis*advantage in the production of that commodity.

The calculations in Table 20.3 show that comparative advantages differ in the two countries. Although absolute costs of production of both goods are lower in A than in B, relative costs are different. The opportunity costs of wheat are lower in A; the opportunity costs of cloth are lower in B.

It is these differences in relative advantages and disadvantages that explain the gains which were shown in Table 20.2, as following specialization by each country in the production of the good in which it enjoys a comparative advantage.

It is important to appreciate that this conclusion rests on relative opportunity costs, and is *independent of the level of absolute costs*. Although we derived the figures of opportunity cost here from an example where we happened to know absolute costs, the gains from specialization arise from the opportunity costs, no matter what absolute costs lie behind them.

A graphic representation of the gains from specialization

The principle of comparative advantage is so important and powerful a tool of economic analysis that we shall restate it with the use of a diagram, which allows direct representation of opportunity costs.

The diagram, Figure 20.1, is similar to that of Figure 1.4 in Chapter 1. Part (i) shows the production possibility curve, AA', for America, which can produce *either* 20w *or* 10c, or indeed any combination of c and w on the curve. Part (ii) shows Britain's production possibility curve, BB'; B can produce *either* 10w *or* 8c, or any combination on its curve.[1]

---

1 Note that costs of production may fall, rather than rise or remain constant with output. In this case the scope for gain from trade becomes greater rather than less.

1 Refer back to pp.9–10 if you have forgotten why the slope of the curve measures opportunity cost.

A enjoys an absolute advantage in cloth and wheat but world output can be shown to increase when specialization takes place because opportunity costs, shown by the slopes of the countries' production possibility curves, are not the same. A's curve is steeper than B's because A's opportunity cost of producing cloth (measured in terms of wheat forgone) is higher than B's. A has a comparative *advantage* in wheat and a comparative *disadvantage* in cloth.

Let us look at the scope for gain from trade from the point of view of America and Britain, in turn. First America. Left to itself, a self-sufficient America could consume only at some point on its own production possibility curve. But suppose it were offered the chance of obtaining cloth by trading with Britain, at the British opportunity cost.

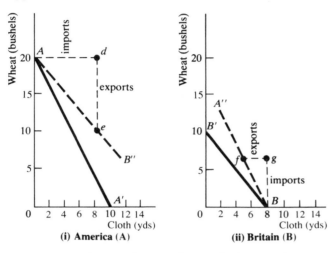

FIGURE 20.1 **The Gain from Trade.** A and B have production possibility curves with different slopes. If A could trade at B's opportunity cost ratio, it could specialize in wheat, producing at A, consuming at *e*, and exchanging wheat for cloth with B. If B could trade at A's opportunity cost ratio, it could specialize in cloth, producing at B and consuming at *f*.[1]

We can show America's consumption possibilities by drawing a line on America's diagram, with the slope exactly the same as the British production possibility curve. We draw it here through point A, which implies that America produces only wheat and exchanges it for British cloth. America's consumption possibilities are now enhanced. It can consume anywhere along AB″. For example, at point *e*, America would produce OA wheat, of which *d − e* would be exported in exchange for *d − A* cloth imported. The consumption level at point *e* is beyond what can be obtained by producing at any point along AA′, America's domestic production possibility curve. Clearly America has gained from trade and, though Britain has not done so in this illustration, it is no worse off, but has broken even.

By similar reasoning, it can be shown that Britain could

gain from exchange, if it were offered the chance to trade at the American opportunity cost, in terms of cloth sacrificed. A″B is drawn, with the same slope as AA′, through point B on Britain's diagram, i.e. assuming Britain specialized completely in cloth production. Britain could then consume anywhere along BA″, such as point *f*, producing OB cloth, of which *g − f* is exported in exchange for *g − B* imports of wheat. B's consumption level at *f* is more favourable than at any point on B's production possibility curve – the best available for B if it were to stay self-sufficient. Clearly, now it is Britain that gains from specialization and exchange.

This exercise has shown that A can gain if it trades at B's opportunity cost, and that B can gain if it trades at A's opportunity cost. In both cases, the second trading partner breaks even, so we may conclude there is a net gain to the world, i.e. to A and B together. Clearly, both cannot happen at the same time. The rate at which A trades wheat for cloth must be the same as the rate that B trades cloth for wheat. This rate must lie between the opportunity cost ratios of the two countries, if *both* countries are to gain. The division of the gain between them depends on the rate at which trade takes place. The closer that rate is to the opportunity cost ratio of country A, the greater the gain will be for B, and vice versa.

The Gains from Economies of Scale

The second source of gain from trade is the reaping of economies of large-scale production made possible by the expansion of the market which trade permits.

In many lines of output, real production costs fall as the scale of output increases. The bases of falling costs (or increasing returns to scale) were given in Chapters 13 and 14. If each country's resource costs fall as they specialize, the resulting increases in output when trade and specialization takes place will be larger than if costs were constant.

We conclude that the potential gain from trade arising from large-scale production is likely to be greater for small countries such as Denmark and Israel, whose domestic markets are too small to allow the exploitation of the full economies of scale, than for countries such as the USA, which have domestic markets large enough for full realization of scale economies. The vast explosion of product diversity in the last couple of decades has greatly increased the size of an industry needed to exhaust all scale economies in the full range of its products. This has, in turn, greatly increased the scope for international specialization in particular product niches. In consequence, we should expect the cost of remaining self-sufficient to be particularly high for small countries, while for large countries the gains from trade arise mainly from specializing in the production of goods in which they have a comparative advantage.

Learning-by-Doing

The discussion so far has assumed that costs vary only with output. However, as we know from Chapter 14, costs can vary not only with output but also over time. The tendency for firms to learn by doing, and acquire expertise

---

1 Note, the diagram illustrates the scope for gains from trade for two countries. It does not show trade equilibrium, i.e. the equality of imports and exports, for which see Figure 20.2.

as they specialize, applies equally to regions and to countries. This is our third source of gains from trade.

When learning-by-doing takes place, the countries' cost curves shift downwards. If it occurred in the example of Table 20.2, it would mean that output of cloth per worker would rise in Britain, and that output of wheat per worker would rise in America, as each country specialized in the production of the commodity in which it had a comparative advantage.

Learning-by-doing suggests that existing patterns of comparative advantage are not immutable. The classical theory of gains from trade, based largely on countries' natural endowments, is to an extent being challenged by a dynamic view of comparative advantage. This view sees some comparative advantages as acquired, rather than nature-given, and changing. Many new industries are seen as depending more on human capital, than on fixed physical capital or natural resources. For example, natural endowments cannot account for the UK's prominence in pop music, nor for US, and later Japanese, successes in the silicon-chip-based industries.

The new view has not replaced orthodox comparative advantage theory, so much as modified it. It means, for example, that when countries lose former dominance based on traditional industries, they need not sit idly by, but can adapt by developing new areas of comparative advantage. There are important policy implications here, which we discuss later in the chapter.

The Terms of Trade

The basis for increasing world production through trade has been shown to lie in the exploitation of the possibilities for specialization by countries in the production of commodities in which they have a comparative advantage. The total gain in world production is shared between A and B when they trade with each other.

How much each country gains depends on what is called the TERMS OF TRADE, which measures the quantity of imported goods attainable in exchange for a unit of exported goods.

The terms of trade depend, therefore, on the prices of imports and exports.

In Figure 20.1 we showed that Britain would appropriate all the gain from trade if she exchanged cloth for wheat at the American opportunity cost of wheat in terms of cloth (and that America would reap all the gain from trade if she exchanged wheat for cloth at the British opportunity cost of cloth in terms of wheat). If trade takes place at any rate of exchange (terms of trade) which lies *between* the British and American domestic opportunity costs, the gain will be shared between the two countries. It is beyond the scope of an introductory textbook to show how the terms of trade are determined. We may, however, mention that the strength of demand for traded goods is a relevant factor.

International trade involves many countries and many commodities. The terms of trade are, therefore, computed as an index number, itself consisting of two price index

numbers: the price of exports and the price of imports:

$$\text{Terms of Trade (index)} = \frac{\text{price of exports (index)}}{\text{price of imports (index)}} \times 100$$

The terms of trade index rises if the price of exports rises *relative* to the price of imports. For example, if the price of exports rises from 100 to 120, while the price of imports falls from 100 to 80, the terms of trade index will rise from 100 in the first period to 150 (120 divided by 80, multiplied by 100).

The terms of trade will also rise even though the prices of exports and imports both increase, providing that the former increases relatively more than the latter – e.g., if export prices rise by 50 per cent and import prices by only 25 per cent, the terms of trade index becomes 120 (150 divided by 125, multiplied by 100). In the opposite case, where import prices rise relatively to export prices, the terms of trade index falls – e.g., if the import price index is 160 while the export price index is 120, the terms of trade index is 0.75.

Rises in the terms of trade are commonly called 'favourable' movements, and falls in the terms of trade 'unfavourable' movements. These adjectives have precise definitions, and should not be taken to mean more than these definitions, i.e. favourable movements in the terms of trade mean that more imports can be obtained per unit of exports, and vice versa.

Whether or not favourable movements in the terms of trade will bring social gain depends on circumstances. For instance, rising relative prices of exports may make them more difficult to sell abroad, and pricing exports out of foreign markets would hardly be regarded as a desirable development. But a favourable change that arose because exports were in increasing demand, so that their prices rose, would more likely entail a net gain for the country.

INTERNATIONAL TRADING EQUILIBRIUM

We take a step towards understanding how supply and demand determine prices, production and quantities traded, by looking at trade for a single commodity. We consider two situations – a two-country and a many-country world.

A two-country world: Assume, as previously, a world with only two countries, this time France and Germany, abbreviated to F and G. The single commodity we shall call onions, which are produced under conditions of rising marginal costs in both countries. (This assumption differs from that lying behind our previous numerical examples, which assumed constant costs).

Part (i) of Figure 20.2 shows the domestic supply and demand curves for onions in France, and part (ii) shows them in Germany.

In the absence of trade, a self-sufficient France will produce and consume q_f onions; while a self-sufficient Germany will produce and consume q_g onions. The price

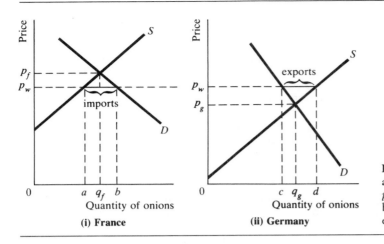

FIGURE 20.2 **Trading Equilibrium for One Commodity in a Two-Country World.** Before trade, domestic prices are p_f in France and p_g in Germany. After trade, price is p_w in both countries; French imports, $b - a$, equal German exports, $d - c$.

of onions will be p_f and p_g in F and G respectively. Since the relative prices of onions in F and G reflect real opportunity costs, there is a potential gain to be reaped from specialization by G, which has the lower unit costs. In the absence of governmental trade restrictions or prohibitive transport costs, profit-seeking businesses would spot the profit to be gained by buying onions in G and selling them in F.

Trade will be profitable so long as there is a difference between the price of onions in the two countries. But the opening up of trade will cause domestic prices in G and F to come closer together. As G exports onions, the quantity available on the domestic market falls, and the price of onions in G will rise. At the same time, as F imports onions, the quantity available in F's market (domestic production plus imports) rises, and the price of onions falls in F. Trade will continue until the domestic price of onions is the same in F and G. When that position is reached, trade is at an equilibrium level, and the quantity of onions that F wishes to import is exactly equal to the quantity that G wishes to export.

The equilibrium position may be seen in Figure 20.2. The price of onions is p_w in both F and G, and is, effectively, the world price. At the price p_w there is excess supply, $d - c$, in Germany; while there is excess demand, $b - a$, in France. Because $b - a = d - c$, imports and exports are equal. This is the equilibrium of two trading countries, *production* having risen in G (by $d - q_g$) and fallen in F (by $q_f - a$), while *consumption* has risen in F (by $b - q_f$) and fallen in G (by $q_g - c$).

A many-country world: The previous section described equilibrium trading conditions in one commodity, for two equal-sized nations. For many commodities, a more realistic assumption is that any one country is a relatively small importer or exporter – small enough to be unable to influence price on the world market.

We need only a minor modification to the diagram we used in the previous section, to show trading equilibrium in a many-country world to deal with this case, where the country is a price-taker. In Figure 20.3 we show the supply and demand curves for, say, apples, for a 'small' country

which takes the world price as given, regardless of the quantity of apples imported or exported.

In the absence of trade, equilibrium would be found at the point of intersection of the domestic supply and demand curves D and S with price p_d. If the world price happened to be the same as the domestic price, no trade would be profitable. We shall, however, examine the nature of equilibrium in two cases – where the world price is (1) lower and (2) higher than what the domestic price would be in the absence of trade.

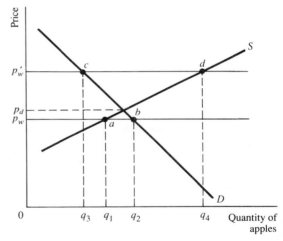

FIGURE 20.3 **Trading Equilibrium for one Commodity in a Small Country.** If world price is p_w, domestic consumers buy q_2, domestic producers produce q_1, and $q_2 - q_1$ are imported. If world price is p_w', domestic producers produce q_4, domestic consumers buy q_3, and $q_4 - q_3$ are exported.

First, assume the lower world price, p_w. Domestic consumers can buy as many apples as they wish at that price. In effect, the world supply curve is perfectly elastic for the small country. Domestic consumers will be in equilibrium at point b, the intersection of their demand curve with the world supply curve. They will buy q_2 at the world price. Who, however, will supply q_2? The answer is that domestic producers will supply some apples, and some will be imported. The supply curve in the diagram tells us that domestic producers will be prepared to offer q_1 apples at the price p_w. They would only offer more than that quantity at prices higher than the world price. The difference between the domestic supply and the domestic demand is, therefore, the quantity of imports $q_2 - q_1$ (or $b - a$).

Now consider the consequences of a world price higher than the domestic price that would obtain in the absence of trade. Suppose it is p'_w. Consider, first, domestic producers. The meaning of the world price of p_w is that domestic producers can sell in foreign markets at that price, all they can produce. In effect, it is now the world demand curve facing the small country which is perfectly elastic. Domestic producers will be in equilibrium at point d, the intersection of their supply curve with the world price. We can see from the domestic demand curve (D) in the diagram, however, that domestic consumers are only prepared to buy q_3 apples at the price p'_w. The difference between domestic supply and domestic demand is the quantity of exports $q_4 - q_3$ (or $d - c$).

THE CASE FOR FREE TRADE

The case for free trade rests on the principle of comparative advantage.

When opportunity costs differ among countries, specialization leads to increased production and consumption on a world scale.

There is abundant evidence that significant differences in costs do exist in real life. Therefore there are large potential sources of gain. It is also clear that nations do not seek complete self-sufficiency. Trade not only exists, it has been growing faster than world production.

Free trade does not mean, however, that *everyone* is better off with trade than without. It means only that it is *possible* for everyone to be better off. Usually, there are gainers and losers from trade, at least in the short run. In the example of Figure 20.2, the gainers are German onion-growers and French onion-eaters. The immediate losers are French onion-growers. German onion-eaters also lose, but they gain when they buy now-cheaper French goods.

Of course, if comparative advantage exists, there will be further compensating benefits to be taken into account in a final reckoning. For example, displaced French onion producers will tend to move into the production of other goods in which France has a comparative advantage and should, therefore, gain in the long run. Because trade creates gainers and losers, free trade does not appeal to the self-interest of everyone. The remainder of this chapter is devoted to a consideration of the case for interference in international trade.

PROTECTIONISM

Methods of Protection

Governments intervene in international trade for economic and non-economic reasons. Such intervention is usually called PROTECTION. The available methods include measures to increase exports, but we shall be concerned mainly with those which hinder imports, and which are commonly called barriers to trade.

There are three principal methods of reducing imports. They are: (i) tariffs, (ii) quotas, and (iii) non-tariff barriers.

Tariffs

Taxes levied by the government on imports of a particular good are known as TARIFFS (or IMPORT DUTIES). A tariff may be either 'specific', i.e. so much money per unit of the good imported, or it may be *ad valorem*, which is calculated as a percentage of the price of the product. Tariffs bring revenue to the government, but our present concern is with the protection they give to domestic producers when they raise the prices of imported goods relative to the prices of competing domestic products.

Import quotas

Limiting the quantity of a good that is allowed into the country over a period of time is done through IMPORT QUOTAS, which provide an upper limit to permitted imports over the given period.

Non-tariff barriers

The term usually employed for protective measures other than tariffs and quotas is NON-TARIFF BARRIERS. (Strictly speaking, quotas are non-tariff barriers.) Non-tariff barriers have provided the most important means of restricting imports since the early 1970s. There is a wide variety of devices that are employed, including the imposition by governments of quality restrictions on imports, or requiring importers to have special licences allowing them to buy goods from abroad.

Figure 20.4 compares the three methods of restricting imports. In each part of the diagram, D and S represent the domestic market demand and foreign supply curves of cars for a small country which takes the world price as given. We assume that foreign producers are willing to supply, at the price p_0, all the cars that are demanded in the UK. Hence the supply curve of imports is perfectly elastic. Equilibrium, before any trade restrictions are introduced, is found at the intersection of the domestic demand and foreign supply curves. Price p_0 and quantity q_0 are the initial equilibrium values.

Now, suppose that the government wishes to restrict imports of foreign cars to, say, q_1. Part (i) shows the effect of doing so with a tariff, part (ii) shows the effect of a quota, and part (iii) the effect when non-tariff barriers are employed.

A tariff: A tariff shifts the supply curve of imports upwards because it adds to the foreign producer's cost of every unit sold in the country imposing the tariff. If the tariff is t per unit, the new supply curve becomes S', horizontally above the original supply curve, by t, for all levels of imports. The intersection of the new supply curve with

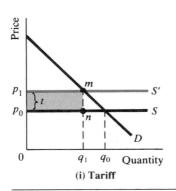

(i) Tariff

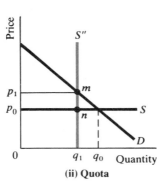

(ii) Quota

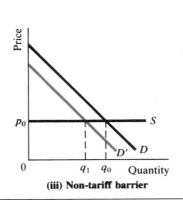

(iii) Non-tariff barrier

FIGURE 20.4 Import Restrictions: A tariff, a Quota and a Non-Tariff Barrier. Imports are restricted to q_1 with all methods. A tariff raises domestic price to p_1, and raises $p_0 p_1 m n$ government revenue; a quota will raise price to p_1 without any government revenue; a non-tariff barrier may lower the demand curve and leave price unchanged.

the unchanged demand curve identifies the new equilibrium position. Imports fall to the targetted q_1, while the domestic price of cars rises to p_1.

A quota: If the government imposes an import quota of q_1 cars, the supply curve becomes vertical at that quantity. The market-clearing price for quantity q_1 is p_1, where the new supply curve, S'', intersects the unchanged demand curve.

A non-tariff barrier: The third method of restricting imports is to resort to one of a variety of non-tariff barriers which reduce the demand for imports. In part (iii), the effect of introducing a non-tariff barrier that acts on demand is seen as shifting the demand curve to the left, from D to D'. Once again, quantity falls to q_1, but this time price stays constant at p_0.

Comparative effects of tariffs, quotas and non-tariff barriers

Figure 20.4 showed that all three methods of protection can succeed in restricting imports to a target. However, that does not mean that all effects are the same. Two important differences require consideration. The first concerns the identity of the gainers from protection; the second turns on the maintenance or severance of international trading links among nations.

An import restriction prevents buyers and sellers from reaching the equilibrium price and quantity that would prevail in a free market. Consequently, there is a difference between the domestic price of imports in the importing country, and the price at which the reduced quantity of imports would be supplied by foreigners.

Who gains?: To illustrate, compare the effects of a tariff and a quota. Under a tariff, the difference between the prices p_0 and p_1 in Figure 20.4(i) accrues to the government in the importing country, as revenue from the tariff. This is shown in the Figure as the shaded area $p_0 p_1 m n$. Under a quota, however, the government receives no revenue. The shortage, resulting from the quota restriction, forces up the market price, so that importers are able to charge p_1 for q_1 cars (that would have been on offer at price p_0).

Our first conclusion from comparing a tariff and a quota, is that the former benefits the Exchequer in the country imposing the tariff, while the quota benefits domestic importers.[1]

The comparison of tariff and quota can be extended to non-tariff barriers. One of the most common forms of non-tariff barriers in the modern world are the Voluntary Export Restraints (VERs), which are arrangements whereby exporting countries agree to limit their exports (in return for some *quid pro quo*). For example, Japanese car manufacturers agree voluntarily to limit their exports to the UK.

A similar difference exists between the price that consumers in the importing country would pay for the restricted volume of imports and the price that the foreign exporters would accept. In the case of VERs, however, a common result is for the exporting country to reap the benefit by charging domestic consumers in the importing country the full price.

International trading links:

The second difference in the effects of tariffs, quotas and non-tariff barriers follows from the fact that only the first of these maintains an automatic link between domestic and international prices.

The effects of the changes in the conditions of supply and/or demand *after* protection has been introduced can differ, depending on the protective device employed. Quotas and non-tariff barriers are similar in their effects. We shall compare tariffs and quotas.

Suppose there is a reduction in costs of production affecting foreign suppliers of cars. In Figure 20.5, we reproduce, in a single diagram, the tariff and quota of Figure 20.4 (i) and (ii). The curves D, S and S' are the same in Figures 20.4 and 20.5. Both tariff and quota reduce imports from q_0 to q_1.

---

1 The text assumes that the quotas are given to domestic importers. If the state auctions licences to import q_1 cars, importers would pay up to p_1 for them. Government revenue would, then, be $p_0 p_1 m n$, the same as with a tariff. Conceivably, foreign suppliers could reap the benefit if they did not compete with each other on sales, but charged the higher price of p_1 for the limited supply.

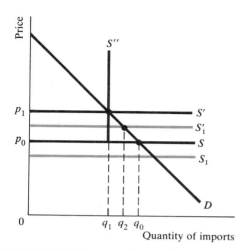

FIGURE 20.5 A Tariff Versus a Quota. The initial effect of both is to cut imports to q_1. A fall in (overseas) costs shifts the foreign supply curve from S_1 to S_1'. With a tariff, imports rise to q_2; with a quota, imports are unchanged.

The reduction in costs of production affecting foreign suppliers now shifts the supply curve of imports down, to S_1, and the supply curve inclusive of the tariff shifts also down, to S_1'. The intersection of the new supply curve S_1' with the demand curve identifies the new equilibrium with a tariff. Imports rise, despite the tariff, from q_1 to q_2.

Compare this result with that under a quota. The changed costs of production do not affect the relevant part of the supply curve. The quota made the supply curve vertical at quantity q_1, so no increase in imports follows the reduction in costs.

This difference between the effects of tariffs and quotas is of considerable importance. Tariffs maintain links between domestic and international prices. Any change in supply and/or demand conditions can therefore affect trade flows. Quotas remove the links between domestic and international prices. The country imposing a quota insulates itself from the rest of the world. Moreover, consumers in that country fail to enjoy the benefits of technological advance elsewhere in the world.

If interference with free trade must occur, economists usually have a preference for tariffs over import quotas in order to retain the signalling functions of prices. On the demand side, the severance of the links between international prices deprives consumers of the opportunity to buy more goods whose costs of production fall. On the supply side, quotas tend to be allocated arbitrarily – e.g. on a first-come first-served basis, thereby failing to give any advantage to producers with the lowest production costs.

Despite the foregoing arguments, tariffs are not always preferred to quotas. The latter are, for example, usually more *certain* in their effects. The choice between methods must depend on the reasons why protection is regarded as desirable at all. It is to the arguments for protection that we therefore turn.

Arguments for Protection

We shall concentrate on arguments for protection based on economic grounds. First, however, we should mention some other arguments better described as non-economic. We concentrate on general issues and ignore the differences between tariffs and quotas just described.

Non-economic arguments for protection

The citizens of a nation may prefer objectives other than maximizing national income and, therefore, choose to maintain policies which interfere with free trade. There are many reasons why; we mention a few. One might be to preserve a peasant farming community, even if it were inefficient. This could justify restrictions on the import of farm products which were obtainable more cheaply from other countries, i.e. as the EC's Common Agricultural Policy. A second example might be protection on grounds of national defence. It has been argued, for instance, that Britain needs an experienced merchant navy in case of war, and this industry should, therefore, be shielded from competition by more efficient foreign vessels, even in peacetime. A third example might be protection in order to diversify. A nation might have comparative cost advantages in a narrow range of commodities. The government, however, might decide that the risks of narrow specialization made the nation politically vulnerable.

All these non-economic arguments may be acceptable, because life has other objectives as well as the maximization of real income per head of population. Economists concern themselves with three aspects of such arguments for protection. First, they look to see if the tariff does achieve the ends suggested. Second, they calculate the cost of the tariff in terms of lost living standards. Third, they check whether there are alternative policies which might achieve the stated goal at a lower cost.

Economic arguments for protection

Arguments for protection which have the objective of raising living standards are here described as economic. We deal with the following arguments for protection: to create comparative advantage; to improve the terms of trade; and against low-wage foreign labour.

Protection to create comparative advantage

Foremost among the economic protectionist arguments are those which assert that *existing* patterns of comparative advantage are not always the best guide for allocating resources in the long run. We explained earlier that economies of scale, and learning-by-doing, are important sources of gain from trade. It follows that a country which does not possess an efficient industry on a scale large enough, or in existence long enough, to have developed a comparative advantage in that sector, might nevertheless find it worthwhile to acquire that advantage deliberately, in order to enjoy the later benefits.

The best known variant of this type is called the INFANT INDUSTRY ARGUMENT. It applies to industries where costs are high when the industry is small and young, but fall as it grows. Protecting such a domestic industry from foreign competition may give it a genuine comparative advantage later.

Three points should be made about the infant industry argument for protection. The first is that it is necessary to identify in advance industries which are currently unprofitable but which will succeed in the long run. If the state must select such industries, we should ask why private businesses are not prepared to invest in them without government help. After all, businesses invest for *future* returns all the time – that is the nature of enterprise. The record of governments in picking future winners is not very satisfactory.

The second point is why private businesses are not prepared to invest for future profits. One answer might be that they would invest if the potential economies of scale are *internal* but not if they are *external*. Firms make planning decisions on the basis of costs and revenues, as they see them. They do not take account of economies of scale which are *external to the firm* – i.e. *those related to the growth of the whole industry*. The infant industry argument for protection is therefore valid when there are external economies of scale.

The last point is that, in practice, it is often difficult to remove protection when the industry 'grows up'. All too frequently, the protected infant grows into a weak adolescent and feeble adult, requiring continued protection for survival.

Protection to improve the terms of trade

A second argument for protection has restricted relevance. It applies only to a country that can exert monopoly (or monopsony) power, by restricting the volume of exports (or imports) of one or more commodities, thereby affecting their prices – effectively improving the country's terms of trade. By restricting its exports it may drive up their prices (as does any monopolist selling in a local market). By restricting its imports, it may drive *down* their prices.

Notice three things about this protectionist argument. First, there is no conflict with the theory of comparative advantage. The reduction of world trade implies a loss of world output and forgone gains for the world as a whole. The benefit accrues entirely to the country imposing the tariff.

Second, it is uncommon for a single nation to have the necessary monopoly or monopsony power. (Perhaps the UK is a sufficiently large importer to have some small effect on the world price of tea.) However, *groups* of nations can collude to influence the price of their products – the OPEC oil-exporting cartel is a good example.

Third, there is the risk of retaliation. In so far as one country succeeds in shifting the terms of trade in its favour, the terms of trade shift, of necessity, against some other country, or countries, who then have an incentive to retaliate. Tariff wars rarely benefit anyone in the long run, as the volume of world trade shrinks with every retaliatory protective restriction.

Protection against low-wage foreign labour

Probably the most common argument for protection for industries facing more efficient foreign producers, is that they have to compete against low-wage foreign labour. It is often put forward as 'job protection' for workers in advanced countries from low-paid labour in the developing world.

Although circumstances can exist to give some partial justification to such arguments, they are, in their typical form, fallacious, denying the very basis for gainful trade – comparative advantage.

To appreciate the fallacy behind the argument, consider it first in a local, rather than in an international, context. Is it impossible for a rich person to gain from trading with a poor one? Would the chairperson of a large corporation be better off if she did all her own typing, gardening and house repairs? No one believes that rich persons must lose by trading with poor ones.

It may, then, be argued, additionally, that poor countries price their goods 'too cheaply'. How on earth do consumers in a rich country suffer from that? Do rich consumers lose from buying a given good at a low rather than a high price? The fact that Koreans pay low wages means that the prices of Korean goods are low. Consumers in the rest of the world, therefore, gain, by being able to import these goods at low cost, in terms of the exports that have to be given up in exchange.

Moreover, many Koreans will be worse off if restrictions are imposed on their exports. Demand for labour in Korean export industries will be lower, leading to even lower wages; and Korean consumers will lose the benefits of importing goods from the rest of the world, in which other countries have comparative advantages. Thus, the lost benefits from international specialization apply not just to one country, but to all.

The grain of truth in the argument for high-wage countries is that factors of production located in industries in which the low-wage country has a comparative advantage will lose. They will suffer until they move to industries in which the high-wage country has a comparative advantage. But this concerns the adjustment costs of liberalizing trade, and it does not apply just to high-wage countries. Factors of production in the low-wage country will also lose when they are located in industries in which that country has a comparative disadvantage. They will only gain after they move to industries where the country has a comparative advantage.

Protection and the distribution of income

Protecting industries against low-cost foreign products denies consumers the opportunity of buying from the cheapest sources of supply. As we explained in the previous paragraph, however, there can be short-term distributive losses to some groups. Generally, it can be said that:

the theory of comparative advantage demonstrates the possibility of universal gain, but does not assert that *everyone* gains.

Within a country, some may gain, while others lose. The gainers from trade are consumers of imports and producers of exports. The losers are inefficient producers of all countries. If the UK textile industry is a high-cost industry, tariff protection will harm textile consumers, but it will safeguard UK textile workers (and shareholders). Is this a sufficient reason for accepting a tariff on textiles?

There cannot be an unequivocal answer to this question, because it involves judgements about the distribution of income. However, most economists assert that, in the long run at least, such arguments are weak. They say this for two reasons. In the first place, it should be possible to redistribute income so that no one ends up worse off under free trade than under protection. In the second place, if there are legitimate reasons for protecting textile workers, there are other ways of protecting them which do not have the detrimental side-effects of tariffs.

One variant of this argument with some short-run validity calls for *limited duration protection*, to allow time for workers displaced by efficient foreign competition to retrain and relocate. However, the argument is not confined to international trade. It applies equally to regions within a country which suffer from competition from other regions. It tends to be strong when declining industries happen to be concentrated in regions with few alternative occupations. We discuss industrial policy towards depressed areas in Chapter 21.

Dumping: Complaints are often heard from businesses that they cannot compete with foreign firms, not because they are less efficient but because the foreigners employ 'unfair' practices, involving selling at artificially low prices, called DUMPING.

Dumping, if it lasts indefinitely, can be a gift to the importing country. Its consumers get goods from abroad at less than their real cost. However, dumping is often a temporary measure to get rid of unwanted surpluses, or to drive competitors out of business. It is also often aided by government subsidies. Such predatory behaviour encourages retaliation, and it is accepted international practice for affected countries to levy offsetting *anti-dumping* duties.

Anti-dumping duties were originally designed to remove the effects of 'unfair' foreign competition. Over time, however, they have themselves been used as thinly disguised protectionist devices. Almost any foreign price competition now risks becoming the object of anti-dumping duties.[1]

Alternative Policies for Protection

Several of the arguments for protection that we have examined contain a certain force. Before tariffs are proposed for such cases, it is important to ask whether their objective could not be attained by other, less costly, means. The answer is, often, yes.

We illustrate with two arguments, protection against low-cost foreign labour and for infant industries. We assume the arguments are valid, and compare the effects of protection by tariff and by a direct subsidy.

You will recall that the main detrimental effect of the tariff to protect an industry from low-wage competition in another country falls on consumers, while the beneficial effect is the safeguarding of workers in the domestic industry. If, instead of the tariff, the government grants a subsidy to the producers, the beneficial effects remain. Note, however, that the detrimental effects of higher domestic prices disappear. There is, therefore, a case for preferring the subsidy to the tariff. Consumers are not disadvantaged. The burden of protecting the industry is widely spread among all taxpayers.

In the case of the protection of the infant industry, the same argument applies. Consumers may enjoy low-price imports while the infant industry is growing up, protected by a subsidy rather than by a tariff on imports. There is, moreover, in this case an additional reason for preferring the subsidy. It is that the domestic industry will have to market its products in open competition with those of efficient foreign producers.

Why, in the face of these considerations, are governments usually reluctant to indulge in much direct subsidization? The answer is that subsidies have to be paid for out of government revenue. Substituting a subsidy for a tariff means giving up a policy which yields revenue, for one that involves paying out. Someone always pays for the protection. In the case of a tariff, consumers pay through higher prices. In the case of a subsidy, taxpayers pay through the tax system. But the former burden may be less noticed and politically easier, even if it is economically less efficient.

International Co-operation

This chapter has argued that, although individual countries may try to protect sectional interests, the gains from international trade are great. Attempts by a single country to gain a narrow advantage can easily be offset by retaliatory action by others, as witness the experience of the 1930s, when nation after nation indulged in protective policies that resulted in a downward spiralling of world trade. All countries have a common interest, therefore, in joint action to prevent a repetition of the history of those inter-war years.

International collaboration takes place at two levels, global and regional.

Global

Global agreements that involve most trading nations in the modern world, are mainly conducted through GATT (the General Agreement on Tariffs and Trade) under whose auspices tariff negotiations have been held. The first GATT meeting in 1947 has been followed by other 'rounds', the most recent being known as the 'Kennedy Round' (completed 1967), the 'Tokyo Round' (completed 1986), and the 'Uruguay Round' (nearing completion). Initially, GATT tariff concessions were negotiated bilat-

---

1 Parallel to anti-dumping duties to offset actions by foreign firms, there are countervailing duties aimed at offsetting foreign govenment subsidies (to create a 'level playing field').

BOX 20.1 Thoughtless Drift into World War

'Europe's leaders imperil us all by ignoring American anger over their mockery of free trade, warns Rosemary Righter.

'The European Community's 12 foreign ministers spent the weekend mulling over the grand theme of "the New Europe in the New World Order" ... gliding with the mindlessness of a sleepwalker towards the most serious breakdown in transatlantic relations since 1945 ... The argument is over the Uruguay round of negotiations to liberalize world trade, conducted since 1984 under the auspices of one of the least visible of international bodies, the GATT.

'The signals have been on red since last December at least, when what were supposed to be final negotiations in Brussels collapsed ... Final breakdown can be averted only by a radical change in EC policy. Unless by next month the EC comes up with an offer capable of breaking the impasse, the talks will almost certainly fail, and Europe will be to blame for the protectionist trade war that follows ... The weapons for a mutually destructive trade war between the world's two largest blocs are ready to be honed. America's 1988 Trade Act requires the administration to retaliate against "unfair"

trade ... The EC has its own equivalent regulation, enabling Europe to hit back.'

(*The Times*, 30 April 1991)

The news item highlights the strains that result from protectionism on a large scale, threatening a major collapse in the volume of world trade. The argument between the EC and outsiders, especially the USA, centres around the use of farm subsidies in the EC, not only to protect Community farmers in their home market, but also to enable EC farmers to dump their surplus produce on the world market.

Questions

1 What are the economic aims of the GATT and the EC? Are they mutually compatible?
2 Who are the gainers in the EC, and in the rest of the world, from the EC policy described in the extract?
3 Which groups would gain from a change in EC policy of the kind called for? Would gainers and losers be different in the short term and the long term?

erally (i.e. between pairs of countries), though agreed in advance to be extended multilaterally to all member states, in what is called the 'most favoured nation' (MFN) principle. In most recent rounds a general percentage reduction in all tariffs has been agreed to by all GATT members.

Regional

Regional co-operation is distinguished from global co-operation, because it involves a limited number of countries. Three types of regional union should be distinguished:

A free trade area: A FREE TRADE AREA is a regional union where members agree to remove tariffs on trade among each other, but allow each country to levy whatever tariffs it wishes on imports from outside countries in the rest of the world.

A customs union: A CUSTOMS UNION is a Free Trade Area where, also, a common tariff is agreed on goods imported from non-member nations.

A common market: A COMMON MARKET is a Customs Union where, additionally, there are no restrictions of the movement of factors of production among union members.[1]

Examples of all three types of union are to be found in Europe since World War II. The European Free Trade Association (EFTA) was formed in 1960. The UK was a member of EFTA until 1973, when she joined the European Economic Community (EEC, later the EC), which started as a customs union but has developed, as intended by the Treaty of Rome (1957), to become a common market. The EC is on track to become a full economic union (see footnote) after 1992, with the passing of the Single European Act which envisages, *inter alia*, the removal of all barriers affecting trade in goods and the complete freedom of movement of all factors of production, in the creation of a 'Single European Market'.

Trade creation and trade diversion

The benefits of economic unions are all the advantages associated with free trade among its members that have been discussed in this chapter – greater opportunities for specialization, greater scope for economies of scale, and greater competition to keep producers on their toes. There are, however, certain detriments to be considered.

To illustrate the source of the detriments, consider a world where there are three countries, A, B and C. Suppose that all three countries trade with each other, but maintain 10 per cent tariffs on imports, regardless of source. Let A and B now form a customs union, abolishing tariffs on each other's goods, but both retaining the 10 per cent tariff on imports from C.

Two effects can be expected. The first, known as

---

1 We do not deal here with a full *Economic Union*, which involves, additionally, the use of a single currency among all union members. See Chapter 41.

TRADE CREATION effects, are those with which we are familiar. Free trade between A and B will improve resource allocation between them. Each will now import from the other some goods which were previously produced at home.

The second effect of the formation of the customs union is known as TRADE DIVERSION. In sharp contrast to the beneficial trade-creation effects, the trade-diversion effects involve a *less* efficient world allocation of resources. This is because the customs union involves *discrimination* against imports from non-member nations, even when real costs of production are lowest outside the union.

An example may help to explain the nature of the trade-diversion effects. Suppose the real cost of soap per tonne is £155 in A, £130 in B and £120 in C. C is, thus, the lowest cost producer in the world. If, before the customs union was formed, all three countries imposed a 10 per cent tariff on imports on each other's goods, regardless of origin, the cheapest source of supply of soap for A and B would be imports from C. In A, for example, the price, inclusive of the 10 per cent tariff, would be £132 for imports from C, £143 for imports from B, compared with £150 for domestically produced soap. A would therefore buy its soap from C.

When the customs union is formed, A and B abolish tariffs on each other's goods, but maintain the 10 per cent tariff on imports from C. The price of soap in A now becomes £130 for imports from B, £132 for imports from C (and, of course, remains at £150 for domestically produced soap). The cheapest source of supply of soap in A is now from country B, its partner in the customs union. So A switches imports from the lowest cost producer, C, to imports from B, which no longer bear import duty.

This result runs counter to comparative advantage. It

(*continued on next page*)

Summary

1 International trade theory is an extension of the theory of specialization among persons and among regions. The distinguishing features of international trade – factor immobility and the existence of national currencies – give governments freedom to follow independent policies.

2 A gain from trade is said to occur if trade results in an increase in the total value of world production.

3 Gains arise from cost differences among nations. A country is said to have an absolute advantage in the production of a commodity if it can produce more than another country, using a given quantity of resources.

4 Gains arise also from comparative advantage, which exists when *relative* (opportunity) costs of production of different commodities are not the same in all countries. Each country specializes in the production of goods where its margin of advantage is greatest.

5 The scope of gains from trade may be limited by high transport costs and by rising production costs.

6 Gains arise also from specialization following the expanding of the market and the realization of economies of scale, and of learning-by-doing, which can alter patterns of comparative advantage over time.

7 The division of the gain from trade among nations depends on the terms of trade, which is the relative prices of exports and imports.

8 International trading equilibrium can be demonstrated with the use of supply and demand curves. In the case of a small country trading with the rest of the world, world supply and world demand curves are perfectly elastic at the given world price.

9 The case for free trade is an extension of the general case for free-market systems. Everyone in trading nations is not necessarily better off with free trade rather than without, because of changes in the distribution of income.

10 Governments can intervene in international trade with tariffs (import duties), quotas or non-tariff barriers. Tariffs are economically preferable to quotas in that they do not sever links between domestic and world prices.

11 Two economic arguments for import restrictions which contain valid elements are to protect an infant industry (when the argument is particularly strong if there are external economies of scale), and to improve the terms of trade (requiring the use of monopoly, or monopsony, power).

12 Arguments for protection against low-cost foreign labour and 'unfair' foreign competition, deny the basis for gainful trade and are fallacious. However, foreign predatory prices and subsidies do exist. Protection affects the domestic distribution of income and may benefit specific groups of individuals.

13 Most of the beneficial effects of protection can be achieved at less cost by other means – e.g. by subsidies, which place the burden more widely, on taxpayers rather than on consumers.

14 Trade may be liberalized by international co-operation on a global basis (e.g. through GATT), or on a regional basis within a customs union (e.g. the EC). Customs unions improve resource allocation among union members ('trade creation'), but worsen allocation between the union and the rest of the world ('trade diversion').

follows from the fact that the customs union discriminates against non-member nations, and in favour of union trading partners.

Exactly the same argument can, of course, be applied to country B, in other goods.

This conclusion does not conflict with the case for free trade based on comparative advantage. It calls, however, for the general case to be qualified. *Complete* free trade throughout the world still leads to optimal resource allocation. But *partially* freeing trade in a part of the world can lower efficiency, even for members of the customs union. For outsiders in the rest of the world, the initial effects are largely negative, in so far as they experience discrimination against their imports, and lower foreign earnings to spend on imports. They may gain, however, if the union brings rising incomes that lead to higher imports from all countries, including those outside the union. There can be a real conflict between the global and regional approaches to trade liberalization. As Box 20.1 shows, the protectionist measures shown to agriculture in the European Community threatened progress of GATT negotiations in 1990–91. They relate to factor immobility and to the existence of national currencies.

Questions

1 With one unit of resources, countries F and G can produce the quantities in the following table:

	F		G	
Question (i)	12 cloth or 8 oranges		10 cloth or 3 oranges	
Question (ii)	4	12	6	18
Question (iii)	4	2	3	2

Which of the following will occur under free trade?
  (a) F exports cloth and imports oranges.
  (b) G exports cloth and imports oranges.
  (c) F exports cloth and oranges.
  (d) G exports cloth and oranges.
  (e) No trade will take place.

2 Refer to Figure 20.3. You are informed that supply conditions and the world market price p_w are as in the diagram, but that the country exports $q_4 - q_2$ apples. What conclusions do you draw?

3 What circumstances prevent a gain from trade?

4 Which One, More or None of the following describes the 'terms of trade'?
  (a) The quantity of imports attainable per unit of exports.
  (b) The quantity of domestic production sacrificed for a unit of imports.
  (c) The price index of imports divided by the price index of exports.
  (d) Customs and frontier rules that have to be observed by importers and exporters.

5 Which One or More of the following tend to make the infant industry argument for protection relatively (i) strong, (ii) weak?
  (a) The industry enjoys external economies of scale.
  (b) Future cost conditions are known with certainty.
  (c) The country possesses a high degree of monopoly power.
  (d) Workers in competing foreign countries are very low paid.

6 Is the following statement True or False? 'The larger is a customs union *vis-à-vis* the rest of the world, the more likely it is that world resources allocation will on balance be improved.'

21 Government and Microeconomic Policy[1]

We have discussed government intervention in the economy in many relevant places in this book, but as we now reach the end of our study of microeconomics we can benefit by drawing together some conclusions about the role of government in resource allocation. These are principles of microeconomic policy. You have met most of them before. We shall begin by reviewing the nature of the microeconomic goals of efficiency and equity, the case for *laissez-faire*, and the causes of market failure. We then consider the methods of state intervention and close the chapter with a review of the causes of government failure.

You should not expect us to conclude that unfettered markets are invariably preferable to alternative methods of resource allocation. All methods have their advantages and disadvantages – which is why mixed economies are so widespread. Most economists feel that each situation should be decided on its merits. We illustrate with a number of case studies, presented in the usual boxes.

THE GOALS OF MICROECONOMIC POLICY

Government economic policy on resource allocation pursues two goals – efficiency and equity (or fairness).[2] We shall be concerned rather more with the former than with the latter, not because efficiency is the more important or urgent goal, but because positive economics has more to say on efficiency, and inefficiency, than it has on equity, where normative judgements cannot be avoided and where useful policy conclusions often call for personal opinions.

The Goal of Efficiency

In Chapter 9, we first defined an efficient allocation of resources as obtaining whenever it is not possible to make any one person better off without making at least one other person worse off. Such an allocation we described as 'optimal' (or 'Pareto optimal'). We should also remind you that full economic efficiency has two components – productive efficiency and allocative efficiency.

Productive efficiency obtains when it is not possible to produce more of any one good without producing less of

any other good. Allocative efficiency involves choosing between productively efficient bundles. It obtains when it is not possible to produce a combination of goods different from that currently being produced, which will allow any one person to be made better off without making at least one other person worse off.

Optimum allocation of resources

We can illustrate diagrammatically the conditions for the achievement of full economic efficiency. Consider Figure 21.1, which shows a production possibility curve, similar to that in Figure 1.2 in Chapter 1, together with two indifference curves. These are similar to the indifference curves of the diagrams in Chapter 11, and represent levels of satisfaction from the consumption of jeans and kebabs by consumers, all of whom we assume, for the purpose of argument, have identical tastes.[1]

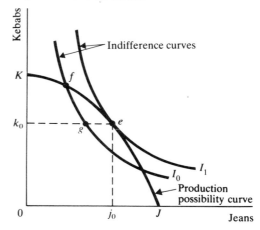

FIGURE 21.1 Economic Efficiency. Productive efficiency obtains at all points on KJ. Full economic (including allocative) efficiency obtains only at e, where the slope of the production possibility curve equals that of the indifference curve I_1.

Consider, first, productive efficiency, which is straightforward to identify. All combinations of the two goods which lie on the production possibility curve are efficient in this sense – it is not possible to produce more of either good without producing less of the other.

Next, consider allocative efficiency. This occurs at point

1 For more detail on the background to many applied economic problems in the UK, see C. Harbury and R.G. Lipsey, *An Introduction to the UK Economy*.

2 These are, of course, the microeconomic goals. The macroeconomic goals are considered in Parts 4 and 5. Although treated separately, for convenience, there is considerable overlap among them – for example, between the macroeconomic goal of economic growth and the micro-economic goal of efficiency.

1 The assumption of identical tastes is purely illustrative, and not necessary for the conclusions reached in the text about what is known as welfare economics, a subject whose detailed exposition is for intermediate rather than introductory courses in economics. More advanced treatments make use of so-called 'community indifference curves' for similar purposes.

e on the production possibility curve which is tangent to the higher indifference curve I_1. The combination of k_0 kebabs and j_0 jeans produced is that which gives the highest attainable level of satisfaction to consumers. Compare it, for example, with point *f*, which also lies on the production possibility curve. The indifference curve which passes through *f* is I_0, which represents a lower level of satisfaction than I_1. Thus, the combination at *e* is preferable to that at *f*, as it is to every other attainable point on the graph.

Note, too, that at *e* the marginal cost of kebabs in terms of jeans sacrificed, given by the slope of the production possibility curve, is equal to the marginal rate of substitution of kebabs in terms of jeans, given by the slope of the indifference curve. In other words, at *e* the benefit to consumers of an extra kebab is equal to the extra cost of producing it. There is no other point in the diagram where this is true. Resource allocation is efficient, or optimal.

Economic efficiency and market forces

We know that both productive and allocative efficiency can result from the operation of market forces, without state intervention. The case for *laissez-faire* has been stated more than once in this book. We refer you back to our exposition in Chapter 9 which laid out the argument for markets where buyers and sellers are price-takers, modified for when some traders are price-makers in Chapter 17. We shall not restate yet again the case for *laissez-faire*. Instead, we list for you a summary of the conditions under which the free working of market forces would lead to an efficient allocation of resources. They are:

1 Buyers and sellers are price-takers.
2 Buyers seek to maximize satisfaction and sellers to maximize profits.
3 There are no public goods, no goods with externalities, no merit or demerit goods.
4 There are no problems arising from information deficiencies, or from dynamic considerations.

The satisfaction of all four sets of conditions listed above ensures that, at the margin, the satisfaction attained by

the production of the last unit of each commodity is equal to the real opportunity cost of producing it.[1]

You will, hopefully, recognize the conditions in items 3 and 4 on the list as causes of market failure when they are not fulfilled. We shall return to them shortly, and to an omission you may have noticed from the list – income distribution. These matters are central to the question of state intervention in the market. First, however, we have an important qualification to make about the conditions for the achievement of economic efficiency.

Optimum allocation of resources and the 'second best'

The conclusion that resources are optimally allocated when marginal cost is equal to marginal utility is correct if, and only if, such equality obtains throughout the entire economy. It is not valid if there are some sectors where marginal cost differs from marginal utility.

To demonstrate this proposition, we assume that at least one sector of the economy is producing optimally while another is, for some reason, not. Any reason would suffice, but let us assume a two-industry world, with one industry (toys) operating under conditions of perfect competition, and the other (films) run by a profit-maximizing monopolist. The argument is illustrated in Figure 21.2. The monopolist (equating MC with MR) would choose to produce q_c films (in the left-hand section of the diagram). Perfectly competitive firms produce q_c toys (in the right-hand section of the diagram). How efficient is resource allocation?

The answer is clearly not efficient, in films. Marginal utility exceeds marginal cost under monopoly; output is suboptimal. But what about the toy industry, where $MU = MC$. On the face of it, that sounds optimal.

---

1 In our familiar symbols, this ensures that the ratios $MC_x/MC_y = MU_x/MU_y$, etc. for all pairs of commodities. This way of expressing the conditions for economic efficiency is an alternative to that of the previous section, which ran in terms of the slopes of production possibility curves and indifference curves.

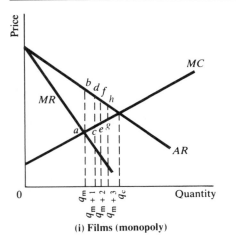

(i) Films (monopoly)

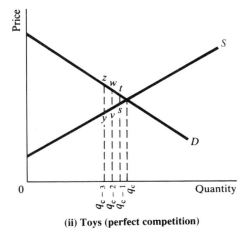

(ii) Toys (perfect competition)

FIGURE 21.2 Second-Best Allocations. If optimum output does not obtain in all markets, it should obtain in none. First best allocation would be (q_c toys + q_c films), but (q_{c-2} toys + q_{m+2} films) is less inefficient than (q_c toys + q_m films).

The superficial answer is, however, the wrong one. Toy output is 'superoptimal', inefficiently large relative to film output. To show this, imagine resources being gradually transferred from toy to film production. As this commences, toy output falls from q_c to q_{c-1}, while film output increases from q_m to q_{m+1}.

Look at the relationship between marginal utility and marginal cost in the two industries. In films, MU is still greater than MC, but the difference has fallen – from the vertical distance $b-a$, to $d-c$. Now, look at the toy industry, where output has fallen to q_{c-1}, resulting in an excess of MU over MC, equal to the vertical distance $t-s$. However the *net* loss ($\Delta MU - \Delta MC$) in toys ($t-s$) is less than the net gain ($\Delta MU - \Delta MC$) in films ($d-c$). The transfer has improved efficiency in resource allocation, by adding more to utility than to cost, measured of course in opportunity cost terms.

The conclusion from this example is that resource allocation is not optimal just because marginal utility equals marginal cost in one industry, unless both are equal in all industries.

This result is an aspect of what is called the THEORY OF THE SECOND BEST.[1] Its implications are considerable, and are not confined to resource (mis-) allocations which are due to monopoly. Any departure from perfectly competitive output, for any reason and in any sectors of the economy, has a similar 'distorting' effect on the most efficient allocations in all sectors.

Indeed, one of the prime causes of such departures are certain activities of the government itself. When the state imposes an output-related tax (or subsidy) on an industry,

---

1 The general rule for such transfers (the proof of which is beyond the scope of this book) is that MUs should stand in the same proportion to MCs in all sectors.

this, normally, results in a change in profit-maximizing output. (See Chapter 10, pp.96–7.) If output without the tax is perfectly competitive, the tax may well be described as 'distorting'.

The implications of the theory of the second best for economic policy can be important. For example, suppose a certain sum is to be raised by taxation. In order to decide how evenly or unevenly to spread the tax burden, the government should have regard to the state of resource allocation in the economy. If resource allocation is close to optimal, it follows that the taxes should be spread evenly. However, if it is known that resource allocation is inefficient, because of competition in some sectors and monopolies in others, it would be better to levy unequal taxes – in order to offset existing distortions.

The Goal of Equity

After that diversion into the theory of the second best, we return to our review of the goals of microeconomic policy. Consider now the second goal – equity, or fairness. There is less to be said about it than about efficiency. However, we remind you of some major conclusions that we drew earlier:

1 Given the distribution of income, there is an advantage in avoiding an inefficient allocation, because everyone can be made better off by moving to an efficient allocation.

2 The collection of resources produced in a market economy depends on the distribution of income and wealth among members of the population. A society with a very unequal distribution of income is unlikely to produce the same collection of goods and services as a society with a more equal distribution.

3 It is not possible to say that one allocation is preferable to another without implying that one distribution of

---

BOX 21.1 Pay-As-You-Drive Trial for City

'Cambridge has been offered as host city for a pilot project on road pricing, a traffic control policy which John Major has put back on the Downing Street agenda.

'Under the Cambridge plan, the council would fit meters, free of charge, to all local cars. Drivers would buy cards, like phone cards, to feed them. Roadside beacons would activate the meters by microwave when the car was being driven in the city centre, with credits being deducted only in heavy traffic. Drivers who ran out of credits would have what they owed recorded on their meters. They would not be allowed into the city centre again until they had bought a new card, from which the debt would be automatically deducted. Daily passes would be available for visitors.'

(*The Independent on Sunday*, 7 April 1991)

New technology is responsible for the Cambridge plan – a new alternative for the UK for the control of traffic congestion. It falls into the category of government policies using the price mechanism, mentioned in the chapter, and is a good example of tax-targeting. In Singapore a comparable system introduced in 1975 is said to have led to a 44 per cent reduction in traffic and a 22 per cent increase in vehicle speeds. It was not, however, electronic. Drivers pay a fee of £1.75 per day or £33 per month for a sticker allowing them into the city centre.

Questions

1 What is, or are, the main cause(s) of market failure that motivate the plan in the news item?

2 What alternative policies are, or might be, used to the same end? Compare them with the Cambridge plan.

3 How would you decide the level to set for the daily visitor's card?

income is, at the same time, preferable to another distribution, both of which statements would be normative and necessarily based on personal value judgements.

4 The goals of equity and efficiency may be related, when a trade-off exists between them. For example, if income redistribution affects efficiency, then taxing certain groups in order to benefit other groups influences the total output available for distribution.

There is one further general point to make about equity and income distribution. There are two aspects of equity – known as horizontal and vertical. HORIZONTAL EQUITY is concerned with giving the same treatment to persons who are, in some major respects, equals – for example, allowing identical treatment for eligibility for state benefits of men and women. VERTICAL EQUITY is concerned with giving different treatment to persons who are recognized as unequals – for example, taxing the rich more heavily than the poor.

MARKET FAILURE

Our final topic for review is of market failure – the reasons why markets can lead to non-optimal allocations of resources. We referred earlier to the causes of market failure as being, implicitly, the absence of one or more of a list of conditions for a market system to work efficiently. They were also described at some length, in Chapters 2 and 9 – for markets where traders are price-takers – and in Chapter 16 – for imperfect markets. Here they are, all together for the first time.

Public goods: Public goods are those which are consumed collectively, being non-rival and non-excludable. Individual consumers cannot be forced to pay for them, hence producers will not offer them for sale. The basic problem with the provision of public goods is that of deciding on the optimum level of their supply. It is exacerbated by what is known as the 'free-rider' problem. In response to government questioning as to how much people would be prepared to pay for a public good, it is in the interest of individuals to understate the sums they would pay, if they think that they will be charged appropriately and that the total responses will be sufficient for the good to be supplied anyway. Each person realizes that if someone else pays for the army, for example, he or she will 'free-ride' – i.e. also benefit from its provision. Hence no one is willing to pay. It has to be provided by the community.

There is one technical point to add. Goods with the above characteristics are sometimes referred to as 'pure' public goods. Others goods may have more or less of an element of 'publicness' about them. One example is provided by television programmes, which are completely non-rival (there is no less of *Coronation Street* for you to watch when your neighbour switches on too), but *not* completely non-excludable, because broadcasts can be scrambled, with unscrambling (pay-as-you-view) devices sold for those who want to watch them.

Merit and demerit goods: Merit and demerit goods occur where individuals are said to be unaware of the true benefits and detriments that follow consumption. Market forces tend to supply too few merit goods, such as preventive medical care, and too many demerit goods, such as addictive drugs. Overriding market allocations in the cases of merit and demerit goods, implies the acceptance of a paternalistic attitude, that the state can better decide than can individuals how they should spend their money.

Externalities: Externalities (positive and negative) exist when private costs and benefits are greater or less than social costs or benefits involved in the production or consumption of particular commodities. Examples of negative externalities are the costs imposed by congestion on roads or by pollution. Examples of positive externalities are education and health, where benefits are more widely spread than among direct users (consumers). The market mechanism, responding to the private costs and benefits, tends to underprovide where there are positive externalities, or overprovide where there are negative externalities, relative to optimal social outputs. Refer back to Figure 9.4, for illustrations of the way in which differences between social and private costs (and benefits) lead to inefficient market allocations.

BOX 21.2 Only the Taxman can Outgun Saddam

'This week the price of oil has risen yet again. Since Saddam Hussein invaded Kuwait, it has gone up by over 15 per cent. It is tempting to claim that higher petrol prices could do more for the environment than the [350] measures in Chris Patten's environment white paper put together. They would if they were permanent. The trouble is that the oil price fluctuates too much to influence people's long-term behaviour.

'To reduce carbon dioxide emissions, what is needed is a permanent increase in the price of energy. Permanently higher petrol prices and electricity prices are an essential component of any serious attempt to tackle global warming.'

(Dieter Helm, *The Times*, 27 September 1990)

The article raises a number of points relevant to state intervention in the allocation of resources.

Questions

1 Can you identify one or more goals for intervention?
2 Can you suggest at least two methods by which the government could try to achieve the goal, or goals, you identified in question 1?
3 Can you argue against the intervention in this case?

Imperfect competition: Imperfect competition may be a cause of market failure if it leads to allocative and/or productive inefficiency as was explained in Chapter 16. Allocative inefficiency arises when profit-maximizing price-makers (e.g. monopolists) restrict output in order to raise price, resulting in equilibrium where marginal cost is less than marginal utility.

Productive inefficiency occurs when competition is imperfect – for example, as a result of managerial slack, otherwise referred to as X-inefficiency. When this happens, businesses fail to minimize costs, with the implication that firms are not profit-maximizing. Note, however, that perfectly competitive output may be unattainable if costs fall over the entire range of relevant output – the case of so-called natural monopoly, which causes difficult policy problems (see below).

Other market shortcomings: Other shortcomings which can impede efficiency include (1) imperfect information about prices and qualities of commodities, (2) dynamic considerations – i.e. the way that markets behave over time. As to (i), accurate and complete information about costs and benefits of different commodities must be available if maximization assumptions are to be meaningful on both sides of the market. As far as dynamic considerations are concerned, some markets may be sluggish, i.e. slow to clear, while others may be excessively volatile, especially when demand and/or supply is determined by *expectations* of future prices rather than by current market price (e.g. the cobweb theorem).

THE METHODS OF STATE INTERVENTION

If there is reason to believe that market allocations are inefficient and/or inequitable, then a case exists for considering government intervention. This does not imply that the state must intervene. Government inefficiency has also to be taken into the reckoning (see below, pp.236–7). Each case should be considered on its merits.

There are dozens of methods available to a government seeking to intervene in the allocation of resources. There are also several ways of classifying them. One classification which fits economic theory is based on a threefold division into:

(1) Policies using the market system
(2) Policies improving the market system
(3) Extra-market policies

Policies using the market system

Policies using the market system seek to change the

BOX 21.3 Taking Work to the Workers or Workers to the Work?

'The stated objectives of UK regional policy have remained broadly unchanged since at least the 1960s. Most recently the 1983 White Paper gave the objective of policy as of 'reducing on a stable long-term basis regional imbalances in employment opportunities', and this was reaffirmed in the 1988 White Paper. These objectives have generally been couched in fairly vague terms, although it can be observed that policy interventions have usually sought to create employment in designated areas in order to reduce the relatively high unemployment levels which help define these areas.

'Traditionally, regional policy was predicated on "taking the jobs to the workers", and in the 1960s job diversion was the major aim of policy. However, the flow of mobile industry began to dry up in the 1970s. . . . By 1988, revisions were of a radical nature, with a shift away from the direct subsidization of employment, towards employment creation through the "strengthening" of firms. Thus, Regional Selective Assistance (RSA) with its emphasis on efficiency was set to become the mainstay of regional policy, and specific schemes were introduced to encourage innovation and improve operating efficiency.'

(Colin Wren, 'Regional Policy in the 1980s', *National Westminster Bank Quarterly Review*, November 1990)

The incidence of unemployment varies greatly from one region in the UK to another. In January 1991 (by no means an untypical time) unemployment rates were 6 per cent in the south of England, $9\frac{1}{2}$ to 10 per cent in Wales and Scotland, 11 per cent in northern England, and 16 per cent in Northern Ireland. Rates in some narrowly defined districts were much higher than any of these. Many interventionist techniques have been tried in regional policy over the years, including the withholding of licences for factory construction, regional employment premium (a kind of negative poll tax), subsidies and grants, and the provision of infrastructure in the form of housing and social capital. Yet the effectiveness of regional policy is regarded as quite weak by most observers, without even counting the costs.

Questions

1 How many microeconomic policy goals can you identify associated with regional policy?
2 What are the costs, mentioned in the last sentence of our comment, that should be included in an assessment of regional policy?
3 Compare the relative merits of policies (i) to help the unemployed move to where there are job vacancies, (ii) to assist industry to move to where there are unemployed workers.

price signals that influence buyers and sellers in order to alter their behaviour.

For example, output-related taxes can reduce production, or consumption, of a commodity. Output-related subsidies can increase them. We saw examples of these policies in Chapter 16, where they were designed to persuade a monopolist to produce optimum output (see Figure 16.6). A second example of the use of taxes or subsidies could be to deal with externalities. In Figure 9.4, we showed how optimal output can follow the use of output-related taxes (and subsidies) which shift private benefit, and/or cost, curves so that they reflect full social and private values, if the two diverge. A third example could be taxes on imports, used to protect an industry from foreign competition (see Figure 20.4).

Policies improving the market system

Policies improving the market system are designed to change the structure of markets to help them function more efficiently.

A prime example is the set of so-called competition policies, described in Chapter 17, laying down rules governing monopolies, mergers and restrictive practices. Other examples include actions aimed at the removal or lowering of barriers to mobility in goods and factor markets – e.g. reductions of tariffs and other trade restrictions, or 'deregulation' measures such as those which hit at monopoly powers of solicitors on the legal transferring of residential property, and of the Post Office on delivery of certain kinds of mail.

Extra-market policies

Extra-market policies work not through the price mechanism, but outside it. One example we noted earlier is the setting of import quotas (see Figure 20.4). Another is the central planning of output of public goods, such as the administration of justice, where the government decides on the quantity and quality of provision. Note, however, that nationalization, the transfer of an industry from private to public ownership, does not necessarily fall into this category, since the price mechanism not only can be, but usually has been, used to some extent to determine resource allocations by the major nationalized industries in the UK.

Policy Instruments

In putting its policies into effect, the government has to choose between two kinds of policy instruments – (i) budgetary policies and (ii) non-budgetary policies.

Budgetary Policies

A major source of government power over the economy lies in what is known as the Budget, which is presented annually to Parliament by the Chancellor of the Exchequer.

The budget contains details of the sources of state income and planned expenditure for the coming year. Taxes, subsidies, etc., can be used in pursuit of microeconomic goals. The main categories are listed in Table 21.1.

Government income

The left-hand side of the Table lists sources of income. About half the total are taxes on incomes of persons and of corporations (on their profits), known as DIRECT TAXES. Included among them are national insurance contributions, paid by employers and employees, and Capital Gains Tax, which is levied on certain increases in the value of assets which accrue during the year.

The second major group of taxes are those levied on expenditure, known as INDIRECT TAXES. They include VAT (Value Added Tax)[1] on the value added on sales of goods and services (other than foods and certain other exceptions), excise duties on petrol, alcoholic drink and tobacco, and customs duties on imported goods.

TABLE 21.1 Government and Expenditure

Income	Expenditure
TAXES	TRANSFER EXPENDITURES
Direct taxes:	Pensions
Income Tax	Social Security benefits
Capital Gains Tax	National Debt interest
Corporation Tax	
National Insurance	EXHAUSTIVE EXPENDITURES
contributions	Education
	Health
Indirect taxes:	Industry
Value Added Tax	Environment
Excise duties	Misc. (law and order etc.)
Customs duties	
Other taxes:	NATIONAL DEBT REPAYMENT
Inheritance Tax	
Community Charge	
BORROWING	

The third category of taxes are not of major importance in revenue terms, though the Community Charge, or 'poll tax', caused a greater furore than any tax in living memory (its abolition was announced within weeks of these lines being written). Inheritance tax is the latest in a long line of taxes, going back 100 years, on personal wealth, as distinct from personal income.

Finally, note from Table 21.1 that taxes are not the only source of government revenue. The state can also borrow, which it does by selling securities offering a fixed, guaranteed rate of interest. This gives rise to some important problems. The total of all past borrowings by the state is known as the NATIONAL DEBT. Additions to the Debt occur when the so-called PBSR (Public Sector Borrowing Requirement) is positive. When the government reduces the Debt, the PSBR is negative, and is called the PSDR (Public Sector Debt Repayment). The PSBR (and PSDR) are important instruments of macroeconomic policy, as you will study in Parts 4 and 5 of the book.

---

1 See p.258 for an explanation of the term 'value added'.

The role of taxes

Taxes are major instruments of economic policy. We have considered their effects in several places already but there remain some further important aspects to discuss.

A convenient way to introduce the following ideas is to ask a simple question – what constitutes a good tax? Simple questions in economics rarely have simple answers, and this one is no exception. It does, however, concentrate the mind on a subsidiary and easier question – what criteria should one use to assess the quality of a particular tax?

Two centuries ago, the groundwork for tax assessment was laid by Adam Smith (originator of the 'invisible hand' you remember), who set out four criteria, which he called 'Maxims' (but which are more commonly called 'Canons') of taxation. They are remarkably relevant today. In Smith's own words (taken from *The Wealth of Nations*):[1]

1 *The subjects of every state ought to contribute towards the support of government, as nearly as possible, in proportion to their respective abilities.*
2 *The tax which every individual is bound to pay, ought to be certain and not arbitrary.*
3 *Every tax ought to be levied at the time, or in the manner, in which it is most likely to be convenient for the contributor to pay it*
4 *Every tax ought to be so contrived, as both to take out and to keep out of the pockets of the people as little as possible, over and above what it brings in to the public treasury of the state.*

Smith's four maxims are often dubbed *Equity, Certainty, Convenience and Economy*. They provide an excellent basis for tax assessment. However, modern economists would be inclined to amplify, qualify and extend them in a number of ways, which are conveniently considered under our twin microeconomic goals of efficiency and equity.

Tax efficiency: Amplifying Smith's goal of economy in taxation, one would nowadays add that a good tax should

---

1 Adam Smith, *The Wealth of Nations* (1776), Book V, Chapter II, Part II.

BOX 21.4

'In the understatement of the decade Michael Heseltine told the Commons that the public had not been persuaded that the community charge was fair.'

(*The Times*, 22 March 1991)

'The replacement of the old domestic rates by the community charge or poll tax has been an economic and, so far, a political blunder. Apart from rebates and charges on owners of second homes, it stands accused of being unrelated to ability to pay: a dustman pays as much as a duke. This violates one of the most important maxims of Adam Smith, Margaret Thatcher's favourite dead economist. Indeed, Adam Smith specifically attacked such "capitation taxes" and specifically praised taxes on ground rents. ... Smith would have been horrified by the poll tax's collection cost.'

(John Muellbauer (Official Fellow, Nuffield College, Oxford), *The Independent on Sunday*, 2 September 1990)

'As I have travelled the country, I have found widespread acceptance of the principle of the Community Charge.'

(Chris Patten, then Environment Secretary, April 1990)

'It will be seen to be a very much fairer system of paying towards the cost of local government than was the old rating system.'

(John Major, then Chancellor of the Exchequer, April 1990)

'The poll tax was a grave error of judgment.'

(Nigel Lawson, ex-Chancellor of the Exchequer, November 1990)

'I have always opposed the poll tax. It is a very unfair tax and a very costly tax to collect.'

(Edward Heath, ex-Prime Minister, February 1990)

The Community Charge (official title and used by supporters) or poll tax (name used by opponents) was introduced as a substitute for 'rates' levied by local authorities on the (rental) values of properties in their areas. Unlike the Community Charge, rates were, to an extent, related to ability to pay. Owners of expensive houses paid more than owners of cheap flats. However, the association between rateable value and income – the most commonly quoted measure of ability to pay – was not as close as many people would have liked. For example, rates bear heavily on elderly pensioners remaining in their old homes but with small cash incomes.

Questions

1 Compare the taxes mentioned in Muellbauer's article by the criteria for a good tax mentioned in the text.
2 Is there any sense in which the concept of economic rent is relevant to the rates issue?
3 At the time of writing, the government had just announced the replacement source of revenue for local government is to be a form of property tax. How does it compare to the Community Charge?

have low *direct* administrative costs, i.e. those incurred by the state (including costs of 'policing' to minimize tax evasion) and low *indirect*, or COMPLIANCE costs, incurred by taxpayers. Putting part of the administrative burden of tax collection on taxpayers, as with the VAT, merely transfers it from the public to the private sector. Complex taxes with multiple tax rates and exemptions tend to be administratively costly. Moreover, *flexibility* is probably a desirable tax quality. Some taxes even change *automatically* in the desired direction. An example is the income tax, which rises as income rises.

A good tax should also be well *targeted* towards its objective. For example, we have identified subsidiary policy goals in connection with various causes of market failure. Hence, an efficient tax for the removal of an externality, e.g. designed to control pollution, would succeed in doing just that. If the pollution were related to the volume of factory output, for instance, a well-targeted tax would be output-related, so that the incentive to reduce the amount of pollution was directly related to the tax burden.

Such a tax would be more efficient than a tax on the profits of a polluter, who might pollute no less. If a polluting firm was using the lowest cost methods of production before the tax, there is no reason why it should not continue to do so, being left merely with lower profits. We might remind ourselves in this connection that the effectiveness of an output-related tax is dependent on the elasticity of supply and demand for the taxed commodity (see Chapter 10, page 98).

The points mentioned above in this section may be regarded as elaborations of the four maxims of Adam Smith. Rather different is the idea, sometimes put forward, that a tax should cause minimum distortion in the allocation of resources, or be *neutral* in its incidence. This quality is desirable sometimes, but not always. It will be desirable if the object of the tax is simply to raise revenue in order to create a budget surplus (e.g. to control inflation), and if resource allocation is otherwise efficient. However, 'distortion' can be a tax objective – as, in the example of the previous paragraph, to reduce pollution. Additionally, a tax may be designed to balance existing distortions in other sectors of the economy, as suggested by the theory of the second best, earlier in this chapter.

Tax equity: Taxes are sometimes imposed to redistribute income or wealth. Even when the prime tax objective is other than this, it is virtually inevitable that some redistribution will follow its introduction, its reduction, or its abolition.

The two dimensions of equity mentioned earlier are relevant to tax assessment – vertical and horizontal equity. Adam Smith's first tax maxim – that taxes should be proportional to ability to pay – is a fair starting point. However, it does not really take us far enough, nor is it necessarily and universally acceptable – though this whole question unavoidably brings in personal value judgements. Should people be taxed in proportion to their ability to pay, as Smith suggested? Some might agree. Others might argue that people should be taxed *more than proportionately*; others *less than proportionately*.

The commonest measure used of ability to pay is income. This is a fairly rough and sometimes imperfect measure, but it allows us to divide taxes into three classes – proportional, progressive and regressive.

PROGRESSIVE taxes absorb higher proportions of income as income rises. REGRESSIVE taxes are the opposite of progressive; they take lower proportions of income as income rises. PROPORTIONAL taxes are the intermediate case, where tax payments rise in proportion to rises in income.

To illustrate, consider a person paying £1000 tax on an income of £10,000. Suppose their income rises to £11,000, and, under three tax regimes, their tax liability was (i) £1200, (ii) £1050, and (iii) £1100. We would decribe the taxes to be (i) progressive, (ii) regressive and (iii) proportional.

Progressivity of a tax is defined in terms of the AVERAGE TAX RATE (ATR), tax paid/income, which must be distinguished from the MARGINAL TAX RATE (MTR), defined as the change in tax paid/change in income. Figure 21.3 displays the relationship between income and tax payments in five cases. The ATR and MTR are measured in a manner similar to other average and marginal values with which we are now familiar. Thus, ATR at income y is the same (t/y) for the three curves which intersect at point a. MTR is given by the slope of the curve.

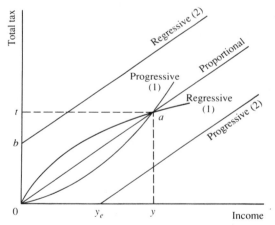

FIGURE 21.3 The Relationship between Taxation and Income. A tax is progressive, proportional, or regressive depending on whether the proportion of income paid in tax (ATR) rises, is constant, or falls as income increases.

The easiest tax to understand is the proportional tax – any straight line going through the origin of the graph, when the slope of the line gives ATR as well as MTR. In the diagram both are 50 per cent.

There are two progressive taxes in Figure 21.3. One is a curve (marked Progressive 1) which shows both ATR and MTR rising with income. The other progressive tax (marked Progressive 2) has the same slope as the proportional tax, i.e. it also has an MTR of 50 per cent. However, the tax is still progressive because ATR rises with income. This is due to the fact that there is a threshold, or exemption limit – a minimum income, y_e, below which no tax is paid. Hence, ATR is zero until income exceeds y_e, after which, MTR is constant at 50 per cent. Thus, half of every increase in income goes in tax, pushing up ATR.

There are two regressive taxes in the diagram. Again one is a curve (marked Regressive 1). As income rises, the slope of the curve decreases, showing a declining ratio of tax to income, so that ATR also falls as income rises. The other regressive tax (marked Regressive 2) has the same slope as the proportional tax (i.e. MTR is also 50 per cent). The regressivity is due to the fact that there is a minimum tax that is levied, b, regardless of income, indeed even if income is zero. As income rises, the total tax burden falls as a proportion of income – the tax is regressive.

It is a useful exercise to classify particular UK taxes according to their progressivity or otherwise. We recommend you to try it. To start you off, (1) the income tax is progressive – rather mildly so compared to income taxes in other countries which have rising marginal tax rates. The UK income tax is levied at only two rates (1991) but 95 per cent of taxpayers pay only at the lower 'standard' rate. Progressivity stems mainly from the exemptions, which cause the ATR to rise with income. (2) Any poll tax, defined as an equal absolute tax per head of the population, is regressive. Hence the Community Charge is/was a regressive tax, though its regressivity was moderated by exemptions for some of the poor. (3) VAT is rather different. Tax paid is approximately proportional to *expenditure* rather than to income (again because of exemptions of certain commodities, outstandingly food, bought by low income groups). However, since the proportion of income spent, rather than saved, tends to be greater for low than for high income groups, VAT is, probably, a mildly regressive tax. Go ahead and try to classify some other taxes. Don't be disappointed if you find it tricky. It is! But the exercise is a good one.

A final and rather different equitable tax principle is that taxes should be based on what is called the 'benefit principle'. The idea is one of relating taxes directly to benefits derived by taxpayers from uses to which tax proceeds are put. For example, a tax imposed specifically for road maintenance might, arguably, be levied on road users. The benefit principle can be used as a substitute for the market system with public goods, which cannot be sold in the market. The applicability of the benefit principle is clearly limited. It conflicts, as a rule, with the principle of ability to pay, and it is clearly irrelevant to taxes deliberately targeted at income redistribution.

Goal conflicts in taxation: Most taxes have multiple effects. Consequently, choosing one for a particular purpose may well involve priorities. The commonest conflict that is usually discussed among tax goals is between efficiency and equity. It arises because of the possible disincentive effects of taxes designed to redistribute income more equally.

Equity versus efficiency in taxation: The effect of tax-rate changes can be analysed in a fashion similar to that for the effect of wage-rate changes. Incentive effects of a tax are related to marginal tax rates. The higher the tax rate, the lower the *net* reward from time spent working, and the stronger the incentive for an individual to substitute leisure for work. However, you may remember that the effect of a fall in the price of labour would include an income effect and a substitution effect, which would pull in opposite directions (see above, pp.190–91). We suggested that the supply curve of labour might contain a backward-sloping section, so that a fall in the *net* wage rate (such as would follow a rise in the marginal tax rate) could lead to a rise, or to a fall, in the amount of work done. The evidence is controversial, despite a great deal of research.

The imposition of an income tax effectively lowers the net return from working, causing a disincentive, substitution, effect (which will be greater, the steeper the marginal tax rate). Whether it is larger or smaller than the income effect cannot be stated, generally, on the evidence.

The poverty trap: One area where the disincentive effects of taxation have received particular attention is at very low incomes, when tax eligibility begins, i.e. when income reaches the top of the range of the personal allowance (below which no tax is payable).

It happens that some of the poorest members of the community with incomes at this level, are also in receipt of social security benefits. As soon as their income rises, this can both take them into the range of tax eligibility, and lead to the loss of social security benefits. In such cases, the effective marginal tax rate, calculated to include loss of state benefit, is greater than the standard rate of income tax. People in such a position can be literally worse off as a result of a rise in income. Their marginal tax rate (including loss of benefit) can, rather startlingly, even exceed 100 per cent. They are said to be caught in what is called the 'poverty trap'.

A negative income tax (NIT): A negative income tax was proposed some years ago, as a way of avoiding the poverty trap while increasing work incentives. The idea of NIT is that individuals with incomes below a predetermined and 'guaranteed' minimum receive a payment from the government – the level being related to income. Table 21.2 below gives an illustration of how a NIT might work, on the assumptions that (i) the guaranteed minimum was fixed at £5000 and (ii) the tax rate was 50 per cent on incomes between £5000 and the breakeven level where income is neither taxed nor supplemented.

TABLE 21.2 An Illustration of a Negative Income Tax (£s)

Earned income (i)	Welfare receipts* [5,000 – 50%(i)] (ii)	Total income [(i) + (iii)] (iii)
0	5,000	5,000
2,000	4,000	6,000
4,000	3,000	7,000
6,000	2,000	8,000
10,000	0	10,000

*Welfare payments reduced by 50 per cent of earnings.

Thus, under NIT, there is no *sudden* rise in the tax rate, which is associated with the poverty trap. As far as incentives are concerned there are two, conflicting, considerations.

For individuals with incomes above the guaranteed minimum, but in receipt of supplementation, work incentives are increased, since they retain half of their earnings. However, for individuals with incomes in the range between the minimum and the level at which welfare receipts become zero (£10,000 in the example), work incentives may decline. This is true for persons not previously liable to tax, but who pay, under NIT, at the 50 per cent rate.

Experiments with real NITs in the USA suggest that their net disincentive effects are likely to be small, though positive. For these reasons as well as others to do with costs of administration and political issues, there is no strong lobby in favour of the negative income tax at the present time in the UK.

Disincentive effects of taxation are not restricted to the supply of labour. We should be on the lookout for any tax disincentive effects – e.g. of income tax on saving; of profits tax on risk-taking. It has even been suggested that there is a maximum level of TAXABLE CAPACITY, such that attempts by the state to exceed it would be counter-productive. This notion received a new lease of life a few years ago, when it became fashionable to refer to a 'Laffer Curve', after the American economist, Arthur Laffer, who claimed to have discovered a relationship between tax rates and government revenue from taxation, such that a cut in tax rates would stimulate the supply of effort and raise national income to such an extent that tax revenue would be greater at the lower level of tax rates.

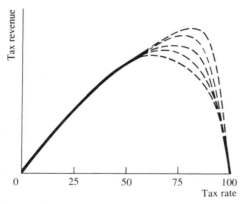

FIGURE 21.4 Laffer Curves, showing relationships between tax rates and total government revenue from taxation. As tax rates rise from zero to 100 per cent, tax revenue first rises and then falls. The curves are dotted because of doubts about where the curve peaks.

It is not in dispute that there must be some point at which the tax rate has this effect. 100 per cent tax rates eliminate any income to tax. However, there is no consensus on the tax level at which the 'Laffer Curve' peaks. That is why in Figure 21.4, we have drawn several dotted lines joining established positive associations between tax

rates and tax revenues and the ultimate certainty of zero tax revenue from 100 per cent tax. Whether the levels of taxation in the USA, to which the Laffer Curve was first applied, or in the UK, are at or anywhere near these levels is a controversial question – though most economists do not think that they are.

Government expenditure

Returning to Table 21.1 on p.228, we now consider the expenditure side of the government's account. There are two categories here – transfers and exhaustive expenditures. TRANSFER PAYMENTS are one-sided transactions, including items such as retirement pensions and unemployment benefit. The state pays out without receiving anything in exchange. Recipients are free to allocate funds as they wish. EXHAUSTIVE EXPENDITURES, in contrast, are double-sided transactions, where the state acquires goods and services in exchange for the money it pays out. The state decides how its funds are to be used, e.g. for roads, education, health, etc.

Government expenditures can be directed at the goals of both efficiency and equity. Subsidies can be used, just like taxes, to 'correct' distortions in resource allocation due to any of the categories of market failure listed earlier – e.g. to control pollution, to supply merit goods, to influence output decisions of firms in imperfect competition.

Both transfers and exhaustive expenditures can redistribute income. They, too, can be categorized into progressive, proportional and regressive groups, in similar fashion to taxes, according to their importance relative to income.[1] With a few relatively minor exceptions (such as subsidies to the arts), the redistributive effect of the expenditure side of the government's account is substantially more egalitarian than is taxation.

For an appreciation of the extent of redistribution by state budgetary measures, we can look at the annual estimates of the Central Statistical Office. Figure 21.5 presents these for a recent year, making use of the technique of Lorenz curves, explained in Chapter 18 (see p.185). Two Lorenz curves are drawn in the diagram. The curve closer to the diagonal (or line of complete equality) is, of course, the one showing the income distribution inclusive of state benefits and net of taxes. In fact, the main beneficiaries of the tax-benefit system as a whole are the lowest income groups. Looking, for example, at the poorest 20 per cent of households, state cash benefits provided about three-quarters of their final income. From the graph itself, we can see that the share of total income of this poorest class rose from 2 per cent to $7\frac{1}{2}$ per cent of total income.

Non-Budgetary Policies

The policy instruments available to the government through the budget are extensive. We must not, however,

---

1 Note a technical difference. The term 'regressive' when applied to expenditure is usually taken to mean that receipts by lower income groups are proportionally greater than receipts by higher income groups, i.e. it is more egalitarian than progressive expenditures. With taxes, as we saw, regressive means more inegalitarian than progressive.

BOX 21.5 Income Inequality and Living Standards: Changes in the 1970s and 1980s

'This country has the highest standard of living that it has ever known. . . . Real incomes have increased throughout all income groups.'

(Margaret Thatcher)

'While the very rich have lost some of their riches to the less rich, over time, the poor have hardly profited proportionally.'

(Neil Kinnock)

Percentage Shares of Total Income

Decile group	1967 (%)	1978 (%)	1988 (%)
Bottom 10%	2.4	2.3	1.6
Second 10%	4.2	3.4	2.6
Third 10%	5.9	4.9	3.8
Fourth 10%	7.2	6.1	5.5
Fifth 10%	8.2	8.3	7.3
Sixth 10%	9.6	9.8	9.2
Seventh 10%	10.9	11.4	11.1
Eighth 10%	12.6	13.4	13.4
Ninth 10%	15.2	16.1	16.8
Top 10%	23.6	23.7	28.7
All	100.0	100.0	100.0

'Lorenz curves for the 1970s and the 1980s indicate that income distribution was more unequal in the mid- to late 1980s than in the early 1980s, and than in the early 1970s. But while inequality has increased, so too have average real incomes, with the gains most marked in the 1980s and amongst the rich; the poorest have gained little. It seems that, according to the data I have examined, there are senses in which both Mrs Thatcher and Mr Kinnock are correct.'

(Stephen P. Jenkins, *Fiscal Studies*, February 1991)

Jenkins's researches produced the table opposite as well as the extract taken from his conclusions. Note, a decile means 10 per cent of the population, i.e. the top decile refers to the group in the top 10 per cent.

Questions

1 Rank the decile groups in the following lists (i) by the percentage increase or decrease in their share of total income (a) for 1967–1978, (b) for 1978–1988; (ii) by the percentage increase, or decrease, in their real income in the same two periods as in (i). What correspondence, if any, do you find?
2 The text above suggests a possible trade-off between two goals of economic policy. What is it?
3 Why do you think Jenkins drew the conclusions that he did about trends in the distribution of income and in average living standards?

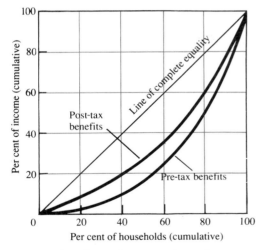

FIGURE 21.5 **The Effects of Taxes and Benefits on Household Income, UK, 1987.** The post-tax-benefit Lorenz curve lies closer to the line of complete equality than the pre-tax-benefit curve (for an explanation of Lorenz curves, refer back to Chapter 18). (Source: *Economic Trends*, May 1990).

ignore non-budgetary policy options, of which we discuss three: (1) rules and regulations, (2) cost-benefit analysis, and (3) state ownership.

Rules and regulations

We have already referred several times to rules and regulations. They can be used in a variety of ways for the pursuit of both efficiency and equity goals. Regulations can be directed at the improvement of resource allocation due to externalities. Examples are the introduction of smoke-free zones, and the requirement of drivers of motor vehicles to buy insurance for the benefit of 'innocent' third parties who suffer in accidents.

Some rules and regulations are directed at improving the market system, e.g. competition policy, and the lowering of barriers to international trade. Other rules operate in the area of merit and demerit goods – e.g. free vaccination against infectious diseases, and banning the sale of heroin. Regulations influence the distribution of income – e.g. laws prohibiting discrimination in employment on grounds of sex and ethnic origin.

One special set of rules is used where alternatives are unsatisfactory. This is the case of natural monopoly, where you may recall (see pp. 168–9 if you don't) that demand is not sufficient to support more than one efficient firm when unit costs of production fall over the entire range of output for which demand is positive. Not only does a single firm enjoy lower costs than any two or more firms, but a natural monopolist would make losses, not profits, if it produced optimum output (where $MC = MU$). The situation commonly affects public utilities, and applies for example to the operation of national grids supplying electricity.

One solution to the natural monopoly problem is for the state to own and operate the industry in the 'public interest'. A second solution is for the industry to be left in private hands, while a state regulatory body tries to ensure that it behaves in the public interest. The first solution was common in the early post-war years.

After 1980, this approach fell out of favour. The 'Thatcherite' Conservative governments of that decade preferred a policy of transferring to the private sector many nationalized industries, in a privatization programme (see below). However, the special natural-monopoly characteristics of some of these ex-nationalized industries led to the establishment of regulatory machinery at the time that they were sold to private enterprise. The regulatory bodies, such as OFTEL, OFGAS and OFWAT, were given certain powers over the telecommunication, gas and water industries, to try and ensure they were operated in the public interest. Regulation of public utilities can take many forms. Elsewhere in the world, controls have concentrated on levels of profit. In the UK, they have focused on prices rather than on profits, though the two are clearly interrelated. Regulation may extend also to other areas, including quality of service.

Note that rules may be *prescriptive*, laying down minimum quality standards, for instance, or *proscriptive*, banning pollution for example. An alternative division of rules distinguishes between *automatic* (or mandatory) and *discretionary*. An example of an automatic rule is the financial grant to students admitted to a first undergraduate degree course at university or polytechnic. Grants for postgraduate study, in contrast, are made at the discretion of awarding bodies.

Cost-benefit analysis

Government policy with regard to public goods, and to other goods with substantial divergencies between private and social costs or benefits, can be aided by a technique known as (social) COST-BENEFIT ANALYSIS. In the case of a private good, market forces determine the quantity supplied. In the case of (non-rival and non-excludable) public goods, and of others with significant externalities, market forces do not value in full all relevant costs and benefits. In such cases, the state may try to judge the optimal social quantity of the good that should be supplied. This is where cost-benefit analysis may come in.

Cost-benefit analysis is a method of calculating the present value of a stream of future social costs and benefits, i.e. those accruing indirectly as well as directly.

It can be applied in cases where social costs are believed to exceed private costs – e.g. environmental matters, involving acid rain, CFCs, atmospheric pollution from lead in petrol. Cost-benefit analysis is also applicable to cases where social benefits exceed private benefits – e.g. in education, health, the provision of public transport.

To illustrate, suppose the state is contemplating the construction of a motorway. It needs to assess the costs and benefits involved. Construction costs will be relatively straightforward to estimate. It is the benefits from the motorway that cause the greater problems. Two steps are necessary: (1) to identify all benefits, and (2) to value them. Identification means counting not only direct beneficiaries, who will use the new motorway, but also indirect beneficiaries, including users of other roads on which congestion is reduced. This step is often accomplished by taking traffic surveys.

The second step of valuing the benefits is, in this case especially, the more difficult one. Some benefits, such as savings in motoring costs due to more efficient use of vehicles, are relatively easy to value, as savings in petrol consumption, tyre wear, etc. Other benefits create more difficulties.

One of the major advantages of a bigger and better road network is time saving. The problem is of the value to place on the, maybe millions, of hours that are estimated would be saved by the new motorway. In practice, official cost-benefit analyses often use national average hourly wage rates for valuing time savings. This approach would be acceptable if time saved were used for additional work. However, many people have little freedom to vary the hours that they work. Hence the hours saved may be used for extra leisure, with the consequence that this method of valuation might be an underestimate or an overestimate.

A second benefit even more difficult to value is of any reduction in the number of accidents, including fewer deaths, that may follow the opening of a new motorway. Of course, there is no unique or satisfactory method of placing a monetary value on human life. Profound moral questions are raised by the very idea. Indeed, some people would argue that the value of a human life is infinite.

If you are tempted by this argument, however, reflect that it unerringly leads to this conclusion: no resources should be used for any purpose in the world other than the saving of human life, until there was not a single preventable death! In fact, decisions are taken all the time that carry an implicit valuation on human life – for instance, when a government decides not to spend money on building a pedestrian bridge over a railway line but spends it instead on public library services (see Box 1.1 on p.7).

The best estimates of costs and benefits having been made, the final step in the analysis is to discount both to compare their present values (see Chapter 19, pp.202–3 for an explanation of this procedure). The decision whether to construct the motorway is made by comparing the present values of costs and benefits. If the latter exceed the former, the investment can profitably go ahead, unless there are alternative projects with even larger net benefits.

Understandably, cost-benefit analysis has its critics, who argue that it can be dangerous (i) because it produces numerical valuations which impart a spurious impression of precision in areas where precision is inherently difficult, and (ii) because it highlights the results of the calculations rather than the assumptions on which they are based. Our view is that cost-benefit analysis is a useful tool for decision-making in awkward areas of policy.

When several estimates of particularly intractable benefits (or costs) are made on a range of assumptions, the results may be less open to criticism. The tool is a useful one for decisions on how much of some public good can usefully be provided with social gain. It is less useful in helping to decide *who* should provide it. The question of private *versus* public provision is a different issue.

State ownership

The final non-budgetary policy available to the government that we discuss is state ownership. Many arguments have been advanced for nationalization of an industry – not all of them on narrow economic grounds. We ignore the merits and demerits of the political arguments, based on moral and ethical motives, because they are beyond the scope of positive economics. Moreover, the case for state *ownership*, on grounds of equity, hardly differs in principle from the case for state intervention to redistribute income by any means, and we shall not waste space repeating it.

The case for nationalization

A case for nationalization on grounds of efficiency must be seen as separate from the case for intervention because of some market failure. The existence of such a failure does not carry the implication that the state should both own and run an industry which is not performing sat-isfactorily. To take up the illustration of the provision of a motorway in the previous section, where the results of a cost-benefit analysis may justify the construction of the motorway, it is a separate matter whether the government should do the building or leave it to private civil engineering businesses.

Let us consider some aspects of the case for nationalization on grounds of economic efficiency. First, note two main differences between privately and publicly owned business operations: (i) their accountability, and (ii) their sources of funds.

On the first of these, private-sector businesses are, in principle, accountable to their shareholders; while nationalized industries are, in principle, accountable through Parliament, to the general population. The practice may, of course, be different. Some large corporations may be controlled by managers rather than shareholders, while nationalized industries in the UK have been organized as 'public corporations' with a considerable autonomy over their operations. Neither organizational form is necessarily preferable to the other. The prime relevant issue, as most economists see it, is whether or not an industry enjoys a degree of monopoly power. Strong competition is a powerful driving force for economic efficiency, whether firms are privately or publicly owned.

Where an industry is a monopoly, it is usually preferable to attack the sources of the monopoly power than to imagine that ownership transfers will increase efficiency. When there is a natural monopoly, unfettered market

---

BOX 21.6 Who Should Control Energy?

'Traditionally energy policy has been concerned with the availability of fuels from all sources, in sufficient quantities to meet national needs. The creation of the public sector monopolies – coal, gas, and electricity in the late 1940s – put the direction of these industries squarely on the political agenda, and at the same time shifted the emphasis in energy policy from demand to supply. When coal, then one of the 'commanding heights' of the economy, was nationalized in 1947, the National Coal Board (NCB) was instructed to modernise the industry and cut every possible ton of coal regardless of the cost. High investment in mechanized coal-cutting machinery and the reorganization of coal-face technology, enabled the NCB to raise productivity and increase output. . . .

'All the fuel industries, except oil, have been in the public sector for the past 40 odd years. This has meant that for most of this period the Labour Party has tended to ascribe their successes to the fact that they were nationalized, while the Conservatives have taken the same line on their failures. The problems attending the introduction of privatization have served to emphasize the complexity of the energy industry. Gas gave the programme a relatively easy start as it was privatized in one large lump, which turned a publicly owned into a privately owned monopoly. . . . A Department of Energy, with its minister in the Cabinet, is necessary to take the across-the-board view which alone can produce and implement a coherent policy for problems which extend well beyond party and country boundaries.'

(Richard Bailey, 'Energy Policy in Confusion', *National Westminster Bank Quarterly Review*, February 1991)

Most of the issues on both sides of the nationalization-privatization debate come close to the surface in this article on the energy industry.

Questions

1 Can you suggest why the industries mentioned were regarded as specially suited for nationalization, and later for privatization?
2 What case could be made against the proposal in the final sentence?

forces will not lead to optimal resource allocations. Nor even can a nationalized natural monopoly produce optimal output without the help of a subsidy to cover the inevitable losses it must make (refer back to p.170 if you cannot remember why this is so). It then becomes difficult to judge the performance of the industry.

Profits, the market indicator of efficiency under competitive conditions, are unreliable when a business is (i) a monopoly and (ii) in receipt of a subsidy. It is well-known that sheltered industries may engage in 'cross-subsidization', i.e. the use of profits in one sector of the business to offset losses in another. Some cross-subsidization may be thought justifiable on social grounds – for example, the cross-subsidization of postal services in rural areas by charging a single scale of rates for mail regardless of origin or destination. It is another matter when cross-subsidization is not open, but concealed in the accounts of large businesses, where it may be difficult to detect.

Before leaving the case for nationalization, there is a point about the sources of funds for public and private enterprises. It has particular relevance to the efficiency argument based on the promotion of innovation-led growth, sometimes made in support of public ownership. The argument is that nationalized industries can afford to spend where private firms cannot, because the latter would not receive the approval of shareholders, who are the ones at risk. However, if private individuals are not prepared to shoulder risks, one ought to ask whether it is proper to risk taxpayers' money. Many would say no, unless there were special circumstances.

The case for privatization

Privatization is a term which often means no more than denationalization. However, in the UK it has been used to describe a package of measures of the Conservative Government led by Margaret Thatcher in the 1980s.

The privatization programme in this country has included:

(1) the transfer to private ownership of nationalized industries;

(2) measures extending market forces, e.g. by 'deregulation' and sub-contracting of state-provided services to the highest bidder;

(3) the promotion of 'popular capitalism', by encouraging wider share ownership, and the sale of council houses to tenants at substantial discounts; and

(4) the generation of substantial budget surpluses, used to lower tax rates and to help achieve the macroeconomic policy goal of controlling inflation (see Chapter 38 below).

Whether private ownership is a more efficient form of organization than public ownership is an open question. We have already expressed the view that the degree of competition within which a business operates is a more significant influence on its efficiency than who actually owns it. There is plenty of evidence to support this view.

The evidence on the relative efficiency of privately owned versus publicly owned natural monopolies is differ-ent and less clear-cut. Some public-sector businesses out-perform comparable private-sector business, and vice versa. It has, moreover, to be said that several nationalized industries in the UK suffered, in practice, from chronic underinvestment in the post-war years. However, when natural monopolies are in private hands, most economists agree that some form of official regulatory machinery is needed to monitor them in sectors such as electricity, gas, telephone services and water.

The relationship between ownership and efficiency always seems to have had an emotive appeal to those with radical political views. Half a century ago, George Bernard Shaw wrote: 'Any State railway service can be made to be punctual, efficient, solvent and profitable, if the Ministry of Transport is determined to make it so.'[1] Shaw's words are as doctrinaire as the views of extreme supporters of market forces of the present day. Serious students of economics are more concerned with assessing the evidence and promoting competition, than with speculative arguments about ownership.

The Costs of Intervention: Government Failure

Much of the tone of the argument in this chapter has put the case rather one-sidedly – presenting causes of market failure and describing the ways in which the government may try to improve resource allocation. We end this chapter by redressing the balance. Governments are far from perfect. This is not because bureaucrats and politicians are more stupid or more corrupt than other people. They are just like others, with flaws as well as virtues.

There is government failure as well as market failure.

Here are a few of its many causes.

Rigidities: Regulations, tax rates and expenditure policies are not easily changed. Market conditions, however, change often, sometimes rapidly. A rule requiring the use of a certain method to reduce pollution may be made obsolete by technical change. Today's monopolies may be transformed into tomorrow's competitive industries by innovation. For example, the falling cost of air travel is providing new and growing competition for surface transport in the movement of many commodities. Centralized decision-taking bodies have difficulty in adapting fast to changing conditions, compared to the speed of adjustment of decentralized decision-takers to market signals.

Decision-takers' objectives: Central authorities surely care about the social good, to some extent, but public officials have their careers, their families and their prejudices too. Their personal needs may not be always wholly absent from their minds when considering the best policies to adopt.

Political constraints: Political considerations may interfere with policy decisions in undesirable ways. Govern-

---

1 *Everybody's Political What's What?* (Constable, 1944), p.254.

ments must face elections every so often, and the implications of alternative policies on the voting behaviour of the electorate cannot be ignored, especially when an election is near. This is a subject where economists should take care not to overstep the line and give what might be taken as authoritative statements on political matters.

What worries some people, however, is the power of a relatively small number of 'floating voters', in whose hands election results often hang.

(continued on next page)

Summary

1 Government microeconomic goals are efficiency and equity. An efficient allocation is where it is not possible to make any one person better off without making at least one other person worse off.

2 Efficient allocations imply equality of marginal costs and marginal utilities. The theory of the second best states that if all sectors are not producing optimal outputs, it may be better that none should be doing so.

3 Choosing among income distributions requires personal value judgements and, therefore, normative statements.

4 Market failure occurs when an unfettered market system fails to bring about an optimal allocation of resources. It can be due to the presence of (1) public goods (which are non-rival and non-excludable), (2) merit and demerit goods (of which individuals are unaware of their true merits and demerits), (3) externalities (where social and private costs and/or benefits diverge), or (4) imperfect competition. Additional market shortcomings may be due to incomplete information, and dynamic considerations leading to sluggish or volatile markets.

5 The methods of state intervention include (i) policies using the market system, (ii) policies improving the market system, and (iii) extra-market policies.

6 Policy instruments available to governments may be either (1) budgetary policies or (2) non-budgetary policies (see 12 below).

7 Budgetary policies operate through the income or the expenditure side of the government's budget, especially the tax system, subsidies and other state-provided benefits.

8 The characteristics of a good tax were suggested by Adam Smith in four maxims of taxation as Equity, Certainty, Convenience and Economy. There are advantages in a tax having low direct and compliance costs as well as being well targeted.

9 Tax equity is related to its incidence. Progressive, regressive, and proportional taxes absorb higher, constant, and lower proportions of income as income rises respectively.

10 Taxes may be more effective in achieving some goals, the less effective they are in achieving others. A common goal conflict is between efficiency and equity. High marginal tax rates are sometimes associated with disincentive effects, though evidence on this is not clear.

11 Government expenditures may be transfers or exhaustive. Both can be used to attack market failures and to redistribute income.

12 Non-budgetary government policies include (1) rules and regulations, (2) cost-benefit analysis, and (3) state ownership (nationalization).

13 Rules and regulations involve no government expenditure other than costs of administration, and may be (1) prescriptive or proscriptive, and (2) automatic or discretionary.

14 Cost-benefit analysis may help assess the efficiency of investment projects, where public goods and goods with significant externalities are involved. The analysis requires the identification and valuation of indirect external benefits and costs, including social items, not satisfactorily valued by a private market.

15 State ownership may be proposed for an industry on a variety of grounds. The question of who owns a business is usually less important than the degree of competition in the industry. Nationalization has particular relevance to natural monopolies, as an alternative to state regulation of private business.

16 Privatization is a term used to describe a range of policies including denationalization, deregulation, the promotion of share ownership and macro-economic goals. The efficiency argument over private *versus* public ownership of natural monopolies is an open question, and depends on evidence, which is not clear.

17 The establishment of a case for government intervention does not imply that the state should always intervene. There are costs of government intervention and types of government failure which must be taken into account.

THE PROPER BALANCE

Our conclusion must be that there is no single ideal system for resource allocation. Markets can fail, but so can governments. Moreover, there are intermediate alternatives, which may at times be preferred to unfettered markets or state intervention. For instance, charities concern themselves with the relief of poverty and other social problems; clubs overcome the free-rider problems associated with semi-public goods, such as golf courses – with members sharing costs among themselves. Indeed there is a body of opinion which thinks that a government would do well to encourage co-operation over costs and benefits which are external to *individuals*, turning them effectively into internal costs and benefits of *groups*.

To be valid, a case for state intervention must pass two tests: (i) there must be a market failure to achieve either efficiency, or equity in the distribution of income and wealth, *and* (ii) the manner by which the government intervenes to reduce inefficiency, or redress inequity, must not generate inefficiencies or inequities at least as great as those it eliminates. Each case for intervention needs to be treated on its merits.

Questions

1 Which of the following One or More characteristics are associated with (i) a public good, (ii) a merit good?
  (a) It gives consumers benefits of which they are unaware.
  (b) It is non-rival in consumption.
  (c) It is subject to increasing returns to scale.
  (d) It is technically impossible to exclude anyone from consuming it.
  (e) The more of it that is consumed by one individual, the less there is for another to consume.

2 Refer to Figure 21.1. Starting from optimum resource allocation, you are told that 'something' has changed so that full economic efficiency obtains at a point lying in the area *gfe*. (i) How would output of jeans and kebabs compare with the previous optimum? (ii) What could the 'something' that has changed be?

3 Which One or More of the following policies would be appropriate (i) to deal with the provision of a public good, (ii) to improve resource allocation in the hands of a profit-maximizing monopolist?
  (a) Lowering import duties.
  (b) Raising the rate of tax on profits.
  (c) Increasing the progressivity of income tax.
  (d) Improving consumer awareness of the benefits of consuming a good.
  (e) Offering a per unit subsidy on output.

4 A person's income rises from $10,000 to $12,000 in each of four countries, A, B, C and D. Classify each tax as progressive, proportional or regressive.

INCOME($s)	TAX PAID($s)			
	Country A	Country B	Country C	Country D
10,000	1,000	4,000	500	800
12,000	2,000	4,500	600	1,200

5 How would you represent a poll tax in Figure 21.3?

6 What budgetary change(s) would help reduce the impact of the poverty trap?

7 Refer to Figure 21.5. Approximately what change in the income of the bottom 40 per cent of households is due to the tax-benefit system?

8 In the text (p.234) it was said in the context of cost-benefit analysis that valuing time saved at the national hourly wage rate might be an underestimate of the true value to those who save it. (i) Why might this be so? (ii) Why might it be an overestimate?

PART 4

Elementary Macroeconomics

Preface to Part 4

In this part you will be introduced to the simple Keynesian model of macroeconomics. Macroeconomics studies the behaviour of broad aggregates, such as total national output, and broad averages such as the general price level.

The Keynesian model deals with total expenditure and divides it into the broad categories of consumption, investment, government expenditure, exports, and imports. The basic assumption of the simple Keynesian model is that these expenditures can be divided into two groups. The first group is composed of those variables that vary with national income and so are endogenous in the sense defined on page 4. The second group is composed of those variables that are determined outside of the model and so can be treated as exogenous constants in the sense also defined on page 4. In the simple Keynesian model, the price level and the interest rate are both assumed to be constant.

In Part 5 the Keynesian model is augmented to allow the interest rate and the general price level to be determined endogenously.

22 An Introduction to Macroeconomics

Inflation, unemployment, recession, economic growth, the balance of payments and the exchange rate are everyday words. Governments worry about how to reduce inflation and unemployment, how to prevent or cure recessions, how to increase the rate of growth, and how to achieve a satisfactory balance of payments. Firms are concerned with how inflation affects their earnings, how to increase their productivity, and how to insulate themselves from the consequences of recessions. Those firms that are engaged in foreign trade also worry about the value of sterling on the foreign-exchange market. Workers are anxious to avoid the unemployment that comes in the wake of recessions and to protect themselves against the hazards of inflation. All of these issues relate to problems studied in macroeconomics.

WHAT IS MACROECONOMICS?

We may define MACROECONOMICS as the study of the behaviour of broad economic aggregates and averages, such as total national output, income, employment and unemployment as well as the average level of all prices. In painting a broad picture of the economy, macroeconomics avoids much of the economy's interesting but sometimes confusing detail. In contrast, microeconomics paints a detailed picture of the economy, dealing with the behaviour of thousands of individual markets, such as those for wheat, coal or apples.

An example will illustrate the difference between the two branches of economics.

A microeconomic problem: Explaining the behaviour of energy prices is a typical microeconomic problem. For decades, energy prices fell in relation to the prices of most other commodities. Then, beginning in the early 1970s, this trend was reversed with energy becoming increasingly expensive relative to most other goods and services. In microeconomics, we seek to understand the causes and the effects of such changes in *relative* prices.

A macroeconomic problem: Over recent decades, as well as changing relative to other prices, energy prices have tended to follow the general trend for all prices to rise. The average behaviour of all prices is called the *general price level*. (Note, however, that the adjective 'general' is often dropped so that reference is made to 'the price level'.) In macroeconomics we seek to understand the causes and effects of changes in the general price level.

This chapter introduces macroeconomics by considering the main variables, whose behaviour we will study throughout Parts 4 and 5. In the course of the discussion, we define a number of important terms which will be used over and over again in the rest of this book. Because these terms are important, and because some of them will not reappear again for several chapters, we urge you to make a list of their names and definitions.

Six Macroeconomic Issues

Six major macroeconomic issues concern: (1) employment and unemployment, (2) inflation, (3) the trade cycle, (4) stagflation, (5) economic growth, and (6) the exchange rate and the balance of payments. We discuss these intuitively in this section. In the section that follows, we give a more detailed discussion which includes formal definitions.

Employment and unemployment: Why did the decades of the 1930s and 1980s see high unemployment, while other decades, such as the 1950s and the 1960s, saw relatively low unemployment? We have seen that all economies are characterized by *scarcity* – not nearly enough goods and services can be produced to satisfy everyone's wants. Why, then, should resources lie idle when what they could produce is very much wanted by consumers?

Inflation: Everyone knows that inflation is a general rise in prices. But why did the pace of inflation accelerate during the 1970s to reach levels not seen before in peacetime in most advanced Western nations? Why was inflation quite low throughout much of the 1980s and then accelerated at the end of the decade? Why should we worry about inflation in any case?

The trade cycle: The TRADE CYCLE refers to the tendency of output and employment to fluctuate over time in a recurring sequence of ups and downs. Boom periods of high output and high employment alternate with slump periods of low output and low employment, often referred to as recessions or, when they are extremely severe, as depressions. In boom periods, unemployment is low and the rate of inflation often accelerates. In periods of recession, unemployment is high and inflation often moderates. What is it about market economies that produces this cyclical behaviour?

Stagflation: The alternating bouts of boom and recession have caused many policy headaches in the past. But the 1970s saw the emergence of a new economic ailment. Why were the recessions of the 1970s and 1980s accompanied, not only by their familiar, and traditional, companion of earlier recessions – high unemployment – but also by an unexpected fellow traveller – rapid inflation? The new disease, called STAGFLATION, is the simultaneous occurrence of a recession (with its accompanying high unemployment) *and* inflation. Will it be a recurrent problem of free-market economies in the future?

Economic growth: In spite of the short-term variations of output that are associated with the trade cycle, the long-term trend of total output has been upward for several centuries in all advanced industrial countries. The trend in the nation's total output over the long term is referred to as ECONOMIC GROWTH. Since rates of economic growth have typically exceeded rates of population growth in all advanced countries, there has also been an increase in per capita output – output per head of the population. Over recent centuries, the rise in per capita output has brought more or less continually rising living standards for the average person. Starting in the mid-1970s, there was a slowdown in worldwide growth rates which left per capita output stagnant. Does this represent a basic change in underlying trends, or is it just a reaction to the prolonged recessions of the 1970s and 1980s?

The problem of bringing sustained economic growth to the world's less developed economies (called LDCs) is referred to as the problem of ECONOMIC DEVELOPMENT. Doing so often requires many changes in the basic structure of the economy as well as in national attitudes to such things as work, competition, and saving. Such changes are often difficult to accomplish.

The exchange rate and the balance of payments: All international transactions are recorded in what are known as a country's balance-of-payments statistics. These transactions are influenced by the exchange rate, which is the rate at which a country's own currency exchanges for foreign currencies. The trend in the value of the pound sterling in terms of many other currencies, including the US dollar, has been downwards until quite recent times when it has risen somewhat. Economists wish to discover the causes and consequences of such changes.

KEY MACRO VARIABLES

Some key variables of macroeconomics are:

- The overall level of employment and unemployment.
- The total national product.
- The general price level.
- The interest rate.
- The balance of payments and the exchange rate.[1]

We hear about them on television; politicians make speeches about them; economists theorize about them. To discuss them in a reasoned fashion, we must first understand several things about them:
1. Precisely how are they defined?
2. Why are we concerned about them?
3. How have they behaved in the past?

Employment and Unemployment

Definitions: The EMPLOYED are those persons working for others and paid a wage or a salary, while the SELF-EMPLOYED are those who work for themselves. The UNEMPLOYED are those who would be willing to accept work if jobs were available – an easier concept to understand than to measure.[1] The WORKING POPULATION, or LABOUR FORCE, is the total of the employed, the self-employed and the unemployed, i.e. those who have a job plus those who are looking for work.

In the microeconomic analysis of Parts 2 and 3, we were concerned with employment and unemployment in individual markets, such as, for example, the market for mechanics in Coventry. In macroeconomics we are concerned with overall employment and unemployment in the whole economy.

The numbers unemployed are often related to the total labour force and expressed as a rate or percentage. We will express it in this form and denote it by the symbol U. Thus

$$U = \frac{\text{number unemployed}}{\text{labour force}} \times 100$$

Why unemployment is a matter of concern: To understand the importance of unemployment, it is necessary to distinguish between voluntary and involuntary unemployment. VOLUNTARY UNEMPLOYMENT occurs when there is a job available but the employed person is not willing to accept it at the existing wage rate. INVOLUNTARY UNEMPLOYMENT occurs when a person is willing to accept a job at the going wage rate, but cannot find such a job. When we are concerned about the undesirable social effects of unemployment in terms of lost output and human suffering, it is involuntary unemployment that mainly concerns us. When we use the word *unemployment* hereafter, we mean involuntary unemployment, unless we say otherwise.

The unemployment rate is important both socially and politically (as well as economically). It is widely reported in newspapers; the government is blamed when it is high and takes credit when it is low; it is often a major issue in elections; and few economic policies are formed without some consideration of their effect on it.

There are two main reasons for worrying about unemployment: it wastes economic resources, and it causes human suffering.

The economic waste is fairly obvious. If a fully employed economy has 25 million people who are willing to work, their labour services must either be used now or be wasted.

---

1 The six macroeconomic problems discussed above relate to four of the variables on this list (all except the fourth). Of the items that do not directly repeat the list of macroeconomic variables, the trade cycle and stagflation relate to the behaviour of employment, national product and the price level, while economic growth concerns the rate at which national product is growing.

1 Many of the definitions given in this chapter were given in earlier parts of the book. We repeat those that are needed for macroeconomics, both for completeness and because some of you will be studying Part 4 before studying Parts 2 or 3.

If only 22 million are used because 12 per cent of the labour force is unemployed, the potential output of three million workers *is lost for ever*. In an economy characterized by scarcity, with not nearly enough output to meet everyone's needs, any waste of the potential to produce that output is a serious matter.

In addition to economic waste, there is the human cost of unemployment. Severe hardship and misery can be caused by prolonged periods of unemployment. Not only do the unemployed lose the goods and services that they could have bought with their incomes from work, prolonged periods of unemployment have been observed to be associated with above average incidences of ill health, alcoholism and divorce among those without work.

Experience of unemployment: Figure 22.1 shows the statistics for UK unemployment since 1930. During the period between the two world wars, UK unemployment was *never* less than 10 per cent in any single year. The 1950s and 1960s provided a sharp contrast. Unemployment was always less than 3 per cent, and it was not until the early 1970s that it exceeded that figure. In the mid-1970s, however, unemployment rose steadily, reaching 5 per cent early in 1976. By 1982 the rate had passed the 10 per cent level – or what is sometimes called the 'two-digit level' – and it had reached a peak of 11 per cent in 1985–6. It then fell steadily in the boom that lasted until the beginning of the 1990s. Then as a new recession set in, the rate began to move upward once again.

Total National Product

Definitions: The nation's total output is loosely described as its *national product, national output* or *national income*. Precise measures and their definitions are discussed in the next chapter. In the meantime, we note that this total product is calculated by adding up the money values of all the goods and services that are produced in the economy over some period of time, usually taken as a year.

A serious problem arises when we want to see how the quantity of the nation's output is changing from year to year while prices are also changing due to inflation. To see the problem, consider an example. Say that, over one year, all prices remain unchanged while the quantities of all outputs increase by 10 per cent. In this case, the value of total output rises by 10 per cent. Then over the next year, all quantities of output remain unchanged while the prices of everything that is produced rise by 10 per cent. Again the value of total output rises by 10 per cent. But the two cases are very different. In the first case, the measured value of output rises by 10 per cent because the *quantities* of everything that is produced rise by 10 per cent. In the second case, the measured value of output rises by 10 per cent because *prices* rise by 10 per cent while quantities remain constant.

Methods exist to distinguish these two cases, and we shall shortly consider them. In the meantime, we merely note that national product can be calculated in two ways.

In the first method, output is valued each year at the market prices ruling in that year. It is then referred to as national product, *valued at current prices*, or as NOMINAL NATIONAL PRODUCT, or as MONEY NATIONAL PRODUCT. In this case, the measured value of national product changes from year to year as a result of changes in both *prices* and quantities. For example if, from one year to the next, all market prices *and* all quantities produced rise by 10 per cent, national product valued in current prices will rise by about 21 per cent.

In the second method, national product is valued at the prices ruling in some fixed year. It is then referred to as NATIONAL PRODUCT VALUED AT CONSTANT PRICES or as REAL NATIONAL PRODUCT. In this case, the prices used to value output do not change from year to year so that all change in the measured value of

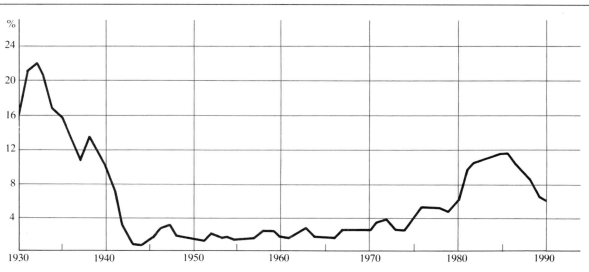

FIGURE 22.1 Unemployment in the UK. The figures show the average numbers unemployed as a percentage of the labour force in each year.

output must be due only to changes in *quantities* of output.

The year whose prices are chosen for this calculation is often referred to as the BASE YEAR. If, for example, the base year is 1982 so that actual prices ruling in 1982 are used as the constant prices, the resulting output figure could be referred to as *national product at 1982 prices*.

A further important output concept is POTENTIAL OUTPUT, or FULL-EMPLOYMENT OUTPUT. This refers to what the economy could produce if all resources were fully employed at their normal rates of utilization. When the economy is producing its potential or full-employment output, the production point is somewhere on the transformation curve shown in Figure 1.2 on page 8. When there are unemployed resources, so that output is less than potential, the production point is somewhere inside the transformation curve. Potential output is a very important concept, and you should be sure you remember both terms that are used for it.

When we wish to contrast the economy's present output with its potential output, we refer to the former as ACTUAL OUTPUT. Thus, for example, saying that actual output is less than potential output means that the economy is currently producing less than it could produce if all resources were fully employed.

Why output is a matter of concern: Short-term fluctuations of national product around its potential level reflect the ebb and flow of economic activity, called the trade cycle. Policymakers care about such fluctuations because they cause unemployment and lost output.

Long-term, trend-changes in national product, valued at constant prices, have generally been upwards in recent centuries. We have already referred to this as the phenomenon of economic growth, and have noted that such growth is the major cause of long-term increases in living standards. The worst horrors of the early industrial revolution are no longer with us, mainly because economic growth has removed the necessity of fourteen-hour days worked in extremely harsh conditions. As long as growth continues, each generation can expect, on the average, to have substantially higher living standards than were enjoyed by all preceding generations.

The long-term effects of growth rates can be dramatic.

A 2 per cent annual growth rate, which is close to what the UK has experienced in the last half of the twentieth century, doubles real national product every 36 years. An 8 per cent growth rate, which is closer to Japan's experience over the same period, doubles real national product every 9 years!

Output experience: Figure 22.2(i) shows the long-term trend of output, while Figure 22.2(ii) highlights the fluctuations from one year to another. (Output is measured by a particular statistic called the GDP, which stands for Gross Domestic Product and which we shall study in Chapter 23.) The two parts are two ways of displaying the same output series. Part (i) shows the level of output each year from 1945 to 1990. Part (ii) shows by how much

output has changed from one year to the next over the same period – i.e. the growth rate of output.

Comparing changes with index numbers: Between 1980 and 1989 American real national income rose from $3,187,000m to $4,102,000m while the UK's rose from £231,901m to £295,022m. How does the growth performance of these two countries compare? The raw data are hard to interpret because they are in different monetary units and because the two countries are quite different in size. For ready comparisons, it is much better to compare percentage changes rather than absolute changes. This is conventionally done using INDEX NUMBERS, which express the ratio of one figure to another multiplied by 100 with the base, or comparison period, taken as 100.

TABLE 22.1 Calculation of Index Numbers of Total Output

	Value of Total Output (constant prices)	Calculation	Index No.
UK			
1980 (Base year)	£231,901m	(231,901/231,901)100 = (1)(100)	100
1989	£295,022m	(295,022/231,901)100 = (1.27)(100)	127
US			
1980 (Base year)	£3,187,000m	(3,187,000/3,187,000)100 = (1)(100)	100
1989	£4,102,000m	(4,102,000/3,187,000)100 = (1.29)(100)	129

Table 22.1 shows the calculation of the index numbers for the two countries. The index for the base year is 100; the index for the new year shows its value as a percentage of the base-year value. The percentage change between the two is the new value minus 100. Thus, in the table, UK income in 1990 is 127 per cent of what it was in 1980, which means a 27 per cent increase. The US income rose just a bit more over the same period, i.e. by 29 per cent.

The General Price Level

Definitions

Macroeconomics uses the concept of the GENERAL PRICE LEVEL, the average level of the prices of *all* goods and services produced in the economy.

Changes in the price level: In practice, we are not interested in the average level of all prices itself but in *changes* in this average. For example, you wouldn't be much the wiser if you were told that the average level of all prices ruling in the UK this year was £121.34. But you would be interested to know that the average level of all prices ruling this year was 7 per cent higher than the average ruling in the previous year. A rise in the price level is called an INFLATION, while a fall in the price level is called a DEFLATION.

Changes in the value of money: By definition, changes in the price level are reflected in changes in what is variously

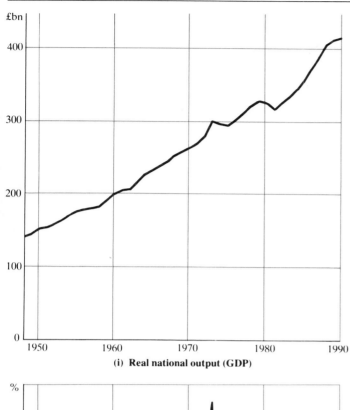

(i) **Real national output (GDP)**

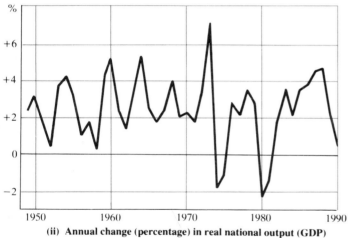

(ii) **Annual change (percentage) in real national output (GDP)**

FIGURE 22.2 **Real National Product since 1945.** The data are for GDP measured at constant 1980 prices. Part (i) gives the level in each year; part (ii) gives the percentage rate of change from one year to the next.

called the PURCHASING POWER OF MONEY or the VALUE OF MONEY. Both terms refer to *the amount of goods and services that can be purchased with a given amount of money*. Inflation, which is a rise in the general price level, reduces the purchasing power of money, deflation increases it.

Say, for example, that all prices rise by 10 per cent. Since a unit of money now buys (about) 10 per cent less than previously, we also say that the value of money (measured by what can be bought with it) has fallen by 10 per cent.

Now consider the opposite case. Assume that all prices fall by 10 per cent. Any given amount of money will now buy 10 per cent *more* than it previously did. Thus, this deflation raises the value of money by 10 per cent.

These examples illustrate the general proposition that the purchasing power of money varies in inverse proportion to the price level, falling when the price level rises and rising when the price level falls.

Measuring changes in the price level – index numbers: In practice, changes in the price level, and in the value of money, are measured by a PRICE INDEX which shows the average percentage change that has occurred in some group of prices over some period of time. The point in time from which the change is measured is called the BASE PERIOD (or base year). There are several aspects to the definition of any price index.

First, what group of prices should be used? The answer

is that one should choose those most appropriate to one's purpose. For example, the RETAIL PRICE INDEX (RPI) covers prices of commodities commonly bought by households. Changes in the RPI are meant to measure changes in the typical household's 'cost of living'. The Wholesale Price Index measures a different group of commodities commonly bought and sold by wholesalers. The 'implied deflator for the GNP' is a price index that covers virtually all of the goods and services produced in the economy: it includes not only the prices of consumer goods and services bought by households but the prices of capital goods such as plant and machinery bought by firms.[1]

Second, what kind of average should be used? If all prices were to change in the same proportion, in what is sometimes called a *pure inflation*, this would not be an important question. A 10 per cent rise in each and every price covered means an average rise of 10 per cent no matter how much importance we give to each price change when calculating the average. But what if – as is almost always the case – different prices change differently? Now it does matter how much importance we give to each price change. A rise of 50 per cent in the price of caviar is less important to the average consumer than a rise of 40 per cent in the price of bread, and this in turn is less important than a rise of 30 per cent in the cost of housing. Why? The reason is that the typical household spends less on caviar than on bread and less on bread than on housing.

To take account of the varying importance of different commodities, government statisticians apply weights to each price change. These weights are based on the proportion of total income that households typically spend on purchasing that commodity. They are obtained from periodic surveys of household expenditures.

The RPI is then calculated in two stages. First an index is calculated for each of about 14 different commodity groups. To do this, price changes within each group are weighted by the proportion of total expenditures devoted to that item. Second, the price indexes for each group are combined into a single RPI by weighting each by the proportion of total expenditure typically allocated to that commodity group. This latter procedure is illustrated in Table 22.2.

TABLE 22.2 Calculation of a Price Index

	price 1990	price 1991	Index	Weight	
A	£1.00	£1.10	110	.6	66
B	£3.00	£3.60	120	.4	48
					114

According to the Table, the prices of A and B rose by 10 and 20 per cent respectively, and these commodities took 60 and 40 per cent respectively of total expenditure. The weighted average price increase is calculated by multiplying the price index of 110 for A by its weight of 0.6 to obtain 66, then multiplying the price index of 120 for B by 0.4 to obtain 48, and finally summing these two numbers to obtain 114. This weighted, average price index says that the average 'price level' for the two commodities rose over the period by 14 per cent.

1 Be careful not to confuse a *deflator*, which is an index number designed to measure average price changes, and a *deflation*, which is a fall in average prices.

Some difficulties with index numbers: An index number is meant to measure the broad trend in prices rather than the details. This means that the information it gives must be interpreted with care. Here are three reasons why.

First, the weights in the index refer to an average bundle of goods. This average will be typical of what each and every household consumes. Rich, poor, young, old, single, married, urban and rural households typically consume bundles that differ from one another. An increase in air fares, for example, raises the cost of living of a frequent traveller while leaving that of a stay-at-home unaffected.

Second, households usually alter their consumption patterns in response to price changes. A price index that shows changes in the cost of purchasing a fixed bundle of goods does not allow for this. For example, a typical cost-of-living index for middle-income families at the turn of the century would have given much weight to the cost of maids and children's nurses. A doubling of servants' wages in 1900 would have greatly increased the middle-income cost of living. Today it would have little effect because middle-income families do not typically employ a group of full-time servants. A household that greatly reduces its consumption of a commodity whose price is rising rapidly does not have its cost of living rise as fast as a household that continues to consume that commodity in an undiminished quantity.

Third, as time goes by, new commodities enter the typical consumption bundle and old ones leave. A cost-of-living index in 1890 would have had a large item for horse-drawn carriages and horse feed, but no allowance at all for motorcars and petrol. The longer the period of time that passes, the less some fixed consumption bundle will be typical of current consumption patterns. For this reason the government makes frequent surveys of household expenditure patterns and revises the weights.

Why inflation is a matter of concern

No economist argues that the price level ruling in Britain in, say, 1892 was intrinsically better or worse than the one ruling in 1992. The reason why one price level is just as good as any other price level is that, if all prices of goods, factors of production and everything else change in equal proportion, no relative prices have changed and there are no real consequences. For instance, if the amount of money you must pay for everything you buy doubles but the amount of money you receive also doubles, you are unaffected. You pay twice as much for everything you buy but, since your money income has also doubled, you can buy just as much as you could before prices rose.

It follows that when every individual price has been fully adjusted, a change in the overall level of prices has no effect.

Another way of seeing this important point is to observe that changing the number of zeros on the prices at which *all* transactions take place has no real effect on anything.

The real effects of inflation occur during the transition from one price level to another.

While the price level is changing, some prices adjust faster than others. As a result, relative prices change and real effects occur. Gainers are those who find the prices of what they buy rising slower than the prices of what they sell. They are powerful, or lucky, or smart enough to keep up to, or even ahead of, the inflation. Losers are those who find the prices of what they sell rising slower than the prices of what they buy. They lack the necessary economic power, the luck, or the needed foresight to keep up with inflation. Thus, inflation causes haphazard redistributions of income.

Fixed money income: The extreme case of the redistributive effects of inflation occurs when some people's incomes do not rise at all as prices rise. For example, if a retirement pension specifies an income as so many £s, a rise in the price level lowers the purchasing power of that income. Anyone who retired on a fixed money income in 1975 found the purchasing power of that income cut in half by 1980 and then by a further 52 per cent by 1991. This meant that the person could buy in 1991 only 23 per cent of what could be bought in 1975. For such people rapid inflation means great suffering.

Note that the problems only arise with pensions, and other payments, that really are fixed in money terms. State pensions in the UK have been adjusted from time to time as the inflation proceeds. Some private pensions, however, remain fixed in money terms, so that their purchasing power shrinks steadily as the price level rises.

Unforeseen inflations:

The most serious effects of inflation occur when the rise in the price level is unforeseen.

Contracts freely entered into when the price level was expected to remain constant will bring hardships to some and unexpected gains to others if the price level unexpectedly starts to rise.

For example, consider a new wage contract that specifies wage increases of 3 per cent and that is made in the general expectation of a constant price level. Both employers and workers expect that the purchasing power of wages paid will rise by 3 per cent as a result of the new contract. Now assume that the price level rises unexpectedly by 10 per cent over the course of the wage contract. The workers' wages will now buy less than they would before the wage increase was negotiated.

Indexing: Some of the redistributive effects of inflation can be avoided by what is called 'indexing' (or 'index linking') which means linking the payments made under the terms of a contract to changes in the general price level. For example, a retirement pension might specify that it will pay the beneficiary £5000 per year starting in 1995, and that the amount paid will increase each year in proportion to the increase in some specified index of the price level. Thus, if the price index rose by 10 per cent between 1995 and 1996, the pension payable in 1996 would be £5500. The great advantage of indexing is that it works automatically and hence the future course of inflation does not have to be foreseen.

Foreseen inflations: Indexation provides an automatic correction that does not require anyone to foresee future changes in the price level. However, even without formal indexation it is possible to allow for the effects of an inflation provided that the rise in the price level is *foreseen*. Wage and price contracts are major examples. If, say, a 10 per cent inflation is expected over the next year, a money wage that rises by 10 per cent over that period will preserve the expected purchasing power of wages. A money wage that increases by 13 per cent will provide for an expected

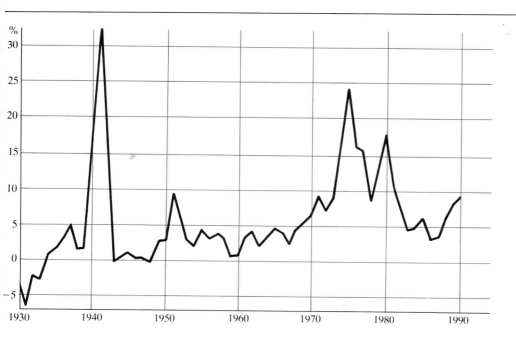

FIGURE 22.3 **The Rate of Inflation in the UK since 1930.** The figures show the percentage increase in the Retail Price Index from one year to the next.

3 per cent increase in the purchasing power of wages (10 per cent more wages to preserve purchasing power in the face of the expected rise in prices and 3 per cent more to increase the real purchasing power of the wages).

So when an inflation is foreseen, many of its effects can be allowed for in contracts that take account of the expected rise in prices.

The experience of inflation

Figure 22.3 shows the UK inflation rate for each year since 1930. Throughout the 1950s and the 1960s the rate, although low by current standards, was high enough to cut the purchasing power of the pound by more than half over those two decades and to be a worry to policy-makers and voters.

Then, in the late 1960s, the United Kingdom, together with the rest of the developed world, moved into a period of *accelerating* inflation. Although there was some variability, the trend was upward and by 1975 the annual rate of inflation reached a peak of approximately 25 per cent in the UK. (This rate halves the purchasing power of money in just over 3 years!) This high rate was not, however, maintained. The trend was downward for the rest of the 1970s and the first half of the 1980s.

The inflation rate over this extraordinary period was such that a household retiring in 1972 with a comfortable income that was fixed in money terms saw 75 per cent of that income's purchasing power eroded over the next ten years.

By 1983, the government had reduced the inflation rate to below 5 per cent, which was low by the standards of the recent past, but high compared with the average inflation rate over the past two centuries. It rose to the 7–8 per cent range in 1984 and 1985 but then fell back to around 5 per cent until 1988 when, once again, it began to rise rapidly, reaching 10 per cent around the turn of the decade. A new bout of strong anti-inflationary policy finally began to work and the rate fell back below 5 per cent before the end of 1991.

The Interest Rate

If a bank loans you money, it will usually ask you to agree to a schedule for repayment. Furthermore, it will charge you interest for the privilege of borrowing the money. If, for example, you are lent £1000 today, repayable in one year's time, you might be asked to pay £10 per month in interest. This makes £120 in interest over the year, which can be expressed as an interest rate of 12 per cent per annum [(£120/1000) × 100 per cent].

The INTEREST RATE is the price that is paid to borrow money for a stated period of time and is expressed as a percentage amount per £1 borrowed. For example, an interest rate of 12 per cent per annum means that the borrower must pay 12 pence per year for every £1 that is borrowed.

Just as there are many prices of goods in the economy, so there are many interest rates. The bank will lend money to an industrial customer at a lower rate than it will lend money to you – there is a lower risk of not being repaid. The rate charged on a loan that is not to be repaid for a long time will usually differ from the rate on a loan that is to be repaid quickly. The former is called the LONG-TERM INTEREST RATE and the latter the SHORT-TERM INTEREST RATE. The relation between the various interest rates in the economy is called the STRUCTURE OF INTEREST RATES.

When economists speak of 'the' interest rate, they mean a rate that is typical of all the various interest rates in the economy. Dealing with one interest rate suppresses much detail, but it allows economists to deal with overall changes in the level of interest rates. The PRIME RATE OF INTEREST, the rate that banks charge to their regular business customers, may be thought of as 'the' interest rate since, when the prime rate changes, most other rates change in the same direction.

Financial Assets

During your study of macroeconomics, you will encounter descriptions of many valuable pieces of paper which their owners count as parts of their wealth. Two of the most important of these are assets which are evidence of part ownership of a firm, called STOCKS or SHARES or EQUITIES, and assets which are evidence of debt. Two general types of the latter are bills and bonds.

A BILL is a promise to pay a stated sum at some future date, usually within a year. The borrower issues the bill and the lender buys it at a discount, which means he pays less than the amount the bill promises to repay. The difference is the lender's interest. For example, assume A issues a bill promising to pay £110 in one year's time and B buys it now for £100. B has lent A £100 and gets 10 per cent interest on that loan because at the end of the year, he gets his £100 back, plus an additional £10. Private firms can issue bills when they borrow short-term, as can the government. Bills issued by the government when it borrows short-term, usually for a 90-day period, are called TREASURY BILLS.

A BOND is a promise to pay a stated sum at some future date, typically many years after its date of issue. It also carries a promise to make a series of fixed periodic payments (usually quarterly or annually) which is the interest on the loan. The person who buys the bond when it is issued is lending money to the person who issues it. In return, she gets a promise to have her money repaid at some stated future date together with fixed, regular interest payments in the interim.

Collectively, shares, bills and bonds and other similar assets are called FINANCIAL ASSETS. We will discuss these in much more detail in Part 5. It is necessary in the meantime to understand only as much about these assets as is presented here.

The Balance of Payments and Exchange Rates

Definitions: If you are going on a holiday in France, you will need French francs to pay for your purchases while you are there. Any bank will make this exchange of currencies for you. If you get 10 francs for every pound you give up, then these two currencies are trading at a rate of £1 = 10F or, what is the same thing, 1F = £0.10. The 'exchange rate' refers to the rate at which different countries' currencies are traded for each other.

The above example suggests that the exchange rate can be defined in either of two ways: (i) the amount of foreign currency that exchanges for one unit of domestic currency (10F for £1 in the above example), or (ii) the amount of domestic currency that exchanges for one unit of foreign currency (10p for 1F in the above example). It is customary in the UK to express the sterling exchange rate in the former way. Thus the exchange rate between the pound sterling and the US dollar was £1 = $1.90 during the latter part of 1991. This means that £1 would buy you $1.90 or, what is the same thing, $1 would buy £0.526.

Thus, in the UK the EXCHANGE RATE between sterling and any one foreign currency is defined as the amount of that foreign currency that must be given up to purchase one pound sterling, i.e. the price of sterling in terms of a foreign currency. Clearly there is a separate exchange rate between sterling and each other currency in the world. FOREIGN EXCHANGE is defined as foreign currencies (or claims to such currencies such as bank deposits, cheques and promissory notes payable in the foreign currency). The FOREIGN EXCHANGE MARKET is defined as the market where foreign exchange is traded (at a price which is expressed by the exchange rate).

If the exchange rate is left free to be determined on the foreign-exchange market by the forces of demand and supply, the country is said to have a FLOATING or a FLEXIBLE EXCHANGE RATE. If the country's central bank intervenes in the foreign-exchange market to hold the exchange rate at some pre-announced fixed value, the country is said to have a FIXED or a PEGGED EXCHANGE RATE.

Now let us turn to the other important international concept that we need to consider at this point, the balance of payments.

In order to know what is happening to the course of international trade and international capital movements, governments keep account of the transactions among countries. These accounts are called the BALANCE-OF-PAYMENTS ACCOUNTS and they record all such international payments. When the accounts are gathered, each transaction, such as a shipment of exports or the arrival of imported goods, is classified according to the payments or receipts that would typically arise from it.

Any transaction that would lead to a payment to other nations is classified as a debit (−) item because it uses foreign exchange. British purchase of foreign goods and services (imports) and of foreign assets (a capital outflow) are classed as debit items.

Any transaction that would lead to a payment by foreigners to UK residents is classified as a credit (+) item because it earns foreign exchange. British sales of goods and services to foreigners (exports) as well as sales of British assets to foreigners (a capital inflow) are classified as credit items.

Consider some examples, first on the side of current transactions. When a British importer buys a Japanese personal computer to sell in the United Kingdom, this appears as a debit in the UK balance of payments because it uses foreign exchange – yen in this case. However, when a Japanese shipping firm insures its cargo with Lloyd's of London, this represents a credit in the UK balance of payments. The shipping firm will have to give up yen in order to buy the sterling needed to pay Lloyd's its premium, so that the transaction earns foreign exchange. Of course a credit item to one country is a debit item to the other, and vice versa. Thus in the Japanese balance of payments, the transaction involving the personal computer is a credit while the insurance transaction is a debit item.

Now look at the capital side. If a British investor buys some shares in a Brazilian mining company, this appears as a debit item in the UK balance of payments because the transaction uses foreign exchange. When a Japanese citizen decides to buy shares in a British manufacturing firm, this is a credit item in the UK balance of payments because it earns foreign exchange. As with current items, so it is with capital items: what is a credit item for one country is a debit item for the other. Thus the sale of the shares is a credit item in the Brazilian accounts because it brings in foreign exchange, while the purchase of the shares is a debit item in the Japanese accounts because it uses foreign exchange.

Interest rates and capital flows: Capital markets have become internationalized, and enormously sophisticated, compared to what they were a mere two or three decades ago. This is partly due to the communications revolution that has made possible fast, cheap, reliable communications on a world-wide basis. As a result, small differences in expected returns on capital in different countries can cause large flows of capital among countries. If interest rates rise in Germany, residents of other countries with money to lend will transfer some of their funds into German marks and then buy German assets. They do this to benefit from the high rates of return in Germany. Similar capital flows occur into any country whose rates of return rise relative to rates available in other countries.

Since different countries are involved, the expected benefit depends not just on differences in interest rates, but also on what is expected to happen to the exchange rate. For example, if the exchange rate between the US dollar and sterling is expected to stay constant for 3 months, then a small positive differential between interest rates in London and New York may cause a large movement of funds from New York to London. If, however, the exchange rate is expected to change over the period of the loan, that will also have to be taken into the calculation.

Sometimes governments fix exchange rates within

BOX 22.1 The UK Economy: Summary Outlook

'We are already in a recessionary phase, with consumer spending declining; investment plans being scaled back further and heavy destocking now underway. At the same time, exports are no longer providing the strong offset to weak domestic demand that was the case earlier this year. [However] the current export weakness has been the result of economic conditions abroad, rather than a problem with competitiveness. The trough in activity may not be reached until the spring of next year but, thereafter, a modest recovery should be underway.'

'The corollary of all this appears to be a turning point of the inflation tide. Cost pressures mount and the Gulf crisis and oil complicates the issue. But manufacturers are increasingly unable to pass costs on in full and producer output price inflation has been held to around 6 per cent.'

(Barclays *Economic Review*, November 1990)

Many of the variables discussed in this chapter are referred to in this passage. Although everything that underlies the analysis will not be fully apparent until later in the book, many of the issues discussed in the quotation have already been briefly touched on.

Questions

1 According to the authors, what categories of expenditures account for the falling off of economic activity?
2 Why might inflation be expected to fall as a result of the forces discussed in the first paragraph?
3 What forces are used to explain the poor export performance of the UK economy at the time, and what forces are dismissed? (Do not just repeat the terms used in the quotation, explain and elaborate on them.)

narrow limits, as in the case with the European Monetary System. Even then, however, rates are allowed to vary within a wide enough band to wipe out the short-term gains resulting from higher foreign interest rates. Say, for example, that the interest rate on short-term bills is 14 per cent in Germany and 10 per cent in London. A holder of sterling with £100,000 to lend for 3 months can earn $2\frac{1}{2}$ per cent in London ($\frac{1}{4}$ of 10 per cent) and $3\frac{1}{2}$ per cent in Germany. He makes £2500 in London and £3500 in Germany. But to earn the extra the investor needs to turn £100,000 into marks at the outset and then back into sterling 3 months later. A very small weakening of the value of sterling on the foreign-exchange market could more than wipe out the whole £1000 gain.

Why policy-makers are concerned about exchange rates and the balance of payments: Most people agree that a *ceteris paribus* rise in either unemployment or inflation is undesirable. There is no obvious reason, however, for feeling the same about a change in either the exchange rate or the balance of payments. Whether or not policy-makers need to be concerned about such changes depends on why the changes occurred. For this reason, it is best to postpone consideration of the reasons why policy-makers are sometimes concerned about these variables until we have studied them in more detail later in this book.

Experience: Figure 22.4 shows the exchange rate between the pound sterling and the US dollar since 1945. The long periods of stability are periods where the exchange rate was fixed. The sudden changes were periods when the rate was altered to a new fixed level. Since 1972 the rate has been left to find its level on the free market, and this shows up as a continuously varying rate on the chart – i.e. a floating exchange rate.

Balance-of-payments experience can be understood only after you have learned more about the meaning of balance-of-payments figures. So we postpone looking at such data until a later chapter.

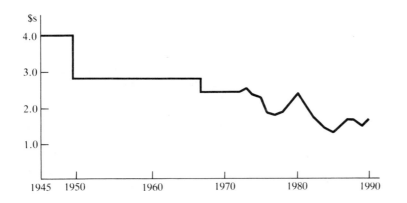

FIGURE 22.4 The Sterling–US Dollar Exchange Rate. The data show the average US$ price of £1 sterling during each year.

THE GOALS OF MACROECONOMIC POLICY

The two main goals of microeconomic policy concern efficiency in the allocation of resources and equity in the distribution of income. In the remainder of this book we shall be concerned with a further set of policy goals, which are related to the five key macro variables discussed above: employment, output, the price level, the exchange rate and the balance of payments.

The remainder of this chapter provides a general survey of much of what we shall study in later chapters. The survey is included here to point the way, and to familiarize you with some important terms. Do not spend too much time trying to understand what follows in every detail. If you return at the end of your study of macroeconomics to reread this chapter, you will then find that nothing here seems at all difficult.

Early Goals

Until the twentieth century, the main government responsibility towards the economy was to provide a stable background of law and order, and security of contracts that would help citizens to get on with the private economic activity on which the material wealth of the nation depended.

Early in the history of economics, it was realized that the amount of money and credit that was available to 'grease the wheels of commerce' was at least partially under the control of the government. It was also realized that mismanagement of the monetary system could, as we shall see in detail later, cause inflation. The government's responsibility was therefore understood to include management of the monetary system in such a way that there was enough money to satisfy the needs of trade, but not so much as to cause inflation.

The macro variables other than the price level were not, however, considered to be the responsibility of government policy. Good times and bad times seemed to follow each other – in the ebb and flow of the trade cycle – for reasons that were assumed, at the time, to be beyond government control.

Modern Goals

In response to the so-called Great Depression of the 1930s, and the decade of heavy unemployment that was a part of it, modern macroeconomic theory was born. Since that time, economists have understood that government policy can have a significant influence on the nation's overall level of economic activity, while governments have, for better or worse, accepted a responsibility for influencing the behaviour of each of the major macro variables that we have discussed above.

The policies with respect to each of these variables are usually stated as full employment, a satisfactory rate of growth of output, a relatively stable price level, and a satisfactory balance of payments.

We shall look briefly at each of these.

Full employment: Between 1945 and the early 1980s the governments of most market-oriented, industrial countries accepted a responsibility for ensuring the existence of something close to full employment. In the UK, this objective was stated in the *White Paper on Employment Policy* (Cmd 6527), published in 1944 by the coalition government of that time.

Achieving the objective of full employment means holding national product at its potential, or full-employment, level. It does *not* mean achieving zero unemployment. Indeed, zero unemployment is an impossibility in any real economy, and here is why.

Any economy has a normal turnover of labour that arises both because people leave one job to take, or to look for, another, and because there are always some people leaving the labour force due to retirement, or death, and others entering it. As a result, there is always a pool of people who are unemployed because they are currently between jobs. Such unemployment, which is due to the normal turnover of labour, is called frictional unemployment. It is the amount of unemployment that exists when output is at its potential level. Thus, full employment does not mean having zero unemployment; instead it means having the amount of frictional unemployment that is associated with potential output.

The 1944 White Paper argued that the irreducible minimum was about 3 per cent in the UK. It therefore defined full employment as existing when the recorded unemployment rate was 3 per cent. For a decade or so, starting in 1950, unemployment rates of 2 per cent, or less, became common. Then in the late 1960s, and throughout the 1970s, the amount of unemployment associated with potential output rose steadily until, by the mid 1980s, it seemed to be somewhere between 6 and 9 per cent (although estimating this number poses some formidable difficulties). The reasons for these changes will be discussed in later chapters.

In the course of the 1980s, the Conservative government in the UK under Margaret Thatcher lowered the priority that was placed on the prevention of unemployment as a macroeconomic policy objective. Employment was left to be whatever the free market produced. The reasons for this dramatic change in policy will be discussed in later chapters. In spite of this policy shift, changes in the government budget are still understood to affect the economy's macroeconomic behaviour in ways which we will study over much of the rest of this book.

A satisfactory rate of growth of output: We have seen that economic growth has been the major cause of long-term increases in living standards. Unfortunately, one of the least successful branches of economics has been the theory of growth. Economic theory does identify some factors, such as investment, and research and development, that are often associated with high growth rates. No one, however, has been able to sort out causes and effects in these relations to the extent that governments can easily influence the growth rates of their economies. We shall discuss these matters further in Chapter 36.

Thus, although many UK governments have had growth targets, few have found the policy tools needed to influence the country's growth rate. Nonetheless governments do, as we shall see, continue to adopt growth policies.

Stable prices: Governments still accept the responsibility, which was established centuries ago, for maintaining a stable price level, or, if that is not possible, for maintaining a low rate of inflation. Figure 22.3 shows that the UK government has had a mixed success in meeting this objective over the years.

A satisfactory exchange rate and balance of payments: Most governments feel that extreme, short-term fluctuations in the exchange rate are undesirable, while also feeling that long-term trends in the exchange rate should not, indeed cannot, be resisted.

Governments differ on how they regard the balance of payments. Some countries have active policies, others leave the balance of payments to be determined by market forces, without any serious government intervention. Because the balance of payments presents no such obvious policy objectives as do employment, output and the price level, balance-of-payments objectives are sometimes said to be *secondary*, in contrast to the *primary* objectives of full employment, economic growth and price stability.

Policy Instruments

There are two major sets of macroeconomic policy tools available to the government. One set, called demand-side policies, works on the demand side of the economy's markets. These are called the policies of DEMAND MANAGEMENT. The other set, called supply-side policies, work on the supply side of these markets.

Demand-side policies

The major policies available to influence the demand side of markets are called fiscal and monetary policies.

Fiscal policy: FISCAL POLICY is the use of the government's budget to influence the total level of economic activity in the country by influencing the *total demand for goods and services*. (This total demand is nothing other than the sum of all of the demands in the nation's individual markets that we studied in the micro half of this book.) An increase in total demand can be achieved either by increasing total government expenditure or by reducing total taxes, or both. Reducing total demand requires reducing government expenditure, increasing taxes, or both.

An increase in government expenditure means that the government is demanding more of the goods and services to which it allocates its extra expenditure. This means that the government is directly causing an increase in total demand. Reducing taxes has a similar, though indirect, effect on total demand. It leaves more money in the hands of the private sector and relies on that sector to increase total demand by spending some of this money.

Monetary policy: MONETARY POLICY is the manipulation of the amount of money and credit available, and the cost of that credit to borrowers (i.e. interest rates) in an attempt to influence total demand. Since business and households borrow to finance much of their expenditure, changing the availability, and the terms, of credit can influence total demand. By making more funds available to be borrowed, and by exerting a downward pressure on interest rates which lowers the cost of borrowing, the government seeks to increase total demand. By making fewer funds available to be borrowed, and by exerting an upward pressure on interest rates, the government seeks to lower total demand.

Monetary policy is administered by a country's central bank – in the UK this is the Bank of England (often called the Bank). How the Bank of England can accomplish these changes in the conditions of credit will be studied in detail in Chapter 34. There we will also study the problems caused by international capital movements: when the Bank wishes to raise UK interest rates for domestic reasons, it may set in motion international flows of capital funds. These can lead to new problems, and may act as constraints on domestic policy.

Supply-side policies

As well as influencing total demand, the government can try to influence total national product by adopting what are called SUPPLY-SIDE POLICIES. These try to influence the total output that the private sector can, and will, produce. The possible policies are too numerous to outline here, but they will be discussed in detail later in this book.

Suffice it to say here that supply-side policies are designed to cause rightward shifts in the supply curves in many individual markets. Consider just two examples. First, let there be a reduction in the rates of personal income taxes. This *may* increase the amount of work that people wish to do. (This possibility is discussed in detail in Chapter 19.) If it does so, then the increased supply of labour will increase the economy's full-employment output. For a second example, let there be a large tax exemption for the research and development done by firms. If this causes an increase in invention and innovation, there will be more output of those goods and services that are affected.

If enough individual supply curves are shifted, the aggregate supply of all goods will be significantly increased.

Macroeconomic Theories and Economic Policies

In this chapter, we have discussed the main variables of macroeconomics and some of the reasons why policy-makers are concerned about them. What determines the size of these variables, and how governments can influence them, is the subject-matter of macroeconomic theory to which we will soon turn our attention. First, however, we must look in more detail at the output and income variables of macroeconomics. This we do in Chapter 23.

Summary

1 Macroeconomics studies the economy in terms of broad aggregates and averages such as total employment and unemployment, total national product, the overall price level and the balance of payments.

2 Six major issues concern: (1) the amount of employment and unemployment, (2) the rate of inflation (changes in the price level), (3) the trade cycle (fluctuations in output and employment), (4) stagflation (the combination of high unemployment and high inflation), (5) economic growth (long-term trend of output), and (6) the behaviour of the exchange rate and the balance of payments.

3 High unemployment is undesirable because of the lost output and human misery involved. High output is desirable because the size of the national product determines (along with the size of the population) the average standard of living of a country's residents.

4 Changes in the price level are measured by an index number of prices. The index shows the percentage change in the cost of purchasing a given quantity of commodities in any year, compared to a base year.

5 Changes in the general price level may be undesirable in so far as they cause the price mechanism to allocate resources less efficiently and/or less equitably than would otherwise occur. This tends to be more likely when changes are unanticipated than when they are anticipated. Anticipated inflation causes less disruption than does unanticipated inflation.

6 The major primary goals of macroeconomic policy are (1) full employment (which does not mean zero unemployment), (2) a satisfactory rate of growth of national product, and (3) a stable price level. A satisfactory balance of payments is usually regarded as a secondary policy goal, since it is not so obviously desirable in itself, but may inhibit attainment of the primary goals if it is not achieved.

7 Two sets of macroeconomic policy instruments are: (1) demand-side policies, which include fiscal and monetary policies; (2) supply-side policies.

Questions

1 Indicate whether each of these events primarily concern microeconomics (MI) or macroeconomics (MA).
  (a) The price of wheat rises due to a poor harvest.
  (b) Inflation breaks out in the USSR.
  (c) Employment falls in the car industry due to a recession.
  (d) Output of computers doubles as demand soars.
  (e) The general level of unemployment reaches 12 per cent (as recession deepens).
  (f) Rapid growth in Hong Kong doubles (real) GDP over the last decade.

2 Consider the following table and then answer the questions that follow.

Retail Prices (1995 = 100)

	Weights	2000	2005	2010
Food	.180	175	190	250
Transport	.160	150	200	250
Housing	.150	200	230	300

  (a) By what persentage did the price of food change between 2000 and 2005?
  (b) Which group had the highest inflation rate between 2005 and 2010?
  (c) Did other items rise faster than food between 1995 and 2010?
  (d) What was the percentage increase in the price of transport between 2005 and 2010?
  (e) How important in consumers' budgets were all items other than F, T and H?

3 Explain the allegation: 'inflation is legalized government robbery' and the reply, 'no one with foresight needs to lose through inflation'.

4 Most films on the list of biggest-ever money-makers have been made recently. Does this mean that the most popular films are the most recent ones?

5 True or False? 'A rise in the general price level causes a rise in the value of money.'

6 Which One or More of the following is a correct statement about rapidly rising general unemployment?
  (a) It is seldom caused by a recession.
  (b) It usually causes output to rise.
  (c) It was typical of the period 1984–9.
  (d) It is wasteful because it causes output to fall below its potential levels.

7 Given these individual RPIs, what is the all-items' RPI?

Item	Weights in base year	Current index
Food	40	115
Clothing	10	96
Housing	30	140
All Other	20	112

23 The Circular Flow and National Income Accounting

In Parts 2 and 3, we studied individual markets, such as those for labour and for wheat. In Parts 4 and 5, we study how these markets fit together into a broader picture.

THE CIRCULAR FLOW OF INCOME

In Figure 23.1, all *producers* of goods and services are grouped together in the lower circle labelled producers. All *consumers* of goods and services are grouped together in the upper circle labelled consumers. Of course, most individuals have a double role. As buyers of goods and services, they play a part in consuming output; as sellers of factor services, they play a part in producing that output.

Those who buy and consume goods include individual consumers, firms and governments. When we speak of an individual consumer, we are referring to someone who buys and consumes goods. A HOUSEHOLD refers to all people who live under the same roof and who make joint financial decisions about, among other things, the purchase and consumption of goods. In microeconomics, we use the term 'consumer' to refer to the basic purchasing unit. In macroeconomics we use the term 'household'.[1]

The interactions between producers and consumers take place through two kinds of markets.

Goods markets: The outputs of commodities flow from producers to consumers through what are usually known as goods (or product) markets. Note the plural in 'product markets'. Just as firms produce many products, so are there many markets in which products are sold. Households constitute one major group of consumers – indeed the largest, by amount consumed. They buy, for their own use, goods and services such as food, clothing, train journeys, record albums and cars. Other 'consumers' are firms who purchase capital goods produced by yet other firms, and foreigners who purchase our exports. For the time being, we concentrate on the first group.

Factor markets: Most people earn their incomes by selling factor services to firms. Exceptions are people receiving pensions, unemployment benefits and income support; they receive an income but not in return for providing their factor services to aid in current production.

Most of those who do sell factor services are employees. They sell their labour services to firms in return for wages. Some people own capital and receive interest or profits for providing it. Some people own land and derive rents from it. Buying and selling of these factor services takes place in factor markets. The buyers are producers. They use the services that they purchase to produce goods that are sold to consumers.

The circular flow: What we have just described involves a circular *flow*. Money flows both to producers as a result of selling goods and services to consumers, and to consumers as a result of their selling factor services to producers.

This concept of a circularity in economic relations is a critical one. It helps us to understand how the separate parts of the economy are related to each other in a system of mutual interaction. For example, what producers do affects households, since the wages they pay affect people's incomes. What households do affects firms, since the goods they buy affect the sales revenues of firms.

The circular flow can be examined at various levels. The first is what is called the MICROECONOMIC level. This is what is covered in Parts 2 and 3 of this book. The microeconomic view stresses the details of the flows within and between the myriad individual markets that form the entire economy.

The second level is termed the MACROECONOMIC level. We shall briefly consider this below, and it is the subject of the second half of this book. The macroeconomic level is painted with a broad brush; it aggregates flows in individual markets to consider flows between various very broad 'sectors' of the economy.

The macroeconomic view of the circular flow

Macroeconomics suppresses the details of the many markets through which the circular flow works. In doing so, attention is concentrated on the total flows shown in Figures 23.1 and 23.2.

Macroeconomics deals with broad aggregates, and may, therefore, be described as *aggregate economics*. In macroeconomics we study such things as the total number of people employed (the aggregate amount of labour flowing through all of the labour markets in the economy), and the total sales of all consumers' goods (the aggregate amount of all goods and services for consumption flowing through all of the economy's relevant markets).

Money flows: Dealing with such aggregates, immediately poses an important measurement problem: how do we add

---

1 When using real-world data, the difference between individual consumers and households can be important. In what follows, we use the term 'household' to describe the basic purchasing unit for consumption goods because that is the term usually employed by macroeconomists. At the introductory level, however, the distinction is unimportant and, for everything that matters in this book, you can take the terms 'individual consumer' and 'household' as interchangeable.

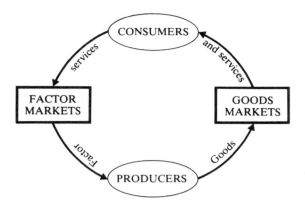

FIGURE 23.1 The Circular Flow of Goods and Services. Factor services flow from consumers to producers, while goods and services flow from producers to consumers.

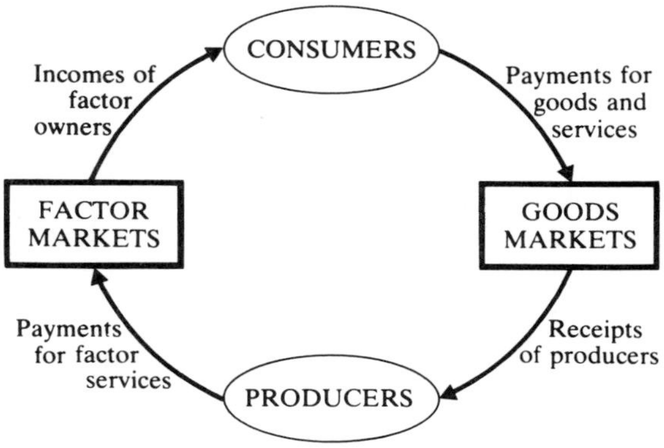

FIGURE 23.2 The Circular Flow of Income. Payments flow from consumers to producers in return for goods and services bought by consumers; payments flow from producers to consumers in return for factor services bought by producers.

up the various amounts to get the total flows that are to be studied in macroeconomics? We can measure total output of wheat in tonnes, of shirts in numbers, and of electricity in kilowatts. But what is the total output of all three taken together? To answer this question, we need a common denominator that we can use to add up such diverse outputs as wheat, shirts and electricity.

The common denominator that economists use is money. Almost all goods and services have money values, which are simply the prices paid to purchase them. The total money *value* of all output is, thus, a meaningful, and a convenient, way of measuring the *size* of the economy's total, or aggregate, output.

Income flows: Figure 23.2 shows how we look at the totals that flow through the economy's markets when we use the measuring rod of money. The two Figures, 23.1 and 23.2, are alternative ways of looking at the same transactions. Every market transaction is an exchange. It has two sides, in the sense that, for every sale, there is a purchase and, for every seller, there is a buyer. The buyer receives goods or services and parts with money; the seller receives money and parts with goods or services.

Figure 23.1 concentrates on the flows of goods and services through markets. These are seen flowing, anti-clockwise, from consumers to producers and from producers to consumers. Figure 23.2 concentrates on the corresponding money flows. Money flows are seen going in the opposite direction, i.e., clockwise. Money flows from producers to consumers to pay for factor services, and from consumers to producers for goods and services.

To distinguish these two sets of flows, each of which is the counterpart of the other, the flows in Figure 23.1 are called *real* flows while those in Figure 23.2 are called money, or *nominal*, flows.

Macroeconomics deals with the money flows that are shown in Figure 23.2 (and many other similar flows that we shall encounter later). When we talk of total output, we refer to the right-hand flow in Figure 23.2: the total value of goods and services produced and flowing through

goods markets to purchasers. When we talk of the total amount of factor services used, and of the total incomes earned by the owners of factors of production, we refer to the left-hand flow in the Figure: to the total value of all factor services flowing through factor markets from the suppliers of factors to producers.

MAJOR TYPES OF PRODUCTION

The circular flow diagrams have identified two main groups, producers and consumers. To avoid confusion, you should note that the whole group of producers is referred to by a variety of names such as the 'production sector', the 'firm sector' or the 'business sector'.

To begin our study, we look at producers and divide their production into three main categories which cover consumption commodities, investment goods, and government production.

Consumption Commodities

The category of consumption commodities, normally referred to as CONSUMPTION, includes the output of all goods and services for consumption by households (except for new houses). These are the economy's outputs of bread, beer, dresses, TV sets, haircuts, concerts, and a host of other goods and services that satisfy people's wants.

Notice three things about consumption commodities.

- First, the category includes only *currently produced* goods and services. For example, the output of new cars is part of the current production of consumption goods, but the purchase of a used car (produced in an earlier year) is merely a transfer of ownership of an existing asset. It is not a part of current car production. Thus the value of all second-hand goods transferred is not a part of the economy's current production.

  It is worth noting before we pass on, however, that the amount paid to the car dealer for the work he does as an 'intermediary', bringing buyer and seller together, *is* a part of current production. After all, the second-hand-car dealer is providing a current service that people are willing to pay for and which is a current output of a service. What does not count is the value of the car that goes to the former owner. Thus, if I sell my old car to a car dealer for £3000, and he sells it to you for £3500, current output is £500 – not £3500, but not zero. The £3000 is merely a payment that goes, in effect, from you to me in return for the transfer of a car that was manufactured at some time in the past. The £500, however, represents the value of the currently produced services of the second-hand-car dealer. He must pay his sales and office staff; he must also pay rent and advertising expenses; and he must earn a return on the capital that he has invested in the firm. This is where his £500 goes, and it will be reported as a current contribution to national product.

- Second, consumer goods and services are included in the measurement of production *when they are produced*, not when they are consumed. With non-durable goods such as haircuts and fresh strawberries, there is no significant difference between the time of production and of consumption, since these two points in time are very close to each other. Indeed with a service such as a haircut or a rock concert, consumption usually occurs at the same point in time as production. With durable goods, such as cars and TV sets, however, there is a marked difference. The good is produced at one time, but it is consumed over the good's lifetime, which may be many years. For example, a 1980 model refrigerator that lasted 10 years was produced in one year but was consumed over the 10 years that it was in service.
- Third, residential housing is the one exception to the general rule that the term consumption commodities refers to the output of all goods and services consumed by households. Housing is counted as investment and is considered below.

Investment Goods

Investment goods, normally referred to as INVESTMENT, are the capital goods that are studied in microeconomics, plus residential housing, which is counted as an investment rather than a durable consumer good by the conventions of national income accounting.

In macroeconomics, investment goods are divided into three main categories: fixed capital, circulating capital, and residential housing. The first two of these categories were discussed in detail in Chapter 19. The *output* of these investment goods in any period is the amount of new capital goods, new additions to circulating capital and new residential housing produced over that period. The total output in these three categories is called total investment.

There is a possible source of confusion arising from the common usage in which a household says it *invests* when it purchases some financial assets such as bonds or shares. This is *not* investment expenditure in the sense in which economists use the term. All that the household is doing is passing funds over to the sellers of these shares or bonds – which in itself creates no output and no employment. It is

the transfer of ownership of an equity or a debt, but it is not a current production of an investment good.

Fixed capital: The current output of fixed capital includes currently constructed factories, and machinery and equipment currently produced. These fixed-capital goods may be used to replace other capital goods that have worn out or become obsolete, or they may be used to make a net addition to the nation's total stock of capital.

Circulating capital: In the UK, circulating capital is called STOCKS, but the American term INVENTORIES is also used. (It is also sometimes called WORKING CAPITAL.) It consists of (1) stocks of materials that firms hold for use in further production, (2) stocks of semi-finished goods in the process of production, and (3) stocks of finished goods ready for sale but not yet sold. Current output of these stocks consists not of the total stocks held, since much of this may be carried over from the past, but rather of the *change* in these stocks over the period in question. For example, assume that £700m worth of stocks are held at the beginning of the year and £780m at the end of the year. This means that total investment in stock accumulation was £80m over the year. This £80m will be a part of the economy's total investment for that period.

To show this relation more generally, let I_s stand for current investment in stocks and write:

$$I_s = \text{End-of-year stocks} - \text{Beginning-of-year stocks}$$

If stocks held at the end of the year exceed those held at the beginning of the year, we say there has been a STOCK ACCUMULATION or 'positive investment in stocks'. If stocks held at the end of the year are smaller than stocks held at the beginning of the year, stocks are being reduced. In this case, valuable things produced in the past have been used up in the current year and not replaced. Several equivalent terms are used to describe such a situation. We may say that there has been a STOCK DECUMULATION or DESTOCKING or 'negative investment in stocks'. As an example, assume that the £700m worth of stocks held at the beginning of the year in the previous example were reduced to £650m by the end of the year. This would represent a negative investment, or decumulation of stocks of £50m over the year.

One final word of caution is in order. The word stock has two distinct, but related, meanings. First, it is used in the restricted sense just described: to denote circulating capital. Second, it is used in the more general sense to denote a quantity that does not have a time dimension. The quantity of circulating capital, the quantity of fixed capital, or the amount of money you have in the bank are all stocks in this more general sense, while the change in circulating capital per unit of time, the change in the quantity of fixed capital per unit of time, and the amount that you add to your bank balance per unit of time are all flows. A stock, in the restricted sense of the quantity of circulating capital in existence at any one time, is but one example of a stock in the more general sense.

Housing: A house is a very durable asset that yields its utility to its user slowly over the lifetime of the dwelling. For this reason, the nation's current output of new housing is treated as an investment item rather than as an item for current consumption.

Gross and net investment: The total production of investment goods that occurs during a period is called the economy's GROSS INVESTMENT. The amount of capital that wears out, or becomes obsolete, is called DEPRECIATION or CAPITAL CONSUMPTION. The amount necessary for the replacement of capital goods that have worn out, or have been discarded as obsolete, is called REPLACEMENT INVESTMENT. The remainder is called NET INVESTMENT:

Net Investment = Gross Investment – Depreciation

A digression on stocks and flows

We must pause for a moment to discuss the important distinction between stocks and flows. This distinction arose in our discussion of investment, and it will arise in other important contexts later.

It is easy to become confused between the nation's *stock* of capital and the *changes* to that stock which arise out of current production. The nation's current *stock* of capital – we are now using 'stocks' in the general sense – consists of all the fixed capital, all the circulating capital, and all the housing that has been produced in the past and is in existence today. The nation's *current output* of investment goods (capital goods) is a *flow* that consists of additions to these stocks that are made in the current period. Thus only *additions* to fixed capital, and only *additions* to stocks of circulating capital, and only *additions* to the nation's stock of housing are counted as the *output* of *current* investment goods.

The possible confusion just mentioned is an example of a general problem of confusing *stocks* (e.g., the stock of capital) and *flows* (e.g., this year's addition to the stock of capital). To study the distinction, further consider, as illustrated in Figure 23.3, a bath half full of water with the tap turned on and the plug removed. You now have in mind a model similar to many simple economic theories.

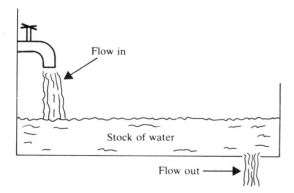

FIGURE 23.3 Stocks and Flows. The amount of water in the bath is a stock, the amounts entering through the tap and leaving through the drain are flows.

The level of water in the bath is a stock – an amount that is just there. We could express it as so many gallons of water. If we replaced the plug and turned off the tap, the stock of water currently in the tub would remain there indefinitely. Now consider the amount of water entering through the tap and the amount leaving down the drain. Both are flows. We could express them as so many gallons per minute or per hour. A flow necessarily has a time dimension – there is so much flow *per period of time*. A stock does not – it is just so many tonnes or gallons or machines.

The flow into the bath tub is an addition to the stock of water in the tub. From the point of view of that stock, it is a positive flow. The flow of water down the drain is a subtraction from the stock of water in the tub. From the point of view of that stock, it is a negative flow. The change in the stock is the difference between these two flows or, stated more formally: the change in the stock equals the difference between the flow into it (additions to it) and the flow out of it (subtractions from it).

The total amount of machinery in the country is part of the nation's *stock* of capital – analogous to the amount of water in the bath tub. The amount of depreciation is a flow that reduces the capital stock – analogous to the amount of water flowing down the drain. Finally, the amount of new capital goods produced, i.e. gross investment, is a flow that increases the capital stock – analogous to the flow of water coming from the tap into the bath. The difference between the two flows, gross investment minus depreciation, is the addition to the country's capital stock, i.e. net investment.

Government Production

To determine government production, we need to look at government expenditure. When doing so, it is important to distinguish between two main types of government expenditure. The first type is expenditure which pays for the current services of factors of production which are used to produce current output. This is expenditure on such things as road building, national health, civil servants' salaries (which pay for the resource of labour), and defence. It is often called EXHAUSTIVE EXPENDITURE, and that is the term we shall use. All government exhaustive expenditure is counted as producing output of goods and services. Government output thus includes the activities of the police, courts of law, traffic wardens, Foreign Office employees, building inspectors, and a host of other activities at all levels of government.

The second type is expenditure which merely transfers purchasing power from one group to another. This is expenditure on such things as retirement pensions, unemployment insurance benefits, disability payments, income support benefits, and a host of other payments made by the modern welfare state. This type of expenditure is usually called TRANSFER PAYMENTS. Such expenditures do not add to current output; they merely transfer purchasing power from those who provide the funds – usually taxpayers – to those who receive them. Transfer payments made by the government are *not*, therefore, regarded as a part of the government's current output of goods and services. For the moment, we confine ourselves to exhaustive expenditures.

OUTPUT, EXPENDITURE AND INCOME IN THE CIRCULAR FLOW

Figure 23.4 is similar to the simple circular flow diagram which was Figure 23.2 on page 255 but with some of the explanatory labels omitted. To find out what is happening to the level of economic activity in the country, we need to measure the amount of this circular flow over some period of time, usually taken as a year. The diagram shows the three ways in which this can be done. These are called the output (or product) method, the income method and the expenditure method. They are methods of measuring the *total market value* of the nation's output. (Later we shall consider measures based on values other than market prices.) We discuss below how total output is measured using each of the three approaches. Figure 23.5 shows the major components of each of the three measures, and it can be referred to as the discussion proceeds.[1]

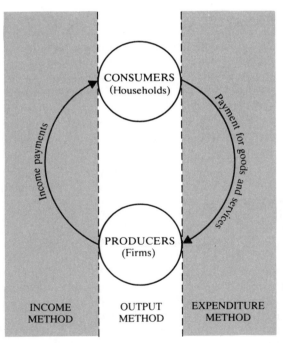

FIGURE 23.4 Three Methods for Measuring the Value of the Nation's Output. The Output Method looks directly at the value of what is produced; the Expenditure Method looks at the expenditure needed to produce the nation's output; the Income Method looks at the incomes generated by the production of that output.

The Output or Product Method

The first method is to go directly to producers and add up

1 Much of the factual detail of the measures discussed here is given in Chapter 7 of Harbury and Lipsey.

the values of all of their outputs. (We noted earlier in this chapter that we can add up the values of different types of production – tonnes of steel, megawatts of electricity, and kilos of strawberries – by adding up their money values.) This method measures the circular flow at the point of production and it is shown by the middle, unshaded section of the diagram.

Double counting

When we measure the value of each producer's output, we encounter a problem which is called *double counting*. Because of the advantages of specialization, the output of virtually every commodity occurs over a series of stages, each stage being carried out by separate firms. Thus coffee spoons may be made by one firm, from stainless steel provided by a second firm, which used iron ore provided by a third firm, and transported by a fourth. If we add up the value of the sales of the mining firm, the steel plant, the transport firm and the spoon manufacturer, we would get a total well in excess of the value of final output of coffee spoons.

The problem of double counting is avoided when the output of each firm is defined as its value added. VALUE ADDED is the output of a firm, minus all inputs that it buys from other firms. It is thus the amount added to the value of the product in question by the firm's own activities.

TABLE 23.1 Value Added Through Stages of Production: An Example

Inter-firm transactions at three different stages of production				
	Firm B	Firm I	Firm F	All firms
1 Purchases from other firms	£0	£100	£130	£230 = Total inter-firm sales
2 Purchase of factors of production (wages, rent, interest, profits)	£100	£30	£50	£180 = Value added
3 Value of sales	£100	£130	£180	£410 = Value of total sales

The sum of the values added by all the firms in the economy is the nation's total output, its national product. The worked example given in Table 23.1 develops this idea further. It uses a simple example in which production moves through three stages, begun by the basic producer, B, through the intermediate firm, I, and ending up with the producer of the final product, F. Firm B produces basic materials valued at £100; the firm's value added is £100. Firm I purchases these raw materials, valued at £100, and produces semi-manufactured goods (often called intermediate products) that is sells for £130. Its value added is £30 as a result of the firm's activities. Firm F purchases these semi-manufactured goods for £130 and works them into a finished state, selling them for £180. Firm F's value added is £50. The value of final goods, £180, is found either by counting the sales of firm F or by taking the sum of the values added by each firm. This value is less than the £410 that we obtain by adding up the market value of the commodities sold by each firm.

The above illustration suggests another important distinction. INTERMEDIATE GOODS are goods and services that are sold by one firm to be used as inputs by another firm. FINAL GOODS are the end-product of economic activity; they are the economy's output. This final output includes all goods for consumption, all investment goods, and all goods and services produced by the government. Each firm's contribution to final output is measured by its value added.

The total value of output

The output method measures the nation's output as the sum of all values added in the economy:

Total output = the sum of all values added

The Expenditure Method

The expenditure method arrives at the nation's total output by adding up the expenditures needed to purchase all of the final output of the economy. This method measures the flow around the right-hand part of the circuit shown in Figure 23.4. The main categories of expenditure are considered below.

Consumption (C):   This includes the value of all consumer goods and services purchased over the year. *We give total consumption expenditures the designation C.*

Investment (I):   This is the value of all capital goods produced over the year. It includes the value of all new, fixed capital, such as plant and equipment, all new housing,

and any net changes in circulating capital. *We designate total investment expenditure by the symbol I.*

Government (G):   When the government spends money to produce goods and services that are sold, the goods and services are valued at market prices. We have already observed, however, that many government exhaustive expenditures do not produce goods or services that are sold on the market. The value of the output resulting from such expenditures is taken to be the amount spent on them. In other words, valuation is at cost. (See below for further discussion of this matter.)

We have also observed that government expenditure on transfer payments is not a part of current output. Thus, *to get at the government's contribution to national income from the expenditure method, we need to count only the government's exhaustive expenditures, which we designate by the symbol G.*

The total value of expenditure on output

A closed economy: A CLOSED ECONOMY is one that does not engage in foreign trade; an OPEN ECONOMY is one that does. In a closed economy, the expenditure approach measures total output as the sum of consumption, investment and government expenditure. In symbols:

A closed economy's total expenditure = $C + I + G$

An open economy: In an open economy part of the expenditure in each of the categories so far considered – consumption, investment and government – goes to purchase commodities produced in other countries. For example, total expenditure on cars bought in the UK

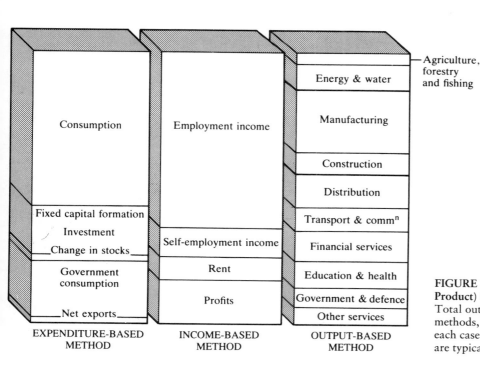

EXPENDITURE-BASED METHOD	INCOME-BASED METHOD	OUTPUT-BASED METHOD
Consumption	Employment income	Energy & water
		Manufacturing
Fixed capital formation		Construction
Investment	Self-employment income	Distribution
Change in stocks		Transport & commⁿ
Government consumption	Rent	Financial services
	Profits	Education & health
Net exports		Government & defence
		Other services

— Agriculture, forestry and fishing

FIGURE 23.5 Total Output (Gross Domestic Product) Calculated from the Three Methods. Total output is the same from all three methods, but the breakdown is different in each case. The relative sizes of the segments are typical of figures for recent years.

includes not only the value of purchases of cars made in the UK but also purchases of parts of those cars that were made abroad plus the purchases of cars wholly produced abroad and imported into the UK. To discover the output produced by the car industry in the UK, we must subtract from total expenditures on cars by UK residents the amount that goes to purchase imported cars. Similar considerations apply to all other categories of expenditure. Some expenditure on investment goes to buy equipment and materials imported from abroad. The same is true for government expenditure; e.g., when a Japanese computer is bought by a local authority, or a foreign selling agent is hired by a government department selling arms abroad.

So, to arrive at *national* output from the expenditure method, it is necessary to subtract from $C + I + G$ the value of all expenditures on imports, which we designate as M.

Exports pose an analogous problem. When Italians, Swedes and Germans purchase British cars and British-made car parts, this is expenditure on UK production. So to calculate UK national output from the expenditure approach, we must add in all expenditures by foreign residents on UK exports. We give these the symbol X.

Net exports: To take account of foreign trade, we must add the value of exports and subtract the value of imports. In symbols this is $+ X$ and $- M$. It is customary to group these into a single term called NET EXPORTS $(X - M)$.

In summary, total output from the expenditure method is the sum of consumption, investment, government expenditure and net exports:

An open economy's total expenditure = $C + I + G + (X - M)$

The Income Method

The income method looks at total output in terms of the incomes generated in the process of producing that output. It measures the flow around the left-hand part of the circuit in Figure 23.4.

Since all market value that is produced must belong to someone, all output generates income for the factors that produce it (plus, as we shall see, an amount that goes to the government as indirect-tax revenue). These incomes must account for, and hence add up to, the total value of this output.

Major classes of measured incomes

Wages and salaries, which national income accountants call income from employment, is by far the largest income share generated. This includes gross pay before income tax, social security and pension fund contributions are deducted. In total, these represent that part of the value of production attributable to labour. Next, in order of size, comes what are called gross trading profits (the incomes of privately and publicly owned producers who sell their outputs on the market), followed by the capital consumption allowance (which is the national income accountants' estimate of depreciation). Smaller items include incomes of the self-employed and rent. The former is

mainly the income of farmers, unincorporated businesses, tradesmen, and professionals who work either on their own or in partnerships. The latter includes rents received by those owning property let to others, and what is called 'imputed rent' of owner-occupied dwellings.

This last term is new and requires some explanation. In general, to 'impute' means 'to attribute to'. In this case, a rental value of housing occupied by its owners is imputed to the owners' income even though no actual rent is paid or received. Let us see why this is done.

When a block of flats is built, the expenditure on it is part of this year's investment. When it is rented out, the rentals appear in national income as part of the gross profits of the owners of the flats. However, a flat may not be let; instead it may be occupied by the owner. In this case, a rental value for the use of the housing services is imputed and included in the total value of output of goods and services. This imputation of rent to owner-occupied housing is needed if all housing, whether owner-occupied or rented, is to be treated similarly.

Government taxes and subsidies

If there were neither taxes nor subsidies, the market value of all output would equal the incomes earned by the owners of the land, labour and capital used in the process of production. Taxes and subsidies, however, introduce a complication, as illustrated by the following examples.

If the government gives a subsidy to the producers of wheat of 50p per bushel of wheat produced, every bushel produced can generate 50p of income to farmers over and above its market value. Say, for example, that wheat sells for £4 a bushel but there is a subsidy to producers of 50p per bushel. Then, those factors used in producing wheat will earn £4.50 for every bushel produced.

Now consider taxes levied on the production or sale of goods and services, so-called indirect taxes. Say, for example, that there is no subsidy but instead a sales tax of 50p for every bushel of wheat sold. While the market value of each bushel produced remains at £4, the incomes earned by the factors used to produce that wheat will be only £3.50; the extra 50p goes to the government as an indirect tax.

The above examples illustrate the following important conclusion. In the case of a subsidy, incomes earned by the factors of production (market value of output plus subsidies) exceed the total value of output. In the case of a tax, incomes earned (the market value of output minus taxes taken by the government) fall short of the total market value of output.

To allow for the effect of indirect taxes and subsidies, two adjustments are needed when we add up incomes generated by production in order to arrive at the total value of production *measured at market prices*. First, we must add the government's taxes on goods and services, since these are part of the market value of output that does not give rise to incomes going to land, labour or capital. Second we must subtract government subsidies on goods and services, since these allow incomes to exceed the market value of output.

In the national accounts, the effects of indirect taxes and subsidies are usually combined into one figure called *net indirect taxes*, which is total taxes minus total subsidies. Students are sometimes confused as to whether this amount should be added or subtracted. If you keep its purpose firmly in mind, you should not get confused. *If you have all factor incomes and want to get the market value of output, you must add in net taxes. If, however, you have the market value of total output and want to get factor earnings, you must deduct net taxes.*

The total value of income generated by output

The income method measures the value of total output at market prices as the sum of all factor incomes generated by the process of production. This is the sum of all wages, interest, profits and rents, plus net indirect taxes.

Why the Three Methods Yield the Same Total: The Identity of Output, Income and Expenditure

In all three methods so far considered, the basic *overall* aggregate being measured is the total value of the nation's output at market prices. This can be looked at directly in terms of the output itself, O, or the expenditure required to purchase it, E, or the income it generates, Y. Although the details of each calculation give us independent information, the totals do not, since all three are defined so that they are identical:

$$O = E = Y$$

The reason for the identity of Y and O is that Y measures the incomes generated by producing O (plus the amount that goes to the government as a result of net indirect taxes). The value of all output must belong to someone: what is not wages, interest and rent becomes either profits of the producers or goes to the government through indirect taxes.[1] Between them they must account for all output.

Now consider the identity between O and E. This follows because E measures the expenditure required to purchase the nation's output, which must equal the value of that output. In calculating expenditure, national income accountants add up the amounts actually spent to purchase what is sold, plus the amount that would have to be spent if the output added to stocks had been sold instead.

The interest in having all three measures lies not in their identical total, which is purely a matter of definition, but in the breakdown of each. In the case of O, the breakdown is by industry, such as electricity generation and car production; in the case of E, it is by type of expenditure, such

as consumption and investment; in the case of Y, it is by type of income, such as wages and salaries.

National income as the general term

We have just seen that, when appropriately measured, output, income and expenditure are identical. They yield a single total that simultaneously measures the market value of total output, the incomes earned by producing that output (plus net government taxes), and the expenditure needed to purchase that output.

The usual term used to refer to this total in theoretical work is NATIONAL INCOME. It is given the symbol Y. Thus, when we refer throughout all subsequent chapters to the national income, we are referring to the total value of income earned in the country, usually over a year, as well as to the total value of output, as well as to the total value of the expenditure needed to purchase that output.

NATIONAL INCOME STATISTICS

In Chapter 25, when we come to the theory of how national income is determined, we shall see that expenditures are the most useful way of looking at national income. For this reason, we now study a series of expenditure measures. Each gives a somewhat different total, and each provides useful and interesting information. The relation between them is illustrated in Figure 23.6 and discussed below.

Various Measures of Total Expenditure

We start with a measure that is the basis from which the most commonly quoted measures are calculated. TOTAL DOMESTIC EXPENDITURE (TDE) is the sum of all domestic expenditure on final output, irrespective of where the output was produced:

$$TDE = C + I + G$$

Next comes TOTAL FINAL EXPENDITURE (TFE), which is the sum of all domestic expenditure on final output, irrespective both of the country in which the goods and services were produced, *and of the country in which they were consumed*. This is TDE plus exports:

$$TFE = C + I + G + X$$

Next, we come to the most widely used measure of the national income. This is GROSS DOMESTIC PRODUCT (GDP) *at market prices*. It is defined as TFE minus imports. Subtracting imports reduces the value of TFE by the amount of expenditure that goes to purchase goods and services produced abroad:

$$GDP \text{ (at market prices)} = C + I + G + (X - M)$$

Recall that it is customary to group exports and imports together into the single term $(X - M)$.

The GDP at market prices tells us the value of all final expenditure on the goods and services that are produced within the nation.

The next measure that we need to consider is called GROSS DOMESTIC PRODUCT *at factor cost*. This

---

1 If firms make losses, wages, interest, rent, etc. exceed the value of output and the losses must be subtracted from other incomes to get the value of output. Also, goods produced and not sold are valued at market prices, and the difference between their value and their cost of production is counted as profits and recorded as part of profit income even though this will not accrue until the goods are sold.

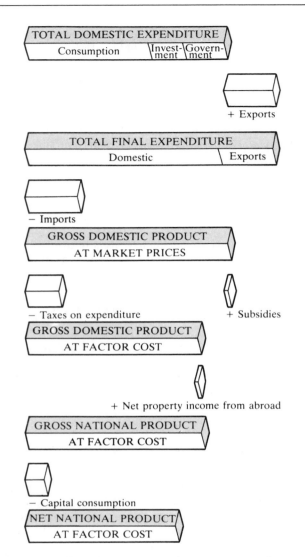

FIGURE 23.6 The Relation Between the Various Expenditure Totals. Of the totals shown, TFE is the largest and NNP is the smallest.

measures GDP at the cost of the factors used to produce it, and hence at the incomes earned by those factors. It differs from GDP at market prices by the correction for *net* indirect taxes. Spelling this out in detail, GDP at market prices must be changed by the *addition* of government subsidies on the production or sale of what is produced, and the *subtraction* of taxes on the production or sale of what is produced. Subsidies, as we have seen, allow factor incomes to exceed the market value of goods sold, while taxes on expenditure force incomes received to be less than the market value of goods sold because some of the proceeds derived from the sale of the product accrue to the government:

$$\begin{array}{l}\textbf{GDP} \\ \textbf{(at factor cost)}\end{array} = \begin{array}{l}\textbf{GDP (at market prices)} \\ \textbf{+ subsidies} - \textbf{taxes on expenditure}\end{array}$$

The next measure is GROSS NATIONAL PRODUCT

(GNP) *at factor cost*. This is the sum of all incomes earned by UK residents in return for contributions to current production that takes place anywhere in the world. We get from GDP to GNP in two steps. First we *add* receipts of interest, profits and dividends received by UK residents from assets that they own overseas. These receipts are part of incomes earned by UK residents, but they are not a part of UK production. Second, we have to *subtract* interest, profits and dividends earned on assets located in the UK, but owned abroad, if we wish to arrive at income earned by UK residents. Although these are part of UK production, they are incomes earned, not by UK, but by *foreign*, residents. The total of these adjustments is called NET PROPERTY INCOME FROM ABROAD.

$$\begin{array}{l}\textbf{GNP} \\ \textbf{(at factor cost)}\end{array} = \begin{array}{l}\textbf{GDP (at factor cost) +} \\ \textbf{net property income from abroad}\end{array}$$

The next measure that we meet is called NET NATIONAL PRODUCT (NNP) *at factor cost*. This is GNP minus the capital consumption allowance (depreciation). NNP is thus a measure of the net output of the economy after deducting from gross output an amount necessary to maintain intact the existing stock of capital. (In the UK National Accounts this is known as *net national income*.)

$$\begin{array}{l}\textbf{NNP} \\ \textbf{(at factor cost)}\end{array} = \begin{array}{l}\textbf{GNP} - \textbf{depreciation (or} \\ \textbf{capital consumption allowance)}\end{array}$$

We have illustrated the *net* concept by discussing NNP. But once we have the idea of deducting the capital consumption allowance to calculate a figure that is net of the amount needed to maintain the country's capital stock intact, we can make this subtraction from any of the 'gross' figures mentioned above. For example, if we take gross domestic product, GDP, and subtract the capital consumption allowance, we obtain *net* domestic product, NDP.

Other measures

PERSONAL INCOME is gross income earned by households, whether as factor payments or transfer payments, before allowance for personal income taxes. A number of adjustments to NNP (at factor cost) are required to arrive at personal income. The most important are (1) subtracting from NNP all income taxes paid by businesses (since these are part of the value of output that is not paid to persons); (2) adding to NNP all transfer payments (since these create incomes for persons that do not arise out of current production); and (3) deducting all *undistributed* business profits (since these are incomes that are not paid out to persons because the firms retain the funds for their own purposes).

PERSONAL DISPOSABLE INCOME is a measure of the amount of personal income that households have available to spend or to save. It is calculated as personal income minus both personal income taxes and national insurance contributions.

INTERPRETING NATIONAL INCOME MEASURES

The information provided by measures of national income is useful, but unless carefully interpreted it can also be misleading. Furthermore, since each specialized measure gives different information, each may be the best statistic for studying a particular problem.

We start with two variations on total national income, each of which gives us useful information.

Money Values and Real Values

We have already studied the important distinction between measures of national income that use current prices and are called *nominal* national income and those that use constant prices and are called *real* national income. (See pages 243–4.)

All we need to do here, therefore, is to summarize the significance of this important distinction.

When nominal national income changes, we know that the market value of total output has changed. This may be the result of changes in either, or both, the *quantities* and the *prices* of final outputs. When real national income changes, we know that this must be the result of changes in the quantities of final output (since the prices at which outputs are valued remain unchanged).

Total Output and Per Capita Output

Both real and nominal national income are measures of aggregate, or total, income. For many purposes, totals are just what we require. For example, to assess a country's potential military strength, we need to know (among other things) the total output of which it is capable. Also if we wish to gauge the importance of a country as a market for our exports, we are interested in its total sales and purchases.

For other purposes, such as studying changes in living standards, we require *per capita* measures, which are obtained by dividing a total measure such as GDP by the population. Comparisons of living standards are often made by reference to per capita disposable income in constant prices. This measure allows for comparisons over time in a single country, and also for international comparisons, if disposable incomes are all measured in terms of the prices ruling in one country.

There are many useful per capita measures, and the division must be made by the appropriate 'population'. Dividing GDP by the total population gives a measure of how much GDP there is on average for each person in the economy; this is called PER CAPITA GDP. It is particularly useful in estimating living standards. Dividing GDP by the number of persons employed tells us the average output per employed person. This is called GDP PER EMPLOYED PERSON. Dividing GDP by the total number of hours worked measures output per hour of labour input. This is called GDP PER HOUR WORKED. These last two measures give us estimates of overall labour productivity.

Measurement Problems

Next we consider three problems connected with getting useful measures of national income: classification, coverage and valuation.

Classification

Our first problem concerns how to classify certain items that are a part of total national income. We illustrate the many problems of classification with the example of residential housing.

Earlier in this chapter, we saw that expenditure on new housing is classified as an investment expenditure, while expenditure on all other consumer durables, some of which last even longer than many houses, is classified as a consumption expenditure. The decision to do so is arbitrary.

Coverage

There is always room for disagreement on what items of expenditure do and do not form a part of national income. Although we know what we mean by national income in a general, theoretical way, no concept is perfectly clear at the margins. Precise definitions of what is, and is not, a part of national income require tough decisions as to whether or not to include particular items. We will illustrate with the case of interest on the public (or national) debt.

Earlier in this chapter we observed that interest on private-sector debt is included in the national income while interest on public-sector debt is not. If a private firm borrows money and pays interest on its debt, this is counted as part of national income. The payment is understood to be in return for the service of private investors in providing productive capital to the firm. However, if the government borrows money to build a new nuclear power plant, the interest that is paid on this debt is counted as a transfer payment and hence not included in national income. In the case of the nuclear power plant, the distinction seems quite arbitrary. If the plant had been owned by a private firm, the interest on its debt would have been counted as a part of national income. But if the government owns the plant, and does exactly what the private firm would have done, the interest is not counted in national income.

The distinction between interest paid by private firms and by the government makes more sense in so far as the government's debt was accumulated to finance current, rather than capital, expenditures made in the past. Say, for example, that five years ago the government could not meet all of its unemployment benefits out of current tax revenue and borrowed money to enable it to make these payments. If the debt still exists, the government will be making current interest payments on it, and there will be no current output that is financed by these payments.

Valuation

Whenever a good is sold on the market, it can be, and is, valued at its market price. Major problems arise, however, with non-marketed output. We shall consider two categories of expenditure which present major valuation problems: government production and stock accumulation.

Consider government non-marketed production first. In many cases, the government's 'output' is not sold. This is the case, for example, with state education, defence and the services of fire departments. Since there is no market price at which to value these goods and services, they are valued 'at cost'. This means that whatever it costs the government to provide the service is taken as the value of the output of the service. Thus, *the government's total production of goods and services is taken to be equal to the total of the government's exhaustive expenditures.*

There is no easy alternative to valuing non-marketed government services 'at cost'. Such a procedure does, however, have one curious consequence in that productivity may appear to rise when it has actually fallen, and vice versa. To see this, consider an example. If one civil servant now does exactly what two used to do, and the redundant worker shifts to the private sector, the government's measured output will fall. This happens in spite of the fact that the things the government does are actually unchanged, and productivity (output per employed civil servant) has risen. Suppose, however, that it now takes two civil servants to do exactly what one used to do, and an extra civil servant is employed for this purpose. The government's measured contribution to output will rise – even though the things the government does remain unchanged, and productivity has fallen.

Another valuation problem arises with stocks accumulated by firms. Since stocks are goods that have *not* been sold, they must be valued by some convention. They could be valued at cost or at current market prices. Valuation at cost means using the amount spent on them so far (net of the value of inputs purchased from other firms to avoid double counting). Valuation at market price means valuing them at what they could be sold for today, which is what has been spent to produce them *plus* the profit margin that will be added to costs to determine selling price. In the UK's official national income statistics, market prices are used to value stocks. (Accounting practices vary, however, among firms.)

Valuation of stocks at market prices causes its own problems. In times of unexpected slumps in sales, stocks of unsold goods may pile up in the storerooms of their producers. Because these are valued at market prices, measured business profits will include the unrealized profits on these stocks. For this reason, an unexpected sales downturn, in which businesses may be in serious difficulty and be realizing few profits, is often accompanied by a high recorded level of profits in the national accounts.

Does the GDP Measure Living Standards?

Great interest attaches to measured values of GDP. Governments, investors, and ordinary citizens measure the success of their economy by how its GDP is changing over time, and how it compares with the GDPs of other countries. How well do the figures for per capita real GDP measure differences in living standards over time, and across countries?

There is no doubt that, by measuring the marketed value of goods and services produced, the GDP does tell us something about living standards. But the measure is far from perfect, both because it includes some things that do not contribute to current living standards, and because it omits many things that do.

Things included that do not contribute to current living standards

The most important item in this category is investment. Investment is important for future living standards but does not contribute to current ones.

Consider, for example, a country whose GDP grows by 3 per cent while its investment grows by more than 3 per cent at the expense of consumption, which falls by 1 per cent. The GDP figure will record 3 per cent growth but people's consumption will be down by 1 per cent. The reduction in their current living standards is freeing resources for investment which may raise living standards in the future. But currently their living standards fall, while this is not reflected in a fall in the GDP.

Things excluded from GDP that do contribute to current living standards

Many items mentioned in the earlier section fall into this category. Activities in the black economy and some illegal activities (such as goods smuggled into the country) do contribute to living standards, whether or not we approve of the manner in which they became available. So also do many non-marketed economic activities. We say no more about these since they were discussed above. Other important omitted matters are mentioned below.

Leisure: Leisure is another example of an omitted item. Although a shorter work week may make people happier, it will tend to reduce measured GDP. Much of the benefits of economic growth over the last 100 years have been taken out in increased leisure. Today's worker works for fewer days each year and for fewer hours each day, and has more holidays, than his or her counterpart in 1900.

Product quality: The GDP does not adequately reflect changes in the quality of products. A 1990 radio is a much superior product to a 1930 radio. It is more reliable and has better reception. But GDP measures do not fully reflect these changes in *quality*. As with radios, so it is with literally millions of products from record players and records, to airplane safety, to hotel rooms, to food preservation, to cars.

Satisfaction: Also, GDP does not allow for the capacity of different goods to provide different satisfactions. A million pounds spent on tanks, or a missile, makes the same addition to GDP as a million pounds spent on a school, a stadium, or sweets – expenditures that may produce very different levels of consumer satisfaction. Are today's children happier with the vast variety of expensive toys than were children in 1900 playing with what they, and their parents, could adapt from what they found around them?

Quality of life: To the extent that material output is purchased at the expense of such things as overcrowded cities and highways, polluted environments, defaced countrysides, maimed accident victims and longer waits for public services, GDP measures only part of the total of human well-being. These undesirable products are often called *bads* to distinguish them from *goods*, which are desirable products.

Illegal activities: The GDP does not measure illegal production, even though many such goods and services are sold on the market and generate factor incomes. The production and distribution of soft and hard drugs are important examples today. As long as the income generated from such activities goes unreported, it is unlikely to show up in the national income statistics. If we wish to measure the total demand for factors of production in the economy, or the total marketable output − whether or not we as individuals approve of particular products − we should include these activities. The main reason for omitting illegal activities is that, because of their illicit nature, it is difficult to find the information needed to include them.

The black economy: An important omission from the measured GDP is the so-called *black economy*. Here the transactions are perfectly legal in themselves. The only illegal thing about them is that they are not reported for income-tax purposes. For example, an unemployed tiler repairs a leak in your roof and takes payment in cash in order to avoid tax. Such unreported transactions are unrecorded in the country's GDP. Thus, measured GDP statistics significantly understate the real values of output and income earned. If we could measure these transactions, they should be included in a measure of total market output.

The black economy seems to have grown rapidly in many countries during the last two decades, particularly in the countries that made up the USSR. Important reasons for this growth are to evade both taxes, such as income tax and the VAT, and regulations regarding such matters as safety, minimum wages, and discrimination by sex or race. Generally, the higher are tax rates, and the greater are the restrictions arising from rules and regulations, the greater the incentive to evade them by 'going underground'.

The growth of the black economy has also been facilitated by the rising importance of services in the nation's total output. It is much easier for a window cleaner or TV repairman to pass unnoticed by the authorities than it is for a large manufacturing establishment, which is hard to hide. Another reason for the growth of this part of the economy is to help some people to claim unemployment

---

BOX 23.1 Reform in Eastern Europe: Italy on the Danube

'Official Hungary is not a pleasant place to live in, say the statisticians: GDP fell by 5% in 1990 after a decade of near-stagnation. Yet officially measured real consumption in the past two years had been stronger than it should have been if the official measurement of GDP were accurate. That suggests that the official measurement is wrong. Count in private-sector output, much of which the statistics ignore, and the depression evaporates.

'In unofficial Hungary, the private (mostly black) economy may provide 25–30% of GDP ... That is up from 16–18% a decade ago and the share is growing fast ... there are as many as three times more losers than winners from the economic transformation. These losers make up the core of the 74% of Hungarians who in a recent opinion poll said they thought the economic situation had worsened. But the winners make up with the size of their winnings what they lack in numbers.'

(*The Economist*, 23 February 1991)

The text discusses the black economy in the British context. In Part 2 you will have met (or will meet, if you have yet to study Part 2) the *black market*, which is the

market for a single product in which goods are sold illegally at prices in excess of a maximum price set by government decree. The above passage deals with the Black economy in Hungary where it has undoubtedly been much larger as a percentage of GDP than in the UK. In general, the greater the severity, and scope, of government regulation and control of economic transactions, the more the incentive to avoid them by entering the black economy.

Questions

1 What is the black economy, and how does it differ from a black market?
2 How will the existence of a black economy affect the official measurements of Hungarian national income? If, as enforcement powers diminish in the transition to a more democratic state, more and more of economic transactions 'go black' so as to avoid the remaining restrictions, what will happen to recorded national income and to its divergence from actual national income?
3 Assuming that the writer means profits by 'winnings', are the 25 per cent who are the 'winners' the only ones who gain from their activities?

benefits while actually earning significant amounts of income.

Non-marketed economic activities: When a bank clerk hires a carpenter to build a bookshelf in his house, the value of the work done enters into the GDP; if the clerk builds the bookshelf himself, the value of his work is omitted from the GDP. In general, any labour service that does not pass through a market is not counted in the GDP. Such omissions include, for example, the services of the housewife, any do-it-yourself activity, and voluntary work such as canvassing for a political party or leading a Boy Scout troup.

Does the omission of these types of non-marketed economic activities matter? Once again, it all depends. For example, we may wish to account for changes in the opportunities for employment for those households who sell their labour services in the market. Here, we are not interested in changes in non-marketed activities, since these do not provide marketable employment opportunities. For this purpose, the omission of the services of the housewife, and unpaid political canvassing, is desirable.

If, however, we wish to measure the total flow of goods and services available to satisfy people's wants, whatever the source of the goods and services, then the omissions are undesirable and potentially serious. In most advanced industrial economies the non-market sector is relatively small, and it can be ignored even if GDP is used for purposes for which it would be appropriate to include non-marketed goods and services.

What it does measure: The philosophy of the national income statistician might be expressed in the observation: 'Man does not live by bread alone, but it is nonetheless important to know how much bread he has.'

The national income figures do not measure everything that contributes to human welfare, nor were they intended to do so.

But what they do measure is an important indicator of much of a nation's economic activity and of many (but not all) of the things that contribute to people's living standards.

International comparisons

International comparisons of GDPs tell us something about the relative abilities of different economies to produce marketable goods and services. However, they provide only imperfect measures of relative living standards.

One important reason is that things that are omitted from GDP may be relatively much more important in some countries than in others. Generally, non-market activities are more important the less rich, and the more rural, the country. Poor farmers may make their own fabrics and use them to make their own clothes as well as building their own sheds and even houses. The 'do-it-yourself' activities will not show up in GDP measures.

For this reason, GDP comparisons between developed and less developed countries may overstate the differences

---

BOX 23.2 The Meaning of Gross Domestic Product

'Gross domestic product is an important entity in its own right, and changes in its real amount are the best estimates available of changes in total UK production. Even so, it must be remembered that it leaves a good deal out of the picture by excluding practically all productive work which is not sold for money ... It is also important to recognize that GDP stands for the production of UK residents, not their expenditure. As an expenditure total it measures the spending of all persons, resident or foreign, on the goods and services produced by the residents of the UK. Thus if national welfare is conceived as spending of UK residents, it is incorrect to represent it by GDP. The total appropriate for this purpose is GDP *plus* imports *minus* exports. This total is referred to as total domestic expenditure . . . , and is equal to the UK's total use of resources, which is the sum of personal consumption, government consumption and gross investment.'

(Prest and Coppock, *The UK Economy*, 12th edn, Weidenfeld & Nicolson, 1989)

This discussion relates to a similar discussion on pages 263–6 of the text. It emphasizes that the difference between what UK residents produce and what they spend is net exports. If imports exceed exports, spending exceeds production and if exports exceed imports, spending is less than production.

Starting in the early 1980s, the United Nations has tried to harmonize the collection of national income data across all of its members. As a result, the GDP, rather than the GNP, has become the main statistic used to report overall national income. (See pages 261–2 for a discussion of the difference between the GDP and the GNP.)

Questions

1 What type of non-market activities are the authors likely to be referring to?
2 Why might expenditure of UK residents, rather than their production, be a better measure of their welfare?
3 Explain how GDP and total domestic expenditure are related.
4 What are some of the factors that might affect welfare but are neither included in GDP nor discussed by the authors?

in real living standards between advanced and less developed countries (which are, of course, still very large).

You should, therefore, be a little cautious in interpreting data from a country with a very different climate and culture from your own. When you hear that the per capita GDP of Nigeria was less than £150 per year in 1990, you should not imagine living in Britain on that income. Certainly the average Nigerian is at a low level of real income compared to the average resident of the UK, but the measured GDP figure does not allow for the fact that many of the things that are very costly to a UK resident are provided to the Nigerian by a host of non-marketed goods and services as well as climate.

Another reason is that in some countries much economic activity is needed to create what in other countries is provided freely by nature. The most obvious example is heat. In cold climates, many resources are devoted to keeping warm while little or no resources are needed to do so in warm climates.

Which Measure is Best?

To ask which is *the* best national income measure is something like asking which is *the* best carpenter's tool. The answer is 'It all depends on the job to be done'. *There are many related national income measures. There is no single true, or best, measure for all purposes. The advantages and disadvantages of each can be assessed only in relation to the particular problem for which it might be used.*

The use of several measures of national income, rather than just one, is common because each provides an answer to a different set of questions. For example, GDP provides the best answer to the question 'What is the market value of goods and services produced for final demand?' NNP answers the question 'By how much does the economy's production exceed the amount necessary to replace the capital equipment used up?' Personal disposable income answers the question 'How much income do households have available to allocate between spending and saving?' Additionally, real (constant-price) measures eliminate purely monetary changes, and allow comparisons of purchasing power over time; per capita measures shift the focus from the nation to the average person.

For yet other purposes, such as providing an overall measure of economic welfare, we may wish to supplement conventional measures of national income. We can do this by considering other welfare measures *alongside* GDP. These can omit investment and other parts of GDP that do not contribute to *current* living standards, while including

(continued on next page)

Summary

1 Production may be divided into four main categories: (i) *consumption* which includes goods and services currently produced for use by households, with the exception of residential housing, (ii) *investment* which covers new construction of fixed capital, residential housing and *changes* in stocks, (iii) *government production* which covers all the government's exhaustive expenditures but excludes its transfer payments, and (iv) *exports* which include everything that is produced at home and then exported.

2 The output method measures the total value of the nation's output by adding up the values of all final goods and services produced or the *values added* by all producers in the economy.

3 The expenditure method measures the total value of expenditure on final output in the categories of consumption, investment, government expenditure and *net* exports (exports minus imports).

4 The income method measures the total value of incomes generated by production plus indirect taxes *net* of subsidies.

5 Although equal in total, each of the three measures is valuable because of the breakdown of output, expenditure or income that it provides. In all the theory of the following chapters, this total is referred to as *national income* and it is usually measured from the *expenditure approach*.

6 When interpreting national income figures, it is important to distinguish between nominal income, measured in current prices, and real income, measured in constant prices. The distinction between measures of per capita and total income is also important.

7 Three important problems in measuring national income are (i) how to classify certain items such as cars (consumption) and housing (investment), (ii) whether or not to include various items such as interest on private-sector debt (included) and public-sector debt (excluded), and (iii) how to value certain items such as government activity (at cost) and stocks (at market value).

8 GDP measures much of what contributes to current living standards, such as consumer goods, but includes some things that do not, such as investment, while excluding (fully or partially) many items that do, such as leisure, changes in product quality, pollution, illegal and black economy production, and non-marketed productive activities.

other aspects such as leisure which are not included in the GDP but do contribute to living standards.

Even if better measures of welfare are developed, economists are unlikely to discard conventional national income measures. Economists and policy-makers who are interested in the ebb and flow of economic activity that passes through markets, and in the variations in employment opportunities for factors of production whose services are sold on markets, will continue to use GDP as the measure that comes closest to telling them what they need to know.

Questions

1 Which One or More of these are part of investment expenditure in the current year's GDP?
   (a) The purchase of Ms Black's cottage by Mr King.
   (b) The purchase of a new printing press by *The Times*.
   (c) The purchase of shares in ICI by Ms Smith.
   (d) The purchase of a government bond by Lloyds Bank.
   (e) The purchase of steel by Rover in order to increase its stock of steel on hand.

2 True or False? 'If we added up the sales of all the nation's producers, the total would exceed the value of the GDP.'

3 In measuring GDP of the UK from the expenditure side, which one or more of the following are included?
   (a) Expenditures on cars by households.
   (b) Expenditures on food by tourists.
   (c) Expenditures on new machinery by UK firms.
   (d) The purchase of one corporation by another.
   (e) Increases in stocks of finished products held by firms.

4 What would be the effect of the following on the real value of GDP for the UK?
   (a) Destruction of thousands of homes and shops in a severe earthquake.
   (b) Passage of a law prohibiting abortion.
   (c) Lifting sanctions on imports from South Africa.

5 A recent newspaper article reported that Switzerland was considered to be the 'best' place in the world to live. In view of the fact that Switzerland does not have the highest per capita GDP in the world, what factors might cause it to be ranked as the 'best' place to live?

6 Calculate the economy's Net National Product given the following figures:

GNP at market prices	30,000
Exports	4,000
Imports	4,500
Indirect taxes	5,000
Subsidies	1,000
Capital consumption	3,000
Net property income from abroad	1,500

24 Consumption and Investment

Why does national income behave the way it does, exhibiting a short-term pattern of increases and decreases and a long-term rising trend? Why have there been long periods in the recent past when Britain's resources of land, labour and capital were more or less fully employed? Why have there also been long periods of heavy unemployment of resources in Britain (and in many of the other countries of Western Europe)?

To answer these and other similar questions, we need a theory to explain the behaviour of national income. Such a theory is called the THEORY OF INCOME DETERMINATION.

In Chapter 23, we studied the national income accounting procedures that allow us to *measure* total national income and its components. Of the three methods studied in that chapter, the expenditure method provides the categories most useful for the theory of income determination. The four key categories are expenditure on consumption, investment, the government's exhaustive expenditures, and exports.

THE KEYNESIAN MODEL

To conduct our study we shall use what is called the simple *Keynesian model of the economy*. This model is named after the great English economist John Maynard (later Lord) Keynes (1883–1946) who was one of the main founders of modern macroeconomics, and who developed the model that is used in this Part in his most famous book, *The General Theory of Employment, Interest and Money*.

You will recall from Chapter 3 that a model is a simplified representation of the economy. A good model ignores less important forces and includes the more important ones. If it does this successfully, it will be useful both in explaining what we see in the world, and in predicting the results of major changes in which we are interested.

The Keynesian model describes the economy's short-term behaviour which is mainly determined by fluctuations in the demand for the nation's output, its GDP. In contrast, the economy's long-term behaviour is mainly determined from the supply side, particularly by changes in the nation's potential output. This behaviour is dealt with by the theory of economic growth, which we study in Part 5.

The main characteristics of the Keynesian model are that total desired expenditure is divided into a number of categories that either depend on national income, or can be treated as exogenous. National income itself varies so as to establish equilibrium between the expenditure flows that depend on it.

This may sound rather abstract at this point, but once

you have studied this Keynesian model, its properties will become fairly obvious.

Keynesian models relate to sectors of the economy. Each sector determines a particular type of expenditure.

A Two-Sector Model

In the next three chapters, we shall study a very simple case in which the only categories of expenditure are consumption, which is made by domestic households, and investment, which is made by domestic firms. The group comprised of domestic households and the group comprised of domestic firms are often referred to respectively as the *household sector*, and the *firm sector*.

To conduct this study, we will build a simple 'two-sector Keynesian model of the economy'. In it the only two categories of expenditure are consumption and investment, there is no government and no foreign trade. (These are considered in later chapters.) Simple though this imaginary economy may be, it allows us to study the forces that determine national income in real economies. Once we understand how these forces work, it becomes a relatively easy matter to allow for the government, and for foreign trade.

We develop this simple model over three chapters. In this chapter we enquire into the determinants of the two expenditure flows of consumption and investment. In Chapter 25 we study the forces that determine the equilibrium size of national income, and in Chapter 26 the forces that cause national income to change.

Categories of Expenditure in the Two-Sector Model

We have already noted that, in the simple economy we are going to study, there are only two categories of expenditure:

(1) expenditure on investment goods, which we assume to be made solely by firms, and

(2) expenditure on consumption goods, which we assume to be made solely by households.

All expenditure, both by firms and by households, is paid to firms in return for their sales of consumption and investment goods. Firms sell the consumption goods that they produce to households, and they sell the investment goods that they produce to other firms. Thus firms have two sources of receipts: they receive payments from households for the consumption goods that they sell to them, and they receive payments from other firms for the investment goods that they sell to them.

All income is paid to households as factor payments in

the form of rent, interest, profits and wages. Households then decide how much they wish to spend on consumption and they save the rest.

Characteristics of Expenditure Flows

At the outset, we need to understand three of the basic characteristics of all the expenditure flows that we will study.

Expenditures are real (not nominal):   Keynesian theory is about *real*, not nominal, expenditures. We saw in Chapter 23 that total national income and its various components can be measured either in current, or in constant, prices. All the values of consumption and investment that we discuss in this chapter are measured in constant prices. Thus when there are changes in the measured flow of consumption or investment, the real output of consumption or investment goods must be changing (since we are holding prices constant).

Of course, if the overall price level is constant, we get the same result whether we use current or constant prices (since prices are not changing). But when the overall price level does change, current and constant price measures will give different results. We choose the constant-price measure because we are concerned with changes in real outputs.

All values are planned values: The term PLANNED EXPENDITURE refers to what people intend to spend; the term REALIZED EXPENDITURE refers to what they actually succeed in spending. The key point to remember is that when we refer to consumption and investment expenditure, we are referring to what households and firms plan to spend on purchasing consumption and investment goods. Realized expenditure will diverge from planned expenditure whenever plans are frustrated. For example, consumers' plans to spend on consumption goods may be frustrated by a strike that interrupts production of those goods. Note that planned expenditure is also described as DESIRED or EX ANTE EXPENDITURE, while realized expenditure is often described as ACTUAL or EX POST EXPENDITURE.

Expenditure flows are aggregate flows: In macroeconomics, we are not concerned with the behaviour of individual households or firms, but with the aggregate behaviour of all households and all firms. Thus, when we talk about consumption expenditure, we mean the total amount that all households desire to spend on consumption; while investment expenditure also refers to the total amount that all firms desire to spend on investment.

THE DETERMINANTS OF INVESTMENT EXPENDITURE

We start by considering why firms make investments in plant and equipment. Later we study the determinants of other types of investment.

Fixed Investment

Profits provide the basic motive driving the investment decisions of private-sector firms. Firms that wish to spend money on investment expect that investment to yield a profit over all its costs. The factors that affect these expectations determine the amount of desired investment expenditure in the economy as a whole.

The main factors that influence investment decisions are:

- **the rate of interest and the availability of credit,**
- **the cost and the productivity of capital goods,**
- **expectations about future profits,**
- **current profits earned by firms and available for re-investment, and**
- **the development of new techniques of production and of new products.**

The rate of interest: The rate of interest measures the cost of capital to the firm. If the firm borrows money to spend on investment, it must pay the rate of interest to its creditors in return for these funds. If the firm uses its own funds, it must forgo the revenue that it could have obtained by lending out those funds to others and earning the rate of interest in return.

The lower is the rate of interest, the lower is the cost of borrowing money, so the lower is the cost of making investment, and the more investment firms will tend to make. To see this, think of the firm's opportunities for investing in new capital being arranged in order of profitability. There will be a few lines of investment that will offer very large returns. There will be further lines that will offer lower, but still quite substantial, returns. There will be yet more lines of investment that will offer moderate returns, and even more lines that will offer only quite modest returns. If the rate of interest is very high so that funds for investment are very expensive to the firm, the firm will only undertake the most profitable investments. If the rate is lower, there will be more investments that will offer a profit after the cost of the investment funds is deducted.

Consider a simple example. Let there be four investment opportunities, each involving spending £100 now and obtaining a single sum one year hence. The most profitable pays £120, the next £115, the next £110, and the least profitable only £105. At interest rates in excess of 20 per cent, none of these four will be profitable. At rates between 15 and 20 per cent, only the first will be profitable. For example, if the rate were 17 per cent, then £100 could be borrowed at a cost of £17. In a year's time the investment would yield £120, allowing a profit of £3 after repaying the £100 borrowed and paying interest of £17. At rates between 10 and 15 per cent, the two best opportunities will be profitable. A rate below 10 per cent makes the third one profitable, while any rate below 5 per cent makes even the fourth opportunity profitable. Thus, as the rate of interest falls, first one, then two, then three, then all four opportunities become profitable, and desired investment expenditure rises from £100 to £200 to £300 to £400 on account of these four investment possibilities.

In general, the lower is the rate of interest, the greater the number of investment opportunities that will be profitable and, therefore, the greater the investment expenditure that firms will wish to make.

There is an important exception to this rule. During very depressed times, investment opportunities are few or non-existent. At such times, changes in the rate of interest have little effect on investment decisions. In more normal times, however, a wide range of potentially profitable investment opportunities does exist. At such times, a change in the rate of interest shifts the line between what does and does not look profitable and hence affects the volume of desired investment expenditure.

Thus, the volume of desired investment expenditure is negatively related to the interest rate, rising as the interest rate falls and vice versa.[1]

Up to now, we have assumed the firm could borrow all it wishes at the going rate of interest. This is not always correct since many firms find that their bankers restrict the amount they will lend to them. Also smaller firms cannot always raise all they wish by selling new issues of bonds. As a result, investment expenditure tends to vary, not only with the cost of credit (the rate of interest), but also with the availability of credit to firms.

The cost and productivity of capital goods: What the firm has to pay to buy any piece of capital that it purchases, as well as the productivity of that capital, will influence the profitability of the investment. A new process that reduces the cost of capital goods will make any given line of investment more profitable because the interest costs involved will be reduced. For example, a machine costing £1000 will have an interest cost of £100 per year at a rate of 10 per cent, but if the machine's cost falls to £800 its interest cost will only be £80 per year.

Also, any new invention that makes capital equipment more productive will make investment more attractive. For example, if the replacement of typewriters by word-processors makes a given amount spent on office equipment more productive, this will lead to a burst of investment expenditure to obtain the new capital equipment.

As a result, a fall in the cost of capital goods, and/or a rise in their productivity, will tend to increase desired investment expenditure.

Expectations of future profits: Expectations of future profits exert a strong effect on investment decisions. Profit expectations in turn depend on expectations of future demand conditions and cost conditions.

Expected demand conditions matter because the profitability of any investment depends on being able to sell the output of the capital goods, and to sell it at a favourable

price. Investment expenditure made now, means producing goods for sale in the future. If firms have favourable expectations about the amount that they will be able to sell in the future and the price that they will be able to obtain, they will be inclined to invest now to create the capacity to sell in the favourable market that they expect in the future. If firms expect sales and prices to be falling in the future, they will be much less inclined to spend on capital equipment now than if they expect sales and prices to be rising.

Expected cost conditions also matter because profits, which are what motivate investment decisions, depend on market prices for output, and on the costs of producing that output. When a machine is bought now, the cost of the machine is known now. But the cost of the labour that will operate the machine, and the cost of the materials that will be used over the lifetime of the machine, depend on prices that will rule in the future.

On occasion, these expectations about the future can change dramatically and suddenly – these are what Keynes called the animal spirits of businessmen – and when they do change, desired investment will also change dramatically. A sudden swing from pessimism to optimism about the future can lead to a large increase in desired investment expenditure, while the opposite swing from optimism to pessimism can lead to a drastic curtailment of investment plans.

On occasion, expectations can change so as to offset the effects of changes in interest rates. For example, in a severe recession, a fall in interest rates may encourage investment, while a fall in profit expectations discourages it. The net result may be little change in investment. The correct interpretation of this observation is *not* that investment is insensitive to the interest rate *ceteris paribus*. The correct interpretation is rather that other things were not equal, so that the effect of the fall in interest rates was offset by the effects of the change in profit expectations.

Current profits: Investment is often financed by borrowed funds. But a great deal of investment is also financed by firms' own money. In this case, current profits are retained – i.e. not paid out to the firms' owners – but instead are reinvested by the firms. Thus an important determinant of investment expenditure is current profits. If these are large, there is a large flow of funds that can be reinvested by the firms who made them. If profits are low or non-existent, there are few funds available from within the firm to finance new investment expenditures.

New techniques and new products: The development of new techniques for producing existing products is called 'process innovation', while the development of new products is called 'product innovation'.

New ways of producing old products are constantly being invented. These new ways are usually embodied in new equipment. For example, robotization has radically changed assembly-line processes. The installation of robots has accounted for large quantities of recent investment expenditures in manufacturing industries in advanced countries.

---

1 We have not discussed the magnitude of the response, only its direction. It is also important to note that fixed investment responds to the *long-term* interest rate. In a later chapter we shall see monetary policy may have more effect on short-term interest rates than long-term rates. Monetary policy that fails to influence the long-term interest rate may have little effect on fixed investment; but this does not upset the proposition that *if* the long-term rate changes, fixed investment will tend to change in the opposite direction.

When new products are developed, new investment is needed to produce the plant and equipment required to produce them. Sometimes existing plant and equipment can be modified, but only at the expense of some expenditure on modification and adaptation, while at other times whole new arrays of capital equipment are needed to make the new product.

Investment in Stocks

Investment in stocks responds to two main variables, the volume of output and the rate of interest. Firms need to keep a proportion of their output as stocks. These allow the firm to meet increases in sales before output can be varied (by reducing stocks) and to hold production steady when sales fall temporarily (thus increasing stocks). As a result, the need to hold stocks varies with the size of the firm's output. The cost of holding stocks is given by the short-term interest rate. The firm has funds tied up in stocks. If the stocks were sold, the money could be used to pay off bank loans or, if no loans exist, could be lent out. In either case, the interest rate measures the cost of having funds tied up in unsold stocks. As a result, stocks tend to vary in the opposite direction to the interest rate.

Residential Housing

Many influences on residential housing construction are non-economic and depend on demographic or cultural considerations, such as new family formation. However, households must not only want to buy houses but also be able to do so. Periods of high employment and high average family earnings tend to lead to increases in housing construction. Periods of high unemployment and falling earnings tend to lead to decreases in such construction.

Almost all houses are purchased with money that is borrowed by means of mortgages. Interest on the borrowed money typically accounts for over one-half of the purchaser's annual mortgage payments; the remainder is repayment of principal. It is for this reason that sharp variations in interest rates have a substantial effect on the demand for housing.

Two of the main economic determinants of expenditure on housing are household incomes and the rate of interest.

INVESTMENT AS AUTONOMOUS EXPENDITURE

In the simple Keynesian theory, we treat desired investment expenditure as a constant. This means we are assuming that the major forces that influence investment such as interest rates, current and expected future profits, and the rate of product and process innovation, are all assumed to remain constant. This allows us to see how national income is determined when desired investment expenditure is a constant.

Then, when we wish to see how national income responds to a change in investment, we assume a given change to a new constant level and study the effects on national income.

Autonomous expenditures

Investment is an example of an AUTONOMOUS or EXOGENOUS EXPENDITURE. This is any expenditure that is not explained within our theory. It is determined outside of our theory, i.e. exogenously. Such expenditures are treated as constants when national income is being determined. Their influence is studied by allowing them to change exogenously, for reasons outside of the theory.

This may sound very abstract at this point, but it will soon become commonplace as practice gives you familiarity with handling autonomous variables.

A graphical representation

Figure 24.1 plots national income on the horizontal axis and investment expenditure on the vertical axis. Because investment does not vary with national income, its graph is a horizontal straight line, labelled I in the Figure, showing the same amount of desired investment, I_1, at all levels of national income.

Note that in this type of graph all autonomous expenditures will be graphed by horizontal lines, showing that the expenditure in question does *not* vary as national income varies.[1]

CONSUMPTION EXPENDITURE

Households make plans about how much to spend on consumption and how much to save. These are not, however, independent decisions. *The* SAVING *of households is defined as all households' income not spent on consumption.* It follows, therefore, that households have to decide on a *single* division of their income between saving and consumption. For example, if one household plans to spend £180 out of its weekly income of £200, it must, by definition, be planning to save the remaining £20.

The main incentives which influence how households in the aggregate divide their incomes between consumption and saving are the following:

- **the level of income,**
- **the rate of interest,**
- **the tastes of households,**
- **the terms of credit,**
- **the level of wealth,**

---

1 The terms lines, straight lines and curves present a possible source of confusion. A line is one-dimensional, having length but no width. Lines may be straight (called straight lines) or curved (called curves). In this book we sometimes deal with straight lines and sometimes with curves. We should, therefore, refer to all of them as lines. Sometimes, however, people understand 'line' to refer to a 'straight line' where straight is understood. For this reason we sometimes use the word curve where line would do just as well.

- **the existing stock of durables,**
- **price expectations.**

Not every household needs to be influenced by all of these factors, but each factor has an important influence on some households. As a result, all of the factors have an influence on aggregate household behaviour.

The level of income: The higher is a household's income the more we would expect it to spend on consumption. If, for example, households always allocate 80 per cent of their incomes to consumption and save the rest, then households with higher incomes would also have higher consumption expenditures.

The rate of interest: The rate of interest provides a reward for saving. If a household saves £100 out of its current income, it will have £105 next year if the rate of interest is 5 per cent, £110 if the rate is 10 per cent, and so on. We would expect the decisions of households on how much to spend now and how much to lay aside for spending in the future to respond to this rate of interest.

The tastes of households: Household tastes determine savings attitudes in many ways. We mention two, 'time preference' and the 'bequest motive'. If people are very impatient and unwilling to postpone present consumption in order to consume more in the future, they will save little; if people are willing to defer present consumption in order (by earning interest on their savings) to consume more in the future, they will save much. These attitudes are described as people's TIME PREFERENCE. A second influence concerns the desire to pass on wealth to one's children and others as well as to make bequests to one's heirs when one dies. The stronger is this desire, the greater the willingness to save. This motive is called the BEQUEST MOTIVE for saving.

The terms of credit: Many durable consumer goods are purchased on credit, whose terms may range from a few months to pay for a radio, to two or three years to pay for a car. If credit becomes more difficult to obtain, many households may postpone their planned, credit-financed purchases. If the typical initial payment required for goods purchased on hire purchase increases from 10 to 20 per cent, households that had just saved up 10 per cent of the purchase price would have to postpone their planned purchases until they saved 20 per cent of the purchase price. There would then be a temporary reduction in current consumption expenditures until these extra funds had been accumulated.

The level of wealth: Households save in order to add to their wealth.[1] If anything happens to reduce wealth unexpectedly, households may increase their saving in order to restore their wealth. If something happens to increase their wealth suddenly, households may lower their saving as they feel less need to add to their now-larger stock of wealth. So we may expect changes in wealth to alter consumption decisions. By discouraging saving, and hence encouraging consumption, a rise in wealth may increase the amount of consumption associated with *each* level of income.

Existing stocks of durables: The emphasis here is on durable goods (e.g. cars and TV sets) because purchases of non-durable consumer goods (e.g. food and clothing) and of services (e.g. car repairs) cannot be so easily postponed. While expenditures on non-durables are relatively steady, purchases of durables are volatile and can be the source of sharp shifts in consumption expenditure.

Any period in which durables are difficult or impossible to purchase will be followed by a sudden outburst of expenditure on durables. Such a flurry of spending will follow a major war, when durables are unavailable, and a period of heavy unemployment, when many families have postponed buying durables.

Price expectations: If households expect inflation to accelerate, they tend to purchase now durable goods they would otherwise not have bought for another one or two years. In such circumstances, purchases made now are expected to be cheaper than purchases of the same good made in the future. By the same argument, an expected deflation may lead to postponing purchases of durables in hopes of purchasing them later at a lower price.

The consumption function

The term CONSUMPTION FUNCTION is used to describe the relationship between households' planned consumption expenditure and all of the determining forces just discussed. To develop a simple theory, we hold constant all but one of these forces. The one force that we allow to vary is income. This allows us to derive a simple relation between consumption expenditure and income. To describe this relation, we say that *consumption is a function of income.* When the other influencing forces change, they will shift the function relating consumption to income.[1]

Consumption as induced expenditure

The assumptions just made have the effect of making consumption what is called an INDUCED or an ENDOGENOUS EXPENDITURE. This is expenditure that is influenced by, and hence varies with, the variable (or variables) our theory is designed to explain – i.e., in this case, variations in consumption are explained by variations in national income.

---

1 We have here the same stock-flow distinction that we earlier raised with respect to capital and investment. Saving is a flow, while wealth is a stock. In our bath analogy, wealth is the stock of water in the bath; saving is the flow of water from the tap into the bath.

1 This is just what was done for demand curves in Part 2. All of the influencing forces except the good's own price were held constant, and a relation called a demand curve was established between the price and quantity demanded. When one of the other influencing forces changed, this *shifted* the demand curve.

BOX 24.1 The Squirrel's Curse

'A recent survey ... argues that the key to savings lies in changes in household wealth. Between 1982 and 1989 the total value of household assets increased by 37% in real terms in America and by 83% in Britain ... In Britain most of this gain was due to the explosion in house prices (houses account for 39% of Britain's personal assets, compared with only 16% in America); in America it was mainly from capital gains on financial assets.

'One consequence of these huge gains was that people felt they did not need to save so much of their current income to accumulate a given stock of wealth for their old age. Another was that households were able to borrow against the increase in property values, encouraging them to spend even more. This was the main reason why America's saving ratio fell in the 1980s from 7% to a low of 3%, and Britain's dropped from 13% to 5%.

'Last year, as the prices of houses and shares slumped, total household wealth fell in nominal terms for the first time since 1962 in America and since 1974 in Britain. The wealth of American households fell by 8% in real terms in 1990, while that of Britons tumbled 15%. This has prompted British consumers to save, not spend, which explains why the recession is much nastier than expected.

'Indeed ... perceived changes in wealth could have an unusually large impact on spending in this economic downturn, not only because of the size of the drop, but also because more people now own homes and shares. And heavy borrowing by households against increasing asset values leaves consumers more exposed to a fall in wealth than in the past. Last, but not least, the slump in asset prices is partly to blame for the so-called credit crunch because it has made banks much more cautious about lending.'

(*The Economist*, 9 February 1991)

In the simple Keynesian model, we assume that current saving and consumption depend solely on current income. This is a useful simplification in order to build a simple and understandable model. As we point out in the chapter, however, consumption and saving depend on a number of important variables in addition to current income. Before we can fully understand events such as are discussed in this article, we often need to allow for these other influences. This is done in later chapters. In the meantime, the passage quoted above emphasizes some of the important influences that are introduced in the text of this chapter.

Questions

1 What determinants of consumption and saving are alluded to in this article?
2 Why might a household that experienced a large, and unexpected, increase in its wealth increase the amount that it borrowed? (Just *being able* to borrow more is not a sufficient explanation.)
3 What is meant by 'the savings ratio' referred to in the article? Could the household savings ratio rise while total household savings fell? Under what circumstances might that be most likely to occur?

Induced or endogenous expenditure flows are to be contrasted with the autonomous or exogenous expenditure flows discussed on page 272. The simple Keynesian theory that we discuss in Part 4 divides *all* expenditure flows into two categories. Those that vary with national income are endogenous (induced). Those that are independent of national income (but vary with other influencing forces) are exogenous (autonomous).

This distinction is basic to the Keynesian model and you should memorize the meaning of the two concepts and the two names that are used to describe each: autonomous and exogenous mean the same thing, as do induced and endogenous.

The aggregate consumption function: Every individual household's desired consumption expenditure varies with its income. In macroeconomics, we are interested in the aggregate behaviour of *all* households. The macro, or aggregate, consumption function shows how the total desired consumption expenditure of all households varies as national income varies.

The aggregate consumption function reflects the behaviour of typical households, with extremes cancelling each other out. To see what is meant by this, consider an example. When income rises, some households – especially very poor ones – may spend all of the extra income, while other households – especially very rich ones – may save all the extra income. But the great majority of households spend some of their extra income and save the rest. Thus the aggregate consumption function will show an increase in national income to be associated with an increase in *both* consumption and saving.

From now on when we speak of 'the' consumption function, we are referring to the aggregate function for the whole economy.

Characteristics of the consumption function: The following four characteristics describe how aggregate consumption behaviour is related to income in the short term.

(1) There is a *break-even level* of income, which is defined as the level of income at which households just plan to consume all of their income, neither more nor less.

(2) Below the break-even level, households plan to consume in excess of their current income. They do this

by borrowing, or by spending out of their accumulated stock of wealth, which is known as DISSAVING.

(3) Above the break-even level of income, households plan to consume only part of their income and to save the rest.

(4) Any change in income causes consumption expenditure to change, but by less than the change in income. For example, an increase in aggregate income of £1m per year might cause households to increase their consumption expenditure by £750,000 per year and to increase savings by £250,000 per year.

Table 24.1 gives an illustration that conforms with the four characteristics listed above. The schedule shown in the Table gives desired consumption and desired saving at each level of income.

TABLE 24.1 Planned Consumption and Savings Schedules (£ million). Both consumption and savings rise as income rises

National income (Y)	Planned consumption expenditure (C)	Planned savings (Y–C)	Reference letter
0	300	–300	a
400	600	–200	b
800	900	–100	c
1200	1200	0	d
1600	1500	+100	e
2000	1800	+200	f
2400	2100	+300	g
2800	2400	+400	h
3200	2700	+500	i

The data in the Table are graphed in Figure 24.2. The line in that Figure is obtained by plotting each national income from the first column of Table 24.1 against its corresponding planned consumption expenditure obtained from the second column of the Table. This graph of the relation between desired consumption expenditure and national income is variously called 'the consumption line', 'the consumption curve' or 'the consumption function'. (Similar designations of 'line', 'curve' or 'function' also apply to the other variables whose relations with national income are plotted on a figure.)

Let us notice some of the things that the Table and the Figure reveal.

Notice first that, unlike the investment function in Figure 24.1, the graph of the consumption function is *not* a horizontal line. Instead it slopes upward, indicating that as income rises so does consumption. This is a graphical expression of the induced, or endogenous, aspect of consumption: changes in consumption are caused by changes in national income.

Notice second that, at an income of £1200m, consumption expenditure is also £1200m. This is the break-even level referred to in point (1) above. It is shown by point *d* on the Figure.

Notice third that, at an income of £800m, £900m is spent on consumption. At this level of income, consumption expenditure exceeds income by £100m. This extra expenditure must be financed by new borrowing or by the using up of past saving. This means that households in aggregate are *dissaving* – which is shown by a negative value in the

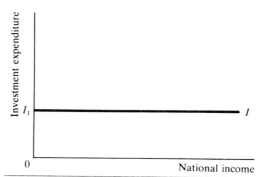

FIGURE 24.1 Investment Expenditure and National Income. Because investment is autonomous, its graph is a horizontal line showing no change as national income changes.

planned saving column. This is an illustration of point (2) above. It is shown by point *c* in the figure.

Notice fourth that, at an income of £2000m, desired consumption is only £1800m (point *f* on the figure). This is an illustration of point (3) above.

Finally notice that, every time income rises by £400m, expenditure rises by £300m. This is an illustration of point (4) above. (We shall illustrate this point graphically later.)

Autonomous and induced consumption: Notice in Table 24.1 that when income is zero, consumption is 300. This amount of consumption is often called *autonomous consumption* since it does not depend on income. The amount by which consumption exceeds its autonomous value is then called *induced consumption*. Since autonomous consumption is always (in this case) 300, induced consumption is actual consumption minus 300.

Figure 24.2 shows that autonomous consumption is given graphically by the intercept of the consumption line with the consumption axis. This gives the amount of consumption when income is zero.

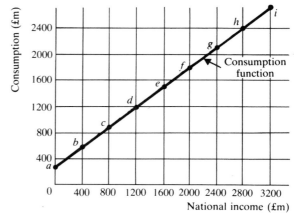

FIGURE 24.2 A Graph of the Consumption Function. This line shows the relation between aggregate desired consumption expenditure and national income. The intercept point *a* is autonomous consumption and the height above *a* of any other point, such as *d*, represents the amount of induced consumption. At *d*, for example, where total consumption is 1200, autonomous consumption is 300, so that induced consumption is 900.

TABLE 24.2 The Calculation of the Average Propensity to Consume (APC) and the Marginal Propensity to Consume (MPC). The *APC* measures the proportion of total income consumed, and the *MPC* measures the proportion of any change in income that is consumed

National income (Y) (i)	Planned consumption (C) (ii)	APC = C/Y (iii)	ΔY (Change in Y) (iv)	ΔC (Change in C) (v)	MPC = ΔC/ΔY (vi)
£m	£m		£m	£m	
0	300	—			
400	600	1.50	400	300	0.75
800	900	1.13	400	300	0.75
1200	1200	1.00	400	300	0.75
1600	1500	0.94	400	300	0.75
2000	1800	0.90	400	300	0.75
2400	2100	0.88	400	300	0.75
2800	2400	0.86	400	300	0.75
3200	2700	0.84	400	300	0.75

(DO SOMETHING FREQUENTLY)

Propensities to consume

Economists use two rather imposing terms to describe the relation between consumption and income. The AVERAGE PROPENSITY TO CONSUME (APC) is defined as the value of total consumption expenditure, C, divided by the value of total income, Y. For example, if total consumption expenditure is £1500m when total income is £1600m, the APC is £1500/£1600 which is 0·93.[1]

More generally, we can write this relation as:

$$APC = \frac{C}{Y}$$

The MARGINAL PROPENSITY TO CONSUME (MPC) is defined as the *change* in consumption divided by the *change* in income that brought it about. For example, if an increase in income of £400m causes consumption expenditure to rise by £300m, then the *MPC* is £300/£400 which is 0.75. More generally, we can use the Greek letter delta, Δ, to stand for changes, so that ΔY means the change in income while ΔC stands for the the change in consumption. This allows us to write

$$MPC = \frac{\Delta C}{\Delta Y}$$

Table 24.2 shows the calculations of the *APC* and *MPC* from the consumption schedule of Table 24.1. It deserves careful study since it illustrates some very important concepts. Notice from the Table that the *APC* in column (iii) exceeds unity below the break-even level of income (£1200). This is because consumption exceeds income. Notice also that, above the break-even level of income, the *APC* is less than unity. The last three columns, (iv), (v) and (vi), are set between the lines of the first three columns to indicate that they refer to *changes* in the levels of income and consumption.

In this example, the *MPC* is constant at 0.75 at all levels of income. This indicates that 75 per cent of any change in income is spent on consumption – consumption expenditure rises (or falls) by 75p for every increase (or decrease) of £1 of income – while saving changes by 25p.

For practice, we may use our new terminology to restate the four characteristics of consumption that we listed on pages 274–5:

(1) At some positive level of income, called the break-even level, APC = 1.

(2) Below the break-even level, the APC exceeds unity (APC > 1).

(3) Above the break-even level, the APC is less than unity (APC < 1).

(4) The MPC is less than unity at all income levels (MPC < 1).

The graphical representation of the propensities

We now wish to illustrate these marginal and average propensities graphically. To make the graph as clear as possible, we consider two points on a *new* consumption function. These are shown as points x and y in Table 24.3 and graphed in Figure 24.3. (All figures are in £000m.) Note that in order to make the graph as clear as possible, we have taken quite unrealistic figures. (Most countries have *MPC*s between 0.75 and 0.95.)

TABLE 24.3 Calculation of the APC and the MPC (£m)

Reference letter	National income (Y)	Consumption (C)	APC (C/Y)	MPC (ΔC/ΔY)
x	5	4	0.80	
				0.40
y	10	6	0.60	

The *APC* is total consumption divided by total income, the *MPC* is the change in consumption divided by the change in income that induced it.

Now consider how the two propensities that are calculated in the Table show up in the Figure. The *APC*s are shown in part (i). Point x shows the case where income is £5 and consumption is £4. The *APC* in this case is 4/5 or 0.80. Graphically, this is the ratio of the length of the vertical line showing the amount of consumption at x, which is 4 units long, to the horizontal line showing the amount of income, which is 5 units long. This ratio is given

---

1 The figures in the text examples are drawn from Table 24.1.

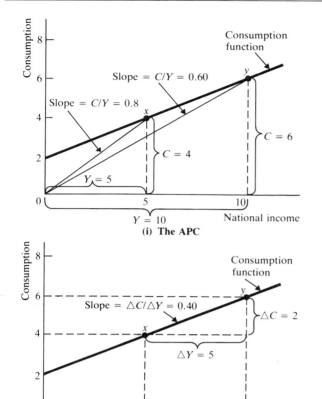

(i) The APC

(ii) The MPC

FIGURE 24.3 The Graphical Representation of the Average and Marginal Propensities to Consume. The APC is the slope of the line between the origin and the point in question, while the MPC is the slope of the line joining the two points in question.

by the slope of the line drawn from the origin to point x. (Note that this is a construction line; it is *not* the consumption function.)

Point y shows the case where income is 10 and consumption is 6. Again, it is clear from the Figure that the ratio C/Y is the slope of the line joining the origin to point y which, when drawn, becomes the hypotenuse of the right-angle triangle whose other two sides have lengths given by the values of C and Y.

Now look at part (ii) of the Figure, which illustrates the MPC. The MPC is the ratio of the change in consumption to the change in income, i.e. $\Delta C/\Delta Y$, measured over the change in income being considered. It is clear from the Figure that ΔC is the vertical distance separating points x and y, while ΔY is the horizontal distance between the two points. This makes $\Delta C/\Delta Y$ the slope of the line joining the two points in question.

In other words, the MPC is the slope of the consumption function between the two points in question.

If the consumption function is linear, its slope is the same at all points between x and y. Real-world consumption functions, however, are sometimes non-linear. We assert

without proving that if the function is a curve – as shown, for example, by the curve C_1 in Figure 24.4 – then the MPC between two distinct points on the function must be understood as the average slope of the consumption function between the points in question.

We have now derived two useful results relating to the graphical representation of these consumption propensities:

(i) the average propensity to consume at any one consumption-income point is measured graphically by the slope of the line joining that point with the origin; and

(ii) the marginal propensity to consume between any two consumption-income points is measured graphically by the slope of the line joining the two points.

Some possible consumption functions

Figure 24.4 shows two consumption functions that are consistent with the four basic hypotheses listed on page 276. The positive vertical-axis intercepts of both curves show that their APCs exceed unity at zero income. The positive slope of both curves shows that their MPCs are positive at all levels of income.

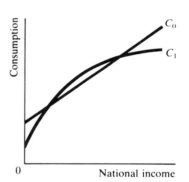

FIGURE 24.4 Two Possible Shapes of the Consumption Function. On C_0 the MPC is constant while the APC declines as income rises; on C_1 the MPC and the APC both decline as income rises.

The consumption function C_0 is linear. This means that the MPC is the same at all levels of income. The APC, however, declines continuously as income rises along the line C_0. (To see this, draw lines from the origin to successive points further and further out on the consumption function and observe that their slopes fall continuously.)

The consumption function C_1 displays not only a declining APC, but also a declining MPC, as shown by the fact that the line C_1 gets flatter as income rises. Thus, successive increases in income cause smaller and smaller increases in consumption.

The saving function

We have seen that households have only one expenditure decision: how to divide their incomes between consumption and saving. It follows that, if we know the dependence of planned consumption on income, we also know the dependence of planned saving on income. Table 24.1 illustrates this. The figures in the third column are implied by the figures in the first two columns. Given the data for consumption and income, the data for saving cannot be other than they are.

We may now define two saving concepts that are exactly parallel to the consumption concepts of APC and MPC already defined. The AVERAGE PROPENSITY TO SAVE (APS) is the proportion of total income devoted to savings. It is the value of total saving divided by the value of total income:

$$APS = \frac{S}{Y}$$

The MARGINAL PROPENSITY TO SAVE (MPS) is the *change* in total saving divided by the *change* in total income that brought it about:

$$MPS = \frac{\Delta S}{\Delta Y}$$

You can now go back to Table 24.1 and calculate for yourself the average and marginal propensities to save. This is done in exactly the same way as the consumption propensities were calculated in that Table. Your own calculations from Table 24.1 will allow you to confirm that, in the example given, the MPS is constant at 0.25 at all levels of income, while the APS rises with income. (For example, APS is zero at Y = £1200m, and 0.10 at Y = £2000m.)

A graphical representation of consumption and saving

Figure 24.5 graphs the consumption and saving schedules given in Table 24.1. The C line relates planned expenditures on consumption to national income. The S line relates planned saving to national income. Both rise as income rises.

Also shown in the Figure is a construction called the 45° line. This line does not plot any planned expenditures; instead it simply joins all those points at which the values measured on the two axes are equal. In other words, it joins all those points where planned expenditure equals income. To remind us of how it is constructed, the line is always labelled E = Y. Provided that we use the same scales on the two axes, the line has a slope of + 1 or, what is the same thing, it makes a 45° angle with both axes. To remind us of its position, one of the 45° angles is usually shown.

The 45° line proves handy as a reference line. For example, it helps locate the break-even level of income at which planned consumption expenditure equals total income. Graphically, this is where the consumption line cuts the 45° line, telling us that this is the point on the consumption function where expenditure equals income. Notice also that the break-even level of income is where the saving line cuts the horizontal axis. This is because at the break-even level of income, saving is zero.

It is important to understand the relation between the three lines shown in the Figure. Since saving is all income

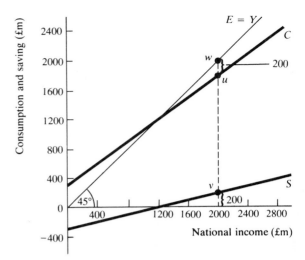

FIGURE 24.5 The Consumption and Saving Functions. Both consumption and saving rise as income rises. The height of the savings line, S, is equal to the vertical distance between the C line and the 45° line. Both distances measure the amount of income not consumed, i.e. saved.

not spent on consumption, the vertical sum of the S and the C lines must, by definition, coincide with the 45° line. Or to put it another way, at any given level of income, saving is the vertical distance between the C line and the 45° line.

Consider an example. If income is £2000m, planned consumption is £1800m (point u), while planned saving is £200m (point v). Note that the £200m of saving is also shown by the gap between the consumption line and the 45° line (the distance from u to w). This is merely another way of saying that at each level of income, total income must by definition be the amount saved plus the amount consumed.

The Aggregate Expenditure Function

The only two kinds of output produced in our simple economy are consumption goods and investment goods. Thus, total desired expenditure on final goods must be the sum of desired consumption expenditure and desired investment expenditure. So, for example, if desired consumption is £4 billion and desired investment is £1 billion, desired aggregate expenditure is £4 + £1 = £5 billion. To state this more generally we can let E stand for total desired expenditure and write:

$$E = C + I$$

We may now ask how changes in national income affect the total desired expenditure of households and firms. The answer turns out to be quite simple. Aggregate expenditure in this simple model is the sum of desired investment and desired consumption expenditure. We have assumed for purposes of this chapter that investment is an autonomous expenditure that does not vary with national income. Hence, the answer is that:

Aggregate desired expenditure varies with national income exactly as does desired consumption expenditure.

Table 24.4 illustrates the calculation of the aggregate expenditure function. The calculation is based on the consumption and income data in Table 24.1, along with the added assumption that investment is constant at £300 million. Column (i) together with column (iv) shows how desired aggregate expenditure varies with national income. These two columns define the AGGREGATE EXPENDITURE FUNCTION, which shows how much firms and households wish to spend on purchasing final output at each level of income. Since the aggregate expenditure function shows the total amount that households and firms wish to spend on the economy's output – i.e. how much output they demand – it is often called an 'aggregate demand function'. For the reason discussed in the footnote, however, we shall use the term *aggregate expenditure function*.[1]

TABLE 24.4 Calculation of the Aggregate Expenditure Function (£m)

Y	C	I	E = C + I
(i)	(ii)	(iii)	(iv) = (ii) + (iii)
0	300	300	600
400	600	300	900
800	900	300	1200
1200	1200	300	1500
1600	1500	300	1800
2000	1800	300	2100
2400	2100	300	2400
2800	2400	300	2700
3200	2700	300	3000

Aggregate desired expenditure at each income level is the sum of the desired consumption and desired investment associated with that level of income.

A graphical representation

Figure 24.6 graphs the consumption and investment function given in Table 24.4, together with the aggregate expenditure function. The Figure shows that geometrically the aggregate expenditure function is the vertical summation of the individual expenditure functions that make it up – in the simple case that we are considering here there are only two such functions, one for consumption and one for investment. Note that vertical summation of the C + I curves is the geometrical equivalent of adding columns (ii) and (iii) in Table 24.4. In both cases we are finding the

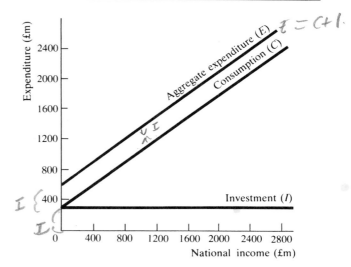

FIGURE 24.6 The Aggregate Expenditure Function. The line labelled E relates total desired expenditure to national income and is derived by vertically summing the lines showing the separate components of desired expenditure.

total amount of C and I associated with each level of income.

Shifts in the aggregate expenditure function

The aggregate expenditure function is the sum of the consumption and investment functions. Anything that shifts either of these individual functions will also shift the aggregate expenditure function.

Consumption: So far we have seen how consumption, and hence aggregate expenditure, varies with national income. Earlier we observed that, to draw a stable relation between total desired consumption expenditure and total national income, we had to hold all of the other determinants of consumption that we listed on page 000 constant. A change in any of these other determinants will shift the functions graphed in Figures 24.5 and 24.6. Let us now briefly consider such shifts.

First, consider upward shifts. Anything that increases the desire to spend on consumption at each level of income, and hence reduces the desire to save at each level of income, will cause an upward shift in the consumption function, and hence also an upward shift in the aggregate expenditure function.

This effect is shown in Figure 24.7(i). The initial consumption function is labelled C. The increased desire to consume shifts the function upwards to C', thus indicating a higher desired expenditure on consumption *at each level of national income*. This also shifts the aggregate expenditure function upwards by the same amount, from E to E'.

The reverse case of a reduced desire to spend on consumption (an increased desire to save) can also be shown on the same Figure. Let the initial consumption and aggregate expenditure functions be C' and E'. The fall in the desire

---

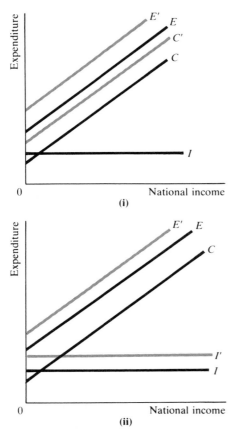

FIGURE 24.7 Shifts in the Aggregate Expenditure Function.
Upward and downward shifts in the consumption and
investment functions cause corresponding upward and
downward shifts in the aggregate expenditure function. In part
(i), the shift in the consumption line from C to C' shifts the
desired expenditure line from E to E'. In part (ii) the shift in
desired investment from I to I' shifts desired expenditure from
E to E'.

to consume lowers the consumption function to C, and
hence lowers the aggregate expenditure function to E.

Factors that can shift the consumption function upwards
are shifts in any of the determinants of consumption that
we listed earlier in this chapter and that we held constant
in order to construct the simple relation between consumption and income.

**Among the most important causes of an upward shift in
the consumption function are the following:**

- **A reduction in the thriftiness of the population.**
- **A fall in interest rates that reduces the reward for
  saving.**
- **Fear of a future inflation that encourages a psychology
  of 'buying now before prices rise'.**
- **An increase in wealth, so that people feel less urgency
  to save in order to add yet further to their wealth.**

The opposite changes will shift the consumption function
downwards.

All of the above are forces that influence each individual

household's consumption-saving decision and hence also
influence their behaviour in the aggregate. Because the
consumption function is the aggregate of the behaviour of
all households, there is one further force that we must
consider. This is

- **a redistribution of income among households.**

Income redistributions can shift the aggregate consumption
function without shifting the consumption functions of the
individual households.

Consider a redistribution that takes income away from
a group of households whose marginal propensity to spend
is 0.80p. These households will cut their spending by 80p
and their savings by 20p for every £1 that is taken from
them. There are now three cases to consider.

First, assume that the income is transferred to a group
of households whose MPC is 0.90. The households who
gain the income spend 90p and save 10p out of every £1
that they receive. The net effect of this income transfer
between the two groups is that an extra 10p is spent on
consumption out of every £1 of income that is transferred.

Second, assume that the income is transferred to households whose MPC is only 0.70. Now the households who
receive the income spend only 70p while saving 30p out of
each £1 they receive. The net effect of this transfer is that
10p less is spent out of each £1 of income transferred.

Finally, assume that the income is transferred to households whose MPC is 0.80, the same as the MPCs of the
households from whom the income was taken. Now the
transfer has no effect on total consumption – those who
lose income cut their spending by 80 per cent of the transfer,
while those who gain income raise their spending by 80
per cent of the transfer. The net effect is zero.

**We may conclude that redistribution of national income
will shift the aggregate consumption function, upwards
if those gaining the income have higher MPCs than those
losing it and downwards if those gaining the income have
lower MPCs than those losing it.**

Investment: In this chapter we have assumed that investment is an autonomous expenditure flow. This is why the
figures in column (iii) of Table 24.4 are constant and the I
lines in Figures 24.1 and 24.6 are horizontal.

A change, however, in any of the forces that influence
desired investment spending will change the amount of
such expenditure. This will change the figures in column
(iii) of Table 24.4 and *shift* the investment function shown
in the Figures.

An illustration is shown in Figure 24.7(ii). The initial
investment, consumption and aggregate expenditure functions are I, C and E. A change in one of the determinants
of investment will cause desired investment to change.
If more investment expenditure is desired, the function
shifts upwards, say to I', taking the aggregate expenditure
function upward with it by the same vertical distance,
i.e. to E'.

The reverse case is shown by setting the initial functions
at C, I', and E'. A reduction in desired investment expenditure shifts the investment function downwards to I,

taking the aggregate expenditure function down with it to *E*.

From our earlier discussion, we can isolate the major changes that will cause the desired investment to increase:

- **a fall in the rate of interest,**
- **a fall in the cost of buying capital goods,**
- **a rise in the productivity of capital goods,**
- **expectations of increased profits in the future,**
- **a rise in current profits which can be used to finance investment,**
- **the development of new techniques and new products.**

Opposite changes will cause a fall in desired investment.

Conclusion

This concludes our study of the determinants of the aggregate expenditure function. In the next chapter we shall study how the relations developed here interact to determine the equilibrium level of national income.

Summary

1 In national income theory, all expenditure flows are (1) aggregates, (2) real (not nominal), (3) planned (or desired), not actual (or realized).

2 Investment expenditure in our elementary macroeconomics is assumed to be autonomous. Its determinants include the rate of interest, the price of capital goods, expectations of costs, sales and profits, and innovations. Changes in any of these shift the investment curve.

3 Determinants of consumption include income, the rate of interest, time preference, terms of credit, the stock of wealth, and expectations of future trends in these variables.

4 The consumption function relates consumption expenditure to income, *ceteris paribus*. A change in income implies a movement along the consumption curve. A change in any other determinant of consumption shifts the entire curve.

5 The consumption function relates desired consumption expenditure to national income on the assumption that all other factors that influence consumption are constant. A change in any of these other factors will shift the consumption function, upwards if it encourages consumption and downwards if it discourages it.

6 The average propensities to consume and to save are C/Y and S/Y, while the marginal propensities are $\Delta C/\Delta Y$ and $\Delta S/\Delta Y$ respectively.

7 In a closed economy without a government sector, the aggregate expenditure curve is the (vertical) sum of the C and I curves. It slopes upwards showing that expenditure and income are positively associated.

Questions

1 Which One or More of these changes will shift the aggregate consumption function upwards?
   (a) redistribution of income from rich to poor
   (b) a rise in income
   (c) a fall in wealth
   (d) a rise in the interest rate

2 Which One or More of the following events can cause the aggregate expenditure curve to shift downwards?
   (a) a fall in wealth
   (b) a rise in national income
   (c) a rise in desired investment
   (d) a rise in desired saving

3 What is the meaning of the positive slope of the aggregate desired consumption curve?

4 If the consumption function shifts upwards, what effect does this have on:
   (a) the savings curve
   (b) the investment curve
   (c) the aggregate expenditure curve

5 A household which was earning £25,000 per year and spending £23,000 has its income rise to £30,000 and now spends £27,000. Calculate its average and marginal propensities to consume.

6 In Figure 24.2, what is the level of national income where all of income is spent on consumption? When income increases from 1200 to 2800, what happens to consumption? What is the MPC over that range of income change? What is the APC at income levels of 1200 and 1800?

7 Choose the correct alternative:
   (a) Savings equals income minus (investment/consumption).
   (b) All expenditure flows in the theory of national income are (planned/actual) expenditures.
   (c) The consumption curve has a slope that is (positive/negative/zero).
   (d) The investment curve is (horizontal/vertical/upward sloping).
   (e) The aggregate expenditure curve has a slope that is (flatter than/steeper than/the same as) the slope of the consumption curve.

8 True or False?
   (a) The savings and the consumption lines necessarily shift upwards together or downwards together.
   (b) The marginal propensity to consume is the change in total consumption divided by average household income.
   (c) A rise in desired investment causes the desired expenditure curve to shift upwards.

In the previous chapters we began our development of the two-sector Keynesian model by making assumptions about the two components of aggregate desired expenditure in our simple two-sector economy. According to that theory, investment is an autonomous, or exogenous, expenditure flow while consumption is an induced, or endogenous, expenditure flow. We are now ready to take the critical step of seeing how the equilibrium size of national income is determined.

When we considered the behaviour of prices and quantities in individual markets in Part 2 of the book, we found that they could be explained by the interaction of demands and supplies. Similarly, when we come to explain the behaviour of the nation's total output (i.e. its national income), we shall find that it depends on the economy's *total* demand and *total* supply.

Some Simplifying Assumptions

The Keynesian model concentrates on total demand. Two key assumptions help to isolate the influence of demand.

- The economy's *potential*, or *full-employment*, national income (defined in Chapter 22) is the *maximum* output that can be produced with the existing resources of labour, land and capital.

- Whenever total output is less than potential output, firms will vary their outputs as demand varies without any change in prices.[1]

The first assumption is a simplification which we shall drop in due course. The second assumption is crucial for everything in this part of the book. When output is below potential, firms have unused capacity and it is assumed that they will utilize this capacity to increase their output whenever there is an increase in the demand for their product. Furthermore, they will do this without any increase in their prices. This second assumption makes the economy's total national output depend on total demand. If demand is sufficient to buy the whole of the economy's potential output, that much output will be bought, so that the economy's actual output will be equal to its potential output. However, if there is only enough demand to purchase, say, 90 per cent of the economy's potential output, only that amount will be bought, so that actual output will only be 90 per cent of potential output.

---

[1] The second assumption means that firms have perfectly elastic supply curves up to potential output. The first assumption means that the supply curves become vertical at potential output.

Equilibrium National Income

Definition: National income is said to be in equilibrium when there is no tendency for it either to increase or to decrease. The particular value of national income that exists in equilibrium is called the EQUILIBRIUM NATIONAL INCOME. In practice the adjective 'national' is often omitted. Thus, in common with accepted practice, we use the terms 'national income' and 'income' interchangeably when it is obvious that national income is intended.

Equilibrium conditions: Any requirement that must hold if equilibrium is to be established is called an EQUILIBRIUM CONDITION. In what follows, we are going to study the equilibrium conditions for national income. We shall see that these can be stated using either of two methods:

- desired purchases equal actual output (the income-expenditure method);
- leakages equal injections (the leakages-injections method).

The determination of equilibrium income: The determination of the equilibrium level of national income in our simple economy can be studied through either of the two methods stated above. Both give the same answer, so they can be used interchangeably; each has different insights, so it pays to study both.

THE INCOME-EXPENDITURE METHOD

We begin our study of the income-expenditure method by looking at Table 25.1, which uses data from Table 24.1. Recall that, in our simple economy, all income generated by production, i.e. all national income, is paid out to households, so that household income is equal to the value of output.

The relation between expenditure and income

Now let us consider how much expenditure is planned at each level of national income. Assume, to begin with, that firms are producing an output of £1600m. Household income is £1600m and, according to Table 25.1, total planned expenditure by households and firms on consumption and investment is £1800m at that level of income. *If firms persist in producing a current output of only £1600m in the face of planned expenditure of £1800m,* something must happen. There are two extreme possibilities: either (1) production plans will be fulfilled and expenditure plans frustrated, or (2) expenditure plans will be fulfilled and production plans will be frustrated. Let us consider each of these extreme cases in more detail.

TABLE 25.1 The Equilibrium of National Income Using the Income-Expenditure Method. National income is in equilibrium where planned aggregate expenditure equals actual output (£m)

National income (Y)	Planned consumption (C)	Planned investment (I)	Planned expenditure ($E = C + I$)	
(i)	(ii)	(iii)	(iv) = (ii) + (iii)	
0	300	300	600	⎫
400	600	300	900	⎪ Pressure on
800	900	300	1200	⎬ income to
1200	1200	300	1500	⎪ increase
1600	1500	300	1800	⎪
2000	1800	300	2100	⎭
2400	**2100**	**300**	**2400**	Equilibrium income
2800	2400	300	2700	⎫ Pressure on
3200	2700	300	3000	⎬ income to
3600	3000	300	3300	⎭ decrease

Unfulfilled expenditure plans: The first possibility is that households and firms will be unable to spend the full £1800m that they wanted to spend, but £200m less. The result will be that shortages of output, and perhaps queues of unsatisfied customers, will therefore appear. These provide signals to firms that they can increase their sales if they increase their production. When they do so, national income rises.

Unplanned changes in stocks: The second possibility is that households and firms will succeed in meeting their expenditure plans by purchasing goods that were produced in the past. Indeed, the only way people could fulfil their plans to purchase more than is currently being produced is by purchasing stocks of goods that are already in existence. In the present case, if plans to buy £1800m worth of commodities are fulfilled in the face of current output of only £1600m, then firms' stocks will be reduced by £200m. As long as stocks last, this situation can persist, with more goods being sold than are currently being produced. Sooner or later, however, stocks will run out. But long before that happens, firms will take steps to increase their output to meet the extra demand. The additional output will then allow extra sales to be made, without a further running down of stocks. Thus, in this case, as well as in the first case, the consequence of an excess of planned expenditure over actual output is a rise in national income.

Whether the excess of planned expenditure over current output manifests itself in queues of unsatisfied customers, as in the first case described above, or in unplanned reductions in the stocks held by firms, as in the second case described above, we may conclude that:

at any level of national income at which aggregate planned expenditure exceeds total output, national income will sooner or later rise.

Now consider the national income of £3200m shown in Table 25.1. At this level of income, households and firms wish to spend only £3000m on consumption and investment goods. If firms persist in producing a total output of £3200m worth of goods, £200m worth must remain unsold. Thus, stocks of goods in the hands of firms must rise. Firms will, however, be unwilling to allow stocks of unsold goods to rise indefinitely. Sooner or later, they will cut back on their output to bring it in line with their current sales. When they do so, national income will fall.

Thus, at any level of national income for which aggregate planned expenditure falls short of total output, national income will sooner or later fall.

Equilibrium income

Now look at the national income of £2400m in the Table. At this level, and only at this level, the planned expenditure of households and firms is exactly equal to national income. Households are able to buy just what they wish to buy without causing stocks to accumulate or to be depleted. Firms are just able to sell all of their current output, so that their stocks neither rise nor fall. There is no incentive for firms to change their total output. Thus, national income remains steady; it is in equilibrium.

The equilibrium level of national income occurs where aggregate planned expenditure is exactly equal to total output.

The results just obtained apply to all Keynesian models of this type; they do not depend on the numbers chosen for this specific illustration. A glance at Table 25.1 will show that there is *always* a tendency for national income to be pushed in the direction of its equilibrium value. This is because aggregate planned expenditure is *less* than national income when income is above its equilibrium value, and *greater* than national income when income is below its equilibrium value. Only when aggregate planned expenditure is equal to actual national income do expenditure plans exactly match output. People plan to spend an amount equal to the value of what is produced. Since what people want to buy is equal to what is produced, there is no tendency for output to change.

We refer to the level of national income where aggregate planned expenditure equals total output as the EQUILIBRIUM INCOME. When that income is actually being produced we say that the economy is 'in a state of equilibrium'. All other levels of national income are called DISEQUILIBRIUM INCOMES and, when any of them is being produced, we say that the economy is 'in a state of disequilibrium'.

Equilibrium income and potential income

It is important to remember that *equilibrium national income* is not the same thing as *potential national income*. The latter is the national income that the economy would produce if all resources were fully employed. The former is the national income at which there are no economic forces exerting pressure for income to change. The amount of unemployment in the economy will depend on the relation between the two: the further below potential income is equilibrium income, the more unemployment there will be at equilibrium national income.

Planned and actual expenditure

Before going on, we need to say a word about the relation between output on the one hand, and planned actual expenditure on the other hand. We saw in Chapter 23 that, as a matter of definition, the value of the nation's output is equal both to actual expenditure on that output and to actual factor incomes generated by the output. These are just different ways of looking at a single number, the value of total output produced.

But what matters for our theory is planned expenditure. We have seen above that *disequilibrium occurs when planned expenditure is not equal to total output*. There is no reason why the amount that households and firms *plan* to spend on purchasing total output should be equal to the value of total output. Indeed we have seen that, if these two magnitudes are not equal, national income must change.

We have also seen that *equilibrium occurs where planned expenditure is equal to total output*. The income-expenditure approach determines the equilibrium level of national income at that point. This means that people are just willing to purchase the total output that is produced.

THE LEAKAGES-INJECTIONS METHOD

On page 255 we defined the circular flow of income as the flow of payments from households to firms (to pay for consumption goods) and from firms to households (to pay for factor services). Figure 23.2 (on page 000) depicts this flow. In the Figure the flow is closed, in the sense that nothing is added to it and nothing is subtracted from it.

The concept of leakages and injections

The circular flow is, however, not fully closed. Instead there are both leakages out of the flow and injections into it. A LEAKAGE, which is sometimes also called a WITHDRAWAL, represents payments received by firms or households that are *not* passed on through their spending. An INJECTION represents payments received by firms or households that do not arise from the spending of the other group. In other words, a leakage is an income receipt that *does not cause* further spending, while an injection is an income receipt that *was not caused by* household spending. Leakages are identified by looking forward to see where the income goes, while injections are identified by looking backwards to see where the income comes from.

In the simple economy that we are currently considering, saving is the only leakage while investment is the only injection. Later we shall consider other leakages and injec-

tions. In the meantime let us see why savings are a leakage while investment is an injection.

Saving is a leakage: Households do much of the saving in any real economy and, for simplicity in building our theory, we assume that households are the only savers. (This means that firms pay out all of their profits as dividends.)

Household saving is income received by households and *not* passed on to firms through household consumption expenditure. Saving thus represents a leakage from the circular flow. That saving is a leakage can be seen by considering an extreme case. Assume that households suddenly go on a wild saving spree and save all of their incomes. All of the income received by households now leaks out of the circular flow; none of it is passed on to firms through consumption expenditure. Firms will receive no income as a result of the consumption spending of households because there is no spending. Being unable to sell anything to households, firms will sooner or later cut their production of consumption goods to zero.

Investment is an injection: Investment creates income for the firms that make the investment goods. However, this income does not arise from the spending of households. It arises instead from the spending of those firms that purchase the investment goods. Investment thus represents an injection of income into the circular flow.[1]

The relation between saving and investment

It is most important to note that *the decision to save is made by one group, households, while the decision to invest is made by another group, firms*. As a result, firms may plan to increase their investment expenditure just at the same time that households plan to reduce their saving (in order to increase consumption). It is also possible, however, that firms may plan to cut their investment expenditure just when households plan to increase their saving. So, although there are many financial institutions that help to channel savings into investment, the key point that matters for our theory is that:

since saving and investment decisions are made by different groups, there is no automatic reason in the Keynesian model why the amount that households plan to save should be equal to the amount that firms plan to invest.

A summary using the circular flow diagram: Figure 25.1 shows a circular flow diagram with expenditure flows going from firms to households (as income payments) and from households to firms (as consumption expenditure). It also shows the leakage of saving (marked with a '−') and the injection of investment (marked with '+'). Between the two lie financial institutions which operate in capital

---

1 Recall the discussion on page 270 of the possible confusion between real investment expenditure, which is referred to here, and the allocation of funds by an individual to his or her various purchases of financial assets.

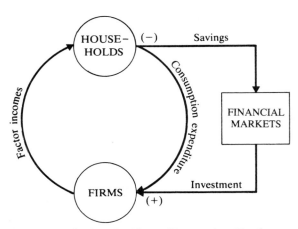

FIGURE 25.1 The Circular Flow of Income in a Simple Economy. Saving is a withdrawal from, and investment is an injection into, the circular flow of income between households and firms.

markets. Because *households* decide on the flow of leakages that they wish to make in the form of saving, while *firms* decide on the flow of injections that they wish to make in the form of investment, there is no reason why, at any moment of time, the flow of planned savings must equal the flow of planned investment.

The influence of saving and investment

We have seen that saving is income received by a household and not passed on by way of further spending. Not surprisingly, therefore, saving exerts a contractionary force on the circular flow of income. It reduces the flow around the income circuit just as a leakage at some point in your garden hose reduces the flow of water through the hose beyond that point.

We have also seen that an investment is revenue received by firms that does not arise out of the spending of households. In the case of investment goods, firms are both the buyers and the sellers. The firms that make and sell investment goods must employ factors of production. This, in turn, creates income for the households that supply the factors. Households can then, in their turn, spend this income on consumption goods produced by firms. Investment thus increases the flow of income just as a second garden hose that is joined to your first hose, and adds its volume of water to that hose, will increase the flow through the hose beyond the point at which the hoses join.

Equilibrium income

In view of the argument in the previous paragraph, we should not be surprised to find that the circular flow is in equilibrium – with national income neither rising nor falling – when the volume of leakages (caused in our present model by saving) is equal to the volume of injections (caused in our present model by investment). Let us see how this comes about.

Look now at Table 25.2, which repeats the data on

planned saving and income from Table 24.1 and on planned investment from Table 25.1. To see how equilibrium national income is achieved through saving and investment, consider what would happen if the value of output were held at £1600m. At this level of national income, households wish to save only £100m, while firms wish to invest £300m. Savings and investment plans are inconsistent with each other.

TABLE 25.2 Equilibrium National Income from the Leakages-Injections Method. National income is in equilibrium when firms plan to invest the same amount as households plan to save (£m)

National income (Y)	Planned saving (S)	Planned investment (I)	
0	−300	300	
400	−200	300	
800	−100	300	Pressure on income to
1200	0	300	increase
1600	100	300	
2000	200	300	
2400	**300**	**300**	Equilibrium income
2800	400	300	
3200	500	300	Pressure on income to
3600	600	300	decrease

We have seen that there are two extreme possibilities if output is held at this level. Either production plans will be fulfilled and expenditure plans frustrated, or expenditure plans will be fulfilled and production plans will be frustrated.

Now consider each of the above possibilities. In the first case, households, which are unable to buy all that they wish to buy, end up by saving more than they planned to save. They are forced to save income that they planned to spend. Firms see that they could sell more, if only they were producing more.

In the second case, firms find their stocks of finished goods being depleted. They find, therefore, that they end up making less than the £300m total investment that they planned to make. They do spend £300m on capital goods but they also have an unplanned depletion of stocks. Actual total investment therefore is £300m minus the reduction in stocks. (Recall that total investment includes investment in fixed capital and changes in stocks.) If stocks fall by £200m – which is what must happen if plans to spend £200m more than current output are fulfilled – then while planned investment was £300m, actual total investment would only be £100m (since the reduction in stocks was unplanned and undesired). Since firms do not wish to deplete their stocks, they will increase their production in order to end this unplanned stock depletion.

In either of the two cases that we have just considered, there is a tendency for output to rise whenever households wish to withdraw less from the circular flow by saving than firms wish to add to it by investing. In other words, *whenever planned saving is less than planned investment, national income tends to rise*.

Now consider a level of national income above the equilibrium, say £3200m. At this income, planned saving exceeds planned investment. If firms insist on holding output at £3200m, they will be unable to sell all of it and stocks will rise. There will thus be unplanned investment in stocks. Firms will cut back their output in an effort to eliminate the unplanned increase in stocks. Thus national income will fall as a result of households wishing to withdraw more from the circular flow by saving than firms wish to add to it by investing.

When the level of national income is £2400m, the plans of firms and households coincide so that both are able to save and invest just what they plan to save and invest at the existing level of income. Thus no one has any reason to alter their behaviour, so there is no reason for national income to change.

Thus national income is in equilibrium when planned saving equals planned investment.

The above discussion may be summarized as follows. Below the equilibrium level of income and output, planned investment injects more spending into the circular flow than planned saving withdraws from it. This imbalance between the income-increasing forces of investment and the income-decreasing forces of saving tends to cause national income to rise. Above the equilibrium level of national income, planned investment is less than planned saving and the opposite imbalance between expansionary and contractionary forces causes national income to fall.

THE EQUIVALENCE OF THE TWO METHODS

We have shown the determination of equilibrium national income by two different methods. Both give the same answer, though offering different insights. It is important to assure ourselves that they really do come to the same conclusion. We do this first graphically and then algebraically.

A graphical demonstration

Figure 25.2 shows the determination of the equilibrium level of national income, first using the aggregate expenditure function in part (i), and then using the saving and investment functions in part (ii). The Figure is plotted using the data in Tables 25.1 and 25.2. The two graphs have the same scales. This allows us to compare desired expenditure and desired saving at any level of national income.

Look first at part (i) of the Figure. The aggregate expenditure function plots the data from columns (i) and (iv) of Table 25.1 and is labelled E.

Below the equilibrium level of income, the E line lies above the 45° line (labelled $E = Y$). This shows that planned expenditure exceeds income. When people wish to buy more than is currently being produced there is, as we have seen, pressure on national income to rise. This pressure is shown by the upward-pointing arrow to the left of income Y_e. Above equilibrium income, the E line lies below the 45° line, showing that planned expenditure is less than

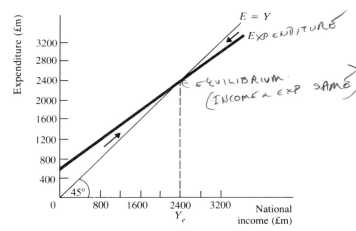

(i) The income-expenditure approach

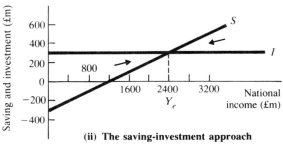

(ii) The saving-investment approach

FIGURE 25.2 The Determination of Equilibrium. Equilibrium national income is the level of income (2400 in this example) where the aggregate expenditure curve intersects the 45° line, and where the saving and investment curves intersect each other.

income. When people wish to spend less than the value of current production, there is pressure on income to fall. This pressure is shown by the downward-pointing arrow to the right of income Y_e.

Equilibrium occurs at the level of income Y_e, where the aggregate expenditure function, E, cuts the 45° line. At this point desired expenditure, measured on the vertical axis, is exactly equal to actual national income, measured on the horizontal axis.

Now look at part (ii) of the Figure. Below the equilibrium level of income, the investment curve lies above the saving curve, indicating that planned investment exceeds planned saving. Above equilibrium income, the saving curve lies above the investment curve, indicating that planned saving exceeds planned investment. Equilibrium occurs where the saving and investment curves intersect each other. At this level of national income, planned saving is exactly equal to planned investment.

We have already seen in Tables 25.1 and 25.2 that both the income-expenditure and the saving-investment approaches give the same solution for equilibrium income. This is also shown in the two parts of Figure 25.2, since the level of income, Y_e, where the aggregate expenditure curve cuts the 45° line, is the same as the level of income, Y_e, where the savings curve cuts the investment curve.

This is, of course, no accident. *Planned saving* is the

difference between income and planned consumption expenditure, which, graphically, is *the vertical gap between the 45° line and the consumption line*. Aggregate planned expenditure is the sum of planned consumption and planned investment expenditures, so that *planned investment is the vertical distance between the expenditure line and the consumption line*. Thus, when the expenditure line cuts the 45° line (i.e. planned expenditure equals income), the saving line must cut the investment line (i.e. planned saving equals planned investment). Put another way, in equilibrium, households plan not to spend on consumption (leakages) an amount that is equal to the amount that firms plan to spend on investment (injections).

The model of the economy

We have just shown the equivalence of the expenditure-income and the leakages-injections approaches using geometry. This section provides an alternative algebraic demonstration for those who find it helpful.

A numerical illustration: Let consumption be given by the relation

$$C = 300 + 0.75\,Y \tag{1}$$

This is the algebraic version of the consumption function shown in Table 25.1. You can check that this is so by letting income first be zero and then be 400. Substituting these values into (1), gives us corresponding consumption values of 200 and 600, which agree with the values shown in the Table on page 284.

Letting planned investment be constant at 300, gives an aggregate desired expenditure function of $C + I$, or $300 + 0.75\,Y + 300$, or:

$$E = 600 + 0.75\,Y \tag{2}$$

Equilibrium income occurs where aggregate desired expenditure, E, equals national income Y and we write this

$$Y = 600 + 0.75\,Y \tag{3}$$

Subtracting $0.75\,Y$ from both sides of (3) gives

$$Y - 0.75\,Y = 600$$

or

$$0.25\,Y = 600$$

Dividing both sides by 0.25 gives

$$Y = 600/0.25$$

or

$$Y = 2400$$

A check of Table 25.1 shows that the result that we have just obtained using elementary algebra agrees with the result we got by inspecting Y and E in the Table.

Equilibrium conditions: Let us now look at the equilibrium conditions for the model more generally using letters for C and I rather than the numerical values of the previous illustration.[1] When we determine equilibrium by

the intersection of the 45° line and the aggregate expenditure curve, we are solving two simultaneous equations. The first, equation (1), tells us about behaviour. It says that total expenditure depends on decisions about consumption and decisions about investment. The second, equation (2), is the equilibrium condition that desired expenditure should equal actual income; it is the equation of the 45° line.

$$E = C + I \tag{1}$$
$$E = Y \tag{2}$$

Substitution of (1) into (2) tells us immediately that the equilibrium condition is:

$$C + I = Y \tag{3}$$

This says that, in equilibrium, desired expenditure (which is $C + I$ in this simple model) must equal actual income (i.e. actual output). This is the equilibrium condition from the income-expenditure method.

We can now show the equivalence of the leakages-injections approach by recalling that households must allocate their income between consumption, C, and saving, S. Writing this in equation form gives us:

$$C + S = Y \tag{4}$$

This equation says that total income must be allocated to saving and consumption.

We now take the equilibrium condition for the income-expenditure method given by (3) above, and substitute into it the relation between income, consumption and saving given by (4) above, which we do by eliminating the common Y term. This gives us:

$$C + I = C + S \tag{5}$$

Subtracting C from both sides of equation (5) yields:

$$I = S \tag{6}$$

This is the equilibrium condition for the leakages-injections method. This shows us that, if (3) is true, (6) must also be true. In other words, if the income-expenditure equilibrium condition is fulfilled, so must the leakages-injections equilibrium condition be fulfilled.

It follows that the income-expenditure and the leakages-injections methods are equivalent because fulfilling the equilibrium condition of one method implies that the equilibrium condition of the other method is also fulfilled.

How General are the Results?

We have now developed a theory of the determination of equilibrium national income. We have done so, however, in the context of a simple model where there are only two expenditure flows, consumption and investment. Nonetheless, we have arrived at a general result that holds in more complex models. This is that national income is in equilibrium where aggregate planned expenditure is equal to actual output (i.e. actual national income). Graphically,

---

1 The general solution for equilibrium income, using letters instead of numbers, is worked out in Appendix 3 on page 512.

this is where the aggregate expenditure line intersects the 45° line.

We have also seen that, in the present model, equilibrium occurs where planned saving equals planned investment. Graphically, this is where the S and I lines intersect. This result always obtains in this model, but it is *not* a general result. The general result, using the leakages-injections approach, is that equilibrium occurs where the sum of desired leakages equals the sum of desired injections. In the present special case, however, saving is the only leakage and investment is the only injection. In this case, saying that leakages equal injections is the same thing as saying that desired saving equals desired investment.

A Link between Saving and Investment?

Earlier in this chapter we stressed that saving and investment decisions were made by different groups, and that there was no necessary reason why households should decide to save the same amount as firms decide to invest. We have just concluded, however, that in the simple economy we are now considering, national income is in equilibrium when planned saving is equal to planned investment. Does this not mean that we have found a mechanism that ensures that households end up desiring to save an amount equal to what firms desire to invest? The answer is 'yes', and the mechanism is in the changes in national income that are induced when desired saving does not equal desired investment. Is there not then a conflict between what we said about the decisions to save and invest and what we have now concluded? The answer is 'no'.

The explanation of the apparent conflict provides the key to the theory of the determination of national income in this simple Keynesian model.

There is no reason why the amount that households wish to save at any given level of national income should be equal to the amount that firms wish to invest at that same level of national income.

This is the meaning of the statement made at the outset.

But when planned saving is not equal to planned investment, there are forces at work in the economy that cause national income to change until the two do become equal.

This is the meaning of the later statement.

The argument of the above paragraph can be expressed graphically. That planned household saving does not have to equal planned investment by firms is shown graphically by the fact that the saving curve does not everywhere coincide with the investment curve. Where it does not, planned saving does not equal planned investment at the indicated level of income. The graphical expression of the point that planned saving will end up equal to planned investment is that the saving and investment lines do intersect somewhere, and the equilibrium level of income occurs at that intersection point.

This graphical discussion can be illustrated by reference

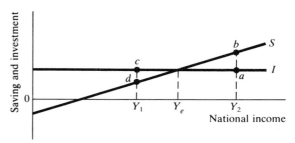

FIGURE 25.3   A Saving and an Investment Function. Planned saving equals planned investment only at the equilibrium level of national income, Y_e.

to the values indicated on Figure 25.3. But before we do this, we need to add a note on how values are indicated on our graphs. Figure 25.3 is the first time we have not been graphing specific numerical examples with specific numerical scales on each axis. From now on, graphs will usually be similar to 25.3 with the variables being specified on each axis, but without specific numerical scales, since the argument is not tied to one numerical illustration. In this case, we have Y, S and I, standing respectively for national income, saving and investment. We then use subscripts to indicate specific values of these variables. In the Figure, Y_1, Y_e and Y_2 all stand for specific, but unstated, values of national income. Since we are not tied to a specific numerical example, we do not know what numbers Y_1, Y_e and Y_2 stand for. But we do know, and this is all we need know, that Y_e stands for the equilibrium value of national income where the saving and investment lines intersect, and also that Y_1 is less than Y_e, while Y_2 exceeds Y_e.

When we wish to indicate values that are not measured from the origin, we show these as the difference between the two relevant values. For example, when income rises from Y_1 to Y_e, the amount of the increase in income is given by $Y_e - Y_1$. In a particular example, where Y_e was £1500m and Y_1 £1000m, the increase would be £1500 − £1000 = £500m (which in symbols is $Y_e - Y_1$).[1]

Now we can illustrate the analysis of savings and investment in Figure 25.3. For example, at income Y_2 in Figure 25.3, planned saving exceeds planned investment by the amount ab, while at income Y_1 planned investment exceeds planned savings by the amount cd. Both of these are disequilibrium situations and if national income is at either Y_1 or Y_2, it will move away from those levels. Only at Y_e is income in equilibrium, and only at Y_e is planned saving equal to planned investment.

In later chapters we shall consider other more elaborate models where there are injections in addition to investment and leakages in addition to saving. Although we shall then have to amend our results somewhat, the basic ideas developed in this chapter will not have to be altered.

Now we know the forces that determine equilibrium national income. Our task in the next chapter is to investigate the causes and consequences of changes in equilibrium income.

1 For an important, and fuller, discussion of alternative ways of expressing the magnitudes of variables on graphs, see Appendix 1, pp.505–6.

Summary

1 In the simple theory of the determination of national income developed in Part 4, national income is demand-determined. (In Part 5 supply-side influences are introduced.) The influence of demand-side forces is isolated by the twin assumptions (i) that firms are willing to supply all that is demanded at current prices up to capacity output (also called potential, or full-employment, output), and (ii) that actual output cannot exceed capacity output.

2 Equilibrium national income occurs where there are no pressures for income to change.

3 According to the income-expenditure method, equilibrium income occurs when aggregate desired expenditure equals actual output. For levels of income greater than equilibrium, desired expenditure is less than current output and output will be reduced. For levels of income less than equilibrium, desired expenditure is greater than current output and output will be increased.

4 According to the leakages-injections method, equilibrium income occurs when aggregate desired leakages equal aggregate desired injections. In the simple model of this chapter (i.e. in a closed economy without a government sector), this is where desired saving equals desired investment.

5 The two methods are equivalent since, in our present simple model, the condition $E = Y$ implies the condition $S = I$.

6 Equilibrium income does not have to equal potential (or full-employment) income. When equilibrium income is less than potential income, there is unemployment of resources.

7 When planned investment does not equal planned saving, national income changes until these two are brought into equality.

Questions

1 Equilibrium national income occurs where:
   (a) desired saving equals national income.
   (b) desired investment equals consumption.
   (c) desired expenditure equals actual income.
   (d) desired saving equals actual income minus consumption.

2 Which One or More of the following are true in the simple Keynesian model of this chapter?
   (a) The MPC is positive but less than one.
   (b) The MPC usually exceeds the APC.
   (c) Investment is an exogenous expenditure flow.
   (d) Desired savings equal desired investment at all levels of income.

3 Determine actual income, actual saving, actual investment and actual consumption when income is in equilibrium given the following data:

Y	I	C
0	200	200
1000	200	900
2000	200	1800
3000	200	2700
4000	200	3600

4 Look again at Figure 25.2:
   (a) What is desired saving and desired investment at a national income of £1200m?
   (b) Why will income change from that level?
   (c) Now assume that with I constant the aggregate expenditure curve E in part (i) shifts to have a new intercept at £400m and an unchanged slope. What must have happened to the Savings curve?
   (d) Given the changes specified in (c), what would happen to national income?

5 Determine the equilibrium level of national income from the following data: (i) Consumption expenditure is £50m when income is zero and it rises by 80p for every £1 increase in income; (ii) investment expenditure is constant at £150m per year.

6 True or False?
   (a) When actual income exceeds potential income, desired savings exceed desired investment.
   (b) When national income is in equilibrium, leakages equal injections.
   (c) When national income is below equilibrium, desired expenditure is less than income.

In Chapter 25 we studied the conditions for national income to be in equilibrium in a simple two-sector Keynesian model. Equilibrium occurs where there is no tendency for national income either to rise or to fall. Figure 22.2 on page 245 shows, however, that the national income of the UK does not remain in an unchanging equilibrium. Instead UK national income changes continually, as do the national incomes of all countries. In this chapter, we use the Keynesian theory of income determination to explain why national income may change.

The distinction between movements along curves and shifts of curves is important to our study. Since failure to make the distinction often causes great confusion, we recommend that you study this section carefully. (Those who have already studied microeconomics will have encountered this distinction with respect to demand and supply curves in Chapters 5 and 6.)

MOVEMENTS ALONG CURVES AND SHIFTS OF CURVES

If planned consumption expenditure rises, it matters whether this is a response to a change in national income or to an increased desire to consume *at each level of national income*, including the present one. The former change is represented by a movement along the aggregate consumption curve. It is the response of consumption to a change in income. The latter change is represented by a *shift* in the consumption curve. It means a change in the proportion of income that households plan to consume at each level of income and it occurs in response to a change in some variable other than income. For example, as we saw in Chapter 24, a rise in wealth may shift the consumption function upwards as people feel less need to save so as to add even more to their wealth.[1]

Figure 26.1 illustrates this important distinction. The lines in the Figure conform to our assumptions about how consumption, saving and investment are related to national income. The consumption and the saving curves have positive slopes, indicating that households plan to consume and save more as income rises. We continue to assume that investment expenditure is autonomous. Thus the investment line is horizontal, indicating that firms plan to make a constant amount of investment expenditure, I_0, whatever the level of national income.

Movements along curves: Each of the lines shows how the flows in question respond to a change in income. To illustrate, consider an example where national income rises from an initial value of Y_0 to a new value of Y_1. Figure 26.1 shows that at national income Y_0, consumption is C_0, saving is S_0 and investment is I_0. Now let national income rise to Y_1 in part (i) of the Figure. Consumption expenditure rises to C_1, while saving rises to S_1, but investment remains constant at I_0. These changes in saving and consumption are in response to a change in income.

This example illustrates a general proposition: the response of any expenditure flow, such as consumption, saving or investment, to a change in national income is shown by a movement along the curve relating that expenditure to income.

These responses are measured by the marginal propensities to save and consume that were defined on pages 276 and 278.[1] *A marginal propensity measures the change in some expenditure flow that results from a unit change in income.* Thus, marginal propensities relate to movements along curves and tell us how much a particular expenditure flow responds to a change in income.

Shifts of curves: Expenditure flows can also change because the curves themselves shift, indicating a new level of expenditure that is associated with *each* level of national income. Such shifts are illustrated in part (ii) of Figure 26.1.

In each case, the curve shifts from the black to the grey line. This change is not a consequence of a change in income, but, instead, it represents a change in the whole relationship with income. The shift from C to C' is a rise in the consumption function – more is spent on consumption *at every level of income*, for example because a rise in wealth makes households less interested in saving more. The shift from S to S' shows a fall in the savings function – less is saved at every level of income, say, for the same reason that more is spent on consumption. The shift from I to I' shows a rise in investment – more is spent on investment at every level of income, say, because of a major fall in the interest rate.

To see what has happened, look at some particular level of income, say Y_0. At that level of income: (i) consumption rises from C_0 to C'_1 as a result of the upward shift of the whole consumption curve from the one labelled C to the

_____

1 Be careful here not to confuse wealth (a stock) with income (a flow), as is sometimes done in common speech. People often say they have become 'wealthier' when their income rises. But wealth refers to a person's *stock* of assets, not to his *flow* of income.

1 So far we have defined marginal propensities to consume and to save. But there can be a marginal propensity for *any* flow, X, defined as $\Delta X/\Delta Y$ and measuring the change of expenditure, X, that results from a change in income, Y. Thus in later chapters, when we distinguish other expenditure flows, we can define other marginal propensities.

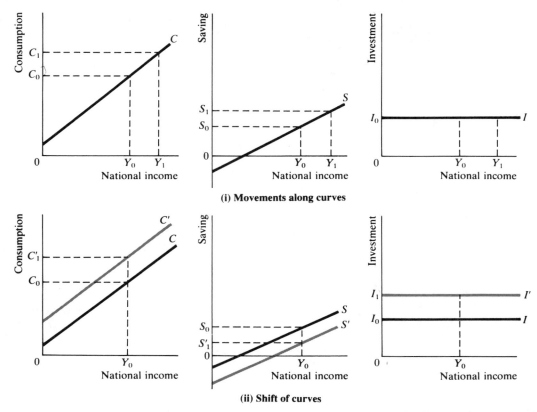

(i) Movements along curves

(ii) Shift of curves

FIGURE 26.1 Movements Along, and Shifts of, Expenditure Curves. In part (i), a movement along each curve occurs in response to a change in income: in part (ii), a shift of a curve indicates a different level of expenditure at each level of income. (The marginal propensities to consume and to save are calculated from the first two panels of part (i) by $\Delta C/\Delta Y$ and $\Delta S/\Delta Y$; these are the slopes of the C and the S curves respectively.)

one labelled C'; (ii) saving falls from S_0 to S'_1 as a result of the downward shift in the whole savings curve from the one labelled S to the one labelled S'; while (iii) investment rises from I_0 to I_1 as a result of the upward shift in the whole investment curve from the one labelled I to the one labelled I'.

These examples illustrate a general proposition: a shift in the curve relating any type of planned expenditure to national income indicates a change in the level of that type of expenditure that is associated with each level of income.

Our next task is to study the effects that such shifts in expenditure curves have on equilibrium national income.

WHY NATIONAL INCOME CHANGES

A Change in Desired Investment

What will happen to national income if there is, say, an increase in the amount of investment expenditure that firms wish to make? For example, a new product may be invented and firms may decide to build new plants in order to serve the new market.

Just as we saw that we can describe equilibrium national income either by the condition that *desired expenditure equals national income*, or by the condition that *leakages equal injections*, so can we use either of these approaches

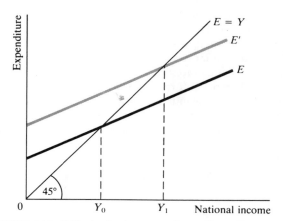

FIGURE 26.2 Shifts in the Aggregate Expenditure Function. Equilibrium is at Y_0 when the aggregate expenditure curve is E, and at Y_1 when the curve is E'. This shows that upwards shifts in the expenditure curve increase equilibrium income, while downward shifts decrease it.

to discover the effects of changes in planned expenditure flows, such as a rise in desired investment.

The income-expenditure approach

The rise in planned investment expenditure shifts the aggregate expenditure curve upwards, indicating that more expenditure is planned at each level of income. The effects are shown in Figure 26.2. In that Figure, the initial expenditure function is E, and the initial equilibrium level of income is Y_0. An increase in planned investment now shifts the aggregate expenditure curve upward to E'. This raises equilibrium income to Y_1. Not surprisingly, if desired expenditure on the nation's output rises, equilibrium national income rises.

The opposite change is a fall in planned investment expenditure. This can be shown by letting the initial expenditure function be E', which produces equilibrium income of Y_1. The fall in planned investment expenditure then causes the aggregate expenditure function to fall to E and, as a result, equilibrium national income falls to Y_0.

The leakages-injections approach

In Figure 26.3 the original saving and investment schedules are S and I. These curves intersect to produce an equilibrium national income of Y_0. Now let the investment schedule shift upwards to I'. There is more planned investment at each level of income and equilibrium income rises to Y_1 as a result.

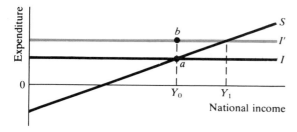

FIGURE 26.3 The Effect on National Income of a Change in Investment. Equilibrium national income is Y_0 when the desired investment curve is I and Y_1 when the curve is I'. This shows that an upward shift in the investment curve increases equilibrium national income, while a downward shift reduces it.

Conclusions

We have now derived two basic conclusions:

- **A rise in planned investment expenditure raises equilibrium national income.**

- **A fall in planned investment expenditure lowers equilibrium national income.**

Economic forces

Let us now ask what economic forces are at work to cause the changes just studied? We can look at this in each of the two approaches.

Income-expenditure approach: We started from an equilibrium where desired expenditure was equal to total output. The expenditure curve then shifted upward, indicating that people now wished to purchase more than total output. In response firms raise output, thus raising national income. Income and output continue to rise until income is once again equal to desired expenditure. Equilibrium is then restored.

The leakages-injections approach: Since the saving curve is unchanged, the upward shift of the investment curve means that, at the initial level of income, Y_0, some decision-makers wish to inject more into the circular flow by way of investment than other decision-takers wish to withdraw through savings. This excess of planned investment over planned saving is shown by the distance ab in Figure 26.3.

As output is increased to meet this extra demand, national income rises. The rise in income causes the amount of desired savings to rise *in response to the change in income*. The rise in income continues until, at income Y_1, desired saving once again is equal to the (new and higher level of) desired investment. In other words, the upward *shift* of the investment curve has induced *a movement along* the savings curve until the flow of desired saving is again equal to the now-higher flow of desired investment.

It is important to remember that we are dealing with continuous flows measured as so much per period of time. An upward shift in the investment curve means that, *in each period*, desired investment is more than it was previously. It is also important to remember that we are dealing with real flows. Our curves relate real national income to real expenditure so they reflect the *quantities* of consumption and investment goods people wish to purchase at various levels of real national income.

A Change in Desired Consumption and Saving

Now consider the effect of an upward shift in the consumption function and, therefore, a downward shift in the savings function. Say, for example, that households in the aggregate decide to spend £500,000 more *at each level of income*. This means that they must save £500,000 less at each level of income. We derive the effects using our two approaches in turn.

The income-expenditure approach

The change in household behaviour is shown by an upward shift in the consumption function, and hence in the aggregate expenditure function, and by a downward shift in the savings function.

The income-expenditure approach has already been shown in Figure 26.2. The only difference between the present and the previous case is the *cause* of the shift in the expenditure curve. In the earlier case, it was an upward shift in the I curve; this time it is an upward shift in the C curve. Both changes shift the aggregate expenditure curve upwards and both thus have similar consequences. The original aggregate expenditure curve is E, and it shifts upwards to E'. This raises equilibrium income from Y_0 to Y_1. The reverse case of a fall in planned consumption shifts the aggregate expenditure curve downwards from E' to E, lowering equilibrium income from Y_1 to Y_0.

The leakages-injections approach

If households plan to spend more at each level of income, they must plan to save less, so the saving function shifts downwards. This is shown in Figure 26.4 where the initial curves of S and I intersect to produce an equilibrium national income of Y_0. The saving schedule then shifts downwards to S' and, as a result, equilibrium income rises to Y_1. Equilibrium is restored because the desire of households to save less, shown by a downward shift in the saving curve, causes income to rise until desired saving returns to its original level. This is shown by the movement *along the new saving curve* from point a to point b.

The reverse case of an increase in planned savings is shown by an upward shift in the savings curve from S' to S. This lowers equilibrium income from Y_1 to Y_0. In this case, the desire of households to save more at each level of income, as shown by an upward shift in the saving curve, causes national income to fall until actual saving returns to its original level. This is shown by a movement along the *new saving curve* from point c to point d.

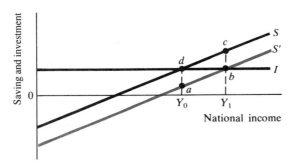

FIGURE 26.4 The Effect on National Income of a Change in Saving. Equilibrium income is Y_0 when the desired saving curve is S, and Y_1 when the curve is S'. This shows that an upward shift in the saving curve decreases equilibrium income while a downward shift increases it.

Conclusions

The above analysis leads to two further conclusions:

- **A rise in planned consumption expenditure, which is the same thing as a fall in planned saving, raises equilibrium national income.**

- **A fall in planned consumption expenditure, which is the same thing as a rise in planned saving, lowers equilibrium national income.**

The paradox of thrift

The results just obtained have one rather surprising application. When *one* individual saves more, his or her savings rise. But when *all* individuals try to save more of their income, total savings may well not rise. This is why economists speak of the 'paradox of thrift'.

We have seen what will happen if all households try simultaneously to increase the amount that they save – for example if the saving curve in Figure 26.4 shifts from S' to S. *The increase in thriftiness will decrease the equilibrium level of national income* – from Y_1 to Y_0 in the Figure. The upward shift in the saving schedule causes planned saving to exceed planned investment at the initial equilibrium level of income. National income falls and this induces a decline in planned saving. Income continues to fall until saving is again equal to investment. But we are assuming that investment is constant. Therefore, saving must fall right back to its original level so that desired saving is, again, equal to the unchanged level of investment. *The attempts to save more are frustrated because income falls until everyone ends up saving just what they were saving initially.*

The opposite case, a general decrease in household thriftiness (an increase in planned consumption), causes a downward shift in the saving function – e.g. from S to S' in Figure 26.4. The attempt on the part of households to reduce saving causes desired leakages to be less then desired injections at the initial level of national income – Y_0 in the Figure. This causes an increase in national income, and the increase continues until the actual volume of saving has been restored to its original level but at a new, higher level of national income. *The attempts to save less are frustrated because income rises until everyone ends up saving just what they were saving initially.*

A paradox?: These results follow directly from the theory of the determination of national income. They seem paradoxical, however, to those who expect the way in which a single household should act if it wishes to raise its wealth and its future ability to consume ('save, save, and save some more') to be directly applicable to the economy as a whole. The paradox is resolved as soon as it is understood that changes in desired saving by the community as a whole *change the level of total demand*. In the present theory, the result is a change in the equilibrium level of national income, which is the major determinant of the amount actually saved.

Applicability of the predictions: The applicability of the predictions just outlined depends critically on the truth of the two basic assumptions of the elementary Keynesian theory of national income determination.

(1) National income is below its potential level. Thus, the available productive capacity will allow output to increase whenever demand increases. Conversely, anything that reduces total demand reduces output. In other words, income is demand-determined. In this case, income is lowered by anything that lowers demand, such as an increased desire to save.

(2) Plans concerning investment are assumed to be independent of plans concerning savings. If the Smiths and the Greens *save* more, or save less, so the theory goes, that does not affect decisions by the National Coal Board or ICI on how much to spend on *investment*.

Let us now consider circumstances in which these two assumptions are not correct, in which case the paradox will not apply.

(1) If actual national income is already equal to potential income, then the first assumption will not be correct. In such circumstances, a decrease in household saving, and an increase in consumption expenditure, will not cause an increase in real output and employment *since full employment already exists*. In such circumstances, the effect of the increase in desired spending will probably be (as we shall see in Chapter 38) to cause an inflation. An increase in saving, however, with its accompanying decrease in spending will tend to reduce output and employment.

(2) If the second assumption is invalid, none of the predictions of the paradox of thrift will hold. Assume, for example, that the amounts of desired saving and desired investment are linked, and that changes in household saving *cause* changes in investment. In this case, there will be an offsetting shift in the investment function whenever the desire to save changes. An increase in the desire to save, for example, would shift the saving function upward but, by permitting more investment, it would also shift the investment function upward. As a result of these two offsetting shifts, no downward pressure on national income would emerge.

There are two reasons why changes in desired saving and desired investment are somewhat related in today's world. First, firms account for a substantial amount of both the saving and the investment that occurs in the modern world. When a firm decides to retain some of its earnings it is saving on behalf of its owners. When it decides to spend these funds on new equipment it is investing funds that it has saved. Second, the rate of interest exerts an influence on both saving and investment decisions. When desired investment exceeds desired saving, the rate of interest may rise, thereby reducing investment and encouraging saving. One condition for the paradox of thrift to apply, therefore, is that interest rates do not adjust quickly so as to bring about an equality between planned savings and planned investment at each and every level of national income.

The paradox of thrift is a property of a simple model in which national income is the only thing that changes when either desired investment or desired saving shifts. To the extent that shifts in either desired investment or desired savings cause shifts in the other (because firms do both and/or because changes in the rate of interest help to equate the two), the paradox of thrift will be less important and, in the limit, non-existent.

Conclusion: What is important about the paradox of thrift is the following insight:

sudden shifts in consumer spending and saving *do* affect total demand and *do*, therefore, exert expansionary or

---

BOX 26.1 Predicting Recession: Will National Income Fall?

'When the chairman of the Federal Reserve, Mr Alan Greenspan, gave evidence to a congressional committee on January 30th, he delivered a cautious ... message about the state of the American economy.

'Mr Greenspan's remarks did justice to the signs of slowdown in many parts of the economy. Car production has fallen sharply since the beginning of the year, he pointed out; the market is in a hollow after the strenuous promotions and price-cutting of last year. Business and residential construction is weak, partly because the rate at which new households are forming is slowing down. Real business spending on equipment fell by more than 4 per cent at an annual rate in the fourth quarter, reflecting the mood of pessimism about sales prospects.

'Against this he stacked [several points] ... The orders backlog in the civilian-aircraft industry is still enormous. Companies have not built up their stocks of material and finished goods in the way they did before some previous recessions. Foreign demand (thanks partly to the depreciated dollar) is strong. Despite job losses in manufacturing, overall employment continues to rise.'

(*The Economist*, 10 February 1990)

In this context, a recession may be taken to be a fall in the equilibrium level of national income. The chairman's remarks point to several items that have been discussed in this chapter, and which cause national income to rise or to fall when they change. He also points to some items that will be discussed in later chapters, such as foreign demand for the country's exports, but whose influences are not hard to guess.

Questions

1 What are the major items to which the chairman points as possible reasons why American national income may fall?
2 What causes that have been discussed in this book so far, does he suggest may lie behind the recession-creating expenditure changes?
3 What possible causes of a decline in equilibrium national income does he ignore?
4 He points to strong order books in the civilian aircraft industry. To what item of aggregate expenditure does this relate?

contractionary demand pressures on the economy in the short term.

As we shall see in Chapter 36, however, over the long run, supply conditions are more important in determining total output than are demand conditions. As a result, it is *not* correct that a reduction in planned savings will increase national income over the long term.

THE MULTIPLIER, OR HOW MUCH DOES NATIONAL INCOME CHANGE?

So far we have considered the direction of the change in national income caused by changes in planned expenditure flows. But what about the *magnitude* of these changes? If the annual flow of investment expenditure changes by £1000m, by how much will national income change?

The Definition of the Multiplier

A major prediction of national income theory is that a change in autonomous expenditure caused by a shift in any desired expenditure function will cause a change in national income that is greater than the initial change in expenditure. We first consider a change in investment expenditure, which gives rise to the well-known INVEST-MENT MULTIPLIER (often given the symbol K, and often just called '*the*' *multiplier*). This is defined as the *ratio* of the change in national income to the initial change in planned investment expenditure that brings it about:

$$K = \frac{\Delta Y}{\Delta I}$$

For example, if a change in investment of £2000 causes a change in national income of £6000, the multiplier is 6000/2000, which is 3.

Thus the multiplier tells us the change in national income for each £1 change in desired investment expenditure.

The value of 3 in the above numerical example tells us that for every £1 increase in desired investment expenditure there will be a £3 increase in equilibrium national income. So when investment increased by £1000m, equilibrium income increased by £3000m.

The Determination of the Multiplier

The importance of the investment multiplier in national income theory makes it worthwhile using more than one approach to develop it and to display its basic characteristics. We will explain the multiplier using an intuitive approach, then a numerical approach, and finally a geometric approach.

The multiplier: an intuitive approach

What would you expect to happen to national income if there were a rise in firms' planned investment expenditure

on new factories of £1000m per year? Would national income rise by only £1000m? The answer is 'No; national income will rise by *more than* £1000m.' There will be an immediate, *direct* rise in income of £1000m due to the rise in autonomous expenditure. This will be followed, however, by further rises in consumption expenditure which will be induced by the increase in national income. In the new equilibrium, the total rise in expenditure, and hence in national income, will be more than the rise in autonomous expenditure by the amount of the rise in induced expenditure.

Remember that we are dealing with flows of expenditure, so that a rise of £1000m in planned investment on new factory construction means an extra £1000m spent on new factories *each period*. The initial impact of the rise in investment expenditure will be felt by the industries that provide the materials for the new factories and those that do the actual construction. Income and the employment of factors of production in those industries will rise by £1000m as a direct result. These newly employed factors will then spend some of their new incomes buying food, clothing, shelter, holidays, cars, refrigerators, and a host of other products. This is the induced rise in consumption expenditure, and, when output expands to meet this extra demand, employment will rise in all of the affected consumption industries. When the owners of factors that are newly employed spend their incomes, output and employment will rise further; more income will then be created and more expenditure induced. Where will this process of new income inducing new expenditure which creates new income, come to an end? The answer is more easily seen if we use the income-expenditure approach.

The initial rise in investment expenditure is a rise in injections. This will increase income, but, as income rises, the volume of leakages (in the form of new saving) will rise. Income will continue to rise until additional saving of £1000m has been generated. At this point, desired saving will have risen by as much as the original rise in investment and, assuming we began from an equilibrium, we will be back in equilibrium, but at a higher level of income. For example, if 20 per cent of all income is withdrawn through saving, then the rise in income will come to a halt when income has risen by £5000m. At this higher level of income an extra £1000m in saving will have been generated, and since the rise in saving equals the initial rise in investment, income will no longer be rising.

Thus, the increase in income does come to a halt. In this example, it halts when national income has risen by £5000m. The multiplier is 5, since a rise in investment expenditure of £1000m causes a rise in national income of £5000m.

The multiplier: a numerical approach

The economy just studied behaves in a simple way: every time any household receives some additional income it promptly spends 80 per cent of it on consumption ($MPC = 0.8$) and saves the other 20 per cent ($MPS = 0.2$). This economy's marginal propensity to spend is 0.8, and its marginal propensity to save is 0.2.

TABLE 26.1 A Numerical Example of the Multiplier.
Where 20 per cent of any increase in income leaks out of the circular flow through new savings

Round	Increase in income at each round (£m)
Round 1: Initial increase in investment expenditure	1000.00
2nd round increase (80% of £1000m)	800.00
3rd round increase (80% of £800m)	640.00
4th round increase (80% of £640m)	512.00
5th round increase (80% of £512m)	409.60
6th round increase (80% of £409.60m)	327.68
7th round increase (80% of £327.68m)	262.14
8th round increase (80% of £262.14m)	209.71
9th round increase (80% of £209.71m)	167.77
10th round increase (80% of £167.77m)	134.22
Sum of 1st 10 rounds	4463.12
11th and all subsequent rounds	536.88
Total	5000.00

Now suppose that injections increase in the form of the £1000m of new investment spending. National income rises by £1000m. But that is not the end of the story. The factors of production involved directly and indirectly in manufacturing the investment goods devote £200m to new saving, and spend an extra £800m each year. The recipients of this £800m in turn spend an extra £640m a year (80 per cent of £800m), which is a further addition to aggregate expenditure. And so the process continues, with each successive set of recipients of new income spending 80 per cent of their new income and saving the rest. Each additional expenditure creates new income and yet another round of expenditure. Table 26.1 carries the process through ten rounds. Notice that the sum of all of this new expenditure approaches £5000m, which is five times the initial new injection of £1000m of investment. This argument thus leads to the same result as did the intuitive argument above. The multiplier is 5, given the numerical assumptions that we have made about consumption and saving.

The results of Table 26.1 are graphed in Figure 26.5. The white bar in each period shows the national income in the previous period. The shaded bar shows the increase in the present period, which is 80 per cent of the increase in the previous period. The total height of the two parts of each bar shows the total income in the period in question.

The multiplier: a graphical approach

In Figure 26.6, income is initially assumed to be in equilibrium at £80,000m.[1] Autonomous investment is then

---

1 Notice the break on each axis of the Figure. This is to show that the scale does not run continuously back to zero. If we showed the whole range from 0 to 85,000, the changes in which we are interested, from 80,000 to 85,000, would be shrunk to such a small segment of the Figure that they would be nearly invisible.

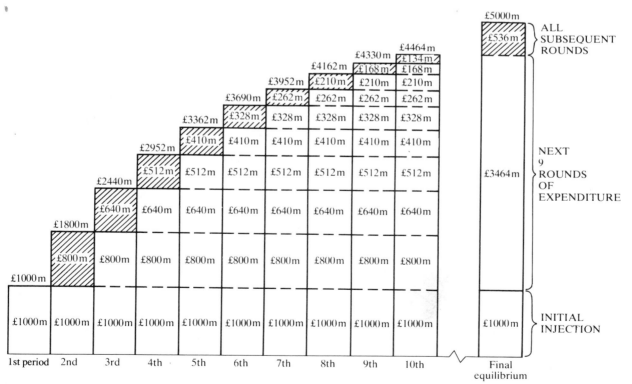

FIGURE 26.5 The Multiplier. The *total height* of each bar shows the full increase in national income as a result of an increase in investment expenditure of £1000m. The shaded part shows the increase over the previous round of expenditure as a result of new induced expenditure; each increase is 80 per cent of the previous increase because the *MPC* is 0.80. (Figures from Table 26.1 have been rounded to the nearest whole number.)

assumed to shift upward from £30,000m to £31,000m because firms increase their spending on new factories. The shift in the investment curve by £1000m from I to I' increases equilibrium income from £80,000m to £85,000m. This increase – which is shown as ΔY in the Figure – is larger than the increase in investment – which is shown by ΔI – which caused the increase in income.

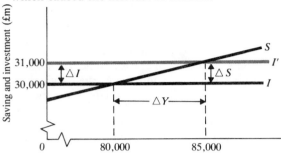

FIGURE 26.6 The Multiplier and the Saving Function. The slope of the saving function, S, is given by $\Delta S/\Delta Y$. The multiplier is defined as $\Delta Y/\Delta I$, which the diagram shows to be equal to $\Delta Y/\Delta S$ in equilibrium. This shows that the value of the multiplier is the reciprocal of the slope of the saving function.

The *ratio* of the increase in income (ΔY) to the increase in investment that brought it about (ΔI) is the multiplier, K. In this case we have:

$$K = \Delta Y/\Delta I = £5000m/£1000m = 5$$

Again this tells us that for every £1 increase in autonomous investment expenditure, equilibrium income rises by £5.

This much is simply definition: The multiplier is the ratio of the change in income to the initiating change in autonomous spending that brought it about.

Next consider Figure 26.7. In that Figure we see that the size of the change in income brought about by a shift in the investment function by £1000m from I to I' differs according to the *slope of the saving curve*. The three lines S, S' and S'' represent three *alternative* saving curves with slopes of 0.40, 0.20 and 0.133. In response to a change in investment of £1000m (i.e. $\Delta I = £1000m$), the respective changes necessary to restore equilibrium are $\Delta Y_0 = £2500m$, $\Delta Y_1 = £5000m$ and $\Delta Y_2 = £7500m$. The mul-

tipliers are thus 2.5, 5 and 7.5 respectively. This shows us that the *flatter* the saving curve, the larger must be the increase in income before saving rises to equal the new level of investment; thus the larger is the value of the multiplier.

Next we need to ask ourselves what the slope of the saving curve measures. This we already know from our discussion of Figure 26.1 above. The slope of the saving curve is the marginal propensity to save, MPS (i.e. $\Delta S/\Delta Y$). It measures the proportion of each new £1 of income that is saved. For example, an MPS of 0.40 means that 40p of each new £1 of income will be saved.

So now we know that the multiplier is *larger* the flatter is the slope of the saving curve; i.e. the *smaller* is the MPS. This means that the value of the multiplier is negatively related to the MPS: the smaller the MPS, the larger the multiplier.

Finally, we wish to show that the exact relation is that the multiplier is equal to the reciprocal of the MPS:

$$\text{The Multiplier } (K) = \frac{1}{MPS}$$

This is most easily seen by referring to Figure 26.6 again, and locating each of the ratios referred to below on that Figure. We know that the multiplier is defined as $K = \Delta Y/\Delta I$. We also know, and the Figure illustrates it, that when the economy has moved from its original to its new equilibrium, the change in saving must equal the change in investment; i.e. $\Delta I = \Delta S$. Thus we can rewrite the multiplier as $K = \Delta Y/\Delta S$. But we have already seen, and once again the Figure illustrates it, that the *slope* of the savings function is $\Delta S/\Delta Y$. Thus the multiplier, $\Delta Y/\Delta S$, is the reciprocal of the slope of the savings function $\Delta S/\Delta Y$. Since $\Delta S/\Delta Y$ is the MPS, the multiplier is the reciprocal of the MPS, which is what we set out to prove.

We have derived two important propositions:

- **The value of the multiplier is equal to the reciprocal of the MPS – i.e. the reciprocal of the fraction of the change in income that is saved, $K = 1/MPS$.**

- **Because MPS is less than 1, K must be greater than 1.**

This completes our study of changes in equilibrium national income in our simple, two-sector model. In the next chapter, we go on to allow for the influence of government on national income.

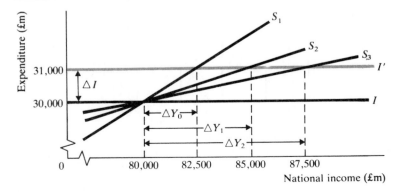

FIGURE 26.7 The Multiplier and Various Saving Functions. Equilibrium income, initially 80,000 on all three savings curves, rises to 82,500 when the saving curve is S_1, 85,000 when the saving curve is S_2, and 87,500 when the saving curve is S_3. This illustrates that the flatter is the saving curve, the higher is the value of the multiplier.

Summary

1 Expenditure may be either income-induced, or autonomous.

2 An increase in autonomous investment increases equilibrium national income, while a decrease reduces equilibrium national income.

3 A downward shift in the consumption line (an upward shift in the saving line) reduces equilibrium national income. An upward shift in the consumption line (a downward shift in the savings line) increases equilibrium national income.

4 The paradox of thrift states that, under certain specific conditions, an attempt to save more (less) will merely reduce (increase) equilibrium national income and

leave actual saving unchanged. These results require (i) that actual equilibrium income is below potential income so that income is demand-determined, and (ii) that desired investment is unaffected by changes in desired saving.

5 The investment multiplier measures the change in equilibrium income that results from a change in autonomous investment expenditure. It is defined as the ratio of the change in income divided by the change in investment ($\Delta Y/\Delta I$). The multiplier has a value greater than unity.

6 In the simple model of this chapter, the value of the multiplier is the reciprocal of the marginal propensity to save ($1/MPS$).

Questions

1 Using the following data, and assuming that all expenditure curves are straight lines, draw two graphs, one showing the investment and saving curves and one showing the consumption, investment, and aggregate expenditure curves and the 45° line. Determine equilibrium income from each and check that they are the same.

Income (Y)	Desired Consumption (C)	Desired Investment (I)
100	80	100
200	160	100

(Hint: if you are given any two points on a straight line, you can plot these, and use a ruler laid on these two points to draw the whole line; you will have to calculate the two points on the savings and the aggregate expenditure lines for the data given.)

2 Add to the graphs just drawn the curves needed to establish the new equilibrium level of national income when desired investment expenditure increases to 150.

3 True or False?
(a) A rise in desired investment increases equilibrium national income.
(b) The rise in income is always less than the rise in autonomous expenditure that brought it about.
(c) An increased desire to save at all levels of national income will reduce desired expenditure at all levels of national income.

4 Answer these questions with respect to the two-sector, Keynesian model considered in this chapter.
(a) Given that the $MPC = 0.80$, what is the value of the multiplier, K?
(b) Given that the MPS is 0.6 (just for fun). What is K?
(c) Given that K is 4, what is the MPC and MPS?

5 Describe the effects on national income of a fully employed economy in which a sudden fear of war leads to an increased desire to save on the part of households and a reduced desire to invest on the part of firms. Which curves will shift?

6 Describe some *pairs* of shifts in desired expenditures that could leave income unchanged.

7 Suppose that in Figure 26.7 desired investment expenditure falls from £31,000 to £30,500. What happens to national income given each of the three savings functions, S_1, S_2 and S_3?

27 Government and the Circular Flow

Government spending adds directly to aggregate expenditure. Government taxes reduce aggregate expenditure by removing from households and firms income that they might otherwise have spent on purchasing goods and services. As a result, total government taxing and spending activities have major effects on the equilibrium levels of national income and employment. The government cannot avoid having a major influence on the circular flow of income, since the government's size makes it one of the largest spenders in the nation.

This chapter shows how equilibrium national income is affected by the government's taxing and spending activities. The following chapter investigates what is called fiscal policy which, as we saw in Chapter 22, is the conscious use of the government's spending and taxing to influence national income.

Simplifying Assumptions

In the simple model used in Chapters 25 and 26, the only expenditures were consumption and investment. They were made by private households and firms, which together are described as the private sector. We are now going to add in government, or as it is often called, the public sector. (Until Chapter 29, however, we continue to deal with a closed economy with neither imports nor exports.)

Governments raise their revenues by many kinds of tax. The three main categories are *taxes on income, taxes on expenditures* (sometimes called direct and indirect taxes respectively) and *taxes on capital assets*, e.g. inheritance taxes, which are levied on the values of sums left at a person's death. We can simplify this introductory treatment without losing anything essential by dealing with only one type of tax, the income tax. For simplicity of exposition we assume that all income taxes are levied on households. As a result of personal income taxes, not all income that is earned by factors of production reaches their hands. Instead, part is taken by the government as tax revenue and only the remainder becomes personal disposable income, a concept we defined on page 262 of Chapter 23, and which we now denote as Y_d.

Although this is a useful simplification for developing our theory, we must not forget that many taxes fall on consumers' expenditure rather than income. This is true for example of the value added tax (VAT). Such taxes exempt investment and consumer saving. They are levied on C (which is $Y_d - S$), *not* on Y.

THE INCOME-EXPENDITURE METHOD

When we add the government to our model of income determination, we must alter the definition of aggregate expenditure to include all of the government's exhaustive expenditures. (If you have forgotten the distinction between exhaustive expenditures and transfer payments, you should reread page 257 of Chapter 23 now.) If we let G stand for exhaustive expenditures, as we did in Chapter 23, our new aggregate expenditure function is:

$$E = C + I + G$$

This tells us that desired aggregate expenditure is the sum of desired consumption, desired investment and desired government expenditure.

The Behaviour of Desired Expenditure

Next we must consider the behaviour of each of these planned expenditure flows.

Investment: Planned investment is still assumed to be autonomous. Investment is determined by many factors other than national income and these factors are assumed, for the moment, to remain constant. Thus firms plan to spend a constant amount each year on investment in new plant and equipment, and to keep unchanged their holdings of stocks of materials and finished goods.

Government: For simplicity, we assume planned government expenditure is an autonomous expenditure flow unrelated to national income. We first study how national income responds to a fixed level of government expenditure. Later we go on to see how national income is affected by exogenous changes in government expenditure.

Consumption: We continue to assume that consumption expenditure is an induced expenditure flow because it is determined by household income. There is, however, one important new consideration. In the earlier model, without a government, all national income accrued to households as their personal disposable income, and all of it was, therefore, available to them to spend or to save. Now, however, government income taxes introduce a gap, or what is often called a 'wedge', between total national income and disposable income.

We now need to use the distinction between national income, Y, and disposable income, Y_d, that was first introduced on page 262 of Chapter 23. National income is the total market value of all final goods produced. Disposable

TABLE 27.1 The Marginal Propensities to Consume out of Disposable Income and out of National Income. Columns (ii) to (vii) show the calculations of the two *MPC*s for cases (1), (2) and (3)

Assumed case	ΔY Change in national income	ΔT Resulting change in tax revenue	ΔY_d Resulting change in disposable income	ΔC Resulting change in consumption	$\Delta C/\Delta Y$ MPC out of national income	$\Delta C/\Delta Y_d$ MPC out of disposable income
(i)	(ii)	(iii)	(iv)	(v)	(vi)	(vii)
(1) Tax rate is zero	100	0	100	80	0.80	0.80
(2) Tax rate is 25%	100	25	75	60	0.60	0.80
(3) Tax rate is 40%	100	40	60	48	0.48	0.80

income is the income that is available to households to spend or to save. Disposable income is reduced below national income by tax payments but increased by transfer payments (described in Chapter 23, page 257). Thus, although transfer payments are not a part of government demand for goods and services, they do affect demand by influencing household expenditure.

For present purposes it is convenient to assume that there are no transfer payments. This gives us a simple model with the following characteristics: (i) all saving is done by households, (ii) all taxes are income taxes on households, and (iii) there are no transfer payments. In these circumstances, disposable income is equal to national income minus the tax revenues raised by the government.[1]

The consumption expenditure and the savings of households respond to their disposable income. For example, if national income remains constant, but the tax wedge is increased so that disposable income falls, both consumption expenditure and saving will fall.

We have seen that consumption expenditure depends upon disposable income. In our theory, however, all expenditure flows must be related to national income. To obtain this relation in the case of consumption, we must now allow for the link between national income and disposable income.

To see what is involved, consider the example shown in Table 27.1. Here households are assumed to have a marginal propensity to consume *out of disposable income* of 0.8. This means that for every increase of £100 in their *disposable income*, they spend an extra £80 (and save the other £20). This defines basic household behaviour: they have a stable relation between changes in their disposable income and changes in their desired consumption. We call this the *MPC* out of disposable income, and measure it by the ratio of the change in desired consumption expenditure to the change in disposable income that induced it: $\Delta C/\Delta Y_d$.

We are interested, however, in how consumption changes as national income changes, which we call the *MPC* out of national income, $\Delta C/\Delta Y$. The example illustrates how the two marginal propensities are related. They show us that the *MPC* out of national income is always less than the *MPC* out of disposable income. The reason is that a £1 increase in national income leads to an increase

of less than £1 in disposable income and so to a smaller increase in consumption expenditure than does a full £1 increase in disposable income.

In the first case, shown in row (1) of the Table, taxes are zero. Thus disposable income is the same as national income, and consumption expenditure rises by £80 for every rise of £100 in national income. In this case, the marginal propensity to consume out of national income (column vi) and the marginal propensity to consume out of disposable income (column vii) are both equal to 0.80.

In the case shown in row (2) of the Table, the government levies an income tax at a rate of 25 per cent. Thus £25 out of every £100 of national income goes in taxes, so that only £75 becomes the disposable income of households. Now when national income rises by £100, disposable income will only rise by £75 and planned consumption will only rise by £60 (= 80 per cent of £75). In this case, the *MPC* out of national income is only 0.60 even though the *MPC* out of disposable income remains unchanged at 0.80.

Row (3) of the Table shows a case where the tax rate is 40 per cent. Thus £40 of each £100 of new national income goes in taxes, and only £60 reaches households as their disposable income. Now if national income rises by £100, disposable income only rises by £60, and consumption only rises by 80 per cent of that amount, i.e. by £48. In this case, the *MPC* out of national income is only 0.48 even though households continue to consume £80 out of each £100 of disposable income that they receive.

The effect of changing tax rates on the consumption and aggregate expenditure functions is shown geometrically in Figure 27.1. Curve C_1 is consistent with the example in row (1) of the Table, curve C_2 with the example in row (2), and curve C_3 with the example in row (3). We see that the function relating consumption to national income shifts from C_1 to C_2 to C_3 as the fraction of income going to taxes is increased. Notice that when the tax rate is increased so as to syphon off a larger proportion of income in taxes, the slope of the consumption function falls. This indicates a smaller proportion of total national income being spent on consumption. This illustrates an important conclusion:

since increasing the tax rate reduces disposable income, it reduces the amount of consumption associated with each level of national income – i.e. it shifts the consumption function relating desired consumption to national income downwards.

Anything that shifts the consumption function downwards also shifts the aggregate expenditure function downwards.

---

1 If we allow for transfer payments, we have $Y_d = Y - T + Q$, where T is total tax payments and Q is total transfer payments to households. In the present case, we let Q be zero for simplicity.

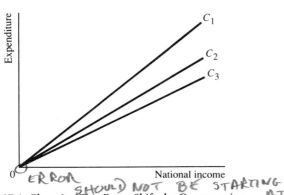

FIGURE 27.1 **Changing Tax Rates Shift the Consumption Function.** The higher the proportion of national income taken in taxes, the lower the slope of the curve relating consumption to national income.

So an increase in tax rates must lower the aggregate expenditure function.

The aggregate expenditure function: Figure 27.2 shows the derivation of the aggregate desired expenditure function for the present model. Investment expenditure, shown by the I curve, is assumed constant at I_0. Government expenditure, shown by the G curve, is assumed constant at G_0. (Don't forget G_0 refers to the distance from the origin to G_0, *not* just the distance from I_0 to G_0.) This means that, when income is zero, total expenditure is I_0 plus G_0. Consumption expenditure, shown by the C curve, varies with national income in a way that is determined, as we have just seen, by the relation between consumption expenditure and disposable income (which depends on household behaviour) and the relation between disposable income and national income (which depends on the government's tax rates).

The aggregate expenditure curve is merely the vertical sum of these three curves. (We add the curves vertically

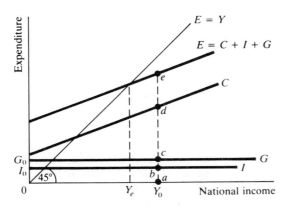

FIGURE 27.2 **The Derivation of the Aggregate Expenditure Function with a Government Sector.** The E curve is the vertical summation of the C, I and G curves. Equilibrium income, Y_e, is where the E curve intersects the 45° line.

because we want E to reflect the sum of I, G and C at each *level of income*.) For example at income Y_0, total desired expenditure is ae, which is the sum of ab (investment expenditure), ac (government expenditure), and ad (consumption expenditure).

Equilibrium National Income

If you look again at Figure 27.2, you will see the usual diagram for the determination of equilibrium national income by the intersection of the aggregate expenditure function and the 45° line (which indicates the equilibrium condition that planned expenditure should equal actual output). In the Figure, equilibrium national income is determined at Y_e.

There are two differences between the present model and the one developed in the previous chapters. First, the aggregate expenditure function now includes the government's exhaustive expenditure. Second, the consumption function (and hence the aggregate expenditure function) has been shifted by the presence of taxes in the manner discussed above.

This is all there is to the determination of equilibrium by the income-expenditure method in our new model. Figure 27.2 is the same as Figure 25.2(i) in all its essential features. All that differs is what underlies the aggregate expenditure function (i.e. the addition of exhaustive government expenditures and the effect of taxes on the consumption function).

The Effects of Changes in Government Taxes and Expenditures

The government may change its taxing and spending policies for many reasons. Whatever the motivation, such changes will affect equilibrium national income. We first consider the changes that increase equilibrium income and then the changes that reduce it.

Fiscal changes that increase equilibrium income: First, consider an increase in the government's exhaustive expenditure, *while tax rates are held constant*. The increase in spending adds to the amount of total desired expenditure that is associated with each level of income – i.e. the aggregate expenditure function shifts upwards. Second, consider a reduction in tax rates while *government expenditure is held constant*. This leaves more disposable income in the hands of households (because the government's tax wedge is reduced). As a result, households increase the amount of their consumption spending that is associated with any given level of national income – the aggregate expenditure function shifts up.

We have already studied the effects of an upward shift in the aggregate expenditure function. If you turn to Figure 26.2 on page 292, you will see these effects summarized. The conclusion that we reached there needs only to be recalled here: an upward shift in the aggregate expenditure function raises the level of equilibrium national income.

This leads us to our first major conclusion which relates to what are sometimes called expansionary fiscal measures: **an increase in government expenditure, or a decrease in tax rates, raises equilibrium national income.**

Fiscal changes that reduce equilibrium income: Now consider the opposite two changes in government policy – ones that will reduce income. First, a reduction in the government's exhaustive expenditures reduces the amount of desired expenditure associated with each level of income – it shifts the aggregate expenditure curve downwards.

Second, an increase in tax rates reduces the amount of national income that becomes households' disposable income. This means that households have less to spend on consumption, so that the amount of planned consumption associated with any given level of national income falls. The consumption function relating consumption expenditure to national income thus shifts downwards. Since the aggregate expenditure function is the sum of C, I and G, this shift in the consumption function also shifts the expenditure function downwards by the same amount.

Again, we already know the effects of a downward shift of the aggregate expenditure function; it lowers equilibrium national income (see p. 292).

This leads us to our second major conclusion, which relates to what are sometimes called contractionary fiscal measures: **a reduction in government expenditure, or a rise in tax rates, reduces equilibrium national income.**

THE LEAKAGES-INJECTIONS METHOD

We now repeat the same analysis using the leakages-injections method. Not only is the repetition good practice in such a key area; this method has some important insights to offer.

We have several times had occasion to observe that government expenditure is an injection into the circular flow of income, while tax payments are a leakage from it. Let us recall the reasoning.

Government expenditure is an injection: Recall that injections (which we symbolize by J) are anything that creates income for households or firms that does not arise out of the expenditure of the other group. Government exhaustive expenditure creates incomes for the firms and households from which it buys goods and services. This income arises from the spending of government, not from the spending of either firms or households. It is clear, therefore, that government expenditure comes within our definition of an injection.

Tax revenue is a leakage: Recall that leakages (which we symbolize by L) are any income received by either households or firms that is not passed on to the other group by way of spending on goods and services. Income taxes create a leakage between the total increases that are earned

by the production of final goods and the disposable income that is actually received by households. Instead of being received by households, the tax revenues go to the government. Clearly, therefore, tax revenues come within our definition of a leakage.

The Behaviour of Taxes and Expenditures

Government expenditure: First, consider government expenditure. We have already made the assumption that planned government expenditure is autonomous – i.e. it is determined by factors other than Y. This means that our two injections are both constant; they do not change as Y changes. Expressing injections in symbols, we have:

$$J = I + G$$

This says nothing more than that total injections are the sum of desired investment and government expenditures.

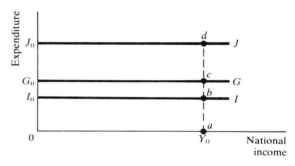

FIGURE 27.3 **Injections with a Government.** The injections function is the sum of investment and government expenditures. Since all are autonomous expenditures that do not vary with national income, the lines showing I, G, and J are all horizontal.

The graphs of investment and government expenditure, and hence the graph of the aggregate injection expenditure function (I + G), are all horizontal lines, as shown in Figure 27.3. They indicate that planned injections do not change as national income changes. Note, in the Figure, that the aggregate injections are the sum of the two separate injections so that, at any level of national income, reading off the vertical axis, I_0 plus G_0 equals J_0. For example, at income Y_0 aggregate injections are *ad*, which is the sum of *ab* investment expenditure and *ac* government expenditure.

Tax revenues: Next consider government tax revenues, which we continue to assume are all raised through personal income tax. If the government keeps its *rates of tax* constant, its actual *tax revenues* will rise as national income rises. For example, income taxes levied at a rate of 15 per cent take 15p out of every new £1 of income earned. They will thus yield an additional £150,000 for every £1,000,000 increase in national income. In general, therefore, provided that the government leaves its tax rates unchanged, its tax revenues will rise as national income rises.

The relation between the government's total tax revenues and national income with constant rates of tax is

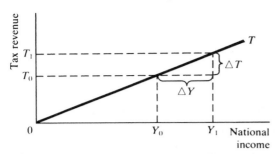

FIGURE 27.4 The Government's Tax Revenue Function. With constant tax rates, tax revenues rise as national income rises.

shown by the tax curve, T, in Figure 27.4. At national income of Y_0, tax revenue is T_0. At national income of Y_1, tax revenue is T_1. In the diagram, the change in national income from Y_0 to Y_1 is indicated by ΔY, while the change in tax revenues from T_0 to T_1 is indicated by ΔT. The slope of the tax curve is $\Delta T/\Delta Y$. This slope tells us the proportion of any increase in national income that goes to the government in the form of increased tax revenue. We refer to this as the MARGINAL PROPENSITY TO TAX (MPT). This is Keynes' term. Some modern treatments describe the same magnitude as the marginal tax revenue (MTR). Both terms mean the same thing: the amount of each new increment to national income that accrues to the government as tax revenue.

Total leakages: In Chapter 24 we studied the leakage of savings (S), drawing a savings function and defining the marginal and average propensities to save. We have now done the same for a second leakage, government tax revenue. The total of these two leakages gives us aggregate leakages in the present model:

$$L = S + T$$

where T stands for total government tax revenue.

The derivation of the aggregate leakage function is shown in Figure 27.5. The aggregate leakage curve, L, is merely the vertical summation of the saving curve, S, and the tax revenue curve, T (where the two curves relate

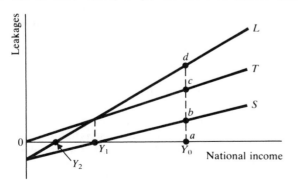

FIGURE 27.5 The Aggregate Leakage Curve. In the present model, aggregate leakages are the sum of savings and tax revenues. Since both savings and taxes are positively related to national income, both the S and the T curves, as well as their vertical sum the total leakage curve, L, have positive slopes.

saving and tax revenue to national income). Thus, for example, at income Y_0 aggregate leakages of ad are equal to the sum of ab savings and ac tax revenues.

Figure 27.6 shows the calculation of the relation between changes in national income and changes in leakages. At a national income of Y_0, leakages are L_0. At national income Y_1, leakages are L_1. The change in income is indicated on the Figure by ΔY and the change in leakages by ΔL. The slope of the aggregate leakage curve is given by the ratio of these two changes, that is by $\Delta L/\Delta Y$. This slope shows the fraction of each £1 change in national income that leaks from the circular flow due to the aggregate of all leakages. But any change in aggregate leakages must be accounted for by a change in saving and/or in tax revenues. Thus $\Delta L/\Delta Y$ must be equal to the sum of the MPS and the MPT (both measured as propensities out of national income). All that this says is that the proportion of national income that leaks out of the circular flow must be the sum of the proportions that leak out through saving and through taxes. We need a term for this fraction. Although ugly, the most obvious term is the MARGINAL PROPENSITY TO LEAK (MPL).

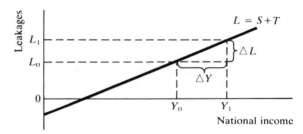

FIGURE 27.6 The MPL is the Ratio of the Change in Leakages to the Change in Income. In the Figure, an increase in income of ΔY from Y_0 to Y_1 causes an increase of ΔL in total leakages from L_0 to L_1. Thus the marginal propensity to leak is $\Delta L/\Delta Y$, which is the slope of the L curve.

In summary: the slope of the leakage curve shows the proportion of any change in income that goes in leakages, $\Delta L/\Delta Y$, and is called the MPL. Where the leakages are saving and taxes, it is also the sum of the MPS and the MPT out of national income.[1]

Equilibrium National Income

Part (i) of Figure 27.7 shows the determination of equilibrium income. The leakage and injection curves intersect to determine equilibrium national income at Y_0. This graph is similar to Figure 25.2(ii) on page 287 except that, in the present Figure, we allow for two leakages of saving and tax revenues and two injections of investment and government expenditure, whereas in Figure 25.2 the only leakage was saving and the only injection was investment.

---

1 A little algebra does wonders here! Leakages are $L = S + T$. This implies that $\Delta L = \Delta S + \Delta T$. Now divide through by ΔY to get $\Delta L/\Delta Y = \Delta S/\Delta Y + \Delta T/\Delta Y$. But the three terms are, in order, the marginal propensities to leak, to save and to tax. This is the same thing as $MPL = MPS + MPT$.

The Effect of Changes in Government Taxes and Expenditures

Fiscal changes that increase equilibrium income: Part (ii) of Figure 27.7 shows the effects of an increase in government expenditure with tax rates held constant. The injection curve shifts upwards to J' – i.e. by the amount of the additional government expenditure. This increases equilibrium income to Y_1.

To show the effects of a cut in tax rates, return to part (i) with the initial curves of L and J. Now a cut in tax rates causes less income to leak out of the circular flow in the form of taxes at each level of national income, and this causes the aggregate leakage curve to shift downwards to L', as shown in part (iii) of the Figure. Equilibrium national income rises from Y_0 to Y_1 as a result.

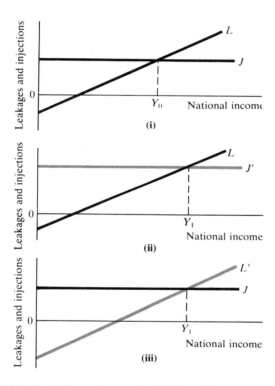

FIGURE 27.7   An Expansionary Fiscal Policy. Government policies to increase equilibrium national income above the initial level shown in part (i) are either an increase in exhaustive expenditures, which raises the injections curve as in part (ii), or a cut in tax rates, which lowers the leakage curve as in part (iii).

Fiscal changes that reduce equilibrium income: Now let us consider the opposite changes in government policy – ones that reduce income. The two contractionary fiscal changes are shown in Figure 27.8. We can be brief, since by now we are covering familiar ground.

The initial curves are J and L, for desired injections and leakages respectively. They intersect in part (i) of the Figure to produce an initial equilibrium national income of Y_0. Part (ii) of the Figure shows a downward shift of the

injection function to J'', brought about by a decrease in government spending. It reduces equilibrium income to Y_2.

Part (iii) shows an upward shift in the leakages function, to L'', brought about by an increase in tax rates. An increased amount of tax revenue is withdrawn at each level of national income. Equilibrium national income falls to Y_2 as a result.

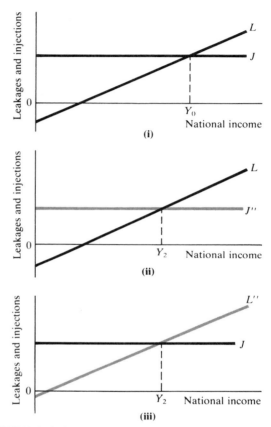

FIGURE 27.8   A Contractionary Fiscal Policy. Government policies to reduce national income below the initial level shown in part (i) are either a reduction in exhaustive expenditure, which lowers the injections curve as shown in part (ii), or an increase in tax rates, which raises the leakage curve, as shown in part (iii).

THE MULTIPLIER WITH A GOVERNMENT SECTOR

Since aggregate injections are just the sum of the separate injections of I and G, it follows that aggregate injections are equally affected by a £1 change in either I or G. If the shift in aggregate injections is the same, so is the change in equilibrium income. So we do not need separate multipliers for each type of injection. Instead we broaden our definition of the multiplier. It is no longer just $\Delta Y/\Delta I$. Instead it becomes the ratio of the change in equilibrium national income, ΔY, to the change in whatever injection brought it about, ΔJ. This makes our new multiplier formula:

BOX 27.1 Japan Halts Budget-Deficit Bonds

'As in Thatcherite Britain, the parsimonious holders of the government's purse strings in Japan have been relentless in purging the country of its bad public-borrowing habits. It looks now as though the Ministry of Finance's "iron fiscal guidelines" – for the government to stop issuing deficit-covering bonds, by 1990 – will be met a year earlier than planned. Thanks to more tax revenue than expected, the government will not need the net £1.3 trillion [a trillion is 1,000,000,000,000] of deficit-financing bonds written into this year's budget . . .

'Even the Bank of Japan's move into the secondary market to become the largest purchaser of government bonds . . . reminds many of Thatcherite Britain. After years of borrowing, the British government had its first reverse auction last January, buying back some £500m of gilts . . .

'Conservative estimates of the country's GNP growth have delivered pleasant surprises with each upward revision of the GNP figures. This year, for instance, the official view is that GNP will grow by no more than 4%, when practically every private forecaster is quoting 5%. Civil servants sheepishly admit that taxes will be bringing in £3 trillion more than they had planned for the year ending March 1990.

'Actually, the surplus is likely to be even larger. Aware of Japan's customary tax-fiddlers, the finance ministry had expected only half of all the companies liable for the new 3% consumption (i.e., value added) tax to have coughed up after even six months. In fact, there has been almost 100% compliance, which is thought to have chipped in an extra £700 billion or so.'

(*The Economist*, 25 November 1989)

The discussion concerns the move from a large government budget deficit, with accompanying borrowing (through what the Japanese call deficit-covering bonds), to a surplus. Comparison is made with the British government which achieved the same fiscal position a few years earlier than did the Japanese. The secondary market is one where securities issued earlier can be bought and sold (as distinguished from the new issues market where newly issued securities are bought and sold).

Questions

1 Use Figure 27.5 to show how a rise in national income and a new 'consumption tax' would increase that government's total tax revenue. In these circumstances, what must happen to government expenditure if the deficit is to be eliminated?

2 If the Japanese fiscal changes discussed in this article were to take place without a major recession (i.e. without a fall in national income), either there must have been some compensating changes in other expenditure flows (*what might these have been?*) or, initially, there must have been a particular relation between actual and potential national income (*what would this have been?*).

3 Explain the relationship between the government's budget deficit or surplus, its sales or purchase of bonds, and the rise or fall in the national debt. (What in this context is meant by a 'reverse auction'?)

$$\text{The Multiplier } (K) = \frac{\Delta Y}{\Delta J}$$

There is nothing profound about this: ΔJ stands for whatever increase in injections that does occur. It may be all an increase in private investment, in which ΔJ is all accounted for by ΔI. It may be all an increase in exhaustive government expenditure, in which ΔJ is all accounted for by ΔG. Or it may be some combination of the two, in which case ΔJ is the sum of the two.

The Size of the Multiplier

We saw that, in the simple model of Chapter 26, the size of the multiplier depended on the *MPS*. We now wish to show that in the present model the size of the multiplier depends on the sum of the *MPS* and the *MPT*. Let us see why this is so.

The reason why the multiplier always exceeds unity is that any increase in income induces new spending, which

further raises income and in turn induces further new spending through a series of rounds of new income and new spending. How much spending rises on each round depends on how much leaks out of the system. The higher the amount of leakages from each round of new income, the lower the induced new spending and the lower the final increase in national income.

For example, say that out of each £1 of new national income 15p is saved, 25p goes to the government as new tax revenue, and the remaining 60p is devoted to new consumption expenditure. Now let there be £1000m of new investment, just as we assumed on page 296 of Chapter 26. This creates £1000m of new income for those who supply the investment goods. According to our present assumptions, this will give rise to only £600m of new spending, as the rest will go to taxes and saving. This new spending creates new income, and this new income will in its turn create another £360m of new spending. And so the process goes on, with each new round of income creating a new round of expenditure of 60 per cent of the new

TABLE 27.2 A Numerical Example of the Multiplier. Where leakages of taxes and savings total 40 per cent of new income

Round	Increase in income at each round	Increase in taxes (2) × 0.25	Increase in savings (2) × 0.15	Induced increase in consumption (2) − [(3) + (4)]
(1)	(2)	(3)	(4)	(5)
1	1000.00	250.00	150.00	600.00
2	600.00	150.00	90.00	360.00
3	360.00	90.00	54.00	216.00
4	216.00	54.00	32.40	129.60
5	129.60	32.40	19.40	77.76
6	77.76	19.44	11.67	46.66
7	46.66	11.67	7.00	27.99
8	27.99	7.00	4.20	16.80
9	16.80	4.20	2.52	10.07
10	10.07	2.50	1.51	6.06
Sum of first 10 rounds	2484.88	621.21	372.70	1490.98
11th and all subsequent rounds	15.11	3.79	2.30	9.02
Final increase in income	2500.00	625.00	375.00	1500.00

Round 1 records the initial injection of £1000 in col. (2). Cols (3) and (4) shows that £250 leaks out by way of taxes and £150 by way of savings. This leaves £600 in new induced consumption expenditure, which creates that amount of new income in round 2. Each further row records the new income, the tax and savings leakages, and the new induced consumption expenditure. This latter figure, which is recorded in col. (5), becomes the new income in the next round recorded in col. (2) of the next row. After 10 rounds of expenditure, the additions to total income of £2484.88 are very close to the final equilibrium value of £2500.

income. Table 27.2 follows this process through 10 rounds of expenditure.

You should now compare this example with the one given in Table 26.1 on page 297. When you have done so, you will see that each new round of expenditure is less in the present case than it was in the previous one. This is because 40 per cent of each new increment of income leaks out of the income flow in the present case, while only 20 per cent leaked out in the case considered in the earlier chapter.

Figure 27.9 looks at this matter graphically. The initial curves of J and L intersect to give an initial equilibrium income of Y_0. The injections curve now shifts upwards to J', which yields a new equilibrium income of Y_1. The change in income from Y_0 to Y_1 is shown in the diagram as ΔY. The change in the injections that caused income to change is shown by ΔJ.

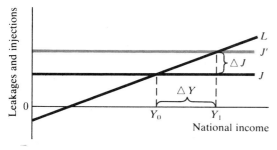

FIGURE 27.9 The Multiplier Related to the *MPL*. The multiplier is the reciprocal of the slope of the leakages function made up of the saving and tax revenue functions.

We already know that the multiplier is the ratio of the change in income to the change in injections that brought it about – i.e. $K = \Delta Y / \Delta J$. A look at Figure 27.9 reminds us of what we have already established: that the slope of the leakage function between Y_0 and Y_1 is $\Delta J / \Delta Y$. (This is because, to restore equilibrium, leakages must change by the same amount as did injections.)

So the multiplier is the reciprocal of the slope of the leakage function.

We have already called this slope, $\Delta L / \Delta Y$, the marginal propensity to leak, MPL. So the multiplier is

$$K = \frac{1}{MPL} \qquad (1)$$

But we have already seen that, in our present model, the MPL is the sum of the MPS and the MPT. (This says nothing more than that the proportion of any income that leaks out of the system in total must be the sum of the proportions that leak out through the separate leakages caused by saving and taxes.) So we may also write the multiplier as:

$$K = \frac{1}{MPS + MPT} \qquad (2)$$

(Where the two propensities measure the amount of savings and tax revenue resulting from a £1 increase in national income.)

The result in (1) is quite general and applies to any model of the type we are dealing with, no matter how many leakages are specified. The result in (2) is specific to this particular model, where there are only two leakages, S and T.

If all of this seems familiar stuff, it should be, because it is a repeat of the argument in Figure 26.6. The only difference is that, where we there spoke of investment and saving, we now speak of injections and leakages.

The Balanced Budget Multiplier

So far, we have considered a change in either government exhaustive expenditure with tax rates held constant, or a change in tax rates with exhaustive expenditure held constant. If the government starts with a balanced budget, then an expansionary fiscal policy that *either* raises spending *or* cuts taxes will lead to a budget deficit. Also starting from a balanced budget, a contractionary policy that lowers expenditure or raises tax rates, will lead to a budget surplus.

What happens if the government alters *both* its expenditure and its tax rates? Specifically, assume that the government raises expenditure and raises tax rates so as to keep its budget balanced. Now for every £1 that it injects through government spending, it withdraws £1 in new tax revenue.

The BALANCED BUDGET MULTIPLIER refers to the change in equilibrium national income caused by an equal (i.e., 'balanced') change in government expenditure and government tax revenue. Such a change leaves the government's budget deficit or surplus unaffected.

At first sight you might think this would leave national income unchanged. This would not, however, be correct. Instead, this balanced-budget increase in expenditure and revenue exerts an expansionary effect on national income. Similarly, a balanced-budget decrease in both expenditure and revenue will exert a contractionary effect on equilibrium income. What is the reason for this somewhat surprising result?

When the government spends an additional £1, aggregate expenditure rises by £1. When the government takes an additional £1 from households by way of income tax, households do not cut their expenditure by £1 because some of what they pay in new taxes would otherwise have been saved. So the net effect is an *increase* in aggregate expenditure by the amount that would otherwise have been saved.

Assume, for example, that the *MPC* out of disposable income is 0.9 while the *MPS* is 0.1. Now let the government raise £1 in new income taxes and spend it on current production. Households lose £1 of disposable income and, in response, they cut spending by 90p and saving by 10p.

The net effect of the cut in consumption expenditure by 90p and the rise in government expenditure of £1 is an increase in aggregate expenditure by 10p.

This net increase in spending creates new employment and income which then sets up further rounds of expenditure in the familiar multiplier fashion.

The effect is similar to the case of a redistribution of income. When income is redistributed from people with lower MPCs to others with higher MPCs, the consumption curve shifts upwards because more is spent out of any given national income. Similarly, when the government taxes people and spends the money, it is transferring income from the private sector, whose marginal propensity to spend is less than one, to the public sector which, by assumption, spends it all.

Notice that the balanced budget multiplier is much less than the simple government expenditure multiplier. When the government spends an additional £1, keeping tax rates constant, the whole £1 is new expenditure which then gets multiplied through rounds of additional induced spending. However, when the government spends £1 of new tax revenue, the new expenditure is only the difference between the £1 the government spends and the amount the private sector would have spent, which is determined by its MPC. This makes the new spending per £1 of tax-financed increase in expenditure, £1 – MPC. If, for example, the MPC is 0.80, the new expenditure is only 20p per £1 of extra tax-financed government expenditure. Only this relatively small amount then gets multiplied through additional rounds of new expenditure.

An Application

The above results may be used to throw light on one real-world issue. The fluctuations in income and employment since the Second World War have been much less in most countries than were the fluctuations before the First World War. (The period between the two wars was so disrupted that it is easier to leave it out of the comparison.) Many economists have wondered why this was so, and, during the 1950s and 1960s, many governments took credit for having brought about this greatly increased stability in their economies.

One important element in the explanation arises from what we have just established. After the Second World War, government expenditure grew to unprecedented heights in many countries, including the UK. To finance this expenditure, taxes also grew to take an unprecedented fraction of national income. Thus the marginal propensity to tax increased greatly. The theory we have just developed tells us that the multiplier would be reduced by this change. Thus, when the economy was hit by fluctuations in such injections as desired investment expenditure over which the government had no control, the induced changes in income and employment would also be correspondingly reduced. By lowering the value of the multiplier, the sheer increase in the importance of the government in the economy helped to reduce fluctuations in income and employment without any conscious stabilization policy on the government's part.

So an important contribution to the increased stability in many post-Second World War economies was the unplanned side-effect of the increased size of government taxes and expenditures. The consequent increase in the marginal propensity to tax reduced the values of each country's multiplier and so reduced the fluctuations in income and employment that accompanied shifts in expenditure functions.

In the 1980s, for efficiency reasons, governments have been reducing their presence in the economy. This may help the price mechanism to function better, but an unfortunate side-effect may be larger cyclical fluctuations because cyclically insensitive government expenditure has been replaced by cyclically sensitive private-sector expenditure.

Summary

1 To incorporate the government into the model of the determination of national income, allowance must be made for the effects of taxes and government exhaustive expenditures (as distinct from government transfers).

2 From the income-expenditure method, government expenditures are an addition to the aggregate desired expenditure function, which becomes $E = C + I + G$. Taxes, which are for simplicity assumed to be only taxes on personal incomes, introduce a wedge between national income and disposable income.

3 An increase in tax rates reduces household disposable income, and, with a given propensity to consume out of disposable income, the propensity to consume out of national income is reduced. Thus, an increase in tax rates shifts downwards the curve relating consumption expenditure to national income, while a decrease in tax rates shifts the curve upwards.

4 In the leakages-injections method, government expenditure is an injection and taxes are a leakage.

5 Both approaches yield the key results that equilibrium national income is positively associated with government expenditure and negatively associated with tax rates.

6 In a Keynesian model with a government sector, the multiplier is $1/(MPS + MPT)$ compared with $1/MPS$ when there is no government sector.

7 In the usual multiplier case, when an injection such as I or G changes, no offsetting change in a leakage such as S or T is assumed. In the balanced-budget multiplier, the government alters its expenditure *and* tax revenues to keep the balance between the two unchanged. In the case of an increase, the net injection of new expenditure is equal to the *increase* in government expenditure minus the *reduction* in consumption expenditure as a result of a lower disposable income. This is $£1 - MPC$ per £1 of new tax-financed expenditure. Only this smaller net injection is then magnified by the multiplier process.

Questions

1 Consider a society in which households always spend 90 per cent of their disposable income and government tax revenues always account for 20 per cent of national income:
  (a) What is the marginal propensity to consume out of disposable income?
  (b) What is the marginal propensity to consume out of national income?
  (c) What is the marginal propensity to save out of national income?
  (d) What is the marginal propensity to tax?
  (e) What is the value of the multiplier?
  (f) What is equilibrium national income if private investment expenditure is 130 and government expenditure is 150?
  (g) What happens to equilibrium national income if government expenditure rises to 290?
  (h) Check your calculation in (e) with that in (g).

2 True or False?
  (a) The marginal propensity to consume out of national income is always less than the marginal propensity to consume out of disposable income.
  (b) The aggregate expenditure curve is the horizontal sum of the I, G and C curves.
  (c) Taxes are a leakage.
  (d) Adding a government sector lowers the value of the multiplier, *ceteris paribus*.

3 Which One or More of these changes will *increase* equilibrium national income?
  (a) Tax rates increase.
  (b) Government exhaustive expenditure rises.
  (c) Private investment expenditure falls.
  (d) Households decide to spend more out of each £1 of disposable income that they receive.

4 What is the value of the multiplier in each of these cases?
  (a) The marginal propensity to leak is 0.5.
  (b) For every increase in national income of £1, total aggregate expenditure increases by 75p.
  (c) The marginal propensity to tax is 0.2 while the marginal propensity to save out of disposable income is 0.25.

5 Look at Figure 27.2. Assume that investment expenditure falls to zero.
  (a) What will happen to each of the lines in the Figure?
  (b) What will happen to equilibrium national income?

6 Look at Figure 27.5:
  (a) At what levels of income are (i) savings, (ii) taxes, and (iii) total leakages respectively equal to zero?
  (b) At what levels of income are (i) revenues equal to total leakages and (ii) savings equal to total leakages?

28 Income Fluctuations and Fiscal Policy

In the first half of this chapter, we use the Keynesian model to study the fluctuations in national income and employment that are known as the trade cycle. In the second half, we consider how the government's fiscal policy might be used to offset some of these fluctuations.

TYPES OF FLUCTUATION

When national income, employment and other similar macroeconomic time-series are studied over time, a number of distinct variations can be disentangled.[1]

Long-term trend: The tendency for a series to change in the long term is called its secular or long-term trend. The long-term trend for income, output and employment has been upward over the last two centuries. Such upward trends are usually referred to as 'economic *growth*.'

Seasonal variations: Many series show variations that take place within a single year. For example, retail sales tend to be high before and low after Christmas. Employment in construction tends to be relatively low during the winter months, when the weather impedes many outdoor construction jobs, compared to the rest of the year, when the weather is less of a hindrance.

The trade cycle: When both the long-term trend and seasonal variations have been accounted for, many economic series show further fluctuations of an up-and-down pattern. We briefly discussed the most prominent of these fluctuations in Chapter 22. It is called 'the trade cycle' or sometimes 'the business cycle'. Cycles lasting, on average, just under 10 years from peak to peak are clearly visible in the pre-1914 data for unemployment. More muted, and somewhat shorter, cycles in both output and employment are evident in the post-1945 data.

Stock cycles: A shorter STOCK CYCLE of about 40 months' duration is sometimes observed. This cycle is associated with the alternating building up, and running down, of stocks held by firms. The desire to accumulate stocks raises the demand for output; the desire to reduce stocks lowers demand. The stock cycle is sometimes also called the 'inventory cycle', which is the American term for the same phenomenon.

Other cycles: A number of other alleged cycles are more controversial. The Russian economist, Nikolai Kondratieff, thought he could identify long waves of 40 to 50 years associated with the introduction of major innovations. The existence of such long-wave cycles, called 'Kondratieffs', is highly controversial – although the depressed decade of the 1980s was 50 years after the depressed decade of the 1930s, which came 50 years after the depressed decade of the 1880s. Also, some economists have argued, as we shall see later in this chapter, that in many Western democracies there exists a political business cycle associated with the pattern of elections. Other economists have identified a 'stop-go' cycle associated with alternating bouts of expansionary and contractionary demand-management policy.

THE TRADE CYCLE

For the moment we concentrate on the trade cycle and start by considering its rich, and sometimes confusing, terminology.

The Terminology of the Trade Cycle

Although recurrent fluctuations in economic activity are neither smooth nor follow a precise, regular pattern, a vocabulary has developed to denote their different stages. The two parts of Figure 28.1 show stylized cycles that will serve to illustrate some terms. Each diagram shows a time-series for the economy's real GDP.

Part (i) shows the crudest distinction, that between boom and slump. When real GDP exceeds its *average performance*, we can talk of a boom; when real GDP falls short of its average performance, we can talk of a slump.

Part (ii) shows more detail and illustrates the more subtle vocabulary of cyclical fluctuations that is defined below.

Trough: The trough is, simply, the bottom. A trough is characterized by high unemployment of labour and low demand for final output. There is a substantial amount of unused capacity. Business profits are low or negative. Business confidence is lacking and, as a result, many firms are unwilling to risk new investments. If a trough is deep enough, it may be called a 'depression'.

Expansion: The recovery of the economy out of a trough is called an expansion. One key influence is that the climate of business opinion swings from pessimism to optimism. The results of this change are many: worn-out machinery will be replaced; employment, income and consumer

---

1 When data for observations of some variable taken at successive points in time are tabulated, the result is a 'time series'. When these data are plotted on a figure, the result is a 'time series graph'.

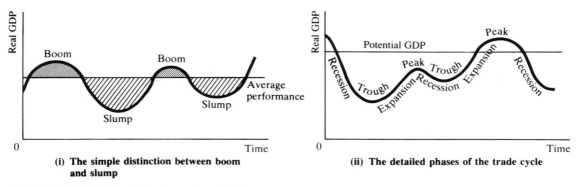

FIGURE 28.1 A Stylized Trade Cycle. While the phases of the trade cycle are described by a set of commonly used terms, no two cycles are exactly the same. The top half of the cycle, shaded in the Figure, is often called a boom, while the bottom half, striped in the Figure, is often called a slump.

spending all begin to rise; investments that once seemed too risky may now be undertaken; as demand expands, production is expanded with relative ease merely by re-employing the existing unused capacity and unemployed labour. In the early stage, favourable business conditions and a good outlook for the future now encourage business activity.

Peak: The peak is simply the top. Sometimes the forces of expansion are weak and the peak occurs before GDP reaches its potential level. At other times the expansion is strong and GDP will reach or exceed its potential level at the peak.

When the peak is a high one, signs of 'overheating' may occur. Labour shortages may become severe, particularly in key skill categories; and shortages of raw materials may develop. Output cannot easily be increased because few resources remain unemployed. Output can be raised further only by means of investment that increases capacity. Because such investment takes time, further rises in demand are now met more by increases in prices than by increases in production. Costs rise, but prices rise also, and business remains generally profitable. Expectations of the future are favourable, and more investment may be made than is justified on the basis of current levels of prices and sales alone.

Recession: When the top of the peak is passed, the economy turns downward, into a period of RECESSION or contraction. Recently the practice began in the UK of recognizing the existence of a recession when real GDP has declined three quarters in a row. (In the US the definition requires a decline for only two successive quarters.) However, this mechanical procedure is arbitrary (and not always helpful).

In a recession demand falls off and, as a result, production and employment fall. As employment falls, so do household incomes; falling income causes demand to fall further. Profits drop, and many firms make losses. New investments that looked profitable on the expectation of continuously rising demand suddenly appear unprofitable. Investment plans are revised downward, and actual invest-

ment spending is reduced to a low level. It may not even be worth replacing some capital goods as they wear out because unused capacity is increasing steadily.

Turning points: The point at which a recession begins is called the 'upper turning point' or 'downturn' while the 'lower turning point' or 'upturn' refers to the point at which a recovery begins.

Explanations of the Trade Cycle

Any explanation of the cycle needs to account for its two basic characteristics. First, there is the *cumulative* nature of economic activity: once started upwards, or downwards, the expansion, or contraction, tends to feed on itself. Second, there are the *turning points*: expansions eventually reverse themselves and become contractions; contractions eventually reverse themselves and become expansions. We shall consider these characteristics in turn.

Cumulative movements: the accelerator theory

An important explanation of the tendency of the economy to show periods of cumulative expansions and cumulative contractions is to be found in the combination of two forces: the multiplier, which we have already studied, and what is called the accelerator, which we must now study. To do this, we must look at the possibility that investment expenditure may be at least partially an induced (endogenous) expenditure rather than an autonomous (exogenous) expenditure, as we have regarded it so far.

Up to now, desired investment expenditure has been autonomous because it has not been related to national income. We are now going to consider a theory that makes investment an induced expenditure by relating it to national income.

Recall from Chapter 23 that gross investment has two components, replacement investment – what is needed to replace existing capital as it wears out – and net investment – investment to expand the productive capacity.

According to the accelerator theory, usually just called THE ACCELERATOR, net investment is related to the *rate of change of national income*. When income is increasing, net investment is needed in order to increase the capacity to produce consumption goods; when income is falling, it may not even be necessary to replace old capital as it wears out, let alone to invest in net additions to the capital stock.

Anything that changes the desired quantity of plant and machinery can generate investment expenditure. The accelerator focuses on one such source of change, changing national income. This gives the accelerator its particular importance in connection with *fluctuations* in national income.

How the accelerator works: To see how the theory works, it is convenient to make the simplifying assumption that an industry has a particular capital stock needed to produce each given level of its output. (The ratio of the value of capital to the annual value of output is called the 'capital/output ratio'.) Given this assumption, suppose that the industry is producing at capacity and that the demand for its output increases. If the industry is to produce the higher level of output, its capital stock must increase. This necessitates new investment.

TABLE 28.1 An Illustration of the Accelerator Theory of Investment

(1) Year	(2) Annual output	(3) Change in output	(4) Required stock of capital (assuming a capital/output ratio of 5)	(5) New investment: increase in the required capital stock
1	£10	£0	£50	£0
2	10	0	50	0
3	11	1	55	5
4	13	2	65	10
5	16	3	80	15
6	19	3	95	15
7	22	3	110	15
8	24	2	120	10
9	25	1	125	5
10	25	0	125	0

Table 28.1 provides a simple numerical example of the accelerator. The Table assumes that, in one particular industry, it takes £5 worth of capital to produce £1 of output per year. (This industry's capital/output ratio is 5.) The industry's sales, which determine its output, are recorded in the second column of the Table. They are constant at first. Thus in years 1 and 2, there is no need for new investment. In year 3, however, a rise in sales of £1 requires investment of £5 to provide the needed capital stock. In year 4, a further rise in sales of £2 requires new investment of £10 to provide the needed new capital stock. When the increase in sales tapers off in years 7–9, investment declines. When, in year 10, sales no longer increase, new investment falls to zero because the capital stock of year 9 is adequate to provide output for year 10's sales. A comparison of columns (3) and (5) shows that the amount of new investment is proportional to the *change* in sales.

This example suggests three conclusions:

- **Rising sales tend to induce investment expenditure.**
- **For investment to remain constant, sales must rise by a constant amount per year.**
- **The amount of new investment will be a multiple of the increase in sales because the capital/output ratio is greater than one.**

The data in Table 28.1 were given for a single industry. If many industries behave in this way, aggregate new investment will bear a similar relation to changes in national income. This is what the accelerator theory tells us.

Note the difference in the influence of national income on consumption and on investment. According to the Keynesian theory of the consumption function, the amount of desired consumption depends on the size of national income. Thus the level of *C* is related to the level of *Y*. According to the accelerator theory, the level of desired investment expenditure is related to changes in national income.

Limitations of the accelerator: The accelerator assumes that for each firm new investment is rigidly related to changes in sales (and thus, over the whole economy, to changes in national income). The actual relation is more subtle than that. Let us see why.

(1) Changes in sales thought to be temporary will not necessarily lead to new investment. It is usually possible to increase the level of output for a given capital stock by working overtime or extra shifts. This may be preferable to investing in new plant and equipment that would lie idle after a *temporary* spurt of demand had subsided. Thus *expectations* about whether changes in national income will be short-lived, or sustained, lead to a much less rigid response of new investment to changes in national income than the accelerator suggests.

(2) The accelerator relates only to the investment in additional capacity that is similar to what is already in existence. It says nothing about the new types of investment needed to install new production processes, or to produce new products. Both of these types of investment may occur even though there is no increase in demand for existing products, the first because it helps to lower costs and the second because it helps to produce new products.

(3) The accelerator does not allow for the fact that investment in any period is likely to be limited by the capacity of the capital-goods industries, so that actual investment expenditure may fall short of desired investment as a result of capacity constraints in the capital-goods industries.

(4) The accelerator can have different values at different stages of the trade cycle. In slumps there is much excess capacity. A rise in demand may thus be met mainly by putting existing capital back to work, and only slightly by adding to new capacity. In booms there is little excess capacity, and a rise in demand will have to be met mainly by increasing capacity, if it is to be met at all.

For these reasons, the accelerator does not, by itself, give anything like a complete explanation of variations in investment in plant and equipment. You should not be surprised, therefore, to learn that, taken rigidly on its own, the accelerator theory provides a relatively poor *overall* explanation of changes in investment.

Yet accelerator-like influences do exist and they do play a role in the variation of investment over the trade cycle.

Upswings and downswings: the multiplier-accelerator mechanism

The combination of the multiplier and accelerator-type influences can make upward or downward movements in the economy cumulative. They can also cause upswings to turn into downswings and vice versa.

The expansion phase: Imagine that the economy is settled into a trough with heavy unemployment. Then, for some reason, a revival of investment demand occurs. Orders are placed for new plant and equipment, which creates new employment in the capital-goods industries. A multiplier process is now set up. The newly employed workers spend most of their earnings, and this creates new demand for consumer goods. The spending of the incomes newly created in the consumption-goods industries induces further increases in demand.

Once existing equipment is fully employed in any industry, extra output will require new capital equipment – and the accelerator theory takes over as an important determinant of investment expenditure. This investment will increase demand in the capital-goods sector of the economy. The resulting rise in expenditure creates new incomes in that sector, and the spending of this new income sets up further multiplier effects. So the process goes on, with the multiplier-accelerator mechanism continuing to produce a rapid rate of expansion.

The downturn: Many forces can bring this expansion to a halt. To start with, supply limitations on the firm's inputs of labour and materials may slow the expansion. For example, when the labour force is fully employed, firms cannot increase output simply by taking on previously unemployed workers.

At this point, the accelerator again comes into play. A slowing down in the rate of increase of output leads to a decrease in the investment in new plant and equipment. To see this, look again at Table 28.1. Between rows 7, 8 and 9, output is still *increasing* but *by ever smaller amounts*. As a result of this *declining rate of increase of output*, the volume of new investment *decreases*. This decline in investment expenditure can cause national income to fall, initiating a recession. Other forces that can cause a downturn are a sudden loss of business confidence, leading to a decline in investment expenditure; a sharp rise in interest rates, leading to a decline in all types of spending that are financed by borrowed money; or such external shocks as sharp increases in the prices of imported materials or sharp decreases in the demand for exports.

The contraction phase: Once a contraction begins, it too tends to feed on itself in a cumulative downward process: falling income causes falling consumption expenditure.

The growing excess capacity leads to further declines in investment expenditure, while the decline in profits leads to a decline in business confidence.

The upturn: Sooner or later, this recession comes to a halt. Once all expenditure that can be postponed has been postponed,[1] expenditure no longer falls further; not all sectors may be caught up in the recession and those that are not may increase their investment expenditure as the recession causes input prices and interest rates to fall; new processes and new products are constantly being invented and new investment is needed to bring them into use. A revival of investment for any of these reasons can cause an upturn.

For whatever the reason, sooner or later an upturn will begin. At this stage, new machines will be bought to replace those that are worn out. The rise in the incomes earned by employees in the capital-goods industries will then cause, through the multiplier, a further rise in income. An expansion, once started, will trigger the sort of cumulative upward movement already discussed.

Conclusion: Given the tendency of expansions or contractions to become cumulative once they have begun, any severe shock such as those that have been discussed above, may be sufficient to cause the economy to turn from expansion to contraction, or vice versa. The characteristic cyclical pattern involves many outside shocks that sometimes initiate, sometimes reinforce, and sometimes dampen the cumulative tendencies that exist within the economy. The fact that so many different shocks can do the job is one reason why different cycles have different durations and amplitudes.

Cycles vary for other reasons as well. In some, full employment of labour may be the bottleneck that slows the expansion. In others, high interest rates and shortages of investment funds may begin a recession, although much of labour is still unemployed. In some cycles, the recession phase is short; in others, a full-scale period of slump sets in.

We have suggested reasons why an economy that is subjected to periodic shifts in aggregate expenditure will tend to generate fluctuations. In the next section, we study how, from time to time, governments have sought to influence the cycle, removing some of its extreme fluctuations through the use of fiscal policy. As a preliminary to this study, you must read pages 251–2 of Chapter 22 now. That earlier section discusses the broad macroeconomic goals of government policy.

FISCAL POLICY

Up until the 1930s, it was generally accepted that a prudent government should always balance its budget. The argument was based on an analogy with what seems prudent behaviour for the household. It is a foolish household

---

1 You can put off repairing machinery for a while but you cannot put off eating.

BOX 28.1 German Economy Reaches the Peak of its Upswing?

'In West Germany, there is increasing evidence that the economy is now in the late phase of an upswing: inflationary pressure from wage costs is mounting, monetary policy is becoming tighter, and profit margins are being squeezed. At the same time, foreign demand has weakened considerably. Yet domestic demand is clearly on the increase, thanks not least to an expansionary fiscal policy. In fact, the growth of domestic demand has been the key factor of West German economic performance in 1990. Private consumption's strong expansion has been spurred by the 1990 tax cuts, the sizeable rise in employment, higher pay settlements, and the strong propensity to consume of German immigrants from the East.'

(*The Economist*, 15 December 1990)

This quotation discusses the state of the German economy at the end of 1990 and uses several of the concepts you have studied in this chapter.

Questions

1 Three types of events are referred to in the article. Which of the events are typical endogenous events associated with the peak of an upswing in the trade cycle; which are exogenous events created by policy decisions to stimulate the economy; and which are private-sector events that might have occurred at any phase in the trade cycle?
2 What might the West German government have done if it wished to prolong the upswing?

whose current expenditure consistently exceeds its current revenue so that it goes steadily further into debt. It was then argued that, if avoiding a steadily rising debt is good for the individual, it must also be good for the nation.

But the paradox of thrift, discussed in Chapter 26, suggests that the analogy between the nation and the household may be misleading. When government balances its budget annually, it must restrict its expenditure during a recession because its tax revenues will necessarily be falling. During a recovery, when its revenue is high and rising, it will increase its spending. In other words, it will roll with the economy, raising and lowering its expenditure in step with everyone else, thus helping to accentuate cyclical fluctuations in expenditure.

By the end of the 1930s, largely because of the lead taken by Keynes, many economists had concluded that the government could stabilize the economy by doing just the opposite of what everyone else was doing – by increasing

its demand when private demand was falling, and lowering its demand when private demand was rising. This policy, which came to be known as Keynesian fiscal policy, sought to stabilize aggregate demand, in the face of fluctuations in its individual components.

Today many people feel that governments have abused the respectability that Keynesian economics gave to budget deficits. Instead of using deficits as an anti-cyclical tool, they have often spent in excess of revenues in good times as well as in bad times. As a result, there are strong pressures in many countries to force a balanced budget policy on their governments. This may or may not be an effective way to restrain those governments who would run deficits at all times. If balanced budgets are enforced, however, they will contribute to cyclical instability by forcing governments once again to *roll with* the rest of the economy rather than, as Keynes *advocated*, rolling against it. In the rest of this chapter, we develop the analysis needed to understand these critically important issues of public policy.

To do this, we will study how fiscal policy can influence the behaviour of national income and employment. But first, we must look at three important concepts – the deflationary gap, the recessionary gap and the inflationary gap.

Three Gaps

Figure 28.2 shows the economy in two alternate situations. In both cases potential, or full-employment, national income is indicated by Y_F. In part (i) of the Figure, the desired expenditure function intersects the 45° line to produce an equilibrium income of Y_1 that falls short of the economy's potential income. The economy is in a recession. In part (ii), the desired expenditure function intersects the 45° line at a level of income, Y_2, that is greater than potential income. The economy is in a boom.

Gaps in times of recession

Figure 28.2(i) illustrates two important concepts. The DEFLATIONARY GAP is the amount by which aggregate desired expenditure would fall short of income *if* full-employment income were achieved. It is thus the amount by which the expenditure function would have to shift upwards if equilibrium income were to coincide with full-employment income. This gap is indicated in part (i) of the Figure by the vertical distance, *ab*, between the E curve and the 45° line at full-employment income, Y_F.

The second gap can also be seen in part (i) of the Figure. It is the RECESSIONARY GAP, sometimes also called the OUTPUT GAP, defined as the difference between full-employment national income and actual national income. This is shown as the horizontal distance between Y_F and Y_1. The recessionary gap is a measure of the output that is lost when actual national income falls short of potential income.

Notice that the deflationary gap measures the *cause* of the economy's unsatisfactory performance, the amount by which aggregate expenditure falls short of what is needed

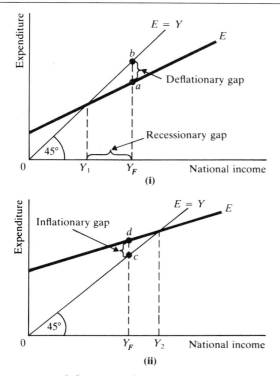

FIGURE 28.2 Inflationary, Deflationary and Recessionary Gaps. The recessionary gap is the horizontal distance between equilibrium income and potential income; it is a measure of output lost because the economy is performing below its potential. The inflationary and deflationary gaps are the vertical distances between the desired expenditure and the 45° line at potential income; they measure the amount by which aggregate desired expenditure exceeds or falls short of the amount needed to produce full employment.

to produce full-employment income. The recessionary gap measures the *consequence* of this shortfall, the amount by which equilibrium income falls short of potential, or full-employment, income.

Gaps in times of boom

Now consider part (ii) of the Figure. The difference between parts (i) and (ii) lies in the position of the aggregate expenditure function. In part (ii), the E curve intersects the 45° line to produce an equilibrium income, Y_2, that is above potential income. The resulting gap is called the INFLATIONARY GAP. It is defined as the amount by which aggregate desired expenditure exceeds income *at potential income*. In the Figure, it is shown as the vertical distance, *cd*, between the 45° line and the E line at Y_F. The inflationary gap is the amount by which the aggregate expenditure line would have to shift downwards if equilibrium income were to equal potential income.

In part (ii), we do not define a horizontal gap between actual and potential income, as we did in part (i) of the Figure. The reason is that (given our assumption on page 283) the national income, Y_2, *cannot* actually be achieved, since to produce that much real output would require

more resources than the nation has available. Thus, if the economy's curves are those shown in part (ii), actual real income will be held at Y_F by the unavailability of the resources needed to produce further output. The economy is thus in a situation of *disequilibrium*, and the inflationary gap measures the amount by which desired expenditure exceeds actual output at the existing level of income, Y_F. In other words, this gap is a measure of the amount of aggregate *excess demand* over and above the amount that the nation can produce when operating at full capacity.

In this situation, demand will exceed supply in most of the economy's individual markets and prices will be rising as a result. If most individual prices are rising, the average of all prices – i.e. the general price level – will also be rising. Hence the term inflationary gap is a good one. Inflations associated with inflationary gaps are often called *demand inflations*, which means a rise in the general price level caused by the existence of general excess demand.

The Government's Budget

If the government is to vary its spending and taxing policies with a view to reducing inflationary or deflationary gaps, it must be willing to let the balance between these two change as necessary. To see what is involved, we look first at the budget balance. The government's BUDGET BALANCE is the difference between all of its current receipts and all of its current disbursements.

The government's CURRENT RECEIPTS are revenues from taxes, and from anything that it sells, including both currently produced goods and services and assets such as nationalized industries being privatized. Current receipts do not, however, include funds that are raised through borrowing. The government's CURRENT OUTLAYS include all the funds that it spends, both for exhaustive and transfer expenditures.

If this balance is positive, we say that the budget is in surplus. If this balance is negative, we say that the budget is in deficit. If receipts are exactly equal to disbursements, we say that the budget is in balance, and we speak of a balanced budget.

Every year in the spring the Chancellor of the Exchequer introduces a Budget for the coming fiscal year. (These days there is often a supplementary 'Mini-Budget' in the autumn.) The government is concerned with how much revenue it expects to receive and how much money it expects to pay out, and with the expected balance between the two. Notice that, since they refer to the coming year, all of these figures are based on estimates. Not surprisingly, these estimates are subject to errors, which are often quite large.

The debt implications of the budget balance

A deficit: If the government's budget is in deficit, the shortfall must be made up by borrowing funds. Thus a deficit is matched by an equivalent amount of government borrowing. This new borrowing adds to the country's NATIONAL DEBT (which is the total of outstanding government debt).

The government may borrow funds from two main sources. First, it may borrow from the private sector. Both households and private-sector banks lend money to the government by buying Treasury bills and government stocks. Second, the government may borrow money from the central bank, the Bank of England. The financial implications of borrowing from these two main sources are quite different. We shall study these in detail in later chapters when we discuss the country's financial institutions.

A surplus: In the opposite case, the government has a budget surplus, its receipts exceed its disbursments. A surplus is used to pay off some existing debt and, thus, to reduce the size of the national debt.[1] It follows that the national debt is the sum of all past government budget deficits, which increase the debt, minus all past budget surpluses, which reduce the debt.

The public-sector borrowing requirement

In the latter part of the 1970s, it was realized that the fiscal influence of the government spreads beyond the confines of the central government's own budget. To assess the total impact of government fiscal activities through government revenues and expenditures, as well as through the nationalized industries, the practice grew up of looking at the budget balance of the whole public sector. This 'public sector' is the government at the national and local levels, plus the nationalized industries. The balance of current receipts minus current disbursements over the whole public sector is called the PUBLIC-SECTOR BORROWING REQUIREMENT (the PSBR) when it is negative, and PUBLIC-SECTOR DEBT RETIREMENT (the PSDR) when it is positive. This is nothing more than the government's budget balance that we discussed above, where the concept of the government is extended to include all levels of government and their nationalized commercial enterprises.

The Goals of Fiscal Policy

From 1945 to the mid-1970s, all UK governments took the reduction of substantial inflationary and deflationary gaps as major objectives of policy. Preventing deflationary gaps was designed to keep the economy operating at close to full employment. Preventing inflationary gaps was designed to prevent the outbreak of demand inflations.

Such a policy is called STABILIZATION POLICY, for the obvious reason that it attempts to stabilize the aggregate expenditure function at levels that would not give rise to large deflationary or inflationary gaps. In Chapter 22 we saw that this policy is also called 'demand management', which alludes to the fact that it seeks to manage the total demand for output – i.e. aggregate desired expenditure.

In this chapter we study how demand management can work through fiscal policy. A second tool of demand management, called monetary policy, is studied in a later chapter.

Eliminating fixed gaps

A relatively easy problem faces the makers of fiscal policy when private-sector expenditure functions for consumption and investment do not shift. What is needed in such circumstances is a once-and-for-all fiscal change to remove any inflationary or recessionary gap. The policies are shown in the two parts of Figure 28.3.

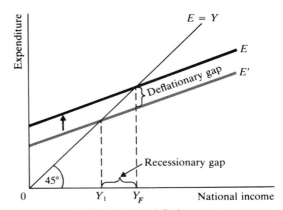

(i) Eliminating a deflationary gap

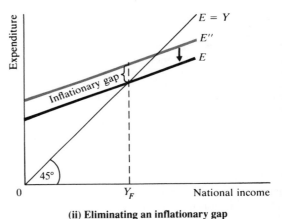

(ii) Eliminating an inflationary gap

FIGURE 28.3 Eliminating Deflationary and Inflationary Gaps. A deflationary gap (and its accompanying recessionary gap) can be removed by fiscal policy that shifts the desired expenditure function upwards from E' to E as shown by the arrow in part (i); an inflationary gap can be removed by fiscal policy that shifts the desired expenditure function downwards from E'' to E as shown by the arrow in part (ii).

In part (i), the initial expenditure function is E', yielding the equilibrium level of national income Y_1. Thus the economy is currently operating at less than full employment, with a recessionary gap of $Y_F - Y_1$, and a deflationary gap which is shown by the vertical distance between the E curve and the 45° line at Y_F. A policy that shifts the aggregate expenditure curve upwards to E, so that it intersects the 45° line at income Y_F, will remove the deflationary gap, returning the economy to full employment. We saw in Chapter 27 that a shift of the desired expenditure function, such as the one from E' to E, can be achieved by an appropriate cut in tax rates or by an appropriate increase in government expenditure.

We conclude that an appropriate reduction in tax rates and/or increase in government expenditure can remove a given recessionary gap.

In part (ii) of the Figure, the aggregate expenditure curve is E''. National income is at its potential level, Y_F, and there is an inflationary gap, shown by the vertical distance between the aggregate expenditure curve and the 45° line at Y_F. A policy that shifts the aggregate expenditure curve from E'' to E, so that it intersects the 45° line at income Y_F, will remove the inflationary gap without reducing national income below its potential level. We saw in Chapter 27 that the shift of the aggregate expenditure line from E'' to E can be accomplished by an appropriate increase in tax rates and/or by an appropriate decrease in government expenditure.

We conclude that an appropriate increase in tax rates and/or decrease in government expenditure can remove a given inflationary gap.

Eliminating variable gaps

So far, we have seen how the government can eliminate a given inflationary or deflationary gap. Having identified the gap, the government would take steps to eliminate it for *once and for all*.

Unfortunately, the more or less *continual shifts* in private expenditure functions that occur in reality make stabilization policy much more difficult than it would be if stable gaps were all that had to be dealt with. What can the government reasonably hope to achieve when private-sector expenditure functions are continually shifting?

Fine-tuning

The policy that was popular over the first two and a half decades following 1945 is called FINE-TUNING – which means trying to use demand management so as to offset every fluctuation in the desired expenditure function.

When fiscal policy is used to fine tune the economy, tax rates and/or government expenditure must be altered continuously in an effort to stabilize national income at its potential level. The 1950s and the 1960s were a period of optimism about a fine-tuning-through-stabilization policy. Fiscal policy was altered frequently, and by relatively small amounts, in an effort to hold national income close to its potential, or full-employment, level.

Careful assessment of the results of fiscal stabilization policies in the 1950s and 1960s showed that the successes of fine-tuning, if any, fell far short of what had been hoped for. The basic reasons lay in the complexity of the economy and the time-lags with which policy has to operate.

Complexity: The economy is a very complex mechanism. Economists, and policy-makers, can usually identify broad and persistent trends. They do not, however, have detailed knowledge at any moment in time of all the forces that are operating to cause changes in the immediate future, nor of all the short-term effects of small changes in the various government expenditures and tax rates.

This makes fine-tuning difficult because it is hard to predict both how the size of any inflationary or deflationary gap will change over the ensuing few months and how small, short-lasting changes in fiscal policy will influence the size of those gaps in the near future.

Time-lags: Time-lags pervade all aspects of economic activity, and therefore of economic policy. Even our understanding of the economy's current position is subject to time-lags. Lags are of various sorts, but two are of special importance.

Lags in knowledge. By the nature of economic statistics, policy-makers only know where the economy was at some point in the past when the statistics were collected. Some statistics are reported with only a short lag, others with lags of many, many months. So policy-makers are in the position of car drivers whose only vision is through their rear-view mirrors – they only know where they were in the past, not where they are at present, let alone where they will be in the future. To compensate somewhat for this disadvantage, economists are able to make use of *leading indicators*. These are particular variables which tend to change ahead of most other variables and hence give advance notice of where the whole economy is going.

Lags in policy. Any policy change takes time to make its effects felt. This can mean that changes designed to remove one gap finally take effect when the economy is suffering from the opposite gap. For example, the building of a new motorway, decided on as an expansionary measure to remove a deflationary gap, may not get into full swing for several years. By the time it does, private expenditure may have recovered to such an extent that the economy's current problem is an inflationary, rather than a deflationary, gap. In this case, the 'stabilization policy' will actually destabilize the economy by increasing, rather than decreasing, the gap from which it is currently suffering.

Conclusion: Of course, if the fluctuations in the economy were perfectly regular, and fully known, the lags could be allowed for without further problems. We have already observed, however, that no two cycles are the same. Thus there is always the danger that either a contractionary or an expansionary fiscal policy, that looked stabilizing when initiated, will turn out to be destabilizing when it takes effect, because the economy will have unexpectedly gone through a turning point.

The conclusion to be drawn from the research in several countries is that efforts at fine-tuning often have done as much to encourage minor fluctuations in the economy as to remove them. In other words, they have often been destabilizing. As a result of such experience, few economists any longer believe that, given the present state of knowledge, fiscal policy can fine tune the economy to hold

BOX 28.2 Rules of Public Finance

'The government has been operating with considerable success since the mid-1980s a rule that public expenditure should rise more slowly than GDP, and thus fall as a proportion of it, leaving a bigger share to the private sector. To avoid distortions due to privatisation of public corporations, they are excluded from the definition of public expenditure, which is called "general government (central and local) expenditure" or GGE.

'Back in 1980, the government was hoping to reduce GGE in real terms; when that proved too difficult, it aimed to hold it constant in real terms. Finally in the mid-1980s, it allowed GGE to rise in real terms, provided that GDP was rising faster. Now the rule has been modified so that it need not be observed in each and every year, but only in the medium term. In fact the Autumn Statement shows the GGE:GDP ratio remaining constant at $39\frac{1}{2}$ per cent this year and for the next two years, then resuming its falling trend.

'This is quite an ambitious objective, because GGE tends to rise, and GDP to fall or remain static, in recessions, while the opposite is true in recoveries ...

'It has been argued, for example, by Professor Sir Alan Walters, that the cyclical nature of unemployment and other such items makes the GGE:GDP ratio an unsatisfactory rule to try to follow. It certainly looked like that some years ago, because on the new basis the ratio rose from 44 per cent in 1970–80 to $47\frac{1}{2}$ per cent in 1982–83, in spite of the government's best attempts to hold down public expenditure. Since then, the ratio has fallen to a low of $39\frac{1}{4}$ per cent in 1988–89; with only a slight increase to $39\frac{1}{2}$ per cent in subsequent years.

'GGE is set to start rising again by over 2 per cent in real terms in 1991–92 and the following year, in line with GDP. If the recession goes on longer, or is deeper than expected, however, the government will have to choose between letting the GGE:GDP ratio rise, and even using public expenditure as a way of reflating the economy, or again cutting back the real increase in GGE to no more than that in GDP. Clearly the preferred solution would be to hold the ratio constant in recessions – rather than allowing it to rise – and let it fall in recoveries.'

(*Lloyds Bank Review Bulletin*, No.44, December 1990)

This article discusses the Conservative government's policy, in the 1980s and early 1990s, of being more concerned with the size of the public-sector debt than with using fiscal measures to stabilize national income. Although accepting the government's general strategy, the writer wonders if some secondary consideration might not be given to the impact of the policy on stabilization.

Notice the use of the concept of the 'general government sector' rather than the 'public sector'. Different concepts are used as circumstances change. For decades, the *central government's* expenditures and borrowing requirements were the main focus. Then, as the importance of the nationalized industries was recognized, the *public sector's* spending and borrowing requirements became the focus of attention. This article now argues that privatization, which (among other things) transfers borrowing from the public to the private sector, is distorting the public-sector figures, and so it goes back to data for government alone, but includes the local government expenditure to get what it calls 'general government expenditure'.

Questions

1 What is the main policy objective of the government's rule described in the quotation?
2 Explain why the GGE is cyclically sensitive.
3 Why might it be difficult, and undesirable, to reduce the GGE *every year* until its long run target was met?
4 What policy conflict is discussed in the last paragraph of the quotation?

---

it at, or very near to, its full-employment level, preventing the emergence of either inflationary or recessionary gaps.

A Policy-Induced Cycle

The critics of policy have sometimes suggested that governments have deliberately used fiscal policy for political ends, and that this has had the effect of creating fluctuations rather than eliminating them. Why should the government cause such disruptive expenditure shifts?

A political trade cycle: Early in the development of the Keynesian theory of stabilization policy, the Polish-born economist Michael Kalecki warned that, once governments had learned to manipulate aggregate expenditure, they might engineer an election-geared trade cycle. In pre-election periods they would raise spending and cut taxes. The resulting expansionary pressures would create rising output and employment that would cause voters to support the government. But the inflationary gap that would ensue would lead to a rising price level. So, after the election was won, the government would depress demand. This would remove the inflationary gap and also provide slack for expansion before the next election.

This theory invokes the image of a cynical government manipulating employment and national income mainly because it wants to stay in office. Few people believe that governments do this all the time, but the temptation to do it some of the time, particularly before elections, may prove irresistible.[1] Since political scientists have identified the state of the domestic economy as a prime determinant of voting behaviour, the tendency to induce an upswing before a national election must be very strong.

A stop-go cycle: One variant of the policy-induced cycle does not require a cynical government and an easily duped electorate. The theory of the STOP-GO CYCLE requires only that both the government and the public be rather shortsighted.

In this theory, when there is a recession and relatively stable prices, the public and the government identify unemployment as the primary economic problem. The government then introduces an expansionary fiscal policy through some combination of tax cuts and spending increases. This, plus such natural cumulative forces as the multiplier-accelerator, expands economic activity. Unemployment falls, but, once an inflationary gap develops, the price level begins to rise.

At this point, the unemployment problem is declared cured. Now inflation is seen as the nation's number one economic problem. A contractionary policy is then introduced. The natural cumulative forces again take over, causing a recession. The inflation subsides but unemployment rises, setting the stage once again for an expansionary policy to reduce unemployment.

Many economists have criticized British government policy over the last few decades as sometimes causing fluctuations by alternately pushing expansion to cure unemployment and then contraction to cure inflation.[2]

Discretionary and Automatic Policies

So far, we have been speaking of deliberate government attempts to remove gaps by altering expenditures or taxes. Such policies are called DISCRETIONARY POLICIES. The government identifies a gap and then makes a conscious decision to alter its policies in an effort to reduce the gap. Discretionary stabilization policy is subject to all of the problems we have just discussed.

Stabilizers

Fortunately, the government's stabilization objective is greatly assisted by what are called AUTOMATIC, or BUILT-IN, STABILIZERS. These are 'automatic tools' of fiscal policy which influence government spending or tax revenues without the need for the conscious exercise of government discretion. For example, if a recessionary

gap opens up, a stabilizer may *automatically* increase government expenditure or reduce tax revenues and so help to reduce the gap.

Any shift in a private expenditure function has its effects on income and employment magnified through the successive rounds of expenditure, that are induced by the initial change, and whose full effects are summarized by the value of the multiplier. For example, fluctuations in investment expenditure of £1000m around its average value will lead to fluctuations in national income of £5000m around its average value when the multiplier is 5, but only £2000m when the multiplier is 2.

In general, a built-in stabilizer may be regarded as anything that reduces the value of the multiplier, thereby reducing the magnitude of the fluctuations in national income that are caused by shifts in autonomous expenditure.

Most importantly, it does so without the government's having to react consciously to each change in private-sector

---

BOX 28.3 A Political Trade Cycle?

'The best time for ... [the Conservatives] to win an election is likely to be October 1991. An election in June 1991 is less likely because the good news on inflation and interest rates will be only just beginning. National output will be recovering only gently; unemployment will be rising strongly ...

'Research into voting patterns by Dr David Sanders of Essex University, has suggested that the Government needs to get inflation down to 5 per cent and interest rates down to 10 per cent to win enough votes for re-election.'

(Andrew Britton and Christopher Huhne, in *The Independent on Sunday*, 14 October 1990)

This article was written while Mrs Thatcher still led the Conservatives, before the Gulf War and, of course, well before the election of 1992.

Questions

1 What kind of a cycle is suggested by the article – one in which economic events drive political ones, or one in which the political timetable drives economic events?
2 Given the date of the 1992 election, what economic events do you think influenced the choice of date?
3 Given the outcome of that election, how important do you think economic events were in influencing actual voting behaviour? (In particular were the interest rate and inflation targets suggested by the writers met, and did the actual rates seem to matter in the election?)

---

1 In the American system, where elections occur on a fixed timetable, the temptation to manipulate booms to coincide with elections is particularly great. In British and European systems, where the timing of elections is at the discretion of the government in power, there is a tendency to manipulate elections to coincide with naturally occurring booms, giving rise to the possibility of an 'economic election cycle' rather than a 'political trade cycle'.

2 In the UK, the stop-go cycle was also associated, in the past, with balance-of-payments problems in ways that we will study in Chapter 42.

spending as it occurs. Although the government may make a conscious decision to introduce some built-in stabilizer, once put in place, the stabilizer adjusts government expenditures or tax revenues automatically as inflationary or deflationary gaps emerge.

The two principal built-in stabilizers are most sources of tax revenues and government transfer payments.

Taxes: Tax revenues are a leakage from the circular flow. Revenues that vary directly with income cause leakages to increase as income rises and to decrease as income falls; this dampens the fluctuations in income that are caused by fluctuations in autonomous expenditure. (On page 000 we saw that the higher the marginal propensity to tax, the lower the multiplier.) Progressive income taxes have a stronger dampening effect on fluctuations than do proportional taxes. They cause the *proportion* of income leaking out of the flow to rise as income rises and to fall as income falls.

Government transfer payments: Although transfer payments are not themselves a part of current national income, they do enter into households' disposable income and hence they affect current consumption expenditure. Many government transfer payments act as built-in stabilizers. They do so by stabilizing disposable income in the face of fluctuations in national income, thereby helping to stabilize expenditure on consumption.

Unemployment and certain other social security measures, such as income support, are the main transfer payments that have this effect. If there were no such benefits, then every fall of £1 in after-tax wage income earned through work would mean a fall of £1 in disposable income. But because of transfer payments, people who become unemployed, and hence lose their wage income, find that their disposable incomes, and hence their ability to spend on consumption, is to some extent maintained. If, for example, a rise in umemployment causes the after-tax earnings of labour to fall by £1000m, but unemployment and other social security benefits give £600m to the newly unemployed, then disposable income only falls by £400m.

The reverse effect occurs in booms. When income and employment rise, people are put back to work. If they had received no disposable income prior to going to work, their incomes and expenditures would rise greatly. Instead, however, their incomes only rise by the difference between the transfer payments they were receiving and their new wage incomes. Their consumption expenditures will then only rise by a correspondingly smaller amount.

Because of transfer payments, variations in national income cause smaller variations in disposable income than in factor income earned from employment. As a result, fluctuations in consumption expenditure are correspondingly reduced.

Discretionary fiscal policy once again

Built-in stabilizers do an important job in reducing fluctuations in income and employment. Such stabilizers, however, cannot be expected to eliminate all fluctuations in income and employment. They work by producing stabilizing tax and expenditure reactions to changes in income that have already occurred. For example, until people become unemployed they cannot receive unemployment benefits. So this stabilizer, like all others, is only activated by a change in income and employment.

Short-term fluctuations that are not removed automatically by built-in stabilizers cannot, given present knowledge, be consciously removed by fine tuning the economy. However, larger and more persistent gaps sometimes occur. For example, there was a severe inflationary gap throughout much of the 1970s, and a severe deflationary gap throughout the first half of the 1980s.

Gaps such as these persist long enough for their major causes to be studied and understood, and for fiscal remedies to be fully planned and executed. Many economists who do not believe in fine-tuning do feel that fiscal policy can aid in removing such persistent gaps. Others believe that, even with persistent gaps, the risks that fiscal policy will destabilize the economy are still too large to be worth taking. They would have the government abandon stabilization policy altogether. Instead, the government would set its taxes and expenditures solely in relation to such long-term considerations as the desirable size of the public sector, and the need to obtain a satisfactory long-term balance between its revenues and expenditures.

Other stabilization policies

In this chapter we have dealt with two major tools of fiscal policy, personal income tax rates and government expenditures. In conclusion, we should note a few other measures.

Any tax rate can be varied to alter equilibrium national income. For example, a rise in the VAT rates will increase the leakage between the expenditures of households and the receipts of firms. This will lower equilibrium national income. In the same way, a fall in the VAT rates will raise equilibrium income.

Also, direct controls can be exercised, particularly on capital expenditures. Any control that decreases investment expenditure lowers equilibrium national income.

Furthermore, fiscal measures are not the only tools of stabilization policy. As we shall see in later chapters, monetary policy may also be used to shift the aggregate expenditure function.

For reasons that we will study in later chapters, fiscal policy is much less in favour as a tool for stabilizing the economy against cyclical fluctuations. Fiscal built-in stabilizers are still understood to be important, but where discretionary measures are called for, other instruments, such as those of monetary policy, are more in favour.

Summary

1 The trade cycle is composed of cyclical fluctuations in national income, which run through alternating periods of expansion and contraction (the latter is called a recession, or a depression if very severe).

2 The accelerator, which relates new investment to *changes* in national income, provides part of the explanation of changes in investment expenditure. The accelerator is determined by the capital/output ratio (i.e. the required stock of capital per unit of output).

3 The accelerator does not explain all investment expenditure. It has nothing to say, e.g., about innovation and replacement investment, or about responses when changes in sales are thought to be temporary.

4 One key force in the cyclical behaviour of the economy is the tendency for *self-reinforcing* upward and downward movements. One explanation of these lies in the multiplier-accelerator process.

5 Stabilization policy refers to attempts by the government to hold national income at its potential level by removing inflationary or deflationary gaps.

6 When equilibrium national income is less than potential income, two gaps can be identified. The deflationary gap measures the amount by which aggregate desired expenditure falls short of income at potential income, Y_F. It is the vertical distance from the E curve to the 45° line at Y_F. The recessionary gap measures the amount by which equilibrium income falls short of potential income. It is the horizontal distance between equilibrium Y and Y_F.

7 An inflationary gap occurs when aggregate desired expenditure exceeds potential income. In the simple model of Part 4 of this book, actual income will then equal potential income, and the gap will be the vertical distance from the 45° line to the E curve at Y_F.

8 A given recessionary gap may be removed by any appropriate combination of increased government expenditure and reduced tax rates. Inflationary gaps are removed by any appropriate combination of decreased government expenditure and increased tax rates.

9 Stabilization policy is complicated by frequent shifts in expenditure functions. Fine-tuning is no longer thought to be desirable due to the complexity of the economy and problems associated with time-lags.

10 In a political trade cycle, booms are generated before elections and restrained afterwards. In a stop-go cycle, alternating concern with unemployment (or the balance of payments) and inflation induces fiscal policies which result in alternating bouts of expansion and recession.

11 Automatic stabilizers exert contractionary pressure as national income rises, and expansionary pressure as national income falls. These help to stabilize the economy without the problems associated with discretionary changes in taxes or government expenditure.

Questions

1 Which One or More of these would be appropriate policies for reducing a recessionary gap?
   (a) A cut in tax rates.
   (b) A cut in government expenditure.
   (c) Any policy that would reduce the PSBR.
   (d) Cutting interest rates charges in an attempt to shift the consumption function upwards.
   (e) Increasing unemployment benefits.

2 Which One or More of the following policies are likely to be built-in stabilizers?
   (a) The provision of free food for the unemployed.
   (b) Index-linking all wages to the Retail Price Index.
   (c) Income supplements to farmers to insulate their incomes from cyclical declines in their sales.
   (d) A wealth tax levied at 1 per cent of a person's wealth.

3 True or False?
   (a) Stock cycles tend to be over a shorter period than trade cycles.
   (b) The accelerator relates changes in income to *changes* in consumption.
   (c) The inflationary gap is the excess of aggregate desired expenditure over potential national income.
   (d) Fine-tuning has become an increasingly popular policy as experience of its use accumulates.
   (e) A political cycle arises from the inefficient use of built-in stabilizers.

4 What might be meant by a built-in destabilizer? Can you give examples of policies that might be classified as such?

5 In Figure 28.2:
   (a) Why is the deflationary gap of *ab* smaller than the recessionary gap of $Y_F - Y_1$?
   (b) Draw the changes in the E curve needed to remove both gaps.

29 The Balance of Payments and National Income

So far we have studied the behaviour of equilibrium national income in a *closed economy*, one that does not engage in foreign trade. We must now extend our analysis to an *open economy*, one that does engage in foreign trade. You should now review pages 249–50 of Chapter 22 concerning the balance of payments and the exchange rate, since the terms defined there will be used throughout this chapter.

INTERNATIONAL PAYMENTS AND EXCHANGE RATES

Our first task is to consider how international payments are recorded in the 'payments accounts' and how they are made in foreign-exchange markets.

The International Payments Accounts[1]

In Chapter 23 we studied the national accounts that are used to record the nation's output, income and expenditure. Another major set of accounts are the international payments accounts, which are also called the 'balance of payments'. These accounts are a record of the payments made as a result of the international transactions of a country's residents. Table 29.1 shows the UK payments accounts for 1990. Note that the accounts are divided into three main categories, the current account, the capital account and what is called official financing.

Current account

The CURRENT (or income) ACCOUNT records payments arising from trade in goods and services and from income in the form of interest, profits and dividends earned on real and financial capital owned in one country and invested in another. This account is divided into the two main sections that are discussed in the two following paragraphs.

The first of these two main sections is variously called the TRADE ACCOUNT, the VISIBLE ACCOUNT, or the MERCHANDISE ACCOUNT. It records payments and receipts arising from the import and export of tangible goods (as distinct from services) – e.g., computers, cars, wheat and shoes. British imports require the use of foreign exchange and, hence, are entered as debit items. British exports earn foreign exchange and, hence, are recorded as credit items on the visible account.

The second main section is called the INVISIBLE ACCOUNT or the SERVICE ACCOUNT. It records payments arising out of trade in services and payments for the use of capital. Trade in such services as insurance, shipping and tourism is entered in the invisible account, as are payments for capital – interest, dividends and profits – owned in one country but used in another. Those items that use foreign exchange, such as purchases by UK residents of foreign insurance or shipping services, travel abroad by UK residents, and payments to foreign residents of interest, dividends and profits earned in the UK, are entered as debit items. Those items that earn foreign exchange, such as foreign purchases of British insurance or shipping services, foreign travel in the UK, and payments to UK residents of interest, dividends and profits earned abroad, are entered as credit items.

Another item in the invisible accounts is remittances of foreign workers to their home countries. These are deficits in the host country's accounts and credits in the accounts of the workers' home countries. Many Italian and Turkish workers come to the UK and send money to their families back home. These are debits in the UK invisible account and credits in the Italian and Turkish invisible accounts.

Beware of the common error of assuming that credit items are good and debit items are bad. No such judgement should be implied, as we shall show later.

Capital account

The second main division in the balance of payments is the CAPITAL ACCOUNT, which records transactions related to international movements of financial capital assets such as bonds and equities. In the UK accounts, the capital account is referred to as 'Investment and Other Capital Transactions'. All exports of capital from the UK are entered as debit items because they use foreign exchange; all imports of capital into the UK are entered as credit items because they earn foreign exchange.

It may seem odd that, while the export of a good is a credit item, the export of capital is a debit item. To see that there is no contradiction in the treatment of goods and capital, consider the export of British funds to purchase a German bond. The capital transaction involves the purchase, and hence the *import*, of the German bond, and this has the same effect on the balance of payments as the purchase, and hence the import, of a German good. Both items involve payments to foreigners and both use foreign exchange. They are thus debit items in the UK's balance of payments.

The capital account often distinguishes between movements of short-term and of long-term capital. Short-term

1 For a more detailed discussion of the issues raised here, see Harbury and Lipsey, Chapter 7.

TABLE 29.1 Balance of Payments of the UK, 1990 (£m)[1]

Current Account

Visibles:		
Exports		102,746
Imports		120,657
Balance of visibles		− 17,911
Invisibles:		
Credits		118,236
Debits		113,119
Balance of invisibles		+ 5,119
Balance on current account		− 12,794

Capital Account

Overseas investment in the UK:		
Direct		17,984
Portfolio		5,324
Bank		45,337
Other inflows (net)		2,469
UK investment overseas:		
Direct		9,475
Portfolio		15,049
Bank		37,092

Official Financing

Reserves (increase)		71

Source: Economic Trends.

capital is money held in the form of short-term assets, such as bank accounts and Treasury Bills. If a non-resident merchant buys sterling and places it in a deposit account in London, this represents an inflow of short-term capital into the UK, and it will be recorded as a credit item on short-term capital account. Long-term capital represents funds coming into the UK (a credit item) or leaving the UK (a debit item) to purchase long-term assets such as a ten-year bond or physical capital such as a new car-assembly plant.

The two major subdivisions of the long-term part of the capital accounts are direct investment and portfolio investment. DIRECT INVESTMENT is the item in the balance-of-payments accounts that records changes in non-resident ownership of domestic firms and in resident ownership of foreign firms. Thus foreign direct investment in the UK is capital investment in a branch plant or subsidiary corporation in the UK in which the foreign investor has voting control. Alternatively, it may be in the form of a takeover in which foreigners acquire a controlling interest in a firm previously controlled by residents. PORTFOLIO INVESTMENT, on the other hand, is investment in securities, such as Treasury bills or bonds issued by governments and firms, or a minority holding of shares, none of which involve legal control.

Official financing

The final section in the balance-of-payments accounts is called OFFICIAL FINANCING. It covers transactions by the Bank of England in the OFFICIAL RESERVES which are held in the form of gold, foreign exchange – i.e.

claims on various major foreign currencies, in particular the US dollar – and in an international currency called SDR (which we study in Chapter 41).

The Bank of England, operating on behalf of the government, intervenes in the market for foreign exchange to influence the exchange rate. If, for example, the Bank intervenes to prevent the price of sterling from falling, it must buy sterling. This means it must sell gold or foreign exchange. It can only do so if it holds reserves of these media. When the Bank wishes to stop sterling from rising in value, it enters the market and sells sterling. In this case, the Bank buys foreign exchange which it adds to its reserves.

The Balance of International Payments

We have seen that the trade statistics show the total of receipts of foreign exchange (called credit items) and payments of foreign exchange (called debit items) on account of each category of payment. It is also common to calculate the *balance* on separate items or groups of items. The balance of payments on particular parts of the payments account refers to the difference between the credit and the debit items on that part of the account.

The concept of the balance of payments is used in different ways. These can be confusing, so we must approach this issue in several steps.

The overall balance of payments must be zero

Every exchange has two sides, something is given up and something is received. In the foreign-exchange market different national currencies are traded. A holder of sterling who sells it on the foreign-exchange market sells (or uses) sterling and buys (or receives) some foreign currency of equivalent value. Since this is true of every transaction, it must be true of the sum of all transactions: the sum of all payments must equal the sum of all receipts.

It follows that the total receipts of foreign exchange arising from current-account transactions, capital-account transactions and the Bank of England's official financing must be exactly equal to the total payments of foreign exchange arising from current-account transactions, capital-account transactions and the Bank of England's official settlements. Since the value of all payments must equal the value of all receipts, the overall balance of all payments minus all receipts *must be zero*.

Although this relation is necessarily true, it often worries students who feel that it need not be so. To help to clarify the issue, let us consider the example of an alleged exception.

An illustration: Say that the sole international transaction by a small country called Myopia was an export to the UK of Myopian coconuts worth £1000 sterling. The Myopian central bank issues its local currency, the stigma, but does not operate in the foreign-exchange market, so there is no official financing, and this year its self-sufficient inhabitants want no imports. Surely, then, you might (wrongly) think, Myopia has an overall favourable balance

---

1 The figures in the balance of payments do not balance exactly because of errors in certain reported totals and rounding.

of £1000, which is a current-account receipt with no balancing item on the payments side? To see why this is wrong, we must ask what the exporter of coconuts did with the sterling he received for his coconuts. Say he deposited it in a London bank. This transaction represents a capital export from Myopia. Myopians have accumulated claims to foreign exchange which they hold in the form of a deposit with a London bank. Thus there are two entries in the Myopian accounts – one a credit item of £1000 for the export of coconuts and the other a debit item of £1000 for the export of capital. The fact that the same firm made both transactions is irrelevant. Although the current account is in credit, the capital account must exactly balance this. Hence, looking at the *balance of payments as a whole*, the two sides of the account are equal. The balance of payments has balanced – as it always must do.

Consider now a slightly more realistic case which would arise if the coconut exporter wants to turn his £1000 into Myopian stigmas so that he can pay his coconut pickers in local currency. To do this, he must find someone who wishes to buy his sterling in return for Myopian currency. But we have assumed that no one in Myopia wants to import, so there is no one wanting to sell him Myopian currency for current-account reasons. Assume, however, that a wealthy Myopian landowner would like to invest £1000 in London by buying shares giving him ownership of a British firm. To do so, he needs £1000, which he gets from the exporter. The coconut exporter sells his £1000 to the landowner in return for stigmas. Now he can pay his local bills. The landowner sells stigmas to the exporter and takes sterling in return. Now he can buy his British shares.

Once again the Myopian balance-of-payments figures will show two entries, equal in size but opposite in sign. There will be a credit item for the export of coconuts (the sale of coconuts earned foreign exchange) and a debit item for the export of capital (the purchase of British pounds used foreign exchange).

A general statement: The balance just illustrated is so important that it is worth going to the trouble of stating it symbolically. We let C, K and F stand for current account, capital account and official financing account, and use a subscript P for payments (a debit item) and R for receipts (a credit item). Now we can write

$$C_R + K_R + F_R = C_P + K_P + F_P \qquad (1)$$

This says, what we have already argued, that if we add up across all transactions, they must balance in total: the sum of receipts on current, capital and official financing accounts, equals the sum of payments made on these three accounts.

Payments on parts of the accounts need not be zero

Although the overall set of payments must equal the overall set of receipts, this does not have to be true on sections of accounts. We now look at such balances, first in relation to particular countries and then in relation to particular sectors of the account.

Regional balances: In the above example, Myopia had what is called a bilateral payments balance with the UK, which means that its payments to, and receipts from, the UK were equal. In general, the BILATERAL BALANCE OF PAYMENTS between any two countries is the balance between the payments and receipts flowing between the two countries. If there were only two countries in the world, their payments would have to be in bilateral balance. But this is not true when there are more than two.

Suppose that next year Myopia again sells £1000 worth of coconuts to the UK, that the landowner does not wish to invest further in the UK, but that the Myopian people wish to buy 10,000 yen's worth of parasols from Japan. (Assume also that on the foreign-exchange market £1 trades for 10 yen.) Finally, assume that a Japanese importer wishes to buy £1000 worth of singles recordings from a London record company.

Now what in effect happens is that the Myopian coconut exporter sells his £1000 to the Japanese record importer for 10,000 yen, which the coconut dealer then sells to the Myopian parasol importer in return for Myopian stigmas. (In the real world the exchanges are all done through specialists who deal in foreign exchange, but the above is what happens in effect.) Now the Myopian payments statistics will show a £1000 bilateral payments surplus with the UK – receipts of £1000 from the UK, and no payments to the UK – and a 10,000 yen (which is equal to £1000) bilateral deficit with Japan – £1000 of payments to Japan, and no receipts from Japan. But when all countries are considered, Myopia's multilateral payments are in balance.

In general, the MULTILATERAL BALANCE OF PAYMENTS refers to the balance between one country's payments to, and receipts from, the rest of the world. It follows from what we have said earlier that, when all items are considered, every country must have a zero multilateral payments balance with the rest of the world – although, as the Myopian example has just illustrated, it can have bilateral surpluses or deficits with individual countries.

Sectoral balances: Let us now look at the balance of payments on individual sectors of the payments accounts.

The *balance* on visible account refers to the difference between the value of UK exports of goods and the value of imports of goods. A surplus, or 'favourable balance', occurs when exports of goods exceed imports of goods, while a deficit, or 'unfavourable balance', occurs when imports exceed exports. The balance on invisibles refers to the difference between the value of receipts from invisibles and the value of payments for invisibles.

The balance of payments on current account is the sum of the balances on the visible and invisible accounts. It gives the balance between payments and receipts on all income-related items.

The balance on capital account gives the difference between receipts of foreign exchange and payments of foreign exchange arising out of capital movements. A surplus on capital account means that a country is a *net* importer of capital, while a deficit means that the country is a *net* exporter of capital.

A credit balance on official settlements means that the

Bank of England has bought more gold and foreign exchange than it has sold. This adds to its reserves of foreign exchange. A deficit balance means that the Bank has sold more gold and foreign exchange than it has bought. This reduces its foreign exchange reserves.

The relation between various balances

Since payments must balance on an overall basis, it is clear that the phrase a balance of payments '*deficit*' or '*surplus*' must refer to the balance on some part of the payments account. Note, too, that, because of the necessity for the balance of payments to balance overall, a deficit or surplus on one *part* of the accounts implies an offsetting surplus or deficit on *the rest* of the accounts. Two particular relations are important.

Current and capital balances: To make the relation between current and capital balances clear, let us assume that the Bank of England does not engage in any foreign-exchange transactions. This means that payments and receipts on official financing, F_R and F_P in equation (1) above, are both zero. It follows that any deficit or surplus on current account must be matched by an equal and opposite surplus or deficit on capital account. For example, if a country has a credit balance on current account, the foreign exchange earned must appear in the capital account. The foreign exchange may be used to buy foreign bonds and equities, or merely stashed away in foreign bank accounts. In either case, there is an outflow of capital from the UK. It is recorded as a debit item because it uses foreign exchange.

We can see this clearly if we make use of the relationship expressed symbolically on page 000. We repeat that equation below.

$$C_R + K_R + F_R = C_P + K_P + F_P \qquad (1)$$

If we set F_R and F_P equal to zero to indicate no official financing transactions by the Bank of England, this gives us

$$C_R + K_R = C_P + K_P \qquad (2)$$

Now subtract C_P and K_R from both sides of the equation:

$$C_R - C_P = K_P - K_R \qquad (3)$$

This expresses, in equation form, what we have just argued verbally: a surplus on current account must be balanced by a deficit on capital account (i.e. an outflow of capital), while a deficit on current account must be matched by a surplus on capital account (i.e. an inflow of capital).

One important implication concerns capital transfers. A country that is exporting capital has a deficit on capital account and so it *must* have a surplus on current account. Also, a country that is importing capital has a surplus on capital account so it *must* have a deficit on current account.

If we allow for Bank of England transactions, the above relations do not need to hold exactly. They must diverge by the balance on official financing ($F_R - F_P$) but, since this

balance is usually small relative to net payments on current and capital account, the relation between the two major accounts shown in equation (3) is usually approximately true.

The relations just discussed are important, and we shall use them in later chapters.

Official financing and the rest of the accounts: When people speak of a country as having an overall balance-of-payments deficit or surplus, *they are usually referring to the balance of all accounts excluding official financing.* A balance-of-payments surplus means that the Bank of England is adding to its holdings of foreign-exchange reserves. A balance-of-payments deficit means that the Bank of England is reducing its reserves.

The Exchange Rate

Although we shall study the determination of exchange rates in detail in Chapter 40, we need to say a little about this subject now. We saw in Chapter 22 that the exchange rate for sterling gives the price of a unit of sterling in terms of some foreign currency. For example, if the exchange rate between sterling and US dollars is $1.25, then it costs $1.25 to buy £1 or, what is the same thing, its costs 80p to buy $1 (1/1.25 = 0.80).

The determination of the exchange rate: The free-market value of the exchange rate is set by demand and supply.

The demands and supplies for foreign exchange arise from the transactions that are recorded in the payments accounts. Holders of foreign currencies demand sterling in order to be able to buy exports of goods and services from the UK, to make payments of interest, profits and dividends to UK residents, and in order to move money into the UK to buy British. Holders of sterling demand foreign exchange in order to buy UK imports, to pay interest, profits and dividends to foreign residents, and to move funds into foreign countries in order to buy foreign assets.

On a free market, the exchange rate moves to equilibrate these demands and supplies, just as the price of carrots moves to equilibrate the demand and supply for carrots.

The effect of changes in the exchange rate: First consider a rise in the sterling exchange rate.

On the one hand, foreigners will have to give up more of their currency to get each £1 that they buy, and UK residents will be able to get more foreign currency for each £1 they offer. For example, if the sterling–dollar rate moves from $1.25 to $2.00, holders of dollars will find it costs them $2.00 instead of $1.25 for each pound that they buy. This will make buying anything whose price is set in sterling more expensive to holders of foreign money. British exports of goods and services will cost more, as will a holiday in Britain. Also it will cost more for any foreigners to buy British assets such as Treasury Bills or shares in British Telecom. This will discourage such purchases and the number of pounds sterling demanded in order to buy British goods and services will fall.

BOX 29.1 How the Balance of Payments Balances

'Since the sum of all credit items must be matched by an equivalent sum of debit items, it follows that the balance of payments must itself balance. This may be explained with reference to the balance of payments of the UK in 1987 ... The current balance was in deficit by £2.5 billion ... This sum would, of necessity, have to be covered either by borrowing or by using reserves of gold or foreign exchange. Indeed, if no borrowing or lending had taken place, the reserves would have fallen by £2.5 bn.

'What actually happened is ... that there was a net inflow of funds from direct and portfolio investment of £7.8 bn. This is £5.3 bn more than was necessary to cover the current account deficit of £2.5 bn ...

'Had there been no other monetary movements, the reserves would have risen by exactly £5.3 bn. However, there were other monetary transactions [such as foreign-currency-denominated lendings and borrowings of UK banks] which, on balance, also resulted in an inflow of funds – of another £6.7 bn ... Hence the reserves ought to have risen by exactly £12 bn, which they did.'

(C. Harbury and R.G. Lipsey, *An Introduction to the UK Economy*)

This discussion deals with the relation between the main items in the balance of payments accounts, showing how individual balances can be in surplus or deficit while the overall accounts must balance.

Questions

1 Given the additional information that the balance on merchandise account was –£10.2 bn during the year in question, draw up as detailed a balance-of-payments statement as can be made from the figures given in this Box.
2 Give illustrations of the kinds of transactions that would be included under each of the main items in your balance-of-payments table.
3 Assume that a newspaper, reporting on these results, had written 'The UK balance of payments reaches serious proportions as the payments deficit passes £10 billion.' In what sense would the paper have been correctly reporting facts, and in what sense might it have been guilty of misinterpreting them?

On the other hand, it will now cost less for holders of sterling to buy foreign currency. When the exchange rate is $1.25, $1 costs 80p, while when the rate rises to $2.00, $1 costs only 50p. When the exchange rate rises, goods, services and assets priced in foreign currency will appear cheaper to holders of sterling. This will encourage British imports of goods and services.

If you have understood all this, you should be able to work out the opposite case for yourself. If the exchange rate goes from $2.00 to the pound to $1.25, British goods and services will seem cheaper to foreigners and they will tend to buy more of them. At the same time, foreign goods and services will be more expensive to holders of sterling, who will tend to buy less of them.

This leads us to an important general conclusion.

A rise in the price of sterling on the foreign-exchange market will tend to discourage UK exports and capital imports and encourage UK imports and capital exports, while a fall in the price of sterling will have the opposite effect.

FOREIGN TRADE IN THE THEORY OF INCOME DETERMINATION

In the next part of this chapter, we extend our theory of income determination to cover foreign trade. As a first step, we must study the forces that influence a country's exports and its imports.

The determinants of exports

The foreign demand for UK exports depends on two main forces:

• the *level of income* in the rest of the world, and
• the *relative prices* of UK and foreign goods; these relative prices, in turn, depend on:
  (a) the *price levels* in the UK and in the rest of the world, and
  (b) the *exchange rate*.

Our first task is to explain how each of these forces work.

Foreign income: We saw in Chapter 24 that consumption expenditure depends on income. When *foreign* incomes rise, foreigners buy more of their own domestically produced goods, and more imported goods, some of which come from the UK. This increases UK exports. As a result, UK exports are positively associated *with foreign incomes – the higher are foreign incomes, the higher are UK exports.*

Relative prices: Those readers who have already studied the microeconomics of Part 2 of the book, will recall that consumers' demands for commodities depend on their *relative* prices. Insofar as UK and foreign goods are substitutes for each other in general, if UK prices rise relative to the prices of competing foreign goods, foreigners will buy fewer UK goods. If UK prices fall relative to the prices of competing foreign goods, foreigners will buy more UK goods. Thus *UK exports are negatively associated with the relative prices of UK goods – the higher their relative prices, the lower are UK exports.*

The prices of UK goods relative to the prices of foreign goods depends on the price levels ruling in the UK and abroad, and on the exchange rate.

Price levels. If we hold the exchange rate constant, a rise in the UK price level, relative to foreign price levels, makes UK exports relatively more expensive and reduces the quantity that will be sold. A fall in the UK price level, relative to foreign price levels, makes UK goods relatively less expensive, and increases the quantity that will be exported.

The exchange rate. If we hold price levels constant, the effects are those that we studied in the section on page 000. A rise in the sterling exchange rate raises the price of UK exports and reduces the quantity sold. A fall in the UK exchange rate reduces the price of UK exports and increases the quantity sold.

An assumption: For the moment it is convenient to assume that all of these influences on the quantity of UK exports remain constant so we can treat exports as autonomous. This does not mean that exports never change, only that for the moment we are holding constant *all* factors that influence UK exports – in particular, we are assuming that price levels, the exchange rate and the level of foreign income are all constant.

The determinants of imports

Not surprisingly, the same general forces that influence UK exports also influence its imports, income and relative prices. What matters now, however, is income in the UK, not foreign income.

Domestic income: UK imports depend on UK demand. We have already seen that UK consumption expenditure varies directly with UK national income. We now make the parallel assumption that UK imports vary directly with UK national income: as UK income rises, firms, households and governments spend more, both on domestically produced goods and on foreign goods.

Relative prices: UK imports also depend on the relative price of UK goods and foreign goods, which in turn depend, as we have seen, on relative price levels and the exchange rate. Because we are dealing with imports, however, the effect of changes in relative prices is reversed. Anything that raises the price of UK goods relative to the prices of foreign goods – a rise in the UK price level relative to foreign price levels, or an increase in the exchange rate – will tend to increase British imports. Anything that reduces the price of UK goods relative to the prices of foreign goods – a fall in the UK price level relative to foreign price levels, or a fall in the exchange rate – will tend to reduce UK imports.

The forces that increase imports and exports are summarized in Table 29.2. A fall in UK exports will be induced by the opposite of the changes listed in the first column. A

TABLE 29.2 Causes of Changes in Imports and Exports

FORCES THAT WILL INCREASE UK EXPORTS	FORCES THAT WILL INCREASE UK IMPORTS
1 A rise in foreign income	1 A rise in UK income
2 A fall in the UK price level relative to foreign price levels	2 A rise in the UK price level relative to foreign price levels
3 A fall in the sterling exchange rate	3 A rise in the sterling exchange rate

fall in UK imports will be induced by the opposite of the changes listed in the second column of the Table.

The Theory of Income Determination

Initial assumptions

We start by assuming that price levels and the exchange rate are constant. This removes the influence of changes in relative international prices by holding them constant. We also treat *foreign* national income as exogenous. It is not affected by anything within our model of the determination of our own country's national income. These assumptions make exports exogenous – they are unaffected by anything in the model of domestic income determination.

Since relative prices are constant, these cannot influence UK imports. But UK national income cannot be held constant, since it is UK national income we are determining. Thus imports are not exogenous; instead they vary with UK national income: the higher is national income, the higher are imports.

Import propensities: In earlier chapters we defined marginal and average propensities to consume, to save and to tax. We can now define similar propensities with respect to imports, M. The average propensity to import, the APM, is total imports divided by total income, i.e. M/Y. The marginal propensity to import, the MPM, is the proportion of any *increase* in national income that is spent on imports, i.e. $\Delta M/\Delta Y$ (where, as usual, the symbol Δ means a change in the variable to which it is attached).

Table 29.3 illustrates the calculation of the average and marginal propensities to import using an example where an increase in income from 100 to 200 causes imports to increase from 20 to 36.

TABLE 29.3 Calculation of the Average and Marginal Propensities to Consume

(1) Income (Y)	(2) Imports (M)	(3) (2)÷(1) APM (M/Y)	(4) Change in Y (ΔY)	(5) Change in M (ΔM)	(6) (5)÷(4) MPM ($\Delta M/\Delta Y$)
100	20	0.20			
			100	16	0.16
200	36	0.18			

The net export function: Our assumptions about exports and imports are illustrated in the hypothetical example given in Table 29.4. Exports are autonomously determined at a value of £240m. Imports rise with income, and the Table uses an example where both the marginal and average propensities to import are constant at 0.10 – i.e. 10 per cent of income is always spent on imported goods and services.

TABLE 29.4 A Net Export Schedule. The schedule assumes that exports are exogenous and that the *MPM* (and the *APM*) are 0.20

(1) National income (Y)	(2) Exports (X)	(3) Imports (M)	(4) Net exports (X – M)
1000	480	200	280
2000	480	400	80
2400	480	480	0
3000	480	600	– 120
4000	480	800	– 320
5000	480	1000	– 520

NET EXPORTS are the difference between exports and imports, i.e. X – M. Because X does not change with income, while M rises as income rises, *net* exports *fall* as income rises. For low levels of income, *net* exports are positive; while for high levels of income, *net* exports are negative.

Figure 29.1 graphs the data from Table 29.4. Part (i) shows how exports and imports vary with national income, part (ii) shows how *net exports* vary with national income. The graph shows that as income rises, exports are unchanged (the X function is horizontal), imports rise in

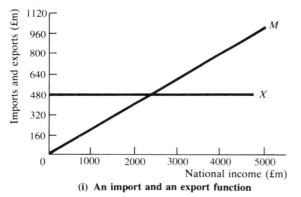

(i) An import and an export function

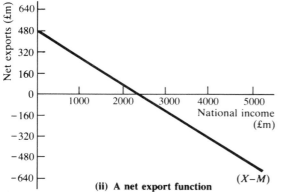

(ii) A net export function

FIGURE 29.1 The Export, Import and Net Export Functions. Part (i) shows the assumptions that exports are constant while imports are positively related to national income. As a result, the net export function is negatively related to national income. This function, which is the difference between the export and the import functions, is shown in part (ii) and labelled (X – M).

direct proportion (the M function is positively sloped and goes through the origin) and net exports fall (the X – M function is negatively sloped).

We now wish to see how imports and exports fit into our theory of the determination of national income. We look first at the income-expenditure approach and then at the leakages-injections approach.

The income-expenditure approach

In the closed-economy model used in previous chapters, aggregate expenditure has three components: consumption, C, investment, I, and government expenditure, G. To put exports and imports into the aggregate expenditure function, we merely recall our discussion in Chapter 23 (see page 260) where we showed that, in an open economy, the aggregate expenditure on UK output was equal to what it would be in a closed economy, C + I + G, plus net exports, X – M:

$$E = C + I + G + (X - M)$$

This tells us that exports add to aggregate demand while imports subtract from it.

From this point on, the argument proceeds exactly as it did in the earlier chapters. The only difference is that the desired expenditure curves in such Figures as 25.2 (p.287) and 26.2 (p.292) contain an added term for net exports.

As a result, equilibrium income is increased by a rise in autonomous exports or a fall in *the propensity to import* which lowers imports. By the same reasoning, equilibrium income will be lowered by a fall in exports or a rise in the propensity to import.

Note that, since exports are autonomous, we can speak of a rise or a fall, meaning that they change from one constant amount to another. But since imports are a function of income, we must speak of a shift in the whole import function, indicating a change in the amount of imports at each level of income.

So we know the direction of the change in equilibrium income caused by a change in either imports or exports. The next question to ask is exactly how much a given change in imports or exports causes equilibrium national income to change. This question is better studied, however, after we have looked at the leakages-injections approach.

The leakages-injections approach

Let us now look at the determination of national income in an open economy using the leakages-injections approach. The first step is to see why imports are a leakage from the circular flow and why exports are an injection.

Imports as a leakage: When a UK resident buys a commodity that was made abroad, this creates income for foreign firms. Imports thus represent income of domestic spending units that was not passed on to domestic firms through the purchases of domestically produced commodities. Imports, therefore, withdraw expenditure from the domestic circular flow. For example, if households reduce their expenditure on domestically produced cars in order to buy more foreign-produced cars, leakages will rise just as they would if the consumption expenditure had been reduced in order to save more.

Exports as an injection: When a foreign household purchases a good manufactured in the UK, it creates income for a UK firm and thus for the factors of production that the firm employs. So exports represent incomes earned by UK firms that do not arise from the spending of UK households. Exports, therefore, inject expenditures into the domestic circular flow.

In our closed-economy model we had two leakages, savings and taxes, and two injections, investment and government expenditure. We now augment that model to allow for the extra leakage of imports and the extra injection of exports. For leakages, we now have

$$L = S + T + M$$

and, for injections,

$$J = I + G + X$$

Equilibrium income: As in all previous models, equilibrium in the circular flow occurs when aggregate desired leakages equal aggregate desired injections, i.e. $L = J$. Spelling this out in terms of the new, augmented components of both L and J gives as the condition for equilibrium:

$$S + T + M = I + G + X$$

The equilibrium is shown in Figures 29.2 and 29.3. Because I, G and X are assumed to be autonomous, the total injection line is horizontal, showing that injections are the same at all levels of national income. Because imports rise with national income, just as do savings, the total leakage line remains upward-sloping.

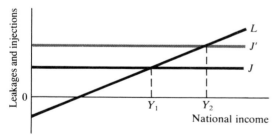

FIGURE 29.2 The Determination of Equilibrium National Income and the Effect of a Rise in Exports. A rise in exports shifts the injections function upwards and raises equilibrium national income.

Assuming that the original injection and leakage curves are J and L, equilibrium income is Y_1 in both Figures. At Y_1 the sum of savings, tax revenues and imports equals the sum of investment, government expenditure and exports.

Changes in exports and imports: Figure 29.2 also shows the effect of changes in exports and imports. A rise in

exports increases the level of injections associated with all levels of national income and so shifts the injections function upwards. This is shown by the shift from J to J' in the Figure. As a result, equilibrium income rises from Y_1 to Y_2. A fall in the export function can be shown by a downward shift in the injection function, taking it from, say, J' to J. As a result, equilibrium income falls from Y_2 to Y_1.

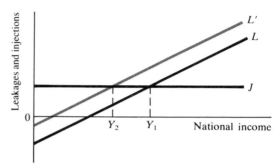

FIGURE 29.3 The Determination of Equilibrium National Income and the Effect of an Upward Shift in the Import Function. A rise in the import function shifts the aggregate leakages function upwards and reduces equilibrium national income.

Figure 29.3 shows the effects of a change in the import function. An increased desire to import at each level of national income shifts the import function upwards, and hence shifts the whole leakage function upwards. In the Figure, the leakage function shifts from L to L' and equilibrium income falls from Y_1 to Y_2. A decreased desire to import causes a downward shift in the leakage function from, say, L' to L. As a result, equilibrium income rises from Y_2 to Y_1.

Except for the introduction of a new injection and a new leakage, the analysis of the leakages-injections approach is identical to that given in earlier chapters. A change of £1 in one type of injection expenditure has a similar effect on aggregate expenditure, and hence on equilibrium national income, as a change of £1 in any other type of injection. Similarly with leakages, an increase in the leakage function reduces equilibrium income, whether the expenditure leaks out through new saving, new tax revenue or new imports, and vice versa.

The Size of the Multiplier

Leakages in induced expenditure: We saw on page 000 that the value of the multiplier is given by the reciprocal of the slope of the leakage function, $1/MPL$, where MPL stands for the marginal propensity to leak. This is a general result in the type of model being used throughout Part 4.

All we need to do now is to note that the increase in total leakages when national income rises by £1 is equal to the sum of the amount of new saving, as measured by the MPS, the amount of new tax revenue, as measured by the MPT, and the amount of new imports, as measured by the MPM. Stating this in symbols gives for an open economy:

$$MPL = MPS + MPT + MPM$$

All that this equation says is that the *total leakages* per £1 increase in national income must be equal to *the sum of the individual leakages*.

The multiplier, $1/MPL$, can now be rewritten as:

$$\text{The Multiplier } (K) = \frac{1}{MPS + MPT + MPM}$$

This tells us that the value of the multiplier in an open economy is equal to the reciprocal of the sum of the marginal propensities to save, tax and import.

The expression also tells us that, *ceteris paribus*, the larger is the marginal propensity to import, the smaller will be the multiplier. Again, there is nothing surprising about this. We saw by comparing Tables 26.1 and 27.2 on pages 297 and 307 that the larger were the leakages out of each round of induced expenditure, the smaller was the final increase in income when the multiplier process had worked itself out completely. Since imports are a leakage, this result applies directly to imports.

For economies such as the UK that engage in large amounts of foreign trade, the *MPM* is quite large. Thus the value of the multiplier is much smaller than it would be if there were no foreign trade (in which case *MPM* would be zero).

Now we know that a £1 change in any injection – investment, government expenditure or exports – will increase national income by the amount given in the above multiplier equation. Let us illustrate with an example using figures that are probably somewhere near those of the UK economy. (The exact estimation of these propensities is, however, a difficult matter.) Let the figures be $MPS = 0.05$, $MPT = 0.40$, and $MPM = 0.25$. This makes the marginal propensity to leak 0.70 and yields a multiplier of $1/0.7$ which is 1.43. Thus, in this example, an increase in invest-

ment, government, or export expenditure by, say, £1m would increase equilibrium national income by £1.43m.

Leakages in the initial injection: The multiplier shows how an initial injection of spending on domestic production causes a magnified increase in national income due to the induced rounds of new spending that it sets up. Now that we have allowed for foreign trade, we must recognize that the initial injection of autonomous expenditure may itself have an import component. Say, for example, that the government spends an extra £1 million per year on a road-building programme, and that £800,000 of that goes to purchase UK inputs, including labour, while £200,000 goes to buy imported materials (such as asphalt). Now, although the government increases its exhaustive expenditure by £1 million, it only injects £800,000 into the domestic circular flow and the rest goes on imports (which create income in other countries).

The important conclusion is that all the multiplier analyses in Keynesian models applies to injections of expenditure on domestic production. If autonomous expenditures have an import content, this must be removed before the initial injection is calculated. Only that part of an increase in autonomous expenditure that goes on domestic production counts as an injection, and only that part gets multiplied by successive rounds of induced expenditure.[1]

An example: Table 29.5 presents an example of the effect of a new injection when there are leakages through savings,

---

1 The multiplier defined as $K = \Delta Y/\Delta A$, where A is that part of autonomous expenditure that goes on domestic production, must exceed unity for reasons laid out several times in the text. If, however, ΔA is defined as the change in autonomous expenditure *including its import content*, the multiplier need not exceed unity. Assume, e.g., that the government spends an extra £1m on some hi-tech activities that have an import content of 0.66 and a domestic content of only 0.34. If the multiplier for an injection of domestic expenditure is 2, income will only rise by £680,000 (£340,000×2) which is less than the initial £1m of new expenditure.

TABLE 29.5 A Numerical Example of the Multiplier where leakages of taxes, savings and imports total 60 per cent of new income

Round	Increase in income at each round	Increase in taxes (2) × 0.25	Increase in savings (2) × 0.15	Increase in imports (2) × 0.20	Induced increase in consumption (2) − [(3) + (4) + (5)]
(1)	(2)	(3)	(4)	(5)	(6)
1	1000.00	250.00	150.00	200.00	400.00
2	400.00	100.00	60.00	80.00	160.00
3	160.00	40.00	24.00	32.00	64.00
4	64.00	16.00	9.60	12.80	25.60
5	25.60	6.40	3.80	5.10	10.30
6	10.30	2.57	1.56	2.06	4.12
7	4.12	1.03	0.63	0.82	1.65
8	1.65	0.41	0.25	0.33	0.66
9	0.66	0.17	0.10	0.13	0.26
10	0.26	0.07	0.04	0.05	0.10
Sum of first ten rounds	1666.59	416.65	249.98	333.31	668.65
11th and all subsequent rounds	0.08	0.02	0.02	0.02	0.02
Totals	1666.67	416.67	250.00	333.33	668.67

The first round shows the initial £1000 of injections creating leakages of £250 in new tax revenues, £150 in new savings, and £200 in new imports. This leaves £400 of induced new consumption expenditure, which becomes new income in round 2. Comparing this Table with Table 27.2, notice how much faster the increments in income tail off because of the larger leakages.

taxes and imports. In this example, total leakages are 60 per cent of any increase in national income (i.e., $MPC = 0.60$). Comparing the results of this Table with those in Tables 26.1 on page 297 and 27.2 on page 307, we see that the addition of the further leakage of imports reduces the effect on income of a change in autonomous expenditure.

The International Transmission of Income Changes

We have developed a multiplier that incorporates the effects of foreign trade. It can now be used to show that the fates of various economies are intertwined. So far in this chapter we have assumed that imports and exports are independent of each other, but this is a simplification that is not exactly correct.

If the UK suffers a fall in national income for some purely domestic reason, UK imports will fall. UK residents will reduce their purchase of such things as German Volkswagens, Irish tweed jackets, Swiss watches, Japanese cameras, and Austrian skiing holidays, as well as many types of raw materials. As a result, the exports, and hence the national incomes, of these countries will fall. Then they, in turn, will buy fewer imports from all countries including the UK. The reduction in British exports further reduces the UK's national income.

Thus, the national incomes of various countries are linked together: any change in income in one country tends to cause the incomes of other countries to change in the same direction, and the changes in the incomes of other countries tend to reinforce the initial change in the first country.

The extent to which changes in income in one country affect incomes in other countries, and the extent to which these changes reinforce the initial change, depends on their marginal propensities to import. In many countries, such as Canada, Japan and the United Kingdom, the marginal propensities to import are relatively high, and fluctuations in income in one of these countries are easily transmitted into fluctuations in the incomes of other countries whose exports are a significant fraction of their total national incomes. This is one reason why booms and slumps are infectious. A boom or a slump in one major trading country is easily communicated to other trading countries.

IMPORTS AND EXPORTS: GOOD OR BAD?

It is commonly argued that exports are 'good' because they raise equilibrium national income, whereas imports are 'bad' because they lower equilibrium income. When we say exports raise national income, we mean that they add to total expenditure and raise equilibrium income (given the assumption in this part that there is unused industrial capacity). But they do not add to the value of domestic consumption. In fact, exports are goods that are *produced* at home but *consumed* abroad, while imports are goods that are produced abroad and consumed at home.

An economy with unemployment: Assume that, faced with a large recessionary gap, the UK government gave a subsidy to exporters and put tariffs and quotas on imports, or depreciated the exchange rate to encourage exports and discourage imports. As we saw earlier in this chapter, both the rise in exports and the switch in domestic expenditure from imports to home goods would reduce any recessionary gap and hence increase equilibrium national income as well as employment. Surely, in a time of recession, this can be regarded as a 'good thing'.

Two points need to be made about such a policy. In the first place, the goods being produced by the newly employed workers in the export sector are not available for domestic consumption and so do not raise domestic standards of living. Would it not be better if, instead of encouraging exports, the government created new employment by increasing its expenditure, for example building more roads, schools and research laboratories? Income and employment would go up, but now there would be something more tangible to show for it than the smoke of ships bearing the subsidized exports to foreign markets disappearing over the horizon.[1]

The second point to be made concerns the effects on other countries of such a policy of fostering exports and discouraging imports in a situation of general world unemployment. Although the policy raises domestic employment, it will have the reverse effect abroad – it will lower incomes and create unemployment abroad. Foreign countries will suffer a fall in their equilibrium national incomes because their exports will fall and their imports rise. If they seek to protect their domestic employment by encouraging their exports and discouraging their imports, this will reduce other countries' national incomes. If all countries adopt such a policy, the net effect will be a fall in the volume of international trade without any rise in the level of employment in any country.

Such policies are often called BEGGAR THY NEIGHBOUR POLICIES because a country tries to deal with its unemployment problem by buying less from, and selling more to, other countries, which raises unemployment in these other countries. One country can operate such a policy successfully if other countries do not retaliate. But as we have seen, if all countries try to 'beggar their neighbours', the employment effects cancel out but the loss of international efficiency implies that each country has ended up 'beggaring' itself.

A fully-employed economy: The situation is different in a fully employed economy because there is no scope for increasing output in response to increasing demand. Now an increase in the production of goods for export requires a reduction in the production of goods for other uses.

The view that, even in these circumstances, exports are beneficial and imports harmful goes back to the eighteenth century to a group of economists called Mercantilists.

---

1 We are here considering the effects of the *initial* rise in employment in either the export or the investment industries. Of course there would be multiplier effects of an increase in exports, and these could contribute to an increase in domestic living standards.

Modern economists reject this view and point out that the standard of living of a person, or of all persons in a country, depends on the goods and services that they consume, not on what they produce. The *average* material standard of living of the residents of a country may be thought of in terms of the following equation:

$$\text{Average standard of living} = \frac{\text{total goods and services consumed}}{\text{number of people}}$$

If exports are really good and imports really bad, then a fully employed economy that obtains an increase in its exports without any corresponding increase in its imports ought to be made better off. This change will, however, result in a reduction in current standards of living because, when more goods are sent abroad and no more are brought in from abroad, the total goods available for domestic consumption must fall.[1] The importance of exports is that they permit goods and services to be imported. This two-way international exchange is valuable whenever more goods can be imported than can be obtained if the same goods were produced at home.

---

1 Those of you who have read Chapter 20 will recall that the gains from trade depend on the ability to import goods at a lower opportunity cost than they could be produced at home. In this view, the gains from trade depend on the terms of trade and the *volume of* trade, not on the *balance* of trade. The more a country exports and imports the more it is taking advantage of the gains from trade.

Summary

1 International transactions are recorded in the balance of payments, which is divided into three sections: the current account, the capital account and official financing.

2 Taking all transactions into consideration, the overall balance of payments must be zero.

3 There may be a positive or a negative balance on payments between two countries and/or on some part of the account. The terms balance-of-payments surplus or deficit usually refer to the balance on current plus capital account (which must be matched by a balance of the opposite sign on official financing).

4 Exports (regarded as autonomous) depend on foreign national incomes and international relative prices. Imports depend on domestic national income and international relative prices (which are assumed constant). International relative prices in turn depend on price levels and the exchange rate.

5 The determination of equilibrium national income in an open economy by the expenditure approach requires that net exports (i.e. X minus M) be added to the aggregate desired expenditure function: $E = C + I + G + (X - M)$. For the leakages-injections approach, exports are added as an injection, $J = I + G + X$, and imports as a leakage, $L = S + T + M$.

6 Equilibrium national income (where $E = Y$, and $J = L$) is increased by a rise in autonomous exports or by a downward shift in the import function. It is decreased by the opposite changes.

7 Foreign trade reduces the size of the multiplier, $1/MPL$, by adding another leakage making the multiplier: $1/(MPS + MPT + MPM)$, (where all marginal propensities relate to national income).

8 A rise in income in one country raises its imports which, being other countries' exports, raises their incomes as well.

9 Policies of trying to raise domestic income by increasing exports and reducing imports are likely to be self-defeating. When followed by many countries, they tend to lower living standards in all countries.

Questions

1 Which One or More of the following changes, *ceteris paribus*, will tend to increase a country's exports?
(a) a local inflation
(b) a depreciation of its exchange rate
(c) a boom in foreign countries
(d) a severe inflation abroad that is not matched at home.

2 Repeat Question 1 for imports rather than exports.

3 Will the following raise (R) or lower (L) equilibrium national income?
(a) a rise in exports
(b) a fall in the average propensity to import.

4 True or False?
(a) Exports of goods are a credit item in the balance of payments.
(b) Imports of capital, as when a Japanese buys a UK Treasury bill, are a credit item in the balance of payments.
(c) Official financing aside, a balance on current account must be accompanied by a balance on capital account that is equal in magnitude but opposite in sign.
(d) The exchange rate compares the cost of borrowing money in two countries.
(e) The marginal propensity to import is the ratio of the change in imports to the change in income that brought it about.
(f) Exports are properly regarded as leakages since the goods leave the domestic circular flow.
(g) The larger is a country's marginal propensity to import, the lower is the value of its multiplier (other things being equal).

5 What will happen to equilibrium national income when investment expenditure rises by £200 million in a country in which each £1 increase in national income leads to increases of 7p in savings, 22p in imports and 21p in government tax revenue?

6 'Trade Deficit Rises Alarmingly' reads a recent headline in the financial press. What other changes might you expect to see in the balance of payments taking place at the same time?

7 Using equation 1 on page 324, what must the official financing have been if the balance of payments was + £1000m?

8 Calculate the multiplier for an economy in which savings, imports and tax revenues always account for 0·05, 0.25 and 0.20 of *national income* respectively.

9 In Figure 29.1, what are imports, exports and net exports when national income is 1000?

10 In Figure 29.2, what would have happened to the L curve if the injection curve had remained at J while equilibrium income rose to Y_2?

One of the most quotable quotes in the English language is that 'the love of money is the root of all evil.' But just what is money, and how is it related to national income, to prices and the price level? We discuss these general issues in this chapter. Later we consider some key aspects of money in more detail.

MONEY

To understand the place of money in the economy, we must understand what money is and the several related functions that it fulfils.

The most important function that distinguishes money from everything else is its use as a MEDIUM OF EXCHANGE. Indeed MONEY may be defined as any generally accepted medium of exchange, which is anything that will be accepted by virtually everyone in exchange for goods and services.

The Functions and Characteristics of Money

Four of the most important functions of money are to act as:
- **a medium of exchange,**
- **a store of value,**
- **a unit of account, and**
- **a standard of deferred payments.**

We shall discuss these in turn. Money must also have several characteristics if it is to be fully satisfactory. It must be: (i) acceptable, (ii) portable, (iii) divisible, and (iv) difficult to counterfeit.

It is best to discuss these characteristics along with the functions of money because they are best understood in terms of the ability of money to carry out each of its functions.

A medium of exchange: Where money does not exist, goods must be exchanged through BARTER, the direct exchange of one good for another. If a wheat farmer wants a winter coat, he must seek out someone else who both has a winter coat and also wants wheat. This need for both sides in a barter transaction to want the good the other has to trade is called the need for a *double co-incidence of wants*. Clearly, locating such double co-incidences can be difficult and time-consuming, and sometimes impossible. As a result, under barter, most people are forced to be relatively self-sufficient – to make both their wheat and their winter coat and, indeed, almost everything else that they consume.

The great advantage of money is that it separates the two sides of the barter transaction. Let us see what this means in the case of the wheat farmer who wants a winter coat. Money allows the farmer to sell his wheat to anyone who wants it, whether or not the purchaser has anything that the farmer wants. Instead, the farmer takes money in exchange for his wheat and then seeks out someone else who has a winter coat for sale, secure in the knowledge that the seller of the coat will accept money in exchange.

A high degree of specialization requires that most of what one produces goes to others, and most of what one consumes comes from others. This requires an efficient exchange of products that is quite impossible under barter. Without money, therefore, our complicated economic system, based on specialization and the division of labour, would be impossible.

To serve as an efficient medium of exchange, money must have the following characteristics.

(i) *It must be readily acceptable*, for if one is to take money in exchange for what one wants to sell, one needs to know that others will, in their turn, take the money in exchange for what one wants to buy.

(ii) *It must be easily portable*, which requires that it must have a high value for its weight, for it would otherwise be a nuisance to carry around.

(iii) *It must be divisible*, for money that comes *only* in large denominations is useless for transactions having only a small value.

(iv) *It must not be easily counterfeited*, for money that can be easily duplicated by anyone will quickly lose its value.

A store of value: Many goods, and all services, cannot be stored up for future needs. Money, however, allows us to store purchasing power: you can sell your goods today and store the money. This gives you a claim on someone else's goods that you can exercise at some future date.

To be a fully satisfactory store of future purchasing power, money must have a stable value in terms of the things that it can buy. If prices are stable, one knows how much command over goods and services has been stored up when a certain sum of money has been accumulated. If there is uncertainty about future prices, one does not know how many goods an accumulated sum of money will command when one comes to spend it.

Thus, aside from the characteristics listed above, the most desirable one for the store-of-value function is that *the purchasing power of money remains stable over time*. This has *not* always been a characteristic of modern money. Later in this chapter we study in more detail how inflation changes the value of money.

A unit of account: Money may also be used purely for accounting purposes, without having any physical existence. For instance, a village commune might say that each person had so many 'roubles' at his or her disposal each month and might then establish these as credits on the books of the village's only shop. Goods would be given prices and purchases would be recorded. Each consumer would be allowed to buy the desired goods until his or her supply of roubles was exhausted. The money would have no existence other than as entries in the shop's books, but it would be serving as a perfectly satisfactory unit of account.

A standard of deferred payments: This is a fourth function that is sometimes distinguished, although it is really implied by the other three. Acting as a standard of deferred payments means that a payment to be made in the future can be denominated in money terms in just the same way as can a payment to be made today. Here, money is acting as a unit of account with the added dimension of time.

The concept of liquidity

Money can be used as a means of payment. Although other monetary assets, such as bills, bonds and equities, cannot be used as a means of payment, they can usually be converted into money if a means of payment is required. The problems in holding monetary assets that one might wish to convert into money relate to ease of conversion, expense of conversion, and uncertainty about the conversion rate.

Ease: There are well-established markets where many monetary assets can be readily bought and sold. Such markets make conversion easy. With assets that are not well known, or not commonly traded, conversion may be more difficult.

Expense: There is a cost, in terms of time and administrative expenses, involved in converting financial assets into money. For most assets in advanced market economies, these costs are quite small. In less developed, and/or less market-orientated societies, these costs can become significant.

Uncertainty: A marketable financial asset is converted into money by selling it on a financial market. How much money is obtained depends on the current price of that asset. Because the prices of most assets fluctuate more or less continually, there is always some uncertainty about the rate at which a given financial asset will be convertible into money at any future date. Most bonds have a MATURITY DATE at which their issue price will be repaid to their current holders. The time to that maturity date is called the TERM of the bond.

These matters will be discussed in more detail in later chapters. In the meantime, all we need to note is that the longer is the term of any bond, the larger are its price fluctuations, *ceteris paribus*, and, hence, the greater the uncertainty about the rate at which it can be converted into money at some date in the future.

Liquidity: The concept of liquidity is meant to capture the above differences between various financial assets. A PERFECTLY LIQUID ASSET is one that can itself be used as a means of payment. Money, therefore, is the only perfectly liquid asset under most circumstances. Other assets are less liquid. Generally, the easier and less costly it is to convert a given asset into money, and the less the uncertainty attached to the asset's conversion rate (as determined by its price), the more liquid is that asset said to be. HIGHLY LIQUID ASSETS are those that are easily converted into money, at low cost, and at rates that do not fluctuate greatly over time. HIGHLY ILLIQUID ASSETS are those that are harder and more costly to convert, and whose conversion rates fluctuate substantially over time.

We can think of a whole spectra of assets running from the perfect liquidity of money to the perfect illiquidity of a valuable asset which could not be sold, and hence could not be converted into money under any circumstances.

The History of Money

A surer understanding of what money is, and what it does, can be gained by studying some of the highlights in the history of money.

Metallic money

All sorts of commodities have been used as money at one time or another, but gold and silver proved to have great advantages. They had a high and stable price, both because their supply was relatively limited and because they were in constant demand by the rich for ornament and decoration. They had the additional advantages that they do not easily wear out, and are divisible into extremely small units. They were also easily recognized and generally known to be commodities that would be readily accepted – their acceptability, of course, being the key characteristic they needed to develop as money.

Before the invention of coins, it was necessary to carry precious metals around in bulk, and to weigh the amount required for each transaction. The invention of coinage eliminated this need. The government made a coin using a fixed quantity of gold or silver for value, mixed with base metals to give the coin durability. It then affixed its own seal to guarantee the amount of precious metal contained in the coin.

This system worked well as long as the government played its part. From time to time, however, when the government had debts that it could not pay, it could *debase* the coinage. Gold and silver coins would be melted down and coined afresh, but, between the melting down and the recoining, further inexpensive base metal was added. If the coinage were debased by adding, say, one ounce of new base metal to every four ounces of old coins, five coins could be minted for every four melted down. With these extra coins the government could pay its debts.

The result was inflation. When the government paid its bills, the recipients of the extra coins would spend some or all of them, and this would cause a net increase in demand. In a fully employed economy, the extra demand would bid up prices. Debasing the coinage thus led to a rise in the general price level. Such experiences led early economists to propound the 'quantity theory of money and prices'. They argued that a change in the quantity of money would lead to a change in the price level in the same direction. (We shall have more to say about this theory later in the chapter.)

Gresham's law: The early experience of currency debasement led to a famous economic 'law' that has stood the test of time. The law states that 'bad money drives out good' and is called GRESHAM'S LAW after the Elizabethan financial expert, Sir Thomas Gresham, who first explained its workings to Queen Elizabeth I. Monarchs before Elizabeth had severely debased the English coinage. Seeking to help trade, Elizabeth minted new coins containing their full face value in gold. But as fast as she fed these new coins into circulation, they disappeared. Why?

Suppose a trader has one new and one old coin, each with the same face value but different gold contents and wishes to settle an account. He would pay with the debased coin and keep the undebased one because he would part with less gold that way. If, however, he wanted to obtain a certain amount of gold bullion by melting down the gold coins (as was frequently done), he would use new undebased coins because to get a given amount of gold, he would part with less 'face value' that way. The debased coins would thus remain in circulation and the undebased coins would disappear. Hence the bad money stayed in circulation and drove the good money out of circulation.

Gresham's law has many modern applications. Here is one for illustration. Until about 25 or 30 years ago, most countries used some silver content in many of their coins, but the market value of silver content was much less than the face value of the coin. Then in the 1960s, the price of silver soared. The value of the silver in the coins exceeded the face value of the coins making them 'good' money. True to Gresham's law, they quickly disappeared from circulation. People melted them down and sold their silver content for more than the face value of the coin while using paper money and non-silver coins for their transactions.

Paper money

Paper money came into use in many ways. One was through the practice of storing gold for safekeeping with goldsmiths – craftsmen who worked with gold. The goldsmiths issued receipts promising to hand over the gold to the bearer of the receipt on demand. These receipts soon became a medium of exchange. A buyer needed only to transfer a goldsmith's receipt for so much gold to a seller, who would accept it, secure in the knowledge that the goldsmith would pay over the gold whenever it was needed. As the receipts became *acceptable* for settling market transactions, they *became* money. The convenience of using easy-to-carry pieces of paper instead of gold is obvious.

Thus, when it first came into being, paper money was a promise to pay on demand so much gold, the promise being made first by goldsmiths who became, in this way,

some of the first bankers. Later as banks evolved, they too undertook to store gold and issued their promises to pay that gold on demand. These promissory notes were called BANK NOTES. As long as the institutions were known to be reliable, their pieces of paper would be 'as good as gold'. Such notes remained an important part of the money supply until the early part of the twentieth century. When a country's money is *convertible* into gold, the country is said to be on a GOLD STANDARD. (Banks are studied in detail in the next chapter.)

Fractionally backed paper money: Such was the convenience of paper money that most people were content to use it for most of their transactions and only occasionally did they demand to convert their notes into gold or silver. They held their deposits in banks and used cheques or bank notes for most of their transactions. At any one time, therefore, some of the bank's customers would be withdrawing gold, others would be depositing it, and the great majority would be using the bank's paper notes without any need, or desire, to convert them into gold. For this reason, the bank was able to issue *more* money, redeemable in gold, than the amount of gold held in its vaults. This was good business, because the banks could use the money to make interest-earning loans. In such a situation, we say that the currency is *fractionally backed* by the reserves.

In the past, the major problem of a fractionally backed currency was to maintain its convertibility into the precious metal by which it was backed. The imprudent bank that issued too much paper money found itself unable to redeem its currency in gold when the demand for gold was even slightly higher than usual. This bank would then have to suspend payments, and the holders of its notes would suddenly find that no one would accept them because they could not be converted into gold.

The prudent bank, which kept a reasonable relation between its note issue and its gold reserve, found that it could meet the normal everyday demand for gold without difficulty. But if the public lost confidence and *en masse* demanded redemption of their bank notes, even prudent banks could find themselves unable to honour their pledges. Banks were sometimes ruined by sudden, 'panic-induced' runs on their reserves.

Central banks: A central bank was a natural outcome of the fractionally backed currency system. Where were ordinary banks to turn when they had good investments but were in temporary need of cash? If these banks provided loans to the public against reasonable security, why should not some other institution provide loans to them against the same sort of security?

In response to such needs, central banks evolved as private institutions acting as banker to the other banks. In time, central banks throughout the world became the main institutions permitted to issue notes. Central banks in turn became governmental institutions.

The UK central bank, the Bank of England, was founded as long ago as the seventeenth century. Although it had close associations with the government from its inception, and eventually became an arm of government policy, it remained technically a private institution until its nationalization in 1946. To distinguish the central bank from all other banks, the others are commonly referred to collectively as commercial banks, while the Bank of England, which is studied in detail in Chapter 34, is called the Bank.

Fiat currencies: Originally, central banks issued currency that was fully convertible into gold. The gold supply thus set some upper limit on the amount of paper money that the central bank could issue. But the central bank could issue (as banknotes) more currency than it had gold because only small amounts of the currency would be presented for redemption at any one time.

During the period between World Wars I and II, virtually all the countries of the world abandoned gold convertibility – the UK did so in 1931. From that time on, paper money has depended for its value on nothing more than its general acceptability – and the fact that the government has ordered it to be accepted. Inconvertible paper money that is declared by government order (or fiat) to be legal tender for settlement of all debts is called FIAT MONEY.

Modern Money

Most of the terms referring to various kinds of money have been introduced already. In view of the large number of terms in use, some of which mean the same thing, it is worth pausing to recapitulate.

COINS refers to all metallic money. Examples are the 10p and 50p coins in your pocket. NOTES refers to paper money. In England, virtually all paper money in circulation consists of notes issued by the Bank of England. In Scotland, notes issued both by the Bank of England and the Bank of Scotland are in common circulation. Examples are the £5, £10 and £20 notes that you carry around to make everyday purchases. Taken together, notes and coins are commonly referred to as CASH or CURRENCY. DEPOSIT MONEY or BANK MONEY refers to deposits held at banks. Which types of bank deposits are properly regarded as money is discussed later in the chapter.

LEGAL TENDER is money that must be accepted if offered in payment for a purchase or settlement of a debt. In the UK, legal tender consists of coins (up to certain maximum amounts) and notes. Cheques drawn on bank deposits are not legal tender, although they are commonly used in purchases and in the settlement of debts.

Money is said to be CONVERTIBLE if it can be converted into some other form of money that is legal tender. In the UK, bank deposits are convertible money since they are convertible into legal tender – and they are so converted every time a customer withdraws currency from his bank account.

Convertible money is said to be BACKED by the legal tender into which it can be converted. It is 'fully backed' if, for every unit of convertible money outstanding, a unit of whatever backs it is held in reserve. Convertible money is said to be 'partially backed' or 'fractionally backed' if

the reserves held to back it are only a fraction of the amount of convertible money outstanding. Money that is not convertible into anything is said to be FIAT or INCONVERTIBLE money. It is legal tender, but it is *not* convertible into anything else of value that backs it.

Modern fiat currencies

Today, all notes and coins in circulation are fiat money. Modern coins, unlike their predecessors, contain a value of metal that is characteristically only a minute fraction of the face value of the coin. Nonetheless, they function satisfactorily as money. Since notes and coins are acceptable, they are a medium of exchange; since their purchasing power remains relatively stable in normal times, they are a satisfactory store of value; and they also serve as a unit of account and a standard of deferred payments.

Modern deposit money

Early in the twentieth century, most private banks lost the authority to issue bank notes. Yet they did not lose the power to create *money*. Let us see how this is done.

Banks' customers frequently deposit coins and paper money for safekeeping, just as in former times they deposited gold. Each deposit is recorded as an entry on the customer's account.

Customers who wish to pay debts might come to the bank to claim their money in notes and coins, and then pay the money to another person. This person might then redeposit the money in a bank. Like the gold transfers, this is a tedious procedure, particularly for large payments. It is more convenient to have the bank transfer claims to the money they hold on deposit. The common 'cheque' is an instruction to the bank to make the transfer. As soon as such transfers became easy and inexpensive, and cheques became widely accepted in payment for commodities, bank deposits on which cheques could be drawn became a form of money called DEPOSIT MONEY. In the UK this type of bank deposit is called a SIGHT DEPOSIT or a CURRENT ACCOUNT DEPOSIT. The deposit can be transferred to others by means of cheque and it can be converted into cash on demand.

Cheques are in some ways the modern equivalent of old-time bank notes issued by commercial banks. The passing of a bank note from hand to hand transferred ownership of a claim against the bank. A cheque on a bank account is similarly an order to the bank to pay the designated recipient money credited to the cheque writer's account. Unlike bank notes, however, cheques do not circulate freely from hand to hand. Thus cheques themselves are *not* money. The cheque balance in the bank deposit is money; the cheque transfers money from one person to another. Because cheques are easily used, and because they are relatively safe from theft, they are widely regarded as being virtually as good as the currency they stand for. Furthermore, the use of cheque-guarantee cards in the UK virtually makes cheques into money for purchases of up to £50–£100.

Thus, when banks lost the right to issue notes of their

own, the form of bank money changed, but the substance did not. Today's banks hold reserves to back the convertibility of their deposit money, just as their predecessors did. Some is held as currency in their vaults, and some as deposits made by the commercial banks with the central bank. These deposits are *claims* to currency that the commercial banks know the central bank will always honour, so they are as good as cash – indeed, they are often referred to as part of their 'cash reserves'.[1]

It is true today, just as in the past, that most bank customers are content to pay their bills by passing among themselves the bank's promises to pay money on demand, which they do by writing cheques. Only a small proportion of the transactions made by the bank's customers is made in cash. Thus today, just as in the past, banks can create money by issuing more promises to pay (deposits) than they hold as reserves to pay out. The details of how this works are laid out in Chapter 31.

Near money

The term NEAR MONEY refers to assets that fulfil some of the functions of money but not all of them. Specifically, near money is anything that fulfils the store-of-value function, and is readily *convertible* into a medium of exchange, but is *not* itself a medium of exchange. Near monies are highly, but not perfectly, liquid financial assets.

As long as all sales and purchases do not occur at the same moment, everyone needs a temporary store of value between the act of selling and the act of buying. Whatever serves the function of a medium of exchange can be held, and thus can also fulfil the function of a temporary store of value. But other assets can also be used for this store-of-value function.

Consider, for example, a deposit (or 'investment') account – often also called a 'time deposit' – at a bank or building society. With such an account you know exactly how much purchasing power you hold (at today's prices). But this deposit is not a medium of exchange because you cannot write cheques on it. However, given modern practices, you can turn your deposit into a medium of exchange – cash, or a sight deposit – at short notice. Additionally, your time deposit will earn some interest during the period that you hold it.[2]

Why then does everybody not keep their money in deposit accounts instead of in sight deposits or currency?

The answer is that the inconvenience of continually shifting back and forth between sight and time deposits may outweigh the interest that can be earned. One week's interest on £100 (at 12 per cent per year) is less than 25p, not enough to cover the time and money costs in transferring money needed in a week into an interest-earning account now, and back out again next week.

Money substitutes

Near moneys are assets that are not themselves media of exchange, but which can be easily converted into such at a secure rate (£1 in a time deposit can always be converted into £1 in a sight deposit). MONEY SUBSTITUTES, on the other hand, are things that serve as temporary media of exchange but are not stores of value. Credit cards are a good example. With a credit card, many transactions can be made without either cash or a cheque. But the evidence of credit, in terms of the credit slip you sign, is not money because it cannot be used to effect further transactions. Furthermore, when your credit card company sends you an account, you have to use money to pay that account which is, in effect, a delayed payment for the original transaction. The credit card serves the short-term function of a medium of exchange by allowing you to make purchases even though you have neither cash nor a positive bank balance currently in your possession. But this is only temporary; money remains the final medium of exchange for these transactions when the credit account is settled.

The Supply of Money

Economists use the terms SUPPLY OF MONEY, and MONEY SUPPLY, to refer to the total amount of money available in the entire economy (defined in one of the ways discussed in Chapter 34). It is a relatively easy matter to collect statistics on the total amount of notes and coins in circulation (since they are issued by the central bank), and the total of bank deposits (since banks must publish their accounts). Thus, we can know with a reasonable degree of accuracy the size of the money supply according to any of its various definitions.

Operational definitions of the money supply: What is an acceptable medium of exchange has evolved over time. Furthermore, new monetary assets are continuously being developed to serve some, if not all, of the functions of money, and these are more or less readily convertible into money.

Economists who wish to measure the quantity of money in existence now find it necessary to define several different measures of money. Each definition includes a different, but overlapping set of monetary assets. The definitions used in the UK are many and various and have changed a great deal over the years. There are two reasons for this.

The first is changing financial structures. For example, in recent times building societies, which used to be quite distinct institutions from banks, have become more and more like banks by taking on many of the functions that used to be the exclusive province of banks. Indeed, one,

---

1 Note the possible source of confusion here. 'Cash' strictly means notes and coins. Although the reserves that commercial banks hold on deposit with the Bank of England are called 'cash reserves', they are not cash. They are only entries on the Bank of England's books. But they are convertible into cash on demand. Furthermore, since the Bank of England is responsible for issuing notes and coins, there is no doubt about its ability to honour the commercial banks' requests whenever the commercial banks wish to withdraw cash.

2 As we shall see in a later chapter, the simple distinction between sight deposits, which earn no interest but which are subject to transfer by cheque, and time deposits, which earned interest but were not transferrable by cheque, has been breaking down over the last decade. Over that time, many different accounts have been developed, some of which have characteristics of both time and sight accounts.

BOX 30.1 Money Substitutes

'The use of new technology has spread to the . . . point of direct contact between banks and clients. . . . Automatic teller machines (ATMs) . . . permit depositors to withdraw cash or carry out other simple transactions automatically and outside normal banking hours. . . . Electronic funds transfer at point of sale (EFT/POS) . . . is a system, already technologically feasible, which is expected, in time, to replace many payments in cash or by cheque. It requires retailers to have specially designed computer terminals at check-outs or cash desks, and it requires banks' customers to have their own personal debit card. When the card is inserted in the retailer's terminal and when, at the same time, the card-holder registers his personal identification number, then payment for purchases is made automatically by the instantaneous debit to the buyer's account and credit to the retailer's account of the sum due.

'It is common for newspaper accounts of EFT/POS to claim that it heralds the advent of the cashless society. This is clearly a gross exaggeration. For interpersonal transactions and for many small purchases, e.g. bus fares, newspapers or packets of chewing gum, cash is likely to remain the cheapest and most efficient means of payment. But EFT/POS may, in time, substantially reduce the number of payments by cash and by cheque, with consequent savings in costs for both banks and retailers. It may also mean new changes in the demand for different types of media of exchange and new difficulties in interpreting movements in statistics of the money supply.'

(Prest and Coppock, *The UK Economy*, 12th edn, Weidenfeld & Nicolson, 1989)

This quotation describes some of the most recent of a series of technological changes that over the last few decades have affected the demand for money by affecting the amount of cash balances that the public needs to hold.

Questions

1 What affect will the increasing use of ATMs have on the demand for notes and coin? Will this reduce the volume of deposits that people will wish to hold?
2 Answer the same questions for EFT/POS.

basis for understanding what are the 'totally liquid assets' to be included as money. These two factors are not unrelated.

These alternative definitions of money are discussed in detail in Chapter 34.

The nominal and the real money supply: It is also useful to distinguish the nominal from the real money supply. The NOMINAL MONEY SUPPLY is the money supply measured in monetary units. The REAL MONEY SUPPLY is the money supply measured in purchasing-power units and expressed in constant prices – prices that were ruling in some base year. To obtain the real money supply, the nominal money supply is deflated by an index of the general price level.

For example, the nominal supply (as measured by M1) was £25,800 million in 1980 and £44,200 million in 1990. The real money supply, measured in 1980 prices, was £25,800 million in 1980 and £21,100 million in 1990. The latter figure is found by dividing the nominal money supply of £44,200m by the index of retail prices for 1990 of 209 (1980 = 100) and then multiplying by 100. Thus, although the nominal money supply nearly doubled between 1980 and 1990, the real money supply – the purchasing power of the existing money supply – actually fell over the period in question.

In everything that follows in this book, we shall deal with the nominal money supply. We mention the distinction because it is often encountered. But for our purposes, we use the nominal money supply.

MONEY VALUES AND RELATIVE VALUES

Money is our measuring rod in most economic activities. We value our wealth, our incomes, what we buy, and what we sell, all in money terms. When we think of a commodity's market value we usually think of its money price. 'What', we might ask, 'is the value of this refrigerator?' 'It costs £X' might go the reply. 'Is this refrigerator worth more than this hi-fi set?', is another type of value question we frequently ask. Assuming the hi-fi set costs £200, the answer is 'yes' if the refrigerator is priced at more than £200 and 'no' if it is priced at less.

'Have I saved enough money this winter to afford a week's holiday in Spain next summer?' is another common type of question. The answer depends on comparing the amount you have saved now with what you expect the Spanish trip to cost you.

Money prices are our measure of economic value. Money prices allow us to compare different values at any point in time, as with the refrigerator and the hi-fi set. They also allow us to compare values over time, as with the amount saved now and the package holiday to be taken later.

Money as a veil

Suppose you tell a man, newly arrived from Patagonia,

Abbey National in 1989, has become a bank. As a result, the deposits in building societies have become more and more like deposits in banks and so have a strong claim to be regarded as money, just as bank deposits are so regarded. The second reason is the changing theoretical that the price of a refrigerator is £200. If he knows no other sterling values, this would convey no useful information to him.

But let us say that he entered Britain with £2000. Now he knows his funds are sufficient to buy 10 refrigerators. He has compared two money values: the market value of the refrigerator and the value of the funds he has brought in with him.

But is the £2000 he has with him a little or a lot? Now he needs to know the prices of all the things he might want to buy, either individually or expressed as an average. This requires that he relate the amount of his funds to the *general level* of prices.

Consider a further example. How much meat, beer and travel can we buy for a day's wages? Such 'exchange rates' – between the labour that we sell and the goods that we buy – are what determine our living standards. If a worker sells his labour for £40 a day and buys a suit for £120, then what matters is that it costs him three days' work to buy the suit. If instead he only received £20 a day while a suit only cost him £60, the *real* exchange rate would be unchanged at three days' work to obtain the suit.

Adam Smith, writing in 1776, saw what the above examples illustrate, that individual sums of money, and individual money prices, each looked at in isolation, convey no useful information. Instead, the comparison of two or more monetary values is what conveys significant information. Such comparisons allow us to look behind individual money prices to find real opportunity costs: how much of one thing must be given up to obtain something else.

The great insight is that value is *relative*; the monetary unit in which values are expressed is irrelevant. If, for example, wheat is worth twice as much as is barley per bushel, it does not matter, as far as their exchange rate is concerned, whether wheat is £2 and barley £1, or wheat £4 and barley £2 or wheat £100 and barley £50. Early economists thus talked of money as a veil behind which real economic relations occurred and were reacted to.

The neutrality of money

Out of this insight grew the doctrine of the *neutrality of money*. Correctly stated, this doctrine is that the units chosen to measure values have no effect on 'real values' – real values are 'relative values', and it is relative values that affect behaviour.

It follows from the doctrine of the neutrality of money that, if we change *all* monetary values by the same proportion, nothing real happens. No economic effects can be expected.

The neutrality of money is most easily seen with a currency reform, such as the one instituted in France in the 1950s. By taking two zeros off the prices of all commodities, all factors of production and all contracts, nothing real was changed. Everyone's money incomes were reduced by a factor of 100, but so were the money values of all debts, and all other contracts, as well as all money prices. As a result, everyone's real income and wealth was unchanged. No new value was created and no existing value was

destroyed. The change was solely in the 'monetary part' of the economy.

Money illusion

A person who understands the real choices facing her will be unaffected by changes that merely add or subtract the number of zeros on *all* prices and all money values. If that person's money income, and money wealth, is multiplied by 10, and all the prices she faces are also multiplied by 10, she will recognize that no real change has occurred. Her economic behaviour will thus be unaffected. Such a person has penetrated the veil of money and is responding to the real choices that lie behind it.

Economists use the term MONEY ILLUSION to refer to behaviour that responds to purely nominal changes in money prices and values in either direction. Say for example that, faced with a tenfold increase in all prices, a second person felt poorer and increased his savings in response, even though his money income and money wealth had also been increased tenfold. That person is experiencing money illusion, altering his behaviour in response to changes in money values that leave all real choices unaffected.

Some people may suffer from money illusion in the short term, feeling harmed by inflation even though their incomes, and the values of all their wealth, rise in step with the rise in prices. Over longer periods of time, however, money illusion seems less common. People may not realize quickly that an inflation that leaves unchanged the relation between the incomes they earn and the prices they pay leaves them unaffected, but they appear to make the adjustment sooner or later. This means that, over the long term, real expenditure decisions are affected relatively little by purely nominal changes in money prices.

The real and the monetary parts of the economy

The doctrine of the neutrality of money leads to a conceptual division of the economy into two parts. In the 'real part', *relative* prices, quantities and the allocation of resources are determined by such things as consumers' tastes, production technology, and the degrees of competition among buyers and sellers. In the monetary part, the *absolute level of prices* is determined by monetary forces.

Thus, for example, the relative price of wheat and barley might be determined in the real part of the economy at 1 bushel of wheat = 2 bushels of barley, their outputs at 3 and 5 million tonnes, and the resources of land and labour allocated to each at 1 and 2.5 million hectares and 10 and 20 thousand person-hours respectively. These are determined by the real forces of tastes and production possibilities operating through the markets for commodities and for factors of production. The monetary part of the economy would then set the price level at which transactions would take place. For example, wheat might be priced at £4 and barley at £2 a bushel, and agricultural wages at £3 an hour; or wheat at £8 and barley at £4 and wages at £6. *Both* of these levels of absolute prices yield the same *price relatives*.

The process of price-level changes: Will changes in the price level always leave real (relative) values unaffected? The answer is 'yes' when all adjustments have been fully made, but 'no' until then – and 'until then' may be a very long time. To see why, compare the French monetary reform referred to earlier with a change in the price level that comes about through the normal workings of the market.

The French currency reform was carried out overnight by the stroke of a pen, and hence had virtually no real effects – the new long-run equilibrium set of money prices was established instantaneously. All prices, and all wealth holdings, were adjusted by legal decree at the same instant.

In most real-world situations, however, a major change in the price level is spread over a great deal of time – sometimes years and even decades. Consider a case in which a rapid doubling of the quantity of money leads to an eventual doubling of the price level. It may take years for this new price level to be achieved through the operation of normal market forces. Some prices will adjust quickly, others will take time. At the outset, all existing contracts – wage contracts, mortgages, loans, orders to buy output not yet produced, etc. – will reflect the old price level. New contracts reflecting the new price level will be written as old ones expire. But many contracts last for years, so it will take years for the full adjustment to be completed. Thus, in the process of moving from one price level to another, real changes in relative prices occur and, hence, the process of inflation has real effects.

The doctrine of the neutrality of money holds as a long-run equilibrium concept: it does not hold in transitory situations when the price level is changing.

Relative and absolute prices: It is important to realize that we are contrasting changes in relative prices with changes in absolute prices. The microeconomics which is covered in Parts 2 and 3 of this book is exclusively concerned with relative prices. Since we assume, however, that all money prices except the one being studied remain constant, all changes in money prices become changes in relative prices. A rise in the money price of a hamburger, for example, also raises its relative price *if all other prices remain constant*.

Determining changes in relative prices is more difficult when all prices are changing at the same time, as during an inflation. Now a rise in the relative price of hamburgers requires that their price rises faster than the average of all other prices. Thus the same real forces of demand and supply that would cause the price of hamburgers to rise by 10 per cent in the context of a stable general price level will cause its price to rise by 21 per cent if the price level rose by 10 per cent at the same time. (No, this is not a printer's error. A 10 per cent rise followed by a second 10 per cent rise, results in a 21 per cent rise over the initial value.)

THE RELATION BETWEEN MONEY AND PRICES: THE CLASSICAL QUANTITY THEORY OF MONEY

The real side of the economy dictates our living standards. Total output of real goods and services divided by the total population determines the average living standards attained in the country. Money prices merely determine the absolute value at which transactions take place.

What then determines the average level of prices at which these real exchanges occur? We observed earlier in this chapter that the relation between money and the price level suggested very early in the history of economics was given by the so-called QUANTITY THEORY OF MONEY. This theory predicts that the general price level is *positively related* to the quantity of money in such a way that changes in the quantity of money cause proportionate changes in the price level. Thus, for example, a doubling of the quantity of money would lead to a doubling of the price level.

The 'Equation' of Exchange

One way to introduce the quantity theory is through the so-called 'equation of exchange' that was made famous by the late American economist Irving Fisher. Although called an equation, it is in fact a definitional identity, which means something which is true simply by virtue of how the terms are defined.

Here are the four terms that appear in the 'equation'.

Y is real national income, i.e. the physical volume of output.

P is the average level of all prices. (Thus P times Y, which is written PY, is the money value of national income.)

M_S is the quantity of money, i.e. the supply of money as indicated by some appropriate measure of that supply.[1]

V is what is called the INCOME VELOCITY OF CIRCULATION, which means the average number of times that the typical unit of money must change hands, in order to accomplish all the sales and purchases involved in producing and selling the national income. (In practice 'income' is often omitted and the term 'velocity of circulation' used instead.)

We are already familiar with the concepts of real national income, Y, the price level, P, and money national income, PY. We have also discussed the concept of the supply of money, M_S, earlier in this chapter. The only new thing we need to notice about M_S is that, since every unit of money in existence must be owned, and hence held, by someone – either in the form of cash or a bank balance – we can call M_S *the total money balances held by the public*.

---

1 In simple developments of the quantity theory it is common to denote the quantity of money by M. We use M_S because we will soon need to distinguish the supply of money in existence, M_S, from the amount of money the public wishes to hold, called the demand for money and indicated by M_D.

Only the last term in the above list, V, has not already been discussed in this book. So we must consider it here. First, consider a simple example. Say in an imaginary economy with only two £1 notes, there are £4's worth of income-creating transactions. In this case, the velocity of circulation is *two* since the two £1 notes must have been used twice on average to effect £4's worth of transactions. If next period's income-creating transactions rise to £8, then the velocity of circulation must have risen to four in order that the £2's worth of money could be used in £8's worth of transactions. This use of the term income velocity in effect defines it as PY/M_S, which is a measure of the average amount of work that a typical £1's worth of money must do to create a money national income of PY.

We can now set out the 'equation' of exchange:[1]

$$M_S V = PY \qquad (1)$$

What this tells us is that the quantity of money multiplied by its velocity of circulation must be identical to the money value of national income. So if, for example, money national income is £10 billion while the quantity of money is £2 billion, then velocity must be 10/2 which is 5. In other words the average £1 unit of money must have been used five times to create £10 billion worth of national income.

Because this relation is a *definitional identity* (i.e. true by definition), it tells us nothing about the real world. But it does provide a useful insight into the working of economic forces, as well as a framework for classifying real-world data. When we see national income measured in current prices rise, we can ask how much of this is accounted for by an increase in velocity. For example, if we observe PY to rise by 10 per cent while M_S only rises by 5 per cent, then there must also have been a rise in velocity of about 5 per cent.

From the Equation of Exchange to the Quantity Theory

The equation of exchange can be turned from an identity into a theory in two steps. First, we must define V independently of P, Y and M_S. Second, we must make assumptions about how the four variables behave.

First divide equation (1) through by V to obtain the following:

$$M_S = \frac{PY}{V} \qquad (2)$$

Now define k as $1/V$ and substitute into (2) for k:

$$M_S = kPY \qquad (3)$$

So far, (3) is still an identity but let us see what k means. We have defined k to be the reciprocal of V. (You will recall from school algebra that the reciprocal of any number x is $1/x$.) k is also the proportion of money national income actually held as money balances in the whole economy, i.e. $k = M_S/PY$. For example, in the case considered above, PY

was £10 while M_S was £2. This makes k equal to 2/10, which is 0.2. This tells that the amount of money balances held by everyone in the economy was, in this example, 1/5th (i.e. 20 per cent) of the money value of national income – which is the same thing as saying that the velocity of circulation of money is 5 in that economy.[1]

What k does is to express the realized quantity of money actually held in the economy in terms of the proportion of PY that people actually hold as money balances.

Now to turn what we have into a theory, we redefine k in *planned* or desired terms. We define the DEMAND FOR MONEY as the amount of money balances that the public wishes to hold (in the form of notes, coins and bank balances). According to the quantity theory, the public wishes to hold an amount of money balances whose value is some proportion of the money value of total national income, PY. This proportion is given by k so, denoting the demand for money by M_D, we can write:

$$M_D = kPY \qquad (4)$$

Expression (4) says that the demand to hold money balances will be some proportion, k, of money national income, PY. To make sure you understand (4), consider an example. Say k is 0.2. This means that the public as a whole wishes to hold an amount of money balances equal to 20 per cent of their income-creating transactions. Now say the money national income is £15bn. Then (4) tells us that the public will wish to hold money balances equal in value to £3bn (i.e. £15bn times 0.2).

But is there any reason for assuming that the demand to hold money balances is related in this way to PY; or indeed, that it is related in any way to PY? To answer this question we must look at what is called the transactions motive for holding money balances.

The transactions motive

We saw earlier in this chapter that money is a medium of exchange. People and firms who use it as such must hold money balances in the form of cash and bank deposits to facilitate their exchanges. Let us see why such balances need to be held.

First, consider a firm. If that firm's payments and receipts were perfectly synchronized, so that every time it had to pay someone, someone else paid it, the firm would not need to hold transactions balances. But payments and receipts are not perfectly synchronized for any firm. As a result, the firm, like everyone else in the economy, must hold balances of money. When its customers pay, the firm's money balance is increased. When the firm settles its accounts, its money balance is diminished. At times when receipts are unusually large, the firm's money balance will rise; at times when payments are unusually large, its money balance will fall.

Similar considerations apply to households. They receive their income in periodic payments – usually every week or

---

1 The symbol T, standing for the volume of transactions, is sometimes used instead of Y. The 'equation' is then $M_S V = PT$.

1 Be careful not to confuse the k being used here with the K that stands for the multiplier. These two, k and K, are unrelated to each other.

every month. They hold these receipts as money balances – currency and, for many, a bank balance as well – in order to finance their payments until the next payday.

We may conclude from the above discussion that, given the way in which payments and receipts are timed, the public – people and firms – need to hold money balances in order to be able to receive and pay out money according to their needs. The amount of money that people wish to hold for these reasons is called the TRANSACTIONS DEMAND FOR MONEY.

On what does the size of this demand depend? The answer is that it mainly depends on the demander's money income. If your income and your expenditures double, you will find yourself holding about twice as much money to finance your purchases between paydays. Similarly, if a firm's business doubles, it will need to hold larger amounts of cash in order to be able to meet its now-doubled volume of payments as they fall due. If we add up this behaviour over all firms and individuals in the economy, we find that *the public's transactions demand for money is positively related to the level of national income measured in current prices.*

This tells that the demand for money balances, M_D, varies directly with PY. But this is exactly what equation (4) above says. The fraction of their annual income transactions that the public wishes to hold as money balances is given by k.

We shall study the demand for money in greater detail in Chapter 32. All we need to note here is that the transactions motive is the only motive for holding money recognized in the simple quantity theory of money described here, which is known as the 'classical quantity theory of money'.

Other assumptions

We have now seen the reasoning lying behind the demand for money given in equation (4) above. Next, let us briefly outline the other assumptions of the theory.

- The supply of money, M_S, is exogenous. It is determined by the banking system, including the central bank, but does not vary as P, Y or k vary.
- k depends on institutional factors, such as the frequency with which payments are made and received. Since these do not vary greatly from one year to the other, k can be taken as a constant.
- P rises when there is excess demand for output (an inflationary gap) and falls when there is an excess supply (a deflationary gap).
- Since we are dealing with long-term trends, departures from full-employment income can be ignored. Y will therefore be assumed to be at its full-employment, or potential, level and, for simplicity, to be constant (no real growth).

Note that the last two assumptions represent a major change in the assumptions we have used so far in Part 4. Up to now, we have assumed that the price level, P, was constant while real income was variable. In these circumstances, changes in aggregate desired expenditure caused real national income (and employment) to change.

These were suitable assumptions for short-run analysis. To study long-run behaviour, however, we reverse these assumptions. We assume that, in the long run, actual national income will be equal to potential income (more precisely, that short-run deviations of Y from potential income can be ignored when studying changes over long-run periods of time). We also assume, however, that the price level can change – which we know it does. In these circumstances, variations in aggregate desired expenditure will affect the price level but not real income.

The assumptions set out above relate to the variables in the theory. We now need to make some assumptions concerning what changes will occur when the demand to hold money balances is not equal to its supply.

- When the demand for money balances is less than the supply – i.e. the public has excess money balances – the excess is assumed to be spent on the purchase of current output. In other words, the aggregate desired expenditure curve shifts upward.
- When the demand for money balances is greater than the available supply – i.e. there is a shortage of money balances – the public is assumed to reduce its purchases of current output, adding the unspent funds to its money balances. In other words, the aggregate desired expenditure curve shifts downward.

Implications

What happens when the demand for money does not equal its supply, i.e. when the public wishes to hold an amount of money balances different from the fixed amount that is available to be held? We have already seen that when there is an excess supply of money balances, aggregate desired expenditure on current output increases. Because Y is fixed at its potential level, the upward shift in the aggregate expenditure curve opens up an inflationary gap and the price level rises. As P rises with Y constant, PY rises and so, therefore, does the quantity of money that is demanded. (See equation (4) above.) The price level goes on rising until all the excess money balances are willingly held.

Now consider what happens when there is a shortage of money balances. People try to add to their balances by reducing their expenditure, which means that the aggregate desired expenditure curve shifts downward, creating a recessionary gap. But, unlike the theory we have considered in earlier chapters, the price level is now assumed to be flexible in a downward direction. Thus Y stays at its full-employment level and the price level, P, falls. As PY falls, less money is demanded to finance the falling value of money income. (See equation (4) above.) The price level goes on falling until the demand for money balances has fallen to equal the available supply.

Only when the demand for money balances equals the available supply, so that there is neither a surplus nor a shortage of money balances, will equilibrium be reached and the price level remain stable.

Let us show what is happening in equation form. Equation (4) above gives the demand for money. Equation (5) below expresses the equilibrium condition just discussed, that the demand for money, M_D, should equal its supply, M_S:

$$M_D = M_S \qquad (5)$$

Note that (5) is not an identity. It does not hold as a matter of definition. Indeed, it only holds in equilibrium. Out of equilibrium either M_D will exceed M_S – an excess demand for money – or M_D will be less than M_S – an excess supply of money.

Now we substitute (4) into (5) to get:

$$kPY = M_S \qquad (6)$$

Equation (6) expresses the equilibrium condition that the demand for money equals its supply just as does equation (5). The only difference is that (6) spells out what determines the demand for money; i.e. kPY.

Next, we divide (6) through by kY to get

$$P = \frac{M_S}{kY} \qquad (7)$$

This is the famous equation of the quantity theory of money. In it, both k and Y are assumed to be constant. Although the quantity of money is exogenous (which means it is unaffected by any of the variables in our theory, k, P and Y), it can be changed by the Bank of England. The equation tells us that the equilibrium price level will vary in the same direction as M_S. Furthermore, the equation also implies that M_S and the equilibrium value of P will vary in direct proportion with each other. For example, a 10 per cent increase in M_S will cause a 10 per cent increase in P.[1]

Conclusion

These, then, are the predictions of the Classical quantity theory of money – which is sometimes also called the 'naïve' quantity theory. We shall see that modern theories of the relation between money and the price level are not quite as simple as this one. Nonetheless, to understand the theory laid out in this chapter is to understand the fundamentals of the relation between the quantity of money and the price level.

Modern economists continue to accept the Classical insight that the quantity of money is closely related to the general level of prices. It is also worth noting that many more complex and satisfactory theories also predict the direct proportionality result of the simple quantity theory.

In subsequent chapters, we will continue our study of the modern theory of money by looking in much more detail at the supply of money in Chapter 31 and at the demand for money in Chapter 32.

---

1 That P and M_S vary in the same direction as each other is obvious from inspecting equation (6): holding k and Y constant, an increase in M_S must increase P. As an exercise in simple algebra, you might like to try to prove for yourself the proportionality result; i.e. that $\Delta P/P = \Delta M_S/M_S$ as long as kY is constant.

Summary

1 The major functions of money are to act as a medium of exchange, a store of value, a unit of account and a standard of deferred payments. To act as a satisfactory medium of exchange, money should be generally acceptable, portable, divisible and not easy to counterfeit. To act as a satisfactory store of value, money should also maintain a stable value over time.

2 Many commodities, including precious metals and convertible paper, have been used as money in the past. Today the principal forms which money takes are metallic coins, bank notes and certain deposits held in banks. The total amount of money in existence is called the money supply or the quantity of money.

3 Banks hold deposits in sight accounts, which can be transferred by cheque, and in deposit accounts, which count as 'near money', but which pay interest to the deposit-holder.

4 There are several measures of the money supply, used for different purposes. All may be expressed in *nominal* and in *real* terms, the latter allowing for changes in its purchasing power.

5 Relative values determine the rate at which different goods and services exchange for each other. The doctrine of the neutrality of money is a long-run equilibrium proposition that real (relative) values are independent of the general price level. The neutrality does not hold in disequilibrium situations when the price level is changing.

6 The equation of exchange $M_S V = PY$, forms the basis for the Classical quantity theory of money, which predicts that, in long-run equilibrium, a given percentage change in the quantity of money will cause an equal percentage change in the price level: $P = M_S/kY$.

Questions

1 Which One or More of the following are normally regarded as functions of money?
  (a) To facilitate the exchange of goods.
  (b) To allow people to carry purchasing power from one point in time to another.
  (c) To allow the foreign-exchange market to work efficiently.
  (d) To assist in equating savings and investment.
  (e) To provide a unit in which firms can keep their accounts.

2 According to the quantity theory of money, what could be the effect on the equilibrium price level, P, of each of the following changes (other things being equal)?
  (a) The quantity of money, M_S, doubles.
  (b) The proportion, k, of the value of transactions people wish to hold in money balances is halved.
  (c) Real national income, Y, is cut in half.

3 True or False?
  (a) Sometimes a commodity that is not a medium of exchange can serve some of the functions of money.
  (b) The real money supply measures the purchasing power of the nominal money supply.
  (c) The doctrine of the neutrality of money holds that variations in the money supply have no significant effects on real economic activity.
  (d) The equation of exchange relates the money value of national income to the money supply and its velocity of circulation.
  (e) The quantity theory of money predicts that the price level varies in inverse proportion to the quantity of money.

4 A Canadian who receives a US coin has the option of spending it at face value or taking it to the bank and converting it to Canadian money at the going rate of exchange. When the rate of exchange was near par, so that $1 Canadian was within plus or minus $0.03 of US$1, American and Canadian coins circulated side by side, exchanging at their face values. Use Gresham's law to predict which coinage disappeared from circulation in Canada when the Canadian dollar fell to $0.75 American. Why did a $0.03 differential not produce this result?

5 Some years ago a strike closed all banks in Ireland for several months. What do you think happened during that period?

6 In prisoner-of-war camps during the Second World War, cigarettes were sometimes used in place of money. What made them suitable?

31 Banks and the Supply of Money

In Chapter 30 we studied how, according to the quantity theory of money, variations in the money supply (also called the quantity of money) can cause variations in the general price level. Although most economists now believe that the version of the quantity theory that we studied in that chapter is overly simplified, they still accept the broad insight that the price level and the money supply are intimately linked.

In this chapter, we study how the nation's private-sector financial institutions help to determine the country's money supply. In a later chapter we will see how the central bank, in pursuit of its monetary policy, seeks to influence the size of the money supply.

TYPES OF FINANCIAL ASSET

As a first step in our study we need to observe the major types of financial asset which are held by one of the country's financial institutions, its banks. These are shown in Table 31.1.

Notes and coins held on their premises and their balances held on deposit with the Bank of England, which can be turned into currency on demand, are perfectly liquid assets. These assets earn no interest. Notice that, although deposits with the Bank of England are not currency, they are as good as cash, since they can be used to settle debts with other banks or, on request, they will be withdrawn as currency by the Bank of England. Thus the banking system's deposits with the Bank of England are often loosely referred to as their 'cash reserves'. A final part of the banks' cash reserves are loans either for very short terms or 'at call', the latter term meaning repayable on demand. These short-term and call loans are called 'market loans'. They are part of the cash reserves because they can

be turned into cash on demand and with virtual certainty.

The next most liquid assets are Treasury and local authority bills, all of which will have terms of less than a year. By far the most important asset is advances to customers. These are loans and overdrafts, called ADVANCES, that are repayable on demand or after a fixed term. Other longer-term, less liquid assets are also held. Of these, bonds and securities issued by commercial establishments (called investments), and by the government, comprise a significant proportion of the banking system's total assets.

Long-term bonds issued by the central government are often referred to as *gilt-edged securities* or just *gilts* for short. This refers to the fact that they are as good as gold, since there is virtually no risk that the central government will default on its debt obligations.

Table 31.1 also shows the banks' major liabilities. Deposits are a liability of the banks, since they are promises to pay currency to customers who wish to withdraw their deposits. Some of these liabilities are denominated in sterling while the rest are denominated in a variety of foreign currencies.

By far the largest of all liabilities are sight and time deposits denominated in foreign currency and held by overseas depositors. The largest sterling liabilities are time deposits, followed by sight deposits. The enormous size of deposits denominated in currencies other than sterling is an indication of the internationalization of the world's banking system that has taken place in the last two decades. Ordinary banks now do a substantial amount of their business in foreign currencies, accepting deposits and withdrawals denominated in these currencies.

TABLE 31.1 Liabilities and Assets of UK Banks December 1989 (millions of £s)

Liabilities		Assets	
Notes outstanding	1,560	STERLING ASSETS	
STERLING DEPOSITS		Notes and coins	3,890
Sight deposits	156,149	Balances with the Bank of England	1,641
Time deposits	270,537	Market loans (call & very short term)	136,242
Certificates of deposit	42,869	Bills (Treasury & local authority)	1,965
		Bank and other bills	10,657
		Advances	334,983
		Net lending to central government	1,321
		Investments	22,471
		Other	28,780
OTHER CURRENCY DEPOSITS	666,667	OTHER CURRENCY ASSETS	691,733
Misc. items in transit	95,901		
	1,233,683		1,233,683

Source: *Annual Abstract of Statistics*, 1991.

THE UK BANKING SYSTEM[1]

The main institutions of the UK banking system are the commercial banks, the building societies, the merchant banks, the discount houses, finance houses, overseas banks, and the Bank of England. The Bank of England is considered in detail in Chapter 34 where we deal with monetary policy, so we say little about it here. In the first part of this chapter, we deal with the commercial banks and their ability to create deposit money. In the second part, we discuss the other main institutions of the banking system.

The Retail Banks

To ordinary people, the most visible units in the present-day banking system are the RETAIL BANKS, which are privately owned banks that deal with the public.

The retail banks have a number of functions:
- **they accept deposits;**
- **they transfer certain kinds of deposits among both their customers and other banks, when ordered to do so (usually by cheque);**
- **they make loans to customers, called advances, charging them interest in return;**
- **they use some of their funds to purchase interest-earning assets on the open market.**

The most important of the retail banks are the so-called London clearing banks, located in England and Wales, and the clearing banks of Scotland and Northern Ireland. (They are called clearing banks because they are members of a clearing house, which institution we discuss in the next section).

The four largest London clearing banks dominate the system in terms of value of deposits held. They have numerous branches throughout the country. For this reason the UK system is called a 'branch banking' system as opposed to the American system, which is a 'unit banking' system and which contains many individual banks (over 15,000 in 1990), each with relatively few branches.

The great advantage of a branch banking system over a unit system is its ability to spread risks. A crop failure in Nebraska could drive a local American bank into insolvency when the farmers who were its major customers became unable to repay their loans. A crop failure in Somerset could not, however, seriously threaten the solvency of any British bank, since its customers in that county account for only a minute fraction of its total customers.

Retail banks are in business to earn profits. They thus have a strong incentive to invest in assets that earn a high return. Generally, however, assets that earn the higher returns tend to be relatively illiquid. This creates a conflict with the bank's need to hold adequate reserves to meet its depositors' demands for cash. To meet these needs, the bank must hold reserves of cash in its vaults or on deposit with the Bank of England, or in very liquid 'near money' assets, such as short-term securities that can easily be redeemed for cash. One of the arts of bank management is to balance the bank's portfolio of assets between revenue and liquidity.

The Bankers' Clearing House

When a depositor in Bank A writes a cheque in favour of someone whose account is with Bank B, Bank A now owes money to Bank B. The cash flow is exactly the same as when one individual withdrew cash from Bank A and gave it to the second individual, who deposited it in Bank B. When the transaction is done by cheque, however, the banks, rather than the individuals, transfer the money. Multibank systems settle interbank debts through a CLEARING HOUSE, where interbank debts are cancelled.

In England, the clearing house is owned and operated by the retail banks. At the end of the day, all of the cheques drawn by Bank A's customers, and deposited in Bank B, are totalled and set against the total of all the cheques drawn by Bank B's customers, and deposited in Bank A. The two banks then only need to settle the difference between these two sums. All of the customers' cheques used to be passed through the clearing house back to the bank on which they were drawn so that each bank could adjust its depositors' accounts by a set of book entries. Today, the operation is computerized, though the result is the same. Payments from one bank to another are unnecessary unless there is a *net* transfer of deposits from the customers of one bank to those of another.

Other Institutions in the UK Financial System

The UK financial system also contains several other financial institutions which we should briefly mention.

Retail banks

Retail banks are defined as those banks that have networks of branches throughout the country and/or participate in a bankers' clearing house. They thus include the clearing banks as well as the Trustee Savings Bank, the National Giro, and a few other more specialized institutions.

There are two large savings banks, the National Savings Bank, operated by the Post Office, and the Trustee Savings Bank. These banks were originally intended as a repository for the deposits of small savers. Money could be deposited and withdrawn but not transferred by cheque. Now, however, the Trustee Savings Bank does offer chequing facilities.

Overseas banks

This class of banks includes branches of foreign banks operating in the UK. The growing importance of foreign trade, and of international capital movements, has led to a steady increase in the number of such banks.

---

1 Further details of UK banking institutions are given in Harbury and Lipsey, Chapter 8.

Merchant banks

These banks, which are also called accepting houses, grew up in the nineteenth century to finance the country's international trade. They still do much of their business in international trade, but they also engage in other specialized work such as managing investment portfolios for other institutions, providing financial advice to companies, handling the issues of new shares and arranging mergers, and dealing in very large deposits with a term of over one year.

Non-banking financial institutions

The UK financial system also includes a number of institutions that are not banks but which play an important part in financial markets. These are called NON-BANKING FINANCIAL INSTITUTIONS.

Discount houses: The DISCOUNT HOUSES are specialized institutions which are peculiar to the UK. They borrow money at 'call' (i.e. repayable on demand) from banks and other lending institutions. They use this money to purchase short-dated financial assets such as Treasury bills. The advantage to the banks of this arrangement is that they can earn interest on a large part of their cash reserves. (Loans to the discount houses are repayable at call and hence are as good as cash.)

The specialization of the discount houses in the short-term money market provides a good example of the division of labour. Institutions that specialize in other forms of loans do not find it worth their while to acquire detailed knowledge of the short-term market. They lend those funds that they can commit only for short terms to the discount houses who, guided by their specialist knowledge, lend them profitably.

Financial intermediaries: Most banking systems also have a variety of other specialized institutions. Some of these accept time deposits from the public and lend money out on a longer-term basis. One of the most important is building societies. These financial institutions, originally engaged in lending money on mortgage for house purchases, have been becoming more and more similar to banks in recent years – because their deposits have been regarded by the public as being almost as liquid as bank deposits. Many now offer a whole range of banking services and at least one (the Abbey National) has changed its charter to become a retail bank.

THE CREATION OF MONEY BY THE RETAIL BANKS

Our main concern in this chapter is with the supply of money. From that point of view, the most important aspect of the banking system is its ability to create and destroy deposit money. Banks have this ability because all customers do not try to convert their deposits into notes and coins at the same time. At any one time, some customers will be withdrawing cash from their accounts while others will be depositing cash to the credit of their accounts. Because these two amounts do not exactly balance, banks must keep reserves to accommodate their customers when withdrawals exceed new deposits. But because in normal times the *net* amount of withdrawals is far less than the total of customers' deposits on their books, the reserves that are required are only a small fraction of total deposits.

The behaviour summarized above is the basis of the fractional reserve system that we first encountered in Chapter 30. In turn, it is the fractional reserve system that allows banks to create money, through a process that we now need to study.

Some simplifying assumptions: To focus on the essential aspects, assume that banks can hold only two kinds of assets, cash and advances to customers. Further assume that there is only one kind of deposit, a sight deposit, which earns no interest and can be withdrawn on demand. The other assumptions listed below are provisional. Later, when we have developed the basic ideas concerning the bank's creation of money, these assumptions will be relaxed.

Fixed reserve ratio: We have seen that retail banks hold their cash reserves partly as notes and coins on hand to meet the day-to-day needs of their depositors, partly as reserves held on deposit with the Bank of England, and partly as call loans to the money market. Dividing total cash reserves by total deposit liabilities gives what is known as the CASH RESERVE RATIO. For example, if a bank has deposit liabilities of £10m and reserves of £2.5m, its reserve ratio is 2.5m/10m, which is 0.25. This figure indicates that reserves held are sufficient to cover 25 per cent of all deposit liabilities.

For purposes of illustration, we shall assume that all banks have a desired reserve ratio of 20 per cent; that is, that banks decide to have at least £1 of reserves for every £5 of deposits. Reserves in excess of their desired reserve ratio are called 'excess reserves'.

No cash drain from the banking system: We further assume that the public wishes to hold a fixed, and unchanging, amount of currency. Thus, any changes in the money supply will take the form of changes in deposit money.

Deposit creation

We give below the balance sheet of a hypothetical bank. This bank's assets consist of reserves of £200, held partly as cash on hand and partly as deposits with the central bank, and £900 of loans to its customers. Its liabilities are

Balance Sheet 1. The initial position

Liabilities		Assets	
Deposits	£1000	Cash and other reserves	£200
Capital	100	Loans	900
	1100		1100

£100 to those who initially contributed capital to start the bank, and £1000 to current depositors. The bank's actual ratio of reserves to deposits is 200/100 = 0.20, and this is exactly equal to its assumed desired reserve ratio.

Now imagine that an immigrant arrives in the country and opens an account by depositing £100 in cash with the bank. This is a new deposit for the bank, and it results in the revised Balance Sheet 2.

Balance Sheet 2. Position after a cash deposit of £100

Liabilities		Assets	
Deposits	£1100	Cash and other reserves	£300
Capital	100	Loans	900
	1200		1200

As a result of the immigrant's new deposit, both the bank's cash assets *and* its deposit liabilities have risen by £100. More importantly, its *actual reserve ratio* has increased to 300/1100 = 0.273. The bank now has excess reserves. With its present level of reserves of £300, it could support £1500 in deposits and just maintain its desired ratio of 0.20 (300/1500). This is £400 more in deposits than it now has.

A one-bank system (mono Bank system)

If this bank were the only bank in the banking system, it would know that any loan that it made would give rise to new deposits of an equal amount *all held at that bank*. It would then be in a position to make a new loan of £400. Assuming that the loan is made to a firm, the bank would do so by adding that amount to the firm's deposit account. The result is the new Balance Sheet 3.

Balance Sheet 3. Position after making £400 of new loans

Liabilities		Assets	
Deposits	£1500	Cash and other reserves	£300
Capital	100	Loans	1300
	1600		1600

The immigrant's deposit initially raises cash assets and deposit liabilities by £100. The new loans to firms then create an additional £400 of deposit liabilities. This restores the reserve ratio to its desired level (300/1500 = 0.20). There are no longer any excess reserves and no further expansion of deposit money will occur. As the bank's customers do business with each other, settling their accounts by cheques, the *ownership* of the deposits will be continually changing. What matters to the bank, however, is that its *total* deposit liabilities, and its *total* reserves, will remain constant.

We conclude that the extent to which a single bank can increase its loans, *and thus its deposits* (which are part of the money supply), depends on its reserve ratio.

Because, in this case, the ratio is 0.20, the bank is able to expend deposits to five times the original acquisition of cash.

Many banks

Deposit creation is more complicated in a multibank system than in a single-bank system, but *the end result is exactly the same*. It is more complicated because, when a bank makes a loan, the recipient of the loan may pay the money to people who deposit it in other banks. How this works is most easily seen under the extreme assumption that every new borrower writes cheques on his new deposit in favour of people who deposit the cheques *in other banks*.

We now assume that the bank illustrated in Balance Sheet 1 is one of many banks in a multibank system. Once again the bank receives a new deposit that puts it in the position shown in Balance Sheet 2. With its new level of deposits at £1100, the bank needs only £220 of reserves (0.20 × £1100 = £220). Since it has £300 in reserves, its excess reserves amount to £80. It cannot immediately create £400 worth of new deposits, as did the monopoly bank, because these will be drained off to other banks. Instead, all it can do in the first instance is to lend out the £80 of excess reserves that it now has on hand. According to our assumption, this £80 finds its way into other banks – as the recipient of the loan pays cheques to people who deposit them in other banks. The bank will then suffer a cash drain to these other banks. The result is Balance Sheet 4 and the bank once again has a cash reserve ratio of 0.20.

Balance Sheet 4. Position of a single bank in a multibank system after it has loaned its excess reserves

Liabilities		Assets	
Deposits	£1100	Cash and other reserves	£220
Capital	100	Loans	980
	1200		1200

So far, deposits in the bank have increased by only the initial £100 of the new immigrant's money with which we started. (Of this, £20 is held as a cash reserve against the deposit and £80 has been lent out.) But *other* banks have received new deposits of £80 because the people receiving payments from the firm which borrowed the £80 deposited those payments in their own banks. The receiving banks (sometimes called *second-generation banks*) receive new deposits of £80, and when the cheques clear, they have new reserves of £80. Because they require an addition to their reserves of only £16 to support the new deposit, they have £64 of 'excess' reserves. They now increase their loans by £64. After this money is spent by the borrowers and has been deposited in other (third-generation) banks, the balance sheets of the second-generation banks will have changed as shown in Balance Sheet 5.

Balance Sheet 5. Position of 'second-generation' banks after receipt of new deposits

Liabilities		Assets	
Deposits	+£80	Cash and other reserves	+£16
Capital		Loans	+64
	+80		+80

Note that Balance Sheet 5 only records *changes* in the balance sheets of the 'second-generation' banks, and it records them *after* the banks have (i) received new deposits of £80, (ii) lent out £64 (keeping the remaining £16 as reserves), and (iii) suffered a cash drain to 'third-generation banks' of £64.

The third-generation banks now find themselves with £64 of new deposits. Against these they need hold only £12.80 in reserves, so they have excess reserves of £51.20 that they can lend out.

Thus the immigrant's new deposit sets up a long sequence of new deposits, new loans, new deposits, and new loans. The stages are shown in Table 31.2. The series in the Table should look familiar, for it is similar to the sequence we met when dealing with the investment multiplier (see Table 26.1 on page 297).

TABLE 31.2 Many Banks, a Single New Deposit. The banking system as a whole can create deposit money whenever it receives new reserves

Bank	New deposits	New loans	Additions to desired reserves
Original bank	£100.00	£80.00	£20.00
Second-generation bank	80.00	64.00	16.00
Third-generation bank	64.00	51.20	12.80
Fourth-generation bank	51.20	40.96	10.24
Fifth-generation bank	40.96	32.77	8.19
Sixth-generation bank	32.77	26.22	6.55
Seventh-generation bank	26.22	20.98	5.24
Eighth-generation bank	20.98	16.78	4.20
Ninth-generation bank	16.78	13.42	3.36
Tenth-generation bank	13.42	10.74	2.68
Total first 10 generations	446.33	357.07	89.26
All remaining generations	53.67	42.93	10.74
Total for banking system	500.00	400.00	100.00

Now consider what has happened. Each bank manager can say 'What, me *create* money? Good gracious no! All I did was invest my excess reserves. I can do no more than manage wisely the money I receive.' Yet the banking *system* as a whole has created new deposits and thus new money.

If *r* is the reserve ratio, the ultimate effect on the deposits of the banking system of a new cash deposit will be 1/*r* times the new deposit.

This is the same as the result reached in the single-bank case (although the 'first-generation' bank that received the initial deposit cannot increase its deposits by that amount).

Many deposits

The two cases discussed above, the introduction of a new deposit first in a single-bank system and then in a multibank system, show that under either set of extreme assumptions, the result is the same. So it is, too, in intermediate situations. A far more realistic picture of deposit creation is one in which new deposits accrue simultaneously to all banks because of changes in the monetary policy of the government. (We shall see in Chapter 34 how the Bank of England does this.)

Say, for example, that the banking system comprises five banks of equal size, and that each receives a new cash deposit of £100. Now each bank is in the position shown in Balance Sheet 2 above, and each can expand deposits based on its own £100 of 'excess' reserves. (Each bank does this by granting loans to customers.)

Now consider what happens to any one bank – call it bank A. Because each bank does one-fifth of the total banking business, an average of 80 per cent of bank A's newly created deposits will find its way into other banks as A's customers pay other people in the community by cheque. However, 20 per cent of the new deposits created by the other four banks will find their way into bank A. The net result is no cash drain from bank A. As it is with bank A, so it is with the other four banks. So what happens is that all banks receive new cash and all begin creating deposits simultaneously, and no bank suffers a significant cash drain to any other bank.

Thus all banks can go on expanding deposits without losing reserves to each other; they need only worry about keeping enough reserves to satisfy those depositors who will occasionally require cash. The expansion can go on, with each bank watching its own ratio of reserves to deposits, expanding deposits as long as the ratio exceeds 0.20 and ceasing when it reaches that figure. The process will come to a halt when each bank has created £400 in additional deposits, so that for each initial £100 cash deposit, there is now £500 in deposits backed by £100 in cash. Now *each* bank will have entries similar to those in Balance Sheet 3 for the single bank after it had expanded deposits on the basis of its new cash deposit.

The destruction of deposit money

The 'multiple expansion of deposits' that has just been worked through applies in reverse to a withdrawal of funds. Deposits of the banking system will fall by a multiple of 1/*r* times any amount withdrawn from the bank and not redeposited at another. We leave it to the reader to work through the previous examples assuming that, instead of a deposit, the initial disturbance is a withdrawal. Instead of having excess reserves, the banks will then have deficient reserves and will have to react by cutting their loans.

The creation of deposit money reviewed

A single bank could immediately expand deposits when it received a new cash deposit because it knew it would suffer no cash drain. Individual banks in a multibanking system cannot do this because they know they may suffer a cash drain to other banks. But the banking system as a whole suffers no cash drain; what is withdrawn from one bank ends up in another.

Thus the banking system as a whole does what no single one of its banks can do: produce a multiple expansion of deposit money on the basis of an initial deposit of new cash arriving from outside the system.

The money multiplier

The examples we have given make it clear that the amount

of deposit expansion that occurs depends on the reserve ratio that banks keep. This relationship is easily seen if we use a few lines of simple algebra.

If r is the bank's reserve ratio, the reserves must be r times the amount of deposits. (Notice that, by the meaning of a fractional reserve system, the reserve ratio r must be less than one.) Letting R stand for reserves, and D for deposits, we can write this as:

$$R = rD \qquad (1)$$

Assume, for example, that r is 0.20 (i.e. 1/5), as in the previous example. If banks have deposits of £1000, they must hold reserves equal to 1/5th of £1000, which is £200. Using the symbols shown in equation (1) we can write this:

$$R = 0.20(£1000) = £200$$

Now let us look at changes. If equation (1) is true, the following must also be true:

$$\Delta R = r\Delta D \qquad (2)$$

All this says is that any *change* in deposits must be matched by the appropriate *change* in reserves – which is r times the change in deposits.

In our numerical example, if deposits change by £200 then reserves must change by 1/5th of that amount, which is £40. Putting these figures into equation (2) we can write this as:

$$\Delta R = 0.20(£200) = £40$$

Next we divide equation (2) through by r to obtain:

$$\frac{1}{r}\Delta R = \Delta D \qquad (3)$$

or, what is the same thing:

$$\Delta D = \frac{1}{r}\Delta R \qquad (4)$$

Equation (4) is the so-called MONEY or DEPOSIT MULTIPLIER, which is defined as the amount of deposits which result from each £1 of new reserves.[1] Equation (4) tells us what we have seen illustrated in the earlier examples: any change in reserves brings about a change in deposits by an amount that depends on the reserve ratio r. What we have now proved is that the exact multiplier is $1/r$. Thus, if r is 0.20, the deposit multiplier is 5: every £1 of new reserves supports £5 of new deposits. If r is 0.10, the deposit multiplier is 10, and so on.

A complication: cash drains from the system

So far we have worked with the simplifying assumption that the public is willing to hold, in the form of deposits, all the new money that is created. A more realistic assumption is that the public wishes to maintain *a constant ratio*

between the two kinds of money, deposits and currency. In this case, if £100 of *new money* is created, most will be held as new deposits, but some will be held as new currency. Assume, for example, that the ratio in which the public wishes to hold currency and deposit money is 1:19. Now when £100 of new money is created, the public will hold £95 in deposits and £5 in cash.

The important change in this case is that, when the banking system creates new deposit money, the whole system will suffer a cash drain as the public withdraws some of this new money to hold. Now the story of deposit creation after the banking system receives new cash deposits becomes slightly more complicated. To illustrate how it works, assume that the public always wishes to hold 5 per cent of its money in currency and 95 per cent in deposits.

When the *whole system* receives new cash deposits, each bank starts creating deposits and suffers no significant cash drain to other banks. But because approximately 5 per cent of all newly created deposits is withdrawn to be held as cash, each bank suffers a cash drain to the public. The expansion continues, with each bank watching its own ratio of cash reserves to deposits. Each bank expands deposits as long as the cash reserve ratio exceeds 0.20 and ceases when the ratio reaches that figure.

Whenever the expansion is accompanied by a cash drain, it will come to a halt with a smaller increase in deposit money than when there is no cash drain.

When the process is finished, each bank's balance sheet will look as in Balance Sheet 6 (assuming each received an initial new cash deposit of £100).

Balance Sheet 6. Deposit expansion of each bank in a multibank system with a cash drain to the public

Liabilities		Assets	
Deposits	£1395.80	Cash and other reserves	£279.17
Capital	100.00	Loans	1216.63
	1495.80		1495.80

Compare Balance Sheet 6 with Balance Sheet 3, which showed the position in a single-bank system. We now see that instead of ending up with £1500 in deposits, the banking system now has just less than £1400. Deposit expansion is less because of the cash drain. The banks have created a little less than £400 of new deposit money, and a little more than £20 of reserves – i.e. 5 per cent of the new deposits – has been withdrawn by the public to circulate as currency.

---

1 The 'money multiplier' is also sometimes called the 'bank deposit 'multiplier', the 'bank multiplier' or the 'credit multiplier'. This multiplier must not be confused with the investment multiplier that links changes in investment to changes in national income.

Summary

1 The retail banks are the most obvious part of the UK banking system. They accept deposits from the general public; they provide chequing facilities to their customers; they make advances to their customers; and they hold various interest-earning assets such as bills and bonds.

2 The major institutions in the UK financial system are the retail banks (which include the clearing banks), overseas banks, acceptance houses, discount houses, finance houses and building societies.

3 Retail banks create money by lending out any 'excess reserves'. Their ability to do so depends on the fractional backing of their deposit money – reserves need only be a small fraction of their outstanding deposit liabilities.

4 The money multiplier gives the value of new deposits that can be created for every £1 of new reserves that becomes available to the retail banking system. Its value depends on the banks' desired ratio of reserves to deposits, called the *reserve ratio* and given the symbol *r*. With no cash drain to the public, the money or deposit multiplier is $1/r$.

5 If the public wishes to hold some fraction of new money as currency, the expansion of deposits will be accompanied by a currency drain to the public and the money multiplier will be less than in the no-cash-drain case.

Questions

1 Which One or More of the following are major functions of banks?
(a) to accept deposits from the public
(b) to hold portfolios of equities
(c) to make advances to customers
(d) to handle the mechanics of clearing cheques among banks
(e) to finance hire-purchase loans

2 Which One or More of the following are *not* a part of the UK banking system?
(a) retail banks
(b) merchant banks
(c) the Overseas Development Corporation
(d) discount houses
(e) the International Bank for Reconstruction and Development (the IBRD)

3 True or False?
(a) There are about a dozen major clearing banks in England.
(b) Retail banks create money by making advances to customers.
(c) The money multiplier refers to the relation between new reserves received by the banking system and new deposit money that it creates.
(d) The money multiplier is larger when there is a drain of some newly created money to the public than when there is not.

4 If a single UK bank begins to expand deposits by making advances on the basis of newly acquired excess reserves, to whom might it suffer a cash drain and why?

Intermediate
Macroeconomics

Preface to Part 5

In Part 5, we go beyond the simple Keynesian model. We first integrate money into the model of the circular flow to see how interest rates are determined and how they affect expenditure flows. We then use a slightly more advanced Keynesian-type model to see how national income and the price level are simultaneously determined by the forces of aggregate demand and aggregate supply. This allows us to study the government's monetary and fiscal policies. We do this, first using a model of a closed economy, and then a model of an open economy – one in which foreign trade and foreign capital movements exert important influences.

Readers are warned that Part 5 uses tools of analysis that are developed in Part 2. For this reason, Part 5 should not be attempted before reading Part 2.

32 The Demand for Money

Chapter 32 is the first in a series of three that are designed to integrate monetary forces into the theory of the determination of national income. In this chapter, we study the demand for money. In Chapter 33, we study what is called the monetary transmission mechanism. This is the mechanism that links the demand and supply of money to aggregate desired expenditure and, through aggregate expenditure, links monetary forces to equilibrium national income and the price level. Finally, in Chapter 34 we study how the Bank of England seeks, through its monetary policy, to control monetary forces and thus to influence equilibrium income and the price level.

BONDS, BILLS AND THE RATE OF INTEREST[1]

In order to understand the nature of the demand for money, it is essential to appreciate that people have a choice between holding money and holding other kinds of financial assets. In Chapter 22, we briefly discussed bills, bonds and other financial assets. Now we need to study these in more detail. To start with, we consider only two such assets, *bonds* and *bills*.

What is a Bond?

A bond is a financial asset that is created by some types of loans. It is similar to an IOU that a borrower gives to a lender; it is evidence of a debt.

One important way in which a firm, or a government, can borrow money, is to issue bonds which it offers for sale to the public. Those who buy these bonds are loaning their money to the firm.

To illustrate, consider a bond issued by D.G. Harsey & Co. on 30 December 1990 that is repayable on 31 December 2000 for £100. This bond is offered on the open market and bought by R.C. Lipbury for £100. In return Lipbury has a piece of paper called a bond. Ignoring all of the small print on the bond, what it says, in effect, is the following:

We promise to pay to the bearer
the sum of £100
on 31 December 2000
and also £5 annually on 31 December until that date.
....
(signed) D.G. Harsey – Treasurer

Notice three things about this bond.

First, the bond promises to pay a certain sum in the future. This is called its FACE VALUE or its PRINCIPAL.

Second, the date at which that sum will be paid is specified – 31 December 2000 in this case. This is called the MATURITY DATE. When that date arrives, the bond is said to have *matured*. The length of time that the bond has to run from its date of issue until its maturity date is called the TERM of the bond or sometimes its 'term to maturity'. When the money is repaid to the bondholder, the bond has been REDEEMED.

Third, the borrower promises to pay a specific sum, called INTEREST, until the bond matures. Interest payments occur periodically. In the case of the Harsey bonds shown above, interest is paid once a year. The annual interest to be paid is usually expressed as a percentage of the value of the bond and called the RATE OF INTEREST. In this case, the rate of interest is 5 per cent, since the £5 interest paid each year is 5 per cent of the £100 face value of the bond.

The Market Value of a Bond

Now let us say that on 31 December 1991, Lipbury wants his money back. He cannot go to Harsey & Co. and demand that his loan be repaid because a bond is evidence of a TERM LOAN – one that will be repaid at some specific future date – not of a DEMAND LOAN – one that is repayable on demand. What Lipbury can do, however, is to find someone else – let us call her A. Student – who has money to lend, and sell the bond to her. When he does this, Harsey & Co. are unaffected. They still owe £100, which must be paid on 31 December 2000 and are obligated to pay £5 a year until then. But Lipbury now has his money back, and Student has become Harsey's creditor.

Now come the critical questions: how much would Student be willing to pay, and how little would Lipbury accept, for the Harsey bond? Let us assume there is no doubt that Harsey will meet his obligation and repay the loan on redemption day. Would Student ever consider paying anything more than £100 for the bond? Would Lipbury ever consider taking anything less? The answer is yes to both questions. The price they will both willingly agree on for the sale of the bond may be more or less than £100, depending on the current market rate of interest.

The Market Rate of Interest

Just above, we encountered a new term, THE MARKET

---

1 For a fuller discussion of debt instruments, see Harbury and Lipsey.

RATE OF INTEREST. This is the rate of interest that can currently be earned on new loans – in other words, it is what borrowers are currently willing to pay to obtain loans.

Let us now see how this relates to Lipbury's sale of the bond to Student. *On the one hand*, if newly issued bonds and other loans are offering 10 per cent, then Lipbury's bond will not be worth £100. This is because £100 used to purchase a newly issued bond would earn £10 per year, so no one would pay £100 for a bond that pays a mere £5 a year. *On the other hand*, if the market rate of interest were only 3 per cent, the bond that Lipbury has will be worth more than £100. This is because £100 used to purchase a new bond would earn only £3 per year, so *everyone* who has money to lend would like to buy the bond that Lipbury has for £100 and earn £5 rather than spend £100 to buy a new bond that yields only £3 per year.

This example illustrates a key proposition:

The value of an existing bond is negatively related to the market rate of interest. The higher the market rate, the lower the value of the bond. In future, whenever we refer to a fall in the rate of interest you must realize that this also means a rise in the price of bonds.

This relation often seems mystifying at first sight, so let us pause over it for a moment. Remember first what a bond is. It is a promise to make a certain set of money payments over some future time-period. These payments are often referred to as a *stream of future payments*, and looked at from the point of view of the bond owners they are a *stream of future incomes*. How much it is worth paying now to obtain such a promise depends on how much must be lent elsewhere to earn an equivalent stream of income. The market rate of interest tells you how much you can earn from £1 invested elsewhere. The higher is the market rate of interest, the *less* must you lend in order to earn some fixed stream of interest payments. Thus, the higher the market rate of interest, the *less* is the value of any existing bond which pays a *fixed* stream of interest.

Present Value

The PRESENT VALUE of a stream of future payments is the amount that stream is worth now. We have seen that this amount depends on the market rate of interest. But exactly *how much* is the future stream promised by a specific bond worth, and exactly *how much* does this value change as the market rate of interest changes?

In the case of the Harsey bond, and any other bond that promises a lump-sum repayment of its face value on redemption date, the calculation of the exact answers to these questions is a little complex. This is because of the need to put a present value, not only on the stream of interest payments, but also on the principal that will be repaid on redemption day. We can, however, discover much of what we need to know now by looking at a different type of bond.

Non-redeemable bonds

The type of bond that we now look at is a NON-REDEEMABLE BOND, i.e. one that has no maturity date. It is a promise to make a specified payment each year forever, but not to repay any face value at a specified maturity date. You might think that no one would be willing to 'lend' money to anyone who stated categorically that he would never repay the loan. You would, however, be wrong. After all, you would surely be willing to pay some sum to obtain the right to receive £1000 each year forever. Indeed the UK government has obtained money from the public by issuing some such bonds, the best known of which are called 'consols' (short for Consolidated Stock), which it stated originally might never be repaid. People bought them *solely for the interest that they were guaranteed* to receive each year. The study of this type of bond will tell us much of what we need to know about bonds in general. After we have completed this study, we can finalize our treatment of redeemable bonds with relative ease.

Let us ask what determines the present value of a bond, such as a Consol, *which promises to pay £100 per year indefinitely*. We can now forget about the face value of the bond. It does not have one, because it will never be redeemed. The present value of this bond depends only on how much £100 per annum is worth to potential purchasers, which depends on the market rate of interest.

Suppose, for example, that this rate is 10 per cent. This means that borrowers will pay 10p in interest each year for each £1 that is currently lent to them. At this rate, £1000 must be lent out to earn £100 in interest per year.

The market value of the Consol is determined by what a purchaser would pay for it and what the existing holder would sell it for. First, let us look at a lender. If £1000 can earn £100 per year on current loans, then lenders will be willing to pay £1000 for the existing bond, but no more. Second, look at what the existing holder would accept. If £1000 can be borrowed for interest of £100 a year, the existing bond-holder would accept £1000 and no less. Say, for example, he was only offered £900. Instead of selling his Consol, he could keep it and borrow £1000 at an interest payment of £100 per year. The £100 he earned on his bond would then just pay the £100 interest on his loan so that he would end up with the use of £1000, instead of only the £900 that he would have had if he had sold his Consol. Since buyers would pay £1000 and no more, and since the seller would accept £1000 and no less, the market price of the Consol will be exactly £1000.

When the price of the Consol that pays £100 per year is exactly £1000, people will be willing to hold it because its rate of return, of 10 per cent, is the same as can be earned on new loans. If the price exceeds £1000, no one will want it, so it cannot be sold. If the price is less than £1000, everyone will want it, so this cannot be an equilibrium price for the Consol.

Now, suppose there is some change in market conditions so that the market rate of interest falls to 5 per cent. In this situation it takes £2000 to earn £100 per year at the market rate of interest. The present value of the Consol that pays £100 per year will now rise to £2000. If anything more is asked for it, no one will want to hold it when 5 per cent can be earned at the market rate of interest. If anything less is asked for it, everyone will rush to buy it, since it offers a rate of return greater than the market rate of interest.

This discussion leads to the conclusion that the present value of a Consol will be that sum of money which, if lent at the market rate of interest, would earn the stream of payments that is offered by the Consol. Since the higher the interest rate, the lower the sum of money that must be loaned to yield a specific flow of interest payments, the lower is the present value of a Consol that offers a fixed stream of future interest payments. This illustrates the conclusion we have already reached: the higher the interest rate, the lower the present value of any bond.

All of this is no unsupported theory. A glance at the investment pages contained in most newspapers will show you bond prices falling when interest rates are rising, and rising when interest rates are falling.

Redeemable bonds

The value of redeemable bonds which have a maturity date at which their face value will be repaid, is also related to the rate of interest. The calculation of present value is a little more complicated than in the case of the non-redeemable bond, because the present value of redeemable bonds depends on the present value of the stream of interest payments from now to maturity *and* the present value of the principal sum that will be repaid on maturity.

The present value of the bond becomes increasingly dominated by the fixed principal, as its maturity date approaches. To illustrate, take an extreme case. The present value of a bond that is redeemable for £1000 in a week's time will be very close to £1000 no matter what the interest rate. Thus its value will not change much, even if the rate of interest leaps from 5 per cent to 10 per cent during that week. This illustrates a second important conclusion:

The closer to the present is the maturity date of a bond, the less the bond's value will change with any given change in the rate of interest.

Notice also that what matters to a lender is the term from the present to a bond's maturity, not its term at the time it was originally issued. Thus a 20-year bond issued in 1975, and redeemable 31 December 1995, starts its life as a 20-year bond but has become a three-month, short-term asset on 1 October 1995. If it is government gilt-edged stock, and hence has no risk of default, it will be similar to a government three-month Treasury bill at that time – although it was quite different in 1975 when it was first issued.

Bills

We need to recall what we said in Chapter 22 about another type of financial asset called a BILL (which is short for a

bill of exchange). A bill is like a bond in that it is a promise to repay a definite sum of money at some fixed date in the future. Unlike a bond, however, it carries no explicit interest payments. Interest arises from a bill because the purchaser buys it for less than its face value. Thus, for example, if a newly issued bill promising to pay £105 in one year's time is purchased for £100 now, the purchaser, in effect, earns an interest rate of 5 per cent on the bill. Furthermore, the issuer pays 5 per cent because she gets £100 now, but promises to pay £105 in a year's time. When a bill is purchased at its time of issue for less than its value at maturity, the bill is said to have been DISCOUNTED.

Capital gains and capital losses

Because changes in the interest rate cause the price of bonds to vary, they confer gains and losses on the current holders of bonds. If the market rate of interest *falls*, the market value of all existing bonds rises. Holders of existing bonds then gain increases in the value of their wealth. Such gains are called CAPITAL GAINS. They increase the value of bond-holders' wealth, while not changing the flow of income yielded by their bonds. If, on the other hand, the market rate of interest *rises*, the market value of all existing bonds falls. The holders of existing bonds then suffer reductions in the value of their wealth. Such losses are *negative* capital gains, and they are more often called CAPITAL LOSSES. They lower the value of bond-holders' wealth, while not changing the income streams yielded by their existing bonds.

Bills are used for short-term debts, usually of less than a year (typically 3 months, as with Treasury Bills used by the UK government), while bonds are used for long-term debts (terms of 10 to 20 years are common).

If the holder of a bill that has some time to go to maturity wants her money now, she is in the same position as a holder of a bond. She must find someone who will buy it from her. The price that will be paid will depend on the current interest rate and the time to go to maturity. When the bill is resold, it is said to have been RE-DISCOUNTED. Let us consider an example.

Say that a bill, payable on December 31st for £105, was bought for £100 on January 1st of the same year. This implies an interest rate of 5 per cent. Now assume that the holder wants his money back on July 1st of that year. If the interest rate is unchanged, he will be able to sell his bill for £102.50. This will yield him £2.50 on a loan of £100 for six months, which is an annual rate of interest of 5 per cent.

Now assume, however, that just before the sale on July 1st, the interest rate rose unexpectedly to 10 per cent. Now the owner of the bill can only sell it for a price that will yield an interest rate of 10 per cent to its purchaser. This price is £100. The bill will yield £5 in six months' time, which is a 5 per cent yield over 6 months, making an annual rate of 10 per cent. Now the seller has received no return on the bill that he has held for six months. He bought the bill for £100 on January 1st, and sold it for £100 on July 1st. So the unexpected rise in the interest rate has wiped out his expected gain.

Liquidity

On page 335, we introduced the concept of liquidity. An asset is more liquid the easier, and less costly, it is to turn it into money, and the lower the uncertainty about the amount of money that can be obtained for it at some future date.

An irredeemable bond that could not be sold (but did yield a stream of interest payments) would be a perfectly illiquid asset – it cannot be turned into money. In between, there are various assets with different terms to maturity. The shorter the term of the bill or bond, the more liquid it is for two reasons: first, the less the time its holder needs to wait to get its principal redeemed, and second, the less its market price will fluctuate as the market rate of interest fluctuates. Thus, 30-day bills are more liquid than 90-day bills, which are more liquid than 2-year bonds, which are more liquid than 20-year bonds.

MONEY AND WEALTH

At any moment in time, households and firms have a given stock of wealth. This wealth can be held in the form of many different kinds of asset, and it is helpful to group these diverse assets under three main headings.

Kinds of Asset

The first group of assets are those that serve as a medium of exchange and a store of value – i.e. coins, paper money and chequing deposits. As we saw in Chapter 30, such assets are called money.

The second group includes all evidences of debt, such as short-term bills, longer-term bonds and gilt-edged treasury stocks. These earn a rate of interest and usually yield a fixed money value at maturity. These are often called debt instruments.

The third group includes all forms of *ownership* of capital goods, either directly in the form, say, of a family business or indirectly in the form of shares in a company. These are often called equities. (In the latter case, the shareholders own the company, and the company owns the capital.)

The first two types of assets are often called 'financial assets' to distinguish them from the third group, which are called 'real assets'.

Money and Bonds

To simplify our discussion of the determinants of the demand for money, it is helpful to group all assets into two classes which we call: money and bonds. By money we shall for now mean any medium of exchange as defined in Chapter 30; and by 'bonds' we shall mean all other assets. Money, therefore, includes currency and all deposits that can be transferred by cheque. Bonds include all interest-earning debt instruments *plus* real capital. *By definition, each individual's total wealth is now made up of the sum of his or her holdings of money and bonds.*

THE DEMAND TO HOLD MONEY AND BONDS

By summing everyone's wealth over the whole economy, we can obtain the total stock of wealth in existence. We can think of that wealth being held in a 'portfolio' of various assets. The decision on how to divide one's wealth between the various available assets is called a 'portfolio balance decision' concerning the allocation of wealth. When wealth-holders hold the portfolio of assets that they wish to hold, we say that they are in portfolio equilibrium. When wealth-holders have too much of some assets and too few of others in their current portfolios, they are in portfolio disequilibrium.

The first step in studying portfolio decisions is to look at the demand for money. The amount of wealth everyone in the economy wishes to hold in the form of money balances is called the DEMAND FOR MONEY.

We should warn you at the outset that students sometimes have difficulty with the concept of the demand for money because they fail to appreciate that it is unlike the demands for goods and services that we considered in Parts 2 and 3. The demands we studied earlier were *flow* demands describing the amount of some commodity that people wish to buy and to consume *in each period of time*. The demand for money describes the demand to hold a given *stock* of money. Once the stock is achieved, no further additions to, or subtractions from, that amount will be made – at least until there is a change in one of the conditions that determines the demand for money.

We now wish to study the conditions that determine the demand for money.

Note first that, because we have grouped all forms of wealth into only two classes called money and bonds, the part of their wealth that households do not hold in the form of money, they must hold in the form of bonds. It follows that households have only one decision to make on how to divide their given stock of wealth. For example, if a group of households having wealth of £5 billion demand to hold £1 billion worth of money, their demand to hold bonds must be for £4 billion worth. If the demand for money rises to £2 billion, the demand for bonds must fall to £3 billion. In this case, people will be trying to reduce their holdings of bonds by £1 billion – by selling them on the open market – and increasing their holdings of money by £1 billion – by adding the proceeds of their bond sales to their money holdings.

It also follows that, *if households are in equilibrium with respect to their money holdings, they must be in equilibrium with respect to their bond holdings.* They cannot, for example, feel that their current wealth is held in just the right amount of money and too many bonds. If too much of their wealth is held in bonds, then too little must be held in cash, since there is, by definition, no other way in which wealth can be held.

Because bonds yield an interest return to their owners, while money held in the form of currency does not, holding wealth in the form of money involves an opportunity cost.

The opportunity cost of holding money is the rate of interest that could have been earned by holding bonds instead.

If wealth can be held in the form of bonds which earn interest income, why hold it in the form of money which does not? Three reasons for doing so are important. They are called the transactions, the precautionary, and the speculative motives for holding money. As we shall learn, the first two relate to the function of money as a medium of exchange, while the third relates to the function of money as a store of wealth.

The Transactions Motive

The first motive for holding money is the one that we studied in connection with the Classical quantity theory of money, and pages 000–0 of Chapter 30 should be reread at this time. Let us recall what we learned in that chapter about the demand for money.

The amount of money that the public wishes to hold in order to finance their transactions is called their TRANS-ACTIONS DEMAND FOR MONEY. The need to hold such transactions balances arises because payments and receipts are not exactly synchronized. The transactions demand for money is positively related to the level of national income measured in current prices, i.e. to nominal national income.

In the simplest theory, the transactions demand for money measured in nominal monetary units is pro-portional to nominal national income (PY):

$$M_D = kPY$$

where M_D is the transactions demand for money, Y is *real* national income, P is the price level, so that PY is nominal national income (i.e. valued at current prices) and k is the fraction of national income that is held as transactions balances.

It follows that the transactions demand for money will be increased by either an increase in real national income with prices constant, or an increase in the general price level with real national income constant, or any combination of the two.

The only reason for holding money in the Classical quantity theory is the transactions motive, and the resulting demand is related soley to nominal national income, which is real income Y multiplied by the price level P and so written PY. In the rest of this chapter, we go beyond the Classical quantity theory by studying other influences on the transactions motive and other motives for holding money.

The transactions demand and interest rates

The modern view of the transactions demand for money makes it depend not only on income but also on interest rates. The reason lies in the opportunity cost of holding money balances which, as we already know, is the interest rate. Because of the interest that is forgone when money

balances are held, people and firms have an incentive to minimize the transactions balances that they hold. One way this can be done is to make frequent switches between money and other assets.

This possibility remained a relatively unimportant adjunct to the theory that the transactions demand depended on income until the late 1970s. Then interest rates soared from rates under 10 per cent to rates well over 20 per cent. At these new higher rates, it paid firms, especially big ones with large transactions balances, to devote much attention to reducing their balances. After all, if a large firm could reduce its average balances by £1 million over the year, this is an extra £250,000 earned, at a 25 per cent interest rate. That sum would pay the salary of a full-time cash-management official and still leave a profit for the firm.

This kind of thing happened on a grand scale in the 1970s with large firms lending out unwanted balances, sometimes for periods of no more than a few hours at a time. As a result the average transactions balances held by the public (firms and households) fell dramatically.

The Precautionary Motive

We have seen that the transactions need for cash arises because the timing of receipts and payments is not perfectly synchronized. The precautionary need arises also from money's function as a medium of exchange, but it arises because the timing and size of receipts and payments are *uncertain*. As with the transactions motive, both firms and households have precautionary motives for holding money which are broadly similar.

To see what is involved, assume that a firm knows for certain that all of its receipts for goods sold during the week will come in on Friday, and that all of its payments for everything it purchases will be made in equal amounts on each day of the week. In this case, a firm would have a large money balance on Friday just after it received its payments. It could then let its money balances run down as it settled its accounts on each day of the following week until its balances reached zero just before it received its payments the following Friday.

Now assume that the firm is *un*certain about the exact timing of its receipts. Possibly on one Friday all its cus-tomers may not settle their accounts. Unless the firm has some additional cash balances, it will be unable to meet all its payments over the following week. Or, to take another case, although it receives all it expects on Friday, the following week there are some extra unexpected pay-ments it has to make. Again, if its money balances were only what it received last Friday, it could not make these extra payments.

As a precaution against unexpectedly high payments, or unexpectedly low receipts, firms (and individuals) often hold more than the minimum balances that they need to accommodate their ordinary, expected flows of receipts and payments. The desire to hold money to accommodate such unexpected fluctuations in receipts and payments is called the PRECAUTIONARY MOTIVE FOR HOLDING MONEY. The precautionary demand for money arises out of uncertainty about the exact timing, and size, of payments and receipts.

Just as with the transactions need, the precautionary need varies directly with the level of money income, which is its prime determinant. If a firm does only £10,000 worth of business each week, it will need to hold, say, an extra £500 to guard against receipts that are 5 per cent below normal or payments that are 5 per cent above normal. But if the firm does £100,000 worth of business each week, it will need to hold £5000 to guard against the same percentage fluctuations in its receipts or payments.

Thus the precautionary demand for money is positively associated with national income valued in current prices. The higher the level of money income, the larger the money balances that will be needed for precautionary (as well as for transactions) purposes.

The Speculative Motive

The first two motives for holding money relate, as we have seen, to the function of money as a medium of exchange. The third motive, which we shall now study, relates to the function of money as a store of wealth. We have seen that money has an opportunity cost in the form of the interest forgone by not using the money to buy some interest-bearing asset (which we call a bond). The cost of holding money provides an incentive for firms, and individuals, to hold no more money than the minimum they need to satisfy their transactions and precautionary motives. We might expect, therefore, that any surplus wealth would be held in the other form that is available, bonds.

A major problem with holding wealth in the form of bonds is that the price of bonds may vary. As we saw earlier in this chapter, the price of bonds is negatively related to the interest rate: high interest rates mean low bond prices, while low interest rates mean high bond prices.

This variability in the price of bonds means that bond-holders can make capital gains by buying when the price is low (i.e. the rate of interest is high) and selling when the price is high (i.e. the rate of interest is low). This means that holding bonds involves a risk not present when money is held. The holder may wish to obtain money for the bond by selling it before its maturity but is uncertain about how much money it will yield. People who expect the price of bonds to rise in the future will be more inclined to hold bonds (expecting a capital gain on bonds) while those who expect bond prices to fall will be more likely to hold money (expecting a capital loss on bonds.)

The motive that leads people to vary their money balances as a result of the knowledge that bond prices change frequently is called the SPECULATIVE MOTIVE.

The first important theory of the speculative motive was developed by Keynes in the 1930s. A later and in many ways more satisfactory theory was developed by the American economist James Tobin in the 1950s. Tobin's theory was path-breaking in creating an entire new branch of theoretical and empirical work that explains the mixture of assets in which wealth will be held. In 1981 he was awarded

the Nobel Prize in economics for, among other things, his fathering of what is now called the 'portfolio balance theory'.

The details of Keynes' and Tobin's theories are given in more advanced textbooks.[1] In the text that follows, we give only the barest outlines which lead to the conclusion that the demand for money will be negatively related to the rate of interest.

Uncertainty: The cost of holding money rather than bonds is the interest forgone by not holding bonds. The advantage of holding money rather than bonds is that the cash value of the money balance is certain. In contrast, the bond earns an interest return but has an uncertain cash value should money be needed before maturity. As a result, wealth-holders will divide their portfolios of assets until the gain in certainty on the last unit of money held just balances the loss of interest. A rise in the rate of interest raises the cost of holding money and reduces the quantity held. A fall will have the opposite result. This is the aspect of the speculative motive emphasized by Tobin.

Expected changes in interest rates: Whenever wealth-owners expect interest rates to rise, i.e. the price of bonds to fall, they expect capital losses from holding bonds, and will be inclined to hold more money. Whenever wealth-owners expect the interest rate to fall, i.e. the price of bonds to rise, they expect capital gains from holding bonds and will be inclined to hold more bonds. We also assume that, *ceteris paribus*, the lower the current interest rate the more likely are people to expect it to rise, and, conversely, the higher the current rate the more likely are people to expect it to fall. It then follows that the rate of interest, and the demand for money, will be negatively related, because the higher the current rate, the greater the expectations of capital gains on bond holdings when the rate falls in the future. This was the aspect of the speculative motive stressed by Keynes.

Both Keynes' and Tobin's theories lead to the important result that the demand to hold money varies negatively with the rate of interest – the higher the rate of interest, the lower the demand to hold money, and vice versa.

This negative relation between the demand for money and the rate of interest is well established empirically and it has, as we shall see in a later chapter, important implications for the theory of income determination.

The Total Demand for Money: A Recapitulation

The demand for money is defined as the total amount of money balances that everyone in the economy wishes to hold. Our discussion of the motives for holding money leads to the following important conclusion:

the demand for money, which is the demand to hold a stock of money balances, varies *positively* with national

---

1 See, for example, IPE, 7th edn, Chapter 31.

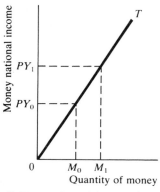

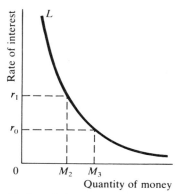

(i) Transactions and precautionary demands are proportional to money national income

(ii) Speculative demand is negatively related to the interest rate

FIGURE 32.1 The Demand for Money as a Function of the Interest Rate and Income. The quantity of money demanded varies positively with national income valued in current prices, part (i), and negatively with the rate of interest, part (ii).

income valued in current prices and *negatively* with the rate of interest.

Figure 32.1 shows the influences of money national income and the rate of interest on the quantity of money demanded. Recall that since Y stands for real national income, we must multiply it by the average level of money prices, P, to obtain money national income, PY.

In part (i) of the Figure, the demand for money is shown as varying directly with money national income, along the curve T. As money national income rises from PY_0 to PY_1, firms and households increase their demand for money from M_0 to M_1. In part (ii), the demand for money varies inversely with the rate of interest, along the curve L. As the rate of interest falls from r_1 to r_0, firms and households increase their demand for money from M_2 to M_3.[1]

Real and nominal value in money demand and supply: Everything that we have done is in terms of nominal values. The current money value of national income determines the nominal amount of money needed for transactions purposes. In equilibrium, the nominal demand for money, measured as so many pounds sterling, must equal the nominal supply of money, also measured in pounds sterling.

It is possible to re-do the whole analysis using real rather than nominal values. In this case, the real demand for, and the real supply of, money is measured in purchasing power units, e.g. as so many months' worth of GDP. In equilibrium, the real demand for money is equal to the real supply. In practice, the real demand is found by deflating the nominal demand by some index of the general price level.

Since we are interested, among other things, in how changes in the price level affect monetary equilibrium, it is simpler to use nominal quantities. In this case, a rise in the price level raises nominal national income, and raises the nominal amount of money needed, and hence demanded, for transactions and precautionary purposes. This creates excess demand for money and sets the transmission mechanism in play.[1]

Liquidity preference for a given level of national income

The function that shows how the total demand for money varies with the rate of interest is called the LIQUIDITY PREFERENCE (LP) FUNCTION. It shows the public's demand to hold the liquid asset money, rather than the illiquid asset bonds. Note that the liquidity preference function is also often called the DEMAND FOR MONEY FUNCTION. In the first of these terms, 'liquidity preference' refers to the choice being made: people are expressing their preferences between holding the liquid asset, money – which usually earns no interest – and the illiquid asset, bonds – which does earn interest. In the

---

1 Beware of a possible confusion in the notation. M_D and M_S are the symbols for two variables, the demand for money and the supply of money. Particular values of the variables are indicated by numerical subscripts. Thus M_0, M_1, M_2, M_3 indicate specific values that are taken by (in this case) the demand for money. These might, for example, be £50,000m, £70,000m, £40,000m and £60,000m respectively. Similarly, Y is the symbol for the variable called real national income, while Y_0 and Y_1 stand for two specific values of real national income, possibly £300bn and £400bn respectively.

---

1 Examiners sometimes ask students to distinguish between the analysis done in real and nominal terms. This footnote is only for those who wish to follow this distinction out. If we wished to do the analysis just given in the text using real demand and real supply, we would find that the rise in the price level reduced the real supply of money (nominal money deflated by the price level), leaving real demand unchanged and creating an excess demand for money which sets the transmission mechanism in play. Both real and nominal analyses are dealing with the same phenomenon, only they deal with it using slightly different concepts.

A few symbols do wonders in showing what is going on here: If M_D and M_S are the nominal demand and supply of money, we have, using nominal variables, the equilibrium condition that $M_D = M_S$. A rise in P increases M_D thus creating excess demand for money. To use real variables, we divide both demand and supply by the price level so that, in equilibrium, $M_D/P = M_S/P$. Now a rise in P lowers M_S/P but creates the same situation of excess demand for money. In other words, it means the same thing to say that a rise in the price level creates excess demand for money by *increasing the nominal demand for money* or by *reducing its real supply*.

second of these terms, 'demand for money' is a straight-forward reference to the amount of money balances that the public wishes to hold.

In subsequent chapters, we shall often show only the function relating the demand for money to the rate of interest, i.e. the liquidity preference function. Since the demand for money actually depends on both the rate of interest, r, and money national income, PY, any given LP function, showing the relation between the demand for money and the rate of interest, must be drawn for a *given level of PY*. Changes in PY thus shift the LP function. This important point is illustrated by relating what we have already studied in Figure 32.1 to Figure 32.2.

Let money national income be constant at PY_0 in part (i) of that Figure. The demand for money that depends on income is then M_0. When the rate of interest is r_0 in part (ii) of Figure 32.1, the demand for money that depends on the rate of interest is seen to be M_3. The total demand for money is then the sum of M_0 and M_3 in parts (i) and (ii) of Figure 32.1, which we plot as M_4 in Figure 32.2. As the rate of interest varies, the total demand for money varies along the line LP in Figure 32.2. For example, if the interest rate rises to r_1, the demand for money falls to M_5, which is the sum of M_0 and M_2 shown in the two parts of Figure 32.1.

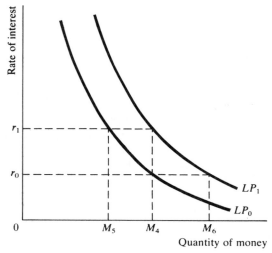

FIGURE 32.2 The Liquidity Preference Curve. This curve shows how the total demand for money varies with the rate of interest; it is drawn for a given level of nominal national income; a change in nominal national income shifts the curve rightwards, as from LP to LP', when income rises, and leftwards, as from LP' to LP, when income falls.

Now, however, let national income increase to PY_1 in Figure 32.1(i). The demand for money that depends on income rises to M_1, as shown in Figure 32.1(i). Now more money is demanded at each rate of interest. This causes the LP function in Figure 32.2 to shift rightwards by the amount $M_1 - M_0$ to LP'. For example, at interest rate r_0 the total demand for money is now M_6, which is the sum of M_3 and M_1 in parts (i) and (ii) of Figure 32.1.

It is important to understand the distinction between movements along and shifts of the LP function. The function itself relates the demand for money to the interest rate. Changes in the interest rate cause changes in the quantity of money demanded, which are shown by movements along the curve, since it is drawn for a given level of money national income. Changes in money income shift the curve: a rise in income shifts the curve rightwards, while a fall in income shifts it leftwards.[1]

Conclusion

The theory of the demand for money is important because, as we shall see in the next chapter, the demand for money provides a key link between the stock of money and the flow of national income. Although you have studied many issues in this chapter, all that you need to know for what follows is that:

Firms and households will wish to hold more money the higher is the money value of national income, which creates their need for it, and the lower is the interest rate, which is the opportunity cost of holding it.

---

1 This is the same point as has been made familiar from demand and supply curves. The demand curve shows the relation between the demand for a commodity and that commodity's price; changes in other variables that influence quantity demanded, *shift* the demand curve.

Summary

1 A redeemable bond is a promise to repay a fixed principal at a given redemption date and to pay a fixed interest payment in the interim. An irredeemable bond (e.g. a consol) has no redemption date.

2 A bill is a promise to pay a stated sum at some future date. Interest arises because the bill is *discounted* by purchasing it at a price below its future redemption value.

3 The market value of any bond or bill, which is called its present value, varies inversely with the rate of interest.

4 The demand to hold money depends on the transactions, precautionary and speculative motives.

5 In the Keynesian theory of the speculative motive, wealth-owners hold their wealth in bonds – in anticipation of capital gains on bond holdings – when the rate of interest is above their normal expected rate

and hold their wealth in money – in expectation of capital losses on bond holdings – when the rate of interest is below their normal expected rate.

6 In Tobin's theory of the speculative motive, people balance the risk in holding bonds, whose prices may change, against the interest forgone by holding money. The higher the interest yield, the greater the proportion of their wealth people will hold in bonds and, hence, the lower the demand for money.

7 The *liquidity preference (LP) function*, also called the *demand for money function*, relates the demand for money to the interest rate along a curve whose negative slope is predicted both by Keynes' and by Tobin's theory of the speculative demand for money. It is drawn for a fixed level of nominal national income. A change in the interest rate is shown by a movement along the *LP* curve, while a change in nominal income shifts the curve – outwards if nominal national income rises and inwards if nominal income falls.

Questions

1 Which One or More of the following are characteristics of (i) a bill, (ii) a redeemable bond, and (iii) an irredeemable bond?
   (a) a fixed redemption date
   (b) a fixed payment of interest each period
   (c) a market value that fluctuates over time
   (d) a risky investment
   (e) a fixed redeemable value

2 A person buys a newly issued three months' £10,000 Treasury bill for £9700. In a month's time she sells it for £9850.
   (a) What was the approximate annual market rate of interest when she bought the bill?
   (b) What was the approximate annual market rate of interest when she sold the bill?
   (c) Did she have a capital gain or a capital loss on her transaction?

3 True or False?
   (a) The rate of interest and the price of bonds are negatively associated with each other.
   (b) The transactions and precautionary motives make the demand for money positively associated with the level of nominal national income.
   (c) The speculative motive makes the demand for money negatively associated with the rate of interest.
   (d) If people expect the interest rate to rise in the near future, they will be inclined to increase the proportion of their wealth held in money now.
   (e) A rise in nominal national income shifts the liquidity preference function leftwards.

4 If interest rates rise a great deal, as they did in the early 1980s, what will happen to the amount of money households and firms wish to hold?

5 In Figure 32.2 what would have to happen to the *LP* function to make the demand for money M_5 when the rate of interest was r_0? What change in real national income or in the price level could bring this about?

6 What do you think the introduction of credit cards did to the liquidity preference function?

In Part 4 we saw that equilibrium national income changes whenever the aggregate expenditure function shifts. This can be caused by a shift in any of its components: C, I, G or $(X - M)$. Consider each of these in turn. The consumption function shifts whenever there is a change in households' propensity to spend and save out of disposable income, or whenever there is a change in tax rates that alters the relation between disposable income and national income. Desired investment shifts whenever there is a change in any of the variables that influence it. Government expenditure shifts whenever there is a change in the government's spending. The net export function shifts whenever there is either a change in the propensity to import or an autonomous shift in exports.

In this chapter we show how the aggregate expenditure function can be shifted by monetary forces. We do this by explaining the rate of interest, which was formerly an exogenous variable, within our theory. This also has the effect of making investment, which is influenced by the interest rate, into an endogenous variable that is explained within our theory.

THE LIQUIDITY PREFERENCE THEORY OF INTEREST

Money demand and money supply: To start our explanation of the determination of the interest rate, let us recall what we have already learned about the demand for, and the supply of, money.

On the demand side, the key point was established in Chapter 32, where we saw that the demand for money depends on the level of national income and on the rate of interest. (See Figure 32.2.)

On the supply side, it is convenient to begin our study with the assumptions that the retail banks have created all the deposit money that they regard as prudent on the basis of their current reserves. As a result, the money supply is an autonomous (or exogenously determined) variable and it remains constant unless changed by some force outside of our theory (such as new cash deposits received by the system as a whole). In Chapter 34 we shall see how the government attempts to change the money supply through its monetary policy.

Monetary equilibrium: Next we need to define what is called MONETARY EQUILIBRIUM. This occurs when the demand for money equals the supply of money. In Chapter 8, we saw that in a competitive market a commodity's price adjusts to ensure an equilibrium where the quantity demanded equals the quantity supplied. We now ask, what does the same job for money? The answer is that *the rate of interest does the job of equating the quantity of money demanded to the available supply; i.e. it does the job of producing monetary equilibrium.*

In Figure 33.1, we see how the interest rate produces monetary equilibrium. The money supply is fixed exogenously at the specific quantity M_0. Because (by assumption) the money supply does not change with the rate of interest, the supply curve of money, M_S, is shown as completely inelastic at the quantity M_0. The curve marked LP is the liquidity preference function that we first met in Figure 32.2. It shows how the demand to hold money varies with the rate of interest, and it is drawn for a specified level of money national income. Monetary equilibrium occurs at the interest rate r_0, where the LP and the M_S curves intersect. At that interest rate, everyone in the economy – households and firms – is just willing to hold all of the money that is available to be held.

Monetary disequilibrium: Now let us ask what happens if the current interest rate is not r_0. First, let the rate be below its equilibrium value. For example, at the interest rate r_1 in the Figure, the demand for money is M_1 while the supply remains fixed at M_0 by assumption. Thus there is an excess demand for money of $M_1 - M_0$. As we saw in Chapter 32, an excess demand for money causes people to offer bonds for sale in an attempt to increase their money holdings. This will force the rate of interest upwards, and it will only stop rising (bond prices stop falling) when the interest rate reaches r_0. At that interest rate, the quantity of money demanded is equal to the available supply of M_0 and people will no longer be trying to turn bonds into money; instead, they will be content to hold the quantities of money and bonds that are currently in existence.

Second, consider what happens if the rate of interest is above the equilibrium rate. For example, at the interest rate r_2, the quantity of money demanded is M_2, while the supply still remains fixed at M_0. Thus there will be an excess supply of money, $M_0 - M_2$. As a result, everyone will be trying to buy bonds with their excess money balances. This behaviour will force the rate of interest down (the price of bonds rises) until it reaches r_0, at which point the quantity of money demanded will have risen to equal the fixed money supply of M_0.

Conclusion: The important conclusion is that *the condition for monetary equilibrium is that the rate of interest will be such that everyone is just willing to hold the existing supply of money.*

In the previous chapter, we described the *liquidity preference theory of the demand for money.* We have

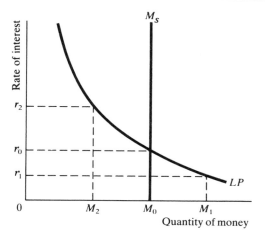

FIGURE 33.1 Monetary Equilibrium and the Rate of Interest. The interest rate rises when there is an excess demand for money and falls when there is an excess supply of money, and reaches equilibrium where LP and M_S intersect.

now developed what is called the LIQUIDITY PREFERENCE THEORY OF INTEREST-RATE DETERMINATION. It is also called the PORT-FOLIO BALANCE THEORY. The first term alludes to Keynes' theory of the demand for money as a function of the interest rate, while the second term alludes to Tobin's theory of the same phenomenon. (See Chapter 32, page 360.) In either case, the mechanism at work is people's decisions on how to divide their portfolios between the two available wealth-holding assets, money and bonds. We have seen that both Keynes and Tobin developed theories to explain the reason why the demand for money is negatively related to the interest rate. Both of these theories are compatible with everything we have said in this chapter so far. The difference between the two lies solely *in the explanations that they give of what lies behind* the down-ward-sloping LP curve. These differences do not need to concern us here because all that matters for the rest of this chapter is that the demand for money is — for whatever reason — negatively related to the interest rate.

THE MONETARY TRANSMISSION MECHANISM

Now that these important preliminaries are behind us, we can turn to the main subjects of this chapter: to understand the mechanism by which monetary changes — changes in the demand and/or the supply of money — are transmitted into changes in desired expenditure and, therefore, alter the equilibrium level of national income. This is called the MONETARY TRANSMISSION MECHANISM.

To understand the transmission mechanism, we study how the economy reacts when it is disturbed by what is called a *monetary shock*. In general, a SHOCK is anything that disturbs an equilibrium. A *monetary* shock is any *monetary* change that disturbs *monetary* equilibrium. One major cause of shocks is a change in any exogenous (autonomous) variable, but there are, as we shall see, other causes as well.

The first monetary shock that we shall study is an increase in the supply of money. Money is still assumed exogenous — i.e. unaffected by anything within our theory — but we now allow for an exogenous change in the money supply.

An Increase in the Supply of Money

There are several links in the transmission mechanism, and we study them one at a time.

Link 1: From money to the interest rate

The first link is based on the liquidity preference theory of interest which we have just studied.

In Figure 33.2(i) the original supply of money is M_0, yielding an equilibrium interest rate of r_0. Now let the amount of money increase from M_0 to M_1. The supply curve of money shifts from M_S to M'_S, and, at the existing rate of interest, r_0, there is excess supply of money. People still wish to hold only M_0 of money balances, but M_1 is now available. What will happen?

In an effort to eliminate their excess holdings of money, everyone attempts to buy bonds. But *everyone* cannot simultaneously buy bonds, because this means that no one

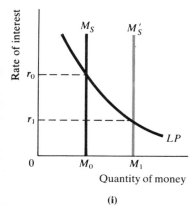

(i)

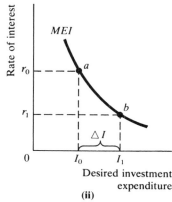

(ii)

FIGURE 33.2 The Effects of Changes in the Money Supply on Desired Investment Expenditure. An increase in the money supply, from M_S to M'_S, reduces the rate of interest, from r_0 to r_1, and increases desired investment expenditure by ΔI from I_0 to I_1; a reduction has the opposite effect.

is trying to sell them. The result of the attempt to turn money into bonds is that the price of bonds rises (i.e. rate of interest falls.) When the interest rate has fallen to r_1, the quantity of money demanded will have risen to equal the available supply of M_1. Monetary equilibrium is thus re-established, though at a lower rate of interest.

Link 2: From the interest rate to investment expenditure

The second link in the transmission mechanism is the one that relates interest rates to desired investment expenditure. On pages 000–0 of Chapter 24 we saw that desired investment expenditure is negatively related to the interest rate: the lower the interest rate, the higher is desired investment expenditure, and vice versa. (This important discussion must be reread now.) This relation is shown in Figure 33.2 (ii). The curve in that Figure is called a MARGINAL EFFICIENCY OF INVESTMENT CURVE (or just a DEMAND FOR INVESTMENT CURVE). It shows that the lower the rate of interest, the larger will be the number of investment opportunities that will show a profit and, hence, the larger the volume of investment expenditure that firms wish to undertake.

Remember that investment includes investment in inventories and new housing construction as well as in fixed capital. Although fixed investment may respond only sluggishly to changes in the interest rate (a matter further discussed in Chapter 34), inventory investment and purchasing of new housing tends to be more sensitive. In any case the evidence is clear that monetary shocks do influence aggregate desired expenditure although the specific channels through which this happens are subject to some debate.[1]

Note that, because both parts of Figure 33.2 have the interest rate on the vertical axis, the interest rate can be compared between the two parts. Both parts show an initial equilibrium with the quantity of money of M_0 (shown by the inelastic money supply curve M_S), and an interest rate of r_0. This gives rise to a level of desired investment expenditure of I_0 in part (ii) (point a).

When this equilibrium is disturbed by an increase in the money supply to M_1 (shown by the money supply curve M'_S), the rate of interest falls to r_1. Part (ii) of the Figure tells us that the fall in the interest rate from r_0 to r_1 increases desired investment expenditure from I_0 to I_1 (point b). This increase is marked ΔI in the Figure.

Interest elasticity of investment: The MEI curve shown in part (ii) of Figure 33.2 relates investment to the rate of interest. Its negative slope shows that, as the inter-

est rate falls, desired investment expenditure rises. The amount by which investment responds is measured by THE INTEREST ELASTICITY OF INVESTMENT, which is defined as the percentage change in investment divided by the percentage change in the interest rate that brought it about.[1] We can write this

$$\frac{\text{per cent change in Investment}}{\text{per cent change in Interest Rate}}$$

If the percentage change in investment exceeds the percentage change in income, we say that the investment relation is *interest-elastic*. For example, a 5 per cent fall in the interest rate might lead to a 10 per cent rise in investment expenditure. In this case, the interest elasticity of investment would be 2.

If the percentage change in investment expenditure is less than the percentage change in the interest rate that brought it about, we say that the investment relation is *interest-inelastic*. For example, a 5 per cent fall in the interest rate might lead to only a 2 per cent rise in investment expenditure. In this case the interest elasticity of investment would be 2/5 which is 0.4.

Link 3: From investment expenditure to aggregate expenditure

So far, we have seen that an increase in the money supply leads to a fall in the interest rate which, in turn, leads to an increase in desired investment expenditure. We know from previous chapters (see e.g. Figure 24.7 on page 280) that an increase in desired investment expenditure causes an upward shift in the aggregate desired expenditure curve.[2] The amount of the shift is given by ΔI in Figure 33.2 (ii).

Other Monetary Changes

A reduction in the money supply: A reduction in the money supply reverses the process just studied.

In Figure 33.2 let the original money supply be M_1. This produces a rate of interest of r_1 in part (i) of the Figure and investment expenditure of I_1 in part (ii). Now let the money supply fall to M_0. This causes a shortage of money at the interest rate r_1. People try to sell bonds to replenish money balances. This pushes the price of bonds down, which means a rise in the interest rate. When the rate has risen to r_0, people are content with holding the smaller money supply and monetary equilibrium is thus restored. The rise in the interest rate to r_0 lowers investment by ΔI in part (ii) of the Figure from I_1 to I_0. The fall in desired investment

---

1 Another important channel by which the interest rate affects aggregate expenditure is by influencing that part of consumption expenditure that is financed through borrowing such as goods bought on hire purchase or with money borrowed from banks. We do not include this in our simple theory of consumption but it is an important factor in the transmission mechanism. For our simple theory, the interest-rate changes affect only investment. To assess the workings of the monetary adjustment mechanism in reality, however, one must take all *interest-sensitive expenditure* into account.

---

1 Elasticity, you will remember from Chapter 7, is the measure used in economics for the responsiveness of any one variable, call it X, to a change in another variable, call it Y. It takes the form: per cent change in X divided by per cent change in Y.

2 Generalizing from the experience of the 1930s, it used to be commonly asserted that aggregate expenditure was almost completely interest-insensitive. The experience of very high interest rates in the 1980s, however, showed that if central banks are willing to let interest rates rise high enough they can bring about major reductions in aggregate expenditure.

expenditure by the amount ΔI shifts the aggregate expenditure curve, downwards by that amount.

A fall in the demand for money: So far we have looked at shocks arising from changes in the *supply of* money. Equivalent disequilibria can be caused by shocks arising from changes in the *demand for* money. On the one hand, a fall in the demand for money – a leftward shift in the liquidity preference function – creates an excess supply of money, just as does a rise in the supply of money. On the other hand, a rise in the demand for money – a rightward shift in the LP function – creates an excess demand for money, just as does a fall in the supply of money.

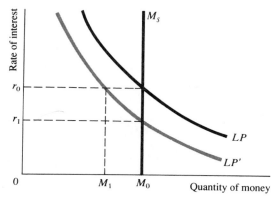

FIGURE 33.3 Changes in the Demand for Money Cause Changes in the Interest Rate. A fall in the demand for money, from LP to LP', lowers interest rates from r_0 to r_1; a rise does the reverse.

Figure 33.3 shows the effects of a decrease in the demand for money. The money supply is held constant at M_0 and the initial demand for money is given by the curve LP. The equilibrium interest rate is r_0. Now let the demand for money fall, taking the LP curve to LP'. This creates an excess supply of money of $M_0 - M_1$ at the original interest rate of r_0. People try to purchase bonds, thus driving up the price of bonds, which means a fall in the interest rate. When the rate falls to r_1, the public is willing to hold the existing stock of money and monetary equilibrium is restored.

The fall in the interest rate then sets the monetary transmission mechanism going. Desired investment expenditure rises, and this raises aggregate desired expenditure as well.

We see from this that a fall in the demand for money has the same effect as a rise in the supply of money. Both create a monetary disequilibrium that reduces interest rates and, by increasing desired investment, shifts the aggregate desired expenditure curve upwards.

A rise in the demand for money: A rise in the demand for money means a rightward shift in the liquidity preference function. The results are shown in Figure 33.3, where the liquidity preference function shifts from LP' to LP. The shortage of money causes the price of bonds to fall as people try to replenish their money balances by selling

bonds. The rate of interest rises from r_1 to r_0, thus restoring monetary equilibrium. This causes desired investment expenditure to fall, thus shifting the aggregate desired expenditure curve downwards.

We see that a rise in the demand for money has the same effect as a fall in the supply of money. Both create a monetary disequilibrium that raises interest rates and, by lowering investment, also lowers aggregate desired expenditure.

The Monetary Transmission Mechanism Summarized

The transmission mechanism provides a connection between monetary forces and real expenditure flows. It has three links – it works (1) from a change in the supply of, or demand for, money, to a change in interest rates and bond prices, (2) through a change in investment expenditure caused by the change in interest rates, (3) to a *shift* in the aggregate desired expenditure curve caused by the change in investment. Increases in the supply of money and decreases in the demand for money shift the aggregate expenditure curve upwards; reductions in the supply of money and increases in the demand for money shift the aggregate expenditure curve downwards.

The mechanism is so important that it is worthwhile summarizing it schematically. The sequence of events summarized in Figure 33.4 is set in motion either by an increase in the supply of money or by a decrease in the demand for money. The shock is called *expansionary* because it raises aggregate desired expenditure. Figure 33.5 shows the opposite case of a *contractionary monetary shock*. Either a decrease in the supply of money or an increase in the demand for money sets up the sequence of events summarized in the Figure. The shock is called contractionary because it lowers aggregate desired expenditure.

MONETARY SHOCKS AT VARIOUS INCOME LEVELS

We can now get some substantial payoff from our theory. To do this, we use Figure 33.6 to investigate the effects of expansionary monetary shocks, first when equilibrium national income is below potential income and, second, when it is equal to potential income.

First look at part (iii) of that Figure. It shows three alternative aggregate expenditure curves, a 45° line, and the level of potential, or full-employment, national income, Y_F. A vertical line is drawn through Y_F to indicate the resource constraints on further output: real national income cannot exceed Y_F because sufficient factors of production are not available.

Unemployed Resources

In the case of unemployed resources we only need to use part (iii) of the Figure. The initial aggregate expenditure

THE TRANSMISSION MECHANISM FOR
AN EXPANSIONARY MONETARY SHOCK

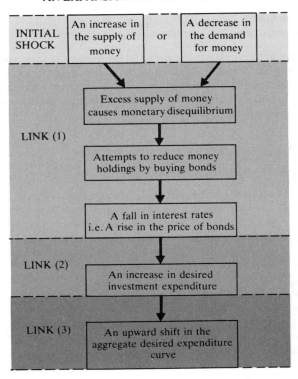

FIGURE 33.4 The Monetary Transmission Mechanism for an Expansionary Monetary Shock. An increase in the supply of money or a decrease in the demand for money sets an expansionary process in train.

THE TRANSMISSION MECHANISM FOR A
CONTRACTIONARY MONETARY SHOCK

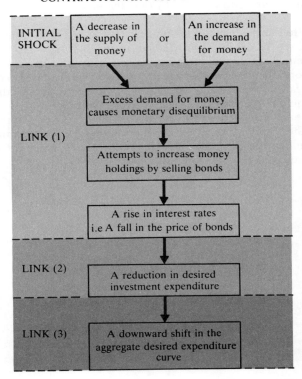

FIGURE 33.5 The Monetary Transmission Mechanism for a Contractionary Monetary Shock. A decrease in the supply of money or an increase in the demand for money sets a contractionary process in train.

function is E. Equilibrium national income is Y_0, which is below potential income of Y_F. The increase in desired expenditure, which we saw follows from an increase in the money supply, shifts the aggregate desired expenditure curve upwards, thereby increasing the equilibrium level of national income. If the rise in E is sufficient to shift the expenditure function all the way to E_F, actual income rises to its full-employment level of Y_F.

This is nothing more than an application of the results that we obtained in Part 4 of this book; the only difference here is in the *cause* of the shift in the aggregate expenditure function. Our conclusion is that, when actual national income is less than potential income, an increase in the money supply can, by reducing interest rates and raising desired investment expenditure, increase equilibrium national income and employment. (Do not forget what we reminded you of earlier in this chapter: 'investment' stands for more than just investment in fixed capital.)

Full Employment

The analysis so far assumes that an increase in aggregate expenditure can increase the level of real national income. But what if equilibrium national income is already at Y_F? We analyse this important case in three steps – initial

equilibrium, the creation of an inflationary gap, and the elimination of the inflationary gap – using all three parts of Figure 33.6.

The initial equilibrium: Initially the money supply is M_0 in part (i) of the Figure. The money supply curve M_S intersects the liquidity preference curve LP, to establish an interest rate of r_0. In part (ii) of the Figure, we see that the interest rate r_0 induces investment expenditure of I_0. This amount of investment, added to consumption, government expenditure and net exports, yields an aggregate desired expenditure curve that we assume takes the position E_F in part (iii) of the Figure. This means that *equilibrium is initially at potential income,* Y_F.

The creation of an inflationary gap: Now let us see what happens when the money supply increases, starting the sequence already summarized in Figure 33.4. Let the money supply increase to M_1 in part (i) of Figure 33.6, shifting the money supply curve to M'_S.

Since the demand for money is still given by the curve labelled LP, the interest rate falls to r_1 and desired investment expenditure rises by ΔI to I_1. This shifts the aggregate desired expenditure function upwards to E' in part (iii) of the Figure.

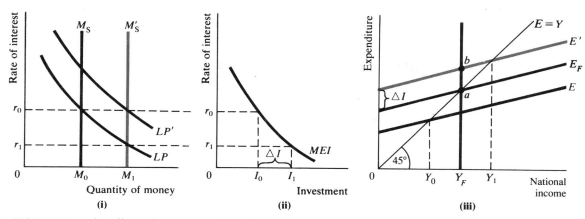

FIGURE 33.6 The Effects of an Increase in the Money Supply with Unemployment and Full Employment. In part (i), the money supply curve shifts from M_0 to M_1, reducing the interest rate from r_0 to r_1. This raises investment by ΔI from I_0 to I_1 in part (i).

In the case of initially unemployed resources, the initial aggregate desired expenditure curve is E and the increase in I shifts the curve to E_F, taking equilibrium national income from Y_0 to Y_F.

In the case of initially fully employed resources, the initial curve is E_F and the increase in I takes it to E'. An inflationary gap of ab is opened up, and the general price level starts to rise. This increases the demand for money. When the LP curve has shifted to LP', the rate of interest has risen to r_0, investment has fallen back to I_0, taking the aggregate expenditure curve back to E_F. At that point, the monetary adjustment mechanism has eliminated the inflationary gap.

If resources were available to produce more output, national income would rise to Y_1 and that would be the end of the story. But in the case we are considering, equilibrium income is initially at the full-employment level. As a result, real national income remains at Y_F and the shift of the aggregate expenditure function to E' opens up an inflationary gap, shown by the distance ab in the Figure.

The removal of the inflationary gap: The next step in the sequence of events is an extremely important one; it is the reason why *single, once-for-all,* monetary shocks cause the price level to rise but *not* forever, or without limit.

The excess demand causes the general price level to rise. The rise in the price level raises the money value of national income, and hence raises the money value of all transactions in the economy. As we saw in Chapter 32, more money will now be demanded at each rate of interest for transactions purposes. This shifts the LP curve to the right in the way that we analysed in Figure 32.2 on page 362.

At the existing rate of interest, there is now an excess demand for money. This starts the monetary adjustment mechanism in motion according to the sequence outlined in Figure 33.5 for a contractionary monetary shock. The interest rate rises, desired investment expenditure falls, and the aggregate expenditure curve starts to shift downwards again. This contractionary process will continue until the inflationary gap has been eliminated, because, as long as there is such a gap, the price level will be rising and the LP curve will be shifting to the right.

When we last looked at Figure 33.6 at the end of the section on the creation of an inflationary gap, the money supply was M_1, the interest rate r_1, investment I_1 and the aggregate expenditure curve E', yielding an inflationary

gap of ab. Now, however, as the price level rises, the LP curve shifts to the right, indicating a larger demand for money at each interest rate. The price level goes on rising and the liquidity preference curve goes on shifting to the right until it reaches LP' in part (i) of the Figure. At that point, the curve LP' intersects with the money supply curve M'_S to yield an interest rate of r_0. This restores desired investment expenditure to its original level of I_0 and, hence, shifts the aggregate desired expenditure function back to E_F. *The rise in the money supply has ended up having no effect other than raising the price level.*

This is the long-run neutrality of money that we first studied in Chapter 30:

Starting from a position of full-employment equilibrium, a once-for-all increase in the quantity of money does have real effects during the period of disequilibrium, altering interest rates and desired investment expenditure. When equilibrium is restored, however, interest rates, and each of the components of desired expenditure, will have returned to their original levels. Real national income is unchanged and the only permanent effect of a change in the quantity of money is a change in the price level.

The Automatic Elimination of an Inflationary Gap

The process that we have just outlined is important. It eliminates any inflationary gap, no matter what its initial cause, *provided that the money supply remains constant.*

The process works as follows:

1　an inflationary gap causes the price level to rise;
2　this increases the level of nominal national income;
3　this increases the transactions demand for money, thus shifting the *LP* function to the right;
4　this raises the interest rate;
5　this lowers desired investment expenditure, thus shifting the aggregate expenditure curve downwards and reducing the inflationary gap.

This self-correcting process is the reason why price levels and the money supply have been linked for so long in economics. We shall see in Chapter 38 that many forces can cause the price level to rise. Yet, whatever the cause, *unless the money supply is continuously expanded*, the increase in the price level will itself set up forces that will remove any initial inflationary gap and so will stop the inflation.

The process by which an inflationary gap is removed is sometimes called the 'monetary adjustment mechanism'. It is, however, just an application of the monetary transmission mechanism operating when there is full employment. The transmission mechanism shows how a monetary shock is transmitted into a change in desired real expenditure. The monetary shocks come from changes in the demand or supply of money which we first took to be exogenous. An inflationary gap causes *endogenous* changes in the demand for money. The excess demand associated with the gap causes the price level to rise, which increases the amount of money demanded for transactions and precautionary purposes, which raises the interest rate, which lowers interest-sensitive expenditure, which reduces the real excess demand.

This shows that an inflationary gap sets up monetary forces which, *if the money supply is held constant*, decrease desired real expenditure sufficiently to remove the gap.

We have twice stated the key qualification to the operation of the self-correcting mechanism that eliminates an inflationary gap: *the money supply must remain constant*. To see why this is such an important provision, let us see how the mechanism can be frustrated.

Frustration of the mechanism for removing an inflationary gap

The self-correcting mechanism for removing an inflationary gap can be frustrated *if* the money supply is increased at the same rate that prices are rising. Say that the price level is rising at 10 per cent a year under the pressure of an inflationary gap. Demand for money balances will then also rise at about 10 per cent per year – i.e. the *LP* curve will be shifting outwards to the right at that rate. If the money supply is held constant, the interest rate will be rising steadily.

Now suppose that the Bank of England also allows the money supply to rise at 10 per cent per year. (Remember we are assuming throughout this chapter that the money supply is fixed, exogenously, by the central bank.) This possibility is shown in Figure 33.7. The initial curves are

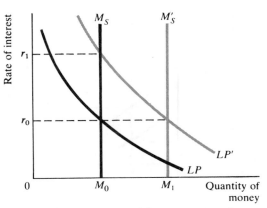

FIGURE 33.7　The Frustration of the Automatic Adjustment Mechanism. A rise in the supply of money that parallels a rise in demand for money can prevent interest rates from rising and so leave real expenditure unchanged as, e.g., when the curves shift from *LP* and M_S to *LP'* and M'_S.

LP and M_S (money supply M_0). The initial interest rate is thus r_0, which is assumed to give rise to an inflationary gap. The resulting rise in the price level shifts the liquidity preference function to *LP'*. If the money supply is held constant, the interest rate rises to r_1. Instead, however, let the money supply be increased to M_1 at the same time as the *LP* curve shifts to *LP'*. No excess demand for money now develops at the interest rate r_0, since the extra money needed to meet the rising demand is forthcoming. The interest rate will *not* rise to reduce desired aggregate expenditure and so the inflationary gap will not be removed.

An inflation is said to be VALIDATED when the money supply is increased as fast as the price level is increasing so that the monetary adjustment mechanism is frustrated. A validated inflation can go on indefinitely although, as we shall see in Chapter 39, possibly not at a constant rate.

Conclusion

Now that we know how changes in the supply of money affect aggregate desired expenditure and hence national income, we understand why policy-makers are concerned about the behaviour of the monetary part of the economy. Our task in the next chapter is to see how the central bank tries to control the monetary sector in a conscious attempt to influence aggregate expenditure.

Summary

1 According to the liquidity preference (or portfolio balance) theory of interest rates, when wealth-holders are content to hold the existing amounts of bonds and money, the interest rate is in equilibrium.

2 If wealth-holders feel that they have too many bonds and too little money, their attempts to sell bonds will drive down the price of bonds (drive up the rate of interest) until everyone is no longer trying to add to their money balances.

3 The transmission mechanism links monetary shocks to shifts in the aggregate desired expenditure curve. The initiating *expansionary* shocks are either an increase in the supply of money, or a reduction in the demand for money.

4 There are three links in the transmission mechanism: (1), the monetary shock drives interest rates down. In step (2), the fall in the interest rate increases desired investment. In step (3), the rise in desired investment shifts the aggregate expenditure curve upwards.

5 The two initiating *contractionary* shocks are a decrease in the supply of money, or an increase in the demand for money. This then (1) drives interest rates up, (2) reduces desired investment, and (3) shifts the aggregate expenditure curve downwards.

6 Contractionary monetary shocks reduce national income. Expansionary monetary shocks increase national income if unemployed resources exist.

7 If resources are already fully employed, an expansionary monetary shock will create an inflationary gap. The price level will then rise until the inflationary gap is removed. In the final equilibrium, the increase in the quantity of money will have driven up the price level but restored national income and the interest rate to their original levels.

8 The transmissions mechanism removes the inflationary gap: given a fixed money supply, the rising money value of transactions increases the demand for money, which increases the interest rate, which reduces aggregate desired expenditure.

9 If the money supply is increased at the same rate as prices are rising, the automatic adjustment mechanism is frustrated because no money shortage develops to drive interest rates upwards. An inflation that is allowed to continue because the money supply is increasing as fast as the price level is increasing is said to be *validated*.

Questions

1 Which One or More of the following would cause an expansionary monetary shock?
  (a) A rise in the quantity of money.
  (b) A fall in the price level (due, say, to a fall in import prices).
  (c) An increase in the precautionary demand for money due to increased uncertainty about payments and receipts.
  (d) A leftward shift in the *LP* curve.

2 Choose one of the bracketed alternatives in each case. A fall in the demand for money is (a contractionary/an expansionary) monetary shock; people will try to (buy/sell) bonds, forcing the price of bonds (up/down) and the interest rate (up/down); this will lead to (an increase/a decrease) in desired investment and (an upward/a downward) shift in the aggregate desired expenditure function; this changes (real national income/the price level) when there are unemployed resources and (real national income/the price level) when resources are fully employed.

3 True or False?
  (a) The rate of interest equates the demand for and supply of money.

  (b) Excess demand for money pushes the rate of interest up.
  (c) Excess supply of money pushes the price of bonds down.
  (d) An expansionary monetary shock occurs when either the money supply increases or the demand for money falls.
  (e) The transmission mechanism links monetary shocks to changes in the distribution of income.
  (f) An inflation caused by an inflationary gap must come to a halt if the money supply is held constant.

4 In the late 1970s and early 1980s a large number of financial innovations allowed the private sector to finance a given volume of transactions with much diminished holdings of money. What kind of a shock did this administer to the economy?

5 In Figure 33.6 let the initial curves be *LP* and M'_s in part (i), *MEI* in part (ii), and *E* in part (iii):
  (a) What are the equilibrium values for national income, the rate of interest and investment?
  (b) Now let an increase in government expenditure shift the expenditure curve to E_F. What happens to income, interest and investment?

34 The Bank of England and Monetary Policy

We saw in the previous chapter how changes in the demand for, and the supply of, money affect aggregate desired expenditure. In this chapter, we study 'monetary policy' which we defined in Chapter 22 as the manipulation of the amount of money and credit available, and the cost of that credit to borrowers (i.e. interest rates), in an attempt to influence total demand.

SOME PRELIMINARIES

Before we begin our study of the Bank of England and its operation of monetary policy, we need to drop a simplifying assumption and allow for some important complications.

Many financial assets

In order to study the monetary transmission mechanism in its simplest form in Chapter 33, we grouped all financial assets into two categories – money, and everything else, which we called bonds. Now, in order to study the details of how monetary policy works, we need once again to distinguish among the many different financial assets that can be held by the public. First, there is currency and non-interest-bearing financial assets such as some sight deposits at banks. Then there is a range of assets running from higher to lower levels of liquidity and usually from lower to higher rates of interest. Included are interest-bearing deposits at banks and building societies, bills of exchange and Treasury bills, medium- and long-term securities, including gilt-edged treasury stocks, and ending with undated or irredeemable securities, which are of infinite term.[1]

The structure of interest rates

In Chapter 22, we distinguished between the long- and the short-term rates of interest. In subsequent chapters, it was convenient to treat all financial assets as a single composite asset called 'bonds'. In that case, there was only one interest rate. Now that we are allowing for many financial assets, there are several rates of interest, one for each type of asset. These rates are, however, closely related to each other. The whole set of relations among these rates is called *the structure of interest rates*.

The link that creates an interrelated structure among these rates is that wealth-owners must willingly hold these assets in their portfolios. This means that the rates of return must vary among assets to compensate for other characteristics that would otherwise make their attractions uneven.

Fully expected changes in the short-term rate: If people were certain of what the short-term rate, say on 3-month Treasury bills, was going to be for each 3-month period in the future, the rate on any longer-term bond, say a 5-year government bond, would merely be the average of these short-term rates. The average would be such that investing in the 5-year bond would yield the same return over five years as investing in a succession of Treasury bills each 3-month period for 20 periods.

For a simple example, if the 3-month bill rate were 9 per cent today and was expected to go to 10 per cent in three months' time, then a 6-month bill would have to yield approximately $9\frac{1}{2}$ per cent to make it equally attractive to buy now when the alternative is to earn 9 per cent on a 3-month bill now and 10 per cent on a 3-month bill bought three months from now.[1]

This illustrates two important conclusions. Other things being equal, (i) when the short-term rate is expected to rise in the future, the long-term rate will tend to be above the current short-term rate, and (ii) when the short-term rate is expected to fall in the future, the long-term rate will tend to be below the current short-term rate.

Uncertainty: Anyone who buys a financial asset may need to sell it before it reaches maturity. If the interest rate changes unexpectedly between the time of buying and the time of selling, the owner of the asset will suffer a capital loss (if the rate has risen) or a capital gain (if the rate has fallen). Many people do not like these risks, even if there is an equal chance of gain or loss. Economists say they are 'risk averse', and they need the compensation of higher interest payments to persuade them to assume this risk. Now recall that the longer the term of the bond, the greater the percentage fluctuation in its price for any given alteration in the interest rate. (See page 357.)

Thus, the longer the term of the bond, the greater the risk of fluctuations in its capital value due to unexpected changes in the interest rate and, other things being equal, the higher the rate of interest it must pay to compensate for this added risk.

---

1 The discussion of liquidity on page 335 is relevant here, as are the several discussions of financial assets on pages 248, 346 and 355–8.

1 Because of the complications of compound interest, the rate earned on the 6-month bill will not be a simple arithmetic average of the two 3-month rates. This detail need not, however, bother us at this point.

Risk of default: Different financial assets carry different risks of default. A UK Treasury bill carries virtually no default risk, while a 20-year bond issued by a Brazilian mining company carries a significant risk. No one would hold the Brazilian bond unless it paid a rate sufficiently above the Treasury bill rate to compensate for the extra default risk. Other things being equal, the higher the default risk, the higher the rate of interest that a financial asset will pay.

Political risk: Countries with unstable political systems or a record of confiscating foreign assets without full compensation will find that their government, and their local firms, will have to pay higher interest rates to compensate investors for the added risk in holding these assets.

Summary: This discussion leads to some important conclusions.

The rate of interest on any particular financial asset will be equal to:

(a) **the average of the expected short-term rates between the present and the asset's maturity date**
(b) **plus an uncertainty premium which is higher the longer the term of the bond**
(c) **plus a risk premium to cover both the commercial risks of default and the political risks of such government actions as confiscation without adequate compensation.**

Movements in the structure of interest rates

Although there are many many different interest rates, we can still think of alterations in 'the' interest rate providing that the whole structure of rates tends to move upwards or downwards together. This is similar to our ability to study 'the' price level, in spite of there being millions of individual prices in the economy. When the price level rises or falls, the whole structure of prices tends to rise or fall together. By the same token, when we speak of 'the' interest rate changing, we mean the whole structure of interest rates is either rising or falling.

The interest rate, which is the average of the whole structure of rates, is determined by the liquidity preference theory. It is the rate at which wealth-owners are satisfied with the division of their portfolio between money on the one hand and the whole range of non-perfectly liquid financial assets on the other.

THE BANK OF ENGLAND

Our next task in this chapter is to study how the Bank of England works. It is the central bank of the UK, and it is often referred to as just 'the Bank' (and sometimes as 'the old lady of Threadneedle Street', where it is located).

The Issue and the Banking Departments

The Bank's activities are divided between two departments, the Issue Department and the Banking Department, whose balance sheets are shown in Table 34.1.

The Issue Department is responsible for controlling the issue of notes and coins (although the actual manufacture of currency is in the hands of the Royal Mint). Notes and coins are put into circulation in return for securities obtained from the Banking Department. These appear as assets on the Issue Department's balance sheet, while the notes and coins appear as its liabilities.

The Banking Department acts as banker to the government and to the retail banks. Deposits of the government (called 'public' deposits), and of the retail banks, appear as liabilities on this department's balance sheet called 'bankers' deposits'. Other liabilities are deposits of nationalized industries, local authorities and the central banks of other countries, included in 'other accounts'. Assets of the Banking Department include government bonds (called securities) and bills (called Treasury Bills), and loans to the banking system (called advances). The item called special deposits among the liabilities, standing at zero in 1990, will be discussed later.

Functions of the Bank of England

The Bank's most important functions are to act as:
• **banker to the government;**
• **banker to the retail banks;**
• **controller of the country's currency;**
• **agent for the government's exchange rate policy;**
• **supervisor of the financial system;**

TABLE 34.1 Bank of England Balance Sheet September 1990 (£million)

ISSUE DEPARTMENT				
Liabilities			*Assets*	
Notes in circulation	15,696		Government securities	12,425
Notes in Banking Department	4		Other securities	3,275
	15,700			15,700
BANKING DEPARTMENT				
Liabilities			*Assets*	
Public deposits	37		Government securities	1,429
Special deposits	0		Advances and other accounts	833
Bankers' deposits	1,770		Premises, equipment, etc.	1,846
Reserves and other accounts	2,305		Notes and coin	4
	4,112			4,112

Source: Bank of England Quarterly Bulletin, November 1990.

- **supporter of financial institutions;**
- **agent for the government's monetary policy.**

Banker to the government

The Bank provides the government with an account into which it can make deposits and against which it can draw cheques.

The Bank also 'manages' the National Debt.[1] When the government issues new bonds, the Bank arranges their actual sale. The Bank also redeems debt issues when they reach maturity. It takes in the bonds and pays the bondholders on behalf of the government.

The Bank also smooths over the effects that might otherwise ensue from uneven borrowing and lending requirements. The Bank purchases any part of new issues of the National Debt that is not taken up by other lenders on the day of issue, at what the Bank deems to be a reasonable price (i.e. interest rate). If it has judged the market correctly, the Bank will be able to sell the remaining part of the new debt over the next week or so. If it has guessed incorrectly, it may end up holding some of the new debt indefinitely. The Bank also enters the market if there is a large issue of government debt due for early redemption. The Bank buys up this issue over a period of time, thus preventing a sudden large accretion of cash to the public on redemption date.

The Bank also makes the interest payments on the government debt on behalf of the government, issuing cheques that go to pay the bond-holders.

Finally, the Bank holds substantial amounts of the National Debt itself. These are bills and bonds that the Bank has purchased from the government, paying with a credit added to the government's account held at the Bank. These assets are the credit side of the financial system's reserves that consitutes MO. Indeed, all money is debt. The Bank of England holds government debt, against which it has issued currency and bank deposits. Together these are MO. In turn, the retail banks create deposit liabilities (debt) which are the other side of the deposit money held by the public.

Banker to the retail banks

The Bank of England acts as banker to the retail banks. It holds deposits of the retail banks and will, on order, transfer these from the credit of one bank to the credit of another. In this way the Bank provides the retail banks with the equivalent of chequing accounts, and with the means of settling debts among themselves. The Bank also ensures that the banking system is able to obtain funds when it is temporarily short of cash. The Bank does this either by lending funds to the system directly or by buying bills from the system in the open market in return for the needed funds.

We shall see later in this chapter that these activities provide the Bank with the channels through which it operates its monetary policy.

Controller of the country's currency

In most countries the central bank has the sole power to issue banknotes. In England this is done by the Issue Department of the Bank of England.[1] The Bank makes no attempt, however, to control the quantity of coins and banknotes in circulation. This is determined by the tastes of the public for holding money as bank deposits or as cash.

Agent for exchange-rate policy

As we saw in Chapter 29, the Bank carries out the government's policy with respect to the exchange rate. It holds the country's official reserves of gold and foreign exchange, and it intervenes from time to time on the foreign-exchange market to influence the exchange rate between sterling and other currencies. These policies are discussed in detail in Chapters 40–42.

Supervisor of the financial system

The Bank of England plays an important role in supervising the entire financial system. In the 1979 Banking Act, the Bank was given the job of licensing deposit-takers which includes vetting of top staff appointments in the banking sector. A few years later the Securities and Investment Board (SIB) was set up. This is an agency established under the 1986 Financial Services Act, with members appointed by the government and the Bank of England, to regulate certain financial transactions in the UK. The SIB does so by delegating powers to a number of self-regulating bodies, such as FIMBRA (Financial Intermediaries, Managers and Brokers' Regulatory Association) and LAUTRO (Life Assurance and Unit Trust Regulatory Association).

Supporter of financial institutions

The Bank is the LENDER OF LAST RESORT to the financial system, which means it is the ultimate supporter of the system. If all else fails, the Bank has a responsibility to support financial institutions that are in a fundamentally sound position, but in need of short-term finance. This lender function is now undertaken with the co-operation of the discount houses, making their assets liquid by buying them on the open market. But routinized or not, the Bank is the ultimate backer for the rest of the system.

Today, the Bank's function as lender of last resort is a part of its more general SUPPORT FUNCTION. This consists of managing the system so as to avoid financial crises that could lead to failures of banks and other institutions that are in a basically sound position.

The two main aspects of the support are to provide financial institutions with sufficient liquidity and to prevent them from being put into difficulties by very rapid shifts in interest rates.

Many financial institutions are in the position of 'bor-

---

1 See Chapter 28 for a discussion of the national debt.

1 Certain Scottish banks are allowed to issue banknotes, but the operation of monetary policy is solely in the hands of the Bank of England.

rowing short' and 'lending long'. This means that they are obliged to pay their depositors and other creditors on demand, or on short notice, but they lend money out for longer terms. Thus if too many depositors demand their money, the banks cannot immediately raise the required funds by recalling loans. This puts the system in temporary need of liquidity. To provide the needed cash, the Bank either makes loans to the system or provides the cash by buying up assets held by the system. Later in the chapter, we shall study in detail how this is done.

If interest rates rise quickly, financial institutions will have to pay more interest to those who hold interest-bearing deposits. This must be done to prevent them from taking their money elsewhere in search of higher rates. The interest that the institutions earn on many of their investments and fixed-interest loans will rise only after the old investments and loans mature. Thus a rapid rise in interest rates may put some financial institutions in financial difficulties. Rather than let this happen, the central bank may try to slow down the rise in interest rates. To do this, the Bank enters the open market and buys bonds, thus preventing their prices from falling as rapidly as they otherwise would.

The support function was one of the prime motives of the Bank's activities in the 1950s and 1960s. The Bank tried to 'lean against the wind', slowing down changes in the interest rate in either direction. Today this motivation is less important, partly because the returns on many of the investments and loans made by the financial system now change as the market rate of interest changes. Nonetheless, the Bank still is the ultimate protector of the monetary system.

The agent for monetary policy

The Bank is responsible for carrying out the government's monetary policy. This function is discussed in detail in a later section.

KEYNESIANS, MONETARISTS AND NEW CLASSICISTS

Before we go on to discuss monetary policy, we need to identify three groups of economists who have taken different positions in debates over many issues, including both monetary and fiscal policies. Only a brief outline will be given here, as the views of these groups will be discussed at several points in later chapters. Many of the points made in this section will be elaborated later in this and in subsequent chapters. What is important now is to get an overall impression of the views of these three groups. Much of the detailed reasoning behind these views will be filled in later.

Keynesians

The Keynesian view of the economy: Keynesian economists use the Keynesian income-expenditure model that

we have developed in Parts 4 and 5 to analyse the economy. Early Keynesians gave little importance to fluctuations in the money supply as a cause of income fluctuations (believing in a very elastic LP curve and a steep MEI curve, as discussed in Figure 34.3 on page 384). Later, Keynesians accepted that money can be a cause of disturbances, but they still stress variations in such real expenditure flows as investment and net exports.

Keynesians stress the importance of non-competitive elements in markets. They believe that prices do not adjust quickly to clear all markets. In particular, they believe that in recessions many firms would be willing to sell more if there was more demand, and many workers would be willing to take employment if only the jobs were available.

Stabilization policy: Keynesians stress the need for short-run stabilization policy to increase demand during recessions and reduce it during booms. They favour fiscal policy but also see a place for monetary stabilization policy.

Inflation: Many Keynesians stress cost-push and other non-competitive elements as a cause of inflation. In more recent times, however, Keynesians have also come to accept monetary mismanagement as a cause of inflation, particularly in countries where central banks have permitted massive increases in the money supply.

Monetarists

The monetarist view of the economy: Monetarists sometimes use the Keynesian income-expenditure model to analyse the economy. However, they also use the quantity theory model that we discussed in Chapter 30, adding the assumption that the velocity of circulation of money is stable. This makes nominal national income vary directly with the quantity of money. Since the price level does not adjust instantly, they see variations in the quantity of money as a major cause of variations in national income.[1]

What characterizes them is (i) the enormous potency they give to the quantity of money as the major determinant of fluctuations in aggregate expenditure, (ii) their belief that a particular group of monetary assets can be identified as 'the' quantity of money, (iii) their belief that there is a stable relation between changes in this quantity of money and changes in money national income, PY.

Stabilization policy: Monetarists would avoid short-term stabilization policy. They believe that fiscal policy is too weak to be useful and that monetary policy is too powerful to risk using! Although they believe that monetary policy has potent effects on the economy, they believe it exerts those effects with a time-lag that is long (twelve to twenty-four months) and variable. Therefore, they believe that the attempt to use monetary policy to stabilize the economy is quite likely to destabilize it.

Inflation: Monetarists believe that inflation is almost

---

1 The equation of exchange, $M_S V = PY$, tells us that, if V is constant, $M_S = \Delta(PY)$ and, if P changes slowly, ΔM_S and ΔY will be directly related.

exclusively caused by overly rapid increases in the money supply. They would focus monetary policy solely on the goal of providing a stable price level. They recommend that central banks ensure enough monetary expansion to satisfy those increases in the demand for money that depend on increases in real income, while preventing the more rapid expansions that cause inflation.

New Classicists

The New Classical view of the economy: New Classical economists use a model of perfect competition for the whole economy. Although they recognize that many markets have non-competitive elements, they believe the economy behaves *as if* it were perfectly competitive. In particular, prices fluctuate in goods and factor markets to equate demand and supply continually. Thus, there are never significant amounts of either unsatisfied buyers or unsatisfied sellers in any market. In particular, there are no firms who would sell more at the prevailing prices if only demand were greater, and there are no workers who would really take a job at the going wage rate if only jobs were available.

Stabilization policy: New Classicists see no need for stabilization policy of either a fiscal or a monetary sort. In their view, markets work best if they are left alone, free of any policy interference. Any attempt to stimulate output and employment by increasing aggregate desired expenditure will merely cause the price level to rise.

Inflation: In their view, all inflations are caused by too much demand. Thus New Classicists agree with monetarists that the sole goal of monetary policy should be to ensure a stable price level by ensuring that the rate of monetary expansion is low enough to prevent the emergence of inflationary gaps.

MONETARY POLICY IN A CLOSED ECONOMY

Monetary policy is based on the central bank's ability to influence monetary variables, changes in which set the monetary transmission mechanism in motion which, in turn, causes aggregate desired expenditure to change. In the previous chapter we saw how the transmission adjustment mechanism worked for exogenous changes in the money supply. In Chapter 31, we saw how deposit money was created by the retail banking system and how, given a constant ratio of deposits to reserves, the size of their reserves determined the size of the money supply (through the money multiplier given on page 351).

Monetary policy affects the size of bank reserves, and, through them, the size of the money supply. There are, however, two possible ways in which this can work.

Strict control of reserves: In the simplest case, the Bank rigidly sets reserves at a desired level and allows the behav-

iour of the retail banks to determine the money supply. This gives the Bank fairly strong control over aggregate expenditure. It sets the money supply at any desired level and then the monetary transmission mechanism does the rest by working as shown on page 368.

Influencing but not controlling reserves: In this case, the Bank cannot set reserves at any desired level and wait for the money supply to adjust. For various reasons which we will study later, when retail banks create more deposit money, the central bank is forced to supply the reserves needed to back these extra deposits. In this case, the central bank seeks to exert an influence on the amount of deposit money that the retail banks create by varying the terms on which it will supply reserves to the system. This gives the Bank power to influence reserves, and the money supply, without the power to set either of these at precise, predetermined levels. Under this system, monetary policy is more difficult to operate and less precise in its effects than under the rigid reserve system. It is, as we shall see, the system that exists as a result of the current institutions of the British banking system.

Instruments, Targets and Goals

In discussing any economic policy, we need to distinguish three types of variables: INSTRUMENTS, often called 'instrumental variables', INTERMEDIATE TARGETS, often called just 'targets' or 'target variables', and GOALS, often called 'policy goals' or 'policy variables'.

Instruments: The INSTRUMENTS of monetary policy are what the Bank can directly manipulate in an effort to achieve its goals.

The main instruments used in the UK today are:
(1) the purchase and sale of financial assets (mainly government securities) in the open market, so-called 'open-market operations' which directly affect bank reserves;
(2) the rate at which it will offer credit to the banking system.

Targets: The intermediate TARGETS of monetary policy are the variables that the Bank monitors, and reacts to. When an intermediate target variable attains a value outside the range that the Bank targets for it, the Bank will use its instruments in an attempt to get the variable 'back on target'.

The two main intermediate target variables that have at one time or another been used in monetary policy are:
(1) the money supply as measured by one or another of the monetary aggregates listed on page 382, and
(2) interest rates.

Goals: There is, as we shall see, some controversy as to what the goals of policy should be.

Traditionally, the goals of monetary policy have been to help to achieve:

(1) a stable price level,
(2) full employment,
(3) a satisfactory foreign exchange rate, and
(4) a healthy financial system.

The first goal refers to long-term price stability, which has traditionally been the most important goal of monetary policy. The second goal is the primary goal of 'short-term stabilization policy' operated through monetary and/or fiscal policy. The third is a secondary goal of stabilization policy, because the exchange rate may at times interfere with the achievement of the primary goal. It also becomes a primary goal when the Bank is committed to sustain a fixed exchange rate, as it is under the European Monetary System (EMS). The complications that this causes are discussed at length in Chapters 40–42. The fourth goal is in pursuit of what is called *support policy*, which refers to the Bank's role of supporter of the financial system.

In the bulk of this chapter, we concentrate on the first two policies. We ignore goal (3), the balance of payments, but return to it later, in Chapter 42. At the end of the chapter, we briefly discuss the goals of support policy.

We now look at each of these three categories, instruments, targets and goals, in some detail.

The Instruments of Monetary Policy

If the Bank can change the reserves of the retail banks, it can lead them to alter the amount of deposit money that they create. This, as shown in Figures 33.4 and 33.5 on page 365, sets the transmission mechanism in motion working through changes in the interest rate to changes in aggregate desired expenditure. The same effect can be obtained somewhat more directly if the Bank can alter interest rates directly.

We first look at the three main methods available to the Bank to operate its policies relating to bank reserves and interest rates – open-market operations, loans to the financial system, and rules and regulations.

Open-market operations

OPEN-MARKET OPERATIONS occur when the Bank purchases and sells financial assets in the open market. We shall see that these operations affect both interest rates and retail bank reserves. To see what is involved, we study in detail the monetary changes that occur first when the Bank purchases, and then when it sells, assets on the open market.

Purchases from the public: Assume that the Bank enters the open market and purchases, say, government bonds. The immediate effect of these purchases is to force up the price of bonds, which means a fall in the interest rate.

A less obvious effect, however, relates to retail banks. To see this effect, let us follow out the consequences of the Bank's purchase of a single £100 bond from a household that maintains an account with one of the retail banks.

The Bank pays for the bond by making out a cheque drawn on itself, payable to the seller. The seller deposits this cheque in its own bank. That retail bank presents the cheque to the central bank for payment. The central bank makes a book entry increasing the deposit of the retail bank at the central bank. At the end of these transactions, the central bank has acquired a new asset in the form of a bond, and a new liability in the form of a deposit by the retail bank. The household will have reduced its bond holdings and will have raised its cash holdings. The retail bank will have a new deposit equal to the amount paid for the bond by the central bank. Thus the retail bank will find its cash assets, and its deposit liabilities, increased by the same amounts. The balance sheets of the three parties concerned will show the changes indicated in Table 34.2.

TABLE 34.2 Changes resulting from the Purchase by the Central Bank of a £100 Bond from a Household

BANK OF ENGLAND	
Liabilities	Assets
Deposits of retail banks + £100	Bond + £100

RETAIL BANKS	
Liabilities	Assets
Deposits of households + £100	Deposits with central bank + £100

PRIVATE HOUSEHOLDS	
Liabilities	Assets
No change	Bonds – £100
	Deposits with retail banks + £100

A retail bank will now be in the position that was originally illustrated by Balance Sheet 2 on page 349 of Chapter 31. It will have received a new deposit of £100 against which it holds £100 of reserves. In Chapter 31 we assumed that the new cash deposit reached the banking system when an immigrant deposited his money in some bank. Now we can see how such new deposits usually arise. They result from open-market purchases by the Bank of England. Whatever its source, however, the new deposit gives the retail banking system reserves in excess of the minimum it wishes to hold, and thus allows banks to engage in the multiple expansion of deposits that we studied earlier.

Notice that everything has been accomplished by a set of book transactions. The retail banks have extra reserves to their credit on the books of the central bank. The household has new deposits recorded to its credit on the books of the retail banks. No new coins or banknotes will be created unless, and until, the public wishes to hold some of its new money in the form of currency.

The important result is that the purchase of bonds (or other assets) by the Bank increases the reserves of the retail banks. This allows the banks to make a multiple expansion of deposits.

Sales to the public: Second, let the central bank enter the open market and sell £100 worth of bonds to the public. The immediate effect is to lower the price of bonds, which means a rise in the interest rate. Once again, however, there is a more subtle effect on the reserves of retail banks. To see this, follow through the resulting set of transactions. The central bank sells a bond to a household that maintains an account with a retail bank. The Bank hands over the bond and receives in return the household's cheque drawn against its deposit at the household's bank. The central bank presents this cheque for payment. The payment is made merely by a book entry reducing the retail bank's deposit at the central bank.

Now the central bank has reduced its assets by the value of the bond it sold, and has also reduced its liabilities in the form of deposits standing in the favour of the retail banks. The household has increased its holdings of bonds, and reduced its cash on deposit with its own bank. The retail bank has reduced its deposit liability to the household, and reduced its cash assets (on deposit with the central bank) by the same amount. The balance sheets of the three parties concerned will initially show the changes indicated in Table 34.3.

TABLE 34.3 Changes resulting from the Sale by the Central Bank of a £100 Bond to a Private Household

CENTRAL BANK	
Liabilities	*Assets*
Deposits of retail banks −£100	Bond −£100

RETAIL BANKS	
Liabilities	*Assets*
Deposits of households −£100	Deposits with central bank −£100

PRIVATE HOUSEHOLDS	
Liabilities	*Assets*
No change	Bonds +£100
	Deposits with retail banks −£100

The important result is that the sale of bonds (or any other financial asset) by the Bank decreases the reserves of the retail banks. If nothing else happens, the banks will then have to make a multiple contraction of deposits in order to restore their desired reserve ratio.

Open-market operations in an inflationary world: Open-market sales designed to force retail banks actually to *reduce* the amount of deposit money are rare in modern times. In a world where national income is rising year by year – due both to growth of real output and inflationary increases in prices – the Bank is usually expanding the reserves of the retail banks continually, so that they can expand the nominal money supply to meet the needs created by the increasing money value of national income. However, by varying the rate at which it purchases bonds, the Bank can vary the *rate* of expansion of the retail banks' nominal reserves. What happens both to real reserves and to the real money supply will depend on whether the nominal values increase faster or slower than the price level.

Transactions with the government: In the examples we have used so far, the Bank dealt with private individuals. However, *any* open-market purchase, or sale, by the central bank has the same effect. For example, if the Bank buys bills and bonds directly from the government, this equally, though less directly, increases the reserve of retail banks. In the first instance, it is the government's account with the central bank that gains the new credit balance. But as soon as the government spends the money, writing cheques

in favour of households and firms, the deposits will find their way into the retail banks, who then obtain new deposits that increase both their reserves and their deposit liabilities by an equal amount. This puts them in the position of the bank shown in Balance Sheet 2 on page 000.

The Bank purchases bonds from the government in order to increase the money supply at the rate required to finance the rising value of transactions that accompany economic growth. If real income is increasing at, say, 2 per cent per year, then a stable price level will be compatible with a money supply that increases at about 2 per cent per year.

Purchase of bonds from the government can also occur if the government is unable, or unwilling, to finance the whole PSBR by borrowing from the private sector. The government then sells its bonds to the Bank. This has the same effect as any other open-market purchase: it puts new reserves into the hands of the retail banks, who can then engage in a multiple expansion of deposits. This is what is loosely referred to as *printing press finance*. Although it is all done by book entries, the effect is the same as if the government had printed pound notes in its own cellars and used them to settle its debts. That part of new debt that is sold to the Bank, rather than to the public, is financed by creating new money.

Providing funds to the financial system

Financial institutions that have sound but illiquid investments often have temporary needs for funds. One way of getting the required funds is to borrow them from the central bank. This has the effect of altering the reserves of the retail banks.

Loans to the discount houses: In many countries, retail banks borrow directly from the central bank. In the UK, however, the discount houses stand between the retail banks and the Bank of England. If the banks find themselves in need of cash, they recall some of their demand loans made to the discount houses. Because (as we saw in Chapter 31) the discount houses use their borrowed money to buy short-term financial assets, they cannot repay the banks out of their own cash reserves. One way they can obtain the money is by borrowing from the Bank of England. They put up approved financial assets (mainly short-term Treasury Bills) as security, and they pay interest on these loans. In these circumstances, the discount houses are said to be 'in the Bank'.

The rate the Bank charges the discount houses used to be set in advance and announced every week by the Bank of England. It was first called BANK RATE, and then the 'Minimum Lending Rate' (MLR). Now, however, the rate is usually determined by the Bank from day to day, though the Bank has the power to set MLR if it chooses to do so. (It did so, for example, in 1984, when the exchange rate was under heavy pressure.)

Direct purchase of bills and bonds: There is a second way in which the Bank can provide assistance when the banking system needs cash. Instead of lending to the discount houses, it can engage in open-market operations to buy their bills directly. If discount houses try to sell a large number of bills on the open market, their prices will be forced down. However, the central bank can enter the market and buy all the bills offered *at their present prices*. This allows the discount houses to obtain the funds they need to repay their loans from the retail banks by selling some of their financial assets. It also prevents interest rates from rising. In the mid-1980s, the Bank of England let it be known that it favoured this method rather than the method of lending money directly to the discount houses.

In summary, the Bank can provide new reserves to the retail banks by engaging in open-market purchases of bonds from the public, or from the government. It can also allow the retail banks to obtain cash by permitting the discount houses to borrow from, or sell to, the Bank enough bills to raise the funds needed to repay their loans that are being called in by the retail banks.

Rules and regulations

In the past, the Bank has used many rules and regulations as instruments of monetary policy. Today, this type of intervention is out of favour. Policy-makers feel that they distort market signals and/or market reactions to those signals. Today the Bank relies on directly influencing bank liquidity and market interest rates.

In the past, however, ceilings have been placed on bank advances, and informal requests to banks to restrict lending have been employed in a procedure sometimes referred to as 'moral suasion'. A system was also in use between 1973 and 1980 whereby the banks were set target rates of growth for their deposits and were penalized if they overshot them. (This was the so-called *supplementary deposit scheme*, otherwise known as the 'corset'.) Also in the 1970s, the Bank imposed a minimum liquid assets ratio on the retail banks. As well as having their own desired ratio of cash to deposits, they were also required to keep a minimum ratio of liquid assets – cash plus short-term bills – to deposits.

Finally we should mention the introduction in 1960 of SPECIAL DEPOSITS. These are 'frozen' deposits of the retail banks held at the Bank of England. These special-deposit requirements can be raised or lowered as a means of influencing the retail banks' liquidity. Special deposits have not, however, been required since 1980. Hence they appear in Table 34.1 as a zero item.

The world's banking system has become vastly more international, and vastly more competitive, over the last two decades. Computers move funds around the world with ease. Would-be borrowers who cannot get funds in London can quickly turn to Paris, New York or Tokyo. As a result, all of these special restrictions are out of favour. They tend to hurt the competitiveness of one country's banks without effectively curtailing borrowing.

Announcement effects

The techniques reviewed so far work through the transmission mechanism which we studied in Chapter 33.

However, since people's expectations are a major determinant of their spending decisions, the monetary transmission mechanism can sometimes be short-circuited.

Assume, for example, that the Bank announces a tightening of monetary policy – in the past, it would have raised the MLR; today it might let it be known that it *intends* to enter the open market and drive up interest rates. If the announcement is taken seriously, people may expect contractionary forces to be felt in the near future and, as a result, may cut their expenditure plans now. For example, investment plans may be curtailed in anticipation of a future fall in national income. There is then a contractionary effect on aggregate expenditure that is felt before the restrictive monetary policy actually creates a money shortage and drives interest rates upwards.

With announcement effects it is not an actual change in the rate of interest that does the job, but an announcement that the rate of interest is going to be changed in the future.

Of course, if the Bank did not usually follow up on its announcements by instituting the expected policy, the announcements would soon cease to be believed. But as long as the Bank usually does what it says it is going to do, it can often get very quick effects that operate through changed expectations to cause planned expenditure to change and hence the aggregate desired expenditure function to shift.

The Targets of Monetary Policy

Targets are the variables that the Bank monitors and reacts to. The Bank will normally have a target range for these variables and will use its instruments in an attempt to keep them within their target ranges.

Requirements for a satisfactory target

If this attempt is to be successful in meeting the Bank's goals of influencing its policy variables in the desired manner, two conditions need to be fulfilled.

(1) The target variables need to be fairly quickly influenced by the Bank's instruments.

(2) The target variables must be closely related *in a stable manner* to changes in the policy variables in which the Bank is ultimately interested. If they were not, then there would be no point in the Bank altering its behaviour in response to change in its intermediate target variables. The circumstances under which this second condition is fulfilled are discussed later in this chapter.

Notice that we have italicized the phrase 'in a stable manner' in the previous paragraph. This is an important qualification. Because of the trade cycle, many economic variables are loosely correlated with each other, rising more or less together on the upswing and falling more or less together on the downswing, even when there is no direct causal link between them. As a result, many economic variables will show some correlation with national income and the price level, which are the policy variables of monetary policy. But most of these other variables will not make good intermediate targets because changes in them do not *cause* changes in national income and prices.

Consider an example. The number of loaded goods trains leaving London is correlated with UK's real national income, but it would not be a good intermediate target. If, in order to restrain a boom, steps were taken to lower rail shipments (the assumed intermediate target), it is very unlikely that the boom would be restrained. Instead, alternative means would be found for shipping goods.

Major targets used

The main intermediate targets that have been used by central banks throughout the world are various measures of the money supply and interest rates.

The money supply: Targetting the money supply as measured by one of the various definitions listed on page 382, means controlling the supply of credit. Deposit money is created when retail banks make loans to their customers. If retail banks do not have sufficient reserves, they cannot expand the supply of new loans, and hence cannot expand the supply of new money, no matter how urgently their customers may want to borrow from them.

Interest rates: Controlling the interest rate controls the demand for credit. The amount that firms will wish to spend on investment, and hence the amount they will wish to borrow to finance such expenditures, will, as we have seen, vary with the rate of interest. Thus high rates of interest will be associated with small demands for new borrowing, and hence new money creation, while low rates of interest will be associated with large demands.

The relation between the money supply and interest rates: Because of what we have just said about interest rates and the money supply, one might think of the Bank having two policies, one influencing the quantity of money and the other influencing the interest rate. This, however, would be a mistake. The reason is that interest rates and the quantity of money are linked to each other through the liquidity preference function. The Bank cannot set independent targets for the quantity of money *and* the interest rate. If it sets a target for one of these variables, it must be content with the value of the other that will allow it to meet its target. Thus, if there is a *stable* demand for money – i.e the *LP* schedule is not continually shifting – the Bank really only has one decision to make: what combination of interest rate and money supply – i.e. what point on the *LP* schedule – to aim at.

Which intermediate target?

It follows from what has just been said that, in a world of perfect stability and perfect certainty, it would not matter whether the Bank chose the quantity of money or the interest rate as its intermediate target variable. If the Bank knew exactly the location of the *LP* curve shown in Figure 34.1 and if the curve never shifted, then the Bank could decide on an intermediate target of either an interest rate

of r_0 or a money supply of M_0, and both decisions would produce identical results. However, both the demand and the supply of money change over time so that the Bank will not know the exact position of the *LP* and the M_S curves. As a result, it does matter which variable the Bank chooses as its intermediate target. We cannot go into all of the reasons here, but we can look at some.

Shifts in the demand for money: The first thing to notice is that the demand for money varies over the trade cycle. The *LP* schedule drawn in Figure 34.1 is drawn for a given national income. As national income rises in a boom, and then falls in a slump, so the *LP* function shifts to the right and then to the left. (The *LP* curve shifts in the manner studied on page 362 because national income varies over the trade cycle.)

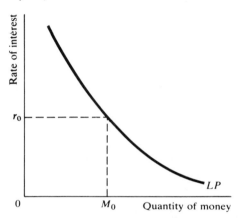

FIGURE 34.1 The Rate of Interest and the Quantity of Money as Intermediate Targets. Choice of a value for either one of the two intermediate variables implies a value for the other.

An example of such shifts is shown in Figure 34.2. The *LP* function that exists at potential income is labelled LP_N, which stands for the normal demand for money. The *LP* functions that exist in booms and in slumps are labelled LP_B and LP_S, which stand for the demand for money typical of booms and typical of slumps.

Stabilizing the money supply. First, let us assume that the money supply is the target, and that the Bank manages to hold it constant over the cycle at the quantity M_N. This means that the money supply curve is M_S. As the demand for money fluctuates over the trade cycle, the interest rate will also vary. It will rise to r_B in booms, when the demand for money is high, and fall to r_S in slumps, when the demand for money is low.

These movements have the effect of making the interest rate act as a MONETARY BUILT-IN STABILIZER. (See Chapter 28, page 319, for a discussion of *fiscal* built-in stabilizers.) In the boom, the shortage of money forces up interest rates and thus tends to reduce interest-sensitive expenditure, and so reduce the high aggregate expenditure that is causing the boom. In the slump, the low interest rates tend to encourage interest-sensitive expenditure, and hence to increase desired aggregate expenditure above the low levels that are causing the slump.

We conclude that stabilizing the money supply over the trade cycle causes the interest rate to rise in booms, discouraging interest-sensitive expenditure, and to fall in slumps, encouraging interest-sensitive expenditure. This effect creates a built-in monetary stabilizer.

Stabilizing the interest rate.   Second, assume that the interest rate is the target, and that it is held constant over the cycle. This means that the Bank must vary the money supply in order to hold interest rates constant in the face of fluctuations in the demand for money. In Figure 34.2, the money supply must vary from M_0 in the slump, through M_N at potential income, to M_1 during the boom.

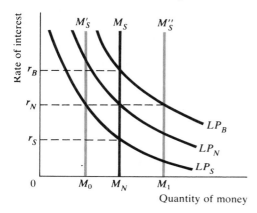

FIGURE 34.2 Alternative Stabilizing Policies when the *LP* Function is Shifting. In the Figure the demand for money is fluctuating cyclically between LP_S and LP_B. If the rate of interest is stabilized at r_N, the Bank must vary the money supply between M_0 and M_1. If the money supply is stabilized at M_N, giving the money supply curve M_S, the rate of interest will fluctuate between a high of r_B and a low of r_S.

The net effect of this is that the built-in stabilizing effect of a fixed money supply is lost. During the boom the increased demand for money puts upward pressure on the interest rate and the Bank must expand the money supply to prevent interest rates from rising. The money supply curve is shifted to M''_S, in combination with LP_B. This yields an equilibrium interest rate of r_N. As a result, there is no monetary mechanism operating to restrain expenditure and so reduce the strength of the boom. During the slump, the decreased demand for money puts downward pressure on the interest rate and the Bank must contract the money supply to prevent interest rates from falling. The money supply curve is shifted to M'_S as the money demand curve falls to LP_S. As a result, the equilibrium interest rate remains at r_N, so there is no monetary mechanism operating to increase expenditure and so reduce the magnitude of the slump.

We conclude that stabilizing the interest rate over the trade cycle requires that the money supply be increased in the boom and decreased in the slump. This eliminates the built-in stabilizing effect of interest-rate changes when the money supply is stabilized.

Uncertainty: In drawing Figure 34.2, we assumed that we knew the exact positions of the M_S and the *LP* curves. But certain knowledge is never given to any policy-maker – nor, unfortunately, to any other person. The Bank does not know exactly where the *LP* function is at any time, nor does it know exactly what its open-market operations will do to the money supply. Under such conditions, the Bank cannot control either the money supply, or aggregate desired expenditure, with any short-term precision, even if it consistently keeps interest rates within their target band.

The evolution of the debate over target variables

From the end of World War II to some time in the 1970s, most of the world's central banks used interest rates as their target. Then, during the 1970s, one central bank after another, including the Bank of England, went over to using some measure of the money supply as their target. It was hoped that using the money supply as an intermediate target would give central banks more consistent control over aggregate desired expenditure than was obtained by using the interest rate.

The switch to the money supply as the intermediate target gave rise to a number of new issues, which are discussed below.

Which money supply as a target?   In our analysis of the monetary transmission mechanism in Chapter 33 we assumed that there is a unique money supply. However, as we observed at the beginning of this chapter, there is a continuous spectrum of monetary assets, ranging from such highly liquid assets as bills with a few days to maturity, to such highly illiquid assets as long-term bonds. Just where to draw the line between money and short-term liquid assets that are not money will always be an arbitrary decision.

There *is no doubt* that money exerts an important influence on the economy. There *is doubt*, however, about the existence of a unique group of assets called money that the central bank can use as a satisfactory intermediate target.

Alternative money supplies: When the money supply was first proposed as a target variable, it was customary to distinguish between only two definitions of the money supply. Narrowly defined money referred to currency in the hands of the public and bank sight deposits which, at the time, were all non-interest-bearing. Money broadly defined referred to the above, plus time deposits in banks and some other financial institutions.

As soon as central banks started to target on one or the other of these money supplies, the strong correlations between them and national income began to weaken. The search then began for a 'right' measure of the money supply, meaning a measure that would continue to be closely related to national income when the Bank manipulated it in an attempt to influence national income. Definitions came and went with bewildering frequency. They differed in one country from year to year, and among countries in any one year. Furthermore, proponents of monetary control differed among themselves as to which was the best measure of the money supply for the Bank to use as its target.

Table 34.4 shows the definitions in use in the UK at the beginning of 1992. These are different from what they were when we wrote the first edition of this book, and very probably they will have changed yet again when we come to write the third edition.

TABLE 34.4 Some Definitions of the UK Money Supply

Notes and coins in circulation	
+ Bankers' operational balances with the *Bank of England*	**M0**
Notes and coins in circulation	
+ Private-sector sterling sight bank deposits (interest and non-interest bearing)	**M1**
+ Private-sector sterling time bank deposits	
+ Private-sector holdings of sterling bank certificates of deposit[1]	**M3**
+ Private-sector holdings of Building Society shares and deposits and sterling certificates of deposit	**M4**
+ Holdings by the private sector (except Building Societies) of bank bills, Treasury bills, local authority deposits, certificates of tax deposits and (some) National Saving instruments)	**M5**

The definitions given exclude M3$_c$ and M4$_c$ which include many additional assets that are similar to those included in the definitions M3 and M4 except that they are denominated in foreign currency. The rapid globalization of the world's banking system has led to an enormous rise in deposits *denominated in foreign currency units* held in UK banks by UK residents.

M0 is sometimes called the 'monetary base' or the 'high-powered money supply' (HPMS). If banks operated on a strict reserve ratio, it would be the magnitude which determined total deposits through the money multiplier. M1 is what used to be understood as *the* money supply: currency plus sight deposits in banks. Higher numbered M's include more and more assets that, if they are not media of exchange, can be quickly liquidated, i.e. turned into media of exchange.

1 A certificate of deposit shows a sum of money deposited for a stated period of time at a given interest rate. It is often saleable.

The details of such measures are not important. What matters is for you to understand that, what we call money, comprises a spectrum of closely related financial assets which their holders regard as highly substitutable for each other. Particular definitions, such as M0 or M5, pick out specific points along that continuous spectrum.

Can the money supply be controlled? If the money supply – however defined – is to be the target variable, the Bank must be able to use its instruments to control that supply fairly closely.

A group of economists called Monetarists believe that the demands for these assets are stable enough that any group of them can be controlled through the high-powered money supply. That is, they believe in a *stable deposit multiplier*. (See page 351.) They therefore urge the Bank to adopt strict money supply targets. One problem with this advice, as Box 34.1 suggests, is the monetarists cannot always agree among themselves as to which is the correct

definition of the money supply on which the Bank should target.

Critics of the monetarists have denied that any correlation between changes in the measured money supply and changes in national income that has been observed in past data represents a reliable relation for policy manipulation. In particular, they have argued that as soon as the Bank altered the money supply with a view to altering national income, the relation between the two variables would break down. There are many closely substitutable monetary assets. The critics reason that if the Bank made some subset of them scarce, people would learn to economize on them and use some other, similar, monetary assets instead.

In practice, something like this did happen and, although central banks managed to meet their monetary targets quite often, the predicted effects on national income did not occur much of the time.

This experience is an example of what is often called *Goodhart's Law*, which states that 'if policy-makers rely on a relation between two variables, the relation will change or even disappear'. Thus, if the money supply and nominal national income seem to be statistically related, and if policy-makers manipulate the money supply seeking to influence nominal national income, the relation between the money supply and nominal national income will change or disappear. The reason is that relations result from human behaviour, and when policy-makers start to manipulate the money supply, human behaviour may change, thus altering the relation between the two variables.

Should some measure of the money supply be the intermediate target? Throughout the world, central banks have tried a variety of money-supply targets in an effort to find the one that bears the closest relation to national income and the price level, which are the policy variables that ultimately interest them. Critics say that there are so many different kinds of liquid assets, and such a high degree of substitutability between them, that no long-term relations will be found that relate any sub-group called 'money' to aggregate expenditure and hence to national income and the price level. Thus they argue that targeting on some measure of the money supply is unsatisfactory.

Those who advocate monetary targeting say that such stable relations do exist. Because they believe that the rate of growth of the money supply is the ultimate determinant of the inflation rate, they say that monetary targeting is the best way in which central banks can fulfil their function of controlling the price level.

There is no serious debate about the insight gained hundreds of years ago that money and the price level are closely related in the long term. The debate is instead on whether or not there is some group of monetary assets that is suitable for central banks to use as their intermediate target in pursuit of their ultimate policy goal of stabilizing the price level in the short or medium term.

In 1981 the Bank abandoned its money-supply targets and announced that its policy would be to try to exercise its influence by stabilizing interest rates within a narrow band. This band would be changed from time to time, whenever the Bank felt that its policies should be more contractionary or more expansionary. In the former case, it would seek to raise interest rates; in the latter case, it would seek to lower them.

We have already noted that the target rate is not stated publicly in advance. The Bank hopes that uncertainty about the interest rate that the financial system will have to pay to obtain funds will make the retail banks more cautious in creating new deposit money. After all, if the system gets short of reserves and has to borrow from the Bank, it may be charged a very high rate – usually referred to as a penal rate – that would cut drastically into profits.

More importantly, in 1981 the Bank removed virtually any reserve requirement for the clearing banks. They now operate with the minimum balances they need to finance their day-to-day clearings of interbank transactions. They

also know that, if they run into serious difficulties, the Bank of England would have to make cash available to them rather than permit widespread failures among financial institutions.

This means that the Bank must use interest rates rather than some narrow definition of the money supply, such as M0, as its major intermediatde target variable.

It watches the various money supply figures; it watches the behaviour of real national income and the price level, as well as a host of international indicators, such as the balance of payments and the exchange rate. If it wishes to tighten monetary policy, it enters the market and sells bills, driving the interest rate upwards. This moves the economy upwards to the left along its liquidity preference curve. Interest rates rise and aggregate desired expenditure falls. If it wishes to be more expansive in its monetary policy, it enters the market and buys bills, driving the interest rate down. This moves the economy downwards to the right along its liquidity preference curve. Interest rates fall and aggregate desired expenditure rises.

Policy Variables

We now consider the Bank's policy goals of full employment, stable prices and stability of the financial system. (The third goal of maintaining the exchange rate at some target value is considered in a later chapter.) The full-employment goal is part of 'stabilization policy': to stabilize national income at its potential, or full-employment, level.

Stabilization policy

The traditional view has been that monetary policy can work along with fiscal policy to help to stabilize the economy. Let us see how this was supposed to work out.

When the economy was suffering from a recessionary gap, an expansionary monetary policy would be followed. The Bank would enter the open market and buy bonds. This would force down interest rates and expand the reserve base. Given a stable money multiplier, the actions of the retail banks would expand the money supply by a predictable amount. The expansionary effects would then work through the monetary adjustment mechanism in the manner laid out in Figure 33.4 on page 368.

When the economy was suffering from an inflationary gap, a contractionary monetary policy would be followed. The Bank would sell bonds, forcing the interest rate up and contracting the reserve base. The resulting decline in the money supply would cause the monetary adjustment mechanism to operate in the contractionary manner outlined in Figure 33.5 on page 368.

The use of monetary policy as a tool of stabilization policy has been criticized along two lines. One line of criticism, stemming from Keynesians, has been that monetary policy is often too weak in its effects to be a useful stabilization device. The other, stemming from Monetarists, has been that monetary policy is too strong in its effects to be a useful stabilization device! In discussing

---

BOX 34.1 Base Rate Hopes Rise as M0 Slows

'A fresh slowdown in banknotes in circulation points to the dramatic deceleration in the money supply continuing this month and next, fuelling the case for an early cut in interest rates.

'Some city economists believe Norman Lamont [the Chancellor] could cut a half point off base rates as early as today, given the expected slowing in M0, the narrow money aggregate, to an annual 3 per cent in November, a percentage point below the October rate and the smallest rise since mid-1986.

'The sharp downturn in M0 reflects the extent of the recession. "The monetary case for a base rate cut is unambiguous", John Shepperd, senior economist at Warburg Securities, said … But Gerard Lyons, chief economist of DKB International, said he expected the authorities would want to keep policy tight to establish the new cabinet's credibility.'

(*The Times*, 30 November 1990)

The quotation was written at the time when the Bank of England was operating a fairly tight monetary policy, trying to bring down an inflation rate that had risen over the previous year.

Questions

1 State in your own words the argument being advanced in the first paragraph, but use the terminology of targets, goals, instruments etc., that has been introduced in this chapter.
2 Why should a serious recession lead to a deceleration in the rate of increase in the money supply?
3 What is the credibility issue referred to by the last person quoted?

these arguments, we assume that the money supply can be controlled by the Bank, and study the results of being able to exercise such control. We will deal with the first criticism here, but postpone consideration of the second criticism until Chapter 39.

The factors that influence the strength of monetary policy are illustrated in Figure 34.3. In both parts of that Figure, the money supply is originally M_0. The perfectly inelastic money supply function, M_S, and the liquidity preference function, LP, combine to yield an interest rate of r_0. The interest rate of r_0 combines with the marginal efficiency of investment (MEI) curve to yield a desired investment expenditure of I_0. (You will recall that the MEI curve relates desired investment expenditure to the rate of interest.)

Now assume that a monetary expansion increases the money supply to M_1, shifting the money supply curve to M'_S. This lowers the interest rate to r_1 and increases desired investment expenditure by the amount ΔI to I_1.

This is the by-now-familiar operation of the monetary transmission mechanism. We shall now see, however, that the strength of the effect that works through that mechanism depends critically on the interest elasticities of the LP and MEI curves – that is to say, on the magnitudes of the effects of changes in the money supply on the rate of interest, and changes in the rate of interest on the volume of investment.

A weak effect: Part (i) of the Figure illustrates the case of a weak monetary effect. The LP function is fairly interest-

elastic so the interest rate does not fall by much as a result of the increase in the money supply. Also the MEI function is fairly interest-inelastic, so desired investment does not respond much to any fall in the interest rate that does occur. Taken together, the effect of the expansionary monetary policy is a small increase in desired investment expenditure, and hence only a small upward shift in the desired expenditure function.

The liquidity trap: An extreme case arises when there is a perfectly elastic LP curve. This is called the case of a LIQUIDITY TRAP: an increase in the money supply leaves the interest rate unaffected and, therefore, has no effect at all on desired investment and hence no effect on aggregate desired expenditure. This case is an unlikely one – indeed, there is some doubt if such a case has *ever* actually occurred. Nonetheless, it does show that conditions are conceivable where, at one extreme, monetary policy has no effect on aggregate expenditure.

A strong effect: Figure 34.3(ii) illustrates the opposite case where monetary policy has a strong effect. The LP function is interest-inelastic, so the interest rate falls quite a bit as a result of the increase in the money supply. Also the MEI function is fairly interest-elastic, so desired investment responds substantially to the fall in the interest rate. Taken together, the effect of the expansionary monetary policy is a large increase in desired investment expenditure and, hence, a large upward shift in the aggregate expenditure function.

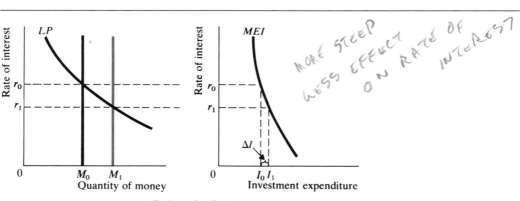

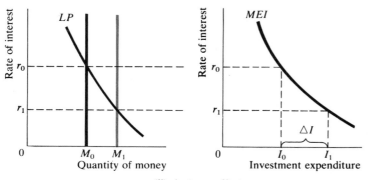

FIGURE 34.3 The Magnitude of the Effects of Changes in the Money Supply Depend on the Slopes of the *LP* and the *MEI* Curves. Comparing part (i) to part (ii), a given increase in the money supply from M_0 to M_1 causes a somewhat smaller reduction in the interest rate and a much smaller increase in desired investment expenditure in part (i), where LP is relatively flat and MEI relatively steep, than in part (ii), where LP is relatively steep and MEI relatively flat.

Summary: The influences of the shapes of the relevant curves can be summarized as follows.

- **The steeper (more interest-inelastic) the *LP* curve, the greater the effect on interest rates of a change in the money supply.**
- **The flatter (more interest-elastic) the *MEI* curve, the greater the effect on investment of any given change in the interest rate.**

Those who believe that monetary policy has strong effects on aggregate expenditure believe that changes in the money supply cause large changes in interest rates, which in turn cause large changes in desired investment expenditure. Those who believe that monetary policy has weak effects on aggregate expenditure believe that changes in the money supply cause small changes in interest rates, and that changes in interest rates cause only small changes in desired investment expenditure. Monetarists have often been associated with the view that monetary policy is strong, while some Keynesians have often been associated with the view that monetary policy is weak.

Will variations in the short-term interest rate really affect investment?:   A quite separate worry about monetary policy is based on the realization that the concept of 'the' interest rate that we have used above, refers to the whole structure of interest rates that we allowed for at the beginning of this chapter. The Bank's open-market operations are all conducted in short-term financial securities, most often Treasury Bills. Their initial effect is, therefore, on short-term interest rates.

If changes in short-term rates are to cause the whole structure of rates to change, longer-term rates must also vary. We saw earlier (see page 248) that long-term interest rates tend to be the average of expected short-term rates. This means that if the Bank drives up the short rate, and everyone expects this to be only a temporary policy, the longer-term rates term will rise by much less than the current short rate. Similarly, if the Bank drives the short rate down in what is expected to be a transitory policy, the longer-term rates will fall by very much less than the current short rate.

This means that, if the Bank wishes to influence aggregate demand by operating a monetary policy that alters the supply of money and short-term interest rates:

- **The effect will be larger the more people believe that the Bank will persist in its policy for as long as is required.**
- **The effect also will be larger on those elements of aggregate expenditure that respond more to short rates than to long rates.**

Stocks held by firms tend to be financed by short-term borrowing and to be quite responsive to variations in short-term interest rates. Mortgages, although for long periods, have interest rates that tend to follow short-term rates, sometimes with a bit of a time-lag. Even a temporary rise in the mortgage rate causes some people to postpone the purchase of new houses.[1]

Long-term investments in new factories, offices and machines tends to be financed for long periods at longer-term rates of interest. They will, therefore, be least affected by monetary policies that are not expected to persist over very long periods of time and thus do not have much effect on longer-term interest rates.

This suggests that, if the public doubts the Bank's determination to stick with some new monetary policy, expecting rather that it may be soon reversed, longer-term rates may be almost unaffected. The influence of aggregate expenditure will then be weak, and confined to easily postponable spending that is financed by short-term credit. This is why modern central bankers put so much stress on credibility. When they announce some major change in monetary policy, they do their best to persuade the public that, whatever the short-term pressures on them to alter their policy, they will stick to that policy until the target change in spending, or inflation, is achieved.

The evidence is strong (with one possible exception noted below) that, under most conditions, the Bank has the power to alter aggregate desired expenditure through a determined monetary policy. When there is an inflationary gap, the Bank operates a tight monetary policy that drives up interest rates. Stock accumulation, and new house construction (and consumers' spending) are the first to respond, while long-term capital investment may be more sluggish to react, both because long-term rates do not rise as much, and because favourable sales outlooks are often a more important determinant than the long-term interest rate. But as the Bank makes clear its determination to break the inflation, whatever the short-term costs in high interest rates and rising unemployment, long-term rates will rise as well, and longer-term investment will fall to some extent.

Countless central banks the world over have allowed inflation to increase to very rapid rates by following highly *expansionary* monetary policies that allowed aggregate expenditure to increase rapidly. In most cases, the Banks have then adopted *contractionary* monetary policies that have driven interest rates up to very high levels, eventually stopping the increases in aggregate expenditure and stopping the inflation. The Bank of England and the Federal Reserve System of the United States both did this at the beginning of the 1980s. Interest rates rose to unprecedented levels, real aggregate expenditure fell, unemployment rose and, eventually, inflation fell dramatically. Many South American countries have gone through several alternating periods of pro- and anti-inflation policies. They first created rapid inflations through expansionary monetary policies; they then reduced those inflations through contractionary monetary policies; they then repeated this policy sequence several times. This may not say much for their policy wisdom, but it provides ample evidence that the transmission mechanism works as described in this book.

---

1 Hire purchase and other types of consumer credit are all financed at short-term rates, so that consumption tends to respond to monetary policy as well as investment. This adds to the strength of the transmission mechanism that turns a monetary shock into a change in real expenditure.

The evidence of history is clear: expenditure (on both investment and consumption) is sensitive enough to interest rates that a really determined monetary policy can either create or remove inflationary gaps.

The one situation where there is doubt about the Bank's ability to alter an output gap is if it wishes to follow an expansionary policy during a full-fledged depression. If consumers are worried that they may lose their jobs, they may not increase their spending on new houses (or on consumers' goods) in response to a fall in short-term interest rates. If firms are worried about their solvency, they may not hold more stocks when short-term rates fall. Furthermore, if they already have substantial excess capacity they may not be willing to make new investments in fixed capital, even if the Bank succeeds in driving the long-term interest rate down.

During very depressed times the Bank may find it difficult to remove a recessionary gap through expansionary monetary policy, both because it may be hard to drive interest rates down very far (because the LP schedule is quite elastic), and because all forms of expenditure may become quite insensitive to reductions in the whole structure of interest rates.

Such circumstances are, however, the exception rather than the rule. In normal times of moderate recession or boom, the evidence is that, *if the Bank is willing to take whatever strong measures are necessary*, it can shift the

Summary

1 Because there are many financial assets, there is a whole structure of interest rates. *Ceteris paribus*, the rate on a particular asset will be higher (i) the greater the risk of default, (ii) the greater the political risk in its country of origin, and (iii) the longer its term to maturity. The long rate will be above (below) the short rate if the short rate is expected to rise (fall) in the future.

2 The Bank of England is the controller of the currency supply, it acts as banker to the government and to the retail banks, it carries out government policy with respect to the exchange rate and monetary policy, and it supports the financial system.

3 An open-market purchase of securities increases the cash reserves of the banking system and leads to a multiple expansion of deposit money. An open-market sale lowers reserves and leads to a multiple contraction of deposit money.

4 The Bank provides funds when the banking system is in need of liquidity, operating as a so-called lender of last resort. These funds are either provided by lending, possibly at a penal rate, or by entering the open market and buying bills so that the banking system can obtain the needed liquidity without borrowing from the Bank. The terms on which the Bank will provide liquidity have an effect on the retail banks' willingness to create deposit money.

5 The Bank's major intermediate target has sometimes been the interest rate, and sometimes the money supply. Currently the Bank seeks to control the economy by setting a band within which it controls interest rates by its open-market operations. If the Bank wishes to expand aggregate demand, it lowers its interest-rate target; to contract aggregate demand, it raises the target.

6 Stabilizing the money supply helps to stabilize the economy because free-market interest rates then vary in the same direction as national income. This helps to dampen down booms and mitigate slumps. Stabilizing interest rates removes the stabilizing force of pro-cyclical variations in interest rates and thus tends to accentuate cyclical swings in the economy.

7 Successful use of some measure of the money supply as an intermediate target requires that the money supply be controllable without overly long lags by the Bank's policy instruments, and that the chosen measure of the money supply maintains a fairly stable relation to the Bank's policy goals.

8 Economists still debate the extent to which the Bank can control any one measure of the money supply and many doubt that, if controlled, that measure will continue to show a stable relation with the target variables.

9 The strength of monetary policy depends on the slopes of the liquidity preference and the marginal efficiency of capital curves. A given change in the money supply will have a small effect if the *LP* curve is interest-elastic while the *MEI* curve is interest-inelastic; it will have a large effect if the *LP* curve is interest-inelastic while the *MEI* curve is interest-elastic.

10 The Bank can exert more influence on short-term rates than on long-term rates. This means that the impact effect of an alteration in monetary policy is likely to be mainly on consumers' credit-financed spending, on stock accumulation or decumulation, and on new house building. A sustained, long-term policy will eventually affect long rates and, through them, spending on capital equipment such as new factories and new machines.

aggregate desired expenditure curve either upwards or downwards by operating a sufficiently tough expansionary or contractionary monetary policy.

The long-term behaviour of the price level

Everyone agrees that a major task of monetary policy is to control the price level by preventing major inflations. Those who believe that monetary policy is not an effective short-term stabilization device go further and advocate control of the price level as the *sole* goal of monetary policy. They believe that the *rate* of monetary expansion should be set in such a way as to provide for the needs of a growing economy but not so as to validate any significant inflation. This view often leads them to advocate a constant trend rate of growth of the money supply – a rate of growth that takes no account of the short-term fluctuations in national income but that is set equal to the rate of growth of potential income. The idea is that the supply of money should be allowed to grow as fast as what the long-term trend-increase in the demand for money would be if the price level were steady. We shall have more to say about this simple monetary rule in later chapters.

Concentrating solely on the behaviour of the price level would represent a major shift in the Bank's policy variables. Influencing the cyclical behaviour of national income to maintain full employment is to be abandoned as a monetary policy variable. The full attention of monetary policy is then to be concentrated on controlling the long-term trend of the price level, i.e. the inflation rate.

This is an increasingly popular view and it is the view of the architects of the policy for a 'common European currency', which we shall study in a later chapter. They would make stabilization of the price level the sole objective of the European central bank that would control the European money supply.

Now that we have studied the Bank's monetary policy, we can move on to a further study of the behaviour of the economy, concentrating on long-term growth, employment and unemployment, and inflation. When this has been done, we shall return to look once again at the workings of both monetary and fiscal policy.

Questions

1 Which One or More of the following are functions of a central bank?
   (a) To operate the government's fiscal policy.
   (b) To control the money supply.
   (c) To be a banker to the government.
   (d) To provide temporary loans to manufacturing firms whose finances are basically sound but which are in temporary financial difficulties.

2 State whether each of the following is primarily an instrument (I), an intermediate target (T), or a goal (G) of monetary policy:
   (a) the money supply
   (b) the price level
   (c) open-market purchases and sales of bonds
   (d) the Bank's lending rate
   (e) full employment
   (f) the interest rate

3 Indicate the correct choice in each case.
Monetary policy will have a strong effect on aggregate desired expenditure the more (interest-elastic/interest-inelastic) is the *LP* curve and the more (interest-elastic/interest-inelastic) is the *MEI* curve.

4 True or False?
   (a) An open-market purchase of bonds by the Bank tends to increase the money supply.
   (b) The Bank cannot simultaneously pursue independent targets with respect to the interest rate *and* the money supply.
   (c) Monetary targets were increasingly favoured by the Bank of England throughout the 1980s.

5 If the Bank wishes to reduce a chronic inflationary gap that is causing a rapid inflation, which One or More of the following would be appropriate?
   (a) Open-market sales of bonds.
   (b) Increase in the rate at which it is willing to lend funds to the discount houses.
   (c) Pressure on retail banks to ease lending requirements.
   (d) Announce drastic reductions in its target rate of monetary expansion.

6 What methods does the Bank have to supply liquidity to the banking system?

7 In Figure 34.2 what would happen to the rate of interest if, with the liquidity preference curve fixed at LP_S, the money supply went from M_0 to M_N to M_1?

35 Aggregate Demand and Aggregate Supply

This chapter introduces two new tools of analysis, the aggregate demand curve and the aggregate supply curve. They will help us greatly in the studies of growth, unemployment and inflation that we undertake in the following three chapters. First, however, we need to review the main tool of analysis that we have used in macro-economics so far.

LIMITATIONS OF THE BASIC KEYNESIAN MODEL

So far our study of equilibrium national income has used the famous Keynesian '45°-line diagram' which graphs the simple *Keynesian model* in which both interest rates and the price level are fixed. This is the diagram that combines the aggregate desired expenditure curve with the 45° line, and determines equilibrium national income at their intersection. This model of the determination of equilibrium national income is often referred to as 'the' Keynesian model, although it is just the simplest version of a series of models all of which are Keynesian in spirit. It is a valuable tool of analysis, but it can only get us so far.

Limitations: One of its major disadvantages is that it cannot deal with any cause of inflation other than an inflationary gap at full employment. The analysis runs in terms of income, output and expenditure, which are *directly* measured on the diagram's axes. Implications for the price level can only be deduced *indirectly* – and then only for cases where a change in the price level is caused by an inflationary or a deflationary gap – i.e. inflations which come from the demand side.

The model cannot explicitly handle any inflation that starts from the cost side, such as would result from increases in the prices of imported raw materials or increases in wages that are not themselves the result of an inflationary gap. For this reason it provides no explanation, for example, of the important phenomenon of *stagflation* – rising prices at times of *high* unemployment.[1]

The crisis of stagflation: When stagflation first became a serious problem in the mid 1970s, it seemed such a mystery that numerous commentators proclaimed the end of Keynesian economics. In response to the challenge of new and surprising observations, theoretical and empirical work on stagflation proceeded at a hectic pace. Within a very few years an understanding of the problem was developed. Although this understanding did not overthrow Keynesian

economics, it did establish two points: (1) the conventional Keynesian 45° model must be amended to take account *explicitly* of the effects of changes in the price level on equilibrium national income; and (2) the conventional Keynesian model emphasized aggregate demand and paid insufficient attention to aggregate supply.

Of course, the full explanation of the events of the 1970s and 1980s is complex. But the essence of the explanation is so simple that it is now incorporated into elementary textbooks. It is to this revision and extension of the simple Keynesian model that we now turn our attention. The theory we are to develop is still Keynesian. This is because it deals with income variations in a model in which (i) expenditures are strongly influenced by income and (ii) where income can come to equilibrium in the short run when either a substantial inflationary or deflationary gap occurs.

THE DEMAND SIDE OF THE ECONOMY

What is now called THE AGGREGATE DEMAND CURVE in most modern economic literature is a curve relating the price level plotted on one axis and *equilibrium* national income plotted on the other. The equilibrium national income plotted in this new diagram is determined by the intersection of the aggregate desired expenditure curve and the 45° line.[1]

Equilibrium National Income when the Price Level Changes

Figure 35.1 shows the by-now familiar determination of national income in the 45° diagram. The initial aggregate desired expenditure curve is $E(P_0)$ and equilibrium national income is Y_0. (We will shortly explain why the P_0 is there.)

Now we ask a key question: what does a change in the price level do to the aggregate desired expenditure curve, given that the money supply is held constant? This question does not require further study, for we have already answered it in Chapter 33 when we discussed the monetary adjustment mechanism. Let us review that discussion now.

A rise in the price level increases the demand for money for transactions and precautionary purposes. This creates

---

1 For a definition and discussion of stagflation, see page 241.

1 Economics is a developing subject and so terminology is never fully agreed at any moment of time. Some economists use the term *macro demand curve* to refer to what we have just defined as the *aggregate demand curve*. They then use this latter term to refer to what we have called the aggregate desired expenditure curve.

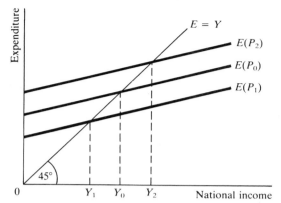

FIGURE 35.1 Determination of Equilibrium National Income when the Price Level is Changed. A rise in the price level from P_0 to P_1 shifts the aggregate desired expenditure curve downwards from $E(P_0)$ to $E(P_1)$ and thus lowers equilibrium income from Y_0 to Y_1. A fall in the price level from P_0 to P_2 has the opposite effect.

an excess demand for money that sets the monetary transmission mechanism in motion along the lines described in Figure 33.5 on page 368. (Since it is critical to everything that follows in this chapter, it is essential that you turn back to pages 365–7 now and review the workings of the monetary transmission mechanism.) The key result is so important that it deserves restating: *a rise in the price level, with the money supply held constant, increases the demand for money, which drives the interest rate up, which lowers desired investment expenditure, which shifts the aggregate desired expenditure function downwards.*

In Figure 35.1 the rise in the price level from P_0 to P_1 shifts the aggregate desired expenditure curve downwards from $E(P_0)$ to $E(P_1)$ and lowers equilibrium national income from Y_0 to Y_1.

A fall in the price level has the opposite effects. Because the money value of transactions falls, so also does the transaction demand for money. This causes a monetary disequilibrium and sets in train the events outlined in Figure 33.4 on page 368. The key result is: *a fall in the price level reduces the demand for money, which drives the interest rate down, which increases desired investment, which shifts the desired expenditure curve upwards.*

A fall in the price level from P_0 to P_2 shifts the aggregate desired expenditure curve upwards in Figure 35.1 from $E(P_0)$ to $E(P_2)$ and raises equilibrium national income from Y_0 to Y_2.

Because a change in the price level shifts the aggregate expenditure curve, each such curve must be related to a specific, and constant, price level. We did not have to worry about this in Part 4 because we were *assuming* a constant price level. Now, to remind us of this assumption, we state in parentheses after each aggregate expenditure curve's label the price level to which it relates.

Derivation of the Aggregate Demand Curve

To derive the aggregate demand curve we merely plot in Figure 35.2 each equilibrium national income as determined in Figure 35.1 against the price level that determined it. Thus income Y_0 is plotted against price level P_0 to yield point *a*, income Y_1 against price level P_1 to yield point *b* and Y_2 against P_2 to yield point *c*. If we imagine changing the price level continuously, we can plot out the curve in Figure 35.2, each point relating a specific price level to the specific equilibrium national income with which it is associated.

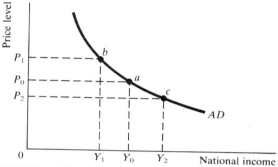

FIGURE 35.2 The Aggregate Demand Curve. The aggregate demand curve plots the equilibrium national income determined in Figure 35.1 against the price level associated with that level of income. The *AD* curve slopes downward to the right because the higher the price level, the lower is equilibrium national income, *ceteris paribus.*

The curve so derived is called an *aggregate demand (AD) curve* and it relates each price level to its associated level of *equilibrium* national income. The curve is negatively sloped because, *ceteris paribus*, the higher the price level the lower the level of equilibrium national income. It is important to remember the qualification of *ceteris paribus*. In particular the money supply is being held constant. The rise in the price level creates a money shortage that drives up the interest rate and lowers interest-sensitive expenditure; that is the process we studied on pages 365–7, and it explains why equilibrium income is reduced. In this instance, the contractionary monetary shock is a rise in the price level which leads to an increase in the demand for money. This sets the transmission mechanism in motion leading to a fall in aggregate desired expenditure and hence in equilibrium national income.

Movements Along, and Shifts of, the *AD* Curve

We now come to a point on which you must take special care: do not confuse movements along the *AD* curve with shifts of that curve.

Movements along the *AD* curve: We have seen that the *AD* curve plots equilibrium national income against the price level. Although changes in the price level *shift* the aggregate expenditure curve in Figure 35.1, they move the economy *along* its *AD* curve in Figure 35.2. The *AD* curve is designed to show how equilibrium national income changes as the price level changes (when the quantity of money is held constant). So when we move along the *AD* curve, we are observing the relation between equilibrium national income and the price level, other things being equal.

Shifts of the *AD* curve: We have seen that the *AD* curve shows the *equilibrium* national income that corresponds to each particular price level. Thus any force that *changes the equilibrium national income that is associated with a given price level* must shift the *AD* curve. These are shifts in desired expenditure on consumption, investment, government exhaustive purchases, and net exports. Increases in any of these will raise aggregate desired expenditure (at any given price level), increase equilibrium income, and hence shift the *AD* curve outwards to the right. Thus, *anything other than a change in the price level that shifts the aggregate desired expenditure curve, and so alters equilibrium national income at a given price level, also shifts the AD curve.*

The above analysis allows us to restate the conclusions we reached in Part 4, as follows.

A rise in the amount of desired consumption, investment, government, or net export expenditure associated with each level of national income shifts the *AD* curve to the right. A fall in any of these desired expenditures shifts the *AD* curve to the left.

Such shifts are shown in Figure 35.3. The original curve is *AD*. A rise in any component of desired expenditure shifts the curve to the right, say to *AD'*. A fall in any component of desired expenditure shifts the curve to the left, say to *AD''*.

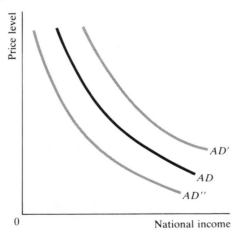

FIGURE 35.3 A Shift in the Aggregate Demand Curve. A rightward shift in the *AD* curve indicates that a higher level of equilibrium national income is associated with each price level; a leftward shift indicates a lower level.

THE SUPPLY SIDE OF THE ECONOMY IN THE SHORT RUN

Everything to do with aggregate demand is referred to as being on the 'demand side' of the economy, while everything to do with aggregate supply is referred to as being on the 'supply side'. We now pass to a consideration of the supply side.

Our first step is to remove an unrealistic assumption that we have used to simplify all of the macroeconomic theory that we have studied so far. This is the assumption that income cannot exceed Y_F. According to this assumption, if the aggregate expenditure curve cuts the 45° line at a national income above Y_F, as in Figure 28.2(i) on page 315, actual income will be at Y_F and the inflationary gap will cause the price level to rise.

From now on, however, we will allow an inflationary gap – desired expenditure exceeds income at Y_F – to cause actual national income to rise temporarily above Y_F, as well as causing prices to rise. (We explain in detail on page 394 why actual income, Y_1, can temporarily exceed potential income Y_F.) Whenever actual income does exceed potential income there must be an inflationary gap – if equilibrium Y exceeds Y_F, the aggregate desired expenditure curve must lie above the 45° line at Y_F.

Next we define a new curve. The AGGREGATE SUPPLY CURVE (AS) shows the total output (i.e. the real national income) that all the firms in the economy will be willing to produce at each price level. It turns out that, although one aggregate demand curve is all we need, we need two aggregate supply curves, one for the short run and one for the long run. We first consider the short-run curve and then, later in the chapter, we study the long-run curve.

The short-run aggregate supply curve: The SHORT-RUN AGGREGATE SUPPLY CURVE (*SRAS*) shows how much will be produced and offered for sale at each price level *on the assumption that the firm's input prices – labour, raw materials, etc. – are fixed.* Two such curves, labelled *SRAS* and *SRAS'*, are shown in Figure 35.4. For the moment, let us concentrate on the curve drawn with a solid line and labelled *SRAS*.

The slope of the *SRAS* curve: The *SRAS* curve is positively sloped indicating that, other things being equal, the higher the price level, the greater will be the total quantity that will be produced, and the lower the price level, the less will be the total quantity produced. *It is important to remember that the other things that are held constant along an SRAS curve include the prices of all inputs.*

Let us now investigate the reasons for this overall upward slope. Suppose that, because of an increase in aggregate expenditure, firms wish to increase their current production. Even if the *prices* of all of the firms' inputs remain constant, this does not necessarily mean that firms' unit costs will remain unchanged. Increasing output may require that less efficient standby machines and plants are used, less efficient marginal workers are employed, and the

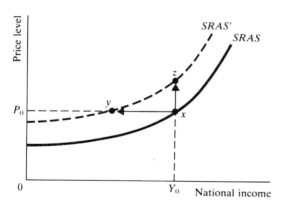

FIGURE 35.4 Two Short-Run Aggregate Supply Curves. *SRAS* curves slope upward to the right. The shift from *SRAS* to *SRAS'* indicates a reduction in aggregate supply because after the shift a given output, Y_0, requires a higher price level, point z, while the same price level, P_0, is associated with a lower total output, point y.

existing workers put in overtime. Thus, even with the restriction that prices per unit of input remain constant, higher output is associated with increased costs per unit of output because it requires the use of more, and more costly, methods of production.

This increase in *cost per unit of output* is referred to as *rising unit costs*. Since expanding output usually implies such higher unit costs, firms will only produce extra output if that output can be sold at higher prices. Thus, as the economy moves to the right along the *SRAS* curve, higher output tends to be associated with higher output prices.[1]

Now consider what happens when firms wish to reduce their output. The forces just discussed then work in reverse. There will be cost savings as the least efficient labour is laid off first, and the least efficient capital is put on standby. Thus, the lower output will be associated with somewhat lower unit costs and with lower output prices.

In summary, the positively sloped, short-run aggregate supply curve shows that, with input prices constant, higher output is associated with higher output prices because unit costs of production vary directly with output.

Shifts in the *SRAS* curve: As the next step in our study, we consider shifts in the *SRAS* curve. Such shifts are often called SUPPLY-SIDE SHOCKS. The short-run aggregate supply curve will shift if there is *any* change which affects the output that firms offer for sale at each given price level. Here we consider two of the most important.

Changes in input prices.   We have assumed so far that input prices are held constant along the *SRAS* curve. If we

now drop this assumption, we can see one important reason for the *SRAS* curve to shift. If input prices rise, firms will find that the profitability of their current production has been reduced. Their response is to raise output prices to cover their increased costs. This in turn causes the *SRAS* curve to shift up and to the left.

Increases in productivity.   If labour productivity rises, meaning that each worker can produce more, the unit costs of production will fall, as long as wage rates do not rise sufficiently to fully offset the productivity rise. Lower costs generally lead to lower prices. Competing firms cut prices in attempts to raise their market shares, and the net result of such competition is that the fall in production costs is accompanied by a fall in prices.

Since the same output is sold at a lower price, this causes a downward shift in the *SRAS* curve.

Using the terminology we used in the theory of price in Part 2, an upward shift in the *SRAS* curve is referred to as a *decrease in supply* because at any given price level, less output will be produced. Putting the same point another way, for any given level of output to be willingly produced, an increase in price will be required. This is illustrated in Figure 35.4.

In the Figure, the initial *SRAS* curve is shown by the black curve. An increase in input prices shifts the curve upward to the grey line, *SRAS'*.

Because the *SRAS* curve is positively sloped, this upward shift also moves the curve to the left. For example, suppose the price level is initially at P_0 and output is arbitrarily assumed to be Y_0 (point x). Following an increase in factor prices that reduces profitability, firms could maintain prices and reduce output, thus moving from point x to point y. They might, instead, maintain output but increase prices, thus moving from point x to point z. Or they could have some combination of price increases and output reductions, moving them to some point on *SRAS'* between y and z. The point to which the firms actually move depends, as we shall see, on the shape of the *AD* curve. But what is important is that *SRAS'* lies above and to the left of the original curve, *SRAS*.

A change in either factor prices, or productivity, will shift the *SRAS* curve because any given output will be supplied at a different price level than previously. An increase in factor prices, or a decrease in productivity, shifts the *SRAS* curve to the left; a decrease in factor prices or an increase in productivity shifts it to the right.

EQUILIBRIUM OF AGGREGATE DEMAND AND AGGREGATE SUPPLY IN THE SHORT RUN

Our next step is to bring the *AD* and the *SRAS* curves together to determine the short-run equilibrium values for national income and the price level.

Figure 35.5 does this. Equilibrium of aggregate demand and aggregate supply occurs where the *AD* and *SRAS*

1 Those who have read Part 3 will realize that we are assuming, as is true for most of manufacturing, that firms do not sell their products in perfectly competitive markets. Instead they are price-makers who sell in oligopolistic markets and we assume that a rise in unit costs will lead the firm to increase the price that it charges for its output. The micro behaviour that lies behind this key assumption is discussed in IPE.

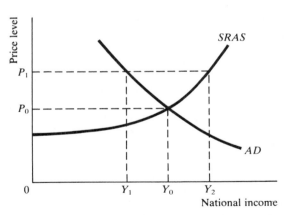

FIGURE 35.5 The Determination of National Income and the Price Level. The aggregate demand and the aggregate supply curves together determine the economy's price level and its total output. Equilibrium output is Y_0 and the equilibrium price level is P_0.

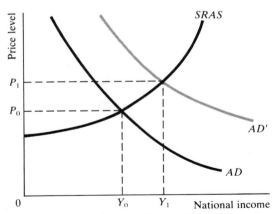

FIGURE 35.6 Aggregate Demand Shocks. Shifts in AD cause the price level and real national income to move in the same direction. A shift from AD to AD' raises income from Y_0 to Y_1 and the price level from P_0 to P_1.

curves intersect. This yields the price level of P_0 and the real national income of Y_0 in the Figure. At higher price levels, aggregate supply exceeds aggregate demand; at lower price levels, aggregate demand exceeds aggregate supply. For example, if the price level were P_1, national income would be in equilibrium at Y_1 (in the sense that purchasers would just be willing to buy that output *if* it were produced). Producers, however, would wish to make and sell Y_2. The resulting surplus would then force prices down from P_1 to P_0.

Shifts in the *AD* and *SRAS* Curves

Next consider what happens when either the AD or the $SRAS$ curve shifts, i.e. when the economy is hit with either a demand or a supply-side shock.

Aggregate demand shocks: Figure 35.6 illustrates the effects of an increase in aggregate demand on the price level and real output. As previously explained, the increase could have occurred because of an increase in any type of autonomous spending – i.e. spending not resulting from a change in income. Examples are increased investment, increased government spending, or greater net exports. For the moment, we are not concerned with the source of the increase; we are interested in its implications for the price level and real output.

A demand shock now hits the economy in the form of a shift in the aggregate demand curve from AD to AD'. The price level rises from P_0 to P_1, and real national income rises from Y_0 to Y_1. Because the increase in aggregate demand causes the AD curve to shift to the right, the new equilibrium entails a movement along the $SRAS$ curve so that both the price level and the quantity of real output increase.

A decrease in aggregate demand causes AD to shift to the left, say from AD' to AD. As a result, the price level falls from P_1 to P_0 while real national income falls from Y_1 to Y_0.

Let us summarize what we have now established:

Because the *SRAS* curve slopes upward to the right, aggregate demand shocks cause the price level and real national income to change in the same direction, both rising or both falling together.

Aggregate supply shocks: Figure 35.7 shows the effect of a supply shock consisting of a shift in the $SRAS$ curve to the left. This might have been caused by a change in costs of production – for example, by a rise in the price of imported raw materials or in the wage rate paid to labour. The shift from $SRAS$ to $SRAS'$ causes the equilibrium price level to rise from P_0 to P_1 while national income falls from Y_0 to Y_1.

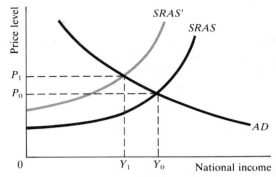

FIGURE 35.7 Aggregate Supply Shocks. Shifts in $SRAS$ cause the price level and real national income to move in opposite directions. A shift from $SRAS$ to $SRAS'$ lowers income from Y_0 to Y_1 while raising the price level from P_0 to P_1.

An increase in aggregate supply caused, say, by an increase in productivity, causes the curve to shift downwards. This can be shown by assuming the initial aggregate supply curve is $SRAS'$ in Figure 35.7, and then letting it shift to $SRAS$. National income then *rises* from Y_1 to Y_0, while the price level *falls* from P_1 to P_0.

The cases we have just studied are caused by shifts in the *SRAS* curve and movements along the *AD* curve. They lead to the following important conclusion:

Aggregate supply shocks cause the price level and real national income to change in opposite directions, one rising and the other falling.

Various output gaps

The output gap is defined as potential income minus actual income ($Y_F - Y_0$ where Y_F is potential income and Y_0 is actual income). We have many times dealt with positive output gaps in which actual income fell short of potential income. We have usually called such gaps *recessionary gaps*. In the simple Keynesian model, output cannot rise above its potential, or full-employment, level. The model we have just constructed is, however, more realistic in allowing income to rise above potential, at least in the short run. When this happens, capital is being worked above its normal utilization rate, and labour is working overtime. As a result, output rises above potential because resources are being worked above their normal intensities of use. This causes a *negative* output gap since actual income, Y_0, exceeds potential income, Y_F. This negative output gap is often referred to as an *inflationary output gap*.

The two output gaps for which we must now allow are illustrated in Figure 35.8.[1]

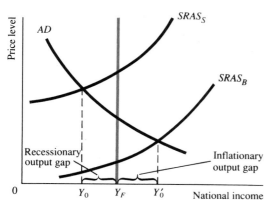

FIGURE 35.8 Output Gaps can be Positive or Negative. The output gap of potential income minus actual income is positive when the *SRAS* curve is at $SRAS_S$ (for slump) and income is Y_0. This gap is also called a recessionary output gap. The gap is negative when the *SRAS* curve is $SRAS_B$ (for boom) and income is Y_0'. This gap is called an inflationary output gap.

---

1 We earlier identified two *expenditure gaps*, a deflationary expenditure gap when desired expenditure would fall short of what is required to buy full-employment output, and an inflationary expenditure gap when desired expenditure would exceed what is required to buy full-employment output. Now we have two related *output gaps*: a recessionary output gap is the amount by which output falls short of full-employment output, and an inflationary output gap is the amount by which output exceeds full-employment output.

The Slope of the *SRAS* Curve Further Considered

So far we have merely said that the *SRAS* curve is positively sloped. We must now consider a somewhat less obvious, but in many ways more important, property of a typical *SRAS* curve: its slope *increases* as output rises, being relatively flat to the left of potential output and relatively steep to the right. This is the first of two important asymmetries related to aggregate supply. We need to consider it in some detail.

The first asymmetry of aggregate supply: the varying slope of *SRAS*

Below potential output, firms will typically have unused capacity – some plant and equipment will be idle. When firms are faced with unused capacity, only a small increase in the price of their output may be needed to induce them to expand production, at least up to normal capacity. Indeed, some firms may be willing to produce and sell more at *existing prices* if only the demand were there. (This is the case where the firm's short-run supply curve is perfectly elastic and output is determined by its intersection with a downward-sloping demand curve.)

Once output is pushed very far beyond normal capacity, however, unit costs tend to rise quite rapidly. Older, higher-cost equipment that normally stands idle may have to be used. Bottlenecks appear in more and more stages of the production process. Overtime and extra shifts may have to be worked. These expedients raise the cost of producing a unit of output more and more as output expands. Many more costly productive techniques may also have to be adopted. These higher-cost methods will not be used unless selling prices can be raised to cover them. Furthermore, the more output is expanded beyond normal capacity, the more do unit costs tend to rise and hence the larger is the price rise associated with each further increase in output.

Below potential national income, changes in output are accompanied by relatively small changes in the price level; above potential national income, changes in output are accompanied by large changes in the price level.

The effects of *AD* shifts further considered

Now that we have learned more about the general slope of the *SRAS* curve, we can be a little more specific about the effects of shifts in the *AD* curve than we were when we first studied them in Figure 35.6.

Figure 35.9 shows an *SRAS* curve that is upward-sloping over its whole range. Its slope gets steeper the further to the right we move along it, being rather flat to the left of Y_F and rather steep to the right of Y_F.

The consequences of this shape are shown by combining the *SRAS* curve with various aggregate demand curves shown in the Figure. The curve *AD* produces equilibrium at income Y_0 and price level P_0. An increase in demand to AD' raises national income by a large amount to Y_1 and

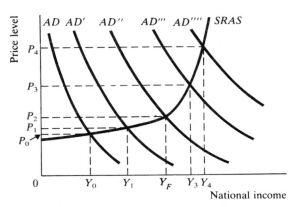

FIGURE 35.9 Shifts in the *AD* Curve with an *SRAS* Curve of Varying Slope. Given shifts in *AD* cause large changes in Y and small changes in P when Y is below Y_F, but small changes in Y and large changes in P when Y is above Y_F.

increases the price level only slightly to P_1. A further increase to *AD″* takes national income to Y_F and the price level to P_2, again a large increase in income and a relatively small increase in the price level. Once potential income is passed, however, the responses of Y and P to shifts in *AD* alter. As aggregate demand rises from *AD″* to *AD‴*, and finally to *AD⁗*, the increase in national income (from Y_F to Y_3 and Y_4) get smaller, while the increases in the price level (from P_2 to P_3 and P_4) get larger.

This leads to an important conclusion: the further is equilibrium income *below* potential income, the more will national income change and the less will the price level change for any given shift in the aggregate demand curve; and the further is equilibrium income *above* potential income, the less will national income change and the more will the price level change for any given shift in the aggregate demand curve.

THE SUPPLY SIDE OF THE ECONOMY IN THE LONG RUN

So far we have concentrated on the short-run aggregate supply curve – a curve that assumes the prices of all inputs used by the firm are constant. Now we need to look at the behaviour of aggregate supply over a longer period of time. The key to understanding the *long-run* aggregate supply curve is to see how changes in aggregate demand *induce* shifts in the *short-run* aggregate supply curve. Thus we will study induced shifts in the *SRAS* curve for the next several sections. When we fully understand these, we will be able to derive, and appreciate the significance of, the long-run aggregate supply curve.

Effects of an Increase in Aggregate Demand on the *SRAS* Curve

To see the long-run effects of an increase in aggregate demand, we assume that the economy starts off in the

happy position of full employment and a stable price level, as pictured in Figure 35.10. In that Figure the initial curves are *AD* and *SRAS*, which produce an equilibrium level of income equal to the economy's potential level, Y_F, and a price level of P_0. A rise in autonomous expenditure, perhaps caused by an investment boom, shifts the aggregate demand curve to *AD′*. The immediate effects are that the price level rises to P_1 while real income rises above its potential level to Y_1.

Firms will now be producing beyond their normal capacity output, so there will be an excess demand for all factor inputs, including labour. Here we concentrate on the cost of labour to the firm, although analogous arguments apply to other factors. Workers will be demanding wage increases to compensate them for the higher cost of living caused by the increase in the price level. Thus the boom generates a combination of conditions – higher profits for firms, greater demand for labour, and a desire on the part of labour for wages to catch up with the price rises – that is, a recipe for increases in wages. Indeed, this sequence is just what past experience of the economy tells us will happen.

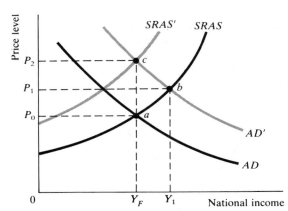

FIGURE 35.10 The Short- and Long-term Effects of a Rise in Aggregate Demand. An upward shift of the *AD* curve from *AD* to *AD′* first raises the price level from P_0 to P_1, and output from Y_F to Y_1, along a given *SRAS* curve. It then induces a shift of the *SRAS* curve to *SRAS′*. This further raises the price level to P_2, but lowers output to Y_F along the curve *AD′*.

Increases in wages mean increases in costs. These, as we have already seen, lead to upward shifts in the *SRAS* curve as firms pass on their increases in unit costs by increasing their output prices. For this reason, the rise in the price level from P_0 to P_1 and real output from Y_F to Y_1 in Figure 35.10 is *not the end of the story*. The upward shift of the *SRAS* curve causes a further rise in the price level, but this time the price rise is associated with a fall in output. The cost increases, and the consequent upward shifts in the *SRAS* curve go on until income returns to its potential level. Only then does the excess demand for labour disappear. At this point, the short-run aggregate supply curve has shifted to *SRAS′* in Figure 35.10, taking equilibrium income back to Y_F and the price level yet higher to P_2.

Starting from full employment and a stable price level

(point *a* in Figure 35.10), the sequence of events following a demand shock can now be summarized.

(1) A rise in aggregate demand raises the price level and raises income above its potential level as the economy expands along a given *SRAS* curve (to point *b* in Figure 35.10).

(2) The expansion of output beyond its *normal* capacity level puts pressure on factor markets; factor prices then begin to rise, shifting the *SRAS* curve upward.

(3) The shift of the *SRAS* curve causes output to fall along the given *AD* curve; this process continues *as long as* actual output exceeds potential output. Therefore, actual output eventually falls back to its potential level. The price level is now higher than it was after the initial impact of the increased aggregate demand, but inflation will have come to a halt (when the economy reaches point *c* in the Figure).

The above reasoning shows that it would be misleading to assume that there is a fixed and unchanging upward-sloping aggregate supply curve. The ability to increase output beyond the economy's potential output is only a short-term success. Achieving real income greater than Y_F sets up inflationary pressures that tend to push national income back to Y_F.

Effects of a Decrease in Aggregate Demand on the *SRAS* Curve

Let us return to that happy economy with full employment and stable prices that we considered above. It appears again in Figure 35.11, which duplicates the initial conditions of Figure 35.10. The initial curves are *AD* and *SRAS*, making actual income equal to potential income at Y_F and the price level P_0 (point *a*).

Now assume a *decline* in the aggregate demand curve from *AD* to *AD″*, perhaps due to a major reduction in investment expenditure.

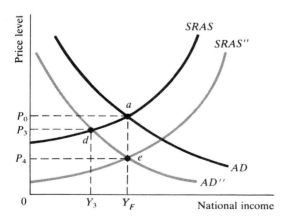

FIGURE 35.11 The Short- and Long-run Effects of a Fall in Aggregate Demand. A downward shift of the *AD* curve from *AD* to *AD″* first lowers the price level from P_0 to P_3 and output from Y_F to Y_3 along the *SRAS* curve. It then induces a (slow) shift of the *SRAS* curve to *SRAS″* that further lowers the price level from P_3 to P_4 but raises output from Y_3 to Y_F along the *AD″* curve.

The impact of this decline is a fall in income to Y_3 and some downward adjustment of the price level to P_3, as shown in the Figure (point *d*). As output falls, unemployment will rise. The resulting recessionary gap is $Y_F - Y_3$.

The importance of the labour market

In the previous section we assumed that excess demand in the labour market caused money wages to rise. There is ample evidence that this is the case in the real world. Now, however, we are considering a case in which there is excess supply in the labour market; there are insufficient jobs to employ everyone who would like to work at the going wage rate.

If the labour market were perfectly competitive, money wages would fall in the face of excess supply of labour so as to clear the market. But trade unions exert substantial monopoly power in the labour market and are often able to resist downward adjustment in wages. At most, wages fall very slowly in the face of excess labour supply; in the limit, they do not fall at all. In other words, unemployment has, *at most*, a weak and sluggish downward effect on wages and may have no effect at all. For this reason we must study two cases – one where wages fall and one where they do not.

Downward wage flexibility: Consider what would happen *if* the resulting unemployment did cause wage rates to fall. Falling wage rates would lower costs for firms, and competition among firms to sell in a depressed market would lead them to cut prices, once their falling costs gave them scope to do so. This in turn would cause a downward shift in the short-run aggregate supply curve. As a result of the shifting *SRAS* curve, the economy would move along its fixed *AD″* curve with falling prices and rising output until the *SRAS* curve reached *SRAS″* in Figure 35.11 and full employment was restored at potential national income, Y_F, and a lower price level, P_4 (point *e*).

We conclude that *if* wages were to fall whenever there was unemployment – a condition called 'downward flexibility of wages' – the resulting fall in the *SRAS* curve would restore full employment. In other words, downwardly flexible wages would provide an automatic adjustment mechanism that would push the economy back toward full employment whenever output fell below potential.

Wages that are flexible in both an upwards and a downwards direction make the economy's adjustment to increases and decreases in demand symmetrical. On the one hand, a rise in demand opens up an inflationary gap and the ensuing rise in wages eliminates the gap, returning national income to its full-employment level. On the other hand, a fall in demand opens up a recessionary gap and the ensuing fall in wages eliminates the gap, returning income to its full-employment level.

Downward wage inflexibility: Unfortunately, the symmetrical world in which flexible wages eliminate both inflationary and deflationary shocks with equal effectiveness does not exist in reality. Instead, the economy's behaviour is asymmetric, in the sense that wages respond rapidly to excess demand but only sluggishly to excess supply. Therefore, although the adjustment mechanism described in Figure 35.10 acts quickly to remove excess demand, the adjustment mechanism described in Figure 35.11 is, *at best*, weak and slow-acting in its removal of excess supply.

Raw material prices, many of which are competitively determined, fall in recessions. This will push the *SRAC* curve downwards. But since wages account for the majority of costs in many lines of production, full employment cannot be restored by forces acting solely on the cost side unless wages fall.

Notice that the weakness of the automatic adjustment mechanism does not mean that slumps must last indefinitely. All that it means is that, if the economy is to avoid a lengthy recession in conditions of downward wage inflexibility, the force leading to recovery must be an upward shift of the *AD* curve rather than a downward drift of the *SRAS* curve.

The second asymmetry of aggregate supply: Varying speed of shifts of *SRAS*

We have now arrived at what may be called the second asymmetry of the supply side of the economy. (The first is the slope of the *SRAS* curve, flat below Y_F and steep above Y_F.)

The second asymmetry runs as follows: boom conditions, with severe labour shortages, do cause wages to rise rapidly, thereby causing rapid upward shifts of the *SRAS* curve; but slump conditions, with heavy unemployment, do not cause wages to fall with a corresponding speed and, hence, do not cause the *SRAS* curve to shift downwards rapidly.

The second asymmetry of aggregate supply behaviour explains two key characteristics of our economy. First, unemployment *can* persist for quite long periods without causing large decreases in wages and prices (which would, if they did occur, help to remove the unemployment). Second, booms, with labour shortages and production beyond normal capacity, *cannot* persist for long periods without causing large increases in wages and prices.

The Long-Run Aggregate Supply Curve

So far our analysis has concentrated on the interaction between the *AD* and the *SRAS* curves. Now we must consider what happens in the long run. Although, as we have seen, the downward adjustment of wages may not remove recessionary gaps fast enough to be acceptable to policy-makers, the *possibility* of automatic adjustments gives rise to an important theoretical concept called the LONG-RUN AGGREGATE SUPPLY (LRAS) CURVE. This curve relates the price level to equilibrium real national income *on the assumption that all input costs,*

including wages rates, have been fully adjusted to eliminate any excess demand or supply. It thus shows the national income that would occur if wages were flexible enough in both directions to eliminate any excess demand or excess supply of labour. Full employment would then prevail and output would be at its potential level, Y_F.

Thus, when all input prices are fully adjusted, the aggregate supply curve becomes a vertical line at Y_F, as seen in Figure 35.12. Along the *LRAS* curve, the prices of *all* outputs and *all* inputs have been fully adjusted to eliminate excess demands or supplies in all markets. Points on the *LRAS* curve thus refer to situations where the prices of *all* outputs and *all* inputs have changed equi-proportionally (i.e. the same percentage change in each price).

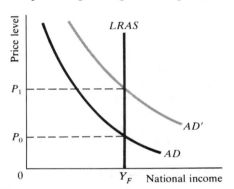

FIGURE 35.12 Long-Run Effects of Shifts in *AD* and *LRAS* Curves. When *LRAS* is vertical, aggregate supply determines Y and aggregate demand determines P. An increase from *AD* to *AD'* raises the price level from P_0 to P_1, while leaving income constant at Y_F.

Equal proportionate changes in money wages and in the price level (which, by definition, will leave real wages unaltered) will also leave equilibrium employment and output unchanged. The key concept is this: if the price of absolutely everything (including labour) changes in the same proportion, then nothing real changes. When the prices of everything bought *and* sold change, everyone's real position is unchanged and, hence, no one has any incentive to alter behaviour. Output, therefore, is unchanged. The level of output will be what can be produced in the economy when all factors of production, including labour, are utilized at their 'normal' levels of capacity.

It follows that the long-run equilibrium level of output is unaffected by the price level.

Equilibrium output and price level in the long run

Figure 35.12 shows the long-run equilibrium output and price level determined by the intersection of the *AD* curve and the vertical *LRAS* curve. The initial aggregate demand curve is *AD*, which intersects the long-run aggregate supply curve to produce the price level P_0. When the aggregate demand curve shifts upwards to *AD'*, *long-run* equilibrium income stays at Y_F but the price level rises to P_1.

One important implication of this analysis is that if the *LRAS* curve is vertical, output is determined solely by conditions of supply in the long run, and the role of aggregate demand is simply to determine the price level.

Note we are here discussing only long-term tendencies. To see the short-term impact of demand shocks and supply shocks, we need to use the short-run aggregate supply curve. The vertical *LRAS* curve is really nothing more than an expression of the long-run neutrality of money (see Chapter 30, page 340). It says that a full-employment equilibrium of the economy *can* be achieved at any price level. The extent to which the *LRAS* curve is useful for applied analysis of the real world is quite another matter. For example, downward pressures on the price level are slow to act. For this reason, the *LRAS* curve is usually a poor guide to practical policy when the *AD* curve shifts left.

Note the sharp difference between the long-term and short-term results that we have obtained. Aggregate demand shocks exert an influence on real income only in the short run. When national income is already at full employment, real income cannot be permanently increased by raising aggregate demand. What is needed to do this job is a rightward shift of the *LRAS* curve, and a major source of such shifts is investment. Many early Keynesians paid little attention to the long-run effect of investment on aggregate supply. Although not an unreasonable thing to do when analysing the severe recessionary conditions of the 1930s, the neglect is serious when the economy is operating at or near full employment. These matters are discussed in detail in the next chapter. First, however, it may be helpful to relate what we have learned in this chapter to the aggregate supply curve that was implicit in everything we did in Part 4.

The Keynesian aggregate supply curve

In Part 4 (and in Part 5, up to this chapter) we used an aggregate supply curve that was so simple that we did not need to draw it. This is the *Keynesian aggregate supply curve* that underlies the simple Keynesian model. (It is also sometimes called the 'J-shaped' or the 'reverse L-shaped' aggregate supply curve because it resembles a J and the mirror image of an L.) It is composed of a horizontal segment for national incomes up to full-employment income, Y_F, and a vertical segment at Y_F. (See Figure 35.13.)

Let us recall how this Keynesian aggregate supply curve arises. In all of our macroeconomics until Chapter 35, we assumed that when firms had excess capacity, they would produce and supply all that they could sell at current prices. *This makes the economy's aggregate supply curve up to Y_F horizontal at the current general price level.*

We also assumed that full-capacity output was the maximum that firms could produce. This means that national income can never exceed Y_F, so that *the economy's aggregate supply curve is vertical at Y_F.*

The resulting Keynesian aggregate supply curve is shown by *KAS* in Figure 35.13.

It can be regarded as a limiting case of the more general

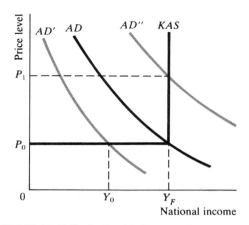

FIGURE 35.13 Shifts in the *AD* Curve with a Keynesian Aggregate Supply Curve. Below potential income, fluctuations in *AD* cause fluctuations only in national income; at potential income, increases in *AD* cause increases only in the price level.

SRAS curve shown in Figures 35.4 and 35.8. The Keynesian curve arises when the flattish portion of the *SRAS* curve below Y_F becomes perfectly flat (horizontal), and the steep portion above Y_F becomes as steep as possible (vertical).

Shifts in *AD* with the Keynesian AS curve: Figure 35.13 shows a Keynesian *AS* curve, together with several aggregate demand curves. Fluctuations in the *AD* curve between *AD* and *AD'* will cause national income to fluctuate between Y_0 and Y_F while leaving the price level constant at P_0. This is the case we studied throughout Part 4. The *AS* curve was horizontal, the price level was fixed, and equilibrium national income was determined by aggregate demand.

Note also that an increase in aggregate demand from *AD* to *AD''* raises the price level from P_0 to P_1 while leaving national income constant at Y_F.

The Keynesian aggregate supply curve was useful in our earlier chapters, but, for a detailed study of the relation between output and prices it represents an over-simplified view of the economy. Two key aspects of the economy that it suppresses are the following:

- First, changes in national income below the level of Y_F are often observed to be accompanied by changes in *both* real income *and* the price level. The horizontal Keynesian *AS* curve denies this possibility.
- Second, potential income is not an absolute constraint on output. At the micro level, firms can, and often do, produce beyond their normal capacity outputs, although the further they try to push output beyond normal capacity, the more costly it usually becomes to do so. At the macro level, the economy is sometimes observed at a level of income in excess of potential or full-employment income. (This gives rise to a situation sometimes called 'over-full employment'.)

Summary

1 The 45° diagram is not suited to studying inflation because it can cope with inflation coming from the demand, but not from the supply, side. Although it can implicitly analyse demand inflations, because it does show the inflationary gap, it cannot handle cost-side inflations.

2 The aggregate demand curve plots the relationship between the general price level and equilibrium national income. It is negatively sloped because increases in the price level lower the equilibrium income through the monetary adjustment mechanism.

3 Anything that shifts the aggregate desired expenditure curve upwards – other than a fall in the price level – shifts the aggregate demand curve to the right. Anything that shifts the aggregate expenditure curve downwards – other than a rise in the price level – shifts the aggregate demand curve to the left.

4 The short-run aggregate supply curve is positively sloped, indicating that the price level rises with output (because unit costs rise with output). The *SRAS* curve is relatively flat to the left of potential income and relatively steep to the right of it.

5 A rise in input prices or a fall in productivity shifts the *SRAS* curve upwards, while a fall in input prices or a rise in productivity shifts it downwards.

6 Aggregate demand shocks cause national income and the price level to rise or fall together.

7 Aggregate supply shocks cause national income and the price level to change in opposite directions. An upward shift in the *SRAS* curve causes stagflation, with income falling and the price level rising.

8 With flexible wages, the initial effects on national income of aggregate demand or aggregate supply shocks are reversed and any final effect is only on the price level.

9 The *LRAS* curve relates income to the price level on the assumption that all prices have been fully adjusted to remove excess demands or excess supplies from all markets. It is perfectly inelastic. This indicates that, in the long run, national income is solely determined by aggregate supply, while aggregate demand only determines the price level.

Questions

1 Which One or More of the following will lead to an increase in the price level in the short run?
(a) a leftward shift in the *SRAS* curve
(b) a leftward shift in the *AD* curve
(c) a rightward shift in the *LRAS* curve
(d) an expansionary monetary policy

2 Select the correct alternatives in each case starting from equilibrium at potential national income.

An increase in aggregate desired expenditure shifts the (*SRAS/AD*) curve to the (left/right), causing equilibrium national income to (rise/fall) and the price level to (rise/fall); this creates (an inflationary/a deflationary) gap, the longer-run effect of which is to cause the (*SRAS/AD*) curve to shift (leftward/rightward), thus causing the price level to (rise/fall) and national income to (rise/fall); comparing the final, long-run equilibrium, with the original position, real national income is (higher/lower/unchanged) while the price level is (higher/lower/unchanged).

3 True or False?
(a) The negative slope of the *AD* curve indicates that a rise in the price level lowers equilibrium national income.
(b) An autonomous increase in desired aggregate expenditure shifts the *AD* curve to the left.
(c) A rise in the price level shifts the *AD* curve to the left.
(d) The *SRAS* curve is positively sloped as a result of the operation of the monetary transmission mechanism.
(e) A rightward shift in the *AD* curve initially increases both national income and the price level.
(f) A leftward shift in the *SRAS* curve initially lowers income but raises the price level.

4 Assuming that only one curve shifted in each of the following cases, is it more likely to have been the *SRAS* or the *AD* curve of the UK? Which way did the curve shift, left (L) or right (R)?
(a) OPEC oil-price rises bring on recession.
(b) Steady business expansion brings no serious inflation pressures.
(c) Bank applies the brakes hard in response to soaring inflation.
(d) Rapid productivity increases help to ease inflationary pressures.

5 In Figure 35.6, let the initial curves be *SRAS* and *AD'*. Now let the aggregate demand curve shift to *AD*. What happens?

6 In Figure 35.9, let the initial curves be *AD''* and *SRAS* while the price level is P_1.
(a) Is the market in equilibrium?
(b) What changes will occur?

The term *economic growth* refers to the increase in the economy's potential or full-employment national income; it is measured as the growth in the nation's potential national income at constant prices or, to use different words to express the same concept, the growth in real, full-employment, national income. It may be shown graphically in either of two ways: (1) by an outward shift in the production possibility curve that we first saw in Figure 1.4, and (2) by an outward shift in the economy's long-run aggregate supply curve. The former is a microeconomic concept. It shows all of the alternative consumption bundles that can be produced in a fully employed economy, and how economic growth increases these possibilities. The latter is a macroeconomic concept. It uses the market value of the particular consumption bundle that is actually produced from all of the alternative possibilities shown in Figure 1.2.

That we can show growth using both micro and macro economic tools, reflects the insight of the last decade or so of economic analysis. This is that the determinants of economic growth are as much micro as macro economic in origin. This will become clear as you read on, finding several references back to the microeconomic parts of this book. Indeed this whole chapter would be no less at home in Part 3 as here in Part 5.

THE TIMESCALES FOR ASSESSING GROWTH

We must be careful at the outset to distinguish forces that affect growth only in the short run from forces that exert their influence over the long run. Consider first the effects of investing and saving in the short and the long runs.

The Short and Long-Run Effects of Investment on National Income

The theory of income determination that we studied in Part 4 is a short-run theory. It takes potential income as constant and concentrates on the effect of investment expenditure on aggregate demand and thus on variations of actual national income around a given potential income. This short-term viewpoint is the focus of Figure 36.1(i).

In the long run, by adding to the nation's capital stock, investment raises potential income. This effect is shown by the continuing rightward shift of the *LRAS* curve in Figure 36.1(ii). The theory of economic growth is a long-

run theory. It ignores short-run fluctuations of actual national income around potential income and concentrates on the effects of investment in raising potential income – i.e. increasing aggregate supply.

Note the important contrast between the short- and long-run aspects of investment. In the short run, any activity that puts income into people's hands will raise aggregate demand. Thus the short-run effect on national income is the same whether a firm 'invests' in digging holes and refilling them or in building a new factory. In terms of growth, however, we are concerned only with that part of investment that adds to a nation's productive capacity.

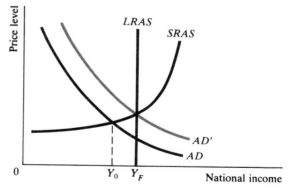

(i) Growth through AD shifts

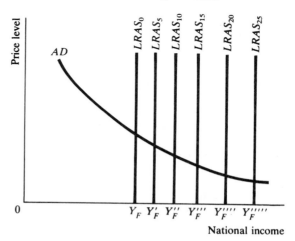

(ii) Growth through LRAS shifts

FIGURE 36.1 Two Ways of Increasing National Income. In the long term, shifts in aggregate supply exert a larger influence than do shifts in aggregate demand. In part (i) a rise in aggregate demand can raise income rapidly if an output gap exists. In part (ii) when output is at its potential level, the main source of increases in income is shifts in the aggregate supply curve.

1 Further descriptive material related to the subject of this chapter will be found in Harbury and Lipsey.

The Short and Long-Run Effects of Saving on National Income

Saving and national income

The short-run effect of an increase in saving is to reduce aggregate demand, because when households elect to save more they must spend less. The resulting downward shift in consumption lowers aggregate demand and thus lowers equilibrium national income.

In the longer term, however, higher savings tend to produce higher investment by providing the funds out of which investment is financed. Firms save and reinvest a significant part of their earnings, while the savings of households pass to firms, either directly through the purchase of shares or indirectly through the financial sector. If full employment is more or less maintained in the long run, then the volume of investment will be strongly influenced by the volume of savings. The higher the savings, the higher the investment – and the higher the investment, the greater the rate of growth due to the accumulation of more and better capital equipment.

It follows from this discussion that in the long run there is no paradox of thrift; societies with high savings rates have high investment rates and, other things being equal, high growth rates.

Financing growth

The above discussion of the place of saving in providing funds for growth-creating investment raises the more general issue of how growth is financed.

The main source of long-term growth is technological innovation, which is of two main types. *Process innovations* provide new, lower-cost ways of producing existing products. *Product innovations* provide new products. Both types of innovation usually require new types of specialized capital equipment. This poses two problems: (i) where to get the factors of production needed to produce these capital goods and (ii) where to get the funds needed to pay for the required factor services. In a market economy, these two questions are closely linked. The answer to the second question is that the funds are provided by the savings of persons and institutions which are then transferred either directly or indirectly to those who wish to spend them on new investment. How this happens answers the first question. By not spending funds on consumption, savers free the factors of production needed to produce the goods they would have consumed. When the saved funds are spent to create capital goods, these freed factor services are redirected out of consumption production into capital-goods production.

This point is both important and subtle, so it bears repeating.

People's savings, which would have been used for the purchase of consumption goods, are transferred to those who spend it on capital goods; this causes a transfer of resources, from the production of consumers' goods to the production of capital goods.

Here are the main sources of the savings.

Household saving: Households save part of their incomes. They may then use their savings (i) to make loans to firms by purchasing bonds issued by firms, (ii) to become part owners of firms by purchasing shares issued by firms, or (iii) to make deposits in financial institutions which, in turn, make the funds available to firms. Households may also lend to governments, who borrow the money either for their own use or on behalf of such bodies as nationalized industries and local transport organizations.

Firm saving: When firms earn incomes, they distribute some to their shareholders by paying dividends. The rest, known as undistributed profits, is retained to reinvest in the firm. In this case, the firms are financing their own investment by saving on behalf of their owners. (If the investments are good ones, the value of the firm will rise and, in return for the earnings held back for reinvestment, the owners will get a capital gain in terms of an increase in the value of their equities.)

Government saving: Governments can force the private sector to refrain from consumption in order to finance investment. They can do this by taxing the private sector and making the revenues available through such channels as investment in the public sector, and granting subsidies for research and development or for investment in certain projects. The use of tax revenues to finance investment will increase total investment to the extent that households cut consumption to pay their extra taxes. However, households may respond in whole or in part to the taxes by cutting their own saving. In this case, total investment is not increased, although it may go in different directions when it is financed by tax revenues rather than by private-sector saving.

Foreign saving: The financing of domestic investment from foreign funds comes from two main sources, portfolio investment, and foreign direct investment (FDI). Portfolio investment occurs when foreign nationals lend to, or buy minority interests in, domestic companies. The foreigners refrain from spending while domestic firms spend the funds on investment. The foreigners do not, however, have control over the firms that are using their savings.

FDI occurs when the foreigners retain control over the activities that are created. They may buy a majority interest in a domestic company, or take it over, or set up a new firm of their own. In today's world of increasingly globalized firms, transnational corporations (TNCs)[1] do much of the investment spending. TNCs raise funds from their own undistributed profits, or by selling fixed-interest securities and equities to savers in countries where savings are high. They invest these funds in countries where the return on capital investment is high. As a result, investment in some countries is financed by savings drawn from other

---

1 A TNC – which is also sometimes called a *multinational* – is a company with a location in more than one country. Many TNCs are globalized companies with locations in most of the world's major countries.

countries. The net effect is usually beneficial for people in both countries. Those who save get a higher return on their capital than if they were restricted to invest only in their own country. Those who live in the investment-receiving country get more growth-creating investment than could be financed from their own country's domestic saving.

THEORIES OF GROWTH

We now pass to a discussion of the causes of economic growth.

Growth Without Learning

Early economists viewed growth as a long-run process which consisted of the growth of the labour force and the growth of the capital stock taking place in the framework of fixed (or at least very slowly changing) technical knowledge. The law of diminishing returns would then operate to bring the growth process to a halt.

To gain some idea of how this happens, assume that the supply of land and labour is fixed, while the capital stock grows.[1] Also assume that there is a known and fixed stock of investment projects that might be undertaken and that nothing ever happens to increase the supply of such projects. Whenever the opportunity is ripe, some of the investment opportunities are utilized, thereby increasing the stock of capital goods and depleting the reservoir of unutilized investment opportunities. Of course, the most productive opportunities will be used first.

Such a view of investment opportunities can be represented by the fixed MARGINAL EFFICIENCY OF CAPITAL curve shown in Figure 36.2. It relates the stock of capital to the productivity of an additional unit of capital. The productivity of a unit of capital is calculated by dividing the annual value of the additional output resulting from an extra unit of capital by the value of that unit of capital. Thus, for example, a marginal efficiency of capital of 0.2 means that £1 of new capital adds 20p per year to the stream of output.[2]

The negative slope of the MEC curve indicates that, with knowledge constant, increases in the stock of capital bring smaller and smaller increases in output per unit of capital. That is, the rate of return on successive units of capital declines. This shape is a consequence of the law of diminishing returns. If more and more capital is used, with land, labour and knowledge all constant, the net amount added by successive increments will diminish and will eventually reach zero.[3]

As capital is accumulated in a state of constant know-

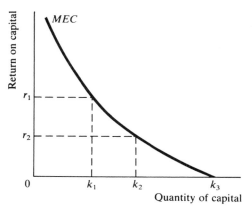

FIGURE 36.2 The Marginal Efficiency of Capital Schedule. A negatively sloped *MEC* schedule shows that successive additions to the capital stock bring smaller and smaller increases in output.

ledge, the society will move down its *MEC* schedule. For example when the capital stock is k_1 in Figure 36.2 the marginal return on new capital is r_1, while when the capital stock has grown to k_2, the return on new capital will have fallen to r_2. When the capital stock finally reaches k_3, the return on capital will have reached zero.

In such a 'non-learning' world, where new investment opportunities do not appear, growth in output will occur but, for a given rate of capital accumulation, the rate of growth of output will fall as the contribution of successive increments of capital falls. Eventually, when the capital stock reaches k_3, no further growth is possible.

Growth With Learning

Modern economists look at the process of growth more optimistically than did economists of the nineteenth century. The main reason lies in the recognition of the importance of *certain changes*: changes in the nature of factor inputs, changes in the nature of outputs, and changes in the technology that links inputs to outputs. Experience has shown that growth theories based on a fixed technology are not very helpful in understanding the changing world in which we live.

The very long run

Those of you who have read Chapter 14 will recall that in the long run, all factor inputs can be varied, but the firm must do the best it can within the confines of known technology – i.e. the production function is fixed. The best the firm can do is to be on, rather than above, its long-run cost curve.

---

1 Early economists were also interested in the consequences of the growth of population, but what we need for our purposes can be shown in the simple case in which capital is the only factor whose supply is increasing.

2 This curve relates the total quantity of capital (often called the 'stock of capital') to the return on another unit of capital. The marginal efficiency of *investment* curve, as shown e.g. in Figure 33.6, relates the amount of investment, which is the *change* in the stock of capital, to the return on that unit of new capital.

3 In some cases, curves of marginal returns have an upward-sloping portion. We ignore this possibility because (1) our assumptions about investment opportunities have ruled it out, (2) no competitive economy can be in equilibrium in the upward-sloping portion, and (3) even if it existed, we are not interested in it, since our concern is with what happens when growth has encountered diminishing returns.

The VERY LONG RUN is defined as a period of time over which the techniques of production, the nature of factors of production, and the products that can be produced, all change. Changes in production techniques cause downward *shifts* in long-run cost curves. Increases in the *quality* of factor supplies increase the output that can be obtained from given quantities of inputs. These two forces, along with the development of new products, are the major sources of economic growth. All three need to be considered.

New techniques: First, consider changes in the techniques available for producing existing products. Over an average lifetime in the twentieth century, such changes have been dramatic. Eighty years ago, roads and railways were built by gangs of workers using buckets, spades and draft horses. Today bulldozers, steam shovels, giant trucks and other specialized equipment have banished the workhorse from construction sites and to a great extent have displaced the pick-and-shovel worker.

Increases in productive capacity can be either of two types, known as embodied and disembodied technical change. Those that are the result of changes in the form of particular capital goods in use are called EMBODIED TECHNICAL CHANGE. The historical importance of embodied technical change is clearly visible: the assembly line, automation, computerization and robotization transformed much of manufacturing, the aeroplane revolutionized transportation, and electronic devices now dominate the communications industries. These innovations plus less well-known but no less profound ones — for example improvements in the strength of metals, the productivity of seeds and the techniques for recovering basic raw materials from the ground — all create new investment opportunities.

Less visible, but nonetheless important, changes occur through what is called DISEMBODIED TECHNICAL CHANGE, which concerns changes in the organization of production that are not embodied in specific capital goods. One example is improved techniques of managerial control.

Changes in the quality of factors: The quality of labour and capital has changed greatly over the years. A given value of capital, say £1's worth, is much more productive today than it was in 1900 (where the values are measured in constant prices). This is mainly due to the kind of embodied technological progress referred to above, so we say no more about it here.

Increases in the quality of labour are reflected in increases in the productivity of labour. One cause of such increases is improvements in health standards. Of course, better health is desired as an end in itself, but it also increases productivity per worker-hour by cutting down on illness, accidents and absenteeism.

A second cause is the accumulation of human capital that we discussed in Chapter 19. Training is clearly required to invent, operate, manage and repair complex machines. More subtly, there are general social advantages to an educated population. Productivity improves with literacy and, in general, the longer people are educated, the more adaptable they are to new and changing challenges — and thus, in the long run, the more productive.

New goods: Finally, consider the changes in outputs. Television, polio vaccine, nylon, pocket calculators, quartz watches, personal computers and even ballpoint pens did not exist two generations ago. Other products are so changed that the only connection they have with the 'same' commodity produced in the past is their name. A 1992 Rover automobile is very different from a 1932 Rover. The European Airbus is revolutionary compared with the DC-3, which itself barely resembled the Wright Brothers' original flying machine which flew on its historic flight within living memory. All such new products are a major source of economic growth in the very long run.

Large firms, small firms and the product cycle

The very-long-run changes discussed above are all found in an important characteristic of a growing economy which is called the PRODUCT CYCLE. The motto of a growing economy could be 'nothing is permanent'. New products appear continually, while others disappear. At the early stage of a new product, total demand is fairly low, costs of production are high, and many small firms are each trying to get ahead of their competitors by finding the twist that appeals to consumers or the technique that slashes costs. Sometimes new products never get beyond that phase. They prove to be passing fads, or else they remain as high-priced items catering to a small demand.

Others, however, do become items of mass consumption. Successful firms in growing industries buy up, merge with, or otherwise eliminate, their less successful rivals. Simultaneously, their costs fall due to economies of large-scale production. Competition drives prices down along with costs. Eventually, at the mature stage, often, although not invariably, a few giant firms control the industry. They become large, conspicuous and important parts of the nation's economy.

Sooner or later further changes bring up new products that erode the position of the established giants. Demand falls off, and unemployment occurs as the few remaining firms run into financial difficulties. A large, sick, declining industry appears to many as a national failure and disgrace. At any moment of time, however, industries can be found in all phases, from new industries with many small firms to declining industries with a few ailing giants. Declining industries are as much a natural part of a healthy growing economy as are small growing ones.

Growth with a shifting *MEC* curve

The steady depletion of growth opportunities in the no-learning case occurred because new investment opportunities never occurred, by assumption. In fact, however, new investment opportunities are created continually. This causes the *MEC* schedule to shift outward over time as illustrated in Figure 36.3.

Such outward shifts can be regarded as the consequences

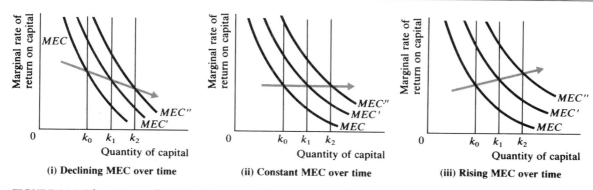

FIGURE 36.3 Three Cases of Shifting Investment Opportunities. When both knowledge and the capital stock grow, their relative rates of growth determine the actual marginal efficiency of capital. In (i), new investment opportunities are developed slower than old ones are used up. In (ii), new investment opportunities are developed at the same speed as old ones are used up. In (iii), new investment opportunities are being developed faster than old ones are being used up. In each case the actual return on capital follows the path shown by the grey arrow as time passes.

of learning either about investment opportunities or about techniques that create such opportunities. When learning occurs, what matters is how rapidly the *MEC* schedule shifts relative to the amount of capital accumulation. Three possibilities are shown in the Figure.

In each case, the economy's capital stock grows by the same amount, from k_0 to k_1 to k_2. In each case, learning shifts the *MEC* curve outwards from *MEC* to *MEC'* to *MEC"*. The cases differ by the speed at which the *MEC* curve is shifting.

Case 1 – gradual reduction in investment opportunities: In part (i) of the Figure, investment opportunities are created, but at a slower rate than they are used up. The rate of return follows the declining arrow while the ratio of capital to output increases.

This case is a slightly more subtle version of the 'no-learning case'. No longer are investment opportunities unchanging because of an absence of any learning. Instead, learning occurs but not at a fast enough rate to counteract the decline in the marginal productivity of capital due to the growth in the capital stock.

Cases 2 and 3 – constant or rising investment opportunities: Parts (ii) and (iii) of Figure 36.3 show cases where invention and innovation create new investment opportunities – seen as an outward shift of the *MEC* curve – as fast, or faster, than these opportunities have been used up through new investment – seen in a movement downwards along any given *MEC* curve. The Figures show that in a world with rapid innovation, despite large amounts of capital accumulation, the marginal efficiency of new capital may remain constant as shown by the horizontal arrow in part (ii), or even increase, as shown by the upward-sloping arrow in part (iii).

The historical record suggests that modern economies have been successful in generating new investment opportunities at least as rapidly as old ones were used up. As a result, modern economists devote more attention to understanding the *shifts* in the *MEC* schedule over time and less to discovering its shape in a situation of static knowledge.

Additional Factors Affecting Growth Rates

We have seen so far that an economy's growth rate is influenced by

- the rate at which capital is accumulated,
- the rate at which new technologies are put in place,
- the rate at which the quality of the labour force increases, and
- the rate at which new products are brought into production.

There are, however, some additional forces that now need to be considered. These are: the size of the population, structural changes, and institutions.

The size of the population

Clearly, for any given state of knowledge and supplies of other factors of production, the size of the population can affect the level of output per capita. Because population size is related to income per capita, we can conceive of an OPTIMAL POPULATION, which is defined as the population that maximizes national income per capita.

A closed economy with a balanced population: We start by assuming a closed society with what we may call a 'balanced' age distribution between children, adults of working age, and old persons.

The optimum population, under these circumstances, is illustrated in Figure 36.4. For given technology and given supplies of land and capital, too small a population will not provide scope for the most efficient division of labour nor for the full exploitation of economies of scale in the nation's industries. Thus, as the nation's population increases, each new citizen adds more to total output than did each previous citizen. Thus the marginal contribution to national income of additional citizens is increasing. As the population goes on increasing, however, all of the opportunities for improving the division of labour and for exploiting scale economies will eventually be exausted.

From that point on, further new inhabitants will add less to total production than did each previous addition to the population. Now the marginal product of further additions to the population will fall. In Figure 36.4, falling marginal product sets in after the population has reached N_1.

Eventually, the falling marginal product of new inhabitants will cause a fall in the average product of all the population. In the Figure, the average product per person begins to fall when the population reaches N_2, which is the population that maximizes output per person.

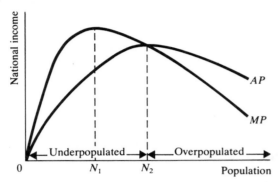

FIGURE 36.4 Optimum Population. The optimum population, N_2 in the Figure, is the one that maximizes per capita national income.

Notice that, to maximize living standards, the population must be increased beyond the point of diminishing *marginal* returns. It does not matter if each new inhabitant raises income by less than did any or all of the previous new inhabitants. What matters is that a new inhabitant raises income by more than the *average* income produced by everyone – i.e. that the marginal product of a new inhabitant exceeds the average product of all existing inhabitants.[1]

Notice that the optimum population is defined for a particular stock of land and capital and given technology. The very-long-run changes that we have already studied will cause *upward shifts* in the average and marginal product curves shown in Figure 36.4. This will certainly increase the size of per capita income when the population is optimal, but it may or may not also increase the size of the optimum population by shifting the maximum point of the *AP* curve to the right.

Structural change

Changes in the structure of the economy's output can cause changes in its measured growth rate. On the one hand, a

decline in such low-productivity sectors as distribution and an expansion in such high-productivity sectors as manufacturing, will temporarily boost the measured aggregate growth rate as labour moves from the declining to the expanding sectors. On the other hand, a decline in the high-productivity manufacturing sector, and a rise in the size of the lower-productivity service sector, will lower the measured rate of growth while the movement is occurring. The first (growth-increasing) shift was typical of the 1950s and the 1960s, while the second (growth-reducing) shift was typical of the 1980s and early 1990s.

Changes in the structure of inputs used in production can also affect growth rates. For example, when one type of energy (say, solar) supplants another type (say, oil), much existing capital stock specifically geared to the original energy source may become costly to operate and will be scrapped. New capital geared to the new energy source will be built. *During the transition*, gross investment expenditure is high, thus stimulating aggregate demand. But there is little if any increase in the economy's potential national income because the old capital goods have been scrapped. Similarly, new pollution control laws will affect investment expenditure but will not lead to growth in capacity. (The reduction in pollution may nonetheless be socially desirable.)

A rise in the international price of *imported* energy will also lower productivity. The higher-priced imported energy means that domestic *value added* falls, and with it GNP per worker. Although the same volume of goods can be produced with a given input of labour, a smaller portion of the output's value is now earned as income by domestic workers and firms, while a larger proportion is used to pay for the energy imports. These changes show up in the statistics as a decline in productivity and a temporary fall in growth rates.

Institutional considerations

Almost all aspects of a country's institutions can encourage or discourage the efficient use of natural and human resources. Social and religious habits, legal institutions, and traditional patterns of national and international trade are all important. Financial institutions can matter. So, too, does the political climate.

BENEFITS AND COSTS OF GROWTH

Our next task is to outline some of the costs and benefits of growth. We start by looking at benefits. Then we go on to consider costs.

Benefits of Growth

Growth and living standards

Economic growth as just defined, refers to the growth of total national income. What happens to living standards depends also on the growth of the number of people among whom this income must be shared. To measure the growth

---

1 Notice that the theory of the optimum population is nothing more than an application, at the macro level, of the law of diminishing returns that is discussed in the microeconomic sections of this book (see Chapter 13.) In the earlier chapter we considered adding more labourers to fixed amounts of land and capital in a particular firm and studied the average and marginal changes in output that resulted in that industry's output. Now we are considering the effects of more population being added to a whole country's fixed stock of land and capital and studying the average and marginal changes in national income that result.

in a country's average material living standards, we use PER CAPITA ECONOMIC GROWTH, which is the rate of growth of per capita national income (national income divided by the population).

In the circumstances facing most countries, the most important single force leading to long-run increases in living standards is economic growth. To see this, let us compare the effects of growth with policies that increase economic efficiency or redistribute income.

Increasing efficiency by pushing the economy closer to its production possiblity curve (e.g. from point v to point t in Figure 1.2 on page 0) can increase national income somewhat. But a once-and-for-all increase of 5–10 per cent would be an extremely optimistic estimate of what could be obtained by making all possible reductions in economic inefficiencies.

Redistributing income can make some people better off at the expense of others; but increasing the incomes of the bottom 20 per cent of the people by, say, 10 per cent, would be an optimistic prediction of what could be done with further redistribution policies. In any case, without growth, the magnitude of the income gains that can be achieved for lower-income groups through redistribution is limited by the size of national income.

Economic growth, however, can go on raising national living standards for as long as it continues at a faster rate than population is growing, which can be for centuries on end. Even the modest rate of growth of 2 per cent per year in per capita income takes a little less than 5 years to raise everyone's incomes by 10 per cent, and just over 9 years to raise the living standards of everyone, including the poor, by 20 per cent. That growth rate doubles average living standards about every 35 years, which means that with no change in economic efficiency or the distribution of income, everyone's living standards will increase by 300 per cent over one biblically allotted lifetime of three score years and ten.

The cumulative nature of growth: The cumulative effects of growth rates are further illustrated in Table 36.1. It compares the real incomes of five different countries that all have national incomes of 100 in 'year zero' but experience different growth rates. Again assuming a constant population, these growth rates may be taken as indicators of rising living standards.

The effects of growth on living standards can be seen by looking down any column. For example, assuming a constant population, a 3 per cent growth rate doubles real national income in about 24 years, and at the end of 70 it has raised national income by over 700 per cent!

The effects of differences in growth rates can be seen by comparing across any row, showing national incomes in one particular year at various growth rates. Although all the countries illustrated start with the same real income at 'year zero', by 'year ten' they have very different real incomes. For example, the country with a growth rate of 1 per cent has a real income of 111, while the country with a growth rate of 7 per cent has a real income of 201! A 7 per cent growth rate doubles real income in 10 years, while a 1 per cent rate only increases it by 10 per cent!

The continued importance of efficiency and redistribution: Do not misunderstand us when we say that, over the long term, by far the most potent force for raising living standards is economic growth rather than reducing inefficiencies or redistributing income. We are *not* saying that policies designed to increase economic efficiency, or to redistribute income, are unimportant.

Consider efficiency first. If at any moment of time we could get a larger national income by removing certain inefficiencies, such gains would be valuable. After all, any increase in national income is welcome in a world where many wants go unsatisfied. Furthermore, inefficiencies may themselves serve to reduce the growth rate. For one example, rent controls, which can cause inefficiency in the housing market, may also reduce the geographic mobility of labour that is necessary if economic growth is to continue.

Now consider redistribution. It may be some consolation for the poor to know they are vastly better off – due to economic growth – than they would have been if they had lived 100 years ago. But this does not make it any the less upsetting if they cannot afford basic medical treatment for themselves, or schooling for their children, that is available to higher-income citizens. After all, what people *see* is how they compare with others in their own society, not how they compare with their counterparts at other times or in other places. Because we care about relative differences between people, we continue to have policies to redistribute income, and to make such basic services as health and education available to everyone, at least at some minimum acceptable standards.

Nonetheless, over the long term, the potential of economic growth for raising living standards of the poor, the middle-income groups, and everyone else, vastly exceeds the potential from removing inefficiencies or redistributing the existing national income.

Interrelations among the policies: One important implication of the above discussion is that policies to reduce inefficiencies, or redistribute income, need to be examined carefully for any effects they may have on economic growth. Any policy that reduces the growth rate may be a bad bargain, even if it increases the immediate efficiency of the economy, or creates a more equitable distribution of income. Consider, for example, a hypothetical redis-

TABLE 36.1 Real National Incomes Over Time at Alternative Growth Rates. Small differences in national growth rates can cause enormous differences in national incomes

YEAR	GROWTH RATES*				
	1%	2%	3%	5%	7%
0	100	100	100	100	100
10	111	122	135	165	201
30	135	182	246	448	817
50	165	272	448	1,218	3,312
70	201	406	817	3,312	13,429
100	272	739	2,009	14,841	109,660

* The figures in the body of the table show real national income at alternative growth rates after the elapse of time shown in the first column.

tributive policy that raises the incomes of lower-income people by 5 per cent but lowers the rate of economic growth from 2 to 1 per cent. In 10 years, those who gain from the redistribution will be no better off than if they had not received the redistribution of income while the growth rate had remained at 2 per cent (and, of course, everyone who did not gain from the redistribution would be worse off from the beginning). After 20 years, those who had gained from the redistribution would have 5 per cent more of a national income that was 12 per cent smaller than it would have been if the growth rate had remained at 2 per cent. Thus, as a result of the lower growth rate, *everyone* will be substantially worse off than if the redistributive policy had not been followed.

Of course, not all redistribution policies have unfavourable effects on the growth rate. Some may have no effect, and others – by raising health and educational standards of ordinary workers – may raise the growth rate.

Other benefits

Although the major benefit of growth is its effect on living standards, some other possible benefits also need to be mentioned.

Growth and income redistribution: Economic growth may make government policies to redistribute income more politically acceptable than when national income is static. If a static national income is to be redistributed, someone's standard of living will actually have to be lowered. However, when there is economic growth, it is possible, by redistributing some of *the increment* in income, to reduce income inequalities without actually having to lower anyone's income. It is thus much easier for a rapidly growing economy to be generous toward its less fortunate citizens – or neighbours – than it is for a static economy.

Growth and lifestyle: As well as producing more of what we already consume, growth changes consumption patterns and lifestyles in more profound ways. A family often finds that a big increase in its income can lead to a major change in the pattern of its consumption – that extra money buys important amenities of life. In the same way, the members of society as a whole may change their consumption patterns as their average income rises. Not only are more cars produced, but the government is led to produce more highways and to provide more recreational areas for its newly affluent (and mobile) citizens. At yet a later stage, a concern about litter, pollution and ugliness may become important, and their correction may then begin to account for a significant fraction of national income. Such 'amenities' usually become matters of social concern only when growth has assured the provision of the basic requirements for food, clothing and housing of a substantial majority of the population.

Growth and national power: When one country is competing with another for power or prestige, rates of growth are important. If our national income is growing at 2 per cent, say, while the other country's is growing at 5 per cent, the other country will only have to wait for our relative strength to dwindle. Moreover, the faster its national income is growing, the easier a country will find it to bear the expense of an arms race, or a programme of foreign aid.

Costs of Growth

The benefits discussed above suggest that growth is a great blessing. Some of the consequences can, however, be a curse. Some of these less desirable effects were considered in Chapter 21, under the heading externalities.

Social and personal costs of growth

Industrialization can cause deterioration of the environment. Unspoiled landscapes give way to highways, factories and billboards; air and water become polluted; and in some cases unique relics of earlier ages – from flora and fauna to ancient ruins – disappear. Urbanization tends to move people away from the simpler life of farms and small towns and into the crowded, sometimes crime-ridden life of urban areas. Those remaining behind in the rural areas find that rural life, too, changes. Larger-scale farming, the decline of population, and the migration of children from the farm to the city all have their costs. The stepped-up tempo of life brings joys to some but tragedy to others. Accidents, ulcers, crime rates, suicides, divorces and murder are often higher in rapidly growing than in static societies.

When an economy is growing, it is also changing. Innovation leaves obsolete machines in its wake, and it also leaves partially obsolete people. No matter how well trained you are at age 25, in another 25 years your skills may well be partially obsolete. Some of you will find that your skills have become completely outdated and unneeded. A rapid rate of growth requires rapid adjustments, which can cause much upset and misery to the individuals affected.

It is often argued that costs of this kind are a small price to pay for the great benefits that growth can bring. Even if that is true in the aggregate, personal costs are very unevenly borne. Indeed, many of those for whom growth is most costly share least in the fruits of growth. Yet it is also a mistake to see only the costs – to yearn for the good old days while enjoying higher living standards that growth alone has made possible.

The opportunity cost of growth

In a world of scarcity, almost nothing is free. Growth requires investments of resources in capital goods and education. These investments absorb factors of production that could otherwise be used to produce goods and services for current consumption – hence current sacrifice. When, after a time, the new capital goods come into use, or the better-educated people enter the labour force, the economy's potential income will rise – hence future gain.

Growth as a Goal of Policy: Do the Benefits Justify the Costs?

Do the already developed countries need yet more growth? Most people think they do. Poverty is now a solvable problem in many of the richer western European countries as a direct result of its enhanced average living standards. Clearly, people in the top quarter of the income distribution in any industrialized country have more opportunities for leisure, travel, culture, fine wines and gracious living than have persons with much lower incomes. Most of those now in the bottom half of the income distribution would like these opportunities too. Only growth can provide the national income needed to give these opportunities to everyone.

Today, many countries that have not yet experienced sustained periods of economic growth are urgently seeking to copy those that have done so in order to obtain the benefits of growth despite its costs.

How seriously people rate the costs of growth depends in part on how many of the benefits of growth have already been achieved. With mounting population problems, the poorer countries are increasingly preoccupied with creating growth. With mounting awareness of pollution, the richer countries are devoting more resources to overcoming the problems caused by growth – at the same time that they are understandably reluctant to give up further growth.

Indeed, a similar conflict can often be seen within the same country at one time: a relatively poor community fights to acquire a new paper mill for the employment and income it will create; another, relatively affluent, community deplores the ruin of its beaches and its air by an existing mill.

GROWTH IN LESS DEVELOPED COUNTRIES

In the civilized and comfortable urban life of today's developed countries, most people have lost sight of the fact that a very short time ago in terms of the life span of the earth, people lived like other animals, catching an existence as best they could from what nature threw their way. It

has been only about 10,000 years since the first agricultural revolution, when people changed from food gatherers to food producers. Throughout most of subsequent human history, civilizations were based on a civilized life for a privileged minority and unremitting toil for the vast majority. It has been only within the last century that ordinary people have been able to expect leisure and high consumption standards – and then only in the economically developed parts of the world.

The Uneven Pattern of Development

Over 5 billion people are alive today, but the wealthy parts of the world – where people work no more than 40 or 50 hours per week, enjoy substantial leisure, and have a level of consumption at or above *half* that attained by Western Europeans – contain around 15 per cent of the world's population. Many of the rest struggle for subsistence. Many exist on a level at or below that endured by peasants in ancient Egypt or Babylon.

Data on per capita income levels throughout the world (as in Table 36.2) cannot be accurate down to the last $100. Nevertheless, such data do reflect enormous real differences in living standards that no statistical discrepancies can hide. The DEVELOPMENT GAP – the discrepancy between the standards of living in countries at either end of the distribution – is real and large.

The consequences of low-income levels can be severe. In a relatively rich country such as the United Kingdom, variations in rainfall are reflected in farm output and farm income. In poor countries such as those of the Sahel area of Africa, variations in rainfall are often reflected in the death rate. In these countries, many people live so close to a subsistence level that slight fluctuations in the food supply bring death by starvation to large numbers. Other, less dramatic characteristics of poverty include inadequate diet, poor health, short life-expectancy, and illiteracy.

For these reasons, reformers in under-developed countries, often called LESS-DEVELOPED COUNTRIES (LDCs), feel a sense of urgency not felt by their counterparts in rich countries. Yet, as the first line of Table 36.3 shows, many of the poorest nations are also the slowest growing nations.

TABLE 36.2 Income and Population Differences Among Groups of Countries, 1989

GNP per capita (US dollars)	(1) Number of countries	(2) GNP (US$000,000) 1989	(3) Population (000,000) 1989	(4) GNP per capita (US$) 1989	(5) Per cent world population	(6) Per cent world GNP
Less than $500	46	970,000	2,915	330	56.1	5.0
$500–$1,499	43	459,000	500	920	9.6	2.4
$1,500–$3,499	34	1,344,000	578	2,330	11.1	6.9
$3,500–$5,999	14	1,554,000	374	4,160	7.2	8.0
$6,000 or more	48	15,170,000	830	18,280	16.0	77.8
World[a]	185	19,497,000	5,197	3,750	100.0	100.0

The unequal distribution of world income is shown in columns (5) and (6). The poorest half of the world's population earns only 5 per cent of world income. The richest 16 per cent earns nearly 80 per cent of world income.

Source: World Bank Atlas 1990, The World Bank, Washington DC.
[a] World Bank staff estimate.

The development gap for many of the very poorest countries has been widening.

What are the causes of under-development, and how may they be overcome?

Barriers to Economic Development

Income per capita grows when aggregate income grows faster than population. Many forces can impede such growth.

Rapid population growth

Population growth is a key problem of economic development. If population grows as quickly as national income, per capita income does not increase. Many less-developed countries have rates of population growth that are even larger than their rates of growth of GDP. For example, in the decade 1980–89 Ecuador, Ethiopia and Papua New Guinea had growth rates of population of 2.7, 2.9 and 2.4 per cent per year alongside economic growth rates of 2.2, 1.8 and 1.8 per cent respectively. Hence, they experienced *negative* rates of growth of GNP *per capita* (of − 0.5, − 1.1 and − 0.7 per cent per year). They have made appreciable gains in aggregate income, but most of the gains have been literally eaten up by the increasing population. This is shown in row 1 of Table 36.3.

The critical importance of population growth to living standards was perceived early in the nineteenth century by the Reverend Thomas Malthus. He asserted two relations concerning rates of increase. First, food production tends to increase in an arithmetic progression (e.g., 100, 103, 106, 109, 112, where the increments in this example are *three units per period*). Second, population tends to increase in a geometric proportion (e.g., 100, 103, 106.09, 109.23, 112.55, where in this example the increments are *three per cent per period*). As a result of these relations Malthus argued that, under conditions of natural growth, population will always tend to outrun the growth in food supply. The difference in the above example may not seem much after only 5 periods. But after 15 periods the arithmetic increase in the food supply has increased it to 142, while the geometric increase in the population has increased it to 151.26.

Malthus argued that the natural tendency for population increases to outrun the increases in the food supply would tend to depress living standards. Unless people voluntarily limited population growth, living standards would be pushed to the subsistence level. Population growth would then be slowed to the same growth rate as that of the food supply by such natural disasters as famine, pestilence and plague.

Malthus' prediction gave economics the name of 'the dismal science'. In some poor areas of the world the predictions seem all too accurate, even today. There, agricultural methods are fairly traditional so that food production increases only slowly while population tends to increase at a more rapid rate. The result is subsistence living, with population held in check by low life-expectancies and periodic famines.

Fortunately over most of the world, Malthus' predictions have been falsified. Two reasons are paramount. First, Malthus underestimated the rate of technological change which has increased productivity in agriculture at a *compound rate* much faster than demand for food has been growing in most advanced countries. Second, he underestimated the extent of voluntary restrictions of population growth due to the widespread use of birth control techniques. As a result, population has grown more slowly than has the production of food (and most other things) in advanced countries. The result has been rising, rather than falling, standards of living.

For the more advanced industrialized countries, Malthusian pressures are not a problem today. For many LDCs, however, the tendency for the growth in population to outstrip the growth in the food supply makes Malthusian pressures a current threat.

Poor natural resources

A country with ample fertile land and a large supply of easily developed resources will find growth in income easier to achieve than one that is poorly endowed with such resources. The United Arab Emirates has a per capita

---

TABLE 36.3 The Relationship Between Population Growth and Per Capita Income, 1980–1989

Growth of GNP per capita 1980–1989	Number of countries[1]	GNP (US$000,000) 1989	Population (000,000) 1989	GNP per capita (US$) 1989
Less than 0%	64	899,000	820	1,100
0%–0.9%	16	654,000	393	1,660
1.0%–1.9%	21	2,209,000	244	9,050
2.0%–2.9%	16	9,575,000	673	14,230
3.0% or more	29	4,384,000	2,441	1,800
No data	39		626	—

The very poorest countries spend much of their increase in income on a rising population. Thus, their increase in income per capita is less than half that of the countries that are already richer. The gap in income between rich and many of the very poor countries is not closing.

Source: as for Table 36.2
[1] Countries with more than 1 million population.

income comparable with that of most European countries because by accident it sits on top of an enormous oil field. A lack of oil proved to be a devastating setback to many LDCs when the OPEC cartel increased oil prices tenfold during the 1970s. Without oil, their development efforts would have been halted, but to buy oil took so much scarce foreign exchange that it threatened to cripple their attempts to import needed capital goods.

The amount of resources available for production is, at least in part, subject to control. Badly fragmented land holdings may result from a dowry or inheritance system. When farmland is divided into many small parcels, it may be much more difficult to achieve the advantages of modern agriculture than it is when the land is available in huge tracts for large-scale farming.

Lands that are left idle because of lack of irrigation or that are spoiled by lack of crop rotation are well-known examples of barriers to development. Ignorance is another. The people of the Middle East lived through recorded history alongside the Dead Sea without realizing that it was a substantial source of potash. Not until after World War I were these resources utilized; now they provide Israel with raw materials for its fertilizer and chemical industries.

Abundant supplies of natural resources can assist growth and poor supplies can inhibit it. However, some countries with large supplies of natural resources have had poor growth performances because the economic structure has encouraged waste and inefficient use of resources. Prime examples are the USSR, Argentina and Uganda. Furthermore, other countries have enjoyed rapid rates of economic growth based on human capital and entrepreneurial ability in spite of a dearth of natural resources. Prime examples are Switzerland in earlier centuries and Singapore, Hong Kong, Taiwan and South Korea in the last half of this century.

Inadequate human resources

A well-developed entrepreneurial class, motivated and trained to organize resources for efficient production, is often missing in less-developed countries. The cause may be that managerial positions are more often awarded on the basis of family status or political patronage; it may be the presence of economic or cultural attitudes that do not favour acquisition of wealth by organizing productive activities; or it may simply be the absence of the quantity or quality of education or training that is required.

Poor health is likewise a source of inadequate human resources. When the labour force is healthy, less time is lost and more effective effort is expended. The economic analysis of medical advances is a young field, however, and there is a great deal to be learned about the drag of poor health on the growth of an economy.

Inadequate financial institutions

The lack of an adequate and trusted system of financial institutions is often a barrier to development. Investment plays a key role in growth, and an important source of funds for investment is the savings of households and firms. When banks and other financial institutions do not function well and smoothly, the link between private saving and investment may be broken and the problem of finding funds for investment may be greatly intensified.

Many people in LDCs do not trust banks – sometimes with good reason, but more often without. Either they do not maintain deposits, or they panic periodically, drawing them out and seeking security for their money in mattresses, in gold, or in property. When banks cannot count on their deposits being left in the banking system, they cannot engage in the kind of long-term loans that are needed to finance investments. When this happens, finance does not become available for investment in a productive capacity.

Developing countries not only must create banking institutions but also must develop enough stability and reliability so that people will entrust their savings to such financial intermediaries.

Inefficient use of resources

Low levels of income and slower than necessary growth rates may result from the inefficient use of resources as well as the lack of key resources.

It is useful to distinguish between two kinds of inefficiency, which have already been discussed extensively in Chapter 21 (see page 223). *Allocative inefficiency* occurs when factors of production are used to make an inefficient combination of goods. There is too much of some goods and too little of others. This means that the society is at the 'wrong' point on its production possibility boundary. If resources are reallocated to produce less of some and more of other types of goods, some people can be made better off while no one is made worse off.

Productive inefficiency occurs when factors of production are used in inefficient combinations. Some production processes use too much capital relative to labour, while others use too little. This means that the society is inside its production possibility boundary. If factor combinations are altered, more of all goods can be produced.

Both of these inefficiencies can occur when firms seek to maximize their profits, and owners of factors seek to maximize their material living standards, provided that either prices are not set in competitive markets or that all firms and factors do not face the same set of prices. Monopolistic and monopsonistic market structures, as well as taxes, tariffs and subsidies, are some important sources of the distortions that lead to both allocative and productive inefficiencies.

There is another kind of inefficiency called *X-inefficiency*. It occurs when either firms do not seek to maximize their profits, or factor owners do not seek to maximize their material welfare. X-inefficiency puts the society inside its production possibility boundary.

X-inefficiency usually means that firms are employing productive techniques that use more of *all* factors than is necessary. A careful analysis of reactions to market prices is not needed, therefore, to identify the existence of X-inefficiency. In this sense X-inefficiency is a cruder type than the other two kinds of inefficiency.

X-inefficiency can arise when firms choose not to max-imize their profits and, instead, follow routines that are dictated by custom or tradition. For example, the family members of a firm may be employed by that firm even when they are less efficient than hired workers would be. The family members may behave inefficiently, not because they are intrinsically less efficient than other workers, but *because* they are employed in their families' firms. Firms may employ more factors than they need, and produce less than these factors could produce, because they are satisfied with their present situations and see no reason to try to increase their profits. Firms may also avoid potentially profitable lines of endeavour because they prefer safe, cus-tomary behaviour to risky, novel behaviour. In this form, X-inefficiency may be the price that societies must pay for giving heavier weight to friendship, loyalty, tradition and the quiet life than to maximizing material living standards.

The American professor Harvey Leibenstein, who developed the concept of X-inefficiency, cites psychological evidence to show that non-maximizing behaviour is typical of situations in which pressure that has been placed on decision-makers is either very low or very high. If the customary living standard can be obtained with little effort, according to this evidence, people are likely to follow customary behaviour and spend little time trying to make optimal decisions. When pressure builds up, so that making a reasonable income becomes more difficult, optimizing behaviour becomes more common. Under extreme pres-sure, however, such as very low living standards or a rapidly deteriorating environment, people become dis-oriented and may not adopt optimizing behaviour.

Thus X-inefficiency may be typical of industries, and whole economies, where life is either too easy or too tough.

Cultural barriers

Traditions and habitual ways of doing business vary among societies, and not all are equally conducive to pro-ductivity. The late German sociologist, Max Weber, argued that the 'Protestant ethic' encouraged the acqui-sition of wealth and hence encouraged more growth than systems of belief that directed activity away from the economic sphere.

Often in LDCs, cultural forces are a source of X-inef-ficiency. Sometimes personal considerations of family, past favours, or traditional friendship or enmity are more important than market incentives in motivating behaviour. One may find a farm that is too small struggling to survive against a larger rival and learn that the owner prefers to remain small because expansion would require use of non-family capital or leadership. To avoid paying too harsh a competitive price for built-in inefficiency, the firm's owners may then spend much of their energies in an attempt to influence the government to prevent larger firms from being formed or to try to secure restrictions on the sale of output – and they may well succeed. Such behaviour will inhibit economic growth.

In an environment in which people believe that it is more important who your father is than what you do, it may take a generation to persuade employers to change their attitudes and another generation to persuade workers that times have changed. In a society in which children are expected to stay in their fathers' occupations, it is more difficult for the labour force to change its characteristics and to adapt to the requirements of growth than in a society in which upward mobility is itself a goal.

Structuring incentives is a widely used form of policy action in market-oriented economies. However, if people habitually bribe the tax collector rather than pay taxes, they will not be likely to respond to policies that are supposed to work by raising or lowering taxes. All that will change is the size of the bribe.

Many of these inefficiency-creating attitudes are also found in such market economies as the UK. They seem, however, to be more prevalent in LDCs. There is, in any case, a lively debate on how much to make of the significance of differing cultural attitudes. Some analysts believe the traditional considerations dominate peasant societies to the exclusion of economic responses; others suggest that any resulting inefficiency may be relatively small.

The fact that existing social, religious or legal patterns may make growth more difficult does not in itself imply that they are undesirable.

Instead, it suggests that the benefits of these patterns must be weighed against the costs, of which the limitation on growth is one. When people derive satisfaction from a religion whose beliefs inhibit growth, when they value a society in which every household owns its own land and is more nearly self-sufficient than in another society, they may be quite willing to pay a price in terms of growth opportunities forgone.

Some Basic Choices

There are many barriers to economic development that, singly and in combination, can keep a country poor. Econ-omic development policy involves identifying the barriers to growth and then devising ways to overcome them. Although the problems and strategies vary greatly from country to country, there are common basic choices that all developing countries must face.

How much government intervention?

How much government control over the economy is necess-ary and desirable? Practically every shade of opinion from 'The only way to grow is to get the government's dead hand out of everything' to 'The only way to grow is to get a fully planned, centrally controlled economy' has been seriously advocated.

The extreme views are easily refuted by historical evi-dence. Many economies have grown with relatively little government assistance: Great Britain in the Industrial Rev-olution; the United States during the nineteenth and twen-tieth centuries. Others have grown through a mixture of free markets and government intervention. Japan, Singapore, Austria and South Korea show various combinations of market determination and government policy direction. Furthermore, the Soviet Union and China showed that some of the early stages of economic growth could be accomplished within a centrally planned system.

Until recently, many LDCs sought to follow the Soviet route to growth. They adopted central planning and directed resources into what were thought to be growth-creating sectors of the economy, in particular infrastructure and heavy industries. They also controlled foreign trade, and by limiting imports, sought to foster local industries that would produce these goods domestically. The failure of the economies of eastern Europe and the uniformly poor performance of those LDCs that adopted the policies of central planning and import substitution have now largely discredited this route to growth. Although a few countries still use such policies, a growing number of LDCs are following the lead of the former Communist countries of eastern Europe in seeking to allow more market determination of both their allocation of resources and their pattern of foreign trade.

Types of government intervention

There is, however, still plenty of room for differences in the degree of the mix between free-market and government control over the allocation of resources. Government action may still be needed to create infrastructure, to remove barriers to growth, to influence the rate of economic growth, and to affect the pattern of growth. We shall look at each of these in turn.

Creating infrastructure: Key services, called INFRA-STRUCTURE, such as transportation and a communications network, are necessary to efficient commerce. Roads, bridges, railways and harbours are needed to transport people, materials and finished goods. Phone and postal services, water supply and sanitation are essential to economic development. The absence, for whatever reason, of a dependable infrastructure can impose severe barriers to economic development.

Many governments feel that money that is spent on a new steel mill or a dam shows more impressive results than money that is spent on such infrastructure investments as automating the telephone system. Yet private, growth-creating entrepreneurial activity will be discouraged more by the absence of good telephone communications than by the lack of domestically produced steel. During the 1970s, for example, the Republic of Ireland spent large sums on an unsuccessful attempt to establish a domestic steel industry, while spending little to modernize its inefficient telephone system. Several successful firms that moved from Ireland to the United States listed the enormous amounts of time wasted on trying to complete telephone calls as a major reason for their move.

Removing barriers: Authoritarian central governments can be particularly effective in overcoming some of the sources of X-inefficiency. A dictatorship may suppress social and even religious institutions that are barriers to

growth, and it may hold on to power until a new generation grows up that did not know and does not value the old institutions. It is much more difficult for a democratic government, which must command popular support during each election, to do currently unpopular things in the interest of long-term growth. Whether the gains in growth that an authoritarian government can achieve are worth the political and social costs is, of course, an important value judgement.

Governments may seek to remove the barrier to growth of per capita income caused by a high rate of population increase. Population policies may increase the knowledge about, and voluntary practice of, birth control techniques. They may also, as in China, create severe disincentives to have large families.

Where natural and human resources are not being fully utilized, governments can seek to improve these. Patterns of land ownership that discourage efficient use of natural resources can be changed. Education and health measures can raise the quantity, and quality, of available human resources.

Affecting the rate of growth: One major appeal of government intervention is to accelerate the pace of economic development. When living standards are low, people have urgent uses for their current incomes, so savings tend to be low. Governments can intervene in a variety of ways and force people to save more than they otherwise would in order to ease a shortage of investment funds.

Compulsory saving has been one of the main aims of most development plans of centralized governments, such as those of the USSR and China. The goal of such plans is to raise savings and thus lower current consumption below what it would be in an unplanned economy. A less authoritarian method is to increase the savings rate through tax incentives and monetary policies. The object is the same: to increase investment in order to increase growth and thus to make future generations better off.

Altering the pattern of growth: An important goal of planning is often to channel growth into sectors that the planners believe will have the greatest chance of long-run success.

Governments may seek to alter the course of a country's pattern of growth for several reasons. First, they may believe that they can evaluate the future more accurately than can the countless individuals whose decisions determine market prices. Sceptics see no reason why government bureaucrats, who are risking taxpayers' money and are responsive to politicians who worry about the next election, can be better at making such risky assessments than private entrepreneurs, who are risking their own and their shareholders' money.

Second, governments may wish to adopt a longer time horizon than would private investors. Usually, private investors require the prospect of a fairly quick pay-off from those risky ventures that do succeed. Governments can worry about the state of their country decades down the line, concerning themselves with the welfare of future as well as present generations. There is a rational case for

BOX 36.1 Rediscovering the Middle of Africa

Development economists sometimes . . . complain about a "missing middle": Africa, they say, has vast state companies and thousands of subsistence hustlers, but virtually nobody in between.

'During the 1980s two-thirds of the countries south of the Sahara embarked on the market-freeing policies advocated by the IMF and the World Bank. They received more than $1 billion a year in aid. Yet private capital has fled. After nearly a decade of reforming, some wonder if banks and businesses will ever return.

'For the foreseeable future, few foreign companies are likely to invest in Africa to produce for the local market. It is simply too poor: the continent's combined GDP is a tenth of that of the seven countries of Eastern Europe.

'Yet some countries have managed to attract investment aimed at export markets. Mauritius has drawn in so much that it no longer depends on huge injections of aid.

'There are plenty of Africans running medium-sized firms. Botswana (population 1.1m) has 13 competing manufacturers of metal furniture; Tanzania has 5,000 registered road-transport companies.

'These medium-sized African firms are efficient. A World Bank study in Kenya in 1986 found that private, Kenyan-owned enterprises earned an average return of 20%, compared with 18% for foreign private firms and 15% for public enterprises.

'. . . entrepreneurs bring more expertise and motivation to such work than government consultants. Public funds, he suggests, are better spent on tax incentives that promote the private sector. In Botswana, for example, new investment projects attract tax relief and selective wage subsidies. This is probably the biggest reason why private employment has grown much faster there than in the highly taxed Ivory Coast.

'Mr Marsden's main recommendation is for more lending to go to entrepreneurs rather than to governments. Many standard sorts of finance are denied to African businessmen: stock exchanges are scarce; banks lend doggedly according to a client's assets, rather than judging his business's potential. On top of all that, government borrowing often crowds out private requests – from institutions both domestic and foreign.'

(*The Economist*, 8 December 1990)

This article reports on a discussion paper called 'Africa's Entrepreneurs' written for the International Finance Corporation by Mr Keith Marsden.

Many countries are learning that private-sector entrepreneurs are often a better engine of economic growth than is public-sector investment. They are also learning that it is important to reduce growth-inhibiting tax policies.

Questions

1 What are some of the reasons why the older style growth policies based on central planning and investment in heavy industries are now discredited?
2 Why is producing for export often a more successful growth policy than encouraging import substitution?

---

planning here. Critics, however, argue two points. First, because they are tied to an election cycle, democratic governments typically adopt a shorter time horizon than does the market. Second, freed from the constraint of showing a profit, governments often make investments that never pay off and therefore waste the country's scarce capital.

Third, investment in changing a country's comparative advantage is in the nature of a public good. As we know from Chapter 21, if the government does not provide a public good, no one will. Many skills can be acquired, some of them by formal education but some of them only through on-the-job training. Fostering an apparently uneconomic domestic industry may, by changing the characteristics of the labour force, develop a comparative advantage in that line of production, as well as in other, similar lines of production.

Supporters of this view point out that the Japanese had no visible comparative advantage in manufacturing when their feudal country was opened to the world in 1854. Nonetheless, the Japanese became an industrial power by the end of the century and now lead the world in a range of high-tech products. Furthermore, the newly industrialized Asian countries (often called NICs), such as Singapore, Taiwan, Hong Kong and South Korea, have grown dramatically under various forms of government growth policies. These successful NICs have used a mix of free market and government intervention. There has been no central planning of the Soviet type, but governments have adopted *industrial policies* that have done several things. First, good infrastructure has been provided to foster transportation and communications. Second, broad policies that encourage industrial development have been adopted, while those that might discourage development have been avoided. These include favourable tax treatment of investment and profits, and assistance to research and development. Third, particular areas have often been targeted for growth and given favourable treatment through taxes, subsidies and government purchasing policies. The emphasis is on targeting and encouraging broad sectors rather than trying to pick individual products and firms as potential winners and backing them with government money.

What sorts of education?

Most studies of less-developed countries suggest that undereducation is a barrier to development and often urge increased expenditures on education. This poses a choice: to spend educational funds on erasing illiteracy and increasing the level of mass education rather than on training a small cadre of scientific and technical specialists.

To improve basic education requires a large investment in school building and in teacher training. This investment will result in a visible change in the level of education only after 10 or more years, and it will not do much for productivity even during that time-span. The opportunity cost of basic education expenditures always seems high. Yet it is essential to make them, because the gains will be critical to economic development a generation later. A major characteristic of many of the rapidly growing countries of Asia, such as Japan, South Korea and Singapore, is the existence of excellent primary and secondary schools that ensure a high rate of literacy and numeracy for all members of the labour force.

The case for the market

Most people would accept that government must play an important part in any development programme, especially in programmes concerning education, transportation and communication. Nevertheless, what of the sectors that are usually left to private enterprise in advanced capitalist countries?

The advocates of relying on market forces in these sectors place great emphasis on human drive, initiative and inventiveness. Once the infrastructure has been established, they argue, entrepreneurs will do vastly more to develop the economy than will civil servants. The market will provide the opportunities and direct their efforts. People who seem lethargic and unenterprising when held down by lack of incentives will show bursts of energy when given sufficient self-interest in economic activity.

Furthermore, the argument goes, individual capitalists are far less wasteful of the country's capital than civil servants. A bureaucrat who is investing capital that is not his own (raised perhaps from the peasants by a state marketing board that buys cheap and sells dear) may choose to enhance his own prestige at the public's expense by spending too much money on cars, offices and secretaries and too little on truly productive activities. Even if the bureaucrat is genuinely interested in the country's well-being, the incentive structure of a bureaucracy does not encourage creative risk-taking. If his ventures fail, his head will likely roll; if they succeed, he will receive no profits – and his superior may get the medal. Thus, he will be cautious about taking risks.

Some developing countries have put a large fraction of their educational resources into training a small number of highly educated men and women, often by sending them abroad for advanced study. Many of the educated elite become dedicated specialists who work hard for their country's welfare. Others, however, regard their education as the passport to a new aristocracy rather than as a mandate to serve their fellow citizens; and an appreciable fraction emigrate to countries where their newly acquired skills bring higher pay than they do at home.

How to acquire capital?

A country can raise funds for investment in three distinct ways: (1) from the savings (voluntary or forced) of its domestic households and firms, (2) by commercially motivated loans or investment from abroad, and (3) by aid contributed by foreign governments.

Capital from domestic saving – a vicious circle of poverty: If capital is to be created at home by a country's own efforts, resources must be diverted from the production of goods for current consumption. This means a cut in present living standards. If living standards are already at or near the subsistence level, such a diversion will be difficult. At best, it will be possible to reallocate only a small proportion of resources to the production of capital goods.

Such a situation is often described as the VICIOUS CIRCLE OF POVERTY: because a country has little capital per head, it is poor; because it is poor, it can devote few resources to creating new capital rather than to producing goods for consumption; because little new capital can be produced, capital per head remains low, and the country remains poor.

The vicious circle is not an absolute constraint on growth rates. If it were, we would all still be at the level of Neanderthal man. The grain of truth in the vicious-circle argument is that some surplus must be available somewhere in the society to allow saving and investment. In a poor society with an even distribution of income, in which nearly everyone is at the subsistence level, saving may be very difficult, but this is not the common experience. Usually, there is at least a small middle class that can save and invest if opportunities for the profitable use of funds arise. Also, in many poor societies today, the average household is above the physical subsistence level. They will find that they can sacrifice some present living standards for a future gain. For example, presented with a profitable opportunity, villagers in Ghana planted cocoa plants at the turn of the century, even though there was a seven-year growing period before any return could be expected.

An important consideration is that in less-developed countries one resource that is often *not* scarce is labour. Profitable home or village investment that requires mainly labour inputs may be made with relatively little sacrifice in current living standards. However, this is not the kind of investment that will appeal to many central planners who are mesmerized by large and symbolic investments, such as dams, nuclear power stations and steel mills.

Imported capital: Another way of accumulating the capital that is needed for growth is to obtain it from abroad.

There are two main ways in which LDCs can obtain foreign capital (other than by aid). In the first way, governments, or agencies and firms that are directly under government control, may borrow it. This method was used

BOX 36.2 Helping the Poorest of the Poor

'More than 1 billion people living in developing countries are in poverty, according to the World Bank's latest World Development Report. With luck and a lot of policy changes in rich and poor countries alike, that might be cut to about 800m by 2000.

'If that goal seems uninspiring, there is a more cheerful way to look at what might be achieved. In 1985 (the most recent year for which useful data can be gathered), the 1.1 billion people reckoned by the World Bank to be "in poverty" made up a third of the developing world's population. If, as the Bank's report argues, the head count can be cut to 800m by 2000, the incidence of poverty would fall dramatically, to 18%. In other words, against a background of growing populations, the right measures can quickly and substantially reduce the probability that any given person in the third world will be condemned to a life of acute deprivation. If that is not an inspiring aim, it certainly ought to be.

'The report's prescriptions fall under two main headings:

'Create new economic opportunities for the poor. Since the poor's main source of income is what they are paid for their labour, this means promoting labour-intensive economic growth.

'Equip the poor to grasp these opportunities. This calls for adequate provision of basic social services such as primary education, health care and family planning.

'Also, one of the most damaging economic distortions in many developing countries is excessive taxation of farming; this hits the very part of the economy upon which most of the poor depend for their livelihood.

' ... much public spending in developing countries (as, no doubt, in developed countries) misses its supposed target by a wide margin. With less but better-targeted spending, governments could offer more help to the poor and balance their books at the same time.

'In sub-Saharan (i.e., black) Africa in 1985, 53% of the people were above the bank's poverty line; but the primary-school enrolment rate was barely higher, at 56%, suggesting that hardly any of the poorest children

were benefiting. Higher-than-primary levels of education are consumed almost exclusively by the middle classes and their bosses.

'It might, at first sight, seem crazy to argue that fees for education and hospital care are a good way to help the poor. In developing countries, however, they can indeed serve that purpose. If governments recovered the cost of higher education and hospital health-care from consumers, they would not be hurting the poor, because the poor never set foot in universities and hospitals. The revenue raised could then be used for spending that really would help the poor – like better provision of cheap primary education and village health-posts.

'It used to be claimed that economic growth hurts the poor – a claim since disproved by the success of the East Asian dragons. Labour-intensive growth helps the poor, rest assured. However, governments do have a trade-off to wrestle with – not between overall growth and the well-being of the poor, but between the poor and the not-poor.'

(*The Economist*, 21 July 1991)

This article stresses the importance of targeting growth efforts to those who most need it. Large investments in heavy industries may do much less to alleviate poverty than encouraging small, labour-intensive enterprises. Social spending on things not consumed by the poor will not help them directly, although most people gain if overall growth is stimulated.

Questions

1 Why might it be appropriate to finance some growth-creating expenditure by user fees while state funds are used in other cases?
2 What types of growth-creating expenditures might be allocated to each class?
3 What is the nature of the trade-off between the poor and the not-poor?

---

extensively after the first OPEC oil price shock in 1974. During the next 12 years, reliance on foreign borrowing exploded to the point where it became a serious international problem for both LDCs and their creditors. During the 1970s the rising cost of oil to many oil-importing, less-developed countries, combined with overly optimistic income expectations, led to massive borrowing by the LDCs. High interest rates during the 1980s greatly raised the cost of servicing this debt and much of the funds were wasted on investment expenditure which proved unprofitable. World recession and rising protectionism in

the developed world made it more difficult to earn the money that was necessary to pay interest on, let alone repay, the principal. For oil-importing countries, the collapse of oil prices in 1985 provided some relief, but for oil exporters such as Mexico the oil price decline made things much worse. This problem reached the dimensions of a crisis by the mid-1980s. Today many LDCs are burdened by immense debts on which they have trouble meeting their interest and which they have little chance of ever repaying in full.

The second way in which foreign, non-gift capital can

be obtained is through capital that has been brought in by foreign companies – the so-called 'transnational corporations' (TNCs). Many LDCs have been suspicious of foreign capital. They have feared that foreign investors will gain control over their industries or their government.

The extent of foreign control depends on the form that foreign capital takes. When foreigners buy bonds in domestic companies, they do not own or control anything. When they buy shares, they own part or all of a company, but their control over management may be minimal. When foreign companies establish plants and import their own managers and technicians, they have much more control. Finally, when foreign firms subsidize an LDC government in return for permission to produce, they may feel justified in exacting political commitments.

Whatever the feelings are about foreign ownership and control, the realities of modern globalized industry are such that no country today can hope to grow from a less-developed into a developed nation without a large presence of foreign transnational corporations. These companies do too much of the world's business to be excluded from any country that hopes to become a significant player in the global marketplace. Today, more and more countries that have development plans are seeking to attract foreign transnational corporations rather than to discourage them.

There are three enormous advantages of using foreign firms to make growth-creating investments. First, foreign owners take the risks. If the investments turn out to be unproductive, domestic citizens are not burdened with debt. Second, the investments are made by private-sector decision-takers who are less likely to be carried away by grandiose schemes with unrealistic expectations than are civil servants. Third, large foreign TNCs have access to technological knowledge that may not be available to small domestic investors. Indeed, the transfer of technological know-how, from those in advanced countries who have it, to those in LDCs who need it, is now seen as one of the most important functions of TNCs.

Aid: Investment funds for development are being received today by LDCs from the governments of the developed countries. These governments sometimes act unilaterally (for example, the programme of the US Agency for International Development) and sometimes act through international agencies, such as the World Bank, the Export-Import Bank, and the OPEC Fund, which was established in 1980. These funds are not really outright gifts but are 'soft' loans on which repayment is not demanded in the near future. It is common to label them *contributed capital* to distinguish them from hard loans, on which repayment is expected under normal commercial terms.

The heyday of contributed capital occurred during the late 1970s and early 1980s, when the United States, the Soviet Union and others sought to win the allegiance of Third World LDCs by making 'soft' loans and outright gifts. Today Japan is the largest single source of contributed capital.

Some Controversial Unresolved Issues

Development economists are currently involved in some important controversies. Among them are the following.

The pace of development

Reformers in less-developed countries often think in terms of transforming their economies within a generation or two. The sense of urgency is quite understandable, but, unless it is tempered by some sense of historical perspective, unreasonable aspirations may develop, only to be dashed all too predictably.

Many underdeveloped countries are probably in a stage of economic development that is analogous to that of medieval England, having not yet achieved anything like the commercial sophistication of the Elizabethan era. It took 500 years for England to develop from the medieval economic stage to its present one. Such a change would be easier now, for much of the needed technology can be imported rather than invented, but what is a feasible pace? To effect a similar growth within 50 or 100 years would require a tremendous achievement of the kind that was accomplished by the United States, Japan and a handful of other countries; to aspire to do it in 20 or 30 years may be to court disaster – or to invite repressive political regimes.

Population policy

The neo-Malthusian view that rapid population growth is a formidable barrier to development is a part of the current conventional wisdom on development.

This view allows little place for the enjoyment value of children by their parents. Critics point out that the psychic value of children should be included as a part of the living standards of their parents. They also point out that in rural societies even young children are a productive resource, and in societies in which state help for the aged is negligible, fully grown children provide old-age security for their parents.

The neo-Malthusian view is also criticized for assuming that people breed blindly, as animals do. Critics point out that traditional methods of limiting family size have been known and practised since the dawn of history. Thus, they argue that large families in rural societies are a matter of choice.

The population explosion came not through any change in 'breeding habits' but as a result of medical advances that greatly extended life-expectancy (which surely must be counted as a direct welfare gain for those affected). Critics argue that, once an urban society has developed, family size will be reduced voluntarily. This was certainly the experience of Western industrial countries; why, critics ask, should it not be the experience of the developing countries?

The cost of creating capital

Is it true that LDCs must suffer by sacrificing current

consumption if they wish to grow? A recent criticism of this conventional wisdom questions the alleged heavy opportunity cost of creating domestic capital. Production of consumption and capital goods are substitutes only when factor supplies are limited and fully employed. However, critics say, the development of a market economy will lead people to substitute work for leisure.

For example, the arrival of Europeans with new goods to trade led the North American Indians to produce furs and other commodities that were needed for exchange. Until they were decimated by later generations of land-hungry settlers, the Indians' standard of living rose steadily with no immediate sacrifice. They created the capital that was needed for their production – weapons and means of transport – in their abundant leisure time. Thus, their consumption began to rise immediately.

This, the argument says, happens in less-developed countries whenever market transactions are allowed to evolve naturally. The spread of a market economy leads people to give up leisure in order to produce the goods that are needed to buy the goods that private traders are introducing from the outside world. In this view it is the heavy-industry pattern of development that is often chosen, rather than development itself, that imposes the need for large sacrifices.

Growth and the Environment

Today the earth's environment is subject to many serious threats, from fluorocarbon emissions that threaten the ionosphere which shields us from the sun's cancer-creating radiation, through sewage and industrial effluent which is threatening whole bodies of water including the Mediterranean Sea, to the destruction of tropical rainforests which hold the topsoil, influence our climate, and provide a significant part of the world's oxygen supply.

One of the biggest threats comes from sheer numbers. It took from the beginning of homo sapiens' time on earth, until about 1800 AD, for the population to reach 1 billion persons. Today, it is close to 6 billion and is expected to reach 10 billion early in the twenty-first century. The earth's natural processes of rejuvenation could cope without assistance with the pollution of all sorts produced by 1 billion people. But 5 billion are putting the ecology under major stress, and 10 billion will threaten to overwhelm it *unless major help is provided by humans.*

Two major schools of thought disagree over the strategy needed to cope with the threat. One school would stop further economic growth and so put less stress on the environment by curtailing resource use. The other would encourage growth and rely on the new technologies that are part of the growth process to develop vastly improved ways of coping with the pollution created by so many people engaged in so much productive activity.

The stop-growth school

People of the stop-growth school would hold world output at its current levels so as to keep resource use from rising. The extreme poverty of the less developed countries would

be dealt with by redistribution policies which would help them at the expense of the richer countries.

One problem with this proposed solution is that any feasible redistribution would still leave mass poverty in much of the world. To see this, consider the extreme (and impossible) case in which per capita income was distributed equally among all the world's countries. An equal distribution of total world income would have given everyone in the world a per capita income of about US$2750 in 1985. This would have given a family of four an income of US$11,000. This was just below the American Department of Commerce's estimate of the poverty level for an American non-farm family of four in that year. Since substantial inequalities of income must persist within each country, having the average household at the poverty level implies that about half would be below it, and a significant proportion well below it.

This redistribution of income might be attempted in either of two ways. First, production could remain in its present locations and an attempt made to redistribute the income generated by it to the LDCs. This would require that income-earners in advanced countries gave up the vast majority of their incomes to citizens in less developed countries, even before they began to pay taxes to support their own government's activities.

The difficulties in doing this would be formidable. Even quite modest redistributions within one country run into serious incentive problems when income-earners pay a large percentage of the incomes as taxes. Serious incentive (and self-respect) problems also arise when people live on money that is transferred to them from income-earners elsewhere. So the *massive* international redistributions of income required to raise living standards of the LDCs to, say, even half the current US poverty level would seem to be quite unfeasible on present knowledge.

The second method would be to attempt to redistribute production to the LDCs, thus transferring much of the current levels of resource utilization to them. This would pose even more impressive difficulties. How would production be wound down in the advanced countries? Western workers would not voluntarily agree to stop working and reduce their incomes to the poverty level in order to allow production to increase in the LDCs. Furthermore, it is certain that many of the LDCs would use the resources with much less efficiency than they are used in advanced countries. So the world's GDP that would be generated by a constant level of resource use would shrink as a result of this transfer.

Such an enormous transfer of production on a scale never before seen, to regions with neither the infrastructure to support it, nor the human capital to drive it, could only be attempted using the techniques of the command economy. It is hard to see how the fate of the Eastern European countries could fail to be repeated, but on a much grander scale as the whole world came under command techniques for allocating resources.

Indeed, it is difficult to see how the policy of stopping growth could result in anything other than condemning much of the world permanently to the poverty from which its people are now trying to escape.

The rely-on-growth school

The second alternative is to rely on further economic growth, constrained by effective environmental controls, to solve the poverty problem by raising output. According to this view, the environmental problems would then be dealt with through effective incentives both to use existing pollution-reducing technology and to develop new technology (which is often quickly developed when incentives to do so are created by making pollution a costly activity for producers).

Those in this school argue that economic growth is best understood in terms of advances in technology that transform our ways of doing and making things, as well as transforming the things we make. Look, they argue, at the complex workings of a living animal, or the human brain, or think of the energy sources alternative to fossil fuels, and you will begin to realize the possibilities of methods not yet invented, to do things we can barely dream of, and in ways that are not yet even imagined.

Whether or not this optimism is justified, there is no doubt that past technological advances have revolutionized almost everything about how we live and do things. Consider just one example.

In 1890, the streets of the major cities in the world were being submerged in smelly, disease-carrying horse manure, and were reaching their capacity to carry transport through horse-drawn vehicles. The internal combustion engine, and its offshoot motor transport, solved the problem of manure pollution. It also allowed a tenfold increase in the volume of traffic before a new environmental problem arose from new types of excretions. Non-fossil energy sources will, in their turn, solve the petroleum-pollution problem, once we are forced to end our use of petrol-driven cars (or earlier, if we are willing to give them up while plenty of petrol is still available).

Here we see a typical sequence in the history of technology. One technology reaches its limits in two senses. First, it cannot do more of the job it is doing because of some physical limits in its ability to produce the results required of it. (No more room on the streets for more horse-drawn vehicles.) Second, its side-effects begin to create serious problems as its use expands towards its limits. (Horse manure begins to be a serious environmental problem.) That technology is replaced by a superior technology that solves the environmental problem and allows a large increase in the amount of output. Then, as growth continues, and the new technology is used more and more intensively, new limits are reached in terms both of the amount of output it can produce and of unacceptable environmental side-effects. A yet newer technology then replaces the old and the cycle is repeated, taking output to higher levels before new limits to output and new environmental problems are met.

Critics of growth often think of it as producing more and more of the same things and then argue that there must be a limit to doing this. 'What could we want with five times as much of all the goods and services we now know?' they ask.

But growth does not produce more and more of the same

The writer is taking one side in the great debate that is going on between those who see the salvation of the environment coming from stopping economic growth and those who see the salvation coming from continued economic growth and the development of superior technologies that are one of the main engines of growth.

Questions

1 What arguments might be advanced to suggest that capitalism is not compatible with good environmental policy? Did the socialist countries of Eastern Europe produce good environmental policy?

2 What arguments might be advanced to suggest that continued growth of free market economies is the best way to alleviate poverty in the less developed countries and to develop more environmentally friendly technologies?

3 What new technologies might allow increased production while reducing pollution? (Hint: think of the major categories of resource use, starting with sources of energy.)

old things. Being based on new ideas and new technologies, growth largely takes the form of new products some of which transform our whole manner of living.

Consider some examples. Victorians could not have imagined the modern dentist's office; doctor services; penicillin; pain killers; bypass operations; modern hospitals; safe births and abortions; personal computers; compact discs; TVs; opportunities for cheap, fast, world-wide travel; universal secondary schooling; affordable universities; safe food of great variety; central heating; elimination of endless kitchen drudgery by either wives or masses of servants through the use of detergents, washing machines, vacuum cleaners, disposable nappies, and a host of other new products. Yet all these, and more, are products that their great grandchildren take for granted. It is safe to say that the success of the women's liberation movement would have been impossible without the technological advances that freed the majority of women from the day-long drudgery of household duties accomplished largely by hand.[1] Many will be thankful that Victorians did not stop growth because they could not imagine what

to do with five times as many units of the products that they knew about.

The point is important. Technological advance transforms our lives by inventing new undreamed of things. Our present-day technologies, based on fish caught from the sea and grain grown on land (in ways not fundamentally changed since the dawn of history), fossil fuels,

---

1 A few higher-income women escaped by being able to employ servants. The vast majority, however, who either could not afford servants or were servants themselves, were condemned to long hours of drudgery.

Summary

1 Growth of national income can result from the once-for-all removal of a recessionary gap through a rightward shift in the *AD* curve. Growth of national income can also result from a continued outward shift of the *LRAS* curve.

2 In the short run, investment increases aggregate demand while, in the long run, it increases aggregate supply as measured by potential income. In the short run, savings decrease aggregate demand while, in the long run, by providing the funds needed for investment, savings help to increase aggregate supply. In the long run, therefore, there is no paradox of thrift.

3 In a world of static technology, the accumulation of capital is the main source of growth. As capital accumulates, however, the capital-output ratio rises while the marginal return on capital falls.

4 In a world of improving technology, the marginal efficiency of capital curve shifts outwards. If it shifts as fast as, or faster than, the capital stock is growing, the return on capital will not fall, and the capital-output ratio will not rise.

5 The major factors affecting the growth rate are the rate at which capital is accumulated, the rate at which new technologies are put in place, the rate at which the quality of the labour force increases, the rate at which new products come into production, the growth of both the population and the labour force, and structural changes in the economy.

6 The optimum population is the population which maximizes a nation's output per capita.

7 The major benefits of growth are rising average living standards, easier redistribution of income, beneficial changes in lifestyle, and its contribution to growing national power. The major costs of growth are all of the costs associated with rapid change.

8 Sustained economic development is relatively recent in history and has been highly uneven. About one-fourth of the world's population still exists at a level of bare subsistence, and nearly three-fourths are poor by Western European standards. The gap between rich and poor is large and not decreasing.

9 Impediments to economic development include excessive population growth, resource limitations, inefficient use of resources particularly those that are related to X-inefficiency, inadequate infrastructure, and institutional and cultural patterns that make economic growth difficult.

10 History has demonstrated that the early stages of growth are possible with many mixtures of free-market and central control. Centralized planning can change both the pace and the direction of economic development; it can also prove to be highly wasteful and to destroy individual initiative. The more complex and developed an economy becomes, the greater are the advantages of decentralized markets over central planning.

11 Educational policy, while vitally important to the long-run rate of economic development, yields its benefits only in the future. Improvement of basic education for the general populace is sometimes bypassed for the more immediate visible results of educating a selected technical and political elite.

12 Capital for development can be acquired from domestic savings, but the vicious circle of poverty is a problem. Importing capital rather than using domestic savings permits large investment during the early years of development. Much foreign capital for LDCs since the 1950s has been in the form of 'soft' loans or contributions by foreign governments and international institutions.

13 Unresolved issues concern the appropriate pace of development, the neo-Malthusian view of population growth as a problem, the cost of creating capital in terms of sacrifices of current consumption, and the compatibility of further economic growth with environmental protection.

and goods produced in noisy, pollution-creating factories, will seem crude beyond measure to *our* great grand-children. Without the technological advance produced by growth, and in the absence of seemingly impossible massive redistribution schemes, the LDCs are condemned to poverty while the advanced countries are condemned to relatively crude technological means for handling their pressing environmental problems.

Conclusion

This is an important debate, one on which our very survival on the planet may depend. If the optimists are right, technological advance may allow the world's environmental problems to be dealt with, while raising the living standards of the mass of the world's people who currently live in poverty. If the pessimists are right, continued growth will cause more problems than it creates. Stopping growth, if that could be done, would then condemn much of the world's population to poverty for ever. The political effects of arriving at this 'solution', and having it generally understood, would be far-reaching indeed.

Questions

1 Is the growth referred to in each of the following newspaper stories likely to be due to a shift in aggregate demand, or a shift in the long-run aggregate supply curve?
   (a) 'Growth reaches 7 per cent as recovery gains strength.'
   (b) 'Tax exemptions for research and development to encourage growth.'
   (c) 'Japan's high savings rate encourages its economic growth.'
   (d) 'Lack of consumer spending will hurt this year's growth rate.'
   (e) 'New innovations raise output but lower jobs in the car industry.'

2 Which One or More of the following are ways of increasing a country's long-term growth rate?
   (a) Increasing domestic savings and domestic investment.
   (b) Removing a recessionary gap.
   (c) Encouraging research and development.
   (d) Establishing a more equitable distribution of income.

3 True or False?
   (a) In the long run there is no paradox of thrift because savings help to raise potential national income.
   (b) Growth in the twentieth century has been associated with major changes in new products and only minor changes in the techniques for making existing products.
   (c) The optimum population occurs where the marginal returns to adding an additional person to the population reaches a maximum.
   (d) Growth usually redistributes income from the more to the less well-off.
   (e) Rapidly increasing the growth rate usually means more consumption in the future at the cost of less consumption in the present.

4 Growth of the capital stock in a world without learning will be associated with a (leftward-shifting/rightward-shifting/static) marginal efficiency of capital curve, a (declining/increasing/constant) marginal return on capital, and a (falling/rising/constant) ratio of capital to output.

5 Assume technological innovations are shifting the *MEC* curve outwards *faster* than capital accumulation is moving the economy downwards along any given curve, and then answer as in question 4.

37 Employment and Unemployment[1]

In the early 1980s worldwide unemployment rose to very high levels, higher than during some of the years of the 1930s although not as high as the peak unemployment rates of that earlier 'Great Depression'. Not only was the overall level of unemployment wastefully large, the structure of unemployment was extremely varied – in Britain in 1990 the unemployment rate was about 11 per cent among males under 25 and $4\frac{1}{2}$ per cent among women over 44. Regional disparities were significant, although not so large as they were a decade or two before. Currently, males seem to be major sufferers compared to females – a phenomenon new in UK history and unusual in foreign countries. Young males have unemployment rates 20 per cent higher than young females, while the rate for older males is a third higher than the comparable age-group among women.

Economic conditions as well as social and economic policies instituted since the 1930s have no doubt made the economic consequences of short-term unemployment less serious than they were in earlier times. But the effects of the current high unemployment, especially for the long-term unemployed in terms of disillusioned groups who have given up trying to succeed within the system, many of whom sow the seeds of social unrest, is a matter of serious concern to those concerned with the long-term health of the society.

Two Views of the Labour Market

In considering labour and unemployment there are two key views that need to be distinguished. The older Keynesian view is that workers can be involuntarily employed because of frictions and structural rigidities in the labour markets. Workers may lose jobs because their factories close. Although there may be new jobs created when other factories open, there will be unemployment while these jobs are located, possibly in different geographical locations. So, to Keynesians, not all frictional unemployment is voluntary.

Keynesians see structural unemployment as largely involuntary. They see the demands and supplies changing throughout the whole economy so those without jobs may be in the wrong place, and have the wrong skills to take the new jobs being created. For Keynesians this sort of unemployment is involuntary.

The other view, called the New Classical view, is held by many in the academic community today. According to this view, all unemployment that is not due to deficient

aggregate demand is voluntary. For these economists, those who are unemployed for frictional or structural reasons are, in some real sense, voluntarily unemployed.[1]

We will see how the debate between these two camps plays out as we study unemployment in this chapter.

KINDS OF UNEMPLOYMENT

For purposes of study, the unemployed can be classified in various ways. We can distinguish among categories of persons unemployed – e.g. youth, women, adult men – among age, sex, occupation, degree of skill, and even by ethnic groups. We may distinguish by location – e.g. unemployment in the South East, the North West, and Scotland. We may also distinguish by the duration of unemployment between, say, those who are out of jobs for long periods of time and those who suffer relatively short-term bouts of unemployment. Finally, we may distinguish the reasons for the unemployment.

In the present chapter we concentrate on the reasons for unemployment. We start with a very basic distinction. A worker is in INVOLUNTARY UNEMPLOYMENT if he or she is prepared to work at the going wage rate but no job is available. A worker is in VOLUNTARY UNEMPLOYMENT if there is a job available at the going wage rate but he or she is not willing to accept it.

We now pass on to consider a different classification based on causes of unemployment. Although it is not always possible to attach a specific cause to each unemployed person, it is often possible to gain some idea of the total numbers of people unemployed for each major cause. Different economists find it convenient to identify different causes, and there is no right or wrong about any system of classification. In what follows we take one common scheme for classifying unemployment by types:

- demand-deficient unemployment
- frictional unemployment
- structural unemployment
- real-wage (or 'Classical') unemployment

Demand-Deficient Unemployment

Unemployment that occurs because there is insufficient total demand to purchase all of the output that could be produced by a fully employed economy is called DEMAND-DEFICIENT UNEMPLOYMENT or sometimes KEYNESIAN UNEMPLOYMENT. The national-income theory that we have studied throughout

---

1 Details of employment and unemployment in the UK may be found in Harbury and Lipsey.

1 See page 375 for a discussion of New Classical views.

the macro part of this book seeks, among other things, to explain this type of unemployment.

When the aggregate demand curve is given by AD in Figure 37.1, short- and long-run equilibrium is at a national income of Y_F. At that level of income, there is no demand-deficient unemployment. If the aggregate demand curve shifts to AD', equilibrium income falls to Y_0. A recessionary gap shown in the diagram by $Y_F - Y_0$ opens up. The accompanying unemployment is called demand-deficient unemployment. It can be eliminated by raising aggregate demand to AD without setting up any inflationary pressures due to excess demand, in the sense that the price level will be no higher than it was before the fall in aggregate demand.

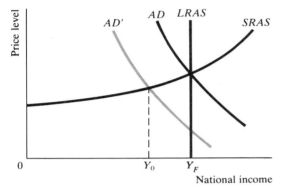

FIGURE 37.1 Demand-Deficient Unemployment. Demand-deficient unemployment occurs when the aggregate demand curve cuts the $SRAS$ curve at a level of national income below potential income, Y_F. It occurs in the Figure when the aggregate demand curve is AD' but not when it is AD.

Full employment: The term 'full employment' generally refers to a situation in which there is no demand-deficient employment. When the economy is 'fully employed', all remaining unemployment is due to other causes. It cannot therefore be reduced, except temporarily, by the tools of demand management. Because the volume of unemployment due to these other causes changes from time to time, so also does the amount of unemployment regarded as full employment.

The brevity of our discussion of demand-deficient unemployment does not reflect any judgement that it is unimportant. Having studied it throughout macroeconomics, however, there is little more that needs to be said about it at this point.

Beyond demand-deficient unemployment: Consider the amount of unemployment that does exist at Y_F in Figure 37.1. This is sometimes called the NATURAL RATE OF UNEMPLOYMENT or the NAIRU,[1] defined as the level

---

1 The NAIRU is further explained on page 452. (There is by definition no room in the Figure for a person who is actively looking for a job at the going wage rate w_e but can't find one. The model is not set up to allow for such persons. Instead they are defined out of existence, which does not help to tell us much about the real world.)

of unemployment at which the aggregate demand for labour equals the aggregate supply of labour so that, *viewed as an aggregate*, the labour market is in equilibrium. At this point, there is some kind of a job available (total demand for labour) for everyone who wants a job at going wage rates (total supply). There can, however, still be substantial unemployment when this aggregate equality exists. We now turn to a study of the unemployment that is additional to demand-deficient unemployment and that persists even when demand-deficient unemployment is zero.

Frictional Unemployment

The term FRICTIONAL UNEMPLOYMENT refers to the unemployment that is associated with the normal turnover of labour. People leave jobs for many reasons, and they take time to find new jobs; old persons leave the labour force and young persons enter it, but often new workers do not fill the jobs vacated by those who leave. Inevitably all of this movement takes time and gives rise to a pool of persons who are 'frictionally' unemployed while in the course of finding new jobs. This unemployment would occur even if the occupational, industrial and regional structure of employment were unchanging.

Is frictional unemployment voluntary?

Some frictional unemployment is clearly voluntary. For example, a worker may know of an available job but may not accept it so she can search for a better one. The new classical view regards all frictional unemployment as voluntary. Critics of that view argue that many frictionally unemployed are in involuntary unemployment because they lost their jobs through no fault of their own (e.g., their factories may have closed down) and they have not yet located a specific case of jobs they know to be available *somewhere*, and for which they know they are qualified.

Structural Unemployment

Structural changes in the economy can cause unemployment. As economic growth proceeds, the pattern of demands and supplies changes constantly. Some industries, occupations and regions suffer declines in the demand for what they produce, while other industries, occupations and regions enjoy increases. These changes require considerable economic readjustment. STRUCTURAL UNEMPLOYMENT occurs when the adjustments are not fast enough, so that severe pockets of unemployment occur in areas, industries and occupations in which the demand for factors of production is falling faster than is the supply. It is defined as the unemployment that exists because of a *mismatching* between the unemployed and the available jobs in terms of regional location, required skills or any other relevant dimension. In Britain today, structural unemployment exists, for example, in Wales, in the car industry, and among machine-tool operators.

Structural unemployment can increase because either the pace of economic change accelerates or the pace of adjustment to change slows down. Natural forces and social policies that discourage movement among regions, industries and/or occupations can raise structural unemployment. Policies that prevent firms from replacing some labour with new machines may protect employment in the short term. If, however, such policies lead to the decline of an industry because it cannot compete with more innovative foreign competitors, they can end up causing severe pockets of structural unemployment.

Is structural unemployment voluntary?

According to the New Classical view, all structural unemployment is voluntary. Say, for example, that there is an excess supply of skilled carworkers and an excess demand for unskilled dishwashers. If an unemployed carworker does not take one of the available jobs as a dishwasher he is voluntarily deciding to stay unemployed in the hopes of finding a job that uses his skills.

Critics reply 'but what if it is the other way around, as it so often is?' What if there is excess supply of unskilled workers and excess demand for those with skills? The unemployed dishwasher cannot accept a job as a computer programmer; his skills do not equip him for this. This mismatching between the skills of those unemployed and the skills required by the available jobs cannot easily be removed by individual actions of the unemployed dishwashers nor can it be blamed on their union since they have none.

Real-Wage Unemployment

Unemployment due to too high a real wage is called REAL-WAGE UNEMPLOYMENT. It is sometimes also called CLASSICAL UNEMPLOYMENT after the many economists who held that unemployment in the 1930s was due to too high a real wage and whom Keynes called 'Classical economists'. Their remedy for unemployment was to reduce wages. Keynes argued that the unemployment of the 1930s was caused by deficient aggregate demand rather than by excessively high real wages.

The Keynesian view of the causes of the Great Depression eventually prevailed. But the debate of the thirties aroused such strong emotions that many modern economists have refused to believe that *any* significant amount of unemployment could be caused by real wages that were too high. There was concern, however, that some of the unemployment that occurred in Britain and Europe during the 1980s was traceable to high real wages.

We can distinguish two types of real-wage unemployment, one associated with relative wages among different groups of labour and one associated with the general level of wages.

Disequilibrium relative wages

Typical microeconomic causes of unemployment are minimum floors to wages, union agreements that narrow wage differentials, nationally agreed wage structures that take no account of local market conditions, and equal-pay laws where employers perceive unequal marginal-value products among the groups concerned. Some of these have already been discussed in Chapters 18 and 19.

Consider, for example, a minimum-wage law. Figure 37.2 is a microeconomic diagram that shows the effect of such a law on the market for unskilled labour. This is the only group that will be affected, since semi-skilled and skilled workers will earn wages above the minimum in any case. Under competitive conditions the forces of supply and demand produce a wage of w_c and employment of q_c. A minimum wage of w_m is now imposed. As a result, wages rise to w_m but employment falls to q_1. The q_1 workers who keep their jobs are benefited by the law: they can earn higher wages. But the $q_c - q_1$ workers who lose their jobs are harmed by the law: they become unemployed. Also, a further $q_2 - q_c$ workers would now like employment at the higher wage, but they cannot find work.

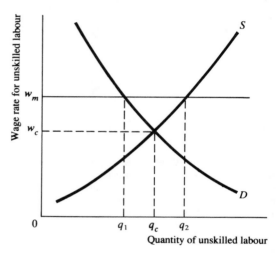

FIGURE 37.2 A Disequilibrium Relative Real Wage. A real wage that is held above its free-market level causes unemployment in that microeconomic market. The wage w_m causes unemployment of $q_2 - q_1$.

There is evidence that minimum-wage laws cause unemployment of young and inexperienced workers. These people tend to have lower marginal productivities than do experienced workers and their low starting wages reflect this. But the young tend to learn quickly, so as they gain experience, their marginal productivities, and hence their free-market wages, rise. If a high legal minimum wage makes it hard for them to obtain their first job, they are delayed in gaining the work experience that would lift their market-determined wage above the minimum.

Consider, for example, a school-leaver who would accept £X for her first job. A potential employer is willing to pay this, but the minimum is £1.5X. So the employer hires someone overqualified for the job on the grounds that, if he has to pay more than he needs to, he might as well get something extra in return.

A disequilibrium average real wage

So far in this book, we have used the term *the real wage* to refer to the purchasing power of money wages. This can be measured by deflating the money wage by the retail price index. Now we introduce a second type of real wage: the REAL PRODUCT WAGE, which is the money wage earned in a particular industry deflated by the value of that industry's product. For example, suppose labour costs £300 a week and each week produces an output whose market value is £400, then the real product wage is £300/£400, which is 0.75. This means that 75p out of every £1 of sales goes to pay for labour inputs.

Note that, since it is *labour costs* in which we are interested, the wage is the full cost to the employer of hiring a unit of labour. This includes the pre-tax wage rate, any extra benefits such as pension-plan contributions, and such government payroll taxes as employers' contribution to national insurance.

The real product wage can affect employment through forces operating both in the short run and in the long run. We shall consider each of these time-periods in turn, assuming the real product wage has risen for exogenous reasons.

The short run: First consider the short run, where the amount of capital is fixed. Past technological changes that are embodied in existing plant and equipment mean that, at any moment in time, an industry will have an array of plants, running from those that can do little more than cover their variable costs through to those that make a handsome return over variable costs. Now assume that the real product wage rises by, say, 15 per cent. This will mean that some plants can no longer cover their variable costs and they will close down. If, for example, a plant originally had wages of 64p and other direct costs of 30p in every sales £1, production would be worthwhile, since 6p of every £1 of sales would be available as a return on already invested capital. If the product wage rose by 15 per cent to 73.6p in every £1 of sales, then the plant would immediately be shut down, since it would not even be covering its variable costs, which would be 103.6p in every £1 of sales. The plant's employees would then lose their jobs.

The long run: Two effects may be noted. First, as real product wages rise, profits fall, making investment in new plant and equipment less and less profitable. Plants may not be replaced as they wear out and new plants that use new production techniques to produce new commodities may not be built. Long-term unemployment can result. Many economists think this was the situation in the UK economy in the late 1970s and early 1980s.

Second, when new plants are being built, their designers will respond to the high wage rate by seeking to substitute relatively cheap capital for relatively more expensive labour. So a given volume of output would employ less labour (and more capital) than before, causing unemployment to grow.

Conclusion: A large rise in the real product wage can lead to persistent unemployment as plants that cannot cover their variable costs close quickly, as long-term investment falls in response to low return to capital, and as new plants are designed to use more capital and less labour in response to high wage rates.

Is real-wage unemployment voluntary?

In so far as wages are held above their equilibrium level by unions, the resulting unemployment can be regarded as collectively voluntary for union members. No single union member can do much about it but, as a group, they elect, or at least tolerate, their union representatives and, therefore, are responsible for the overly high wage. As a group, they have chosen not to cut their wages and have, therefore, chosen the unemployment consequences.

Critics reply that since it is the least senior who lose their jobs when supply exceeds demand, it is quite possible that all the unemployed would have voted for a lower wage but were outvoted by the more senior majority who voted for the higher wage knowing that someone else would suffer the unemployment consequences.

So, in one sense, the unemployment is voluntary since it was accepted by the majority of union members as a consequence of their high wage. In another sense, however, it is involuntary in the sense that those unemployed would not only be willing to work at the going wage, but would work at a lower one. Only their union agreement prevents them from doing so. Moreover, it may well be involuntary for non-members of the union who find themselves discriminated against by employers.

Is the NAIRU all Voluntary Unemployment?

Many examiners will want you to answer 'yes' to the question stated in the title to this section. Thus you should understand the argument: (1) All frictional unemployment is voluntary because people are voluntarily unemployed while looking for a job they think suits their needs and abilities. (2) All real-wage unemployment is voluntary because collectively, even if not individually, all workers are responsible for not cutting the real wage negotiated by their unions. (3) All structural unemployment is voluntary because there is always some menial job available that anyone could take (provided there is no excess of total supply of labour over total demand, i.e. no Keynesian unemployment).

The argument that all of the NAIRU is voluntary is illustrated in Figure 37.3, which shows a single aggregate labour market for the economy. The wage rate is determined 'competitively' in the sense that it equates quantity demanded and quantity supplied.

The total number of people willing to work at each real wage rate is given by the curve S. The number of people in the labour force is given by the curve LF. The difference between S and LF is assumed to be made up of people who are voluntarily holding their labour off the market, either because they are between jobs, or because they are looking for something better than they can now find. In this example, the labour market clears at a wage of w_e, with employment at q_0. Unemployment is $q_1 - q_0$, which is the NAIRU. All of these unemployed persons are, *by definition*, voluntarily unemployed.[1]

This New Classical view argues that the millions of UK workers out of work in the 1980s, and the many in a similar position today, were *voluntarily refraining from going to work*. If their unemployment was voluntary, they presumably did, and do, not deserve the sympathy, and state help, that would be extended to people who were *involuntarily* unemployed.

Critics of the New Classical view argue that the new classical result that all of the NAIRU is voluntary is merely a matter of definition. As already observed, the critics argue that some of the people in frictional unemployment are not voluntarily unemployed since, with the best will in the world, it takes time to find a new job when one has lost one's old job.

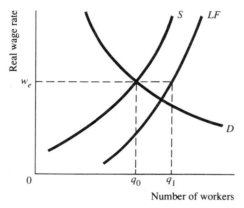

FIGURE 37.3 The New-Classical View of Unemployment in which all of the NAIRU is Voluntary Unemployment. Let S be the supply of people willing to work at the going wage. LF is the labour force, so that the difference between S and LF is people in the labour force but not willing to work at the going wage. If there is one labour market for the country, and if it clears at the equilibrium wage of w_e, $q_1 - q_0$ are unemployed. According to the New Classical definition, this amount of unemployment is the NAIRU and, as the aggregate national labour market shown in the Figure has been defined, all of this unemployment is voluntary.

More importantly, they argue that to compress the entire labour market into one competitive market shown in Figure 37.3, is highly unrealistic. Structural unemployment occurs because there are *many labour markets* whose prices adjust slowly, and among which labour takes time to move. The critics argue that to say that a decline in the car industry in the Midlands that throws people out of work for some months, even when there is work in the South East, causes *voluntary* unemployment is to stretch words well beyond their normal meaning. Be that as it may,

to explain structural unemployment in a model of *one* aggregate competitive labour market containing homogeneous labour (as Figure 38.3 assumes) is to *assume away* the important problems associated with the structure of unemployment among imperfectly linked markets.

The New Classical economists define the NAIRU as the amount of unemployment existing when the labour market illustrated in Figure 37.3 is in equilibrium. The critics, allowing for the many labour markets that exist and are only imperfectly linked, define the NAIRU as the amount of unemployment existing when the *total* demand for labour is equal to the *total* supply. This is the same thing as saying that the number of unfilled vacancies is equal to the number of unemployed. There are many labour markets and excess demand in some may be matched by excess supply in others. This allows a macro balance in the sense that for every unemployed person there is some unfilled vacancy. But if the unemployed are in different places, and/or have different trainings, than is required by the available jobs, many may be unable to locate a job at the going wage rate. This structural imbalance between the characteristics of the available labour and the characteristics of the available job is ruled out *by assumption* in the simple aggregate model of Figure 37.3.

If you are asked to explain why everyone who is unemployed at the NAIRU is *voluntarily* unemployed, you must show that you understand the arguments, even though you may feel, as we do, that these arguments do not fully describe unemployment that we see in the real world. There we often see genuine suffering associated with people who would like to work at the prevailing wage rate in jobs for which they are qualified but who cannot currently find such jobs.

THE MEASUREMENT OF UNEMPLOYMENT

There are two main problems of measurement that need to be addressed: the measurement of the overall rate of unemployment, and the measurement of different types of unemployment.

When we measure the overall rate of unemployment, what we would like to discover is the extent of *involuntary* unemployment. Problems arise both because we may not count some of those who are involuntarily unemployed, and because we may count some who are voluntarily unemployed and others who are actually working.

The number of persons unemployed in the UK is estimated from a monthly count of those who are eligible to claim unemployment benefits.

There are reasons why this measured figure for unemployment may not reflect the number of people who are truly unemployed in the sense that they would accept the offer of a job for which they were qualified. On the one hand, the measured figure may *understate* involuntary unemployment by missing people who are genuinely willing to work at going wage rates. For example, some people who have worked in the past are not eligible for unemployment benefits and, therefore, are not counted.

---

1 The reason for the use of this latter term, which stands for *non-accelerating inflationary rate of unemployment*, will be explained in Chapter 39.

BOX 37.1 Unemployment, NAIRUles OK

'How high must unemployment rise to squeeze inflation out of the economy? Higher than its current rate of 1.8m (6.2%), but probably not as high as it had to in the mid-1980s. That is not just because inflation is raging less fiercely than it was in the early 1980s, but also because of improvements in the way the labour market works. Economists talk of the "non-accelerating inflation rate of unemployment" (NAIRU) – or, in simple English, the unemployment rate which stops inflation taking off. The interaction between inflation and unemployment depends upon how well the labour market works. The better it works, the lower is the rate of unemployment compatible with stable inflation – ie, the lower the NAIRU.

'Putting an exact figure on Britain's NAIRU is rather like chasing a mirage, but changes in unemployment and inflation give clues to its general area. In the halcyon days of the 1960s, ... inflation and unemployment shuffled along together comfortably within ranges of, respectively, 0.8%–6.3% and 1.5%–2.6%. By the early 1980s it took an unemployment rate of 11% to bring inflation down. In the second half of the decade the NAIRU seemed to become much less daunting, as unemployment fell without provoking much rise in inflation.... There are two possible explanations for that pleasant interlude. The NAIRU may, as the figures imply, have fallen sharply. Or the link between inflation and unemployment may simply have been operating on a long lag, with the old, high NAIRU returning after several years to smack ministers in the face.

'The answer is probably a bit of both. Certainly, it takes time for workers and employers to react to changing conditions in the labour market.... But the NAIRU is indeed likely to be lower these days – partly because the labour market works better, and partly because some of those out of work will not show up in the figures.'

(*The Economist*, 5 January 1991)

The title NAIRUles, a play on words, combines the term NAIRU and the word rules. The article itself defines, and then discusses, the NAIRU. Its rise in the 1970s is noted, and several reasons why it might have fallen during the latter part of the 1980s are advanced.

Questions

1 Why might the NAIRU have risen from low figures in the 1960s to much higher figures by the early 1980s, and what specific policies might have reduced it by the late 1980s?
2 To what is the writer referring when he says one reason for the NAIRU to have fallen is that some of the unemployed may not show up in the figures? Should macroeconomic policy-makers take credit for such a change?
3 What effects would long lags in the reactions of workers and employers to changing conditions have on estimates of the NAIRU made by observing the reaction of inflation to changes in unemployment?

Also, those who have not worked before are not eligible for benefits. School-leavers and housewives who would work if a booming economy offered them jobs, will not show up on the statistics as unemployed. In contrast, the measured figure may *overstate* unemployment by including people who are not truly unemployed in the sense we have just defined. Some people cheat on the system by collecting unemployment benefits when they are employed. Some people do not really wish to work because the difference between their unemployment benefits and what they can earn in work is not sufficient to compensate them for the disutility of work. These people have voluntarily withdrawn from the workforce, but they register as unemployed in order to collect their benefits. Others, for reasons of age or disability, are unemployable but register in order to receive benefits.

The measured rate of unemployment has been reduced in the UK by making several changes in the method of measurement during the 1980s. Prior to 1982, the unemployed were counted at Job Centres. The change to the basis described in the text caused an apparent fall of nearly a quarter of a million in the number of jobless. In 1986,

the self-employed, and people in the armed services, were added to the labour force. This accomplished a further reduction of about $1\frac{1}{2}$ per cent in measured unemployment. This time, the trick was to add to the labour force people who are seldom counted as unemployed.

CURES FOR UNEMPLOYMENT

Demand-Deficient Unemployment

We do not need to say much more about cures for this type of unemployment since its control is the subject of demand management which we have studied in several earlier chapters. A major recession that occurs as a result of the operation of market forces can be countered by monetary and fiscal policy to shift the aggregate demand curve so as to reduce demand-deficient unemployment.

Frictional Unemployment

The labour turnover which causes frictional unemployment is an inevitable part of the functioning of the economy. There will always be some turnover as people of all ages change jobs for any reason. Furthermore, some frictional unemployment is an inevitable part of the learning process. One reason why there is a high turnover rate, and hence high frictional unemployment, among the young is that one has to try jobs to see if they are suitable. New entrants – whether the young or older women who have just decided to take a job rather than stay at home – often try several jobs before settling into the one that most satisfies, or least dissatisfies, them.

Insofar as frictional unemployment is caused by ignorance, increasing the knowledge of labour-market opportunities may help. But such measures have a cost, and it is not clear how much is to be gained by further expenditure at the margin here.

Finally, policy changes that make it easier for youths to find jobs from which they can learn, and hence raise their productivity, could help. Youth training, and schemes aimed at subsidizing the wage rate for young workers, may also help.

Structural Unemployment

The changes in the structure of the economy that cause short-term bouts of structural unemployment are an inevitable result of economic growth which is the main cause of long-term increases in average living standards. Although this does not make structural unemployment any the less unpleasant, it does put such unemployment into some perspective.

Two basically different approaches can be taken to reducing structural unemployment, and to alleviating the hardship that it causes. The first, which has sometimes found expression in British economic policy, is to try to prevent, or at least to slow, the changes in the economy that cause structural unemployment. The second, which has been pioneered in Sweden, is to accept the economic change that accompanies economic growth and to adopt policies designed to make the economy more flexible and adaptive to such change.

Reducing the amount of change: Throughout the centuries many governments and workers have sought to combat the threat of structural unemployment by preventing, or slowing, structural changes.

One way in which this has been done in the past is through *manning agreements*. These seek to prevent people from being declared redundant, and thus becoming structurally unemployed, because of new innovations. For example, the replacement of coal by diesel in railway engines forty years ago made firemen who shovelled coal into the boiler unnecessary, but existing firemen were kept on by agreement between British Rail and the firemen's union. A second way is through the support of declining industries by public funds. For example, if the market would support an output of X but subsidies are used to support an output of $2X$, then jobs are provided for a large part of the industry's labour force who would otherwise become unemployed and then have to find jobs elsewhere.

Both of these policies will be attractive to the people who would otherwise become unemployed. It may be a long time before they can find other jobs and, when they do, their skills may not turn out to be highly valued in their new industries. If such policies are used to manipulate the rate at which jobs disappear in particular categories or in whole industries, they can be successful. If, however, they are used to resist change indefinitely, they will not in the end be sustainable. Manning agreements raise costs and hasten the decline of an industry threatened by competitive products. An industry that is declining due to market forces but supported by government subsidy, becomes an increasingly large charge on the public purse as the market becomes less and less favourable to its success. Sooner or later, public support is withdrawn and an often precipitous decline in output and employment then ensues.

In assessing the above remedies for structural unemployment, it is important to realize that, although not viable in the long run for the economy, they may be the best alternative for the affected workers. Thus, there is often a real conflict between those threatened by structural unemployment, whose interests lie in preserving their old jobs, and the general public, whose interests lie in encouraging economic growth and change.

Increasing adaptability to change: The conflict just stated can be reduced by accepting the decline of some industries and the destruction of some jobs, as well as the rise of other industries and the creation of other jobs, that accompany economic growth and then employing policies that reduce the costs, and increase the speed, of the adjustments that must be made.

For example, retraining and relocation grants can make it easier for labour to move among jobs and between geographic areas. They can also reduce the hardship involved in making these movements. Such policies have the advantage of helping the economy adjust to inevitable change and, by speeding up the change, of reducing the pool of people who are structurally unemployed at any one time.

Avoid policies that inhibit adjustment: For most of the past fifty years, British housing policy has inhibited the geographic reallocation of labour and hence increased structural unemployment. Rent controls have discouraged the private construction of rental accommodation in expanding areas. By thus contributing to a housing shortage, they make it harder for people to move. Geographic movement was also discouraged by the provision of council housing at low rents accompanied by an inadequate supply of such housing in expanding centres. To leave a declining area often meant giving up cheap, and available, council housing in return for only a place on a long waiting list in the expanding area. Due to some major changes in housing policy in the 1980s, and due to the poor market for selling new houses, the private rental market has greatly recovered in the 1990s and no longer acts as such an important

BOX 37.2 Aspects of Unemployment

Structural Unemployment: 'Britain's labour market may be working better, but it is still not working well. Western Germany manages to maintain an inflation rate of 3% with an unemployment rate of 6.7%. One obvious failing in Britain is the gap between the skills the workforce offers and those employers want. That mismatch seems worse than the was ten years ago. According to the Confederation of British Industry, in 1980 when unemployment was at the same level as now, around 5% of firms were reporting skill shortages; the equivalent figure in 1990 was around 25%.'

Why Recorded Unemployment misses many of the truly unemployed: '1. Many jobs are marginal part-time jobs held by women. Many do not earn enough to pay national insurance, so do not qualify for unemployment benefit and so do not show up as "unemployed" when they lose their jobs. 2. Changes in the benefit system keep ineligible claimants out [of the recorded unemployment statistics].'

Why wages are more flexible than in the past: 'Weaker unions tend to mean that wages are more flexible. Without unions fighting to keep up wages, employers are free to cut back costs by squeezing pay rather than by sacking marginal workers. The rise in self-employment is also likely to increase the flexibility of earnings. A company will lay off workers in bad times, the self-employed are likely to stay at work and work less hours as orders dwindle.'

(*The Economist*, 5 January 1991)

This article deals with some of the aspects of unemployment that we have discussed in this chapter.

Questions

1 *Ceteris paribus*, would each of the three factors mentioned in the article increase or decrease the NAIRU?
2 Some theories say that the NAIRU is made up entirely of voluntarily unemployed persons. Are the unemployed whose skills do not match the skills required by the jobs that are vacant (referred to in the first quotation), voluntarily unemployed? What type of unemployment do they constitute?
3 How might workers with different types of jobs, and with different seniority levels, evaluate policies designed to lower the NAIRU by making wages more flexible?

---

inhibitor of regional mobility.

Unemployment and other benefits sometimes make the margin between the income from unemployment in contracting areas and the income from employment in expanding areas less than the costs, and risks, of moving. Such benefits discourage geographic mobility and so contribute to structural unemployment. This is not to say that policies that reduce the suffering from involuntary unemployment are undesirable. But if they are designed with no concern about their potential for increasing structural unemployment, they can be self-defeating in the long run. Some countries require that those on benefits enter training schemes that will fit them for new jobs. Others give strong incentives to move to expanding areas, and disincentives to stay in contracting ones in the form of movement bonuses to those who move and reduced payments to those who do not.

Real-Wage Unemployment

Whenever this type of unemployment exists, it is not easy to cure. Basically what is required is a fall in the real product wage, combined with measures to increase aggregate demand so as to create enough total employment. But the cure is a slow one, requiring enough time to build the new labour-using capital. The steps would run as follows.

First, the real product wage would be cut substantially.

Two approaches are possible. First, a direct attack on union power could reduce the ability of unions to hold wages above equilibrium levels. This was the approach taken by the Conservative government in the UK during the 1980s. There is no doubt that the unions were very strong during the 1970s, and that their power was substantially curtailed during the 1980s.

An alternative, tried in some other countries, and in the UK in earlier decades, was to reach some form of 'social contract' whereby unions, employers and the government agreed to allow this to occur, or at least to allow the real wage to fall slowly as money wages rose less fast than the price level. Alternatively, employers' contributions to unemployment insurance or to employees' pensions schemes could be cut, thus reducing the overall labour cost of producing each unit of output. The reduction would provide the incentive to create more employment by using more labour-intensive methods of production.

Second, since wages determine disposable income, and disposable income determines consumer demand, the cut in wages will tend to reduce aggregate demand and hence reduce equilibrium national income. This contractionary force could be offset by fiscal and monetary policies.

Third, it must be accepted that unemployment is likely to remain relatively high until new capital capacity is built to employ the surplus labour. Any attempt to push aggregate demand beyond the capacity output of the current capital stock will create the conditions for a demand inflation.

Conclusion

Most economists agreed that, throughout the first half of the 1980s, there was significant demand-deficient unemployment. This unemployment was accepted by government policy-makers as a necessary, although unfortunate, consequence of their anti-inflationary policies and their drive to reduce the public-sector borrowing requirement. Some economists felt that these policies were not worth the price that was entailed in terms of unemployment. They called for expansionary demand-management policies to eliminate the demand-deficient unemployment.

Most economists agreed that there was more structural unemployment in the UK in the 1980s than there had been at any time since the end of the Second World War. Many called for policies to increase the adaptability of the economy and reduce inhibitions to the movement of labour. Others were more attracted by government intervention, mainly in the form of moving work to the places where unemployment was highest. Grants to encourage unemployed persons to start regional service-oriented industries had a bit of both approaches in them.

Whether or not real-wage unemployment was a serious problem in Britain and Europe throughout the 1980s was probably the most contentious issue concerning unemployment. Advocates of the real-wage explanation argued that British real wages were some 10–15 per cent too high at the beginning of the 1980s and, as a result, significant amounts of capital were being scrapped. Economists who held this view argued that the unemployment could not be eliminated until the real product wage fell significantly – as it did in many American industries in the early 1980s.

In the last part of the 1980s, unemployment fell temporarily due to a rapid expansion in the economy which eliminated much of the demand-deficient unemployment. Then in the early 1990s unemployment rose once again, as a new recession increased demand-deficient unemployment.

Summary

1 Unemployment normally refers to those who are involuntarily unemployed – i.e. willing to work at the going wage rate but unable to find a job. Unemployment is traditionally divided into four categories: frictional, structural, real-wage, and demand-deficient unemployment.

2 Demand-deficient unemployment can be removed by using the tools of demand management to raise equilibrium national income to its potential level.

3 Frictional unemployment is the amount of unemployment due to labour turnover as new people enter the labour force and look for jobs and existing workers change jobs. Structural unemployment occurs because changes in the regional, occupational and industrial structure of the demand for labour are not matched by equivalent changes in the structure of the supply of labour. Real-wage unemployment occurs when the real product wage is too high. Demand-deficient unemployment is due to a lack of sufficient demand to raise equilibrium income to potential income.

4 The measured unemployment rate overstates unemployment because some people may be eligible to claim unemployment benefits while having withdrawn from the labour force, and because others claim benefits while working surreptitiously. It understates true involuntary unemployment by recording only those eligible for unemployment benefits rather than all those who would be willing to work at the going wage rate if jobs were available.

5 Frictional unemployment can be reduced by reducing the amount of time taken between jobs.

6 Structural unemployment can be reduced by measures that increase the degree of labour mobility among regions, occupations and industries.

7 Real-wage unemployment can be reduced by lowering the real product wage, adopting expansionary fiscal and monetary policies to offset the expenditure-decreasing effects of lower wages, and waiting until new plants are built to employ a higher ratio of labour to capital.

Questions

1 True or False?
(a) Full employment means effectively zero unemployment.
(b) Frictional unemployment occurs because people are not trained for the jobs that are available.
(c) Demand-deficient unemployment occurs when the aggregate demand curve cuts the $SRAS$ curve to the left of Y_F.
(d) Increasing knowledge about available jobs is a way of reducing structural unemployment.
(e) Other things equal, a rise in the rate of economic growth is likely to increase the amount of frictional and structural unemployment.

2 Interpret the following statements from newspapers in terms of types of unemployment:
(a) 'Recession hits local factory, 500 laid off.'
(b) 'A job? I've given up trying', says mother of two.
(c) 'We closed down because we could not meet the competition from Taiwan', says local factory manager.
(d) 'When they raised the minimum wage, I just could not afford to keep these retired policemen as security guards', says the owner of a local shopping centre.
(e) 'Slack demand puts local foundry on short time.'
(f) 'Of course I could take a job as a dishwasher but I am trying to find a job that makes use of my six GCSE passes', says a young person in a survey of the unemployed.
(g) 'Retraining the main challenge in the increased use of robots.'
(h) 'The owner and I couldn't get along, but I shouldn't have any trouble finding another place that wants a chef.'

3 In many countries the unemployment figures are derived from a sample survey that counts as unemployed those who are without a job but who were actively searching for one during the week. Why is this likely to produce a higher figure for unemployment than the British practice of relying on those who are eligible to claim unemployment benefits?

4 Which type of unemployment is most likely to be reduced by each of the following measures?
(a) Retraining schemes for long-term unemployed.
(b) A large volume of open-market purchases of bonds by the Bank of England.
(c) Increased numbers and efficiency of job centres.
(d) Agreements between unions and employers to hold the increases in money wages to less than the increase in the firms' product prices.
(e) A reduction in the standard rate of income tax.
(f) A building boom greatly increases the supplies of rental accommodation in expanding parts of the UK.

38 Inflation

This chapter deals with the important topic of inflation, which we defined in Chapter 22 as any increase in the general price level. As a preparation, the introductory material in Chapter 22 on the price level that begins on page 000 must be reread.

The analysis of this chapter builds on what you learned in Chapter 35 on aggregate demand and aggregate supply. Indeed, much of the early analysis of the initial effects of demand and supply shocks repeats what we studied in that earlier chapter. We repeat it here, rather than merely referring you back, because the review should be helpful and because the later analysis of sustained inflations builds on the study of isolated demand-side and supply-side shocks that we first cover.

CAUSES OF INFLATION

Anything that tends to drive the price level upwards is often referred to as an inflationary shock, while anything that tends to drive the price level downwards is often referred to as a deflationary shock. We start by making four important distinctions concerning these shocks.

- Inflations that are caused by shifts in aggregate demand – which are referred to as demand-side shocks – must be distinguished from inflations that are caused by shifts in aggregate supply – which are referred to as supply-side shocks.
- Isolated, once-and-for-all demand- or supply-side shocks must be distinguished from repeated shocks. The former cause temporary bouts of inflation as the general price level moves from one equilibrium level to another. The latter cause continuous or 'sustained' inflations.[1]
- Increases in the price level that take place when the money supply is held constant must be distinguished from those that take place when the money supply is being increased at the rate at which the price level is rising. When an increase in the money supply accompanies supply-side or demand-side shocks, the resulting inflation is said to be VALIDATED (or sometimes 'accommodated') by the monetary expansion. When the money supply is held constant in the face of demand-side or supply-side shocks, the resulting inflation is said to be *non-validated*.[2]

- For shocks that produce recessionary gaps, it matters whether wages are flexible enough to reduce unit costs in the face of a persistent recessionary gap (called flexible costs) or whether they are so inflexible in a downward direction that unit costs do not fall (called rigid costs). Both 'flexible' and 'rigid' refer to downward adjustments in the face of recessionary gaps; ample evidence shows that wages and costs are flexible upwards in the face of inflationary gaps.

These distinctions seem to give rise to many potential cases: (i) demand or supply shock, (ii) isolated or sustained, (iii) validated or non-validated, and (iv) flexible or non-flexible costs. If all combinations of these four either-or situations were possible, there would be 16 cases to study. Fortunately, the number of cases is much less. For example, as we shall see below, sustained shocks can only occur if the resulting inflation is validated, so the combination *sustained and non-validated* is not one we need to consider. Also as we shall see below, although an isolated supply shock can be validated or non-validated, the validation of an isolated demand shock turns it into a sustained demand shock. So the combination *isolated, validated demand shock* need not detain us.

Figure 38.1 illustrates all the combinations that can occur, and it should be studied as the analysis of the various possible cases unfolds. Do not try to follow it all through now, just use it as a guide for the discussion that follows.

Supply-Shock Inflation

When an inflation is caused by supply-side shocks, it is called a 'supply-shock inflation', a 'supply-side inflation' or, most commonly, a COST-PUSH INFLATION. Such an inflation is defined as any rise in the price level originating from increases in costs *that are not caused by excess demands in the markets for factors of production*. Examples are a rise in the cost of imported raw materials, and a rise in wage rates caused by the exercise of union power in the absence of any excess demand for labour.

Initial effects

The initial effects of a single cost-push shock were already

---

1 Some economists reserve the term 'inflation' for sustained changes in the price level, using other words such as a *rise in the price level* to refer to once-and-for-all changes. As long as one understands the distinction, the choice of words used to describe it is not a substantial matter.

2 Some economists have reserved the term *accommodated* for when a money supply increase accompanies a supply-side shock and *validated* for when a money supply increase accompanies a demand-side shock. This distinction no longer seems to be in general use, so we no longer use it. We now use the terms *accommodated* or *validated* as interchangeable, both describing a situation in which a rise in the price level is matched by an increase in the money supply.

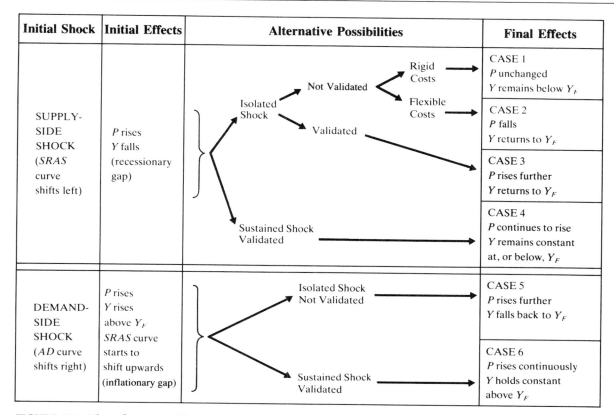

Initial Shock	Initial Effects	Alternative Possibilities		Final Effects

FIGURE 38.1 The Inflationary Effects of Demand-Side and Supply-Side Shocks. The Figure follows through the various possible shocks, assuming that in the initial situation the price level is stable and national income is equal to potential income ($Y = Y_F$).

---

analysed in Figure 35.7 on page 392.[1] Since these effects are important, we repeat, and extend, the analysis in Figure 38.2. The original curves are AD and $SRAS$, which produce an equilibrium income and price level of Y_F and P_0. A rise in costs now occurs – say, a general increase in wage rates achieved by a particularly aggressive round of union bargaining. This shifts the short-run aggregate-supply curve upwards from $SRAS$ to $SRAS'$ in the Figure. As a result, equilibrium income falls from Y_F to Y_1, while the price level rises from P_0 to P_1.

The initial effect of a supply-side shock is to cause stagflation: the price level rises while national income falls.

What happens next depends on how the monetary authorities react. Do they validate the supply-shock inflation or do they not?

Final effects

No monetary validation: In this case, the rise in the price level is non-validated. The money supply is held constant, so that the aggregate demand curve remains at AD. What then happens depends on the behaviour of costs of production.

Rigid Costs: We have seen that the supply-side shock increases the price level and lowers equilibrium income. If wages and other costs do not fall, even in the face of excess supply – i.e. if there is complete downward inflexibility of costs – that is the end of the story. This possibility is listed as case 1 under 'Final Effects' in Figure 38.1. The economy remains in the equilibrium given by the curves AD and $SRAS'$ in Figure 38.2.

Flexible Costs: As we saw in Chapter 35, if money wages rise less rapidly than productivity is rising, unit costs will fall. This shifts the $SRAS$ curve downwards, increasing equilibrium income while reducing the price level. As long as wages and other costs fall whenever there is excess supply, this continues until the short-run aggregate supply curve has been restored to its initial position or $SRAS$ in Figure 38.2. The equilibrium income is returned to Y_F and the price level to its initial value of P_0.

---

1 Notice that we have stylized the $SRAS$ curve by giving it a nearly constant upward slope. This makes the Figure easier to follow than if we had given it the more accurate slope shown in Figure 35.4. We can do this because all that matters in the subsequent analysis is the upward slope. If we wished to analyse the *proportions* in which Y and P were changing in response to various shocks, we would need to use a more accurate $SRAS$ curve that is quite flat below potential income and quite steep above it.

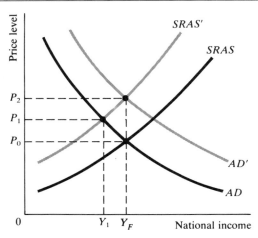

FIGURE 38.2 The Effects of a Supply-Side Shock. A shift from *SRAS* to *SRAS'* reduces equilibrium income to Y_1, and increases the equilibrium price level to P_1. A shift in *AD* to *AD'* restores full employment but at the cost of a further rise in the price level to P_2.

Given the fact that money wages fall only slowly (if at all) in the face of excess supply, the recovery from a non-validated supply-shock inflation back to full employment will take a very long time.

This possibility is shown as case 2 under Final Effects in Figure 38.1.

Monetary validation: Now let us see what happens if the money supply is changed in response to the isolated supply shock. This takes us beyond what we have previously studied.

The initial supply-side shock established the short-run equilibrium of Y_1 and P_1 in Figure 38.2. Now suppose the Bank reacts to the recessionary gap by increasing the money supply in an effort to restore full employment. We know that such an increase works through the monetary transmission mechanism to increase aggregate desired expenditure. (The monetary transmission mechanism is outlined in Figure 33.4 on page 000.) This increases the equilibrium level of national income associated with any given price level and thus shifts the aggregate demand curve to the right.

The rise in aggregate demand causes both the price level and national income to rise, as equilibrium moves along the fixed aggregate supply curve *SRAS'* in Figure 38.2. A sufficiently large increase in the money supply will shift the *AD* curve to *AD'*. This eliminates the recessionary gap completely by restoring full-employment income Y_F, but it also further increases the price level to P_2. We have now reached an important conclusion:

Monetary validation of an isolated supply shock can restore full employment, but at the cost of a further increase in the price level.

Nonetheless, the Bank might decide to validate the supply shock because, if it waits for unit costs to fall, a major slump will ensue. This case is shown as case 3 in Figure 38.1.

Sustained supply shocks

So far, we have considered the effects of a single supply shock, distinguishing between the case in which the shock is, and is not, validated. We now consider the case of sustained supply shocks caused, say, by powerful unions which are able to push up money wages year after year, even when there is a recessionary gap. Since the cost push is often attributed to wage increases, this case is often referred to as WAGE-COST-PUSH INFLATION.

What happens next depends on how the Bank reacts to this behaviour.

No monetary validation: In the case in which the Bank does not validate these shocks, the aggregate supply curve will shift upwards continually. This takes equilibrium upwards along the fixed *AD* curve, with national income falling while the price level rises, i.e. a stagflation ensues.

If unions continue with their wage-cost push, *and the AD curve does not shift*, the process will eventually drive national income towards zero. Long before this happens, however, everyone will come to realize that the rising wages in the face of unchanging demand are the cause of the falling employment. Unions will realize that they face a trade-off between wages and employment – they can have more of one only if they accept less of the other. Long before everyone is unemployed, unions will cease forcing up wages in order to maintain jobs for those who are still employed.

Thus we see that repeated non-validated supply shocks must come to an end. This means that the results are identical to those of a single, isolated supply shock. Whether the situation in Figure 38.2 is the result of a single isolated supply-side shock or of a series of repeated shocks, the end result is the same: when the non-validated shocks come to an end, the price level is higher and national income is lower than in its initial, pre-shock equilibrium.

What happens next is just a repeat of what we have already studied for an isolated shock; it all depends on whether costs are rigid or flexible.

First, if the unions succeed in holding onto their high wages the economy will come to rest with (i) a stable price level, (ii) a large recessionary gap, and (iii) substantial real-wage unemployment. This is case 1 in Figure 38.1.

Second, if the persistent unemployment erodes the power of the unions, wages will fall, thus reversing the supply shock. Eventually, full employment will be restored and the price level will return to its original value. This is case 2 in Figure 38.1.

Recall, however, that the very slow pace with which wages fall, even in the face of very heavy excess supply, means that this adjustment process would at best take a very long time – and at worst it might never be completed. This is case 2 in Figure 38.1.

The conclusion is that unvalidated supply-shock inflations caused by wage-cost push have natural correctives, both in the restraining pressures of rising unemployment on further wage push and in the possible erosion of the power of unions to hold wages above the level that would produce full employment. But these correctives may take a long time to operate and, hence, a wage-cost push can cause a long and sustained inflation and recession.

Monetary validation: Now suppose that the Bank validates the initial supply shock with an increase in the money supply, thus shifting the aggregate demand curve to the right. This is just what we showed in Figure 38.2. There the initial equilibrium was at Y_F and P_0; the shift in the supply curve to $SRAS'$ took equilibrium to Y_1 and P_1; and the monetary validation took equilibrium income and the price level back to Y_F and to P_2. This case is shown again in Figure 38.3, which duplicates the curves $SRAS$, $SRAS'$, AD and AD' from Figure 38.2.

In the new full-employment equilibrium of Y_F and P_2 (point a in the Figure), the initial rise in money wages has now been fully offset by a rise in prices. Workers are no better off than they were originally at Y_F and P_0 – although those who remained in jobs were better off in the transition period, after wages had risen but before the price level had risen from P_1 to P_2.

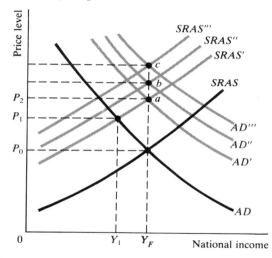

FIGURE 38.3 A Repeated Cost-Push Validated by Monetary Expansion. Starting from AD and $SRAS$ which determine equilibrium at Y_0 and P_0, an upward shift in $SRAS$ alone takes equilibrium upwards along the fixed AD curve. However, upward shifts in both the AD and the $SRAS$ curves cause the price level to rise continuously while income remains constant at Y_F.

The stage is now set for the unions to try again. If they succeed in negotiating a further increase in money wages, they will hit the economy with another supply shock. If the Bank again validates the shock with an appropriate increase in the money supply, full employment can be maintained but at the cost of a further round of inflation.

This process is illustrated in Figure 38.3. The second round of wage-cost push takes the aggregate supply curve to $SRAS''$, while the second round of monetary validation takes the aggregate demand curve to AD''. The next round of wage push takes the aggregate supply curve to $SRAS'''$ while the accompanying round of monetary validation takes the aggregate demand curve to AD'''. If this process

continues, with the monetary validation more or less synchronized with the wage-cost push, the inflation can go on indefinitely with national income remaining at, or below, its full-employment level. Successive equilibrium points are at a, b, c, and so on.

So now we know the two things that are required for wage-cost-push inflation to be sustained over a long time. First, powerful unions must ask for, and employers must grant, increases in money wages, even in the absence of excess demand for labour and goods. Second, the central bank must validate the resulting inflation by increasing the money supply and so prevent the emergence of a *growing* recessionary gap.

This possibility is shown as case 4 in Figure 38.1.

Is wage-cost-push inflation a real possibility?

As far back as the 1940s, early Keynesians were worried that, once the government was committed to maintaining full employment, much of the discipline of the market would be removed from wage bargains. They felt that the scramble of every group trying to get ahead of other groups would lead to a wage-cost-push inflation. The government's commitment to full employment would then lead it to validate the inflation through increases in the money supply. In these circumstances, cost-push inflation could go on indefinitely without any market mechanism to bring it to a halt.

Many economists believe this process actually occurred in those countries of Western Europe where unions were very strong. The enormous decline in union power in the UK in the early 1980s, greatly reduces the possibility of a sustained wage-cost-push inflation occurring today.

Is monetary validation of supply shocks desirable?

Once started, the spiral of wage-price-wage increases can be halted only if the Bank stops validating the shocks. The longer it waits to do so, the more ingrained will be the expectations of wage and price-setters that the Bank will continue to validate. Many economists believe that these firmly held expectations will make wages more resistant to downward pressure arising from unemployment. Thus, if the government ever stops validating the wage-cost-push inflation, the AD curve will stop shifting upwards but the $SRAS$ curve will continue to do so as unions carry on with their customary behaviour. The economy then enters the stagflation phase, with rising prices and rising unemployment. If the wage-cost-push behaviour is firmly entrenched, a very deep recession may have to develop before the cost push ceases so that the $SRAS$ curve can be stabilized.

Hence, the argument runs, in order to stop inflation from getting established, it is best never to let the process of a validated wage-cost-push inflation get started. One way to ensure this is to refuse to validate any supply shock whatsoever.

To some people, caution dictates that no supply shocks

be validated lest a wage-price spiral be set up. Others would be willing to risk validating obviously isolated shocks in order to avoid the severe and prolonged recessions that otherwise accompany them.

Demand-Shock Inflation

When an inflation is caused by demand shocks, it is sometimes called a 'demand-shock inflation' or a 'demand-side inflation'. The two most commonly used terms, however, are DEMAND-PULL INFLATION or, more simply, DEMAND INFLATION, defined as any inflation that is caused by general excess demand in the economy's markets for final output and for factors of production. Demand inflation occurs when a demand shock causes aggregate demand to exceed aggregate supply at full-employment income.

Initial effects

The initial effects of a demand inflation were analysed in Figure 35.6 but we repeat and elaborate the analysis in Figure 38.4 because of its importance. The original curves are AD and $SRAS$. They produce an original equilibrium at the point labelled a, with income of Y_F and a price level of P_0.

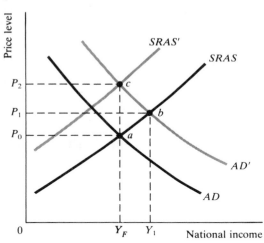

FIGURE 38.4 A Non-Validated Demand-Side Shock. Starting from AD, $SRAS$, Y_F and P_0, a shift in the AD curve to AD' causes national income and the price level to rise initially, to Y_1 and P_1 respectively, along the fixed $SRAS$ curve. The price level then rises further to P_2, while income returns to its potential level, Y_F, along the fixed aggregate demand curve AD' as the $SRAS$ curve shifts from $SRAS$ to $SRAS'$.

The aggregate demand curve now shifts to the right. This shift could have occurred for either of two quite distinct sets of reasons. First, it may have been caused by an autonomous increase in aggregate desired expenditure. The desired amount of expenditure on consumption, investment, government purchases, or net exports that is associated with each level of national income may have increased. Second, there may have been an increase in the money supply. As we saw in Chapter 33, an increase in the money supply works through the monetary transmission mechanism – via excess supply of money, higher price of bonds, lower interest rates, increased investment expenditure – to increase aggregate desired expenditure, and hence shifts the aggregate demand curve upwards.

The demand shock shifts the aggregate demand curve in Figure 38.4 from AD to AD'. The initial effect of this shift is for equilibrium national income to increase to Y_1 and the price level to rise to P_1 (point b).

But this is not the end of the story. The rise in the price level to P_1 is a reaction of the goods market to the excess demand created when the aggregate demand curve shift from AD to AD'. The $SRAS$ curve is, however, based on a given set of factor prices. The excess demand associated with income Y_1 occurs in factor markets as well as in goods markets. This causes wages to rise, shifting the $SRAS$ curve upwards. (Note that the rise in wage costs is not the result of wage-cost-push shock, but the result of general excess demand.) What happens next depends on whether or not the demand shock is validated.

Final effects

No monetary validation of an isolated shock: The upward shift in the $SRAS$ curve in Figure 38.4 raises the price level above P_1. As long as the Bank holds the money supply constant, the rise in the price level brings the transmission mechanism into play: the economy moves upward to the left along the fixed aggregate demand curve AD'. This rise in the price level acts to reduce the inflationary gap. Eventually the gap is eliminated as equilibrium is established at a higher, but stable, price level, with income returned to its potential level. In this case, the initial period of positive inflation is followed by further inflation that lasts only until the new equilibrium is reached.

This is shown in Figure 38.4 by the upward shift in the $SRAS$ curve to $SRAS'$, which takes equilibrium income back to Y_F and the equilibrium price level further upward to P_2 (point c). This is case 5 in Figure 38.1.

Monetary validation: Next suppose that, following a demand shock that created an inflationary gap, the Bank increases the money supply when output starts to fall. Two forces are now brought into play. The wage increases that are fuelled by excess demand cause the $SRAS$ curve to shift upward. The monetary expansion causes the aggregate demand curve to shift upward. If the shift in the aggregate demand curve exactly offsets the shift in the $SRAS$ curve, the inflationary gap will remain constant.

Monetary validation of an isolated demand-side shock turns it into a sustained shock because it allows the inflationary gap to persist in spite of the rise in the price level.

This process is shown in Figure 38.5. As before, the initial equilibrium is at a and the initial demand shock takes the short-run equilibrium to b. But now, as the $SRAS$ curve starts to shift upwards, the validating increase in the money supply means that the AD curve shifts upwards as well

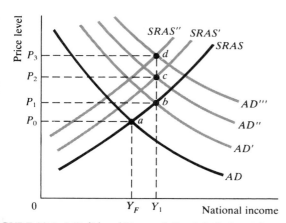

FIGURE 38.5 A Validated Demand-Shock Inflation. The *AD* curve initially shifts to *AD'*. After this initial shock, the *AD* curve continues to shift upwards because of monetary validation while the *SRAS* curve shifts upwards because the inflationary gap causes wages, and hence unit costs, to rise. As a result, equilibrium goes from *b* to *c* to *d*, maintaining the inflationary gap while the price level rises continuously, reaching P_3 when the curves reach *AD'''* and *SRAS''*.

This frustrates the mechanism that would have worked from rising demand for money, through rising interest rates, to falling aggregate desired expenditure.

When the *SRAS* curve has reached *SRAS'*, the money supply is increased sufficiently to take the *AD* curve to *AD''*. Equilibrium is then at *c*. When the *SRAS* curve reaches *SRAS''*, *AD* is shifted to *AD'''*. Equilibrium is then at *d*, with income still at Y_1, but with a price level of P_3. This process takes the economy on the path of a continuously rising price level and a persistent inflationary gap. In other words, there is a sustained inflation. We have now reached an important conclusion:

Validation of an initial demand shock turns what would have been a transitory inflation into a sustained inflation fuelled by monetary expansion. The subsequent shifts in the *AD* curve that perpetuate the inflationary gap are caused by monetary forces.

This is shown as case 6 in Figure 38.1.

ISSUES CONCERNING INFLATION

The distinction between changes in aggregate demand and in aggregate supply as causes of inflation allows us to resolve some persistent confusions. Let us consider three.

Is Inflation a Monetary Phenomenon?

There has sometimes been heated debate among economists about the extent to which inflation is a monetary phenomenon with purely monetary causes – i.e. changes in the supply of (or demand for) money – and purely monetary consequences – i.e. only the price level is affected by inflation. One slogan by economists who have taken an extreme position on this issue is that 'inflation is *every-*

where and *always* a monetary phenomenon'.

In order to consider these issues, let us summarize what we have learned. First, look at the *causes* of inflation:

(1) We have seen that many forces can cause the price level to rise. On the demand side, anything that shifts the *AD* curve to the right will cause the price level to rise. This includes the expenditure changes of an autonomous increase in *I* and *G* (and an upward shift in the *C* and $(X - M)$ functions). It also includes the monetary changes either of an increase in the supply of money, or a decrease in the demand for money. On the supply side, anything that increases costs of production will shift the *SRAS* curve upwards and cause the price level to rise.

(2) We have also seen that such inflations can continue for some time without being validated by increases in the money supply.

(3) Furthermore, we have seen that the rise in prices must eventually come to a halt unless monetary expansion occurs.

Points (1) and (2) provide the sense in which a temporary burst of inflation need not be a monetary phenomenon: it need not have monetary causes, and it need not be accompanied by monetary expansion. Point (3) explains the sense in which a sustained inflation must be a monetary phenomenon. If a rise in prices is to go on continuously, it must be accompanied by continuing increases in the money supply, regardless of the causes that set it in motion.

Second, let us look at the *consequences* of an inflation:

(4) We have seen that, in the short run, a demand-shock inflation tends to be accompanied by an increase in national income above its potential level.

(5) We have seen that, in the short run, a supply-shock inflation tends to be accompanied by a decrease in national income below its potential level.

(6) We have also seen that, when *all* adjustments are fully made so that the relevant supply-side curve is the *LRAS* curve, shifts in *AD* or *SRAS* leave national income unchanged and only affect the price level.

Points (4) and (5) provide the sense in which inflation is *not*, in the short run, a purely monetary phenomenon: it affects such real variables as total output and employment. Point (6) provides the sense in which inflation is, in the long run, a purely monetary phenomenon: it only affects the price level.

Does Inflation Reduce Excess Demand?

One of the most important conclusions reached in our study of inflation is this. In the absence of monetary validation, a demand shock causes a temporary burst of inflation accompanied by an inflationary gap, but the gap is removed as wages rise, returning income to its potential level but at a higher price level. This proposition is sometimes denied on the argument that rises in the general price level do not choke off excess demand because labour's reaction is merely to demand higher wages, which means higher incomes, which means higher demand. Let us see what is wrong with this argument.

Assume that there is an inflationary gap such as is shown by point *b* in Figure 38.4. A rise in wages, as well as in all other money incomes, shifts the *SRAS* curve upwards. As long as the money supply is held constant, the equilibrium moves along the fixed aggregate demand curve, *AD'*, until it reaches point *c*. At that point, the excess demand has been eliminated.

Thus the removal of excess demand through a rise in the price level does not depend on what happens to wages and prices, but on what happens to the money supply.

If the money supply is held constant, the rise in the price level brings the transmission mechanism into play. The transactions demand for money rises, interest rates rise, interest-sensitive expenditures fall and aggregate desired expenditure falls. This reduces equilibrium national income, as shown by a movement upwards, and to the left, along a fixed *AD* curve.

Are Rising Interest Rates Anti-Inflationary?

We have seen that, when the money supply is held constant, the monetary transmission mechanism serves to eliminate excess demand as the price level rises. However, this proposition is frequently denied, whenever a tight monetary policy is instituted. Critics note that, although rising interest rates may reduce demand, they also increase costs and hence drive up prices. They then assert that the two effects offset each other.

To see what is wrong with this argument, consider a continuing inflation such as the one illustrated in Figure 38.5. Costs are rising and driving the *SRAS* curve leftwards. But the inflation is being validated by a monetary expansion so that the *AD* curve is shifting rightwards. The two shifts are offsetting each other, so that the price level is rising and the inflationary gap is holding constant at $Y_1 - Y_F$.

Now, when the economy is at point *c*, let the Bank institute a tight monetary policy. For purposes of illustration, say it holds the money supply completely constant. This fixes the aggregate demand curve at *AD"*. The tight monetary policy will indeed cause a money shortage as the price level rises further, and this will indeed drive interest rates upwards. The rising interest rates are a sign that the monetary validation has stopped.

If interest rates enter into current costs of production, this will help to drive the *SRAS* curve upwards. But because the *AD* curve is being held constant, the rising costs shift the equilibrium upwards *and to the left* along a fixed aggregate demand curve. The result is that the excess demand is eliminated. The rise in interest rates confers a *once-and-for-all* increase in costs and therefore a *once-and-for-all* upward shift in the *SRAS* curve. But it is also a necessary accompaniment to the tight monetary policy that stops the *AD* curve from shifting upwards *continuously*. A one-time upward shift in the *SRAS* curve that permits the ending of a continual upward shift in the *AD* curve is indeed anti-inflationary.

The key point to understand in the fallacious arguments considered in this and in the previous section, is that it does not matter how much the *SRAS* curve shifts upward as long as the *AD* curve does not also shift upwards.

As long as the *AD* curve can be held constant (or allowed to shift upwards by less than the *SRAS* curve shifts), excess demand will be reduced by a rise in the price level.

What is the Relation Between Desired Saving and Inflation?

We saw in Chapter 36 that, in the short run, saving tends to reduce national income by reducing aggregate expenditure while, in the long run, it tends to increase national income whenever those savings find their way into productive investment.

Saving affects inflation: An increase in saving tends to reduce the pressure of inflation in the short run by reducing desired aggregate expenditure and thus shifting the aggregate demand curve to the left. In the long run, it also has an effect on reducing inflationary pressures if it results in investment that shifts the *LRAS* curve to the right.

Inflation affects saving: But what of the reverse influence – i.e. that of inflation on saving? The dominant influence here is that inflation reduces the value of all wealth that is denominated in money terms. For example, a bond with a £1000 redemption value would lose half of its real value in terms of purchasing power if the price level should double. If people try to maintain their real wealth in the face of this inflationary erosion, they will increase their savings in money terms. This is one of the reasons why the volume of saving usually rises as the inflation rate rises.

What is the Relation Between Investment and Inflation?

Investment affects inflation: On the investment side similar considerations apply. An increase in investment adds to aggregate demand in the short run and, hence tends to add to inflationary pressures. But in the long run investment adds to productive capacity and, by shifting the *LRAS* curve outwards, tends to alleviate inflationary pressures.

Inflation affects investment: As with saving, inflation tends to influence the amount of investment expenditure. For instance, when income-tax laws allow depreciation only on the historical rather than the replacement cost of capital, inflation acts as a tax on real capital unless offset by other compensating measures. If, for example, the price level doubles, a firm must put aside twice as much money just to replace its existing capital stock as it wears out. But tax laws usually allow depreciation to be deducted as a cost only on the basis of the original money price of the capital equipment. Therefore, the additional sums needed just to maintain capital must first be reported as profits, then taxed, then saved. So inflation, by taxing capital, tends to reduce real profits and makes less available for investment.

Because of inflation, recorded investment must be increased just to hold one's own against shrinking real values. As a result, a lot of what is really replacement investment, shows up in the national accounts as new investment merely because some accounting procedures do not easily handle changes that inflation causes in the real value of assets denominated in monetary units.

The above are only two of the links between investment and inflation. Depending on the provisions in the tax laws, inflation exerts many pressures to increase or decrease investment. Inflation certainly does influence investment, but in different ways at different times.

This concludes our study of the basics of inflation. In the rest of this chapter, we go behind the *SRAS* curve to study the speed with which that curve shifts in the face of inflationary or recessionary gaps. We do this by studying a remarkable relationship called the Phillips curve.

THE PHILLIPS CURVE, OR HOW FAST DOES THE *SRAS* CURVE SHIFT?

We have seen that when the short-run equilibrium level of national income is not at its potential level, the *SRAS* curve tends to shift due to changes in input prices. When there is an inflationary gap, demand pressures in factor markets tend to push input prices down and shift the *SRAS* curve downwards.

We have also stated that input prices can rise very rapidly when there is excess demand but that they tend to fall only very slowly when there is excess supply. On page 396 we called this the second asymmetry in the behaviour of aggregate supply. (The first asymmetry is in the shape of the *SRAS* curve, flat to the left of Y_F and steep to the right of it.)

The nature of the Phillips curve

The PHILLIPS CURVE, named after the late Professor A.W. Phillips, refers to a graph in which the level of unemployment is plotted on the horizontal axis and the rate of change in money wage rates on the vertical axis. Thus, any point on the curve relates a particular level of unemployment to a particular rate of change of money wages. (It is important to understand that the vertical axis of the Phillips curve measures changes in *wage rates* and not changes in the general *price level* of goods and services.

A numerical example of a Phillips curve is shown in Figure 38.6. For the moment ignore the horizontal line labelled *g*, which is explained later. We stress that the numbers on the Figure are hypothetical – although they are not totally unrealistic.[1] This is a new and unfamiliar type of curve, so a numerical example may help you to

understand. In this example, point *a* on the curve shows that an 8 per cent unemployment rate is associated with a rate of increase in money wages of 3 per cent per year.

The Phillips curve must be carefully distinguished from the *SRAS* curve. The *SRAS* curve has the price *level* on the vertical axis. The Phillips curve does not have the *level* of money wages on the vertical axis; instead its vertical axis plots the *annual rate of change* of money wage rates.

The shape of the Phillips curve

A negative slope: Note first that the Phillips curve has a negative slope, showing that the lower is the level of unemployment, the higher is the rate of change of money wages. This should not surprise us, since low rates of unemployment are associated with boom conditions when excess demand for labour will be bidding money wages up rapidly. High rates of unemployment, on the other hand, are associated with slump conditions when the slack demand for labour will lead to low increases in money wages, or possibly even to decreases.

A flattening slope: Moving along it from left to right, the Phillips curve gets flatter. This shape of the curve is a reflection of the second asymmetry of the behaviour of aggregate supply that we mentioned above – namely that input prices change more rapidly upwards than downwards. Let us see why.

First, assume that a growing boom is increasing the excess demand for labour. As the boom develops, the unemployment rate will decrease towards, but never reach, zero (there will always be *some* frictional unemployment). At the same time, the growing excess demand for labour will be bidding up wage rates more and more rapidly. This behaviour is shown when the Phillips curve gets very steep and lies far above the axis at its left-hand end. The further is the curve above the axis, the faster are wages rising. In Figure 38.6, a fall in unemployment from 8 to 6 to 4 per cent increases the rate at which wages are rising from 3 to 7 to 14 per cent (points *a* to *b* to *c*). By the time that unemployment has fallen as low as 4 per cent, wages are rising at a very rapid rate of 14 per cent per year, and it is clear that further small cuts in unemployment will increase the rate of wage inflation very much. The steepness of the curve in this range shows that even a very small reduction in unemployment will lead to a large increase in the rate of wage inflation.

Second, consider a growing recession that raises unemployment. This recession restrains wage increases. As a result, the Phillips curve comes closer and closer to the horizontal axis, indicating less and less upwards pressure on wages at higher and higher levels of unemployment. If the curve fell below the axis, then money wages would actually be falling at the associated levels of unemployment. We do not show this case in the Figure but assume that, as unemployment gets very large, the change in money wages approaches zero but never becomes negative. As unemployment rises from 8 to 10 to 12 per cent in the Figure, wages go from a 3 to a 2 to a $1\frac{1}{2}$ per cent annual rate of increase. *The flatness of the curve over this range*

See Harbury and Lipsey for some real data on the Phillips curve relationships.

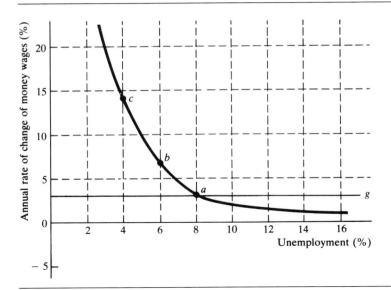

FIGURE 38.6 A Phillips Curve. The curve relates the level of unemployment to the rate of change of money wages. The horizontal line labelled 'g' shows the rate of growth of output per worker. To the left of the intersection point *a*, money wages are rising faster than productivity so unit costs are rising. (The *SRAS* curve, which is not shown here, must be shifting upwards.) To the right of *a*, money wages are rising slower than productivity so that unit costs are falling. (The *SRAS* curve must be shifting downwards.) Only at the level of unemployment where wages and productivity are rising at the same rate will the *SRAS* curve be stable. (See Chapter 39 for the expectations-augmented versions of this curve.)

shows that it takes a larger rise in unemployment to reduce the rate of wage inflation even slightly.

The Phillips curve and unit labour costs

We have seen in earlier chapters that increases in costs of inputs increase unit costs of production and thus cause the *SRAS* curve to shift upwards. To see what is happening to unit costs of production, we need to relate the increase in wage rates to the increase in labour productivity (which we have earlier defined as output per unit of labour employed). For simplicity in the rest of the discussion, we will assume that labour is the only variable factor used by the firm. This allows us to associate the labour costs of each unit of output with total variable costs per unit of output. (We could equally well assume that all input prices change at the same rate as does the price of labour.)

What happens to unit costs of production now depends only on the *difference* between what labour costs the firm and what labour produces for the firm. Let us see why.

Assume, for example, that labour is *paid* 10 per cent more per hour but that it also *produces* 10 per cent more per hour. In this case, the firm's costs of production per unit of output – its unit costs of production – are unchanged. In general, unit costs of production rise if wage rates rise faster than productivity is rising. Thus, for example, a 5 per cent increase in money wage rates combined with a 3 per cent increase in labour productivity means a 2 per cent increase in unit costs of production; while the same increase in productivity combined with only a 1 per cent increase in money wage rates means a 2 per cent *decrease* in unit costs of production.

To illustrate what is involved, we add to the graph in Figure 38.6 a horizontal line labelled *g*, for growth in output per hour of labour input. This line shows the rate at which labour productivity is growing year by year. In the hypothetical example of the Figure, we have assumed that productivity is rising at 3 per cent per year.

The intersection of the Phillips curve and the productivity line at the point *a* now divides the curve itself into an inflationary and a deflationary range.

(1) At unemployment rates lower than the intersection point – lower than 8 per cent in our example – wages are rising faster than productivity and, thus, unit costs of production are rising. If unit costs are rising, the *SRAS* curve must be shifting upwards and so, *ceteris paribus*, the price level will be rising.

(2) At unemployment rates greater than 8 per cent, money wage rates, although rising, are rising slower than productivity is rising and, thus, unit costs of production are *falling*. If unit costs of production are falling, the *SRAS* curve must be shifting downwards, and so, *ceteris paribus*, the price level must be falling.

This is really all we need in order to determine the rate at which the *SRAS* curve is shifting. For example, if unemployment is 6 per cent, then Figure 38.6 tells us that money wage rates are rising by 7 per cent per year. Since productivity is rising at 3 per cent, unit costs are rising at approximately 4 per cent per year. This means that the *SRAS* curve is shifting upwards at that rate. To take a second example, let unemployment be 12 per cent. Now money wages are rising at $1\frac{1}{2}$ per cent. Combined with a 3 per cent increase in labour productivity, this means a 1 per cent *decrease* in unit costs of production. This means that the *SRAS* curve will be shifting downwards at that rate.

Notice that, although we have assumed downward inflexibility of money wages, this does *not* imply complete downward inflexibility of prices. As long as money wages rise less than productivity rises, then unit costs of production will be falling, and the *SRAS* curve will be shifting downwards. Complete downward inflexibility of prices – and thus the total absence of the equilibrating mechanism that comes from downward shifts in the *SRAS* curve – requires more than the downward inflexibility of money wages; it requires that money wages *never* rise by *less than*

BOX 38.1 Flexible Pay Can Ease the Fitness Test

'Sadly the rise in unemployment is an inevitable result of dealing with the ... boom. High interest rates and a strong pound have gradually squeezed demand with the aim of curbing price rises and imports. This creates pressure on profit margins and on company finances. Managers react by cutting costs.

'One of the biggest costs they control is the pay bill. Faced with stagnant demand, companies stop hiring, encourage early retirement and lay people off. The alternative is pay flexibility: deferred pay rises, pay freezes, even pay cuts. The more flexible is pay, the less likely are job losses.

'The sharpness in the rise in unemployment can be interpreted in one of two ways. It may be again that pay has not become more flexible. If so, we are in for a nasty and prolonged recession.... Alternatively, the sharp unemployment rise may be a sign that managers are reacting to their predicament quickly, with pay deferrals, and cuts to follow. If so, unemployment may rise more quickly now but more slowly later.

'The key figures to watch are those for pay settlements. A collapse would be extremely good news....

'Meanwhile, the best response to the rise in unemployment would be new training measures. The mistake

of the 1979–81 recession was to allow many unemployed to languish so long on the dole that they became unemployable.'

(*The Independent*, 21 April 1991)

During the recession occurring at the beginning of the 1990s, the government was particularly anxious to bring down the rate of inflation, which had climbed to an annual rate of 10 per cent (from $3\frac{1}{2}$ per cent in 1986). The article deals with the use of demand management to curb inflation at the cost of rising unemployment and then goes on to discuss how the recession that usually follows the breaking of an inflation may vary in its intensity, depending on the flexibility of wages.

Questions

1 Does the article suggest that fiscal or monetary policy has been used to deflate the economy?
2 The article discusses a Phillips curve without using that name. Explain how the Phillips curve enters the discussion.
3 Why would pay flexibility lead to a shorter recession than pay inflexibility?
4 What kinds of unemployment are discussed in the article, and in which paragraphs?

---

the increase in productivity, so that unit costs of production can never fall.

Conclusion

The Phillips curve, although much misunderstood when it was first introduced, has become an integral part of the Keynesian model of income determination. It explains the speed at which the SRAS curve is shifting when actual income does not equal potential income. We have introduced this relation in this chapter. In Chapter 39 we see that we need to augment it to take account of some additional inflationary forces that we have not yet included in our analysis of the Phillips curve. These additions produce what is called an 'expectations-augmented Phillips curve'.

Questions

1 Which One or More of the following shocks could cause an inflation combined with falling output?
   (a) A rightward shift in the AD curve
   (b) A rightward shift in the SRAS curve
   (c) A leftward shift in the AD curve
   (d) A leftward shift in the SRAS curve
   (e) A rightward shift in the LRAS curve
   (f) A leftward shift in the LRAS curve

2 (a) In Figure 38.2, what is the name and size of the gap when the curves are AD and SRAS'?
   (b) In Figure 38.5, what would happen if the SRAS curve stayed fixed at SRAS while the AD curve shifted to AD' to AD" to AD'''?
   (c) In Figure 38.6, what is the rate of wage inflation when unemployment is 10 per cent and what is the amount of unemployment when wages are rising at 10 per cent per year?

3 Choose the correct alternative in each case:
   Starting from equilibrium at potential income, let there be a large increase in the money supply. This will shift the (AD/SRAS) curve to the (left/right), which will (raise/lower) the price level and (raise/lower) national income. The resulting (inflationary/deflationary) gap will

Summary

1 A once-and-for-all supply-side shock raises the price level and lowers equilibrium income. Without monetary validation, full employment will be restored only if costs fall sufficiently to restore the pre-shock equilibrium. With monetary validation, the AD curve can be shifted sufficiently to the right to restore full employment but at the cost of a further increase in the price level.

2 Repeated supply shocks without monetary validation cause continued rises in the price level and falls in national income. With monetary validation, repeated supply shocks can cause a steady inflation at a constant level of national income.

3 A once-and-for-all demand shock leads in the short run to a rise in the price level and a rise in output. If the rise in the price level is not validated by a corresponding increase in the money supply, the inflationary gap will cause factor prices to rise, shifting the SRAS curve upwards and pushing equilibrium national income back to its potential level.

4 If the rise in the price level following a demand shock is validated, the increases in the money supply frustrate the monetary transmission mechanism and provide the shocks needed to sustain the inflation. The inflationary gap causes the SRAS curve to shift left, but the repeated increases in the money supply cause the aggregate demand curve to shift right, so that the net effect is a continually rising price level without any fall in equilibrium national income.

5 A sustained inflation at a constant level of national income requires an increase in the money supply at the same rate that prices are rising.

6 Inflation is a monetary phenomenon in the senses that it can be caused by excessive monetary expansion on the part of the central bank, that it cannot continue indefinitely without monetary validation and, when it is finished, its only effect is on the price level. Inflation is a real phenomenon in the senses that it can be caused by increases in real expenditure flows, it can persist for some time without monetary validation, and, while it is in process, it has effects on such real variables as output and employment.

7 A policy to stop inflation requires an increase in the interest rate. An attempt to reduce the interest rate in a fully employed economy will cause an inflation which will *increase* the nominal interest rate.

8 An increase in savings reduces demand and is deflationary in the short run. An increase in inflation tends to increase money savings. An increase in investment increases demand and is inflationary in the short run. In the long run it increases potential output, which is anti-inflationary. The effect of an increase in inflation on investment is uncertain.

9 In its original form the Phillips curve relates the rate of change of money wages to the level of unemployment. The rate of change of money wages minus the rate of growth of productivity determines the rate at which unit costs are increasing, which in turn determines the rate at which the SRAS curve is shifting upwards.

cause the (AD/SRAS) curve to shift to the (left/right), which will cause national income to (rise/fall) and the price level to (rise/fall). When full equilibrium has been restored, the price level will be (higher/lower/the same) and national income will be (higher than/lower than/the same as) it was in its pre-shock equilibrium.

4 To which sources of inflation do the following statements refer?
   (a) 'The one basic cause of inflation is governments spending more than they take in; the cure is a balanced budget.'
   (b) 'Wage settlements currently being negotiated in several basic industries will soon lead to an acceleration of inflation.'
   (c) 'As the boom grows, inflationary pressures are being manifested throughout the economy.'
   (d) 'Oil shock threatens inflation as oil prices soar.'

5 True or False?
   (a) Supply-side shocks tend to cause unemployment and national income to change in the same direction.
   (b) Demand-side shocks tend to cause national income and the price level to change in opposite directions.
   (c) When all markets are fully restored to equilibrium, a demand shock affects only the price level and neither national income nor employment.
   (d) When all markets are fully restored to equilibrium, a supply shock coming from a change in money costs affects only the price level and neither national income nor employment.

39 Macroeconomic Policy in a Closed Economy

In this chapter we are going to draw together much of what you have studied in the earlier chapters on macroeconomics. Chapters 27, 28, 34 and 38 are particularly important. Although we shall review some of the main results of these chapters, we must assume that you understand these earlier discussions.

Our main concern here is with macroeconomic policy in the context of a closed economy. (International complications are discussed in Chapter 42.) The chapter is divided into two main parts, of unequal size. The first, and by far the largest part, looks at demand-management policies. The second, and much shorter part, studies supply-side policies. The first part is in turn divided into four main subsections. The first two of these consider fiscal and monetary policies, which are the main tools of demand management. In the third part, we look at the two main goals of demand management, which are to maintain low rates of inflation and unemployment. The fourth subsection looks at some limitations of demand management. Knowing what demand management cannot accomplish is as important as knowing what it can accomplish. The second main part of the chapter examines supply-side policies, both of the market-oriented and the interventionist variety.

Figure 39.1 summarizes how each of these various policies work through a chain of variables to end up affecting real national income, Y, and the general price level, P. It is there to guide you through the chapter. You should not study it in detail yet. Instead, you should use it as a guide as you work through the details of the chapter.

DEMAND MANAGEMENT POLICIES

Demand management relates to all policies that seek to shift the aggregate demand curve. These include both fiscal and monetary policies as shown on the lefthand-side of Figure 39.1.

Fiscal Policy

We studied the working of fiscal policy at some length in Chapter 28. Here we merely summarize its workings by outlining what may be called *the fiscal transmission mechanism*: how fiscal changes are transmitted into changes in national income.

The fiscal transmission mechanism

The fiscal transmission mechanism is outlined in the lefthand part of Figure 39.1, labelled Fiscal Policy. The two major instruments are the government's exhaustive expenditures, G, and its tax policy, labelled t in the Figure.

The arrow with the plus sign running in Figure 39.1 from G to E indicates that government expenditure, G, increases aggregate desired expenditure, E. Aggregate desired expenditure in turn helps to determine the aggregate demand curve AD. An increase in G raises aggregate demand while a decrease in G lowers aggregate demand, operating in both cases through the linkages shown in the Figure.

Tax rates, shown by t in the Figure,[1] determine, in combination with the level of national income, the size of the government's tax revenue, T. This revenue reduces aggregate expenditure (as shown by the minus sign on the arrow joining T to E). Once again, aggregate desired expenditure helps to determine aggregate demand. An increase in tax rates reduces aggregate demand, while a reduction in tax rates increases aggregate demand – in both cases through the linkages shown in the Figure. Aggregate demand and aggregate supply interact in the manner discussed in Chapter 35 to determine real national income, Y, and the price level, P.

Alternative tools of demand management

So far in our discussion of demand management, we have emphasized the role of direct changes in income-tax rates and government expenditures. It is also possible for the government to use fiscal incentives to influence specific types of expenditures. A prime example is investment incentives, the most common of which are called investment (or depreciation) allowances. These can take various forms but they usually work by the government sacrificing some current tax revenues by giving favourable tax treatment to private investment expenditures in the hope of greatly increasing that expenditure.

Many other policies may shift desired expenditure functions. For example, we observed in Chapter 24 that wealth and consumption tend to be positively related. It follows that a once-and-for-all tax on wealth, by reducing households' present wealth, may reduce their desired consumption expenditure as households save more in order to recoup their lost wealth. A continuing tax on wealth reduces the after-tax return to saving – since part of the savings get taxed away by the wealth tax – and so will have a similar effect as a fall in the interest rate, which can work either to raise or to lower saving.

---

1 By tax rates we mean the whole schedule of the terms of the taxes. This includes threshold levels of income below which various taxes do not apply and rates at which they apply above the thresholds.

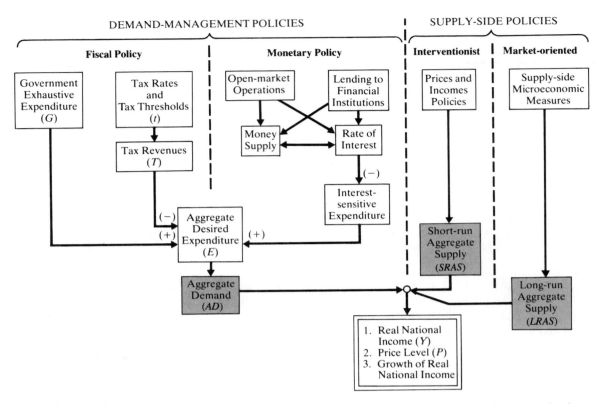

FIGURE 39.1 Macroeconomic Policies. The Figure follows the text discussion of the various policies. Fiscal policy affects aggregate desired expenditure through government expenditure, which adds to aggregate expenditure, and tax revenues, which subtract from it. Monetary policy has slightly more complex routes of influence. The Bank's open-market operations, and its lending to financial institutions, affect both the money supply and interest rates. Interest rates in turn affect interest-sensitive expenditure with a negative relation (the higher are interest rates, the lower is such expenditure). Interest-sensitive expenditure, in turn, adds to aggregate expenditure. Aggregate expenditure helps to determine aggregate demand, which interacts with aggregate short-run and long-run supply, to determine the level and rate of growth of real national income, and the behaviour of the general price level.

Government prices and incomes policies are interventionist supply-side policies that attempt to slow the rate of upward shift in the *SRAS* curve. Market-oriented supply-side policies attempt to increase the rate at which the *LRAS* curve is shifting outwards, and, therefore, to affect the rate of growth of national income over time.

Tax changes versus expenditure changes

As we saw on pages 319–20, many fiscal measures work as automatic stabilizers. In this section, we deal with the important issues that arise whenever the government decides to reduce a persistent recessionary gap by adopting an expansionary fiscal policy. The government must now choose many aspects of its discretionary fiscal policy. In particular, should tax rates be reduced, or should government expenditures be increased? Four of the points of comparison that are relevant to the answer are discussed in the sections that follow.

The size of the changes: A given change in national income can be achieved either by cuts in tax rates or by increases in exhaustive expenditures. However, the magnitudes of the changes required by these two policies are different, because the multiplier effects differ.

First consider an increase in government expenditure. If the government spends an extra £1000m, this much is added directly to aggregate demand. If the multiplier is 2,

then the final increase in equilibrium national income is £2000m.

Next consider a tax cut. First assume that the government cuts its tax rates in such a way that, at the initial level of national income, its revenues fall by £1000m. This leaves an extra £1000m in the hands of the private sector. But aggregate expenditure will rise by less than £1000m, because part of that new disposable income will be saved. Say, for example, that the marginal propensity to spend out of disposable income is 0.75. In this case, the first impact of the tax cut of £1000m will be to increase income-creating expenditure by only £750m. Combined with a multiplier of 2, this means a final increase in equilibrium income of £1500m.

Thus we see that, with an increase in government expenditure or an equal reduction in tax revenues, the rise in income is greater with the expenditure increase than with the tax cut. This can be put slightly differently as our first important comparison:

Bringing about a given increase in equilibrium national

income through fiscal policy requires a larger reduction in tax revenue than an increase in government expenditure.

The location of the effects: The *impact effect* of any fiscal change refers to where the effects are initially felt. The full effect refers to what happens once adjustments to it have worked themselves out.

The impact effects of tax cuts, such as for example a cut in income-tax rates, tends to be spread over the whole economy. All taxpayers get an increase in disposable income and the demands for most consumer goods increase as a result. This is an advantage if the slump is a general one affecting the whole economy. However, if the slump has severely localized characteristics, with a few areas or industries being particularly hard hit, expenditure increases have some advantage. Their initial impact effects can be localized by the decisions on how the money is to be spent. Expenditure can be concentrated in particular areas or in particular industries. For example, if the construction industry has been particularly badly hit, then new expenditures on roads, schools and hospitals may be appropriate. Of course, the induced multiplier effects will spread out over the whole economy, but at least the impact effects can be partially localized in the construction industry.

The amount that £1's worth of government expenditure in a region adds to regional income is measured by a REGIONAL MULTIPLIER. Most regional multipliers tend to be *less than one*. How could this be? There are two main reasons.

First, only a part of each £1 spent in a region adds initially to regional income. For example, of each £1 spent on roads in some region, well over 50p may go for materials made in other regions and, hence, will create incomes in those other regions. Only the amount that goes to local labour and local contractors increases local incomes. The second reason is that there are leakages out of a region at each and every round of induced expenditure. For the *regional* multiplier, imports are all expenditures made on goods and services produced in other regions, and in most modern industrial economies these regional import leakages are large. So, in summary, only a fraction of each £1 of expenditure creates income in the region, and the multiplier that is applied to this fraction tends to be smaller the smaller the region.

Our second point of comparison, then, is:

Expenditure increases have some advantage over income-tax cuts if it is desired to localize some of the effects of the expansionary fiscal policy.

Time-lags: Discretionary fiscal policy, which is involved with tax and expenditure changes, is subject to at least two 'policy lags'. First is a *decision lag*. The problem must be identified, studied, and appropriate action decided upon. These lags can be long for both tax cuts and expenditure increases.

Once the measure has been authorized, there is an *execution lag*. For example, after funds have been allocated for a new road-building programme, some considerable time will pass before substantial income payments are made to private firms and households. Routes must be surveyed, land must be acquired, public protests must be heard, bids must be called for and contracts let. All of this takes time, a very long time for certain types of expenditure programmes.

Some expenditures, however, are not subject to such long lags. Funds can often be released quite quickly for education and health expenditures. Also cash limits placed on certain expenditures can operate with dramatic suddenness.

The execution lag for tax cuts is mainly due to the fact that Parliament normally enacts tax changes only once or twice a year, at Budget times. Once Parliament has agreed to cuts in personal income-tax rates, however, households will very soon find themselves with more disposable income.

So our third point of comparison is:

Certain forms of tax cuts and expenditure increases have advantages over others because they have a much shorter lag between the time when action is decided upon and when the effect is felt on aggregate expenditure. No general presumption exists, however, favouring tax cuts over expenditure increases or vice versa; instead, each measure must be judged on its merits as far as lags are concerned.

The change in the role of the government in the economy: Many people have strong feelings about the size of the government sector. One measure of the importance of the government's use of productive resources can be obtained from the ratio G/Y, i.e. the ratio of government exhaustive expenditure to national income. Some would like to see this ratio reduced, while others would like to see it increased.

The policy that is adopted will certainly affect this ratio. If the government chooses the expenditure-increasing policy, then it will increase the amount of the nation's resources whose allocation is decided by the government. If the government chooses the tax cut, the government will hold constant the amount of the nation's resources whose allocation is determined by the government's exhaustive expenditure (G).

Our final point of comparison, then, is:

Tax cuts leave the amount of the nation's resources whose allocation is determined by the government's exhaustive expenditures unchanged; expenditure increases raise this amount.

Problems associated with the use of fiscal policy

We now consider a number of problems that arise with the use of fiscal policy.

Fiscal drag: If government expenditures and tax rates are held constant over several years, one might think that fiscal policy was exerting a constant effect on the economy. Although this might be true *ceteris paribus*, other things do not remain equal over any long period of time. Economic growth increases potential income at anything from 1 to 4 per cent per year in typical industrialized countries. As a result, with *tax rates* constant, government *tax revenues* will tend to grow at that rate. If expenditures are held constant, any deficit will shrink, and eventually turn into a surplus. Fiscal policy will thus exert a growing contractionary pressure when the economy is operating *at potential income.*[1]

This tendency for the budget surplus at potential income to grow as potential income itself grows, is called FISCAL DRAG. To counteract it, the government must either raise expenditures or lower tax rates to hold its deficit or surplus at Y_F constant as Y_F itself rises.

The fiscal implications of privatization: Transfer of ownership of major national industries, from the public sector to the private sector, was a major part of the programme to increase the power of market forces instituted by the Thatcherite governments of in the 1980s. While the expressed motives were the pursuit of microeconomic efficiency, there have been some important macroeconomic effects.

First, the large revenues obtained from the sale of nationalized industries to private owners have made it possible for the UK government to reduce its deficit and then turn it into a budget surplus. In 1987–8 the PSBR became negative. Instead of borrowing to add to debt, some past debt was retired. People began to speak of the Public Sector Debt Retirement (PSDR). In the downturn of the early 1990s, however, the PSBR again returned to a positive requirement (although modest by standards of earlier decades). Once all nationalized industries that are candidates for privatization have been sold off, the government will need a substantial cut in expenditures, or increase in tax rates, if it wishes to maintain an unchanged budgetary position.

Second, the transfer to the private sector of industries which need to borrow money has significantly reduced the PSBR. As a result, a government that wishes to have a given expansionary or contractionary effect on the economy can borrow substantially more than it did 20 years ago while leaving the total PSBR more or less unchanged.

The crowding-out effect: The next limitation applies only to expansionary fiscal policy and works through the monetary transmission mechanism laid out in Figure 33.5 on page 368. The increase of national income following a fiscal expansion tends to create a money shortage due to increased transactions demand for money. This money shortage then puts upward pressure on interest rates. The rise in interest rates tends to reduce interest-sensitive expenditure and partially offsets the expansionary effect of the increases in expenditure brought about by the initial tax cuts or government expenditure increases. This tendency for an expansionary fiscal policy to induce a partially offsetting contractionary monetary shock is called the

CROWDING-OUT EFFECT. It is defined as an offsetting decrease in private-sector expenditure caused when an expansionary fiscal policy increases interest rates. It is analysed graphically in Figure 39.3.

Although the strength of crowding-out tendencies will vary from case to case, depending on the state of the economy, there is no doubt that, *ceteris paribus*, a fiscally induced expansion does put upward pressure on interest rates, particularly as the economy nears full employment. There is no need, however, for the other things to remain equal. The Bank, acting on behalf of the government, can adopt an expansionary monetary policy sufficient to offset the induced contractionary monetary effects.

The crowding-out effect can be avoided if the Bank accompanies any fiscal expansion with a sufficient monetary expansion to prevent interest rates from being driven up.

If the money supply is increased at about the same rate as the demand for money is increasing, the crowding-out mechanism does not operate because no money shortage develops to drive up interest rates.

The Bank must be careful, however, not to bring about so much monetary expansion that an inflation breaks out. Since we are discussing validating only the increased demand for money that accompanies an expansion in real income when a large recessionary gap is reduced, the *appropriate* monetary expansion will not cause an inflation.

The responsiveness of consumption to tax changes: The theory of the consumption function that we have used throughout this book, and which is basically due to Keynes, relates current consumption expenditure to current national income. An alternative theory of the consumption function, called the PERMANENT INCOME THEORY, relates consumption to what people regard as their 'permanent' income. It states that people form expectations about the long-run trend in their incomes, and then make their consumption decisions on the basis of these expectations. They do not let *short-term* fluctuations in their current incomes affect their consumption. According to this theory, if people find themselves with temporarily low incomes, they either reduce their current savings or borrow, in order to maintain their expenditure on current consumption. If they find themselves with temporarily high incomes, they save the extra income.

This theory has been used to question the effectiveness of short-term tax changes to act as a fiscal stabilizer. To see what is involved, consider cuts in personal income-tax rates that people expect to be temporary, because people see them as part of a short-run fiscal policy designed to provide temporary stimulus to the economy. According to the permanent income theory, this temporary increase in income will mainly be saved. Thus consumption expenditure will not rise as much as is predicted by the Keynesian theory which relates consumption to current income. Similarly, temporary tax increases, meant to reduce a transitory inflationary gap, will be paid mainly out of savings with little reduction in consumption.

---

1 The government surplus is $T - G$. Taxes depend on income, so we can write the surplus at potential-income as $tY_F - G$, where t is the proportion of income going as tax revenue. If Y_F is growing steadily, so will this surplus grow, *unless* either G is raised or t is lowered.

Evidence suggests that consumers sometimes behave in this way. But the effects on consumption may not be as small as a simplistic reading of the permanent-income theory might suggest. For one thing, many people have neither sufficient liquid assets, nor the borrowing power to maintain consumption in the face of a temporary fall in their disposable income, even though they might want to do so. For another thing, many people 'save' their temporary increases in income by 'investing' in durable consumer goods that they will 'consume' over subsequent years. Although such purchases count as saving in the permanent-income theory, they are, nonetheless, expenditures on currently produced goods which add to current aggregate demand.

The need for reversibility: A policy that is not easily reversible can easily turn out to have perverse effects. To see what is involved, consider Figure 39.2. There we *assume* that the average, or normal, position of the aggregate expenditure function is E_N. This implies that, on average, national income will be at its full-employment level, Y_F. Now assume, however, that a *temporary* slump in private investment shifts the aggregate expenditure function downwards to E_S, thus opening up a large deflationary gap (*ab* in the Figure). Equilibrium income falls to Y_S. Assume, furthermore, that the gap persists for some time.

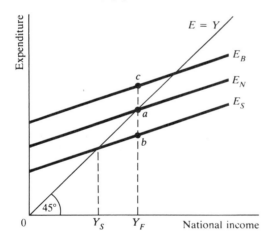

FIGURE 39.2 The Need for Reversibility of Fiscal Policies. Fiscal policies designed to remove temporary gaps will open up gaps if they are not quickly reversed when private expenditure returns to a more normal level.

Now assume that the government decides to take action. Its expansionary fiscal policy shifts the expenditure function back to E_N, thereby restoring full employment.

But the slump in private investment spending is, by assumption, only temporary. When private investment expenditure recovers, the desired expenditure function shifts upwards and, unless the government responds quickly, an inflationary gap will be opened up. The government has already shifted the expenditure curve up to E_N and, if nothing else is done, the revived private-sector investment expenditure will shift the aggregate expenditure

function up to E_B, thereby opening up an inflationary gap (*ac* in the Figure).

To avoid this, the government must reverse its expansionary policy when investment expenditure recovers, allowing the reduction of the government's expenditure to offset the revived private expenditure. Done perfectly, the expenditure function will be held at E_N, with the government's contribution to aggregate expenditure diminishing as the contribution of private investment increases. This, however, is no easy task.

The above analysis leads to a very important conclusion:

Fiscal policies designed to remove inflationary or deflationary gaps resulting from temporarily high or low levels of private expenditure will lead to overshooting when national income moves back towards potential income unless the policies can be rapidly reversed once private expenditure functions return to their more normal levels.

Lags and forecasting errors: Finally recall that fiscal policy acts with lags – as does monetary policy. These lags, combined with the difficulty in forecasting what private-sector aggregate demand will be when the fiscal measures take effect, raise the possibility that stabilization policy will actually destabilize the economy.

Monetary Policy

We now move to a brief discussion of monetary policy. This tool of demand management has already been analysed in detail in Chapter 34. First let us recall the transmission mechanism of monetary policy.

The monetary transmission mechanism

The transmission mechanism that works for monetary policy is outlined in detail in Figures 33.4 and 33.5 on page 368. The mechanism works by putting pressure on interest rates. The contrast with fiscal policy is important when in the next chapters we consider the issues that arise in the context of an open economy.

On the one hand, *expansionary fiscal policy*, which increases national income, causes an increase in the transactions demand for money. This puts upward pressure on interest rates. In contrast, an *expansionary monetary policy* increases the supply of money. This puts downward pressure on interest rates, which then leads to an increase in aggregate expenditure and national income.

On the other hand, *contractionary fiscal policy* reduces national income which causes a reduction in the transactions demand for money. This puts downward pressure on interest rates. In contrast, *contractionary monetary policy* reduces the supply of money. This puts upward pressure on such rates, which leads to a decrease in aggregate expenditure and national income.

In summary, fiscal policy causes national income and interest rates to move in the same direction, rising or falling together, while monetary policy makes them move in opposite directions, one rising while the other is falling.

The broad outlines of monetary policy are shown in Figure 39.1. The arrows are a little more complex than those for fiscal policies because of the mutual interaction between monetary variables. The Bank's two main monetary instruments are open-market sales and purchases and lending to financial institutions to provide reserves when these are needed. Each of these has an effect on both interest rates and the money supply (by altering bank reserves, they influence bank credit creation). Changes in the money supply can affect interest rates (by altering the supply of money) and changes in interest rates can affect the money supply (by altering the amount that people wish to borrow). Interest-rate changes affect interest-sensitive expenditure, which includes purchases of new housing, inventory accumulation and (often to a lesser extent) fixed capital investment. (It also affects consumption expenditure to the extent that such expenditure is financed with borrowed funds.) Changes in investment (and other interest-sensitive expenditure) cause changes in aggregate desired expenditure which, in turn, cause the aggregate demand curve to shift.

Interest-rate changes with a recessionary gap and full employment

We have seen that the transmission mechanism of monetary policy works through the interest rate, lowering it in the case of an expansionary policy and raising it in the case of a contractionary policy. If the economy has unemployed resources, this mechanism works as we have described it.

Some observers have drawn from a correct appreciation of the monetary transmission mechanism the erroneous conclusion that an expansionary monetary policy can lower interest rates, *even in times of full employment.*

In Chapter 33 we studied the effects of an increase in the money supply in a fully employed economy. The increase puts transitory downward pressure on interest rates, but the ensuing rise in the price level returns interest rates to their original level. So the sole effect, once equilibrium is re-established, is a rise in the price level. (See pp. 368–9.) This result is one aspect of the long-run neutrality of money that we studied in Chapter 30: in a fully employed economy, the rate of interest is *independent* of the quantity of money as long as the price level is at its long-run equilibrium value.

But what if the policy-makers seek to maintain the disequilibrium by creating new money as fast as prices rise in an attempt to maintain the lower interest rates induced by the initial monetary expansion? They will then be creating a fully validated inflation and the economy will be in the state illustrated in Figure 38.5 on page 435. The initial monetary expansion creates an inflationary gap, and the subsequent monetary expansions frustrate the monetary adjustment mechanism, thus maintaining the gap. To study this possibility further, we need to make the important distinction between real and nominal interest rates.

Real and nominal interest rates: The rate of interest, like many of the other variables we have been considering in this book, can be measured in real or in nominal values.

The NOMINAL or MONEY INTEREST RATE is the one we have been considering so far. It is the annual money value of interest paid, divided by the principal of the loan. Thus, for example, a bond that can be purchased for £100 per year and that pays £5 interest per year has a nominal interest rate of 5 per cent.

The REAL INTEREST RATE is the rate of interest earned after deducting an amount necessary *to maintain the purchasing power of the principal invested.* When an inflation is occurring, the real purchasing power of any money is falling at the rate of inflation.

For example, the purchasing power of £100 falls by 5 per cent each year in the face of a 5 per cent inflation. Thus it will take £105 next year to buy what £100 will buy this year. If £100 invested only yields £5 over the year, all of that sum is needed just to maintain the purchasing power of the principal. In this case the real interest rate would be zero, while the nominal rate was 5 per cent. To see why, note that if the investor saves the entire 5 per cent interest and adds it to his principal, he will have just maintained its purchasing power. If the money rate of interest had been 7 per cent, he could have deducted 5 per cent to maintain the purchasing power of his principal and had 2 per cent left over as a real return on his investment. In this case, the money rate is 7 per cent while the real rate is 2 per cent. Finally, consider an example in which the money rate of interest is only 3 per cent in the face of a 5 per cent inflation. If the investor saves the whole 3 per cent interest and adds it to the principal, his principal will be eroding at about 2 per cent per year. He will have received a negative real return; the real rate of interest will be −2 per cent in this case.

These examples illustrate the following general proposition:

$$\text{The real rate of interest} = \text{the nominal rate of interest } \textit{minus} \text{ the rate of inflation}$$

Notice that, if the rate of inflation is zero, the nominal and the real rates are the same. If there is no inflation, there is no need to make a deduction to maintain the purchasing power of the principal. This is why we did not need to distinguish the real and the nominal rates up until now. But, when there is a continuing inflation, the distinction becomes important.

Lenders who do not suffer from money illusion are concerned with the real, not the nominal, rate of interest. They want to know, before parting with their money, how much they will earn after maintaining the purchasing power of the amount lent. If investors expect a negative real rate, they would be better off not lending at all. Rather, they could buy some physical asset, such as a piece of land, or a machine, whose money value is expected to rise along with all other prices – to rise, that is, at the general rate of inflation. In that case, they would be obtaining a zero rate – instead of a negative rate – since the market value of the assets would, by assumption, rise at the same rate as the price level, thus preserving the purchasing power of the sum invested.

The real forces in the economy, such as the willingness

of people to borrow and lend, tend to determine the real rate of interest. The nominal rate then becomes the real rate *plus* the expected rate of inflation. It follows that an inflation generated by policy-makers in an attempt to lower interest rates will end up *increasing* money interest rates by the amount of the inflation that they create.

We have now reached two very important conclusions:

- **In a fully employed economy, a once-and-for-all increase in the money supply will, *once equilibrium is re-established*, have no effect on the real rate of interest or real income, only on the price level.**

- **In a fully employed economy, a continuing expansion of the money supply will, *once the ensuing inflation comes to be expected to continue*, increase the nominal interest rate; however, *once full adjustment to the expected inflation has taken place*, it will have no effect on the real interest rate.**

Limitations of monetary policy

We now pass to a brief consideration of some of the limitations of monetary policy.

Difficulties with respect to instruments: The Bank attempts to control aggregate demand working through the monetary transmission mechanism. It uses its open-market operations, and its loans to the discount houses, to influence interest rates both directly and indirectly. It uses its purchases of bonds from the government to expand bank reserves at some desired rate without reducing bonds in the hands of the public. These actions cause changes in interest rates and influence interest-sensitive expenditures and, through them, aggregate desired expenditure.

Although the Bank has only a loose control over the money supply, it can control short-term interest rates with a reasonable degree of precision. At various times in the past, however, some economists have argued that this is not enough to be able to control aggregate expenditure. The problem, as they see it, is twofold: (i) that controlling short-term interest rates may not control long-term interest rates, and (ii) expenditure on fixed investment may not be very responsive to variations in long-term rates. These problems have already been discussed on page 385, and we need only briefly reiterate the arguments given there.

- Many expenditures do respond to variations in the short-term rate of interest. These include firms' expenditures on stocks, and people's expenditures on new housing and on consumer goods where these are financed by credit.
- The long-term interest rate will respond to the short rate if markets are convinced that the Bank is determined to stick to its monetary policy until the desired results are achieved.
- Fixed investment does respond, to some extent at least, to variations in the long-term rate of interest. However, if the transmission mechanism had to rely solely, or even mainly, on influencing fixed investment expenditure, it would be unreliable. As it is, the evidence of history is

clear: (i) a determined contractionary monetary policy can bring aggregate expenditure down enough to stop an inflation no matter how high is the current inflation rate – although usually at the cost of a significant recession; (ii) the same can be said for a determined policy to remove a recessionary gap, with the sole exception that during a really severe depression, in which unfavourable expectations dominate all changes in interest rates, aggregate desired expenditure may not respond swiftly to expansionary monetary policy.

Intermediate monetary targets: The problem of intermediate targets, such as various measures of 'the' money supply, arises because the Bank is interested in controlling aggregate demand and, through that, national income and the rate of inflation. However, as we saw in Chapter 34, the linkages between what the Bank can control – bank reserves, and short-term interest rates – and national income and the price level take a long and a variable time to work out. For this reason, central banks have sought to identify an intermediate target that responds fairly quickly to MO and interest rates, and that correlates with their ultimate targets of national income and the price level.

The major problem is that no intermediate monetary target seems to maintain a stable relation with income and the price level over a long period of time. One reason is associated with the rapid changes in the nature of financial institutions over the last decades that we discussed in Chapter 34. These changes have allowed households and firms to reduce the transactions balances that they must hold. This means that neither M1, nor any of the other measures of the money supply, have held a stable relation to the central bank's ultimate targets.

Fiscal *vs.* monetary policy

Depending on the circumstances, fiscal policy may be more or less potent than monetary policy. Let us see what these circumstances are. In Figure 34.3 we saw that the strength of monetary policy depended on the slopes of the liquidity preference and the marginal efficiency of capital curves. An elastic *LP* curve, and an inelastic *MEI* curve, makes fiscal policy very potent, while an inelastic *LP* curve, and an elastic *MEI* curve, makes it relatively impotent.

Figure 39.3 shows that similar considerations apply to fiscal policy, because the slopes of the *MEI* and *LP* curves determine the magnitude of any crowding-out effect. The left-hand sides of parts (i) and (ii) show monetary forces determining the interest rate. The original money supply is M_0 and the demand curve for money is *LP*, yielding an interest rate of r_0. An expansionary fiscal policy increases national income and hence increases the transactions demand for money. We know from Chapter 32 that this shifts the *LP* function to the right, say to *LP'* in the Figure. The additional demand for money, in conjunction with a fixed supply, causes the interest rate to rise to r_1 in the Figure. This then reduces investment (and all other interest-sensitive expenditures). This is shown by the fall in investment of ΔI, from I_0 to I_1 in the right-hand sides of both parts of the Figure. Now compare the effects when the

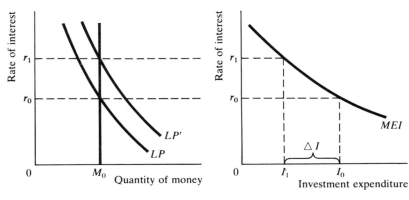

(i) Fiscal policy is effective

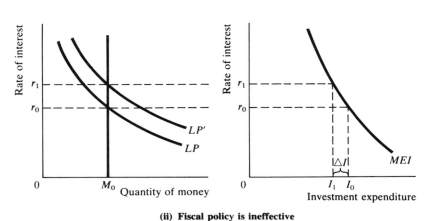

(ii) Fiscal policy is ineffective

FIGURE 39.3 The Crowding-Out Effect Reduces the Efficiency of Fiscal Policy. These Figures come into play after the expansionary fiscal policy has raised national income and led to an increased demand for money (from LP to LP' in the Figures). This drives up the interest rate from r_0 to r_1 which in turn curtails private investment by ΔI from I_0 to I_1 in both parts of the Figure. This reduction in investment offsets the initial expansionary effects of the fiscal policy. In part (i), the combination of a steep LP curve and a flat MEI curve leads to a large crowding out and hence a weak fiscal policy. In part (ii), the combination of a flat LP curve and a steep MEI curve leads to a small crowding-out effect and a strong fiscal policy.

LP and MEI functions are interest-elastic and interest-inelastic.

In part (i), the LP function is inelastic, so the interest rate is driven up a lot. Also the MEI function is interest-elastic, so investment falls a lot. The crowding-out effect is large and much of the original fiscal stimulus will be offset.

In part (ii), the LP function is interest-elastic, so the interest rate does not rise much. Also the MEI function is inelastic, so the rise in the interest rate does not reduce investment by much. The crowding-out effect is small, so that the original fiscal stimulus will not be much reduced.

We now see that the same combination of elasticities that makes monetary policy relatively impotent makes fiscal policy relatively potent, and vice versa:

• **the effect of a given fiscal stimulus is weaker and the effect of a given monetary stimulus is stronger: (i) the more inelastic is the *LP* function, and (ii) the more elastic is the *MEI* function;**

• **the effect of a given fiscal stimulus is stronger and the effect of a given monetary stimulus is weaker: (i) the more elastic is the *LP* function, and (ii) the more inelastic is the *MEI* function.**

Goals of Demand Management: Full Employment and Stable Prices

In this section we assume that, by one means or another, policy-makers can manipulate aggregate demand, and we look at the problems that they then face in pursuing the two major goals of short-term stabilization policy in the context of a closed economy. These goals are traditionally described as achieving *full employment* and *stable prices*.

When UK full-employment policy was first adopted as a primary goal in 1944, total unemployment was thought to be divided between frictional and demand-deficient unemployment. Any demand-deficient unemployment could, it was widely believed, be dealt with by demand-management policy, and the remaining frictional unemployment seemed small enough to be acceptable. The 1944 White Paper on *Employment Policy* (Cmd. 6527) set a 3 per cent unemployment rate as a 'full-employment' target, thus accepting 3 per cent as the acceptable amount of frictional unemployment. Experience over the next two decades suggested that even this figure was unduly pessimistic, since the unemployment rate in the 10 years after 1947 was below 2 per cent in all but a single year. Under these circumstances, the conduct of short-term stabilization policy seemed relatively simple.

Stabilization policy with a Keynesian aggregate demand curve

The J-shaped, Keynesian aggregate supply curve, first discussed on pages 397–8, was thought at the time to be a reasonable description of reality. It is shown again in Figure 39.4. Given such a curve, the problem of stabilization policy is to achieve point x where full employment and stable prices occur simultaneously. This is done by keeping the aggregate demand curve in the position shown by the curve labelled AD_F. First, assume that aggregate demand is too low, say at AD'; there is a recessionary gap of $Y_F - Y_1$, in the Figure. If aggregate demand is increased to AD_F, full employment and stable prices are restored. Second, assume that aggregate demand is too high, say at AD'' in the Figure. If nothing is done, an inflation will take the price level to P_1. However, if a contractionary policy can be introduced fast enough, the aggregate demand curve can be shifted back to AD_F, thus eliminating the inflationary gap and restoring full employment and stable prices.

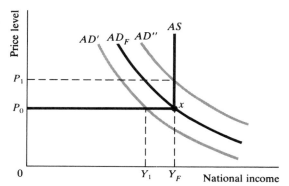

FIGURE 39.4 Stabilization Policy with a Keynesian Aggregate Supply Curve. By stabilizing aggregate demand at the appropriate level, AD_F in the Figure, full employment and stable prices could be achieved at point x.

So stabilization policy was designed to hold the aggregate demand curve at AD_F, thereby assuring full employment and a stable price level, with no more than 2–3 per cent of the labour force unemployed for frictional reasons.

Stabilization policy with a stable Phillips curve

The Keynesian aggregate supply curve describes a world where inflationary pressures only develop at full employment. Thus, *either* there is demand-deficient unemployment *or* there is inflationary pressure, but *never* both at the same time. In such a world, policy-makers know for sure whether aggregate demand is currently too low or too high. The development of the Phillips curve was a major step in upsetting this simple view of the world.

The Phillips curve describes a world where less unemployment can be obtained at the cost of more inflation, and less inflation can be obtained at the cost of more unemployment. When it came to be believed that the Phillips curve was a better description of reality than the

Keynesian aggregate supply curve, the possibility of a 'trade-off' between unemployment and inflation came to dominate stabilization policy. This domination continued for more than a decade. Today, economists no longer believe that such a trade-off exists in the long run, but it clearly does exist in the short run and this greatly complicates stabilization policy. Let us see what is involved in the 'trade-off issue'.

One of the key points about the Phillips-curve view of the world is that potential income ceases to be the maximum attainable level of income. Figure 39.5 shows a Phillips curve similar to the one drawn in Figure 38.6 on page 438. It relates the rate at which money wages are changing to the level of unemployment. The line labelled g shows the rate of productivity growth.

In the diagram, we indicate two key levels of unemployment. The first, labelled U_N, is the amount of unemployment (all of it frictional and structural) that exists when the economy is operated at normal rates of capacity utilization. It is the amount of unemployment associated with the economy's potential income. We saw in Chapter 37 that U_N is called the *natural rate of unemployment* or the NAIRU.

The second level of unemployment, U_{min}, is associated with the maximum level of national income that can be achieved by working the economy flat out as happens during such emergencies as major wars. People are then patriotically motivated to work for long hours at demanding jobs and all available capital equipment is pressed into use. Thus U_{min} is the economy's minimum achievable level of frictional unemployment; it occurs when there are so many job vacancies that job leavers can find a new job almost immediately.

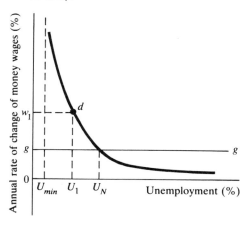

FIGURE 39.5 Minimum and Natural Rates of Unemployment. The natural rate of unemployment, or NAIRU, shown as U_N, occurs when income is at its potential level, and the minimum rate of unemployment, shown as U_{min}, occurs when income is at its absolute maximum level. At point d there is unemployment U_1 and inflation because the rate of increase of money wages, w_1, exceeds the rate of increase of productivity, g.

Finally, note that any unemployment rate between U_N and U_{min} requires that firms operate at more than normal-capacity output. The labour needed to produce more than potential income comes from a fall in frictional unemployment as people take less time between jobs, and by an expansion of the labour supply as people are attracted into the labour market by both the ease of finding work and the rapidly rising wage rates.

The recognition that unemployment could be driven below U_N presented policy-makers with a possibility not allowed for by the older, J-shaped, Keynesian, aggregate supply curve. They could run the economy in the situation given by some point such as d in the diagram. At that point, unemployment of U_1 is below U_N (national income exceeds Y_F) *but unit costs are rising at the rate of $w_1 - g$ per period*. For example, U_1 might stand for a 5 per cent annual rate of increase of money wages, while g stood for a 2 per cent annual rate of increase in productivity. In this case, unit costs would be rising at the rate of 3 per cent per year.

As a result of the rising unit production costs, the $SRAS$ curve will be shifting upwards. As we saw in Figure 38.4, this will tend, *other things being equal*, to eliminate the inflationary gap and reduce national income to Y_F and increase unemployment to U_N.

A stable Phillips curve, however, seems to open up a new policy option. The central bank could ensure that other things do not remain equal. The Bank could validate the inflation by increasing the money supply at the same rate that prices are rising. This frustrates the automatic adjustment mechanism that works through a contractionary monetary shock. (This is the case we analysed in Figure 38.5 on page 435 and if you are in any doubt about it, you should review that discussion now.)

By following such a policy, a trade-off would have been made between inflation, on the one hand, and national income and unemployment, on the other. Instead of trying to stabilize national income at Y_F with U_N unemployment and zero inflation, the policy-makers have accepted a positive inflation rate as the cost of lowering unemployment to U_1 and raising national income above Y_F.

Throughout the 1960s, this type of trade-off decision was made by many governments. Then in the 1970s something happened. Instead of being associated with a constant rate of wage inflation, a given level of unemployment came to be associated with an ever rising rate of wage, and hence unit-cost, inflation. In other words, the curve shown in Figure 39.5 began to shift upwards. As a result, the inflation rate began to accelerate in spite of there being no obvious increase in the inflationary gap or decrease in the level of unemployment.

Stabilization policy with a shifting Phillips curve[1]

To explain this acceleration of inflation we must first study a phenomenon called expectational inflation.

Expectational inflation: An EXPECTATIONAL INFLATION is one that continues, and even accelerates, because of expectations of price and wage increases. Wage- and price-setters in both the markets for commodities and for labour (and other factors of production) form expectations about what the general price level will be over the lifetime of any contract currently being negotiated. They then seek to set their own price or wage in relation to the price level they expect to persist over this time-period.

Suppose, for example, that *both unions and firms* expect that a 10 per cent inflation will occur next year. Unions will tend to start negotiations from a *base* of a 10 per cent increase in money wages (which would hold their real wages constant). They will argue that firms will be able to meet the extra 10 per cent on the wage bill out of the extra revenues that will arise because product prices will go up by 10 per cent. *Starting from this base*, unions will then negotiate in an attempt to obtain some desired increase in their real wages. Firms will also be inclined to begin bargaining by conceding at least a 10 per cent increase in money wages, since they expect that the prices at which they sell their products will rise by 10 per cent. The bargaining between unions and employers will thus centre on how much money wages will be increased in excess of 10 per cent.

The conclusion is important and needs emphasis.

If both workers and employers expect an inflation of *x* per cent, their behaviour in wage- and price-setting will tend to bring that rate of inflation about, whatever the state of monetary and fiscal policy.

Accelerating inflation: Expectational inflation proved to be a major part of the explanation of the acceleration of world inflation throughout the 1970s. To see how it explains the problem, look at Figure 39.6. The Phillips curve labelled P reproduces the curve from Figure 39.5. It tells us the increase in wage rates due to demand pressure in labour markets *on the assumption that people expect the price level to remain constant*.

Now assume that the government has chosen a trade-off indicated by point d in the Figure. This yields a high level of national income, above Y_F, *and a correspondingly low level of unemployment*, U_1. With productivity increasing at the rate g and money wages at the rate w_1, unit costs are rising by the difference between the two, i.e., $w_1 - g$. The resulting inflation is then validated by the appropriate rate of monetary expansion. The net result is that the $SRAS$ curve and the AD curve are both shifting upwards, leaving national income and unemployment constant while the price level rises continually.

After a while, however, firms and unions will come to expect this rate of inflation to continue. As a result, all

---

1 The sections on accelerating inflation and breaking an entrenched inflation contain what is probably the most difficult material in the whole of Part 5. Do not worry if it does not seem perfectly clear on first reading. After all, it took professional economists over a decade to figure it out! All you need to learn from it is (i) that inflation will tend to accelerate if the government attempts to hold national income permanently above its potential level and fully validates whatever inflation that ensues, and (ii) that when the Bank stops validating a demand inflation it will be replaced by an expectational inflation until entrenched expectations of further inflation are revised.

BOX 39.1 Wage Bargaining: Poles Apart

'Both main parties at Westminster now see membership of the European exchange-rate mechanism (ERM) as the best available remedy for Britain's chronic vulnerability to inflation. But the British way of wage bargaining, with its I'm All Right Jack disdain for consensus, means the new discipline will almost certainly entail a sharp rise in unemployment.

'This works in two ways. British trade unionists tend to be sceptical, with good reason, about government promises of lower inflation. So a fall in the national level of wage claims tends to lag behind any slowdown in the rate of inflation, squeezing corporate profit margins.... two-thirds of the pay deals struck in Britain so far this year have been worth 9% or more, though latest estimates of inflation predict 5–7% by June....

'[Second, the us-versus-them attitude] pulls most negotiations towards more pay, less caution. Britain's car makers were handing out rises of 12% and more in the last weeks of 1990, reflecting hopes of a fairly gentle recession. Now sales have plummeted and they are laying off workers in droves.'

(*The Economist*, 19 March 1991)

This quotation alludes to the ERM which will be discussed in a later chapter. All that needs to be known here is that the ERM makes it difficult for British firms to raise prices to cover increased wages (since higher prices cannot be compensated for under the rules of the ERM merely by devaluing sterling on the foreign-exchange market).

Questions

1 What view of inflation is alluded to in this quotation?
2 Do the writers suggest a trade-off between higher wages and higher employment? Why might this exist? For how long might it exist? Who gains and who loses when higher wages are chosen, and when lower unemployment is chosen?

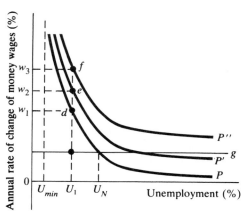

FIGURE 39.6 Accelerating Inflation and Expectations-Augmented Phillips Curves. Each curve refers to a specific expected rate of inflation. The expected rate of zero gives the Phillips curve P, which shows money wages rising at the same rate as productivity when unemployment is at U_N. The persistence of a validated demand inflation with unemployment held at U_1, causes the inflation rate of wages and unit costs to accelerate, as the continual upward revision of expectations cause the Phillips curve to shift upwards continually. If the rate of productivity growth remains constant at g, the *gap* between it and the rate of growth of money wages (which determines the rate of growth of unit costs) grows continually.

at 5 per cent. If the ensuing inflation is fully validated by monetary expansion, the AD curve will also rise at 8 per cent per year instead of at 5 per cent. The result will be that the inflation rate accelerates from 5 to 8 per cent per year.

After a further lapse of time, the new rate of price inflation will come to be expected and that rate of wage increase will occur, just to 'hold one's own' against the general inflation. The curve then shifts upwards to P'', causing inflation to accelerate once again. To keep the economy located at unemployment U_1 and its associated level of national income above Y_F, a very rapid rate of monetary expansion is needed to validate the inflation that is now driven by the rate of increase of unit costs of $w_3 - g$ in the Figure.

Of course, if the policy-makers are determined to maintain unemployment at U_1, they must increase the rate of monetary expansion every time the Phillips curve shifts upwards.

Expectations-augmented Phillips curves: The set of curves shown in Figure 39.6 are called EXPECTATIONS-AUGMENTED PHILLIPS CURVES. Each curve shows how money wage rates vary as unemployment varies *for a given expected rate of inflation*. The curve that cuts the productivity line g at the NAIRU, U_N in the Figure, refers to a *zero expected rate of inflation*. It shows the actual inflation at each level of unemployment, *if no inflation is expected*. The higher the expected rate of inflation, the higher the relevant Phillips curve. This shows that, for a given rate of unemployment, inflation will be higher the higher the expected rate of inflation.

wage- and price-setters will raise their wages and prices by the current rate of inflation just to hold their relative prices and wages constant. The result is to shift the Phillips curve upward by the expected inflation rate, as shown by the shift from the curve P to P' in Figure 39.6. At unemployment U_1, the rate of wage inflation has accelerated to w_2 in the Figure. With the rate of productivity growth constant at g, the increase in unit costs is now at a rate of $w_2 - g$. This pushes the $SRAS$ curve upwards *more rapidly*, accelerating the rate of inflation.

Consider an example. Assume that every point on the $SRAS$ curve is now rising at 8 per cent per year instead of

It follows, as we have already seen, that trying to hold national income and unemployment at levels where the rate of inflation is constantly being revised upwards, is an unsustainable policy.

This result is important, so it is worth reiterating what is happening.

When national income is held above its potential level, excess demand persists in goods and factor markets and the inflation continues *because of the demand pressures*, as shown by the original curve labelled *P* in Figure 39.6. When the inflation comes to be expected, people will seek to raise wages and prices by the expected inflation rate just to hold their own against the rising price level. Thus, an expectational inflation is added to the already-existing demand inflation. But the expectational inflation by itself will always tend towards the existing rate of inflation. Since demand pressures add to expectational inflation, the actual rate due to expectations *and* demand pressures will tend to accelerate. A stable rate of inflation is impossible because expectational inflation will tend to approach the existing inflation rate *as that rate comes to be expected,* but the actual rate is always expectational inflation *plus* the inflation due to demand pressures.

Like the dog chasing its tail, the accelerating spiral continues with expectations chasing the actual rate, but the actual rate being above the expected rate by the amount of demand inflation.

All of this can only occur, of course, as long as the accelerating inflation is validated by an ever-increasing rate of monetary expansion.

We now see why the level of unemployment U_N, which corresponds to national income Y_F, is called the *Non-Accelerating Inflationary Rate of Unemployment*, the NAIRU. It is the minimum rate of unemployment at which the inflation rate can be held constant. At all lower rates of unemployment, not only will the price level be rising but the rate of inflation will tend to rise as well.

Breaking an entrenched inflation: Faced with an accelerating inflation that had been validated for some time, government after government in the industrial countries finally decided in the late 1970s and early 1980s that the inflation rate had to be brought down. If inflation depended only on excess demand, there would be no problem. All policy-makers would do is to stop validating the inflation through monetary expansion. They would hold the money supply constant, allowing the automatic adjustment mechanism to work as shown in Figure 38.4 on page 434. A problem arose, however, because the inflation had continued so long that expectations that it would continue were firmly held. This is what is meant by an EN-TRENCHED INFLATION, an inflation with firmly held expectations on the part of wage- and price-setters that it will continue.

Once the inflationary gap has been removed, expectations of inflation still drive wages upward. What was a demand-side inflation becomes a supply-side inflation, driven by expectations of further inflation.

The Bank now faces a dilemma. Either it validates the inflation, in which case full employment can be maintained, or it continues with its tight monetary policy and allows unemployment to develop. If it is determined to break the inflation, it holds the rate of monetary expansion below the rate of inflation thus reducing aggregate demand. As demand falls, income falls and unemployment rises in the process analysed in Figure 38.2 on page 000. Sooner or later the resulting recession becomes severe enough that people no longer expect inflation to continue. They cease marking up wages and prices in expectation of general inflation, and the actual inflation falls. Once the inflation reaches zero, or some low acceptable rate, the authorities can then cautiously increase demand to take the economy back towards full employment – being careful, however, not to overshoot and allow inflationary pressures to start up once again.

Policy objectives

Short-run goals: How does the replacement of a single, stable Phillips curve with a set of expectations-augmented curves affect views of stabilization policy? In the short run, policy-makers can, if they wish, still aim to stabilize the economy by reducing its cyclical fluctuations around Y_F and U_N. In doing so, they will encounter a short-run trade-off between inflation and unemployment:

The short-run effects of expanding aggregate demand will be to reduce unemployment and increase inflation. The short-run effects of contracting aggregate demand will be to lower inflation but to increase unemployment.

Long-run goals: The theory of accelerating inflation, and the shifting Phillips curve, suggests that demand management cannot be used to sustain a level of unemployment below U_N, which means it cannot be used to sustain national income above its potential level, Y_F. In the long run, demand management must aim at U_N and Y_F. Long-run demand policy *can*, however, influence the rate of inflation and hence the price level. If policy-makers adopt expansive policies that create inflationary gaps more often than deflationary gaps, the price level will tend to rise and the average experience over the years will be inflationary.

Limitations of Demand Management Policies

In this section we discuss the limitations of demand-management policies. Whether fiscal or monetary policy is used, demand management has limitations in that *many variables in which policy-makers are interested do not respond to variations in aggregate demand.*

Limitations of fine-tuning

This case has been fully explored for fiscal policy in Chapter 28, pages 317–18, and analogous reasons apply to monetary policy: it takes time to diagnose the state of the economy, time to institute policy changes, and time for these changes to take effect. In the case of monetary policy, it can take up to 18 months for a given policy change to have its full effects on aggregate demand. By that time, the state of the economy may be very different from the state that led to the policy change. For example, a monetary expansion designed to reduce a recessionary gap may have its full effects felt after the economy has already developed an inflationary gap. These long lags make short-run stabilization policy of dubious value, and can even make it act perversely in the sense of increasing rather than dampening cyclical fluctuations.

Limitations in achieving full employment

The full-employment goal: Providing a job for everyone who wishes to work is a goal that most people accept. The problem is, however, providing a job *at what wage rate?* For example, in the 1980s, the UK had heavy unemployment in many sectors and many vacancies for lower-skilled, lower-paid jobs. Guaranteeing everyone the jobs for which they were trained is an impossible goal in a world of change. Guaranteeing everyone the jobs at high real wages is also impossible, since the average real wage that can be paid depends on the size of the employed labour force and total national output.

So although most people accept some form of a full-employment goal as important, there has been substantial rethinking of what precisely is meant by such a goal.

Structural and frictional unemployment: Demand management can remove demand-deficient unemployment but it is an ineffective tool for dealing with the remaining amount of unemployment which is called the NAIRU and is made up of structural and frictional unemployment. The NAIRU can at times be disturbingly high. What can be done about it?

Structural unemployment is, as we saw in Chapter 37, the result of economic change and the slowness of labour and product markets to bring about the necessary adjustments to that change. This type of unemployment, which seems to have risen in most countries over the last two decades, arises because individual markets do not work well enough and it therefore requires microeconomic policies for its cure. Policies to increase labour mobility are one example. Reform of labour-market institutions is a second.

If an attempt is made to reduce such unemployment by increasing aggregate demand, labour will not be in the right places with the right training to meet the extra demand. Inflation will then ensue because the increased demand cannot be matched by increased output.

BOX 39.2 Destabilizing Fiscal Policies?

'Although the economy was growing rapidly [the Chancellor in his 1988 Budget] cut taxes drastically and eased monetary policy, believing that the fast growth rates achieved from 1987 onwards had been due to structural improvements in the economy and not to an old fashioned macroeconomic boom. . . . In the event . . . his conviction turned out to be false. Inflation accelerated . . . the tax cuts, which were supposed to affect only the supply side of the economy, instead stimulated demand and produced unsuspected trade deficits and credit growth.

'Consider the key [1991] budget measures: the huge shift of tax burden on to consumption; the total rejection of any role for discretionary macroeconomic policy to steer the economy out of recession; the quest for "fiscal neutrality", even at the expense of demand for cars and housing, the two cyclical industries on which the hope for spontaneous recovery from recession would above all depend. *The central objective of the government's macroeconomic policy continues to be the defeat of inflation.*

'[In his 1991 budget, the Chancellor] seemed intent on repeating the blunders made in the Budget three years ago – intensifying the economic cycle, but this time on the downswing instead of on the way up.'

(Anatole Kaletsky in *The Times*, 25 March 1991)

This article argues that fiscal policy has accentuated fluctuations in national income in the years under discussion. This can happen either when policies, which are designed to stabilize, act with too long a time-lag, or, as in the present case, when policies are chosen with other goals in mind and without consideration of their effects on stabilization.

Questions

1 According to the article, what measures were introduced in the 1988 Budget and what were the results that surprised the Chancellor? Would they seem surprising to someone who had just studied the present chapter?

2 What macroeconomic goal was the government emphasizing in 1991, and what goal was it de-emphasizing? Would the policies it adopted in recent years have stabilized or destabilized national income, according to this commentary? Why?

3 If the Chancellor had been mainly concerned to stabilize national income and employment, what measures might he have introduced in 1988 and in 1991?

Limitations in achieving price stability?

Insofar as inflation is caused by demand pressures, it can be controlled by demand management. This is a powerful tool for inflation control. Many people doubt that aggregate-demand tools can produce full employment and stable prices even under conditions where demand can be quite precisely regulated. The main concern is with cost-push inflation.

Insofar as there is an upward push on wage costs that does not respond to the state of aggregate demand, there is an inflationary pressure that does not respond to demand management. This gives rise to the behaviour of the economy analysed in Figure 38.2 on page 432.

Such wage-cost-push inflation presents demand-management policy-makers with a cruel dilemma. Either they validate the resulting supply-side inflation, and produce something close to full employment, or they refuse to do so and accept a high, and possibly a rising, level of unemployment.

Wage-cost-push inflation can only be dealt with by removing the cost push. Three major alternative reforms have been suggested. The first is to refuse to validate the cost push and rely on a long period of unemployment to eliminate the wage-push force. If this stems from union power, for example, the prolonged unemployment may weaken the unions and lead to a decline in their cost-push pressures. The second is to change bargaining practices so as to make wage costs more responsive to conditions of demand and supply, as was done in the 1980s. The third is to have an incomes policy that seeks to control wage inflation by government intervention, which bypasses market forces, as was repeatedly tried in the 1960s and 1970s.

The third reform, prices and incomes policies, takes us to supply-side policies which are the subject of the next main section.

Limitations in influencing economic growth

In Chapter 36, we observed the importance of economic growth as a long-run determinant of living standards. The long-term growth rate does not seem to respond greatly to short-term demand-management techniques. People who are concerned with growth emphasize what are called supply-side policies to shift the long-run aggregate supply curve to the right. If the aggregate demand and the aggregate supply curves were independent of each other, then demand-management policies and supply-side policies could be carried out independently of each other. But many economists who emphasize the supply side maintain that many demand-management policies can be detrimental to growth. We shall consider this controversy further in the last chapter.

SUPPLY-SIDE POLICIES

The issue of growth just raised takes us to the second major part of this chapter, SUPPLY-SIDE POLICIES.

These policies are of two main sorts. First, prices and incomes policies work mainly through the short-run aggregate supply curve and attempt to supplement demand-management policies. Second, there are market-oriented, supply-side policies that are intended to be mainly long-term in effect. They seek to influence national income by shifting the long-run aggregate supply curve.

Interventionist Supply-Side Policies: Prices and Incomes Policies

Demand management seeks to influence the level of aggregate demand, and then allow individual prices and wages to be set by market conditions. Over the years, some economists have recommended an alternative called prices and incomes policies and many governments have experimented with them. A PRICES AND INCOMES POLICY is defined as an attempt by the government to influence directly the setting of wages and prices.

Because these policies attempt to act directly on prices and/or wages, they operate through the short-run aggregate supply curve. Their purpose is to come closer to the twin goals of full employment and stable prices by intervening in market behaviour.

There is a wide range of possible measures. First, the government could simply set voluntary guidelines for wage and price increases. By stating such guidelines, the government hopes to influence wage- and price-setting decisions.

A slightly more 'activist' form of incomes policy is consultation on wage and price norms among unions, management and government. The more centralized a country's wage-and price-setting mechanism, the more easily such consultation is accomplished. An even more activist approach is compulsory controls on wage and/or price increases. Another, as yet untried, proposal is TIPs (tax-related incomes policies), which introduce penalties or rewards that operate through the tax system in an attempt to induce desirable wage- and price-setting behaviour.

To evaluate these additional methods of controlling inflation, we need to distinguish the various circumstances in which they might be used. We can distinguish three main uses of prices and incomes policies: (i) to suppress a demand inflation, (ii) to break an expectational inflation, and (iii) to control a persistent wage-cost-push inflation.

Applied to demand inflations

One reason why incomes policies have bad reputations throughout the world is that they have often been used in futile attempts to stop demand inflations. To see why such attempts are futile, consider the situation shown at b in Figure 38.5 on page 435, where there is an inflationary gap of $Y_1 - Y_F$. If nothing else is done, the inflationary gap will cause wages to rise, shifting the $SRAS$ curve upwards to $SRAS'$. The price level will then rise to P_2 and the inflationary gap will be removed. Direct government intervention could, however, be used to hold the price level at P_1. But once the intervention ceases, the excess demand will cause prices to rise. Thus, in the face of an inflationary gap, prices/incomes policies can postpone an inflation. However, once the policies are removed, the price level will rise to the value it would have attained had the intervention never occurred.

Wage drift: Even while they last, wage-restraint policies tend to have more success controlling legal wage rates than they do controlling unit labour costs. Say that an incomes policy successfully limits money wage increases this year to 2 per cent, which is the same as the rate of productivity increase. If nothing else happens, unit costs will remain constant. If there is an inflationary gap, however, labour markets will be very tight and employers will be bidding against each other to gain access to the available labour. If they cannot raise wage rates because of the incomes policy, they can adopt many other measures that have the same effect. They can promise overtime that is credited without being worked, they can offer generous bonuses, they can increase such 'fringe benefits' as pensions, generous holiday pay, and daycare for working mothers. All of these add to the employers' labour costs and raise unit costs of production. This in turn shifts the *SRAS* curve upwards and contributes to inflation.

This tendency for the true *earnings* of labour, and the true cost of labour to employers, to rise even though wage *rates* are legally constrained by incomes policy is called WAGE DRIFT.

Applied to expectational inflations

When there are firmly entrenched expectations that an existing inflation will persist, prices and incomes policies provide a possible way of forcing the inflation rate down and helping to lower expectations of future inflations. Such policies may be used *in conjunction with a reduction in the rate of growth of the money supply* to what is compatible with the target rate of inflation. The hope is that they would reduce the depth and duration of the recession that must occur until expectations of further inflation are adjusted.

Once a stable price level is achieved, the incomes policy can be removed. If everyone then expects the new low rate of inflation to persist, expectations will have been broken while the recession that follows from the use of monetary restraint alone will have been avoided.

Supporters of incomes policies contend that such policies can break an expectational inflation. Opponents disagree, offering several arguments.

1. *After the policies are removed, people will expect a resurgence of inflation, and so incomes policies merely postpone inflation.* This depends on whether or not the Bank's accompanying tight monetary policy convinces people that inflation will not break out again, and on there being no inflationary gap when the controls are removed.

2. *Incomes policies are unnecessary because inflationary expectations will be adjusted downwards as soon as an anti-inflationary policy is adopted.* Some economists have argued that inflationary expectations would adjust quickly

once the Bank stopped validating the inflation. But the worldwide experience of 1980–83 showed that although the recession that normally accompanies the breaking of an entrenched inflation did not last as long as some pessimists had predicted, it lasted quite long enough to be very costly.

3. *Prices and incomes policies themselves would do much damage by inhibiting the operation of the price system.* This is a valid point, whose importance grows the longer the policies remain in force. A temporary bout of incomes policies lasting for a year or two, however, need not do long-term damage to the efficacy of the price system.

Applied to permanent wage-cost push

The third and final use of prices and incomes policies is to deal with an alleged permanent wage-cost push. Some economists contend that upward pressure on wages will constantly shift the *SRAS* curve upwards even when there is no inflationary gap. Unlike expectational forces, this wage-cost push will not be eliminated, even if the inflation rate is held at a very low level for several years. Instead, inflationary pressure will always be present when the economy is anywhere near full employment. These economists thus advocate *permanent* prices and incomes policies as the only way to achieve anything approaching full employment and relatively stable prices.

Here the problem of interfering with the price mechanism becomes serious. Whereas a bout of administered price- and wage-setting by governments may not do too much harm for a year or two, experience shows that its harmful effects grow the longer it persists because administered prices and wages get further and further away from the equilibrium prices and wages. The signalling functions of prices and wages are thus upset, and this has serious long-run effects on the efficient functioning of the economy.

Long-run prices and incomes policies come close to instituting some key aspects of a planned economy. Since such economies have proven to be failures in the long run, permanent government intervention into wage and price setting does not have a strong appeal these days.

Supply-side prices and incomes policies are shown under supply-side interventionist policies in Figure 39.1. They are shown as operating directly on the short-run aggregate supply curve which then interacts with the aggregate demand curve to determine the values of real income and the price level in the short run.

Market-Oriented, Supply-Side Policies

The supply-side policies that we now discuss are market oriented in their philosophy and look to long-term gains in increasing the rate of economic growth. (See Figure 39.1.) They have also been discussed in Chapter 22 of Part 4.

The origin of the modern interest in supply-side policies lay in the increasing realization that economic growth is influenced by microeconomic, as well as macroeconomic, forces. At the macro level, the overall amounts of saving and investment are undoubtedly important. At the micro level, however, a key factor affecting growth is entrepreneurial activity, both to develop new techniques for producing old products and to produce new products. So also is the ability of the economy to adjust to the inevitable changes caused by growth. If relative wages cannot change to reflect excess demands in some sectors and excess supplies in others, and if labour cannot – or will not – move from jobs, industries and geographic areas that are declining to those that are expanding, the overall growth process will be inhibited. Tax policy, education policy, housing policy, labour-market policy and a host of other microeconomic policies that once were looked at only from the point of view of static efficiency and equity in income distribution, are increasingly being scrutinized for their effects on long-term growth rates.

Supply-side economics is not new. Indeed much of it is in Adam Smith's *Wealth of Nations*. In its modern version, like many general but catchy terms, it sometimes means all things to all people. Basically, however, as a growth policy it means putting emphasis on pushing the long-run aggregate supply curve rightward rather than on manipulating aggregate demand. The motto here might be, 'It

is more important to increase full-employment national income than to try to reduce the temporary lapses from full employment that the market economy produces.'

There is little doubt that many government policies do have output-restricting effects. Thus some policy changes could do some of the things alleged by supply-side economics. If even a small increase in the growth rate of full-employment income could be achieved, the long-term effects on living standards would be high.

Here are some of the major items that were on the supply-side agenda in the late 1970s together with an account of what was done about them by the Conservative government during the 1980s.

Revise tax system to reward rather than penalize saving: Consider a woman in the 40 per cent tax bracket who earns an extra £1000 and pays £400 income tax. If she spends her after-tax income, she will be able to buy £600 worth of goods. If she saves the income instead, she will be able to buy a £600 bond. If the bond pays, say, a 4 per cent real return, she will earn £24 interest per year. But a 40 per cent tax must then be paid on the interest earnings, leaving only a £14.40 annual income. This is a 1.44 per cent after-tax return on the original £1000 of income earned. Supply-side advocates allege that this 'double taxing' is a serious disincentive to saving. They advocate taxes on consumption, not on income, so that any income saved would be tax-free. A tax would be levied only when the interest earned on the savings was spent on consumption.

A major move to change the balance between taxes on income and taxes on consumption was made through the reduction in personal income-tax rates and then making up the lost revenue by increasing the rate of VAT which falls only on consumption. During the 1980s, the basic rate of income tax was reduced from 30 to 25 per cent and the maximum rate from 75 (60 per cent on earned income plus an investment income surcharge of 15 per cent) to 40 per cent.

Ending 'double taxation' of business income: Business income is taxed first as the income of firms when it is earned and, second, as the income of households, when it is paid out as dividends. This, and other policies that reduce business profits, and hence diminish the return to investing in company shares, are alleged to discourage households from saving and investing in growing but risky businesses that are the mainspring of economic growth.

The main concession in this area was to change the rate of corporation tax on business profits from 52 per cent to 33 per cent in 1980.

Encourage work by ending high rates of income tax: Supply-side advocates allege that high taxes discourage work. But depending on the relative strengths of the substitution and the income effects, high taxes may actually make people increase *or* decrease the amount that they work. Theory is silent on which is more likely, and no hard evidence has yet shown that lowering current tax rates will usually make people work harder. (The effect of any tax-reducing policy on the distribution of income needs also to be considered.)

As already mentioned, rates of personal income tax at the high end were substantially cut during the 1980s from a maximum rate of 60 per cent to one of 40 per cent.

Encourage competition: Most economists tend to agree with this recommendation, although there is disagreement over how much competition is desirable, and possible, in certain industries. For example, those who believe in the efficacy of market forces tend to support complete deregulation of fare- and route-setting by airlines, while those who are more sceptical tend to worry that cut-throat competition may reduce airline quality and safety.

Much was done on these lines in the 1980s. Laws and regulations relating to competition and monopolies have been revised. Nationalized industries have been sold to private owners as part of the privatization programme. Unfortunately, however, the opportunity to break these industries into smaller competing units was often lost so that, while ownership changed, the degree of competition was not increased. Many industries were deregulated – for example, the dispensing of spectacles and the conveyancing of real estate. It was felt that the regulation encouraged joint profit-raising, monopolistic action, and that deregulation would encourage competition.

Labour market reforms: Making labour markets more competitive was alleged to have many advantages, from reducing inflation by reducing cost-push elements, to encouraging growth by having wages become more flexible, and reducing the monetary incentives to stay out of work.

Over the 1980s, the power of trades unions was substantially reduced through a number of government policy initiatives. Furthermore, unemployment benefits were made more difficult to obtain. One major reform that is still being discussed is to make a portion of wages depend on profits, as is common in Japan. This introduces substantial flexibility into the wage bill and leads to less unemployment in time of recession. Instead of the whole burden falling on a small fraction of the labour force who lose their jobs, the burden of recession is more evenly spread among workers whose pay falls somewhat (while employment remains fairly constant).

Encourage people to have a stake in the market economy: It is argued that if people have a stake in the success of the economy they will be more inclined to make it work. One policy in this direction was the sale of council houses to their occupiers at quite favourable prices.[1] This created many new home-owners in place of renters. The policy of making wages partly dependent on profits, discussed above, is also presented as a way of increasing people's stake in the success of the market economy.

---

1 The downside of this policy became apparent in the early 1990s when a rise in interest rates caused many buyers to default on their mortgage payments, thus losing the housing they had purchased. This forced them back to the rental market where cheap council housing was harder to obtain (because much of it had been sold).

Encourage adjustment by ending support for declining industries: The policy of supporting declining industries reduces resource mobility. Resources that could be more productively employed elsewhere leave the industry more slowly than they would under free-market conditions. Most economists agree that such policies are costly, harmful to growth and, in the end, self-defeating. Such support has become much rarer than it was in the past.

There is still room, however, to disagree on how much transitional adjustment help should be given to labour and capital in declining industries. Supply-side advocates tend to worry that transitional aid will become *de facto* permanent aid and thus cause the necessary adjustment to be postponed. Others feel that reasonable help could be given to those whose lives are disrupted by the changes associated with growth without inhibiting the growth process itself.

POLICY TRADE-OFFS: A CONCLUDING WORD

People often ask: Is one policy goal more important than another? This question is interesting only in so far as there are conflicts among the various policies – if they are unrelated to each other, all may be pursued simultaneously. In so far as conflicts exist, so that getting closer to one objective implies getting further from another, the question is interesting. There can, however, be no final answer to the question of relative importance, since any answer depends on both factual judgements about the effects of each and on value judgements about various goals.

Where there are important trade-offs between goals, choices must be made. Most economists today accept a *short-run* trade-off between inflation on the one hand and output and employment on the other. A reduction in inflation is usually bought at the cost of a temporary fall in output below its potential level. A temporary rise in output above its potential level can be bought at the cost of a rise in the price level. Many economists also believe, however, that there is no long-run trade-off. They believe that potential income, which is the maximum sustainable level of income, is independent of the economy's rate of inflation. Other economists, however, believe that cost-push forces create a permanent conflict between achieving full employment by demand-management techniques and maintaining a stable price level. They believe that a choice must be made between full employment and stable prices as long as demand management is the only available tool.

Most economists also believe that there is a relation between full employment and growth, but that no choice is required in this case. Low levels of income, employment and capacity utilization are not conducive to the savings and investment which are an important determinant of growth. High levels of income, employment and capacity utilization are. So with full employment and growth, we can have our cake and eat it too! Getting closer to the former tends to give us more of the latter.

Possibly one of the most serious domestic trade-offs, and one that as yet we know too little about, is between equity and growth. It is clear that some measures introduced for reasons of equity, such as rent controls and high unemployment benefits, inhibit the adjustments needed for a high growth rate – rent controls by discouraging geographic mobility of labour, and high unemployment benefits by reducing the incentive to move to, or train for, new jobs when old jobs disappear. (A further important trade-off between domestic objectives and the exchange rate arises when the exchange rate is fixed by the Bank.

The important issues involved here are discussed in the next three chapters.)

To make an intelligent choice on trade-offs, where they do exist, we need much more positive knowledge than we now have about just how much each policy affects growth. Then each of us needs to exercise our value judgements to decide how much reduction in growth it is worth accepting – if this proves necessary – to get a given increase in equity.

Summary

1 One major tool of demand management is fiscal policy.

2 When initiating an expansionary fiscal policy, a key issue is whether to increase expenditure or to cut taxes. This choice is influenced by such considerations as the size of the change, the location of the impact effects, the time-lags involved, and the effect on the size of the government in the economy.

3 Some major limitations of fiscal policy are the following: (i) the crowding-out effect, which occurs when an expansionary fiscal policy increases interest rates and the resulting reduction in investment partially offsets the initial fiscal stimulus; (ii) the permanent-income hypothesis, which suggests that temporary changes in disposable income may cause savings to change and leave consumption expenditure relatively unaffected; (iii) an expansionary or contractionary policy must be rapidly reversed when private expenditure functions resume their more normal positions.

4 The second major tool of demand management is monetary policy. This works through interest-rate changes and then onto interest-sensitive expenditures. An expansionary monetary policy puts downward pressure on interest rates, while a contractionary policy applies upward pressure.

5 When there is a recessionary gap, interest rates can be forced down by an expansionary monetary policy and real income increased as a result. When national income is at its full-employment level, the long-run effects of an expansionary monetary policy are to raise the price level but to leave income, employment and real interest rates unchanged once a new equilibrium is established. In a fully expected inflation, the nominal interest rate will exceed the equilibrium real interest rate by the amount of the inflation.

6 The major goals of short-run stabilization policy in a closed economy are full employment and a stable price level.

7 With a Keynesian aggregate supply curve of the J-shape, the problem of stabilization policy appears easy: stabilize the aggregate demand curve to achieve full employment and a stable price level.

8 A stable Phillips curve gives policy-makers a trade-off between inflation on the one hand and unemployment and national income on the other hand. This trade-off is, however, illusory in the long run. An attempt to hold unemployment below the natural rate, which means income above its potential level, leads to an accelerating inflation rate as the Phillips curve shifts upwards continually.

9 Limitations of demand-management policies are: (i) demand management cannot stabilize income completely because time-lags and other uncertainties make fine-tuning potentially destabilizing; (ii) demand management cannot eliminate frictional, structural or real-wage unemployment; (iii) demand management cannot deal with permanent wage-cost-push inflation if it exists; and (iv) economic growth is more influenced by micro supply-side rather than macro demand-management policies.

10 Interventionist supply-side policies seek to influence aggregate expenditure through direct intervention into wage and price setting. These are usually referred to as prices and incomes policies. They work through the *SRAS* curve. They are unable to suppress a demand inflation indefinitely, but could shorten the recession that accompanies the breaking of an entrenched inflation. Some economists feel that such policies are needed as a permanent check to wage-cost-push inflation without which full employment and stable prices would prove incompatible.

11 Market-oriented supply-side economics seeks to achieve economic gains by long-term measures designed to raise the rate of growth by shifting the long-run aggregate supply curve to the right. Some specific policies are designed to encourage saving, raise mobility and labour-force participation, and encourage entrepreneurial activities.

There are many ways of classifying macroeconomic policies. We have chosen in this chapter to focus attention on demand-management (fiscal and monetary policies) and on supply-side policies. An alternative classification would be to group policies on more political criteria – whether they tend to be interventionist or market-oriented in character. We shall consider such a classification in Chapter 43. Meanwhile, however, we need to consider the complications that arise in an open economy, and that we have assumed away in this chapter.

Questions

1 Which One or More of the following are typical supply-side policies?
  (a) Measures to increase the mobility of labour.
  (b) Increasing government expenditure to increase national income.
  (c) Shifting the tax burden from income taxes to value added taxes.
  (d) Using an expansionary monetary policy to force down interest rates and so encourage business investment.
  (e) Abolishing the corporation income tax.

2 For removing a recessionary gap, fiscal policy will have an advantage over monetary policy in which One or More of the following situations?
  (a) The current PSBR is worryingly high.
  (b) The economy is in a severe, and persistent, recession.
  (c) The government would like to see interest rates rise for reasons connected with policy goals other than full employment.
  (d) The private-sector demand for investment is thought to be highly elastic.

3 True or False?
  (a) The same increase in aggregate desired expenditure can be accomplished either through a tax increase or an expenditure increase of equal size.
  (b) Expenditure changes are normally capable of having more regionally localized impact effects than tax changes.
  (c) The permanent-income hypothesis suggests that government expenditure changes may be a more potent tool for influencing aggregate expenditure in the short run than tax changes.
  (d) An expansionary fiscal policy tends to push interest rates upwards while an expansive monetary policy tends to push interest rates downwards.
  (e) Prices and incomes policies are likely to be more effective when they are used to control an inflation due to entrenched expectations of inflation, rather than an inflation due to excess demand.
  (f) Demand management is a particularly potent tool for influencing the rate of economic growth.

4 The combination of elasticities that tends to make fiscal policy relatively effective is an (elastic/inelastic) liquidity preference curve and an (elastic/inelastic) marginal efficiency of investment curve.

5 Repeat question 2 for monetary policy.

6 An attempt to hold national income above its potential level implies that unemployment is to be held (above/below) its natural rate and that the money supply must be (increased/reduced/held constant). This will lead to expectations of inflation being revised (upwards/downwards) and to an (upwards/downwards) shift in the Phillips curve, leading to (an acceleration/deceleration/constant rate) of inflation.

40 Exchange Rates

In Chapter 29, we integrated foreign trade into the model of income determination. (Pages 326–31 of that chapter should be reviewed now.) We observed that the main determinants of imports and exports are national income and international relative prices. In that earlier discussion, we held international relative prices constant by assuming each pair of countries' price levels to be unchanged, as well as the exchange rate between their two currencies. This leaves income as the only variable that can maintain equilibrium in international payments. A change in exports causes the home country's national income to change in the same direction, while a change in that country's import function causes its national income to change in the opposite direction: an upward shift in the import function leading to a reduction in equilibrium national income, and vice versa.

We are now ready to see how prices influence exports and imports. To do this, we first allow the exchange rate to change and then we allow international price levels to change as well. We then see that the main variable that maintains equilibrium in international payments is the exchange rate – i.e. changes in relative prices, rather than changes in national income, do the main job.

To get some idea of what is involved, consider the case in which the home country suffers an exogenous fall in its exports, which means the same fall in its *net exports*. (If X falls with M constant, then X − M falls by the same amount.)

We already know from Chapter 29 that, *ceteris paribus*, a fall in net exports will reduce the home country's national income. But the fall in exports will also mean less demand for the country's currency on foreign-exchange markets. This will tend to cause its exchange rate to fall which, as we shall see, encourages exports and discourages imports through a relative price effect. These changes increase net exports and tend to offset the intial effect of the exogenous fall in exports. If the fall in net exports is reduced because of the exchange-rate changes, then the fall in national income needed to restore equilibrium is less than it would have been if the exchange rate had been fixed.

In this chapter we study the detailed workings of this exchange-rate mechanism. In the next chapter, we consider the regimes for determining exchange rates that have been used by the world's trading countries at various times during the twentieth century. Then, in Chapter 42, we take both income and price changes into account to complete the study of how international equilibrium is restored after it is disturbed by various shocks, and to make a further reconsideration of fiscal and monetary policies.

Two Important Distinctions

At the outset we need to introduce two important distinctions that we will need at various points over this and the next chapter. We distinguish between small and large open economies, and between tradeable and non-tradeable commodities.

Large and small open economies[1]

As those who have already read Chapter 19 will recall, a LARGE OPEN ECONOMY is one whose imports and exports are so large in relation to the total volume of trade in those commodities that it can affect their prices by changing the quantities that it buys or sells. A SMALL OPEN ECONOMY is one whose imports and exports are too small in relation to the total volume of trade in those commodities to affect their prices by changing the quantities that it buys and sells. A small open economy must accept the internationally determined *prices* of the goods that it trades and adjust the *quantities* that it trades in response to *given* prices.

Imports: As far as imports are concerned, the UK is a small open economy. Total UK demand for most of the commodities that it imports is too small a part of the total world demand for these commodities to exert a significant influence on their price. UK demand for any of these goods could rise or fall by 10 or 20 per cent with little appreciable effect on their prices.

The UK is a price-taker in most of its imports. The prices are set on foreign markets, and UK purchasers can buy as much as they wish at those prices.

Exports: The situation is a little more complicated with regard to exports. In so far as the UK exports homogeneous commodities that are the same the world over, such as coal, oil and rape seed, the UK is a small open economy whose own demands and supplies are too small to affect the world prices of these commodities. Manufactured goods, however, are differentiated so that no two products produced by different competing firms are identical. Goods such as Rolls-Royce aircraft engines, Ford Fiesta cars and Hotpoint washing machines are differentiated from other competing products. As a result, their producers face downward-sloping demand curves: if they cut their prices, they will sell more both at home and abroad; if they raise their prices, they will sell less both at home and abroad.

---

1 These concepts were first introduced in Chapter 19.

Since most UK exports are of differentiated products, we will make the large-open-economy assumption for all UK exports. This is something of a simplification. However, enough UK exporters can alter their sales by altering their prices that it is realistic to assume that:

UK exporters face downward-sloping demand curves, implying that UK export prices can be altered by UK producers.

Most UK exports are sold in competition with similar goods produced in other countries. This severely limits the power of UK exporters when setting their prices. Although they can raise prices somewhat without losing all of their sales, if their prices get seriously out of line with those of their foreign competitors, they will lose substantial sales. In other words, although most UK exporters face downward-sloping demand curves for their goods in foreign markets, these curves tend to be quite elastic in most cases.

Tradeable and non-tradeable commodities: We can conceptually divide all commodities into two types. TRADE-ABLES are goods and services that enter into international trade, such as cars and wheat. NON-TRADEABLES are goods and services that are produced and sold domestically but do not enter into international trade, such as haircuts and gravel.[1] Their prices are set on domestic markets by domestic supply and demand and these prices are unaffected by market conditions for the same products in other countries.

THE MECHANISM OF INTERNATIONAL TRANSACTIONS

With these preliminaries settled, we can begin our study of exchange rates.

When British producers sell their products, they require payment in pounds sterling. They need this currency to meet their wages bills, pay for their raw materials and reinvest or distribute their profits. If they sell their goods to British purchasers, there is no problem, since they will be paid in sterling. However, if British producers sell their goods to Indian importers, either the Indians must exchange rupees to acquire sterling to pay for the goods, or the British producers must accept rupees – and they will accept rupees only if they know they can exchange the rupees for the sterling that they require. The same holds true for producers in all countries; they must eventually be able to receive payment in the currency of their own country for the goods and services that they sell.

In general, trade between nations can occur only if the currency of one nation can be exchanged for the currency of another.

---

[1] Sixty years ago, many goods were too perishable or too costly to transport to be traded internationally. Today, with refrigeration and high-speed, low-cost transport, there are relatively few goods that do not routinely move across international borders. The majority of non-traded commodities are now services which must be consumed where they are produced. Many services, however, are also traded – e.g., banking, insurance and shipping.

An illustration of how transactions in foreign exchange are carried out is given below and summarized in Table 40.1. Suppose that an American firm wishes to purchase a British sportscar to sell in the US. The British firm that produced the car requires payment in pounds sterling. If the car is priced at £15,000, the American firm will go to its bank and ask for a cheque for £15,000. How many dollars the firm must pay to purchase this cheque will depend on the exchange rate between US dollars and pounds sterling. Let us suppose the firm is required to pay $26,250. In other words, the exchange rate for this transaction is $1.75 to the pound (26,250/15,000), or, what is the same thing, £0.571 to the dollar (15,000/26,250). The American purchaser will send the cheque to the British car firm, which in turn will deposit the cheque in its bank.

TABLE 40.1 Changes in the Balance Sheets of Two Banks as a Result of International Payments

UK BANK		AMERICAN BANK	
Liabilities	*Assets*	*Liabilities*	*Assets*
(1) Deposits of car exporter + 15,000	No change	(1) Deposits of car importer –$26,250	No change
(2) Deposits of computer importer –£15,000	No change	(2) Deposits of computer exporter +$26,250	No change
(3) Net change	0	(3) Net change	0

The American importer of British sports cars reduces his US bank balance by $26,250 in order to buy a sterling cheque for £15,000 at an exchange rate of $1.75 to the pound; the British exporter deposits this cheque in his UK bank. The British importer of US computers reduces his deposit in his UK bank by £15,000 in order to buy a US dollar cheque for $26,250 at a price of £0.571 per dollar; the US exporter deposits this cheque in his US bank. All the transactions are effected by transferring dollar deposits among US residents and sterling deposits among UK residents.

Now assume that, in the same period of time, a British firm purchases five American personal computers for sale in the UK. If the computers are priced at US $5,250 each, the American seller will have to be paid $26,250. To make this payment, the British importing firm goes to its bank and writes a cheque on its account for £15,000 and receives a cheque drawn on an American bank for $26,250. The cheque is sent to the US and deposited in an American bank.[1]

The American import of a British car reduces the deposit liabilities of the American bank to American residents and increases its deposit liabilities to British residents. The two transactions cancel each other out, and there is no net change in international liabilities. No money need pass between British and American banks to effect the transactions; each bank merely increases the deposit of one domestic customer and lowers the deposit of another. Indeed, as long as the flow of payments between the two countries is equal (Americans pay as much to British residents as British residents pay to Americans), all payments

---

[1] The whole set of transactions can be done without even having cheques issued. Instead, the banks can telegraph to their correspondents in the other country with orders to pay. This would give rise to the same set of book entries as those shown in Table 40.1.

can be managed as in these examples. There will be no need for a net payment between British and American banks. What in effect has happened is that the American personal computer manufacturer received the dollars the American car purchaser gave up to get a British-made car, while the British car manufacturer received the sterling that the computer importer gave up.

Two ways of expressing the exchange rate

In our discussion so far, we have compared magnitudes measured in different currencies. These comparisons are made using the exchange rate. As a first step in studying such exchange rates we look at the two ways in which any exchange rate can be expressed.

The exchange rate of £1 = $1.75 expresses the *dollar price of £1* – i.e. it costs $1.75 to buy £1. The same information can also be expressed by quoting the *sterling price of $1*. If it costs $1.75 to buy £1, it also costs £0.571 to buy $1 (1/1.75 = 0.571).

In what follows it is necessary to move back and forth between these two ways of expressing the exchange rate. Because this can be confusing, we show their equivalents in Figure 40.1. On the left-hand scale, we give the exchange rate as it is normally expressed in the UK, the price of one unit of sterling in terms of some foreign currency – the US dollar in this case. On the right-hand scale, we give the reciprocal of this rate, the sterling price of one US dollar.[1]

A fall in the sterling exchange rate – say from £1 = $1.75 to £1 = $1.50 – is called a DEPRECIATION of sterling or of the exchange rate. It takes fewer American dollars to buy £1. Looked at the other way around, the dollar has become more expensive, in terms of sterling. In the case just considered, instead of costing £0.571, a US dollar now costs £0.667. This means that the relative value of sterling has fallen, while the relative value of the dollar has risen.

A rise in the sterling exchange rate – say from £1 = $1.50 to £1 = $1.75 – is called an APPRECIATION of sterling or of the exchange rate. It takes more US dollars to buy £1. Looked at the other way around, the dollar has become cheaper relative to sterling. In this case, it now takes only £0.571 to buy a dollar instead of £0.667. As a result, the relative value of home currency, sterling, has risen while the relative value of foreign currency has fallen.

The direction of changes in the prices expressed in both ways, when sterling appreciates or depreciates, is shown in Figure 40.1. Moving up the page on both scales indicates an appreciation of the sterling exchange rate, while moving down the page on both scales indicates a depreciation. Of course, the situation looked at from the point of view of the US dollar is the other way around. Whenever sterling appreciates relative to the dollar, the dollar depreciates relative to sterling. Whenever sterling depreciates relative to the dollar, the dollar appreciates relative to sterling.

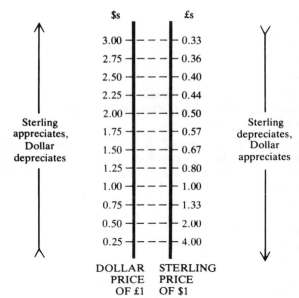

FIGURE 40.1 Two Ways of Expressing the Exchange Rate. The exchange rate between sterling and US dollars can be expressed as the dollar price of one pound sterling or the sterling price of one US dollar. The two arrows show the terminology used to describe a movement upwards on the scale (left-hand arrow) or downwards on the scale (right-hand arrow).

For practice, let us follow through one further movement along both scales. If the pound is worth three dollars (as it was, not too many years ago), then the scale tells us – reading across – that the dollar is worth 33p. If the pound now falls to $2.50, the scale tells us – again reading across – that the dollar is worth 40p. The arrow now tells us that, since we are moving downwards along the scale, sterling is depreciating (it is worth fewer dollars), while the dollar is appreciating (it is worth more sterling).[1]

Internal and external value of a currency

The exchange rate describes what is called the EXTERNAL VALUE of a country's currency, which means how much the currency is worth *in terms of the currencies of other countries*. For example, a rise in the exchange rate from $1.50 to $1.75 to the pound sterling means that the external value of sterling has risen. The external value of a currency must be clearly distinguished from what is called its INTERNAL VALUE, which means how much the currency is worth *in terms of domestic purchasing power*. For example, an inflation that doubles the UK price level would cut the internal value of sterling in half because each

---

1 Although equal distances indicate equal price changes in the left-hand scale, they do not do so on the right-hand scale. This is because the figures on the right-hand scale are the reciprocals of the figures on the left-hand scale. (Because the figures on the right-hand scale are derived from those on the left-hand one, they do not all come out even, and they are quoted correct to two decimal places.)

---

1 Readers should be warned that in international economic theory the exchange rate is almost always expressed as the number of units of domestic currency needed to buy one unit of foreign currency (the price of foreign exchange). In the UK, however, the exchange rate is usually expressed as the number of units of foreign currency needed to buy one pound sterling (the foreign-currency price of sterling). We use the standard UK terminology in which a depreciation of the sterling exchange rate means that the price of a pound sterling, measured in some foreign currency, has fallen.

unit of currency would only buy half as much as it did previously.

THE DETERMINATION OF THE EXCHANGE RATE

The theory that we develop here applies to the exchange rates between any two currencies, but for convenience we shall deal with the example of trade between the US and the UK, and with the determination of the rate of exchange between their two currencies, dollars and pounds sterling. To make the treatment general, the US can be thought of as *all foreign countries* and the US dollar as *all foreign exchange*.

We shall assume, just for the moment, that the Bank of England does not intervene in the foreign-exchange market, and that there are only trade items in the balance of payments, so that there are no capital account transactions.

We start with an important relation with respect to the market for foreign exchange.

Because one currency is traded for another on the foreign-exchange market, it follows that to desire (demand) dollars implies a willingness to offer (supply) pounds, while an offer (supply) of dollars implies a desire (demand) for pounds.

For example, if at an exchange rate of £1 = $1.80, a British importer demands $9.00, he must be offering £5.00. If an American importer offers $9.00 at that exchange rate, she must be demanding £5.00. For this reason, the theory of the foreign-exchange market can be expressed in either of two ways: (i) we can deal either with the demand for, and the supply of, dollars, *or* (ii) with the demand for, and the supply of, pounds sterling. Both need not be considered.

It turns out to be simpler to deal with the demand and supply of sterling on the foreign-exchange market, so we use this approach. The demand and supply of sterling refers to what is required for foreign-exchange transactions. It has nothing to do with the demands of those who wish to hold sterling for domestic trading purposes.

In our two-country world, there are only two groups of private traders on the foreign-exchange market: people who have sterling and want dollars, and people who have dollars and want sterling.

The demand for sterling: The demand for sterling on the foreign-exchange market arises because holders of dollars wish to make payments in sterling. It arises therefore because of British exports of goods and services to the US.

The supply of sterling: The supply of sterling to the foreign-exchange market arises because holders of sterling wish to make payments in dollars. It arises therefore because of British imports of goods and services from the US.

The Exchange Rate Determined Graphically

We now wish to draw demand and supply curves for sterling on the foreign-exchange market. These curves will allow us to study the determination of exchange rates.

Until one gets familiar with this kind of diagram, these ratios can be confusing, so it is worth emphasizing what is being plotted on Figure 40.2. As we move *upwards* on the vertical axis, the numbers on the axis tell us that the dollar price of sterling is rising. Looked at the other way around, this means that the sterling price of the dollar is falling. In other words, relative to each other, sterling is becoming more expensive while the dollar is becoming cheaper. So when we move upwards on this axis, sterling is *appreciating* while the dollar is *depreciating*.

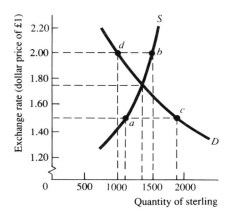

FIGURE 40.2 The Foreign-Exchange Market. The demand and supply curves for sterling on the foreign-exchange market intersect to determine a US dollar price of sterling of $1.75. At this exchange rate, the US dollar is worth £0.571. When the pound is undervalued at $1.50, there is excess demand for sterling of *ac* on the foreign-exchange market. This will tend to cause sterling to appreciate. When the pound is overvalued at US$2.00, there is excess supply of sterling of *db* on the foreign-exchange market. This will tend to cause sterling to depreciate.

Conversely, when we move downwards on the vertical scale, the numbers on the axis tell us that the dollar price of sterling is falling. Looked at the other way around, the sterling price of the dollar is rising.

The slopes of the demand and supply curves for dollars

Next we must determine what the slopes of the demand curve and the supply curve for sterling will be when we plot them on a diagram such as Figure 40.2. We have seen that the demand and supply of sterling on the foreign-exchange market arise out of imports and exports. To determine the slope of these curves, we must first see what a change in the exchange rate does to the *quantities* of imports and exports, and then to their *values* in terms of sterling.

TABLE 40.2 The Effect on the Supply of Sterling of Changes in the Exchange Rate

Case	US dollar price of UK import	Dollar price of £1	Sterling price of UK import	Quantity of import	Sterling value of import (= supply of sterling)	Figure reference
1	$10	$1.50	£6.67	170 units	£1140	a
2	$10	$2.00	£5.00	300 units	£1500	b

Going from Case 1 to Case 2, sterling has appreciated in value. One pound sterling is worth $1.50 in Case 1 and $2.00 in Case 2. In Case 1 it costs £0.667 to buy one US dollar and in Case 2 it costs only £0.50. This change lowers the sterling price of any import whose price is fixed in US dollars. Given the normal negative slope of the demand curve for the imported good, more of it will be bought and (assuming the demand to be elastic) more sterling will have to be spent to purchase it. The actual change in quantity is assumed for purposes of illustration.

The supply of sterling: First consider imports: Table 40.2 illustrates the effects using hypothetical data. Because UK demand is too small to affect the price of its imports, these prices are fixed exogenously in foreign currency. We assume the foreign price is US$10 for each unit of imports. In what we call Case 1, the exchange rate is US$1.50 to the pound which means that a US dollar costs £0.667. In this case, the imported good must sell for £6.67 each on the UK market. (When the sale price of £6.67 is converted to US dollars at the prevailing exchange rate, the world selling price of US$10 is obtained.) We assume that 170 units of the good are imported, making a total sterling cost of £1140. Thus this amount of sterling is supplied to foreign-exchange markets to buy dollars to pay for the imports.

Turning now to Case 2, where the exchange rate changes to US$2.00 to the pound, this makes a US dollar cost £0.50. The sterling price of this good falls to £5.00. We assume that, in response to the fall in the sterling price, 300 units are now imported into the UK. This means that £1500 must now be supplied in order to purchase the dollars needed to pay for imports.

The appreciation of sterling has led to an increased supply of sterling on the foreign-exchange market.

Now let us state in more general terms what is happening. When the pound appreciates, the sterling price of imports falls in the UK market. Thus, more imports will be purchased. If the demand for these imports is elastic, more sterling will be spent on them.

Demand for sterling: Now consider UK exports. We assume that the UK exporters set their prices in sterling at levels sufficient to cover their costs and yield them profits. The prices that they must charge in the US market depend on the exchange rate. For example, a British good priced at £5 must sell in the US for $7.50 when the exchange rate is $1.50 to the pound. When the good is sold for $7.50 in the US, that amount can be exchanged for £5 at the going exchange rate.

A numerical example is shown in Table 40.3. When sterling appreciates, it takes more US dollars to buy one pound. Thus a British export must sell at a higher dollar price if it is to yield an unchanged sterling price to its producers. As a result, fewer units can be sold on the export market. In the Table, we assume the fall is from 373 to 200 units. Since less is sold at an unchanged sterling price, there is a fall in the demand to buy sterling on the foreign-exchange market to pay for these UK exports.

Now let us state what is going on in this case more generally. When the pound appreciates, the price of UK exports rises in terms of dollars. In response, less is exported. As a result, less sterling is demanded on the foreign-exchange market in order to buy UK goods.

The foreign-exchange market

Figure 40.2 plots the dollar price of sterling on the vertical axis and the quantity of sterling on the horizontal axis. To familiarize you with this diagram, we plot a numerical example. The four points labelled a, b, c and d in the Figure are plotted from Tables 40.2 and 40.3. Each point plots an exchange rate against a quantity of sterling sup-

TABLE 40.3 The Effect on the Demand for Sterling of Changes in the Exchange Rate

Case	UK export	Exchange rate (US$ price of £1)	US$ price of UK export	Quantity of export	Sterling value of exports (= demand for sterling)	Figure reference
1	£5	$1.50	$7.50	373 units	£1865	c
2	£5	$2.00	$10.00	200 units	£1000	d

In this example the price of UK exports is fixed in sterling and the US$ price is determined by the exchange rate. The demand for sterling on the foreign-exchange market is given by the number of units sold multiplied by their sterling price. That is the amount of sterling US importers must purchase in order to pay for the British goods that they buy.

Going from Case 1 to Case 2, sterling has appreciated in value. It costs $1.50 to buy £1 in Case 1 and $2.00 in Case 2. This change raises the dollar price of any export whose price is fixed in sterling. Given the normal negative slope of the US demand curve for the exported good, less of it will be exported and less sterling will be demanded to buy these exports (because the quantity has decreased and the sterling price is unchanged). The actual change in quantity is assumed for purposes of illustration.

plied. Point *a* is from Case 1 of Table 40.2, and point *c* is from Case 1 of Table 40.3. They show the quantities of sterling supplied and demanded at an exchange rate of US$1.50. Points *b* and *d* are from Case 2 in Tables 40.2 and 40.3 respectively. They show the quantities supplied and demanded at an exchange rate of US$2.00 to the pound.

The two curves follow the general rules we have established. The negatively sloped demand curve indicates that, as sterling appreciates, less sterling is demanded to pay for British exports. The positively sloped supply curve indicates that, as sterling appreciates, more sterling is supplied to buy dollars to pay for British imports.

Now look at how the market will determine the equilibrium exchange rate. Where the two curves intersect, which is at the price of US$1.75 in Figure 40.2, quantity demanded equals quantity supplied, and the exchange rate is in equilibrium. The equilibrium exchange rate of £1.00 = US$1.75 also means that US$1 is worth £0.571. To show why this is the equilibrium exchange rate, we need to do no more than we did in the early microeconomics chapters; we follow the consequences of the exchange rate being at any other level.

Assume first that the exchange rate is below equilibrium – say it is US$1.50 in the Figure. In this case the demand for sterling exceeds the supply. Because sterling is in excess demand (*ac* in the Figure), some people who wish to convert dollars into pounds will be unable to do so. Sterling will appreciate.

What will happen if the current price of the sterling is above equilibrium, say US$2.00? At this exchange rate, the supply of sterling exceeds the demand. Because sterling is in excess supply (*db* in the Figure), some people who wish to sell sterling in order to make payments to the US will be unable to do so, and the price of sterling will fall – i.e. sterling depreciates on the foreign-exchange market.

CHANGES IN THE EXCHANGE RATE

We now use the theory we have developed to understand the effects of some important changes in the conditions that determine exchange rates.

Price-level changes

A change in the price level of one country: Consider, for example, the case of a localized inflation in the UK. A local British inflation will raise the price of all non-traded goods and services and of all factors of production in the UK. This will raise the sterling price of British exportables, but, until the exchange rate changes, the sterling price of *importables* will not change. (Their dollar price is unchanged and if the exchange rate is unchanged, their sterling price will also be unchanged.) What will happen to the quantities of *imports* and *exports*? Since non-tradeables and exportables rise in price, *imported* goods will now be relatively cheaper than they were, and more imports will be bought. As far as *exports* are concerned, their price must rise in the foreign market and less of them will be sold. Assuming the demand for them is elastic, as it is for most differentiated goods that are in close competition with other similar goods, the percentage fall in quantity will exceed the percentage rise in price. As a result, the sterling value of these exports will fall and there will be a decline in the amount of sterling demanded on the foreign-exchange market in order to pay for British exports.

A local British inflation raises the quantity of imports and lowers the quantity of exports at each given exchange rate.

This means that, at the original exchange rate, more sterling will be supplied in order to buy dollars to pay for increased imports while less sterling will be demanded to pay for British exports. In other words:

A local British inflation shifts the supply curve for sterling on the foreign-exchange market to the right and the demand curve to the left.

The effects are shown in Figure 40.3, where we drop the numerical example and use letters to indicate amounts of sterling demanded and supplied at various exchange rates. As a result of the forces just considered, the supply curve for sterling will shift to the right – from, say, *S* to *S'* – while the demand curve shifts to the left – from, say, *D* to *D'*. The exchange rate must now fall – i.e. sterling depreciates. In the Figure, the price of one pound falls from $1.75 to $1.50. This fall in the pound's external value is the same thing as a rise in the external value of the dollar from £0.571 to £0.667. (Don't forget that Figure 40.1 is there to help you turn any exchange rate around the other way.)

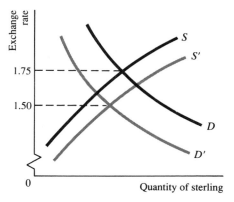

FIGURE 40.3 The Effect of a Localized Inflation. An inflation that raises UK prices will shift the demand curve for sterling to the left (because less is exported) and the supply curve for sterling to the right (because more is imported). This will cause sterling to depreciate on the foreign-exchange market. In the example, the exchange rate goes from $1.75 to $1.50 to the pound.

An equal percentage change in the price level in both countries: Once again, the UK prices of non-traded commodities, UK factors of production, and UK exportables, rise by the amount of the inflation. This time, however, the prices of imported commodities (whose prices are set on world markets) also rise, because price levels rise abroad as well as at home. Since these changes are exactly offsetting, relative prices of British and US goods are unchanged, both in the UK and in the US markets. There is, therefore, no change in the volumes of either imports or exports.

The equal rate of inflation in Britain and abroad leaves the relative prices of non-traded commodities, plus imported and exported commodities, all unchanged in the British market (and in foreign markets) and hence has no effect on the pattern of trade. There is no reason to expect any change in the UK's demand for imports or its supply of exports at the original exchange rate, and hence no reason to expect any shifts in demands and supplies of foreign exchange.

Equal rates of inflation in the two countries leave the equilibrium exchange rate unchanged.

Differing rates of inflation in the two countries: Consideration of the last two cases of changes in the price levels, shows that what matters is the relative rates of inflation between any two trading countries. Differences in the inflation rates will cause changes in imports and exports and hence changes in demands and supplies on the foreign-exchange market. Thus the exchange rate between the two currencies will change.

The conclusion that follows from a simple extension of the two cases just studied is important:

If the price level in one country is rising faster (falling slower) than that of another country, the first country's exchange rate will be depreciating (ceteris paribus).

Structural Changes

'Structural change' as we use the term in this chapter is an omnibus expression for anything that affects the patterns of international competitiveness, such as changes in cost structures and the invention of new products. For example, the firms in one country might lose out in the continued race to develop new, or improved, products. As a result, at the initial set of prices, consumers' demand would shift slowly away from that country's products and towards those of foreign countries. This would cause a slow trend-depreciation in the home country's exchange rate.

Dramatic changes, such as major shifts in OPEC pricing policies, will have similar effects, except that they may occur suddenly over a space of months rather than gradually over a space of years.

The general conclusion from what has been established so far is an important one.

Long-term changes in exchange rates can be accounted for mainly by the relative inflation rates and structural changes.

Capital Movements

Finally, we must consider the effects of capital flows on exchange rates. First, consider UK capital imports. If holders of US dollars wish to transfer funds to the UK for any reason, they will be demanders of pounds on the foreign-exchange market. This is equally true whether they wish to buy UK goods and services or UK financial assets. So capital imports, whether to put money into UK (sterling-denominated) bank accounts, to buy short-term Treasury or commercial bills, longer-term bonds, shares in joint-stock companies, or to build factories in the UK, all add to the demand for pounds on the foreign-exchange market. It follows that increased capital exports into the UK will increase the supply of dollars and cause their price to fall on the foreign-exchange market and hence cause sterling to appreciate.

Now consider UK capital exports. When holders of sterling wish to invest their funds abroad for any of the reasons listed in the previous paragraph, they become demanders of foreign exchange – US dollars in our simple case. This adds to the demand for dollars. It follows that, *ceteris paribus*, an increase in capital exports from the UK will increase the demand for dollars and hence bid up their price, causing sterling to depreciate.

This statement is true for short-term and long-term capital movements. However, since the motives that lead to capital movements often differ between the short and long terms, each needs to be considered.

Long-term capital: Long-term capital movements are mainly related to different prospects for real earnings on capital in various countries. A country that offers persistently high returns on capital will attract inflows of long-term capital. Expectations of long-term earnings also depend on the expectations that conditions will continue to be favourable to such earnings in the future. Thus expectations about the general political and economic stability of a country will influence its long-term capital flows.

Short-term capital: The owners of capital that moves from country to country for short periods are not interested in the long-term outlooks of various countries. Instead their main concerns are short-term interest rates and expectations of movements in exchange rates over the short term. If exchange rates are not expected to change over the short term, capital will tend to search out the highest short-term interest rates. A rise in one country's rates will, *ceteris paribus*, tend to cause an inflow of short-term capital (and hence an appreciation of the value of its currency on the foreign-exchange market).

Expected changes in exchange rates will also exert an influence. An expected fall in the country's exchange rate will mean capital losses when short-term capital is eventually moved out of a country, and this will tend to cause an exodus of short-term capital immediately. An expected rise in the exchange rate will mean capital gains when the capital is moved out of the country after the exchange adjustment occurs. This will tend to cause an influx of short-term capital so that its owners can be holding the country's currency when its value rises.

Changes in the Exchange Rate: a Summary

Figure 40.4 shows the demand and supply shifts that can cause the exchange rate to change. In all cases, the original price is p_0, the curve that shifts is indicated with a prime mark, and the new price is p_1. In each case, the horizontal axis measures the quantity of sterling demanded or supplied on the foreign-exchange market, while the vertical axis measures the dollar price of one pound sterling, i.e. the sterling exchange rate. Part (i) shows that sterling depreciates when there is an increase in the supply of sterling coming onto the foreign-exchange market. Part (ii) shows that the exchange rate also depreciates with a decrease in the demand for sterling. Parts (iii) and (iv) show that sterling appreciates when either the supply of sterling to the foreign-exchange market falls or the demand rises.

If you list all the causes of demand and supply curve shifts discussed in the previous sections, you can combine them with Figure 40.4 to show the effects of each of these on the exchange rate. For example, an outflow of capital from the UK increases the supply of sterling on the foreign-exchange market and, according to part (i), depreciates sterling. Conversely, an inflow of capital into the UK increases the demand for sterling on the foreign-exchange market and, according to part (iv), appreciates sterling.

From now on, we drop the specific example and refer to 'all foreign countries', instead of just the US, and to 'foreign exchange', instead of just the US dollar.

The Relation Between the Exchange Rate and the Balance of Payments

There is an important relation between the balance of payments and the exchange rate that is taken for granted in most policy discussions. To see what is involved, consider the determinants of the demand and supply of sterling on the foreign-exchange market.

The demand for sterling comes from three main sources: (i) UK exports, (ii) credit earnings on the UK invisible account, and (iii) UK capital imports. The reasons in these three cases are (i) to buy UK exports, holders of foreign currency must obtain sterling; (ii) to repatriate foreign earnings back to the UK, foreign currency must be turned into sterling; (iii) for foreigners to make investments in the UK, they require sterling.

The supply of sterling on the foreign-exchange market comes from three parallel sources: (i) UK imports, (ii) debit items on the invisibles account, and (iii) UK capital exports. The reasons in these three cases are (i) to buy foreign goods, UK importers must sell sterling on the foreign-exchange market; (ii) to send UK earnings abroad, sterling must be sold for foreign exchange; and (iii) for holders of sterling to make foreign investments, they must sell sterling and buy foreign exchange.

When the foreign-exchange market is in equilibrium, the quantity of sterling demanded is equal to the quantity supplied – where both the demand and supply come from the sources just identified. It follows that, when the foreign-exchange market is in equilibrium, with no intervention by the Bank of England, overall payments must be in balance with official financing at zero.

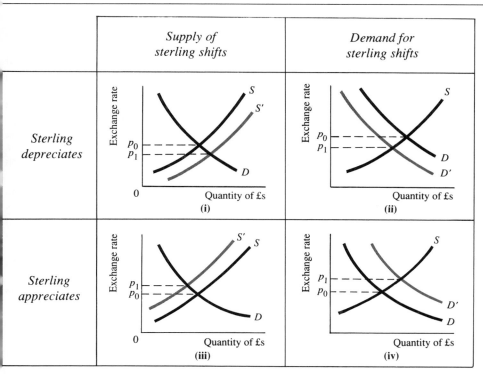

FIGURE 40.4 Causes of Changes in the Exchange Rate. The Figure shows the demand and supply curves for sterling on the foreign-exchange market plotted against the price of £1 sterling measured in US dollars (i.e. the sterling exchange rate).

In each panel, the original curves are D and S, which give the equilibrium exchange rate P_0. In each panel, one curve shifts to the position given by a grey curve. Comparing the new equilibrium exchange rates of P_1 with the original rate of P_0, gives the following conclusions. Sterling is depreciated by an increase in the supply of sterling on the foreign-exchange market (panel (i)) and/or a decrease in the demand for it (panel (ii)). Sterling is appreciated by a decrease in the supply of sterling on the foreign-exchange market (panel (iii)) and/or an increase in the demand for it (panel (iv)).

Now assume that the demand for sterling falls. We have seen that this will lead to a depreciation of the equilibrium price of sterling on the foreign-exchange market. Assume, however, that the Bank of England enters the market to stop sterling from depreciating. To do this, it must buy up the excess amount that is supplied. This means that the Bank will be buying sterling and selling foreign exchange, which will lead to a decline in its foreign-exchange reserves. The balance of payments will now show an overall deficit on current plus capital account (payments exceed receipts). That deficit will be covered by official financing, causing the Bank's foreign-exchange reserves to fall.

This leads to three important conclusions:

- **When the foreign-exchange market is in equilibrium with no government intervention, there will be an overall zero balance of payments on current plus capital account with no official settlements.**

- **When there is pressure on the exchange rate to fall that is being resisted by the Bank, there will be an overall balance-of-payments deficit on current plus capital account, and the Bank's foreign-exchange reserves will be falling.**

- **When there is pressure on sterling to appreciate which is being resisted by the Bank, there will be an overall balance-of-payments surplus on current plus capital account, and the exchange reserves of the Bank will be rising.**

The Value of the Exchange Rate in the Long Run

So far in this chapter we have shown how demand and supply determine exchange rates. We have also shown how various forces can shift demands or supplies on the foreign-exchange market and so cause exchange rates to change.

We now ask why is the average value of the exchange rate taken over several years what it is, rather than something else? Why, for example, was the average sterling-dollar exchange rate, around $1.50 between 1980 and 1986, well down from what it had been a decade and a half previously? Why did it rise to around $1.75 in the early 1990s?

The simple answer is that the relevant demand and supply curves intersected at a sterling price of around US$1.50 in the 1980s, but at higher prices in earlier decades. But why did these curves intersect at those prices rather than at other very different ones? One theory that tries to answer this question seeks to explain the long-run trend around which the actual market rate fluctuates. It is called the PURCHASING POWER PARITY (PPP) THEORY, and the long-term exchange rate predicted by this theory is called the PURCHASING POWER PARITY (PPP) EXCHANGE RATE.

The PPP rate is the one that equates the costs of purchasing a representative bundle of traded goods and services between two countries. Thus, if a representative bundle costs $100 in the US and £62.50 in the UK, the PPP exchange rate is $1 = £0.625 or, looked at the other way around, £1 = $1.60. At this exchange rate, it would cost the same for a holder of sterling to buy the bundle for £62.50 in the UK or to convert sterling into dollars and buy the bundle for $100 in the US.

We now need to explain a number of important points about the PPP rate.

(1) *If the exchange rate between two countries is at the PPP rate, neither will have an overall competitive advantage over the other since, on average, each country's goods have the same prices as the other's.* In these circumstances, each country will export to the other the goods that it can produce at home at a *relatively* lower price and will buy from the other the goods it can produce at home at a *relatively* high price.[1]

(2) *Changes in relative price levels change the PPP exchange rate.* To illustrate, say that in the above example an American inflation increases the price of the bundle of goods from $100 to $125 in the US while prices are unchanged in the UK. Now the PPP rate changes to $1 = £0.50 or, what is the same thing, £1 = $2. In other words, the pound appreciates and the dollar depreciates. (Don't forget Figure 40.1 is still there on page 000 to help you if you are bothered by these ratios or by which changes are a depreciation and which are an appreciation.) Notice that, if the actual rate follows the PPP rate, the American inflation does not put its firms at a competitive disadvantage. The rise in the US price level raises all of its costs and prices, but the depreciation of the exchange rate exactly offsets this so that the prices of the bundle of commodities remain the same in both countries. Indeed, the PPP rate has the effect of holding the relation between the price levels of the two countries constant when they are measured in a common currency.

(3) *If the external value of a country's currency is overvalued relative to its PPP rate, that country will tend to have a deficit on the balance of trade while, if it is undervalued, the country will tend to have a surplus.* Assume in the previous example that, although the cost of purchasing the representative bundle in the US rose from $100 to $125, the actual US exchange rate remained constant at $1 = £0.625. Now the US dollar is overvalued relative to its PPP rate. Converting the cost of the representative bundle from £62.50 to US dollars at the existing exchange rate yields $100 but, because of the inflation, the bundle costs $125 in the US. The same goods are, on average, cheaper in the UK than in the US. This will encourage Americans to buy more goods from the UK and discourage UK residents from buying American goods. American imports will rise and exports will fall, opening up a balance-of-trade deficit.

By the same argument, the UK exchange rate undervalues sterling relative to its PPP rate. (£1 is still only worth $1.60 when its PPP value is $2.) As we have seen, the UK will increase its exports to the US while reducing its imports from that country.

(4) Finally, consider capital movements. We saw on page

---

1 Those of you who have read Chapter 20 will recognize this as the workings of the law of *comparative* advantage.

325 of Chapter 29 that when a country is a net importer of capital (i.e. has a 'favourable' balance of payments on capital account) it also has a matching deficit on current account. Combining this with what we have just learned, leads to the conclusion that *capital-importing countries will tend to have exchange rates that are overvalued relative to their PPP rates – this will produce the deficit on current account needed to balance the surplus on capital account.*

Now consider countries that are net exporters of capital. Such countries have a deficit on capital account, which must be balanced by a surplus on current account. We have seen that surpluses are generated by having the country's actual exchange rate below its purchasing power parity rate. It follows that *countries that are net exporters of capital will tend to have exchange rates that are undervalued relative to their PPP rates.*

Different Exchange-Rate Concepts

Real and nominal rates: In Chapter 23, we discussed real and nominal values for national income. A similar distinction can be made with the exchange rate. The nominal exchange rate refers to the rate we have just been discussing, i.e. how much foreign currency does it take to buy a unit of home currency, or how much home currency it takes to buy a unit of foreign currency. It is expressed in nominal monetary units. For the sterling–US dollar rate, it is so many dollars in the first case above, and so many pence in the second case.

Real rates refer to purchasing power, i.e. to changes in the internal value of the domestic currency *relative to* its external value. Say, for example, that a local British inflation doubled the sterling prices of all domestic goods.

This is a halving of the internal purchasing-power of sterling. Assume also that the external value of the pound also halved, from being worth, say, US\$2 to US\$1. Now the nominal exchange rate has halved because the pound is worth only half as many US dollars as before. But the real exchange rate is unchanged because the relative prices of UK and US goods are unchanged. To see this, consider a British good that initially cost £1, and a US good that initially cost \$2. At the exchange rate of £1 = \$2, these goods have the same price when either the price of the US good is translated into sterling or the price of the British good is translated into dollars. After the local UK inflation the British good will cost £2, but at the exchange rate of £1 = \$1 the good still has the same dollar price as the US good (and the US good has the same sterling price as the British good).

In summary, a change in the nominal exchange rate means the domestic currency exchanges for a different amount of foreign currency, while a change in the real exchange rate means that the relative prices of domestic and foreign goods change when they are converted into a common currency unit at the prevailing nominal rate.

The trade-weighted exchange rate: We have seen how to calculate the exchange rate when we consider only two countries. When we consider foreign exchange in general, how do we calculate the appropriate exchange rate for sterling? One answer is to use what is called A TRADE-WEIGHTED EXCHANGE RATE. This rate is an average of the exchange rate between sterling and each of the UK's major trading partners, with each rate being weighted by the amount of trade between the UK and the country in question. As a result, a movement in the sterling

(continued on next page)

Summary

1 Exchange rates are the price of one national currency in terms of another. Their free-market values are determined by demands and supplies in the foreign-exchange market.

2 The demand for foreign exchange arises from the importing of goods and services and the exporting of capital. The supply of foreign exchange arises from the exporting of goods and services and the importing of capital.

3 A country's exchange rate will be depreciated by a rise in its relative price level, by structural changes that make it harder to export, and by the export of capital. The opposite changes will appreciate its rate.

4 The long-term trend value of the exchange rate is determined by purchasing power parity: the exchange rate will tend to change so as to hold

constant between countries the price of a bundle of internationally traded commodities expressed in a common currency.

5 The nominal exchange rate measures the number of units of foreign currency it takes to buy a unit of domestic currency. The real exchange rate corrects for changes in internal purchasing power and, therefore, measures changes in the amount of foreign goods that can be brought by a unit of domestic currency.

6 The trade-weighted exchange rate is a composite of the exchange rates between the domestic currency and each foreign currency where each rate is weighted by the volume of trade between the two countries. The effective exchange rate is similar to the trade-weighted rate but the weights reflect the importance of each rate in influencing the country's competitive position in foreign markets.

exchange rate with a major trading partner has a big effect on the trade-weighted exchange rate, while the equivalent movement with a minor trading partner has only a little effect.

The effective exchange rate: Changes in the trade-weighted exchange rate are valuable indicators of changes in a country's international price competitiveness, but they do not tell the whole story. To illustrate, note that Sweden does little trade with Canada, so changes in the Swedish kroner–Canadian dollar exchange rate will have little effect on the Swedish trade-weighted exchange rate. But Sweden and Canada compete strongly in the sale of a number of commodities, such as pulp and paper, to the United States. If the kroner depreciates against the Canadian dollar, Swedish exports to the US will gain a price advantage over Canadian exports.

The International Monetary Fund calculates a series called the effective exchange rate. This attempts to weight changes on individual exchange rates by their importance in influencing competitiveness against each other's products and against those from other countries. Thus a change in the Swedish kroner–Canadian dollar rate would be weighted by the importance of Swedish sales to Canada *and* of Swedish sales to other countries that are made in competition with Canadian products.

Questions

1 What would be the effect on the external value of sterling of each of the following?
   (a) A rise in UK interest rates.
   (b) A local recession in the UK.
   (c) A large inflation in the rest of the world, unmatched in the UK.
   (d) The discovery of large new oil supplies in the North Sea.
   (e) An unexpected rise in outputs and incomes in Eastern Europe raises their demands for imports.

2 Choose the correct alternatives: A local UK inflation will (increase/decrease) the demand for US dollars on the 'UK' foreign-exchange market. It will also (increase/decrease) the supply of US dollars being offered in exchange for sterling. Both of these changes will tend to (appreciate/depreciate) the value of the US dollar against sterling.

3 True or False?
   (a) The equilibrium exchange rate is the one that equates the demands and supplies on the foreign-exchange market.
   (b) The purchasing power parity exchange rate alters as a country's price level alters relative to those of its trading partners.
   (c) If the price of sterling rises from US$1.60 to US$1.80, more sterling will be demanded because it has become more valuable.
   (d) A rise in the price of sterling on the foreign-exchange market will tend to make UK exports more expensive in foreign markets.

4 Look at Figure 40.2. What curve shifts would be required to shift the exchange rate to $2.00 to the pound? What internal changes in the UK might cause either of these shifts?

41 Exchange Rate Regimes

A system for determining exchange rates is called an EXCHANGE-RATE REGIME. Although the nations of the world have tried many different regimes, no system has proved fully satisfactory.

TWO MAIN TYPES OF REGIME

Among the principal payments regimes that the world has used, two main groups can be distinguished, 'fluctuating' and 'fixed' exchange rates. We briefly introduce these in turn. Then we give a brief historical sketch of how the schemes in use have varied over the twentieth century. After that, we consider in more detail the theory of how each main type of system works, and the relative merits of each.

Fixed exchange rate regimes

Under a regime of FIXED EXCHANGE RATES, the rates are fixed at some PAR VALUE (called, as we shall see, the *central value* in the European system). Under a truly fixed-rate regime, these rates are determined exogenously and are not subject to easy change by the central bank.

The only truly fixed system seen in this century was the gold standard. Under this system, each country's currency had a fixed value set by the amount of gold into which it could be converted, called the currency's gold content. The exchange rate between two currencies was then set by their relative gold contents. For example, the British pound sterling was convertible throughout most of the nineteenth century into 4.86 times as much gold as was the US dollar. Thus the exchange rate was £1.00 sterling = US $4.86. As long as the gold content of each national currency was fixed, exchange rates were fixed.

The second form of a fixed exchange rate is the one found in the world today. It is often called an ADJUSTABLE-PEG REGIME. In it, the central bank fixes the exchange rate within a publicly announced, narrow band by buying and selling foreign exchange whenever the free-market rate threatens to go outside of that band. It accepts, however, that in the face of a persistent disequilibrium, it will alter the rate that it is maintaining. When a pegged exchange rate is altered, the currency is said to be DEVALUED when its external value is lowered, and REVALUED when its external value is raised. When a whole system of pegged rates have their values changed, the rates in the system are said to have been 'realigned'.

The difference between the gold-standard version of fixed rates and the adjustable-peg version is that, under the gold standard, the exchange rates between currencies were set by the relative intrinsic values of the two currencies which could not easily be changed; while, in the adjustable-peg system, the exchange rates are set by government decree (and supported by central-bank market intervention) and can readily be changed when that seems warranted.

Fluctuating rate regimes

The second major category of regimes is called one of FLUCTUATING EXCHANGE RATES. In the pure or FLOATING form of this regime, called a system of 'freely fluctuating rates', exchange rates are determined by market demands and supplies, as described in the previous chapter. There is no central bank intervention into these markets, and exchange rates are determined wholly by free-market forces. This pure form of fluctuating rates is seldom found in the world today. When a fluctuating exchange rate rises on the free market, it is said to be APPRECIATING; when it falls, it is said to be DEPRECIATING.

When rates are allowed to fluctuate in today's world, there is almost always some substantial central bank intervention into these markets. The intervention is designed to stabilize the rates to some extent. This gives rise to a system called MANAGED FLOATS. In this regime, the central bank seeks to have some stabilizing influence on the exchange rate, but does not try to fix it at a publicly announced par value. It generally has its own target range for the exchange rate and intervenes to hold the rate within that target. But the range is not publicly announced and can be changed without fanfare, whenever that seems advisable to the central bank.

The difference between the freely fluctuating and the managed floating versions of fluctuating exchange rate regimes is that, in the former, there is no central bank intervention into exchange markets while, in the latter, the central bank intervenes in the market to stabilize the rate around its own target values, which are not publicly announced and which can be changed at will.

TWENTIETH-CENTURY REGIMES

The world has worked under several exchange regimes in the present century. In this section, we briefly outline them, after which we study the theory that explains the behaviour of each type of regime.

The gold standard

When the twentieth century began, the world had been working for more than a century under a payments system called the GOLD STANDARD. In this system, each country tied its own national currency to gold by guaranteeing that holders of a unit of its paper currency could convert it on demand into a stated amount of gold. The gold convertibility of different national currencies established a fixed rate of exchange between them.

The gold standard broke down under a series of crises that rocked the world's financial systems during the 1920s and early 1930s. Country after country dropped the gold convertibility of their currencies and thus removed the force that fixed the exchange rates between them. The gold standard finally came to an end when, in September 1931, the UK, then the world's most important trading nation, suspended the gold convertibility of sterling. There followed a period of fluctuating exchange rates. Some countries pegged their rates to the currencies of one of their major trading partners. The currencies of most of the major trading countries, however, fluctuated freely on foreign-exchange markets where their rates were determined by the demands and supplies of foreign exchange.

With the outbreak of the Second World War in 1939, virtually all of the world's trading nations pegged their exchange rates and regulated foreign-exchange markets so as to use funds earned from exports for their war efforts.

Bretton Woods:　In 1944, representatives of the allied countries, who were by then obviously winning the war against Germany and Japan, met in the town of Bretton Woods in New Hampshire, USA to design the postwar payments regime. The system that emerged was an adjustable peg system. The system was also called the BRETTON WOODS SYSTEM after the town where it was born. This was the world's first payments system to be designed wholly by conscious acts of policy. The earlier gold standard arose because each country made its domestic currency convertible into gold and the fixed rates followed as a consequence. The regime of fluctuating rates that followed arose without central design, and currencies were allowed to find their own levels on free markets.

The functioning of the Bretton Woods system was helped by a new international organization, the International Monetary Fund (IMF). This organization was designed to provide assistance to countries who were having difficulty maintaining their exchange rates in the face of fluctuations in demand and supply that, although severe, were thought to be temporary. The Bretton Woods system served the world well for two decades. Then in the late 1960s, financial markets were once again rocked by a series of crises and the regime of fixed exchange rates became increasingly difficult to defend. Finally, in the early 1970s, the system was abandoned as country after country announced that it would no longer defend a fixed par value for its exchange rate. Although the Bretton Woods system is long gone, the IMF continues in existence. It offers considerable assistance to countries with balance-of-payments problems.

Fluctuating rates

A period of freely fluctuating exchange rates followed. However, fluctuations turned out to be more extreme than had been expected, and slowly, central banks in many countries increased their degree of intervention into foreign-exchange markets. As that happened, the payment system evolved from something close to freely floating rates, to one of managed floats.

The European exchange rate mechanism

As a result of the unsatisfactory experience with the regime of fluctuating exchange rates, the countries of the European Community decided to establish a regime of fixed rates among their own currencies which would then fluctuate as a block against the other currencies of the world. In doing this they operated within the EUROPEAN MONETARY SYSTEM (EMS) which has the broad aim of promoting European monetary stability.

In 1979 they set up, as a key part of this system, the *European Exchange Rate Mechanism (ERM)*. The system is designed to stabilize exchange rates between its members, in a manner broadly similar to what was done under the Bretton Woods system. In 1990, there were nine members, Germany, France, Italy, Netherlands, Denmark, Belgium, Luxembourg, Ireland, and Spain. In 1991 the UK became the tenth member.

The basic principle of the system is that each country agrees to stabilize the external value of its currency around a value called the CENTRAL RATE. The central rate between sterling and the German Mark was DM2.95 when the UK joined the ERM. These central rates are actually fixed against the EUROPEAN CURRENCY UNIT (ECU), which is an average of EC currencies with each one given a specified weight in line with that country's economic importance. (The ECU is discussed later in this chapter.)

Each currency is allowed to fluctuate around its central rate within specified margins. In 1992, these margins were 2.25 per cent for eight of the members, and 6 per cent for the UK and Spain. The wider bands for the UK and Spain were due to the uncertainties on joining the new arrangement. Over time, as the exchange rates of these new members settle down, the bands may be narrowed for them.

The bands are defined against all other currencies in the EMS so that sterling cannot get more than 6 per cent above the weakest currency in the group, nor more than 6 per cent below the strongest. When these limits are reached for any pair of countries, the central banks of both countries must intervene in the foreign-exchange market to prevent the two rates from diverging further.

When the central rates get permanently out of line, as measured by the EMS's 'divergence indicators', realignments are permitted. But such changes in exchange rate must be agreed by all members. To prevent these from occurring so frequently that the advantages of exchange rate stability are lost, member countries are expected to pursue broadly similar macroeconomic policies. This is to ensure that the free-market rates stay close to the central rates most of the time.

In the first decade of the EMS, there were no less than twelve realignments of exchange rates. Such realignments have, however, become less and less frequent as the macroeconomic policies of member countries began to converge.

In conclusion we note that managed floats is the system operated by most of the world's countries. Although the countries of the ERM have rates that are fixed among themselves, their currencies float against the other currencies of the world. So the system found in Europe is a mixture of fixed rates within the ERM, and a managed float between their currencies as a block and the currencies of the rest of the world.

After this brief historical review, we turn our attention to a discussion of the two most important regimes in use in the world today, fixed and fluctuating rates, noting however that the version of fixed rates is the adjustable peg and the version of fluctuating rates is the managed float.

FIXED EXCHANGE RATE REGIMES

Since there are no longer any truly fixed-rate regimes in the world, adjustable peg systems are usually referred to as fixed-rate systems. In this usage, fixed-rate systems have exchange rates that are stabilized by central bank intervention but the rates can be adjusted occasionally when the free-market rate is considered to have departed from the fixed rate by too much.

Intervention to fix the exchange rate: When a country fixes its exchange rate, its central bank must intervene in the foreign-exchange market whenever its exchange rate threatens to go outside of an agreed narrow band on either side of its 'central rate'.

Having agreed on the central value of its exchange rate, the Bank must then manage matters so that the chosen rate can actually be maintained. In the face of short-term fluctuations in market demand and supply, the Bank can maintain its fixed exchange rate by entering the exchange market and buying and selling foreign exchange as required. It offsets imbalances in demand and supply by its own sales or purchases of foreign exchange as shown in Figure 41.1.

To do this, the central bank has to hold reserves of acceptable foreign exchange or be able to borrow them when they are needed. When there is any abnormally low demand for its country's currency on the market, the Bank supports the exchange rate by selling foreign-exchange and buying up domestic currency. This depletes its reserves of foreign exchange. When there is an abnormally high demand for its country's currency on the foreign-exchange market, the Bank prevents the currency from appreciating in value by selling domestic currency in return for foreign exchange. This augments its reserves of foreign exchange.

As long as the central bank is maintaining an exchange rate that equates demand and supply on average, the policy can be successful. Sometimes the Bank will be buying and other times selling, but its holdings of foreign exchange (i.e. its reserves) will fluctuate around a constant average level.

Pressure to alter the fixed rate: If, however, there is a long-lasting shift in demand or supply of a nation's currency on the foreign-exchange market, the long-term equilibrium rate will move away from the pegged rate. It will then be difficult to maintain the pegged rate. For example, if there is a major inflation in the UK while prices are stable in the other EC countries, the purchasing power parity (PPP) value of the sterling exchange rate will fall. In a free market the pound would depreciate. But a fixed exchange rate is not a free-market rate. If the Bank of England persists in trying to maintain the original exchange rate, it will have to meet the excess demand for foreign exchange by selling from its reserves. This policy can persist only as long as it has sufficient reserves of its own, or that it can borrow from the various sources available to it. These reserves must be sold to hold the exchange rate

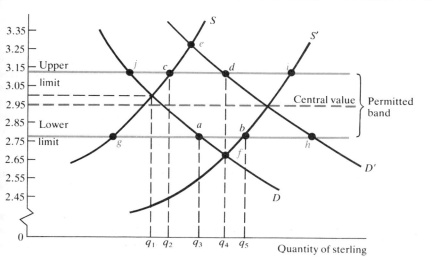

FIGURE 41.1 Central Bank Action to Fix the Exchange Rate. In the Figure, the central value of the pound against the German mark is DM2.95 to the pound. The rate is permitted to fluctuate within a band from DM3.13 and DM2.78. When the demand and supply curves are D and S, no action is needed. If, however, the supply curve shifts to S' while the demand curve stays at D, the Bank must enter the market and buy ab of sterling (selling marks or other foreign exchange) to prevent sterling's price falling below the lower band. If, instead, the demand curve shifts to D' while the supply curve stays at S the Bank must sell cd of sterling (and buy marks) to prevent sterling from rising above the permitted upper band.

above its long-run equilibrium level. The central bank cannot do this indefinitely. Sooner or later the reserves that it has, and those that it is willing and/or able to borrow, will be exhausted. At that point the exchange rate will have to be devalued.

Policies to sustain a fixed rate: The art of running a fixed exchange rate without the need for frequent devaluations or revaluations, lies in having the central bank run its monetary policy so as to keep the equilibrium exchange rate at, or near, the pegged rate. This means avoiding major inflations or deflations that are not matched in other countries. If one member of the EMS, say the UK, has a major inflation not matched in the other EC countries, this will, as we saw earlier in the chapter, lower its equilibrium exchange rate. It will then be difficult for the Bank of England to maintain the original exchange rate even when it gets the type of assistance from other EMS members described below. Sooner or later, sterling will have to be devalued to match the change in its PPP rate.

Under a flexible exchange rate, a country can run its domestic demand-management policy primarily with domestic objectives in mind. Say, for example, that a significant recession has occurred along with a 2 per cent inflation rate. The government may be willing to adopt expansionary fiscal and monetary policies to counter the recession even at the risk of an acceleration of inflation, say to 5 or 6 per cent. If the resulting rise of UK prices causes a deficit on merchandise trade, the exchange rate can be allowed to depreciate to offset the higher UK prices. (See the discussion on pages 465–6.) The flexible exchange rate allows the country independence to adjust its fiscal and monetary policy with domestic goals in mind. If these cause prices to get out of line with those of foreign competitors, the free-market exchange rate will adjust to maintain the country's international competitiveness.

Under fixed rates, however, this policy independence is seriously compromised. If the domestic expansionary policies put downward pressure on sterling, the Bank must resist this. It must buy sterling on the foreign-exchange market to support its price. The Bank can only do this for as long as is permitted by its reserves of foreign exchange. Sooner or later, if devaluation is ruled out, it will have to depress domestic demand to remove the pressure on sterling. Indeed, to prevent UK prices from getting far out of line, it will probably not engage in the expansionary policy in the first place.

In other words, with a fixed exchange rate, the prime policy objective must be to prevent balance-of-payments problems from arising by never letting the country's inflation rate get out of line with those of the country's trading partners.

Membership of the ERM, or any other regime of fixed exchange rates, means that the goals of domestic policy must be subjugated to the goals of maintaining a fixed exchange rate – which means keeping international payments in balance at that rate.

It was this 'sovereignty issue' that upset the opponents of the UK's membership of the EMS. They wished to keep domestic policy goals as the prime goals of UK monetary and fiscal policy.

Ironically, it was this same 'sovereignty issue' that appealed to many of the supporters of the UK's membership of the EMS. They felt that the UK's domestic performance would be improved by having to keep its inflation rate in line with those of Germany and France. They welcomed the loss of policy independence if that meant being forced to have an inflation record about as good as Germany's.

Advantages of Fixed Exchange Rates

Advocates of fixed exchange rates feel that a regime of fixed rates has many advantages.

- They feel that secure knowledge of what rates will be encourages international trade.
- They also wish to prevent speculation, which they fear would destabilize rates under a regime of floating rates as speculators rushed alternately to buy and sell a currency as a result of waves of optimism and pessimism about what was going to happen to its market value.
- They worry that nations will try to gain competitive trading advantages over each other by engaging in bouts of self-defeating devaluations and counter-devaluations of their currencies. They feel that fixed rates, with only occasional changes in the face of a clear disequilibrium, would prevent such beggar-thy-neighbour policies from breaking out again as they had in the 1930s. (See Chapter 29, page 331.)
- They feel that the need to prevent the exchange rate from being devalued will act as a major restraint on policies that encourage inflation. When devaluation is an easy option, there is no internal restraint on following expansionary monetary and fiscal policies that end up causing rapid inflations.

Problems with Fixed Exchange Rates

The fixed-exchange-rate system has three characteristic problems, which we discuss below.

The provision of reserves

We saw on page 466 of Chapter 40 that fluctuations in current- and capital-account payments cause the free-market exchange rate to fluctuate. To prevent such fluctuations when rates are fixed, the central bank buys and sells foreign exchange in the necessary amounts. These operations require the authorities to hold reserves of foreign exchange, without which they cannot maintain a pegged rate.

European countries hold their reserves in many forms, including gold, foreign currencies, SPECIAL DRAWING RIGHTS (SDRs), and European currency units (ECUs).

SDRs have been issued by the International Monetary Fund (IMF) since 1969. Each IMF member is assigned a SDR quota which can be used to obtain an equivalent amount of foreign currencies from other member countries. SDRs can be used to cope with short-term balance-of-payments problems.

These SDRs are available for operating managed floats with currencies of the rest of the world. For stabilizing rates within the EMS, several lines of credit are available, beyond each central bank's normal reserves of foreign exchange. The most important is the VERY SHORT TERM FACILITY (VSTF). With this arrangement, each central bank must make available unlimited short-term credit facilities in its own currency for any other Bank that must intervene in markets to stop its currency from breaking through its lower margin. This ensures that no forced devaluation will take place. (Of course if support of a currency at its lower margin persists, the central banks will try to agree on a currency realignment among themselves.)

The other facility is the ECU which, like the SDR, is a pure unit of account. ECUs are a credit on the books of the European Monetary Cooperation Fund given in return for payments of gold or foreign exchange. They can be used to settle accounts between central banks arising when a Bank intervenes to stop its currency breaking through its margin.

The rest of the world would still have problems in finding adequate reserves if it were to adopt a fixed exchange rate system that required intervention to stabilize rates at pre-announced central values. The countries of the ERM have solved this problem for stabilizing rates among themselves (but not against the rest of the world) by agreeing to provide unlimited reserves to each other.

Coping with long-term disequilibria

With fixed exchange rates, long-term disequilibrium can be expected to develop because of lasting shifts in PPP exchange rates. There are three important reasons for such shifts. First, different trading countries may have different rates of inflation. Second, changes in the demands for, and supplies of, imports and exports are associated with long-term economic growth. Third, structural changes, such as major new innovations or a change in the price of oil, cause major changes in imports and exports.

The associated shifts in demand and supply on the foreign-exchange market imply that, even starting from a current-account equilibrium with imports equal to exports, there is no reason to believe that equilibrium will exist at the same rate of exchange 5 or 10 years later. Indeed, the rate of exchange that will lead to a balance-of-payments equilibrium will tend to change over time; over a decade the change can be substantial.

Governments may react to long-term disequilibria in at least three ways.

First, the exchange rate can be changed whenever it is clear that difficulty in maintaining the existing pegged exchange rate is the result of a long-term shift in the PPP exchange rate, and not the result of some transient factor.

Second, the country's overall price level can be changed to make the present fixed exchange rate become the equi-

librium rate. To restore equilibrium, countries with overvalued currencies need to have deflations and countries with undervalued currencies need to have inflations. But countries with overvalued currencies find deflations difficult and costly to accomplish – e.g. reductions in aggregate demand intended to lower the price level are likely to raise unemployment.[1] Countries with undervalued rates often have explicit policies of avoiding inflation.

Third, restrictions called EXCHANGE CONTROLS can be imposed on trade and foreign payments. Imports and foreign spending by tourists and governments can be restricted, and the export of capital can be slowed or even stopped. (The UK did this from 1940 to 1979.) As world trade and investment have become more globalized, developed countries have been increasingly reluctant to use exchange controls. For one thing, they are upsetting to a country's trade and investment position. For another thing, today's capital markets are so sophisticated, and many firms so international, that it is difficult to make such controls on the movement of short-term funds effective. Many countries do, however, have restrictions on foreign direct investment. It is not easy for foreigners to buy equities in the firms of many European companies. These restrictions, however, are to control foreign ownership, not to restrict payments to maintain a disequilibrium exchange rate.

Coping with speculative crises

The most important reason for speculative crises is that, over time, equilibrium exchange rates get further and further away from any given set of fixed rates. When the disequilibrium becomes obvious to everyone, traders and speculators come to believe that a realignment of rates is due. There is a rush to buy currencies expected to be revalued and a rush to sell currencies expected to be devalued. Even if the authorities take drastic steps to maintain rates at their current pegged values, there may be doubt that these measures will work before the exchange reserves are exhausted. Speculative flows of funds can reach very large proportions, and it may be impossible to avoid changing the exchange rate under such pressure.

As the PPP value of a country's exchange rate changes over time, possibly under the impact of high inflation, it becomes obvious that the central bank is having more and more difficulty holding the pegged rate. So when a crisis arises, speculators sell the country's currency. If it is devalued, they can buy it back at a lower price and earn a capital gain. If it is not, they can buy it back at the price at which they sold it and lose only the commission costs on the deal. This asymmetry, with speculators having a chance to make large profits by risking only a small loss, was what eventually destroyed the Bretton Woods system of pegged but adjustable exchange rates.

---

1 In a world in which all countries have positive inflation rates, 'deflating' to reduce a payments deficit requires holding one's inflation rate below those of most other countries – rather than actually reducing one's own price level. The domestic implications remain, however, that aggregate demand needs to be restrained, usually with the consequence of rising unemployment.

BOX 41.1 British Interest Rates Fall

'But it is always possible to reduce British interest rates by comparison with German ones, and stay within the ERM, if the markets believe that UK inflation is falling.... The main reason why the gap between British and German interest rates has halved... is that the markets believe British inflation will fall.'

(Christopher Huhne in *The Independent on Sunday*, 7 April 1991)

This short quotation refers to a debate about the advisability of lowering UK interest rates in early 1991. As mentioned in this chapter, membership of the ERM implies some loss of autonomy in monetary policy for the UK. The quotation argues, however, that the ERM will not constrain the Bank from lowering UK interest rates, if expectations of UK inflation are falling at the same time.

Questions

1 Why might the UK's membership of the ERM constrain the Bank of England in its policy with respect to UK interest rates?
2 Why will UK interest rates fall relative to German rates if people expect the UK inflation rate to fall?
3 What influence would varying expectations of the German inflation rate have on the 'interest rate gap'?

or be able to borrow them, in order to stabilize the exchange rate.

- When exchange realignments are needed, destabilizing speculations are likely to occur.
- The need to operate domestic policies so as to hold the free-market exchange rate near to the existing fixed rate. This is often referred to as the loss of sovereignty over domestic monetary and fiscal policy. It was a major reason for the reluctance of Mrs Thatcher, and some of her advisors, to allow the UK to join the EMS.

FLEXIBLE EXCHANGE RATE REGIMES

Under a system of flexible exchange rates, demand and supply determine exchange rates without any government intervention. Since the foreign-exchange rate varies to ensure that the demand and supply of foreign exchange is always equal, governments can turn their attention to such domestic problems as lowering inflation and unemployment, leaving the exchange rate and the balance of payments to take care of themselves – at least so went the theory before flexible rates were introduced.

Unfortunately, this optimistic picture did not materialize when the world went over to flexible exchange rates in the early 1970s. Free-market fluctuations in exchange rates were far greater – and hence potentially more upsetting to the performance of national economies and to the flow of international trade – than many economists had anticipated. As a result, central banks have felt the need to intervene quite frequently and extensively to stabilize exchange rates.

Speculative behaviour

During the Bretton Woods period of fixed exchange rates, the advocates of floating rates argued that speculators would stabilize the actual rate within a narrow band around the PPP rate. The argument was that, since everyone knew the long-term equilibrium exchange rate was the PPP rate, deviations from that rate would quickly be removed by speculators seeking a profit when the rate returned to its PPP level. To illustrate, suppose the PPP rate is US$2.00 = £1.00 and that the actual rate falls to $1.90 = £1.00. The argument was that speculators would rush to buy pounds at $1.90, expecting to sell them for $2.00 when the rate returned to its PPP level. This very action would raise the demand for sterling and help push its value back towards $2.00. Such behaviour is called STABILIZING SPECULATIVE BEHAVIOUR.

Such behaviour could be relied upon to stabilize the exchange rate near its PPP value *if* speculators could be sure that the deviations would be small and short-lived. But as we have noted, the swings around the PPP rate have been wide and have lasted for long periods. Under these circumstances, speculation can no longer be relied on to stabilize the exchange rate at, or near, its PPP rate.

To understand this last point, consider an example. Assume that sterling fell to US$1.90 when its PPP rate

The problem under Bretton Woods was that governments were very reluctant to change their fixed rates. Instead, they tried to defend existing rates well beyond the time that it was obvious to everyone that adjustments were necessary. As a result, there was an enormous incentive to speculate on the inevitable, and *large*, adjustments which were sure to come before too long.

European governments who belong to the EMS have been better at coping with these speculative problems. They have been willing to readjust fixed rates well before balance-of-payments problems became so obvious as to set up vast amounts of destabilizing speculations. By changing the rates more frequently, and by smaller amounts, and by having larger reserves through various intergovernmental arrangements, speculative crises of large proportions have been avoided. Whether this can be continued in the future remains to be seen.

Summary

The main disadvantages of a fixed rate system are:

- **Central banks need to hold large quantities of reserves,** was $2.00. If speculators knew that deviations were short-lasting, they would rush to buy sterling hoping to sell it back at $2.00 for a profit. However, when experience showed that rates could deviate from their PPP rates a great deal, and for long periods of time, speculators came to understand that the rate could go far below $1.90, possibly as low as $1.60, and that it could stay there for quite a while before returning to $2.00. In that case it might be worth speculating on a price of $1.80 next week rather than a price of $2.00 in some indefinite future. This would lead speculators to sell sterling and thus drive its price down even further. This is called DESTABILIZING SPECULATIVE BEHAVIOUR.

The extremely important conclusion is that the wide swings in exchange rates that occur show that speculative buying and selling cannot always be relied on to hold exchange rates very close to their PPP values.

Exchange-rate overshooting

A second reason for exchange-rate volatility under flexible rates stems from the response of holders of short-term funds to variations in monetary policy.

Assume that the central bank of one country is trying to reduce a current inflation through tight monetary policy. This will, as we saw in Chapter 42, cause that country's interest rates to rise. Higher interest rates will attract those with money to lend for short periods of time. So if, for example, the Bank of England drives up the UK interest rate in pursuit of an anti-inflationary policy, those with funds lent out in New York, Tokyo and Paris will want to move their funds to London to take advantage of the higher rates.

This will mean a large extra demand for sterling on the foreign-exchange market and, as we saw earlier in this chapter, sterling will appreciate. Money will continue to flow in until the advantages of lending in London are no more than the advantages of lending elsewhere.

But how can that be if interest rates are higher in the UK than elsewhere? The answer lies in exchange-rate risk.

Lenders know that sterling is high on the exchange market only because of the movement of funds to take advantage of the high interest rates. Once the Bank has inflation under control, it will allow interest rates to fall and the funds will move out once again. This means that the exchange rate can be expected to depreciate in the

---

BOX 41.2 A Long Dark Winter

'Evidence that Britain is in recession mounts by the day. Some economists and newspapers are already panicking. The *Sunday Times*, for example, argues that "the high pound is a job destroyer", and wants an immediate cut in interest rates and a devaluation – barely two months after Britain joined the ERM. Mr Lamont, the Chancellor of the Exchequer, ... has ruled out devaluation and warned that interest rates will not be cut until sterling picks up from its current position at the bottom of its exchange-rate band.

'Mr Lamont is right. ... to devalue now would defeat the main purpose of entering the ERM. This was not, as some seem to believe, to give industry a competitive edge, but to defeat inflation. True, for every month that Britain's inflation rate remains above Germany's its competitiveness worsens, but devaluation would be quickly wiped out by price rises. The only permanent cure is for industry to restrain cost rises.

'The pound's present weakness is attributable not to an unsustainable high exchange rate, but to a continuing scepticism in the financial markets about the government's commitment to the ERM and high interest rates, in the face of a recession and an approaching election. A devaluation would only confirm that scepticism. Mr Lamont's task is to convince the markets and companies that devaluation is off the menu. They may take some convincing, which will mean a longer and deeper recession.'

(*The Economist*, 22 December 1990)

This chapter discussed the loss of sovereignty over monetary policy implicit in the UK's membership of the ERM. This quotation suggests that the loss may have been seen by some as an advantage. The reason is that it may force UK monetary policy to keep the UK inflation rate in line with the German rate, which has been much lower than the UK rate over the last forty years. The article also asserts that the effects of a devaluation would be quickly cancelled out by a rise in domestic prices. Economic theory does not predict that this result will necessarily follow a devaluation. (If it always followed, devaluations would never remove payments imbalances.) But it would follow, *if* UK wages rose in line with the devaluation, causing prices to rise as wage costs rose.

Questions

1 In what sense is a high inflation rate combined with a fixed exchange rate 'a job destroyer'?
2 Why should scepticism about the government's commitment to the ERM lead to a weakness in the value of the pound on foreign-exchange markets?
3 Why should membership of the ERM impose stiff anti-inflationary monetary policy on the Bank of England?
4 The quotation in Box 41.1 was written four months *after* the above quotation. Can you guess what happened in the meantime? Does *The Economist* appear to have been right in the advice it was giving?

future. When it does, funds invested in London will be worth less in terms of the currencies of other countries. As a result, funds continue to flow into the UK now, driving sterling up in the foreign-exchange market, until the *expected depreciation in the future* just compensates for the *extra interest to be earned in the present*.

This process can take a year or more, depending on how long the tight monetary policy is needed, which in turn depends on how fast the inflation rate responds. In the meantime, the high exchange rate puts the country's export industries under extreme competitive pressure. They may lose foreign markets which are hard to regain after the exchange rate returns to its PPP value.

Under flexible exchange rates, tight anti-inflationary monetary policy that drives up domestic interest rates, leads to an inflow of short-term capital, which appreciates the exchange rate until the expected future depreciation just counterbalances the current interest premium.

A REGIME OF MANAGED FLOATS

As a result of the early experience with floating exchange rates, and the discovery that speculation could not be relied on to hold actual rates near their purchasing power rates, most countries quickly adopted a system of managed floating rates.

A major difference between the system of managed floats and the Bretton Woods system is that central banks no longer publicly announce par values for exchange rates that they are committed in advance to defend even at heavy cost. Central banks are thus free to adjust their exchange-rate targets as circumstances change. Sometimes they leave the rate completely free to fluctuate, and at other times they interfere actively to alter the exchange rate from its free-market value.

Although under managed floats, central banks do intervene in the foreign-exchange market in an effort to reduce some of its fluctuations, they have not always had sufficient reserves to stop major exchange-rate fluctuations and overshootings of the sort discussed above. Of course, they can never hope to resist a shift in the PPP rate permanently.

So some of the main advantages and disadvantages of systems of flexible exchange rates are as follows:

Advantages:
- Governments do not need to subjugate domestic policies to the concerns of maintaining the existing exchange rate, nor do they need, unless they wish to for domestic reasons, to co-ordinate their macroeconomic policies with those of their trading partners.
- Governments need not worry about being caught in speculative runs from (or towards) their currency; if these happen, they just let the exchange rate take the pressure until the speculation stops.
- The exchange rate will slowly adjust as international differences in inflation rates, and structural changes, cause the PPP rate to alter.

Disadvantages:
- Short-term fluctuations in the exchange rate can be a source of uncertainty that harms trade.
- Speculation can cause wide swings in the exchange rate which can do harm to the export, and import-competing sectors.
- Variations in the domestic policies that cause variations in interest rates can set up large movements of funds that drive the exchange rate away from its PPP rate for long periods of time.

Summary

1 The members of the European Exchange Rate Mechanism (ERM) fix the exchange rates among their currencies by allowing the actual rate to fluctuate only within narrow margins on either side of a *central value*. This establishes a regime of fixed rates among their currencies, while they have a joint, flexible rate against other currencies, against whom the European currencies fluctuate as a block.

2 Major advantages of an exchange regime of fixed rates are greater short-run security of international values and the avoidance of some speculative capital movements that cause foreign-exchange rates to diverge far from the PPP rate, and the pressure it creates to prevent a country's inflation rate from exceeding those of its trading partners. The disadvantages are the need to adjust domestic policy to maintain external balance, the difficulty of providing adequate reserves, the difficulty of making adjustments of the rate when the PPP rate begins to diverge significantly from the pegged rate, and the enormous speculative movements of capital that occur when people come to feel that the pegged rate must be changed.

3 Major advantages of flexible rates are that policymakers do not have to subjugate domestic policy to the needs of external balance. The major disadvantage is that the actual rate can diverge greatly from the PPP rate because of capital movements.

4 Managed floats attempt to get some of the best of both worlds by allowing the exchange rate to vary so as to achieve a payments balance (and so freeing domestic policy for domestic objectives) while maintaining enough intervention to stop the most extreme of speculative swings in exchange rates.

Managed Floats

- Managed floats share all of the above advantages and disadvantages, with the added advantage that the central bank can intervene to stop undesirable short-term fluctuations when it seems sensible to do so. In principle, this regime could combine much of the stability of fixed rates with the steady adjustability of flexible rates to changing economic circumstances. In practice, fluctuations under managed flexible rates are still large enough to worry policy-makers.

The worry expressed in the last sentence is enough to guarantee that the debate over changes in the exchange regime will continue over the next decade.

Questions

1 Which One or More of the following is a characteristic of a regime of fixed exchange rates?
   (a) The inflation rate must be constrained to be close to those of major trading partners.
   (b) Exchange-rate overshooting will periodically put pressure on the country's export sector.
   (c) The target rate is a secret known only to the central bank and its advisor.
   (d) Having access to sufficient reserves is a key problem.

2 Look at Figure 41.1:
   (a) How much will the Bank have to buy or sell to stabilize the exchange rate within the permitted range if the demand and supply curves are (i) D and S', (ii) S' and D', (iii) S and D'?
   (b) How much would the Bank have to buy or sell if it wished to stabilize the pound at (i) its *lower limit* if the curves were S and D', and (ii) at its *upper limit* if the curves were D and S'?
   (c) What would the free-market exchange rate be if the curves were (i) D' and S, (ii) S' and D', and (iii) D and S'?

3 True or False?
   (a) The gold standard was a regime of managed floating rates.
   (b) The currencies of European countries who belong to the EMS are linked by an adjustable-peg version of a fixed-exchange-rate regime.
   (c) The 'central rate' is the term used in the ERM for the rate around which the exchange rate of a participating country must be stabilized.
   (d) An abrupt change in a country's monetary policy that drives up its interest rate will cause its exchange rate to appreciate but to undershoot its final equilibrium value.

4 Choose the correct alternatives: The Bank of England seeks to increase aggregate demand by open-market operations that (increase/decrease) UK interest rates. This will have the effect of (increasing/decreasing) the UK money supply and (appreciating/depreciating) sterling on the foreign-exchange market. If sterling approaches its permitted (upper/lower) band, the Bank will have to enter the exchange market and (buy/sell) foreign exchange. This will tend to (increase/decrease) the UK money supply, thereby (reinforcing/offsetting) its original monetary policy.

42 Macroeconomic Policy in an Open Economy

In Chapter 29, we saw how shifts in the values of imports and exports could cause national income to change in order to restore equilibrium. In Chapter 40, we concentrated on the equilibrating effects of relative price changes operating through the exchange rate. In the present chapter, we combine income and price changes into a more general view of how the international equilibrating mechanism works, and of the problems it causes for macroeconomic policy-makers. Allowing for the openness of the economy, introduces some new policy goals that may be in conflict with policy goals arising solely from domestic considerations.

GOALS AND INSTRUMENTS

We start by studying two key *goals* of macroeconomic policy, called internal and external balance. We then briefly consider two major classes of policy *instruments*, called expenditure-changing and expenditure-switching policies. After that, we show that conflicts can arise among goals and then study how these may be resolved.

Policy Goals: Internal and External Balance

Internal goals refer to conditions that macroeconomic policy-makers are seeking to achieve within the domestic economy, such as full employment and price stability. *External goals* refer to conditions that the policy-makers are seeking to achieve with respect to the balance of payments and the exchange rate. The former are, as we have previously stressed, *primary goals* in the sense that full employment and price stability are desirable in their own right. In contrast, the latter are *secondary*, because the balance of payments and the exchange rate, while not goals in their own right, may pose problems which interfere with the primary goals.

Internal balance

INTERNAL BALANCE is said to occur when policy-makers have achieved their goals with respect to the domestic economy.[1] In the short run, these goals are to achieve low rates of unemployment and inflation. In discussing these objectives, it is important to notice both what can,

and cannot, be accomplished through macroeconomic policy, the main tool of which is demand management.

Inflation: As far as inflation is concerned, the long-term goal of demand management is to avoid *demand* inflations, which means avoiding inflationary gaps. Wherever wage-cost-push inflation exists, it must be dealt with by tools other than demand management. The most important alternative tools, called prices and incomes policies, were discussed in Chapter 39.

Unemployment: As far as unemployment is concerned, the long-term goal of demand management is to achieve as little unemployment as is consistent with the absence of any inflationary gap. If significant structural and frictional unemployment exists at that level of unemployment, micro labour-market policies are needed. These alternative policies were discussed in Chapter 37.

Overall goals: The internal goals of demand management that we assume in this chapter may be summarized as achieving (i) the full-employment, or potential, level of national income, and (ii) stable prices. Both goals will normally be achieved by eliminating both inflationary and recessionary gaps. It must be noted, however, that if an entrenched demand inflation currently exists, the temporary goal of macro policy may be to produce a recessionary gap, with current income falling well below potential income, in order to break the existing inflation.

In the simple illustration used in this chapter, *internal balance* means that the policy-makers' target level of potential national income has been achieved.

External balance

EXTERNAL BALANCE is said to have been achieved when *the policy-makers' targets with respect to the balance of payments and exchange rates have been achieved.* With respect to external conditions, policy-makers will, depending on the conditions in which they operate, be concerned with the balance of payment on various accounts and the exchange rate. Here are some of the possibilities.

- If the country is on a fixed exchange rate, as is the UK within the ERM, policy-makers will need to keep the exchange rate within the appropriate margins. This can

---

1 The term 'balance' is due to Nobel Prize-winning British economist, James Meade, whose pioneering analysis brought to light the issues discussed in this chapter. 'Balance', in this context, is not be confused with other concepts of balance, such as 'balance of payments' or 'balanced growth'. In the present context, balance means that *the policy-makers' goals, whatever they may be, have been achieved.* Internal balance is when internal goals have been achieved, and external balance when external goals have been achieved.

be done in the short run with Bank intervention, but, in the long run, conditions need to be created that make the market equilibrium exchange rate fall within the permitted range. This requires that the nation's overall payments be in balance with no official financing. (If this last sentence causes you any trouble you should reread the passage in the preceding chapter that explains it; see pages 473–4.)

- If it is thought desirable that the country be a long-term importer or exporter of capital (see page 000 above), policy-makers will wish to target for the appropriate deficit or surplus on the current-account balance of payments.

The above are no more than illustrations of the goals of external balance that policy-makers may have. For the analysis of this chapter, all that matters is that policy-makers have some reasons leading them to adopt a goal for the balance of payments on the current account.

For the first part of this chapter, we focus, *for purposes of illustration only*, on the current account of the balance of payments as the external policy goal. You will recall from Chapter 29, that the current account has two parts: (i) the visible account, which comprises trade in goods, and (ii) the invisible account, which comprises trade in services plus returns on overseas assets in the form of interest, dividends and profits. Trade in goods and services responds to relative international prices, which in turn depend on relative domestic price levels and the exchange rate. Interest, dividends and profits depend on the amounts already invested abroad, and on the profit and interest rates that these investments earn. In the present discussion, we will concentrate on the trade (visibles) account. What we say, however, is equally applicable to the traded-services part of the invisible account.

Internal and external balance illustrated graphically

The conditions for internal and external balance are illustrated in Figure 42.1. Because, for purpose of illustration, we are assuming only one internal goal, achieving some target level of national income, and one external goal, achieving some target value for the current account balance of payments, we can illustrate the relation between internal and external balance on a two-dimensional graph. To do this, we plot national income on the horizontal axis and net exports $(X - M)$, on the vertical axis.

In the graph, we give two examples of the targets for income and the balance of payments.

In case 1, the target for real national income that defines internal balance is indicated by the vertical grid line drawn at Y_1.[1] The target for external balance is indicated by the horizontal grid line drawn at a trade balance of B_1. In the Figure, this target is a small trade-account surplus, which is consistent with a desire to finance some capital exports.

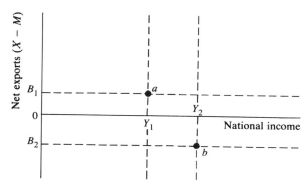

FIGURE 42.1 Internal and External Balance. In the Figure, the internal goal of Y_1 and the external goal of B_1 imply that internal and external balance can only be achieved at point a. Given the different goals, Y_2 and B_2, internal and external balance can only be achieved at point b.

The level of the target is, however, unimportant for anything that follows. The two lines intersect at a, which indicates the only combination of income and balance of payments that simultaneously achieves both targets. At a both internal and external balance are achieved.

In case 2, the income target is larger at Y_2 while the external target is for a current-account balance-of-payments deficit, consistent with capital imports, and indicated by the point B_2. The two grid lines drawn from these new targets intersect at b, which indicates the only combination of national income and balance of payments that simultaneously achieved both targets. At b, given the new targets, both internal and external balance are achieved.

Policy Instruments: Expenditure-Changing and Expenditure-Switching

Governments seeking to maintain internal and external balance can choose from two major classes of policy instruments. The first set is called EXPENDITURE-CHANGING policies. They cause an increase, or a decrease, in aggregate desired expenditure, $C + I + G + (X - M)$, and hence alter equilibrium national income. They must change some of the components of aggregate desired expenditure without causing offsetting changes in the other elements. An example would be a policy that increased G leaving the other components unchanged.

The second set of policies are called EXPENDITURE-SWITCHING policies. These maintain the *level* of aggregate desired expenditure, but influence its *composition* between expenditure on domestic output and net exports. They either increase $C + I + G$ while reducing $(X - M)$, or reduce $C + I + G$ while increasing $(X - M)$.

Expenditure-changing

Policies that change expenditure, and hence alter equilibrium income, include all the tools of demand management. We have studied their impact on *internal* balance

---

[1] Usually, but not always, the income target will be full-employment national income, Y_F, but to allow for the possibility that the target might be some other level of income, we do not use that symbol for the target.

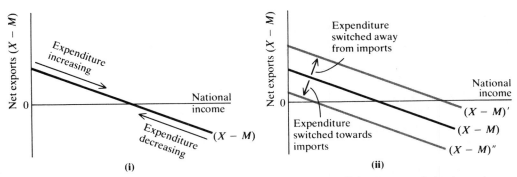

FIGURE 42.2 Expenditure-Changing and Expenditure-Switching Policies Compared. As shown in part (i) of the Figure, expenditure-changing policies move the economy along a given net export function, causing national income and net exports to change in opposite directions. As shown in part (ii), expenditure-switching policies cause the net export function to shift. It shifts upwards, e.g. from $(X-M)$ to $(X-M)'$, when expenditure switches from imports to domestic production, and downwards, e.g. from $(X-M)$ to $(X-M)''$, when expenditure goes from domestic production to imports.

at length earlier in this book: they alter equilibrium national income and, if they cause it to reach the policy-makers' target level of income, internal balance has been achieved.

Their effect on *external* balance is shown in the first part of Figure 42.2. This Figure relates net exports $(X-M)$ to national income (Y), and is called a net export function. Why is it drawn sloping downward to the right? First, exports are exogenous (i.e. X is a constant). Second, a rise in income increases imports. If exports are constant and imports rise as income rises, their difference, $X-M$, must fall as income rises. (This type of Figure was first introduced in Chapter 29, and if you feel at all unsure about it, you should reread pages 327–8 now.)

Now consider how expenditure-changing policies show up on this Figure. They work by altering national income. They thus move the economy *along* its net-export function. A rise in national income causes a movement to the right, and hence a fall in net exports. A reduction in national income causes a movement to the left, and hence a rise in net exports.

Expenditure-switching

Expenditure-switching policies change the amount of net exports associated with each level of national income. They, therefore, *shift* the net export function shown in Figure 42.2(ii).

Consider first a policy that *shifts* expenditure from imports to domestically produced goods. Possibly quotas on the import of Japanese cars cause a reduction of imports and an increase in domestic consumption expenditure as people switch their purchases from Japanese to British-made cars. This policy lowers the amount of *imports*, M, associated with any *given* level of national income, Y. This has the effect of raising the amount of net exports, $X-M$, associated with any given level of national income. Graphically, this is shown by an *upward shift* in the net-export function in part (ii) of the Figure (from $(X-M)$ to $(X-M)'$).

Next, consider a policy that *shifts* expenditure from domestically produced commodities to imports. Possibly the quota in the above example is removed and consumers switch a certain amount of their expenditure from buying British-made to buying Japanese-made cars. Everything is now put into reverse. The amount of imports, M, associated with any given level of national income rises. This causes the net exports $(X-M)$ associated with each level of national income to fall. Graphically, this *shifts* the net export function downwards (from $(X-M)$ to $(X-M)'$ in the Figure).

In summary, policies that shift expenditure from imports to domestically produced goods, shift the net-export function upwards; while policies that shift expenditure from domestically produced goods to imports, shift the net-export function downwards.

Expenditure-switching policies include devaluation or revaluation of the exchange rate, restrictions on international trade such as tariffs and quotas, and measures designed to change the domestic price level relative to foreign price levels. In this discussion, we shall concentrate on changes in the exchange rate.

Mixed effects: Changes in the exchange rate are expenditure-switching policies because they switch expenditure between domestic and foreign goods. For example, a depreciation of sterling discourages imports by raising their prices expressed in domestic currency (as we established on page 464 of Chapter 40). Purchasers will then substitute domestically produced goods for imports. This is a switch of expenditure from imports to domestically produced substitutes.

However, this switch also increases domestic aggregate demand as expenditure on home-produced goods and services increases.

In the reverse case, an appreciation of the exchange rate tends to encourage imports by making them cheaper when expressed in domestic currency. Consumers substitute some imports for domestically produced goods. The rise

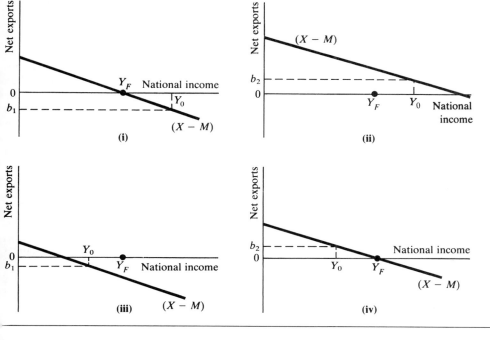

FIGURE 42.3 The Relation Between Internal and External Balance. In part (i), lowering income from Y_0 toward Y_F will reduce the inflationary gap and the trade deficit. In part (iv), increasing income from Y_0 toward Y_F will reduce the recessionary gap and reduce the trade surplus. In part (ii), reducing income from Y_0 toward Y_F will reduce the inflationary gap but increase the trade surplus. In part (iii), increasing income from Y_0 towards Y_F will reduce the recessionary gap but worsen the trade deficit.

in imports is a *switch* of expenditure from domestically produced goods to imported goods.

The change, however, also decreases domestic aggregate demand. Expenditure on domestic goods declines, causing a decline in aggregate desired expenditure.

Recap

We are now ready to study macroeconomic policy. Before we do, however, it is worth noting that this chapter may seem so far to contain more new material than it really does because it uses some new names for some familiar ideas. *Internal balance* is just a new name for achieving a familiar goal. This is a target level of national income, usually taken to be potential income, combined with a stable price level. *Expenditure-changing policy* is just a new name for all of the fiscal and monetary tools of demand management which serve to alter aggregate desired expenditure and hence equilibrium national income.

The *new* concepts introduced in this and the previous chapter are *external balance*, which means achieving some goal on the external side, usually a balance of payments or an exchange rate target, and *expenditure switching*, which refers to policy instruments which switch expenditure between domestic and imported commodities (and also have expenditure-changing effects).

INTERNAL AND EXTERNAL BALANCE WITH A FIXED EXCHANGE RATE

For the next part of this chapter, we assume that the exchange rate is fixed, as it is within the ERM.[1] Later in the chapter, we will study the complications that arise when a flexible exchange rate (and the capital account) are allowed for.

For simplicity, we now assume (i) that the target level of real national income is potential income (which makes the target equal to Y_F), and (ii) that the target for the trade account is a 'zero balance' (by which we mean that the value of imports should be exactly equal to the value of exports, making the balance on trade account zero). This policy combination is shown by the point T in part (i) of Figure 42.3. *Hence, we can identify the initial situation relative to the targets simply in terms of the sign of the trade-account balance and the difference between actual income and potential income.*

Expenditure-changing policies only

When the exchange rate is fixed, the simplest way of *shifting* expenditure between domestic production and imports is denied to the policy-makers. They cannot alter the exchange rate to induce substitutions between imported and domestically produced goods. We shall begin, therefore, by studying the policy-makers' problem when only expenditure-changing policies can be used.

The analysis also applies to the type of managed float that we studied in Chapter 41. As long as the central bank has some reason for wishing to hold the exchange rate steady over the time-span that we are considering, then the problems that it encounters over that period of time under a managed float can be studied by assuming a fixed rate (i.e. the rate that the Bank is trying to maintain under the managed float).

Achieving external balance: Look at the net export curves labelled $(X - M)$ in each of the four parts of Figure 42.3. They relate net exports to national income. The target level of a zero trade balance, which we are assuming to define external balance, is achieved at the level of national income where the net export line cuts the income axis, indicating that $(X - M)$ is zero.

Achieving internal balance: The problems of using fiscal and monetary policy to change aggregate demand, and thus to change equilibrium income, were discussed in Chapter 39. Here, we assume that the policy-makers are capable of altering equilibrium national income by using their fiscal and monetary instruments. This means they are capable of achieving internal balance at Y_F.

The relation between the two goals: We now focus on what further problems arise when seeking the *twin* goals of internal and external balance. The problems arise because national income and the trade balance are related to each other; if one is changed then the other changes as well. This can be seen by inspecting the net export function. It slopes downwards to the right. This means that, as national income rises, the trade balance declines. So any policy that increases the equilibrium value of national income will lower the value of the trade balance by causing a movement to the left along the negatively sloped, net export function.

Thus, rising income is associated with a declining trade balance.

One set of tools, two goals: The problem we now discuss arises because policy-makers have only one set of tools they can use in order to reach two goals. These are expenditure-changing tools which alter equilibrium national income. Internal balance is approached by moving actual income in the direction of potential income. External balance is approached by moving actual income towards the point where the net export function cuts the horizontal axis – i.e. the level of income at which the balance of trade is zero.

Conflict or harmony: The two goals are in harmony if a change in equilibrium national income moves the economy closer to internal and to external balance. This requires that if there is a recessionary gap, so that current income is too low, there should also be a trade surplus, so that raising income would move the economy towards external balance. It also requires that if there is an inflationary gap, so that current income is too high, there should be a trade deficit, so that lowering income also moves the economy towards a trade balance.

The two goals are in conflict if a change in equilibrium income needed to move the economy towards potential income increases the trade deficit. This occurs if a recessionary gap is combined with a trade deficit, or an inflationary gap with a trade surplus.[1]

A graphical analysis of conflict and harmony

Four of the possible cases are shown in Figure 42.3. In all four parts of the Figure, potential income is at the same level, indicated by Y_F. In each part of the Figure, the net export function is shown by the line labelled $(X - M)$ while current equilibrium income is assumed to be at Y_0. The Figures differ from each other in the position of the net export curve and in the value of current equilibrium national income, Y_0. In parts (i) and (iii) of the Figure, there is a current-account deficit of b_1, while in parts (ii) and (iv) there is a current-account surplus of b_2.

Case 1. A deficit combined with an inflationary gap: In part (i) of Figure 42.3, the economy's current income of Y_0 is assumed to be greater than its potential income of Y_F. Thus the economy is suffering from an inflationary gap, measured by $Y_0 - Y_F$ in the Figure. There is also a balance-of-payments deficit, measured by b_1. In this case, there is harmony between the two objectives since reducing the inflationary gap and reducing the payments deficit both call for contractionary policies to reduce equilibrium national income.

Case 2. A surplus combined with an inflationary gap: In part (ii) of the Figure, actual income is again assumed to be above potential income so that in the initial position at Y_0 there is an inflationary gap, $Y_0 - Y_F$. This time, however, there is a trade-account surplus of b_2. Now there is a conflict, since a contractionary policy designed to reduce the inflationary gap will increase the trade surplus, while an expansionary policy designed to reduce the trade surplus will increase the inflationary gap.

Case 3. A deficit combined with a recessionary gap: In part (iii) there is a recessionary gap because current income, Y_0, is less than potential income, Y_F. There is also a trade deficit of b_1 at the current level of income, Y_0. In this case, there is a conflict. An expansionary policy of increasing national income to remove the recessionary gap will worsen the payments deficit, while a contractionary policy of reducing national income to remove the payments deficit will increase the recessionary gap.

Case 4. A surplus combined with a recessionary gap: In part (iv) there is also recessionary gap of $Y_F - Y_0$. This time, however, there is a trade surplus at current income. Now the current situation combines a deflationary gap, $Y_F - Y_0$, with a balance-of-trade surplus of b_2. In this case there is no conflict. An expansionary policy designed to raise income will also reduce the payments surplus. As we have drawn the Figure, the expansion of the economy can proceed until both internal and external balance are achieved at Y_F.

The four possible cases are set out in Figure 42.4. Harmony arises when an inflationary gap is combined with a trade deficit, and a recessionary gap with a trade surplus.

---

1 In the text we confine ourselves to conflicts with respect to small changes in national income. With large changes, it is clearly possible that one goal will be overshot before the other is achieved, in which case a conflict will arise where one did not exist originally.

POLICIES FOR EXTERNAL BALANCE		
	Balance of payments deficit **reduce Y**	*Balance of payments surplus* **increase Y**
POLICIES FOR INTERNAL BALANCE — *Inflationary gap* **reduce Y**	Policy harmony (Case 1)	Policy conflict (Case 2)
Deflationary gap **increase Y**	Policy conflict (Case 3)	Policy harmony (Case 4)

FIGURE 42.4 Harmony and Conflict Between Policies for Internal and External Balance under Fixed Exchange Rates and Expenditure-Changing Policies. Harmony occurs where moving towards internal and external balance require that national income changes in the same direction; conflict occurs where moving towards the two balances requires opposite changes in national income.

Conflict arises when an inflationary gap is combined with a trade surplus, and a deflationary gap with a trade deficit.

Conflict cases

In Case 3, the trade-account deficit calls for a decrease in national income, but the recessionary gap calls for an increase. In Case 2, the trade-account surplus calls for an increase in national income, but the inflationary gap calls for a decrease.

Case 3 has traditionally attracted the most attention, perhaps because a trade deficit is generally viewed as being a more serious problem than a trade surplus, and – at least in the past – unemployment was considered a more serious problem than inflation. Case 3 is often referred to as a situation in which there is a 'balance-of-payments constraint' on domestic full-employment policy.

Case 3 described Britain's position during much of the period from 1950 to 1970, while fear of Case 2 strongly influenced German policy-makers during most of the 1960s and 1970s. As a result, not only did each country face its own conflict between internal and external balance, it also faced a political conflict between the policies that each country urged on the other.

Countries that belong to the ERM will find Cases 2 and 3 equally embarrassing. In Case 2, the country's currency will be tending to appreciate and steps that reduce the inflationary gap will tend to make the external situation worse. Lowering income to reduce inflationary pressures, will lower imports and hence increase the upward pressure on the currency. In Case 3, the currency will be tending to depreciate and measures to prevent its value from breaching the lower margin are required. Steps taken to reduce the recessionary gap to get closer to internal balance will, however, worsen the balance of payments and put more downward pressure on the exchange rate.

Policy Combinations

One important way in which these policy conflicts can be removed is by adding a second set of instruments to the policy-maker's toolkit.

Now we can discuss combinations of expenditure-changing and expenditure-switching policies needed to remove the policy conflicts that we earlier analysed. We take deficits first and refer to cases summarized, each of them numbered above.

A trade-account deficit

Case 1. A deficit combined with an inflationary gap, no conflict: If the economy already has an inflationary gap, an expenditure-reducing policy is needed to reduce national income. The trade-account deficit indicates that domestic expenditure is above the current level of national output and above the full-employment level of national income. To eliminate the deficit, expenditure must be lowered. In other words, if net exports are to rise, the resources needed to produce the necessary export goods must be released through a reduction in domestic usage. This calls also for expenditure-reducing policies. No conflict for expenditure-changing policies arises in this case, because the reduction of expenditure both reduces the inflationary gap and improves the trade account (the latter by inducing a movement along the net export function).

Case 3. A deficit combined with a recessionary gap, conflict: When national income is below its potential level, achieving internal balance calls for expenditure-increasing policies to raise national income. But an increase in national income, with a given net export function, will worsen the current account. So expenditure-increasing policies run into a conflict between internal and external balance. What is needed is a switch of domestic expenditure away from foreign goods (thus reducing the trade deficit) and towards domestic goods (thus reducing the recessionary gap).

This can be done using expenditure-switching policies. If expenditure can be switched from foreign goods – thus reducing imports – to domestic goods – thus increasing domestic expenditure – the payments deficit can be reduced and national income increased.

These policies are shown in Figure 42.5. The initial aggregate expenditure curve is labelled *E* in part (i) of the

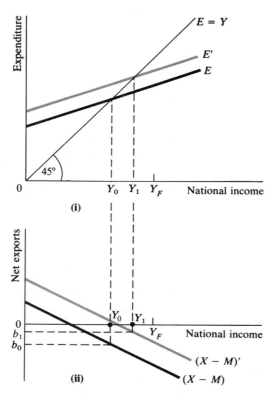

(i)

(ii)

FIGURE 42.5 A Trade Deficit and a Recessionary Gap. A policy to switch expenditure away from foreign goods and toward domestic goods can be used to resolve the conflict posed by a trade deficit combined with a recessionary gap. This policy shifts both the E and the $(X-M)$ curves upwards and so allows a movement towards both potential national income and a trade balance. Let the expenditure curve shift from E to E' and the net export curve from $(X-M)$ to $(X-M)'$. Income will rise from Y_0 to Y_1, reducing the recessionary gap by $Y_1 - Y_0$ and the trade deficit by $b_0 - b_1$.

Figure. This yields an equilibrium national income of Y_0. Since potential income of Y_F exceeds current income, there is a recessionary gap. In part (ii) of the Figure, the initial net export function is labelled $(X-M)$. At equilibrium income of Y_0, there is a payments deficit of b_0.

Now assume that an expenditure-switching policy is adopted in the form of a devaluation of the exchange rate. This increases the exports and reduces the imports associated with any given level of national income. The net export function thus shifts upwards, say to $(X-M)'$ in part (ii) of the Figure. The expenditure-switching policy also raises aggregate expenditure, since exports increase while imports decrease. Say that the curve shifts to E' in part (i) of the Figure. The new equilibrium level of national income is Y_1 and the current-account deficit is now b_1. Both the recessionary gap and the current-account deficit have been reduced.

A trade-account surplus

Now let us look at cases involving a payments surplus, which are Cases 2 and 4 outlined above. In these cases, an

increase in equilibrium national income will cause a move toward external balance by reducing net exports.

Case 4: In Case 4, where there is a recessionary gap, there is no conflict between internal and external balance. Expenditure-increasing policies will lead to movement toward both targets. By raising national income, they will move the economy towards Y_F and, by lowering the payments surplus, they will move the economy towards a zero trade balance.

Case 2: In Case 2, there is an inflationary gap combined with a payments surplus, and a conflict does arise. Achieving external balance calls for expenditure increases, but achieving internal balance calls for expenditure reductions. What is needed is a switch in expenditure away from domestic goods (thus reducing the inflationary gap) and towards foreign goods (thus reducing the trade-account surplus).

The policies are illustrated in Figure 42.6. The initial expenditure function is E. Equilibrium income is Y_0, which exceeds potential income, Y_F. Thus there is an inflationary gap. Given the net export function of $(X-M)$ in part (ii) of the Figure, there is a trade-account surplus of b_1.

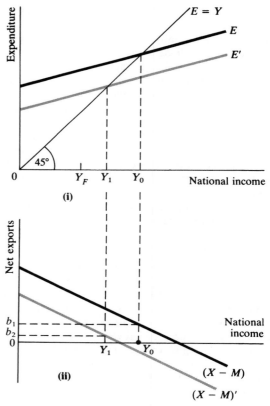

(i)

(ii)

FIGURE 42.6 A Trade Surplus and an Inflationary Gap. A policy to switch expenditure away from domestic goods and toward foreign goods can be used to resolve the conflict posed by a trade surplus combined with an inflationary gap. The policy shifts the E and the $(X-M)$ curves downwards, thus simultaneously reducing equilibrium national income and the trade surplus.

Now assume that the authorities adopt an expenditure-switching policy in the form of a revaluation of the exchange rate. This will shift expenditure from domestic to imported goods and hence will lower net exports at each level of income – i.e. the net export function shifts downwards to $(X - M)'$. The policy also lowers aggregate expenditure because less is spent on home-produced goods and more on imported goods. Thus the aggregate expenditure curve shifts downwards, say to E'. The equilibrium national income falls to Y_1 and at that lower income, the trade balance falls to b_2. Hence both the inflationary gap and the trade surplus are reduced.

A general statement

We have now seen the difference in the effects of the two types of policies in an open economy.

The important point is that to achieve internal and external balance, some appropriate combination of expenditure-changing and expenditure-switching policies is called for.

Here are the key policy implications concerning expenditure-switching policies that are suggested by the previous discussion.

- Expenditure-switching policies should be directed towards the policy of external balance.

- Expenditure-switching policies should be combined with the appropriate expenditure-changing policies that focus on internal balance.

As an example of the second point, consider an economy that is currently at its potential income but has a trade imbalance which it wishes to cure by using expenditure-switching policies. If the trade imbalance is a payments deficit, it needs to depreciate its exchange rate in order to switch expenditure from imports to domestic production. It must, however, accompany that expenditure-switching policy with an expenditure-reducing policy in order to prevent an inflationary gap from developing. This is because switching expenditure from imports to domestic production also increases domestic aggregate demand. In contrast, if the initial payments imbalance is a surplus, then a revaluation is called for to shift expenditure away from domestic production to imports. This must be accompanied, however, by an expenditure-increasing policy to prevent a recessionary gap from opening up.

Lags in the Adjustment Process

So far we have spoken of the effect of exchange-rate changes on sales and purchases without considering how long these effects might take to work out. In fact, it takes time for the full effects to be felt, and different lags in different parts of the payments accounts give rise to a characteristic pattern for large countries called the *J curve*.

This curve plots the balance on the trade account on the vertical axis and time on the horizontal axis. It looks like a J with its top tilted to the right. The curve shows how the balance changes over time following a devaluation of the exchange rate. The balance first worsens, which is the falling part of the J, and it then improves, which is the upward-sloping part of the tilted J.

The cause of the J-curve phenomenon is that the exchange rate changes prices immediately, while quantities take time to adjust. If, say, the country's export prices are fixed *in sterling*, a depreciation of the exchange rate lowers the dollar price of these exports. While the quantity remains constant, foreign earnings will fall, worsening the balance of payments measured in foreign currency. If the prices of imports are fixed in *foreign prices*, the value of imports will be unchanged at first. Overall, therefore, the balance of payments will worsen, measured in foreign currency, so that foreign-exchange earning will be reduced. This is the falling part of the J curve. Over time, however, the quantity of exports will rise, increasing the value of exports, while the quantity of imports will fall, reducing their value. Eventually, the balance of trade measured in foreign prices will change favourably, so that net earnings of foreign exchange will increase.[1] This is the upward-sloping portion of the J curve.

Expenditure-Switching under Fixed Exchange Rates

The main tool for switching expenditure is the exchange rate. When exchange rates are fixed, the most important remaining tools are controls on spending of foreign exchange and changing international relative price levels.

Controls on spending: Controls on spending are mainly used to deal with a balance-of-payments deficit. It is difficult to force people to spend more in the case of a payments surplus, but they can be forced to spend less in the case of a payments deficit. Such controls can be seen as attempting to shift the supply curve for sterling on the foreign-exchange market to the right. (Less sterling is supplied in return for foreign exchange because not everyone who wants to is allowed to purchase foreign exchange.)

In Figure 41.1 on page 473, let the free-market demand and supply curves be D and S'. In order to prevent the exchange rate from breaching its lower margin, restrictions on the purchase of foreign exchange could be used to shift the supply curve of sterling to S, thus making the market-determined exchange rate fall within the target range.

One major tool for controlling spending is EXCHANGE CONTROLS. These are government controls on the use of foreign exchange. In a tight regime of exchange controls, all foreign exchange earned by exporters must be sold to the central bank and all foreign exchange needed by importers must be purchased from the Bank. (Recall that the central bank is the agent that carries

---

1 This will happen providing a famous condition, called the Marshall–Lerner condition, is fulfilled. This takes several forms, the simplest of which is that the *sum* of the foreign elasticity of demand for exports and the domestic elasticity of demand for imports should exceed unity. Derivation of this condition is beyond the scope of this book.

out the government's policy with respect to the exchange rate.) By limiting the use of foreign exchange to specified importers and purposes, the exchange rate can be maintained in spite of the pressure to devalue that would occur if all exchange-market transactions were free of government control.

A second method is the use of import quotas and licences. These were used by European governments in the aftermath of the Second World War, but they are no longer in favour for influencing the exchange rate.[1] They are, however, still in common use for maintaining exchange rates in some less developed countries. Their central banks can switch expenditures between domestic production and imports by altering the total amount of imports allowed through their quotas and licences.

Today, quantity controls on imports are in disfavour for many reasons: (i) government quantity controls are inconsistent with a free-market approach to resource allocation; (ii) quotas create shortages, and large profits due to the supply restrictions go to those who obtain the quotas; (iii) the very sophisticated nature of modern international payments mechanisms, plus the growing importance of transnational corporations (TNCs), who do much international trade between divisions of a single company, make government control of international payments much more difficult than it was 30 or 40 years ago.

Control of the price level: In Chapter 40, we observed that relative international price levels are a determinant of imports and exports. If a country with a fixed exchange rate inflates faster than its trading partners, it will run into balance-of-payments difficulties because its imports from cheaper foreign sources will rise while its exports will fall as they become increasingly expensive. In contrast, a country that inflates slower than its trading partners will find its balance of payments improving as it imports less, because foreign goods are becoming increasingly expensive relative to domestically produced goods in the domestic market, and because its exports will be getting increasingly less expensive relative to foreign goods in foreign markets.

A country on a fixed exchange rate with a balance-of-payments deficit, and unwilling to devalue its exchange rate (or unable to because of international agreements), may choose to initiate a very tight monetary policy that will reduce its rate of inflation below those of its trading partners. Eventually, this will have effects similar to a devaluation. One country's payments deficit is another country's surplus. The deficit country's adjustment process is made easier if the surplus country is willing to inflate a bit more rapidly. It is made much more difficult if the surplus country does everything it can to hold its inflation rate as low as possible.

From the point of view of the deficit country there are at least two disadvantages of using price-level adjustments

as an equilibrating mechanism. First, they can take a long time to have effect. For example, if the average rate of inflation abroad is 4 per cent, and one country manages to hold its rate to 2 per cent, five years are needed to accomplish the same change in relative prices as could be done overnight by a 10 per cent devaluation. Second, the tight monetary policy is likely to depress domestic national income and conflict with the goal of internal balance.

Nonetheless, many countries which have been in that situation have chosen external balance over internal balance. They have instituted tight monetary policies to keep their inflation rates below their trading partners' at the cost of experiencing substantial, and persistent, recessionary gaps.

Neither of the policies discussed in this section are very attractive to modern governments, and the possibility of having to adopt them provides a major disadvantage of a regime of fixed rates in addition to those discussed in the last chapter.

The countries of the ERM have avoided forcing such unattractive policies on their members by their willingness to realign rates when persistent balance-of-payments deficits and surpluses seem to be arising. They do, however, expect their members to keep their monetary policies sufficiently in line so as to prevent the emergence of major misalignments of exchange rates due to divergent inflationary experiences. This is the 'loss of sovereignty' over domestic stabilization policy that we discussed in Chapter 41.

MACROECONOMIC POLICY AND THE CAPITAL ACCOUNT

We start our study of the influence of capital flows with two important background matters: the target of external balance and the effects on the money supply of intervention in the foreign-exchange market.

An alternative target for external balance

So far in this chapter, external balance has meant achieving a target balance on the trade account. We now consider extending this target to incorporate the capital account. To do this we now specify external balance in terms of a target level of the balance of payments on current and capital account, *excluding the official financing*. For simplicity, we take this target to be a zero balance. This means that the exchange rate is in equilibrium without any need for intervention by the Bank, which leaves the Bank's foreign-exchange reserves constant.[1] Any other target would do just as well for our study. What matters is that the authorities have some target that can be expressed in terms of a value for the overall balance of payments.

Box 42.1 Monetary Policy Debated

Urgent Need for Interest-Rate Cut

'We are deeply concerned about the state of the economy. The principles of good monetary policy imply that interest rates should have been cut significantly by now in response to the clear evidence of recession from monetary and indeed all other indicators.

'Failure to cut them is increasing the risks of a depression which would get out of control and from which recovery would be long delayed . . .

'As interest rates fall there should also be a sharp depreciation in sterling which is seriously overvalued against the average of our world competitors . . .

'The exchange-rate mechanism [ERM] obstructs this course. Ideally we should leave it, in order to adhere to soundly-based monetary targets, the best long-term guarantee of a sound currency . . .

'Yet, even within the ERM, we and others in it have been pressed by the Bundesbank to realign, so that we should not be penalised by their domestic need for high interest rates. Even if others will not realign, it is still open to Britain to do so.'

(Letter to *The Times*, 13 February 1991 signed by Tim Congdon, Bill Martin, Patrick Minford, Gordon Pepper, Alan Walters, Peter Warburton)

Discordant Note in the Siren Song of the Six

'The six economists do not help. The more political pressure on the Chancellor to debauch the currency, the more difficulty he will have persuading the market that he will resist their siren voices. The refrain is particularly ironic coming from the six, both because they are people who in the past recognized the importance of low inflation and because they respected markets. The ERM is an anti-inflationary mechanism whose discipline is exerted by the financial markets. Yet Sir Alan and his friends do not like it.

'They argue, of course, that we "should adhere to soundly based monetary targets". The snag is that they

are no more able today to agree on which money supply measures they should be targeting than they were then: Tim Congdon believes in broad money measures such as M4; Bill Martin . . . believes in the middle money measure M2; Sir Alan and Patrick Minford believe in the narrow money measure M0. . . . neither the broad nor the narrow money measures successfully track inflation.

'We should all promise ourselves not to take them seriously until they agree precisely which money supply measure we should target. Meanwhile, a commitment to maintain the link with the German mark will reduce inflation – and even reduce interest rates, eventually.'

(Christopher Huhne in *The Independent*, 17 February 1991)

The six signatories are well-known monetarists. They are arguing for a change in monetary policy to be less restrictive and they hold out the possibility of a severe recession if this does not happen. They are also opposed to the ERM but if the UK must remain within it they advocate a devaluation.

Christopher Huhne states that good monetarist principles would require holding to a tight monetary policy as long as inflation is not fully brought under control. He also castigates them for not being able to agree on which monetary aggregate they would choose as a target.

Questions

1 What would be the effects on UK aggregate demand of a sharp fall in UK interest rates?
2 Why would sterling be expected to depreciate if interest rates were driven down?
3 Would you expect a monetarist who sees a stable price level as the main goal of monetary policy to support or oppose Britain's membership of the ERM?
4 Why might a 'commitment to maintain the link with the German mark . . . reduce inflation – and even reduce interest rates, eventually'?

The monetary effects of exchange-rate stabilization

We shall see below that, once we allow for capital movements, we must distinguish sharply between the effects of fiscal and monetary policies. Because of this, we must study the effect on the money supply of open-market purchases of foreign exchange made by the Bank.

Suppose that the UK experiences a balance-of-payments deficit, and that the Bank of England intervenes in the foreign-exchange market to prevent a fall in the exchange rate. The Bank will be selling foreign currency in exchange for sterling, thereby running down its stock of official reserves. This is an open-market operation, and its effects are exactly the same as if the Bank had bought domestic

TABLE 42.1 Balance Sheet Changes Caused by a Sale of Foreign Currency by the Central Bank. The money supplied is reduced when the central bank sells foreign currency

NON-BANK PRIVATE SECTOR		
Assets (£s)		*Liabilities (£s)*
Foreign currency (equivalent) value in domestic currency	+ 100	No change
Deposits	− 100	

RETAIL BANKS		
Assets		*Liabilities*
Reserves (deposits with central bank)	− 100	Demand deposits − 100

CENTRAL BANK		
Assets		*Liabilities*
Foreign currency	− 100	Deposits of retail banks − 100

bonds. Because we have analysed open-market operations in detail in Chapter 34, we can be brief here.

The effects of a purchase of foreign exchange are summarized in Table 42.1. A balance-of-payments deficit of £100 leads to an excess demand for foreign exchange of £100, which is met by a sale of some of the central bank's official reserves by that amount. When the central bank receives payment in the form of a cheque drawn on a retail bank, central bank reserves fall by £100. There will then be a multiple contraction of deposit money through the process analysed in Chapter 31.

We conclude that, if there are no offsetting transactions, a balance-of-payments deficit will lead to a decrease both in bank reserves and in bank deposits equal to the amount of foreign exchange sold by the central bank.

A surplus will have the opposite effects. Stated briefly, the Bank will buy foreign exchange, paying with cheques drawn in domestic currency. The retail banks will find themselves with new deposits and new reserves equal to the amount of the central bank's open-market purchases.

Sterilization: We have seen that a balance-of-payments deficit tends to cause a contraction of the money supply. The central bank has the option, however, of preventing this from happening by undertaking offsetting transactions. The decrease in bank reserves shown in Table 42.1 can be offset by an open-market purchase of domestic bonds, which will have the effect of increasing bank reserves. The increase in bank reserves that would result from a balance-of-payments surplus can be offset by open-market sales of domestic bonds, which decreases bank reserves.

A balance-of-payments surplus requires that the Bank buy foreign exchange and this open-market operation lowers bank reserves. The increase in bank reserves that would result from a balance-of-payments surplus can be offset by open-market sales of domestic bonds, which decrease bank reserves.

This procedure of insulating the domestic money supply from the effects of balance-of-payments deficits or surpluses is known as STERILIZATION.

Interest rates and international capital flows

When we allow for capital-account transactions, we find that flows of short-term international capital have important effects on the outcomes of monetary and fiscal policies. We have discussed some of these effects several times

BOX 42.2 UK Balancing Act Collapses

'The balance of payments deficit has taken second place in the government's priorities to getting the rate of inflation down. Indeed, the high interest rates and high exchange rates now being used to reduce inflation, in or out of the EMS exchange rate mechanism, may make the current account of the balance of payments worse, after a short-term boost to overseas earnings. They also make it easier to finance the deficit by attracting short term foreign funds, thus avoiding the worse case in which a falling exchange rate increases inflation, even if it later helped the balance of payments.

'The current account has been roughly in balance only twice in the period under review, in 1979 and again in 1986. There was a large swing into a surplus of £6.7bn in 1981 (3.1 per cent of gdp), then into a deficit of £19.1bn (4.4 per cent of gdp) in 1989. The surplus was caused as much by the effect of the 1980–81 recession on imports as by rising net exports of North Sea oil, which did not reach the peak of £8.1bn until 1985. The 1989 deficit was caused by the excess of domestic demand in the UK relative to other countries, as well as by the decline of the oil surplus.

'Britain has in the past been able to remain in external balance only by growing more slowly than other countries. The UK's matching of the growth of other countries in the 1980s has caused the balance of payments to move into deficit, and the UK will again have to grow more slowly than other countries to return to balance.

'British industry regained the competitiveness it lost in 1980, but can remain competitive in the EMS exchange rate mechanism only if it checks the rise in unit labour costs. The parts of the balance of payments that do not depend on manufacturing competitiveness are unpredictable, so that UK must aim to remain competitive in manufacturing.'

(*Lloyds Bank Economic Bulletin*, October 1990)

The quotation discusses the reasons for the variations in the UK balance-of-payments deficits and surpluses on current account. By 'competitiveness', the author is referring to the prices of UK goods relative to foreign prices. The competitiveness of UK goods can be changed by altering the UK rate of inflation relative to inflation rates in its trading partners and/or by altering the exchange rate (assuming that domestic wages and prices do not alter to offset exactly the exchange-rate change).

Questions

1 Discuss the conflicts between internal and external balance mentioned in the quotation, and the policy choice that the government has made.
2 What mechanisms for maintaining external balance are mentioned in the article? Classify each as expenditure-switching or expenditure-changing.
3 Why might a falling exchange rate help the balance of payments 'only later'? Why might it increase inflationary pressures?

before, but a short summary is in order at this important juncture.

Short-term capital is extremely mobile, moving rapidly from country to country as conditions change. As it moves, it has major effects on free-market exchange rates. An inflow of capital causes an increased demand for domestic currency on the foreign-exchange market, which tends to appreciate the exchange rate. If the rate is fixed, the Bank must react to this by selling sterling and buying foreign exchange to hold the rate down. An outflow has the opposite effects, with the exchange rate tending to be driven down on a free market. Under fixed exchange rates, the Bank must enter the market and sell foreign exchange to hold the value of sterling up.

What are the main factors that influence these movements of short-term capital?

First and foremost, are differences in short-term interest rates between major countries. If rates rise in London over what they are in other major financial centres, capital will flow into London to take advantage of the higher rates. When rates fall in London, the capital will flow out again to some other centre where rates are higher.

A second major factor is expectations about exchange rates. Consider, for example, a Japanese firm with money that it does not need for three weeks. If interest rates are 2 per cent higher in London than elsewhere, it will consider lending its money out in London for the three weeks. But this will not be a good deal if the exchange rate falls slightly over that three weeks, and all the funds, interest and principal, must be converted back into yen at a lower exchange rate.

Exchange risk is one reason why all short-term capital does not flood into the country that currently has the highest interest rates. There is always the risk of losses when funds are repatriated because the exchange rate may have moved unfavourably. To hedge against the possibility of these losses, owners of large amounts of short-term capital tend to spread their funds around different centres. They will favour countries with higher interest rates and put less in countries with lower rates. But insurance against unexpected exchange-rate fluctuations makes them spread their money over several different currencies.

It follows from the international mobility of short-term capital that monetary and fiscal policies, that affect the interest and the exchange rates both in the present and in the near future, will have major effects on capital flows into and out of the country. These, in turn, will exert major influences on interest rates and exchange rates. The consequences of these movements are a major theme in what follows.

Fiscal and Monetary Policy Compared

In discussing the trade account in the first part of this chapter, we did not distinguish between the effects of monetary and fiscal policy, since both have similar effects on *national income*. However, when we come to the capital account, we must distinguish between the two policies, since they have opposite effects on *interest rates*. We saw this in Chapter 39. In a closed economy, expansionary

monetary policy exerts its influence on income by *reducing* interest rates. However, fiscal policy influences aggregate demand directly, and fiscal-policy-induced increases in national income create an excess demand for money, which *increases* interest rates.

Fiscal policy and the capital account: The effects of fiscal policy on the capital account of an open economy operate via induced changes in interest rates. For example, an expansionary fiscal policy tends to cause interest rates to rise in a closed economy. In an open economy, a rise in interest rates attracts short-term capital. So the capital-account sequence is: an expansionary fiscal policy will put upward pressure on interest rates, and this will lead to an inflow of foreign capital, thereby moving the capital account toward a surplus. A contractionary fiscal policy will have the opposite effects: domestic interest rates will fall, capital will flow out, in search of higher returns elsewhere, and the capital account will move towards a deficit.

Monetary policy and the capital account: Since monetary policy influences interest rates in a closed economy, it will influence the capital account in an open economy. An expansionary monetary policy will put downward pressure on interest rates and lead to an outflow of short-term capital. This will move the balance of payments on the capital account toward a deficit. A contractionary monetary policy will put upward pressure on interest rates and cause an inflow of short-term capital. This will move the balance of payments on the capital account towards a surplus.

So the effects of the two policies on the capital account are the opposite of each other. Expansionary fiscal policy tends to cause a capital-account surplus, while an expansionary monetary policy tends to cause a capital-account deficit. Contractionary policies have the opposite effects.

Fixed exchange rates

We now consider the implications of these capital-account forces for fiscal and monetary policies that attempt to alter aggregate desired expenditure and hence equilibrium national income, first with fixed, and then with flexible, exchange rates.

Monetary policy: Monetary policy has only a limited effect on aggregate demand under a fixed exchange rate. Consider the following sequence of events. Suppose UK interest rates are at levels similar to those in the rest of the world, and that there is equilibrium in international capital markets. Suppose now that the Bank of England, faced with a large recessionary gap, seeks to stimulate demand through an expansionary monetary policy. The Bank buys bonds in the open market, thereby increasing the money supply and reducing interest rates.

The lower interest rates, however, induce an outflow of capital and thus cause a deficit on the capital account. To the extent that national income rises, the imports will rise, creating a deficit on the trade account. Thus the overall balance of payments moves into deficit, putting downward pressure on the exchange rate. To maintain the fixed exchange rate, the Bank will have to intervene in the foreign-exchange market and sell foreign currency. This open-market operation in foreign exchange will have the effect of reducing the money supply and thus reversing the increase brought about by the initial open-market operation.

If no other transactions are initiated by the Bank, national income and the money supply will fall and domestic interest rates will rise until they all return to their initial levels. Thus the induced balance-of-payments deficit will be self-correcting, and the Bank's expansionary policy will be nullified.

Suppose now that the Bank attempts to sterilize the impact on the money supply of the balance-of-payments deficit. The difficulty with this strategy is that it can be continued only as long as the Bank has sufficient reserves of foreign exchange. If capital flows are highly sensitive to interest-rate changes, as a great deal of evidence suggests is the case, these reserves will be run down at a rapid rate, and the Bank will be forced to abandon its expansionary policy.

This leads to an important conclusion:

Under a fixed exchange rate, there is reduced scope for the use of monetary policy for purposes of reaching internal balance because of the sensitivity of international capital flows to interest rates. The Bank will be forced to maintain domestic interest rates close to the levels existing in the rest of the world, and it will not be able to bring about substantial changes in the domestic money supply for expenditure-changing purposes.

Fiscal policy: Consider now the effectiveness of fiscal policy under fixed exchange rates. Suppose again that UK interest rates are in line with those in the rest of the world when an expansionary fiscal policy is introduced, aimed at reducing a large recessionary gap. The fiscal expansion tends to raise the level of domestic interest rates and national income.

Higher interest rates stimulate an inflow of short-term capital, thereby leading to a surplus on the capital account. If the capital flows are large, the surplus on capital account will exceed the current-account deficit arising from the increased national income. Hence there will be an overall balance-of-payments surplus, putting upward pressure on the exchange rate.

To maintain the fixed exchange rate, the Bank will have to intervene in the foreign-exchange market and buy foreign exchange. This will have the effect of increasing the money supply, thus reinforcing the initial fiscal stimulus with an induced monetary expansion.

This leads to another important conclusion:

Under a fixed exchange rate, interest-sensitive international capital flows stabilize the domestic interest rate and enhance the effectiveness of fiscal policy as a tool for altering expenditure.

Combining monetary and fiscal policy: Consider an attempt to increase national income with expansionary monetary policy intended to reduce interest rates and thereby stimulate investment and other interest-sensitive expenditures. The decline in domestic interest rates causes short-term capital to move abroad to be invested at more attractive rates in foreign financial centres. This worsens the balance of payments on the short-term capital account. Of course, if the expansionary policy succeeds in raising income, there will also be a movement towards deficit on the current account as a consequence of the increased expenditure on imports caused by the rise in income.

In principle the conflict can be removed by an appropriate combination of monetary and fiscal policy. Consider a country that has full employment combined with a balance-of-payments deficit. The country could eliminate the deficit by following a tighter monetary policy to increase domestic interest rates and attract short-term capital. At the same time, the contractionary effect of tight money on domestic expenditure and employment could be offset by raising government expenditures or cutting taxes. Thus both goals can be achieved through a combination of tight monetary policy and expansionary fiscal policy.

The temporary nature of the strategy: This strategy is unlikely to be a satisfactory solution to a persistent current-account deficit. The reason is that it is difficult to maintain the exchange rate by importing short-term capital over long periods of time.

Short-term international capital flows are extremely volatile, *and they are particularly sensitive to shifts in expectations concerning exchange rates.* If investors lose confidence in a country's ability to maintain its existing exchange rate, capital outflows will build up and ultimately a devaluation will be required to reduce the deficit and restore confidence.

Flexible exchange rates

A major advantage of a flexible exchange rate is that it reduces conflicts between domestic stabilization objectives and the balance of payments, because balance-of-payments deficits or surpluses tend to be automatically reduced through movements in the exchange rate.

Fiscal policy: Suppose the government seeks to remove a recessionary gap by expansionary fiscal policy. An increase in government expenditures, and/or a reduction in taxes, will increase income through the multiplier effect and reduce the size of the recessionary gap. This will also tend to cause a movement along the net export function, leading to a deterioration of the trade account. This, however, is not the whole story, for there will also be repercussions on the capital account and the exchange rate.

Capital flows and the crowding-out effect: In a closed economy, an expansionary fiscal policy causes domestic interest rates to rise. This causes interest-sensitive private expenditures to fall, thus partially offsetting the initial expansionary effect of the fiscal stimulus. As we saw in

BOX 42.3 EMU Means More Than Losing The Queen's Head

'The potential benefits of the EMU ... consist of cost savings on transactions associated with changing European currencies. This may result in further economic advantages with the greater integration of European economies and increased trade, and, arguably, to higher investment. If European monetary management were "successful" (in the way the Bundesbank has been successful), there would be the added advantage of surrendering our less successful system, plagued by high inflation and high interest rates, for something better.... the tangible benefits, (the saving on transactions costs) are relatively minor. The less secure benefits are the potentially large ones.

'The case against rests on two pillars – the usefulness of exchange-rate variations and the degree of political, as well as economic, independence. Exchange rates are a (sometimes) vital part of the price mechanism.

'Exchange rate alterations can be a substitute for domestic price changes. A 10 per cent fall in sterling prices (including wages) against German mark prices is equivalent in its effect on competitiveness to a 10 per cent devaluation of sterling against the mark. But if all prices were as flexible as exchange rates, we might as well do away with exchange rates and have a single currency.

'For the retention of exchange rates to make sense, it has to be true that domestic prices cannot fall sufficiently in reaction to adverse shocks and that when the exchange rate is allowed to take the strain instead, domestic prices (and wages) will not rise sufficiently to offset the effects. That is to say, that it is possible to change the real exchange rate by changing the nominal rate.'

(Roger Bootle, in *The Independent on Sunday*,
16 December 1990)

European economic and monetary union (EMU) is the target for co-operation in economic and monetary policy towards which members of the EC are committed. EMU

includes membership of the ERM (part of the EMS) which the UK joined in 1991 (see Chapter 41, page 472) and, almost certainly, the eventual replacement of sterling, francs, deutschmarks etc. by a single European currency unit.

The writer is discussing the debate over the proposal to create a single European currency. He argues that the certain benefits are small, while the risks in giving up the ability to adjust relative international prices through alterations in the exchange rate may be significant. If UK prices are too high, a fall in the exchange rate will adjust these, but this gain will be wiped out if domestic wages and prices rise in the same proportion as the exchange rate is depreciated. The pressure to raise wages comes from the rise in import prices caused by the depreciation, but there is little evidence that the wage increases are typically sufficient to wipe out the whole of the favourable effect on international competitiveness from devaluing sterling.

Questions

1 Assuming that UK prices were non-competitive across the board, explain how an adjustment could be made either through a deflation or through a devaluation of sterling on the foreign-exchange market.
2 What are the relative advantages and disadvantages of relying on each of these adjustment mechanisms?
3 Why would a single European currency remove the worry that poor UK monetary policy would lead to an inflation that would cause British goods to become non-competitive across the board in European markets? Would it then be impossible for British goods to become non-competitive across the board in Europe under an EMU?

Chapter 39, this crowding-out effect can play an important role in the analysis of fiscal policy in a closed economy. In an open economy, the crowding-out effect will operate differently, due to international capital flows.

Higher domestic interest rates that result from an expansionary fiscal policy will induce a capital inflow and cause the exchange rate to appreciate. If capital flows are highly interest-elastic, there will be a large capital inflow, which will cause the exchange rate to rise substantially. This will reduce aggregate demand by discouraging exports and encouraging the substitution of imports for domestically produced goods. (The switch in expenditures reduces net exports, $X - M$, and reduces aggregate desired expenditure.) The initial fiscal stimulus will be offset by

the expenditure-switching effects of currency appreciation.

We have now reached another important conclusion:

Under flexible exchange rates, a fiscal expansion will crowd out net exports and this reduces its effectiveness.

It is possible, however, to eliminate the crowding-out effect by supporting the fiscal policy with a validating monetary policy. Suppose that the central bank responds to the increase in the demand for money, induced by the fiscal expansion, by increasing the supply of money so as to maintain domestic interest rates at their initial level. There will then be no capital inflow, and no tendency for the currency to appreciate. Income will expand by the usual multiplier process.

The conclusion is as follows:

The effectiveness of fiscal policy under flexible exchange rates can be maintained by use of a validating monetary policy.

Monetary policy: We have seen that there is little scope under fixed exchange rates for the use of monetary policy for domestic stabilization purposes. Under flexible exchange rates, the situation is reversed; monetary policy becomes a very powerful tool.

Suppose the Bank seeks to stimulate demand through an expansionary monetary policy. The Bank buys bonds in the open market, thereby increasing the reserves of the retail banking system. This in turn increases the money supply and puts downward pressure on interest rates. Lower interest rates will cause an outflow of capital and thus tend to open up a deficit on the capital account.

Under a fixed rate, we saw that the Bank may be forced to reverse its policy in order to stem the loss of foreign reserves. Under a flexible rate, however, the exchange rate can be allowed to depreciate. This will stimulate exports and discourage imports so that the deficit on the capital account will be offset by a surplus on the current account.

National income will be increased not only because the fall in interest rates stimulates interest-sensitive expenditure, but also because the increased demand for domestically produced goods brought about by a depreciation of the currency increases aggregate demand. The initial monetary stimulus will be reinforced by the expenditure-switching effects of currency depreciation.

This leads to one further conclusion:

Under flexible exchange rates, monetary policy is a powerful tool for stabilizing domestic income and employment. If capital flows are highly interest-elastic, the main channel by which an increase in the money supply stimulates demand for domestically produced goods is a depreciation of the currency.

Conclusion

The main message of this chapter is that macroeconomic policy looks rather different when viewed from the perspective of an open rather than a closed economy, especially if the overseas sector is large. Under fixed

Summary

1 Internal balance occurs when the target level of national income has been achieved; external balance occurs when the target level on the balance of payments has been achieved.

2 Expenditure-changing policies are the tools of demand management; they cause the level of national income and the balance of payments to change in the opposite directions. Expenditure-switching polices switch expenditure between domestic goods and imports; they cause the balance of payments and national income to change in the same direction.

3 A fixed exchange rate prevents one of the major expenditure-switching tools – exchange-rate variations – from being used. If only expenditure-changing tools are available, internal and external balance objectives may be in harmony, or in conflict. Harmony occurs when a recessionary gap is combined with a payments surplus or an inflationary gap is combined with a payments deficit. Conflict occurs when a recessionary gap is combined with a payments deficit or when an inflationary gap is combined with a payments surplus.

4 When the exchange rate cannot be used as a tool of expenditure-switching, exchange controls may be used or else the domestic price level can be varied relative to foreign price levels to effect the same switches.

5 Irrespective of where the goods and services were purchased, a trade-account deficit means that total expenditure on consumption, investment and government ($C + I + G$) exceeds current output; a surplus means that ($C + I + G$) is less than current output. If both expenditure-changing and expenditure-switching measures are available, expenditure-changing techniques can be used to make equilibrium income equal to potential income (internal balance), and expenditure-switching policies can be used to shift the net export function so that the desired balance-of-payments target is achieved (external balance) at potential income.

6 Although changes in the exchange rate are an expenditure-switching policy, they also have expenditure-changing effects: depreciations increase domestic expenditure, and appreciations reduce it. A pure expenditure-switching effect – no change in aggregate expenditure – requires that the expenditure-changing effects of an alteration in the exchange rate be offset by the expenditure-changing effects of fiscal and monetary policies.

7 When significant international capital movements can occur, the relative effectiveness of fiscal and monetary policy must be reconsidered. On a fixed exchange rate, monetary policy is relatively impotent while fiscal policy is potent. On a flexible exchange rate, monetary policy is potent while fiscal policy is relatively impotent.

exchange rates, problems arise because use of the major tool of expenditure-switching – changes in the exchange rate – is sometimes ruled out. Conflicts of policy goals then arise when achieving internal balance calls for changing national income in one direction while achieving external balance calls for changing it in the other direction. When exchange rates are changed to get the benefit of their expenditure-switching effects, then their expenditure-changing effect must be allowed for as well – depreciations tend to increase domestic expenditure while appreciation tends to reduce it. If these changes move the economy away from internal balance, the Bank can try to offset their effects by appropriate expansionary or contractionary demand-management policies.

Under flexible exchange rates, a policy package that includes monetary and fiscal policy changes, aimed at internal balance, and exchange-rate changes, aimed at external balance, can normally achieve internal and external balance simultaneously.

Questions

1 When the exchange rate is fixed, policy conflicts between internal and external balance are likely to arise in which One or More of the following circumstances?
  (a) A severe recession is combined with a tendency for sterling to breach its lower ERM margin under the impact of poor export figures.
  (b) The Bank is trying to break a serious local inflation while sterling remains strong on the foreign-exchange market.
  (c) With roughly full employment, sterling is tending to breach its upper margins under the influence of expanding exports.
  (d) The developing economic union between the two former Germanys leads to expanding exports and inflationary pressures.

2 In Figure 42.5, let the initial curves be E' and $(X-M)'$ and the target level of national income Y_0 rather than Y_F and let national income currently be Y_1.
  (a) What is the current situation with respect to internal and external balance?
  (b) What sort of conflict, if any, is there between the two goals?

3 Classify each of these measures as primarily expenditure-changing (C) or expenditure-switching (S):
  (a) devaluation of a currency that is on a fixed exchange rate
  (b) driving up the domestic interest rate
  (c) increasing government exhaustive expenditures
  (d) cutting the tax rate
  (e) quotas on key imports
  (f) exchange controls
  (g) major reductions in tariffs

4 Classify the effects on aggregate desired expenditure of each of the measures mentioned in question 3 above as either increasing it (I) or decreasing it (D).

5 True or False?
  (a) An exchange rate well away from its target value is evidence of a lack of internal balance.
  (b) An expenditure-switching policy designed to cure a persistent balance-of-payments deficit will cause a conflict with internal balance if the economy is currently at or above potential income.
  (c) Fixed exchange rates in the ERM mean that the Bank is constrained in its use of monetary policy to achieve internal balance.
  (d) The J curve arises because prices respond much more slowly than do quantities when exchange rates alter.

6 If the Bank of England drives up domestic interest rates in an attempt to curb an entrenched inflation, what will be the effect on the external value of sterling? Why might this be of concern to a government concerned about internal balance?

7 Assume that the UK, a member of the ERM, wishes to fight a severe recession with demand management. Would you recommend fiscal or monetary policy as the main tool to be used? Why? (Hint: consider the effects of each on the interest rate.)

43 Macroeconomic Controversies

How well do markets work? Can government improve market performance? In various guises, these two questions are the basics of most disagreements over economic policy. Indeed, they were the main questions that we asked on the first page of the first chapter of this book, and now we pose them again 43 chapters later at the end of the book. We shall see that, although these are microeconomic questions, the different answers that are given to them imply big differences in macroeconomic policy prescriptions as well.

In this, the last chapter of our book we shall review two extreme positions on the state of the economy. In doing so, much of what we have learned in earlier chapters will be reviewed.

ALTERNATIVE VIEWS

We have seen that macroeconomics is mainly concerned with employment (and unemployment), the price level and the rate of economic growth on the domestic side, and with the balance of payments and the exchange rate on the international side. Broadly speaking, we can identify a non-interventionist and an interventionist view with respect to each of these policy goals. The non-interventionist view says that the unaided market economy can best achieve the goal. The interventionist view says that government policy can improve the economy's performance regarding that goal. Since one can take a non-interventionist or an interventionist position with respect to each of these three goals, there are six different possible policy combinations.[1]

Consider two extreme policy stances. For lack of better names we will identify these extremes as market-oriented and 'interventionist'. Advocates of market orientation are non-interventionist on every issue, while pure interventionists support government intervention in all cases. A few people may actually be pure market oriented or pure interventionist in this sense. Most, however, would find themselves favouring intervention on some issues and opposing it on others. They might still, however, identify themselves as being, on overall balance, market-oriented or interventionist because they were more often on one side than the other.

It is popular to identify Monetarist and New Classical with market-oriented and Keynesian with interventionist. It is true that many Monetarists are on the market-oriented side, while many Keynesians are on the interventionist side. But this is not always so. It is, for example, quite possible to be Keynesian in accepting the Keynesian macro model as a reasonable description of the economy's macroeconomic behaviour, but market-oriented in believing that, in the absence of major externalities, the unaided market usually does the best job of allocating resources at the microeconomic level.

The market-oriented view

Advocates of market orientation believe that the free-market economy performs well when left to itself. They believe that the economy is inherently self-equilibrating, and that the adjustment forces are strong enough to eliminate both inflationary and recessionary gaps fairly quickly and fairly completely – as long as the government does not adopt policies that frustrate these forces.

While all manner of unexpected changes may impinge on the system from time to time, they are, in this view, followed rather quickly, and often relatively painlessly, by the equilibrating adjustments dictated by the market system. For example, relative prices in booming sectors rise, drawing in resources from declining sectors or regions. As a result, whenever the market is allowed to work, resources (and particularly labour) usually remain fully employed, so there is no need for interventionist, full-employment policies. Heavy unemployment is blamed on poor interventionist policies. The market-oriented solution is to remove the intervention, not to intervene more effectively.

Of course, few but the most extreme advocates of market orientation believe that the unaided market system would function perfectly, thereby ensuring *continuous* full employment – although many New Classical economists come close to this view. But the view is that the market system works well enough to preclude any role for government economic policy. The important substantive debate concerns market-clearing. Do markets adjust fast enough so that quantity demanded is equal to quantity supplied most of the time?

In addition, many believe that the available instruments of fiscal and monetary policy are so crude that their use is often counter-productive. A policy's effects may be so uncertain, with regard to both strength and timing, that it may impair, rather than improve, the economy's performance.

In a modern economy, some government presence is generally regarded as inevitable because of public goods, major externalities, imperfect competition and the possibility of merit (and demerit) goods. Thus a stance of *no*

---

1 Since each of the three issues breaks up into hundreds of different sub-issues, there are thousands of different policy stances available on one side or the other of each major issue. Considering these two extreme cases is useful in identifying issues but does not necessarily identify two major groups.

intervention is impossible; so we may reinterpret our extremist market-orientation policy as one of *minimal* direct intervention in the market system. This involves little more than government's bearing responsibility for providing a *stable environment* in which the private sector can function.

The government's provision of a stable environment is important in the market-orientation programme, and it needs some explanation. The belief is that private decision-takers, risking their own or shareholders' money, will provide the best guarantee of rising living standards through economic growth in the long run as well as something close to full employment in the short run. These beneficial results will only occur, however, if economic activity takes place in the context of a stable environment where contracts are enforceable and enforced, where theft and other crimes against persons and property are minimized, where tax rates are reasonable and not subject to capricious changes, where failure is punished by loss of investment (that is not then refunded by the government) and success is rewarded by profit (that is not then confiscated by the government), where the country is secure against aggressive foreign powers, where the transportation routes are secure for foreign trade, and where the price level is relatively stable. The advocates of market orientation see the important functions of the government as providing the necessary backdrop against which private initiative can get on with the job of achieving economic prosperity.

The interventionist view

Interventionists believe that the functioning of the free-market economy is often far from satisfactory. Sometimes markets show weak self-regulatory forces and the economy settles into prolonged periods of heavy unemployment. At other times, markets tend to 'overcorrect', causing the economy to lurch between the extremes of large recessionary and large inflationary gaps.

This behaviour can be improved, argue the interventionists. They believe that, even though interventionist policies may be imperfect, they are often good enough to improve the functioning of the unaided market with respect to all three main goals of macro policy.

DIFFERENT DIAGNOSES

The economy's performance is, of course, often less than perfectly satisfactory. Serious unemployment has been a recurring problem. Inflation was a serious problem throughout the 1970s and early 1980s. Throughout most of the same period, growth rates have been low in many of the industrial countries of Western Europe and North America. Interventionists and non-interventionists differ in diagnosing the causes of these economic ills.

The Trade Cycle

We saw in Chapter 28 that cyclical ups and downs can be observed as far back as records exist. Monetarists and Keynesians have long argued about the causes. *For purposes of the debate about the trade cycle, as well as about inflation, Monetarists can be identified with market orientation and Keynesians with interventionists.*

Monetarist views: Monetarists believe the economy is inherently stable because such private-sector expenditure relations as the consumption and the investment functions are relatively stable. In addition, they believe that shifts in the aggregate demand curve are mainly due to policy-induced changes in the money supply.

The view that trade cycles have mainly monetary causes relies heavily on disputed evidence concerning a relation between changes in the money supply and changes in real activity. A strong correlation does seem to exist, at least for the United States, between changes in the money supply and changes in the level of business activity. Major recessions have been associated with absolute declines in the money supply and minor recessions with the slowing of the rate of increase in the money supply below its long-term trend.

The correlation between changes in the money supply and changes in the level of business activity appears to be supported by the experience of many countries. There is controversy, however, over how this correlation is to be interpreted; do changes in money supply *cause* changes in the level of aggregate demand and hence of business activity? Is the association merely statistical, or is there (as many believe) a much more complex causal chain, or even, does the causal chain turn the other way around, with the changes in aggregate demand causing changes in the money supply? Also given the problems mentioned earlier in measuring the money supply, it is hardly surprising that economists are able to hold (and hold strongly) different views about what is apparently a question of fact.

Monetarists maintain that changes in the money supply cause changes in business activity. They argued, for example, that the severity of the Great Depression was due to a major contraction in the money supply that shifted the aggregate demand curve far to the left. This led them to advocate a policy of stabilizing the growth of the money supply. In their view this would avoid policy-induced instability of the aggregate demand curve.

New Classical views: New Classical economists combine their view that markets always clear with the theory of rational expectations to produce the conclusion that changes in the money supply have no effects on income and employment. Here, briefly, is how they do this.

The theory of RATIONAL EXPECTATIONS assumes that people look to the government's current macro-economic policy to form their expectations of future cost and price inflation. They understand how the economy works, and they form their expectations rationally by predicting the outcome of the policies now being followed. In an obvious sense, such expectations are *forward-looking*. They are usually called rational expectations. Rational expectations are not necessarily always correct; instead, *the rational-expectations hypothesis merely assumes that people do not continue to make persistent, systematic errors in forming expectations.* Thus, *if the economic system about which they are forming expectations remains stable,* their expectations will be correct *on average.* Any individual's expectations at any moment of time about next year's price level can thus be thought of as the actual price level that will occur next year, plus a random error term.

We have seen that the long-run effect of an increase in the money supply is solely on the price level. (See, for example, Figure 35.12 on page 396.) The real effects on income and employment occur only in the transitory period. If market prices always adjust instantaneously to equate demands and supplies, if people always know when a monetary shock is coming, and if they rationally predict its effects, they will immediately raise all prices and wages. The net result is that any monetary policy that does not come as a surprise will only affect the price level, since markets will quickly adjust to it.

While Monetarists would avoid monetary stabilization policy because its powerful effects are too unpredictable, New Classical economists would avoid it because it is totally impotent! This is because rational people see its effects coming and adjust their prices and wages to the new long-run equilibrium instantly. (Keynesians accept the Monetarists' view as a possibility, even if they do not see it as likely – but they dismiss the New Classical view as theory totally devoid of evidence.)

Keynesian views: The Keynesian view on cyclical fluctuations in the economy has two parts. First, it emphasizes variations in investment as a cause of trade cycles and stresses non-monetary causes of such variations.

Keynesians reject what they regard as the extreme Monetarist view that only money matters in explaining cyclical fluctuations. Many Keynesians believe that both monetary and non-monetary forces are important. Although they accept monetary mismanagement as one potential source of economic fluctuations, they do not believe that it is the only or even the major source of such fluctuations. Thus they deny the monetary interpretation of trade-cycle history. They believe that most fluctuations in the aggregate demand curve are due to variations in the desire to spend on the part of the private sector and are not induced by government policy. Such variations in private-sector desired expenditure functions are held by the Keynesians to be due to large shifts in expectations about the future – what Keynes himself called 'animal spirits' – which are uncontrollable by government policy. These fluctuations in desired expenditure in turn mean that fluctuations in aggregate demand will always occur, and the best thing that the government can do is to try to mitigate some of their most harmful consequences on employment and income through an active stabilization policy.

Keynesians also believe that the economy lacks strong natural corrective mechanisms that will always force it easily and quickly back to full employment. They believe that, although the price level rises fairly quickly to eliminate inflationary gaps, the price level does not fall quickly to eliminate recessionary gaps. Keynesians stress the asym-metries noted in earlier chapters which imply that although prices and wages rise quickly in response to inflationary gaps, they fall only slowly in response to recessionary gaps. As a result, Keynesians believe that recessionary gaps can persist for long periods of time unless eliminated by an active stabilization policy.

The second part of the Keynesian view of cyclical fluctuations is acceptance that, while there does exist a correlation between changes in the money supply and changes in national income, the causality often runs from changes in income to changes in the money supply. They offer several reasons for this, but only the most important need be mentioned.

Keynesians point out that from 1945 to the early 1970s many of the world's central banks often sought to stabilize interest rates in pursuit of their support function rather than seeking to vary rates in pursuit of their stabilization function. To do this, they had to increase the money supply during upswings in the trade cycle (so that a shortage of money would not cause interest rates to rise) and decrease the money supply during downswings (so that a surplus of money would not cause interest rates to fall). (This policy was analysed in Figure 34.2 on page 381).

Thus we see that, according to Keynesians, fluctuations in national income are often caused by fluctuations in expenditure decisions, while fluctuations in national income cause fluctuations in the money supply. Nevertheless, most Keynesians also agree that policy-induced changes in the money supply, particularly when they are large and rapid, can cause major shifts in aggregate demand.

The Price Level

As we saw in Chapter 38 sustained inflation requires sustained expansion of the money supply. (A *sustained inflation* is one that has been going on for a long time, while an *entrenched inflation* is one that is expected to continue for a long time. Although one type of inflation often goes with the other, they are not the same thing.)

Excessive monetary expansions have usually come as the indirect effects of policies directed to other ends. If the expansion persists, however, the other objectives are swamped by the harmful effects of the rapid inflations that result. Consider three such policies.

- Sometimes, central banks have tried to hold interest rates well below their free-market levels. To do this, they buy bonds to hold bond prices up. We have seen that these open-market operations increase the money supply and so help to produce a demand inflation.

- Sometimes, central banks have tried to hold the exchange rate below its equilibrium level. The resulting purchase of foreign exchange is an open-market policy that expands the reserves of the banking system and leads to a demand inflation.

- Sometimes, central banks have helped governments finance large budget deficits by buying up the new public debt. These open-market operations provide what is popularly known as 'printing press finance'. The steady increase in the money supply fuels a continuous inflation. This third case has been by far the most common cause of sustained inflations over the centuries.

Monetarist views: Many Monetarists hold that inflation is everywhere and always a monetary phenomenon. (See Chapter 38, page 499, for an assessment of this contention.) They thus focus on changes in the money supply as the key source of shifts in the aggregate demand curve. Many also believe that supply shocks, which cause *some* prices to rise, do not lead to inflation because, unless the money supply is also raised, some other prices will have to fall. This will cause changes in relative prices but no significant change in the price level. Thus, according to many Monetarists, all inflations are caused by excessive monetary expansions and would not occur without them.

Keynesian views: Keynesians accept the view that a *sustained* rise in the price level cannot occur unless it is accompanied by continued increases in the money supply. To this extent, they agree with the Monetarists. Keynesians also emphasize, however, that temporary bursts of inflation can be caused by shifts in the aggregate demand curve brought about by increases in private- or public-sector expenditure functions (consumption, investment, exports and government expenditure). If such inflations are not validated by monetary expansion, they are brought to a halt by the monetary adjustment mechanism. Even when not validated, they can, however, persist long enough to worry policy-makers and governments concerned about the next election.

Keynesians also accept the importance of supply-shock inflations. They accept that such inflations cannot go on indefinitely unless validated by monetary expansion, but believe that they can go on long enough to be a matter of serious concern. Indeed, we have seen that such inflations can present the central bank with agonizing choices: whether to validate the shocks, thereby accepting a bout of inflation but avoiding unemployment, or not to validate the shocks, thereby accepting a period of unemployment but avoiding further inflation.

Many Keynesians also accept the existence of more or less permanent wage-cost-push inflation that we studied in Chapter 39. This type of inflation, if it exists, makes full employment incompatible with a stable price level. Again the Bank is faced with the agonizing choice of whether or not to validate such a wage-cost-push inflation.

Growth

Marked-oriented views: Advocates of market orientation, and indeed most Monetarists, feel that in a stable environment free from government interference, growth will take care of itself. Large firms will spend much on research and development. Where they fail, or where they suppress inventions to protect monopoly positions, the genius of backyard inventors will come up with new ideas and will develop new companies to challenge the positions of the established giants. Left to itself, the economy will prosper as it has in the past, provided only that inquiring scientific spirit, and the profit motive, are not suppressed. Advocates of market orientation point out that much of the increase in employment in the 1980s has come from small businesses that embody the essence of the entrepreneurial spirit.

Interventionist views: Interventionists, and indeed most Keynesians, are less certain about the ability of market forces to produce growth. While recognizing the importance of invention and innovation, they fear the stultifying hand of monopoly, and conservative business practices that choose security over risk-taking. Therefore they believe that the government needs, at the very least, to give a nudge here and there to help the growth process along.

THE DIFFERENT PRESCRIPTIONS

The market-oriented and the interventionist diagnoses of the economy's ills lead, not surprisingly, to very different prescriptions about the appropriate role of economic policy.

Market-Oriented Prescriptions

It is not necessary to distinguish market-orientation policies with respect to the three objectives of full employment, stable prices and economic growth. This is because advocates of market orientation believe all three goals will be achieved by the same basic policy: provision of a stable environment within which the free-market system can operate.

Providing a stable environment

We earlier mentioned market-oriented policies for creating a stable microeconomic environment. Creating the stable macroeconomic environment may, however, be easier said than done. We focus on the prescriptions for establishing stable fiscal and monetary policies.

One major problem to keep in mind is that macro variables are interrelated. The stability of one may imply the instability of another. In such cases, a choice must be made. How much instability of one aggregate should be tolerated in order to secure stability in another related aggregate?

Assume, for example, that people are so worried about budget deficits that the government decides to balance the budget as part of producing a stable macroeconomic environment.

This 'stability' would require *instability* in tax and/or expenditure policy. As we saw in Chapter 39, although governments can set tax *rates*, their tax revenues depend on the interaction between these tax rates and the level of national income. With given tax rates, tax revenues change with the ebb and flow of the business cycle. A stable budget balance would require that the government raise tax rates and cut expenditures in slumps, and lower tax rates and raise expenditures in booms.

Not only would this eliminate the budget's potential to act as a stabilizer, but great instability of the fiscal environment could be caused by continual changes in tax rates and expenditure levels. A stable fiscal environment requires reasonable stability in government expenditures and tax rates. Stability is needed so that the private sector can make plans for the future within a climate of known patterns of tax liabilities and government demand. This in turn requires that the budget balance should fluctuate cyclically, showing its largest deficits in slumps and its largest surpluses in booms.

Advocates of a stable macroeconomic environment are usually concerned to achieve a stable, and low, inflation rate – zero if possible. To accomplish this, the central bank is urged to set a target rate of increase in some measure of the money supply, often MO or M1, and hold to it. To establish the target, the central bank estimates the rate at which the demand for money (which depends on nominal income and the interest rate) would be growing if actual income equalled potential income and the price level were stable. As a first approximation, assuming no radical changes in the interest rate, this rate of growth in the demand for money can be taken to be the rate at which potential income itself is growing. This then becomes the target rate of growth of the money supply.

The key proposition is that the money supply should be changing gradually along a stable path that is independent of short-term variations in the demand for money caused by cyclical changes in national income. This is sometimes referred to as a 'k per cent rule', where k stands for the target rate of growth of the money supply.

Will the k per cent rule really provide monetary stability? The answer is 'not necessarily'. Assuring a stable rate of monetary growth does not assure a stable monetary environment because monetary shortages and surpluses depend on *the demand for* money as well as its supply.

Problems for the k per cent rule arise when the demand for money shifts. For example, payment of interest on sight deposits – a development seen in several countries in recent years – increases the demand for M1 (as people hold fewer sight deposits and more demand deposits). In this event, if the central bank adheres to a k per cent rule, there will be an excess demand for money, interest rates will rise and contractionary pressure will be put on the economy.

Should the central bank commit itself to a specific k per cent rule or merely work toward unannounced, and possibly variable, targets? The pre-announced target makes it easier to evaluate how well the central bank is doing its job. It also helps to prevent the central bank from trying to fine tune the economy with repeated changes in its monetary policy.

One disadvantage of such a rule is that the central bank, in order to preserve its credibility, may fail to take discretionary action that would otherwise be appropriate. For example, after an entrenched inflation is broken, the economy may come to rest with substantial unemployment and a stable price level. There is then a case for a once-and-for-all discretionary expansion in the money supply to get the economy back to full employment. The k per cent rule precludes this, condemning the economy to a prolonged slump unless other means of stimulating the economy can be found.

Despite such problems, advocates of market orientation believe the k per cent rule is superior to any known alternative. Some would agree that, in principle, the central bank could improve the economy's performance by occasional bouts of discretionary monetary policy to offset such things as major shifts in the demand for money. But they also believe that, once given any discretion, the central bank would abuse it in an attempt to fine tune the economy. The resulting instability would, they believe, be much more than any instability resulting from the application of a k per cent rule in an environment subject to some change.

Advocates of market orientation also want to let growth take care of itself. They argue that governments cannot improve the workings of free markets and that their interventions can interfere with market efficiency. Thus they advocate reducing the current level of government intervention.

Given the complex web of government rules, regulations and tax laws that have grown up over many years, the market-oriented agenda for reducing government intervention is usually a long one. Such an agenda was adopted by Thatcher governments from 1979 to 1990 in the UK. Some similar supply-side policies were also adopted in the United States by so-called *supply-siders* during the late 1970s and early 1980s.[1]

Some of the most important aspects of supply-side economics were reviewed in Chapter 39 (see pages 000) and these should be reviewed at this point. Once again, support of supply-side measures can be associated with market orientation, and hostility with interventionists. However, supply-side policies cover a wide range and many economists in many philosophical camps support at least some of them.

Interventionist Prescriptions

Full employment

Interventionists call for discretionary fiscal and monetary policies to offset significant GNP gaps. Some of the major problems associated with discretionary stabilization policy have been discussed in earlier chapters. Interventionists feel that in spite of lags and uncertainties of knowledge, the weakness of the forces leading to recovery from recessions will lead to the occasional occurrence of prolonged recession. These last long enough for expansionary fiscal and monetary policies to be employed without the instability issues that arise with fine-tuning in the face of continual shifts in the aggregate demand curve.

A stable price level

Some interventionists believe that the k per cent rule may not be enough to achieve full employment and stable prices simultaneously. This is because they accept the wage-cost push theory of inflation also discussed in Chapter 39. These

---

1 See earlier discussions on pages 455–7.

economists call for prices and incomes policies to restrain the wage-cost push and so make full employment compatible with stable prices. They believe that such policies should become permanent features of the economic landscape.

Prices and incomes policies: Permanent prices and incomes policies might be of two types. The first type, commonly used in Europe in earlier decades but now out of favour, is often called a *social contract*. Here labour, management and the government consult annually and agree on target wage and price changes. These are calculated to be non-inflationary, given the government's projections for the future and its planned economic policies. Such a scheme is most easily initiated in an economy such as West Germany's, where a few giant firms and unions exert enormous power. It has sometimes been possible in Britain, especially under a Labour government whose strong links with unions have sometimes helped it to gain union co-operation in an incomes policy. But so far, such agreements have never been long-lived. They have tended to break down after some time when the feeling grew that wage restraint was acting to reduce real wages because it failed to produce as much restraint on prices and profits as on wages.

The other main type of incomes policy is the 'tax-related incomes policy', or as it is often called, TIPs. This policy, which we encountered in Chapter 39, provides tax incentives for management and labour to conform to government-established wage and price guidelines. Advocates of TIPs argue that their great advantage is in leaving decisions on wages and prices in the hands of labour and management while seeking only to influence behaviour by altering the incentive system. Critics argue that they would prove to be an administrative nightmare.

Growth

Policies for intervention to increase growth rates are of two sorts. Some policies seek to alter the general economic climate in a way favourable to growth. They typically include subsidization, or favourable tax treatment, for research and development, for purchase of plant and equipment, and for other profit-earning activities. Measures to lower interest rates are urged by some as favourable to investment and growth. We saw in Chapter 38 that monetary policy cannot be used to reduce the real rate of interest permanently in a fully employed economy – but subsidies on interest payments would do the job. Many interventionists support such general measures.

Some also support more specific intervention, usually in the form of what is called 'picking and backing winners'. Advocates of this view want governments to pick the industries, usually new ones, that have potential for future success and then to back them with subsidies, government contracts, research funds and other incentives at the government's command.

Opponents argue that picking winners requires foresight, and that governments do not have better foresight than private investors. Indeed, since political considerations inevitably get in the way, the government may be less successful than the market in picking 'winners'. If so, channelling funds through the government rather than through the private sector may hurt rather than help growth rates. Many economists are sceptical of the government's ability to spot, and then back, potential winners. Sceptics point, for example, to the Concorde aircraft, which continued to absorb large amounts of investment expenditure, channelled to it for political reasons, long after any profit-maximizing firm would have dropped the project.

THE LONG-RUN PROSPECTS FOR GROWTH

We end this chapter, and this book, with a brief consideration of the long-run prospects for world growth. We have already observed several times that raising living standards depends critically on sustained economic growth (and also on controlling population). So many of the world's people live at extremely low living standards that little could be done to raise average living standards by redistributing existing income from the few 'have' countries to the many 'have not' countries. There are things that the rich countries can do by way of providing money and knowledge to encourage economic growth in poorer countries, but, in the long run, the prospect for raising living standards in those countries depends on the growth rates that they themselves can sustain. Similarly the prospect for raising living standards in the richer countries depends on their own growth rates.

It has been popular since the 1970s to argue that sustained growth is an impossible objective for the world. People who hold this view argue that the growth process will soon reach natural limits, and real incomes will then cease to grow throughout the world. Everything terrestrial has some ultimate limit. The ultimate of ultimate terrestrial limits will come when, as astronomers predict, the solar system itself dies with the burning out of the sun in another 6 billion or so years. To be of practical concern, therefore, a limit must be within some reasonable planning horizon. Best-selling books of the 1970s by Jay Forrester (*World Dynamics*, 1973) and D.H. Meadows *et al.* (*The Limits to Growth*, 1974) predicted the imminence of a 'growth-induced doomsday'. These books both contributed to and reflected the fear, prevalent in the 1970s, that growth was coming to a permanent halt due to resource limitations.

But these disaster models were purely mechanical. They took technology as given – i.e. they did not allow for the very long run. The early models did not allow prices of materials to rise as scarcities grew, nor did they consider all the market reactions to such increases in relative prices. Some of the forms taken by market reactions turned out to be conservation of scarce materials, substitution of other materials within known technology, discovery of new sources of the materials and, most important of all, the development of new technologies that substituted abundant materials for the scarce, high-priced materials. A parallel can be drawn with the famous pessimistic predictions of population growth outstripping food supplies, by the Revd. Thomas Malthus, almost 200 years ago, who failed to foresee the massive improvements in nineteenth-century technology.

After a decade of the world's adjustment to high oil prices, from the mid-1970s to the mid-1980s, people now realize that such adjustments can, and do, occur on a massive scale. The sequence is growing shortage, rising prices, then the adaptations mentioned above – some of which will be spread over a decade or more. The biggest threat to such market-induced adjustments is, perhaps, that government will frustrate them by holding down the price of the increasingly scarce commodities through subsidies and price controls. Many governments tried to do this with oil prices after the first OPEC shock in 1974. (The motives were partly anti-inflationary and partly redistributive to protect lower income groups from rapidly rising prices of heating and transportation.) Only later, when governments allowed oil prices to rise to their market values, did a host of adjustments finally begin – adjustments that eventually relieved the world from its heavy dependence on OPEC oil.

The power of market signals, and market reactions, in inducing adaptations to major shortages is now much more clearly understood than it was two decades ago. Human ingenuity, directed by market incentives, is capable of making vast, almost undreamed of, adjustments within the short space of a decade or two. The market mechanism undoubtedly has inefficiencies, and it certainly causes inequities, but no one has yet succeeded in devising an alternative with anything like the same power to induce, and co-ordinate, long-run adjustments. The adaptation that has eroded within the short space of 15 years the near-monopoly of OPEC countries over the world's energy supplies – when in the mid-1970s contemporary observers could see no escape from the monopoly – is testimony to the power of the market to induce and co-ordinate millions of individual adaptations. This experience does not necessarily provide a case for pure *laissez-faire*, but for a mixed economy with significant reliance on markets for efficiency reasons even if there is substantial intervention for distributive reasons.

Oil, however, is not the world's only exhaustible resource and the years since the Second World War have seen a rapid acceleration in the consumption of many resources. We are all familiar with one reason for this accelerated consumption – world population growth. World population has increased from under 2.5 billion to over 5 billion in that period and this alone has greatly increased the demand for the world's resources.

A second major reason is growth in living standards for a *given* total of world population. Calculations have focused on the resources used by those people throughout the world who have living standards equal to the standards enjoyed by 90 per cent of the people in Western Europe and the United States. This so-called 'middle class', which today includes about one-sixth of the world's population, consumes 15 to 30 times as much oil per capita and, overall, at least 5 times as much of the earth's scarce resources per capita, as do the other 'poor' five-sixths of the world's population.

Economic growth has added nearly 4 per cent per year to the number of people throughout the world who achieve this 'middle class' standard over the post-war period. The number of persons realizing these living standards is estimated to have increased from 200 million to nearly one billion between 1950 and 1990. (Box 36.2 on page 414 is relevant here.)

Economic growth is a major cause of projected shortages of many natural resources: the increases in demand of the last three decades have outstripped discovery of new supplies and caused crises in energy, and in the supplies of many minerals, as well as food shortages. Yet the 4 per cent growth rate in the size of the 'middle class', which is probably too fast for present resources to sustain, is too slow for the aspirations of the billions who live in underdeveloped countries and hope for economic growth to relieve their poverty. Thus the pressure on world resources of energy, minerals and food is likely to accelerate even if population growth is reduced.

Another way of looking at the problem of resource pressure is to note that present technology, and resources, could not possibly support the present population of the world at the standard of living of today's average Western European or North American family. For example, the demand for oil would increase nearly tenfold. Since these calculations (most unrealistically) assume no population growth anywhere in the world, and no growth in living standards for the richest sixth of the world's population, it is evident that resources are insufficient.

A Tentative Verdict

Most economists agree that conjuring up absolute limits to growth, based on the assumptions of constant technology and fixed supplies of known resources, is unwarranted. Yet there is surely cause for concern. Most agree that any single barrier to growth can be overcome by technological advances – *but not in an instant, and not automatically*. Clearly, there is a problem of timing: how soon can we discover, and put into practice, the knowledge required to solve the problems that are made ever more urgent by growth in population, growth in affluence, and by the aspirations of the billions who now live in poverty? There is no guarantee that a whole generation may not be caught by the transition, with social and political consequences that would certainly be enormous, and possibly cataclysmic.

The nightmares conjured up by the doomsday models may have served their purpose if they helped to focus attention both on the power of the market mechanism to induce and co-ordinate adjustments to change, and on the severe limitation that the existing supply of known resources puts on the possibilities of rapidly raising world living standards.

Summary

1 In current policy debates, micro and macro issues are intertwined. The micro performance of the economy affects its macro performance, and vice versa.

2 On every policy issue, two extreme positions can be defined. The market-oriented view would leave the issue to be settled by the free market, while the interventionist view would look to government intervention to produce a better result than would be produced by the unaided free market.

3 On the trade cycle, the market-oriented view (which is roughly the Monetarist view) is that, in practice, stabilization policy worsens cyclical swings and it should not be used. The interventionist view, while wary of precise fine-tuning, holds that serious and prolonged slumps will occur from time to time and that these can be alleviated by conscious stabilization policy.

4 On the price level, the market-oriented view calls for stable monetary targets consistent with a long-run, low-inflation target and for no monetary fine-tuning. The interventionist view emphasizes non-monetary causes of changes in the price level and holds that non-monetary cures may be needed. Both sides accept, however, that the money supply and the price level are intimately associated.

5 On growth, the market-oriented view is that governments should provide a stable background of law and order, and a steady price level, leaving private initiative, acting through free markets, to achieve a satisfactory growth rate. Supply-side economics includes measures designed to raise the growth rate by reducing government intervention and so increase the scope for private effort and initiative operating through free markets. The interventionist view emphasizes poor entrepreneurial performance and an alleged lack of risk-taking by large monopolistic firms and calls for government intervention to increase growth rates.

6 Sustained economic growth is required if the poorest of the world's population is to achieve anything like the living standards enjoyed by the richest. Achieving this result would put impossible strains on present resources under existing technology. The experience of the world's adjustment to high oil prices over not much more than ten years suggests, however, that market adjustments would occur and new technologies would be developed to avoid the severe restraints on long-term growth that would otherwise be exercised by growing scarcities of materials heavily used under present conditions.

Questions

True or False?
(a) Enforcing an annually balanced budget would remove the built-in stabilizing effects of fixed expenditures and tax rates.
(b) Following the k per cent rule would prevent monetary policy from being used as an instrument of short-term stabilization policy.
(c) It would be difficult or impossible to raise the real incomes of the LDCs to those of the advanced nations using known technologies.

Typical interventionist views include which of the following?
(a) Markets have strong self-regulatory powers.
(b) The trade cycle has many real causes such as the volatility of investment expenditure.
(c) Once-and-for-all supply-shock inflations should be accompanied by monetary expansion to prevent heavy unemployment from persisting for a long time.
(d) Inflation should be controlled through prices and incomes policies.
(e) Strong growth of potential income is the normal outcome of the operation of the market economy.

3 Discuss the pros and cons of encouraging further rapid economic growth in the advanced nations as a means of raising *world* living standards and dealing with world environmental problems.

Appendix 1
Graphs in Economics

Economics is about quantities, and the relation between different quantities. In this appendix we deal with the method of showing these relations graphically. For some readers this appendix will be unnecessary; for others it will be a useful review; for yet others it will be a way of learning some of the topics covered in GCSE maths that are needed to read this book.

Representation of the values of variables on a line

First, recall an important term that was introduced in Chapter 1. A *variable* is some quantity, such as the price of wheat, that can take on various values. For example, the price of wheat might be £90 per tonne at one time, and £110 per tonne at another time.

Part (i) of Figure A1.1 shows a line. The arrowheads show that the line can be extended in either direction as far as we need. To represent on this line the value of some variable, which we call X, we start by choosing a point on the line and label it O to indicate the situation in which the value of X is zero. Next we mark off equal distances to the right to indicate positive values, running from 0 to 10. (We could extend the line further if necessary.) We also mark off equal distances to the left of the zero point to indicate negative values of X, running up to -10. (Again, we could go further if necessary.)

The SCALE of the line is the amount of distance corresponding to one unit of the variable's value. In this particular line the scale is 3mm = 1 unit.

To show the value of any item, we locate the point corresponding to its value. For example, if X is 2, we plot a point at the spot labelled 2. For ease of reference, we call this point a. If X is -3.5, we plot a point at -3.5. We call this point b.

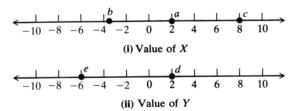

(i) Value of X

(ii) Value of Y

FIGURE A1.1 Measuring the Values of a Variable on a Line.

So far, we have started with values of the variable and plotted them on the line. We can also reverse the process. If we start with point c in the Figure, we can see that this represents a value of 8 for the variable X.

In part (ii) of the Figure we draw another line and use it to represent values of a second variable that we call Y. The procedure is the same as we used in part (i). For example, the value of 2 is plotted as point d and, if we are told that there is a point at e, we know that this means a value for Y of -6.

Notation for specific but unspecified values of variables

Let our variable, X, be a person's age. We now want to indicate

that the person has some specific age, but do not want to specify what age. Using a subscript to indicate that specific, but unspecified, age, we write it as X_1. Next, we want to indicate another person's specific, but again unspecified, age. We let Y be the variable for that person's age and indicate the specific value as Y_1. Some years later, the two persons have different specific, but once again unspecified, ages and we write these as X_2 and Y_2. The subscript, therefore, tells us that we are referring to a specific value of the variable, and a second, different, subscript that we are referring to another specific value.

A co-ordinate graph

Often we want to know if there is a relation between two variables which we may call X and Y. To do this, we can create what is called a *co-ordinate graph* by placing the line Y in Figure A1.1 at a right-angle to the line for X, so that the two points indicating zero for X and zero for Y coincide. This is done in Figure 1A.2.

The Figure now has two lines, one of which measures values of X and one of which measures values of Y. These two lines are called AXES. The horizontal line is called the HORIZONTAL AXIS or the X AXIS, and the vertical line is called the VERTICAL AXIS or the Y AXIS. The point where the two axes intersect, which corresponds to zero values of both X and Y, is called the ORIGIN.

This way of depicting two variables on one graph was invented some 350 years ago by the great French mathematician and philosopher René Descartes. To this day the diagram shown in Figure A1.2 is called a Cartesian diagram.

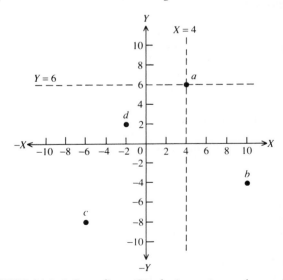

FIGURE A1.2 A Co-ordinate Graph. Any point on the graph refers to a pair of values, one for X and one for Y.

The vertical distance to some point located in this diagram indicates its Y value. For example, *every point on the broken line* drawn through the value 6 on the *Y axis* indicates that *Y* has a value of 6. Also, *every point on the horizontal line drawn through 4 on the X* axis indicates that *X* has a value of 4. Now look at the *point* labelled *a*, where the vertical and the horizontal lines that we have just constructed intersect. This point indicates the combination of values *Y* = 6 and *X* = 4.

Every *point* on the co-ordinate graph corresponds to a *pair of values* called the co-ordinates of the point. The vertical distance of the point from the *X* axis tells us its *Y* value, while the horizontal distance of the point from the *Y* axis tells us its *X* value. For example, if you were told that *X* = 10 while *Y* = −4, you would plot this as point *b* in Figure A1.2. If you were given points in *c* and *d* on the Figure, you would read off from the scales on the axes that *X* = −6 and *Y* = −8 at *c*, and *X* = −2 and *Y* = +2 at *d*.

Notice that the two axes divide the graph into four segments. These are called QUADRANTS. This division is illustrated in Figure A1.3. In the upper right-hand quadrant, both *X* and *Y* are positive; in the lower right-hand quadrant, *X* is positive while *Y* is negative; in the lower left-hand quadrant, both *X* and *Y* are negative; and, finally, in the upper left-hand quadrant, *X* is negative while *Y* is positive.

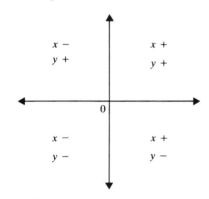

FIGURE A1.3 The Four Quadrants of the Cartesian Graph. The two axes divide the graph into four quadrants.

The upper right-hand quadrant, where both *X* and *Y* are zero or positive, is often called the POSITIVE QUADRANT. Many economic variables can only take on zero or positive values. For this reason many, although not all, economic diagrams only use the positive quadrant. Such a diagram is shown in Figure A1.5. The other quadrants are still there; we just do not bother to draw them in because we do not need to consider negative values of the variables being plotted.

Alternative ways of showing quantities on charts

The Cartesian diagram unites algebra, with its numbers and equations, with geometry, with its distances and angles. This means that the values of variables can be indicated in either of two ways, when specific numbers are not to be specified. One of these is algebraic in concept, and the other is geometric. Parts (i) and (ii) of Figure A1.4 illustrate these for point *a*, which was plotted against the numerical values of its co-ordinates in Figure A1.2. (The broken lines drawn vertically and horizontally from *a* to the *X* and *Y* axes are referred to as *grid lines* or *guide lines*.)

In part (i), the representation of algebraic quantities is stressed. Thus, the symbols X_1 and Y_1 refer to the algebraic values of the *X* and *Y* co-ordinates of the point *a*. In the case of point *a*, X_1 is 4 and Y_1 is 6. If we only had Figure A1.4(i) and not A1.2, we would refer to the value of the variable *X* as X_1, and to the value

of the variable *Y* as Y_1. This usage is algebraic in conception, using letters to stand for numerical values.

In part (ii), the representation of geometric distances is stressed. The points where the grid lines drawn through point *a* cut the two axes are indicated by letters, in this case *M* and *N* respectively. These letters are regarded as identifying two points on a geometrical diagram. The value of point *a*'s *X* co-ordinate is then indicated geometrically as a *distance* from the origin to the point *M*. The value of the *X* co-ordinate of *a* is thus *OM*. Similarly, the value of the *Y* co-ordinate of point *a* is *ON*.

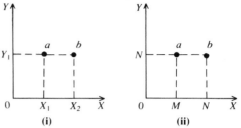

FIGURE A1.4 Alternative Ways of Plotting Numerical Values. Parts (i) and (ii) plot point *a*, whose co-ordinates as *x* = 4 and *Y* = 6, which was first plotted in Figure A1.2. However, in this new Figure the numerical scale is surpressed. Instead the two parts of the Figure show alternative ways of indicating the values of the co-ordinates in general terms. In part (i), X_1 and Y_1 stand for the values of the *X* and Y_1 co-ordinates, which are 4 and 6 in this example. In part (ii), the geometric distances *OM* and *ON* stand for these same values of the *X* and *Y* co-ordinates.

These are two different ways of showing the same thing: the values of the variables *X* and *Y* that define the point *a*. In part (i), the notation refers to specific algebraic values indicated as points on the *X* and *Y* scales. In part (ii), the notation refers to distances measured from the origin which stand for the values of the variables *X* and *Y*.

Differences between two magnitudes: Often it is necessary to indicate the difference between two magnitudes measured on a graph. We may want to know, for example, by how much *X* and *Y* increase when we move from one point on a line drawn on a graph to another point. Once again, we have a choice between two different types of notation, one algebraic, the other geometric.

The difference is illustrated in the two parts of Figure A1.4. In both parts, the point *b* has the same *Y* value as the point *a*, but it has a larger *X* value. Now let us ask: By how much does *X* increase when we move from *a* to *b*?

Look first at part (i), which shows the algebraic representation of the values of *X* and *Y*. The value of *X* increases in the Figure from X_1 to X_2 when we move from *a* to *b*. The increase in the value of *X* is the difference between the two values. This is $X_2 - X_1$. Notice that, to make the difference positive, we take the larger value, X_2 in this case, and subtract the smaller value, X_1 in this case. In a particular numerical example where X_1 is 4 and X_2 is 6, the increase in *X* caused by going from *a* to *b* is $6 - 4 = 2$.

Using the algebraic notation, the difference between two values measured on either the *X* or the *Y* axes is given by the larger value minus the lesser value, i.e. $X_2 - X_1$ or $Y_2 - Y_1$, where the first number in each pair is the larger of the two.

Now look at part (ii), which shows the geometric representation of values of *X* and *Y*. In this part, the value of *X* increases from *OM* to *ON* when we go from point *a* to point *b*. The increase in the value of *X* is the difference between these two values. This is the distance *ON* minus the distance *OM*, which is the distance *NM*. Thus the segment of the axis from *M* to *N* has a distance which corresponds to the difference between the value of *X* indicated by point *a* and the value of *X* indicated by point *b*.

Using the geometric notation, the difference between two values measured on either the *X* or the *Y* axes is given by the length of the segment of the axis between the point indicated by the larger of the values and the point indicated by the smaller of the values. It is indicated by quoting the letters at each end of the line segment in question.

It is important to realise that these are two ways of indicating exactly the same thing, the difference between two values of some variable. On a graph, this difference is shown by the length of the line segment between the two points on the axis that represent the two values taken by the variables. In the geometric notation, the letters attached to the two end points of that segment are used to indicate it. In the algebraic notation, the length of the line segment is indicated by writing a symbol for the higher of the two values that the variable takes minus the symbol for the smaller value.

In this book, we use the algebraic approach given in part (i). In many other British books, and in many examination papers, you will find the geometric approach of part (ii) used. You will not have any trouble *as long as you remember that any value of X plotted along the X axis can be indicated either by a symbol for its value at a point on that axis, such as X_1 or X_2, or by a symbol for its distance measured from the origin, indicated by a pair of letters such as OM or OP.*

Alternative ways of indicating distances: It is natural to measure distances along the two axes, since that is where their scales are plotted. However, it is sometimes convenient to measure distances in the interior of a diagram. It is important to understand that these are two equivalent measures of the same thing.

Consider, for example, the *X* co-ordinate of point *a* in part (ii) of Figure A1.4. The geometric expression of this value is *OM*, but the identical distance is measured by *Na*. Both of these distances measure the distance from the origin to point *a*, in a horizontal direction. Similarly, the value of the *Y* co-ordinate of point *a* is either measured as *ON* or *Ma*. Both of these measure the vertical distance from the origin to point *a*.

Graphs and schedules

A SCHEDULE is a list of values of particular variables. Assume, for example, that we have studied eight households and observed their annual incomes and the amount that each household saves. These values are listed in the schedule shown in Table A1.1.

We wonder if these two variables are related, and to 'see' any

TABLE A1.1 Annual Income and Annual Saving for Eight Selected Households

Househould	Annual income (£s)	Annual saving (£s)
1	7,000	1,500
2	3,000	1,000
3	10,000	3,000
4	6,000	2,000
5	8,000	3,000
6	1,000	0
7	2,000	500
8	5,000	1,500
9	4,000	500
10	9,000	2,500

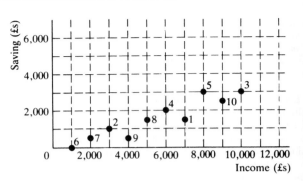

FIGURE A1.5 A Scatter Diagram for Income and Saving. Each point on the diagram shows the income and the saving of a particular household.

possible relation we plot them on a co-ordinate diagram. We plot income on the *X* axis and saving on the *Y* axis. Each household then becomes a point on our diagram. The point tells us that household's income and its saving. This is shown in Figure A1.5. Each household has been given a reference number in the above Table and this number is written in over its corresponding point in the Figure. The Figure suggests a tendency that is used at length in this book: the higher is a household's income, the larger the amount that the household tends to save. This type of graph is called a SCATTER DIAGRAM.

Graphs and equations

In the above graph, we plotted an observed relation between two variables. We can also use co-ordinate graphs to plot relations between variables that are expressed in algebraic equations. This is important because much of economics deals with relations between variables that can be expressed either in equations or in graphs.

Let us say that some economic theory of the relation between two variables *X* and *Y* predicts that *Y* will always be twice as large as *X*. We can write this as the following equation:

$$Y = 2X$$

The equation says just what we said in words above: the value of *Y* is always the value of *X* multiplied by 2.

We can investigate this relation by drawing up a schedule. To do so, we take selected values of *X* and calculate the corresponding values of *Y*. This is done for a few values in Table A1.2.

TABLE A1.2 Values of Y Corresponding to Selected Values of X in the Equation $Y = 2X$

Reference point	Values of X	Values of Y
a	2	4
b	4	8
c	8	16
d	12	24

These four points are plotted on a co-ordinate diagram in Figure A1.6.

To graph the whole relation, we graph the line that corresponds to the equation $Y = 2X$. This line is shown by the solid line going through the four points that we have already plotted in Figure A1.6.

Note that this line goes through the origin. This tells us that when *X* is zero, *Y* is also zero, which can be confirmed by setting

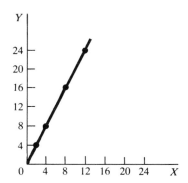

FIGURE A1.6 **The Graph of a Straight Line** $Y = 2X$.

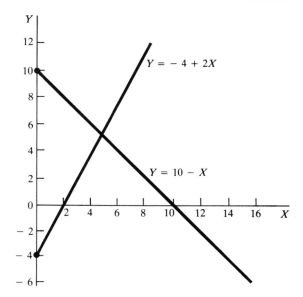

FIGURE A1.7 **The Graph of Two Specific Linear Relations.** The graph of a positive association between two variables slopes upward to the right; the graph of a negative association slopes downward to the right.

X at zero in the above equation. Notice also that the line slopes upward to the right. This indicates that as X increases, Y also increases. This is an example of what is called a positive association between the two variables; as one increases, so does the other. In such a case we say that the two variables are POSITIVELY RELATED to each other.

A linear relation

The equation $Y = 2X$ is an example of what is called a LINEAR RELATION between the two variables. The general equation of a linear relation is as follows:

$$Y = a + bX$$

We must now look at this relation in some detail.

The *variables* in this equation are X and Y. As X takes on various values, Y takes on specific associated values.

The magnitudes a and b are called PARAMETERS. Parameters take on particular fixed values to define some specific example of the general relation. They are constants for that relation, but they take on other fixed values for other examples. For example, in the equation given earlier, a was zero and b was 2. This gave rise to the graph shown in Figure A1.6. Two other examples are given by first letting a equal -4 and b equal 2, and then letting a equal 10 and b equal -1. These give rise to the two following equations:

$$Y = -4 + 2X$$

$$Y = 10 - X$$

These two equations are graphed in Figure A1.7.

Now we can show the key characteristics of the graph of the general linear relation, of which the above are two examples.

(1) The constant term a gives the value of the intercept of the graph on the Y axis. The Y INTERCEPT is the value of Y where the graph of the equation cuts the Y axis. It is found by letting X equal zero (as it is everywhere along the Y axis). Putting X at zero in the above two examples tells us that $Y = -4$ in the first example and $Y = 10$ in the second example.

(2) The sign of the parameter b tells us whether the slope of the line is positive or negative. In the first equation above, Y is positively related to X because the larger is Y, the larger is X. The graph of a positive relation between two variables slopes upward to the right. In the second equation above, Y is NEGATIVELY RELATED to X because the larger is X, the smaller is Y. The graph of a negative relation between two variables slopes downward to the right, i.e. it is *negatively sloped*.

(3) The magnitude of the parameter b tells us how much Y changes every time X changes. The *larger* is the magnitude of b, the *more* does Y change every time X changes. The graphical

expression of this is that the larger is the magnitude of b, the steeper is the line expressing the relation between the two variables. To be precise, b gives the slope of the line that graphs the equation. To show that this is so, we need to use a little algebra.

The slope of a linear relation

First, look at the example given above where $Y = -4 + 2X$. Let X take on the value of 2. Y is then $(2 \times 2) - 4$, which is 0. Now let X take on the value of 3. Y is now $(2 \times 3) - 4$, which is $+2$. This illustrates that the increase in Y for a unit change in X is 2, which is the value of the parameter b.

Now let us do this more generally. Let X take on any specific value, X_1, and calculate the corresponding value of Y, which we obtain by multiplying X_1 by b and adding a:

$$Y_1 = a + bX_1 \tag{1}$$

Now let X take on a second specific value, which we call X_2, and calculate the corresponding value of Y, called Y_2:

$$Y_2 = a + bX_2 \tag{2}$$

Next subtract the first equation from the second. To do this we subtract the LHS (which stands for the left-hand side) of (1) from the LHS of (2) and the RHS (which stands for the right-hand side) of (1) from the RHS of (2). This gives us:

$$Y_2 - Y_1 = (a + bX_2) - (a + bX_1) \tag{3}$$

This simplifies to:

$$Y_2 - Y_1 = bX_2 - bX_1 \tag{4}$$

Notice that the constant term a has now disappeared. It only determines the intercept, and has nothing to do with how Y *changes* as X *changes*.

Equation (4) can be further simplified by factoring out the common term b from the right-hand side to obtain:

$$Y_2 - Y_1 = b(X_2 - X_1) \tag{5}$$

('Factoring out' merely means that, since Y appears in both terms, the two terms can be shown grouped together – in brackets – and multiplied by the common Y term.

This tells us that the change in Y is equal to b times the change in X. We now use a common device of symbolizing *the change in* any variable by the Greek letter delta, Δ. Thus we can rewrite the above as

$$\Delta Y = b\Delta X \qquad (6)$$

Equation (6) says exactly the same thing as equation (5), only it says it in our new notation where Δ means 'the change in' the variable to which it is attached.

Finally, if we divide both sides of (6) by ΔX, we obtain:

$$\Delta Y/\Delta X = b \qquad (7)$$

This tells us that the parameter b expresses the ratio of the change in Y to the change in X. In other words, it tells us the change in Y *per unit change in X*.

Finally, look at the graph of this equation, $Y = a + bX$. A specific case is shown in Figure A1.8. The original point on the line is shown by the values X_1 and Y_1. The new point is shown by the values X_2 and Y_2. The change in Y, which is $Y_2 - Y_1$, is indicated in the Figure by ΔY, while the change in X, which is $X_2 - X_1$, is indicated by ΔX. In geometry, the SLOPE of a line is given by the ratio of the change in Y divided by the change in X, which is $\Delta Y/\Delta X$ in the Figure. But we have already seen that this ratio is equal to b.

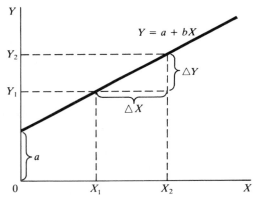

FIGURE A1.8 The Slope of a Straight-Line Graph. The slope of a straight line measures the change in Y per unit change in X.

We conclude, therefore, that the parameter b in a linear equation gives the slope of the line that plots that equation, and that this is the ratio of the change in Y to the change in X. This ratio tells us how much Y changes *per unit change in X*.

On a straight line, the slope is constant over its whole length. This is shown algebraically by the fact that the slope parameter b is a constant.

Non-linear relations

So far we have dealt only with linear relations – relations in which Y changes by the same amount every time X changes by one unit no matter where we are on the line. Many economic relations, however, are non-linear. An example is shown in Figure A1.9. This curve relates the output of a large firm to the revenue that it can gain from selling that output. On the curve, the X axis refers to the firm's output and the Y axis refers to its sales revenue.

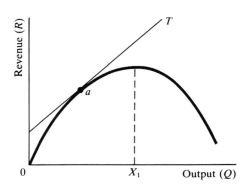

FIGURE A1.9 A Non-Linear Function.

We will study how this relation arises later in this book; in the meantime we merely study its properties.[1]

Notice that when X increases from zero to X_1, Y also increases. Over this range, Y is positively related to X. But also notice that as X increases beyond X_1, Y decreases. Over this range, Y is negatively related to X. Also note that, as X increases from zero Y increases a great deal. This is shown by the steepness of the curve when X is close to zero. Note further that, as X approaches the value of X_1, Y increases less and less as X increases, until when X reaches X_1, Y is no longer increasing as X increases. This is shown by the flatness of the curve just to the left of X_1.

Tangents to curves

To carry the discussion further, we need a precise measure of how steep or flat a curve is at some point. We do this in two steps.

A TANGENT to a curve at a particular point is a straight line that just touches the curve at a particular point. In Figure A1.9 we have drawn a tangent to the curve at point a. The tangent is labelled T.

The second step is to measure the slope of the tangent. This is done in the manner discussed above. The tangent is a straight line, so its equation is $Y = a + bX$ and its slope is b. We saw above that this slope parameter b measures the ratio of the change in Y to the change in X (i.e. $\Delta Y/\Delta X$) along the line.

Thus the slope of any curve at a particular point is measured precisely by the slope of the tangent to the curve at that point, and it can be interpreted as showing how Y is tending to change *per unit change in X* at that point of the curve.

Marginal values and incremental ratios

Economic theory makes much use of what are called 'marginal' concepts. Marginal cost, marginal revenue, marginal rate of substitution and marginal propensity to consume are a few examples that we will meet later in this book. MARGINAL means on the margin or border, and the concept refers to what would happen if there were a small change from the present position.

Marginals refer to relations that can be expressed in curves. We draw the curve relating Y to X and we wish to know what would be the change in Y if X changed by a small amount from its present value. The answer is referred to as the marginal value of Y and is given various names depending on what economic variables X and Y stand for.

---

1 The equation of this particular curve is $Y = a + bX + cX^2$, where a is zero, b positive, and c is negative.

There are two ways of measuring the marginal value of Y. One is exact and the other is an approximation. Because the exact measure uses differential calculus, introductory texts in economics usually use the approximation, which depends only on simple algebra. Students are often justifiably confused because much of the language of economic theory refers to the exact measure while introductory examples use the approximation. For this reason it is worth explaining both now.

Consider the example shown in Figure A1.10, in which a firm's output, Q, is measured on the X axis and the total revenue earned by selling this output, R, is measured on the Y axis.

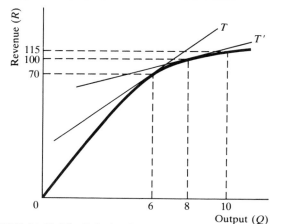

FIGURE A1.10 The Relation Between a Firm's Output and its Revenues.

The marginal concept that corresponds to this function is *marginal revenue*. It refers to the change in the firm's revenue when sales are altered slightly from their present level. But what do we mean by 'altered slightly'? There are two answers, depending on which marginal concept we use.

The approximation to marginal revenue is called the INCREMENTAL RATIO. Let sales in Figure A1.10 be 6, with a corresponding revenue of £70. Now increase sales to 8, so that, according to the Figure, revenue rises to £100. The increase in sales is 2 and the increase in revenue is £30. Using the Δ notation for changes, we can write this as

$$\Delta R/\Delta Q = £30/2 = £15$$

This tell us that sales are increasing at an average rate of £15 *per unit of commodity* over the range of sales from 6 to 8 units. We may call this the marginal revenue at 6 units of output but, as we shall see, it is only an approximation to the true marginal revenue at that output.

Graphically, incremental revenue is the slope of the line joining the two points in question. In this case they are the two points on the revenue line corresponding to outputs of 6 and 8. This is shown in Figure A1.11, which is an enlargement of the relevant section of the curve in Figure A1.10. Now look at the triangle created by these points. Its base is 2 units long and its vertical side is 30 units in height. The slope of the hypotenuse of the triangle is $30/2 = 15$, which is the incremental revenue. Visually it is clear that this slope tells us the average gradient or steepness of the revenue function over the range from $Q = 6$ to $Q = 8$. It thus tells us how fast revenue is changing as output changes over that range of Q.

Incremental revenue will be different at different points on the curve. For example, when output goes from 8 to 10, revenue goes from 100 to 115 and this gives us an incremental revenue of

$$\Delta R/\Delta Q = £15/2 = £7.50$$

This calculation confirms what visual inspection of the Figure suggests: the larger is output (at least over the ranges graphed in the Figure), the less is the response of revenue to further increases in output.

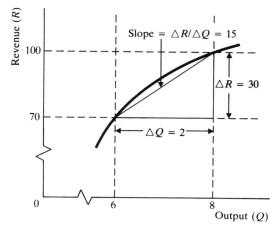

FIGURE A1.11 Calculation of the Incremental Revenue on a Non-Linear Curve. The incremental revenue shows the average change in revenue per unit change in output over a range of the revenue curve.

The incremental ratio is an approximation to the true marginal concept, which is based on the derivative of differential calculus. The derivative is symbolized in general by dY/dX, and, in the case of the relation we are now considering between the two variables R and Q, it is symbolized by dR/dQ. It measures the tendency for R to change as Q changes *at a precise point on the curve* (whereas the incremental ratio measures the average tendency *over a range of the curve*).

The value of the derivative is given by the slope of the tangent at the point on the function in which we are interested. Thus 'true' marginal revenue at 6 units of output is given by the slope of the tangent, T, to the curve at that point. This slope measures the tendency for R to change *per unit change in Q* at the precise value at which it is evaluated (i.e. the point on the function at which the tangent is drawn).

We saw in the example of Figure A1.10 that the incremental ratio declined as we measured it at larger and larger values of Q. It should be visually obvious that this is also true for marginal revenue in that particular curve: the slope of the tangent to the curve will be smaller the larger is the value of Q at which the tangent is taken. Two examples are shown in Figure A1.10; one, T, for $Q = 6$ and the other, T', for $Q = 8$.

Now try measuring the incremental ratio, starting at 6 units of output but for smaller and smaller changes in output. Instead of going from 6 to 8, go, for example, from 6 to 7. This brings the two points in question closer together and, in the present case, it steepens the slope of the line joining them. It is visually clear in the present example that as ΔQ is made smaller and smaller, the slope of the line corresponding to the incremental ratio starting from $Q = 6$ gets closer and closer to the slope of tangent corresponding to the true marginal value evaluated at $Q = 6$.

Let us now state our conclusions in general for a curve relating the variables X and Y.

(1) The marginal value of Y at some initial value of X is the rate of change of Y per unit change in X, as X changes from its initial value.

(2) The marginal value is given by the slope of the tangent to the curve showing the relation between the two variables drawn at the value of X.

(3) The incremental ratio $\Delta Y/\Delta X$ measures the average change in Y per unit change in X over a range of the curve starting from the initial value of X.

(4) As the range of measurement of the incremental ratio is reduced (i.e. as ΔX gets smaller and smaller), the value of the incremental ratio eventually approaches the true marginal value of Y. Thus the incremental ratio may be regarded as an approximation to the true marginal value, the degree of approximation improving as ΔX gets very small.

Appendix 2
The Derivation of Elasticity of Demand at a Point on a Linear Demand Curve

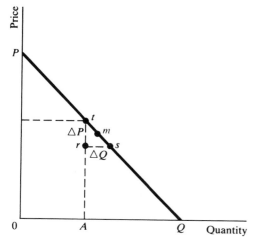

FIGURE A2.1

We are given the demand curve in Figure A2.1 and required to find the elasticity of demand at point t. The formula for elasticity of demand is

$$\eta = \frac{\Delta Q}{\Delta P} \times \frac{P}{Q}$$

We use the geometric method of indicating prices and quantities by naming the parts of each end of the line segment whose distance measures the amount in question.

At price At, the value of η in the formula is

$$\eta = \frac{\Delta Q}{\Delta P} \times \frac{At}{OA} \tag{1}$$

The triangles trs and POQ are similar. Therefore the ratio of any two sides of those triangles are similar.

Thus

$$\frac{\Delta Q}{\Delta P} = \frac{AQ}{At} \tag{2}$$

Substituting (2) in (1) to give

$$\eta = \frac{AQ}{At} \times \frac{At}{OA}$$

The At's cancel out, leaving

$$\eta = \frac{AQ}{OA}$$

Since At and OP are parallel,

$$\frac{AQ}{OA} = \frac{Qt}{tP}$$

Therefore

$$\eta = \frac{Qt}{tP} \tag{3}$$

At any point on a linear demand curve,[1] the value of elasticity of demand is equal to the length from the point to the quantity axis divided by the length from the point to the price axis. Therefore, at the mid-point, m in the diagram, elasticity equals unity.

---

1 For curvilinear demand curves, draw a tangent to the point at which demand is to be measured. The statement above is now applicable to the tangent to the curve.

Appendix 3
Derivation of Equilibrium Values for Simple Micro and Macro Models

(A) Micro Market Equilibrium

Market equilibrium was derived in Chapter 8, using demand and supply schedules, and graphs. It is also possible to derive the equilibrium price and quantity using algebra.

As explained in Appendix 1, a line on a graph is an expression of a relationship between two variables, which can also be expressed in the form of an equation. Hence, we can find equations which are represented by the supply and demand curves for bottles of cider, which are drawn on Figure 8.1 (see page 73). These are as follows:

The demand equation is

$$Q_d = 21 - 5p \qquad (A.1)$$

The supply equation is

$$Q_s = -6 + 10p \qquad (A.2)$$

(You might like to check these for yourself. Assume a value for p and, using equation (A.1), calculate the quantity demanded. For example, if $p = 3$, $q_d = 21 - (5 \times 3) = 6$. $p = 3$, $q = 6$, is one point on the demand curve. The supply equation can be similarly checked.)

To find the market equilibrium price and quantity, using the supply and demand equations, we need to bring in our definition of market equilibrium. This is that quantity demanded equals quantity supplied. In symbols this is:

$$Q_s = Q_d \qquad (A.3)$$

To find the value of p which will make the quantity demanded equal to the quantity supplied, we need, therefore, to solve equation (A.3), after substituting equations (A.1) and (A.2) for the simple $Q_s = Q_d$. In other words we must solve:

$$-6 + 10p = 21 - 5p \qquad (A.4)$$

Equation (A.4) contains only a single unknown, p. So we solve it in the usual manner, by bringing all the terms with p to one side of the equation, leaving the terms without p on the other side (remembering to change the sign of any term which we transfer from one side of the equation to the other side).

Thus, equation (A.4) may be rewritten:

$$10p + 5p = 21 + 6$$

which simplifies to

$$15p = 27$$

and, therefore, also to

$$p = \frac{27}{15} = 1.8$$

The solution to the equation for market equilibrium is that price is therefore 1.8.

The final step in the analysis is to find the quantity supplied and demanded at price 1.8. The quantity supplied at that price is found by substituting 1.8 for p in the supply equation (A.2):

$$Q_s = -6 + 10p$$
$$= -6 + (10 \times 1.8)$$
$$= -6 + 18$$
$$= 12$$

The quantity demanded at the price 1.8 is found by substituting 1.8 for p in the demand equation (A.1):

$$Q_d = 21 - 5p$$
$$= 21 - (5 \times 1.8)$$
$$= 21 - 9$$
$$= 12$$

Thus we have found that if price is equal to 1.8, the quantity demanded and the quantity supplied are each equal to 12. This confirms that the market is in equilibrium when price is 1.8.

We may note, too, that the equilibrium we have found using algebra is exactly the same as the equilibrium we found using graphical methods in Figure 8.1. The intersection of the supply and demand curves in that diagram occurs at price £1.80 and quantity supplied and demanded 12.

(B) Macroeconomic Equilibrium

The macroeconomic model may be handled algebraically in a manner similar to what we just used for the micro model. We shall do this first for a numerical example and then in more general terms.

A numerical example: Consider the simple Keynesian model of Chapter 25 in the text, in which the autonomous component of consumption is £100m, and the induced component is always 80 per cent of national income. We can write this as:

$$C = 100 + 0.8Y \qquad (B.1)$$

Next, we assume that exogenous investment is £400m, which we write as:

$$I = 400 \qquad (B.2)$$

In this simple model, there are only two elements of desired expenditure, consumption and investment. Thus we can write:

$$E = C + I \qquad (B.3)$$

If we substitute equations (B.1) and (B.2) into (B.3), we get:

$$E = 100 + 0.8Y + 400$$

Next we consolidate the autonomous component in consumption with autonomous investment by summing the two constant terms to get:

$$E = 500 + 0.8Y \qquad (B.4)$$

To find equilibrium income, we note that, in this model, the condition for national income to be in equilibrium is that desired expenditure should equal actual income:

$$Y = E \qquad (B.5)$$

If we substitute (B.4), which gives expenditure in our numerical example, into (B.5), which gives the general condition for equilibrium, we get:

$$Y = 500 + 0.8Y \qquad (B.6)$$

This is solved in a few simple steps. First, subtract $0.8Y$ from both sides to get:

$$Y - 0.8Y = 500 \qquad (B.7)$$

Next, factor out the Y that is common to the two terms on the left-hand side of (B.7) to get:

$$Y(1 - 0.8) = 500 \qquad (B.8)$$

'Factoring out' merely means that, since Y appears in both terms, the two terms can be shown grouped together – in brackets – and multiplied by the common Y term. Consolidating the two numerical values in (B.8) gives:

$$0.2Y = 500 \qquad (B.9)$$

Next divide both sides by 0.2 to get:

$$Y = \frac{500}{0.2} \qquad (B.10)$$

Finally, divide through by 0.2 to get

$$Y = 2500 \qquad (B.11)$$

A more general treatment: We can go one step further by substituting letters for the numbers in the above numerical example. We then follow out exactly the same procedure as done in the numerical example.

$$C = a + cY \qquad (B.1')$$

$$I = I_0 \qquad (B.2')$$

The prime marks indicate that these equations are the equivalents of the same-numbered equations in the numerical example used above. The only difference is that letters now replace the specific

numbers. (The term I_0 stands for some specific, but unspecified, value of I.)

Substituting these equations for desired consumption and investment expenditure into the definition of desired aggregate expenditure given in equation (B.3) above, gives:

$$E = (a + I_0) + cY \qquad (B.4')$$

Compared with (B.4) above, all we have done is to group the two exogenous terms together and put them in brackets. (When we had specific numbers for them, we could do the addition and reduce them to one term as in (B.4).) We can save time by not writing out both these terms all the time; instead we use the letter A to stand for all autonomous expenditure. Thus in place of $(a + I_0)$ we now write A. Thus (B.4') becomes:

$$E = A + cY \qquad (B.4'')$$

Next we substitute (B.4'') into the equilibrium condition given in (B.5) above to get:

$$Y = A + cY \qquad (B.6')$$

Now all we have to do is to duplicate the few simple operations made in the earlier numerical example to get an expression for the equilibrium value of Y:

$$Y - cY = A \qquad (B.7')$$

$$Y(1 - c) = A \qquad (B.8')$$

$$Y = \frac{A}{(1 - a)} \qquad (B.10')$$

We cannot go further until we have actual numbers, but if you substitute into (B.10') the actual numbers of our numerical example you will get the solution stated in (B.11). (The numerical values are 100 for the constant in the consumption function and 400 for investment, making 500 for total exogenous expenditure, and a marginal propensity to consume of 0.8.)

Finally, note that, if you let A change by one unit, Y changes by $1/(1 - a)$, which is the value of the simple multiplier given on page 298 of the text.

Appendix 4
Choice of Techniques: an Alternative Analysis Using Isoquants[1]

In the main body of Chapter 14, we showed how a firm decides on the most efficient combination of inputs to produce a given output. The rule for cost minimization is that the marginal products of every factor, per unit of money spent on them, shall be equal. In the case of two factors labour (L) and capital (K), this occurs when

$$MPL/P_L = MPK/P_K$$

where MP stands for marginal product and P stands for price. This condition can be expressed also as

$$MPL/MPK = P_L/P_K$$

There is an alternative, graphical, way of reaching this conclusion making use of what are called isoquants and isocost lines.

Isoquants

An isoquant shows all the technically efficient ways of combining factors of production to produce a given output. Continuing the case with two inputs, labour and capital, an isoquant appears as a curve on a graph, the axes of which measure quantities of the two factors. The curve shows the efficient alternative techniques of production that can produce a given output.

TABLE A4.1 Alternative Methods of Producing 6 Units of Output

Method	Units of K	Units of L
a	18	2
b	12	3
c	9	4
d	6	6
e	4	9
f	3	12
g	2	18

Table A4.1 illustrates, using hypothetical numbers, the various methods of producing 6 units of output. These alternatives are shown also in Figure A4.1 as represented by the curve IQ = 6. Thus the firm could choose combination a (18K + 2L), combination g (2K + 18L), or any intermediate combination.

Just as there is an isoquant for an output of 6 units, so there are isoquants for larger and smaller outputs. Two others are drawn in the diagram, IQ = 8 and IQ = 10, each of which shows the alternative combinations of labour and capital that would produce 8 and 10 units of output respectively.

Isocost Lines

To find the least-cost combination of inputs to produce a given output, we need information about the prices of factors of production. This can be shown by what are known as ISOCOST LINES. An isocost line shows the alternative combinations of

1 The technique closely parallels the use of indifference curves and budget lines in Chapter 11. The treatment here is brief, but if you refresh your memory by rereading pp.111–15 and 117–18, in particular, before embarking on this Appendix you will probably find it helpful.

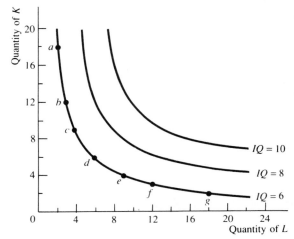

FIGURE A4.1 Isoquants

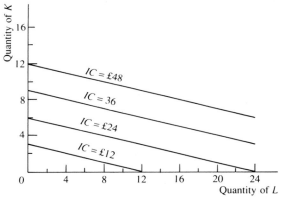

FIGURE A4.2 Isocost Lines

factors that can be purchased with a given total outlay. For example, suppose the price of labour is £1 per unit and the price of capital is £4 per unit, then an outlay of £36 could buy 9K + 0L, 36L + 0K, or other combinations such as 5K + 16L. All these, and other intermediate combinations, are shown in Figure A4.2 by isocost line IC = £36. Isocost lines IC = £12, IC = £24 and IC = £48 show the alternative combinations of capital and labour that can be bought by expenditures of £12, £24 and £48 respectively.

Cost Minimization

To find the cost-minimizing combinations of factors for given outputs we combine Figure A4.1 and Figure A4.2 in Figure A4.3. Suppose we want to produce 6 units of output. We could do so using the combinations represented by points A, B or C on the graph. For example, the cost would be £48 at C, £36 at B and £24 at A. The cheapest method is at A. It is no accident that this is where the isoquant for output of 6 (IQ = 6) is tangent to an isocost line (IC = £24). The minimum-cost methods for other outputs in the Figure are also at points of tangency of isoquants and isocost lines, at points D and E. These may be called equilibrium factor combinations for maximizing output with given factor prices.

The slopes of isoquants and isocost lines: The meaning of the tangency points giving equilibrium input combinations can be appreciated from the meaning of the slopes of isoquants and isocost lines. The slope of an isoquant gives the MARGINAL RATE OF FACTOR SUBSTITUTION, defined as the increase in the quantity of one factor that is required to replace a unit decrease in another factor, when output is held constant along any isoquant.

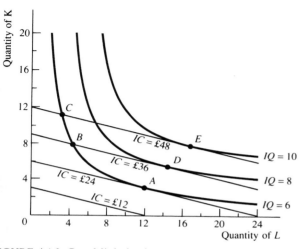

FIGURE A4.3 Cost Minimization

interpreted as indicating that the ratio of the prices of factors is the same as the ratio of their marginal products. Symbolically for the two factors' case, this means

$$MPL/MPK = P_L/P_K$$

which is the conclusion reached in the main body of the chapter and repeated at the opening of this Appendix.

The marginal rate of factor substitution is in fact the ratio of the marginal products of the factors. To see this, consider an example. Assume that output is such that the MPL and the MPK are both equal to 2(units of output), i.e. MPK = MPL. If the firm is to maintain output constant while reducing capital by one unit, it needs to replace the unit of capital by 1 unit of labour. If at another point on the same isoquant, the MPL = 2, while the MPK = 1, the firm needs to replace a unit of capital with only $\frac{1}{2}$ unit of labour.[1]

An isocost line shows the alternative quantities of factors that can be purchased with a given total expenditure. Its slope is given by the ratio of the prices of the factors. Thus in Figure A4.2, given the prices of labour and capital at £1 and £4 per unit respectively, the slope of IC = £12 is determined by drawing the line joining points 3K + 0L (which represents outlay of £12 entirely on capital) and 12L + 0K (£12 spent entirely on labour). All the isocost lines in the diagram have the same slope because the relative prices of labour and capital are the same. If labour were relatively more expensive, the isocost lines would be steeper in Figure A4.2.[2]

The conclusion reached earlier, that cost minimization occurs when an isoquant is tangent to an isocost line, can now be

---

Isoquants have two important characteristics: they slope downwards and are convex to the origin. The downward slope indicates that both factors have positive marginal products. For example, if the quantity of labour is reduced, holding the quantity of capital constant, output falls. Convexity relates to the marginal rate of substitution (the ratio MPL/MPK) at different points on an isoquant. If units of one factor are reduced one at a time, the quantities of the other factor needed as replacements increase continually, if we assume that diminishing returns apply to each factor. The reason is similar to that for the convexity of indifference curves, explained at length on page 14.

Since an isocost line is, in effect, a budget line for a producer, the meaning of the slopes of both lines is similar. See pp.111–12 for a fuller description.

Appendix 5
Exposition of the Basic Dilemma of Oligopoly Using Game Theory

In Chapter 17, we stated that it is in the joint interest of oligopolists to co-operate so as to behave as a monopolist would, in order to share monopoly profits. At the same time, it is in the interest of any one firm to cheat on the agreement, provided that other firms do not retaliate. We now demonstrate these propositions, using the theory of games. We show also that the outcome when all firms cheat, may result in the worst situation for all.

Assume that there are two firms, A and B, in the industry. (An oligopoly with two firms is called a DUOPOLY.) To keep things simple, assume that there are only two strategies – Low output and High output – available to A and B. (You may think of low output as representing co-operation to restrict output as would a monopoly.)

A's Pay–off Matrix

		OUTPUT BY A	
		Low	High
OUTPUT BY B	Low	20	22
	High	15	17

B's Pay–off Matrix

		OUTPUT BY B	
		Low	High
OUTPUT BY A	Low	20	22
	High	15	17

FIGURE A5.1

The profits from adopting different strategies are shown in two so-called 'pay-off matrixes', one for A and one for B, given in Figure A5.1. There are four possible outcomes, depending on which strategies each firm adopts. Look, first, at A's pay-off matrix. The number 20, in the top left-hand cell, shows A's profits if it adopts a low-output policy and B does likewise. The number 15, in the bottom left-hand cell, shows A's profits if it sticks to low output, while B adopts a high-output policy. The numbers 22 and 17 in the cells in the right-hand column of A's pay-off matrix show its profits when A has a high output, while B has low and high outputs, respectively.

Consider, now, B's pay-off matrix, which shows the profits for B of different size outputs by the two firms. For example, the bottom right-hand cell in B's matrix shows that B's profits are 17, when both B and A adopt high-output policies.

The two matrices are, of course linked in that any cell in one of them implies a particular cell in the other. This may be seen by considering how to find the total joint profits for A and B together for each combination of strategies by the two firms. Total profits of A + B are found by adding the profits of each firm in the appropriate cells in the two matrices. They are set out in Table A5.1.

The best result for A and B jointly is when they both behave as output-restricting monopolists and adopt low-output strategies. Total joint profit of 40 is then higher than with any other combination of strategies. A and B both maximize profits, each gaining 20 (as shown in the top left-hand cells of the two pay-off matrixes).

Let us suppose A and B collaborate and reach the joint optimum position, both producing low outputs. Each can now raise its own profits by 'cheating', *provided the other firm does not cheat.* Consider the magnitude of A's temptation to cheat. *Provided B does not cheat* (i.e. stays with a low output), A can increase its profits, from 20 to 22, by moving to a high-output policy, shown in the top right-hand cell of A's pay-off matrix. However, this means that B's profits fall from 20 to 15 (bottom left-hand cell in B's matrix). Total profits of A + B, therefore, fall – from 40 (20 + 20) to 37 (22 + 15), but A gets a larger share of the smaller total.

Consider, now, the magnitude of B's temptation to cheat. Start again at the joint optimum – low outputs by both A and B. *Provided A does not cheat* (i.e. stays with a low output), B can increase its profits from 20 to 22 – by moving to a high-output policy, shown in the top left-hand cell of B's pay-off matrix. However, this means that A's profits fall from 20 to 15 (bottom left-hand cell in A's matrix). Total profits of A + B, therefore, fall again from 40 to 37, but it is now B that gets the larger share of the smaller total.

The final stage in the argument is to show that once one firm cheats, it pays the other to cheat as well. Suppose A cheats, as in our first example, while B maintains a low output. A gets 22, but B gets only 15. However, B could get 17, by following A with a high output. If both A and B cheat, both end up in their bottom right-hand cells. Both produce high outputs, and total profits (17 + 17) are lowest.[1]

TABLE A5.1 Profits from Different Combinations of Strategies

Output strategy		Cell		Profits		
A	B	A's matrix	B's matrix	A	B	A + B
Low	Low	Top left	Top left	20	20	40
High	High	Bottom right	Bottom right	17	17	34
Low	High	Bottom left	Top right	15	22	37
High	Low	Top right	Bottom left	22	15	37

---

1 The non-cooperative equilibrium (where both A and B produce high outputs) is known as a 'Nash equilibrium' (after the American mathematician John Nash), defined as the outcome when each firm adopts its best strategy on the assumption that the strategies of other firms are unchanged.

Answers

CHAPTER 1
1 (c). **2** F. **3** (a), (b), (c). **4** (a) and (b). **5** (d). **6** Figure 1.4, by 40k.

CHAPTER 2
1 (a) F; (b) W; (c) and (d) W *and* F and possibly H. **2** Specialization and division of labour. **3** (c). **4** Resources would flow towards the production of goods bought by the young and away from those bought by the old. **5** In some ways it would be better, since profits are related to prices. Profits are affected by costs as well as by prices, so the word 'prices' *is* adequate so long as, when prices change, costs do not change as well. **6** False.

CHAPTER 3
1 (i)P, (ii)A, (iii)N. **2** Work is discouraged by high rates of tax on incomes (or similar, without the value judgement). **3** True. **4** (dv) factory building; (iv) confidence; (ba) the decision on whether or not to build factories, which depends on confidence. **5** $C = 0.8Y$. **6** (a) only.

CHAPTER 4
1 (a), (c) and (d). **2** The area *oaf*. **3** True. **4** (i) (a) 0, (b) $\frac{3}{4}$; (ii) 5. **5** (d). **6** £3.

CHAPTER 5
1 Hold constant prices of substitutes, complements, consumers' income, tastes, or others listed on page 000. **2** (i)R, (ii)N, (iii)L, (iv)L, (v)L. **3** Change vertical axis to consumer income. **4** (i) inferior good, (ii) complements. **5** False. **6** upward-sloping.

CHAPTER 6
1 (a) all zero, (b) (i) 750, (ii) 225, (iii) 975. **2** (i) R, (ii) L, (iii) N, (iv) N, (v) L. **3** Marginal cost equals price. **4** £20. **5** It would be a horizontal straight line parallel to the quantity axis. **6** Because S_S extended would cut the quantity axis at a positive amount, implying that amount would be supplied even if price were zero.

CHAPTER 7
1 e.g. X has more good substitutes, is more narrowly defined or is measured over a longer time-period. **2** Bread, potatoes (and pork, just). **3** None of them. **4** a, infinity; b, 4; c, $1\frac{1}{2}$; d, $\frac{2}{3}$; e, $\frac{1}{4}$; f, 0. **5** (i) and (ii) minus infinity, extremely highly, but negatively, related for consumers. **6** (a) S in Figures 6.1 and 6.4 and S_L in Figure 6.5; (b) S in Figure 6.4; (c) S_S and S_M in Figure 6.5; (d) S_M in Figure 6.5; (e) none.

CHAPTER 8
1 (i) £1.80, where both are zero, (ii) £21,600, (iii) £3.00, (iv) £1.80. **2** There are no errors in the statement. **3** (i) SL, (ii) DR, (iii) DR, (iv) none. **4** (b). **5** (i) Price rises by $p_0 - p_1$ less in the long run, (ii) No change in quantity, (iii) No change in price. **6** (i) remains the same, (ii) increase (in proportion to the increase in quantity sold).

CHAPTER 9
1 They are substitutes on the supply side. **2** True. **3** (a). **4** (b). **5** (i) an amount halfway between q_0 and q_2, (ii) make the supply curve

steeper than the demand curve. **6** Because fairness (equity) is a matter of personal opinion.

CHAPTER 10
1 (i) C2, (ii) neither, (iii) C1. **2** Zero elasticity of supply (see Figure 10.2(iv)). **3** False. A black market might develop. **4** Figure 10.2(iv), assuming the tax cannot be avoided by deciding not to trade on that day. **5** Demand perfectly inelastic or supply perfectly elastic. **6** (ii) (assuming the government are better forecasters than are farmers) or (iii) of quotas set at the equilibrium value.

CHAPTER 11
1(b). **2** Budget line shifts (i) to between AB and EF, parallel to both. (ii) Budget line pivots around B, intersecting the eggs axis at 10. **3** True. **4** $a - h$ (or $e_1 - e_0$). **5** 7 lbs. of bacon and 2 dozen eggs; I_1. **6** (i) $+ (q_2 - q_1)$ bacon. (ii) A normal good, because a line parallel to AC will be tangent to I_2 at a point to the right of q_1 (showing that quantity bought rises as real income rises, relative prices remaining constant).

CHAPTER 12
1 (i) oligopoly, (ii) monopsony. **2** (b). **3** Differentiated products give the firm greater freedom of manoeuvre. **4** Shareholders in public companies (plc's) enjoy the benefit of limited liability. **5** (i) (a) and (b); (ii) (c), (d), (e) and (f).

CHAPTER 13
1 In the short run, at least one factor of production is fixed; in the long run, all factors are variable; in the very long run, techniques of production can be changed. **2** (i) 15, 20, 25, 25, (ii) 10. **3** (i) 60, (ii) 10, (iii) 210. **4** The level indicated by the point of intersection of SAP_1 and SAP_2. **5** (a) and possibly (e). **6** (i) Decreasing, (ii) 30 and 20 for the 2nd and 3rd units of labour, (iii) 170.

CHAPTER 14
1 (c) and (d). **2** (i) The slopes are the same (both represent marginal cost). (ii) $a - b$ represents average fixed costs. **3** Both describe the level of output at which average cost is at a minimum; but Capacity refers to the short run and MES to the long run. **4** (i) True; (ii) False. **5** (e).

CHAPTER 15
1 Only difference is that total costs must be covered in the long run and only variable costs in the short run (because in the long run $TVC = TC$). **2** (i) True (the two are the same), (ii) True, (iii) True. **3** (a) and (e). **4** (d). **5** Firms in the industry are earning subnormal profits. **6** (i) TR would have to shift so as to lie below TC at every output; (ii) and (iii) b/q_0.

CHAPTER 16
1 (i) (e), (ii) (c) and (d). **2** (i) that where MC cuts AR, (ii) q_2. **3** Where it is greater than unity, because MR is negative where elasticity of demand is less than unity. **4** Falling long-run costs, leading to a natural monopoly. **5** A price (i) below p_m which cuts the MC curve

to the right of q_m; (ii) which cuts the MC curve to the left of q_m. **6** (a), (b) and (c).

CHAPTER 17

1 (i) (b) and (c) and possibly (e); (ii) (a) and (e); (iii) (d) and (e); (iv) (a), (b) and (c) and possibly (e). **2** (i) horizontal or vertical mergers, (ii) conglomerate mergers. **3** Either (because there are two points at which $AR = ATC$). **4** (i) None, (ii) None. **5** (i) (d), (ii) (a), (b) and (c). **6** Price stickiness under oligopoly.

CHAPTER 18

1 In both (i) and (ii) demand is MPP multiplied by marginal revenue, i.e. MRP; but in (i) only it is also equal to VMP. **2** (i) (a) 10 per cent, (b) 30 per cent; (ii) all income accrues to the richest person. **3** The greater the mobility, the faster any factor price differences will be eliminated. **4** (e). **5** (c) and (d). **6** Figure 18.7: (i) Op_0dq_0, (ii) nil; Figure 18.8: (i) nil, (ii) Op_0dq_0.

CHAPTER 19

1 Working population is the same as the labour force – those persons of working age seeking work; the dependent population is the rest of the population. **2** P will have a more unequal distribution than A. **3** Earnings before the union are greater ($Ow_cvq_c > Ow_umq_u$). **4** (i) (b) and (d), (ii) (a) and (c). **5** (i) £1250, (ii) £200, (iii) 20 per cent. **6** (a), (b), (c) and (d).

CHAPTER 20

1 (i) (b), (ii) (e), (iii) (a). **2** The domestic demand curve has shifted to the right, and now intersects the domestic supply curve at output q_2, directly above point b. **3** When opportunity costs of all goods are the same in all countries; when transport costs or import duties are at least as great as comparative cost differences; when quotas or non-tariff barriers eliminate comparative cost differences. **4** (a); (c) is the reciprocal of the UK's terms of trade, and is a definition used in some countries. **5** (i) (a), (ii) (b). **6** True.

CHAPTER 21

1 (i) (b) and (d), (ii) (a). **2** (i) More kebabs and fewer jeans; (ii) e.g. reduction in productivity causing the curve KJ to shift towards the origin of the graph. **3** (i) (e), (ii) (a). **4** A and D progressive, B regressive, C proportional. **5** By a horizontal straight line. **6** Lowering the marginal tax rate, removing the tax allowances, removing the coincidence of level of income for loss of eligibility for state benefits and that of commencement of liability for income tax. **7** Approximately 10 percentage points more – rising from 9 to 20 per cent. **8** Both (i) and (ii) arise when people cannot vary their hours of work; (i) when they would prefer to work less, (ii) when they would prefer to work more.

CHAPTER 22

1 (a) MI (b) MA (c) MI (d) MI (e) MA (f) MA. **2** (a) 10.86%, (b) food, (c) yes housing, (d) 25%, (e) they accounted for 51%. **3** The first refers to the government's responsibility to maintain a stable price level and the second to the fact that many of the consequences of inflation can be avoided if the inflation is foreseen. **4** Inflation means that recent films will earn more nominal income than films distributed in earlier decades even if they do not attract larger audiences. **5** F. **6** (d). **7** 120.

CHAPTER 23

1 (b), (e). **2** T. **3** (a), (b), (c), (e). **4** (a) *no direct effect*, (b) *lower*, (c) *no effect* if they replace other imports, but *lower* if new imports from South Africa replace home production. **5** This is possible if Switzerland rates 'tops' in factors, such as climate and a low crime rate, that are not included in the GDP. **6** 27,500.

CHAPTER 24

1 (a). **2** (a) and (e). **3** For households in the aggregate, a rise in income induces a rise in desired consumption. **4** (a) shifts down, (b) no change, (c) shifts upward. **5** $APC = .92$ when income is £25,000 and .90 when income is £30,000; $MPC = .8$ over the income range £25,000–£30,000. **6** 1200; $\Delta C = 1200$; $MPC = 1200/1600 = .75$; APC at 1200 is 1.0 and at 2800 is 2400/2800 = 0.857. **7** (a) consumption, (b) planned, (c) positive, (d) horizontal, (e) the same as. **8** (a) F, (b) F, (c) T.

CHAPTER 25

1 (c). **2** (a), (c). **3** income = 2000, saving = investment = 200, and consumption = 1800. **4** (a) desired $S = 0$, desired $I = £300m$; (b) Y will rise because total desired expenditure exceeds total income; (c) the S curve in part (ii) shifts upwards to an intercept of $-£100m$ because, if with desired I constant, total desired expenditure falls by £200m for each level of Y then total desired saving must rise by the same amount (total desired consumption falls by that amount); (d) equilibrium national income changes to 1600, which can be found by carefully redrawing the graph or solving the equation $I + C = Y$ for the new data $300 + (100 + 0.75Y) = Y$ for $0.25Y = 400$, or $Y = 1600$. **5** Desired expenditure is $150 + (50 + 0.8Y)$ and this equals actual income when $200 + 0.8Y = Y$, or $Y = £1000m$. **6** (a) T, (b) T, (c) F.

CHAPTER 26

1 To get the two points on the savings curve, subtract consumption from income to get 20 and 40. The E and 45° lines on one graph and the I and S lines on the other intersect to yield an equilibrium Y of 500. **2** The I and the E curves both shift upwards by 50 at each level of Y. This increases equilibrium Y to 750. **3** (a) T, (b) F, (c) T. **4** (a) $K = 1/(1 - 0.80) = 1/0.20 = 5$; (b) $K = 1/0.60 = 1.666$; (c) $4 = 1/MPS$, so $4MPS = 1$ or $MPS = 1/4 = 0.25$ and $MPC = 0.75$. **5** The increased desire to save shifts the S curve upwards and the C and E curves downwards thus lowering equilibrium Y. The diminished desire to invest shifts I and E curves downwards and further lowers equilibrium Y. Since both effects are to reduce income, the effect on Y is the same whether the economy begins with full employment or with some unemployment. **6** C up and I down, I down and C up (note that C up and S up is impossible). **7** Income falls to £81,250 (S_1), £82,500 (S_2) and £83,750 (S_3).

CHAPTER 27

1 (a) 0.90; (b) 0.72; (c) 0.08; (d) 0.20; (e) $1/0.28 = 3.57$ (correct to two decimal places); (f) using $Y = C + I + G$, we have $Y = 0.72Y + 150 + 130$, or $0.28Y = 280$, or $Y = 1000$; (g) now we have $Y = 0.72Y + 290 + 130$, or $0.28Y = 420$, or $Y = 1500$; (h) in (g) ΔG is 140 while ΔY is 500, making the multiplier 500/140 which is 3.57 correct to two decimal places, which agrees with (e). **2** (a) T, (b) T, (c) T, (d) T. **3** (b) and (d). **4** (a) 2, (b) 4, (c) careful with this one: Y_d is 0.8 of Y and saving is 0.25 of Y_d or 0.20 of Y. Thus the multiplier, $1/(MPS + MPT)$, is $1/(0.20 + 0.20) = 1/0.40 = 2.5$; using the income–expenditure approach we have $C = 0.6Y$ and $K = 1/(1 - MPS) = 1/(1 - 0.4) = 1/0.40 = 2.5$. **5** (a) The I curve now coincides with the income axis, showing I to be zero, the G curve is unchanged, the E curve falls by I_0; (b) equilibrium income falls to where the new E curve cut the 45° line, or by I_0 times the multiplier K. **6** (a) (i) Y_1, (ii) 0, (iii) Y_2; (b) (i) Y_1, (ii) zero.

CHAPTER 28

1 (a), (d) and (e). **2** (a) (and (c) and (d) in so far as the value of wealth varies cyclically). **3** (a) T, (b) F, (c) T, (d) F, (e) F. **4** Anything that makes injections rise or withdrawals fall as income rises on the upswing of a cycle (and vice versa). Question 2(b) would be an example since prices tend to rise near the top of a cycle and the rise in indexed wages would feed back to *increase* disposable incomes; a requirement that the budget be balanced annually would be another example: as tax receipts fell during a recession, the government would be forced to cut its expenditures. **5** (a) The deflationary gap is the amount by which expenditure, E, has to increase to produce full employment. The effect of this on income is given by the recessionary gap which is the *multiplied* effect on Y of the increase in E. (b) In part (i), shift the E curve up to pass through point b; in part (ii), shift it down to pass through point c.

CHAPTER 29

1 (b), (c), (d). **2** (a). **3** (a) R, (b) R. **4** (a) T, (b) T, (c) T, (d) F, (e) T, (f) F (it is expenditure flows, not goods flows, that are the subject of the theory), (g) T. **5** $MPL = 0.50$, so $K = 2$, so $\Delta Y = £400$ million. **6** There must be an increased surplus on some other part of the accounts; it could be on invisibles, but it is more likely to be on the capital account or in official financing. **7** $1/(0.05 + 0.25 + 0.20) = 1/0.50 = 2$. **8** 160, 480 and 320. **9** The L curve would have shifted downwards to intersect the J curve at a national income of Y_2.

CHAPTER 30

1 (a), (b) and (e). **2** In all three cases an excess supply of money is created and the price level doubles as a result. **3** (a) T, (b) T, (c) F (this is only true in full and complete equilibrium), (d) T, (e) F (it varies in *direct* proportion). **4** When a C$ is only worth US$0.75, the Canadian currency is the 'bad' money which drives out the 'good' US money. (Any Canadian who gets US coins will take them to a bank and get a 25c premium instead of using them in place of a Canadian coin to buy something. A 3 per cent differential is not enough to cover the time and effort of gathering the coins and taking them to the bank, so they circulate at par.) **5** Money substitutes were quickly invented. For example, people wrote IOUs in public houses where they were known to the publican. The publican, who was in turn generally known by most local people, also signed the note. This added his back-up promise to pay if the original writer defaulted once the banks responded. Such IOUs circulated freely as money. **6** Cigarettes were readily acceptable, had a stable value which was not too high per cigarette, were reasonably durable and could not be counterfeited.

CHAPTER 31

1 (a) and (c). **2** (c) and (e). **3** (a) F, (b) T, (c) T, (d) F. **4** To other banks, as its account holders who receive advances write cheques to people who have accounts in other banks, and to the public if the public wishes to hold some part of its new money in currency (and only a proportion in the form of deposit money).

CHAPTER 32

1 (i): (a), (c), (d), (e); (ii): (a), (b), (c), (d), (e); (iii): (b), (c), (d). **2** (a) (300/9700)100, which is just over 3 per cent for 3 months or *approximately* 12 per cent per year; (b) 150/9850, which is just over 1.5 per cent for 2 months or *approximately* 9 per cent per year; (c) the rate of interest has fallen, driving up the price of her bill so she gets a capital gain. (If the rate had remained at 12 per cent she would have sold her bill for just less than £9800.) **3** (a) T, (b) T, (c) T, (d) T, (e) F. **4** People will economize on cash balances because the opportunity cost of holding money has risen; this is indicated by a movement upwards to the left along the LP curve. **5** The LP function must shift to the left to pass through the point of intersection of the grid lines from M_5 and r_0; a fall in either real national income or the price level would cause the shift by reducing the transactions and precautionary demands for money. **6** Credit cards are a money substitute and in particular mean that people did not have to carry large precautionary balances to meet unexpected payments; this reduced the demand for money and shifted the LP curve to the left.

CHAPTER 33

1 (a), (b) and (d). **2** expansionary, buy, up, down, an increase, upward, real national income, the price level. **3** (a) T, (b) T, (c) F, (d) T, (e) F, (f) T. **4** This reduced the demand for money and set up the expansionary shock followed through in question 2 above. **5** (a) Y_0, r_1 and I_1. (b) Income rises to Y_F, the demand for money rises, increasing the interest rate and reducing investment. (The extra government expenditure crowds out some part of private-sector investment expenditure.)

CHAPTER 34

1 (b) and (c). **2** (a) T, (b) G, (c) I, (d) I, (e) G, (f) T. **3** interest-inelastic, interest-elastic. **4** (a) T, (b) T, (c) F. **5** (a), (b), (d). **6.** Buying bonds and Treasury bills and making loans to the discount houses on favourable terms. **7** The interest rate would fall from r_N to r_S to the low rate where LP_S intersects M''_S.

CHAPTER 35

1 (a) and (d) ((d) by shifting AD to the right). **2** AD, right, rise, rise, inflationary, $SRAS$, leftward, rise, fall, unchanged, higher. **3** (a) T, (b) F (to the right), (c) F (no shift), (d) F (this mechanism relates to the slope of the AD curve), (e) T, (f) T. **4** (a) $SRAS-L$; (b) $AD-R$; (c) $AD-L$ (or its rightward shift is slowed); (d) $SRAS-R$. **5** The price level and national income fall to P_0 and Y_0. Since income is at Y_F the $SRAS$ curve need not shift and those values can persist. **6** (a) No, there is excess demand; (b) the price level must rise to P_2.

CHAPTER 36

1 (a) AD, (b) $LRAS$, (c) $LRAS$, (d) AD, (e) $LRAS$. **2** (a) and (c). **3** (a) T, (b) F (both have changed drastically), (c) F (average not marginal), (d) F, (e) T. **4** static, declining, rising. **5** rightward, increasing, falling.

CHAPTER 37

1 (a) F, (b) F (this is structural), (c) T, (d) F (this reduces frictional unemployment), (e) T (there will be more people moving between jobs at any one time and hence unemployed while doing so). **2** (a) Demand-deficient; (b) she will not be *recorded* as unemployed but she is unemployed in the sense that she would probably take a job if one were available; (c) the unemployment will be frictional if the workers find other comparable jobs easily but structural if they have to move to different areas, industries or occupations; (d) real-wage unemployment; (e) demand-deficient if some are laid off but if everyone just goes on short time they will not be recorded as unemployed; (f) structural unemployment; (g) structural unemployment; (h) frictional unemployment. **3** The British system does not count those who want a job enough to be searching for one but who are not currently eligible for unemployment benefits; the difference between the two methods can be substantial. **4** (a) structural, (b) demand-deficient, (c) frictional, (d) real-wage, (e) demand-deficient, (f) structural (the unemployed will find it easier to move to where the jobs are located).

CHAPTER 38

1 (d) and (f). **2** (a) recessionary gap of $Y_F - Y_1$; (b) the price level, national income and the inflationary gap would all grow, finally reading the amounts indicated by the intersecton of $SRAS$ and AD'''; (c) about 2 per cent, about 5 per cent. **3** AD, right, raise, raise, inflationary, $SRAS$, left, fall, rise, higher, the same as. **4** (a) Demand shock coming from a high level of government expenditure (which may also cause the money supply to increase if the government uses 'printing press finance'); (b) supply shock coming from a wage-cost-push; (c) demand inflation due to an outward expansion of the AD curve; (d) supply shock coming from an increase in the price of all petroleum products. **5** (a) F, (b) F, (c) T, (d) F (if the adjustment restores the original level of national income it also restores the original price level).

CHAPTER 39

1 (a), (c), (e). **2** (b) and (c). **3** (a) F, (b) T, (c) T, (d) T, (e) T, (f) F. **4** elastic, inelastic. **5** inelastic, elastic. **6** below, increased, upwards, upward, acceleration.

CHAPTER 40

1 (a) to (e) all work to appreciate sterling. **2** increase, decrease, appreciate. **3** (a) T, (b) T, (c) F, (d) T. **4** Either the *D* curve shifts right to pass through point *b* or the *S* curve shifts left to pass through point *d*. The *D* curve might shift because the UK inflation rate falls below the rates in its major trading partners. The *S* curve might shift because there was a major reduction in the flow of UK investment going to foreign countries.

CHAPTER 41

1 (a) and (d). **2** (a) (i) It must buy sterling in the amount *ab* each period using its foreign-exchange reserves, (ii) nothing, (iii) it must sell sterling, adding to its reserves of foreign exchange in the amount *cd* each period; (b) (i) it must sell sterling in the amount *gh* each period (adding to its foreign-exchange reserves), (ii) buy sterling in the amount *ji* each period (running down its reserves of foreign exchange); (c) (i) equilibrium is at *e*, making the rate about DM32.28, (ii) DM2.95, (iii) equilibrium is at *f*, making the rate about DM2.66. **3** (a) F, (b) T, (c) T, (d) F. **4** decrease, increasing, depreciating, lower, sell (to buy sterling), decrease, offsetting.

CHAPTER 42

1 (a), (b), (c) and (d). **2** (a) Neither in balance, because income exceeds target and payments are in deficit. (b) There is no conflict because reducing national income will move the economy closer to both goals. **3** (a), (e), (f) and (g) are S; (b), (c) and (d) are C. **4** (a), (c), (d), (e), (f) and (g) are I; (b) is D. **5** (a) T, (b) T, (c) T, (d) F. **6** Sterling will tend to appreciate as short-term capital flows into the UK attracted by the high interest rates; the government might be concerned about the effect of the high value of sterling on UK exports. **7** It will partly depend on the current pressure on sterling. If the balance of payments is favourable, so that sterling is tending to appreciate, then an expansive fiscal policy, which drove interest rates down and caused some capital outflow, might be acceptable. If the balance of payments were unfavourable, so that sterling was tending to depreciate, then fiscal policy which would drive interest rates up and lead to a capital inflow might be more desirable.

CHAPTER 43

1 (a)–(c) all T. **2** (b), (c), (d). **3** *Some pros*: incomes cannot be raised to the levels of advanced economies using known technology; new technologies will allow environmental problems to be better coped with; new technologies have transformed our way of life, usually for the better, every half century or so (few would want to go back to the common worker or housewife's lot of 1900). *Some cons*: life would be easier, and pollution less, if people in advanced countries would learn to live with much less material consumption; new technologies can cause great harm before their risks are appreciated; growth causes many dislocations and leaves people with obsolete skills in its wake.

Index

References to notes are indicated by 'n' and to Boxes by 'B'.

A-F framework, for supply and
    demand analysis, 94–107
ability, relation to earnings, 198
absolute advantage, *defined*, 209
absolute level of prices, 340–341
absolute necessities,
    indifference curves, 117
accelerating inflation, 449–452
accelerator, *defined*, 311
accelerator theory, 311–313
accepting houses (merchant
    banks), 348
accidents, road, social costs,
    86B
accommodated inflation, *see*
    validated inflation
accountability, of private and
    public companies, 235–236
accounting, national income,
    254–268
accounting costs, *vs.* opportunity
    costs, 143
active population, *see* labour
    force
activity rates, *defined*, 5, 189
'acts of God',
    effect on demand, 48
    effect on supply, 57
acts of the state,
    effect on demand, 48
    effect on supply, 57
actual expenditure, *defined*, 270
actual output, *defined*, 244
actual price, *see* market price
AD curve, *see* aggregate demand
    curve
ad valorem tariffs, protectionism,
    defined, 215
adjustable-peg regime, *defined*,
    471
administered prices, *defined*,
    177
advances, *defined*, 346
advertising, oligopoly, 179–180
AFC (average fixed cost),
    defined, 144
Africa, command economies, 17,
    24
age, relation to earnings, 197
age distribution of population,
    196–197
aggregate consumption
    function, 274
aggregate demand, 388–398
aggregate demand curve, 388–
    390
    defined, 388
aggregate demand function,
    279n
aggregate demand shocks, 392
aggregate economics, *defined*,
    254
aggregate expenditure function,
    278–281, 302
    defined, 279
aggregate supply, 388–398
aggregate supply curve, *defined*,
    390
aggregate supply shocks, 392
AGMs (annual general
    meetings), of firms, 130
agriculture,

supply-demand analysis, 104–
    107
technical efficiency, 125–126
    see also cobweb theorem
aid, for development, 415
air travel market, deregulation,
    179B
algebraic equations, economic
    models, 30
allocative efficiency, 223–224
    defined, 82, 223
    under perfect competition,
    167–168
allocative inefficiency,
    defined, 409
    under monopoly, 168
amalgamations, *see* mergers
analytic statements, *defined*,
    27
announcement effects, 379
annual general meetings, of
    firms, 130
anti-dumping duties, 219
AP (average product), of variable
    factor, *defined*, 135
APC (average propensity to
    consume), *defined*, 276–277
APM (average propensity to
    import), *defined*, 327
appreciation, exchange rate,
    defined, 462, 471
APS (average propensity to
    save), *defined*, 277
AR (average revenue),
    defined, 152
    under monopoly, 161
arbitrary prices, 94
arc elasticity of demand, *defined*,
    65
arms manufacturers, change of
    product, 149B
art works, utility, 40B
AS curve, *see* aggregate supply
    curve
assets,
    financial,
        of banks, 346
        defined, 248, 358, 372
    real, 358
'at call', *defined*, 346
ATC (average total cost), *defined*,
    144
ATMs (automatic teller
    machines), 339B
ATR (average tax rate), *defined*,
    230
attitudes to work and risk,
    relation to earnings, 198
automatic rules, *defined*, 234
automatic stabilizers, *defined*,
    319
automatic teller machines
    (ATMS), 339B
autonomous consumption,
    defined, 275
autonomous expenditure,
    defined, 272
AVC (average variable cost),
    defined, 144
average cost, 144
average elasticity of demand,
    defined, 65

average fixed cost, *defined*,
    144
average output per person, 4
average product, of variable
    factor, *defined*, 135
average propensity to consume,
    defined, 276–277
average propensity to import,
    defined, 327
average propensity to save,
    defined, 277
average revenue,
    defined, 152
    under monopoly, 161
average standard of living, 4
average tax rate, *defined*, 230
average total cost, *defined*, 144
average variable cost, *defined*,
    144
avoidable costs, *see* variable
    costs

backed money, *defined*, 337
backward integration, 130
backward-sloping supply curve,
    191
'bad money drives out good', 336
bads, distinction from goods, 265
balance, *see* internal balance;
    external balance
balance of payments,
    and macroeconomic policy,
    252, 490B
    and national income, 322–333
    relation to exchange rate, 249–
    250, 467–468
balance-of-payments accounts,
    defined, 249
balanced budget multiplier,
    defined, 308
bank deposit multiplier, *defined*,
    349–350
Bank of England,
    administration of monetary
    policy, 252, 372–387
    cash reserves, 346
    central bank, 336–337
    official financing, 323
bank money, *see* deposit money
bank multiplier, *defined*, 349–350
bank notes,
    Bank of England issue, 374
    defined, 336
bank rate, *defined*, 378
Bank of Scotland, issuer of notes,
    337
bankers' deposits, Bank of
    England, 373
banks, supply of money, 346–352
bargaining,
    trade unions and employers,
    200–201
    wage, 451B, 451
barriers,
    cultural, effect on
    development, 410
    non-tariff, *defined*, 215–217
barriers to entry,
    defined, 128
    under monopoly, *defined*, 163–
    164
    under oligopoly, 176, 179

barriers to exit, under monopoly,
    164
barter, *defined*, 18, 334
base period, *defined*, 245
base year, *defined*, 244, 245
baskets of commodities, *see*
    combinations of
    commodities
beef market, 59B, 68B
beggar-thy-neighbour policies,
    defined, 331
behaviour,
    human, 28–29
    price-taking, 37
    speculative, *defined*, 476–477
behavioural assumptions, 29
behavioural theories of firm,
    defined, 132
benefit principle, tax equity,
    231
benefits,
    of growth, 404–406
    social and private, 86–87
bequest motive, *defined*, 273
bilateral balance of payments,
    defined, 324
bilateral monopoly, *defined*,
    201
bills, 355–358
    defined, 248, 357
birth rates, 196
black economy,
    contribution to current living
    standards, 265–266
    Hungary, 265B
    see also moonlighting
black markets, for limited supply,
    85, 101, 102
black workers, in labour market,
    197–198
Boards of Directors, 130
bonds, 355–358
    defined, 248, 355
borrowing,
    government, 316–317
    see also imported capital;
    loanable funds
borrowing short and lending
    long, 375
boundary, production possibility,
    see production possibility
    curves
branch banking system, *defined*,
    347
break-even level of income,
    defined, 274
Bretton Woods system, 475–
    476
    defined, 472
British Rail, resource allocation,
    7B
Budget, government, 228, 315–
    316
budget balance, *defined*, 315
budget-deficit bonds, Japan,
    306B
budget line, 111–113, 118–119
    defined, 111
budgetary policies, 228–232
building societies, financial
    intermediaries, 348
built-in stabilizers, *defined*, 319

bundles of commodities, *see* combinations of commodities
Burton Group, 131B
business concentration, 172–173
business cycle, 310–313, 497–498
defined, 241, 310
business decisions, 125–133
business organization, 128–132
business rates, 159B
business sector, *see* suppliers
buyers,
in factor markets, 128
see also consumers
bygones are bygones, 143

CAP (Common Agricultural Policy), European Community, 106
capacity, excess, *defined*, 174
capacity output, *defined*, 146
capital, 201–205
acquisition for development, 413–415
circulating,
defined, 5
investment, 256
defined, 5
fixed,
defined, 5
investment, 256
human, 198, 204–205
defined, 5
opportunity cost of, *defined*, 152
capital account,
defined, 322
fiscal *vs.* monetary policy, 491–494
macroeconomic policy, 488–495
capital assets taxes, 300
capital consumption, *see* depreciation
capital consumption allowance, 260
capital flows, effect of interest rates, 249–250
capital gains, *defined*, 357
Capital Gains Tax, 228
capital goods, cost, influence on investment, 271
capital-intensive industries, 15, 125
capital losses, *defined*, 357
capital market, 201–207
capital movements, effect on exchange rate, 466
capital/output ratio, *defined*, 312
capital transfers, 325
capitalism, *defined*, 22
cardinal measure, *defined*, 113
cars, price differences, 165B
cartels, 175–176, 181, 182B
defined, 175
cash, *defined*, 337
cash reserve ratio, *defined*, 348
cash reserves, 346
defined, 338
causal relations in economics, 32–33
central banks, 336–337
see also Bank of England
central rate, European Monetary System, *defined*, 472
central value, *defined*, 471
centrally planned economies, 16–17, 24
defined, 16
ceteris paribus assumption, *defined*, 31, 38
CGT (Capital Gains Tax), 228
chain reactions, 82

Chamberlin, Edward, on monopolistic competition theory, 173
chance allocations, in limited supply, 85, 101, 102
chance correlations, 32
cheques, deposit money, 337
China, command economy, 17
choice, *defined*, 6
circular flow of income, 254–268
defined, 254
influence of government, 300–309
saving and investment, 285–286
circulating capital,
defined, 5
investment, 256
Classical quantity theory of money, *defined*, 341
Classical unemployment, 422–423, 427–428
defined, 422
clearing banks, *defined*, 347
clearing houses, *defined*, 347
closed economy,
balanced population, 403–404
defined, 259
macroeconomic policy, 441–459
monetary policy, 376–387
closed-shop agreements, *defined*, 200
cobweb theorem, *defined*, 88–90
coins, 335–336
defined, 337
collectively consumed commodities, *see* public goods
combinations of commodities, budget line, 111–112
defined, 9
command economies, *defined*, 16–17
commercial banks, 347
commodities,
defined, 4
composite, *defined*, 117
consumption, 255–256
see also combination of commodities; goods markets; output decisions
Common Agricultural Policy (European Community), 106
common market, *defined*, 220
communications revolution, 180B
communist economies, 17
Community Charge, 228, 229B, 231
community indifference curves, 223n
companies,
joint-stock, 129–130
see also firms
comparative advantage,
creation by protection, 217–218
defined, 209–210
free trade, 215
competition,
encouragement, in supply-side policy, 457
imperfect, 172–184
defined, 172
in goods market, 188
market failure, 227
perfect,
defined, 154
in goods market, 187–188
output and price, compared with monopoly, 167
profit maximization, 152–160
competition policy, 169, 181–183, 228

defined, 181
competitive employers, *vs.* trade unions, 200
competitive factor markets, 185–195
competitive supply, *defined*, 56
complements,
defined, 47–48
indifference curves, 117
completely elastic demand, *defined*, 64
completely inelastic demand, *defined*, 64
compliance costs, of taxation, *defined*, 230
composite commodity, *defined*, 117
composite demand, 40n
compound interest, 202
concentration,
of economic power, 23
of industry, 172–173
concentration ratios, *defined*, 173
conditions of demand, *defined*, 49
conditions of supply, *defined*, 58
conglomerate mergers, 172
defined, 130
conservation, of non-renewable resources, 4–5, 204B
consols (Consolidated Stock), *defined*, 356
constant long-run costs, 149
constant returns to scale, 137, 139–140
consumer co-operatives, 129
goals, 131–132
consumer demand, *see* consumers, individual demand; demand
consumer durables, *see* durables
consumer equilibrium, 117–123
consumer goods and services, in measurement of production, 256
consumer sovereignty, 84n
consumer surplus, *defined*, 43–44
consumers,
defined, 37
distinct from households, 254n
individual demand, 38–41
consumer's budget line, *see* budget line
consumption, 269–282
defined, 255
desired, changes, 293–296
see also desired expenditure
consumption commodities, 255–256
consumption expenditure, 272–281
consumption line/function/curve, *defined*, 275
consumption possibility line, *see* budget line
contestable markets, *defined*, 180
contraction phase, 313
contractionary fiscal policy, 445
contractionary monetary policy, 445
contractionary monetary shock, 368
defined, 367
contractions,
of demand, *defined*, 49
of supply, 59
control,
by monopoly, 164–166
in economic systems, 16
of firms, 130–131, 132
convergent cobwebs, 89–90

convertible money, *defined*, 337
co-operation, international, 219–222
co-operatives, 129, 131–132
co-ordinate graph, *defined*, 504
corporations, 129–130
large, concentration of industry, 172
public, 235
correlation, *defined*, 31–33
'corset', *defined*, 379
cost advantages, natural barrier to entry, 163
cost-benefit analysis, *defined*, 234–235
cost curves,
long-run, 147–150
short-run, 145–146
under oligopoly, 176–177
cost-push inflation, *defined*, 430
costs,
minimization, 21, 146–147
see also average cost; marginal costs; opportunity costs; production costs; transport costs
CR (concentration ratios), *defined*, 173
'creative destruction', and monopoly profits, 164
credit multiplier, *defined*, 349–350
credit terms, influence on household behaviour, 273
cross elasticity of demand, *defined*, 68
cross-subsidization, by sheltered industries, 236
crowding-out effect, 447–448
capital flows, 492–493
defined, 444
cultural barriers, effect on development, 410
currency,
devalued, *defined*, 471
internal and external value, 462
national, 208–209
see also coins; exchange rates
current account, *defined*, 322
current account desposit, *see* sight deposits
current outlays, *defined*, 315
current receipts, *defined*, 315
curves,
defined, 272n
indifference, 111–124
positive and negative slope, 8
production possibility, 8–11
see also consumption curve; cost curves; demand curves; Laffer curve; Lorenz curve; supply curves
curvilinear demand curves, 66
customs union, *defined*, 220–222
cycles,
product, small firms, 150
defined, 402
trade, 310–313, 497–498
defined, 241, 310

data reliability, 32, 33B
DCF (Discounted Cash Flow), 202
death rates, 196
debentures, *defined*, 129
debt,
implications of budget balance, 315–316
of less-developed countries, 414
debt instruments, 358
decentralized decision-taking, 17–18

decision lag, fiscal policy, 443
decision-takers' objectives,
   cause of government failure,
   236
decision-taking,
   centralized, 16–17
   decentralized, 17–18, 19
decisions,
   business, 125–133
   coordinated by price system,
   19
   on output, 14–16, 20–21, 125,
   126
declining industries, support for,
   457
decrease in demand, 50
decreasing long-run costs, 147–
   148
decreasing returns, bases, 139–
   140
decreasing returns to scale, 138
default, risk, 373
deficit-covering bonds, Japan,
   306B
deficits, government's budget,
   315
deflation, *defined*, 244, 246n
deflationary gap,
   defined, 314
   elimination, 316
deflator, *defined*, 246n
degradation of environment, 17
demand,
   aggregate, 388–398
   for capital, by firm, 203
   composite, 40n
   excess, *defined*, 73
   for factor, 187–189
   laws, 51–52, 76–79
   for money, 355–363
      defined, 342, 358
   relation to income, 46–47
   relation to price, 37–45
demand curve, macro-, 388n
demand curves,
   aggregate, 388–390
   defined, 38
   elasticity, 66
   firm's, under perfect
      competition, 155
   individual consumer, 38–41
   market, 42–43
   shifts and movements, 49–52
demand-deficient
   unemployment, 420–421,
   425
   defined, 420
demand elasticity, 62–68
   for factor, 188–189
   and marginal revenue, 161–
   162
   under monopoly, 164
demand inflation, *defined*, 434
demand for investment curve
   (marginal efficiency of
   investment curve), 266
demand loan, *defined*, 355
demand management, *defined*,
   252
demand management policies,
   441–454
   see also stabilization policy
demand for money function
   (liquidity preference
   function), 361
demand-pull inflation, *defined*,
   434
demand-shock inflation
   (demand-side inflation),
   434–435
demand-side policies, 252
demand-side shocks, 430
demergers, 130
demerit goods,
   defined, 22–23

source of market failure, 86,
   226
demographic factors, effect on
   demand, 48, 49
dependent population, *defined*,
   197
deposit creation, 348–351
deposit money,
   defined, 337–338
   destruction, 349
deposit multiplier, *defined*, 349–
   350
depreciation, 142–143
   defined, 142, 257
   exchange rates, *defined*, 462,
   471
depreciation allowances, 441
depression, *defined*, 310
deregulation, 179B, 236
deregulation measures, 169
derived demand, *defined*, 187
desire to buy, *defined*, 37
desired consumption, changes,
   293–296
desired expenditure,
   defined, 270
   income-expenditure method,
   300–302
   relation to equilibrium, 284
desired investment, changes,
   292–293
desired saving, changes, 293–
   296
destabilizing speculative
   behaviour, *defined*, 476
destocking, *defined*, 256
destruction of non-renewable
   resources, 17
development,
   capital acquisition for, 413–415
   defined, 242
   pace of, 415
   see also less developed
      countries
development gap, *defined*, 407
DGFT (Director-General of Fair
   Trading), 181, 182B
diagrams, *see* graphs
differential wage rates, 197–198
differentiation, of products,
   under monopoly and
   oligopoly, 164, 179
diminishing marginal rate of
   substitution, *defined*, 114
diminishing marginal utility, 39–
   41, 114n
   defined, 39
diminishing returns,
   law of, *defined*, 135
   to variable factor, 138
direct costs *see* variable costs
direct investment, *defined*, 323
direct taxes,
   defined, 228
   see also income taxes
Director-General of Fair Trading,
   181, 182B
directors,
   of firms, 130–131
   goals of, 131–132
disaster models, 501–502
discount houses,
   defined, 348
   loans to, 378
discounted bill, *defined*, 357
Discounted Cash Flow, 202
discounting, *defined*, 202
discretionary policies, 320
   defined, 319
discretionary rules, *defined*, 234
discrimination, in labour market,
   defined, 198
disembodied technical change,
   defined, 402

disequilibrium,
   defined, 74–76
   monetary, 364
disequilibrium average wage,
   423
disequilibrium incomes, *defined*,
   284
disequilibrium relative wages,
   422
disincentive effect of taxation,
   231
disposable income, *defined*, 262,
   300–301
dissaving, *defined*, 275
distribution,
   of income, 48–49
      effect of protection, 218–219
      in market system, 21, 23, 91–
      92
   theory, *defined*, 185
   unequal, 23
divergent cobwebs, 90
diversification, 148
division of labour, 18
DIY (do-it-yourself) activities,
   contribution to current living
   standards, 266
dollar price, exchange rate, 462
dominant firms, number,
   oligopoly, 176
double co-incidence of wants,
   defined, 334
double counting, 258
double taxation of business
   income, *defined*, 456
downswings, 313
downturn, 313
   defined, 311
downward wage flexibility and
   inflexibility, 395
downward-sloping curves, 8n,
   39
drink-driving accidents, social
   costs, 86B
dumping, *defined*, 219
duopoly, *defined*, 175n, 516
durables,
   defined, 37
   existing stocks, influence on
      household behaviour, 273
   in measurement of production,
   256
   prices, effect on price changes,
   50
duties,
   anti-dumping, 219
   import, 215–217

earnings,
   differentials, 197–198
   relation to age, 197
   see also transfer earnings
Eastern Europe, command
   economies, 17
EC, *see* European Community
econometrics, *defined*, 31–33
economic cost, *see* opportunity
   costs
economic development, *see*
   development
economic efficiency, 82–85
   goal of microeconomic policy,
   223–225
   nationalization, 235–236
   under monopoly, 167–169
economic forces, cause of
   changes in national income,
   293
economic growth, 399–419
   benefits of, 404–406, 417–418
   costs of, 406, 416
   defined, 242
   demand management, 454
   goal of macroeconomic policy,
   251–252

in less developed countries,
   407–416
long-run prospects, 501–502
long-term trend, 310
theories of, 401–404
'economic juggernaut', 88
economic models, *defined*, 29–
   34
economic policy, *see* policy
economic power, concentration,
   23
economic rent, *defined*, 192–194
economic systems, *defined*, 16–
   19
economic theory, 29–33
economic union, *defined*, 220
economies of scale,
   gains from, 212
   sources of falling costs, 148
   under monopoly, 168–169
ECU (European Currency Unit),
   475
   defined, 472
education,
   for economic development,
   413
   see also human capital
EEC, *see* European Community
effective demand, *defined*, 37
effective exchange rate, 470
effective supply, of labour,
   189
efficiency, 82–85
   goal of microeconomic policy,
   223–225
   of market, 22, 81–93
   of production, 21
   in relation to growth, 405
   in relation to ownership, 236
   of resource allocation, 91–92
   defined, 82
   in taxation, 229–230, 231
   technical, *defined*, 125
   under monopoly, 167–169
   under nationalization, 235–
   236
   under oligopoly, 178–180
EFTA (European Free Trade
   Area), 220
EFTPOS (electronic funds
   transfer at point of sale),
   339B
elasticity,
   of demand, 62–68
      derivation on demand curve,
      511
      for factor, 188–189
      and marginal revenue, 161–
      162
      monopoly, 164
   of demand and supply, 77–79
   of supply, 69–70
      defined, 69
electronic funds transfer at point
   of sale, *see* EFTPOS
embodied technical change,
   defined, 402
empirical evidence, *defined*, 27
empirical question, *defined*, 40
employed, *defined*, 242
employers,
   monopsony, 199
   vs. trade unions, 200, 200–201
employment, 241, 242–243, 420–
   429
   defined, 242
   effect of imports and exports,
   331–332
   full, goal of macroeconomic
   policy, 251
   see also unemployment
employment seekers, 197
EMS (European Monetary
   System), 250, 377, 474
   defined, 472

EMU (European economic and monetary union), 493B
endogenous expenditure (induced expenditure), *defined*, 273–275
endogenous variable, *defined*, 4
energy industry, nationalization and privatization, 235B
Engel's Law, 121B
enterprise (entrepreneurship), *defined*, 5
enterprises, *defined*, 129
see also suppliers
entertainers, economic rent, 193B
entrenched inflation, *defined*, 452
entrepreneurs, in Africa, 412B
defined, 5
effect on economic development, 409
entrepreneurship, *defined*, 5
entry, freedom of, *see* freedom of entry and exit
entry conditions, goods markets, 128
envelope curve, *defined*, 147
environment, conservation, 4–5
degradation in command economies, 17
effect of growth on, 416–419
equality, distinction from equity, 23
equation of exchange, *defined*, 341–342
equations, in economic models, 30
on graphs, 506–507
equibrium condition, *defined*, 283
equibrium income, *defined*, 284
equilibrium, 74–76
aggregate demand and aggregate supply, 391–394
changes, 41, 75–76
consumer, 117–123
defined, 72
of firm, under perfect competition, 154–156
of industry, under perfect competition, 156–158
international trading, 213–215
monetary, *defined*, 364
in perfect factor markets, 191–192
under monopolistic competition, 174–175
under monopoly, 162–164
equilibrium analysis, *defined*, 81
equilibrium national income, *defined*, 283–290
income-expenditure method, 302
in leakages-injections method, 304
relation to price level, 388–389
equilibrium price, *defined*, 72–73, 74
equilibrium quantity, *defined*, 72
equilibrium values, derivation, 512–513
equipment, fixed capital, 5
equities, *defined*, 129, 248
equity, goal of microeconomic policy, 225–226
in market system, 22, 91–92
in taxation, 231
ERM (Exchange Rate Mechanism), 209, 451B, 472–473, 476B, 477B
defined, 472

establishments, *defined*, 129
European Community, 220B, 220
Common Agricultural Policy, 106
competition policy, 182
Exchange Rate Mechanism, 209, 451B, 472–473, 476B, 477B
European Currency Unit, *see* ECU
European economic and monetary union, 493B
European Free Trade Area, 220
European Monetary System, 250, 377, 474
defined, 472
evidence, empirical *defined*, 27
ex ante expenditure, *defined*, 270
ex post expenditure, *defined*, 270
excess capacity, *defined*, 174
excess demand, *defined*, 73
excess reserves, *defined*, 348
excess supply, *defined*, 73
exchange controls, *defined*, 475, 487
exchange rate, 242, 325–326
defined, 249
goal of macroeconomic policy, 252
Exchange Rate Mechanism, *see* ERM
exchange rate regimes, 471–479
defined, 471
exchange rates, 249–250, 460–470
execution lag, fiscal policy, 443
exhaustive expenditure, *defined*, 232, 257
exit, freedom, *see* freedom of entry and exit
exogenous expenditure (autonomous expenditure), 272
exogenous variables, *defined*, 4
expansion, *defined*, 310–311
external economies of scale, 148–149
expansion phase, 313
expansionary fiscal policy, 445
expansionary monetary policy, 445
expansionary monetary shock, 368
defined, 367
expectational inflation, 455
defined, 449
expectations, cause of volatile markets, 90–91
effect on demand, 48
effect on supply, 57
of future profits, influence on investment, 271
influence on household behaviour, 273
expectations-augmented Phillips curves, *defined*, 451
expenditure, autonomous, *defined*, 272
in circular flow, 258–261
consumption, 272–281
of government, 232, 257–258
relation with national income, 283–284
in two-sector model, 269–270
expenditure changes, demand management, 441–443
expenditure-changing policies, 481–482, 483–484
defined, 481
expenditure flows, 270
expenditure-switching policies, 482–483, 487–488

defined, 481
expenditure taxes, 300
expenditures, in leakages-injections method, 303–304, 305
experimental method, *defined*, 27
experimental sciences, 27–28
expertise, *see* learning-by-doing
Export-Import Bank, 415
exports, 250B
determinants of, 326–327
good or bad, 331–332
as injection, 329
net, *defined*, 260, 328
open economy, 460–461
see also balance-of-payments accounts; trade
extensions, of demand, *defined*, 49
of supply, 59
external balance, *defined*, 480–481
fixed exchange rate, 483–488
external costs, *defined*, 87
external economies of scale, *defined*, 148–149
infant industry argument, 218
external goals, macroeconomic policy, *defined*, 480
external value of currency, *defined*, 462
externalities, *defined*, 23
source of market failure, 86–87, 226
extra utility *see* marginal utility
Ezekial, Mordecai, cobweb theory, 90

face value, of bonds, *defined*, 355
factor distribution of income, 185–186
factor immobility, international trade, 208
factor markets, 20–21, 254
business decisions, 128
competitive, 185–195
defined, 127
factor mix, 125
factor mobility, *defined*, 20, 190
factor prices, 146–147
in competitive markets, 186–187
effect on supply, 56
factor productivity, 134–141
factor services, *defined*, 5–6
factors, single-use, 7
factors of production, 4–6
defined, 4
demand and supply, 187–191
markets *see* factor markets
productivity, 134–141
failure, *see* market failure; organizational failure; quality control, failure
fair trading, *see* Office of Fair Trading
fairness, in market system, 23, 91–92
farming, *see* agriculture
favourable balance, 324
favourable movements, terms of trade, *defined*, 213
FDI (foreign direct investment), 400–401
fiat money, *defined*, 337
FIMBRA (Financial Intermediaries, Managers and Brokers' Regulatory Association), 374
final goods, *defined*, 259
financial assets, of banks, 346
defined, 248, 358, 372

financial economies of scale, *defined*, 148
financial institutions, effect on economic development, 409
financial intermediaries, 348
Financial Intermediaries, Managers and Brokers' Regulatory Association (FIMBRA), 374
fine-tuning, *defined*, 317
limitations, 452–453
firm saving, financing growth, 400
firm sector, in two-sector model, 269
see also suppliers
firms, *defined*, 130
dominant, under oligopoly, 176
goals of, 131–132
in monopolistic competition, 173
ownership, 130–131
profit-maximizing, 152–160
small, 150
see also corporations; monopoly; suppliers
fiscal changes, effect on equilibrium national income, 302–303
effect in leakages-injections method, 305
fiscal drag, *defined*, 443–444
fiscal policy, 313–321, 441–445, 453B
defined, 252
vs. monetary policy, 447, 491–494
fiscal transmission mechanism, 441
Fisher, Irving, equation of exchange, 341
fixed capital, *defined*, 5
investment, 256
fixed costs, business rates, 159B
defined, 144
fixed exchange rate, *defined*, 249
fiscal *vs.* monetary policy, 491–492
internal and external balance, 483–488
fixed exchange rate regimes, 473–476
defined, 471
fixed factors, *defined*, 134
fixed investment, 270–272
fixed money income, effects of inflation, 247
fixed reserve ratio, 348
flexible costs, 430, 431
flexible exchange rate, *defined*, 249
flexible exchange rate regimes, 476–478
flexible exchange rates, fiscal *vs.* monetary policy, 492–494
floating exchange rates, *defined*, 249, 471
'floating voters', 237
flows, distinction from stocks, 257
expenditure, 270
see also circular flow
fluctuating exchange rate regime, *defined*, 471
foods, elasticities of demand, 68B
see also beef market
forecasting, 33

foreign direct investment (FDI), 400–401
foreign exchange, *defined*, 249
  see also exchange rate
foreign exchange market, 18
  defined, 249
foreign labour, protection against, 218, 219
foreign saving, financing growth, 400
foreign trade, *see* trade
foreseen inflations, 247–248
forward integration, 130
fractionally backed money, *defined*, 336, 337
free goods, opportunity cost, 7
free market system, *see* market economies; price system
'free-rider' problem, 226
free trade, case for, 215
free trade area, *defined*, 220
freedom of entry and exit,
  effect of communications revolution, 180B
  under monopolistic competition, 174
  under perfect competition, 154
frictional unemployment, 251, 426
  defined, 421
  demand management, 453
full capacity output, *defined*, 146, 176
full cost pricing, 177
full employment,
  defined, 421
  goal of demand management, 448–452
  goal of macroeconomic policy, 251
  limitations on, 453
full-employment output, *defined*, 244
fully backed money, *defined*, 337
functional distribution of income, 185–186

gains,
  from economies of scale, 212
  from specialization, 209–213
  from trade, 209–213
Galbraith, John K., on advertising, 179
game theory, 516
'gateways', Restrictive Practices Court, 182
GATT (General Agreement on Tariffs and Trade), 219–220
GDP (gross domestic product), 244, 259, 266B
  defined, 261
  per employed person, *defined*, 263
  per hour worked, *defined*, 263
gearing, *defined*, 129
General Agreement on Tariffs and Trade, 219–220
general equilibrium analysis, *defined*, 81
general government expenditure, 318B
general price level, 244–248
  defined, 241, 244
general unemployment, 7–8
geographical location, *see* location
geometrical statements, in economic models, 30
GGE (general government expenditure), 318B
giant companies, 172, 173
Giffen goods,
  defined, 52
  price effects, 123

gilt-edged securities (gilts), *defined*, 346
global co-operation, 219–220
globalization, of production and competition, 180B
GNP (gross national product), *defined*, 262
goals,
  defined, 376
  in economic systems, 16
  of firms, 131–132
  of macroeconomic policy, 251–252, 480–481
  of microeconomic policy, 223–226, 226B
  of sellers, 57
  of taxation, 231
gold, *see* metallic money; official reserves
gold standard, 471
  defined, 336, 472
good, nature of, determinant of elasticity of demand and supply, 66–67, 70
Goodhart's Law, *defined*, 382
goods,
  defined, 4
  in measurement of production, 256
  output decisions, 14–16, 20–21, 125, 126
  see also demerit goods; durables; free goods; inferior goods; merit goods; normal goods; public goods
goods markets, 20, 254
  business decisions, 127–128
  competitive, 187–188
  defined, 127
Gorbachev, Mikhail, *perestroika*, 24B
government,
  creation of barriers to entry, monopoly, 164
  influence on business decisions, 132
  influence on circular flow, 300–309
  intervention, 23–24
    for economic development, 411–412
    in industry, 181–183
    methods, 227–237
    in trade, 215–219
  microeconomic policy, 223–238
government budget, 228, 315–316
government expenditure, 232, 257–258
government failure, 236–237
government income, 228
government production, 257–258
government regulation,
  effect on demand, 48
  effect on supply, 57
government saving, financing growth, 400
Government Statistical Service, 33B
government taxes and subsidies, 260–261
graphs, 504–510
  of economic models, 30
  of elasticity of demand, 63–66
  of elasticity of supply, 69
  of marginal rate of substitution, 115
  of production possibility, 8–11
  of utility, 39–40
  see also curves; scatter diagrams
Great Depression (1930s), 251
Gresham's law, *defined*, 336

gross domestic product, 244, 259, 266B
  defined, 261
  per employed person, *defined*, 263
  per hour worked, *defined*, 263
gross incomes, 15
gross investment, *defined*, 257
gross national product, *defined*, 262
gross trading profits, class of income, 260
growth, *see* economic growth

Halpern, Sir Ralph, 131B
heterogeneous products, *defined*, 128
high-powered money supply (MO), 383B
  defined, 382
highly illiquid assets, *defined*, 335
highly liquid assets, *defined*, 335
historical costs, *defined*, 142
  see also sunk costs
holding companies, *defined*, 129
homogeneous products, *defined*, 128, 154
horizontal equity, *defined*, 226
horizontal mergers, 172
  defined, 130
hostile takeovers, mergers, 130
Hotelling, Harold, 204B
household, *defined*, 254
household expenditure, UK, 121B
household income, 15
household saving, 272–273
  financing growth, 400
  as leakage, 285
household sector, in two-sector model, 269
housing, investment, 256–257, 272
housing market,
  barrier to labour mobility, 198–199
  volatility, 91B
housing stock, location, barrier to labour mobility, 198
HPMS (high-powered money supply) (MO), 383B
  defined, 382
human behaviour, 28–29
human capital, 198, 204–205
  defined, 5
human resources,
  effect on development, 409
  see also labour
Hungary, black economy, 265B

illegal activities, contribution to current living standards, 265
IMF *see* International Monetary Fund
immobility, factor, international trade, 208
impact effect, of fiscal changes, 443
imperfect competition, *defined*, 172–184
  in goods market, 188
  market failure, 227
import duties, 215–217
import quotas, *defined*, 215
imported capital, for economic growth, 413–415
imports,
  determinants of, 327
  good or bad, 331–332
  as leakage, 328–329
  in open economy, 460
  see also balance-of-payments accounts; trade

imputed costs, *defined*, 142
imputed rent, *defined*, 260
incentives,
  lack of, in command economies, 17
  to work, 197
income,
  break-even level, *defined*, 274
  in circular flow, 258–261
  disposable, *defined*, 262, 300–301
  distribution,
    in competitive markets, 185–186
    effect of protection, 218–219
    effects on market demand, 48–49
    in market system, 21, 23, 91–92
  effects on budget line, 111–112, 118–119
  effects on demand, 46–47
  government, 228
  household, 15
    effects of taxes and benefits, 232, 233
  producers', effect on supply, 57
  proportion spent on food, 121B
  redistribution, relation to growth, 405–406
  relation to tax, 230–231
  see also national income
income account, *defined*, 322
income-consumption line, *defined*, 119
income determination theory, foreign trade in, 326–331
income effect, of price change, *defined*, 120–123
income elasticity of demand, *defined*, 68
income-expenditure approach, 293, 293–294
  and foreign trade, 328
income-expenditure method, 283–285
  government and circular flow, 300–303
income flows, 255
income fluctuations, and fiscal policy, 310–321
income inequality, 233B
income level, influence on household behaviour, 273
income taxes,
  effect on incentives, 231
  negative, 231–232
  supply-side policies, 456–457
income velocity of circulation, *defined*, 341
inconvertible money, *defined*, 337
increase in demand, 50
increased dimensions, principle, *defined*, 139
increasing long-run costs, 149–150
increasing returns to scale, 137–140
incremental ratios, *defined*, 509
index-linking (indexation), against inflation, 247
index numbers,
  changes in price level, 245–246
  defined, 244
indifference curves, 111–124, 223n
  defined, 114
indifference maps, *defined*, 115–117
indirect costs, *see* fixed costs
indirect taxes, 260–261, 300
  defined, 228
individual factor supply, 190–191
indivisibilities, *defined*, 138–139

induced consumption, *defined*, 275

induced expenditure, *defined*, 273–275

industrial policies, newly industrialized countries, 412

industry,
concentration of, 172–173
declining, support for, 457
equilibrium, under perfect competition, 156–158
government intervention in, 181–183
infant, *defined*, 217–218
related, 148
sheltered, cross-subsidization, 236
size of, in oligopoly, 176

industry demand for factor, 188

inefficiency,
of market system, 22–23
in use of resources, effect on development, 409–410

inefficient output combinations, 9

inelastic demand, *defined*, 64

inequity of market system, 23

infant industry argument, *defined*, 217–218

inferior goods,
defined, 46–47
price effects, 122–123
see also Giffen goods

infinitely inelastic demand, *defined*, 64

inflation, 246–248, 250B, 430–440
defined, 244
entrenched, *defined*, 452
Keynesian, monetarist and New Classical views, 375–376
validated, *defined*, 370, 430

inflationary gap,
creation and removal, 316, 368–370
defined, 315

inflationary output gap, 393n

information, perfect, 154

information deficiencies, cause of market failure, 23, 87–88

infrastructure, *defined*, 411

inheritance, 186
taxes, 228, 300
see also bequest motive

injection, *defined*, 285

innovations,
defined, 5, 140
influence on investment, 271–272
lack of, in command economies, 17
source of long-term growth, 400

input decisions, 125–127

instantaneous period, *defined*, 59

institutions, effect on growth rate, 404

instrumental variables, *see* instruments

instruments,
of policy, 228–236, 252, 376–379, 447, 481–483
defined, 376

intercepts, *defined*, 54, 507

interest,
on capital, 205
compound, 202
defined, 355
liquidity preference theory, 364–365
relation to money, 364–371

interest elasticity of investment, *defined*, 366

interest rates,

defined, 248, 355–358
effect on capital flows, 249–250, 490–491
effect on inflation, 436
influence on household behaviour, 273
influence on investment, 270–271
monetary policy, 380, 446–447
speculative motive, 360
structure, 372–373
and transactions demand, 359

interest rates gap, 476B

intermediate goods, *defined*, 259

intermediate monetary targets, 447

intermediate targets, *defined*, 376

internal balance,
defined, 480–481
fixed exchange rate, 483–488

internal economies of scale, *defined*, 148–149

internal goals, macroeconomic policy, *defined*, 480

internal value of currency, *defined*, 462

international comparisons, GDPs, 266–267

international co-operation, 219–222

International Monetary Fund, *defined*, 472
effective exchange rate, 470
Special Drawing Rights, 474–475

international payments, 322–326

international trade, 208–222

international trading equilibrium, 213–215

international transactions mechanism, 461–463

interpersonal trade, 208

interregional trade, 208

intersection, equilibrium price, 72

intervention, *see* government intervention; paternalistic intervention

interventionist *vs.* market-oriented view, 496–503

inventions, *defined*, 140

inventories, 256
defined, 5
see also stock cycle

investment, 269–282
defined, 256
desired, changes, 292–293
and desired expenditure, 300
determinants, 270–272
direct, *defined*, 323
effect on circular flow, 286
effects on national income, 399
in human capital, 204–205
as injection, 285
relation to current living standards, 264
relation to inflation, 436–437
relation to saving, 285–286, 289
see also portfolio investment

investment allowances, 441

investment goods, 256–257

investment incentives, 441

investment multiplier, *defined*, 296

invisible account, *defined*, 322

'invisible hand', 19, 22, 84

involuntary unemployment, *defined*, 242, 420

isocost lines, *defined*, 514

isolated shocks, 430

isoquants, *defined*, 514–515

Japan, budget-deficit bonds, 306B

job protection, against foreign labour, 218

joint demand, *defined*, 48

joint-stock companies, 129–130

joint supply, *defined*, 56

judging quality by price, 51–52

Kalecki, Michael, on political trade cycles, 318

'Kennedy Round', GATT, 219

Keynes, John Maynard, 88, 269–270, 360

Keynesian aggregate demand curve, stabilization policy, 449

Keynesian aggregate supply curve, 397

Keynesian model, 269–270, 375
limitations, 388
see also interventionist view

Keynesian view,
of the economy, 375
of labour market, 420
of price level, 499
of trade cycle, 498

kinked demand curve, *defined*, 178

know-how, *see* learning-by-doing

knowledge-intensive industries, 5

Kondratieff, Nikolai, on long-wave cycles, 310

laboratory experiments, 27–28

labour,
defined, 5
division of, 18
factor prices, 186–187
foreign, protection against, 218, 219
quality, source of economic growth, 402
total supply, 189

labour force, 196–199
defined, 5, 242

labour-intensive industries, 15, 125

labour market, 196–207, 395–396, 420
reforms, 457

labour mobility, 198–199

Laffer, Arthur, Laffer curve, 232

lags,
effects of exchange rate changes, 487
of fiscal policy, 445
in knowledge, in fine-tuning, 317
of policy, in fine-tuning, 317

laissez-faire,
defined, 19
market efficiency, 82–84
market failure, 22

land,
defined, 4–5
factor mobility, 190
total supply, 189

large open economy, *defined*, 460

LATC (long-run average total cost) curve, *defined*, 147, 149

LAUTRO (Life Assurance and Unit Trust Regulatory Association), 374

law of demand, *defined*, 51–52

law of diminishing returns, *defined*, 135–137

law of large numbers, 29n

law of variable proportions *see* law of diminishing returns

laws,
economic, 79–80
of supply and demand, 76–80

LDCs, *see* less-developed countries

leading indicators, *defined*, 317

leakage, *defined*, 285

leakages-injections approach, 285–287, 293–294, 303–305, 328–329

lean production revolution, 139B

learning-by-doing,
gains from trade, 212–213
source of falling costs, 148

least-squares regression analysis, 31n

legal barriers to entry, monopoly, 164

legal barriers to labour mobility, 198–199

legal tender, *defined*, 337

legislation,
effect on demand, 48
effect on supply, 57

Leibenstein, Harvey, on X-inefficiency, 410

leisure, contribution to current living standards, 264

lender of last resort, *defined*, 374

less-developed countries, *defined*, 407
GDP measurement, 266–267
growth in, 407–416

less-developed economies, 242

liabilities, banks', 346

licences, state, 170

licensing, 183

Life Assurance and Unit Trust Regulatory Association, 374

life expectation, 196

lifestyle, effect of growth, 406

limited duration protection, 219

limited liability, *defined*, 129

Limits to Growth, The, 501

line, *defined*, 272n

linear curves, 10

linear demand curves, 66

linear production possibility curves, 10

linear relations, *defined*, 507

liquidity, 358
defined, 335

liquidity preference function, *defined*, 361

liquidity preference theory of interest, *defined*, 364–365

liquidity trap, *defined*, 384

living standards, 4, 332
and growth, 404–406
measurement by GDP, 264–267

loan stock, *defined*, 129

loanable funds, 203–205
see also interest rates

location,
advantages, natural barrier to entry, 163
input decision, 126–127
of labour force, 198–199

logic, of analytic statements, 27

London clearing banks, 347

London Metal Exchange, 18

long run,
costs and output, 146–150
defined, 59–60, 134
real product wage, 423
returns to scale, 137–140
shut-down conditions, 153
value of exchange rate, 468–469
see also very long run

long-run aggregate supply curve, *defined*, 396–397

long-run average total cost curve, *defined*, 147, 149

long-run disequilibria, of industry, 157

long-run effects of investment, on national income, 399
long-run effects of saving, on national income, 400–401
long-run equilibrium,
  under monopolistic competition, 174
  under perfect competition, 156–157
long-term capital, effect on exchange rate, 466
long-term disequilibria, fixed exchange rates, 475
long-term interest rates, 372
  defined, 248
long-term trend, income fluctuations, 310
Lorenz curve, 232, 233B
  defined, 185
low-wage foreign labour, protection against, 218, 219
lower turning point, *defined*, 311
LP function, *see* liquidity preference function
LRAS curve, *defined*, 396, 396–397

M0, 374, 383B
  defined, 382
M1, *defined*, 382
M3, *defined*, 382
M4, *defined*, 382
M5, *defined*, 382
macro demand curve, 388n
macroeconomic controversies, 496–503
macroeconomic equilibrium, derivation, 512–513
macroeconomic policy,
  in closed economy, 441–459
    goals, 251–252
  in open economy, 480–495
macroeconomic view, of circular flow, 254–255
macroeconomics,
  defined, 241
  elementary, 239–352
  intermediate, 353–503
'mad cow disease', effect on demand and supply, 59B
Malthus, Thomas, on population growth, 196, 408
managed floats, 478–479
  defined, 471
management buy-outs, 130
managerial economies of scale, *defined*, 148
managerial efficiency, under monopoly, 168
managerial theories of firm, *defined*, 132
mandatory rules, *defined*, 234
manning agreements, 426
many-country world, trading equilibrium, 214–215
margin, 44
marginal cost pricing, monopoly, 170
marginal costs, 55–56
  defined, 10, 55, 144
marginal efficiency of capital, *defined*, 203, 401
marginal efficiency of capital curve, 402–403
marginal efficiency of investment curve, *defined*, 266
marginal physical product, *defined*, 187
marginal product,
  of capital, 203
  of factor, *defined*, 187
  of variable factor, *defined*, 135

marginal productivity theory, *defined*, 187
marginal propensity to consume, 276–277, 291, 301
  defined, 276
marginal propensity to import, *defined*, 327
marginal propensity to leak, 304
marginal propensity to save, 291
  defined, 277
marginal propensity to tax, *defined*, 304
marginal rate of factor substitution, *defined*, 515
marginal rate of substitution, *defined*, 114–115
marginal rate of time preference, 204
marginal revenue,
  defined, 152
  under monopoly, 161–162
marginal revenue product, *defined*, 187
marginal tax rate, *defined*, 230
marginal tax revenue, *defined*, 304
marginal utility,
  defined, 39–41
  under monopoly, 168
marginal values, *defined*, 508
market, mechanism, 19–24
market allocations, 84–85, 102n
market-clearing price (equilibrium price), *defined*, 74
market concentration of industry, 173
  defined, 172
market concentration ratios, *defined*, 173
market conditions, goals of firm, 132
market considerations, determinant of business decisions, 127–128
market demand,
  effects of income distribution, 48–49
  effects of prices, 41–44
market-determined prices, 18–19
market economies, 17–23
  defined, 17
market efficiency, 81–93
market failure, 22–23, 85–93, 225B
  defined, 22
  microeconomic policy, 226–227
  under monopoly, 169–170
market forces, 73–74
  for development, 413
  effect on efficiency, 224
market interactions, 81
market loans, *defined*, 346
market-oriented supply-side policies, 455–457
market-oriented view,
  vs. interventionist view, 496–503
  see also monetarist view
market period, 60
  defined, 59
market price,
  defined, 73
  determination, 72–80
market rate of interest, *defined*, 355–356
market sector, *defined*, 24
market supply, 57–60
market supply curves, *defined*, 57–58
market supply schedules, 58
market value, of bond, 355
marketing economies of scale, *defined*, 148

markets,
  black, 85, 101, 102
  contestable, *defined*, 180
  defined, 18, 72
  see also factor markets; goods markets
Marshall-Lerner condition, *defined*, 487n
mass production, 139B
mathematical statements, in economic models, 30
maturity date of bond, *defined*, 335, 355
maximization of profit *see* profit maximization
maximization of satisfaction (utility), 37, 41, 118
maxims of taxation, 229
maximum price, A–F analysis, 100–103
maximum-price control, 84–85
MBO (management buy-outs), 130
MC (marginal cost), *defined*, 10, 55–56, 144–146
Meade, James, on balance, 480n
measures, cardinal and ordinal, *defined*, 113
MEC, *see* marginal efficiency of capital
medium of exchange, 18
  defined, 334
Mercantilists, 331–332
merchandise account, *defined*, 322
merchant banks, 348
mergers, 172, 182B
  defined, 130
  see also Monopolies and Mergers Commission
merit goods,
  defined, 22–23
  source of market failure, 86, 226
MES (minimum efficient scale), *defined*, 149
metallic money, 335–336
MFN (most favoured nation) principle, GATT, 220
micro market equilibrium, derivation, 512
microeconomic policy, 223–238
microeconomics,
  defined, 36
  elementary, 35–107
  intermediate, 108–238
migration, 196
'Mini-Budget', 315
minimum-cost method, 146–147
minimum efficient scale (MES), *defined*, 149
Minimum Lending Rate, *defined*, 378
minimum prices, agriculture, 105–106
minimum resale prices, 182B
mixed economic systems, 23–24
MLR (Minimum Lending Rate), *defined*, 378
MMC, *see* Monopolies and Mergers Commission
mobile factors, *defined*, 20
mobility,
  of factors, *defined*, 190
  of labour, 198–199
  see also immobility
models, economic, *defined*, 29–34
momentary period, *defined*, 59, 60
monetarist view,
  of monetary policy, 375–376, 489B
  of price level, 499

of trade cycle, 497
  see also market-oriented view
monetary adjustment mechanism, *defined*, 370
monetary base, *see* M0
monetary built-in stabilizer, *defined*, 380
monetary disequilibrium, 364
monetary equilibrium, *defined*, 364
monetary policy, 445–448
  of Bank of England, 372–387
  defined, 252
  and the ERM, 488, 489B
  vs. fiscal policy, 491–494
monetary shocks, 367–370
  defined, 365
monetary transmission mechanism, 365–367, 445–446
  defined, 365
money,
  changes of value, 244–245
  costs of, 142
  creation by retail banks, 348–351
  defined, 334
  demand for, 355–363
  medium of exchange, 18, 334
  purchasing power, *defined*, 245
  relation to national income, 364–371
  relation to price level, 334–345
  value of, *defined*, 245
  see also currency
money flows, 254–255
money illusion, *defined*, 340
money interest rate, *defined*, 446
money multiplier, *defined*, 349–350
money national product, *defined*, 243
money substitutes, 339B
  defined, 338
money supply,
  defined, 338–339
  definitions used in UK, 381–383
  increase, 365–366
  role of banks, 346–352
  target of monetary policy, 380
money values, 263, 339–341
monopolies,
  defined, 181
  goods markets, 127
Monopolies and Mergers Commission, 169, 182B
  defined, 181
monopolistic competition, *defined*, 173–175
monopoly,
  defined, 161–171
  natural, government regulation, 234
  vs. monopsony, in labour market, 201
monopoly equilibrium, 162–164
monopoly policy, *see* competition policy
monopoly trade unions, 199–201
monoposonist, monoposony, *defined*, 128, 199
monopsony, *vs.* monopoly, in labour market, 201
monopsony employers, 199
moonlighting,
  defined, 198
  see also black economy
moral suasion, *defined*, 379
'most favoured nation' principle, GATT, 220
motivations,
  consumer, 37
  suppliers', 53
  see also profit motive

movements,
  along curves, national income, 291–292
  along supply and demand curves, 49–52, 58–59, 77
MP, *see* marginal product
MPC, *see* marginal propensity to consume
MPL, *see* marginal propensity to leak
MPM, *see* marginal propensity to import
MPP, *see* marginal physical product
MPS, *see* marginal propensity to save
MPT, *see* marginal propensity to tax
MR, *see* marginal revenue
MRP, *see* marginal revenue product
MRS, *see* marginal rate of substitution
MTR, *see* marginal tax rate
MTR (marginal tax revenue), *see* marginal propensity to tax
MU, *see* marginal utility
multibank system, deposit creation, 349–350
multilateral balance of payments, *defined*, 324
multinationals *see* transnationals
multiplier,
  defined, 296–298
  foreign trade, 329–331
  with government sector, 305–308
  regional, *defined*, 443

NAIRU, *see* non-accelerating inflationary rate of unemployment
'naive' quantity theory of money, *defined*, 341
Nash, John, Nash equilibrium, 516n
national currencies, 208–209
National Debt, 374
  defined, 228, 315
national income, 243–244
  and balance of payments, 322–333
  changes, 291–299
  classification, 263
  defined, 261
  relation to money, 364–371
  short-run and long-run effects of investment, 399
  short-run and long-run effects of saving, 400–401
  see also equilibrium national income; theory of income determination
national income accounting, 254–268
national income statistics, 261–262
national insurance contributions, direct taxes, 228
national output, 243–244
national power, relation to growth, 406
national product, 243–244
national product valued at constant prices, *defined*, 243
national sovereignty, *see* sovereignty, national
nationalization, nationalized industries, 22, 235–236
natural barriers to entry, 163–164
natural monopoly,
  defined, 163
  economies of scale, 168–169

government regulation, 233–234
price mechanism, 170
natural rate of unemployment, (or NAIRU), 425B, 427B, 449, 453
  defined, 421
  see also non-accelerating inflationery rate of unemployment
natural resources, effect on development, 408–409
near money, *defined*, 338
necessities,
  absolute, indifference curves, 117
  vs. luxuries, 67
negative demand elasticity, *defined*, 64
negative income tax, 231–232
negative investment in stocks (stock decumulation), 256
negative slope of curve, 8n, 38–39
negative utility goods, indifference curves, 117
negatively related variables, *defined*, 507
negotiating, 200–201
net export function, 327–328
net exports, *defined*, 260, 328
net indirect taxes, 261
net investment, *defined*, 257
net national product (net national income), *defined*, 262
net property income from abroad, *defined*, 262
neutrality of money, *defined*, 340
New Classical view,
  of labour market, 420, 424
  of monetary policy, 376
  of NAIRU, 424
  of trade cycle, 497–498
new goods, source of economic growth, 402
new products and techniques, 271–272
NICs (newly-industrialized countries), 412
NIT (negative income tax), 231–232
NNP (net national product), *defined*, 262
nominal exchange rate, 469
nominal flows, money, 255
nominal interest rate, *defined*, 446
nominal money supply, *defined*, 339
nominal national income, 263
nominal national product, *defined*, 243
non-accelerating inflationary rate of unemployment, (NAIRU), 421, 425B, 427B, 449, 453
  defined, 452
  voluntary or not, 423–424
  see also natural rate of unemployment
non-banking financial institutions, *defined*, 348
non-budgetary policies, 232–236
non-competing groups, in labour market, *defined*, 198
non-durables (consumer goods and services), 256
  defined, 37
non-excludable good, *defined*, 85
non-market activities, exclusion from GDP, 266B
non-market allocations, 84–85, 103B
non-market sector, *defined*, 24

non-marketed economic activities, contribution to living standards, 266
non-pecuniary advantages and disadvantages of occupations, *defined*, 198
non-price competition, *defined*, 178
non-profit maximization, small firms, 150
non-redeemable bonds, *defined*, 356–358
non-renewable resources, *defined*, 4–5, 204B
non-rival goods, *defined*, 85
non-tariff barriers, *defined*, 215–217
non-tradeables, *defined*, 461
normal capacity output, *defined*, 176
normal goods, *defined*, 46
normal profits,
  defined, 152
  monopoly, 164–165
normative statements, *defined*, 26–27
notes (paper money), *defined*, 337

objectives,
  in economic systems, 16
  see also goals
occupied population *see* labour force
Office of Fair Trading, 169, 182B
  defined, 181
official financing, *defined*, 323
official reserves, *defined*, 323
official statistics, 33B, 261–262
OFGAS, 234
OFT, *see* Office of Fair Trading
OFTEL, 234
OFWAT, 234
oligopoly, 175–181
  defined, 173, 175
  goods markets, 127
oligopsony, *defined*, 128
one-bank system, deposit creation, 349
OPEC, petrol price cartel, 50, 176, 409
OPEC Fund, source of development aid, 415
open economies,
  defined, 259–260
  large and small, *defined*, 460
  macroeconomic policy, 480–495
open-market operations,
  defined, 376, 377–378
opportunity costs, 6–8, 142, 149B
  of capital, *defined*, 152
  defined, 6
  effect on comparative advantage, 211–212
  graphical representation, 9–11
  of growth, 406
  vs. accounting costs, 143
  of work, 190
optimal allocation, 223–225
  defined, 82
optimal population, *defined*, 403
optimum output,
  defined, 154
  discriminating monopolist, 166
  for firm, 155–156
optimum output rule, *defined*, 153–154
  under monopoly, 162
optimum position of consumer satisfaction, *defined*, 37
ordinal measure, *defined*, 113
ordinary shares, *defined*, 129

organization, of businesses, 128–132
Organization of Petroleum-Exporting Countries, *see* OPEC
organizational failure, in command economies, 17
output, 4
  actual, *defined*, 244
  in circular flow, 258–261
  control by monopoly, 164
  relation to long-run costs, 146–150
  under monopoly, 167
  variation of short-run costs, 143–146
  see also national product; optimum output
output decisions, 14–16, 20–21, 125, 126
output gaps, 393
  defined, 314
output-related subsidy, under monopoly, 170
overall concentration of industry, *defined*, 172
overhead costs, *see* fixed costs
'overheating', *defined*, 311
overseas banks, 347
overshooting, 88
own price,
  defined, 38
  determinant of demand, 38
  determinant of supply, 54
ownership,
  by state, 235–236
  in economic systems, 16
  of factor services, 6
  of firms, 130–131, 132
  in relation to efficiency, 236
  under capitalism, 22

paper money, 336–337
par value, *defined*, 471
paradox of thrift, 294–296
paradox of value, 44
parameters, *defined*, 507
Pareto, Vilfredo, 82
Pareto-optimal allocation, *defined*, 82
partial equilibrium analysis, *defined*, 81
partially backed money, *defined*, 337
participation rates, *defined*, 5, 189
partnerships, 129
patents, law, 182–183
paternalistic intervention, 22
peak, *defined*, 311
pegged exchange rate, *defined*, 249
per capita economic growth, *defined*, 405
per capita GDP, *defined*, 263
per capita output, 4
perestroika, 24B
perfect competition,
  defined, 154
  in goods market, 187–188
  output and price, compared with monopoly, 167
  profit maximization, 152–160
perfect complements, indifference curves, 117
perfect factor markets, equilibrium, 191–192
perfect information, 154
perfect substitutes, indifference curves, 116–117
perfectly competitive market, *defined*, 154
perfectly elastic and perfectly inelastic demand, *defined*, 64

perfectly liquid asset, *defined*, 335
permanent income theory, *defined*, 444
personal costs, of growth, 406
personal disposable income, *defined*, 262
personal income, *defined*, 262
Phillips, A. W., 437
Phillips curve, *defined*, 437–439
stabilization policy, 449–452
place, *see* location
planned expenditure, *defined*, 270
relation to equilibrium, 284
planned investment, *defined*, 288
planned saving, *defined*, 287–288
planning, centralized, 16–17, 24
plant, *defined*, 129
fixed capital, 5
policy,
competition, 169, 181–183, 228
defined, 181
discretionary, 319, 320
economic, disagreements about, 33
macroeconomic, goals, 251–252
microeconomic, 223–238
see also fiscal policy; monetary policy
policy instruments,
macroeconomic policy, 252, 481–483
microeconomic policy, 228–236
policy lags, fiscal policy, 443
political constraints, cause of government failure, 236–237
political risk, 373
political trade cycle, 318–319
poll tax (Community Charge), 228, 229B, 231
pollution, *see* conservation; environment; externalities
'popular capitalism', 236
population base, determinant of labour force, 5, 196–199
population factors,
effect on demand, 48, 49
effect on economy, 196, 403–404, 408
effect on environment, 416
population policy, for development, 415
portfolio balance decision, *defined*, 358
portfolio balance theory, 360, 365
portfolio investment, 400
defined, 323
portfolios of assets, 358
positive economics, 26–28
positive investment in stocks, 256
positive opportunity costs, 7, 8
positive quadrant, *defined*, 505
positive slope of curve, 8n
positive statments, *defined*, 26–27
positively related variables, *defined*, 507
potential national income, *defined*, 284
potential output, *defined*, 244
poverty, 414B
vicious circle, *defined*, 413
poverty trap, 231
power,
bargaining, of trade unions, 201
of monopoly, 164–166
national, relation to growth, 406

organizational, effect on market, 23
see also control
ppc (production possibility curves), *defined*, 8–11
ppp (purchasing power parity), *defined*, 468
precautionary motive, *defined*, 359–360
predictability of market demand, 42–43, 48
preferences, sellers', 85, 100–101, 102
prescriptive rules, *defined*, 234
present value, *defined*, 356–358
present value of capital, *defined*, 202
price changes, income and substitution effects, 120–123
price-consciousness, 50
price-consumption line, *defined*, 119–120
price controls,
agriculture, 104–106
under monopoly, 169–170
price differences, 165B
price discrimination, *defined*, 165–166
price elasticity of demand, *see* elasticity, of demand
price elasticity of supply, *see* elasticity, of supply
price expectations, influence on household behaviour, 273
price floor, agriculture, 105–106
price index, *defined*, 245
price level, 244–248, 334–345, 498–499
defined, 241, 244
price-level changes, exchange rate, 465–466
price mechanism, 20
under monopoly, 169–170
see also 'invisible hand'; price system
price stability, demand management, 454
price stickiness, 177–178
price system, *defined*, 18–19
price-takers, *defined*, 37, 53
under perfect competition, 154
price-taking behaviour, *defined*, 37
prices,
of capital, 201–202
factor, *see* factor prices
influence on demand, 37–45
judging quality by, 51–52
market-determined, 18–19
maximum, 84–85
under monopoly, 164, 167
see also administered prices; arbitrary prices; equilibrium price; market price; own price; relative prices
prices and incomes policies, 454–455, 501
defined, 454
primary goals, macroeconomic policy, 252, 480
prime costs, *see* variable costs
prime rate of interest, *defined*, 248
principal, of bonds, *defined*, 355
principle of increased dimensions, 139
printing press finance, *defined*, 378
'Prisoners' dilemma', 175n
private companies, 129
private property, under capitalism, 22
privatization, 22
case for, 236

fiscal implications of, 443
of public utilities, 234
probabilities, 31
process innovations, *defined*, 5, 400
influence on investment, 271–272
producer supply curves, 57
producers,
income, effect on supply, 57
see also suppliers
product,
nature under oligopoly, 176
types in goods markets, 128
product cycles, *defined*, 402
small firms, 150
product differentiation, 164, 173–174, 179
product innovations, *defined*, 5, 400
influence on investment, 271–272
product quality, contribution to current living standards, 264
product specific resources, *defined*, 7
product 'switching', 149B
production,
factors, *see* factors of production
government, 257–258
mass, 139B
major types of, 255–258
production costs, 142–151
effect on gains from trade, 211
effect on markets, 19–20
effect on supply, 56
production decisions, 14–16, 20–21, 125, 126
production methods, 20–21
lean, 139B
new, source of economic growth, 402
production possibility curves, *defined*, 8–11
production sector, *see* producers; suppliers
production techniques, *see* production methods
productive efficiency, *defined*, 82, 223
under monopoly, 168–169
under perfect competition, 168
productive inefficiency, *defined*, 409
productivity,
of factors of production, *defined*, 134–141
relation to costs, 143–145
productivity changes, effect on production possibility curves, 10–11
productivity deals, power of trade unions, 201
products,
homogeneous, *defined*, 128, 154
new,
influence on investment, 271–272
source of economic growth, 402
profit maximization, 55–56
defined, 53
see also non-profit maximization
profit-maximizing firm, 152–160
profit-maximizing output, monopolist, 161–164
profit motive,
under capitalism, 22
see also goals, of firms
profits,
on capital, 205

current and expected, influence on investment, 271
monopoly, 164–165
normal, supernormal and subnormal, *defined*, 152
taxation, 170n1
progressive taxes, *defined*, 230–231
promissory notes, *defined*, 336
propensities to consume, 276–277
proportional taxes, *defined*, 230
proscriptive rules, *defined*, 234
protection,
arguments for, 217–219
defined, 215
protectionism, 215–219, 220B
PSBR, *see* Public Sector Borrowing Requirement
PSDR, *see* Public Sector Debt Retirement
psychological barriers to labour mobility, 198
psychological factors,
effect on demand, 48
effect on supply, 57
public companies, 129
public corporations, 235
public deposits, Bank of England, 373
public goods,
defined, 22
sources of market failure, 85–86, 226
Public Sector Borrowing Requirement, 228, 316
defined, 316
Public Sector Debt Retirement, 444
defined, 316
public utilities, 169
privatization, 234
purchase price, of captial, *defined*, 201–202
purchasing power of money, *defined*, 245
purchasing power parity, *defined*, 468
purchasing power parity exchange rate, *defined*, 468
pure inflation, 246
'pure' public goods, 226

quadrants, *defined*, 505
quality,
assumed relation to price, 51–52
of factors, source of economic growth, 402
of life, contribution to living standards, 265
of products, contribution to living standards, 264
quality control, failure in command economies, 17
quantity, equilibrium, *defined*, 72
quantity demanded, *see* demand
quantity supplied, *see* supply
quantity theory of money, *defined*, 341
quasi-rents, *defined*, 194
queues, for limited supply, 84–85, 100, 102
quintiles, *defined*, 15
quotas,
EC Common Agricultural Policy, 106
import, 216–217
defined, 215

R&D (research and development), 5
race, relation to earnings, 197–198
railways, resource allocation, 7B

rank order of preference (ordinal measure), *defined*, 113
rate of interest, *see* interest rates
rate of return on capital, *defined*, 202
rates,
  domestic, 229B
  unified business, 159B
rational expectations, *defined*, 497
rationing, of limited supply, 85, 100, 102
raw materials, circulating capital, 5
real assets, 358
real cost *see* opportunity costs
real exchange rate, 469
real flows, money, 255
real interest rate, *defined*, 446
real money supply, *defined*, 339
real national income, 263
real national product, 245
  defined, 243
real opportunity cost, *see* opportunity costs
real product wage, *defined*, 423
real values, 263
real-wage unemployment, 422–423, 427–428
  defined, 422
realigned exchange rates, *defined*, 471
realized expenditure, *defined*, 270
recession,
  defined, 311
  effects on national income, 295B
  see also contraction phase
recessionary gap, *defined*, 314
recessionary output gap, 393n
rectangular hyperbolas, 63n
recycling of waste products, 4–5
redeemable bonds, 357
redeemed bonds, *defined*, 355
rediscounted bill, *defined*, 357
redistribution, stop-growth school, 416
redistribution of income, relation to growth, 405–406
regional balances, 324
regional co-operation, 220
regional multiplier, *defined*, 443
regional specialization, 208
regressive expenditures, 232n
regressive taxes, *defined*, 230–231
regulations,
  Bank of England, 379
  government, 233–234
related goods, 81–82
related industries, 148
relative prices, 340–341
  effect on demand, 47–48
  effect on supply, 56
  effects on budget line, 112–113, 119
  price-consciousness, 50
relative values, 339–341
reliability of data, 32, 33B
rely-on-growth school, 417–419
renewable resources, *defined*, 4–5
rent,
  economic, *defined*, 192–194
  housing market, effect on labour mobility, 198–199
  imputed, *defined*, 260
rental value, of capital, *defined*, 201–202
replacement investment, *defined*, 257
research and development (R&D), 5
reserves, *see* cash reserves; official reserves

resource allocation, 6–11
  efficient, *defined*, 82
  through price mechanism, 20
resources,
  natural, effect on development, 408–409
  non-renewable, conservation, 4–5, 204B
  optimum allocation, 223–224
  product specific, *defined*, 7
  renewable, *defined*, 4–5
  see also factors of production
restrictive practices, 181
Restrictive Practices Court, 169, 181–182
restructuring (*perestroika*), 24B
retail banks,
  Bank of England as banker to, 374
  defined, 347
Retail Price Index, *defined*, 246
retail sector, supply and demand, 77B
retirement pensions, *see* transfer payments
returns to scale,
  defined, 137
  long run, 137–140
revalued currency, *defined*, 471
revenues,
  defined, 152
  see also marginal revenue
reversibility of fiscal policies, 445
Ricardo, David,
  on comparative advantage, 210
  on economic rent, 192–193
rigid costs, 430, 431
rigidities, cause of government failure, 236
risk,
  on capital, 205
  political, 373
risk-averse people, *defined*, 372
risk aversion (and risk preference), effect on earnings, 198
risk-bearing economies of scale, *defined*, 148
risk of default, 373
rivalrous behaviour, *defined*, 175
road accidents, social costs of, 86B
Robinson, Joan, on imperfect competition, 173n
roundabout production process, *defined*, 203
Royal Mint, 373
RPI (Retail Price Index), *defined*, 246
rules,
  Bank of England, 379
  government, 233–234
  optimum output, 153–154
  shut-down, 152–153

salaries, class of income, 260
sales tax, A-F analysis, 96–99
sample, 31
SATC curves, 147
satisfaction, *see* utility
satisficing, *defined*, 132
saucer-shaped cost curves, 176
saving,
  defined, 272
  desired, changes, 293–296
  effects on circular flow, 286
  effect on national income, 400–401
  government intervention, for development, 411
  as leakage, 285
  relation to inflation, 436
  relation to investment, 285–286, 289

  see also desired saving
saving function, 277–278
scale of line, *defined*, 504
scarcity, 7B
  defined, 6
scatter diagrams, 31–32
  defined, 31, 506
schedules,
  defined, 506
  in economic models, 30
  of market demand, 42
  of market supply, 58
  of supply, 54
  of utility, 39–40
Schumpeter, Joseph, on creative destruction, 164
sciences,
  experimental and non-experimental, 27–28
  social, 3
scientific method, 27–28
SDR (Special Drawing Rights), *defined*, 474
seasonal variations, income fluctuations, 310
second best, theory, *defined*, 225
second best allocations, 224–225
second-generation banks, 349
secondary goals,
  macroeconomic policy, 252, 480
secondary market effects, A-F procedure, 99, 101, 102–103
sectoral balances, 324–325
Securities and Investments Board, 374
segmentation, of labour market, *defined*, 198
self-employed, *defined*, 242
self-employment, risk preference, 198
self-sufficiency,
  in traditional economic systems, 16, 18
  vs. specialization, 208, 209
sellers,
  goals, 57
  in goods markets, 127–128
  in industry, oligopoly, 176
  preferences under limited supply, 85, 100–101, 102
  under perfect competition, 154
  see also suppliers
service account, *defined*, 322
services,
  defined, 4
  factor, 5–6
  fixed capital, 5
  markets, *see* goods markets
  in measurement of production, 256
'Set Aside', EC Common Agricultural Policy, 106
sex of workers, relation to earnings, 197–198
shareholders, 130–131
  defined, 129
shares,
  defined, 248
  ordinary, *defined*, 129
  ownership, dispersion, 130–131
sheltered industries, cross-subsidization, 236
shifts,
  in supply curve, long-run, 157–158
  in national income curves, 291–292
  in production possibility curves, 10–11
  in supply and demand curves, 49–52, 58–59, 77–79
shocks,
  aggregate demand and

  aggregate supply, 392–393
  defined, 365
  inflationary, 430
  monetary, 367, 368
shops, productivity of, 77B
short run,
  costs and output, 143–146
  defined, 59–60, 134
  monopoly equilibrium, 162
  real product wage, 423
  returns to variable factor, 135–137
  shut-down conditions, 153
short-run aggregate supply curve, *defined*, 390–391
short-run effects of investment, on national income, 399
short-run effects of saving, on national income, 400–401
short-run equilibrium, under monopolistic competition, 174
short-run goals, monetary policy, 452
short-term capital, effect on exchange rate, 466
short-term interest rates, 372
  defined, 248
shut-down rule,
  defined, 152–153
  monopoly, 162
SIB (Securities and Investments Board), 374
sight deposits, 338n
  defined, 337
signals, in price system, 19, 20
silver (metallic money), 335–336
Simon, Herbert, on satisficing, 132
Single European Act, 220
single proprietorships, 129
single-use factors, opportunity cost, 7
site, *see* location
size distribution of income, 185–186
skills, *see* human capital
slope,
  of indifference curves, 114–115
  positive and negative, 8n
sluggish markets, cause of market failure, 23, 88
small firms, 150
small open economy, *defined*, 460
Smith, Adam,
  on 'invisible hand', 19, 22, 84
  on monetary values, 340
  on paradox of value, 44
  on supply-side economics, 456
  on taxation, 229
snob demand, *defined*, 51
social barriers to labour mobility, 198
social behaviour, 28–29
social contract, 427, 501
social costs,
  cost-benefit analysis, 234–235
  defined, 87
  of drink-driving accidents, 86B
  of growth, 406
social factors,
  effect on demand, 48
  effect on development, 410
  effect on supply, 57
social organization, influence on economic system, 16
social sciences, 3
socialist economies, 17
sociological factors, *see* social factors
sovereignty,
  consumer, 84n
  national, 209, 474, 477B

Soviet Union,
  command economy, 17
  perestroika, 24B
special deposits, *defined*, 379
Special Drawing Rights, *defined*, 474
specialization,
  gains from, 209–212
  in production, 18–19, 208
speculative behaviour, *defined*, 476–477
speculative crises, exchange rates, 475–476
speculative demand, *defined*, 51
speculative motive, *defined*, 360
spillover effects (externalities), *defined*, 23
  source of market failure, 86–87
SRAS (short-run aggregate supply curve), 393–396
  defined, 390
stabilization,
  of interest rate, 381
  of money supply, 380–381
stabilization policy, 383–387, 449–452
  defined, 316
  Keynesian, monetarist and New Classical views, 375–376
stabilizers, *defined*, 319
stabilizing speculative behaviour, *defined*, 476
stable environment, 499–500
stable equilibrium, *defined*, 75
stable price level, 500–501
stable prices,
  goal of demand management, 448–452
  goal of macroeconomic policy, 252
stagflation, 241–242, 388
  defined, 242
standard of deferred payment, function of money, 335
standard of living, *see* living standards
state intervention, *see* government, intervention
state ownership, 235–236
statistical association, *defined*, 31–33
statistics,
  economic, 31–33
  government, 261–262
  reliability, 33B
sterilization, *defined*, 490
sterling price, exchange rate, 462
sticky prices, 177–178
stock, *defined*, 256
stock accumulation, *defined*, 256
stock of capital, 401n
stock cycle, *defined*, 310
stock decumulation, *defined*, 256
Stock Exchange, 18
stocks,
  defined, 248
  distinction from flows, 257
  goods and materials, circulating capital, 5
  investment in, 272
stop-go cycles, 310, 319
  defined, 319
stop-growth school, 416
store of value, function of money, 334
straight lines, *defined*, 272n
stream of future income, *defined*, 356
stream of future payments, *defined*, 356
street markets, 18

structural changes,
  effect on growth rate, 404
  exchange rate, 466
structural unemployment, 421–422, 426–427, 427B
  defined, 421
  demand management, 453
structure of interest rates, 372–373
  defined, 248
subsidiary companies, 129
subsidies,
  government, 228, 260–261
  for agriculture, 104–105
subsidy, output-related, monopoly, 170
substitutability in production, 56
  effect on elasticity of supply, 70
substitutes,
  defined, 47–48
  effect on elasticity of demand 66–67
  indifference curves, 116–117
  market interactions, 81
substitution, of factors of production, 146–147
substitution effects, *defined*, 120–123
sunk costs, *defined*, 142, 180
supplementary deposit scheme, *defined*, 379
suppliers,
  defined, 53
  goals, 57
  see also producers
supply, 53–61
  aggregate, 388–398
  of capital, 203–205
  determinants of, 53–57
  elasticity, 69–70
  excess, 74
  defined, 73
  of factor, 189–191
  laws of, 76–79
supply curves, 54–56, 57–60
  aggregate, 388–398
  firm's, under perfect competition, 156
  industry, long-run shifts, 157–158
supply of effort, *defined*, 190
supply elasticity, 69–70
supply of money, *see* money supply
supply schedules, 54
supply-shock inflation, 430–434
supply side, 390–391
  long run, 394–397
supply-side inflation, *see* cost-push inflation
supply-side policies, 454–457
  defined, 252, 454
supply-side shocks, 430
support function, Bank of England, *defined*, 374
support policy, 377
surplus, *see* consumer surplus; government surplus
sustained inflation, 430
sustained supply shocks, 432–433

tabulations, *see* schedules
takeovers, 130–131
tangents, *defined*, 508
target variables, *defined*, 376
targets,
  defined, 376
  of monetary policy, 379–383
tariff wars, 218
tariffs, protectionism, *defined*, 215–217
tastes,
  effect on demand and markets, 19, 48

indifference curves, 113–117
influence on household behaviour, 273
tax changes, demand management, 441–443
tax efficiency, 229–230
tax equity, 230–231
tax rates, fiscal transmission mechanism, 441
tax-related incomes policy, 501
taxable capacity, *defined*, 232
taxation, double, *defined*, 456
taxes,
  categories, 300
  on commodities, A–F procedure, 96–99
  direct, *defined*, 228
  on economic rents, 194
  government, 260–261
  indirect, *defined*, 228
  in leakages-injections method, 303–304
  role of, 228–232
  as stabilizers, 320
  see also fiscal policy
TC, *see* total cost
TDE (total domestic expenditure), *defined*, 261
technical change, source of economic growth, 402
technical economies of scale, *defined*, 148
technical efficiency, *defined*, 125
techniques,
  new, influence on investment, 271–272
  production, changes, 140, 147
technological innovation, source of long-term growth, 400
technology, 'state of the art', effect on supply, 56
tennis championships, ticket allocation, 103B
term of bond (term to maturity), *defined*, 335, 355
term loan, *defined*, 355
terms of trade,
  defined, 213
  improvement through protection, 218
testability,
  of positive statements, 26
  see also econometrics
tests, of economic models, 31–33
TFC (total fixed costs), *defined*, 144
TFE (total final expenditure), *defined*, 261
theory,
  of distribution, *defined*, 185
  economic, 29–34
  of firm, 131–132
  of income determination, *defined*, 269
  of the second best, *defined*, 225
third-generation banks, 349
Third World, industrialization, 24
thrift, paradox of, 294–296
time deposit, *defined*, 338
time-lags,
  in cobweb theorem, 88–89
  in fine-tuning, 317
  fiscal policy, 443
time period, effects on supply and demand, 37, 58–60, 98–99, 101
time preference, marginal rate, *defined*, 204, 273
TNCs (transnationals), 400–401
Tobin, James, on speculative motive, 360
'Tokyo Round', GATT, 219
top 100 companies, 172

total cost,
  defined, 144
  long-run monopoly equilibrium, 163
  perfect competition, 158–160
  see also social costs
total demand, 41–44, 48–49
total domestic expenditure, *defined*, 261
total final expenditure, *defined*, 261
total fixed costs, *defined*, 144
total national product, 243–244
total output, *see* gross domestic product
total product, of variable factor, *defined*, 135
total revenue,
  defined, 152
  long-run monopoly equilibrium, 163
  under perfect competition, 158–160
total supply of factor, 189
total utility, *defined*, 39–40
total variable costs, *defined*, 144
TP, *see* total product
TR, *see* total revenue
trade,
  accompaniment to specialization, 18
  international, 208–222
  in theory of income determination, 326–331
trade account, *defined*, 322
trade-account deficit, 485–486
trade-account surplus, 486–488
trade creation, *defined*, 220–222
trade cycle, 310–313, 497–498
  defined, 241, 310
  political, 318–319
trade diversion, *defined*, 220–222
trade-offs,
  opportunity cost, 6
  policy, 457–459
trade unions,
  monopoly, 199–201
  wage-cost push, 456B
trade-weighted exchange rate, *defined*, 469
tradeables, *defined*, 461
traditional economic systems, 18
  defined, 16
training, *see* human capital
transactions demand for money, *defined*, 343, 359
transactions motive, 342–343, 359
transfer earnings,
  defined, 192
  see also quasi-rents
transfer payments,
  defined, 232, 257
  stabilizers, 320
transformation curves (production possibility curves), *defined*, 8–11
transnationals, 400–401
  defined, 129
  imported capital, 415
transport costs, effect on gains from trade, 210–211
Treasury bills, *defined*, 248
Treaty of Rome (1957), 182, 220
trough, *defined*, 310
turning points, *defined*, 311
TVC (total variable costs), *defined*, 144
two-country world, trading equilibrium, 213–214
two-sector model, 269–270

unavoidable costs, *see* fixed costs

uncertainty,
  about interest rates, 372
  business decisions, 127
  control of money supply, 381
  speculative motive, 360
  see also risk
undershooting, 88
unemployed, *defined*, 242
unemployment, 241, 242–243,
    420–429
  defined, 242
  effect of imports and exports,
    331
  frictional, 251
  opportunity cost of, 7–8
  zero, 251
  see also demand-deficient
    unemployment; natural rate
    of unemployment; real-
    wage unemployment;
    structural unemployment
unemployment benefits, 427
  see also transfer payments
unemployment rates, 243
  effect of labour immobility, 199
  measurement, 424–425, 427B
'unfair' foreign competition, 219
unfairness of market system, 23
unfavourable balance, 324
unfavourable movements, terms
    of trade, *defined*, 213
unforeseen inflations, 247
unified business rates, 159B
unions, *see* trade unions
uniqueness, natural barrier to
    entry, 163
unit of account, function of
    money, 335
unit banking system, *defined*,
    347
unit cost, *defined*, 144
unit elastic demand, 63
  defined, 64
unpaid activities, contribution to
    living standards, 266
unstable equilibrium, *defined*, 75
upper turning point, *defined*, 311
upswings, 313
  Germany, 314B

upturn, 313
  defined, 311
upward slope of curve, 8n
upward-sloping demand curve,
    unstable equilibrium, 75n
'Uruguay Round', GATT, 219
US Agency for International
    Development, 415
USSR,
  command economy, 17
  perestroika, 24B
utility (satisfaction), 39–41
  contribution to living
    standards, 264–265
  defined, 39
  maximization, 37, 41, 118–119

validated inflation, *defined*, 370,
    430
validation, monetary, 432, 433,
    434
valuation, for national income,
    263–264
value, paradox of, 44
value added, *defined*, 258
Value Added Tax, *defined*, 228
value judgements, 27, 33–34
value of the marginal product,
    defined, 188
value of money, *defined*, 244–245
variability of earnings, 198
variable costs, 159B
  defined, 144
variable factors,
  defined, 134
  diminishing returns to scale,
    138
  short-run returns, 135–137
variables, 3–4
  defined, 3
  determining quantity, 37–38
  in economic models, 29–31
  in graphs, 504
  of macroeconomics, 242
  positively and negatively
    related, *defined*, 507
  statistical association, 31–33
VAT, *defined*, 228
velocity of circulation, 341

VER (Voluntary Export
    Restraints), 216
verbal statements, in economic
    models, 30
vertical equity, *defined*, 226
vertical mergers, 172
  defined, 130
very long run, 401–402
  defined, 140, 402
very short term facility, European
    Monetary System, *defined*,
    475
vicious circle of poverty, *defined*,
    413
video market, 47B
visible account, *defined*, 322
VMP (value of the marginal
    product), *defined*, 188
volatile markets, cause of market
    failure, 23, 88–91
voluntary employment, *defined*,
    420
Voluntary Export Restraints, 216
voluntary unemployment,
    defined, 242
voting behaviour, implications of
    alternative policies, 237
VSTF (very short term facility),
    EMS, *defined*, 475

wage bargaining, 451B
wage-cost push, 455, 456B
wage-cost-push inflation,
    defined, 432
wage drift, *defined*, 455
wage flexibility, 395–396, 439B
wage rates,
  differential, 197B
  effects on labour supply, 190–
    191
  influence of trade unions, 200
wages,
  class of income, 260
  factor distribution of income,
    185–186
  factor prices, 186–187
wants,
  double co-incidence of,
    defined, 334

human, 6
wealth, 358–362
  defined, 291n
  distribution, 186
  see also inheritance
wealth level, influence on
    household behaviour, 273
wealth tax, 441
Wealth of Nations, The, see
    Smith, Adam
weights and measures
    inspectorates, 182
welfare economics, 223n
*White Paper on Employment
    Policy* (Cmd 6527), 251
Wholesale Price Index, *defined*,
    246
Wimbledon tennis
    championships, ticket
    allocation, 103B
withdrawal (leakage), *defined*,
    285
women,
  earnings, 197–198
  in employment, 5, 197–198
work, attitudes to, determinant of
    earnings, 198
worker co-operatives, 129, 131
workers, *see* labour
working age, 5
working capital, 256
  defined, 5
working population, *defined*, 5,
    242
World Bank, 415
WPI (Wholesale Price Index),
    defined, 246

X-inefficiency, 409–410
  defined, 168, 409

yield, of capital, *defined*, 201–202

zero elasticity, of demand,
    defined, 64
zero opportunity cost, 7–8
zero unemployment, 251
zero utility goods, indifference
    curves, 117